The History of the Sufferings
of the Church of Scotland

Volume One

Solid Ground Christian Books
Birmingham, Alabama USA

Engraved by Page

JOHN MAITLAND,
DUKE OF LAUDERDALE.

Published by Blackie & Son, Glasgow.

THE

HISTORY OF THE SUFFERINGS

OF THE

CHURCH OF SCOTLAND

FROM THE

RESTORATION TO THE REVOLUTION.

BY THE

REV. ROBERT WODROW,
MINISTER OF THE GOSPEL AT EASTWOOD.

WITH

AN ORIGINAL MEMOIR OF THE AUTHOR, EXTRACTS FROM HIS CORRESPONDENCE
A PRELIMINARY DISSERTATION, AND NOTES,

BY THE

REV. ROBERT BURNS, D.D. F. A. S. E.
MINISTER OF ST. GEORGE'S, PAISLEY; AUTHOR OF HISTORICAL DISSERTATIONS ON THE POOR
OF SCOTLAND; TREATISE ON PLURALITIES, ETC.

IN FOUR VOLUMES.

VOL. I.

GLASGOW:
BLACKIE & SON, 38, QUEEN STREET,
5, SOUTH COLLEGE STREET, EDINBURGH;

MDCCCXXXVII.

Solid Ground Christian Books
715 Oak Grove Road
Homewood AL 35209
205-443-0311
sgcb@charter.net
www.solid-ground-books.com

The History of the Sufferings of the Church of Scotland
From the Restoration to the Revolution
Volume One

Rev. Robert Wodrow (1679-1734)

First Solid Ground edition in June 2008

Taken from 1837 edition by Blackie & Son, Glasgow

Cover design by Borgo Design, Tuscaloosa, AL
Contact them at borgogirl@bellsouth.net

Set ISBN: 978-1-59925-186-8
Volume One ISBN: 978-1-59925-182-0

TO

HIS MOST GRACIOUS MAJESTY,

KING WILLIAM THE FOURTH,

WHO HAS SO NOBLY FORWARDED

THE GREAT CAUSE OF HIS PEOPLE,

AND WON THEIR AFFECTIONS, BY SYMPATHISING IN THEIR WANTS, AND
SUPPORTING THEIR RIGHTS,

THIS EDITION OF A WORK,

RECORDING

THE STRUGGLES AND SUFFERINGS OF THE PEOPLE OF SCOTLAND,

UNDER THAT SYSTEM OF ECCLESIASTICAL TYRANNY

WHICH PRECEDED AND HASTENED THE REVOLUTION OF 1688,

IS, BY SPECIAL PERMISSION,

MOST HUMBLY AND RESPECTFULLY DEDICATED.

BATTLE OF BOTHWELL BRIDGE.

Copied (with permission) from the original Painting in possession of His Grace the Duke of Buccleuch, at Dalkeith House.

CONTENTS OF VOLUME FIRST.

MEMOIR of the Author, i—original Letters, xix—the Author's Dedication, xxxiii—the Author's Preface to vol. i. of the original edition, xxxvii—the Author's Preface to vol. ii. of the original edition, xlv—preliminary dissertation, li.

INTRODUCTION—Short view of the public resolutions, 1650, 1—General Monk takes measures to restore the king, 4—instructions to Mr. Sharp, February 1st, 1660, 5—desires of the city ministers, 8—the judgment of some sober-minded men, 13—letter to the king from Messrs. Douglas, Dickson. &c., May 8th, 1660, 22—instructions for Mr. Sharp, May 8th, 1660, 23—letter to the king from Mr. Douglas, &c., May 10th, 1660, 24—letter, ministers of Edinburgh to some ministers at London, May 12th, 1660, 26—particulars to be propounded to the king by Mr. Sharp, 36—draught of a proclamation for an assembly, 47—letter from Messrs. Calamy, &c. ministers at London, to Messrs. Robert Douglas, &c. ministers at Edinburgh, 54.

BOOK I. FROM 1660 TO 1666.

CHAP. I. Of the state and sufferings of Presbyterians, 1660, 58.

Sect. 1. Of Scots affairs, to the meeting of the committee of estates, August 23d, 1660, 59.

Sect. 2. Of the proceedings of the committee of estates, 1660, 65—declaration at Dumfermline, August 16th, 1650, 66—ministers' (designed) supplication, August 23d, 1660, 68—act for securing Mr. James Guthrie and others, August 23d, 1660, 71—letter, from Mr. John Stirling to his session, September 11th, 1660, 73—proclamation against Lex Rex, and the Causes of God's Wrath, September 19th, 1660, 75—proclamation against remonstrators, &c. September 20th, 1660, 76.

CHAP. II. Of the state and sufferings of Presbyterians, 1661, 87.

Sect. 1. Of the laws and acts of the first session of parliament, with remarks, 87—act 1st parl. anent the president, and oath of parliament, 1661, 92—act 7th concerning the league and covenant, 1661, 95—Abernethie (Jesuit), account of the popish government in Scotland, 1661, 96—act 11th parl. for taking the oath of allegiance, &c. 1661, 99—act 16th, concerning religion and church government, 1661, 102—act 17th, for a solemn anniversary thanksgiving, 1661, 103—act abolishing patronages, March 9th, 1649, 104—act 36th parl. anent presentation of ministers, 1661, 105.

Sect. 2. Of the efforts made by ministers during the sitting of the parliament, for preserving the church, 109—petition of the Presbytery of Edinburgh, 1661, 112—synod of Fife's exhortation and admonition, April 2d, 1661, 119—synod of Galloway's supplication, 1661, 123.

Sect. 3. Of the sufferings and martyrdom of the marquis of Argyle, 130—marquis of Argyle's petition, with reasons for a precognition, February 12th, 1661, 132—marquis of Argyle's speech, April 9th, 1661, 143—marquis of Argyle's speech after reading of his process, April 16th, 1661, 146—the king's proclamation concerning church affairs, 10th June, 1661, 151—marquis of Argyle's speech upon the scaffold, May 27th, 1661, 155.

Sect. 4. Of the sufferings and martyrdom of Mr. James Guthrie, 159—summons to the ministers of Edinburgh, August 20th, 1655, with their declinature, 170—Mr. James Hamilton's declinature at the same time, 170—indictment against Mr. James Guthrie, February 7th, 1661, 174—Mr. James Guthrie's defences, 176—minutes of the process against Mr. James Guthrie, 190—Mr. James Guthrie's speech at his death, June 1st, 1661, 192—captain William Govan's speech on the scaffold, June 1st, 1661, 195.

Sect. 5. Of the sufferings of other ministers and gentlemen, 1661, 196.

CONTENTS.

Sect. 6. Of the erection and procedure of the privy council against Presbyterians, 1661, 217.

Sect. 7. Of the regal erection of bishops, 223 --act of council, September 6th, 1661, 231.

Sect. 8. Some other remarkable events this year, 242.

Chap. III. Of the state and sufferings of Presbyterians, 1662, 247.

Sect. 1. Proceedings against Presbyterians before the meeting of the parliament, with the consecration of the bishops, 248—act of council, January 9th, 1662, 249—draught of the Presbytery of Kirkcudbright's address to the parliament, 253.

Sect. 2. Of the acts of the second session of parliament, 256—act 1st parl. for restitution of archbishops and bishops, 1662, 257—act 114th, parl. 12th, James VI., 1592, ratifying the liberty of the true kirk, 1662, 260—act 2d parl. for preservation of his majesty's person, authority, and government, 263—act 3d parl. concerning patronages, 1662, 265—act 4th parl. concerning masters of universities, ministers, &c. 1662, 266 —act 5th parl. concerning the declaration, &c. 1662, 266—list of fines imposed by Middleton in parliament, 1662, 271.

Sect. 3. Of the procedure of council after the parliament rose, with the act at Glasgow, 280— act of council, September 10th, 1662, anent diocesan meetings, 280—act of council, December 23d, 1662, 285.

Sect. 4. Of particular sufferings preceding the parliament, 287.

Sect. 5. Of Presbyterians' sufferings after the parliament was up, 297—Mr. Livingstone's letter to his flock, April 3d, 1663, 313.

Sect. 6. Other remarkable events this year, 318.

Chap. IV. Of the state and sufferings of Presbyterians, 1663, 323.

Sect. 1. Of the ejection of near 400 ministers, 323—list of non-conformist Presbyterian ministers ejected, 1662, 1663, and the following years, 324—list of ejected ministers in Ireland, 324.

Sect. 2. Of the more general acts of council this year, 336—act of council, August 13th, 1663, 340.

Sect. 3. Of the acts of the third session of parliament, 346—act 1st parl. against separation and disobedience to ecclesiastical authority, 350— act 4th, for establishment and constitution of a national synod, 353.

Sect. 4. Of the sufferings and martyrdom of the lord Warriston, 355—lord Warriston's speech, July 22d, 1663, with some account of his carriage, 358.

Sect. 5. Of the sufferings of particular persons this year, 362.

Sect. 6. Some other occurrences this year, 375.

Chap. V. Of the state and sufferings of Presbyterians, 1664, 383.

Sect. 1. Of the erection and powers of the high commission, 383.

Sect. 2. Of its actings and persecution, 390.

Sect. 3. Of the procedure of council this year, 395.

Sect. 4. Of the sufferings of particular persons, 403.

Sect. 5. Of other incidental matters this year, 414—Rothes's patent to be commissioner to the national synod, October 14th, 1664, 419.

Chap. VI. Of the state and sufferings of Presbyterians, 1665, 420—proclamation for a fast, May 3d, 1665, 420—act of council against ministers, December 7th, 1665, 428—proclamation against conventicles, December 7th, 1665, 430.

MEMOIR OF THE AUTHOR.

MR. JAMES WODROW, the father of the Historian, was born at Eaglesham in the neighbourhood of Glasgow, on the 2d of January 1637. He passed through the regular course of study at the university of Glasgow, and took his degree of A. M. in 1659, with the high approbation of principal Gillespie, and the other members of the senatus. He forthwith entered on the study of divinity under professors Baillie and Young, and was soon distinguished by his high attainments in theological literature. Although ready for license in the course of a few years, his ideas of the sacred office were so solemn, and the difficulties attending its right discharge appeared to him so numerous and so great, especially in those days of persecution, that it required the earnest expostulations of some of the most eminent ministers of the day to induce him to become a candidate for the holy ministry. Among those who urged him to take license in the presbyterian church, then passing into the vale of tears, was the justly venerated Mr. Robert Blair, one of the ministers of St. Andrews, who after hearing one day from Mr. Wodrow the reason of that self-diffidence which kept him back from the public service of the church, thus addressed him in reply; "Be not discouraged: your timidity will gradually lessen, and although it should not entirely wear off, yet it will not mar you," adding in an easy facetious manner, "I'se tell you for your encouragement, I have been now nearly forty years in the ministry, and the third bell scarce ever begins to toll when I am to preach, but my heart plays dunt, dunt, dunt." A solemnly affecting interview which he had with Mr. James Guthrie of Stirling, in the tolbooth of Edinburgh, on the night before his execution, appears to have had a very salutary effect on the mind of Mr. Wodrow; and although the persecuted state of the church, consequent on the restoration of the Stuarts, opposed additional obstacles to his entrance on the public ministry, he was most usefully employed in the prosecution of his private studies, while residing for some considerable time at Car-donald near Paisley, as tutor to the young lord Blantyre. It was not till the 29th February, 1673, that he received license from a class of persecuted presbyterian ministers in the west of Scotland; whose high testimony to his eminent attainments and character is recorded in the memoirs of his life, and stands as a very interesting memorial of the good men of those troublous times. He preached with great acceptance and usefulness among the persecuted presbyterians of the west; associated freely with ministers of both the well known classes of indulged and not indulged; and met with much opposition from the common enemy, making many very narrow escapes from his iron grasp. In 1687, he settled in Glasgow, at the request of the synod of the bounds, and took charge of a small class of students in divinity who were preparing for the ministry among the presbyterians of Scotland. In May 1688, he was called to be one of the ministers of the city, and this office he held with distinguished reputation for four years. In 1692, he was elected to be professor of divinity in the college; and in consequence of this, resigned his pastoral charge. The same diligence and pious zeal which distinguished his ministrations, continued to characterize him as a theological professor. In the various departments of public lecturing examination of students, hearing and criticising discourses, discussing cases of casuistry, daily conference with students on the subject of personal religion, and correspondence with them when absent, on the progress of their studies;—he found enough, and more than enough, to engage all his powers and all his time. From 1692 to the

MEMOIR OF THE AUTHOR.

period of his death in 1707, nearly 700 students passed through his hands, exclusive of nearly 200 from England and Ireland. In order to lessen the burden of the laborious office of the professorship, the college were pleased to elect his son Alexander, a most promising young man, to be his colleague. While the process for his induction or installation was going on, death deprived the church of the services of one who promised to prove the worthy successor of an eminent father. The professor continued to discharge the duties of the chair with growing reputation, till the 25th September, 1707, when he died full of hope, and leaving a noble testimony to the faith which he adorned by his life, and whose principles he had so ably inculcated by his preaching and by his professional labours.*

ROBERT WODROW, the second son of the professor, was born at Glasgow in the year 1679. His mother's name was Margaret Hair, daughter of William Hair, proprietor of a small estate in the parish of Kilbarchan, who married a daughter of James Stewart, commonly called tutor of Blackhall. Mrs. Wodrow was a woman of considerable strength of mind, great discretion, and eminent piety. The year of Mr. Wodrow's birth is perhaps the most eventful in the annals of the history of the Covenanters, and the violence of persecution raged during this period with more than ordinary fierceness. At the time of the birth of her son, Mrs. W. was in the 51st year of her age; and her death, though it did not happen for several years after, was then fully expected. Her excellent husband, obnoxious to a tyrannical government, narrowly escaped imprisonment or something worse, in attempting to obtain a last interview with her. As he passed the town guard-house he was watched, and soon followed by the soldiers into his own house, and even into his wife's bedchamber where he was concealed. The officer on command checked this violence; sent the men out of the room, and left the house himself; placing however sentinels both within and without till the critical event should be over. In half an hour after, Mr. Wodrow, at his wife's suggestion, assumed the bonnet and great-coat of the servant of the physician then in attendance; and carrying the lantern before him, made an easy escape through the midst of the guard. They soon renewed their search with marks of irritation, thrusting their swords into the very bed where the lady lay; who pleasantly desired them to desist, " for the bird," said she, " is now flown."

Our author went through the usual course of academical education at Glasgow, having entered the university in 1691; and studied the languages and different branches of philosophy, according to the method then generally adopted in the colleges of Scotland. *One* master or regent was in the habit of carrying his pupils through the whole of the university curriculum; a custom long ago changed for the more rational and useful plan of assigning to each professor his own appropriate field. In this way, each science obtains its own suitable kind and measure of talent and learning; while the student in the course of his studies enjoys the benefit of profiting by the diversified labours of different minds. Condensation of energies on the part of the teacher, thus secures, or may be reasonably expected to secure, a higher measure of literary qualification; while the pupils may be expected to profit by the concentration of talent thus wisely diversified.

While a student of theology under his father, Mr. Wodrow was chosen librarian to the college, an office which he held for four years. He had very soon displayed a peculiar talent for historical and bibliographical inquiry; and this recommended him as a person admirably qualified for the situation. He accepted of it not from considerations connected with its pecuniary emoluments, then exceedingly slender; but because it gave him a favourable opportunity of access to books and other facilities for his favourite studies. It was immediately on his nomination to this office, he entered with ardour on those researches which in the course of his life he prosecuted to such an extent,

---

* The above particulars of the life of professor Wodrow, are selected from a MS. life of him by the Historian ; a valuable document, which ought, beyond all question, to be given to the world.

into every thing connected with the ecclesiastical and literary history of his country. Here also he imbibed that taste for the study of medals, ancient coins, inscriptions, and whatever tended to throw light on Roman, Celtic, and British antiquities. His collections of this kind were very extensive and valuable; and it is matter of deep regret, that in his case as in that of others, the results of uncommon research and antiquarian skill, should not have been preserved entire for the benefit of posterity.

The study of natural history, then scarcely known in Scotland, seems to have attracted him with no ordinary interest; and before he had arrived at the years of majority, he had opened a correspondence with a number of celebrated men in this and the kindred departments. Among his correspondents we find the names of bishop Nicolson, the distinguished author of the "Historical Libraries;" Mr. Edward Lhuyd, keeper of the Ashmolean closet at Oxford; Sir Robert Sibbald, so well known as a naturalist and antiquarian of the first order; lord Pitmedan; Messrs. James Sutherland, professor of Botany at Edinburgh; Lauchlan Campbell minister of Campbeltown, and many others. With these gentlemen he was in habits of intimacy, and they exchanged with each other their curiosities in natural history and geology. In a letter to Mr. Lhuyd, dated August 1709, Mr. Wodrow tells him that his manse was but at a little distance from a place where they had been lithoscoping together during a visit of Mr. Lhuyd to Scotland. "My parochial charge" he continues " does not allow me the same time I had then for those subterranean studies, but my inclination is equally strong, perhaps stronger. I take it to be one of the best diversions from serious study, and in itself a great duty to admire my Maker's works. I have gotten some fossils here from our marle, limestone, &c. and heartily wish I had the knowing Mr. Lhuyd here to pick out what he wants, and help me to class a great many species which I know not what to make of." He informs him in the end of the letter, that he had 5 or 600 species of one thing or another relative to natural history. His collections were at his death divided among his friends, or found their way into the cabinets of private collectors or of public institutions.

The physical and historical pursuits of Mr. W. were all subordinate to his great business, the study of theology and the practical application of its principles in the discharge of the duties of the pastoral office. To these he showed an early and a decided partiality, and he desired to consecrate all his talents, and all his varied pursuits, to the glory of God and the good of his church. From a pretty extensive examination of his correspondence, it appears that his pursuits in natural science engaged his leisure hours only during the earlier part of his life, and that after he had framed the design of writing the history of the church of Scotland, every thing seems to have been relinquished for the sake of an undivided attention to that great subject.

Mr. Wodrow when he left the library ot Glasgow, and on finishing his theological career, resided for some time in the house or a distant relation of the family, Sir John Maxwell, of Nether Pollock, then one of the senators of the college of justice, a man of great vigour of mind, and exalted piety. While resident in his house, he offered himself for trials to the presbytery of Paisley, and was by them licensed to preach the gospel in March 1703. In the summer following, the parish of Eastwood, where lord Pollock lived, became vacant by the death of Mr. Matthew Crawfurd, the pious and laborious author of a history of the church of Scotland, yet in MS. Mr. Wodrow was elected by the heritors and elders, with consent of the congregation, to supply the charge; and he was ordained minister of that parish on the 28th October, 1703. While he did not feel himself called on to relinquish his favourite studies in history, and antiquities, he nevertheless devoted the strength of his mind, and of his time, to the more immediate duties of the pastoral office. The parish of Eastwood was at that time one of the smallest in the west of Scotland; and it was, on this account more agreeable to Mr. Wodrow, inasmuch as it afforded him more time to prosecute his favourite studies, in perfect consistency with a due regard to his official vocation It was for this very good reason that he never would consent to be removed from the retirement and leisure of a small country parish, to the more conspicuous, but at the same time more laborious and difficult situation, of a clergyman in one of our larger cities. Glasgow in 1712, and Stirling, first in 1717, and again in 1726, did each solicit and with earnestness, the benefits of the pastoral services of this excellent individual; but after serious deliberation, accompanied with earnest prayer for divine direction, he saw it to be his duty to decline all these solicitations. In a letter, from the gallant and worthy Colonel Blackadder, the deputy governor of Stirling castle, there occurs towards the end, the following passage: "There is no place you will be more welcome to than the castle of Stirling, and you may come freely now, without being suspected to be *reus ambitus;* for you will have heard that Mr. Hamilton is transported and to be settled here on the 2d of February next. My wife joins with me in our kind respects to you and spouse. She regrets your obstinate temper (as she calls it) that you resolve to live and die at Eastwood; but we see that every minister is not of that stiff temper." He also felt attached to Glasgow as the field of his father's life and labours; and the scene of his earliest and dearest associations. The advantages which its university library gave him, also influenced him in his wish to remain where he was; and he enjoyed the singularly strong affection of a loving and beloved people.

While he was assiduous and constant in all the duties of the pastoral office, preaching the gospel publicly, and from house to house, and going in and out before his people, in all the affectionate intercourse of Christian and ministerial service; his character as a preacher rose remarkably high in the west of Scotland. Good sense; distinct conception and arrangement of his thoughts; scripturality of statement and of language; solemn and impressive address; these constituted the charms of his public character as a preacher. He composed his sermons with great care; and the frequent habit of regular composition gave him, in this, a remarkable facility. Besides his regular labours on Sabbath, he frequently preached week day sermons and lectures, and even these were the result of accurate and well arranged study. His countenance and appearance in the pulpit were manly and dignified; his voice clear and commanding; his manner serious and animated; and the whole impression on the minds of his hearers, was heightened and sweetened by the complete consciousness of his perfect sincerity, in all he spoke and in all he did for their benefit. He became one of the most popular preachers of his day; and the crowds which resorted on sacramental occasions to Eastwood, proved the eagerness with which these seasons were hailed and enjoyed as a kind of spiritual jubilee. To quote the words of the author of his life inserted in the Encyclopedia Britannica: " Humble and unambitious of public notice, he was well entitled to distinguished reputation by his conscientious and exemplary piety; his learning, not only in professional, but in other branches of knowledge; his natural good sense and solid judgment; his benevolent obliging spirit to all; his warm attachment to his friends, who formed a wide circle around him; and especially his deep concern for the best interests of his people, and active exertions for their instruction and improvement."

The sentiments of cotemporaries regarding him, may be safely appealed to as valid evidences in his favour. The repeated invitations which he received from large and respectable congregations to become their pastor, afford very clear proofs of his extended reputation, and the letters of his correspondents both in this country and in other countries, speak the same language of affectionate veneration. As a small specimen, I shall quote the following passage from the letter of a pious and excellent young minister then newly settled in a small country parish in the south of Scotland, the reverend Mr. Thomas Pollock, minister of Ednam. It bears date, May 23d, 1726. " You, with others of my very reverend fathers, were encouraging to me, in setting forward to the work and office of the ministry, and therefore, I hope, will be concerned for me, that I may be both diligent and successful in it. 'Tis required of a servant that he be found faithful and diligent, and if my heart deceives me not, I would be at approving myself, to my great Lord and Master, by a patient continuance in well doing: for 'blessed shall that servant be, whom, when his Lord cometh, he shall find so doing. Their labour shall not be in vain in the Lord.' Sir, it is now a considerable while, since you, by a kind Providence, entered upon that great work, which (blessed be God) you are continued in, and take pleasure in, and have been successful in; and long may you live to be useful and successful, in making ready a people for the Lord, and espousing them to Jesus Christ: and I hope, that when the Lord comes to count the people, you shall have many to be your ' crown of rejoicing in the day of the Lord.' The lively sermons, the close and earnest calls, the pressing invitations, which you have been helped to deliver in the parish of Eastwood, in and about sacramental occasions, is what some remember and look back upon with pleasure. I need not tell you, that you have been remarkably assisted at these times; and no doubt, you have given the glory of it to him that makes his grace sufficient for us."

As became a conscientious and enlightened clergyman of the church of Scotland, he was most punctual in his attendance on her various courts of presbytery, synod, and general assembly. Of the assembly, he was very frequently chosen a member; and on occasions of public interest, such as the union of the kingdoms in 1707, he was nominated as one of a committee of presbytery to consult and act with the brethren of the commission in Edinburgh, in order to avert the evils which that measure was supposed to portend to the church and people of Scotland. On occasions of this kind, he took a lively interest in the proceedings; kept regular notes of them; corresponded with friends of influence in London and elsewhere; and has preserved in his manuscript records, most authentic and interesting details of the whole procedure of the courts. His desire to search the records in the public offices, and the MSS. and ancient documents in the Advocates' Library, rendered his visits to Edinburgh, necessarily frequent, and this naturally pointed him out as a very proper person to aid in conducting the public concerns of the church. On occasion of the accession of George I. he. was the principal correspondent and adviser of the five clergymen, who were deputed by the assembly to go to London, for the purpose of pleading the rights of the church, and particularly for petitioning the immediate abolition of the law of patronage, which had been revived two years before, by the influence of an ultra tory ministry, aided by a large Jacobite party in the country, hostile to the interests of the Hanoverian succession. The third volume of his MS. letters contains several long and able statements and reasonings on this and collateral topics; and these throw no small light on the views of both parties at the time regarding this momentous question. No man could be more decided than he was on the "unreasonableness and unscripturality" of the law of patronage; and he contended for its abolition, and for the revival of the act 1690, as essential to the faithful maintenance of the terms of the union, and as necessary to the preservation and usefulness of our ecclesiastical establishment. *A man of peace*, as Mr. W. beyond all question was, would never have argued and struggled in this way, had he known, and know it he must, if true, that the mode of settling ministers by the act 1690, was productive, as its enemies affirmed, of "endless tumults and contentions."

It is the part of candour at the same time to notice, that when, contrary to his solemn and matured judgment, the law of patronage was revived, and a decided disinclination to abrogate it, manifested by the highest legal tribunal in the kingdom, he did not think it either right or expedient, to resist the execution of the law, by popular force or by ecclesiastical insubordination. He yielded to the storm which he could not avert, and on one or two occasions, he thought it his duty to countenance the settlement of an unpopular preacher. At the same time, he never hesitated to declare his sentiments on the matter, and he did not despair of the return both of the country and of the church, to sounder constitutional principles.

The same enlightened zeal for the public interests of his church and country, which led him to take such a deep interest in the question of patronage, influenced him in his sentiments and measures regarding the political state and government of Great Britain. Tenderly alive to the liberties of the people; intimately acquainted with the genius of that execrable system of church and state policy, which, during the reign of the Stuarts, had deluged his native land with the blood of her noblest citizens; and alarmed at the ascendancy of tory and Jacobitish principles during the latter part of Queen Anne's reign, he, in common with the great body of zealous Scottish presbyterians, resisted the imposition of what was termed the *abjuration oath*, whose terms and language, seemed to them hostile to the elector of Hanover's newly acquired right to the crown, conferred on him by the parliament and people; and at variance with their avowed sentiments on the subject of ecclesiastical polity. They steadily refused to take this oath, and thus exposed themselves to considerable peril and difficulty. But Mr. Wodrow was of too catholic and liberal a mind, to take offence at those whose consciences allowed them to comply with the order; and he exerted all his influence in attempting to reconcile the people at large to such of the clergy as had gone into a measure thus peculiarly unpopular. With the firmness of the recusant clergy, the forbearance of the public officers admirably harmonized. The obnoxious oath, was, after an ineffectual struggle, not keenly pressed on scrupulous minds. The penalties for noncompliance were remitted; and the Scottish administration seemed to rest satisfied with the assurance that the loyalty of the recusants was beyond all question. Twenty-five years had effected a wonderful change in public feeling; and bigoted intolerance, it was now at length discovered, was not the most likely way of securing the attachment of the subjects, and the stability of the throne.

The rebellion in 1715, was to Mr. Wodrow a subject of deep and painful interest. In common with all truehearted Scottish presbyterians, he stood forward as one of the warmest defenders of the Hanoverian interest; and the deep anxiety of his mind at this critical era, may be fairly inferred from the voluminous collection of letters to him, by correspondents in all parts of the country, which remain among his MSS. There are at least four quarto volumes of these; and the minute and curious details which many of them contain, throw no small light on what may be termed the *internal* history of that momentous struggle.

To a man thus admirably qualified by principle, by extensive information, by a habit of persevering and accurate research, and by a native candour of soul, which bade defiance to all the arts of chicanery, no literary undertaking could be more appropriate, than that of the "History of the Sufferings of the Church of Scotland," during the days of prelatical persecution. To the undertaking of this work, he seems to have been led at a pretty early period of his life; and from the year 1707, down to the time of its publication, all his leisure hours seem to have been devoted to it. His friends encouraged the laborious undertaking, convinced of the incalculable value of such a work, if properly executed, both as a record of the sufferings and of the worth of many excellent men, and as filling up an important niche in the ecclesiastical and political annals of the country. There had been published, it is true, various authentic details of the leading events of the covenanting period, and biographical sketches of the principal characters who figured in it. But there was still wanting a comprehensive digest of the whole into chronological order; together, with what might be held up to future ages, as a fair and impartial exhibition of events, which could not fail to interest the feelings of the immediate actors in them. Mr. Wodrow lived at a time sufficiently distant from the persecuting era, to allow of his forming an unbiassed opinion of its scenes, under the moderating influence of more liberal times, and a more tolerant administration. He had access to the best sources of information, and his ardent but temperate zeal in the great cause for which his forefathers suffered, presented an edifying contrast to that cold, and supercilious, and infidel temper, which has led some other historians to look upon the whole scene either with absolute contempt, or with the frigidity of a cold-blooded Stoicism. The design of the history, was, not so much to give a regular, connected narrative of the events of the period, as to exhibit a distinct sketch of the characters, both of the principal sufferers and their persecutors; the springs of the persecution, in the unjustifiable plans and measures of an arbitrary government; with the motives of its chief advisers and executors. " The unfortunate, but innocent sufferers, our author viewed in the light, not of a set of wild fanatics, as they were called by their cotemporaries, and frequently too by later historians. Many of them were most respectable for their rank in society, as well as for their talents and virtues; but even those in the lower ranks, our author thought worthy of some public notice, as confessors and martyrs in the noble cause which they had espoused, the supporting of the rights of conscience, and of national liberty."

Among the friends to whom Mr. Wodrow was indebted for encouragement and aid in the preparation of his grand work, we may particularly notice his venerable patron lord Pollock, who had himself suffered in the covenanting interest, and who nobly exemplified in his character, the holy principles of the religion he professed; lord Poltoun, one of the senators of the college of justice, and the representative both of the *Durham* and *Calderwood* families; lieutenant colonel Erskine of Carnock; lord Grange; Mr. James Anderson, the celebrated author of *Numismata*, and other well known works in history and antiquities; and particularly Mr. George Redpath, esteemed at the time, as the author of several very able tracts on the union, and who is entitled to more notice than he has obtained, as a severe sufferer in the cause of independence and Scottish nationality.

This person seems to have been an indefatigable collector of old records, and he is said to have possessed one of the largest collections of the kind, of any private individual in Britain. To this friend, Mr. Wodrow submitted his proposal, and a specimen of the history, in autumn 1717. Mr. Redpath embarked with all his soul in the undertaking, and in the following letter, gave Mr. W. every encouragement to proceed, while he suggests some hints that well deserve the attention of every inquirer into ecclesiastical antiquities, and the value of which, was no doubt duly estimated by his amiable and candid friend.

"London, August 3d, 1717.
" Reverend and worthy Sir,

" I have perused your manuscript, sent by Colonel Erskine, with very great satisfaction, and am heartily glad that a person of your ability and industry, has undertaken that necessary part of our history, which has been so long wanted, and nothing yet done in it that can be thought complete or sufficiently vouched. As I am very ready to give you what assistance is in my power, I presume that you will not take it amiss, if I give my advice freely, as I should be willing in the like case that another should use freedom with me.

" I need not inform you, that the style of our country is not what is acceptable here; nor indeed grateful to those of rank at home; which is not our crime but our misfortune, since our present language is derived from our neighbours in England, who alter theirs every day; and it is not to be supposed that our countrymen, who live at home, should be sufficiently versed in it. Therefore, though I am of opinion that our own way of expression is more emphatical, yet as it is the interest of our church and country, that the history should be writ in a style, which will give it a greater currency here, and may be equally well understood at home, I shall be very ready to contribute my endeavours for that end; and though I never studied what they call a polite style, yet I doubt not to make it intelligible, for a plain and natural way of writing is what is fittest for a historian: what is called flowers and embellishments must be left for poets; which humour prevails so much here, that the language has become too periphrastical, and has already lost a great deal of what was masculine.

"As to the *matter*, my opinion is thus;—that it is like to swell too much upon our hands, because the subject is copious. As this will make the history too bulky and chargeable, it must be avoided as much as possible. To this end I would humbly propose —

"First, That what is merely circumstantial, might be left out, except where it is necessary, for illustrating the matter, or aggravating the crimes of our enemies.

"Secondly, That the names of meaner persons may be omitted in the course of the history, except where the case is very flagrant, or of special note; and yet that none of our sufferers may want having justice done them, I think it would be a good expedient either at the end of the work, or of some remarkable period when sufferers abounded most, to draw up their names and abodes in one column, and the causes and time of their sufferings in another, so that the same may be seen at one view in due chronological order.

"Thirdly, That acts of parliament being matters of record, and already in print, a short abridgment of those acts so far as they relate to the case in hand, may be inserted in the body of the history; and not at large in the appendix, unless such acts be not already in print.

"Fourthly, That the same method be taken as to proclamations, except such as are extraordinary; and the same as to acts of council.

"Fifthly, I am of opinion, that though many of the speeches of our martyrs be printed in Naphtali, &c. the most remarkable of them should be inserted in the appendix; because those books may come to wear out of print, and it is a pity that any of those noble speeches should be lost. But for others that are less material, I conceive it will be enough to give a short hint of them in the catalogue of the sufferers, or in the course of the history, viz. that such and such persons gave their testimony so and so, when the subject of their testimonies agrees.

"Sixthly, That where matters of fact are not well attested they should be entirely left out, or but slightly touched as common reports, and not even noticed but where the case is extraordinary.

"Seventhly, I think it necessary that the state or cause of the sufferings, in every period should be distinctly, though briefly set down. I need not hint, that there are very great helps to be had in the *Apologetical Relation, Naphtali, The True Nonconformist*, supposed to be the late Sir James Stewart's, *Jus Populi, The Hind Let Loose*, and other accounts of those named Cameronians; though the latter should be touched with great caution, as I find you have done the unhappy controversy about the indulgence, wherein I applaud your moderation and judgment.

"These things I conceive will be necessary, both for the information of posterity and our neighbours in England, who are very great strangers to the state and causes of our sufferings.

"Eighthly, I judge it highly necessary that a brief account, of what has been done against religion and liberty, in this country, and likewise in Ireland, should be intermixed in their proper periods with our sufferings: for that will not only make the book more acceptable to the dissenters and the state whigs, here and in Ireland, but give more credit to the history, when the reader sees that the designs of popery were uniformly carried on in all the three nations, though with variety of circumstances. To that same end some brief hints of the persecution in France, and elsewhere, and particularly of the war of our court, and Louis XIV against Holland, will be necessary.

"I have made some progress in forming a part of your manuscript according to this model, towards which I have the assistance of manuscripts, writ by the late reverend Mr. David Hume, from 1658 till after Bothwell bridge (1679): if you don't know his character, 'tis proper to inform you that he was minister at Coldingham in the Merse, a person of known zeal, piety, courage, and ability. His manuscripts are by way of Journal, and contain many remarkable things; but as that way of writing oblige-a man to take in many current reports, which are not sufficiently recorded, I have put a query in the margin, upon such things as I doubt, that you may either continue or cancel them as you shall think fit, upon further inquiry. He was himself at Bothwell bridge, and is very particular in his account of that fatal affair, and of the reasons of its miscarriage. I shall transmit the specimen of what I have done to you, with the first opportunity, and submit to what alterations or amendments you and others of your brethren shall think fit to make.

"There are some of the records of our council here, with letters to and from our princes, which perhaps may not be found with you. I doubt not of an opportunity to consult them at our secretary's office, and therefore should be glad to know what you want upon that head." (Here follow some suggestions as to the style of printing, &c. which are omitted as of secondary moment.)

"Mr. Crawford wrote to me some years ago, about helping him in the style of his father's manuscripts. I agreed to it, but never had any return: therefore should be glad to know what is become of those manuscripts, and whether you have the use of them. Mr. Semple of Libberton was likewise about a history, and had encouragement from the Treasury here to go on with it, but I have heard nothing of that matter since, and should be glad to know whether he goes on. You are best able to judge whether either of these interfere with your design, and I doubt not that you will take your measures accordingly."

In another letter of the 10th of the same month, he expresses his sentiments farther in the following terms: "I wish you had commenced from the reformation, for that necessary part of our history has never been well done. Buchanan, Knox, and Calderwood, are very brief and lame on that subject. Petry gives some good hints, but still imperfect. I have many original papers that set it in a clearer light; such as letters from queen Mary and her ministers, besides some things in print that are very scarce. These, with the MSS. of Calderwood, would make the thing as complete as can be expected at this distance of time. I have a MS. of Spottiswoode's that was the duke or Lauderdale's, and differs much from the print; the interlineations are in the archbishop's own hand. I have also an authentic copy of the acts of our general assemblies, from the reformation to 1609, signed by T. Nicholson their clerk; Mr. William Scot of Couper's MS. history; and many other things which would be great helps. I can also have access to the lord Warriston's MSS. in the hands of his son, formerly secretary; so that we might carry on the thread through king James VI. time, to the restoration, especially through that important period, 1638 to 1660."

The idea of "a complete history" from the reformation in 1560, to the revolution in 1688, was strongly urged on Mr. Wodrow's attention both by Mr. Redpath, and by a very intimate literary friend of both, principal Stirling of Glasgow; but the plan, however magnificent and interesting, opened a field by far too wide for any one man to undertake. Later historians have successfully occupied a part of it, but a "history of the Covenanters" in Scotland, upon something like the plan of Neal's "History of the Puritans" in England, still remains a desideratum in the literary and ecclesiastical annals of our country.

Another literary friend with whom Mr. Wodrow particularly consulted regarding his history, was the learned and amiable Dr. James Fraser of London, formerly of Aberdeen, and so well known as the liberal patron of King's college and university in that city. It does not appear indeed that Dr. Fraser was consulted by Mr. W. previous to the actual composition of a large part of the work; for this very good reason, that Dr. Fraser was not at that time so particularly conversant in the history of MSS. and ancient records, as to render his services so necessary in the earlier periods of the undertaking. His patronage was of more importance in the way of a successful introduction of the work when finished, to the notice of those, who, from their stations in society, and extensive influence in public life, had it in their power to give it a most wide circulation. Few Scotsmen in London, I mean in private life, have ever had more in their power in this respect, than Dr. Fraser. His talents and varied accomplishments and polite manners, united with liberality of sentiment and most correct moral deportment, combined with favourable local circumstances to introduce him to the society of some of the first men of the age, and to render him a favourite at the court of George I. To this gentleman Mr. W. transmitted the MS. of the history for inspection, and he received from him an answer bearing date, at Edinburgh, September 25th, 1718, from which the following is an extract.

" Reverend and much honoured sir,

" This is in short with all thankfulness to acknowledge the favour you were pleased to do me when at Glasgow, in trusting me with so valuable monuments of your great labour and useful pains, as the three volumes of the history of the persecutions the presbyterians suffered from the restoration to the revolution; all which I have read with great attention and satisfaction: wherein I cannot but observe the sincerity, honesty, and faithfulness, requisite in a historian; and that the methods invented and practised in those times to distress and ruin that party, do by much exceed the severities used by the heathens against the primitive Christians; or by the Goths, Huns, Vandals, Saracens, or Turks, in succeeding ages; or even by the papists, or inquisition in Spain and Portugal, in many things. So that in the general sentiment of all persons that I have conversed with on that matter, it is very necessary that so useful a work should be published to the world, as soon as possible: considering the clamour the other party make daily about their present sufferings, which they say far exceed any known in former reigns, and that all who suffered before the revolution was on the account of rebellion, and not of religion and conscience, as Sir George Mackenzie in his book of the vindication of the government in king Charles and king James II. reigns, does confidently assert and endeavour to prove. And besides that there are many now alive who were witnesses of these cruelties then exercised and suffered under them: and if delayed till this generation is gone, they will not be ashamed to deny there were any severities used. I think it is proper and useful, that when your occasions oblige you to come to Edinburgh, that you would allow yourself some time to see some honest and knowing persons that frequently meet at the Low Coffeehouse here, where you may receive certain information of very remarkable instances of unheard of severities in those times, that may have escaped your knowledge, very well attested. And also to make a visit to the good and worthy lady Cardross, the earl of Buchan's mother, with whom I had the honour of an hour's conversation last week; from whose mouth you may receive a most distinct information of all the particular steps and circumstances relating to her and her husband's sufferings. There is one Mr. James Nisbet son to Nisbet in Hardhill, who was executed in December, 1685, and is now sergeant in the castle of Edinburgh, and has lately published the history of his father's sufferings, and his last testimony and dying speech; wherein there is a remarkable prediction of the abdication of the name of Stuart from ever reigning in Britain. I have had some hours' conversation with the said James Nisbet, who told me many remarkable things of persons and actings in that time, he having been intimately acquainted with Mr. Peden, Cargill, and others of the suffering party, having been several years in the woods, caves, and deserts, with them. And Mr. Johnston minister at Dundee, told me some surprising instances of the barbarity used in Dunfermline, by one Mr. Norry, now a Jacobite and virulent conventicle preacher at Dundee, which I have communicated to some of your friends here to be imparted to you at meeting. I could heartily wish a way could be found of printing, as soon as possible, so useful and so necessary a work; and I shall not be backward in contributing all in my power towards the promoting it."

Specimens of the history were submitted also to a variety of eminent literary and religious characters in England, and particularly to the celebrated Dr. Edmund Calamy, then at the head of the Dissenting interest, and who from his intimacy with many of our countrymen both on the continent and in

Scotland, was considered a most impartial judge of the merits of the work. Although the correspondence regarding the critical inspection of the work is on record, and abounds with a number of important particulars, it does not appear that the critics of the south contributed any thing material to its improvement, or attempted to dispute the accuracy of the statements it made. Nor does it appear that Mr. Wodrow was indebted in any considerable degree to those ministers in various parts of Scotland, to whom he applied as probable sources of information. With the exception of a few venerable individuals, who from personal experience, or immediate relationship to the sufferers themselves, took a peculiar interest in the work, and most readily lent their acceptable assistance, in the furnishing of materials; it would seem from the complaints which the historian makes in some of his letters, that in his expectations of help from a variety of quarters, he had met with a painful disappointment; so that for the work such as it is—and "admirable and faithful" Dr. Fraser justly terms it—we must consider ourselves as indebted to the single exertions of its indefatigable author. In May, 1719, the matter was submitted to the general assembly, when that venerable body gave their cordial and unanimous approbation to the work, and recommended it to ministers and presbyteries, as richly deserving of encouragement; and instructed their commission to correspond with presbyteries on the subject, and to report their diligence to next assembly. With all these encouraging considerations, the work had many obstacles to surmount, before it made its appearance from the press; and this will not be surprising to any one who knows the real state of Scotland, in what may be called, the infancy of her literary progress. The idea of pecuniary advantage by literary labour, would have been held in those days as a chimera; and some of our ablest treatises on divinity and moral philosophy, would never have seen the light, had it not been for the fostering aid of wealthy patrons, and of a society formed for the encouragement of learning. In these circumstances it was not to be expected that a work of such size and price as the "History of the Sufferings of the Church of Scotland," would all at once be ushered into the world without one serious obstacle to overcome. Very little did the worthy author receive by way of compensation for all the labour and expense he had bestowed upon it;—but to him the satisfaction that he had done something to serve his God "in his generation," and that he had reared a monument to his country and to his church, on which was inscribed in legible characters, "Ære perennius,"—was to him a better return than the gains of fine gold.

The work was published in two large volumes at separate times, in 1721 and 1722; and it soon met with exactly that kind of treatment which might have been anticipated, as the likely portion of an impartial, unvarnished, and independent, historian of the persecuting period. With the exception of a few worthy individuals belonging to the Cameronian class, who thought, and perhaps with some measure of truth, that the author had not on some occasions shown sufficient decision of mind, and on others had awarded rather a measured meed of praise to the noble heroes of the olden time;—the general and high approbation of all the friends of liberty and of presbyterianism, both in Scotland and in Britain, cordially went along with the work; and the value of it was felt by all who had learned to prize the civil and religious interests of their country. On the other hand, the abettors of persecution and the fierce adherents of the Stuart dynasty, smarted keenly under the exposé which was made of the "mystery of iniquity," and felt the more tenderly, because, alas! it was "no scandal." "Facts," observes Mr. Wodrow in one of his letters to a friend in London, " facts are *ill natured things ;*" and it was precisely because the facts of the case could not be set aside, that the assault became the more fierce against the temper and spirit and style of the author. Anonymous and threatening letters were sent to him. Squibs and pasquinades were liberally discharged, under masked batteries, against the obnoxious book that told so much unwelcome truth. Various attempts were made before and after its appearance, to vindicate the reign of the Stuarts: but Sir george Mackenzie is, I believe, the single hapless individual, at least of Scottish name, who to this day enjoys the "base glory," of having fallen in the trenches of such an inglorious cause.

Dr. Fraser had the honour of presenting copies of the work to their Majesties, and the Prince and Princess of Wales. These were most graciously received. The book was, by these illustrious individuals, carefully read and studied; and the king, to whom the work was dedicated, generously ordered £105 sterling, to be given to the author, in token of his cordial approbation. The order for this sum on the exchequer of Scotland, is still preserved, and we give it entire, for the satisfaction of our readers:—"George R. Trusty and well beloved, we greet you well. Whereas, our trusty and well beloved * * * Robert Wodrow, minister of the gospel in Glasgow, did some time since, dedicate and present unto us, his History of the Persecutions in Scotland, from the Restoration to the Revolution, consisting of two large volumes in folio: now, we being minded to certify our esteem of the said author and his works, by bestowing on him some mark of our favour and bounty: in consideration thereof, our will and pleasure is, that we do hereby authorize and empower you, to issue your warrant to the receiver general of our treasury, to pay, or cause to be paid, out of any monies, that are, or shall be in his hands, for the use of our civil government, unto the said Robert Wodrow, or his assigns, the sum of one hundred and five pounds, as of our royal bounty, for the consideration aforesaid, and for so doing, this shall be, not only to you, but also to our said receiver general, and to all others that shall be concerned in passing and allowing the payment upon his account, a sufficient warrand. Given at our court at St. James', the 26th day of April, 1725, in the eleventh year of our reign.

By his majesty's command,
R. WALPOLE.

To our trusty and well beloved, our Chief Baron, and the rest of the Barons of our court of exchequer in Scotland.

GEORGE BAILLIE, WILLIAM YONGE, CHARLES TURNER, GEORGE DODINGTON."

Thus, while the bigoted adherents of a persecuting dynasty, were crying out most lustily against the humble Scottish presbyter and his book, the highest personage in the empire was publicly conferring on the said presbyter, a most substantial mark of his regard, *just because* he had written a book, which at once exposed the horrors of former reigns, and displayed by reflection and by contrast, the blessings connected with the Hanoverian succession.

The work, is beyond all question, exactly what it undertakes to be, a faithful and impartial record of facts and of characters. Its extreme accuracy has been tested by the best of evidence, that of documents, public, official, and uncontradicted. Its facts will not be relished by timeserving historians, who have prostituted the dignity of history to the low ends of a mean and drivelling partisanship; and the proud march of the smooth surface narrator, may not stoop to the minutiæ of its private and domestic details. Nevertheless, its value as a record is beyond all praise; and the picture which it gives of the manners and spirit of the age is graphical and instructive. Says Chalmers, the learned author of the Biographical Dictionary—"It is written with a fidelity that has seldom been disputed, and confirmed at the end of each volume, by a large mass of public and private records." "No historical facts," says Mr. Fox, in his historical work on the reign of James II., "are better ascertained, than the accounts of them which are to be found in Wodrow. In every instance where there has been an opportunity of comparing these accounts with the records and other authentic monuments, they appear to be quite correct."

Mr. Wodrow did not discontinue his historical researches after the publication of his great work. His indefatigable and persevering mind, acting on the suggestions of his friends Redpath and Stirling, planned the scheme of a complete history of the church of Scotland, in a series of lives. With this view, he set to work in enlarging and completing his already ample collection of manuscripts, ancient records, and well authenticated traditions; and actually drew out at great length, and with minute accuracy, biographical sketches of all the great and good men, who had figured from the earliest dawn of the reformation, down to the period when his history takes its rise. These lives are extremely valuable. They form the principal mine of information regarding their several subjects; and taken together, exhibit a comprehensive and accurate view of the leading events in one of the most interesting periods of our national history. It does not appear that they had received the finishing stroke of the author, although they bear all the marks of uncommon research, and most minute specification. The manuscripts of this voluminous work, partly in the handwriting of the author, and partly copied by an amanuensis, are preserved in the library of the university of Glasgow.

It was a favourite wish of our author, that biographical memoirs should be regularly drawn up and preserved, of all the more eminent ministers and private Christians in Scotland who had been distinguished for their piety and the faithfulness and success of their Christian labours. Acting on this idea, he employed his leisure moments in writing down the various articles of information, which his own times brought within his reach, regarding the lives and labours of eminent individuals, together with the ordinary or more remarkable occurrences of the period, during which he lived. These memoranda are preserved in six small and closely written volumes, under the general name of *Analecta*, and they embrace a period of twenty-eight years, from 1705, down to 1732. The information they contain, is, as might have been expected from the nature of the work, exceedingly various, both as to subject and degree of importance. The notices are often exceedingly curious; and taken as a whole, the work exhibits an interesting picture of the history and manners of the period. It is in such private and unsophisticated memoranda as these, we often meet with those minute and undesigned coincidences, and those unstudied allusions to matters of a more public nature, which throw light on subjects otherwise dark and mysterious. To bring out these private memorials to the light of open day, would be extremely injudicious; but the occasional consultation of them for the purpose of historical or general illustration, is not beside the province, or beneath the dignity of the most fastidious analytical inquirer.

Besides writing the "history," the "biography," and the "analecta;" the labours of his parish, and two days every week regularly appropriated to his preparation for the pulpit; much of his time must have been occupied in epistolary correspondence. Many of his letters resemble rather dissertations on theological and literary and historical subjects; and he corresponded with a very wide circle of acquaintances and friends in Scotland, England, Ireland, America, and the continent of Europe. With regard to the continent, his anxiety to become thoroughly acquainted with its literary and religious state was peculiarly great, and he frequently imported at his own expense, the best publications that could be obtained, particularly those in the Latin and French languages. He also transmitted, from time to time, lists of queries respecting the state of matters in the different countries. Of these I shall insert a very small specimen, out of many now before me.

"Memorandum of Inquirenda in Holland, to G. B. April 21st, 1731. What is the state of the protestant churches in Silesia? What numbers of the reformed may be there? if they are Calvinists? if they have judicatories, discipline, &c.? what is the state of the protestants in Hungary—what number of ministers may be there,—and protestant schools? If there be any Socinians among them? what are their present hardships from the papists,—every thing as to their government, discipline, doctrine, judicature and usages. The same as to the churches in Bohemia. The same as to Transylvania. The same as to the Palatinate, as also an account of their present grievances from the papists. All you can learn as to the state of things in Geneva,—their doctrine, discipline, government, and learned men. All the accounts you can get as to the protestants in the valleys of Piedmont,—what numbers are of late in the valleys,—the hardships of the king of Sardinia upon them,—the pretences he uses in his own defence,—and if any number of ministers and protestants continue in the valleys?—The character of the present pope,—what you can learn of the differences between him, and the king of Sardinia.—How the difference stands betwixt the court of Rome and the king of Portugal.—The state of learning in Portugal and Spain.—What is in the accounts we have in the prints, of the manuscripts 12 or 1400 years old, found in an island in the Red Sea by some Portuguese, and sent, I think, to Lisbon, or extracts of them. What may be expected from the press at Constantinople, and the copies of manuscripts taken by the king of France's interest there and brought to Paris? All the accounts you may have of the state of Christianity in the Dutch settlements in the East Indies.—The translation of the Bible into the Malayan tongue,—the success of the Danish missionaries in the East Indies. What you can gather as to the state of the Greek churches in Asia under the Turks; the Greek Christians in Egypt, Palestine, Syria, &c.—Is learning and knowledge penetrating into Muscovy?—All the discoveries made of Greek MSS. by the late Czar, and the progress made by the academy at Petersburg.—Let me have a list of the professors at Leyden and Utrecht; and the most considerable men at Franeker and Groningen; and the most famed learned men in the Protestant universities in Germany. Let me have a hint of the new books, that are most talked of, &c. &c." It is certainly matter of regret that the replies to these queries, were by no means so full as might have been wished; and yet there are in the MS. letters entitled " Foreign Literature," many valuable articles of miscellaneous information.

His chief correspondents in America were the celebrated Dr. Cotton Mather, the friend and patron of Benjamin Franklin; Mr. Benjamin Colman, president of Harvard college, Boston; Mr. Wigglesworth, professor of divinity there; together with the ministers of the Scots churches in Pennsylvania, New Jersey, and New York. The intelligence communicated by these correspondents embraces chiefly the state and progress of literature, religion, and manners in the states,—the disputes regarding political and theological questions,—the relations of the states to the mother country—and the history of the Scottish presbyterian churches in the new world. The letters of Mr. Wodrow to these individuals, and their replies, form together a mass of correspondence that is extremely interesting. Not the least curious of these documents, are, a letter of some length, from a converted Jewish Rabbi who taught Hebrew in Harvard college, together with a most truly Christian reply by our excellent author. The name of the Jew was *Rabbi Judah Monis;* and of his future history one would wish to obtain some farther information. The letter is written in *pure Hebrew*, and also in *Rabinnical characters* and *dialect.* The original is now before me. It is a beautiful specimen of penmanship; and forms altogether a literary curiosity. Its date is " Cambridge 4. 5tæ mensis 1723." The reply bears date, July 23, 1724.

There is one subject which engaged the mind of Mr. Wodrow, in common with all the zealous friends of evangelical truth throughout the empire, for a considerable number of years; I allude to the well known case of professor Simpson of Glasgow. This gentleman was the immediate successor of Mr. Wodrow's venerable father; and this circumstance seems to have touched the delicacy of our author's feelings, while it by no means prevented him from taking a very active share in the ecclesiastical process, which was instituted against the professor. It would be foreign to the design of this brief sketch, to enter at all into the merits of the controversy, either in regard to its subject matter, or the mode in which it was carried on. Professor Simson appears from his defences to have been a man of considerable acuteness; and in learning probably not inferior to his opponents. He seems to have been a decided Arian; but his wish to retain his place led him to throw a veil of mystery over his sentiments. After a tedious and disagreeable process, he at length succumbed to the general voice of the church, and avowed his belief in the catholic doctrine of the trinity, as held in our public standards. Still an impression remained on the minds of all parties in the question, that he was either not sincere in his averments, or that he had not capacity sufficient, to draw the exact line of distinction between opposite systems. The tardiness also, with which he brought out his real creed, and the dubious complexion, to say the least of it, which his theological prelections had long exhibited, convinced the general assembly, that he was not a fit person to be charged with the theological tuition of the sons of the church, and he was therefore suspended from his charge, while the emoluments of the office were still reserved, with an amiable, but mistaken liberality, to the man, who was, with one voice, declared unfit to do that duty, which forms the only claim to these emoluments. During the period of his suspension, and even to the day of his death, the whole duties of the professorship devolved on principal Campbell, who was ex officio, primarius professor of theology.

Mr. Wodrow was a very efficient, and certainly a most moderate and judicious member of the assembly committee for purity of doctrine, to whom the case of professor Simpson was referred; and both by correspondence, and by personal exertion, he contributed much to save the church of Scotland from a tide of heterodoxy, which threatened to overwhelm it. Among clerical coadjutors, he had very able assistants in Mr. John M'Laurin of Glasgow, and Mr. James Webster of Edinburgh; and amongst the lay brethren, on this trying occasion the names of lord Grange, and lieutenant colonel Erskine of Carnock, both elders of assembly, stand conspicuous. The letters addressed by the former to Mr. Wodrow, and which form a leading part in his voluminous correspondence, display a talent of no ordinary kind, combined with a profound knowledge of divinity, and a power of clear and discriminating statement. Mr. W.'s own accounts of the various steps of the process, in his private minutes of committees, and assemblies, throw much light on the minutiæ of the controversy, and still afford a rich repast to any one who intends to write a history of that interesting, but critical period of our church.

On the 10th and 11th June, 1727, Mr. Wodrow preached two sermons in the Barony church of Glasgow, on Isaiah ix. 6. in which he took occasion to illustrate at length, the great doctrine of the divinity of our blessed Saviour, in opposition to the sentiments of Arians and Socinians. These sermons seem to have made a considerable noise at the time; for on the day following, a challenge to a public or private disputation or to a written controversy, was sent him by one Mr. William Paul, a student of theology, and known to be tinctured with Arian sentiments. The letter is on the whole, respectfully written; but while it "wisheth to Mr. W. charity and impartial reasoning," it throws out some dark but harsh insinuations against Mr. John M'Laurin and Mr. George Campbell, two of the ministers of Glasgow; the latter of whom was well known and respected as a zealous and pious labourer in the vineyard; while the former, by the confession of all parties, stands at least as high in the ranks of theology, as his brother Colin does in the scale of mathematics. It is pretty certain that Mr. W. did not accept the challenge, but whether he made any return to it, or what measures he felt it his duty to pursue, we have no means of determining. He was not at all fond of disputation; and he probably saw, that the mind of the young man was not in a proper tone for the serious and successful investigation of spiritual truth.

On the subject of the *Marrow controversy*, which was keenly agitated at this period, and which indirectly led the way to the secession in 1733, Mr. Wodrow held a middle course. He thought that Mr. Boston, and the other divines who patronized the doctrines contained in "the Marrow of Modern Divinity," went rather far in their attempts to vindicate sentiments and modes of expression, which seemed to him somewhat unscriptural and antinomian in their complexion. On the other hand, he thought that the assembly had busied themselves too much in the criticism and condemnation of the book, and had anticipated evil too readily. He disliked the whole controversy; and recommended those virtues of which his own example afforded a most consistent pattern, charity and mutual forbearance.

On the grand question about *subscription to articles of faith*, then keenly agitated in Ireland and in England, our historian assumed a more bold and determined part. The Marrow controversy, he deeply deplored, because it tended to divide the friends of the Redeemer, who, in the main, were "of one heart and of one mind." The question regarding subscription, he, along with all the tried friends of orthodoxy in Scotland, held to be a vital one. He saw ranged on opposite sides, with very few exceptions, the friends and the enemies of the Deity of the Saviour; and the design of the *nonsubscribers* he knew could not be favourable to the cause of evangelical Christianity. With eminent ministers both in England and in Ireland, he held on this, as on other topics, a regular and extensive correspondence. Dr Fraser, who seems in his latter days to have gone in to the Arian hypothesis; Dr. Calamy, Dr. Evans, Dr. Abraham Taylor of London; Mr. Masterton, Mr. Samuel Smith, Mr. M'Racken, Mr. William Livingston, Mr. Iredale, Mr. Gilbert Kennedy, Mr. M'Bride of Ireland, are among his leading correspondents on this and kindred subjects. The letters from these gentlemen are very numerous, and in general very minute, and apparently candid in their statements. The minutes of Irish presbyterian synods are given at length, together with private accounts of the transactions of committees. Any person who wishes to write a narrative of presbyterianism in Ireland—a desideratum in ecclesiastical history—will find a treasure of information in these letters. The results of the controversy are highly instructive. The Arians and Unitarians, ranging themselves under the banners of the nonsubscribing and liberal party, have for upwards of a century displayed the deadening tendency of their system in the annihilation of many flourishing churches: while evangelical doctrine, taking an opposite direction, has shed upon the north of Ireland, those purifying and ennobling influences which contributed so powerfully to render Scotland in her better days, "a praise in the whole earth."

It need not surprise us that labours so numerous and severe, as those in which Mr. Wodrow was incessantly engaged, should have told upon his bodily health and even shortened his days. His constitution was naturally good, and in the earlier part of life he enjoyed excellent health. But his studious habits of constant reading and writing, together with the vast variety of concerns both public and domestic, which pressed upon his mind, would soon have told upon a frame even more robust than his. It appears that in the course of the year 1726, he first began seriously to complain, for in that year we find his friend colonel Blackadder inviting him to Stirling, by way of relaxation and for the recovery of his health; and farther recommending air and exercise on horseback, as among the most likely restoratives. It is interesting to see the affectionate sympathy of his friends on this occasion. His correspondent the Rev. Thomas Mack, minister of Terregles, after noticing the symptoms of his disorder, and strongly recommending a trial of the Bath waters, thus expresses himself: "Your letter does signify to me you are yielding too much to despondence. I hope you will guard against melancholy, the fruit of too much confinement. None that love our cause will neglect to have sympathy with you, and if my letters can divert you, you shall always have the use of them. I am sorry for your affliction. I hope you bear it patiently, and study a resignation to the will of God. My advice is, you divert from all study as much as possible, and if you can go out, preach to your people, though you do not write: it will ease your mind. Suffer not your spirits to sink. Prepare to go to the Bath, or to some mineral water."

"I saw," says Mr. John Erskine, afterwards professor of Scots law, and the father of the late venerable Dr. Erskine of Edinburgh, "I saw Mr. Warner (of Irvine) this night with my father (colonel Erskine) who came to town this evening. I'm exceedingly concerned to hear from him that your trouble is not abated; and though I'll make no promises, I may venture to say this, that if I was to follow my inclinations, I would be at Eastwood this spring, to bear you company for some days in your distress." (Edinburgh, 15th January, 1726.) "I am heartily sorry" says Mr. Walter Stewart "to hear by yours, that your indisposition still continues. I pray God may restore you to your wonted health, and preserve you a lasting blessing to your friends and charge." (January 19th, 1726.)

It is not unlikely that Mr. Wodrow took the advice of his friends in regard to his health, but, although he so far recovered as to be able to go on with his usual labours for several years after this period; it does not appear that he ever completely recovered his former strength. A species of rheumatism or gout seems to have given him great uneasiness, while it occasioned many interruptions in his favourite studies. In the latter end of the year 1731, a small swelling appeared on his breast, which gradually increased till April 1732, when an unsuccessful attempt was made to remove it by caustic. The effect on his bodily frame was very injurious. He became greatly emaciated, and gradually declined till his death, which happened on the 21st of March, 1734, in the 55th year of his age. He bore this long continued distress with admirable fortitude, and unabated piety. The faith of the gospel supported his mind "in perfect peace;" and he gave a testimony in his practical experience to the efficacy of those holy truths, which he had preached so faithfully, and vindicated so nobly by his writings. His dying scene was truly edifying. The day before his death, he gathered his children around his bed, gave each of them his dying blessing, with counsels suitable to their age and circumstances. The two youngest boys, (James, afterwards minister of Stevenston, and Alexander who died in America,) were both under four years of age at this time, and of course too young to understand and feel those marks of his affection; yet after the example of the venerable patriarch, (Gen. xlviii. 15.) he drew them near to him, laid his hands upon their heads, and devoutly prayed, "that the God of his fathers, the Angel who had redeemed him from all evil, would bless the lads." He carried with him to the grave the affectionate regrets of a strongly attached people; of a large circle of friends; and of the whole church of God. His death was felt as a public loss; and the removal of such a man in the critical state of the church of Scotland at the time, was felt as a severe dispensation of the Almighty. His growing infirmities had prevented him from taking any part in the disputes which had just arisen relative to the secession. His views were directed to a better country; and the rising troubles of the church militant on earth, led him to pant with greater ardour of spirit after the serenity and peace of the church triumphant in heaven.

Mr. Wodrow was married in the end of 1708, to Margaret Warner, grand daughter of the venerable William Guthrie of Fenwick, author of the "Trial of a Saving Interest in Christ;" and daughter of the Rev. Patrick Warner of Ardeer, Ayrshire, and minister of Irvine; a man who had borne his full share in the troubles of the persecuting era, and whose name stands deservedly high among the worthies of our church. Mrs. Wodrow was the widow of Mr. Ebenezer Veitch, youngest son of the celebrated Mr. William Veitch of Dumfries; and a young minister of uncommon piety. He was settled minister at Ayr, in 1703; and died after a short but severe illness, when attending his duty at the assembly commission in Edinburgh, December, 1706. His wife, afterwards Mrs. Wodrow, was a lady remarkable at once for personal accomplishments, and for exalted piety; she had sixteen children to Mr. Wodrow, nine of whom with their mother, survived their venerable parent. The following is a brief, but authentic account of the family.—There were surviving at the time of the historian's death, *four* sons, and *five* daughters. The eldest son, *Robert*, was his successor in the parish of Eastwood, but retired from the charge by reason of bad health, and other infirmities. He was twice married, and had six or seven children. His eldest son settled early in America, and his only surviving daughter went there also about 20 years ago, with her husband and family. The second son, *Peter*, was minister at Tarbolton; married the youngest daughter of Mr. Balfour of Pilrig, near Edinburgh; and left one son. His third son, *James*, became minister of Stevenston; married Miss Hamilton, daughter of Mr. Gavin Hamil ton, a distinguished bookseller in Edinburgh, and son of Mr. William Hamilton, professor of divinity, and afterwards principal of the college of Edinburgh; and left one daughter, Miss Wodrow, now residing at Saltcoats in the parish of Ardrossan. His fourth son, *Alexander*, settled in America, had an estate there, and died about the end of the first American war. After the death of the historian his widow and daughters lived in Glasgow, and were much respected for their enlightened piety, and agreeable manners. Mrs. Wodrow died in 1759; leaving behind her in her eminently Christian example, a legacy to her family, far more valuable than all that the wealth of India can command. After her death, the eldest daughter, *Mary*, acted as the head of the family, and managed its concerns with great prudence and discretion. She was confined mostly to bed seven years before her death, and exhibited to all around her, a distinguished pattern of cheerful resignation and lively hope. The second, *Margaret*, was married to Mr. Biggar, minister of Kirkoswald, and left four daughters; the youngest of whom is at present the amiable spouse of Mr. Inglis, the worthy pastor of the parish. The third daughter, *Marion*, kept house with her brother at Stevenston, till his marriage, when she returned to her sisters in Glasgow, whom she attended with affectionate care through life and in death. She had a literary turn; corresponded in the magazines of the day; and wrote some popular Scotch songs, a small collection of which are still extant in manuscript. The fourth daughter, *Janet*, was a most singular character in those days, though Mrs. Fry, and some other distinguished daughters of benevolence in modern times, render her character not so uncommon now. Her days and nights were devoted to the poor, to whom she gave her personal but unostentatious attendance, as her deeds were not known, even to her sisters, till after her death. She visited the haunts of the poor, the sick, the helpless, and the dying; and kindly ministered both to their temporal comforts, and their spiritual welfare. She died at the early age of forty, and her funeral was attended by an unusual crowd of afflicted mourners. The youngest daughter, *Martha*, died early, after a long course of very infirm health, during which she exhibited much amiable and Christian resignation.—The surviving *male* representative of the family in this country, is Mr. Wodrow of Mauchline, Ayrshire; whose son *William* is at present the accomplished and pious pastor of the Scots church, Swallow-street, London.

Mr. Wodrow's mortal remains lie interred in the church-yard of Eastwood, where no stone as yet appears to mark the sacred deposite. Be it so. " The memory of the just is blessed," and to our venerable ecclesiastical Historian, may the sublime words of the Apocalypse be emphatically applied— " Blessed are the dead which die in the Lord, from henceforth; yea, saith the Spirit, they rest from their labours, and *their works do follow them*."

R. B.

Paisley, January 17*th*, 1828.

ORIGINAL LETTERS

OF

MR. WODROW.

From the voluminous and valuable correspondence of the Historian still in MS. we have selected a few specimens for the gratification of our readers.

Letter I.

To Mr. George Redpath, London, in reply to the letters inserted in the body of the Memoir.

Dear Sir,

When I had answered yours of the 3d., and was waiting an opportunity to send it to you, I am favoured with yours of the 10th of August, which is a new tye laid on me; and our common friend the Principal of Glasgow (Stirling) tells me, I shall have an occasion of sending my answers to both these safe to you by some acquaintances of yours to be in this country in a few days.

I forgot in my former to desire you, when you got access to the Secretary's office, particularly to look after that letter of the king in the time of the Pentland executions, ordering a stop to be put to the executions. It is December 1666. It is generally believed here, that such a letter was writ, and came to the Archbishop of St. Andrews as President of the Council in the Chancellor's absence, and that he kept it up till a good many more were execute.

No doubt you may fall upon a great many important papers there, which we can have no access to here, and you are fully able to judge which of them will be proper for the design of the History of the Sufferings: and what are not here, you will know by my papers, in which I took care to insert every thing of importance I found in the registers; and I shall, as soon as occasion offers, and I have your address, send up some more of them to you.

It is most certain, our History, since the Reformation, is not writt as were to be wished. A great many very considerable discoveries have been made since the Revolution, and some before; which Buchanan, Knox, and Calderwood, had not access to know; and many helps are now in our hands these good men had not. Besides, we have a long blank from the death of James the VIth. to this day, during which interval we have nothing of a History. But I never entertained any thoughts of beginning so high, or essaying any thing like a complete History. The account of our Sufferings from the Restoration to the Revolution, was truly too much for my share, and only undertaken with a view to set matters under a just light as to Presbyterians' Sufferings, and not to be a complete History even of that very period. Indeed, there was little thing else but oppression, barbarity, and perfidy, in that black interval; and the account of Presbyterians' Sufferings is almost all that a Church Historian has for his subject for these 28 years. Wherefore, despairing almost to see any tolerable History of our church, and having my spirit a little stirred with the thoughts that posterity would not credit the one half of what was fact, and that since the Revolution we have been so much in the wrong to ourselves, the cause we own, and our children, in not giving the world some view of what this church underwent for religion, reformation rights, and the cause of liberty; and likeways the vile aspersions of our malignant and Jacobite enemies, who will be a dead weight on the government as well as this church, if not looked after;—wants not its weight. These things made me essay a work of this nature.

Sometimes I have thought, the History of this Church is too vast a field for one man to enter upon, unless he could give himself wholly to it; and could it be parcelled out in its different periods among proper persons, it would certainly be the best way of doing it. You see, the black part, I don't well know how, hath come among my hands.

Far be it from me to dissuade you from what you propose in your last, of completing our History. Since I heard of your design of continuing Buchanan, I still reckoned you had your heart on this necessary work; and I was extremely pleased to hear it was among your hands, and grieved that other things had so long diverted you from it. We must certainly do things as we can, when they are not like to be as we would, in a time when the public interests are but too little regarded; and I beseech you to go on to do all you can this way for your mother-church and country.

If ever my History of the Sufferings comes to

any bearing, so as friends think it worth the publishing, it will shorten your work from the Restoration to the Revolution. The design of it being precisely upon the Sufferings, I can scarce think it will be out of the road to publish it separately when ready for that; and I wish it may stir up others to give us the other branches of our History we need so much.

You may assure yourself of the outmost assistance in the work of our complete History I am capable to give you, and you shall want nothing I have in my small collection this way. Since I was capable of remarking this lamentable defect, I still picked up any thing that came in my way which I thought might give light to our History, without any thoughts of ever being in case to do any thing myself; but mostly from an Athenian spirit, and, I hope, some regard to the interests of this church and the Reformation; and if you desire, you shall have a complete list of what I have got in my hands this way.

In your former letter you desired to know what is become of Mr. Crawford and Mr. Sempill's Histories, and I shall give you what I know anent them. Mr. Crawford was my immediate predecessor in this congregation, and a zealous, worthy, and diligent person, for whom I shall still have a great value. His History I read over many years ago. I hear nothing of his son, who is co-presbyter with me, his publishing it now, these several years. The largest half of it, as far as our printed historians go, contains not much, which I observed, distinct from them, except a few remarks upon Spotswood here and there. Neither do I remember, and I talked with its author upon his materials, that he had any papers of that time come to his hands, distinct from our printed historians, except Scot of Coupar, and the MSS. of Calderwood, at Glasgow; and I dont remember if his many infirmities of body suffered him to go through them all either. This made me advise his son to shorten that part of his father's work, and give us only an abstract of the History already in print, referring to the authors and principal papers in them, which would have reduced the first volume to a few sheets; and to intersperse a good many things that have not yet been published. But nothing of this is yet done so far as I know.

After king James' death, Mr. Crawford is very short till the 1637; and from thence to the lamentable division, 1650, he gives a very distinct and large account of matters, which I heartily wish had been long since published. Indeed, his style needs to be helped very much: but he hath many valuable things, and a good many of them from Mr. Robert Baillie's Letters, which I shall speak somewhat of before I end. He overleaps from 1650 to the Restoration, as unfit to be raked into at the Revolution, and a little after it when he wrote, lest these unhappy divisions should kindle again by dipping into them. From the Restoration to Bothwell, where he ends, he hath not completed; and there are but a few hints of things which he would no doubt have extended, had he been spared to finish the work.

What Mr. Semple hath done I cannot give you so good an account of, having never seen any part of it. He told me about a year ago, that he had the first volume, if my memory fail me not, to the union of the crowns, perfected, and ready for the press; and that he designed speedily to publish it. But since I hear nothing of it. This I know, he hath had very great advantages in point of material. One night I was his guest, and he let me see a vast many papers, upwards of thirty quire, he had caused copy out of the Bodleian and Cotton libraries, and other collections in England. I looked over an Index of them he had formed, and found they related mostly to our civil affairs. Besides this, I know he hath got great assistances from Sir James Dalrymple, Sir Robert Sibbald, Mr. James Anderson, and others about Edinburgh; but I imagine they relate mostly to the period before the union of the crowns. What his materials are since, I cannot say; only I know he hath had the advantage of Mr. Baillie's Letters. I showed him a list of what papers I then had relative to our History, and it was but very few of them he had met with, and he designed to come and stay some weeks with me, and go through them: but though this be six or seven years since, I have not had the benefit of his company. He knows of my design upon the Sufferings, and has had a copy of the first part from the Restoration to Pentland, to read, and presses me to go on. This is all I know a doing here as to our History. And after all, I am ot opinion, you ought to go on in your design. If you should be prevented by another well writt History, I promise myself it will be satisfying to you; and if not, it were good to have things in readiness, and still be going on.

It is, perhaps, too much for me to propose any thing upon the method of this work to one who is so good a judge, and hath far more ripeness in this matter than I can pretend to. But according to my plain rough way with my friends, I just dash down what strikes me in the head when writing. In an Introduction, I would have the matter of our Culdees handled, which I own nobody yet hath done to any purpose, save the hints Sir James Dalrymple hath given us in his collections; and yet I am assured by one who has considered this matter, and understands that old part of our History as well as any in this country, that much more might be gathered about them; and I am assured, Mr. Anderson, our General Post-master, whom I suppose you know, hath made some valuable advances with regard to them. I take them to have entertained a noble struggle, not only for religion and its purity, against Rome, but even for liberty, against the encroachments of our princes; and I sometimes fancy, that brave manly temper that appeared before and after the Reformation, and till the union of the crowns, among Scotsmen, was in part owing to them, and the seeds and principles they left before their utter extirpation; of which you have given so good evidences from our old constitution in the valuable paper you published about the 1703.

As to the period from the Reformation to the union of the crowns, I would not be for reprinting much of what we have already in Calderwood and Knox, (whom I should have begun with) Petrie and Spotswood. The line and thread of matter of-fact would be continued, and references for fuller accounts made to them. But I wish the unlucky turns that Spotswood gives to matters, and the facts which, as a complete party man, he suppresseth, were to be taken notice of, and his disingenuity exposed; which you will be in case to do from the MSS. of his you have. Besides the large MSS. of Calderwood, you may have considerable helps in this period from several accounts writt in that time, and before king James' death. I have Mr. James Melvil's Memoirs, of forty or fifty sheet; another History, said to be Mr. John Davidson's, about thirty sheet; Mr. John Forbes' Account of the Assembly at Aberdeen, and the trial of the ministers at Linlithgow, with the reasonings at full length, about twenty sheet; Mr. John Row of Carnock's History, which is pretty large, and contains many valuable hints as to the lives and characters of our ministers and others, before the union of the crowns, I have not met with elsewhere. You have Mr. Scot of Coupar's Apologetical Narration; and the Authentic Acts of Assembly. Balfour's Annals are at Glasgow, but it is mostly as to civil matters. I have just now got copies of a good many letters 'twixt queen Elizabeth and king James, which Sir James Balfour doubled of the originals, with some other papers relative to that time. I have likewise a large History from the Reformation to the 1610, writt at that time, I know not by whom, of near two hundred sheet, which is only ecclesiastical, and has the proceedings of our Assemblies imbodied with it; and Archibald Simson, minister at Dalkeith, his *Annales Ecclesiæ Scoticanæ*, written in a noble style of Latin, about thirty sheet. It reaches from the Reformation to king James' death.

There are some hints, not despicable, in Mr. Blair and Livingston's Life for the period 'twixt the 1625 to the 1637. And in the 1637-8-9, we have great numbers of papers, narratives, and controversies, about the Service Book. I have the Proceedings of the Assemblies 1638 and 1639, with the reasonings at great length, twenty to thirty sheet each. From thence to the 1660, there is no want of materials. I have the Autograph Acts of Assembly from the 1642 to 1646, in two folios, but wanting some leaves. The rest of them are at Edinburgh with the Registers of the Commission. I have a large account of the Assembly at Aberdeen, 1640 or 1641. Bishop Guthrie's Account of this period is printed; and I have Sir James Turner's remarks upon him, which are but short. A valuable MS. is lately come to my hands, which was once in Mr. Robert Douglas's possession, A History of the Church and State of Scotland, from the 1638 to 1647, upwards of one hundred sheet, in a fair hand; and two volumes in folio, entitled, "Register of Letters, Actings, and Proceedings," from 1654 to 1661, copied by Mr. Ker, the church clerk. It contains nothing but copies of letters 'twixt our Scots noblemen and ministers, and Cromwell and the English managers and ministers. It came to me only within this fortnight; and I can only say, it's a rich treasure. Out of it I hope to get some considerable accounts of the overturning of our religion and liberty at the Restoration. The two volumes will contain about five hundred sheet.

After the Restoration I mind nothing save Mr. Kirkton's MS. History, which I have, and it was of use to me as far as he goes, which is only to Bothwell. Thus you have a list of what is in my hands. I have forgot what I reckon the most valuable thing we have remaining 'twixt the 1638 and 1660, and that is, four large folios of Mr. Robert Baillie's Letters, and the most considerable public papers, not in print, interspersed, which I have by me, from his grandchildren. He wrote almost every post when in England, and you know he was much there from the 1641 to 1648, and he gives the best account of the Assembly at Westminster I ever saw. Wherein I can be helpful to you from any of these you may freely command me, and I shall most cheerfully communicate with you copies of any of them that are my own, or copy for myself, and extracts out of others of them in any point you desire to be satisfied in; and I'll presume you'll not grudge me copies of any things you have that are communicable; and as large an account as you can give me of the MSS. and papers in your hands. My Lord Warriston's papers, if they be his Diary, which I am told is in his son's hands, were I as loose footed as I have been, I could come to London to have the benefit of reading it, not so much for the historical hints, which no doubt are valuable, but especially for his religion, and close living with his God, and his rare experiences in prayer. I have a good many of his letters and papers about the unhappy differences, in MS.

To be sure by this time I have wearied you with two long scrawls. I very much long to hear from you, and will assure myself you cannot weary me. Principal Stirling tells me you are beginning the Atlas for Scotland, and if I can give you any assistance from a collection I made long since of fossils and formed stones, curious enough in their kinds, I gathered hereabouts, and some Roman coins and instruments, in my hands, dug up here, they shall be communicate to you. I must break off with my best wishes that you may be preserved in health long to be useful for your God and country;— and am, dear Sir, yours most sincerely and affectionately.

Sept. 23, 1717.

LETTER II.

To the Rev. Mr. James Hart, one of the Ministers of Edinburgh.

R. D. B.

I was much pleased to have another letter from you the 4th of Oct. though it contains a reproof. You have writt so seldom these ten or twelve months, that I fancied you had some other from whom you expected accounts of matters here; and when I am for some time out of the road of writing, I find myself ready to forget my friends even when matter offers, which makes me earnestly wish to have my correspondence with you more stated and customary. I know well you can never want matter, though many times I may.

The visitors of the College, in September, declared the election of a new Rector irregular and unwarrantable; admonished Mr. Dick, one of the Regents, to be more diligent in his work; and received and read a paper of grievances against the Principal, but went through only two articles of them: the *first* about a bond of 2500 merks, which was paid in the time of the confusions at Glasgow in the framing of the Union, and no distinct account can be given of the money. It lands on Mr. Law and the Principal. All the masters who signed the accompts that year are found liable to the College, and to have their relief as law accords. The other article was an act of faculty, excluding Mr. Loudon from meddling with the College accompts, because of some things he insisted on before he would engage in approving or disapproving them, in which the rest would not yield. This act is rescinded. The management of affairs, till a new Rector be chosen, at the ordinary time next year, as to their tacks, accounts, &c. is committed to the Principal, Professor of Divinity, and Dean of Faculty, and Mr. Carmichael and Mr. Loudon. The rest of the grievances are reserved to the meeting of visitors at Edinburgh, Oct. 28th. None of the sides, they say, are entirely pleased at what is done, and therefore such as pretend to be indifferent say the determination is the juster. But the main points are yet to come, and what is done is preliminary.

Our Synod, last week, had the Presbytery of Glasgow's reference of Mr. Anderson's call before them; the Ministers' reasons of dissent and the Town's answers were read, and the Ministers' answers to them heard, *viva voce*. The advice given at the close of the last Synod, when the house was thin, (to fall from Mr. Anderson) was disliked by the Synod now when full, and it was agreed not to be recorded. It appeared plain, that the particular and general Session were for Mr Anderson, but the debate ran upon the form of the call. The Ministers are not named in it, because they had dissented. The Magistrates call, in name of the whole town; and some other singularities not used in former calls. The Ministers disclaimed a negative, and yet insisted on a share in calling, as colleagues. We had long debates upon the nature of *particular* and *general Sessions*, and the ministers (except Mr. Clerk) insisted mostly on this reason, that the general Session, not the particular Session, were the proper callers; whereas, in this case, they are but consenters, because when particular sessions were set up, 1649, the power of calling was reserved to the general Session, till altered by the Assembly; and allege they have still been callers since. They insisted further, that the particular Session being but nine or ten, and the Council thirty-two, if the power of calling were lodged in the Council as heritors, and the Session, the last would still be overruled, and the magistrates might bring in whom they pleased. The magistrates declared they never had (nor would) overruled the particular Session; that they still allowed them to meet and agree on the persons to be called, whom they had still agreed to; and alleged in the present case, both the Council, general and particular Session, were agreed; and the ministers, by their standing out, were essaying to overrule them all. The vote came to be stated,—concur with the call, and transmit it to the Presbytery of Dumbarton, or refer to the Assembly; and it carried;—concur 63; refer 41; whereon the ministers and four or five of the Presbytery appealed to the Assembly, and gave in a complaint verbally against Mr. Anderson, which the Synod obliged them to bring in in write, signed, to-morrow. To prevent this, a committee for peace was proposed for to-morrow, who heard the ministers and Mr. Anderson upon the heads of the affair, but in vain; when their complaint was given in in Synod, and referred to the next Synod to be considered. It runs all on Mr. Anderson's printed letter to Pardovan, which no doubt you have: the ministers deny all the marginal notes, and Mr. Anderson offers to prove them.

Thus you have an answer to both queries. I have writt to our brethren as you desire. Pray send me an account of that soldier in Flanders who had occasion to see king William at his private devotions. My service to Mr. Flint, Millar, Maclaren. Write frequently to me. I hope to see you in November. I am yours most affectionately.

Eastwood, Oct. 8th, 1717.

LETTER III.

To Mr. James Anderson, General Post-master for Scotland.

Dear Sir,

It is with the utmost pleasure that I send you the coins we were talking about, P. Ch. Baptisme piece; one of James the I. very rare; and another of James the II. with odd hair and crown.

The old seal of ivory seems to have been the buckle of a belt. It was found in a grave in the Isle of Tyrie. I read *Sigillum Ducis*, but can make no more.

If any of these can be any way useful to you in your noble design, *De Re Diplomatica*, I'll be mightily pleased. I'll have a copy of Mr. Martin's History of Saint Andrews for you as soon as may be. Any other MSS. I have you may freely command as if they were your own.

When you get Whiston's papers, and have done with Bradbury's Sermon, I'll be fond of them and of any other Pamphlets you get from London, when you and your friends have perused them. I own this is too much to propose; but my Athenian spirit makes me impudent.

Above all, allow me to put you in mind of sending me all you can recollect about that great man Jerviswood. I am just now essaying some account of him.

Accept of my humble thanks for all your favours, and give my humble duty to your lady; and am impatient to hear from you. I am yours, &c.

Eastwood, Nov. 19, 1717.

LETTER IV.

To Mr. James Trail, Minister at Montrose.

Feb. 27, 1718.

R. D. B.

I return you my kindest thanks for your communicating to me what you know of a new projected rebellion; and had it been with fewer apologies, it had been so much the more kind. I have accounts from several other places, of the extraordinary stirrings of the Jacobites, and their elevation, especially since our wrath-like divisions at court.

It was a little after harvest, that I was both fretted, vexed, and alarmed, with an account I had (when the bird was flown, and no reaching him,) of a Highlandman, who came into a country house in a neighbour parish, in habit mean enough, and got lodging. There happened to be a Highland servant in the house, and according to their clannish way, in some few hours they turned very big; and next day when he went off, he took out a pock, as she says, which would have held a peck of meal, full of letters, and told her he was come from their king, and he would be here against next May or summer; and was going to their friends in the Highlands, that they might make ready for him. This the servant discovered that day to a sister of hers in great concern, but too late, for some days passed before it came to my hands.

When our unhappy divisions broke out in a flame, which, by a line from your brother William, I find some in that country take for a politick, but if so, it is from hell and Rome; my fears increased, and now your distinct account of matters heightens all to me. I have not got much time to reflect on things since sending my answer with our friend. We have been supporting one another with things of which we are not good judges: the good terms Spain and king George are in, and how much it will be against the Regent's interest, who appears no great bigot to any religion, to connive at such a design; with the late accounts we have of Sweden's being off his former projects and on a new lay.

These are all guesses, and scarce so much, and moral prognosticks in our case, for dreadful judgments, I own, do more than outbalance them. To those indeed I have no answer, but what for my share I tremble to misapply, and I fear we have too little observed it, and I am sure far less improved it: Its Hosea xl. 8. "I will not execute the fierceness of mine anger: for I am God and not man: the Holy One in the midst of thee."

I am ready enough to hope, that our Jacobites do magnify matters and all they can to support one another in their wickedness; especially now that they have so promising a game from our own divisions. And I cannot but wonder that the government, who you seem to apprehend are apprized of the danger, do not think fit to take other measures; and none of our parliament men come down, when some of them have parts where their presence is necessary.

But if the Lord be to send us to the furnace, our sins are great enough to provoke him to infatuate us, and leave us to our own councils. However, Dear B. let us be still at our proper work, that when he comes, we may be found so doing, and essay to keep up our trembling confidence in Scotland's God, who, I hope will not make an utter end, but correct us in measure.

All the improvement I can make of your accounts is, to stir up myself, and any of God's praying remnant I have access to, to stand in the gap, and earnestly beg you may not despond, nor faint under your many damps. I know your soul is among fierce lions; and I assure you, you want not some here who allow themselves to bear burdens with you, and get leave to do it. I fear the Lord has a peculiar reckoning with the west of Scotland, and we may come as soon to feel the fruit of sin as you. However we are in God's hands, and let us still venture our all upon him.

I have some letters lately from New England and Holland, which I must defer till my next. Only let me beseech you by our friendship to write as soon as possible again with all freedom, and to write as frequently as may be; let us at least, while we may, have the satisfaction of unbosoming ourselves one to another. Great grace be with you. I am yours most affectionately.

LETTER V.

To the very Reverend and learned Cotton Mather, D. of D. and Minister of the Gospel at Boston, (N. E.)

R. and D. Sir,

Your most obliging letter of the 4th day of the 10th month came to my hand some weeks ago, with the valuable packet of what you published since I had the favour of hearing from you.

Your "Malachi," with its companions, were most acceptable to my lord Pollock, who returned to his country-seat here some weeks ago, entered into his 70th year, and is very much refreshed with yours to me, and gives his kindest respects to your venerable parent and yourself. He is much weakened through his close and conscientious application to the business of the nation; and I fear we shall be in some little time, may it be late, deprived of this excellent person.

It refreshes my spirit to find your hope still continuing, that anon we shall see Joel's prophecy fulfilled. I remember, about the 1713, or thereby, you assured me Obadiah's prophecy was near to its execution upon the highfliers, and in part we have seen it verified; and the great thing we want after such wonderful deliverances, you have so graphically described in your *Token for Good*, is the downpouring of the Spirit from on high. May it be hastened! O why do the chariot wheels of our Lord tarry!

The tendencies in popish countries to shake off the yoke of popery, are indeed very remarkable; and we have strange accounts from France, which, I persuade myself, you have from better hands than mine. Sometimes it's damping to me, that at the appearance of Jansenius, there was no small stir, and the appearances of a break of the day then, yet all was stopped by politicks, which I wish may not be the event of the present commotions there also.

I have presumed once more to pay my duty to your very reverend and excellent parent, and enclosed it in yours.

Some years ago, I had the pleasure of reading in the Transactions of the Royal Society, some extracts of your Letters, 1712 and 1713, to Dr. Woodward, in whom I presume to have some interest, and Mr. Waller, which, indeed, raised my appetite rather than satisfied it; and I don't know how, but till this time it still escaped me to write to you anent some of them, of which larger accounts would be extremely satisfying. Some things pointed at there I think I met with in your excellent " Magnalia," and your father's Essay on Remarkable Providences. But such is my Athenian temper, that I covet much to have many of the things of which we have but scanty accounts, from yourself, when your leisure allows. It is my loss, and that of many others, that we have not the full copies of your valuable Letters referred to in that short abstract.

Next to the things accompanying salvation, I have been for some time wishing earnestly for some account of Remarkable Providences; and next to these, the Wonders of God in his Works, as we call them, of Nature. The hints at the *maculæ maternæ;* the particular discoveries made in dreams, which the publisher of the abstract of your Letters very much overlooks; the Indians' knowledge of some constellations by the names we use, before the accession of any European knowledge; your peculiar method of finding out the Julian period;—are subjects I would be most fond to have large hints of, but am ashamed to ask them. And especially the inscription on a rock at Taunton, in unknown characters that seem hieroglyphical, and of kin to the Chinese; with your latter remarkables of nature and providence. I have for some time been much endeared to Natural History, and the wonders of our God in his works of creation and providence, and take both to be a noble $\pi\alpha\varrho\epsilon\varrho\gamma o\nu$, and accessory to our more important studies.

It is high time I should come to give you some hints of matters with us; and it is but a very melancholy account I can offer in many respects. We have mismanaged our wonderful deliverances, and forgotten God's wonders at the sea, even the Red Sea. Iniquity abounds, and the love of many waxeth cold. Unheard of provocations abound in this country these five or six months past. A flood of impurity and whoredoms prevails in city and country; and since I wrote to you last, there have fallen out, in, and about our neighbouring city, eight or ten murders, and attempts that way; and "blood toucheth blood" in a frequency we have known nothing of since the Reformation. Satan is come down in great wrath. O may his time be short!

All societies among us almost are miserably torn, and the anger of the Lord hath divided us. We are biting and devouring one another, and like to be consumed one of another. In our neighbouring city of Glasgow, where, since the Revolution, unity and harmony, and consequently vital religion, flourished, *now*, heat and strife, and every evil work abound. The University is split and broken. The magistrates and ministers are at present in no good terms: and in other societies through this nation we are but too much in the same circumstances; and what of this sin and shame is in our most elevated societies, no doubt you have the melancholy accounts. These open a door for new attempts of our enemies, and the Jacobites have taken new life from those favourable symptoms as to them Multitudes of them are returned from abroad, and they are meditating new disturbances; and the clemency of the government is so far from moving them, that the rebels are more uppish than before this last attempt.

Such things among us call aloud for your sympathy and prayers, and it is for this end I lay before you what otherwise I would choose to draw a veil over. I know we have had your deep concern, when formerly brought low for our iniquity, and now we need it as much as ever.

Dear Sir, I rejoice matters are in better bearing among you. May the kingdom of our Lord be upon the growing hand, and may the accounts you shall be in case to send support me and others under our sorrows here. May the Lord preserve you long for eminent services, and strengthen you more and more for them.

I'll presume to hope you'll take all occasions which offer to this country, and oblige me with as large notices of matters with you, and communications from your learned and extensive correspondence, and favour me with the productions of Boston from time to time. Meanwhile believe that I am, reverend and very dear Sir, your very much obliged, and most affectionate brother and servant, R. W.
April 8, 1718.

Letter VI.

To the very Reverend and Venerable Mr. Increase Mather, Minister of the Gospel at Boston.

Very Reverend Sir,

It was with a great deal of pleasure that by your son the doctor's last kind letter, I find that you are still labouring in our Lord's vineyard, and bringing forth much fruit in your old age; and I could not but once more presume to acquaint you how much I take myself to be indebted to our common Lord for his preserving in his churches such old disciples and faithful ministers, who have seen the glory of the former house; as you, through grace, are.

And besides the valuable blessing there is in this providence to the dear churches of New England, I have now for several years since I had the honour of writing to you and your son promised myself a share in your prayers and sympathy.

I should take it as a peculiar favour to have another line from you with your directions and advices, and your ripe and mature thoughts upon the present appearances of providence as to the Reformation, and the state of things through all the protestant churches, and your hopes of the coming kingdom of our Lord, before you get to heaven.

We have many melancholy appearances among us in this country; and as to these I have unbosomed myself in part in mine to your son. I could add much to you. In short, serious piety among us is under a sensible cloud, and our God is in a great measure removed from us. O! importune him to return with healing under his wings!

The controversy 'twixt the bishop of Bangor and his adversaries is what hath made much noise, and is like to make more in our neighbouring nation; and as the Bishop's papers are sensibly inclining to some of the worst parts of popery, so amidst many excellent advances towards liberty, and against persecution, I am mightily apprehensive the Bishop's tenets flow from, or incline to, libertinism, and smell rank to me of the author of the "Rights of the Christian Church." No doubt you have the papers *pro* and *con*, and I would most willingly have your sentiments upon it. I hear likewise Whiston's abominable heresy spreads mightily in England.

But I fear I may be consuming your valuable time, which you employ so well; and must break off with my earnest requests, that your comfort and usefulness may be as the path of the just, still growing more and more until the perfect day, that you may be long a burning and a shining light. It will be a great comfort to me to hear from you while you are able. Any thing you have published since your last valuable present, of which you have doubles by you, will be most acceptable; and if you will lay your commands upon me as to any thing in this country wherein I can serve you, you'll extremely oblige me. I am, reverend and very dear Sir, your most humble and very much obliged, R. W.

Letter VII.

To Mr. John Erskine, at Edinburgh, (afterwards Professor of Scots Law, and the father of the late venerable Dr. Erskine.)

Dear Sir, Feb. 7, 1718.

Yours of the 4th was more than satisfying. Without any compliment, I never had any account that satisfied me so much as this; and I now understand more of the constitution of the church of Holland than ever. Their Synods are delegate meetings, like our General Assemblies; and they have delegates of delegates, like our commission, which I own is the branch of our constitution most liable to exception. Let me know how many Presbyteries, or classes, there may be in every Synod. Are there ruling elders from every congregation in their classes? Do their parochial Sessions agree with ours? Do their appeals lie from the *Deputati Synodi* to the next Synods? Let me have the minister's name, and subject of the book at Rotterdam that hath made such noise. Give all you can further recover as to Fagel's Testament, and the foundations alleged for patrons. It seems, being so very late, they cannot found on the old claim, *Patronum faciunt dos edificatio donum*. I would likewise know their method of calls; if heads of families consent, and the Session call; if they have written and signed calls; if there be presentations by the magistrates or the *Ambachtsheers* in write.

Give me the state of the Universities; the balance 'twixt Cocceians and Voetians, the state of real religion in the provinces; the success of the East India Company in propagating Christianity; the method of dispensing the Sacrament of the Supper; if at tables, the minister speaks at the time of communicating; if the words of institution are pronounced at the distribution;—the accounts of the care of the poor; their correction houses; if any societies for reformation of manners, or charity schools; and whatever you remarked singular in their civil policy and economy; their present divisions, and the strength of the Barnevelt and Arminian party.

You'll have heard of Mr. Anderson's affair at Dumbarton, and that he was countenanced. I am yours most affectionately.

LETTER VIII.

To the Reverend Mr. Benjamin Coleman, Minister of the Gospel at Boston, N. A. (afterwards President of Harvard College.)

R. Dear Sir,

With great satisfaction I received yours of the 9th of December, transmitted by Mr. Erskine to me, and with grief I perceive that your favour to me hath lost its way; for nothing ever came to my hand but the note Dr. Mather sent me, else I had not failed to have acknowledged it. * * * There is too much occasion in one place or two, for the accounts have been given you, of the unfrequency of public baptism among us. In Edinburgh, I mean, there is a scandalous compliance with a custom, I don't know how, come down to us from the South, of baptizing the infants of most people of fashion in their houses and this method is creeped in too much in Glasgow our neighbouring city. In the first named place, our brethren go entirely into the ill habit, and have brought themselves under no small toil; under which I sympathize very little with them. In Glasgow our brethren stand firmly out against this innovation, and baptize no children but in the church, or at public teaching; however, some ministers come in from the country and do it in private houses. Except in these two cities, we know nothing of private baptism. Through this national church we have witnessed against it since the reformation, and since the revolution we have a standing act of Assembly against it, which I am sorry is in any measure disregarded. The great pretext some make use of for complying is, that if we refuse to baptize in families, people will go to the tolerated party and the exauctorate episcopal clergy, and leave our communion; but really by our compliance with their humours we have brought this yoke upon ourselves; and had we all stood our ground, there could have been no hazard this way, but many times we raise difficulties, and then turn them over into arguments against plain duty.

I am sorry to add, that we have got a greater irregularity among us than even those private baptisms, and that is, especially in cities, parents are not dealt with in private, and admonished and exhorted before they be permitted to present their children, and ministers in our principal towns know not who are to be admitted to that solemn ordinance till the name be given up after sermon is over. This is quite wrong, and what I have been regretting for several years. Other sponsors I cannot away with, when parents mediate or immediate can be had. But enough of this. I hope it will raise your sympathy with us, and accent your prayers for us. You have reason to be very thankful to God, for the free choice the Christian people among you still enjoy with respect to their pastors. When we had this before the miserable turn of affairs 1712, I cannot say we improved it as we should. There were parties and combinations sometimes of the heritors and people of rank against the meaner people in a parish. And sometimes these last would oppose a worthy entrant, because people of sense were pleased with him; yet I must say, these were but rare. But now, if the Lord open not a door of relief, we are in the utmost hazard of a corrupt ministry; and our noblemen and gentlemen, members of the British parliament, *being all patrons*, we are in the worst case possible, for our judges are parties.

For several years I have had very little save general accounts of the state of religion in the dear churches in New England, from my very worthy friend Dr. Mather. His correspondence is very extensive, and I reckon myself extremely in his debt for the short hints he favours me with, and the notices he refers me to in some of his printed sermons. But I earnestly beg you'll favour me with every thing you'll please to think, were you here and I at Boston, you would wish to have; the success of the gospel; the state of real vital religion; the number of your churches; the progress of Christianity among the Indians; the order and method of teaching in the college; the number of students; remarkable providences; conversions, and answers of prayer; and multitudes of other things I need not name; and let me know wherein I can satisfy you, in any thing relative to this church, and I shall not be wanting, in as far as my information goes, to give you the state of matters with us.

I bless the Lord with all my heart for the new set of worthy young ministers God is sending to his vineyard among you. It's certainly one of the greatest tokens of good you can possibly have. I thank you for the printed account you sent me, a copy of which, in manuscript, I had sent me from London about a year and a half ago, with a letter, which came along with it to your friends at London, whereat with pleasure I observe my dear brother Coleman's hand.

Please to accept my most hearty thanks for the valuable sermons you send me. I have read them with delight, and should I speak my sentiments of them, perhaps you would suspect me of flattery; and I shall only pray that there may be a blessing upon them, and upon your further labours in the pulpit and press. I had none of them before, but I take care to communicate what of this kind I receive to my dear brethren in the neighbourhood; and you'll favour me very much if you send me any other thing. Since my last I mind very little published in this country, unless it be the three letters I with this send you, designed against a set of people which withdraw from our communion, because of ministers their taking and holding communion with such as have taken the oath of abjuration. I beg you'll let me know wherein I can serve you in this country.

I have very lamentable accounts of the prevalency of Cocceianism and Roel's opinions in Holland; and from France of the affairs of the constitution, its being turned to a politick. But of those matters, I doubt not, you have better accounts than I can pretend to. I beg you'll miss no occasion you have coming to Scotland without giving me the pleasure of hearing from you, and you may expect the like from, reverend and very dear brother, your very much obliged and most affectionate brother and servant,

April 8, 1718. R. W.

Letter IX.

To the Right Honourable my Lord Rosse at London.

My Lord,

I have the honour of yours of the 9th instant, for which I return my most hearty thanks; and I am satisfied that my last came to hand. At the close of it, I remember I did express my fears with respect to new flames in this church upon any new stir about the reimposition of the oaths. I thought I had expressed myself with all softness in this matter; and if I have erred, in running to any excess upon it, I am heartily sorry for it, but I thought I had let a word fall upon it only by the by. I own, my Lord, it was my opinion, and still is, till I see ground to alter it, that were matters let alone among us, our miserable rents would very soon dwindle to nothing; and if we that are ministers be not such fools as to mix in with parties in the state, and political differences that lie not in our road, we shall very soon be entirely one. When I say this, I hope your Lordship will not think I in the least mean we should not appear against the pretender and Jacobitism in all the shapes of it. I reckon he does not deserve the name of a protestant, and ought not to be in the holy office of the ministry, who will not renounce, and declare in the strongest terms against the popish pretender, and all papists whatsomever their claim to any rule over these reformed nations; and I know of no presbyterian minister of this church, (if there be any, sure I am they ought to be thrown out) who do not in the greatest sincerity own and acknowledge our only rightful and lawful sovereign king George, and pray for him in secret and in public, and bear all the love and regard for him that the best of kings deserves from the most loyal subjects. But the longer I live, the more I grow in the thoughts, that ministers should closely mind their great work, and keep themselves at distance from all parties, save protestants and papists, and the friends to king George, and his enemies.

For my own share, if my heart deceive me not, I have no other views before me but the peace and unity of this poor church, from which, if we swerve, we counteract the divine law and our great work as ministers, and extremely weaken this church, and sink her reputation in the eyes of such who wait for our halting; and I join heartily with your Lordship in blaming any who run to excesses, affect strictness beyond others, or instil notions to their people which all their interest cannot remove again, and as far as I am conscious to myself, I have still abhorred such courses.

Yet, my Lord, when I wrote last, and still, I cannot altogether get free of my fears, though I wish I may be mistaken in them. Whenever a bill is brought in relative to our church, I cannot help being afraid that some clause or other may be cast up that may be choking to severals, even though at first the bill may be framed in the best way that friends can propose it. When the reference is taken out which so many stick at,

I cannot but be concerned lest something may be put in its room that may be straitening, not only to such as did not formerly qualify, but even to some who did take the oaths. And I have heard some of them say very publicly, that if the reference were removed, they would have a difficulty, because it was then an illimited oath.

Besides, in conversation I have had occasion to observe several persons of great worth, and as firm friends to the government as in the kingdom, who want not enthusiasts either, who want not their difficulties as to all public oaths in this degenerate age, as being no real tests of loyalty to the king and government; and no proper marks of distinction 'twixt the king's friends and foes; neither necessary for such who every day attest their loyalty by their hearty prayers for king George and his family; and I need not add their thoughts of an unnecessary oath.

Those and many other things I have observed now these six years since our breaches began upon this head, too long to trouble you with, will lessen your Lordship's surprise, that I was afraid of new flames, and in my own mind wished that there were no reimposition, but our differences suffered to die away. I know the strait with regard to the Jacobite nonjurors in the north, of the Episcopal way. But the difference is vast, and the laws we have against such who don't pray for king George *nominatim*, (or if the laws be not plain, they may be made clearer) do effectually reach them; and there is not among that set who will pray for his majesty, but will take the oaths too; though that is not the case of the west and south, or of any presbyterian nonjurors that I know of. My great ground of expressing my fears in the event of reimposition was, that after I have considered this matter as far as I could, I did not perceive that form of an oath, but what would divide the real and hearty friends of the king in their practices, and so endanger the peace of the church, while at present, as far as I can judge, if mixing in with different state parties do not prevent it, we are upon the point of healing among ourselves, and all differences will be buried. I am very sensible, my Lord, how tender a point this is that I have presumed to write upon, and should not have ventured upon it if your Lordship had not signified your desires, which shall still be commands upon me, to have full accounts from me upon this head.

What the reverend moderator of the commission writes to your Lordship, that we are all agreed in the draught sent up from the commission, I make no doubt, is according to the information he hath; and I do not doubt, but the form sent up from the commission will satisfy the greatest part of such who did not formerly qualify; and if this tend to the healing of the rent of this poor church, as I am persuaded it is designed, can say I am as heartily for it as any minister of the church of Scotland; though some few should be brought to hardship under a government they heartily love, and bless God for. But I cannot go so far as to think that we are all agreed in what is desired. And your Lordship will bear with me when I lay before you some matters of fact which I know are true, otherwise I would not presume to write them. There are about ninety or a hundred who have signified their assent to what is sent up from the commission; and your Lordship will remember that there were upwards of three hundred formerly who did not qualify. You'll further notice, that all who signify their consent to what the commission have sent up expressly, and in so many words, desire there may be no reimposition; but if there be one, that it may be in the manner proposed. And further, probably, by this time, your Lordship will know, that another form of an oath was proposed to the commission from a considerable number of ministers in Fife and Perth, met at Kinross, with some restrictions and explications which the reverend commission did not think fit to go into. And as I think I hinted to you when I had last the honour to converse with your Lordship, in October, we had, what is now sent up by the commission before our Synod at Glasgow, and all the Presbyteries considered it; as far as I know, it was the unanimous opinion of each Presbytery, that we should lie still, and make no application that might draw down new difficulties upon us; and in our Presbytery all our brethren were as one man against it.

These facts I lay before you not to counter any information sent you, which I dare not doubt was according to the view matters appeared in there; but to give you a full state of the matter as it stands; and after all, as I said just now, and my friend colonel Erskine has informed you, I do sincerely think, that what the commission has sent up will satisfy the most part of those who stood out; but fearing that severals may remain under their difficulties, not in renouncing the pretender, or in owning the king's only lawful and rightful title, but from their apprehensions of homologating the laws about patronages, and other burdens on this church, by engaging in public oaths, and their doubts of their being proper tests of loyalty, and I did express my concern to your Lordship lest new flames might arise.

Thus, my Lord, I have wearied you, I fear, upon this subject; what I write is only for your Lordship's information; and it's my earnest prayer to the Lord, that you and all concerned may be under the Divine conduct, and led to such an issue in this matter as may be for the union and peace of this church, and the interest of true religion; and then, I am sure, the king's interests will be promoted. For my share, I resolve ever to lay out myself to my small utmost for these great ends. What my practice will be in case of a reimposition, I cannot determine myself, and ought not till I see the shape it comes in. But I cannot help wishing there may be one.

So long a scroll needs a very long apology, which I was never good at, and must entirely rely on your Lordship's goodness. I humbly thank your Lordship for your kind promise of the Bishop of Bangor on the Sacramental Test. I thought it had been but a pamphlet that might have come by post; but I was never wearied with any thing that came from that masterly pen; and when any occasion offers of transmitting it, it will be most welcome. I am sorry to hear that the clause about the Sacramental Test is out of the Bill, and it only relates to the schism and occasional acts, which, whatever ease it gives to our dissenting friends, I fear don't answer what I earnestly wished and hoped would strengthen the protestant interest, and his majesty's service, as well as do justice to the dissenters.

I'll be glad to know this comes safe to your Lordship's hands, and presume to give my best wishes to your Lordship and your noble family. Your neighbours at Pollock are all very well. I hear my Lord keeps his health very well this winter. Permit me, my Lord, to assure you, that I am, in the greatest sincerity, your Lordship's most humble and very much obliged servant.

Jan. 14, 1719.

LETTER X.

To Mr. Samuel Semple, Minister at Libberton.

R. D. B.

I blame myself that I have been so long in fulfilling my promise to you and Mr. Eliot of London, who spoke to me in name of the Rev. Mr. Neal, who, it seems, is forming somewhat about Mr. Henderson; and who desired me to correspond with you on this subject. The throng of communions and my parochial work is what really put this out of my head, till this day it came in my mind, when you have not been so kind as write to me, as I think you promised to do. It is a loss to me when I begin to write to you upon this, that I know not precisely the subject these gentlemen at London would have our help about; whether it be precisely the pretended declaration Mr. Henderson had palmed upon him after he was dead; or whether they desire an account of what remains of his we have. I shall touch at both to you, and you'll know probably better than I which of them, or if both, these gentlemen desire.

As to the declaration pretended to be made by him on his deathbed, against Presbyterian government, and in favour of Episcopacy, I had it once in my hands, in 4to. printed at London, 1648, and it is at present in our friend Mr. James Anderson's hands. When I glanced it over, this spurious paper appeared to me to be very dully written, about two years after Mr. H.'s death; at least it did not appear till then. There is nothing in the style that in the least resembles the nervous, solid, sententious, style of Mr. Henderson; and it was certainly framed by some of the Scots Episcopal scribblers, who had fled to England for shelter, and lived by what they could earn by their pen. As soon as it appeared, you know, the General Assembly, by their act, August 7, 1648, gave a public declaration of the spuriousness of this pamphlet, and insert the strongest reasons that we can wish for, taken from his constant adherence to our work of Reformation to his last breath, and that from witnesses present. I could add some things I have from very good hands to the same purpose. But the declaration of the Assembly is so authentic, that it needs no support. This declaration (pretended) was, I suppose, reprinted by Dr. Hollingsworth in 1693, in his Character of King Charles the I. at least (for I have only the answer to it) he is severely taken to task for his imposing a spurious paper on the world, by Ludlow, in a printed answer to him, 4to, 1693, which I have, where he brings some good remarks from the style, and the Assembly's act, and the inscription on Mr. Henderson's monument, both which he hath printed at length, to expose this imposition. I mind no more I have seen upon it, unless it be the editor of Mr. Sage's, (one of our Scots Episcopal clergy at London) 8vo. London 1714, publishes two letters of his; one containing an idle story of Buchanan; and the other anent a verbal declaration made by Mr. Henderson to Mr. R. Freebairn; no doubt you have the pamphlet, and it can bear no faith, being published by a nameless author, who may have forged it for Mr. Sage; and though it should be genuine, and Mr. Sage's, it depends both on Mr. Sage's and Mr. Freebairn's authority and memorie; and that which is higher, Mr. Freebairn's father's memory; and some circumstances in the tale look a little childish, and can never be laid in the balance with the contrary accounts given by the General Assembly. This is all I mind I have met with as to the spurious declaration.

As to Mr. Henderson's Remains, in print and in manuscript, if our friends at London want an account of them, I shall give you a hint of what is in my hands. Beside his parliament Sermons, printed at London in 4to. and his valuable Essay upon the government and order of the Church of Scotland, 4to. 1640, or 1641, which I can vouch to be Mr. Henderson's; and his Discourse at the taking of the covenants, 4to. Lond. 1643,

and the letters which passed 'twixt him and the king on Episcopacy, in which, out of decency to the king, he is allowed the last word, though Mr. Henderson, as I am well informed, sent an answer, and kept a copy of it, to the king's last paper: I have in MS. Mr. Henderson's Sermon at the Excommunication of the Bishops, 1638; his Instructions about Defensive Arms; Directions about Voicing in Parliament, 1639; Answers to some Propositions in Defence of Episcopacy; with some original Letters of his to Mr. Douglas. If these hints can be of use to you or the gentlemen at London, it will be a particular pleasure to, reverend dear brother, yours most affectionately. R. WODROW.
Eastwood, July 4, 1726.

P. S.—D. B. You'll oblige me extremely if you'll write me all your accounts of literature and new books and discoveries you have from England and elsewhere in your learned correspondence; and particularly, I hope you'll let me know what you have in your valuable collection of manuscripts, and scarce books and pamphlets relating to the lives of our reformers, learned men, ministers, and Christians since; Mr. Knox, Willock, Craig, the Melvils, Rollock, R. Boyd, Durham, Gillespie, Rutherford, and hundreds of others I need not name to you: their original Letters, Memoirs, &c. Pray send me a list of any thing you have this way. You may command what I have. I am again yours.
R. W.

Letter XI.

To my Lord Grange.

My Lord,

Having the opportunity of Mr. Maxwell's coming in, as his duty is, to wait on my Lord Pollock home, I could not but signify the deep sense I have of your goodness and singular favours to me. I have gone through my good Lord Poltoun's papers, though I cannot say I have perused almost any of them, and sorted them the best way I could. I found what I was extremely pleased to find, in the bottom of the chest, the volume that was wanting in the original Calderwood, that is, the fifth volume, from the 96 to King James his death, which I'll take special care of, and have laid with the other four volumes my Lord favoured me with the loan of. The Glasgow copy, and a copy which now I have got from the College of Glasgow (it was designed for poor Mr. Redpath,) in exchange, were very incorrect, especially in this last part, and I hope this shall set us right. The pleasure of that useful work being yet preserved in the original, was more than a balance to some disappointments I met with in going through the rest of the papers, where I have not yet met with what I hoped for, though there are several things that will be of no small use to me, I hope, in the lives of our reformers, and their successors; and several scattered hints as to Mr. Calderwood himself, and a great many papers which are in the large History; yet the bulk are rough draughts and collections, and imperfect papers, sadly erased, of which little can be made. I would fain hope, that if further search be made, some other papers may be fallen upon, that may make up many of those that are incomplete; and when my Lord Poltoun, to whom I repeat my most humble acknowledgments, finds leisure, he may happen to fall on them. Meanwhile, I hope from thir to give some tolerable account of the great Calderwood.

Since my last, which I doubt not you received, I had a short line from Ireland in the time of the Synod, which I shall transcribe, that your Lordship may have all I yet know in the matter. In a little time I may be in case to give you larger accounts; and you'll find it on the other side. I have sent a dozen of M'Bride's pamphlets to Mr. James Davidson to sell, which give a tolerable view of matters before the Synod sat down. If your Lordship have glanced Niven's case, it may come with my Lord Pollock's servant when he comes west. There being some things in it which are like to cast up among ourselves; which brings me to acquaint your Lordship, that nothing is yet done at Glasgow as to Mr. Simpson. In the end of May he went to the country for his health. In June most of the ministers of Glasgow were out of town at the goat milk. Last week the Presbytery met, and appointed their committee to have their remarks on his letter ready against their first meeting, the first Wednesday of August; and Mr. Simpson is sent to be present that day. I pray the Lord may direct all concerned in that important matter. If it shall happen to be the occasion of your Lordship's being in this country, and if your other affairs allow you, it will be a peculiar pleasure to me to see you here, where I hope I shall be in case to entertain you for some time, though not as I could wish, yet, I am sure, the best way that I possibly can. I shall not have the pleasure of waiting on your Lordship at the commission, since the harvest will oblige us to have our communion, if the Lord will, on the 14th of August, when I will be placed in need of much sympathy and concern. Were it not for this, though I be not a member, I might probably be in at Edinburgh, since riding, I find, agrees much with my trouble, which I am not altogether free of. Meanwhile, I'll be fond to hear from your Lordship at your leisure, and am, my Lord, your very much obliged, and most humble servant, ROBERT WODROW.
July 19, 1726.

LETTER XII.

To Mr. Henry Newman, Secretary to the Honourable Society for Propagating Christianity, Bartlett's Buildings, London.

Dear Sir,

I had yours of the 16th curt. last post. It is satisfaction enough to me (could they any way answer the end of my being honoured to be one of your corresponding members,) that my letters come to your hand; though you be not at the drudgery of making returns, except when your leisure permits. I can form some notion of the load of letters you have to answer, and only wish I may not be a troublesome correspondent.

It pleases me to hear that the new account of workhouses is so near to be published. I am sorry that I cannot tell you of the opening of that at Glasgow. The most active gentlemen in that matter, and indeed the wealthiest people there, are in the country from May to November, and any thing of that nature, (in its beginning) is, as it were, limited to the winter season. But I hope I may acquaint you, that that good design is still going on, though still but in embryo; and whether it will be proper to take any notice of it in the papers now printing, I must entirely leave to your judgment. I sent you last spring the paper printed upon that subject, to give some view of the necessity of such a design. That did not seem disliked by you, and had a good effect here. In some few weeks there were voluntary subscriptions cheerfully given to the amount of twelve hundred pounds English money, and more will certainly be given when the money is called for; I hope several hundred pounds more. This is for the building and providing the house and necessaries. This last fall and winter, when those concerned came to meet, they have made a considerable progress. The annual funds for that charitable design are agreed to, and fixed at about nine hundred pounds, of your money, per annum. There are twelve directors agreed upon for each of the four societies who advance the nine hundred pounds, and the burden of direction and regulations will lie on a smaller committee to be chosen out of these. At their last meeting they seemed to agree that two hundred poor should be taken in at first, and their house fitted up for them; but so as, if need be, and funds answer, it may be enlarged, were it to three or four hundred. This is all I know as yet relative to this, and at your desire I have given you the trouble of it by the first post. You desire to know the methods used here for the instruction of prisoners for debt, and especially the condemned in our gaols. In the country where I live, it is our mercy there are but very few of these. You know we fall vastly short of you in numbers, and it's not very often that debtors lie long in prison ; where they do, the minister or ministers of the place where they are take care of them ; and it is not unusual, if they desire, that with one of the town servants they have allowance to come to public worship, and return when it's over to their prison; but this is not ordinarily the case. When they are confined long, the minister visits them in prison. For criminals under sentence of death, a great deal of pains is taken with them. Those are generally at Edinburgh, Glasgow, Aberdeen, &c. where there are several ministers. These, by turns, go to the prison, and take much pains on them to prepare for death, generally once, or oftener, every day. And after sentence, the prisoners, under a guard, are ordinarily brought together on the Lord's day, and publicly prayed for in all the churches of the city; and on the day of execution, a minister or two attends them to their execution. There is no need of funds, you see, in this method of instruction; and many such extraordinaries, if I may call them so, fall under the hands of ministers in our considerable towns and cities.

I suppose Mr. William Grant, advocate, who succeeds Mr. Dundas as advocate for the church, and clerk to the General Assembly, shortly will be chosen secretary at their annual meeting in January to our society. He is a valuable man. But I have not yet heard any thing certain about it.

I am longing for your circular letter, and conclude with my best wishes to the laudable designs of the Society, and my most affectionate regards to you, and am, dear Sir, your most humble and affectionate servant, R. W.

Eastwood, Dec. 23, 1732.

THE preceding Letters have been selected from a collection of nearly *five hundred* in my possession, all, or nearly all, in the handwriting of the Historian. The Reader will observe, that the subjects treated of in these Letters are various and important; and the good sense, accurate information, and sound judgment of the Writer, will be readily acknowledged. Besides the Letters by the Historian, there are still unpublished, upwards of *five thousand*, addressed to him by his various correspondents in all parts of the world; and these embrace, more or less, all the great questions, political, religious, and literary, which occupied public attention during the important period from 1700 down to 1732. The Life and Correspondence of Robert Wodrow, judiciously arranged, and accompanied with suitable Supplementary Illustrations, would form a most valuable present to the Republic of Letters.

R. B.

Paisley, Feb. 25, 1828.

TO

THE KING.*

SIR,

THE History of the Church of Scotland, under a long series of sufferings, from which it was rescued by that great instrument of Providence, King William of immortal memory, is, with the profoundest humility, laid at your Majesty's feet.

Permit me to observe the adorable and just retributions of the righteous Judge of all the earth. Your Royal Progenitòrs, the excellent King and Queen of Bohemia, had the grace and honour vouchsafed them, to suffer for our holy Reformation, while they were too much neglected by those in Britain, who ought to have supported them: your sacred Majesty, with all your dominions, now reap the fruits of those glorious sufferings; and your happy subjects cannot but hope that there are many rich blessings in reserve to your Majesty and your House, for a great while to come.

Your illustrious Father joined counsels with his highness William Prince of Orange, for bringing about, under God, that wonderful turn of affairs, at the late happy Revolution, which put an end to the sufferings I have described. A period of time never to be forgotten by Protestants! when our Reformation from Popery, with all the religious and civil interests of Europe, were in the utmost danger: Popery had made formidable advances; a bigotted Papist had seated himself upon the throne, and was in the closest concert with the French King, who, after he had, contrary to solemn promises and treaties, ruined a glorious and numerous Protestant Church, was strenuously carrying on his darling project of rooting out the northern heresy, and grasping hard at the universal monarchy. " Then the Lord did great things for us, whereof we were glad."

We had not long enjoyed our religious and civil liberties, till the time approached, when our great deliverer, worn out with cares, was ripe for heaven, and called to enjoy the glorious reward of the eminent service he was honoured to do for God and his generation. It was then kind Providence put him upon securing and perpetuating those great things our gracious God had wrought for us, by entailing the Crown, and settling the Protestant succession in your illustrious House. And we were at a loss to determine, whether the Revolution itself, or the securing all the blessings of it to us and latest posterity, was the greatest appearance of Providence for us and all the churches of Christ.

Your Majesty's subjects could not but humbly and gratefully observe the only wise, powerful, and good God, preserving this his own work, amidst all the artful and open efforts, made afterwards to weaken and even overturn that happy settlement; till we had the inexpressible pleasure of seeing the same Almighty arm, at a season when our dangers were only equalled by those we had been in at the Revolution, bringing your

* George I.

excellent Majesty to the possession of that throne you now so much adorn. May our gracious God, who performeth all things for us, preserve you long long upon it.

One can scarce help envying the happiness of that historian, who shall have the honour faithfully, and in a manner worthy of so great a theme, to transmit to future ages the glories of your Majesty's Government, and of such a lasting and happy reign, as all good men most ardently wish you: but the share fallen to me, is to give some account of a management, perfectly the reverse of the beauties of your Majesty's administration; in which we see an happy temperature of the exercise of that prerogative, which all good Kings ought to have, with the liberties of the subject, and a just regard to the Constitution, a steady firmness and resolution necessary to all great actions, mixed with that goodness and wisdom requisite to so great a trust. The exalted and noble views which fill your Majesty's eye, are the glory of God, the promoting of real religion, the felicity of your subjects, and the good of mankind; and we know not which most to admire, your extensive and paternal goodness to your subjects, or your mildness to your enemies, which, to their lasting shame, is not able to reclaim them: but my mean pen is, at best, every way below this noble subject, and of late is so blunted with the melancholy matter of the following history, and our miseries under preceding reigns, that it is perfectly unfit to enter upon the blessings of your Majesty's government. May I presume to hope, that the uncontestable facts recorded in this history, the arbitrary procedure, oppression and severities of that period, the open invasion upon liberty and property, with the hasty advances towards popery and slavery, must, as so many shades, be of some use to set forth the glories of your Majesty's reign, even with some greater advantage than the best expressions of the happiest pen.

Persecution for conscience' sake, and oppression in civil liberty, flow from the same spring, are carried on by the same measures, and lead to the very same miserable end; so that they could scarce miss going together in a far better reign than those I describe. When Asa put the Seer in prison, he oppressed some of the people at the same time: but your Majesty's just and conspicuous regard to tender consciences among your Protestant subjects, perfectly secures them from the most distant fears of any invasion upon what is valuable to them, as men and members of a civil society.

Great Sir, you have the glory of making a noble stand, in a manner worthy of yourself and the great interests of Religion and Liberty, against the unmanly and antichristian spirit of persecution, oppression, and tyranny, so peculiar to Papists, and such who have been guided by their counsels. All the Protestant Churches are daily offering up their thanks to God, for your generous and truly Christian appearances in behalf of our oppressed brethren in Germany, and cannot cease from their most fervent prayers for success to your Majesty's endeavours this way, in conjunction with the King of Prussia, your Majesty's son-in-law, and other Protestant powers. The Church of Scotland must be nearly touched with the hardships put upon any of the Reformed Churches abroad: in worship, doctrine, government, and discipline, she is upon the same scriptural bottom with them. The Palatine Catechism was adopted by us, till we had the happiness to join with the venerable Assembly at Westminster, in that excellent form of sound words contained in our Confession of Faith, ratified by law, and our Larger and Shorter Catechisms. We suffered the hardships I relate, for adhering to our Reformation blessings, and humbly claim the character of contending and suffering for revolution Principles, even before the revolution was brought about. And it was, when appearing for the liberties of the nation, as well as the principles of our reformation, that Presbyterians in Scotland were harassed and persecuted; and yet they maintained their loyalty, and just regard to the civil powers, even when oppressed by them. They have been indeed otherwise represented by their enemies; but whenever your Majesty's greater affairs permit you to look upon the following history, I flatter myself you will have satisfying evidence, that they suffered for righteousness' sake, and not as evil-doers. This they were taught by their Bibles. And now, when we are relieved from such hardships, our plain duty and highest interests are happily combined in an inviolable attachment to your most excellent Majesty's person, family, and government. The least inclination unto a Popish pretender to the crown of these realms, is a crime so black in our eyes, and so contrary to our principles and interest, that we want words to express our abhorrence of it. The succession in your Majesty's person and Protestant heirs, the very crowning stone of the revolution, is what we ardently prayed and contended for, before it took place; and from our very souls we bless the Lord for making it effectual in your Majesty's accession, and reckon ourselves happy in the honour of avouching our inviolable duty, affection and fidelity to your sacred Majesty, our only rightful and lawful Sovereign.

Permit me, in the most sincere and unfeigned manner, to join with the Church of Scotland, in adoration and praise to our gracious God and Redeemer, who because he loved us, made you King over us, to do judgment and justice, and hath raised up your Majesty to maintain what he hath wrought for us, to preserve our valuable privileges, and redress our remaining grievances, brought upon us under the former unhappy administration. May the same glorious God kindly lead you through such difficulties as the manifold sins of those nations bring in your way, support your sacred Majesty under the fatigue and cares with which your imperial crown is surrounded, pour out his best blessings upon your Royal Person and Family, and, in his great goodness to us and those parts of the world, preserve you long the Arbiter of Europe, and Head of the Protestant interest; and after an happy and glorious reign over your kingdoms, and an extensive and useful life to the church of God, mankind, and those lands, receive you graciously to his blessed and eternal mansions above.

Meanwhile, great Sir, in the most submissive manner, I beg your Majesty's patronage, and the liberty to inscribe this History to the best, as well as greatest of kings, and presume, with your allowance, upon the honour of subscribing myself in this public manner, with the greatest humility and sincerity,

May it please your most excellent Majesty,
Your Majesty's most faithful,
most dutiful, most devoted, and obedient subject,
ROBERT WODROW.

THE

AUTHOR'S PREFACE

TO THE

FIRST VOLUME OF THE ORIGINAL EDITION.

It must appear strange to all disinterested persons, who know any thing of Scottish affairs from the restoration to the revolution, that there is a party among us who deny there was any persecution of presbyterians for conscience' sake in that period, and yet raise a terrible cry of severity and cruelties exercised upon the episcopal clergy at and since the happy revolution. Presbyterians are loudly called upon, to give an instance of persecution during that time, except for the crimes of rebellion and treason. It is boldly asserted, and published to the world, that no man in Scotland ever suffered for his religion. Libels have been printed, and carefully handed about, containing these glaring untruths; and no small pains is taken, and many artifices used, to impress the English nation with them. Multitudes of pamphlets were going about after the revolution, larded with these and such like aspersions upon the church of Scotland, to which some just answers were at that time given. A new cry was raised, to the same purpose, upon the death of our glorious deliverer king William, when a design was formed to strengthen the anti-revolution party, and weaken this church, by a boundless toleration, and the re-introduction of patronages: but the last four years of queen Anne's reign were thought a most proper juncture for propagating those falsehoods, gradually to prepare the way for overturning our revolution establishment, and consequently the glorious settlement of the protestant succession, and with those the religion and liberties of Britain and Ireland. Sir George Mackenzie's Vindication of the Reigns of King Charles and King James, was reprinted, and carefully spread, with many other pamphlets, containing facts, assertions, and representations of things, perfectly contrary to the knowledge and experience of multitudes yet alive. The authors, abetters, and grand promoters whereof were the Jacobites, who threw off the mask at the late unnatural rebellion, equally enemies to his most excellent Majesty King George, and the church of Scotland: and nothing could move them to publish facts they could not but know were false, save their engagement in a party with foreign papists, their virulent malice at our present establishment, and obstinate zeal for the pretender, who is educated and confirmed in Romish idolatry, contradictions and tyranny, and therefore the fittest hand to re-act the tragedies of the unhappy period I am to describe, and worse, if worse can be supposed.

I wish the prelatic party among us have not been tempted to venture upon such methods, by the culpable silence of presbyterians, who have been so far from rendering evil for evil, or measuring out to them according to their measure, that, it must be owned, they have been much wanting to themselves, their neighbours, and posterity, in not representing true matter of fact, for their own vindication. As this negligence hath no doubt given considerable advantage to the other side, so it hath been much lamented by many, who, at this distance, want distinct accounts of the unparalleled severities of the former times: and now it is, with some colour of reason, improven in conversation and otherwise, as an argument that presbyterians have nothing to say for themselves; and silence is taken for confession in persons so nearly concerned. It appears high time then, to let the world know, that presbyterians have not been so long silent from want of matter, but from a regard to the reputation of our holy religion, and common interests of the reformation. They were unwilling to seem in the least to stir up the government to deal with the persecuting party in a way of retaliation; and, till forced, in their own necessary defence, to set matters in their true light, and expose the severe treatment they met with, they could have wished the inhumanities of professed protestants, towards those who were really such, had been buried in oblivion.

The following work being extorted by the impudence of those who are no friends to the present establishment of church and state, they ought to bear the blame of any misimprovement the enemies of our reformation may make of that persecuting spirit, so peculiar to papists, when it discovers itself among protestants. I am assured by a worthy friend of mine, who was present at a conversation betwixt Mr. Jeremiah White, well known at London, and some persons there of the first rank, some few years ago, that Mr. White told, he had made a full collection of all who had suffered by the penal laws in England, from the restoration to the revolution, for nonconformity, their names, the fines imposed, the gaols where they were imprisoned, &c. That the number of persecuted protestant nonconformists exceeded sixty thousand, whereof above five thousand died in gaol. King James, after his accession, came to be informed of this collection, and offered Mr. White a large sum for it, which he generously refused, knowing the design a popish prince probably had in getting such papers in his hand, to expose the church of England, and to extenuate the just charge of the tyranny and persecution of those of his own religion, if popery deserves that name. But the spirit of tyranny, imposition, and persecution, ought to be abominated wherever it is: nor do I see what handle papists can have to insult protestants from the severities narrated in the following history, since it is plain these proceeded from themselves. The duke of York, and his party, several of whom turned papists, were at the bottom of our persecution in Scotland: our prelates were heartily in his interests; his dependants were the chief managers; and any relaxation allowed in his reign, was to serve his own purposes, though presbyterians happily improved it to the strengthening of the protestant interest; which, by the good providence of God, made way for the revolution.

An attempt is made, in the following history, to give a well vouched narrative of the sufferings of the church of Scotland, from the (year) 1660, to the never to be forgotten year 1688, a work much wished for by the friends of the reformation, and lovers of our valuable constitution; the want of which hath been matter of regret to the members of this national church, and improven to her disadvantage by enemies. The fittest season for a performance of this nature had undoubtedly been thirty years ago, when the particular instances of oppression and barbarity, now much forgotten, were recent, and the witnesses alive. At that time somewhat of this nature seems to have been designed: narratives were gathered, some of which have come to my hands, but many of them are lost; yet the public registers, and the severe laws made by our parliaments, and not a few well attested instances of their terrible execution, still remain. Indeed the courts held in several parts of the country, even those clothed with a council and justiciary power, either kept no registers, or, if they did, they are since lost. It was the interest of those who exacted fines, and pocketed them, to suppress what they got; and, in most cases, they were not bound to give accounts of what they extorted. Innumerable cases occur in this melancholy period, where we cannot expect accounts of the exorbitant exactions and oppressions then so common, such as subsistence money, dry quarters, riding money, bribes, vast sums paid by the friends of the persecuted, compositions, and the like; to say nothing of the barbarities committed by the officers of the army, soldiers, and tools of those in power, by virtue of secret instructions, blank warrants, illimited powers, and unwritten orders, for supporting the government, and encouraging the orthodox clergy, as was pretended. At this distance then, and when most of those who were persecuted, and many of the witnesses to what passed, are removed by death, it is plain, the following history must appear with not a few disadvantages, and cannot be so full and particular as it might have been at, or a little after the happy revolution.

How the author came to engage in this attempt, what were his motives and views, are matters of so little importance to the world, that it is not worth while to take up the reader's time with them: it may be of more use to give some account of the materials I had, and somewhat of the method I have followed in putting them together.

Our public records, the registers of the privy council and justiciary, are the great fund of which this history is formed: a great part of it consists of extracts from these, and I have omitted nothing in them which might give light to the state of the church of Scotland in that period; though, in perusing and making extracts out of ten or twelve large volumes, several things may have escaped me.

It is with pleasure I observe a growing inclination in this age to have historical matters well vouched, and to trace up facts to their proper fountains, with a prevailing humour of searching records, registers, letters, and papers, written in the times we would have the knowledge of. If this temper degenerate not into scepticism, incredulity, and a groundless calling in question such things as, from their nature and circumstances, we cannot expect to meet with in records, I hope, it may tend very much to advance the great interests of religion and liberty: but such is the frailty and corruption of our present state, that men are too ready to run from one extreme to the other, and, because they are imposed upon in some relations, to believe nothing at all, although the evidence brought is all the subject is capable of, and no more can be reasonably demanded.

Now, when I am insensibly led into the subject of drawing history from public papers and records, I cannot altogether pass some beautiful strokes, to this purpose, in that noble historian Josephus. It will be of little use to most of my readers to give the original Greek; and therefore I shall insert the passages from the last English translation. Many things lie scattered through the works of that great man, to this purpose; but, in the entry of his first book against Apion, he insists directly upon the necessity of forming history from records. Having taken notice of the lameness of the Greek writers this way, he says, "The Egyptians, Chaldeans and Phenicians, to say nothing of ourselves, have from time to time recorded, and transmitted down to posterity, the memorials of past ages, in monumental pillars and inscriptions, according to the advice and direction of the wisest men they had, for the perpetual memory of all transactions of moment, and to the end that nothing might be lost.——It is most certain, that there is no Greek manuscript extant, dated before the poem of Homer; and as certain, that the Trojan war was over before that poem was written: nay, it will not be allowed either, that Homer ever committed this piece of his to writing at all, but it passed up and down like a piece of a ballad song, that people got by rote, till, in the end, copies were taken on it, from dictates by word of mouth. This was the true reason of so many contradictions and mistakes in the transcripts."—— He enlargeth, in what follows, upon the faults of the Greek historians, and observes their plain clashing and disagreement. "It is evident (adds he,) that the history they deliver is not so much matter of fact, as conjecture and opinion; and that every man writes according to his fancy, their authors still clashing one with another. The first and great reason of their disagreement, is the failing of the Greeks, in not laying a timely foundation for history, in records and memorials, to conserve the memory of all great actions; for, without these monumental traditions, posterity is left at liberty to write at random, and to write false too, without any danger of being contradicted."—He further notices, that this way of keeping public registers had been neglected in Greece, and even at

Athens itself: and adds, "without these lights and authorities, historians must necessarily be divided and confounded among themselves." A multitude of other things, to the same purpose, follow, too large to be here transcribed.

The council and criminal court had most of the persecuted people before them; from their books I have given my accounts: and the passages taken from the records are generally marked with commas; this hath drawn out the history to a far greater length than I could have wished. Every body will observe, that several of the passages might have been shortened, and the principal papers themselves abbreviated, and some repetitions and matters of common form omitted; yet I have chosen to give every thing as it stands in the registers and other vouchers, and to insert the principal papers themselves in the history or appendix, rather than abstracts of them, for several reasons. As they now stand, they are self-vouchers: had I shortened them, and given them in mine own words, perhaps, such as know me might have the charity to believe, I would not knowingly have falsified or misrepresented matters; but it is much better things stand as they are in the records. I design, that as little of this history as may be should lean upon me: let every one see with his own eyes, and judge for himself, upon the very same evidence I have; this is certainly the fairest and justest way. And I am of opinion, even the necessary repetitions, and some lesser circumstances, which might have been omitted, had I compendized the registers, and other public papers, will not want their own use. This method may seem a little to the disadvantage of those whom I would not willingly have misrepresented. It is plain, very harsh names and epithets are given to presbyterians; and the sufferers are represented in the most odious colours, in the registers, proclamations, indictments, and the ordinary course of the minutes of the council. Many facts are set in a very false light; a vast deal of misrepresentations, ill grounded and idle stories, are inserted; and every thing unaccountably stretched against the persecuted side. Some notice is taken of this in the body of the history, and matters set in their true and just light, as briefly as I could. Had I been writing a defence of the sufferers in this period, much more might have been said: but, as an historian, I was chiefly concerned to represent facts; and having given the representation of matters, in the very terms used by the persecutors themselves, their severity, and the innocence of the persecuted, will appear the more brightly.

When searching the books of parliament, I was much discouraged upon finding the processes against the marquis of Argyle, Mr. James Guthrie, and the lord Warriston, quite left out; and therefore, generally speaking, I have confined myself to the printed acts. It had been a labour too great for me, to have gone through all the warrants; and the iniquitous laws stand full enough in print. Had the council warrants been in order, no question but considerable discoveries might have been made of the iniquity of this time; but those being unsorted, and in no small confusion, I was obliged to keep myself by what the managers have thought fit to put into the registers; and it is surprising to find some things there, which we shall afterwards meet with. The rest of the history is made up of particular well vouched instances of severities through several parts of the kingdom, which cannot be looked for in the records: some of them are attested upon oath; others come from the persons concerned, their relations, or such who are present at the facts narrated. In this part, I have taken all the care I could to get the best informations, and have been reckoned by some a little over nice as to my vouchers: if I have erred here, I hope, it was the safest side; and I could not prevail with myself to publish to others, any thing but what I had as full evidence of as the subject would bear at this distance.

In the first and second books, the reverend Mr. James Kirkton's Memoirs were useful to me, and some short hints of the reverend Mr. Matthew Crawford, my worthy predecessor in the charge where I serve; these he did not live to complete, as he had done the former part of the history of this church to the restoration. I had communicated to me likewise a considerable collection of informations, and other papers relative to the persecution of this church, lodged, after the revolution, in the hands of the reverend Mr. David Williamson, late minister of the west kirk. I have had access also to some valuable papers belonging once to the reverend Mr. Alexander Sheils, mostly written before the revolution. Not a few gentlemen and ministers, relations of the sufferers in this period, have sent me well attested accounts of the hardships particular persons met with. My brethren and friends, who have been helpful to me in procuring those materials, and the gentlemen by whose favour I had access to the records, will please to accept of this public and general acknowledgment of their goodness. I am a debtor to so many, as renders it impracticable for me to be more particular; if the following history in any measure answer its design, I know this will be the best return my friends wish for.

Any thing further necessary to be observed, as to my vouchers and materials, will fall in upon the history itself. My part, in putting those together, is what I should next speak of, though I reckon myself the unfittest of any to say much upon this head. Since I began to reflect upon things, I still judged writing of history a very difficult work, and now I find it so: It is a harder province still, to write accounts of times a man hath not personally known, and when the greatest part of them were elapsed before he was born; the task grows, when one has none going before him, nor any thread to guide himself by; especially when the times are full of heat, rents, and divisions, and any accounts that remain are various, according as the several parties stood affected; which occasions very different representations of facts themselves: in such a case, nothing but honesty and integrity, with labour and diligence, can carry a writer through. My style, I know, is what cannot answer the taste of this age; apologies for it are of no great use. I never affected, or had much occasion to attain any delicacy of style; all I purpose to myself, is to be understood. A country life for eighteen years, with my necessary converse among my people, and discoursing to them in my sermons, as much as I can, according to their capacity, hath brought me insensibly to express myself in a manner which in print may appear low and flat: besides, such a heap of informations from different persons, and in various styles, as I was obliged to make use of in this work, may be supposed would have altered a better expression than ever I was master of. Indeed I have kept as much by the papers I made use of, as possibly I could; and there is but a small part of the history in my words, which, I presume, may be understood even by English readers, who, it is hoped, will bear with me, though I come not fully up to the propriety of the English language, nor to the accuracy and neatness of their writers.

The general method I have used in this work, was what I was some way obliged to take, and to me it appeared most natural. In this period which I have described, I had no line to direct me, or any history of affairs in Scotland during those two reigns: I walked in an untrodden path, and was obliged to make a road for myself the best way I could. All left me to do, was to class my materials, informations, acts of parliament and council, with my transcripts from the registers, and to join together what the agreement of the matter required to be connected. This led me to divide the work in chapters and sections, and those obliged me to make some repetitions and resumptions, which otherwise might have been spared. Had I been permitted to keep this history some longer time by me, I might have pared of those, and cast the matter in one continued discourse, without such breaks; but even these may perhaps not want their advantage, and may be breathing places to stop at, in so great a heap of matter as is here collected.

After I had formed this history, and published my proposals for printing it, many informations were sent me, and I had access to some records I wanted before; yea, even during the time of printing this volume, some papers of consequence came to my hand: the inserting of what was necessary from these, in the proper places, hath not a

f

little altered this work, and made the connection of purposes in some parts less natural than it might have been, if all my materials had been under my view at first. And my later informations being fuller and more circumstantiate, there may perhaps be some seeming differences betwixt them and the shorter hints given in other places; but, I hope, no real inconsistency will be found, truth being what I had still in mine eye.

In this collection, I have taken in many things which might have been omitted, had there been any history of church or state affairs published, relating to this interval; but when gathering materials, and searching our records, I thought myself at liberty to insert every thing that offered, which might afford any light to the history of this period. This hath indeed considerably enlarged the bulk of the work: yet, I flatter myself, it may be of some use to supply our want of a history of this time, at least be materials for others to work upon with less labour than I have been at: it will likewise render the melancholy history of sufferings and persecution a little more pleasant to the reader, when other things are mixed with it.

Most part of the principal papers, and the facts here inserted, have never yet been published; and therefore, I am ready to apprehend, they may be the more entertaining to this inquisitive age: from those judicious readers cannot but have the best view of this unhappy time. If, in my inferences from them, I have any where erred, I shall take it most kindly to be set right. I have been very sparing in any thing which might bear hard upon persons or families; but, when narrating facts, it was impossible to evite giving the names and designations of the actors. This is what needs offend nobody, and they stand open to every one's view, in our public records and proclamations. I have charged our prelates with being the first movers of most parts of the persecution of these times: this is a matter of fact, fully known in Scotland; and I could not have written impartially, had I not laid most part of the evils of this period at their door. If I have anywhere used any harshness in speaking of this subject, it hath proceeded from a peculiar abhorrence, I cannot help entertaining at a persecuting spirit, wherever it discovers itself, especially in churchmen.

Since we want a Scots biography, and have nothing almost of the lives of eminent ministers, gentlemen, and private Christians in this church, I have been the larger in my accounts of such worthy persons as fell in my way, since I cannot but reckon that one of the most useful and entertaining parts of history: this has led me to give several instances of sufferers upon the very same account, when fewer examples might otherwise have answered the ends of this history; but I thought it pity that any thing, which might do justice to the memory of those excellent confessors and martyrs, should be lost. From the same consideration, some principal papers are inserted in the history and appendix, relative to the same subject, where, it may be, fewer might have sufficed; but I judged it worth while to preserve as many of the valuable remains of this time, as I could. All of them contain something or other different; and the true sentiments, deliberate views, and undissembled principles of good men, appear most naturally in their own words and papers. Such as think them tedious and irksome, may overlook them with less pain than I have been at in collecting and inserting them.

In the following work, I have taken some notice of the accounts of our Scottish affairs, during the interval before me, by the most noted English historians, Dr Sprat, Bishop Kennet, Mr Collier, Mr Archdeacon Eachard, and others of lesser name. This, I hope, is done with a temper and deference due to their merit. Their gross escapes in our affairs I could not altogether overlook: no doubt, most of them have written according to the information they had; and I am sorry we have been to blame, in part, for their want of better information. This nation and church have suffered not a little by this: I persuade myself, our neighbours will do us more justice, when they have a fuller view of our affairs.

There is another writer, the author of the Memoirs of the Church of Scotland, 8vo. London, 1717, who deserves some consideration by himself. As far as he had our printed historians to guide him, he hath given a very distinct and fair account of matters; he hath likewise done the sufferers in the period before me, some justice, in stating the grounds of their sufferings: but how he hath fallen into some very gross blunders I cannot imagine. He talks of the indulgence, as a contrivance of the prelates and their friends; which is a plain mistake. His making the indulged ministers to accept a license from the bishops, is yet much worse; and indeed, his whole account of this matter seems to be a satire upon some of the most eminent ministers of this church, who had freedom to fall in with it. In other places, this writer bewrays an uncommon ignorance of our Scottish affairs: he speaks of the Highland host as brought down upon the west some time after Bothwell-bridge, and says, that the reverend professor Hamilton and Mr. Mitchell were sent up to London, 1717, to get the act for Yule vacance repealed; whereas that was done some time before. These are of a piece with several misrepresentations of fact, in the History of the Union, generally believed to be written by the same hand. A great number of other mistakes might be noticed, as to the circumstances of the risings at Pentland and Bothwell, yea, even as to our printed acts of parliament; but, I hope, those flow from inadvertency, whereas his account of the indulgence looks like somewhat worse; and the following history will sufficiently set the facts he hath misrepresented, in their true light.

Perhaps, an apology will be here expected for the imperfections in this history; but I see very little use of this in a preface, however fashionable it may be. As I am sure there are no wilful and designed mistakes in it, so any that may have happened in so great a heap of materials, through haste or misinformation, and in the transcribing a vast multitude of papers, shall be cheerfully acknowledged and corrected. Indeed I could have wished this work had remained by me some time longer, that I might have smoothed it a little, cut off some things, necessary in the first forming of it, from a heap of unconnected papers, and brought it to a little better bearing: but, after the proposals were printed, the subscribers pressed my publishing of it; and I found, the longer I delayed, the more it was like to swell on mine hand. Since that time near a hundred sheets have been added, and I did not know where this would end; so that it comes abroad very much as it dropt from my pen, in the midst of other necessary parochial and ministerial work, and without those amendments I would have desired. I know well enough this lands upon myself, but necessity hath no law, and, I can sincerely say, I have more ways than one crossed mine own inclinations in this affair. I did very much incline, both in the proposals and history, to have concealed my name, as conceiving this of very little consequence in a work of this nature; but my friends overruled me in this, and would not have the History of the Sufferings of this Church, published in an anonymous way. The work now comes to the public view, and must have its fate according to the different tempers and capacities of its readers.

Some of my friends have urged me to draw down the thread of our history, in the introduction which follows, from the time where our printed historians end, and in some measure to fill up the gap we have from the death of king James VI. to the restoration. I have been of opinion now of a considerable time, that the whole of our church history since the reformation, is too large a field for one hand, if he have any other business or employment; and that it ought to be parcelled out among different persons, if we have it done to any purpose. Even that period, already described by Mr. Knox, bishop Spotiswood, and Mr. Calderwood, is capable of great improvement. Many valuable original papers, memoirs, and some formed histories, either not known to those historians, or overlooked by them, are recovered since the revolution, and will afford a just light to that time: and there is no want of excellent materials for forming full accounts from king James his death to the restoration. Several of my very good friends have large collections of papers during both those periods, and more may be gotten: I hope, ere long a full account shall be given, by better hands than mine, of our affairs before the restoration; and they have my best wishes. The blackest part of our history in this church has fallen into my hands; and I did not think it necessary for me to go any further back than the time whereof I give the general hints in the introduction, which may suffice to let the reader in to what is immediately connected with the period I have undertaken. I own, I am not much in love with abstracts and compends in historical matters, in which I would have all the light possible: the largest accounts, with their vouchers from original papers and records, are still most satisfying to me; and a short deduction of the former period of our history would have been of no great use, and scarce have answered the toil and labour it would have cost me.

This history, or rather collection of materials for a history, contains a large number of facts, and well attested accounts, which will set the circumstances of presbyterians, during twenty-eight years, in a clearer light than hitherto they have appeared, and, if possible, may stop the mouths of such who have most groundlessly aspersed this church, and do justice to the memory of those excellent persons of all ranks, who, as confessors and martyrs, were exposed to the fury of this unhappy time. It may, also, through the divine blessing, be of some use to revive our too much decayed zeal for our reformation rights, to unite all the real friends of the church of Scotland, from the observation of the various methods used by enemies to divide and ruin her, and serve to quicken our just warmth against popery and every thing that tends to bring us back to the dismal state described in the following history.

Eastwood, Dec. 29, 1726.

AUTHOR'S PREFACE

TO THE

SECOND VOLUME OF THE ORIGINAL EDITION.

However fashionable prefaces are to books of this nature, the author of this history is not so fond of them, as to take up either his own time, or the reader's with any thing of this sort, when nothing of moment offers. What appeared necessary to hand the reader into this work, hath been given before in the former volume; since the publishing of which, the necessary encumbrances with this volume, and other business, have been task enough for me.

Any remarks, additions, and corrections, come to my hand, relative to the first volume, shall be added at the end of this;* I do not question many others might have been made, considering the great heap of matter in this collection, and other things I have formerly noticed. Those undesigned, and, in such a multitude of facts, almost unavoidable mistakes, and those that shall be observed to me in this volume, shall be rectified upon due information: and I want not my fears, that in this third book, where particular instances of severity cast up in great numbers, which cannot be expected to be found in records and public papers, I may have been insensibly led to some things that may be excepted against.

It is with pleasure that I observe the method I have taken, in giving much of the history of this period, by inserting what stands in our records, and the principal papers relative to the several years, either in the body of the book, or appendix, is approven by some of the best judges: those I would have the reader still chiefly to observe, and they are decisive arguments of the harshness of the times I have described; and though there should be some misinformation in the circumstances of particular instances, in the execution of iniquitous laws, and severe and terrible orders, I do not see how this affects the general truth, fully made evident from the registers, and original papers. Indeed, as I have inserted none of the particular facts without vouchers, the best the matters allowed of, and I could reach at this distance, so I shall be heartily sorry, if, after all the pains I could take, I have been led into mistakes even as to those; and I presume to hope, they are few and inconsiderable, and, upon better information, I shall most cheerfully rectify them. This I take notice of, to prevent any little cavils that may be raised, and to save a little pains to some people, who have more spare time upon their hand than I am master of, if they bestow their leisure in forming inferences from any escapes I may have been led into, in circumstantial and less important matters, to weaken the force of this history, which leans in all its important parts, upon undeniable vouchers: and as I shall be ready to set every escape right, upon just information, so I will not reckon it worth while, to enter the lists of debate, about matters that don't affect the principal parts of this work.

I find it complained of, and, I fear, not without ground, that the names of persons and places, especially in the list of Middle-

---

* The additions and corrections, &c. here referred to, have, in this edition, been inserted in the form of notes, at those places in the body of the work to which they refer: an arrangement obviously calculated to promote their usefulness.—*Ed.*

ton's fines, are not so correct as were to be desired:* had the amendments been sent me, they should have been added. All I have to say, is, that the copy from which that list was published, was the best I could have, and was written much about that time; and, even in the registers themselves, I observe much haste, and incorrectness as to the names of persons and places, which nevertheless I durst not adventure to alter.

There is another complaint I hear of, which lands not so much upon me in particular, as the work in general, which I have now got through, and I cannot altogether pass it, that a History of the Sufferings of this church tends to rip up old faults, and may revive animosities, and create resentments against persons and families concerned in the hardships and severities of the time I have described: for my share in this, if I know myself, I am heartily against every thing that may raise or continue differences and animosities; and if ever I had entertained one thought, that a work of this nature would have such effects, I should have been the last man to engage in it. But, as far as I can perceive, there is nothing in this history, that, without perverting it to the utmost degree, can have a tendency this way: and if any thing here should be improven to such vile purposes, I have this support, that the best of things and writings, and many better composures than ever can drop from my pen, have been perverted; and it is well enough known where such misimprovements must land. I hope, the rules of Christianity are better known, than there can be any danger this way, at least among real Christians; and surely they have not learned Christ as they ought, and his holy religion, which every where breathes forth love, meekness, and forgiveness, who can make such a wicked use of the follies and crimes of former times: there are many natural and noble improvements directly contrary to this, which may and ought to be made, even of cruelty and persecution itself, too obvious for me to insist upon. The naming of persons who were active in the sufferings of presbyterians, was what could not be avoided; and this falls in necessarily, more frequently in this than the former volume. Could I have given particular instances without this, I should have chosen to do it, but every body will see this was impracticable. The share such as are named had in the evils of the former times, is no secret, but fully known, and they stand in many of the public papers and records of that period. As this is a natural, just, and necessary consequent of their own deeds, so I shall only wish it may be a warning to all in time coming, to abstain from such arbitrary and unchristian methods, at least for the sake of their own reputation, if they will forget the superior laws of God nature, and society: and if it reach this good end, there appears no reason, why any concerned in the persons named, ought to take this in ill part, which is really unavoidable in narratives of this nature. After all, I hope it will appear, that all aggravating and personal reflections are avoided; and if, at any time, I have, by the narratives I have made use of, been insensibly led into any of those, which I as much as possible guarded against, I shall be heartily sorry for it. In short, were there any thing at all in this objection, we must never more after this, have a history written, for what I can see; since a faithful narrative of any period, will have persons' names and designations in it, and some side or other must be in the wrong, and the alleged consequence of reviving heats, may still be cast up: but there is so much unfairness, not to say ill nature, in this pretext, that I shall leave it. I hope, upon solid consideration, it will be found to be altogether groundless.

More than once, in this second volume, I have pointed at the necessity of an abbreviate of the fines and losses through the different shires and parishes, as far as they have come to my hand, and somewhere I almost promised it: once I designed to have brought it into the appendix, but, upon second thoughts, it seems as naturally to come in here. I may assure the reader, that this abstract of fines and losses throughout the kingdom, hath cost me more labour than many sheets of the History: it is

---

* Not a few corrections of the kind here mentioned, have been made in this edition.—*Ed.*

formed out of several hundred sheets of informations, from different parishes through the kingdom; many of them were gathered at and before the revolution; yet, as will appear by the lists themselves, no informations are come to my hand, from the far larger part of the parishes where the persecution raged; and there are even several shires where there were very sore sufferings, from whom I have nothing almost, as Argyleshire, Dumbarton, Stirling, Linlithgow, &c. Had informations come to me from those, my abbreviate had been much larger. Further, it would be observed, that, save in the shires of Roxburgh, Renfrew, Fife, and Perth, the fines I give the abstract of by the papers in my hands, most of them signed, were actually exacted from the country, and, generally speaking, in a few years of the black period I have described, mostly from the (year) 1679 to 1685. When I went through this vast heap of informations, I found the fines uplifted from the more common sort, country people, tenants, and cottars, save in a few instances from gentlemen, and meaner heritors. The forfeitures and exorbitant fines from particular gentlemen, and others narrated in the history, are omitted, save the sheriff fines last spoken of, those by Middleton's parliament, and the losses at Pentland, and by the Highland host, which I have added, that the reader may have them all together in his view. I would willingly have inserted the names of the persons who were fined, and sustained those losses in every parish, according to the lists I have; but that was impracticable, without adding a third volume to this history; and, in my opinion, would have been of no great use, save to preserve some sort of memory of the persons, most of them truly religious; and, could this have been done easily, I should not have grudged it, since 10, 20, 40, or 100 pounds from a tenant, or cottar, was as heavy to them as a thousand to a landed person.

All those fines, even those accumulated by the sheriff courts, were in terms of law and indeed are chargeable upon the iniquitous laws narrated in the history, excepting a few losses by the rudeness of the soldiers, and the severe courts, where very often the hard laws themselves were exceeded. Upon every turn, I find it observed in the papers before me, that, for want of full information, the accounts given in them are defective and lame; and, considering this, and the comparatively small number of parishes here insert, at a moderate computation, this abbreviate may be reckoned to fall short at least one half. How much of these fines which stand in the decreets in the sheriff books, which I have inserted, were uplifted, I cannot say; but, by particular vouched accounts, come to my hand from the shire of Fife, and that only in twelve or fourteen parishes, I find upwards of fifty thousand pounds actually paid; and, considering the expenses in attendance, the money given to the attendants on these courts, and the exorbitant compositions the sufferers were at length obliged to, we may well reckon them near the sums here. I shall now insert this abbreviate of fines, if once I had noticed that none of the fines imposed upon every turn by the council decreets, upon multitudes, for conventicles, noncompearance, &c. are insert in this account: these the reader hath scattered up and down the history, and I have not had time to gather them up; neither have I cast in innumerable instances of losses of horses, kine, sheep, and whole years' crops, in the informations that are in my hands, those not being liquidate, and I wanting leisure for this, though I am persuaded they would amount to a prodigious sum. Perhaps some of the parishes may be inserted in other shires than they belong to, but I have kept by the lists before me.

Abbreviate of Fines and Losses in the different Shires and Parishes, from particular information in the Author's hands.

SHIRE OF EDINBURGH.

Parishes of West-Calder............................L.2,958	16 8
Livingstone........................... 1,787	17 8
Abercorn 1,243	0 0
Temple 3,713	6 8
9,703	1 0
Shire of Forrest........................... 50,649	0 0
Parishes of Eskdale and Ettrick 2,480	0 0
53,129	0 0

THE AUTHOR'S PREFACE

SHIRE OF BERWICK.

By the Earl of Hume	L.26,666	13	4
Parish of Gordon	3,328	4	C
Lassiden	137	13	4
	30,132	10	8

Shire of Roxburgh, by Letters of Horning, executed August 11, 1684.	253,654	0	0
Parishes of Ancrum	3,349	6	8
Hassindean	11,231	13	4
Bowden	430	14	0
Smallholm	612	0	0
Melrose	40,823	12	0
Stow and Heriot-muir	8,332	13	4
Selkirk-forest	26,666	13	4
Stitchil	9,413	14	0
Logerwood	1,666	13	4
Earlston	781	16	8
Hownam	747	12	0
Oxnam	2,484	0	0
Jedburgh	6,480	0	0
	366,774	8	8

SHIRE OF PEEBLES.

Parish of Peebles	978	6	0
Traquair	374	2	0
Kirkwood, Eddleston, Linton	506	16	0
Tweedmuir	1,130	0	0
	2,989	4	0

SHIRE OF ANNANDALE.

Parish of Johnston	7,512	1	8
Lochmaben	4,460	5	0
St. Mungo	1,178	0	0
Tunnergirth, Hutton, Wamfrey, &c.	2,134	14	8
	15,285	1	4

SHIRES OF NITHSDALE AND DUMFRIES.

Parish of Closeburn and Dalgerno	3,006	5	8
More in Closeburn	665	13	4
Morton	333	6	8
Keir	159	0	0
Kirkmaho	2,142	0	0
Tindram	2,473	6	8
Kirkmichael and Garil	343	0	0
Tinwald	968	5	0
Torthorwald	4,192	11	0
Carlaverock	372	0	0
Glencairn	2,313	6	8
Penpont	182	13	4
	41,152	8	4
More from this Shire at Pentland	9,517	9	10
	23,669	18	2

SHIRE OF GALLOWAY.

In the Stewartry	2,869	14	0
Burgh of Stranraer	2,365	5	4
Kirkcudbright	2,184	18	4
Parish of Borg	6,472	0	0
Twinam	813	0	0
Anworth	333	6	8
Kirkmabrick	563	12	8
Lochrooton	519	13	4
New abbay	948	0	0
Old Luce	6,871	0	0
New Luce	6,506	14	4
Balmughie	363	16	0

Burgh of Partan	L. 5,087	0	0
Orr	889	13	4
Corsmichael	300	0	0
Carsfairn	18,597	0	0
Balmaclellan	2,126	0	0
Dalry	3,200	0	0
Kells	9,511	10	8
Penningham	4,490	0	0
	74,832	4	8
More fined before Pentland, besides Middleton's fines	41,982	0	0
	116,814	4	8

SHIRE OF AYR.

Parish of Ballantree	3,619	14	0
Colmonel	6,545	16	8
Dalmelington	15,780	0	0
Barr	20,856	10	4
More in that Parish	417	6	4
Straiton	6,748	0	0
Kirkmichael and Maybole	5,953	0	0
Muirkirk	5,726	6	8
Kirkoswald	8,104	0	0
Sorn	1,800	0	0
Dalgen	1,118	6	8
Cumnock	5,366	13	4
Auchinleck	1,646	0	0
Loudon	2,713	12	4
Kilmarnock	31,700	0	0
Other Parishes here	6,715	0	0
By the Highland Host, 1678,	137,499	6	0
	258,309	13	2

SHIRE OF RENFREW.

Parish of Eaglesham	3,645	0	0
Cathcart	1,256	1	0
Eastwood	650	0	0
Lochwinnoch	4,579	13	4
By Decreet against Gentlemen, about 1673,	368,031	13	4
	378,162	7	8

SHIRE OF LANARK.

Parish of Libberton	232	8	0
Whatwhan	182	0	6
Biggar	1,071	5	0
Walston	308	8	0
Dunsyre	177	12	0
Carmichael	266	13	0
Carnwath	6,739	19	8
Lanark	5000	0	0
Cambusnethan	6,947	0	6
Dalziel	35	0	0
Shotts	1,708	10	8
Bothwell	11,206	0	0
New Monkland	16,674	5	4
Old Monkland	2,666	13	4
Cambuslang	3,864	19	0
Hamilton	22,681	6	4
Glassford	911	13	0
Dalserf	773	6	8
Evandale or Strathaven	54,085	0	0
Kilbride	19,570	6	8
Carmunnock	23,299	2	4
Rutherglen	2,171	6	4
Govan	1,444	6	8
Calder	837	0	0
Kirkintilloch	700	0	0
	183,554	3	4

TO THE SECOND VOLUME.   xlix

SHIRE OF FIFE, BY THE SHERIFF BOOKS OF CUPAR.			
Parish of Scoonie	L.6,800	0	0
Cameron	8,268	0	0
More from the same	13,600	0	0
Deninno	1,400	0	0
St. Andrews	10,400	0	0
Cairnbee	5,712	0	0
St. Fillans	13,419	0	0
Leuchars	16,340	0	0
Cleish	8,700	0	0
Portmoak	32,700	0	0
Aberdour	2,100	0	0
Dalgety	8,400	0	0
Markinch	5,000	0	0
Falkland	3,300	0	0
Auchterdeering	5,040	0	0
Kinglassie	11,800	0	0
Carnock and Dovehill	6,700	9	0
Dysart	12,000	0	0
Beith	600	0	0
Auchtertool	4,500	0	0
Abbotshall	10,700	0	0
Kinghorn	1,500	0	0
Largo	17,400	0	0
Newburn	2,700	0	0
Burntisland	22,500	0	0
Inverkeithing	13,400	0	0
Aberdour more	1,200	0	0
Kilrinnie	4,200	0	0
Anstruther-wester	4,800	0	0
Anstruther-easter	8,100	0	0
Pittenweem	3,300	0	0
St. Minnan	5,500	0	0
Ely	2,700	0	0
Kilconquhar	8,500	0	0
Munzie	900	0	0
Logie	6,100	0	0
Ceres	12,506	0	0
Orwel	1,500	0	0
Ferry	2,700	0	0
Balmerino	700	0	0
Kembach and Darsie	1,800	0	0
Cult	4,500	0	0
Lesly	10,600	0	0
Kennoway	300	0	0
Cupar	3,700	0	0
Kirkaldy	10,600	0	0
Colesse	1,200	0	0
Kettle	1,500	0	0
Hindlie	2,100	0	0
Auchtermuchty	1,800	0	0
Dunfermline	9,600	0	0
Ballingie	600	0	0
Tory	5,000	0	0
Stramiglo	5,071	0	0
By the Sheriff books of Falkland, S. J. Cal.	30,000	0	0
	396,050	9	0

SHIRE OF PERTH.

By the Sheriff books there, where the extracts do not many times distinguish the parishes.			
Persons, without parishes named	107,400	0	0
Parish of Forgundennie	11,335	10	0
Fossoquhie	3,000	0	0
Kippen	2,000	0	0
Town and Parish of Perth	44,000	0	0
Perth	167,735	10	0
Summa totalis	1,743,999	18	8

Middleton's Fines in the History	L.1,017,353	6	8
Gentlemen in Renfrewshire, 1684, as in History	237,333	6	8
Gentlemen in Dunbartonshire, as in the History	55,200	0	0
Gentlemen in the shire of Murray, as in the History, 1685,	120,933	6	8
	1,430,820	0	0
Summa totalis	3,174,819	18	0

This is the shortest view I could give the reader of the fines, during this period; a vast number of others are to be found in the history itself, and far greater numbers of fines imposed and exacted, are not come to my knowledge.

Since, in this history, I have frequent occasion to name the persons I speak of by their offices, I thought it might be convenient for the reader to subjoin here a list of persons, in such offices, from the restoration to the revolution, as ordinarily come to be spoken of in this work, and I may well begin with the bishops, they being, as I have often remarked, the springs of much of the persecution I have described, though the share of some of them was greater than that of others.

ARCHBISHOPS OF ST. ANDREWS.
1662. Messrs. James Sharp.
1679. Alexander Burnet.
1684. Arthur Ross.

BISHOPS OF DUNKELD.
1662. Messrs. George Halyburton.
1675. Henry Guthrie.
1677. William Lindsay.
1679. Andrew Bruce.
1686. John Hamilton.

ABERDEEN.
1662. Messrs. David Mitchell.
1663. Alexander Burnet.
1664. Patrick Scougal.
1682. George Halyburton.

MURRAY.
1662. Messrs. Murdoch Mackenzie.
1677. James Atkin.
1680. Colin Falconer.
1686. ―― Ross.
1688. William Hay.

BRECHIN.
1662. Messrs. David Strachan.
1671. Robert Lawrie.
1678. George Halyburton.
1682. Robert Douglas.
1684. Alexander Cairncross.
1684. James Drummond.

DUNBLANE.
1662. Messrs. Robert Leighton.
1671. James Ramsay.
1684. Robert Douglas.

g

THE AUTHOR'S PREFACE TO THE SECOND VOLUME.

Ross.
1662. Messrs.	John Paterson, Father.
1679.	Alexander Young.
1684.	James Ramsay.

Caithness.
1662. Messrs.	Patrick Forbes.
1662.	Andrew Wood.

Orkney.
1662. Messrs.	Thomas Sydserf.
1665.	Andrew Honneyman.
1677.	Murdoch Mackenzie.
1688.	Andrew Bruce.

Edinburgh.
1662. Messrs.	George Wishoart.
1671.	Alexander Young.
1679.	John Paterson, Son.
1688.	——— Ross.

Archbishops of Glasgow.
1662. Messrs.	Andrew Fairfoul.
1664.	Alexander Burnet.
1670.	Robert Leighton.
1674.	Alexander Burnet restored
1679.	Arthur Ross.
1684.	Alexander Cairncross.
1686.	John Paterson S.

Galloway.
1662. Messrs.	James Hamilton.
1673.	John Paterson S.
1680.	James Atken.
1688.	John Gordon.

Argyle.
1662. Messrs.	David Fletcher.
1666.	William Scrogie.
1675.	Arthur Ross.
1679.	Colin Falconer.
1686.	Hector Maclean.

Isles.
1662.	Messrs. Robert Wallace.
1677.	Andrew Wood.
1680	Archibald Graham.

In this list I have marked the year of the admission of each bishop, and the entry of his successor; and, save the time of vacancy, which generally was very short, the intermediate space is the time of their continuance in their sees.

The lord high chancellors in this interval were as follows:

1660.	The Earl of Glencairn.
1665.	Rothes.
1680.	Aberdeen.
1684.	Perth.

I might go on to the rest of the officers of state, secretaries, justice general, advocate, and others; but the time of their admission and continuance, may be found in the history itself, from which I shall no longer detain the reader.

Eastwood, May 1, 1722.

Edinburgh, May 16, 1722.

When I resolved to publish this history I could not but expect attacks from the advocates for the bloodshed and severity of the reigns here described; and it was a little strange to me, that my first volume has been now abroad for a year, and nothing this way hath appeared. After my history was printed off, this day I had a printed letter put in my hand, dated May 10th, and signed Philanax.

This performance is so indiscreet, low, and flat, that I can scarce prevail with myself to think it deserves any public notice, yet having room for a few lines in this place. I shall observe once for all, that I don't look on myself as obliged to take any notice of unsupported assertions, scurrilous innuendos, and unmannerly attacks of this nature; they do a great deal of more hurt to the authors and publishers, than to me or this history. I pretend to no talent in railing and Billingsgate, and shall never be able to make any returns this way.

When the letter-writer's friend publishes his history, though recriminations don't affect me, yet I doubt not but it will be considered. The sketch he is pleased to communicate, seems to be taken from the unsupported and ill natured memoirs published under bishop Guthry's name. Any thing that will set the period spoken of in a true and just light, will be acceptable to me and all lovers of truth; but for the historian's own sake, I hope he will take care not to copy after his friend's indiscreet and indecent way, else I am of opinion nobody will reckon themselves obliged to lose time in reading his large work.

PRELIMINARY DISSERTATION.

WERE we to form an estimate of Mr Wodrow's History, by the rules which rhetoricians have laid down for historical composition, we should be apt to draw most unfavourable conclusions. If that alone is entitled to the name of History which bears its reader along with the flow of a regular and well-compacted narrative; which descends not to the minutiæ of private and domestic life; and which gives us the substance and the results of information acquired, rather than the information itself; then, most assuredly, will the work of our venerable author be found to occupy no very lofty niche in the gallery of historical portraiture. But it is the part of candour to judge of a work, not by a standard of our own, however just and equitable it may be, but by a fair and impartial estimate of the object which the author had in his eye at the time, and of the fidelity with which that object has been realized. Had the "History of the Sufferings of the Church of Scotland" been composed according to the rules laid down by the critics, and so admirably exemplified by many ancient and many modern names, we might unquestionably have had a better written narrative; but the church and the world would have lost much by the exchange. As the case actually stands, we have presented to us a most valuable depository of minute and well-authenticated facts, bearing with more or less aptitude on the general character of the period. We have a most exact and vivid picture of the manners of the age; and sketches of the leading individuals drawn to the life, in their actions and habits. We are admitted behind the scenes, and favoured with a view of the ever shifting agency by which the machine of public affairs is kept in play. We see passing in array before us, not only the great actors on the stage, but their less prominent, though not less important minions; while the great public men themselves are stripped of their assumed disguise, and exhibited exactly as they are. The stately march of national events is so associated with the incidents of private and familiar life, as to produce a result not altogether in harmony with the established rules of historical composition, and yet singularly advantageous to the real student of human character. It is not the political, nor the literary, nor the constitutional, nor even the merely ecclesiastical history of the period that is given; but while there is a mixture more or less of them all, there is what the author had professedly in his eye throughout, the internal "history of the sufferings of the church," both in its associated capacity, and in the experience of individuals. The rigid historian might have confined himself almost exclusively to the *first* of these, and on this principle an interesting narrative might have been formed. But it is by the union of both objects that our historian has realized his own judiciously selected plan, and now stands forth to our merited regard as the only minute, and comprehensive, and faithful annalist of the period. *Such another* historian of the eventful era, from 1638 to 1660, is still a desideratum in our national literature; and I verily believe, that with all their prejudices, the Scotts and the Sharpes, and the Russels, and the Pearsons, of anti-covenanting celebrity, would be quite overjoyed to meet with such another.

That the editor of Kirkton's History, and the editor of archbishop Leighton's works, opposite as they are in all matters of a religious and ecclesiastical bearing, should unite in terming Wodrow a "disingenuous" historian, may at first view surprise us. But let it not be forgotten, that these two authors coincide in all those politico-ecclesiastical sentiments, which necessarily induce a cordial dislike of such a work as that in question. A thousand times more astonishing would it have been, to find *praise* lavished on such a work by the high-toned adherents of the hierarchy; or by the patrons of arbitrary power, passive obedience, and the *jus divinum* of kings. Wodrow's history is the work of a man who breathed the air of freedom, and who wished that all men should breathe it along with him. He wrote professedly for the purpose of supporting the interests of civil and religious liberty; and the tendency of every page of his work is, to endear to our hearts the blessings secured to us by the revolution settlement and the Hanoverian succession. He wrote under the influence of a well-grounded attachment to the presbyterian form of church government, not only as the most scriptural, but also as the most advantageous to all the best interests of the people. That such principles and attachments should show themselves in his work; nay, that they should pervade it in every part, and give to it, as a whole, a peculiar tone and texture, is not at all surprising. And the only thing to surprise us would be, to find that a book so constructed and so characterized, should pass, without censure, the ordeal of men, who can have no cordial sympathy with such principles and such attachments.

As an appropriate set-off against the combined opinion of Messrs Sharpe and Pearson, we have it in our power to present the united suffrages of men who differed also in sentiment among themselves, and from the author whose work they praise. Mr Laing had little in common with Wodrow and his heroes in regard to their marked and peculiar sentiments on religion, and he seems to have looked upon both as rather over-keen and enthusiastic; but he bears a clear and oft-repeated testimony to the pains-taking fidelity of the historian, while he finds in his printed and in his manuscript records, a never-failing mine of accurate and valuable information.* Lord Holland, in his biographical notice prefixed to his uncle's posthumous historical work, has given us some most striking and satisfactory instances of Mr Fox's extreme, and even anxious accuracy, as to facts even the most minute; and yet this distinguished individual has, without any regard whatever to existing controversies, given it as his undisguised opinion, that "no historical facts are better ascertained, than the accounts of them which are to be found in Wodrow." Mr Alexander Chalmers, the laborious and learned author of the "Biographical Dictionary," says of the same work; "It is written with a fidelity that has seldom been disputed; and confirmed by a large mass of public and private records." Mr Dibdin, in his "Bibliography," gives to this "valuable" work, as he terms it, "his strong recommendation." Dr Robert Watt, the indefatigable compiler of that stupendous work, the "Bibliotheca Britannica," reports of Wodrow's history, that it has been "written with a fidelity seldom equalled." Need we appeal to the united sentiments of two such writers as Dr M'Crie and Dr Cook, who, though differing materially on many topics, both political and ecclesiastical, do combine most cordially in their high estimate of the merits of Wodrow, as a faithful and accurate historian? Or need we, in addition to the recorded testimonies of such individuals, appeal to the august tribunal of public opinion, which has justly awarded to Wodrow the meed of incredible industry, minute fidelity, and the most commendable candour?

In order to vindicate successfully the high claims of Wodrow to the best qualities of a historian, and to show the groundlessness of the charge which has of late been brought against him, we beg the attention of our readers to some important particulars. —In the *first* place; the statements of our historian were not questioned at the time of

---

* Hist. of Scotland, vol. ii. p. 398.

their first publication. We do not deny that a deep sensation was excited by the work; and that a spirit of violent hostility was roused; and that there was every wish felt and expressed to have its testimony set aside. Nor do we deny that the author was rudely assailed with violent pasquinades and threats of personal violence; while the friendly reception which his majesty and the members of the royal family gave to the book, galled exceedingly the still sanguine adherents of the old dynasty.* But we beg to know, was any formal attempt made to rebut or to controvert its statements? When the advocates of presbyterianism had recourse to *argument* in support of their polity, there was no lack of replies on the part of their opponents. In covenanting times we find a Maxwell and a Baillie in close combat together; and immediately after the revolution settlement we find the learning and the acuteness of Forrester, and Rule, and Jameson, and Anderson, met in battle array by the respectable talents and literature of Bishop Sage, and Dr Monro; † and never was the episcopal and presbyterian controversy managed on both sides with greater ability.‡ Whence then is it that when the unpretending historian comes forth with his two overwhelming folios of facts and documents illustrative of the Sufferings of the Church of Scotland under the episcopalian ascendancy, no pen was drawn to vindicate the *good old cause*, and no effort was made to prove an *alibi* for the pannel at the bar? Reasonings for presbyterianism might be opposed by counter reasonings for episcopacy; and the records of a distant antiquity might admit of varied interpretations. But "facts," as Wodrow says, are " stubborn, ill-natured things" and will not easily be set out of the way.

It is rather a curious circumstance, that while the publication of Wodrow's History was beheld by the episcopalian party with silent dismay, the work was most furiously attacked from a quarter the most remote from episcopacy. The more keen adherents of the ultra-presbyterian interest, such as Patrick Walker and John Macmain, commenced a most furious onset upon the worthy historian. § Why? Because in their opinion he had not done sufficient justice to the characters and the deeds of those worthies who, in their zeal for what they held to be pure presbyterianism, had gone perhaps a little beyond the bounds of moderation. With the merits of *that* controversy we have at present nothing to do; and the notes which accompany this edition of the history will present a fairer opportunity of noticing some of the minuter features of the questions at issue. But we beg particular attention to the fact that the only opposition which was made to Wodrow, was from a quarter *the very antipode* of the episcopalian hierarchy. He was not charged with saying *too much against* the dominant system of prelacy; but he was charged with *saying too little in favour* of the more stanch adherents of suffering presbyterianism. And this we hold to be a very fair presumption in favour of the

---

* In the MS. volume of Wodrow's correspondence for 1722, 23, (Adv. lib.) there are some curious specimens of the manner in which the author was met by his opponents, with threats both of *literary* and of *personal* revenge; none of which appear ever to have been put in execution. There is also an interesting series of letters from Dr Fraser, descriptive of the reception which was given to the work by his majesty and the members of the royal family, and other august personages; a reception sufficiently flattering to have elevated with no common emotion the mind even of the humble and self-denied presbyter of Eastwood.

† Principal of the university of Edinburgh, but deprived at the revolution for his adherence to James.

‡ I allude not here of course to those miserable attacks that were made upon the constitution and discipline of the church of Scotland, by such wretched drivellers as Hickes, Calder, Caddel, Rhind, and others; and the malignant effusions of these men I had thought were long ago consigned to the " tomb of all the Capulets," when lo! the editor of Kirkton and of Law, like a true resurrection-man, has brought them before an insulted public in the shape of numerous references to such books as Ravilliac Redivivus, Scotch Presbyterian Eloquence, &c. &c. This last work the late lord Woodhouselee in his Life of Lord Kaimes, has characterized as " *an infamous libel.*"

§ Walker was the author of the Lives of Peden, Cargill, &c., lately republished under the name of " Biographia Presbyteriana;" and Macmain was the editor of M'Ward's "Earnest Contendings," &c. where specimens of the controversy may be seen.

moderation and candour of our author.—Nor let it be thought that such individuals as Walker and Macmain were *the only kind of persons* who would think it worth *their while* to attack the obscure pastor of Eastwood. His "history" was *not obscure;* and the man who for years was the regular correspondent and personal friend of bishop Nicolson and Dr Lloyd; and the clergyman whom the Bartlett's Buildings' Society, with all the bishops at its head, did not think it discreditable to associate with them as an honorary member, was certainly not *beneath the notice* of the very proudest adherent of episcopacy.

In the *second* place; It is a singular and a most valuable feature in Mr Wodrow as a historian, that he has not only given us *his own* narrative of events, but likewise the *original documents* whence that narrative has been drawn. With the *opinions* of a historian we have, properly speaking, nothing to do; and every reader is at perfect liberty to accord with the sentiments which Wodrow has expressed, or to differ from them precisely as he pleases. When we speak of a historian as "ingenuous" and candid, we do not mean to say of him that he is in all his judgments of things perfectly exact and true; or that even in his statements of facts he possesses all the infallibility of inspiration. Our meaning is to be ascertained by the established usage of language in such cases; and we claim for Wodrow the character of ingenuousness, on this specific ground among others, that the statements of the text he has put it in our power to verify by an actual production in the notes and in the appendix, of the great and leading documents on which his statements are grounded. It is true, he has not published *all* the original papers from which he obtained information, but most of them have been preserved; and after a frequent and rigid examination of these both by friends and by foes, what mighty discoveries have been made to the discredit of the historian? Perhaps it is to be regretted that the venerable author adhered so rigidly to his plan of abridging and condensing the substance of his originals, rather than giving the articles themselves entire. * But as most of these documents are still in preservation, frequent opportunities have been taken both by Mr Laing and others, to examine the originals, and to compare them with the copies or abridgments given of them by Wodrow; and the result has been in every instance highly to the credit of the historian. Within these few weeks we have examined with particular care the largest collection of archbishop Sharp's letters perhaps in existence, that namely among the Wodrow MSS. in the library of the University of Glasgow. We have compared with these the printed copies or abridgments as published in the Introduction to Wodrow's History. While in a considerable number of instances an exact copy has been taken; in others, no little talent and judgment have been displayed in the business of abridgment and condensation. As a general result of the inquiry we would say without hesitation, that while the historian does by no means conceal his design of exposing Sharp's treachery, he had it in his power from these documents to have held him up to detestation in still blacker colours, had he quoted all the expressions of affected devotion—all the solemn protestations of attachment to presbytery—all the specimens of mean adulation—and all the bitter vituperations against

---

* Wodrow's plan of *abridging* papers does not necessarily injure either side; and he applies it to both. Whatever were his grounds of preference, it was his deliberate choice. In Redpath's letter, 3d August 1717, (MS.) he refers to a MS. which had been sent him for review. This was a copy of the *Introduction* to the History of the Sufferings; which copy is now in the Advocate's library with corrections and hints in Redpath's hand, of which the author has availed himself. Among these hints Redpath observes: "I think the letters should have been extracted in the first person. It would be more natural, smooth, and intelligible, and carry more authority, especially where the extracts are long." Yet, in the face of this opinion, with all his estimation of Redpath's judgment, and while adopting many of his alterations, he adheres to his own plan.

his opponents, which these letters contain.* We have also examined the parochial and other returns, from which Wodrow compiled his accounts; and the result has been favourable alike to the laborious industry, and the minute fidelity of the author. It is true, that a considerable number of documents have been brought to light since the history was published; but with the exception of the account of the earl of Argyle's expedition, on which the narratives of Mr Bryson and Sir Patrick Hume have thrown some new light, the discovery of these documents has not effected any material change on the statement of transactions as given by Wodrow; and even although it had, is an author responsible for not availing himself of the use of documents whose very existence was unknown to him?

In the *third* place; The veracity of Wodrow has been farther established by the testimony of historians at the time, and other published sources of evidence. Bishop Burnet published his History of his Own Times immediately after our author had given to the world his History of the Sufferings of the Church of Scotland; and these two works, however different and even opposite were the sentiments of their authors, confirm each other in all the material transactions of the period. Varieties of statement there no doubt must be; and we know that the particular leanings of an author will imperceptibly influence more or less the character of his narrative. But it is extremely interesting to mark the harmony in all the leading transactions of the period, between two writers who were altogether independent of each other, and who belonged to opposite communions. With the bishop's *sentiments* indeed either regarding matters of government in general, or the character of the covenanters in particular, we have nothing to do; but we appeal to his corroborative testimony as to an unexceptionable witness.

Among later publications we may notice the " Secret and True History of the Church of Scotland," by Kirkton; the " Memorials of Remarkable Things," by Mr Robert Law; Sir George Mackenzie's History of the Affairs of Scotland from 1660 to 1677; Lord Fountainhall's Notes on Scottish Affairs from 1680 to 1701; and the lately published Memoirs of Sir James Turner, written by himself. In the works of various individuals differing from one another in sentiment, we are not to expect an exact harmony of statements or of estimates formed of individual character. But with every allowance for such necessary varieties, it is highly creditable to the character of Wodrow as a historian, that there is so little in these publications which is at variance with the substantial features of his narrative. We believe that some of these works were given to the public professedly with the view of bringing discredit on Wodrow and the Presbyterians; and the notes with which some of them are accompanied place this beyond question.† The disappointment must have been exquisite. Presbyterianism is not responsible for all the vices and all the follies of those who have ranged themselves under her banner; and her best friends will feel no regret that such publications, even with the filthy accompaniments of some of them, should from time to time be given to the world. Truth can never suffer from the most rigid examination; and Wodrow and the covenanters will, when tried in the crucible of a most rigid and not over liberal investigation, "come forth like gold."

There is reason to think that the real objections to Wodrow's History have their origin not so much in the history itself as in the *subject matter* of it.

1. We fear that many cherish a dislike to presbyterianism and the covenanters, from

---

* From the MS. letters in Glasgow college, together with a few more which are preserved in the Advocate's library, and in the MS, collections belonging to the church of Scotland, a very curious and valuable work, with notes and historical illustrations, might be produced under the name perhaps of—*Sharpiana.*

† I refer particularly to Kirkton and Law.

a rooted aversion to that system of theology which is commonly denominated Calvinism. We are not sure whether Mr Pearson himself, though he belongs to what is called the evangelical party in England, is altogether free of this fatal prejudice: and it is perhaps on this account we feel more gratified in thinking that he has been so very successful in furnishing a most satisfactory refutation of the very prejudice in question. Archbishop Leighton in Scotland, like archbishop Cranmer in England, and archbishop Usher in Ireland, was a stanch adherent of Calvinism. In the very opening of his exposition of the first epistle of Peter he makes a clear avowal of his theological sentiments, and he is too candid an expounder, to leave it at all a matter of doubt whether the doctrine of election finds a place in the first chapter of that comprehensive and most valuable epistle. The same system of theology indeed pervades all his writings; and the justly esteemed works of Leighton exhibit a pleasing specimen of what Calvinism is when scripturally explained and practically applied.

Now, the system which the archbishop embraced was precisely what he found embodied in the articles of the church of Scotland; and generally, may we not say universally, embraced throughout the kingdom? In proof of this we have only to look into the writings of presbyterians during the covenanting period—of Binning—of Dickson—of Brown—of Wedderburn—of Hutcheson—of Durham—of Gray—and others likeminded with them; and we find that amid a vast variety of talent, and of style, the same scheme of doctrine predominates in them all. Indeed it is a well established fact, although strangely overlooked by too many modern readers of church history, that in the period of the Stewart persecutions, there was no controversy in Scotland about theological opinions. Amid the contest for modes of government, there was a harmony on all matters of doctrine. In proof of this, we find that so early as 1616 the bishops and a certain number of the clergy were specially empowered to revise "*the Confession of Faith* presented to the assembly, and after mature deliberation to take order that the same may be published." They forthwith proceed to their work, and the result was, a revised edition of the Confession of Faith; and that of the *most rigidly Calvinistic* complexion.*

But perhaps it may be thought that the influence of Laud and the Arminian divines of England, gradually introduced a *modified system* among the adherents of the episcopal interest, and that the theology of that class during the period embraced by Wodrow was very different from the theology of their predecessors in the days of James. We have simply to state in reply, that in 1680 when the obnoxious test was attempted to be forced on the people of Scotland, the oath in which it was embodied ran in the following terms: "I ———, solemnly swear in the presence of the eternal God, whom I invocate as judge and witness of my sincere intention in this my oath; that I own and sincerely profess the true protestant religion contained in the Confession of Faith, recorded in the first parliament of king James VI., and that I believe the same to be founded on and agreeable to the written word of God; and I promise and swear, that I shall adhere thereunto during all the days of my life-time, and shall endeavour to educate my children therein, and shall never consent to any change or alteration thereunto; and that I disown and renounce all such principles, doctrines, or practices, whether popish *or fanatical*, which are contrary unto and inconsistent with the said protestant religion and Confession of Faith."† Thus it appears that in 1680 and in the estimation of the hierarchy of Scotland, the doctrines of a strictly Calvinistic creed were held to be neither "popish" nor "fanatical;" and they are avowed on oath *for the very* purpose of guarding

---

* Calderwood's History, p. 668, 669, where the confession is inserted at full length. *It is far more rigidly Calvinistic than the old confession by Knox in* 1560.

† See the oath at length in Wodrow, vol. II. pp. 193, 194, fol.

the more effectually against these supposed extremes! Indeed the question as to the Anti-Calvinism of the church of England is quite of a modern date. In her purer and better days the Anglican church gloried in being associated in doctrine with the Helvetic and Scottish churches, and *our Knox* was one of the persons employed in revising her articles.* Moreover it is extremely worthy of remark, that while in 1680 the episcopal clergy generally went into the test oath, we find so late as 1692 a very large proportion of them craving admission into the church under the promise, "that they would subscribe the said Confession of Faith and larger and shorter catechisms, confirmed by act of parliament as containing the doctrine of the protestant religion professed in this kingdom." " Such is a short history of all the confessions of faith that were ever received in Scotland since the reformation. All of them were formed upon the Calvinistic scheme, and all of them have been assented to by the episcopal clergy.†" Let us no longer hear, therefore, of the Calvinism of the covenanting age as a butt of ridicule or as a ground of dislike.

Of the *practical effects* of Calvinistic doctrine on the people of Scotland in the days of its greatest ascendancy we have the following description by an eye witness, and one too whose honesty has never been impeached. " At the king's return," says he, "every paroche had a minister, every village hade a school, every family almost had a bible; yea, in most of the country all the children of age could read the scriptures, and were provided of bibles, either by the parents or by their ministers. Every minister was a very full professor of the reformed religion, according to the large confession of faith framed at Westminster by the divines of both nations. Every minister was obliged to preach thrice a-week; to lecture and catechise once, besides other private duties in which they abounded, according to their proportion of faithfulness and abilities. None of them might be scandalous in their conversation or negligent in their office, so long as a presbyterie stood; and among them were many holy in conversation and eminent in gifts; nor did a minister satisfy himself except his ministry had the seal of a divine approbation, as might witness him to be really sent of God. Indeed in many places, the Spirit seemed to be poured out with the word, both by the multitude of the sincere converts, and also by the common work of reformation upon many who never came the length of a communion; there were no fewer than sixty aged people, men and women, who went to school, that even then they might be able to read the scriptures with their own eyes. I have lived many years in a paroch where I never heard an oath, and you might have ridde many a mile before you had heard any: also you could not for a great part of the country have lodged in a family where the Lord was not worshipped by reading, singing, and public prayer. Nobody complained of our church government more than our taverners, whose ordinary lamentation was, their trade was broken, people were become so sober." (Kirkton's History, pp. 68, 69.) When the church of Scotland was restored to her rights at the revolution, we find a candid English writer thus bearing testimony to her moral character. " When we view the soundness and purity of her doctrine, the strictness and severity of her discipline, the decency and order of her worship, the gravity and majesty of her government; when we see the modesty, humility, yet steadiness of her assemblies; the learning, diligence, and faithfulness of her ministers; the awful solemnity of her administration; the obedience, seriousness, and frequency of her people in hearing, and universally an air of sobriety and purity on the whole nation; we must own her to be at this time the best regulated national church in the world, without reflection on any of the other nations where the protestant religion is established and professed." ‡

II. Leighton was a man of a gentle spirit, and he shrunk from the controversy regard-

---

* Burnet's Hist. of the Reformation, III. 212. Strype's Cranmer, p. 273.
† Anderson's Defence of Presbyterianism, pp. 7, 8, 4to.
‡ Defoe's Memoirs of the Church of Scotland, p. 2.

ing *forms of church government.* His residence among the Jansenists on the Continent, and his familiarity with their devotional writings, fostered in him a kind of mystical quietism, not over creditable either to his strength of mind or extent of learning. He fell into the notion that real piety might flourish with equal vigour under any form of ecclesiastical regime; and he renounced his earlier principles and attachments, with a precipitation which his best friends feel it no easy task to vindicate. There is reason to fear that a principle substantially the same with that of the archbishop, prevents not a few from entering with interest into the contests of the persecuting times. They cannot think that a struggle for one form of administration rather than another involved the essentials of Christianity; that a question about hoods and tippets is in other words a question about Christianity itself; or that the command to say, "God bless the king"—was in other words a command to renounce allegiance to the Lord Jesus Christ. They forget that these were rather the symbols of the controversy than the controversy itself; that the first question asked, or the first command given, was uniformly the precursor of other questions and other commands infinitely more stumbling to the conscience; that our forefathers nobly acted on the great rule of all moral contests *obsta principiis;* and that the *principle* involved in all these points of the controversy was one which no consistent protestant can renounce or violate with impunity.

Nothing is more fatally erroneous than the notion, that forms of ecclesiastical polity are all equally favourable to the culture of personal religion. On this principle the reformation would have been crushed in its cradle. What the infinite wisdom of God may see meet to accomplish even in opposition to the strongest resistance of a secularized hierarchy; and what attainments in true godliness individuals may be honoured to make even under the worst form of spiritual domination, it does not become us to define. But of this we are assured by the testimony of ages, that the mightiest barriers that have ever been opposed to the progress of knowledge and religion, have owed their existence principally to the agency of corrupt institutions. The "mighty episcopacy" of Rome has in every age proved itself to be the strongest instrument in extending and perpetuating the corruptions of Antichrist; and just in proportion as the lesser episcopacy of England and of Scotland approximated to it in character, has its influence been more or less malignant. Who were the grand agents in the persecution of the protestants of France? They were the bishops and the priests of an over-bearing hierarchy. And who were the prime movers in the persecution of the covenanters in Scotland? They were the bishops and the priests of a hierarchy substantially the same in spirit, and equally overbearing in its tyrannical control. And what was the reason why the Stuart dynasty displayed such an attachment to the government of prelates? Beyond all question, it was the deeply-rooted conviction—a conviction founded in truth—that episcopacy is far more friendly to absolute monarchy than the genius of what Mr Pearson in his alarms would designate, a *levelling presbyterian democracy.* And is not this a clear evidence that if civil liberty is to flourish in the land, it cannot be under such a system as that which the Stuarts enforced by the rack and the screw; a system nevertheless which the amiable Leighton *in effect* supported, and which too many modern writers seem to look upon with something approaching to complacence. And will Mr Pearson maintain in the face of the nineteenth century, that religion,—spiritual, evangelical, experimental religion,—*can* flourish to any extent on that soil from which the genius of civil liberty has been compelled to take her flight? Deeply indented are the lines which record the fact, that civil and religious liberty have ever gone hand in hand. Despotism in the state has ever cast a withering blight over religion in the church; and the spirit which can tamely succumb to the will of a tyrant, is not the spirit which is most likely to rise in lofty aspirations.

It is painful to think of the real injuries which have been done to the best interests of mankind, by the weak compliances of some of the most amiable of men. The Melancthons, the Cranmers, and the Leightons of the reformed church, possessed not the high qualifications which fitted for the labours and the trials of a radical reformation; and had not bolder spirits taken the lead in the work, a compromise would in all probability have been made of all that is substantially valuable in the reformed cause, on the altar of a misguided liberality.

III. Let it not be thought that considerations of this kind, formed the *only* reason why our covenanting ancestors contended so zealously for what to such men as Leighton and his admirers, may appear to be of inferior importance. Whatever may be the ideas now entertained on the subject, our forefathers cherished an attachment to presbytery, which no considerations, merely human, could set aside. They held it to be the divinely constituted plan of ecclesiastical polity, and therefore obligatory on every one who regarded the scriptures as the oracles of heaven. Even from such an early period as the days of the Culdees, this attachment to presbyterianism had been characteristic of Scotsmen. In the economy of these venerable fathers, we find that a humble abbot, holding no higher rank than that of a presbyter, had the precedence even of bishops; and that while the rest of the world were fast sinking under the load of Romish superstition, an obscure colony in one of the smallest of our western Isles, maintained, in some good degree of purity, the doctrine and the discipline of the New Testament.* When, after a long night of ignorance and superstition, the standard of reformation was erected in Scotland, the spirit of the Culdees revived; and the same zeal for a scriptural system of truth and of discipline, displayed its active energies. In the infancy of the reformed church, it is true, an order of men superior to presbyters was constituted; but this arrangement was expressly declared in the terms of the first book of discipline to be merely a temporary measure; and the superintendants held their power at the will and subject to the review of the general assembly.† Even this limited form of ministerial superintendance was found to be productive of no essential advantages; and in place of nominating successors to the primitive superintendants, the assembly adopted the preferable plan of granting temporary commissions to individual ministers to visit and plant or water the churches. From this period indeed down to the era of the revolution, an incessant struggle was maintained between the two forms of ecclesiastical polity; but there can be no question among those who know any thing of the history of the times, that the general voice of the people of Scotland was in favour of presbytery. Even after the sword of persecution had for not less than twenty-eight years been thinning the ranks of its genuine adherents the presbyterian interest was found to be all-powerful in Scotland; and while it was de clared in the " claim of rights" that " Scotland was reformed by presbyters," it was irrevocably fixed that prelacy shall be laid aside as a national grievance, and that presbyterianism " shall be the only recognized government of Christ's kingdom, in these realms."

---

* See Jameson on the Culdees.

† " We consider that if the ministers whom God hath endowed with his singular graces amongst us, should be appointed to several places there to make their continual residence, that then the greatest part of the realm should be destitute of all doctrine ; which should not only be the occasion of great murmur, but also should be dangerous to the salvation of many : and *therefore*, we have thought it a thing *most expedient at this time*, that from the whole number of godly and learned men now presently in this realm, be selected ten or twelve (for in so many provinces we have divided the whole), to whom charge and commandment should be given to plant and erect kirks, to set, order and appoint ministers to the former order prescribes to the countries that shall be appointed to their care where none are now." First Book of Discipline, chap. VI. *Of Superintendants.*

" They," the Scottish reformers, " intended and designed from the beginning, the government of the church by assemblies and presbyteries, although they could not attain that perfection at first in the infancy of reformation, but gave place to necessity, which in such cases is universal, and in this they followed the example and practice of the churches planted by the apostles." Reformation of Church Government in Scotland cleared from Mistakes ; by the commissioners of Assembly now in London, 4to. 1644, p. 11.

In order to form a just estimate of the value of those interests for which our fathers contended, it is of vast importance to keep in view the leading principle in the contest. Under the papacy, all power ecclesiastical and civil was derived from the ghostly pretended successor of St Peter; and the votaries of this unhallowed usurpation were held bound, by the chains of a most dastardly vassalage, to every iota which the autocrat of Rome was pleased to dictate. Under the secularized hierarchy of the Stuarts, again, the power thus claimed by the pope, was transferred to the supreme chief magistrate of Great Britain, and the right to modify the church and to regulate its concerns, was imperiously claimed by the members of his executive government. In opposition to the pretensions of both parties, our reforming and covenanting ancestors, with a steadiness and a consistency which reflect on them immortal honour, asserted the sovereign majesty of the Divine Head of the church as its lawgiver, and the authority delegated by him to the representatives of his church, to explain and to promulgate his laws, and to enforce their observance. The kingdom of Christ they held to be a *spiritual* kingdom; and although they maintained the grand principle of a church establishment as at once expedient and scriptural, they most decidedly anathematized the doctrine, that the power implied in the exercise of church government was a power created by the state. The opinions propagated by one Erastus, a learned Swiss philosopher and physician, in the sixteenth century, and since his days currently known by the name *Erastianism*, they detested and renounced not less firmly than the opposite, yet parallel system, which derived all power from the spiritual head of the Roman Catholic church. They held, and justly, that the church is a spiritual society, whose members are associated together for spiritual purposes, and regulated by spiritual laws, derived immediately from him whom they revered as their Lord. The leaders or office-bearers of this society they held to be intrusted with a delegated power to interpret and to apply these laws, subject to the inspection of their own courts, and not at all amenable to civil authority. While they asserted these rights, and contended for them, they gave a very decided evidence that they had no wish to *go beyond* them, in the uniform pertinacity with which they refused that " *court power and place to kirkmen*," which their opponents of the hierarchy so ardently prized.

Is Mr Pearson prepared to contest these principles as either irrational or unscriptural? or will any consistent believer in the Old and New Testament, as the only supreme standard of faith and duty, venture to impugn them? And yet these are the very principles for which our venerable forefathers endured trials of " cruel mockings, imprisonments, and death." It was for nobly asserting these principles, and acting on them, that Pont, and Balcanqual, and Black, at an earlier period of the Scottish reformation, were obliged to fly from their native country; and it was this which constituted the crime, and the only crime for which not fewer than six of the best clergymen of whom Scotland could boast, were by James VI. condemned to be executed, although considerations of expediency prevented the execution of the sentence.* And what, we ask, formed the " head and front" of the accusation against Mr James Guthry of Stirling? It was his declinature of the king's jurisdiction in things sacred, while he was willing and ready at all times to discharge the duties of civil obedience. Among the first and most prominent acts of the first parliament held in Scotland after the restoration of Charles II. we find the " act concerning religion and church government, in which his majesty " makes it his care to settle and secure the government of the church, in such a frame as shall be most agreeable to the word of God, most suitable to monarchical government, and most complying with the public peace and quiet of the kingdom." Following up this stretch of the royal prerogative, different acts were

---

* Calderwood's Hist. A. D. 1606.

passed asserting "the royal supremacy, in all matters and over all persons, ecclesiastical as well as civil;" and the proceedings of the court in consequence, furnish an affecting comment on the principles thus avowed. The tendency of such enactments was to lay the church at the feet of an absolute monarch; and had our fathers yielded to such usurpations, they would have at once renounced their characters as independent men and as consistent Christians, and forfeited their claim to the gratitude of posterity. Sir George Mackenzie seems to select it as the highest crime that churchmen could commit;— their presuming " to hold meetings of synodical and general assemblies without being called or sanctioned by the king."* In the present day we deem it no heresy and no treason to hold the doctrine that church courts, as deriving their being and their rights from the Lord Jesus Christ, have an *inherent title* to convene for the transaction of their appropriate business, whenever they shall see cause. Our church acknowledges *no earthly head.* She holds directly of her Divine Lord; and every deviation from this principle is in so far a dereliction of her dearest and most essential interests.

IV. We are not prepared to maintain that, in no instance did our forefathers deviate from their first principles, either on the one hand by *falling below* them, or on the other, by carrying them to an *undue length.* In troublous times, and when men's minds are disturbed by painful apprehensions, and when oppression distracts the spirits even of the wisest of men, we are not to be surprised if in some instances things were carried to an extreme. It is certain that throughout the whole period which Wodrow's history has embraced, the persecuting party acted *systematically* on the principle of setting at nought the essential privileges and rights of the presbyterian church as a corporate body; and if in the noble struggle for the maintenance of these, a few excesses were committed, this is nothing more than might have naturally been expected in the order of things. At no time does it appear that the idea of taking up arms in opposition to the government of the country was regularly and systematically resolved on by the general body of presbyterians; and it is clear beyond all question, that the rising, first at Pentland, and afterwards at Bothwell, was the result of circumstances unpremeditated and unforeseen. Previously to the affair at Pentland, the country had groaned for six years under the grossest tyranny, and her sons had seen their dearest rights, civil and ecclesiastical, torn from them and trampled under foot. Prior to the affair of Bothwell Bridge, nearly twenty years of insult, oppression, and cruelty, had passed over unhappy Scotland; and our wonder is, not that such skirmishes as those of Drumclog and Bothwell should have been the issue, but that the people did not rise up as one man to inflict summary vengeance on their wicked oppressors.†

That resistance to lawful authority—even when that authority, so called, has in point of fact set at nought *all law*—is in no instance to be vindicated; will be held by those only who are the devotees of arbitrary power and passive obedience. The principles of Mr Rutherford's *Lex Rex,* however obnoxious they may be to such men, are substantially the principles on which all government is founded, and without which the civil magistrate would become a curse rather than a blessing to a country. They are the very principles which lie at the basis of the British constitution, and by whose tenure the house of Brunswick does at this very moment hold possession of the throne of these realms.‡ All government is established for the good of the people who are under it. Between a king and his subjects there is an implied and virtual contract; and the

---

* Vindication of the Government of Charles II.
† With an obvious intent to blacken the presbyterian interest in Scotland, Sir G. Mackenzie in the appendix to his " Vindication," includes among the generally recognized expressions of the sentiments of the presbyterians, the Sanquhar and Queensferry declarations, and the mad ravings of the notorious John Gibb! " This is too bad."
‡ See a scarce but able pamphlet entitled, " An Inquiry into the measures of submission to supreme authority," published at London in 1688, in defence of the revolution settlement.

duties of allegiance and submission carry along with them the corresponding duties comprehended in government according to law. The king is not the legislator; he is only the executor of law, and is himself amenable to the laws of his country with the humblest of his subjects. It is, indeed, a very delicate matter to determine *in the abstract* the precise point at which obedience to a tyrannical government is no longer binding, and resistance becomes a duty. Perhaps it is well for all parties that such a question should have difficulties thrown around it, and that its solution should be hid amid the obscurities of doubt. But surely there *is* a limit, and blessed be God our country has on more than one occasion found it out and nobly acted on it.* The conduct of the actors in the scenes at Rutherglen, at Sanquhar, and at Torwood, in disowning the king and excommunicating him and his adherents, is, indeed, justly censurable, as rash and unwarranted. But we beg to know, wherein did the primary principles avowed and acted on these occasions, differ from those principles which, in the course of a very few years thereafter, roused the dormant spirit of the country, and chased the oppressor from the throne? " When the Lord," says the author of *Lex Rex*, " shall be pleased to grant that to us which concerns religion, the beauty of his house, the propagating of the gospel, the government of the Lord's kingdom, without popery, prelacy, unwritten traditions and ceremonies—*let his majesty try our loyalty with what commands he shall be pleased to lay on us, and see if we be found rebellious.*"† " A king," said king James in his speech to the parliament, 1609, " a king governing in a settled kingdom, *ceaseth to be a king*, and descendeth into a tyrant, so soon as he leaveth to rule by his lawes, much more when he begineth to invade his subjects, persones, rights, and liberties; to set up an arbitrary power, to impose unlawful taxes, raise forces, and make warre upon his subjects, whom he should protect and rule in peace; to pillage, plunder, waste, and sporte his kingdom; imprison, murder, and destroy his people in a hostile manner, to captivate them to his pleasure." It is well known that our king James, and Charles I., and likewise queen Elizabeth, did, with the consent of parliament, assist the protestants in Germany, the Netherlands, and France, when struggling against their unprincipled oppressors in these kingdoms; and it is also well known, that the conduct of the covenanting brethren in Scotland was vindicated at the revolution, when the parliament of Scotland "in prosecution of the *claim of right*" rescinded all the forfeitures and fines passed against those who had been in arms at Pentland and Bothwell, and pronounced them void and null from the beginning. After mentioning a vast number of names, the act proceeds; " likeas, their majesties and their estates, rehabilitate, reintegrate and restore so many of the said persons as are living, and the *memory of them that are deceast*, their heirs, successors, and posterity, to their good fame, and worldly honour."‡ Of even the most violent of the Scottish covenanters, we may say in the language of an eloquent writer, " Their standard on the mountains of Scotland indicated to the vigilant eye of William that the nation was ripening for a change. They expressed what others thought, uttering the indignation and the groans of a spirited and oppressed people. They investigated and taught, under the guidance of feeling, the reciprocal obligations of kings and subjects, the duty of self-defence and of resisting tyrants, the generous principle of assisting the oppressed, or, in their language, *helping the Lord against the mighty*. These subjects, which have been investigated by philosophers in the closet, and adorned with eloquence in the senate, were then illustrated by men of feeling in the field. While lord Russel, and Sydney, and other enlightened patriots in England, were plotting

---

* " It was the great principle of the house of commons, that the power of the king, like every other power in the constitution, was limited by the laws, and was legally to be resisted when it trespassed beyond them." *Tales of a Grandfather* by Sir Walter Scott, vol. i. p. 181.
† Rutherford's Letter on the Restoration of Charles II. dated St Andrews, 1660.
‡ M'Crie's Vindication of the Covenanters.—Christian Instructor, vol. xiv. p. 192.

against Charles, from a conviction that his right was forfeited, the Cameronians in Scotland, under the same conviction, had the courage to declare war against him. Both the plotters and the warriors fell; but their blood watered the plant of renown, and succeeding ages have eaten the pleasant fruit."*

In the history of Scotland two things are very remarkable, as illustrative of the political bearings of the presbyterian system. The one is, that during the period when England was rent by endless divisions of political sentiment, the presbyterians of Scotland were, almost to a man, the staunch friends of a monarchical government. The other is, that the experience of nearly a century and a half has proved beyond contradiction, not only that presbyterianism, whether established or only tolerated, is perfectly consistent with the best interests of the British constitution, but likewise that in times of danger and alarm, presbyterians have ever been foremost in manifesting loyalty to their king, and patriotic attachment to their country.

V. But "THE COVENANT!" says Mr Pearson, "*that bitter morsel!*"—not so "bitter" as he would persuade us.—While it was relished by men of all ranks and classes in Scotland itself, it was not disliked by those whose sentiments Mr P. and his adherents must treat at least with respect. The "national covenant" was first subscribed by the king's majesty and his household in the year 1580, and thereafter by persons of all ranks in the year 1581, by ordinance of the lords of secret council, and acts of the general assembly. In 1590 it was subscribed again by all sorts of persons; and along with it a general band for maintenance of the true Christian religion, and the preservation of the king's person. In 1638, 1639, it was repeatedly subscribed by "lords and gentlemen, burgesses, ministers, and commons," and if it shall be contended that this was not a "lawful deed," we beg to notice that it was very soon ratified by solemn act of parliament, first in 1638, then in 1640, and thereafter by king Charles I. himself in 1641.† His son Charles II., subscribed the national covenant, and at the same time the solemn league and covenant at Spey, in June 1650, and at Scone on the day of his coronation in 1651. The solemn league and covenant was likewise ratified by parliament in 1644 and 1649. Thus, these several deeds acquired all the authority of public documents, and may be regarded as the expression of national sentiment. The object of the national covenant, and of the solemn league and covenant, was substantially one, namely, as king Charles I. in his $E_{ι κ ω ν}$ $B α σ ι λ ι κ η$ terms it with great propriety, " to establish religion in purity and the kingdom in peace." " Although," says Dr M'Crie, " covenants have often been condemned as unwarranted in a religious point of view, and dangerous in a political, yet are they completely defensible upon the principles both of reason and of revelation; and by cementing union, by producing mutual confidence, and strengthening the motives to fidelity and diligence, among those who are embarked in the same cause, they have frequently proved of the greatest utility for promoting reformation in churches and nations, for maintaining open profession of religion after it had been attained, and for securing the religious and political privileges of men. The misapplication of them, when they are employed in a bad cause, and for mischievous ends, can be no argument against them when they are used in a legitimate way, and for laudable purposes. A mutual agreement, compact, or covenant, is virtually implied in the constitution of every society, civil or religious; and the dictates of natural light conspire with the declarations of scripture in ascertaining the warrantableness and propriety of entering into explicit engagements, about any lawful and important matter, and of ratifying these even in the most solemn manner, if

---

* Charters' Sermons, pp. 275, 277. edit. 1816.
† On this solemn occasion Charles declared himself to be " a contented king with a contented people."

circumstances shall require it, by formal subscription, and by an appeal to the Searcher of hearts."*

It may not be uninteresting to the reader to see the deliberate sentiments of majesty itself on this subject, as recorded in the accredited archives of the kingdom. The " charge" delivered by James VI. and " subscribed with our hand at Halyroodhouse, 1580, the 2nd day of March, the 14th year of our reign," runs in the following strain : " seeing that we and our household have subscribed, and given this public profession of our faith to the good example of our subjects, we command and charge all our commissioners and ministers to crave the same confessions of their parishioners, and proceed against the refusers according to our laws and order of the kirk, delivering their names and lawful process to the ministers of our house with all haste and diligence, under the pain of forty pounds, to be taken from their stipend, that we, with the advice of our council, may take order, with sik proud contemners of God and our laws." From this document it appears that the covenants were viewed not merely as ecclesiastical deeds, but also and principally as instruments of civil obedience to lawful authority. On this principle subscription was enforced by the laws of the state, as well as by the ordinances of the church; and what is very remarkable, the ministers were to act in the capacity of civil prosecutors, and, under a severe penalty, to enforce the instrument. The declaration of Charles I. to his parliament, 1643, was certainly not expressed in very strong terms, but they are sufficiently strong to intimate the sense then entertained of the meaning and intent of the " Solemn League and Covenant." " As things now stand," says his majesty, " good men shall least offend God or me, by keeping their covenants in honest and lawful ways, since I have the charity to think that the chief end of the covenant in such men's intentions was, *to preserve us in purity and the kingdom in peace.*" The " declaration by king Charles II. at Dunfermline, August 16th, 1650," is expressed in language more strong, and as it is a document singular in itself, and still more so by the affecting contrast in which it stands to the conduct which it so solemnly pledged, I shall quote a portion of it for the edification of the reader. " His majesty taking in consideration, that merciful dispensation of divine providence, by which he hath been recovered out of the snare of evil counsel; and having attained so full persuasion and confidence of the loyalty of his people in Scotland, with whom he hath too long stood at a distance; and of the righteousness of their cause, as to join in one covenant with them, and to cast himself and his interests wholly upon God; and in all matters civil, to follow the advice of his parliament, and such as shall be entrusted by them; and in all matters ecclesiastic, the advice of the general assembly, and their commissioners; and being sensible of his duty to God, and desirous to approve himself to the consciences of all his good subjects, and to stop the mouths of his and their enemies and traducers, doth in reference to his former deportment, and as to his resolutions for the future, declare as follows :

" Though his majesty as a dutiful son be obliged to honour the memory of his royal father, and have in estimation the person of his mother; yet doth he desire to be deeply humbled and afflicted in spirit before God, because of his father's hearkening to, and following evil counsels, and his opposition to the work of reformation, and to the Solemn League and Covenant, by which so much of the blood of the Lord's people hath been shed in these kingdoms; and for the idolatry of his mother, the toleration whereof in the king's house, as it was matter of great stumbling to all the protestant churches; so could it not but be an high provocation against him, who is a jealous God, visiting the sins of the fathers upon the children: and albeit, his majesty might extenuate his former carriages and actions, in following of the advice, and walking in the way of those who are opposite to the covenant, and to

---

* Life of Knox, vol. i. pp. 181, 182.

the work of God, and might excuse his delaying to give satisfaction to the just and necessary desires of the kirk and kingdom of Scotland, from his education, and age, and evil counsel, and company, and from the strange and insolent proceedings of sectaries against his royal father, and in reference to religion, and the ancient government of the kingdom of England, to which he hath the undoubted right of succession; yet knowing that he hath to do with God, he doth ingenuously acknowledge all his own sins, and all the sins of his father's house, craving pardon, and hoping for mercy and reconciliation, through the blood of Jesus Christ. And as he doth value the constant addresses that were made by his people to the throne of grace on his behalf, when he stood in opposition to the work of God, as a singular testimony of long-suffering patience and mercy upon the Lord's part, and loyalty upon theirs; so doth he hope, and shall take it as one of the greatest tokens of their love and affection to him and to his government, that they will continue in prayer and supplication to God for him; that the Lord who spared and preserved him to this day, notwithstanding of all his own guiltiness, may be at peace with him, and give him to fear the Lord his God, and to serve him with a perfect heart, and with a willing mind all the days of his life."*

Such covenant transactions as those under which our reforming ancestors acted, were not at all uncommon in former or in later times. The Waldenses in defending themselves against the oppressions of their enemies, bound themselves by solemn oath to one another, and to the cause in which they were embarked.† In the year 1530, the smaller confederate princes of Germany formed the famous *League of Smalcald*, for mutual defence against the emperor, and for maintaining vigorously their religion and liberties against the dangers and encroachments with which they were menaced by the edict of Augsburg.‡ In 1572, the prince of Orange and his adherents in the Netherlands, entered into a solemn covenant to defend their " religion, their lives, and their liberties," against the tyranny of the duke of Alva and the Spanish inquisition.§ In 1608, the protestants of Hungary took up arms in their own defence, and sent a protestation to the estates of Hungary, requiring assistance, conform to the offensive and defensive league that had been previously formed.|| In 1641, a solemn protestation was taken by the members of the house of commons, and afterwards by all sorts of persons in England, " that they will defend religion and civil rights, &c."¶ and this was done at a time when the king and parliament were at open variance.** In 1688, and immediately before the landing of the prince of Orange, two solemn covenants were entered into and extensively subscribed; one at Exeter, and another in the northern counties of England; to the effect that the subscribers shall support the claims of the prince against the then existing tyranny of James.†† I shall close these notices in the words of Charles I., in the famous " acts of oblivion and pacification," and this royal testimony will go far to free our covenanting ancestors from the charge of disloyalty or high treason. " The Scots in taking up arms against the king and his counsellors, in defence of their religion, laws, and privileges, is no treason or rebellion, and they are his true and loyal subjects, because they had no evil nor disloyal intentions at all against his majesty's person, crown, and dignity, but only a care of their own preservation, and the redress of their enormities, pressures, and grievances in church and state, which threatened desolation to both." ‡‡

* Collection of Sermons by Henderson and others at renewing the covenants, vol. I. pp. 534–536.
† Morland's History of Piedmont, pp. 252, 253. and Fox's Acts and Monuments, vol. ii. pp. 208, 209.
‡ Mosheim, vol. iv. pp. 98, 99.
§ General History of the Netherlands, lib. 9. p. 369.
|| Grimston's Imperial History, p. 730, &c.
¶ See copy of it in Free Thoughts on Popery, p. 441. appendix.
** Clarendon's History, vol. I. p. 251. Neal's History of the Puritans, vol. ii. p. 381.
†† Wodrow, vol. ii. p. 60. of this edition.
‡‡ Apologetical Relation, p. 149.

"It has been objected," says the very intelligent editor of "the Life of Alexander Reid," "that the enforcing of religious duties by civil pains and penalties, and in too many instances the blending together of the affairs of church and state, are inconsistent with the spiritual nature of Christ's kingdom. But it should be remembered, that the sacred rights of conscience were not at that time so fully understood, nor so clearly ascertained as they have been since. Charity requires us to allow that our fathers acted conscientiously, and according to the best of their knowledge, in what they accounted their duty; and there can be no doubt that to their exertions under God we are indebted for the privileges civil and religious which we now enjoy."* We are mistaken if we suppose that the covenants were ever designed as deeds *exclusively ecclesiastical.* No doubt the church frequently interposed her authority to enforce these documents; but still the documents themselves are not to be viewed in the light of terms of communion. They are rather to be considered as tests of patriotic attachment to the constitution in church and state; and it is by adverting to this their *mixed character* that we are enabled, in some measure, to see the reason why their reception was so rigorously enforced. Our fathers had not yet learned the perfect consistency betwixt an ecclesiastical establishment closely interwoven with the civil constitution, and a most free and liberal toleration of all classes of dissenters; and this is the reason why hostility to the church was uniformly identified with treason to the state, and arms accordingly taken up in defence of both. The world had not yet learned the true principles of religious liberty. The settlers of New England, although just escaped from the fire and faggot of persecution at home, and in general professing the free principles of independency, did not refrain from persecuting one another; and it is a very striking fact, that the only country where the true principles of freedom seemed to flourish in vigour, was one in which presbyterianism in her strongest character had taken up her abode; we mean the states of Holland. There, our persecuted countrymen found a secure asylum. There, the varieties of sentiment among the refugees proved no bar in the way of a most liberal protection and encouragement by the civil rulers: and there is reason to believe that from that country were afterwards imported into Great Britain those principles of toleration which ever since the era of the revolution have blessed and fructified our beloved land. †

While we readily acknowledge that the covenanters did not possess the most liberal and enlightened views of religious liberty and freedom of conscience, we maintain a very different opinion in regard to their ideas on *civil liberty* and the rights of free men. On this subject they cherished the most just and enlarged conceptions; and while a few solitary individuals in England asserted and suffered for the same principles, the covenanters of Scotland were the only associated body then known in Great Britain, or even in Europe, who nobly stood forward as one man to vindicate and to seal them. In proof of this we appeal to those very *covenants* which have been so absurdly decried by ignorant or prejudiced moderns, but which in reality constituted at the time the only *magna charta* of Scottish freedom. In these documents, the subscribers, while "they promise and swear to stand to the defence of our dread sovereign, the king's majesty, his person and authority," declare at the same time that they shall stand up "in defence of the *liberties and laws of the kingdom*"—that they complain of those evils "which sensibly tend to the subversion and ruin of our *liberties, laws, and estates*"—that "they had before their eyes, next to the glory of God," "the true public liberty, safety, and peace of the kingdoms"—that they would seek to "preserve the rights and privileges of

---

* Appendix to the Life of Alexander Reid by his great grandson, p. 77.
† For an able illustration of the statements regarding toleration, we beg to refer our readers to an admirable Review of Orme's Life of Owen in the Edinburgh Christian Instructor for the year 1821. On the subject of the covenant some additional remarks will be found in a note to the following History, vol. I. p. 269—271.

the parliaments and the liberties of the kingdoms;" and one reason assigned for their procedure is, that "some among themselves had laboured to put into the hands of the king an *arbitrary* and *unlimited* power, destructive to the privileges of the parliaments and the liberties of the subject." * We appeal to the incontestable fact that in the period in question there were only *two parties* struggling for the ascendancy; and therefore, if the interests of civil liberty were not to be found on the one side, they certainly could not be found on the other. We appeal to another fact equally striking; that while the covenanters were divided among themselves in regard to certain questions of an ecclesiastico-political character, they were united hand and heart in their views of civil interests and in the measures necessary to secure them. We appeal further to the writings of those men, the Lex Rex by Rutherford, the Apologetical Relation by Brown of Wamphray, Naphtali by Mr Stirling of Paisley, and Sir James Stewart of Goodtrees, and indeed to the whole strain of their writings; and we ask, are not the principles contained in these works precisely the principles which lie at the foundation of the British constitution, and which secure at once the honour of the sovereign in subordination to law, and the rights of the people in close connexion with the honours of the throne? Moreover, it is of vast moment to observe that the leading principle for which, as we have noticed in a previous part of this essay, the presbyterians contended, involves in it the safety of civil rights as well as of ecclesiastical. Had the erastian principle been given into, that the king has the exclusive right of dictating in matters which concern the government of the church, how easy would have been the transition to a similar claim in regard to civil matters, supported as that claim would naturally be by the whole bench of bishops and a large proportion of other "creatures of his majesty?" Well did the presbyterians see, and well do we now see, that had not such a struggle been made against the encroachments of royalty, or rather of tyranny, under that name, the most essential of all rights would have been prostrated at the feet of an absolute monarch.

On the principles now stated, it is no difficult matter to give a rational explanation of some things in the history of those times, which at first view appear somewhat singular and strange. In the *first* place, we have a very sufficient reason for the *uncommon keenness* with which the Stewart dynasty maintained episcopacy in opposition to presbytery. Abstractly speaking, forms of church government were to [them matters of absolute indifference; but episcopacy they knew well to be a far more convenient instrument for accomplishing the object nearest to their hearts, the subjugation of the people. The bold republicanism of presbytery stood as an iron barrier in their road; and could the Guthries, and the Browns, and the Camerons been put to silence, the flexible spirit of the bishops would have gone sweetly along with the schemes of despotism.—In the *second* place; we find no difficulty in assigning a reason why in those times *England* presented so very different a picture from *Scotland*, in regard to the struggles for liberty. In England an unfortunate separation had been made between the *civil* and the *religious* rights of the people; and the prevalence of independent principles tended at once to detach the ministers from all concern in the civil questions at issue, and to destroy that union which is so essential to prompt and efficient exertion. In addition to this, we must not forget the well-known fact, that most of the leading dissenting clergy in England were gained over to the side of the court by liberal pensions from the royal purse; and it is painful to record that Richard Baxter was the only individual amongst all the recipients who refused acceptance of a boon so degrading. † In the *third* place; on the

---

* Covenants of 1639, 1643, and 1648.
† Burnet's History of his Own Times, vol. I. p. 172. "There was an order to pay a yearly pension of £50 to most of them, and of £100 to the chief of the party. Baxter sent back his pension and would not touch it. But most of them took it." How different was the conduct of the Scottish presbyterians when an offer of £20 a-year out of their benefices was made to them! While some accepted an indulgence *to preach*, not one of them all would accept this *regium donum*.

principles above noticed, we find a rational explanation of the reason why the taking of the covenant was made a matter of compulsory obligation. It was held to be the only safeguard of civil rights, and subscription to it was the only valid test of loyalty and civil obedience. As a matter of ecclesiastical regulation, or as a part of the discipline of the church, we know too much of the parliaments of both kingdoms in those days, to suppose that its enforcement would have given them a moment's concern; but involving *in gremio* the substantial rights and liberties of the nation, no wonder that they rallied round it as the only palladium of national interests.

VI. After all—asks Mr Pearson and those likeminded with him—why did our covenanting ancestors refuse so pertihaciously to accept the boon that was so repeatedly offered them, first in the shape of an *indulgence;* and afterwards in the shape of a *liberal accommodation?* With regard to the indulgence, we reply, that a considerable number or very respectable and pious presbyterians did accept of it, clogged as it was with most galling conditions. Those who declined its acceptance acted, we apprehend, on the most consistent and independent principles. The very acceptance of such a boon, implied, in some sense, a recognition of the reigning order of things in the church. The indulgence came in the shape of a commission to hold a spiritual charge granted by a civil power; and the reception of such a thing as this, was, in so far, a practical renunciation of the grand principles of presbyterianism. Besides, the indulgences were generally clogged with many objectionable clauses. Ministers, though tolerated in certain parishes, were prohibited from exercising many of their essential functions, such as lecturing, catechising, exercising discipline, and sitting with their ruling elders in church courts. Moreover there can hardly be a doubt, that although Leighton and Burnet were actuated with moderate views in obtaining the *first* indulgence for the presbyterians, it soon appeared to Lauderdale and other secular politicians, that the granting of such boons was one of the most likely means to injure the covenanting interest, as it divided the friends of presbyterianism. It was on this account that those enemies of the presbyterian church, who, in the first instance, violently opposed the indulgences, at length came not only to allow, but to press them with eagerness. They formed a *bone of contention* among the adherents of the covenanting interest; and never was a persecuting dynasty more successful in prosecuting their measures than the dominant party in Scotland were, by means of these deceitful indulgences.* Even archbishop Sharpe, immediately after the attempt on his life, by James Mitchell, having been called up to London to receive some mark of the royal favour, professed to approve, " in general terms," as Burnet says, " of the methods of gentleness and moderation then in vogue." When he came back to Scotland, he moved, in council, that an indulgence might be granted to " some of the more resolute men, with certain restraints, such as that they should not speak nor preach against episcopacy, and that they should not admit to either of the sacraments any belonging to the neighbouring parishes without the concurrence of the ministers of these parishes," &c. all with an evident intention to render any liberty that might be conceded unavailing to the presbyterians, and all in the issue adopted to the fullest extent. So far as we have been able to discover, however, this motion of Sharpe in the council was productive of nothing farther on the subject at the time, than preparing the council for prelimiting any indulgence that might be granted. Burnet unequivocally claims the merit (we may, perhaps, rather say the *demerit*) of having brought about that measure, so hurtful to the presbyterian interest. " I," says he, " having got the best information I could of the state of the country, wrote a long account of all I had heard, to the lord Tweeddale, and concluded it with an advice to put some of the more moderate of the presbyterians into the vacant churches. Sir Robert Murray told me the letter was so well liked that it was

---

* Those who wish to examine this subject more fully, may read, with advantage, Brown s History of the Indulgence, with the Answer to it; and the Apologetical Relation.

read to the king. Such a letter would have signified nothing if lord Tweeddale had not been fixed in the same notion. He had now a plausible thing to support it. So my principles and zeal for the church, and I know not what besides, were raised to make my advice signify somewhat. And it was said I was the man that went most entirely into Leighton's maxims. So, this indiscreet letter of mine, sent, without communicating it to Leighton, gave the deciding stroke. And it may easily be believed it drew much hatred on me from all that either knew it or did suspect it." The cunning scheme of Burnet did not at first meet the views of the more violent persecutors; but there can be no doubt that the scheme, as proposed by Leighton and Burnet, was, from the very outset, designed to promote the ends of episcopacy, by moderate means. The letter which was written to Lord Tweeddale on this occasion, was probably the letter which is alluded to by Wodrow in his first notice of the affair, and the writer of that letter thus goes on to state the result of it. "The king wrote a letter to the privy council, ordering them to indulge such of the presbyterians as were peaceable and loyal, so far as to suffer them to serve in vacant churches, though they did not submit to the present establishment; and he required them to set them such rules as might preserve order and peace, and to look well to the execution of them; and for such as could not be provided in churches at that time, he ordered a pension of £20 sterling, a-year, to be paid every one of them as long as they lived orderly. Nothing followed on the second article of this letter. The presbyterians looked on this as the king's hire to be silent and not to do their duty, and none of them would accept of it."* On occasion of the *second* indulgence, Burnet's advice was, that " all the outed ministers should be employed, and kept from *going round the uninfected parts of the kingdom;*" and " that they should be confined to their parishes, not to stir out of them without leave from the bishop of the diocese or privy councillor; and that upon transgressing the rules that should be set them, a proportion of the benefice should be forfeited and applied to some pious use. Lord Lauderdale heard me," says he, " to an end, and then without arguing one word upon any one branch of this scheme, he desired me to put it in writing, which I did; and the next year when he came down again to Scotland, he made me write out my paper, and turned it into the style of instruction."† After this simple and candid statement of the origin and design of the indulgence, we apprehend it would be superfluous to say a word more about its nature. That *the terms* on which it was granted were utterly subversive of presbyterian principles, we presume will be disputed by no man who thoroughly understands them. Whatever he may think of the truth of these principles, he must allow that the scheme of indulgence was really a *snake in the grass;* and his only wonder must be, that any sound-headed and sound-hearted presbyterian was ever gulled into the acceptance of it. Even Burnet himself speaks of it as " probable that Lauderdale had *secret directions to spoil the matter, and that he intended to deceive them all.*"‡

In the present day there is not, we believe, a Christian of any denomination who does not lament the differences which arose among the presbyterians, or who does not think that all diversities of opinion ought to have been merged in one common zeal for the cause in which all were so deeply interested. In tracing the history of those differences, however, we must look to a period long prior to the era of the first indulgence. The grand source of them is to be found in the famous question between the resolutioners and the protesters, which, for ten years previous to the restoration, had divided the church, and the miserable result of which was strikingly exemplified in the want of united and hearty co-operation, at a time when Charles and his Scottish parliament were razing the very foundations of presbyterianism. Beyond all question, these differences of

---

* Burnet's History of his Own Times, vol. i. pp. 512, 513.
† Burnet, vol. ii. pp. 3, 4.
‡ Burnet, vol. i. p. 526.

sentiment ought to have been entirely forgotten at a period when all were called to unite in opposition to a common enemy. The feeble and disjointed measures of the resolutioners presented a melancholy contrast with the firm unanimity of the earlier reformers of Scotland; while the boldness of the protesters failed of its laudable object, by reason of the jealousies between them and their brethren on the other side; and thus both became an easy prey to the common foe. Still there is reason to think that both parties, when called to suffer together in the fire of a common persecution, would soon have been melted into a close and indissoluble union, had not other causes of disunion been originated. Among these, the indulgence is by far the most prominent, and the enemy, in applying it as an instrument of division among the presbyterians of Scotland, was, alas! but too successful. In looking at the indulgence itself, we have cause to lament that the bait which it held out was so readily laid hold of by the friends of the good cause; but in looking at the question which it involved, we have reason to blame the violence and obstinacy of those who would not make common cause with the indulged against a party who were bent on the destruction of both. To this unreasonable pertinacity we have to ascribe not only the fatal issue at Bothwell, but likewise most of the evils which, from that period, befel the interests of presbyterianism in Scotland. On this subject I have peculiar pleasure in quoting the judicious remarks of an author to whom the literature and the religion of Scotland are under obligations of no ordinary kind. Speaking of the quarrels among the presbyterians, previous to the battle at Bothwell Bridge, Dr M'Crie thus expresses himself:—" This dissention was a main cause of the failure of the present attempt to redress national grievances. Hamilton and his party acted on the principle, that it was unlawful to associate, for vindicating their civil and religious rights, with any but those with whom they could join in church-communion; or, which amounts to the same thing, that it behoved them to introduce into the state of their quarrel, as appearing in arms, a condemnation of every thing in relation to the public interests of religion which was sinful or unscriptural; a principle which, while it involved them in that very confounding of civil and ecclesiastical matters against which they inveighed so loudly under the name of Erastianism, tended to rivet the chains of servitude on themselves and the nation. Into this error they appear to have been betrayed partly by mistaken notions of the controversy which had formerly arisen respecting the Public Resolutions. What the more honest party at that period opposed was, the admitting to places of power and trust of such as had shown by their previous conduct that they were enemies to the reformation introduced into church and state, and would use the power intrusted to them to overturn it. This could not be said of those who had accepted of or acquiesced in the Indulgence, and still less of those whom Hamilton's friends wrangled with so fiercely, who protested solemnly that they disapproved of the Indulgence, and whose former conduct vouched for the sincerity of their protestations. Another remark is suggested by the facts here referred to. If ministers of the gospel would preserve their usefulness and respectability, they must guard their independence on the side of the people as well as of civil rulers. Provided they become " the servants of men," it matters not much whether their masters wear a crown or a bonnet; and if, instead of going before the people to point out to them the path of duty, and checking them when they are ready to run into extremes, they wait to receive directions from them, and suffer themselves to be borne along by the popular stream, the consequences cannot fail to be fatal to both. Firm and tenacious of his purpose, the servant of the Lord, while gentle to all, ought to hold on the even tenor of his way, unmoved equally by the frown of the tyrant, the cry of the multitude, and the dictates of forward individuals, good and well-meaning men it may be, but who " cannot see afar off," and just need the more to be led that they think themselves capable of being leaders. An opposite conduct on the part of two or three ministers tended to foster those extravagant opinions and practices adopted by some presbyterians at this period, which discredited the cause for which they appeared, and which their best friends, though they may excuse, will not be able to defend, and should not seek to vindicate."*

The *scheme of accommodation* was very near akin to that of the indulgence. As it originated with Leighton and Burnet, and as the latter of these writers may be justly held as the most likely person to give an impartial account of it, we shall quote largely from his history of the whole transaction. We strongly suspect that, after perusing what follows, some readers will be ready to think that the archbishop and his friend Burnet, while they drank at the comparatively pure streams of Jansenist theology on the Continent, had quaffed also a little of the nectar of jesuitism.

"The king (in England) was now upon measures of moderation and comprehension So these were also pursued in Scotland. Leighton was the only person among the bishops who declared for these methods; and he made no step without talking it over to me. A great many churches were already vacant. The people fell off entirely from all the episcopal clergy in the western counties; and a set of hot fiery young teachers went about among them, inflaming them more and more. So it was necessary to find a remedy for this. Leighton proposed that a treaty should be set on foot, in order to the accommodating our differences, and for changing the laws that had carried the episcopal authority much higher than any of the bishops themselves put in practice. He saw both church and state were rent—religion was like to be lost—popery or rather barbarity was like to come in upon us, and, therefore, he proposed such a scheme, as he thought might have taken in the soberest men of presbyterian principles; reckoning that, if the schism could be once healed, and order be once restored, it might be easy to bring things into such management that the concessions then to be offered should do no great hurt at present, and should die with that generation. He observed the extraordinary concessions made by the African church to the Donatists, who were every whit as wild and extravagant as our people were; therefore he went, indeed, very far in extenuating the episcopal authority; but he thought it would be easy afterwards to recover what seemed necessary to be yielded at present.

"He proposed that the church should be governed by the bishops, and their clergy mixing together in the church judicatories; in which the bishop should act only as a president, and be determined by the majority of his presbyters, both in matters of jurisdiction and ordination; and that the presbyterians should be allowed, when they sat down first in these judicatories, to declare, that their sitting under a bishop, was submitted to by them only for peace sake, with a reservation of their opinion with relation to any such presidency; and that no negative vote should be claimed by the bishop—that bishops should go to the churches, in which such as were to be ordained were to serve, and hear and discuss any exceptions that were made to them, and ordain them with the concurrence of the presbytery—that such as were to be ordained should have leave to declare their opinion, if they thought the bishop was only the head of the presbyters. And he also proposed that there should be provincial synods, to sit in course every third year, or oftener, if the king should summon them, in which complaints of the bishops should be received, and they should be censured accordingly. The laws that settled episcopacy, and the authority of a national synod, were to be altered according to this scheme. To justify, or rather to excuse these concessions, which left little more than the name of a bishop, he said, as for their protestation, it would be little minded, and soon forgotten; the world would see the union that would be again settled among us, and the protestation would lie dead in the books and die with those that made it. As for the negative vote, bishops generally managed matters so that they had no occasion for it—but if it should be found necessary, it might be lodged in the king's name with some secular person, who

---

* M'Crie's Life of Veitch and Bryson, p 452—454.

should interpose as often as the bishop saw it was expedient to use it; and if the present race could but be laid in their graves in peace, all those heats would abate if not quite fall off. He also thought it was a much decenter thing, for bishops to go upon the place where the minister was to serve, and to ordain after solemn fasting and prayer, than to huddle it up at their cathedrals, with no solemnity and scarce with common decency. It seemed also reasonable, that bishops should be liable to censure as well as other people, and that, in a fixed court, which was to consist of bishops and deans, and two chosen from every presbytery. The liberty offered to such as were to be ordained, to declare their opinion, was the hardest part of the whole. It looked like the perpetuating a factious and irregular humour. But few would make use of it. All the churches in the gift of the king, or of the bishops, would go to men of other principles. But though some things of an ill digestion were at such a time admitted, yet, if by these means the schism could be once healed, and the nation again settled in a peaceable state, the advantage of that would balance all that was lost by those abatements that were to be made in the episcopal authority, which had been raised too high, and to correct that was to be let fall too low, if it were not for the good that was to be hoped for from this accommodation—for this came to be the word, as comprehension was in England. He proposed farther that a treaty might be set on foot, for bringing the presbyterians to accept of these concessions. The earl of Kincardine was against all treating with them—they were a trifling sort of disputatious people—they would fall into much wrangling, and would subdivide among themselves; and the young and ignorant men among them, that were accustomed to popular declamations, would say, Here was a bargain made to sell Christ's kingdom and his prerogative. He therefore proposed, that, since we knew both their principles and their tempers, we ought to carry the concessions as far as it was either reasonable or expedient, and pass these into laws—and then they would submit to a settlement that was made, and that could not be helped, more easily than give a consent before hand to any thing that seemed to intrench on that which they called the liberty of the church. Leighton did fully agree with him in this. But lord Lauderdale would never consent to that. He said, a law that did so entirely change the constitution of the church, when it came to be passed and printed, would be construed in England as a pulling down of episcopacy, unless he could have this to say in excuse for it, that the presbyterians were willing to come under that model. So he said, since the load of what was to be done in Scotland, would fall heaviest on him, he would not expose himself so much, as the passing any such act must certainly do, till he knew what effects would follow on it. So we were forced to try how to deal with them in a treaty.

" I was sent to propose this scheme to Hutchison, who was esteemed the learnedest man among them. But I was only to try him, and to talk of it as a notion of my own. He had married my cousin-german, and I had been long acquainted with him. He looked on it as a project that would never take effect—so he would not give his opinion about it. He said, When these concessions were passed into laws, he would know what he should think of them—but he was one of many, so he avoided to declare himself. The next thing under consideration was, how to dispose of the many vacancies, and how to put a stop to conventicles. Leighton proposed that they should be kept still vacant while the treaty was on foot; and that the presbyterians should see how much the government was in earnest in the design of bringing them to serve in the church, when so many places were kept open for them.

" The earl of Tweeddale thought the treaty would run into a great length, and to many niceties, and would perhaps come to nothing in conclusion. So he proposed the granting some of the outed ministers leave to go and serve in those parishes by an act of the king's indulgence, from whence it came to be called the indulgence. Leighton was against this. He thought nothing would bring on the presbyterians to a treaty, so much as the hopes of being again suffered to return to their benefices—whereas, if they were once admitted to them, they would reckon they had gained their point, and would grow more backward. I was desired to go into the western parts, and to give a true account of matters, as I found them there. So I went, as in a visit to the duke of Hamilton, whose dutchess was a woman of great piety and great parts—she had much credit among them, for she passed for a zealous presbyterian, though she protested to me, she never entered into the points of controversy, and had no settled opinion about forms of government, only she thought their ministers were good men, who kept the country in great quiet and order. They were, she said, blameless in their lives, devout in their way, and diligent in their labours. The people were all in a phrenzy, and were in no disposition to any treaty. The most furious men among them were busy in conventicles, inflaming them against all agreements—so she thought that if the more moderate presbyterians were put in vacant churches, the people would grow tamer, and be taken out of the hands of the mad preachers that were then most in vogue. This would likewise create a confidence in them—for they were now so possessed with prejudices, as to believe that all that was proposed, was only an artifice to make them fall out among themselves, and deceive them at last. This seemed reasonable, and she got many of the more moderate of them to come to me, and they all talked in the same strain."*

The following sentences speak volumes on the subject. "Sharp cried out that episcopacy was to be undermined since the negative vote was to be let go. The inferior clergy thought that if it took effect, and the presbyterians were to be generally brought into churches, *they* would be neglected, and that their people would forsake them. So they hated the whole thing. The bigotted presbyterians thought it was a snare, and the doing that which had a fair appearance at present, and was meant only to lay that generation in their graves in peace; by which means episcopacy, that was then shaking over all the nation, would come to have another root, and grow again out of that. But the far greater part of the nation approved of the design; and they reckoned, either we should gain our point, and then all would be at quiet; or, if such offers were rejected by the presbyterians, it would discover their temper, and alienate all indifferent men from them; and the nation would be convinced how unreasonable and stubborn they were, and how unworthy they were of any farther favour." † How far the "*bigotted presbyterians*" were warranted to think of the accommodation as a "snare," may be very fairly inferred from the bishop's own statements above. But in case there should be any dimness of vision yet remaining in any quarter, we shall favour Mr Pearson and his readers with a few sentences from an authority which they will not lightly set aside. "Although the concessions to which Leighton was prepared to proceed went near to vacate the episcopal office, yet he thought them justified by *the improbability of their permanence;* for he counted that when the present race of *untameable zealots* was laid in the grave, and an era of peace had allowed scope for a revival of good sense and charity, there would be a readiness on the part of the people to *reinvest* the bishop with such prerogatives, as he had been *unreasonably* compelled to sacrifice at the shrine of religious concord!" ‡ Moreover, mark what follows, and cease to wonder that men of less penetration than our sharp-sighted covenanting friends should have rejected the overtures as hollow-hearted and insincere: "The most ardent promoters of the accommodation, and among them the king, were men whom it were dotage to imagine under the influence of religious principle; and the whole project was undisguisedly detested by the bench of

---

* Burnet's History, vol. i. p. 502—506.
† Burnet, vol. I. p. 536.
‡ Life of Archbishop Leighton, prefixed to his works, by *John Norman Pearson*, A. M. p. lxxiii.

bishops, and by the mass of the episcopalian clergy. Under these circumstances, the jealousy of the covenanters admits of some palliation. They might apprehend that however sincere Leighton himself was, they still had no guarantee for those stipulations being fulfilled, the execution of which depended on others more than on himself. They might fear that episcopacy, like the *Vishna of Hindostan*, if, by creeping in under a pigmy form, it should wheedle them out of just room enough to stand upon, would straightway dilate into a giant bulk, touch the heavens with its head, and bestride 'the narrow world;' and tread to the dust that venerable structure within the pale of which it had been rashly admitted." *

Of this "venerable structure," king James himself did *once* entertain a very fair opinion, when, in the general assembly at Edinburgh, August 1590, with uplifted hands, and uncovered, he thus gave vent to his feelings :—" I praise God I was born in such a time as in the time of the light of the gospel; to such a place as to be king of such a kirk, *the sincerest kirk of the world*. The kirk of Geneva keep pasche and yule. What have they for them? They have no institution. As for our neighbour kirk of England, their service is an ill said masse in English; they want nothing of the masse but the *liftings*. I charge you, my good people, ministers, doctors, elders, nobles, gentlemen, and barons, to stand to your purity, and to exhort the people to do the same. And I, forsooth, so long as I breuk my life and crown, shall maintain the same against *all deadly*."

Paisley, December 18, 1828.

---

* Pearson's Life of Leighton, p. c.

APPENDIX.

No. I.

Testimonies from Sir Walter Scott.

SINCE writing the above I have perused the second series of the " Tales of a Grandfather," by Sir Walter Scott. It was not to be expected that the covenanters of the persecuting age should be *very particular favourites* with the distinguished baronet; nor need we wonder that he should have lavished on such men as the marquis of Montrose and the viscount Dundee an admiration and a praise which the voice of impartial history will not warrant. Still it is agreeable to find that Sir Walter does not venture to question the fact that there actually was a persecution; while he crowns with the laurels of a well-merited fame the deeds and the sufferings of the Guthries, and the Mackails, and the Browns, of our presbyterian martyrology; and on the whole, the book does leave on the mind of the reader an impression by no means unfavourable to the memory of our covenanting forefathers. I shall select a few specimens illustrative of the author's sentiments regarding some of the most prominent subjects of the following history.

The first extract respects the character of the presbyterian clergy in the reign of James VI. and the earlier part of the reign of Charles I. If, as Sir W. thinks, their successors were deteriorated by means of the politico-theological contests of the times, this was the result of circumstances which they could not control. The *substratum* was the same; and presbyterianism was equally favourable in both periods to excellence of character.

" They," the presbyterian clergy, " were endeared to the people by the purity of their lives, by the depth of learning possessed by some, and the powerful talents exhibited by others; above all, perhaps, by the willingness with which they submitted to poverty, penalties, and banishment, rather than betray the cause which they considered as sacred." p. 82.

" The presbyterian preachers, in throwing away the external pomp and ceremonial of religious worship, had inculcated in its place, the most severe observation of morality. It was objected to them, indeed, that as in their model of church government, the Scottish clergy claimed an undue influence over state affairs, so in their professions of doctrine and practice, they verged towards an ascetic system, in which too much weight was laid on venial transgressions, and the opinions of other Christian churches were treated with too little liberality. But no one who considers their works, and their history, can deny to those respectable men, the merit of practising, in the most rigid extent, the strict doctrines of morality which they taught. They despised wealth, shunned even harmless pleasures, and acquired the love of their flocks by attending to their temporal as well as spiritual diseases. They preached what they themselves sincerely believed, and they were believed because they spoke with all the earnestness of conviction. They spared neither example nor precept to improve the more ignorant of their hearers, and often endangered their own lives in attempting to put a stop to the feuds and frays which daily occurred in their bounds." " The clergy of that day were frequently respectable from their birth and connexions, often from their learning, and at all times from their character. These qualities enabled them to interfere with effect, even in the feuds of the barons and gentry; and they often brought to milder and more peaceful thoughts, men who would not have listened to any other intercessors. There is no doubt, that these good men, and the Christianity which they taught, were one of the principal means of correcting the furious temper and revengeful habits of the Scottish nation, in whose eyes bloodshed and deadly vengeance had been till then a virtue."

" Besides the precepts and examples of religion and morality, the encouragement of general information and knowledge is also an effectual mode of taming and subduing the wild habits of a military and barbarous people." " The preachers of the reformation had appealed to the scriptures as the rule of their doctrine, and it was their honourable and liberal desire, that the poorest as well as the richest man should have an opportunity of judging by his own perusal of the sacred volume, whether they had interpreted the text truly and faithfully." After noticing honourably the exertions of the church to obtain a proper system of national education, he thus writes: " At length the legislature, chiefly by the influence of the clergy, was induced to authorize the noble enactment, which appoints a school to be kept in every parish of Scotland, at a low rate of endowment indeed, but such as enables every poor man within the parish to procure for his children the knowledge of reading and writing; and affords an opportunity for those who show a decided taste for learning, to obtain such progress in classical knowledge, as may fit them for college studies. There can be no doubt, that the opportunity afforded, of procuring instruction thus easily, tended, in the course of a generation, greatly to civilize and humanize the character of the Scottish nation; and it is equally certain, that this general access to useful knowledge, has not only given rise to the success of many men of genius, who otherwise would never have aspired above the humble rank in which they were born, but has raised the common people of Scotland in general, in knowledge, sagacity, and intelligence, many degrees above those of most other countries," vol. i. pp. 169, 174.

Charles' first parliament in Scotland after the restoration, is thus described: "Their parliament when they met were generally, many of them, under the influence of wine, and they were more than once obliged to adjourn, because the royal commissioner (Middleton) was too intoxicated to behave properly in the chair." vol. i. p. 178. This was the parliament that abolished presbytery, established episcopacy, and began the long career of desolating persecution.

Of the horrible system of *intercommuning* he thus speaks: "The nearest relations were prohibited from assisting each other, the wife the husband, the brother the brother, and the parent the son, if the sufferers had been intercommuned. The government of this cruel time applied these ancient and barbarous laws to the outlawed presbyterians of the period, and thus drove them altogether from human society. In danger, want, and necessity, the inhabitants of the wilderness, and expelled from civil intercourse, it is no wonder that we find many of these wanderers avowing principles and doctrines hostile to the government which oppressed them, and carrying their resistance beyond the bounds of mere defence. There were instances, though less numerous than might have been expected, of their attacking the houses of the curates, or of others by whose information they had been accused of nonconformity; and several deaths ensued in those enterprises, as well as in skirmishes with the military." vol. ii. pp. 224, 225.

Of Mitchell's case we read as follows: "It is shameful to be obliged to add, that the duke of Lauderdale would not permit the records of the privy council to be produced, and that some of the privy councillors swore, that no assurance of life had been granted, although it is now to be seen on the record. The unfortunate man was therefore condemned. Lauderdale, it is said, would have saved his life; but the archbishop demanding his execution as necessary to guard the lives of privy councillors from such attempts in future, the duke gave up the cause with a profane and brutal jest, and the man was executed, with more disgrace to his judges than to himself, the consideration of his guilt being lost in the infamous manœuvres used in bringing him to punishment." vol. ii. pp. 252, 253.

His opinion of Sharpe's death is as follows: "Such was the progress and termination of a violent and wicked deed, committed by blinded and desperate men. It brought much scandal on the presbyterians, though unjustly; for the moderate persons of that persuasion, comprehending the most numerous, and by far the most respectable of the body, disowned so cruel an action, although they might be at the same time of opinion, that the archbishop, who had been the cause of many men's violent death, merited some such conclusion to his own. He had some virtues, being learned, temperate, and living a life becoming his station; but his illiberal and intolerant principles, and the violences which he committed to enforce them, were the occasion of great distress to Scotland, and of his own premature and bloody end." vol. ii. pp. 259, 260.

In addition to the interesting details of the following history, those who desire to have a full and impressive view of the real character of those times, and the sufferings of our forefathers, may be referred to such valuable works as the following:—Blackadder's Memoirs—Lives of Alexander Reid—James Nesbit—Hugh Mackail, and John Brown—Kirkton's History—M'Crie's Lives of Veitch and Bryson, and the two volumes of the Scots Worthies. I beg also, particularly to notice, and to recommend the Review of the First Series of the " Tales of my Landlord," in the *Christian Instructor,* for 1817, and afterwards published as a separate work with additions, under the title of a " Vindication of the Covenanters." This truly valuable and triumphant work is well known to be the production of Dr M'Crie. In addition to the references which have been made to it in the previous part of this dissertation, we shall give the following valuable extract:—" What did our presbyterian ancestors do, but maintain their religious profession, and defend their rights and privileges, against the attempts which were made to wrest these from them ? This was the body and front of their offending. And were they not entitled to act this part ? Were they not bound to do it ? What although, in discharging this arduous duty, in times of unexampled trial, they were guilty of partial irregularities, and some of them of individual crimes? What although the language in which they expressed themselves was homely, and appears to our ears coarse, and unsuitable to the subject? What although they gave a greater prominence to some points, and laid a greater stress on some articles, than we may now think they were entitled to? What although they discovered an immoderate heat and irritation of spirit, considering the barbarous and brutal manner in which they had long been treated? What although they fell into parties, and quarrelled among themselves, when we consider the crafty and insidious measures employed by their adversaries to disunite them—and when we can perceive them actuated by honesty and principle, even in the greatest errors into which they were betrayed? These, granting them to be all true, may form a proper subject for sober statement, and for cool animadversion; but never for turning the whole of their conduct into ridicule, or treating them with scurrilous buffoonery. No enlightened friend to civil and religious liberty—no person, whose moral and humane feelings have not been warped by the most lamentable party-prejudices, would ever think of treating them in this manner. They were sufferers—they were suffering unjustly— they were demanding only what they were entitled to enjoy—they persevered in their demands until they were successful—and to their disinterested struggles, and their astonishing perseverance, we are indebted, under God, for the blessings which we enjoy."

No II.

Mr Wylie's Thoughts on the Indulgence and Accommodation.

THE following paper, which has been copied from the autograph of its able and venerable author, may not be uninteresting to the reader. Mr Wylie was a distinguished actor in the scenes of those times; and is frequently spoken of by our historian. He was the father of Mr Robert Wylie of Hamilton, one of the most respectable ministers of his day, and many of whose letters are among the Wodrow MSS.

" 1. Is yr not many presumptiones of it, that the prime-presser of this vnion is favourably inclined to popery: as may appear by his converse with men of that persuasion: by his high esteeme of Romish doctoris and such as are pillars of the Romish church: by his affection to ye liturgie, etc: by his way its evident when ye opportunity offereis he will be as fordward and more cordiall for ane vnion with poperie, nor he is for ane vnion with presbytrie.

" 2*dly*, His designe in this vnion wold be considered: which is not to weaken much less to extirpate episcopacy: it being the *conditio sine qua non* (Episcopacy alwayis standing) and if so, neyther is it to restore presbytrie, or to strenthen the presbyterian party. But the reall design is either to corrupt them to a walling (cementing) with Episcopacy and so to divid them from ye honest people, and party in the land to whom such a complyance as is stood for is most hateful: or if they prevail not thus, then by calumny and reproach to expose them to the hatred of the magistrat as ane humorvs vnpeaceable pack that cannot be endured: so the intended vnion is to be wrought either by a subtill reduction and bringing back of the presbyterian to that Egypt from whence he was delivered, or be ane overturneing or outturneing of him, if he will not returne. And shall any thing els be expected, whiil as these Cassanderis speak magnefyingly of their owne, and slightingly of the presbyterian way.

" 3*dly*, Have wee not looked vpone Episcopacy as a plant not of Godes planting, and hes not our Lord said that every plant which his heavenly Father hes not planted shall be plucked vp. Why then should any incline to be insert in the same stock with them, when the on is pulled vp the other will be in hazard? Is there not to all (who know wherein the essence of one and other consistes) a manifest incompatibility of the two together. Certainely as it is a sin to separat these thingis that God hes put together so it is a sine to joyne these things that God hes separat, both in the essence of the thinges, and by his expresse command: it shall not be so amongst you etc. and is it not also manifest, that there is such ane antipathie betwixt things of human invention and of Godes appointement, that where so ever they are planted together the thriveing of the one is the killing of the other.

" 4*thly*, May not experience teach vs that persons and places most addicted and obsequious to Episcopacy hath least of the trueth of religion, and power of Godliness: and such of the ministry that way basely and servilely inclyned, and most conformable, do least good by thair ministry in the church for the saveing and building vp of menes soules vnto eternall lyfe; and that partly threw the dislik and prejudice of people against them, and partly throw the curse of God vpon them. Its the generall acknowledgement of the Godly that they are not edified by such as fall in with them, and its to be hoped that no indulged brother will desire to be vnder the same curse.

"5thly, Its also remarkable that where these bishopis have had, or have any persones or places vnder their aspect or shaddow, there proceides from them such a malignant influence, and such pestiferous distillationis towardes the same, that very hardly can true religion, and the power of Godlines be there preserved alive, vpone which they cast always a squint eye of malice to keep the same either from rooting there, or that they may kill it with their overdressing of it, or by their power weed it out.

"6thly, The way taken at this present tyme exactly and punctually homologates the way taken by the prelatick party in former tymes, which was their vseing of cuning trickes of dividing of their precisian opposites (as they called them, at K. J. his entry to England) by qualifying or taking aff some by favour and preferment: and exasperating others by severity, whereby these who should have joyned foot to foot and widden throw the swellings of Jordan in otheris handis ran severall wayes and crossed one anotheris endeavoures and designes: I need not instance the lyk practice now, which is palpable to all: whill some are indulged and subtily dealt with for a complyance: whill otheris are not only slighted but cited and put to great extremityis: But doe wish that there be a joyning of hand in hand etc.

"7ly, Yealding brethren (if any such, as God forbid, there be) wold seriously consider whither or not by their example they will. 1. confirme the wavering mynded conformitantis: who with much doubting and reluctancy (out of feare) hath slipped on in the backslyding course: 2ly, reduce some (as yet) vnconformable, and incline them not to stand out any more vpon poyntis of that nature as these who were looked upon as champions do so easily come and gang vpon. 3ly, And adde more to the greife and smart of the peremptory adherers to the presbyterian way, who will be accounted wild, refractury, and rebellious. 4ly, And justifie, both the severity of prelatis, and otheris afterward, against these that shall stand out vnconformable: as proceiding equaly and doeing bot their duty, to God, to his church, and to his maiestie:

"8ly, The brethren called to this communing (standing as wee hop and suppose for reformation) wold consider their capacity: and how they should carry in their capacity: as for their capacity its certainly bot private (tho the subiect matter of their communing be of publick concernment and does very eminently concerne the publick work of reformation) and so should not be medled with by any out of a public capacity: next as they are not chosen generally by those that adhere to the reformatioun, which begetis a prejudice; so they are papped out (as more plyable and yeelding persones) by those who are against the reformation, just as in a tryall by collusion; which thing is apt in its owne nature, to-beget a deeper and a blacker prejudice; and tho wee have not the least jealousie of our faithfull brethren, yet this shewes the subtillty of the adversary and the aptness of the way taken to beget prejudice and divide. But with all it may show the adversary too that tho he should gaine a persone or two to his way, yet he will not gaine much to his cause, their capacity being bot privat engageing none bot themselfes. As to their carriage and behaviour, they wold consider [1.] whether or not it were their best (as no doubt it were their best) to say nothing in a publick cause without a free generall Assembly, wherein all concerned may have liberty to speak. 2ly, as privat persons they may be 1. complaineris of wrong, 2ly, petitioneris at the Magistratis handis for right. 3ly, by argumentis stoutly challengs and defend the churches right; for every privat man may defend, and plead for a public canse tho they may not enter vpon communing in order to comeing and goeing vpon a public cause."

THE INTRODUCTION,

CONTAINING,

After a short view of the public resolutions in 1650, a Narrative of General Monk's management after his departure from Scotland, an Account of the steps taken for the King's restoration, his Majesty's return, and what was done in relation to the Church of Scotland, till the meeting of the Committee of Estates in August, 1660.—Collected from original letters of Mr. James Sharp, afterward Archbishop of St. Andrews, the Reverend Mr. Robert Douglas, and other Presbyterian Ministers, this year.

ONE of the blackest periods of the history of the church of Scotland being fallen to my share, it would not be out of the road, if I should continue the thread of our ecclesiastical history, from the demise of king James VI. where our printed historians end, to the restoration of king Charles II. where my attempt begins, and do somewhat to fill up that blank. Indeed several important memoirs and written accounts of that remarkable period, in my hands, with not a few original papers of that time, would afford me matter enough for such an introductory essay; but it is enough for me to venture upon the twenty-eight years following; therefore I choose rather to communicate any thing of this nature, in my small collections, as to our history, to my worthy friends who have that part among their hands, and can manage them much better than I can pretend to. I shall here, then, very much confine myself to the year wherein the public imprisonments, and other hardships upon presbyterian ministers, gentlemen, and noblemen, began. If once I had remarked, that when matters were going smoothly on after king James's death, the tory high-flying Laudean faction, whose successors, headed by chancellor Hyde, put king Charles II. upon all the heights he ran to in England, and the encroachments he made upon the church and state constitution in Scotland; that violent party, I say, put king Charles I. upon palming books and bishops, and other innovations upon us here. This issued in the strange turn affairs took, at our second and glorious reformation in 1638, when this church was again settled upon her own base, and the rights she claimed from the time of the reformation, were restored, so that she became "fair as the moon, clear as the sun, and terrible as an army with banners." It is hard to manage a full cup, and I shall not take upon me to defend every step in that happy period; the worst step I can observe, was their unhappy and unchristian divisions upon the head of the public resolutions. And because in the following period, there will be occasion to mention those resolutions several times, I shall give a view of the matter of fact relating to them, as succinctly as I can, without dipping at all into the unhappy debates on either side.

When king Charles II. was, in the year 1649, invited home, upon settling the conditions of government, or claim of right, and he had taken the national covenant as explained, together with the solemn league, and was thereupon solemnly crowned at Scone; a considerable number of noblemen and gentlemen, complained of the hardships put upon them, who were his father's friends, and, as they alleged, well disposed to his majesty, in their being excluded from the

A

army and judicatories, by the act of classes, and other laws now made. But although the king did reckon a good many of them well disposed for his service, and fit enough to maintain and extend the prerogative; yet these people, now called malignants, and very justly, from their violent opposition to the liberties and rights, civil and ecclesiastical of the church and kingdom, were suspected by such as had all along appeared firm for our reformation in the church, and a limited management in the state; and those apprehended the other would soon possess the king's ear, and lead him to such measures, as would overturn all that had been done since the year 1638, and therefore for some time, they opposed their coming in. But the king soon fell upon measures to divide these who had the management at his accession, and to gain a majority for taking off the former restrictions, and to let his friends come into the army and judicatories, under some conditions that were never kept. The church, whose judgment, as to sin and duty in public matters, was now much regarded, must next be gained to make some declarations in favour of this design; and, as it always fares with churchmen, when they side into parties, according to the different factions of politicians, and go beyond their line to please great men, they split, according to the two different parties at court; whereas hitherto they had been most united and harmonious.

The English had invaded the kingdom, and obtained a victory at Dunbar. This occasion was improved, to push the taking off restraints, lying upon those who were reckoned the king's friends, though they had opposed the work of reformation since the year 1637, in their admittance to the army and judicatories, while a part of them are up in rebellion in the north. Accordingly the king published an indemnity, and wrote to the committee of estates, and commission of the kirk, that these men might be intrusted and employed. This was then refused. The defeat at Hamilton falling out soon after, that was made a new argument for admitting of malignants; and it was urged, that the standing forces were too weak for defending the kingdom against the enemy, unless the whole fencible men* without distinction, were raised. And the moderator of the commission was importuned by letters from the king, now at Perth, where the parliament then sat, to call a commission *pro re nata*, to give their judgment in this matter. The ministers against the resolutions, allege, that many members were not advertised, that the diet was so short, the members could not come up. A quorum of the commission met at Perth, where the parliament put the following question to them in cunning enough terms. " What persons are to be admitted to rise in arms, and to join with the forces of the kingdom, and in what capacity, for defence thereof, against the armies of the sectaries, who, contrary to the solemn league and covenant and treaties, have most unjustly invaded, and are destroying the kingdom? The commission of the General Assembly, December 14th, 1650, gave the following answer:—" In this case of so great and evident necessity, we cannot be against the raising of all fencible persons in the land, and permitting them to fight against this enemy, for defence of the kingdom; excepting such as are excommunicated, forfeited, notoriously profane or flagitious, or such as have been from the beginning, or continue still, and are at this time, obstinate, and professed enemies, and opposers of the covenant and cause of God. And for the capacity of acting, that the estates of parliament ought to have, as we hope they will have, special care, that in this so general a concurrence of all the people of the kingdom, none be put in such trust and power, as may be prejudicial to the cause of God; and that such officers as are of known integrity and affection to the cause, and particularly such as have suffered in our former armies, may be taken special notice of."

As soon as this answer was given, the parliament in their act of levy, did nominate some of the most considerable of those reckoned formerly malignants, who had been excluded from the renewing the covenant, places of trust, and even access to sacraments,

---

* *i. e.* Men able to bear arms.

for their opposition to the work of reformation; and more than half of the colonels of this sort, and some of the general officers, and great numbers of the soldiers, were such as had been with Montrose, and M'Donald. In short, the bulk of the officers and army, had been either involved in the engagement, or in some respect or other, had opposed the work of reformation, since the year 1638. Many ministers being dissatisfied at those resolutions and actings, a good many presbyteries signified their dissatisfaction with such courses and resolutions, particularly those of Stirling and Aberdeen. Upon this, the commission did, January 7th, publish a warning and large answer to the letter from the presbytery of Stirling, in which they vindicated their answer to the parliament's query, which increased the contention, drew forth new answers and replies, and the flame rising, the opposers of the answer to the query were branded with the character of malignants. All ministers and preachers, were by the commission discharged to speak or write against these resolutions, and an act was made, ordaining presbyteries to proceed with the censures of the kirk against such as did oppose the resolutions; and in May, the commission transmitted the copy of another act to presbyteries, ordaining such who opposed the resolutions, to be cited to the next assembly at St. Andrews, by which a good many, who opposed the resolutions, were kept from being members of that assembly. To give the whole of this matter together, though the former answer to the query, and what followed upon it, be strictly called the resolutions, and the ministers who approved this answer, the brethren for the public resolutions, and the opposers of this way, antiresolutioners and protesters; yet the gentlemen, who by these methods, were got into the army, did not stop here, but pushed their design to get into judicatories, from which they were excluded by the acts of classes, 1646, and 1649, which debarred such as had joined Montrose, and were in the engagement, from public offices of trust, and in short, all malignants. In order to get this act of classes rescinded, the king and estates of parliament, proposed to the commission of the kirk the following query. " Whether or not it be sinful and unlawful, for the more effectual prosecution of the public resolutions, for the defence of the cause of the king and the kingdom, to admit such to be members of the committee of estates, who are now debarred from the public trust, they being such as have satisfied the kirk for the offence, for which they were excluded, and are since admitted to enter into covenant with us?"

The commission, upon some considerations, found it proper at first to delay giving an answer; but upon the 3d of April, the moderator received a letter from the king and parliament, earnestly desiring a meeting of the commission to be called at Perth, the 17th of April, 1651. " That after a due consideration of the acts and declarations emitted by the church, and the other grounds contained in the narrative of the acts of classes, in so far as conscience can be concerned therein, his majesty and parliament have a positive answer, not only to the query in the terms wherein it was propounded, but likewise their clear and deliberate judgment and resolutions, if it be sinful and unlawful to repeal and rescind the act of classes:" and upon the 23d of April, another letter came to the commission, much to the same purpose. To both, the commission, after some previous cautions, gave this answer. " As for the solemn league and covenant, the solemn acknowledgment and engagement, and former declarations emitted by this church, (which are set down as grounds in the narrative of the act of classes,) we do find they do not particularly determine any definite measure of time, of excluding persons from places of trust for bypast offences; but only bind and oblige accordingly to punish offenders, as the degree of their offences shall require or deserve, or the supreme judicatories of the kingdom, or others having power from them for that effect, shall judge convenient, to purge all judicatories, and places of power and trust, and to endeavour that they may consist of, and be filled with such men, as are of known good affection to the cause of God, and of a blameless and christian conversation, (which is a moral duty commanded in the word of God, and of perpetual obligation; so that nothing upon the account of those grounds doth hinder, but that persons formerly debarred from places of power and trust for their offences, may be admitted to be members of the committee of estates, and the censures inflicted upon them by the act of classes, may be taken off and rescinded without sin, by the parliament, in whose power it is to lengthen or shorten the time of those censures, according as they shall find just and necessary) providing they be men who have satisfied the kirk for their offences, have renewed and taken the covenant, and be qualified for such places according to the qualifications required in the word of God, and expressed in the solemn acknowledgment and engagement," &c. As soon as the court had this return, the parliament rescinded the act of classes in all its articles, by which great numbers formerly excluded, were brought into parliament, and nominate as members of the committee of estates, and made capable of places of trust. And in a little time, the malignant party, at least the bulk of them, were admitted to the chief places of trust, and got the management of all into their hand.

The General Assembly met at St. Andrews in July, where the brethren against the resolutions, protested against the lawfulness and freedom of the assembly. Three of the subscribers were, after citation, deposed, and one suspended, and the actings of the commission approven. The same heats continued in the next assembly, 1652; and when Cromwell had effectually prevented the meeting of any more assemblies, and the debates had been carried on in synods and presbyteries, and in print before the world, at length, in 1655, and 1656, conferences were agreed on for union, and the matter was carried to London, before the usurper. At length some sort of union was made up in most synods and presbyteries after Cromwell's death; and things went pretty smooth, till the king, upon his return, declared his displeasure with the opposers of the resolutions, and some of them were first fallen upon; and in a little time, the whole honest presbyterian ministers were struck at, and sent to the furnace to unite them.

Having premised this, I come now to hand myself and the reader into the beginning of our direct persecution, August, 1660, by giving a short view of matters from the time of general Monk's leaving Scotland, till the meeting of the committee of estates, where I will have occasion to take notice of several matters of fact both in Scotland and England, as to the restoration of the king, which I have not met with any where else but in the letters before me, which are mostly betwixt Mr. James Sharp and Mr. Robert Douglas, and some from Mr. Sharp to Mr. John Smith, one of the ministers of Edinburgh, and others. From the very words of those letters, (which shall be marked thus ") I shall endeavour to form an account of the great turn of affairs this year, whereby the reader will have most plain evidences of the reverend Mr. Douglas, and the rest, their integrity and faithfulness, and discoveries how careful they were to preserve our valuable constitution upon the king's return; and as sensible proofs of Mr. Sharp's juggling, prevarication, and betraying the church of Scotland, and his treachery to the worthy ministers who intrusted him. The reader is entirely indebted to the reverend and worthy Mr. Alexander Douglas, minister of the gospel at Logie, for what is in those letters, which in a most obliging manner he communicated to me, with a short narrative of the re-introduction of episcopacy, writ by his venerable father Mr. Robert Douglas, of which I shall make some use in the following history.

In November, 1659, general Monk left Edinburgh, where he had been since the usurper's reduction of Scotland, and by slow marches reached London in January, and soon gave a turn to public affairs in favour of the king's restoration. It appears very probable to me, that he was encouraged secretly by Mr. Robert Douglas; but I come to the matters of fact in the letters, which I exhibit according to their dates.

January 10th, Mr. David Dickson and Mr. Robert Douglas, in their letter to general Monk, signify their entire confidence in him as to the affairs of Scotland, and the necessity of one from them to be near his person, to put him in mind of what is necessary, and acquaint them with the state of things; and

INTRODUCTION.   5

they ask his pass for Mr. James Sharp. Before the receipt of theirs, the general ordered Mr. auditor Thomson to write from York to Mr. Sharp; and in his name he, (January 15th,) desires Mr. Sharp "to undertake a winter journey, and come to him at London with all speed; defers the communicating the reasons till he be there, wishes he may communicate this with Mr. Douglas only, because the general does not desire this to be made too public." And January 16th, the general himself writes a letter from Ferry-bridge to Messrs. Dickson and Douglas in the following words.

"I received yours of the 10th instant, and do assure you, the welfare of your church shall be a great part of my care, and that you shall not be more ready to propound, than I shall be to promote any reasonable thing that may be for the advantage thereof: and to that end I have herewith sent you, according to your desire, a pass for Mr. Sharp, who the sooner he comes to me, the more welcome he shall be, because he will give me an opportunity to show how much I am a well-wisher to your church and to yourselves.

A very humble Servant,

GEORGE MONK."

Upon the 6th of February several ministers met at Edinburgh, and agreed to send up Mr. Sharp with instructions to this effect, that he endeavour that the church may enjoy her privileges, that he testify against the late sinful toleration, that he essay to get the abuses of vacant stipends rectified, that ministers may have the benefit of the act abolishing patronages; and, that in case any commission be granted for settling ministers' stipends, he endeavour to have it in good hands, which I have annexed.* At the same time they write to general Monk, and "recommend Mr. Sharp to him, as one whom they have instructed, and who is to communicate his instructions with his lordship, and they have sent him up to prevent any bad impressions that may be given of them at London. They add, that though it be not their way to intermeddle with civil affairs, yet the miseries of the sinking nation, make them humbly request his lordship may endeavour to ease them of their grievances." By another letter they recommend Mr. Sharp to colonel Wetham; and by a third, to Messrs. Calamy and Ash, to be communicate with Messrs. Manton and Cowper, and any others they think fit; wherein they desire them to be assisting to him in the management of his trust, for the best advantage of this afflicted church.

Mr. Sharp's first letter, of February 14th, takes notice of his arrival at London the 13th, his kind reception by Mr. Manton, who signified to him the large character the general gave of the ministers in Scotland, and Mr. Douglas in particular; "that he had immediate access to the general, who recom-

---

* Instructions to Mr. Sharp, from Messrs. David Dickson, Robert Douglas, James Wood, John Smith, George Hutchison, and Andrew Ker, February 6th, 1660.

1. You are to use your utmost endeavours that the kirk of Scotland may, without interruption or encroachment, enjoy the freedom and privileges of her established judicatures, ratified by the laws of the land.

2. Whereas, by the lax toleration which is established, a door is opened to a very many gross errors, and loose practices in this church; you shall therefore use all lawful and prudent means to represent the sinfulness and offensiveness thereof, that it may be timeously remedied.

3. You are to represent the prejudice this church doth suffer by the interverting of the vaking stipends,* which by law were dedicated to pious uses; and seriously endeavour, that hereafter vaking stipends may be intromitted with by presbyteries, and such as shall be warranted by them, and no others, to be disposed of and applied to pious uses, by presbyteries, according to the 20th act of the parliament, 1644.

4. You are to endeavour that ministers, lawfully called and admitted by presbyteries to the ministry, may have the benefit of the 39th act of the parliament, intituled, act anent abolishing patronages, for obtaining summarily, upon the act of their admission, decreet, and letters conform, and other executorials, to the effect they may get the right and possession of their stipends, and other benefits, without any other address or trouble.

If you find that there will be any commission appointed in this nation, for settling and augmenting of ministers' stipends, then you are to use your utmost endeavours to have faithful men, well affected to the interests of Christ in this Church, employed therein.

DAVID DICKSON.
MR. ROBERT DOUGLAS.
MR. JAMES WOOD.
MR. JOHN SMITH.
MR. GEORGE HUTCHISON.
MR. ANDREW KER.

* The stipends of vacant parishes.

mended him to Sir Anthony Ashly Cowper, and Mr. Weaver, two parliament men. He adds, that the city, who, two days ago, were much saddened by the unhandsome act put upon the general, with a design to bring him into an odium with the city, is now mightily pleased with the general's letter to the parliament."

Upon the 16th of February, the general sends an answer to what was written to him with Mr. Sharp, importing, " that Mr. Sharp is dear to him as his good friend, but much more having their recommendation, and he cannot but receive him as a minister of Christ, and a messenger of his church; that he will improve his interest to his utmost for the preservation of the rights of the church of Scotland, and their afflicted country, which he loves, and had great kindness from; that it shall be his care, that the gospel ordinances, and privileges of God's people may be established both here and with them. He seeks their prayers for God's blessing upon their counsels and undertakings, entreats them to promove the peace and settlement of the nations, and do what in them lies to compose men's spirits, that with patience the fruit of hopes and prayers may be reaped; and assures them he will be careful to preserve their profession in the honour they so much deserve."

Mr. Douglas, February 23d, "acquaints Mr. Sharp with the receipt of his and the general's letters, desires he may mind what he spoke about the lords Crawford and Lauderdale, and promises to write about them to the general, if need be: he desires Mr. Sharp to encourage the general in his great work, for the good of religion, and peace of the three nations, through all the difficulties he may meet with. He adds, you yourself know what have been my thoughts from the beginning of this undertaking, which I have signified to himself; though I was sparing to venture my opinion in ticklish matters, yet I looked upon him as called of God in a strait, to put a check to those who would have run down all our interests."

" By a letter from London, February 21st, Mr. Sharp signifies to Mr. Douglas, that the secluded members of the long parliament are restored, to the joy of all honest people: that he is satisfied he is come up, since that, though little can be done at present for the cause we own, effectually, yet one from the church of Scotland bears a construction that will be for the reputation of the church. He says, friends are satisfied with our late proceedings with Monk, and bless God we were not wanting in such a juncture; that on Saturday he had a private conference with the general, and so far sounded him as he got encouragement for some of the most eminent secluded members to apply to him. Upon Monday, four of them sent him with some propositions to the general, to which he brought them a satisfying return. He adds, that ministers and good people look upon it as the only expedient for securing religion, and dashing the designs both of cavaliers and sectaries, that the secluded members be restored, rather than that a parliament should be called with qualifications which would only tend to the securing of the interest of the rump, which is now the third time the derision and scorn of all men: that with no small difficulty the general was brought to admit the secluded members, which was kept very close till this morning. Yesterday the rump voted their seclusion, and this morning the secluded members entered the house with the acclamations of the people, seventy-three in number to eighteen of the rump. Mr. Manton was called to pray to them; and they made void all done against them these eleven years, appointed the general commander in chief of the forces of the three nations, took off the imprisonment of the committed citizens, and liberate Sir George Booth: that they are to appoint a council of state to sit till the Parliament be called, April 20th. After four or five days they design to dissolve themselves, and so make void the title and claim of the long parliament: that the general, in his speech, declares for presbyterian government not rigid, and hath writ to the officers of the army: that both contain expressions which will not be pleasing, but the present necessity of affairs causeth some to put a fair construction upon them. Once more the public cause of those nations is like to be in honour, fanatic fury quelled, the expectations of all sober men raised, and Scotland somewhat better reputed. In this great turn providence is remarkably seen. The rump intended to bottom themselves upon the sectarian interest, and are now dashed upon that account, and the almost dying hopes of God's people revived. Mr. Sharp desires to be recalled, since nothing can be done till the parliament sit; and the general told him, nothing could be done, till there be a full house, as to his instructions. He adds, that 'tis surmised by some, that before those who now sit, rise, somewhat will be started concerning the covenant, others think it will not be yet time; but however (says he) the public covenanted interest, and our concernment in it, ought not to be neglected. I hope this week our noble prisoners will be released, and I am next day or Thursday to pay them a visit."

"In answer to this, Mr. Douglas writes to Mr. Sharp, February 28th, and signifies, that he may be sure it soundeth harsh in the ears of all honest and understanding men, to hear presbytery, the ordinance of Jesus Christ, reflected upon by the epithet of rigidity. We confess (adds he) rigidity may be fault of men, and may be the fault of those among ourselves, who weakened the unity and authority of this kirk; but the faults of men ought not to be charged upon the ordinance of God, nor upon others who have disallowed and disavowed those actings. I still entertain hopes that presbyterial government will be better known to be well consistent with, and helpful to the government of the state. And as to his return, leaves it to himself, with the advice of the general."

Upon March 1st, Mr. Douglas writes to general Monk, thanking him for his kind reception of Mr. Sharp, and encouraging him to go on in the great work he had among his hands. He adds, "I have been very much satisfied from time to time, to hear what good opinion your lordship entertained of presbyterial government; and I am confident you shall never have just cause to think otherwise of it. There is no government so good in itself, but it may be abused by the corruptions of men; yet the faults of persons are not to be fixed upon the government, nor ought it to be rejected because of the rigid miscarriages of some, whose irregular actings have been hateful to true presbyterians, as the issue of men's corruptions, and not the genuine fruit of the government. It is a blessed mean appointed of God for the preservation of truth and verity in the kirk, and singularly useful to preserve and press obedience to magistracy. It was no small contentment to all here, when we heard of your lordship's grave advice for abstaining from multiplying oaths and engagements, as a way to attain sooner unto settlement. Honest men will follow their duty without such engagements; and they who fear not an oath, will be forward enough to take it when it is imposed, and as forward to break it when occasion is offered. Determinations will be without doubt, more kindly entertained, and bear the more weight with men, when they are known to flow, not from an imposed constraint, but from an unconstrained freedom and inclination, bottomed upon conscience and right reason."

Mr. Sharp's letter of March 1st, to Mr Douglas, apologizes for his so seldom writing, and signifies he is so much engaged in business, that he is deprived of his rest; that people observing the great countenance the lord general gives him, press him so, that he is forced to abandon his chamber all the day, and much of the night; that he declines altogether meddling in the business of particular persons; that though little is yet done to the church and nation, yet his being at London, hath not been useless as to the public cause: "That the cavaliers point him out as the Scottish presbyter, who stickled to bring in the secluded members, to undo all by the presbyterian empire; that before the admission of the secluded members he had spoke to the general concerning the Windsor prisoners, and signified his commission from Mr. Douglas so to do; and after pressing the vote of the house relating to them he went to Windsor, and advised their writing to the general, and carried their letter, which he promised to answer; and every day since, he had been with some of the most considerable of the house, who have promised to move effectually for their coming to London, which will be speedily;

that the general tells him, his being at London, is of use to him; that the house hath yet a fortnight to sit, and have resolved to spend the first hour every day about settling religion, and the rest of their time upon settling the militia; that the city ministers have offered some desires to be made use of by some members of the house, a copy of which he sends. He adds, that worthy Mr. Ash tells him, that three months ago, when the commissioners came down to general Monk, he wrote to you, (Mr. Douglas,) by one of them, which it seems, was not delivered; that in the letter, I (Mr. Sharp,) wrote to Lauderdale about that time, I had this expression, that he might be confident general Monk would be for a good parliament. Upon this, he (Lauderdale,) sent to Messrs. Calamy, Ash, and Taylor, which encouraged the flagging city. He sent also to Oxford and elsewhere, which gave the first occasion of addresses from the city and counties, to the general, for a free parliament."

The desires of the city ministers, mentioned in this letter, I have annexed.* They are for suppressing papists, for sanctification of the Sabbath, against the disturbance of ministers, for a committee to approve ministers, for a declaration of adherence to the confession, catechisms, directory, and form of church government, presented by the late assembly, against molestation of ministers, and for a national assembly of divines.

In Mr. Sharp's letter to Mr. John Smith, March 4th, he regrets the death of Mr. Law at Edinburgh, and tells him, " That the house have voted the confession of the assembly, to be the doctrine of the church of England, except the two chapters about church discipline and censures, which are remitted to a committee, where 'tis thought, they will sleep till the parliament sit. They have appointed Dr. Owen to be before them on Thursday, in order, as 'tis thought, to restore his deanery to Dr. Reynolds. This day the house have released our Scots prisoners, who have given security to the council for their good behaviour, and their estates will soon be restored; that Ireland is secured, and all quakers, anabaptists, and sectaries banished; that some judges are appointed for Scotland, but the parliament will not meddle with them. He adds, he is in a peck of troubles to get the city ministers set about their business. That day a large meeting named four of the fastest and honestest to sit on Monday, and Mr. Sharp with them, and afterwards to meet when he sees fit. He names five, whom he calls warping brethren, and no friends to the covenant interest, whom a member of the house of commons hath undertaken for; but (says he,) they must not be trusted. He adds, I tell what your mind is as to the civil business; and honest people here, who are but few, either in the city or house, are of one heart with you. The great fear is, that the king will come in, and that with him, moderate episcopacy, at the least, will take place here. The good party are doing what they can to keep the covenant interest on foot, but I fear there will be much ado to have it so. They dare not press the voting

---

* Desires of the city ministers, February 1660. It is humbly desired,
1. That there may be a speedy course taken against Jesuits, papists, priests, and all popish emissaries.
2. That an effectual course also be taken for the better sanctification of the Sabbath, and to prevent the opening of shops by quakers, and all other profanation of the Sabbath, and, in order thereto, a certain act, bearing date September 27th, 1651, intituled, an act for relief of religious and peaceable people from the rigour of former acts of parliament in matters of religion (whereby many have taken encouragement to neglect the public ordinances) may be considered and repealed.
3. That the disturbance of the ministers, in the public worship of God, may be prevented and punished.
4. That certain ministers may be appointed for the approbation of all ministers who shall be admitted into livings, till the next parliament take further order.
5. That they would be pleased to declare, that they still own the confession of faith, the catechisms, directory, and form of church government presented to them by the late assembly of divines, and approved of by several ordinances of parliament.
6. That care may be taken, that godly ordained ministers, who are in sequestered livings, may not be molested, through the want of some formalities in law as to their institution.
7. That they would please to consider what may be done in order to the calling of a national assembly of divines, to be chosen by the ministers of the respective counties, with due qualifications, that so, by the blessing of God upon this ordinance, we may have hope for the healing of our sinful and woful divisions.

for presbyterian government, lest it bar them from being elected next parliament. Our friends in the city think it were not amiss, that from the nation of Scotland, were published a declaration; but I think it not yet seasonable. It were good you have your thoughts upon it in time, and the intent would be, to guard against sectaries upon the one hand, and cavaliers upon the other. For God's sake take care that our people keep themselves quiet, and wait till the Lord give a fit opportunity. Matters here are in a very ticklish discomposed condition. They say Ireland hath sent for the king, but I do not believe it."

March 6th, Mr. Sharp writes to Mr. Douglas; and with reference to the complaint in his of the 28th of February, upon the general's declaring himself to be for presbytery, but not rigid, he says, " As to the reflection upon presbytery, by the epithet of rigidity, the carriage of the true friends of it hath given sufficient proof of the causelessness of that aspersion, yet upon all occasions you see it doth not fence against it. The consistency of it with the civil government, seemeth to be clear from the present parliament, who, if they sit a little, intend to ratify what they enacted about it, (in) 1647, though the buzz of some is loud enough, No bishop, no king. The house yesterday, in their preface to the act owning the confession of faith as the doctrine of the church of England, did mention the covenant as one of the grounds upon which they were induced to make such an ordinance: whereupon the motion was stated, that the solemn league and covenant should be revived, and an order made for printing it, and setting it up in all the churches of England and Wales, and the doors of the parliament house: to which none in the house offered to make any contradiction. And this day the league and covenant, in great Lombard paper, is to be sold in all the shops in London. This hath given a great alarm to the sectarian party, who centre in Lambert, who, refusing to give security for keeping the peace, was yesternight laid in the Tower; and they are proceeding against others of that party. Waristoun hath been with me; his drift is, that I may deal with the general, that he may have a personal protection, payment of his debts, or enjoy his places at least. I have declined to meddle in it."

In his postscript to this letter, he tells Mr. Douglas, " that Mr. Calamy, Mr. Ash, and Mr. Taylor, are honest, and after his own heart. They say, I (Mr. Sharp) am useful to them; sure they put me to toil enough in speaking to parliament members, the general and his officers. Honest men are at a stand what to think or do. If this parliament rise, and another sit, they conclude we can have no security for religion or liberty: the following will bring in the king immediately. This cannot sit longer, unless a house of lords be called, and this the army will not give way to. Most of the members have no inclination to sit longer. This clashing of parties is like to cast all in confusion; and the cavaliers and sectaries are waiting their opportunity. All that wish well to religion apprehend that if this parliament do not continue to sit, the king must come in without terms, and therefore do judge it best to call him in time. I never saw England in such a posture. God knoweth how to interpose. The papist and sectary will join issue, expecting toleration; and the honest party are like to be swallowed up."

Mr. Douglas answers the former, March 13th, and tells him, he is refreshed with the reviving the league and covenant, (and) recommends Mungo Murray to Mr. Sharp's counsel and assistance.

March 10th, Mr. Sharp signifies that he had Mr. Douglas's to himself and the general, of March 1, which the general received, and said he would make a return. He adds, that the general hath much countenanced presbyterian ministers, and still professeth to be for that way; "that the sectarian interest is on the waning hand, and moderate episcopacy setting up its head; that upon Thursday our noble prisoners were liberate upon security to keep the peace, and not to return to Scotland without leave of council or parliament; that they are highly esteemed by the English. He wisheth a commission were immediately sent up from Scotland, to Crawford and Lauderdale,

B

to act in capacity of commissioners for the kingdom of Scotland. The parliament are this night upon settling the militia of the city and nation, with this proviso, that all in it shall own the cause of the parliament against the late king to be just. He adds, that several parliament men and the lord Manchester, think he hath privacy with the general, and send him (Mr. Sharp) to him on all occasions, and the general by him communicates his mind to his friends in the city, and he is employed in all that relates to religion, so that he hath scarce any time to write; that he had met with reports once and again, that you (Mr. Douglas) Messrs. Hutchison, Dickson, Wood, and himself, should have said, we could wish to be settled in a commonwealth way, and were against the king's coming in on any terms. Whereupon he went to the earl of Manchester, lord Wharton, and several parliament men, to whom it was buzzed by colonels Wetham and Gumble, and flatly contradicted it as a slander; declaring that nothing would satisfy Scotland but the king on covenant terms, and that it was contrary to their mind he should be brought in on cavalier terms; that he, finding many possessed with the belief, that the king, while in Scotland, broke all terms, and the engagements he was under by treaty, and was vicious, and unclean, and a scorner of ordinances, and a discountenancer of ministers, had detected those great lies and malicious forgeries, and declared he could not say the king broke to us, and that the honest party were well satisfied with him; that by covenant and treaty he engaged by all lawful and peaceable ways to endeavour uniformity in doctrine, discipline, &c. in the three nations. The difficulties, adds he, from the army, are overcome; the militia is so settled that general Monk hath the absolute power of the army, and the agitators and army cannot now stop the design on foot. There is no satisfying the people without the king; a treaty with him will soon be set on foot. The general and leading men in the house are now settled in a mutual confidence. The great thing now is, Whether this house shall continue or dissolve: if they continue, they lose their reputation, and will not be able to act for a settlement; if they dissolve, they fear the next parliament will bring in the king, without security to religion and the public cause. But, adds he, I apprehend they must dissolve themselves, and set that on foot before the sitting of the next parliament which will secure the honest interest; however they are resolved on that which will upon the matter settle presbyterian government.

To this letter Mr. Douglas answers, March 15th, and signifies his satisfaction that the general supports presbyterian government and ministers. He adds, " It is best that presbyterian government be settled simply; for we know by experience, that moderate episcopacy (what can it be other than bishops with cautions) is the next step to episcopal tyranny, which will appear very soon above board if that ground once be laid. You know the old saying, *Perpetua dictatura via ad imperium.* Our constant moderators was a step to bishops, and they once entered, soon broke all caveats." He adds he had thoughts of a commission to Crawford and Lauderdale three weeks ago, but knows not how a meeting shall be got to give it, and to add others if necessary. Further, Mr. Douglas that same day writes to Mr. Sharp about the calumnies cast upon them, and says, " The report of their being for a commonwealth is a mere forgery; that they professed any settled government better than anarchy, and submitted to providence in their present condition; that it may be they were mistaken for some of their brethren the protesters, to whom, says he, the king's return is matter of terror, because of their miscarriages to him. You know, adds he, that the judgment of honest men here is, for admitting the king upon no other terms but covenant terms, wherein religion, the liberties of the nation, and his just greatness, are best secured; that as to the king he never broke, but at the short start at St. Johnstoun, which was occasioned by the remonstrance; that his countenance was favourable to the ministry; and if Mr. Gillespy and others were not so cheerfully looked upon by him, it was because of their opposing the resolutions for the defence of the kirk and kingdom against an unjust invasion. As to his personal faults, they did not appear to

them; that he heard him say, in reference to the settling presbyterian government in England, that, by advice of parliament, and a synod of divines, he would endeavour the uniformity whereunto the league and covenant engages. All this he offers to get attested, if need be, and wishes a meeting were warranted to authorize commissioners to act for poor Scotland; and does not doubt but the noble persons he (Mr. Sharp) speaks of, being prisoners of many prayers, will be cordial for the good of the kirk and kingdom, and not suffer themselves to be deceived again, by admitting those to counsels and actings who have undone all." And, March 17th, Mr. Dickson, Mr. Douglas, and Mr. Hutchison, write a joint letter to Mr. Sharp, vindicating themselves from being for a commonwealth, and meddle with no other parts of the letter he wrote. The same day they write a letter to general Monk, encouraging him to go on, and thanking him for his countenance.

March 13th, Mr. Sharp writes to Mr. Douglas, and tells him, "The house have resolved to do nothing in prejudice of what passed in favour of religion before the 1648. To what before he had said on the covenant, he adds, That it was ordered to be read in all the churches, once in the month, every year; that they have appointed a committee for approbation and ordination of ministers; and therein upon the matter have approven the directory and form for church government; that this day Dr. Owen was outed of his deanery of Christ's church, Oxon, and Dr. Reynolds put in his room; that the house had further ordered, that none suffer any more for the sake of the engagement, and voted it to be utterly void henceforth. By the above named clause in militia act, ordering all to declare the parliament's justice in their war against the king, they have guarded against the cavaliers; and, by their adding, that magistracy and ministry are ordinances of God, they guard against sectaries and levellers. Last Sunday, says he, I went to Mr. Calamy's church with our noble prisoners, where Messrs. Calamy and Taylor gave public thanks for their liberation. This day, the form and order of the king's coronation, with Mr. Douglas's sermon, and the speeches made, are printed, and selling at London, printed according to the first edition at Aberdeen. He adds, the difficulties about sitting or not sitting of this house continue; but sit or not, they will declare for king, lords, and commons. The militia is in the hand of those who are enemies to a commonwealth. He adds, that Sunday last, the general sent his coach for Messrs. Calamy, Ash, and me; and we had a long conversation with him in private; and convinced him a commonwealth was impracticable, and to our sense beat him off that sconce he hath hitherto maintained; and came from him as being satisfied of the necessity of dissolving this house, and calling a new parliament. We urged much upon him, that the presbyterian interest he had espoused, was much concerned in keeping up this house, and settling the government on terms; but in regard he had so lately declared against the house of lords, and continuing of this house, he could not do it so reputably. The secluded members, though they could outvote the rump, yet cannot so well proceed against the rumpers in this as in another parliament."

Upon the 15th of March, Mr. Sharp writes to Mr. Douglas, "that yesterday the house passed the bill for approbation of ministers, granting this power to one and thirty ministers, all presbyterian, save three or four. This, (says he) in a church constitute as ours, were not more tolerable than Mr. Patrick's (Gillespy's) parchment; but here 'tis looked on as a very advantageous act. They have confirmed all ordinances in favours of presbyterian government, extending them to all counties in England. The house will dissolve on Saturday or Monday. The commonwealth party are now for any thing but the king's coming in; they would set up Monk, but he will not be induced to it. The cavalier spirit breaks out very high, and is like to overturn all. We scarce see how a war can be avoided. The general is confident to carry his point. The popish party are at work, and the Jesuit provincial, Bradshaw, who came over from Spain to Lambert and Vane, with above a hundred thousand pounds sterl. is still here, and very busy."

INTRODUCTION.

March 20th, Mr. Douglas writes to Mr. Sharp, that he had his of the 13th, and is well pleased that the parliament's defensive war is vindicated. He says, anarchy and tyranny, and likewise contempt of magistracy, are to be guarded against; and as hierarchy hath been the bane of the kirk of God, so decrying the ministry, and a lawless liberty, hath poisoned the kirk with heresy and error. He tells Mr. Sharp of a meeting of the protesters at Edinburgh very unfrequent; but that 'tis said they wrote a letter to the general in favours of Waristoun. The same day Mr. Douglas writes a letter to the earl of Crawford, wherein he congratulates him on his liberation, and his firm adherence through his sufferings to his principles, and takes the freedom to tell him and the lord Lauderdale, "That on their deliverance they will, like wise Scotsmen behind the hand, be careful not to suffer themselves to be befooled again by fair pretexts and promises, to admit to their counsels, and public employments, men that never loved their master, their country, themselves, or the cause they owned and suffered for; but by their rigidity, and precipitancy, and ambition to set up themselves and followers, had ruined king, kirk, and country; and, if re-admitted, will play the same game over again; 'Burnt bairns dread the fire:' and adds, He is not against compassion to such as deserved the contrary, but would never trust them with places. He beseeches them to improve their enlargement in a solid settlement of the nations, according to our obligations by the solemn oaths of God. And he begs his lordship and Lauderdale may write down to their acquaintances in Scotland, to avoid divisions, and leave off their plottings for their private interest, and let all give way to the public interest of kirk and state." That same day a common letter signed by Messrs. Dickson, Douglas, Hamilton, Smith, and Hutchison, is sent to Crawford, Lauderdale and Sinclair, congratulating them on their liberation.

Mr. Sharp writes to Mr. John Smith, March 17th, that yesterday the parliament did dissolve themselves, after they had issued writs for another parliament to meet 25th of April. Mr. Sharp seeks to be home, and declines coming to be minister of Edinburgh. He says, some sudden rupture of the sectarian party is feared, and those who are against the king's coming in, seem desperate.

March 22d, Mr. Douglas answers Mr. Sharp's last of the 17th, and signifies his great concern in the new parliament; and wishes that the late parliament, in a consistency with their declarations to the country, and promises to the general, could have continued sitting. This he takes to have been the method that would have brought matters to the best issue. And he expects and hopes the general, whose honour now is engaged, will keep all in peace till the parliament sit down. He desires Mr. Sharp to stay as long as he can be serviceable to the general or lords lately released.

Upon the 12th of March, the lord Broghill, colonel Georges governor of Ulster, and Mr. John Greig, in name of the presbyterian ministers of Ulster, write letters to Mr. Douglas, with a gentleman, Mr. Kennedy, whom they send over to reside at Edinburgh, desiring a close correspondence with Scotland, and showing their hearty concern for settling religion, and liberty, and uniformity in the three nations, in concert with general Monk; and desiring Mr. Sharp, or Mr. Wood, or some trusty friend, to be sent over to Ireland, to concert measures for the settlement of all those upon righteous and solid foundations. The 28th of March, Mr. Douglas and the ministers of Edinburgh write answers to those letters, accept of their kind offer, and signify they have writ to Mr. Sharp by his brother, whom they send up express to London to him, as one who is well acquaint with their affairs, signifying their desire to him, and entreating Mr. Sharp or his brother to come over from London to them. How Mr. Sharp ordered this affair at London, we shall find from the detail of the letters before me.

March 29th, Mr. Douglas writes to Mr. Sharp with his brother, that if the general be jealous of Ireland, he needs not acquaint him with their desire to him to go thither, that they know nothing, but they agree in one thing; and leaves it to Mr. Sharp to take what course he thinks fittest; and if he find that the proposal either feed or breed jealousies, the least he can do is, to let my lord Broghill understand that the affair was communicate to him (Mr. Sharp,) and that he excuse himself the best way he can. Mr. Douglas signifies, he sends him up the rude draught of a paper, which might be fit to be published at the meeting of the parliament. This paper I insert,* as the sense of so great a man as Mr. Douglas, on the present juncture of affairs.

Mr. Sharp writes to Mr. Douglas, March 24th, declining his being called to be minister of Edinburgh, and pressing another may be pitched upon. In his postscript he acquaints him, that Lauderdale and he had been dealing to stop the English judges from coming down till the parliament meet: that the English are willing Scotland be as

---

* The judgment of some sober-minded men in Scotland, concerning the settlement of the government in the three nations.

For the settlement of government, two things are mainly considerable; the one is concerning the power of settling it, the other is concerning the form of the government to be settled.

Concerning the power of settling government, it is in the three respective parliaments of England, Scotland, and Ireland. It is matter of no small contentment to us, that there is a full parliament to meet in England, of whom we have the confidence that they will do right for themselves; yet we must plead that *de jure* belongs to the three nations to consult and conclude, in their respective representatives, that wherein all of them are severally concerned; for *quod omnes tangit, ab omnibus tractari debet*. In which purpose it may be considered, 1. That England is but a part, and their representative doth only represent that part; now no part can conclude and determine the whole. 2. All the three nations have always had their respective parliaments, until the unhappy changes under the late usurpation, which hath overthrown the liberties of all the three nations. 3. If any thing be determined by a part, which is not agreeable to the mind of the rest, it must be imposed without a free consent, and by force; and this is the continuance of that very bondage upon others, under which both they and we have lien this while bygone. 4. A greater freedom of expression is required in this particular, in so far as concerneth Scotland, which is in a worse case than any of the other two, because the power that is in the other two, by divine providence, puts them in a capacity to act for themselves; whereas Scotland is, by that same power, impeded from acting toward their own liberty. If the force upon the secluded members, that hindered them from acting according to their trust, was unjust, and was taken off according to justice, then all the acts of violence thereafter committed by these who acted that force, upon these who enjoyed their own freedom before, are unjust, and cannot, without owning the injustice of others, be still continued unto their sad restraint from acting as a free nation. It were to be wished that the injustice thereof were a little better considered, upon which account let it be remembered, 1. How well Scotland hath deserved of England; for being entreated for, and by their commissioners, they took their lives in their hand, and hazarded themselves, to deliver their brethren from a fearful threatened bondage; and yet the recompense that they have gotten, hath been, to be unjustly invaded, and many thousands of them killed, starved, imprisoned, and removed to the far parts of the world: unto this matter, the words which the Lord commanded to be spoken before the host of Israel, by the prophet Oded, may be well applied, 2 Chron. xxviii. 9, 10, 11. "Behold, because the Lord God of your fathers was wroth with Judah, he hath delivered them into your hand, and ye have slain them in a rage that reacheth up unto heaven. And now ye purpose to keep under the children of Judah and Jerusalem, for bond-men and bond-women unto you: but are there not with you, even with you, sins against the Lord your God? Now hear me therefore, and deliver the captives again, which ye have taken captive of your brethren; for the fierce wrath of God is upon you." 2. That that unjust invasion was never imputed unto the nation of England, but unto a party which then and thereafter kept England in bondage, as well as others: but if now, when the Lord hath opened a door of hope unto them for their own liberty, they keep their brethren still in bondage, and do not behave themselves toward their oppressed brethren, in their speeches to the army, and in their actions toward their brethren, as the heads of Israel spake and did, 2 Chron. xxviii. 12, 13, 14, 15. They will add one trespass to another, and make it to be a national sin, which will draw from the avenging hand of divine justice a national judgment. 3. That the body of this nation evidenced their willingness and readiness to hazard themselves unto the utmost, and to lay out themselves above their ability, toward the promoting of the generous intentions of general Monk, whom the Lord raised up, to put a stop unto the violent actings of those that were in a way of undoing religion and liberty, and to make way for the meeting of a full and free parliament. These things, being well weighed in the balances of an impartial judgment, will strongly plead, that Scotland ought to be a sharer with England and Ireland, in the settling of government.

Concerning the form of the government, it is either civil, or ecclesiastical.

As to the civil government, it may be supposed to be intended either in a commonwealth, or in a single person.

The civil government of these three nations cannot be settled in a commonwealth for these reasons. 1. The people of these nations have been so accustomed unto monarchy, that they can hardly put their neck under another form of government. 2. However it be pretended to be a commonwealth, yet it is really and in effect but an oligarchy, the carrying on of the interests of some few particular persons. 3. Such a commonwealth is but introductory to a single person, as late experience had made it evident in the practice of the protector, who turned

INTRODUCTION.

free a nation as they are; but the general is for keeping us in subjection, till he see how matters go in the parliament: that they will essay to delay the instructions and commissions to them, as long as may be.

March 31st, Mr Douglas writes to Mr. Sharp, pressing a meeting in Scotland, either of shires and burghs, or of a select committee, for choosing commissioners to deal in these matters that concern Scotland in general, and to see to the nation's interest. He adds, "he cannot but admire God's hand, in moving the late parliament to revive the solemn league and covenant, which is the only basis of settling these distracted nations. The league and covenant, says he, is hated by many in England and Scotland, because it puts a restraint upon malignants, the prelatic party, the fanatics, and those who are loose and pro-

---

their republic unto government of a single person, viz. of himself. 4. It is held as a maxim in the politics, that it is dangerous to change the government of a kingdom, so long as there are righteous heirs of the crown to plead their right, lest the kingdom be continually vexed with new wars and broils, and involved in blood, so often as they have will and power to endeavour the forcible possession of that which is known to all neighbouring princes, to be their undoubted right. 5. If the settlement of government be in a commonwealth, it will necessitate the keeping up of armies, to impose that form upon these of the nations, who cannot in conscience give way thereto; and how disadvantageous and dangerous this is, may be seen. 1. By the vast expenses which they will draw to, and these must be wrung out of the estates of people: a taste of this the nations have had these few years bygone, wherein there hath been more imposed upon the people, than in hundreds of years before. 2. What security can be had from these armies, but they may act over again what the armies before them have lately acted, and model the government to their own pleasure, or make themselves the rulers of all. 6. A commonwealth, out of a preposterous desire of securing civil interests, useth to bring with it no small disadvantage to the true reformed religion, by toleration of errors and heresies. A sad proof of this these nations have had in late times under the essays for a commonwealth, wherein errors of all sorts, heresies and blasphemies have abounded, more than they have done in any such time since the days of Christ. 7. It seems that God is not pleased with such a change in these nations: for since it began, they have been tossed, like a tennis-ball, from hand to hand, without any settlement, which hath made the government to be like washing floods, overflowing the banks, when once it hath gone out of the right channel; and though men have been framing a government upon the wheel, yet the Lord hath broken it all, intimating this very thing, that a commonwealth is not the foundation wherein these nations can safely rest.

As to the settling of a civil government in a single person, reason and conscience plead that that single person be the righteous heir of the crowns. For, 1. Though the nations were necessitate to undertake a lawful defensive war, to preserve religion and their civil rights and liberties, against the breaches made upon both, by wicked counsellors misleading the father, yet since the parliament found reason to have re-admitted the king, whereupon by force, so many members were secluded, his son who hath never acted any thing of that kind, should not be reputed to be in a worse condition than himself, and so manifestly injured as to be denied re-admission to his just right. 2. However the father was engaged in war against England, yet his son was never so engaged, but only against a prevailing party which kept England under bondage, and kept him under banishment. 3. The three nations are not at liberty to make choice of any single person that they please, but have determined themselves in the solemn league and covenant, which hath been solemnly sworn in them all, professing in the sight of Almighty God, that one main end they aim at is the honour and happiness of the king and his posterity; which was afterward renewed in many declarations, wherein they profess their integrity and sincerity, in pursuing of the war, without any prejudice intended to the king's power and authority, or his posterity. 4. It is expected, that the ensuing parliament (the happy and peaceable meeting whereof is earnestly desired) will endeavour to redress the wrongs which themselves and the nation have received, by the practices of these that violently oppressed them; and it is no less expected, that they will restore persons to their due rights, who were outed of them by the same violence which oppressed the nation, lest the parliament's injustice, in denying *Suum cuique tribuere*, become the sin of the nation. *Non tollitur peccatum, nisi restituatur ablatum.* 5. The setting up of the righteous heir will secure the nation against the fears of invasion from abroad, or insurrections from within, upon the account of any interest to the government, and so take away the necessity of keeping up standing armies, to the exhausting of the country, and endangering of a settled government. 6. All the well affected to government in Scotland can give this testimony unto him who is righteous heir, that he was faithful in his treaties, did countenance the honest ministry, and religious duties, and was without any known scandal in the course of his conversation, which are qualifications desirable in a single person for settling of government. 7. The good hand of divine providence doth lead, as it seems, unto that single person, by keeping the government unsettled until the sitting of a free parliament, by instructing and fitting him for a just and moderate government in the school of affliction, and by mercifully inclining the hearts of the body of the people toward him, whereas for a while there was an alienation of affection in many from that family, that coming out of the furnace of affliction, as a vessel fitted for honourable employments, he may be called unto the throne by the representative, and heartily embraced by the body of the people.

Self-seeking men will not want objections against the settling of the government in this

INTRODUCTION.

fane; which ought so much the more to increase the affections of all honest men to it, as the only mean of effecting a religious and righteous settlement. He tells Mr. Sharp, that there is a great noise of one Hardie, who hath preached before the general in the Babylonish fashion, and vehemently cried up the English hierarchy, and the rest of the Romish relics that remained in England after the first reformation: which is made use of here (Edinburgh) to the general's disadvantage." In the postscript to this letter, Mr. Douglas urgeth further a warrant for a meeting at Edinburgh, to choose commissioners to look after the nation's interest, and adds, "there is now a generation risen up, which have never been acquainted with the work of reformation, nor with the just proceedings of this nation, and therefore would condemn them, the

way. 1. Purchasers of crown lands and of other casualties and emoluments belonging thereto, out of fear to be deprived thereof, will be great sticklers in opposition to this settlement. This objection were easily answered, if covetousness were not both unsatiable and unreasonable. For, 1. The rent of the lands, and other things of that nature during the years of their possession hath equalled, if not exceeded the price which they laid forth upon the purchase. 2. It were most unjust that the three nations should suffer, and be at the expense of keeping up armies for maintaining a few private men in an unrighteous purchase: the nations had far better buy out their purchases than be at the expense of maintaining armies. 3. To deny him admittance to the crown, that he may not be admitted to the possession of his lands, were to add sin to sin, and to maintain a lesser sin by committing a greater. No man will suffer it to enter into his mind that the parliament will make this their sin. 2. Such as have been accessory to the grand injuries done to his father, will fear that he prove vindicative against them if he should be admitted; but an act of oblivion will secure them, and an act of indemnity will secure all others in reference to the actings of these latter times; and as to the defensive war undertaken by the parliaments of the three nations, the lawfulness thereof may, and ought be declared and secured in law. 3. The honest and sober party may, upon sinistrous information, be possessed with fears that he shall introduce an arbitrary government, but his admittance is not pleaded for upon any terms but upon the terms of the league and covenant, wherein all the rights and liberties of the parliaments and people of the three nations respectively are secured, and which he hath most solemnly sworn and subscribed in Scotland.

Whatever other objection may be moved from the fears of men, it may be considered that what is incumbent upon the nations, whereunto they are obliged before God and men, should be done, committing the ordering of contingent events to the good and wise providence of the Lord of the whole earth.

For the government of the kirk in Scotland, they are determined unto presbyterial government, as that which is most agreeable to the word of God, being thereto obliged by their national covenant and by the solemn league and covenant; and the other two nations are obliged by the league and covenant to endeavour the preservation of the reformed religion in the church of Scotland, in doctrine, worship, discipline and government, according to the word of God and the example of the best reformed churches. 2. For England it is expected from the parliament thereof that is shortly to sit, that they will ratify the 30th and 31st chapters of the Confession of Faith, as well as the late parliament hath ratified all the rest of it.

Though there may be some in England for episcopacy, and some for other forms, yet presbyterial government ought to be pitched upon, for these reasons.—1. Episcopacy and other forms are men's devices, but presbyterial government is a divine ordinance. 2. The three nations are tied by the league and covenant to endeavour the extirpation of prelacy, that is, church government by archbishops, bishops, &c.; and to endeavour the nearest conjunction and uniformity, as in religion, Confession of Faith, Directory for Worship, and catechising, so in form of church government. 3. The maintenance of the episcopal hierarchy requireth huge and vast rents, which might be employed to far better uses; more is laid out for the upholding the lordly grandeur of one of that hierarchy, than many able, faithful, and laborious ministers of the gospel live upon. 4. It is known by sad experience in England, that episcopacy hath been the inlet unto popery, Arminianism, and other errors which were on foot, and fomented by them before the late troubles; and other forms which men have been modelling, have brought forth swarms of errors, schisms, and unhappy divisions in these nations; only presbyterial government being Christ's ordinance, stands as a wall and an hedge against all these, as Scotland hath tried by experience, in which, so long as presbyterial government stood in vigour, no error in doctrine, worship, discipline, and government, durst set out the head. 5. Presbyterial government doth well agree with any lawful civil government, though presbyterians have no reason to be indifferent to any form of civil government, since they know what good hath been enacted towards the establishment of presbyterian government in the three nations under kingly government; and it may be truly said of it, that in the right exercise thereof, it is the best school to teach subjects due obedience to the lawful magistrate. It is maliciously suggested by the enemies thereof, that it is intolerably rigid in the exercise of it, which may take with good people who are unacquainted therewith; for removing whereof it may be considered: 1. That the errors of men in abusing of this ordinance of God ought no more to reflect upon it, than the errors of men abusing other divine ordinances ought to reflect upon them. 2. Presbyterial government hath within itself a sufficient guard against the aberrations of men; for inferior kirk judicatories

covenant, and all their honest and loyal actings, according to the covenant principles. You will not believe what a heart-hatred they bear to the covenant, and how they fret that the parliament should have revived it. What can be expected of such, but the pursuing of the old malignant design, to the marring and defacing of the work of reformation settled here, and well advanced in the neighbouring nations? I am informed, that those are to have a meeting here on the 5th of April, and have no purpose to wait upon a warrant, but go on upon such an election, as will be dissatisfying to the sober and well affected of the nation. 'Tis matter of admiration that they are unwilling that Crawford and Lauderdale (being upon the place, and having given such proofs of their honest and loyal affections) should be employed in matters of that concernment; but those worthy noblemen may be assured that the affections of all honest men are upon them. There are three parties here, who have all of them their own fears in this great crisis: the protesters fear that the king come in; those above mentioned, that if he come in upon covenant terms, they be disappointed; and those who love religion and the liberty of the nation, that if he come not in upon the terms of the league and

---

are in their actings liable to the trial and censure of the superior judicatories, until it come at length to the general assembly, which useth to take a course for redressing all abuses, so that there is nothing needful but the authority of the civil magistrate to countenance them in their proceedings. 3. It is so far from being rigid that all tenderness is used toward the ignorant to bring them to knowledge, meekness toward the restoring of those that are fallen through infirmity, painfulness to reclaim these that are of a different judgment, and patient forbearance even toward the obstinate, that, if possible, they may be reclaimed before they be proceeded against by the highest censure of the kirk; and yet it being a divine ordinance, which restrains looseness, profanity, and error, it needs not be wondered by men of judgment, that it be reckoned as rigid by these who love a lawless liberty in opinion and practice.

Seeing it is now both the desire and hope of all honest and sober men, that the Lord, in his good providence, will bring the parliament to sit in peace and freedom, they would seriously consider how much it concerneth them to look well unto the building and ordering the house of the God of heaven; for it hath been observed by very godly and judicious men, that because there was no care taken to settle the affairs of the kingdom of Christ, but by a vast toleration, a way opened for a flood of errors to enter upon the kirk, the Lord justly permitted confusions to come upon the state, and made the various vicissitudes of state mutations to be the astonishment and derision of all about. That abomination which hath provoked the Lord to jealousy must be removed, as they would expect God's blessing upon the nation, and upon their endeavours for the solid settlement of righteous government.

That there is a free parliament to sit in England, is a matter of no small comfort, and giveth good hope to the well affected in the nations; only it is their earnest desire that it may be free indeed, and not as it hath been in these late times. To make a free parliament a threefold freedom is requisite. 1. That there be a freedom in reference to the matters therein to be handled; and in particular, that they be not predetermined in that which is the main matter, by the army, or any other in place or power, toward the settling of any government contrary to the minds and inclinations of the bulk of that body which they represent. 2. That there be a freedom in their voicing, without being overawed. It was thought most absurd, and an encroachment upon the freedom of parliament, when the king seized upon some members of the house; what shall be then thought if a whole parliament should be raised, and not permitted to sit? But this usage is not to be feared, since it hath pleased the Lord in his providence to make my lord general instrumental for their meeting; it is expected that he will also prove vigilant and faithful for their peaceable sitting. 3. There is a freedom requisite for the subjects to present their desires and overtures for the government, that they may be more kindly accepted than hath been the use in late times, wherein a man hath been accounted an offender for a word. The people of Scotland have all this while, under the variety of changes, lived peaceably, submitting unto providence, and do yet in a peaceable way wait patiently for relief and enjoyment of their just liberties. If they shall happen to be frustrate of their expectation, they must in patience possess their souls till God appear for them; but better things are hoped for from this parliament, which God hath raised up to act for public interests and common liberty. It is time in their endeavours to settle these distracted nations: they will meet with many difficulties; but if all the well affected were to speak unto them, they would speak in the words of Azariah the son of Oded, 2 Chron. xv. spoken to Judah in those times, when "there was no peace to him that went out, nor to him that came in, but great vexations were upon all the inhabitants of the countries, and nation was destroyed of nation, and city of city, for God did vex them with all adversity. Be ye strong therefore, let not your hands be weak; for your work shall be rewarded." Upon the hearing of which words of Oded, they took courage, reformed religion, put away all these things that were abominable in the sight of God, and entered into a covenant to seek the Lord God of their fathers, with all their hearts, and all their souls.

covenant, his coming in will be disadvantageous to religion and the liberty of the three nations: therefore I exhort Crawford, Lauderdale, and yourself, to deal with all earnestness, that the league and covenant be settled, as the only basis of the security and happiness of these nations."

Upon the 27th of March, Mr. Sharp writes to Mr. Douglas, desiring to be recalled. He signifies, "that the elections are mostly of the royal party, which causeth fear of mind among the sober party; that Warriston that day took journey for Scotland. He excuseth the general's letter to them, as having some expressions in it not so favourable, put in by Gumble, who is at the bottom for episcopacy. He tells Mr. Douglas, that the printing of his sermon at king Charles's coronation, at London, hath offended the episcopal party, which doth not much matter; that the declaration at Dunfermline, bearing the king's acknowledgment of the blood shed by his father's house, is what he knows not how to excuse; that Lauderdale and he endeavour to vindicate Scotland's treating with the king upon the terms of the covenant, from the necessity England now find themselves in, of treating with the king upon terms, before his return. He adds, some of the episcopal party have sent messages to me twice or thrice, to give them a meeting, which I have refused; and upon this I am reported, both here and at Brussels, to be a Scottish rigid presbyterian, making it my work to have it settled here. They sent to desire me to move nothing in prejudice of the church of England, and they would do nothing in prejudice of our church. I bid tell them, it was not my employment to move to the prejudice of any party; and I thought, did they really mind the peace of those churches, they would not start such propositions; but all who pretend for civil settlement, would contribute their endeavours to restore it, and not meddle unseasonably with those remote cases. The fear of rigid presbytery is talked much of here by all parties: but, for my part, I apprehend no ground for it; I am afraid that something else is like to take place in the church than rigid presbytery. This nation is not fitted to bear that yoke of Christ; and for religion, I suspect it is made a stalking horse still."

April 3d, Mr. Douglas answereth Mr. Sharp's last, and signifies, "that if it be not offensive to the presbyterians at London, he sees no cause but Mr. Sharp might have met with some of the prelatic party. Since presbyterial government, says he, is settled in Scotland, you were not to capitulate with them about that; but it had been worth the pains, if you could have, by fair dealing, persuaded them not to obstruct the settling of the civil government, and to leave the ecclesiastic government to the parliament, who, as it is to be hoped, being men of conscience, will find themselves bound to settle according to the covenant. You might have showed them likewise how falsely presbyterial government is charged with rigidity, and with how much meekness and long-suffering patience it labours and waits for the reclaiming of delinquents that lie under the scandal of transgressing known and unquestionable laws; whereas the lordly dominion of prelacy doth rigidly impose laws on men's consciences, about the observance of ceremonies, and severely censureth, both civilly and ecclesiastically, men who out of conscience dare not conform to them: so that the challenge of rigidity may be justly retorted on episcopacy. Those things you might have calmly debated with them; but herein I would have you do nothing without the advice and allowance of presbyterians, who, being upon the place, can best judge of the expediency of such a meeting. In the postscript to this letter, Mr. Douglas again urgeth, that warrants be sent down for the choosing commissioners to appear from Scotland. He says, Glencairn is much for the committee spoken of before; and he wonders the general can forget Scotland's ready offers of their service to and with him, in his first undertaking, which he hath often acknowledged: (and) adds, "I do not like that we should be so often put to make apologies. Our faith and integrity, both to monarchy and presbyterial government, is more to be valued than theirs who call them in question. It will be strange, if the affections of these people be more enlarged to those great interests, than ours who have been suffering for them, and were active for them, when none of them durst appear. If they think it be a fault, that we laboured to have presbyterial government established with them, and were as tender of their concernments as of our own, they would do well to be plain, and show us wherein the fault lieth; for we supposed, that we were engaged thereunto by the league and covenant: if that oath, which was so solemnly sworn at the coronation, be left out of the form of coronation, it seems purposely done, to hide and keep in oblivion the care that hath been taken here of their concernments in England, because they resolve to mind nothing of our concernments."

Mr. Sharp writes to Mr. Douglas, March 31st, "that there is no fear of any disturbance from the army; and as the general declared at first, so he hath laid things effectually, that the military power shall not maintain a separate interest from the civil: that all people he is among are Englishmen, and incline to keep Scotland at under, and either incorporate, or make us distinct, as they shall find most serviceable to their interest: that he is of opinion, the king, both in point of honour and interest, will restore us, and make us a distinct kingdom. No man questions now the king's being called in; that the real presbyterians in the city hath desired a meeting with the earl of Lauderdale and Mr. Sharp, on Monday, to concert matters against sectaries and cavaliers; which they design to keep."

April 5th, Mr. Sharp signifies to Mr. Douglas, " that the general was positive that he (Mr. Sharp) should not leave him; that a warrant for sending commissioners could not be obtained, for reasons to be communicate to him at Edinburgh; that my lord Lauderdale, and the noble prisoners, are very useful for their country. In his postscript he says, Warriston had applied to him, to deal with the general, that he might have his office, and his debts paid, but I declined; that his wife gives it out, that, had it not been for Mr. Sharp, the general would have restored him to his office; but after the general heard he was gone, he told me (Mr. Sharp) that Warriston would have little use of his grant of six hundred pounds, and, ere three months ended, he would not be worth a groat; that he (the general) would take care, none of the remonstrants should have any trust in Scotland; that the judges were only sent down for the fashion, and in a month or two there would be a change; that it was necessity put him on it, and a little time would show, it was not for Scotland's hurt; that as for sending commissioners from Scotland to the parliament, it was neither for our reputation or advantage; and that, if we be quiet, our business would be done to our mind. He adds, that he behoved to stay at London; that the general had told him, he would communicate his mind to him, and none else, as to Scots affairs; and that in civil things he might signify his (the general's) judgment to such whom he could trust. He adds, that, according to their appointment, they had a meeting with ten presbyterian ministers, whom they could trust, where Lauderdale, they, and he, agreed upon the necessity of bringing in the king upon covenant terms, and taking off the prejudices that lie upon some presbyterians against this. There are endeavours for an accommodation between the moderate episcopalian party, and the presbyterians; but, says he, at our meeting, Lauderdale and I obtained of those ministers that they should not give a meeting to the episcopal men, till they first met among themselves, and resolved on the terms they would stick to. The king is acquainted with all proceedings here, and wants not information of the carriage and affection of Scotland. The parliament will address him, some say, in hard, others upon honourable terms. I see not full ground of hope, that covenant terms will be rigidly stuck to. The paper you sent me by my brother, anent the settlement of the government, will be of good use to me."—By his letter, April 7th, he signifies to Mr. Douglas, that all further applications for commissioners from Scotland must sleep; and adds, " the Lord having opened a fair door of hope, we may look for a settlement upon the grounds of the covenant, and thereby a foundation laid for security against the prelatic and fanatic assaults; but I am dubious if this shall be the result of the agitations now on foot. The story of Hardie's preaching before the general, in the Babylonish habit, is a mere forgery. We intend to publish some letters from the French protestant ministers, vindicating the king from popery, and giving him a large character. The sectaries will not be able to do any thing to prevent the king's coming in; our honest presbyterian brethren are cordial for him. I have been dealing with some of them to send some testimony of their affection for him; and yesternight five of them promised, within a week to make a shift to send a thousand pieces of gold to him. The episcopal party are making applications to the presbyterians for an accommodation; but the presbyterians resolve to stick to their principles. I saw a letter this day under " the king's hand, exhorting his friends to moderation, and endeavours for composing differences amongst his good people."

April 12th, Mr. Sharp writes to Mr. Douglas, that his work is not lessened by the interval of parliaments; that the general had left it on Mr. Calamy and him, to name such as should preach before him; that the fanatics will essay their worst on Lambert's escape, but the general is on his guard. " It was resolved, adds he, that in this juncture, we may speak one by one with any of the episcopal party; and I having told them, that some motions had been made to me of speaking with them, they prayed me not to decline it. To-morrow I have promised to meet with Doctor Morley who came from the king. The king is at Breda. The parliament at its first sitting will, " 'tis expected, call him in. Some say the sectarian party have made application to him, to bring him in without terms. The Dutch have offered to prepare lodgings, and defray his charges during the treaty. The French ambassador presses his going to France, but he refuses." Again, Mr. Sharp writes to Mr. Douglas, April 13th, that the elections are mostly of antirepublicans; that Lauderdale and he had been visiting Mr. Baxter. The insolencies of the cavaliers are so great, that the sober part of that name emit declarations against them. He adds, " there is some talk that for the more reputable settling of the church of England, a synod will be called from all the reformed churches. All that were upon the parliament's side, are gone into the calling in of the king, and they are now only intent upon terms. The general will admit of no other way of treaty, but by a parliament. The council fearing that the parliament may bring him in without sufficient security to such who acted in the war against his father, are now upon framing propositions to propose to the parliament; this is kept secret, but I am promised a copy when they are agreed unto. I continue in my opinion, that Scotland should make no applications till the king come in. I have received letters from Mr. Bruce at the Hague, and the king is satisfied that Scotland keep quiet. I have sent yours, and one from myself, to my lord Broghill."

Mr. Douglas writes to Mr. Sharp, April 21st, that commissioners are coming up, against his mind, and that of others; yet wishes that the general may put respect on them; that Glencairn is following, and wishes there may be a good correspondence betwixt him and Lauderdale, and the rest of the noble prisoners. He adds, " I am engaged to believe that he will do any thing that may be for the liberty of the nation, and for our covenanted interest here, and I have so much from him myself; and my only desire is, that all who truly mind the nation's interest, may not divide, but concur unanimously without by-ends, and self-respects."

April 19th, Mr. Sharp writes to Mr. Douglas, "that the plot of the fanatics appears to be broke: that a messenger from Lambert going to the king is taken, who was to assure the king, if he will trust to the army Lambert could make, they would bring him in without any conditions. Lambert is sculking, nobody knows where. Most of the army have yielded to bring in the king upon terms. If the cavalier party do not drive him on precipitant measures, the parliament will bring him in upon terms, honourable to himself, and safe to the nations. Most of the members of parliament are thought to be for moderation. I find they incline not to put him upon justifying the late war. The business of religion will be altogether waved in the treaty, and referred to be settled by a synod. I have certain accounts this day, that one Mr. Murray came on Saturday to London from Scotland, and went on Monday beyond sea. He told some persons here, that he had letters from the nobility in Scotland to the king, showing they were in readiness to rise for him. This is a divisive way, which will prove foolish and destructive to the nation, if persisted in. I apprehend the gentleman hath been sent by Middleton, and hath brought those stories from some of our sweet lords." To this last Mr. Douglas answereth, April 24th, and tells him, that Mr. Murray came from Middleton, and is returned with a general answer by the lords; that he believes no information that comes that way, will be for their concernments, and the bearer can give little information of the carriage of honest people in Scotland. " But, adds he, if the king be settled, I do not value misrepresentations, for then I hope our religion and civil interests will be settled, which will be sufficient to all, who singly mind the public. As to what Mr. Sharp had writ, that the king was not to be urged to justify the war made against his father, Mr. Douglas says, they would do well, when they do not put him to a direct justifying of it, to provide against his quarrelling the lawfulness of it; that he conceives that war will come under an act of oblivion; and that it does not appear convenient to touch much upon the lawfulness of defensive war; and since it is passed, it ought not to be meddled in, and that whatever hath been in the prosecution, and close of it, evil, yet it was undertaken upon necessary grounds, for our civil and religious interests. He wishes that instead of a synod of foreign divines, the bottom of all were to be the assembly at Westminster their procedure, and there is little need of the help of foreigners in that matter."

Mr. Sharp writes to Mr. Douglas, April without date, that all care is taken against risings; that he gave the general a full account of what he had sent him from Ireland, and he is fully satisfied: that some of the king's party are for bringing him in without terms, but his more sober friends are against it. The general will only have him in by a parliament; and the best accounts from himself bear, that he is desirous to come in upon terms, and by a parliament, whose addresses he will attend. The council have gone through the most sticking part of the articles to be laid before the parliament for a treaty; that of an indemnity, and sales and purchases, which the king will agree to. There is another rub like to rise from the house of lords, that some say Northumberland and Manchester design to engross all offices to themselves and dependants, and to exclude the young lords from sitting, till the treaty be finished. He adds, " no notice is taken of Scotland in the treaty: we shall be left to the king, which is best for us; God save us from divisions and self-seeking. I have acquainted Mr. Bruce how it is with you, and what you are doing, and advised him to guard against Middleton's designs, and those who sent that Murray over to the king. If our noblemen, or others, fall upon factious ways, and grasp after places, they will cast reproach upon their country, and fall short of their ends. I fear the interest of the solemn league and covenant shall be neglected; and for religion, I smell that moderate episcopacy is the fairest accommodation, which moderate men who wish well to religion, expect. Let our noble friends know what you think fit."

A letter from Mr. Douglas to Mr. Sharp, April 26th, bears, " that he hopes the nation will not suffer by the commissioners coming up against all advice. He fears the king hath but slender information of the carriage of the honest party in Scotland, and their disposition; that he wishes the general would permit him (Mr. Sharp) to go over and give the king information concerning his and our carriage. He wishes the king may know who were and are his real friends. He is content that Scotland be not mentioned in the treaty, providing we have the liberty of a free nation, to deal for keeping what we already have both in church and state. So long as this party that now acts get their will, we will never be without divisions and animosities. I fear Mr. Bruce hath not sufficient credit for us. If the solemn league and covenant be neglected, it seems to me that the judgment on these nations is not at an end. The greatest security for the king and those nations, were, to come in upon that bottom. If it shall be neglected, I fear it shall give too great advantage to our ranters here, who are crying it down. If moderate episcopacy shall be the result of all the presbyterians' endeavours, it will be a sad business, for moderate episcopacy is two steps of the ladder, to climb up to the highest prelacy; no caveats will keep them in such a moderation, but ambitious spirits will break all bonds. It is very well known what endeavours king James VI. had here to get a moderate episcopacy settled in constant moderators, with their own consent to caveats, to keep them in subjection to their own presbyteries and synods, and to lay down their places every year at the feet of the general assembly; as appears by the meeting at Montrose, where honest men did protest against it, and tell the king, they did see constant moderators stepping up to the height of prelacy, which fell out in a few years; they broke all caveats, and came to that height of tyranny, which was compesced* with very much ado; and this was the beginning of all the stirs in our nation. You may be assured, that England is better acquaint with, and more inclined to episcopacy, than Scotland was at that time; they need not think that it will stop at moderate precedency, but will take on pomp, dignity, and revenues to uphold it, and all other supports of the hierarchy; then it will be too late to aim at another frame of government. It appears to me, that God has put this fair opportunity in their hand, that they may fall upon the government of his own institution, which would prove a strong defence against errors, heresies, and profanity, that they talk so much of. The time is so favourable, that it will be their own fault if they want a settled government in the kirk; it is not probable that the king will deny it; it will not lie upon him, but upon the kingdom, who will neither seek it, nor have it. If the presbyterians in England shall find the smart of the want of that government, it is just with God that it should be so; seeing they reject his ordinance, and will have a plant of their own settling, which God never planted. Whatever kirk government be settled there, it will have an influence upon this kingdom; for the generality of this new upstart generation have no love to presbyterial government; but are wearied of that yoke, feeding themselves with the fancy of episcopacy, or moderate episcopacy. Our desire is, that presbyterial government be settled; if not, we shall be free of any accession to the breach of a sworn covenant."

April 28th, Mr. Sharp signifies to Mr. Douglas, that the design of closing with the king now appeareth above board. Yesterday the young lords came to the house, who, with those of the year 1648, made up thirty-six. There will, 'tis thought, be no notice taken of qualifications in the house of commons. Both houses are adjourned till Tuesday, when a message will come from the king. By his next letter, May 1st, Mr. Sharp acquaints Mr. Douglas, that a letter was presented to each house, from his Majesty, by Sir John Greenfield, the general's cousin; and refers for other news to the diurnal: that those three days the general had been speaking to him to take a trip to the king at Breda, and he knew not how to decline it, and is sorry he cannot stay till he have Mr. Douglas's mind. If he thinks fit to send over any congratulation to the king, or orders to himself, it may come up in my lord Crawford's packet. In his postscript he adds, "General Monk has been these ten days pressing me to go over to the king, to deal that he may write a letter to Mr. Calamy, to be communicated to the presbyterian ministers, showing his resolution to own the godly sober party, and to stand for the true protestant religion, in the power of it; adding withal, that it will be fit you were there, were it but to acquaint the king with the passages of my undertaking, known to Mr. Douglas and you, and to tell him of matters in Scotland. He spoke to me three several times this last week, and now I am resolved to go, I hope, to do some service to the honest party here, and indeed to ours at home. If you think fit to write to the king, the sooner the better. I have spoken to Glencairn, and showed him what you wrote to me about him." May 4th, Mr. Sharp again writes from London to Mr. Douglas, that he could not get off to Breda

---

* Stayed, repressed.—*Ed.*

to this day. "The presbyterian ministers of the city, after several meetings, have resolved to send over next week some ministers from the city, Oxford, and Cambridge, to congratulate the king: and I am desired to acquaint the king with their purpose, and dispose for their reception; or, if it be possible, that he would write to both houses by way of prevention, that they would secure religion in reference to some points. Some particulars of secrecy the general hath recommended to me, and given orders to transport me in a frigate. I have got a large letter to the king, and another to his prime minister. Providence hath ordered it well, that my going carries the face of some concernment in reference to England; but I shall have hereby the better access and opportunity to speak what the Lord shall direct as to our matters, and give a true information of the carriage of business. I think I need not stay above ten days. It will be best to address the king by a letter. Presbyterians here are few, and all are Englishmen, and these will not endure us to do any thing that may carry a resemblance in pressing uniformity: for my part, I shall not be accessory to any thing prejudicial to the presbyterian government; but to appear for it in any other way than is within my sphere, is inconvenient, and may do harm, and not good."

Mr. Robert Douglas writes to Mr. Sharp, May 8th, that he durst not write of his going to Holland, till his last, of April 26th, and observes now, that his motion and the general's came together. He adds, " I perceive by all that you write, that no respect will be had to the covenant in this great transaction, which if neglected altogether, it fears me that the Lord will be highly provoked to wrath. It will be the presbyterians' fault, if they get not as much settled, at least, as was agreed on by the synod of divines, and ratified by parliament; for I perceive that the king will be most condescending to the desires offered by the parliament: but I leave that. However our desires may be for uniformity in doctrine, worship, discipline, and government; if they will not press it themselves, we are free. Your great errand will be for this kirk. I am confident the king will not wrong our liberties, whereunto he himself is engaged. He needs not declare any liberty to tender consciences here, because the generality of the people, and whole ministry have embraced the established religion by law, with his majesty's consent. It is known, that in all the times of the prevailing of the late party in England, none here petitioned for toleration, except some inconsiderable naughty men. Whatever indulgence the king intends to persons who have failed under the late revolutions, yet he would be careful to do it so as they shall be in no capacity to trouble the peace of the land, as formerly they did. I doubt not but you will inform the king of the circumstances and condition of our kirk: it is left wholly upon you to do what you can for the benefit of this poor distracted kirk, that the king's coming may be refreshful to the honest party here; since no directions from us can well reach you before you come back to London. Receive the enclosed to his majesty, a true copy of it for yourself." —The letter of this day's date to the king, signed by Messrs. Douglas, Dickson, Hamilton, Smith, and Hutchison, I have inserted,*

---

* Letter to the King's Majesty, from Messrs. Robert Douglas, David Dickson, James Hamilton, John Smith, and George Hutchison, Edinburgh, May 8th, 1660.

May it please your Majesty,

We cannot but admire the faithfulness and tender compassions of the Lord our God, who keepeth covenant and mercy, in that it hath pleased him to have respect to the long and sad afflictions of your majesty, and of your faithful subjects, and to the many prayers put up to him, in great trials of affliction, by opening so comfortable and promising door of hope, that he will repossess your majesty in your just rights, and restore unto your people their rulers as at the first, and their counsellors as at the beginning, and that probably (which we hear your majesty so much desires) without effusion of blood : this is the Lord's doing, and it is wonderful in our eyes, that we may not only enjoy the liberty (whereof we have been long, to our great grief, deprived,) to tender our faithful service at such a distance, but are filled with hopes to enjoy your majesty's presence in your own dominions, as a bright sunshine after a long and tempestuous night, to prove a shelter and encouragement to all those who delight to walk in the ways of truth and peace. And, when we abstract from instruments in all the late revolutions, we cannot but further adore the holy and wise providence of God, who, having preserved your majesty's royal person in imminent hazards, hath seen it fit to breed you (as another David)

and shall make no large abbreviate of it. They put him in mind of his covenant, and expect protection in their establishment, and that he will settle God's house in all his dominions, according to God's word. In short, it differs not far from Mr. Guthrie's address, for which he was seized August 23d, as we shall hear. With this letter they send instructions to Mr. Sharp, which I likewise have annexed.*

---

in the school of affliction, that you may be an eminent instrument, in his right hand, to promove the interests of his Son, Jesus Christ, and to rule for him; whereof your majesty's moderation of spirit, and stedfastness in the truth, in all your sharp trials, have been comfortable and refreshing evidences to all who have heard thereof. Sir, as the condition of your majesty, and of your dominions, have been no light affliction of spirit to us, and to the Lord's faithful servants in this church with us, these years bygone, while we have been forced to encounter with difficulties, both from among ourselves, and from without; so it hath been no small addition to our affliction, that we could not any other way express our duty to your majesty, than by our endeavours to sympathize with you, and our prayers to God for you; for any comfortable account whereof, we do heartily bless him, and do resolve, in the power of his grace, to give him more employment, till it please him to perfect that good work which he hath begun. But now, since it hath pleased God to open a door, (which we have long desired,) for our brother Mr. Sharp, to come and wait upon your majesty, we could not any longer forbear to present by him this our humble address, in testimony of our loyal affection to your majesty, and our humble acknowledgment of the Lord's goodness to these your dominions, in this comfortable revolution of affairs, making way for your majesty's re-instalment. If it had been expedient in this juncture of affairs, your majesty might have expected an address from the generality of the ministers of this church, who, we assure your majesty, have continued, and will continue, in their loyalty to authority, and the maintenance of your just rights, in their stations, according to these principles by which your majesty left them walking in opposition both to enemies from without, and disturbers from within: but doubting that, such an application is not yet seasonable, we have desired Mr. Sharp to inform your majesty more fully of the true state of this church; whereby we trust your majesty will perceive our painfulness and fidelity in these trying times, and that the principles of the church of Scotland are such, and so fixed for the preservation and maintenance of lawful authority, as your majesty needs never repent that you have entered into a covenant for maintaining thereof: so that we nothing doubt of your majesty's constant resolution to protect this church in her established privileges, and are no less confident, (though we presume not to meddle without our sphere,) that your majesty will not only hearken to the humble advices of those who are concerned, but will also, of your own royal inclination, appear to settle the house of God, according to his word, in all your dominions. Now the Lord himself bless your majesty; let his right hand settle and establish you upon the throne of your dominions, and replenish your royal heart with all those graces and endowments necessary for repairing the breaches of these so long distracted kingdoms; that religion and righteousness may flourish in your reign, the present generation may bless God for the mercies received by you, and the generations to come may reap the fruits of your royal pains. So pray,

SIR,

Your Majesty's faithful Subjects,
and humble Servants,

Directed,
For the King's Majesty.

MR. ROBERT DOUGLAS,
DAVID DICKSON,
MR. JAMES HAMILTON,
MR. JOHN SMITH,
GEORGE HUTCHISON.

* Instructions for Mr. James Sharp, in reference to the king, May 8th:

1. You shall fully inform the king of the constant fidelity of the body of the ministry of Scotland, to him; and that (however some endeavours were of necessity used, to prevent prejudices to the government of the kirk, yet) conscience hath been made, of not complying with any that have been in power, nor seeking or receiving any benefit from them, notwithstanding many hazards to which they were daily exposed by reason of their fidelity, many temptations from these who would gladly have conciliate their favour, and many trials and temptations from those among ourselves, who, to drive their own designs, did fall off to those in power, and did endeavour to irritate them against us, as constant adherers to the king, and enemies to them.

2. If need be, you may inform the king of the testimony to the government of the kirk of Scotland, and the constant adherers thereunto, extorted even from adversaries; in that, however they did own that party in this church who did homologate their way, yet they were forced to acknowledge that we were the men of sober and rational principles, and therefore did endeavour to gain us, but in vain.

3. In informing of our constant adherence to the king, and our dealing with God for him, if any occasion be offered, to clear our forbearing to express his name in our public prayers, you may clear, that it was only a forbearing to express royal titles, lest thereby greater prejudice might have ensued, both to the work of the gospel, and to the king's affairs; but the thing itself was constantly kept up by us, even in public, in so far that it was still charged upon us, that though we forbare the name, yet we did the equivalent.

4. When ye have occasion to sound the king's inclinations concerning religion, ye may inform, that all honest men have their eyes much upon his majesty's self, that he will not only be ready to hearken to wholesome counsel, but will of himself give eminent proof of his being taught in the school of affliction to be an eminent pro-

I shall scarce break the thread of this account, by taking notice that, May 8th, Mr. Douglas answers a letter dated April —, from the governor of Ulster, wherein is signified the governor's joy to hear of the unanimity in Scotland on covenant principles; that he hopes the prevailing party in Ireland will carry on their work of reformation; that the army is right, as appears by their declaration enclosed; that they are in great fears, some about the king may persuade him to come in otherwise than upon the call of his people in parliament upon a covenant account. To this Mr. Douglas, in return, acquaints the governor how refreshing his was; regrets so few mind the main business of reformation; hopes that God will appear for his own interests, and is persuaded that if the parliament mind the business of religion the king will accord to their proposals.

As soon as the ministers of Edinburgh were acquainted with the earl of Rothes' going over to Breda, May 10th, Mr. Douglas and Mr. Hutchison write a letter to him, signifying, they are glad his lordship is repairing to the king, and that he will have opportunity to give an account of the true state of affairs during the late revolutions. They beg he may lay out himself for the good of the church, that she may enjoy all her liberties established by law. That he knows the constant adherence of the body of ministers to the king during the late revolutions, and how cordial they have been in the late change; that he knows likewise how much the people adhere to the establishment of the church, so that there is no pretext for an indulgence to such as shall recede from it, but many inconveniences would ensue upon the granting it. Those things they beg his lordship may lay before the king, that he may not hearken to any advice to their prejudice, though they hope there is none such. Likewise they send over a letter with the earl to the king, the purport of which is to congratulate his majesty, and to express their thoughts of the gracious message he had sent to the parliament of England, as the reader will see from the letter itself. *

---

moter of reformation, as another Josiah; and particularly, you may inform, that as we doubt nothing of his constancy in adhering to what he is engaged unto by covenant, as to us; so, whatever motives he may have to take another course in England, either to incline to an episcopacy, or to give a latitude to variety of ways (wherein, beside our judgment of the things themselves, and the consideration of the king's engagement, we cannot but foresee many inconveniences; and, for your further instruction in this particular, we refer you to the letter of April 26th, and a paper of March 27th,) yet there is no show even of conveniency or advantage, to alter any thing of the settled government of the kirk of Scotland, wherein all the people are generally principled, and do acquiesce.

You may also inform how necessary it is, that the king, in dealing with this kingdom, do give an equal countenance to all who have adhered to him, in these late revolutions; and that care be taken, that no factions made by any, upon any thing, be allowed to the prejudice of others no less faithful. You know, that, among the king's real friends, some have taken more liberty to make the best they could of the late times, who now seem to set themselves among those who would be greatest courtiers; and we have nothing to say against any particular favour the king may please to put upon them; yet, if those, and others with them, should be only countenanced, and others under a cloud who have made conscience to abstain from the least shadow of compliance, it cannot but sadden honest men much, give occasion to real compliers to insult over them, and exceedingly prejudge the king's affairs, who, we trust, will hold to his old principle, that he came not to be a head to a faction, but a king to all.

As for those among us, with whom you know we have had so much vexation, you may inform, if you find cause, that we really wish no evil to their persons, nor shall, for our part, stumble, if the king exercise his moderation toward them; yet we apprehend their principles to be such, (especially their leaders) as their having any hand in affairs cannot but breed continual distempers and disorders.

When you have occasion to speak concerning the settling of religion in England, you may further remember to inform the king how many presbyterians are in England who have cleaved to him, who cannot acknowledge episcopacy to be of God's institution, and cannot but expect hard things if that yoke be imposed upon them: also you may inform of what stamp divers of the later episcopal divines are, who not only run that length in affecting episcopacy, as to acknowledge the patriarchates of Rome in the western church, but, in point of doctrine, have published many strange tenets, contrary to the doctrine of the reformed churches, and of the church of England, and orthodox bishops in former times. The settling of the interest and way of men of such principles, would give sober and orthodox men cause to fear the overturning of all religion. You may also inform what errors, Arminianism, popery, &c. were hatched under episcopacy, in the latter times thereof.

* Letter to the King's Majesty, from Messrs. Robert Douglas, David Dickson, and George

That same day, May 10th, Messrs. Douglas and Hutchison write to the earls of Crawford and Lauderdale at London, and signify how satisfying it is to them to understand that their lordships endeavour to keep an entire union and good understanding among us in this kingdom. They recommend the earl of Selkirk as very much for this. They add, " there is another particular we are necessitate to trouble your lordships about, concerning the worship of God in the king's family, when it shall please the Lord to bring him to England. We are sensible how he hath been necessitate to make use of the Service-book abroad, which if it should be set up at his return, your lordships know what may be the consequences. We judge it will trouble many of this kingdom, who will account it their duty to be about his majesty, and yet are engaged against that way of worship : it will give a great dash to the hopes of many in that kingdom whose judgments are against it, and yield advantage to many who malign this happy change; and probably upon that practice it may be again generally set up in

---

Hutchison, Edinburgh, May 10th, 1660, with the earl of Rothes.

May it please your Majesty,

While your majesty's faithful subjects in this kingdom were waiting upon the Lord for a comfortable account of the late promising revolution of affairs, it pleased him, who remembereth his people in their low estate, to refresh their spirits, which have so long groaned under so much bondage, with the news of your majesty's gracious message to your houses of parliament of England, and their proceeding thereupon toward the instalment of your majesty in your just right. Upon the first hearing thereof, such of your majesty's faithful subjects, ministers in this city, as had occasion at any time to be near your royal person, did hold it their duty to make their humble address, which they desired Mr. Sharp to present to your majesty : and now the earl of Rothes having made us acquainted with his purpose to come and wait upon your majesty, we have taken the opportunity again to express our humble and sincere affection to your majesty, and our hearty rejoicing in the Lord, who hath filled our mouths with laughter, because of this change of his right hand. This noble lord (a true lover of your majesty, and his country, and the true interests thereof) can inform your majesty with many of our afflictions of spirit under our bondage, and how often our griefs have doubled upon us, while we looked for peace, and behold, trouble, and while many endeavours to put a period to our miseries have been blasted, and contributed only to the augmenting thereof: but now we are like men that dream, while we consider how eminently the Lord himself hath appeared in turning again our captivity. Hereby we are encouraged to trust our faithful God in all exigents, who, after so many years' success, hath fulfilled what he hath recorded in his word against oppressors and usurpers; and we cannot but look upon his doing all these great things for your majesty, and your kingdoms, as a token for good, and pledge of much further kindness to be manifested. We may assert it to your majesty, that as the Lord hath kept our hearts from fainting during our long captivity, and made us confidently expect a revolution, and overturning of all the designs of bloody men; so no small part of our refreshment did flow from our hopes, that your majesty, being restored to your kingdoms, after that God hath for a long time trained you in the school of affliction, shall give singular proofs of your proficiency therein. Your faithful subjects do expect, that the Lord's so wonderful preserving and restoring of your majesty, will produce no ordinary effects; but as the case is singular, so the consequences thereof shall be proportionably comfortable. And in all the hazards to which religion may be exposed, their eyes are fixed upon your majesty as the man of God's right hand, who will not only give your royal assent to what your subjects shall humbly propose, in order to the security and settlement thereof, but will, by your majesty's own example, and by improving the royal power, make it appear unto the world that it is in your heart to order the house of God according to his word, who hath been pleased to respect your majesty and your royal house; so that your subjects may be excited to their duty, and encouraged to walk after such a pattern. Your majesty's constant adherence to the protestant religion amidst so many temptations, and the moderation of your royal spirit, expressed in your late gracious message, are pledges of our hope that religion shall flourish in your majesty's reign, and that all good men shall reap the fruit of those many desires and prayers put up to God in behalf of your majesty and your royal family; and, in particular, this church do nothing doubt of your majesty's royal protection and countenance to the religion therein established, wherein it hath pleased the Lord so to confirm and establish all ranks of persons, notwithstanding all the delusions of the time, that (beside the justice of the thing itself) there will be no hazard to any interest to preserve all the privileges thereof inviolable. We have briefly laid open these thoughts of our heart, which our sincere desire of your majesty's happiness and prosperity doth suggest unto us; and we trust the Lord will give your majesty understanding in all things, and instruct you to judge and esteem of counsels, according as they shall be found consonant to the will of him who is the supreme Lawgiver. To his rich grace and wise direction your majesty is recommended by,

SIR,

Your Majesty's humble and faithful
Subjects and Servants,

Directed,   Mr. ROBERT DOUGLAS,
For the King's   Mr. DAVID DICKSON,
Majesty.   GEORGE HUTCHISON.

that kingdom, and so may prejudge all future settlement of religion. In this exigent, we could find out no better expedient than to recommend this particular to your lordships' wisdom and prudence, that if you think fit, by dealing with his majesty himself, with fit persons in both houses, and with honest ministers, this may be prevented, and some appointed to attend his majesty, for performing family worship till there be a settlement. And it is our humble opinion, that (abstracting from our judgment of the thing itself) his majesty's forbearance, till there be a settlement, is the most safe course. Since the episcopal divines themselves have many of them forborne it in England these years bypast, we can see no prejudice following upon his majesty's keeping his way which he observed in Scotland, till there be some establishment in matters of religion to a more general satisfaction. We shall no further trouble your lordships at this time, but to request that whatever his majesty hath been pleased to declare concerning England, yet care may be had, that no liberty may be granted in this church to overturn the established religion, wherein there is so general and harmonious agreement among us." The same persons, that same day, write to Mr. Sharp, signifying, " that beside the former instructions they sent him by way of London, he may remember the great inconvenience that will ensue upon the king's using the Service-book when he returns, and use all fit means to prevent it; and mind to inform the king, that no such concession is necessary to Scotland, as he hath given in his declaration as to England."

May 12th, The above written ministers of Edinburgh, write a letter to Messrs. Calamy, Ash, and Manton, which, because of its importance, is referred to frequently afterward, and added (below). *

May 22d, Mr. Douglas writes to Mr. Robert Alison of Newcastle, member of parliament, in return to one he had received from him, in which he appears to have pressed Mr. Douglas to undertake a London journey at this juncture. After Mr. Douglas hath expressed his satisfaction with this great turn of affairs, and showed how solicitous all honest men are for the settlement of the church of England; he adds, " these worthy men who revived the league and covenant, gave great encouragement to all lovers of religion, and of lawful authority. I am not without hopes there are many worthy patriots with you, who may be able to persuade the parliament of the inexpediency, to say no more, of returning to prelacy and the Service-book. I apprehend that indeed you do rightly take up the case, that if yourselves do accord to a settlement of presbytery, and the directory, the king will willingly grant it. I trust, the Lord who hath done so great things for us, and particularly England, in this revolution, will not so far leave them, as they shall forget the covenant, and what in pursuance thereof hath been done by the assembly and parliament, and neglect such an opportunity, whereof they never had the like; and it is to be doubted if ever the like return. I am unclear as to the expediency of my coming up at this time. I have frequently spoken and written to the lord general, and doubt not of his willingness to concur with honest men, and have written lately to the ministers of London, and you have Mr. Sharp with you at London ready to join. Much will lie in the parliament's own inclinations, and they have the prayers of all honest men, that they may be directed to settle that government, which we by experience have found the most effectual mean for restraining error and suppressing profanity. And I judge the activity of honest men should be

---

* Letter to Messrs. Calamy, Ash, and Manton, from Messrs. David Dickson, Robert Douglas, James Hamilton, John Smith, and George Hutchison, Edinburgh, May 12th, 1660.

Right reverend and dear brethren,

As we often had occasion of comfortable correspondence with our brethren in England, and under our late distresses have several times given you an account of our case, and have been refreshed with your tender respects toward us, so we held it our duty to pour out our hearts unto you, upon occasion of this signal revolution of affairs, wherein the Lord's hand hath so eminently appeared, that our mouths are filled with laughter, and our tongues with singing. We are indeed as men who dream, when we con-

exerted to deal with members, and if need be I shall write again to the general, if Mr. Sharp shall advise it."

Mr. Douglas writes the same day, May 22d, to Mr. Sharp, signifying what they had done since his departure, contained in the above letters sent with the earl of Rothes. He doubts not but Mr. Sharp hath managed his being with his majesty for the interests of Christ; and wishes he may be helpful to the ministers of London, with all caution and wariness, that, adds he, " your doing for them tend not to the undoing of ourselves. We are very hopeful that his majesty will be mindful of us, and will be loath to entertain suggestions to the prejudice of the established doctrine, worship, discipline, and government of this church; and if the violence of some press an alteration, we are confident he will graciously repress that insolence, and vouchsafe us the enjoyment of the liberties and privileges of this kirk, ratified by the laws of this kingdom, which we have stood for against the opposition of those who plied the usurping powers for the overthrow thereof, by the plausible argument of their compliance with them against monarchy, whereunto they affirmed we adhered, as indeed we did. We hope his majesty will be in case to distinguish betwixt these, who, for their own interest, have struck in with all changes, and those who were fixed in their principles for lawful government."

It is high time now to return to Mr. Sharp at Breda, where Mr. Douglas, in his

---

sider how the Lord hath so ordered this dispensation, as to give us hopes to see our lawful magistrate possessed in his just rights, in so harmonious and peaceable a way. And though we doubt not but many will now be active to have reformation of religion at least obstructed; yet we cannot but hope, that the Lord, who hath done all these things for us, is so far from a purpose to destroy us, that he is putting in our hands a blessed opportunity of advancing his kingdom, if we were fitted for such a mercy, and the dispensation be rightly improved. Though it hath pleased the Lord so far to advance his work in this church, as that all the privileges and interests thereof are established by law, with the king's royal consent, whereunto the people have generally submitted, even in our late confusions, and though we purpose not to stretch ourselves beyond our line; yet our tender sympathy with honest men there, and even respect to the welfare of this church (experience having taught how much influence the condition of affairs with you had upon us) makes us apprehensive of the sad consequences of setting up episcopacy, and the use of liturgy again, under which religion hath suffered so much, as yourselves do well remember. We hope the Lord is putting it in your and your brethren's hearts to lay forth yourselves at this time for preventing those evils, and what may have a tendency thereunto, or may encourage people to look toward these ways. We may assure you, that you have to do with a moderate prince, who is ready to hearken to sound and wholesome counsel, whereof we had large experience, in that his majesty was not only content to ratify the religion as it was established among us, as to the subjects, but did readily condescend to lay aside the Service-book, and observed the Directory of Worship in his own practice and family, all the while it pleased God to continue his majesty with us. You have now the advantage of humble dealing with a prince long trained in the school of affliction, and preserved therein, and (we trust) fitted thereby to be an eminent instrument in God's right hand for the advancement of his Son's kingdom: and therefore we trust his majesty will hearken to what humble advice God shall put in your hearts for him, that he may be exemplary in his own practice, and put forth his royal power for satisfaction of honest men in the matters of religion. We are far from prescribing unto you our reverend and dear brethren, or from being any thing doubtful of your vigilance and activity in this juncture of affairs; but it flows only from our abundance of affection, and the conscience of our obligation by covenant, that we have given you the trouble of these few lines. We know how incumbent it is to us in our stations, to forbear to intrude upon the work of others, and do purpose to demean ourselves accordingly; yet we are most confident that this expression of our brotherly love will not be unacceptable unto you. And we shall pray, that the Lord may give you understanding in all things, and may lead you forth in his right hand, to act in your stations at this time for the good of religion, and for the settling of that government in the church, which you have so solidly asserted by writing, and which is the most effectual mean to stop the current of profanity, and damnable errrors and heresies, as we have found by experience: for we fear that if this opportunity, which God hath put in our hands, be lost, it will hardly (if at all) be recovered. And if the Lord be pleased to assist you in the managing thereof, it shall be your rejoicing to have been instrumental in refreshing the spirits of honest men in all the three nations, and your labour shall be acceptable to God, through Jesus Christ, and tend to the advantage of the true religion in the present and succeeding generations. We add no more, but that we heartily recommend you to the Lord's rich grace, and are

Directed
To the right Reverend
Mr. Edmund Calamy,
Mr. Simeon Ash, and
Mr. Thomas Manton,
Ministers of the Gospel
at London.

Your very loving Brethren,
David Dickson,
Mr. Robert Douglas,
Mr. James Hamilton,
Mr. John Smith,
George Hutchison.

Account of the Introduction of Prelacy, is of opinion he was corrupted. Perhaps the reader may be pleased to have what Mr. Douglas says there, in his own words, and they are as follow: " I profess, I did not suspect Mr. Sharp, in reference to prelacy, more than I did myself, no more than the apostles did Judas before his treachery was discovered: I did not suspect him for that, more than I did suspect him for taking the tender, after he came out of the Tower so long before us. But since I find that has been his truckling; and when he went over to Holland, he had a letter from a prime nobleman to the king, signifying that he was episcopal in his judgment. This was revealed to me after he was made a bishop. The first thing that gave me a dislike at him was, when he was in Holland he wrote to me in commendation of Hyde, an enemy to our nation and presbyterial government. I durst not as yet believe myself in this, having no more save his commendation of Hyde: but it appeared afterwards, that in Holland he was a great enemy to the presbyterian interest; and when we wrote a favourable letter for the earl of Rothes, and with him a letter to the king, he dissuaded the earl from delivering the letter. When at London, he was enraged that we had written to the ministers of London. He dealt also treacherously with the brethren who came from Ireland, in dissuading their addresses to the king. When he came to Scotland, he dealt earnestly against all addresses made to the parliament against prelacy. He dealt treacherously with the king, making him believe that there were no considerable persons against prelacy; but would have persuaded the king that all our lives were in his hand, and he might do what he pleased; and the man never rested till he was brought himself to a chair." This passage I thought proper here to insert from Mr. Douglas' own original copy now before me, both to show the hypocrisy, in what of Mr. Sharp's actings we have seen, if his treacherous design was a forming all this while, as we may suspect from his taking the tender; and to evince it fully, as well as lay open some springs of what he says and does in the following letters.

Mr. Sharp's only letter from Breda to Mr. Douglas, in this collection, is dated May 11th, where, after he hath given him an account of his voyage, and that on the 8th, at night he got to Breda, where he was led to the court by Alexander Bruce, where the marquis of Ormond introduced him to the king, to whom he delivered his letters, and next morning at nine, had an hour and an half with the king alone in his bedchamber. In the evening the king took him to walk in the garden near an hour. He adds, "he found the king's memory perfectly fresh as to all things in Scotland; that he asked by name, how it was with Mr. Douglas, Mr. Dickson, Mr. Hamilton, Mr. Hutchison, and Mr. Wood; and having asked how Mr. Smith was, he said laughing, Is his broadsword to the fore?* I answered, I knew it was taken from him when he was made a prisoner, but his majesty might be persuaded Mr. Smith would be provided of one when his service required it. The king said, he was sure of that, and of the affections of all honest men, to whom he bid me remember him. He further asked how Mr. Bailie was, and said, he heard Mr. Law, and Mr. Knox of Kelso, was dead, adding, that both he and the kingdom had a loss by their removal. The king, adds Mr. Sharp, surpasseth all ever I heard or expected of him. I gave him an account of my management at London, and congratulate his majesty in your name, which he took very kindly. The states are to congratulate him, and it is happy he is acknowledged by so great a protestant state: he is little obliged to France and Spain."

May 26th, Mr. Sharp writes from London to Mr. Douglas, that he is returned to that place that day; that he came in one of the king's frigates with the London ministers: he gives the particulars of the king's landing, general Monk's meeting him at Dover, and the parliament's congratulatory letter, and their desire he may come to the city by water. He adds, " I find the sober presbyterian party have no reserve but in

---

* *i. e.* Has he his broadsword still?

his majesty's clemency, of which they have no cause to doubt; that he received all their letters since the 3d, at London, and would take the first opportunity to present their letter to the king; had it come to him in Holland, he would have presented it there, where he had opportunities to have spoken to the full as to the matter of it. I find the king very affectionate to Scotland, and resolved not to wrong the settled government of our church. For settling religion here, I apprehend they are mistaken who go about to settle the presbyterian government."

Mr. Douglas, by his letter May 29th, acquaints Mr. Sharp, that many of all sorts are thronging to London. " I trust, adds he, the king will not fall upon Scots affairs, but remit them to the ordinary way agreeable to the laws of the land. I suspect counsel may be given to do that which may dissatisfy many, for there are many who seek their own private good; but I am not afraid his majesty will give way to what may be prejudicial to the nation. Cassils, and Mr. James Dalrymple of Stair, are coming up; the first is beyond all exception. The protesters think to obtain somewhat by their means, but I believe the king will not meddle with that which concerns the kirk's interest, but refer all to a general assembly, which he must call for taking away those differences. You know the public resolutions are for the king's interest, and we have nothing standing as a testimony of our loyalty to magistracy, but those actings by the commission of the kirk and general assembly in defence of our lawful magistrate, against the attempts made upon the government. Those have been the ground of our sufferings from the day of his majesty's departure to that of his return. Before his majesty do any thing he will let us have a favourable hearing. We intend nothing against men's persons, only we desire our proceedings may be seen to the world, and that our integrity and respect to lawful magistracy may appear. It will be grievous to all honest men here, if England miss this occasion of settling religion and government. Whatever may be pretended for us, and the securing of our government, it cannot be thought but England's condition in ecclesiastic matters will have a great influence upon this nation, at least, the troubling our peace. We have great hopes his majesty will grant in matters of religion what his parliament desires. The strain of too many protesters in their preachings is, that we are in hazard of episcopacy and a Service-book, and press private meetings as necessary to uphold the power of godliness. It is looked on strangely here that there is never so much as an advertisement from our brethren in England, concerning the estate of their kirk, or any desire to us to deal for the good of it; not that we have thoughts to go without our own line to meddle with the affairs of another kirk, though we might plead some more interest in them than any other by virtue of our solemn league and covenant. If they prudently foresee our doing any thing in their business might relish ill, and resolve to do for themselves: if the Lord shall keep them from the Service-book, and prelacy, and settle religion among them according to the solemn league and covenant, we have all we desire, and shall look on it as a gracious return to our prayers on their behalf."

May 29th, Mr. Sharp writes to Mr Douglas, and gives him a large account of his going to Breda. He says, " general Monk's design in my going was, that I might give his majesty an account of all the passages of his undertaking, from his coming from Scotland to the parliament's owning the king; that I might acquaint him how necessary it was to follow moderation in his after-management; and to move the king to write to some of the city ministers, by them to be communicate to all presbyterians, intimating his majesty's design to suppress profanity and countenance religion in its power. I insisted on several things in yours to me, and was the first minister of the three kingdoms who avowedly addressed the king. I made my address in name of the ministry of the church of Scotland. I was most kindly entertained, and the king hath a great affection for our country and kirk. After I had been several times with his majesty, and he naming a particular time to me to wait on him for his despatches to England, and letter to the city ministers, I began to speak about Scotland, when he told me, he would reserve a full communing about that till his coming to England. I found his majesty most willing to restore our kingdom to its ancient privileges, and preserve the settled government of our church, in both which, I was bold expressly to move, and had a very gracious satisfying answer. The English ministers were much satisfied with the king's receiving of them. I kept much company with the ministers that came over, and returned to England with them; and by conversation I can make a probable conjecture of the tendency of matters as to religion in England. I have much to say on this head, which I cannot write at present; I shall only say this, that for me to press uniformity for discipline and government upon the king and others, I find would be a most disgustful employment, and successless: for though the king could be induced to be for it, it were not in his power to effectuate it, the two houses of parliament, and body of this nation, being against it; and if I may speak what I know, and can demonstrate to you, 'tis already past remedying. I know very few or none who desire it, much less appear for it. And whoever do report to you, or believe that there is a considerable party in England, who have a mind for a covenant-uniformity, they are mistaken; and as you say in yours, May 8th, if they will not press, we are free. I see no obligation by covenant to impose that upon them which they care not for. If you knew what I know, I am persuaded you would not be very urgent upon that point. For my part, I shall have no occasion to what may cross that uniformity, but I have no freedom to an employment which can have no other effect but the heightening an odium upon our church, which is obnoxious already to many upon such an account, though I know causelessly. I have heard of your letter to Mr. Ash, who only has seen it, and Mr. Calamy and Manton. The rumour goes in the city, I know not if occasion be taken by that letter, that the ministers of Scotland have declared their dissatisfaction that the king is brought in but upon the terms of the covenant. I am afraid that such rumours are at this time studiously raised, and I see more and more the need of using caution with those here who have had large experience of Anglorum, &c. And I have cause to think, that we shall have a discovery of it, as much now as ever. I shall present your letter to his majesty as soon as the throng upon his coming to Whitehall is a little over."*

---

* In the preface to an anonymous Memoir of archbishop Sharp, written by a Scottish episcopalian, and published 1723, the writer says: "I find that Mr. Wodrow, in the Abbreviate he gives us of Mr. Sharp's letter to Mr. Douglas, dated the 29th of May, 1660, hath, if not wilfully perverted, yet grossly mistaken, the meaning of the writer, as may be evident to any man who will take the pains to compare the letter itself set down in the Appendix with the said Abbreviate, in Mr. Wodrow's Introduction," preface, p. 10.—We have made the comparison without being able to discover any ground for the charge here preferred. On the contrary, we think it impossible to read the letter itself without feeling that it reflects much more severely on the prelate's subsequent conduct than Mr. Wodrow's Abbreviate does. But for the reader's satisfaction, and because the letter is somewhat curious, we subjoin it entire. —*Ed.*

Letter from Mr. Sharp, to Mr. Robert Douglas, Minister at Edinburgh.

Reverend Sir,

Yours, that, May 22d, and of the 8th, with other letters, I received; by the last Saturday's post I could only give you notice of my safe return to London. General Monk gave the occasion for my journey to Holland, and I did observe a providence in it, that his motion did tryst with your desire, which gave me encouragement to follow the Lord's pointing at my going thither, which for any thing doth yet appear hath been ordered for good. General Monk's intent for my going was, that I might give his majesty an account of all the passages of his undertaking, from the beginning of it in Scotland, to the progression he had made at the time of the parliament's owning his majesty's title; and that I might acquaint the king how necessary it was to follow the counsels of moderation in the future management of his affairs. And, 3dly, That I might move his majesty for writing a letter to some of the eminent city ministers, to be by them communicated to the presbyterian ministers throughout the kingdom, intimating his majesty's resolution, to bear down profanity, and to countenance religion in the power of it. My own special motive for going was, to give a timous information of the condition of poor Scotland, as to the several particulars, which yours of May 8th, doth bear. My thoughts at my going

INTRODUCTION.

June 2d, Mr. Sharp writes to Mr. Douglas, "Upon Thursday night the king called me into his closet, where I presented yours of the 8th of May to him. Having read some of it, and looked on the subscriptions, he told me he was glad to see a letter from your hands; and it being late, and being to go to the house to-morrow, he would after- over did run upon diverse of these, which digestedly and fully that letter doth mention, and it hath much satisfied me, that upon the perusal of yours at my return, I remembered I hit upon some of those you touched. I came very seasonably in the beginning of the growth of the court, and was the first minister of the kingdoms, who made an address avowedly to the king, since his exile; which I did with the more confidence, that having your warrand before my going, I made it in name of the body of the ministry of the church of Scotland, who had persevered in their integrity and loyalty in all revolutions. I cannot express what welcome I had, and with how kindly an acceptance my application was entertained by his majesty, who was graciously pleased to put such a respective usage upon me, all the time I was there, as it was noticed by all at court. I do not mention this out of a tickling vanity, but as an evidence amongst others of our prince's affection to our country and kirk, of which I am abundantly satisfied, though before my going over, he was falsely represented, even to some of the presbyterian judgment, as an enemy and hater of both. He did at Breda, at his table upon occasion, give his public testimony to the fidelity and loyalty of his kingdom of Scotland, and to me in private more than once or twice; and I am persuaded, a sweeter and more affectionate prince never a people had. The first time he allowed me to speak to him in private, which was for the space of one hour and half, I took it up, in giving a full account of general Monk's proceedings, and of the activity of those of our nation to improve that opportunity for his majesty's service. The next time he called me to him in the garden, where he caused me walk with him, almost 200 gentlemen being at his back, almost two hours, was employed in his moving questions and my answering, about the affairs of the parliament; and in the close, somewhat in reference to Scotland, and asking kindly how it was with the ministers who had been in the Tower, and with Mr. Hutchison, Mr. Wood, Mr. Bayly, of which I gave you some touch in my letter from Breda. The third time he spoke to me (doing it upon every occasion he saw me) was in the princess royal's room, where I was amazed to hear him express such knowledge and remembrance, both as to persons and things relating to Scotland, while he was there, as if the passages had been recently acted. He mentioned ministers south and north, and other persons, not forgetting John Boswel of Kinghorn, and another in Crail, where, he said, himself was provost, asking how it was with them. There was opportunity of speaking of those with whom we have had so much vexation, and of the condition of our kirk, and the carriage of honest men in it; and, had he not been taken up by the interposing of a lord come straight from England, I think I had said all was then upon my heart in reference to that matter. After this the court thronging by multitudes from England, and the crowd of his affairs growing upon him, it was unbecoming for me to press for private conference, but when he did call to me; which he was pleased to do twice more before his coming from Breda: and both those times he asked me only about some of his concernments with general Monk, bidding me at the last time meet him at his first coming to the Hague, which was upon May 15th, wait upon, to receive my despatch immediately to England, both as to general Monk, and the letter to the city ministers. When I offered to speak a word in reference to Scotland, he told me, he would reserve a full communing about that till his coming to England. And indeed it had been unseasonable and impertinent for me to have urged further, finding the necessity of his affairs in England so urgent: but this I can say, that by all these opportunities I had, in every of which I did not omit the moving about Scotland, I found his majesty resolved to restore the kingdom to its former civil liberties, and to preserve the settled government of our church; in both which I was bold expressly to move, and had a very gracious satisfying answer. Upon the apprehension that I might be sent into England presently upon his majesty's arrival at the Hague, I hastened from Breda by the way of Dort, Amsterdam, Harlem, and Leyden, to take a transient view of those goodly towns; and came the next day after the king to the Hague, about the very time of the reception of the commissioners from the two houses and the city, to which I was an eye-witness. Dr. Reynolds, Mr. Calamy, Dr. Spoistre, Mr. Case, Mr. Manton, were received privately in his bedchamber: they delivered a letter signed by above 80 ministers met at Sion College: I am promised a copy thereof, which I shall send unto you (and had done it before this, could they have given me one, because they had left it in the city:) they expressed much satisfaction with his majesty's carriage towards them, speaking him to be a prince of a deep knowledge of his own affairs, of singular sweetness and moderation, and great respectiveness towards them; but they were much more satisfied as to these, after they had spoke with him two by two, in private, three days after, in so far as they speak highly to his commendation to all their friends, as a most excellent prince, restored for a public blessing to these nations; and do profess it to be their duty to promote his interest amongst their people. They have often since said to me, they have no reserve nor hope, but in his majesty's good disposition and clemency. At my coming to the Hague, when I had gone to the lord chancellor, who by the king's order was to give me my despatches, he desired me to stay so long as the London ministers staid, telling me he would send by another the king's pleasure to general Monk. I was ready to lay hold upon this motion, knowing that the king was speedily to go for England, and so kept in company with those ministers, and thereby had occasion to know what may give me ground of a probable conjecture of the tendency of matters, as to the

wards consider it, and send a return; and desired me to come to him two or three days after, when the throng was over. I had yours of the 10th of May, with that to the king, which is not yet delivered, by the earl of Rothes. I shall look on the earl of Selkirk and lord Lorn as noble patriots, well affected to the interest of religion. I shall never espouse the interest of any person or party; 'tis our common interest to keep an equal way with all who mind the good of kirk and country: and my endeavour is to prevent animosities, and to beget and keep harmony. Cementing and piecing will be our mercy, and dividing more our reproach than we are aware of. The king hath allowed the noblemen who are here, to meet and consult what is proper to be offered for the good of the nation; they meet on Monday: it is in his heart to restore us to our liberties and privileges if our folly do not mar it. Yesterday the king went to the house of peers, passed some bills, and emitted a proclamation against profaneness. There is a day of thanksgiving appointed in England: I wish we may give some public testimony of our sense of the mercy of the king's return in Scotland. In the house of peers, upon a motion made, that the form of prayer appointed in the Liturgy to be used in that house, be practised, 'tis done. The Service-book is not yet set up by both houses, but they will probably soon do it in all churches. I shall next week send a copy of the letter of the city ministers to the king in Holland. They resent his father's murder, but not one word of the Directory or Confession of Faith. I gave a hint by the Tuesday's post, how it concerneth us to use caution, in offering to any here what may seem to be meddling or imposing; and I am every day more and more confirmed, that it will be a prejudice upon us, both in our religious and civil rights. I was at a meeting yesterday at Sion College, with about sixty ministers, where it was very solemnly debated, whether they should petition his majesty and the two houses, that the exercise of religion by the ordinance of lords and com-

---

ordering of religion in England. I have much to say of this purpose, which I cannot communicate in this way. At present I shall only say this, that for me to press uniformity for discipline and government upon the king and others, I find, would be a most disgustful employment, and successless: for though the king could be induced to be for it, it were not in his power to effectuate it; the two houses of parliament, and the body of this nation, being against it, and, if I may speak what I know, and could demonstrate to you, it is already past remedying: I know very few or none who desire it, much less appear for it, and whoever do report to you, or believe, that there is a considerable party in England, who have a mind for a covenant-uniformity, they are mistaken; and, as you judge, by what you write in that of May 8th, if they themselves will not press it, we are free. I see no obligation by covenant, to impose that upon them, which they care not for. If you knew at a distance, what I have occasion to know since my coming hither, of this matter, I am confident you would not be very urgent in that point; for my part, I shall have no accession to what may cross that uniformity; but I have no freedom to an employment, which can have no other effect, but the heightening of an odium upon our church, which is obnoxious already to many upon such an account, though, I know, causelessly. I have heard of your letter to Messrs. Calamy, Ash, and Manton; which Mr. Ash only hath seen, Calamy and Manton not being in town; and the rumour goes up and down the city (I know not if occasion be taken by that letter) that the ministers of Scotland have declared their dissatisfaction, that the king is brought in, but upon the terms of the covenant. I am afraid, that such rumours are at this juncture studiously raised, and I see more and more the need we have of using caution with those here: we have had large experience of Anglorum, &c., and I have cause to think, that we shall have a discovery of it, as much now as ever.

I shall present your letter to his majesty, at the first opportunity, which, I think, I cannot have till some days pass over, because of the great press upon him, at his first entry into Whitehall. God hath done great things for him, I pray he may do great things by him. It hath been observed, that never any prince did enter upon his government with such a general repute and applause. The satisfaction expressed by the Dutch could not be more, if he had been their sovereign: and for England, the expressions of ecstatic joy, and universal exultation, are admirable. This day from morning till seven o'clock I have been a spectator of what the magnificence and gallantry of England could bring forth in testimony of the greatest reception, was, they say, ever given to their king; the manner whereof you will have by the Diurnal; and it hath taken up so much time to me, that, the post calling, I have confusedly writ this, and must break off till the next, with commending you to the Lord's grace, who am,

Yours, &c.

JA. SHARP

London, May 29th.

mons, according to the Confession of Faith, and Directory for Worship, and Form of Church Government, might be continued, until the parliament shall provide otherwise. This, after long debate, was referred to a committee, to be considered of against next week. There is a conference on Monday, to be betwixt six presbyterians and six moderate (as they call them) episcopals; but I resolve not to be at it. From any observation I can make, I find the presbyterian cause wholly given up and lost. The influencing men of the presbyterian judgment are content with episcopacy of bishop Usher's model, and a liturgy somewhat corrected, with the ceremonies of surplice, cross in baptism, kneeling at the communion, if they be not imposed by a canon, *sub pœna aut culpa.* And for the Assembly's Confession, I am afraid they will yield it to be set to the door; and that the articles of the church of England, with some amendments, take place. The moderate episcopalians and presbyterians fear, that either the high episcopal men be uppermost, or that the Erastians carry it from both. As for those they call rigid presbyterians, there are but few of them, and these only to be found in the province of London, and Lancashire, who will be inconsiderable to the rest of the nation. A knowing minister told me this day, that if a synod should be called by the plurality of incumbents, they would infallibly carry episcopacy. There are many nominal, few real, presbyterians. The cassock men do swarm here; and such who seemed before to be for presbytery, would be content of a moderate episcopacy. We must leave this in the Lord's hand, who may be pleased to preserve to us what he hath wrought for us. I see not what use I can be any longer here; I wish my neck were out of the collar. Some of our countrymen go to the common prayer. All matters are devolved into the hand of the king, in whose power 'tis to do absolutely what he pleases in church and state. His heart is in his hand, upon whom are our eyes."

In another, dated likewise June 2d, Mr. Sharp acquaints Mr. Douglas that he had received his note of May 26th. " As to yuor coming up, when I was with the king on Thursday night, I moved, upon some considerations, his majesty might write for you. He answered, pray you, let it be done; and calling upon Lauderdale, ordered him to draw a letter for him to sign, that you might come up to him speedily. This letter Lauderdale promised to have ready this night, but it will be Monday ere he get it done. The rumour is here, that there are several ministers coming as commissioners from Scotland and Ireland: I know not who hath given occasion to it, but I apprehend it will not be seasonable at this time; we would wait a little, till we see how matters frame. I am confident if ministers come here at this juncture they will be discountenanced, and give suspicion of driving a disobliging design. I find our presbyterian friends quite taken off their feet, and what they talk of us and our help is merely for their own ends. They stick not to say, that, had it not been for the vehemency of the Scots, Messrs. Henderson, Gillespy, &c. set forms had been continued; and they were never against them. The king and grandees are wholly for episcopacy; the episcopal men are very high. I beseech you, sir, decline not to come up. It will be necessary you come and speak with his majesty for preventing of ill, and keeping our noblemen here right. Your coming will certainly do much good; and though I know the temper of the brethren, yet I see not what their coming will signify at this time, and am apt to think they will not get content. I have no design in this; I speak my heart to you, that you may do more alone for the good of kirk and country than they all. Few or no Scotsmen will be about the king in places of significancy. Lauderdale is of the bedchamber; he promises to keep Rothes with himself. The parliament when it meets will make all void since 1639, and so the king will be made king, (that is, absolute there as here,) and dispose of places and offices as he pleases."

Mr. Douglas and Mr. Smith write a return to those two last of Mr. Sharp's, June, without the date:—" That they are refreshed with his majesty's safe arrival. As to that part of your letter about *uniformity*, we thought fit, say they, to give you this return of our thoughts. 1. It is not our opinion to impose any thing upon his majesty; yet humbly to represent to him that he and the parliament may settle religion there according to the terms of the covenant, we think it no crime, yea, we count it a duty for our own exoneration, though it should not prove successful; and if it be held a crime to make known to his majesty so innocent a desire, it may be feared that the keeping of it here may come under the same account. 2. We cannot be induced to believe that it were unfeasible if his majesty would be pleased to intimate his royal inclinations thereunto; but we conceive it would find acceptance when we remember that the reviving of the league and covenant by the ordinance, after the restoring the secluded members, was acceptable and refreshing. 3. The question is not, Whether there be many or few for it? but, whether it be our duty, whereto we are obliged by the oath of God in such an opportunity, when settlement of religion is intended, humbly to desire that it may be done according to the terms of the covenant? And though, if they slight the matter, we cannot impose it upon them, yet, for our own exoneration before God and men, we are obliged to desire it. 4. We cannot but be affected with grief to consider that it should heighten an odium upon our kirk, to desire that ministers may carefully endeavour, by their humble addresses to his majesty and parliament, to prevent the reintroduction of those once rejected relics, episcopacy and the Liturgy, which have bred so much trouble and persecution to the faithful ministers and professors of the gospel there, and have had such a bad influence upon this kirk. 5. Our letter to some brethren there is so innocent, that we are not afraid of the judgment of sober men, though it were printed; and for any misrepresentation that hath been raised, whether upon it, or otherwise, it is a mere calumny; for we were, and are, and could not but be well satisfied with his majesty's restitution to his kingdoms, for which we so heartily prayed, and so seriously longed. Nor can it be interpreted dissatisfaction with his majesty's restitution, that when he is restored, we humbly represent to his majesty our desires for settling of religion according to the terms of the covenant. There is just ground of suspicion, that such reports are raised by some of our own countrymen there, who are enemies to the reformation established, and labour the abolishing of the covenant of the three nations. Dear brother, we have writ these things to you, for your information and encouragement against those discouraging rencounters you meet with in this juncture, from men that are either downright enemies to the reformation of religion, or are but friends of Gallio's temper. Yours of the 2d of June holds forth that there is a great defection there from the grounds of the league and covenant, which continued in, cannot but highly provoke the Lord."

By this plain and full letter of Mr. Douglas and Mr. Smith, we may see how roundly they deal with Mr. Sharp, how fixed they stand to the principles and profession of the church of Scotland; and the reader cannot but regret, that they had such a person to correspond with, as this betrayer of the church of Scotland. Whether Mr. Douglas' jealousies of him by this time were fully formed, I know not; but a great deal of plainness is used with him; and had he followed those instructions and principles laid down in this letter, and formerly, I doubt not but much more might have been done for the work of reformation at this time. However, these worthy persons did lay the matter candidly before him, whom they had unhappily confided in as their commissioner; and what could they do more in the present circumstances? Other letters were sent, much to the same purpose.

Accordingly, June 7th, Messrs. Dickson, Douglas, Hamilton, Smith, and Hutchison, send a joint letter to Mr. Sharp, in which they say, " That, upon the occasion of the late wonderful and comfortable revolution, we held it our duty, upon the account of our solemn engagement to God, and our brotherly affection, and our respect to the quiet of the established interests of this church, to express the thoughts of our heart to some of the reverend ministers of London, for our exoneration, resolving to intermeddle no further in the affairs of others, save to express our humble opinion. But having learned, by your last, of your being present at the meeting in Sion College, and other conferences of our reverend brethren; as we do thankfully acknowledge the respects hereby put upon you, so we have appointed, that your being at these consultations may, through the Lord's blessing, not prove unprofitable for the good of the common interest of religion, which, we know, is most dear to all honest men; and therefore we hope and desire, that (as you have opportunity to express your judgment before these reverend and worthy men) you will not omit to acquaint them how much it lieth on the hearts of all good men here, that God may lead them forth to a right improvement of this opportunity, after which many, who now sleep in the Lord, did so much thirst and long. We suppose it is not a desperate work, humbly to deal with his majesty (who is so excellent and moderate a prince) for the preventing of episcopacy and the Liturgy, which by experience they have found so bitter and prejudicial to themselves and many others in England, and which, if they once be established, may very speedily revive the complaints of godly men. And we hope, that the great pains of the learned assembly of divines (so heartily and unanimously approven in this church, and so much owned in England,) will not be so easily lost; but that godly honest men will endeavour what they can to have those good beginnings entertained, and yet further advanced, as need requires. The condition of the times does necessitate us again to apologize for what we thus write unto you: if we could satisfy our own consciences, and approve ourselves to God and posterity, who will reap the fruit of our improvement of this opportunity, we are so far from any pragmatical humour, that we could with much ease to ourselves sit down in silence, as if no such matters were in agitation about us; but apprehending that your being on the place in this juncture, and it being known that you are owned in your employment there by the body of the ministry of this church, we conceive that it may be looked upon as if we were satisfied with any proceedings prejudicial to our former engagements, unless you express our sense of affairs as you have occasion, with that prudence, respect, and discretion, that becometh, whereof we hope you will be careful so long as you stay there."

The prudent and yet zealous concern of those faithful watchmen, the reverend ministers of Edinburgh, at this juncture, appears yet further by their letter next post, signed by the last named persons, to Mr. Sharp, of the date June 9th, which likewise deserves to be transcribed here, and follows: —" By our last to you of the 7th instant, we acquainted you, that however the conscience of our obligation by covenant, and our sense of the hazards to which this church hath been exposed by the former settlement of England, do put us on earnestly to desire an acceptable settlement there, yet fear of offence hath persuaded us to move no further in that business (after our exoneration by letter to some there) than to desire you so to walk in it, as might not conclude us, by reason of our silence, in an approbation of what may be established there contrary to our covenant. Yet, amongst our solicitudes, we cannot apprehend that we will offend any, if we humbly lay before his majesty our thoughts of those affairs; and therefore have sent you an enclosed paper containing the sum of our thoughts and motives inducing us to use that humble freedom; whereof (and of what else may occur to yourself to the same purpose) we seriously entreat you to make prudent use in laying the particulars therein contained before his majesty. He is gifted to his people in return of their prayers, and their expectations are fixed on him, as the man of God's right hand, who will refresh the hearts of all the lovers of Zion; and honest people (whatever be represented to their fears) can never be persuaded but his majesty will perform all things according to the covenant. His majesty hath been pleased so much to respect faithful and honest men in their humble freedom, that we will not doubt of his acceptance of this mite from your and our hand, which floweth from much real zeal for his majesty's happiness, and without which we could not be satisfied we had dealt faithfully. Be strong in the Lord, and wait for him who hath done great things for us, whereof we are glad, and hath hereby encouraged us to wait for mercy to his Zion. To his grace we commend you, and are," &c. The paper sent along with this letter is subjoined,* and I go on in my abstract of this remarkable correspondence.—

June 5th, Mr. Sharp writes to Mr. Douglas, that he had his of the 29th of May; that the Scotsmen at London had concurred in a paper, containing their desires to his majesty as to Scotland, which was that week

---

* Some few particulars which Mr. Sharp is desired to propound to the king's majesty by conference, at fit opportunities:

1. Albeit we doubt not of his majesty's being satisfied of our loyalty and good affection to his service; yet you may, from time to time, further assure his majesty, that our gracious God hath eased our spirits of a long and sad pressure, by overturning all these bloody usurpers, and restoring his majesty to rule over us, and hath hereby sent us a gracious return of these many petitions we have put up to him in times of deep distress on that behalf, which hath raised our expectations, that the Lord, who hath done all these things for us, hath a purpose of doing much good to these kingdoms by his majesty's means.

2. You may signify unto his majesty, how much we are refreshed with intimations we have received of his resolution to restore us unto our civil liberties, and to preserve the doctrine, worship, discipline, and government of this church. This we look upon not only as an acceptable service to the King of kings whose interests we believe these are, and as an act of special kindness and favour in his majesty, to look to the preservation of their just rights, civil and ecclesiastical, who did expose all to hazard, and much need and sad suffering, in pursuance of their duty and loyalty to his majesty, and who have made it their study in these trying times, to give evidence that their religion and reformation doth teach them loyalty: but we look upon it also as a notable advantage to his majesty's own interests, who shall hereby give proof, that (notwithstanding the rigid dealing of some toward his majesty in some particulars, which you know we do heartily disapprove,) no afflictions or temptations have prevailed with his majesty, to withdraw him from his first voluntary engagement to his people, and the oath of the covenant, and shall also fix unto his majesty an interest which, we are persuaded, will cleave fast unto him and his interests in all exigents; for you may assure his majesty (which we entreat may be understood without reflecting on any, without any desire in us to continue factions among loyal subjects,) that among the various tempers of his subjects, he will find none more fixed for him than men of the principles of the church of Scotland are, and will be.

3. As to the settling of religion in his majesty's other dominions, you may inform his majesty that we are very far from intruding ourselves upon the affairs of others, or meddling without our sphere; and therefore have been very sparing to communicate counsels with any there, as yourself knows; yet there are not a few considerations (beside our judgments of the things themselves) which prevail with us humbly to pour forth our hearts before his majesty himself, such as our cordial and sincere desires (as the Searcher of hearts knoweth) to-

wards the prosperity of his majesty's throne and the completing of this so glorious a work, our fear to be found unfaithful to his majesty, who as he hath been pleased graciously to admit of our freedom formerly, so, we believe, doth still expect it from us, having by his gracious letter since the late sad separation, not only invited, but conjured some of us to it, our knowledge of the temper of many people here and elsewhere, whereof possibly his majesty may not be so fully informed, and our hearty desire that this blessed revolution may be completely comfortable to all honest and loyal subjects who have suffered under the late tyranny, and have been earnest dealers with God for the accomplishment of what they now see with their eyes: these are some of the motives which prevail with us, to desire that his majesty may be informed in these few particulars.

1. How much it will concern his majesty to reflect upon the proceedings at his majesty's coronation here, and seriously consider what is incumbent now to be done thereupon, that being his first public transaction with his subjects.

2. His majesty would be informed, how suitable it would be for a prince, so educated by God, and preserved and restored by him, not only to agree to the humble desires of his subjects, but to let forth somewhat of his own inclination toward an acceptable settlement of religion. As his majesty's practice in Scotland, and his resolution to preserve these things with us, do assure us of his majesty's approbation thereof in his judgment; and of his readiness to give his royal assent to what shall be proposed agreeable thereunto: so his majesty's royal inclination being known, we doubt not of a more general concurrence, than while good people are kept in suspense.

3. You may inform his majesty, that we humbly propose this expedient of his majesty's prudent putting forth himself in this business, not only upon the account of conscience as to the thing itself, but upon point of prudence also, for the good of his majesty's affairs. We shall not concern ourselves to dive into the temper of independents and other sectaries, and how they may relish episcopacy and the Liturgy in this recent settlement of affairs, nor trouble you with an account of what noise is raised upon the very appearance thereof by others whom you know: but if his majesty knew what grief of heart the fear of episcopacy and the Service-book is to many loyal and honest subjects, who have much and often mourned in secret for him, and do now rejoice in his wonderful restitution, and how much it would refresh them to be secured against these fears; we are confident he would be most ready to satisfy such subjects, who will count nothing temporal too dear to be laid forth as his majesty's affairs shall require: and though it may be con-

to be presented. He hath not yet had opportunity to speak to the king: that he reads that day in the newspaper, that Mr. Douglas and Mr. Dickson are repairing to London, and wishes it may hold, and designs to move to the king, that some brethren best known to his majesty may be sent for. He does not perceive the ministers at London design to give them any advertisement concerning the state of the church: and adds, " I pray the Lord keep them from the Service-book and prelacy. If the king should be determined in matters of religion by the advice of the two houses, 'tis feared that covenanted engagements shall not be much regarded. All sober men depend more upon the king's moderation and condescensions, than what can be expected from others. The episcopalians drive so furiously, that all lovers of religion are awakened to look about them, and to endeavour the stemming of that feared impetuousness of these men: all that is hoped is to bring them to some moderation and closure with an episcopacy of a new make. You may easily judge how little any endeavour of mine can signify to the preventing of this evil; and, therefore, how desirous I am to be taken off, and returned to my charge. I am still full of fears, that England shall lose this opportunity of settling religion. It is broadly rumoured in the city and at court, that Scotland are all in arms for the covenant: this is a pretext made to keep us under force. There is talk of a petition from the city in reference to the covenant, and that we from Scotland are the promoters of it; but I apprehend that it will come to nothing. However, the high carriage of the episcopal men gives great dissatisfaction: the Lord may permit them thus to lift up themselves, that thereby they may meet with a more effectual check. Bishop Wren preached last Sabbath in his lawn sleeves at Whitehall. Mr. Calamy and Dr. Reynolds are named chaplains to his majesty. I hear Mr. Leighton is here in town in private."

Mr. Douglas, June 12th, answers the former, and tells Mr. Sharp, there was never an intention of Mr. Dickson and his coming to London. " If," says he, " our brethren, after what we have writ to them and you, lay not to heart the reformation of their kirk, we are exonered, and must regret their archness (backwardness) to improve such an opportunity, and be grieved for the relapse into the sickly condition, and grievous bondage of the hierarchy and ceremonies. If the presbyterians would deal effectually with those concerned, making use of the advantages of a good cause far advanced in the former parliament, the covenant engagements, the gracious disposition, and moderation of the king, and of the high and furious drivings of the episcopalians, they might, by the blessing of God, be in a far better condition, than 'tis probable they shall be, considering their neglect. That Scotland is in arms for the covenant, is a broad lie, when broadly rumoured; if such pretexts be forged for keeping an army on us (and they are daily coming with more forces) it will be a sin against God, and a dishonour to his majesty. But we are persuaded his majesty will defend us, and our

---

ceived that the affairs of England do nothing concern them; yet they cannot but remember, from former experience, what influence the state of the church of England hath had upon this church. Beside this, as we know there is a very considerable plantation in Ireland of loyal and honest presbyterians, who will be ruined by episcopacy and the Liturgy, so we apprehend that in England, however people, fearing the worst, be content of any thing that is better than it, yet when they shall see a settlement of these things wherewith they are dissatisfied, it cannot but be very grievous to them.

4. His majesty is to be humbly informed, that at least (if these humble intimations from us have no weight) it would be expedient not to conclude and determine in these things suddenly; but that his majesty and his parliament take time till he know the true temper of his subjects, and what will be his real interest, which will be better known afterward when his majesty shall have leisure to understand his people's inclinations by himself, and his good people shall have confidence, knowing his majesty's disposition, freely to represent the true state of things.

These things have lien upon our hearts, to have them freely imparted to his majesty, out of no other design, next unto the glory of our Lord, but that we may witness our zeal to his majesty's prosperity and happiness. And we shall not cease to pray that God may guide his majesty, and make him wise as an angel of God, to do these things that shall be well pleasing in his sight, and which may happily settle these long distracted kingdoms.

ancient privileges. 'Tis much to be lamented, that such men as Wren, whose corrupt principles, and wicked practices, in persecuting conscientious ministers, though conform, are too well known to be so soon forgotten, should have the impudence to appear in public with these Babylonish brats. The excommunicate Sydeserf, pretended bishop of Galloway, and Mr. James Atkin, a deposed minister and excommunicate, took journey hence on Friday last, for London, persuading themselves, that prelacy will come again in fashion here; but I hope they shall never see that day, or rather eclipse of our day. I doubt not but you will carefully guard against all that is intended to the prejudice of the established doctrine, worship, discipline, and government, of this kirk."

June 9th, Mr. Sharp, in his to Mr. Douglas, signifies, that he has little pleasing matter to write of: " That he is pleased with my lord Cassils' coming up; he fears we have not many like him to look to. My lord Loudon is not yet come up. That he himself endeavours not to mingle in their particular interests and differences, but presses union. There are none (adds he) here, but disclaim the protesters: that he visited the earl of Selkirk, lord Lorn, and Tweeddale, who professeth his abandoning the protesters: that twenty-eight Scots noblemen, and some gentlemen, had presented a petition to the king for withdrawing the forces and calling a parliament; the king received it graciously. It is thought the committee of estates will first meet, in order to the calling a parliament. The French ambassador is commanded forthwith to remove. Those who are incumbents in sequestrate livings are left to the course of law, whereby above a thousand* in the country and universities will be ejected. I can (says he) do no good here for the stemming of the current for prelacy, and long to be home: whatever dissatisfaction may be upon good people, yet no considerable opposition will be made to prelacy. I hope the Lord will see to the preservation of his interests among us. I gave some hints formerly about this, and by what yet appeareth, I see no ground to alter my thoughts, that our meddling with affairs now will be useless, and of no advantage to our cause. The sad apprehensions I have of what I find and see as to these matters, bring me into a languishing desire to retire home and look to God, from whom our help alone can come. I hope you will consider of what is fit to be done. If you see cause of application in this critical juncture, you will take me off, after my long continued toil."

Mr. Douglas answers this last, June 14th, and signifies to Mr. Sharp, he wishes all were as fixed as Cassils. " You may," adds he, " let the protesters sleep, for they are not to be feared, they are to be pitied rather than envied. Concerning prelacy, we have delivered our mind fully in former letters; and when we have exonered ourselves, we must leave that business on the Lord, who will root out that stinking weed in his own time, whatever pains men take to plant it and make it grow. We expect at your conveniency you will give us an account of what letters and papers you have received since your return to London; after which, we shall give you an answer about your abiding there, or coming home."

In another letter without date, but by a passage in it, I conjecture it is writ June 10th, Mr. Sharp tells Mr. Douglas, " I now begin to fear the long contended for cause is given up. Three months ago, some here were pressing upon the presbyterian party, both in the house and city, to make themselves considerable by conjunction of counsels, and pursuing in a united way the same end and interest: this could not be compassed. Then the dissolving of the secluded members, (which some attribute to some of themselves, others to general Monk, I know both had a hand in it,) and jealousies mutual between army and parliament, made way for the king's coming in without conditions; whereupon the episcopal party have taken the advantage: and they finding now that the influencing men of the presbyterian party are content to yield to a moderate episcopacy and a reformed Liturgy, craving

---

* This number seems too great.—*Wodrow.*

only that ceremonies be not imposed by canon, do shift all offers for accommodation, and do resolve to set up their way, and under pretext of fixing and conforming all to their rule, for avoiding of disorder and schism, (as they say,) give cause to apprehend, that matters ecclesiastic in England will be reduced to their former state. This does exceedingly sadden and perplex the hearts of sober good people, and episcopal men carry as if they concluded nothing could stand in their way. There were, last week and this, some endeavours for getting a petition in name of the city, that religion might be settled according to the league and covenant; but the inconsiderate and not right timeing of that motion has exceedingly prejudged that business, if not totally crushed the design, so as it occasioned a cross petition by the most considerable of the city, that in all petitions hereafter there might be nothing mentioned which had a relation to the league and covenant, and that nothing should be moved of this nature to the common council, till their meeting be full. It hath been generally bruited here, and had belief with some, that the petition for settling religion according to the covenant, was set on foot and influenced by the Scots, and commissioners were coming from the church: they name in the Diurnals, Mr. Douglas and Mr. Dickson, with a gibe. This was so openly spoke of, that, in their meeting at the common council, it was moved by one, that they might put off their petition till the Scots commissioners came to town, they being upon the way; and currently it was talked of in and about the city, and I inquired by divers, if I knew any thing of it? I apprehend this rumour has been industriously raised and spread by some, to cast the greater prejudice upon us, who will have it still believed that we are sticklers to inflame all, and will not *rest till* we have our presbytery imposed upon England, (this is their strain,) and therefore it will be necessary for the king to keep on a force upon us. I have done what I could for vindicating us from giving any ground to that malicious report, professing, that whatever the judgment of the church of Scotland might be as to these matters (which is sufficiently known), yet we had no hand or meddling in that petition: for my own part, I knew nothing of it till the morrow after it was framed, (as indeed I heard not of it till the Monday, when the talk was, that it was to be presented to the house,) neither had I heard of any commissioners coming from the church. I said further, that from the northern counties and other places, there had been endeavours used to draw petitions for the settling of presbyterian government; and this hath been by an underhand way set on foot, by some of the house of commons, giving this encouragement, that the church of Scotland would join with them. But the crushing of the city petition will render all these motions ineffectual, and, I fear, give advantage and ground to the episcopal party, who now make it their work to put off the meeting of a synod, which hitherto hath been in the talk of all, seeking to settle their way before a synod can be called. I see generally the cassock men appearing every where boldly, the Liturgy in many places setting up. The service in the chapel at Whitehall is to be set up with organs and choristers, as formerly. No remedy for this can be expected from the parliament, who, for the majority, are ready to set up episcopacy to the height in matters ecclesiastical; and with the rest moderate episcopacy will go down. The sober party have no reserve but in the king, whose inclinations lead him to moderation; God bless him, and prevent the sad consequences which may come upon this way.

" Our noblemen and others here keep yet in a fair way of seeming accord, but I find a high loose spirit appearing in some of them, and I hear they talk of bringing in episcopacy into Scotland; which, I trust, they shall never be able to effect. I am much saddened and wearied out with what I hear and see. Some leading presbyterians tell me they must resolve to close in with what they call moderate episcopacy, else open profanity will upon the one hand overwhelm them, or Erastianism (which may be the design of some statesmen) on the other. I am often thinking of coming away, for my stay here I see is to little purpose. I clearly see the general will not stand by the presbyterians. Mr. Calamy is at a stand whether to accept of being king's chaplain, and I think it will not be much pressed upon him. The king has taken into his council divers who were upon the parliament's side, but none of them are against moderate episcopacy. The general took me to his majesty on Thursday last; but the throng is so great, I could have no opportunity for private communication.

" As to your coming up, though upon my motion, upon Thursday was se'ennight, that you should be sent for, the king did most willingly yield to it, and desired a letter might be drawn to that purpose by Lauderdale; yet I am tossed in my thoughts about it since, which I have communicated to Crawford and Lauderdale; and they are at a stand in it. Upon the one hand, I consider your coming might be of great use to the church and country at this time; his majesty bearing a great respect to you, would certainly be much swayed with your advice: upon the other hand, when I weigh how much the prelatical men do here signify, and what a jealous eye they will have upon you and your carriage, bearing no good will, I perceive, to you; and the public affairs not yet put in a way of consistency; I fear your coming at this time, which will be attended with charge and toil, may give you small content, when you will find that you can have but little time with the king, and it is not your way to deal with any body else; so that in ten days you will weary. When matters come to a greater ripeness, two or three months hence, your coming may be of more use and satisfaction to yourself, and advantage to the public. I know the king will not be desirous as yet to send for any other of the brethren. And if I thought you would come hither before the instructions for the king's commissioner to the parliament were drawn, you might do much good; else I know a little of your way, and am so tender of your content, that I fear it will not be so convenient. However, I have put all off till I speak with the king, and know his mind fully in it. If I find him positive in his desire of your coming, immediately you shall have notice; if not, I shall give you an account accordingly. Pardon my writing thus confusedly my heart unto you. Your coming at this time can do no good, I am persuaded, to the presbyterian interest here, but you will expose yourself and our government at home to more jealousies and sinister construction; and for our church government, I trust it shall be preserved in spite of opposition, and I would have you reserved from inconveniences on all hands, that you may be in better capacity to act for it. As for myself, I see that here which gives me small content, and were you here, I believe you would have less; and therefore I entreat I may have leave speedily to return. I know you are not capable of being tickled with a desire of seeing the grandeur of a court, and you would soon tire were you here; and the toil and charge of coming hither, and returning in so short a time, (it being necessary you be at home against the sitting of the parliament,) will be in my apprehension, much more than any good can be done at this time. The protesters' interest cannot be kept up, and I apprehend the parliament will handle them but too severely. The design is to overturn all since the year 1640, and to make the king absolute. Elisha Leighton is not so significant a person as that by his means his brother can do us hurt."

June 12th, Mr. Sharp answers Mr. Douglas his letter of the 5th, and tells him, that since a thanksgiving is ordered in England, they will consider what is to be done in Scotland; that he has not yet got any return from the king to their letter, he is so throng. That two days ago my lord Rothes told him he was taking an opportunity to deliver that letter sent by him. That the ministers of London will make a return to that letter sent them. That letter, adds he, may be owned, and contains only a testimony of your affection to this church; I wish they may repay the like to you. What use they will make of it, he knows not. He adds, " For my part, whatever constructions may be put on my way here, I have a testimony that my endeavours have not been wanting for promoting the presbyterian interest according to the covenant. I cannot say they have been significant, as matters are now stated. There are few ministers of the presbyterian persuasion of any note here, to whom I have not communicated your readiness to concur in your sphere, for advancing the ends of the covenant; and upon several occasions both here and in Holland, I have acted with them in order thereunto. I have spoke also with some of another judgment, and given them an account of our principles and way, to evidence we are not persons of that surly temper, nor our profession so inconsistent with magistracy and peace, as hath been represented. Possibly thereby I have not avoided that fate which is incident to men of such employment, in this ticklish time; and therefore must prepare for a lash from both hands. But I am the less solicitous what usage I meet with, that I am assured my ends have been straight, and if I have failed in any mean, it hath been through mistake, and not any dishonest purpose: I leave my reputation to the Lord. It is my duty to acquaint you from time to time with the condition of affairs, as they relate to our cause, and according to my apprehensions, to give you my collections from them. Others may be of another opinion, but I am still of the mind, that our interposing in their matters here, further than we have done, will not bring any advantage to our cause, nor further those ends we think ourselves obliged to pursue at this time. I have not yet come to know his majesty's resolution, for sending for some of the ministers of Scotland: but for what I can learn, it is not his purpose to do it till his affairs here take some settlement. He was pleased last week to say to me before general Monk, that he would preserve our religion, as it was settled in Scotland, entirely to us. My stay here will be of no use upon many accounts; it is most necessary I come home, and speak with you before resolution be taken what is incumbent to be done by you. I am not edified by the speeches and carriage of divers of our countrymen in reference to the covenant and ministry, when they are come up here. I have small hopes the garrisons in Scotland will be removed; the Lord's controversy is not yet at an end with us."

Mr. Douglas answers this in his to Mr. Sharp, June 19th, and says, that before they heard of the thanksgiving in England, they had appointed the day he writes upon, as a day of thanksgiving for the king's return, in the presbytery of Edinburgh, and wrote of their appointment to other presbyteries, who, he hears, are to keep the same day. He adds, " I suspect the king's coronation is delayed upon a prelatic interest. I wish the king were crowned before any thing of that nature be concluded upon, that his majesty may not run to a contrary oath; my heart trembles to apprehend any thing of that kind. It were a happy thing to have religion settled upon covenant terms, that prelacy, so solemnly cast out, may not creep in again under pretext of a moderate episcopacy. This will be found a playing with the oath of God, seeing moderate episcopacy, as they call it, is unlawful, and a step to the highest of episcopacy. Ministers there need not deceive themselves by thinking that it will stand there without the ceremonies, that is impossible; and it is a received maxim, no ceremony no bishop, they having nothing to uphold their pomp but the ceremonies. You know I am against episcopacy, root and branch. I wish the king would put that business off himself, upon the parliament and synod of divines; and if they will have that moderate episcopacy, let it be a deed of their own, without approbation by his majesty. I fear our gracious prince meet with too many temptations from the generality of that people, who love prelacy and the Service-book. I pray he may be kept from doing that which may offend God, who has delivered him."

June 14th, Mr. Sharp writes to Mr. Douglas, " This day the king called for me, and heard me speak upon our church matters, which I perceive he does thoroughly understand, and remembered all the passages of the public resolutions. He was pleased again to profess, that he was resolved to preserve to us the discipline and government of our church, as it is settled among us. When I spoke of calling a general assembly, he said he would call one how soon he could; but he thought the parliament would be called and sit first. I found the end of his majesty's calling for me, was to give me notice that he thought it not convenient to send for ministers from Scotland at present: when his affairs were here brought to some settlement, he would then have time and freedom to speak with them, and to send for them to come to him. He thought it was fit for me to go down and give you notice of this, and the state of his affairs here, and that he would write by me to you; and called to one of his bedchamber to seek for your letter, which I delivered, saying, it would be found in one of his pockets, and a return should be sent, and my dispatch prepared this next week. I find his majesty speaking of us and our concernments most affectionately. There hath been some talk in the city of a petition from the ministers about religion; but some leading men not thinking it expedient, it was waved. Mr. Calamy, Mr. Manton, and Dr. Reynolds, are sworn chaplains: some say Mr. Baxter is to be admitted likewise, and when it is their course to officiate, they are not tied to the Liturgy, but others having performed that service, they shall only preach till they be clear to use it. The king hath ordered a letter to Dr. Reynolds and Mr. Calamy, ordering them to nominate ten to themselves, of their judgment, to meet in a conference with twelve of the episcopal party whom he will nominate."

Messrs. Dickson, Douglas, Wood, Hamilton, Smith, and A. Ker, write to Mr. Sharp, June 21st, that since the king desires he should come down, they are willing he come. They are confident he will refresh them with the tidings of his majesty's constant purpose, to preserve to them their liberties and privileges, so solemnly engaged to, and advantageous to his majesty's greatness and government: they profess they never intended, nor do intend, to press presbyterian government on other kirks, otherwise than by laying before them the warrantableness thereof from God's word, and the efficaciousness of it, being God's ordinance, by his blessing to suppress errors and profaneness. And particularly, they thought it incumbent on them to lay before their brethren their duty, to endeavour by addresses to king and parliament, that the sin of a party who laid aside the covenant, may not now be made the sin of the nation. Since the Lord in his gracious and wise providence has restored the king's majesty and parliament to their just rights and privileges, so notoriously and wickedly wronged against the express obligation of the third article of the covenant; they wish, and it may be in equity expected, that the rights of God and of religion, unto which there is an obligation in the other articles, should be established; that what is God's may be given unto him, as what is Cæsar's is and ought to be given to him: that their tenderness to his majesty makes them desire that he may be kept free from giving his royal approbation to prelacy and the Service-book, and may rather lay the whole matter upon a synod of divines, who, by peaceable debates, may come to resolve upon that which is most agreeable to the word of God and upon his parliament, who may come to further clearness upon the result of their debates.

Mr. Sharp, June 16th, acquaints Mr. Douglas he had received by that post one of the 7th, and two of the 9th, with the enclosed paper, " which," adds he, " contains matters of such ample and important consequences, as will take larger time to manage, than I have in this place, and give work for employing more than one or two: considering the king's present throng, 1 would take three or four months to propose them in a way effectual, or becoming the grandeur of so great a prince. These are materials, I hope, will be laid up for more solemn addresses. I have a testimony, that I have not been wanting to improve any opportunity I had during these transactions for the interest of our country and the covenant. This will bear me up under the constructions my employment at such a ticklish juncture lays me open to. I trust when I return to make it appear, I have pursued the public ends of religion, as far as the condition of affairs would bear; and I have been biassed by no selfish ends. If informations you have received about the state of affairs here, have come from better grounds than what

I have given, I shall not justify my mistake; but for any observation I can make, I profess it still to be my opinion, that I know no considerable number, and no party in England, that will join with you for settling presbyterian government, and pursuing the ends of the covenant. And albeit I am persuaded that our engagements are to be religiously observed; and of all concernments, that of religion ought to be secured, yet, with all submission and reverence to your judgments, I am not satisfied that it is incumbent to me (as the present state of affairs is circumstanced) to press further than I have done the matter of the coronation oath in Scotland, and settling of presbyterian government upon this nation, which I know will not bear it on many accounts. And under correction, I apprehend our doing of that which may savour of meddling or interposing in those matters here, will exceedingly prejudice us, both as to our civil liberty and settlement of religion. It is obvious how much the manner of settling religion here may influence the disturbing and endangering of our establishment: yet providence having concluded us under a moral impossibility of preventing this evil; if, upon a remote fear of hazard to our religious interests, we shall do that which will provoke and exasperate those who wait for an opportunity of a pretext to overturn what the Lord hath built among us, who knows what sad effects it may have? The present posture of affairs looks like a ship foundered with the waves from all corners, so that it is not known what course will be steered: but discerning men see, that the gale is like to blow for the prelatic party; and those who are sober will yield to a Liturgy and moderate episcopacy, which they phrase to be effectual presbytery; and by this salvo, they think they guard against breach of covenant. I know this purpose is not pleasing to you, neither to me. I shall, if I find opportunity before my coming away, acquaint his majesty with as many of your desires as conveniency will allow. I shall also make them known to such ministers as I meet with; and at present, till a door be opened for a more effectual way, this will be a testimony, that you are not involved in an approbation of what may pass here in prejudice of the covenant. Parliament men know that I have often spoke to them of our firm adherence to the covenant; and if any of them would excuse their not taking notice of it, by our not clamouring by papers to the house about it, I am doubtful they think what they speak: but more of this upon my return, which I so much desire, when I have so much dissatisfaction with the course of affairs here. The king speaks to our countrymen about the affairs of Scotland on Monday next: I wish we were all soon home, for little good is either gotten or done here. The Lord fit us for future trials, and establish us in his way."

June 19th, Mr. Sharp writes again to Mr. Douglas, acquainting him, " that he had his of the 12th, and had little to add: that he had been with some city ministers, and Mr. Gower of Dorchester, an eminent presbyterian minister, who speaks with regret of the neglect of the covenant; but, says he, I see no effectual way taken to help this; your exoneration is sufficiently known to them, and I wish I could write you had any encouragement from them to go further. I see little the presbyterians can, or intend to do for the promoting that interest. The surest friends to our religion and liberty of our countrymen, since they came here, are of opinion, that your further interposing can do no good, but will probably bring hazard to the settlement among us. I hope this week to have his majesty's letter signifying his resolution to preserve the established doctrine, worship, discipline, and government of our kirk, and that we shall have a general assembly; and then I shall come home with your leave. If we knew how little our interests are regarded by the most part here, we would not much concern ourselves in theirs. If we cannot prevent the course taken here, we are to trust God with the preservation of what he hath wrought for us. Yesterday his majesty gave audience to the commissioners from Ireland, who, among other desires, moved, that religion might be settled there as it was in the days of the king's grandfather and father, that establishment being the only fence against schism and confusion. From this we may guess what our presbyterian brethren may meet with. In the evening our lords attended the king, and general Monk was present. Crawford and Lauderdale spoke so before the king for the removing garrisons, that the general could not answer them. At the end the king desired they would consult among themselves, and give their advice about calling a parliament, and till then how the government of the kingdom was to be settled. This day they met frequently, and, after some debates, not without heat and reflections, it was referred to a committee of twelve to draw up a petition to his majesty, that the government might be managed by his majesty, and the committee of estates nominated by the parliament at Stirling, until the sitting of the parliament, which, they thought, might be called by proclamation legally; and they humbly desired that all the forces might be withdrawn, and, if it seem good to his majesty, he might, in the place of the English garrisons, put in Scottish. This paper in a day or two they are to present. By the temper that appeared in the generality of this meeting, I know not what may be expected by us; the Lord fit us for the trials that abide us. Mrs. Gillespie is come up to petition the king for the continuance of her husband's place, and he is thought not to be far off."

June 21st, Mr. Sharp writes to Mr. Douglas, that his of the 14th was come to him: " that the course of prelacy is carrying on without any opposition; so that they who were for the moderation thereof, apprehend they have lost their game. No man knows what this overdriving will come to. The parliament complain of his majesty's moderation, and that he does not press the settling all *sicut ante*. God only knows what temptations and trials are abiding us. I have made such use of your papers as is possible. You stand exonered as to any compliance with the times, or betraying the common cause by your silence, in the judgment of all to whom I have communicate what you have ordered me to do. Our task is to wait upon God, who hath done great things we looked not for, and can make those mountains plains."

June 23d, he writes to Mr. Douglas, " all is wrong here as to church affairs; episcopacy will be settled here to the height; their lands will be all restored: none of the presbyterian way here oppose this, or do any thing but mourn in secret. We know not the temper of this people, to have any thing to do with them. All the bishops in Ireland are nominate. Dr. Bramble is archbishop of Armagh : and they are to sit down next session of parliament. I am divers times with Cassils and Lorn, who are fixed to us. I suspect, the general bent of our countrymen carries them to Erastianism among us. I hear your pulpits ring against the course of affairs here, and your sermons are observed particularly. All persons in England, who have acted in the public contests since the (year) 1640, are like to suffer one way or other; and this will cast a copy to the proceedings in Scotland. I find some very eager to prosecute such at the next meeting of the committee of estates or parliament."

June 26th, Mr. Sharp writes to Mr. Douglas, that he had received his of the 19th; " that the king's coronation is thought to be delayed, upon the reason he spoke of Dr. Gauden hath written against the covenant. Petitions come up from counties, for episcopacy and Liturgy. The Lord's anger is not turned away. The generality of the people are doting after prelacy and the Service-book. Dr. Crofts, preaching before the king last Sabbath, said, that for the guilt he had contracted in Scotland, and the injuries he was brought to do against the church of England, God had defeated him at Worcester, and pursued his controversy with a nine years' exile; and yet he would further pursue him, if he did close with his enemies, meaning those of the presbyterian persuasion, who are of the privy council. The king expressed his dislike after sermon, calling him a passionate preacher. The episcopal party take all methods to strengthen themselves: they have reprinted Mr. Jenkins's Petition in the Tower, and Recantation Sermon. Some ministers of the city tell me they are endeavouring to promote a petition, that religion may be settled with moderation; yet, for avoiding offence they will not take notice of the covenant, or presbyterian government."

By another letter of the same date, Mr. Sharp tells Mr. Douglas, " That he had seen a paper of Sir John Chiesly's, in his vindication, wherein he declares, that by the remonstrance they intended not to exclude the king, but proposed, if they had carried the victory at Hamilton, to have joined him: in it, Sir John insists upon his not complying with the English, and refusing offices under them. Lauderdale and Cassils are both convinced we ought not to meddle with the affairs of England. We thought best to put off the speaking to the king of a general assembly, till he signify his pleasure about calling a parliament. Some of our noblemen here are against the covenant and a general assembly, men of no principle railing against the ministry; but the leading sober men are for both; only they differ about the time of calling the assembly: if it should be before the parliament, it would have no authority; and they fear you would be too tender of the remonstrators, for they are resolved to take order with the remonstrance at the parliament. Some think the assembly might sit before the parliament, but most are for its sitting afterwards. In the king's declaration for calling a general assembly, Lauderdale and I were thinking it is fit the assemblies at St. Andrews and Dundee be mentioned as what his majesty owns; which will put a bar upon the elections of remonstrators, or else they must renounce their judgment. We were speaking whether it were fit that the assembly which was interrupted by Lilburn, 1653, should be called to sit again. These hints I give you, that you may send your mind, and a draught for calling an assembly in the way you would have it. When it shall please God to give it us, it will be expected that the remonstrance, protestation, and all that has followed, be disclaimed. Cassils thinks you went too far in your propositions for peace; and that they not being embraced, you ought not now to stand to them, but, for the vindication of the government of our church, you ought to disown all the absurdities of the protesters. I know no call nor shadow of reason for us to mingle with what relates to the English church. The presbyterian ministers are now busy to get terms of moderation from the episcopalians. There are discontents and grumblings, but the episcopal men have the wind of them, and know how to make use of it. I am convinced your coming up, either before this, or now, would have been to no advantage, but much to your discontent afterwards the opportunity, I believe, will be far more seasonable. A friend of Lambert's did move, that the king should send Lauderdale to the Tower, to speak with him privately, and he would discover all the treacheries in Scotland, which he knows better than any Englishman: he promised he would send Lauderdale to Lambert, to know these villanies. I find the king bears no respect to Loudon or Lothian. Dr. Reynolds, Mr. Manton, and Baxter, were this day with the king. Mr. Calamy is ill of the gout. Mr. Ash tells me they will write an answer to yours. The king, after the general and chamberlain had spoke to him of endeavouring reconciliation betwixt episcopal men and others, said, he would make them agree. The calling of a synod is put off. The king having spoke the other night of Mr. Cant's passionateness, fell a commending of you. I have spoke with Broghill to the full, and cleared his mistake of any stirs among us; he professeth great friendship for us."

By his next to Mr. Douglas, June 28th, Mr. Sharp tells him, " I cannot see how it is possible for me, or any one else, to manage the business committed to me by your letters of the other week, with any shadow of advantage; but a certain prejudice will follow upon our further moving in these particulars, that are so disgustful here. I am baited upon all occasions with the act of the West-kirk, and the declaration at Dunfermline. The protesters will not be welcome here; their doom is dight, unless some, upon design of heightening our division, give them countenance, which I hear whispered among some noblemen. No good will follow on the accommodation with the episcopal party; for these who profess the presbyterian way, resolve to admit moderate episcopacy; and the managing this business by papers will undo them: the episcopal men will catch at any advantage they get by their concessions, and, after all, resolve to carry their own way. Those motions, about their putting in writing what they would desire in point of accommodation, are but to gain time, and prevent petitionings, and smooth over matters till the episcopal men be more strengthened. I find that there is a conjecture, and not without ground, that Middleton will be commissioner to the parliament. The garrisons will not be taken off till next summer. The committee of estates will sit down, and make work for the next parliament, which will be soon called. The king hath declared his resolution not to meddle with our church government; which hath quieted the clamourings of some ranting men here, as if it were easy to set up episcopacy among us. I saw this day a letter from one in Paris, that some learned protestants in France, and of the professors at Leyden, were writing for the lawfulness of episcopacy; and, if the king would write to the assembly in Charenton, July next, there would be no doubt of their approving his purpose to settle episcopacy in England. Our noblemen who are of any worth, are fast enough against episcopacy amongst us; but I suspect some of them are so upon a state interest rather than conscience, and all incline to bring our church government to a subordination to the civil power. The committee of estates and parliament will exercise severity against the protesters. It will be yet ten days before I get off."

Mr. Sharp writes another letter to Mr. Douglas, June 28th, and signifies his receipt of that of the 21st, and his satisfaction that they have given him leave to return; and runs out upon the great mercy of the king's restoration; and adds, " although we want not our fears, let us procure what is wanting by prayer, and not dwell too much on fear, lest we sour our spirits:" that he writes this, because he hears some in Scotland cast down all that is done, because the great work of reformation is not done. He adds, " yesterday I asked our friends, honest Mr. Godfrey and Mr. Swinton, what they thought was fit for us to do at present? They answered they saw nothing remaining, but prayer and waiting on God. The other day, Mr. Calamy, Dr. Reynolds, Mr. Baxter, and Mr. Ash, had a conference with the king, whose moderation and sweetness much satisfied them. It issued in this, that the king desired them to draw up in writ the lengths they could go for meeting those of the episcopal way; and promised he would order the prelates and their adherents to draw their condescensions, and after he had seen both, he would bring them to an accommodation, in spite of all who would oppose it. Some friends of the presbyterian way are very solicitous about this business, fearing that what they do now may conclude all their party, and lest they fall into an error *in limine*, which cannot be retracted, that is, if they give in their paper of concessions, those will be laid hold on, and made use of by the other party as granted; and yet they remit nothing of their way, and so break all with advantage: I spake to them to guard against those inconveniences. Mr. Calamy sent to me yesterday, to tell me of their proceedings; but I told him and others I would not meddle in those matters; that their accommodation, and falling in to moderate episcopacy and reformed Liturgy, was destructive to the settlement among us. Next week they are to have meetings on these heads; but I see not through them, and expect no good of them."

July 3d, Mr. Douglas acknowledges the receipt of Mr. Sharp's of the 23d, 26th, and 28th, and notices, that Crofts's seditious sermon before the king is much like the way of the usurpers, who justified all their procedure by the signal providence of God against the royal family. Crofts's sermon, and Gauden's book, says he, may stir up men to speak for presbytery against prelacy. He desires him, when he comes off, to appoint some to receive letters from them, and deliver them to Lauderdale. " After this," adds he, " assemblies are not to interweave civil matters with ecclesiastic; and he wisheth that the king were informed of this, that, after our brethren went from us, our proceedings were abstract from all civil affairs; and he is confident, when the assembly sits, all those former ways will be laid aside." That same day he writes another letter to Mr. Sharp; and as to his and others preaching against the course carrying on in England, he says, " except it be to pray that the kirk of England be settled according to the word of God, and the king and parliament directed, we meddle not with England; neither can it be thought that we should preach against prelacy in England, where there are none of that way to hear us. Some indeed here make it their work to possess people with the king's purpose to bring in prelacy to Scotland, which hath necessitate me often in public to vindicate his majesty, and signify he hath never discovered any such purpose, but rather professed the contrary, which hath satisfied honest people here who were discouraged with such apprehensions. If it be your mind at court that we should not speak of presbyterial government in Scotland, and that our covenant may be kept here, then I hope never to be of it, for we had never more need, considering the temper of many here, and our countrymen with you. Mr. John Stirling and Mr. Gillespie came to me from a meeting of the protesters, desiring us to join with them in a representation to the king, but I declined this, as I hinted before in one of mine. I think an assembly cannot sit till the government of the nation be settled; but when the parliament has sit, it will be necessary. I have sent you the draught of a proclamation for a free general assembly; or if his majesty will have the assembly that was raised, 1653, a small alteration will make it answer. (This draught is annexed.*) I think it necessary, that when the king intimates a parliament, a petition come from this to his majesty, for his convening that assembly *pro re nata;* upon which petition, a proclamation may be issued. Let our noble friends know of this, and such a petition may be soon got.

" As to what you write of the declaration at Dunfermline, I was one who went to his majesty with it first, before any commissioners were sent; and, after hearing his scruples, he knows, if he remember, that I did no more press him with it; and when I returned, I endeavoured to satisfy the commissioners; and when they were naming other commissioners to send again to his majesty, I said, I would not go; and they thought me too favourable a messenger for such an errand, and sent good Mr. Hamilton, with some whom they thought would press it more: and after his majesty had signed it, and written a very honest letter to the commission, to alter some expressions in the declaration, the protesters carried it by multitudes, that not one word of it should be altered.

" As for the act of the West-kirk, I shall declare to you the truth of that business, for none can do it better than Mr. Dickson, Andrew Ker, and I. We met first at Leith, Mr. Dickson, Mr. Hamilton, Mr. Thomas Kirkaldy, and I only, all the rest were protesters. When such an act was offered, we debated on it about the space of three hours, and finding them obstinate, I being moderator, dissolved the meeting. After that, the officers being dealt with by them, a great many of them professed that they would not fight at all, except they got something of that nature, and upon that there was a meeting at the West-kirk drawn on for accommodation, where the quorum was twenty-three ministers, eighteen of whom were for satisfying the officers with such an act; and nine ruling elders, six of

---

* *Draught of a Proclamation for an Assembly.*—Charles, by the grace of God king of Scotland, England, France, and Ireland, defender of the faith, to our lovites, heralds, messengers, our sheriffs in that part, conjunctly and severally, specially constitute, greeting:—Forasmuch as, through and upon occasion of the looseness and distraction of these late times, divers disorders have broken forth in the church of this our ancient kingdom of Scotland, which we do hold it our duty, in our royal station, to heal and restrain by proper and fit remedies: and considering that national and general assemblies are the most proper and effectual remedies for preventing and curing such distempers within this church; and that notwithstanding there are divers laws and acts of parliament of this kingdom, warranting and securing the national as-

whom were violent for it. Messrs. Dickson, Hamilton, Kirkaldy, and I, were still against it, till after conference, two of us, with some of them, after solemn protestation, that there should be no use made thereof, but to show it to the officers for satisfaction, it was agreed on by that plurality that it should be enacted, which was carried to the committee of estates by them; and approven there; and it was by me enclosed in a letter to David Lesly, in which I declared it was merely for satisfaction of some officers, that now they might fight against the common enemy. My memory serves me not to declare what further was in it, yet, notwithstanding of all professions to the contrary, it was published that night in print, without either my hand at it as moderator, or Mr. Ker's as clerk; which afterwards was made evident at Perth, and the chancellor being posed, who gave warrant to print it? he professed publicly he gave none. The king's subscribing the declaration at Dunfermline, made the act null: but that did not satisfy us, after we saw their way which they took, notwithstanding of his majesty's subscription, continuing to oppose all the resolutions which were taken for his majesty's preservation, and the kingdom's defence; and in the assembly at St. Andrews and Dundee, where his majesty's commissioner was present, the assembly took to their consideration that act of the West-kirk, and put an explication upon it. It is not full enough, because by the enemy's coming to Fife, we were forced to go to Dundee. Thereafter our troubles growing upon us, after much hot debate about the condemning it altogether, having so many to deal with in that troublesome time, the assembly only came this length; I hope the next assembly shall make it full enough.

"Two things would be well considered: these men now called protesters were not then discovered to be such enemies to the proceedings of the kingdom as afterward they appeared; and therefore pains was taken to condescend in some things to keep them fast: and next, they had infected many of the officers, who were made unwilling to fight, except they were satisfied in their scruples, and we behoved to condescend in some things to engage them, as in granting a warrant to raise an army in the west, to encourage them to fight. But after they were found to fall on the remonstrance, and those ways, there was never any thing in the least yielded to them, as all our procedure will make evident when seen by a general assembly, which will be to us a standing testimony of our honesty and reality in pursuing his majesty's interest and the kingdoms, in our sphere, against

---

semblies within the same, and it hath been the laudable practice of our royal predecessors to authorise and countenance these meetings, and we ourselves were graciously pleased to honour the assembly at St. Andrews and Dundee with the presence of our commissioner; yet the armed violence of the late usurper did not spare to make forcible interruption to these meetings, so that the same have been intermitted for a long time: and seeing it hath pleased God graciously and wonderfully to restore us to our just and ancient right and government, and to hear and satisfy the earnest prayers and desires of the good people of this nation in that behalf, we are resolved to improve the power and authority he has given us, to his honour, and for promoting and advancing religion and piety, and repressing error, profaneness, and disorder within this kingdom, and, in order to these ends, to apply and restore these remedies, which have been so long wanting and withholden upon the occasion foresaid. Therefore we have thought fit to indict and call a general assembly, and, by these presents, we do indict, appoint, and ordain a free general assembly of this church, to be kept and holden at Edinburgh the   day of

next, at which time we purpose, God willing, that a commissioner from us shall be there, to represent us and our authority; and we will and ordain, that presbyteries, and others concerned, may choose, elect, and send their commissioners to that meeting.

Our will is herefore, and we charge you straightly, and command, that, incontinent these our letters seen, you pass, and make publication hereof at the market-cross of Edinburgh, and other burghs of this kingdom, wherethrough none pretend ignorance; and that you warn thereat all and sundry presbyteries, and others concerned in the election of commissioners to general assemblies, to the effect aforesaid, and also all commissioners from presbyteries, and others having place and vote in assemblies, to repair and address themselves to the said town of Edinburgh, the said   day of   and to attend the said assembly during the time thereof, and aye and while the same be dissolved; and to do and perform all which, to their charges, in such cases appertaineth, as they will answer to the contrary.

Per Regem.

all opposers. The misconstructions of those with you, made me at such length lay before you what may inform you in these matters."

July 5th, Mr. Douglas adds, " In my last I overlooked the matter of the accommodation. My thoughts of it are, 1. That the matters of offices and ordinances, which ought to be of Christ's appointment, admit not of a latitude to come and go upon: which they suppose, who by way of trysting, give commissions and condescensions in the matter of episcopacy, and the Service-book. 2. By their accommodation they yield up what they had gained through the blessing of God by the labours of a learned assembly, and was agreed to by the parliament. 3. Not only their concessions will be improven, as you well observe, but also whatever the hierarchists may happen to condescend to at present, *ad faciendum populum*, they will not keep longer than they find a convenience to step over at their own ease, to their wonted height. Their present carriage, and the open appearances of the most violent of them, makes this plain. 4. I believe those learned men will, on second thoughts, perceive that it is a task, if not impossible, yet very difficult to propose concessions, which may satisfy the presbyterians in England, without conference with them, and communication of counsels. For which effect, and that the odium of the miscarriage lie not on them, it may be expected from their wisdom that they will endeavour a meeting of the honest and learned men of the ministry to consider of the matter. 5. Whatever be the event and effects, it will be a comfort to honest men, they had no hand in the re-introduction of those things they cannot be free of in a way of treaty and condescension. Those things being considered, we cannot approve of that way, and you do well not to meddle in it."

Mr. Sharp writes to Mr. Douglas, July 3d, and says, " I lately spoke with some who have the chief management, and had opportunity to clear the integrity of honest men, from the year 1651, to this. For any thing I can observe, the king and his ministers have such a resentment of the protesters' way, that we shall need rather to plead some indulgence, than fear any favour. Lauderdale denies he sent any letter to Mr. Patrick Gillespie; and all his eloquence will scarce secure him from being accountable, when an inquisition is made into the affronts he put upon the king and his authority, and his intrusions upon the town and university. The king told the four presbyterian ministers at their last conference, he would have the church of England governed by bishops. And when it was replied, that they were not enemies to regulated episcopacy, he bid them put in writ their concessions, and what regulations they thought needful. He promised that none of them should be pressed to conformity, until a synod determined that point, and that all who had entered into livings whose incumbents are dead, should be continued, and others, before they were outed, should be provided for. They have had several meetings since. At their first, they voted they would treat with the episcopal party upon bishop Usher's reduction; but I apprehend they will go a greater length, and to-morrow I shall know of Mr. Calamy the particulars. I trust you will not think it convenient I be present at meetings where such concessions are made. The king will give our countrymen their answer very soon; and it is, that the committee of estates will speedily sit down, with limitations as to the time, and their proceeding as to sequestrations, or finings, till the parliament sit. If the accounts here of expressions ministers use in their pulpits be true, I wish ministers would moderate their passions at such a time."

By another letter, same date, Mr. Sharp acquaints Mr. Douglas, " That he sees no ground to think undeserving men will be in request, as is reported with them in Scotland. I have, adds he, acquainted the king's prime minister with Mr. Gillespie's character in case he come here: I have also acquainted that great man with your deservings of the king. The king hath not yet considered how to manage his affairs as to Scotland, and all he says to our countrymen here will be but for the fashion. That which will be effectual, must proceed from his cabinet council, consisting of three persons, whom he will call in a few days, and set apart some time with them on purpose to manage Scots affairs. Middleton will be commissioner, who professeth a great regard to you. I apprehend Glencairn will be chancellor, Crawford treasurer, Newburgh secretary, Sir Archibald Primrose register, Mr. John Fletcher advocate. General Monk desires you may write to the presbyterian ministers in the north of Ireland, to leave off their indiscreet preaching against the king, and not praying for him. I hope these reports are aggravated, but since the commissioners of that kingdom have petitioned for episcopacy, I am afraid they be persecuted. Cassils is honest, but not for this court."

Mr. Douglas answers the two last, July 12th. As to the expressions in pulpits, he says, some men take a liberty to speak, which will not be remedied but by a general assembly; and if this be meant of others who have been all along for the king, 'tis but a calumny. 'Tis another forgery which you write, of the ministers of the north of Ireland: Mr. Peter Blair is just now come over, and assures us they all pray most cordially for his majesty. I hear of some protesters in the north of Scotland who pray not for the king, but none in Ireland. A general assembly will help us, and give them advice in Ireland. Your matters at London are yet a mystery to me.

July 7th, Mr. Sharp writes to Mr. Douglas he had his June 28th. " The ministers have had several meetings at Sion College since my last: they have many debates, and are not all in one mind; yet they have all agreed to bishop Usher's model, to set forms, and an amended Liturgy; they desire freedom from the ceremonies. Some yesterday spoke in the house for episcopacy, and Mr. Bainfield speaking against it, was hissed down. The English lawyers have given in papers to show that the bishops have not been outed by law. The cloud is more dark than was apprehended. Messrs. Hart, Richardson, and Kays, are to be in town this night from the ministers of the north of Ireland. Their coming is ill taken by the commissioners from the convention there, who have petitioned for episcopacy.

Affairs begin to be embroiled here; many fear a break. The presbyterians are like to be ground betwixt two millstones. The papists and fanatics are busy. Argyle is this day come to town, and he will not be welcome."

July 10th, Mr. Sharp writes to Mr. Douglas, that Crofts is discharged the court. The episcopal men are bowing a little; the presbyterians have finished their concessions; the issue will be the emitting of a declaration by the king about moderate episcopacy, amended Liturgy, and dispensing with the ceremonies. They will subject to any episcopacy; they will act under moderate episcopacy, and own bishops may be acknowledged as civil officers imposed by the king. I find no inclination in the king to meddle with our church government The marquis of Argyle was sent to the Tower last Lord's day. He adds, " He is not of their mind, who would not have you preach for presbyterial government, holding up the covenant, and keeping out prelacy from Scotland; but I am still of the opinion, that there is neither necessity, nor advantage to meddle with the settlement, whether civil or ecclesiastic, here in England. Dear bought experience should make us wary of mingling with the concerns of a people, who bear no regard to us. You'll have many letters as to the manner of Argyle's commitment, and I say nothing of it. His warrant mentions the cause to be high treason, whether for past actings, or what he may do at this time against the king's interest, I know not. This day the lord Lorn was permitted to see his father. I'll endeavour to move that one of the instructions to the committee of estates may be to see to the preserving the government of the kirk, and particularly of the acts of the general assembly at St. Andrews and Dundee, and then that after the parliament a general assembly be called. I doubt if the motion, for the king's taking notice of the assemblies since the interruption of his government, take. I have frequently observed in converse here for our vindication that by the influence of the protesting party among us, we were led out to some exorbitancies not chargeable on us or our kirk. Honest Cassils, Loudon, Lothian, and Lorn, have been pressing a conference before the king, with Crawford, Lauderdale, Rothes, and Glencairn, to debate the expediency of a committee of estates; but this, savouring of faction and division, is not liked by the king. The motive of Cassils and the rest for avoiding the committee, is the apprehension they have of the others' design to quarrel the parliament, 1649, and so to render their actings culpable. I engage in no party, while I am here, that I may know how the wheels move. There is a necessity I get and keep acquaintance with the episcopal party, as well as presbyterians, and with those about court who manage the king's affairs though they be no friends to presbyterians, though I will hereby be exposed to the constructions of men. I am confident the king hath no purpose to wrong our church in her settlement; my greatest fear is their introducing Erastianism. Chancellor Hyde, and those of that party, will have Middleton commissioner, and some of our noblemen have told the king it is their desire he be the man. 'Tis probable Lauderdale will be secretary."

July 19th, Mr. Douglas answers the last, and tells Mr Sharp, " That there is no fear of their meddling with civil affairs in their judicatories: we, adds he, have reason to know that these are to be kept distinct without encroachment. When the king grants a general assembly, it will be seen how consistent presbytery is with monarchy I was never urging for an assembly before, or in time of parliament. It shall be sufficient to us, that nothing be done in parliament to the prejudice of our established kirk government, and that the assembly be indicted shortly after. I think it will do as well, that the members of the assembly be chosen after the established order, as that the last assembly be called. Some of the protesters are here met, they will get none of us to join them in what they do."

July 21st, Mr. Douglas writes again, and desires Mr. Sharp to give the lady Argyle all the comfort and assistance he can when she comes up to see her lord. He adds, " When Sir James Stuart and Sir John Chiesly were seized, Mr. Gillespie was here at the meeting of protesters, and saw fit to remove. Two came to me from the meeting, and desired we would join them in a letter to the king anent episcopacy in England. I told them we could not join with them in any thing of that kind; and wished them to consider that the circumstances they stood in, with reference to the king, were not good. When they asked me, if I thought not it requisite to bear testimony against prelacy there? I answered, I thought not; and told them, I was afraid it might be hurtful to them; and we could not, to any advantage, press any thing now for England. I hear they have resolved to do nothing at this time; but, if any thing were done in reference to the remonstrance, they would give their testimony."

Mr. Sharp writes to Mr. Douglas, July 14th, " that he had communicate his thoughts upon the accommodation to the brethren of the city. They have some sense of the inconveniencies you mention; but they excuse themselves from the present necessity they are under, and the duty they owe to the peace of the church. They gave in their paper to the king on Tuesday last, which he ordered them not to communicate, till he made his pleasure known. After he heard them read it, he commended it, as savouring of learning and moderation, and hoped it might give a beginning to a good settlement in the church. When I heard of the contents of that paper, I asked if they thought it consistent with their covenant engagements? They said they judged so, for they had only yielded to a constant precedency and a reformed Liturgy. I fear they have hereby given a knife to cut their own throats, and do find the episcopalians prosecute their own way. This morning the king called me to his closet alone, where I had the opportunity to give a full information, as to all those particulars you by your former letter did desire; and, I must say, we have cause to bless the Lord for so gracious a king. A letter will be writ in a day or two, and I will get off. Ere long the parliament will restore the bishops' lands. There are universal complaints of the ejection of many honest ministers throughout the land, and the re-admission of many not well qualified."

Next post, Mr. Sharp writes to Mr. Douglas, and acquaints him, " That upon Monday there was a long and a hot debate in the house of commons about religion. The high episcopal men laboured to put to the question the whole complex business about doctrine, worship, discipline, and government of the church of England, that none other should take place, but what was according to law. The other side, consisting of presbyterians, *i. e.* for the most part moderate episcopal men, urged, that the particular about doctrine might only at that time be put to the question. After debates till night, it came to this issue, that the house should adjourn the taking the matter of religion into their consideration until the 23d of October; and, in the mean time, they should desire his majesty to take the advice of some divines about the settling and composing of differences about church matters. Thus all is put into his majesty's hands. Whether this shall contribute to the regulating or heightening the episcopal way, there are different conjectures: however, all offices in the church and universities are just filling with men of that way. Two ministers from Ireland, Mr. Kays, an Englishman, and Mr. Richardson, a Scotsman, came to town some time since; they have been several times with me, and let me see their address, signed by sixty ministers and upwards, and their letter to the London ministers. Their address is well penned, and contains nothing which can give offence, unless the episcopalians except against the designing the king to be our covenanted king, and engaged against error and schism, popery and prelacy; and therefore pray, that reformation may be settled according to the covenant. The London ministers civilly received them, but I do not hear of their assisting them. I have given them advice as to the managing of their employment, and have made way for them to the general, if by him they may have access to the king. I have brought them to my lord Cassils, and am to take them to Crawford and Lauderdale. I am afraid their success be little; but it is well they are come over, to vindicate the aspersions cast upon them as to undutifulness, and to obtain some abatement of the rigour and persecution they have cause to fear from the prelates. They have need, honest men, of our prayers; for the crushing of them will blast the Lord's work, in that kingdom, in the bud. I told you in my last, that on Saturday I was with the king: the sum of what he is graciously pleased to grant as to church matters, was by his order cast into a letter, which was read to him on Monday, and approven, I being present, and ordered to be put *in mundo*, for signing with his hand, and affixing his privy seal. I trust it shall be refreshing to all honest men, (and he gives the heads of it, which need not be here insert.) He adds, This is all I could desire, as matters are stated; and I adore the goodness of God, who hath brought my six months' toilsome employment to this issue. I have asserted our cause to his majesty and others, and pleaded for pity and compassion to our opposers. I have not spoke of any thing savouring of severity or revenge. I had almost forgot my urging his majesty to call a general assembly, which he told me, could not now be resolved upon as to the time, till he should more fully advise about ordering his affairs in Scotland. And, upon the motion of his owning the assembly at St. Andrews, 1651, he readily yielded to it, as the fittest expedient to testify his approbation of our cause, and his pleasure that the disorders of our church be remedied in the approven way. You will easily see why he could not own these assemblies, that were holden after the interruptions of his government."

July 26th, Mr. Sharp acquaints Mr. Douglas, that several of our countrymen are not satisfied with the king's gracious declaration as to the preserving our government. I am advised to put off my journey two or three days, that I may take care that, by instructions to the committee of estates, the king's assurance in his letter may be made good; and probably those instructions will be perfected this week. The king's condescension, that the acts and authority of the general assembly at St.

Andrews and Dundee be owned, doth take in the acts of the commission preceding it. Upon my motion of it to his majesty, he was satisfied with the reasons I gave, from his own concernments and ours. After the parliament, the assembly, I hope, will be indicted. As soon as the king hath nominated a secretary, I shall leave the copy of the proclamation you sent with him, for calling the assembly. I gave you account, on the 24th, of the large opportunity I had with his majesty to clear you from all mistakes and aspersions, according to the particulars of the information you sent me; and the king is sensible the stretches came from the overbearing sway of those men. We hear here of another meeting of theirs: I wish they would forbear them; and if they forbear them not in time, they will draw a check upon themselves. You will have had notice of the king's answer to the paper presented by our lords: after insinuations of his great regard for Scotland, he tells them, the field forces shall be withdrawn presently, the garrisons as soon as may be, and the garrison of Edinburgh, as soon as a Scottish garrison can be raised. The committee of estates sits down, August 23d, and is not to meddle with persons or estates, and to fill up their number with those, who, by remonstrance or otherwise, have not disclaimed the king's authority: the proclamation for this committee is preparing. The proceedings to settle episcopacy in England and Ireland go on apace: the bishops will be speedily nominate for England, as they are mostly already for Ireland. The brethren from Ireland are at a great stand what to do: the general, Manchester, or any person of interest, refuse to introduce them to the king, if they present their address. They have writ to their brethren for advice. The most they can expect, will be a forbearance a little in the exercise of their ministry, but they will not be permitted to meet in presbyteries, or a synod. I give them all the assistance I can, though they get none from the city ministers.

Mr. Sharp writes next, July 28th, and tells Mr. Douglas, that Argyle will be sent down to the parliament, to be tried: his friends wish rather he were tried before the king. No petition from the protesters will be acceptable to the king. I wonder how they expect you should, by a conjunction with them, involve yourself in their guilt and hazard. Their remonstrance will be censured. Yesterday the king went to the house, and, in an excellent speech, pressed an indemnity to all who had not an immediate hand in his father's murder. I spoke this day with our brethren from Ireland, who tell me, by the advice of their best friends here, they are resolved to expunge out of their address the expressions which might be most offensive, and to tender a smooth one to his majesty, without mentioning their exception against prelacy, or craving reformation according to the covenant; and the drift of their desires are, to be permitted the exercise of their ministry, and such a discipline as may guard against error and profaneness. By his next, of August 4th, to Mr. Douglas, he tells him, That the two brethren from Ireland had been with him, and signified, that yesterday they had been introduced to the king, who received their address and petition, (which they did smooth,) and caused read them, and spoke kindly to them, bidding them be confident, they should be protected in their ministry, and not imposed upon; he would give orders to the deputy of Ireland to have a tender regard of them. They are going home much satisfied with this answer.

August 11th, Mr. Sharp signifies, " That the apprehensions of Scotsmen here are much altered, since his majesty hath been pleased to yield to what I humbly offered, by his condescensions in that letter. I thought, it was not amiss to acquaint several here with it; and their expressions about the government of our church are much moderated. The letter of the ministers of London, in answer to yours, is, after much belabouring, signed by them; and I am to have it to-morrow. The episcopal party here are still increasing in number, as well as confidence. Some think, they fly so high, that they will undo their own interest." This collection of letters ends with a letter from Messrs. Calamy, Ash, and Manton, in answer to that of the ministers of Edinburgh, of June 12th, and it is insert,* and with this I shall conclude this extract, and large abbreviate of this correspondence. The king's letter to Mr. Douglas, to be communicated to the presbytery of Edinburgh, with what followed thereupon, will come in upon the history itself.

I have chosen to give this introduction mostly in the very words of the letters themselves, and I have omitted nothing in them I thought necessary to give light to this great change of affairs. Some things minute, and of no great importance in themselves, are inserted, because they tend to give light to other matters of greater weight.

---

* Letter from Messrs. Calamy, Ash, and Manton, to Messrs. David Dickson, Robert Douglas, James Hamilton, John Smith, and George Hutchison, London, August 10th, 1660.

Reverend and beloved brethren,

We had sooner returned our thanks to you, for your brotherly salutation and remembrance of us, but that we expected the conveniency of Mr. Sharp's return, hoping by that time things would grow to such a consistency, that we might be able to give you a satisfactory account of the state of religion among us. We do, with you, heartily rejoice in the return of our sovereign to the exercise of government over those his kingdoms; and as we cannot but own much of God in the way of bringing it about, so we look upon the thing itself as the fruit of prayers, and a mercy not to be forgotten. Hitherto our God hath helped us, in breaking the formidable power of sectaries, causing them to fall by the violence of their own attempts, and in restoring to us our ancient government after so many shakings, the only proper basis to support the happiness and just liberties of these nations, and freeing us from the many snares and dangers to which we were exposed by the former confusions and usurpations: therefore we will yet wait upon the Lord, who hath in part heard us, until all those things, concerning which we have humbly sought to him, be accomplished and brought about. We heartily thank you for your kind and brotherly encouragements, and shall in our places endeavour the advancing of the covenanted reformation, according to the bonds yet remaining upon our own consciences, and our renewed professions before God and man; and though we cannot but foresee potent oppositions and sad discouragements in the work, yet we hope our God will carry us through all difficulties and hazards, at length cause the foundations now laid to increase into a perfect building, that the top-stone may be brought forth with shoutings, and his people cry, Grace, grace unto it.

We bless God on your behalf, that your warfare is in a great measure accomplished, and the church of Christ, and the interests thereof, so far owned in Scotland, as to be secured, not only by the uniform submission of the people, but also by laws, and those confirmed by the royal assent, a complication of blessings, which yet the kingdom of England hath not obtained and (though we promise ourselves much from the wisdom, piety, and clemency of his royal majesty) through our manifold distractions, distances and prejudices, not like suddenly to obtain: therefore we earnestly beg the continuance of your prayers for us, in this day of our conflict, fears and temptations, as also your advice and counsel, that, on the one side, we may neither by any forwardness and rigid counsels of our own, hazard the peace and safety of a late sadly distempered, and not yet healed nation, and on the other side, by undue compliances, destroy the hopes of a begun reformation. We have to do with men of different humours and principles; the general stream and current is for the old prelacy in all its pomp and height, and therefore it cannot be hoped for, that the presbyterial government should be owned as the public establishment of this nation, while the tide runneth so strongly that way; and the bare toleration of it will certainly produce a mischief, whilst papists, and sectaries of all sorts, will wind in themselves under the covert of such a favour: therefore no course seemeth likely to us to secure religion and the interests of Christ Jesus our Lord, but by making presbytery a part of the public establishment; which will not be effected but by moderating and reducing episcopacy to the form of synodical government, and a mutual condescendency of both parties in some lesser things, which fully come within the latitude of allowable differences in the church. This is all we can for the present hope for; and if we could obtain it, we should account it a mercy, and the best expedient to ease his majesty, in his great difficulties about the matter of religion; and we hope none that fear God and seek the peace of Sion, considering the perplexed posture of our affairs, will interpret this to be any tergiversation from our principles or apostasy from the covenant: but if we cannot obtain this, we must be content, with prayers and tears, to commend our cause to God, and, by meek and humble sufferings, to wait upon him, until he be pleased to prepare the hearts of the people for his beautiful work, and to bring his ways (at which they are now so much scandalized) into request with them.

Thus we have, with all plainness and simplicity of heart, laid forth our straits before you, who again beg your advice and prayers, and heartily recommend you to the Lord's grace, in whom we are

Your loving brethren,
and fellow-labourers in the work
of the Gospel,

Directed,   EDM. CALAMY,
To our reverend and highly   SIMEON ASH,
esteemed brethren,   THO. MANTON.
MR. DAVID DICKSON,
MR. ROBERT DOUGLAS,
MR. JAMES HAMILTON,
MR. JOHN SMITH, and
MR. GEORGE HUTCHISON,
these present, Edinburgh.

And though this abbreviate be larger than what at first I hoped it might have been, yet containing a summary of upwards of thirty sheets of paper, and a great variety of matter, both as to the church of Scotland, and matters in England at this critical juncture, and nothing being left out that might clear this part of our history, I flatter myself, it will not be unacceptable to the curious reader. I could not avoid some repetitions, neither could I, without spending more time than I had to allow, reduce this narrative to any other method than what it lies under in the letters themselves; and by this, the reader hath the benefit of having it in the very words of the writers. Some passages in them need to be explained, yet I was not willing to write notes upon them, but let them continue in their own native dress. A few warm passages, relative to the late unhappy debates, I thought good to bury, as of no great use to us now.

Upon the whole, this abstract will give a fuller view, than I have any where seen, of the apostasy of that violent persecutor Mr Sharp, and how inconsistent he proved with his own pretensions and professions. I suspect, and there seems ground for it from what is above, that Mr. Sharp, Mr. Leighton, bishop Sideserf, and others at London, were concerting the overthrow of the church of Scotland, with the high-fliers in England, when Mr. Sharp is writing such letters as we have seen, and, in the mean time, waving and burying the applications made to him by the reverend ministers of Edinburgh. And here we have an undoubted proof of the diligence, activity, and faithfulness, of worthy Mr. Douglas, and the rest of the ministers who joined him: and, when we compare what is above insert, with what shall occur in the body of the history, as to the letter to the presbytery of Edinburgh, and the senses put upon it, the reader must observe the disingenuous and base trick put upon the church of Scotland therein. I come now to the history itself.

THE HISTORY

OF THE

SUFFERINGS

OF THE

CHURCH OF SCOTLAND.

BOOK FIRST.

FROM THE RESTORATION 1660, TO THE PENTLAND ENGAGEMENT 1666.

1660. The heavy persecution of presbyterians in Scotland, from the restoration 1660 to the revolution 1688, is as amazing in the springs of it, as surprising in its nature and circumstances: and the following narrative of it will open a very horrid scene of oppression, hardships, and cruelty, which, were it not incontestably true, and well vouched and supported, could not be credited in after ages. I am persuaded the advocates for the methods taken during the two reigns I am to describe, must be put hard to it, to assign any tolerable reason of so much ungrateful and unparalleled severity, against a set of persons who had, with the greatest warmth and firmness, appeared for the king's interest, when at its lowest, and suffered so much, and so long, for their loyalty to him, in the time of the usurpation.

The violences of this period, and the playing one part of protestants against another, in my opinion, can no way be so well accounted for, as when lodged at the door of papists, and our Scots prelates; who, generally speaking, were much of a spirit with them. Indeed so much of the cruel, bloody, and tyrannical spirit of antichrist, runs through the laws and actings of this period, as makes this very evident to me. I am not so uncharitable as to charge with popery all the prelatists, who held hand to, and were the authors of this persecution; but I am very sure they played the game of Rome very fast, and bewrayed too much of one of the worst branches of popery, a cruel persecuting temper, towards such who differed from them for conscience' sake.

It is useless, and in some cases unfair, to load princes with all the iniquity committed under their reign: how far king Charles II. was chargeable with all the steps taken by those he made use of in Scotland, is not my business to determine. It is probable he wished, when it was too late, that he had less followed the counsels of France and his brother. Whether the two brothers, in their exile, or almost with their milk, drunk in the spirit and temper of popery; whether both of them in their wanderings were present at mass, and assisted at processions; whether the eldest died as really in the communion of the church of Rome, as his brother gave out, I do not say: but to me it is evident, and, ere I end, will be so to the reader, that under their reigns, matters, both in Scotland and England, were ripening very fast toward popery and slavery. Every

1660. thing pointed this way, and favoured the darling project of Rome and France, the rooting out of the northern heresy. The hasty dissolution of the parliament of England, which had so cheerfully invited the king home, most of whom were firm protestants; the gradual putting of the most important posts and trusts in the hands of such as were indifferent to all religions, and no enemies to that of Rome; the breaking in upon the constitution, liberties, and excellent laws of Scotland; the evident caressing and showing favour to every person and course that tended to advance arbitrary government and the enlargement of the prerogative, and served to abridge the power of parliament and liberty of the subject; the open toleration of papists; the plain spite and hatred which appeared against the Dutch and Holland, the great bulwark of the reformation abroad; the burning of London; the Dover league; the mighty efforts made to compass a popish succession, and many other things, put it beyond all question, that papists were not only open, but very successful in their designs, during this period.

Among all their projects, they succeeded in none more than that of playing our Scots bishops, and their supporters, against the presbyterians. And nothing could more advance the hellish design, than the removing out of the way such zealous protestants and excellent patriots, as the noble marquis of Argyle, the good lord Warriston, and the bold and worthy Mr. James Guthrie. Nothing could gratify the papists more than the banishing such eminent lights, as the reverend Messrs. M'Ward, Livingstone, Brown, Nevoy, Trail, Simpson, and others; together with the illegal imprisoning and confining, without any crime, libel, or cause assigned, such excellent gentlemen as Sir George Maxwell of Nether Pollock, Sir William Cunningham of Cunningham-head, Sir Hugh Campbell of Cesnock, Sir William Muir of Rowallan, Sir James Stuart, provost of Edinburgh, Sir John Chiesly of Carswell, major-general Montgomery, brother to the earl of Eglinton, major Holburn, George Porterfield and John Graham, provosts of Glasgow, with several others who will come to be noticed in this book. By such steps as those, and others to be mentioned in the progress of this history, popery mounted the throne, and our holy religion and excellent constitution were brought to the greatest danger and the very brink of ruin; from which, by a most extraordinary appearance of providence, the Lord delivered us at the late happy revolution, which, under God, we owe to the never-to-be-forgotten king William, of immortal memory.

In my accounts of the barbarities of this unhappy time, I shall go through the transactions of each year as they lie in order, as far as my materials and vouchers will carry me. This appears to me the plainest and most entertaining method; and though now and then some hints at other affairs besides the persecution of presbyterians will come in of course, and I hope will be the rather allowed, that as yet we have no tolerable history of this period, as to the church and kingdom of Scotland; yet I shall still keep principally in my view the sufferings of Scots presbyterians in their religious and civil rights. Agreeably therefore unto the three most remarkable eras of the period I have undertaken, I have divided this history, as in the title, into three books: and for the reader's easier access and recourse to every particular, and the help of his memory, as well as my better ranging the great variety of matter come to my hand, it will not be improper, however unfashionable, to divide every book into chapters, and those again into sections, according as each year offers more or less matter. This book, then, I begin with

CHAPTER I.

OF THE STATE AND SUFFERINGS OF PRESBYTERIANS, DURING THE YEAR 1660.

When the king was restored to his dominions, May 29th, 1660, no part of his subjects had a better title to his favour than the presbyterians. English writers can tell what influence the London ministers had upon the city petition, which, by papers I have seen, appears to have had a very considerable branch of its rise from Scotland; as also what interest the presbyterian ministers in the city had with the prime managers there, and what return they very quickly had for their share in the restoration. In Scotland, Mr. Robert Douglas was the first, as far as I can find, who ventured to propose the king's restoration to general Monk, and that very early: he travelled, it is said, *incognito*, in England, and in Scotland engaged considerable numbers of noblemen and gentlemen in this project. From his own original papers, I find, that when Monk returned from his first projected march into England, Mr. Douglas met him, and engaged him again in the attempt; and when at London, the general appeared to him slow in his measures for the king's restoration; Mr. Douglas wrote him a very pressing letter, and plainly told him, "that if he lost time much longer, without declaring for the king, there were a good number in Scotland, with their brethren in Ireland, ready to bring his majesty home without him." Yea, the ministers in Scotland were all of them vigorous asserters of the king's right, and early embarked in his interest. Yet all this was soon forgot, and Mr. (afterwards chancellor) Hyde, a violent zealot for the English hierarchy, is made chief favourite, and lord chancellor of England; and Mr. James Sharp, who was the earliest, and most scandalous complier with Cromwell, and the only one he had for some years, not only signed his owning of the commonwealth, and that neither directly nor indirectly he should ever act for the king, but by taking the tender he solemnly abjured the whole family of the Stuarts, this infamous and timeserving person, by Middleton's means, is put at the head of affairs in the church of Scotland, and managed matters entirely to Hyde, and the high-flying party in England, their satisfaction.

Upon the king's return great was the run of our nobility and gentry to London. It was impossible to satisfy all their expectations: such who missed posts were entertained with promises, and for a while behoved to please themselves with hopes. The chief offices of state were soon disposed of: the earl of Middleton was to be commissioner when the parliament should meet; the earl of Glencairn is made chancellor, the earl of Lauderdale secretary, the earl of Crawford lord treasurer, Sir John Gilmour president of the session, Sir Archibald Primrose clerk-register, and Mr. (afterwards Sir) John Fletcher king's advocate.

1660.

Some view hath been given in the introduction of the transactions of the former part of this year, yet it may be of some use to draw down an abstract of matters from general Monk's leaving Scotland, until the king's putting the government of affairs in the hands of the committee of estates, who sat down in August; and next, to consider their proceedings, and the hardships they put upon ministers, gentlemen, and others, till the sitting down of the parliament. Thus this chapter will fall in two halves.

SECT. I.

Containing a short deduction of our affairs in Scotland, from general Monk's leaving it, to the sitting down of the committee of estates at Edinburgh, August 23d, 1660.

HAD we any tolerable history of this church and kingdom, since the union of the two crowns, I should have come straight to the proper subject of this history: but I shall, till a larger account be given, hand myself and the reader into it, by the following short hint of things in Scotland.

After the death of Oliver Cromwell, there was nothing in England but one confusion upon the back of another. April 1659, his son Richard dissolved the parliament; and in a little time he is forced to demit, and things fall into a new shape almost every month: several of the counties in England run to arms, and matters were in the greatest disorder imaginable. Meanwhile general Monk manages all in Scotland; and, during these risings in England, apprehended and imprisoned the earls Marishal, Montrose, Eglinton, Selkirk, Glencairn, and Loudon, lord Montgomery, lieutenant-general David Lesly, viscount of Kenmure, the lord Lorn, earl of Seaforth, Sir James

1660. Lumsden, colonel James Hay, earl of Kelly, major Livingstone, and the earl of Rothes. Such of them as took the Tender, and gave bond for their peaceable behaviour, were soon liberate.

In October, Lambert threatened to attack the parliament then sitting at London, but was repulsed, and by them divested of his command, and seven persons appointed to govern the army, whereof Monk was one. But in a little time Lambert returned, dismissed the parliament, and shut the doors of the parliament-house. October 19th, Monk called together all the officers of the army in Scotland, and engaged them by oath, to submit to, and serve the parliament, cashiered all he suspected, imprisoned some, and modelled all according to his mind.

The army now prevailing in England, chose first a council of state, consisting of ten persons, and next a council of twenty-four, made up of the officers of the army: Monk was left out of both; and they sent down orders for the meeting of the session, exchequer, and other courts in Scotland, which had not met since Richard Cromwell's demission. General Monk refused to put those orders in execution, as coming from an incompetent authority, and resolves to march up with his army to London and restore the privileges of parliament. Before his departure, he called together to Edinburgh the commissioners from most part of the shires in Scotland, the magistrates of burghs, and a good many of the nobility and barons, who met in the parliament house, November 15th, 1659. The general had a speech to them to this purpose:—" That it was not unknown to them what revolutions were happened; that some of the army had put a force on the parliament of England, which he was resolved with God's assistance to re-establish, and for that end was going with his army to England; that with respect to the nation of Scotland, his regard to them was such, that if he had success in his design he would befriend them in all their just liberties, and study the abatement of their cess: if the business went contrary to his expectation, then his fall should be alone to himself, and not to their prejudice, whose help he was not to take; but desired, as they loved their country and their own standing, that they would live peaceably, and see to the peace of their several shires and burghs, according to their stations; and if any rising should fall out during his absence, that they should suppress the same, let the pretext be what it would; and that he would leave orders with the garrisons he left, to assist them in so doing, and give his mind more fully to them in writ."

November 22d, Monk and his army marched off to England; and when at Haddington he received articles from the council in England, which not being satisfying, he returned with his officers to Edinburgh, where, after consultation, they rejected the articles as contrary to their principles, which were to be governed not by the sword, but a parliament lawfully called, in the maintenance of which they were engaged by oath. Accordingly an answer was returned to England, November 24th; and December 2d, he marched with his army to Berwick, where he continued some time; and December 12th, the commissioners of the shires received from him their commissions for keeping the peace in his absence.

The city of London, and many other places, having declared for a parliament, and against the army, Lambert marches up from the borders, whither he had come with the army to oppose Monk; the parliament sit down December 25th, and Monk is declared general over all the forces of the three kingdoms. And January 1st, 1660, he follows Lambert, Fleetwood, and their armies, and marches straight to London. The daily melting away of the army under Lambert and the rest, and the almost general cry through England and Ireland for a free parliament, with Monk's successful arrival at London, and his management till the king's return, is at full length to be found in the English historians; and some hints have been given of what concerns Scots affairs in the introduction, so that I may pass over the former part of this year very briefly.

February 21st, the secluded members

took their places in the parliament, to the number of about eighty, and of the rump there were but twenty-one; so the former carried all as they pleased. General Monk is made commander-in-chief by sea and land. Writs are issued for a free parliament to meet April 25th. Meanwhile they confirmed the solemn league and covenant, and ordered it to be set up and read in all the churches of England. Thus, as bishop Kennet remarks, the solemn league and covenant did really conduce to the bringing in of the king. They ratified the assembly's Confession of Faith, with a reservation of chap. xxx. and xxxi. to further consideration. Colonel Morgan, whom Monk had ordered in January to return to Scotland with a thousand of the army, when he saw all going so well in England, is appointed commander of the forces and garrisons in Scotland. March 13th, they rescind the engagement taken by all ranks, to be faithful to the commonwealth of England, without king and house of lords; and in room of this, ordain all in office to declare the war undertaken by both houses of parliament against the late king, just and lawful, and that magistracy and ministry were the ordinances of God.

In Scotland, Edward Moyslie, Henry Goodyear, —— Crook junior, John Howie, esquires, and Sir John Wemyss, Sir James Hope, James Dalrymple, John Scougal of Humbie, James Robertoun, and David Falconer, were appointed to be civil and criminal judges, their quorum five, and to go in circuits: but this order took no effect, every body now expecting the king's return. The parliament at London likewise liberate the earl of Lauderdale, the earl of Crawford, and lord Sinclair, whom the usurper and the rump had kept prisoners in the Tower now near ten years. A day of fasting and prayer was also appointed to be kept, April 6th, for conduct to the parliament.

April 25th, the parliament sat down, and upon the 1st of May came to several resolutions, "that the government of England is by king, lords, and commons; that the king of Scotland is king of England," and others, which the reader will meet with in the printed accounts of this great turn of affairs;

and I shall not repeat them. May 1660. 8th the king was proclaimed at London, and May 14th, at Edinburgh. Sir John Granvil went over to his majesty with money; Lauderdale and Crawford went over with him; and we have seen that Mr. Sharp went about the same time, and there probably concerted the ruin of this church, and the measures very soon now entered upon against presbyterians. May 29th, the king entered London with great solemnity, and published a proclamation against profaneness. I shall only take notice of a few more hints relative to the state of affairs in Scotland, before the settling the government in the committee of estates.

In April and May, the synods met, where there appeared a very good disposition towards healing the rent betwixt the resolutioners and protesters; and had not Mr. Sharp, by his letters from London, diverted this upon the king's return, and put him, and the managers about him, upon beginning the persecution, with attacking the remonstrators, and the ministers who were antiresolutioners, a little time would have completed the union. But Mr. Sharp had his own private resentments against Mr. Rutherford, Mr. James Guthrie, the lord Warriston, and others of the protesters, to gratify; and by that was to pave the way to ruin all firm presbyterians, and therefore he put the government upon the measures we shall hear of, in which some of our noblemen, fretted at the discipline of the church, willingly joined him; and we have seen by his letters, so dunned Mr. Douglas and others at Edinburgh, with his accounts of the king's dislike of the protesters, and the approaching evils upon them, all of his own procuring, that those good men kept off from compromising matters, and nothing in the affair of the union was effectually done, till all were cast to the furnace together.

May 1st, the synod of Lothian met. Mr. Douglas opened it with a sermon from 1 Cor. iv. 1. the notes whereof are in mine eye. Therein, after many judicious remarks against prelacy, from ministers being stewards, he warns his brethren to keep equally at distance from malignancy and sectarianism; he compares profaneness and malignancy to

1660. rocks at sea, which appear; and sectarianism to quicksands on the shore, which swallow up people, before they are aware. He notices that kingly government in the state, and presbyterian in the church, are the greatest curbs to profaneness. He explodes the foolish saying, No bishop, no king. "Shall," says he, "kings, which are God's ordinance, not stand, because bishops, which are not God's ordinance, cannot stand? The government by presbytery is good, but prelacy is neither good in Christian policy or civil. Some say, may we not have a moderate episcopacy? But 'tis a plant God never planted, and the ladder whereby antichrist mounted his throne. Bishops got caveats, and never kept one of them, and will just do the like again. We have abjured episcopacy, let us not lick it up again. Consider the times past, how unconstant men have proven, like cockboats tossing up and down; leave them, and come into the ship, walk up to the way of the covenant; and if this be not the plank we come ashore upon, I fear a storm come and ruin all."

The presbyterians in Scotland were extremely lift up with the king's safe return, and in a little time were but ill handled for their hearty concern in the restoration.*

Mr. Douglas preaching in Edinburgh, upon the Monday after the parliament of England agreed on the above resolutions, gave his auditory an account of the great turn of affairs, adding, that "it hath pleased the Lord to roll away all difficulties which hindered the king from his crown, and he who sold us for our iniquities without price hath restored us without money." A day of thanksgiving was kept at Edinburgh, June 19th, for the king's restoration. After sermons were over the magistrates came to the Cross, where was a covered table with sweetmeats; the Cross run with wine, three hundred dozen of glasses were broke, the bells tolled, trumpets sounded, and drums beat. There were fire-works upon the Castle-hill, with the effigies of Cromwell, and the devil pursuing him, till all was blown up in the air. Great solemnity, bonfires, music, and the like, were in other places upon this occasion. But very quickly a good many who had been sharers of those public rejoicings found they had hardships to reap from the restoration, and perhaps that they had exceeded a little in them. We shall afterwards hear, that upon the 8th of July, the marquis of Argyle is seized at London; and upon the 14th of July, orders came down to major-general Morgan, to secure Sir James Stuart,

---

* The following graphic description, by a cotemporary writer, of the state of Scotland at the period of the restoration, and the immediate effects of that event, will, we doubt not, be very interesting to the reader.—*Ed.*

"The king's return from his miserable exile into his languishing, confounded country, was both the object of many fervent desires, and the foundation of very many high expectations; nor am I able to judge whether he longed more to enjoy his royal palace, or his people to see him established upon his throne. Indeed his exile was very comfortless to himself, for, in France, first he was coldly entertained by his nearest neighbours and relations, and thereafter shamefully banished, and partly upon Mazarine's base pick. In Colen he quickly found himself a burdine to his host, and thereafter became the publick object of his dishonour, the boys in the city making a solemn anniversary mock pageant to the scorn of the king without land. And when he was driven to seek shelter and rest in the Spanish Netherlands, where he made his longest abode, yet was he still hunted by his enemies, betrayed by his servants, and most unsuccessful in all his attempts, besides his continual sorrow for his loss, his fear from his hazard, and the poor shift he was constrained to make among strangers for his supply. And there he learned to believe kings might have reason to pray for their daily bread from the Lord, which he could never believe from his tutor, inculcating into his mind the petitions of the Lord's prayer, while he was yet a young child. All these, and many more, you may think were enough to make him long for what might attend the command of Brittain. Upon the other side, his people were most impatient under the grief from his absence, partly from their discontent with, and disdain they hade towards their present lords, and partly from the love they bore to his unknown person. Indeed the nations were brought under and kept under by a party of men, small for their number, being only the rump of that body of people who commenced the warr against Charles the First; and likewayes inconsiderable for their parts, few of them being men of either birth or breeding; and though they were wonderfully successfull, yet their victories smelled alwayes more of ane admireable air of prosperity, than ordinary military valor. And, lastly, that party was despicable for their quality in the world, being almost all of them citizens or husbandmen, which the nobles of Brittain disdained very much. Moreover, tho' these men were of the most sober behaviour of any that ever commanded by the sword, yet you may expect something would

provost of Edinburgh, Sir Archibald Johnston of Warriston, and Sir John Chiesly of Carsewell, who was knighted in the Isle of Wight, and protested against the death of king Charles. The first and last were catched, but Warriston got off for a little: whereupon he was summoned by sound of trumpet to render himself; and

1660.

happen in their administration that would be grievous: forasmuch as even justice and courtesie both were disdained from their hand. Besides, they were constrained to keep up an army for their own support, and heavily to burdine the nations for the maintenance of the same; which was the more odious, being from those who called themselves patrons of the people's liberty. And nothing made the nations roar louder for their king, than that a people, that had taken arms upon a pretence of conscience to purge the reformed religion of superstitions of the episcopal church, should not only tolerate, but also encourage, the vilest blasphemies: and tho' it was sore against the heart of their head (Oliver Cromwell), yet so much did that whole party adore the idol of liberty, he was necessitate to forbear what he durst not suppress. It is also to be considered that it is ane easy matter for a man in discontent to imagine any condition sweeter than the present case, so very many considerations drawn from the king's case and personal character heightened much the desire of the nations after their king's return. The compassions the world had for his father's misfortunes and sufferings, and his own youth being spent in continual toyle, attended with losse, dishonour, and grief, were enough to make a gentle nature to pity him. He was known to be of a meek temper, which he could well improve by his wonderfull reservedness, courtesie, and dissimulation, for every man had at least fair words and big promises: so compassion begat affection, and affection heightened every shadow of virtue in him. Few conversed in his court except these who were full of the same spirit with himself; all those suppressed all noise of his imperfections, and proclaimed his virtues, so he was made to the world a paragon of virtue, as well as an example of pity. The people of Scotland had no correspondence with him, or what they had came from those courtiers who study more to be smooth than faithfull. He wrote indeed a friendly letter to Mr. Hamilton, the minister in Edinburgh, (whom in a special manner he seemed to affect,) assuring him he was the same in France that he had been in Scotland, by which ambiguous expression he seemed both to defend his own constancy and outreach the minister: yet was that letter looked at by many in Scotland as if it hade been a renewing of the covenant. And tho' it be now confidently affirmed that he corresponded with the pope, and no crime now to say he was then a papist, yet was it at that time high laese majesty to doubt he was any other thing than a sincere covenanter. If it were told them he used the English Liturgy in his chapel, it was excused as being rather necessity than choice, people believing he could have no other; so their affections to his person were equal to their discontent with the republican governors. And to compleat the people's appetite for the king's return, the hopes founded upon his restauration were nothing behind either the discontent under Cromwell, or the affection to his person: for then did every fellow that hade catched a scarr in a fray among the tories (though perchance pillaging ane honest house) expect to be a man all of gold. All that had suffered for him in his warr, lossed for him of their estate, or been advocates for him in a tavern dispute, hoped well to be noticed as his friends, or to receive not only a compensation from his justice, but a gratuity from his bounty. I believe there were more gaping after prizes than his sufficiency, hade it been ten times greater than it was, could ever have satisfied. All believed it would be the golden age when the king returned in peace; and some of our Brittish divines made the date of the accomplishment of the glorious promises in the apocalypse, not doubting he was assuredly to be the man should distroy Rome as sure as he was Constantine's successor. In fine, the eagerness of their longing was so great, some would never cut their hair, some would never drink wine, some would never wear linen, till they might see the desire of their eyes, the king.

"Weell: when time was ripe, a sort of parliament conveened in England by the authority of the committee of council, upon which the rump of the long-successfull parliament hade derived their power, before their voluntary dissolution, as general Monk and his cabal had resolved; and immediately upon their first assembling the king thought good, by Sir John Greenvile, to address to them ane obliging letter, wherein he engadged to preserve every man in his profession, and protect every man in the freedom of his conscience, with many other large promises: upon which the parliament (being mostly made of presbyterians) thought fitt to invite him home by a splendid legation of lords and commons, among whom was the lord Fairfax, that he who had ruined the father in the field might do the world reason by restoring the son in peace. Accordingly the king, accompanied with his two brothers, his triumphant court, and many a poor maimed cavaleer, having sett sail from Schevelin, took land at Dover upon the 25th of May, 1660, where he was received with all the honour and reverent splendor England could strain in the highest degree. From thence he was conveyed through London to Westminster, upon the 29th of May, 1660, which was the so much celebrated date of the blessed restauration.

"Now before we speak of the alteration court influences made upon the church of Scotland, let us consider in what case it was at this time. There is in all Scotland some 900 paroches, divided into 68 presbyteries, which are again canton'd into fourteen synods, out of all which, by a solemn legation of commissioners from every presbytrie, they used yearly to constitute a national assembly. At the king's return every paroche hade a minister, every village hade a school, every family almost hade a Bible, yea, in most of the countrey all the children of age could read the Scriptures, and were provided of Bibles, either by the parents or by their ministers. Every minister was a very full professor of the reformed religion, according to the large confession of faith framed at Westminster by

1660. a printed proclamation was published with tuck of drum, discharging all persons to reset him, and offering a reward to such as should apprehend him, as follows:

"*By the commander-in-chief of his majesty's forces in Scotland.*

"Whereas I have received an order from his majesty, for apprehending the lord War-

the divines of both nations. Every minister was obliedged to preach thrice a-week, to lecture and catechise once, besides other private duties in which they abounded, according to their proportion of faithfulness and abilities. None of them might be scandalous in their conversation, or negligent in their office, so long as a presbytrie stood; and among them were many holy in conversation and eminent in gifts; nor did a minister satisfy himself except his ministry hade the seal of a divine approbation, as might witness him to be really sent from God. Indeed, in many places the Spirit seemed to be poured out with the word, both by the multitudes of sincere converts, and also by the common work of reformation upon many who never came the length of a communion; there were no fewer than sixty aged people, men and women, who went to school, that even then they might be able to read the Scriptures with their own eyes. I have lived many years in a paroch where I never heard ane oath, and you might have ridde many miles before you hade heard any: also, you could not for a great part of the country have lodged in a family where the Lord was not worshipped by reading, singing, and publick prayer. Nobody complained more of our church government than our taverners, whose ordinary lamentation was, their trade was broke, people were become so sober. The great blemish of our church was, the division betwixt protesters and resolution-men (as they were called); but as this was inconsiderable upon the matter, so was it also pretty well composed by express agreement among brethren, even while the English continued our governours.

"Now, in the midst of this deep tranquility, as soon as the certainty of the king's return arrived in Scotland, I believe there was never accident in the world altered the disposition of a people more than that did the Scottish nation. Sober men observed, it not only inebriat but really intoxicate, and made people not only drunk but frantic; men did not think they could handsomely express their joy, except they turned brutes for debauch, rebels and pugeants; yea, many a sober man was tempted to exceed, lest he should be condemned as unnatural, disloyal, and unsensible. Most of the nobility, and many of the gentry and hungry old soldiers flew to London, just as the vulture does to the carcase. Then when they were come to court, they desired no more advice than to know the king's inclinations, and he was the best politician that could outrun obedience, by anticipating a command. Always at their arrival almost all hade good words, some hade pensions never to be paid, and some who came in time had offices for a while. Glencairn was made chancellor for his adventure among the tories, Crawford theasurer for his long imprisonment, Lauderdale was made secretary, and the only one Scottish gentleman of the bed-chamber, that he might be always near his very kind master. Sir William Fleeming was made clerk of the register, a place of great gain, for which he was as fitt as to be professor of the metaphysics in ane university; but he was so wise as to sell it to Sir Archibald Primrose, who could husband it better, as indeed he did, for in a few years he multiplied his estate, by just computation, from one to sixteen. Sir John Fletcher was made king's advocate, though he hade been one of the first in Scotland who forsware the king, that he might find employment under the English. But partly by Middleton's procurement (of whose affinity he was), and partly because he was ane honest man of the mode (that is a man void of principles), he was placed in that dangerous office, in which he hade the opportunity to make all the subjects of Scotland redeem their lives at his own price, from his criminal pursuit, upon the account of their old alleadged rebellions, and their late compliances with the English, in which he had been a ringleader. Middleton was judged a fitt man to act the part which afterward he did discharge over and above. He hade, from the degree of a pickman in colonel Hepburn's regiment in France, by his great gallantry, raised himself to the chief command, sometimes in the parliament's armies, and afterwards in the king's, though he was as unhappy under the latter, as he was successful under the first. Always because of his constant adherence to the king, even in his exile, (wherein he suffered much) and the great adventures he hade made among the tories in the Highlands, when the English commanded Scotland, and most of all because of his fierce soldier-like disposition, he was judged a fit instrument to cow Scotland, and bring that people down from their ancient freedom of spirit, (so much displeasing to their late king) to that plian' softness which might better suit with the designs of a free (despotic) prince. The earle of Lithgow he was made colonel of the regiment of foot-guards, a place in which he feathered his nest well; but no man could give the reason of his promotion, unless the descent of a popish family might perhaps promise satisfying inclinations toward hidden designs. The poor old maimed officers, colonels, majors, and captains, who expected great promotion, were preferred to be troopers in the king's troop of life-guards, of which Newburgh was made captain. This goodly employment obliged them to spend with one another the small remnant of the stock their miseries hade left them, but more they could not have, after all their hopes and sufferings. Gentlemen and lords came down from court with empty purses and discontented minds, having nothing to put in place of their flown money, except the experience of a disappointment, which uses to be a bitter reflection on a man's own indiscretion, in mistaking measures, and making false judgment upon events as they hade done. There remained only one comfort among them, which was, that when the fanatic should be fined and forfaulted they would glut themselves with the spoil; and this was enough to some thoughtless minds, but was indeed as groundless as fruitless, for never one of them ever tasted that much desired fruit."
—Kirkton's History of the Church of Scotland, pp. 59—69.

riston, and securing his person in the castle of Edinburgh; and he being withdrawn, and obscuring himself, as also making refusal to yield obedience to his majesty's commands: these are to authorize and empower any person or persons, in his majesty's name, to use their utmost endeavours for apprehending the said lord Warriston, to keep him in safe custody, and bring him in to me; for which exercise they shall receive one hundred pounds Scots. And in case any person or persons shall harbour and conceal the said lord Warriston, and not make speedy discovery of him, they will be deemed guilty of treason; and will be proceeded against accordingly. Given under my hand at Edinburgh, July 16th, 1660.
"THOMAS MORGAN."

This is the first public arbitrary step, and in the progress of this work we shall meet with a great many of this nature. Without libel or cause given, by a private order, not only a worthy gentleman is attacked, and a reward offered, though a very mean one, to his apprehenders; but resetting him is declared treason, and those guilty, to be proceeded against to the death. No doubt the English commander had warrant from our Scots managers at court for so severe a proclamation, and it is of a piece with the after-steps we shall see were taken.

July 20th, Sir John Swinton of that ilk, one of the judges under Cromwell, and called the lord Swinton, was taken out of his bed, in a quaker's house, in King's street, London, and sent in fetters to the Gate-house. We shall afterwards hear he was sent down to Scotland with the marquis of Argyle. He had been once a zealous professor of reformation, and a covenanter; but falling in with the usurper and English sectaries, he first turned lax, and of late took on the mask of quakerism. It is said, the queen mother and papists took a care of him, and brought him off; and indeed quakerism is but a small remove from popery and Jesuitism. He was no more a presbyterian, and the present run was against such, as being chiefly opposite to the designs in hand.—Upon the 26th of July, one William Giffen, or Govan, whom we shall find execute the same day with Mr. James Guthrie, was seized, upon a false information, that he had been present upon the scaffold when king Charles I. was beheaded, and imprisoned in the castle of Edinburgh; and for what I know, he continued in prison, till next year he was brought to a public death. Those are some of the previous steps, as an introduction to the committee of estates, in whose hands the king lodged the government of Scotland, by his proclamation August 2d, till the parliament should meet and a council be named; and their procedure will take in what is further remarkable this year. This will be the subject of the next section.

1660

SECT. II.

Of the proceedings of the committee of estates, their imprisoning Mr. James Guthrie and other ministers, August 23d; the king's letter to the presbytery of Edinburgh, and other things this year.

IT was some time before the throng of English and foreign affairs allowed the king to consider the case of Scotland; and after several meetings of those who were now in great numbers from this kingdom at court, his majesty came to a resolution to lodge the government in the hands of the committee of estates, named by the last parliament we had in Scotland. This he signified by the following proclamation:—

" Charles R. To all our loving subjects of the kingdom of Scotland, or others whom these do or may concern, greeting. Forasmuch as it hath pleased Almighty God to remove that force and armed violence, by which the administration of our royal government, among our people there, was interrupted; and we being desirous to witness our affection to, and care of that our ancient kingdom, of whose loyalty we have had many testimonies, have resolved, that until a meeting of parliament, which we are presently to call, the government shall be administrate by us, and the committee of estates named by us and our parliament, 1651; and therefore do hereby call and authorize the

1660. said committee to meet at Edinburgh, the 23d of August instant. And we do hereby require our heralds, pursuivants, and messengers at arms, to make publication hereof at the market-cross of Edinburgh, and all other places, &c. Given at our court at Whitehall, August 2d, 1660, and of our reign the twelfth year."

The members of this committee had all of them appeared hearty in profession for the constitution of this church and our reformation; they had concurred with the king, in taking the national and solemn league and covenant; and some of them had advised the king to make that remarkable declaration at Dunfermline, August, 1650, which since has made such a noise, as being a hardship put upon the king, and is so diametrically opposite to the course now entering on, that I thought it worth the inserting.* I have seen no exact list of the members of this committee, but I little doubt persons were named upon it, 1651, who did not now meet with them. The earl of Glencairn came down, and was received with great parade as high chancellor of Scotland at Edinburgh, August 22d; and next day, August 23d, the committee sat down, nine noblemen, ten barons, and as many burgesses; and the chancellor presided. The members were all of one kidney, and hearty in prosecuting the designs now on foot.

That same day Mr. James Guthrie, minister at Stirling, Mr. John Stirling, and Mr. Robert Trail, ministers at Edinburgh, Messrs. Alexander Moncrief at Scone, John Semple at Carsfairn, Mr. Thomas Ramsay at Mordington, Mr. John Scott at Oxnam, Mr. Gilbert Hall at Kirkliston, Mr. John Murray at Methven, Mr. George Nairn at Burntisland, ministers, with two gentlemen, ruling

---

* Declaration at Dunfermline, August 16th, 1650.

By the KING.

CHARLES R.

His majesty taking into consideration that merciful dispensation of divine providence, by which he hath been recovered out of the snare of evil counsel, and having attained so full persuasion and confidence of the loyalty of his people in Scotland, with whom he hath too long stood at a distance, and of the righteousness of their cause, to join in one covenant with them, and to cast himself and his interest wholly upon God, and in all matters civil to follow the advice of his parliament, and such as shall be intrusted by them, and in all matters ecclesiastic the advice of the general assembly and their commissioners, and being sensible of his duty to God, and desirous to approve himself to the consciences of all his good subjects, and to stop the mouths of his and their enemies and traducers; doth, in reference to his former deportments, and as to his resolutions for the future, declare as follows:

Though his majesty as a dutiful son, be obliged to honour the memory of his royal father, and have in estimation the person of his mother; yet doth he desire to be deeply humbled and afflicted in spirit before God, because of his father's hearkening to, and following evil counsels, and his opposition to the work of reformation, and to the solemn league and covenant, by which so much of the blood of the Lord's people hath been shed in these kingdoms; and for the idolatry of his mother, the toleration whereof in the king's house, as it was matter of great stumbling to all the protestant churches, so could it not but be a high provocation against him, who is a jealous God, visiting the sins of the fathers upon the children: and albeit his majesty might extenuate his former carriage and actions, in following of the advice, and walking in the way of those who are opposite to the covenant, and to the work of God, and might excuse his delaying to give satisfaction to the just and necessary desires of the kirk and kingdom of Scotland, from his education and age, and evil counsel and company, and from the strange and insolent proceedings of sectaries against his royal father, and in reference to religion, and the ancient government of the kingdom of England, to which he hath undoubted right of succession; yet knowing that he hath to do with God, he doth ingenuously acknowledge all his own sins, and all the sins of his father's house, craving pardon, and hoping for mercy and reconciliation through the blood of Jesus Christ. And as he doth value the constant addresses that were made by his people to the throne of grace in his behalf, when he stood in opposition to the work of God, as a singular testimony of long suffering patience and mercy upon the Lord's part, and loyalty upon theirs; so doth he hope, and shall take it as one of the greatest tokens of their love and affection to him and to his government, that they will continue in prayer and supplication to God for him, that the Lord, who spared and preserved him to this day, notwithstanding of all his own guiltiness, may be at peace with him, and give him to fear the Lord his God, and to serve him with a perfect heart, and with a willing mind, all the days of his life.

And his majesty having, upon the full persuasion of the justice and equity of all the heads and articles thereof, now sworn and subscribed the national covenant of the kingdom of Scotland, and the solemn league and covenant of the three kingdoms of Scotland, England, and Ireland, doth declare that he hath not sworn and subscribed these covenants, and entered into the oath of God with his people, upon any sinister intention and crooked design for attain-

CHAP. I.] OF THE CHURCH OF SCOTLAND. 67

elders, Mr. Andrew Hay of Craignethan, near Lanark, and James Kirkco of Sundiwell, in the parish of Dunscore, in Nithsdale, were met and convened in the private house of Robert Simpson in Edinburgh, to draw up an humble address

1660:

ing his own ends, but so far as human weakness will permit, in the truth and sincerity of his heart, and that he is firmly resolved in the Lord's strength to adhere thereto, and to prosecute to the utmost of his power all the ends thereof in his station and calling, really, constantly, and sincerely all the days of his life. In order to which, he doth in the first place profess and declare, that he will have no enemies but the enemies of the covenant, and that he will have no friends but the friends of the covenant. And therefore, as he doth now detest and abhor all popery, superstition, and idolatry, together with prelacy, and all errors, heresy, schism, and profaneness, and resolves not to tolerate, much less allow any of these in any part of his majesty's dominions, but to oppose himself thereto, and to endeavour the extirpation thereof to the utmost of his power; so doth he, as a Christian, exhort, and, as a king, require, that all such of his subjects who have stood in opposition to the solemn league and covenant, and work of reformation, upon a pretence of kingly interest, or any other pretext whatsoever, to lay down their enmity against the cause and people of God, and to cease to prefer the interest of man to the interest of God, which hath been one of those things that hath occasioned many troubles and calamities in these kingdoms, and being insisted into will be so far from establishing of the king's throne, that it will prove an idol of jealousy to provoke unto wrath him who is King of kings and Lord of lords: the king shall always esteem them best servants, and most loyal subjects, who serve him, and seek his greatness in a right line of subordination unto God, giving unto God the things that are God's, and unto Cesar the things that are Cesar's; and resolveth not to love or countenance any who have so little conscience and piety, as to follow his interest with a prejudice to the gospel, and the kingdom of Jesus Christ, which he looks not upon as duty, but as flattery, and driving of self designs, under a pretence of maintaining royal authority and greatness.

2. His majesty being convinced in conscience of the exceeding great sinfulness and unlawfulness of that treaty and peace made with the bloody Irish rebels, who treacherously shed the blood of so many of his faithful and loyal subjects in Ireland, and of allowing unto them the liberty of the popish religion, for the which he doth from his heart desire to be deeply humbled before the Lord; and likewise considering how many breaches have been upon their part, doth declare the same to be void, and that his majesty is absolved therefrom, being truly sorry that he should have sought unto so unlawful help for restoring of him to his throne, and resolving for the time to come, rather to choose affliction than sin.

3. As his majesty did, in the late treaty with his people in this kingdom, agree to recall and annul all commissions against any of his subjects who did adhere to the covenant and monarchical government in any of his kingdoms; so doth he now declare, that by his commissionating of some persons by sea against the people of England, he did not intend damage or injury to his oppressed and harmless subjects in that kingdom, who follow their trade of merchandise in their lawful callings, but only the opposing and suppressing of those who had usurped the government, and not only barred him from his just right, but also exercise an arbitrary power over his people, in those things which concern their persons, consciences, and estates; and as, since his coming into Scotland, he hath given no commissions against any of his subjects in England or Ireland, so he doth hereby assure and declare, that he will give none to their prejudice or damage; and whatever shall be the wrongs of these usurpers, that he will be so far from avenging these upon any who are free thereof, by interrupting and stopping the liberty of trade and merchandise, or otherwise, that he will seek their good, and to the utmost employ his royal power, that they may be protected and defended against the unjust violence of all men whatsoever. And albeit his majesty desireth to construct well of the intentions of those (in reference to his majesty) who have been active in counsel or arms against the covenant; yet being convinced that it doth conduce for the honour of God, the good of his cause, and his own honour and happiness, and for the peace and safety of these kingdoms, that such be not employed in places of power and trust; he doth declare that he will not employ, nor give commissions to any such, until they have not only taken or renewed the covenant, but also have given sufficient evidences of their integrity, carriage and affection to the work of reformation, and shall be declared capable of trust by the parliament of either kingdom respective. And his majesty, upon the same grounds, doth hereby recall all commissions given to any such persons, conceiving all such persons will so much tender a good understanding betwixt him and his subjects, and the settling and preserving a firm peace in these kingdoms, that they will not grudge nor repine at his majesty's resolutions and proceedings herein, much less upon discontent act any thing in a divided way, unto the raising of new troubles, especially since, upon their pious and good deportment, there is a regress left unto them in manner above expressed. And as his majesty hath given satisfaction unto the just and necessary desires of the kirk and kingdom of Scotland, so doth he hereby assure and declare, that he is no less willing and desirous to give satisfaction to the just and necessary desires of his good subjects of England and Ireland; and in token thereof, if the houses of parliament of England sitting in freedom, should think fit to present unto him the propositions of peace agreed upon by both kingdoms, he will not only accord to the same, and such alterations thereanent, as the houses of parliament, in regard of the constitution of affairs, and the good of his majesty and his kingdoms, shall judge necessary; but do what is further necessary for the prosecuting the ends of the solemn league and covenant, especially in those things which concern the reformation of the church of England, in doctrine, worship, discipline, and gov-

1660. and supplication to the king, "congratulating his return, expressing their entire and unfeigned loyalty, humbly putting him in mind of his own and the nation's covenant with the Lord, and earnestly praying that his reign might be like that of David, Solomon, Jehoshaphat, and Hezekiah." As may be seen in the paper itself.*

ernment; that not only the Directory of Worship, the Confession of Faith and Catechism, but also the Propositions and Directory for Church Government, accorded upon by the synod of divines at Westminster, may be settled, and that the church of England may enjoy the full liberty and freedom of all assemblies and power of kirk censures, and of all the ordinances of Jesus Christ, according to the rule of his own word; and that whatsoever is commanded by the God of heaven, may be diligently done for the house of the God of heaven. And whatever heretofore hath been the suggestions of some to him, to render his majesty jealous of the parliament, and of the servants of God; yet as he hath declared that in Scotland he will hearken to their counsel, and follow their advice in those things that concern that kingdom and kirk; so doth he also declare his firm resolution to manage the government of the kingdom of England by the advice of his parliament, consisting of a house of lords, and of a house of commons there; and, in those things that concern religion, to prefer the counsels of the ministers of the gospel to all other counsels whatsoever: and that all the world may see, how much he tenders the safety of his people, and how precious their blood is in his sight, and how desirous he is to recover his crown and government in England by peaceable means, as he doth esteem the service of those who first engaged in the covenant, and have since that time faithfully followed the ends thereof, to be duty to God, and loyalty to him; so is he willing, in regard of others who have been involved in these late commotions in England against religion and government, to pass an act of oblivion, excepting only some few in that nation, who have been chief obstructors of the work of reformation, and chief authors of the change of the government, and of the murder of his royal father: provided that these who are to have the benefit of this act, lay down arms, and return unto the obedience of their lawful sovereign.

The committee of estates of the kingdom, and general assembly of the kirk of Scotland, having declared so fully in what concerns the sectaries, and the present designs, resolutions, and actings of their army against the kingdom of Scotland, and the same committee and assembly having sufficiently laid open public dangers and duties, both upon the right hand and upon the left, it is not needful for his majesty to add any thing thereunto, except that in those things he doth commend and approve them, and that he resolves to live and die with them and his loyal subjects, in prosecution of the ends of the covenant.

And whereas that prevailing party in England, after all their strange usurpations, and insolent actings in that land, do not only keep his majesty from the government of that kingdom by force of arms, but also have now invaded the kingdom of Scotland, who have deserved better things at their hands, and against whom they have no just quarrel; his majesty therefore doth desire and expect that all his good subjects in England, who are and resolve to be faithful to God, and to their king, according to the covenant, will lay hold upon such an opportunity and use their utmost endeavours to promove the covenant and all the ends thereof, and to recover and re-establish the ancient government of the kingdom of England (under which for many generations it did flourish in peace and plenty at home, and in reputation abroad) and privileges of the parliament, and native and just liberty of the people: his majesty desires to assure himself, that there doth remain in these so much conscience of their duty to religion, their king and country, and so many sparkles of the ancient English valour which shined so eminently in their noble ancestors, as will put them on to bestir themselves for breaking the yoke of those men's oppressions from off their necks. Shall men of conscience and honour set religion, liberties, and government at so low a rate, as not rather to undergo any hazard, before they be thus deprived of them? Will not all generous men count any death more tolerable than to live in servitude all their days? And will not posterity blame those who dare attempt nothing for themselves and for their children in so good a cause, in such an exigent? Whereas if they gather themselves and take courage, putting on a resolution answerable to so a noble and just an enterprise, they shall honour God, and gain themselves the reputation of pious men, worthy patriots, and loyal subjects, and be called the repairers of the breach, by the present and succeeding generations, and they may certainly promise to themselves a blessing from God, upon so just and honourable undertaking for the Lord and for his cause, their own liberties, their native king and country, and the unvaluable good and happiness of the posterity. Whatever hath formerly been his majesty's guiltiness before God, and the bad success that these have had who owned his affairs whilst he stood in opposition to the work of God, yet the state of the question being now altered, and his majesty having obtained mercy to be on God's side, and to prefer God's interest before his own; he hopes that the Lord will be gracious, and countenance his own cause in the hands of weak and sinful instruments, against all enemies whatsoever. This is all that can be said by his majesty at present, to these in England and Ireland, at such a distance; and as they shall acquit themselves at this time in active discharge of their necessary duties, so shall they be accepted before God, endeared to his majesty, and their names had in remembrance throughout the world.

Given at our court at Dunfermline, the sixteenth day of August, 1650, and in the second year of our reign.

* Ministers' [designed] supplication August 23d, 1660.

Most gracious and dread sovereign,
We your majesty's most humble subjects, considering the duty which, as Christians, we owe unto our Lord Jesus Christ, who is King of kings, and Lord of lords, and which, as

CHAP. I.] OF THE CHURCH OF SCOTLAND. 69

The occasion of this meeting, upon which so much followed, was this:—the brethren and ministers, who in their sentiments could not approve of the public resolutions, did very much fear and jealouse (suspect) Mr. James Sharp, now at London, by the allowance, and at the desire of a good many of the brethren for the resolu- 1660.

subjects, we owe unto your majesty as our lawful and native king under him; we hold ourselves bound to tender unto your majesty this our most humble address and supplication. How hateful the actings of the late usurping powers, in offering violence unto the parliament of England, in their unchristian and barbarous murder of your royal father, in their insolent changing of the ancient civil government of the kingdom of England, and by armed violence unjustly secluding your majesty therefrom, in their unjust invading of the kingdom of Scotland, and enthralling the same in subjection to themselves, and beyond all, in their impious encroachings upon the kingdom of Jesus Christ, and the liberties thereof, and in promoting and establishing a vast toleration in things religious throughout these nations, unto the perverting of the precious truths of the gospel, and defacing of the ordinances of Jesus Christ, in opening a wide door to all sorts of errors, heresies, schisms, impiety, and profaneness; how abominable and hateful these things were unto us, the Lord, who searcheth the reins and trieth the hearts, doth know; against which we gave many public testimonies before the world, to witness our abhorrency thereof: and the same Lord knoweth, that as we did earnestly pray for and breathe after his appearing to witness against these, so (saving that christian pity and compassion that we owe unto the persons of men, though our very enemies) we do rejoice in his putting down of them that did lift up themselves, and staining of the pride of their glory, and breaking the yoke of their power off the necks of these kingdoms. We hold ourselves also bound thankfully to acknowledge the Lord's signal preserving of your majesty's person, in the midst of manifold dangers and designs threatening the same these years past, and that after a long exile from your own house and people, he hath been pleased to bring you back to the same; and when the foundations of the ancient civil government of these kingdoms were overthrown, again to make way for repairing the ruins, and building up the breaches thereof, for establishing of the same upon right and sure foundations, in your majesty's person and family, and to do these things when they were so little expected, in so quiet and peaceable a way, and without the effusion of christian blood, and embroiling of these kingdoms in the miseries and calamities of a new war: and as we do adore the wonderful and wise hand of God, and bless his name who hath done these great things; so it is not only our practice for the present, but our sincere purpose and resolution also for the time to come, to pour forth the fervent desires and supplications of our souls, unto the most High, by whom kings reign, for the preservation and safety of your majesty's person, and for the multiplication and increase of his Spirit upon you, that you may employ your power unto his praise and the comfort of his people, and for the establishing of your just power and greatness, and, in subordination to him, to be faithful and loyal in tendering of all the duties of honour, and sub-

jection, and obedience to your majesty, that are due from humble and loving subjects to their native and lawful sovereign. And we desire to be persuaded, and with confidence to promise to ourselves, that your majesty will accept of these our professions as proceeding from honest and loyal hearts, and allow us that protection, countenance, and encouragement, in our stations and callings, that may be expected from a gracious king. And considering the great happiness that ariseth both to kirk and state, and all the members thereof by the mutual embracements of religion and righteousness, of truth and peace, and from the mutual good understanding betwixt the supreme magistrate and the faithful of the land, when it pleaseth divine providence so to dispose, and the many calamities and miseries that, in the holy justice and indignation of God, do attend the separating or violating of these only sure foundations of states and kingdoms; we are bold, in the integrity of our hearts, and in the zeal of the glory of God, and of the good of his church, and of your majesty's honour and happiness, and from the sense of the manifold and great obligations that be upon us, before the Lord, so to do, and particularly that of the covenant, that what lets we are not able ourselves to suppress or overcome, we shall reveal and make known, that it may be truly prevented or removed, humbly to represent unto your majesty the great danger that threatens religion, and the work of reformation in the churches of God in these kingdoms, from the designs and endeavours of the remnant of the popish, prelatical, and malignant party therein, which is beginning again to lift up the head, and, not only to render hateful and bear down many of your majesty's good subjects, who have been employed as instruments in that work, and have kept within the bounds of their duty in promoting and pursuing the same, so far as human infirmity would permit; but also to overthrow that blessed work itself, and to re-introduce prelacy, and the ceremonies, and the Service-book, and all these corruptions which were formerly cast out, as inconsistent with that pure and spotless rule of church government, and discipline, and divine worship, delivered unto us in the word of God, and as a yoke of bondage which neither we nor our fathers were able to bear. Although we know that that spirit will not want specious pretences, and plausible and subtile insinuations for compassing these ends; yet as there cannot readily be greater disservice to the church of God, and to your kingdoms, and to your majesty's honour and happiness, than actings of that nature, so we cannot without horror of heart, and astonishment of spirit, think upon what dreadful guiltiness, kings, princes, ministers, and people shall be involved into, and what fearful wrath shall attend them from the face of an angry and jealous God, if after all the light that he hath made to shine in these kingdoms from his blessed word, for discovering the error and impiety of these things, and after his hand lifted up so high for casting out of the same, and after such

tions. They were apprehensive of designs hatching just now against the church, not from the public resolutioners, but Mr. Sharp, and others who struck in with them. Whereupon once and again they wrote to the ministers of Edinburgh of the other side, that they might join with them in a dutiful address to his majesty at such a solemn vows and engagements taken upon themselves before God, angels, and men, against them, they should again lick up the vomit thereof. God forbid that ever we should hear or see such heart-astonishing things, which would turn the mirth of the Lord's people into mourning, and their songs into most sad and bitter lamentation. Neither are we less apprehensive of the endeavours of the spirit of error, that possesseth sectaries in these nations, which, as it did at first promote the practice of a vast toleration in things religious, and afterwards proceeded unto the framing of the mischief thereof into a law; so we doubt not, but it will still be active unto the promoting and procuring the same, under the specious pretence of liberty for tender consciences; the effects whereof have, in a few years past, been so dreadful, that we cannot think of the continuing of it, but with much trembling and fear: therefore knowing that to kings, princes, rulers, and magistrates, appertains the conservation and purgation of religion, and that unity and peace be preserved in the church, and that the truth of God be kept pure and entire, that all blasphemies and heresies be suppressed, all corruptions or abuses in discipline and worship prevented or reformed, and all the ordinances of God duly settled, administered, and observed; and that nothing can more contribute unto the preserving and promoting of religion, and of the work of reformation, than that all places of power and trust be filled with men of a blameless and christian conversation, and of approven integrity, and known affection to the cause of God: we your majesty's most humble subjects do, with bowed knees and bended affections, humbly supplicate your majesty, that you would employ your royal power unto the preservation of the reformed religion in the church of Scotland, in doctrine, worship, discipline, and government; and in the reformation of religion in the kingdoms of England and Ireland, in doctrine, worship, discipline, and government; and unto the carrying on of the work of uniformity in religion in the churches of God in the three kingdoms, in one confession of faith, form of church government, directory for worship and catechising, and to the extirpation of popery, prelacy, superstition, heresy, schism, profaneness, and whatsoever shall be found contrary to sound doctrine, and the power of godliness: and that all places of power and trust under your majesty may be filled with such as have taken the covenant, and are of approven integrity and known affection to the cause of God, if in a matter that so much concerns the honour of God, and the good of this church, and your majesty's honour and happiness, we be jealous with a godly jealousy, we know your majesty's wisdom and piety to be such, as will easily pardon it. The sense of our duty to God, and to your majesty, with the importunity of men of a contrary mind, who seek to make your majesty and these kingdoms transgressors, by building again the things that were formerly warrantably destroyed, constrain us to be petitioners against the same, and earnestly to entreat that any beginnings of stumbling which have already been given in these things, especially in the matter of prelacy, and the ceremonies, and Service-book in your majesty's chapel and family, and in other places of your dominions, may be removed and taken away, and that there may be no further proceedings in these things which grieve the Spirit of God, and give offence to your majesty's good subjects, who are engaged with you in the same covenant and work of reformation: and that your majesty, for establishing the hearts, and strengthening the hands of these who are faithful in the work of the Lord, and for quashing the hopes and endeavours of adversaries, will be pleased to give public signification of your approbation of the covenant, and of your purpose to adhere unto the same, and to carry on the work of God in these kingdoms according thereto; and that your majesty's eyes may be upon the faithful of the land, that they may dwell with you. We hope that your majesty will not take offence, if we be the Lord's remembrancers to you, that you were pleased, a little before your coming into this kingdom, and afterwards at the time of your coronation, to assure and declare by your solemn oath, under your hand and seal, in the presence of Almighty God, the searcher of hearts, your allowance and approbation of the national covenant, and of the solemn league and covenant, faithfully obliging yourself to prosecute the ends thereof in your station and calling: and that your majesty, for yourself and successors, shall consent and agree to all acts of parliament enjoining the national covenant, and the solemn league and covenant, and fully establishing presbyterial government, the Directory of Worship, Confession of Faith, and Catechisms, in the kingdom of Scotland, as they are approven by the general assemblies of this kirk, and parliaments of this kingdom; and that your majesty shall give your royal assent to acts and ordinances of parliament, past or to be past, enjoining the same in your other dominions, and that you shall observe these in your own practice and family, and shall never make opposition to any of these, or endeavour any change thereof. And we desire to be persuaded, that no length of time hath made your majesty to forget, or weakened upon your heart, the sense of the obligation of that great and solemn oath of God in the covenant; yea, that the afflictions wherewith God hath exercised your majesty these years past, and the great and wonderful deliverance that of late he hath granted unto you, hath fixed deeper impressions thereof upon your spirit, and that amongst all the kings of the earth, religion and reformation shall have no greater friend than your majesty; yea, that as you are more excellent than the kings of the earth, in regard of purity of profession and solemn engagements unto God, and long exercisedness with manifold afflictions, and in the Lord's setting you over these kingdoms, which were not only through grace amongst the first-fruits of the gentiles, but also, in your princely station and dignity, are, amongst all

juncture. We have seen the occasion of the coldness and delays made in this affair, by the ministers of Edinburgh, in the introduction. They were excellent men, but it must be owned that they trusted too much to Mr. Sharp, and by his suggestions and letters every thing of this nature was crushed.

Two former meetings had been concerted at Edinburgh, of ministers from the different corners of the church, but the brethren had not come up to them. Matters seemed still to grow more and more threatening to the church establishment, and no other way appeared to be left them but to act in this manner. There were no assemblies to be expected, there was no commission, and synods were not to meet till October; therefore the above-named persons, a small part of many who were to have met, found themselves under a necessity to do somewhat in such a crisis: so they formed the foresaid supplication, which they designed to have communicate to a larger meeting before it was sent to court. The chancellor and others coming to the knowledge of this meeting, the committee of estates were acquainted with it; and some persons were immediately sent, who came upon the meeting, when the scrolls and other papers were before them, which are mentioned in the Act of Confinement, and seized all. I find those papers were the first draughts of letters to some brethren, desiring another meeting at Glasgow, in September, about the supplication, with instructions to some of their number, when they went west with a draught of the supplication, that it might be considered by the brethren of the synod of Glasgow, that if they found cause, they might join in it: such as came from the committee, asked for the supplication itself, which the ministers gave them a copy of, without any difficulty.

1660.

When the unfinished scrolls and the supplication were read in the committee of estates they were sent straight to court; and all who had been present at the meeting, save Craignethan, who happily escaped, were committed to close prison, in the castle of Edinburgh, by the act of this day's date,* without ever calling the minis-

---

that we know in the world, the most eminent for the purity and power of the gospel; so shall your majesty excel them in zeal for God, and for the kingdom of Jesus Christ, and that by how much your majesty is, by the constitution and hand of the Almighty, lifted up above the sphere of that of your subjects, by so much shall your motions be more vigorous and active unto the carrying about, by the influence of your royal commands and example, all the orbs of inferior powers and persons in these kingdoms, in subordination to God and your majesty, in the practice of godliness and virtue. It is the desire of our souls, that your majesty may be like unto David, a man according unto God's own heart; like unto Solomon, of an understanding heart to judge the Lord's people, and to discern betwixt good and bad; like unto Jehoshaphat, whose heart was lifted up in the ways of the Lord; like unto Hezekiah, eminent for goodness and integrity; like unto Josias, who was of a tender heart, and did humble himself before God, when he heard his words against Jerusalem and Judah, and the inhabitants thereof; and not only made a covenant before the Lord, to walk after the Lord, and to keep his commandments with all his heart, and with all his soul, to perform the words of the covenant; but also caused all that were in Jerusalem and Benjamin to stand to it, and took away all the abominations out of all the countries that pertained to the children of Israel, and made all that were present in Israel to serve, even to serve the Lord their God: so shall your majesty inherit the honour and blessings of these kings upon the earth, and their happiness in heaven; so shall your majesty's person be preserved, and your government established over these kingdoms; which is the unfeigned desire, and fervent supplication of

Your majesty's most humble
and loyal subjects.

* Act for securing Mr. James Guthrie and others.

At Edinburgh the 23d day of August, 1660. The committee of estates, now presently convened by his majesty's special warrant and authority, upon information given to them of a conventicle and private meeting of some remonstrator and protesting ministers and others at Edinburgh, for which they had neither warrant from the ordinary, civil, or ecclesiastic courts, and the said committee, being by his majesty's special commission and commands, intrusted and empowered with the caring, ordering, and providing for what may conduce for the peace of this his majesty's ancient kingdom, and support of his power and authority therein, finding such unlawful conventicles, upon what pretence soever, without public lawful authority, expressly derogatory to his majesty's royal prerogative, and tending to the disturbance of the present peace of his majesty's dominions; gave order and command to some of their number, to search and make trial after the occasion and reason of their meeting, who in the said inquiry, found them with petitions subscribed, and some papers and letters scrolled, to be sent for convo-

1660. ters before them, or hearing what they had to say in their own defence. This illegal and unprecedented step, the first act of our committee of estates, was a preamble to that horrid scene of arbitrary proceeding, oppression, and cruelty, which now began to open. Mr. James Guthrie was never liberate till a glorious martyrdom, and the truth made him free, and the rest underwent very great hardships. It hath been observed that this was done that very day, a hundred years after, in which the idolatrous, tyrannical, contradictory, and cruel religion of popery was abolished in Scotland, and the reformation was established. Indeed from this day and forward, for twenty-eight years, we were going very fast back to Babylon, and wide steps were taken to re-introduce popery and slavery.

A careful comparing of the supplication with the committee's act will sufficiently expose the last. The ministers were chiefly attacked because they were protesters; and yet such as were of that denomination most firmly asserted the king's title under his exile; and Mr. James Guthrie and others of them suffered much from the English for their loyalty, when Mr. Sharp, who now managed all, took the tender, and fell in with the usurper. Ingratitude, however, was but a lesser aggravation of this violent procedure; it was plainly illegal: besides the known privilege of all subjects to address the sovereign, there were then laws unrescinded, to which the members of the committee themselves had assented, warranting them to meet and supplicate. The usurpers, when Scotland was under their feet, did not hinder ministers to meet, except in their general assembly. In short, this step was very unequal as well as ungrate and illegal, since that very same day the committee liberate several persons imprisoned for murder and other atrocious crimes. But those were not the things at present they were in quest of.

Under their confinement in the castle the ministers agreed upon a supplication, and sent it to the committee of estates, whereof I have not seen a copy; but by other papers of this time, I find in it, "They promised no more to prosecute the remonstrance, 1650, and expressed their sorrow for giving their lordships any offence by the unseasonableness of their late meeting, at which they were seized." The chancellor insisted they should acknowledge their fault in meeting upon such a matter: but the ministers, apprehending this would be a receding from their designed testimony, and such a declaration affecting not only the manner and time of their meeting, but the business and important matter upon which they met, might have very ill consequences at this juncture, refused to go this length, though the advocate, who had taken the tender when many of them were suffering for their loyalty and firmness to the king, threatened to found a process of treason upon their supplication.

The people under the pastoral charge of the now imprisoned ministers were extremely afflicted with their confinement, and ready to make all proper applications. I find Mr. Stirling's session at Edinburgh, and no doubt Mr. Trail's also, acquaint him with their design to supplicate in his behalf, which is delayed till they know the issue of their own supplication. All I have of this, is in the following letter from Mr. Stirling to his session at this time, who breathes much of a Christian and ministerial

---

cating all of their own judgment, containing many particulars reflecting upon his sacred majesty, the government of our neighbour church and kingdom of England, and constitution of this present committee, and many other things directly tending to seditions, raising of new tumults, and (if possible) rekindling a civil war amongst his majesty's good subjects. Therefore, the said committee have thought fit, and hereby ordains the persons subscribers of the said papers, and these in company at the updrawing thereof; they are to say, Mr. James Guthrie, Mr. Robert Trail, Mr. John Stirling, Mr. Alexander Moncrief, Mr. John Semple, Mr. Thomas Ramsay, Mr. Gilbert Hall, Mr John Scot, Mr. George Nairn, Mr. John Murray, ministers, and John Kirko ruling elder, to be committed prisoners within the castle of Edinburgh, therein to remain, until his majesty's pleasure shall be further made known; and gives warrant to the present captain of the said castle, to receive them prisoners, and to keep them in safe custody.

Extracted forth of the books of the said committee by me,   Jo. HAY, cler. com.

CHAP. I.] OF THE CHURCH OF SCOTLAND. 73

spirit, and states the cause of their sufferings; and therefore I have insert it,* as what deserves a room in this collection. There was a motion likewise in the synod of Glasgow, at their meeting in October, this year, for a supplication in favour of the imprisoned ministers; but it was much opposed by some ministers who turned bishops, and their undertakings, and some worthy members who exercised too much charity for their false brethren. Thus they continued a considerable time in prison, till at 1660.

---

* Letter, Mr. John Stirling, minister at Edinburgh, to his session, when imprisoned by the committee of estates, 1660.

Dearly beloved,

I hear there are some thoughts among you, of petitioning the honourable committee of estates, for my releasement. I confess it is no small refreshment to me, to think that I have so much room in your affections, as you are ready to look after me, or desire that I might yet continue to serve you, in the work of the gospel: and though I be your debitor on this account, and do most heartily thank you, and all those in whose hearts this motion hath been entertained, yet I dare not advise you to follow it any further at present. My brethren and I are jointly to petition this week, and we shall see what issue that may take, before we desire our people to be engaged in suiting for us. If the Lord have any more service for me among you, he can bring me to you again (I trust) in the spirit and power of the gospel; and this testimony of your affection, shall, I hope, put a new edge upon my spirit, to be more willing than ever to spend and be spent, for the advantage of your souls: but if otherwise, the will of the Lord be done. I am hopeful, that he who ministereth seed to the sower, shall minister to your necessities; and I shall never forget you, by his grace, but ever bear you upon my heart, to hold you up before the Lord, so long as I am in this body.

I know the cause of our sufferings is strangely represented to you; and, I confess, we were miserable men, and unworthy of the room we bear either in the church or kingdom, if that were true that is said of us. The personal sufferings I am under, nor the reproaches that are upon my name, are not a very great trouble, in comparison of the fear I have that Satan may thereby take advantage to cause the Lord's people stumble at the gospel I have preached among them: yet this is my comfort, that whatever the world say or believe, the cause I suffer for is the Lord's, and no less than the avowing of his marriage contract, in a sworn covenant, betwixt the three kingdoms: and albeit we have not now liberty to vindicate ourselves from the aspersions cast upon us, but must lie under the reproaches of seditious persons, and raisers of a new war, (which, God knoweth, our hearts do abhor,) and enemies to our king, (whom our souls do honour, and I dare take you witnesses of my good wishes towards him,) yet this is no new thing; you know who was counted an enemy to Cesar, even Christ our Lord, and Paul was a seditious fellow, and went up and down the world as a deceiver, and yet was true. Yet all we were about, was an innocent supplication, that his majesty might mind the oath of God, and oppose those abjured corruptions of prelacy, and ceremonies that are coming in, and that he might, for advancing of reformation, employ fit instruments in places of power and trust, who are friends thereunto; and we should desire no other vindication, but that our supplication might be printed.

Always, dearly beloved, till I be able, if the Lord will, to speak face to face, I shall desire no other favour of you, but that you will endeavour that the people may not stumble, but retain somewhat of charity to me, till God shall fulfil his promise, in making righteousness appear, that the upright in heart may follow after it. I beseech you, in the bowels of Jesus Christ, take heed to yourselves, and to the flock over which the Holy Ghost hath made you overseers: much more lieth upon you now, than formerly when I was with you. Remember, I beseech you, that you watch as those that must give an account, and that the adversary is going about as a roaring lion, continually seeking whom he may devour. Ah! my heart bleedeth to think how much he prevaileth with the most part, and how few there are who will lay hold on the free offers of grace and salvation through a redeemer, and come to Jesus that they may have life. Edinburgh hath long had the plenty and purity of the glorious gospel, but ah! who hath believed our report, and to whom is the arm of the Lord revealed? It is true the Lord hath a remnant, yea, a precious remnant, among us, else we should have been like to Gomorrah; but yet alas for the blindness and hardness, the looseness and profanity of the most part, who live, in effect, without God in the world: ah, that in their day they might know the things that belong to their peace, before they be hid from their eyes! I know there are many such under your charge, but let me beseech you to be serious with them, while you have occasion, and to walk exemplarly before them. It is not to preachers only, but to all Christ's followers, in their own place and station, that he saith, Let your light so shine before men, that they seeing your good works, may glorify your Father which is in heaven. As for me, the Lord knoweth, that as I have no greater grief by this restraint, than my absence from you, (which would be a deep sorrow indeed, but that I am persuaded of the call of God to this piece of service that is now put in my hands) so can I have no greater joy and comfort, than to hear of all your happiness, and of your love to the gospel, and care to adorn the same by your holy and blameless conversation. I shall add no more, but my earnest request for your prayers before the throne of grace; and so recommending you and all the flock, to him who is the great shepherd and bishop of your souls, I rest,

Your servant for Christ's sake,
Jo. STIRLING.

Edinburgh, Sept. 11.

P. S. If it be possible, that your care and mine together, could provide preaching in your own church, till we know whether the Lord will shorten this trial unto me, I wish we could do it.

K

1660. length a good many of them were let out of the castle, but still confined to their chambers at Edinburgh, till the sitting down of the parliament; some of them had only their prison changed; and several other ministers were seized, as we may hear in the further accounts of the procedure of the committee, which I come now to hint at.

Mr. Archdeacon Eachard's account of the imprisonment of those ministers, vol. iii. p. 39, deserves our notice. In the progress of this history, we shall find him once and again giving very indistinct and unfair representations of our Scots affairs during the period before me, in the short and lame hints he hath. Here he speaks of those ministers as the prime managers of the church of Scotland; whereas though they were excellent persons, yet at this juncture they were far from being the prime actors in the church. We have seen that they could scarce prevail to have any meeting among brethren of their own sentiments, and how thin the meeting they had was. But this innuendo must be made, that they were the prime ministers of the kirk party, that the odium of the remonstrance, unlawful meetings, and seditious papers, and other hard names now made use of against the remonstrators, might lie upon all presbyterian ministers. It would seem to be with some such view as this, that he says, They met and drew up a remonstrance. I can scarce think this author is so absolute a stranger to the Scots history, as to blend the remonstrance formed ten years before, with the petition drawn up by Mr. Guthrie and the rest at this time, though we shall meet with as gross mistakes in the celebrated English writers when they treat of Scots affairs. But one must think he would have his reader believe, that all those excellent ministers were remonstrants. An historian ought to give every thing he speaks of its own name, and not talk of a supplication under that of a remonstrance. It was a piece of greater justice in Mr. Eachard, a few lines below, to take notice of the king's proclamation concerning the carriage of his subjects, November 1st, 1660, and candidly to insert the clause discharging addresses to his majesty, except by the parliament or committee of estates, with the promise of an indemnity, which for private ends was long delayed.

Next day after the ministers were seized, the committee of estates go on to somewhat that was more extensive, and discharge all meetings without the king's authority, and seditious petitions. The proclamation will stand best in its own light.

Proclamation by the committee of estates, against unlawful meetings, and seditious papers. At Edinburgh, August 24th, 1660.

"The committee of estates, in obedience to his majesty's proclamation, being met and taking to their serious consideration, the goodness of God, who in his great mercy hath restored the king's majesty to the exercise of his royal government; and withal considering his majesty's great care of, and affection to his ancient kingdom of Scotland, in calling and authorizing the said committee of estates to meet; and they finding it their duty to prevent all unlawful meetings, which may tend to the prejudice of his majesty's service, or may again involve his majesty's subjects into new troubles, have thought fit, in his majesty's name and authority, to prohibit, and by these presents do prohibit and discharge all unlawful and unwarrantable meetings and conventicles, in any place within his majesty's kingdom of Scotland, without his majesty's special authority; and likewise all seditious petitions and remonstrances, under what pretext soever, which may tend to the disturbance of the peace of this kingdom, or alienating or diminishing the affections of his majesty's subjects from their due obedience to his majesty's lawful authority; and that under all highest pains. And for that effect appoints all sheriffs of shires, and magistrates of burghs, to be careful within their respective bounds, that no such pernicious and dangerous meetings be permitted; but that they may be prevented, hindered, made known, and discovered, to the committee of estates: and ordains these presents to be printed and published. Signed in the name, and by warrant of the committee of estates. "GLENCAIRN, Chancellor." I. P. D. Com."

I shall not stay to make any observes upon this proclamation. We need not be critical upon the narrative and style; this was a great and sudden change, and that by people who had been acquainted with, yea, active in a quite other method of speaking and doing than this, which puts all into the king's hand. Our people seem to be cautious at first, *nemo repente fit turpissimus;* and they only discharge unlawful and unwarranted meetings, which all sides must own should be discharged: but then the question is, what are these? and all seditious petitions and remonstrances are discharged. Indeed the first seems to be understood of all meetings not called and authorized by the king; but it is not time yet to speak out, till the great work and excellent laws made after the year 1640 be rescinded; and there is no doubt this proclamation was very much against the present laws, in the sense in which it is designed, though the double and extensive phrases, unlawful and unwarrantable, &c., screened the members from attacks.

When the king's letter to the presbytery of Edinburgh came down, September 3d, of which more just now, it rather heightened than slackened the committee's procedure against gentlemen and ministers. The brethren for the public resolutions made too much of it; and all who favoured the protest and remonstrance were looked upon almost as rebels and enemies to the king, and accordingly dealt with by the committee, who went on to censure, harass, and imprison them. Upon the 14th of September, by their order, John Graham, provost of Glasgow, and John Spreul, town-clerk there, were imprisoned in Edinburgh tolbooth. Both of them had been reckoned favourers of the remonstrance, and yet they were pious and excellent persons. The committee sent an order to the magistrates of Glasgow, to oblige Mr. Patrick Gillespie, principal of the college, to compear before them; which he did: and September 15th, was made prisoner in the castle of Edinburgh.

From thence he was sent to the castle of Stirling, and continued in confinement till the parliament sat. Mr. Gillespie indeed had fallen in very much with the usurper, and was in this very much alone, and few or none of the ministers followed him. That same day, the committee of estates confined Mr. Robert Row, minister at Abercorn, and Mr. William Wiseheart, minister at Kinneil, to their chambers at Edinburgh. Both of them were excellent persons, but suspected to favour the brethren who were for the protestation, and had used some freedom in their sermons. Upon Thursday, September 20th, Mr. Wiseheart, and with him provost Jaffray, director of chancellary, were imprisoned in Edinburgh tolbooth. About the same time Mr. James Guthrie was sent from Edinburgh castle to Stirling, by order of the committee, where he continued till the parliament called for him in order to his trial, or near about that time, when we shall again meet with him.

September 19th, a proclamation is published against two known books: the first writ, and long before printed, by the reverend and learned Mr. Samuel Rutherford, entitled *Lex Rex*. The other supposed to be drawn up by Mr. James Guthrie,—the Causes of God's Wrath. I have insert the committee's proclamation about them.* We

1660

---

* A proclamation against two seditious books or pamphlets, the one entitled Lex Rex, the other, the Causes of God's Wrath, &c.

The committee of estates, now presently convened by his majesty's special warrant and authority, taking into their consideration, that there are two books, the one entitled Lex Rex, and the other, the Causes of God's Wrath, &c. printed and dispersed by some rebellious and seditious persons within this kingdom, cunningly, and of purpose to corrupt the minds of his majesty's loyal subjects, to alienate and withdraw them from that duty of love and obedience, that they owe unto his sacred person and greatness, stirring them up against his majesty and kingly government, and containing many things injurious to the king's majesty's person and authority, laying the foundation and seeds of rebellion, for the present and future generations: therefore, in consideration of the premises, the said committee of estates do declare the said two books to be full of seditious and treasonable matter, animating his majesty's good subjects to rise up in rebellion against their lawful prince and sovereign, and poisoning their hearts with many seditious and rebellious principles, prejudicial to the king's majesty's person,

1660. shall meet with a good many papers of this nature afterwards. The committee introduce a phraseology, pretty much out of doors for some time in Scotland, but very much followed in the period I am upon, how properly I am not to consider, " the king's sacred greatness." Very liberally they determine the authors of those books, and the printers and dispersers of them, to be rebellious and seditious persons, " that they contain many things injurious to the king, and laying the foundation and seeds of rebellion, that they are full of treasonable matter," with many other hard words. They call in the copies, and order them to be delivered to Mr. Robert Dalgleish, his majesty's solicitor, in less than a month's time; and declare, that all and every one who, after the 15th of October, shall have any copies of them, shall not only be esteemed enemies to the king, but punished accordingly in their persons and estates. Such summar declarations coming so near the popish index *prohibitorius*, and their inquisition, especially when pointed at books, which will still be valued, where a sense of religion and liberty prevails, may surprise the reader; but in a little time he will find them turning common. Mr. Sharp, now come down, had a particular quarrel with Messrs. Rutherford and Guthrie, and prosecuted it a little further than this public mark upon those two books. In short, the principles laid down in the first, never yet disproven, and the plain facts in the last, were diametrically opposite to the course now entering on, and therefore they must be prohibited.

The day following a more general thrust is given against all whom the committee were pleased to name remonstrants and their adherents, in their proclamation, September 20th, which I have likewise added.* The paper speaks for itself with-

---

his royal authority, and to the peace of this kingdom: and that the foresaid two books ought not to be read, perused, nor kept in the hands or custody of any of his majesty's lieges; but that the same be called in, and delivered up, that his majesty's good subjects be not longer infected or poisoned thereby. And for this effect they do ordain all and whatsoever persons, havers of the said books in their hands or custody, to bring and deliver the same to Mr. Robert Dalgleish, his majesty's solicitor in Scotland, betwixt and the sixteenth day of October next to come: with certification to all and every one of these who shall refuse to do the same, and with whom any of the said books shall be found after the said day, they, and each one of them, shall not only be esteemed enemies to the king's majesty, his authority, and the peace of this kingdom, but also they shall be punished accordingly in their persons and estates, as the king's majesty and estates of parliament, or the said committee, shall think fit. And ordain these presents to be forthwith printed and published at the market-crosses of Edinburgh and head burghs within the shires of this kingdom, that none pretend ignorance hereof. Extracted forth of the books of the said committee, by me,

Jo. HAY, Clev. Com.

* A proclamation against all seditious railers and slanderers, whether civil or ecclesiastic, of the king's majesty and his government; and against remonstrators and their adherents, and against all unlawful convocation of his majesty's lieges.

At Edinburgh, the 20th of September, 1660. The committee of estates, presently convened by his majesty's special warrant and authority, laying seriously to heart the great trust committed to them, for carrying on, ordering and using of all means which may tend to the securing of the peace of this kingdom, and maintaining and furthering his majesty's power and authority therein; considering, that by many acts of parliament, all leasing-makers, and tellers thereof, makers of evil information, or engendering discord betwixt the king and his people, all reproachers or slanderers of his majesty, government, or realms, depravers of his laws, misconstruers of his proceedings, meddlers in the affairs of his estate; as also, all hearers of any such leasings, calumnies, or slanders, by word or writ, and concealers thereof, should be punished as seditious persons, enemies to his majesty, and the pain of death to be executed upon them, as at length is contained in the 43d act of king James I. his 3d parl. the 83d act of king James V. his 6th parl. the 134th act, parl. 8th, the 10th act, parl. 10th, the 205th act, parl. 14th, of king James VI. and the 27th act of the 2d parl. of his sacred majesty's umquhile dearest father, of blessed memory; which, more particularly in relation to any such reproaches, lies, or calumnies, concerning the kingdom of England, and his majesty's worthy subjects therein, is expressly prohibited by the 9th act of king James VI. 20th parl. holden in anno 1609, under the pain specified in the said act: likeas, all convocation of his majesty's lieges, without his majesty's special command, or express license, whatever quality, estate, or function the persons be of, spiritual or temporal, is expressly prohibited by the 131st act, parl. 8th, king James VI. under the pains therein contained. As also, the remonstrance presented to the committee of estates, in anno 1650, declared by his majesty and parliament, in July 1651, seditious and treasonable: nevertheless, and albeit it hath pleased the Almighty God, of his wonderful goodness and providence, happily to restore his sacred majesty to the peaceable government of his ancient kingdoms, and all his majesty's subjects to their wonted peace, freedom, and privilege, which is

OF THE CHURCH OF SCOTLAND.

out any commentary. A large enumeration is made of the laws and acts against leasing-making, and particularly calumnies against his majesty's kingdom of England, and his worthy subjects there. This pointed at such, who in preaching or conversation regretted the establishment of the hierarchy and ceremonies there, contrary to the covenants. The laws against all convocations and meetings without the king's command, which, if I mistake not, were rescinded expressly by the parliaments, approven by king Charles I., and all ratified by the present king, are next set down, with the declaration of the parliament, July, 1651, that the remonstrance presented to the committee of estates, 1650, against 1660. malignants being employed in offices, was seditious and treasonable. Then the committee having information, " that those laws are contravened, by slanders on his majesty and government, unlawful conventions of the lieges, owning the remonstrance, meddling in the affairs of his majesty, and his estate, present and bygone, they discharge the same under the pains contained in the said laws, and declare that all who hear any such leasings, calumnies, or slanders, and reveal them not, shall incur the same punishment with the principal offender. And that the lieges being most easily ensnared by seditious and treasonable courses

(as it ought to be) a matter of great rejoicing to all good Christians, and loyal subjects whatsoever, both at home and abroad: yet the said committee of estates, certainly knowing, and receiving daily information, that several of his majesty's lieges, and subjects within this kingdom, do, contrary to the said acts of parliament, convocate, convene, and assemble themselves, without his majesty's special command and license; and that there are several scandalous seditious speeches uttered and preached in sermons, declamations, and otherwise, and several calumnious pasquils, libels, rhymes, and other writs, devised, vented, and published, to the reproach or slander of his majesty's person, estate, or government: as also, that several his majesty's subjects do own, adhere to, avow, abet, or assist the foresaid remonstrance, whereby his majesty's loyal, well meaning subjects, may be drawn from their due allegiance, and ensnared in such seditious combinations and meetings, and involved in their said treasonable plots and practices, unless timous remedy be provided: therefore, the committee of estates, in his majesty's name and authority, command and charge, that no subject, or subjects within this kingdom, of whatsoever quality, estate, or function they be of, spiritual or temporal, presume, or take upon hand, to convocate, convene, or assemble themselves together, for holding of councils, conventions, or assemblies, to treat, consult, or determinate in any matter of estate, civil or ecclesiastic (except in the ordinary judicatories), without his majesty's special command and express license, had and obtained to that effect: as also, that none of them, of whatsoever function, degree, or quality, presume, nor take upon hand, privately or publicly, in sermons, preachings, declamations, speeches, or otherwise, by word or writ, to utter, devise, or vent any purpose of reproach, or slander, against his majesty's person, estate, or government, his parents, or progenitors, or to deprave his laws and acts of parliament, or misconstrue his proceedings, whereby any misliking may be moved betwixt his majesty, and his nobility, and loving subjects, or to meddle in the affairs of his majesty and his estate, present, bygone, and in time coming; or to own, abet, or assist the foresaid remonstrance: with certification, they shall be proceeded against, conform to the tenors of the said respective acts of parliament. Likeas, the said committee of estates declare, that any person or persons, who hear any such leasing, calumny, or slanderous speech, or shall see or have any such pasquils, or writs, as aforesaid, and reveal not the same to his majesty, or one of the said committee, or to the sheriff, steward, or bailie of the shire, stewards in regality or royalty, or to the provost or one of the bailies within burgh, as with best conveniency he may, by whom the same may come to the knowledge of his majesty, his parliament, the said committee of estates, or his majesty's privy council, by whom the said leasing-makers, and authors of such slanderous speeches, may be called, tried, and punished, according to the said acts; in that case they shall incur the like censure or punishment, as the principal party offender. And the said committee of estates considering, that his majesty's lieges are subject more easily to be ensnared and enticed to any such seditious or treasonable courses and practices, by ministers in their sermons, prayers, declamations, and private discourses; the said committee do declare, that upon information given to them of any thing uttered or spoken, contrary to the tenor of the preceding act, the same being lawfully proven in presence of the said committee, or parliament, or his majesty's privy council, they summarily will sequestrate their whole stipend, and imprison their person, until his majesty, parliament, or committee of estates, or any other judge competent, shall proceed to the final cognition and sentencing of their said crime or crimes. And to the effect that this act and ordinance may come to the knowledge of all his majesty's lieges, ordain publication to be made thereof, at the market-cross of Edinburgh, and at the market-crosses of the head-burghs of the shires; and ordain the magistrates of the several head burghs to send so many of the said proclamations to each collector of the assessment of every shire, requiring the said collector to send the same to the several parishes, that the foresaid proclamation may be read after sermon, and fixed upon the kirk-doors of each parish, and upon the market-cross of each head burgh. Extracted forth of the book of the said committee, by me, Jo. HAY, Cler. Com.

1660. and practices by ministers in their sermons, prayers, declarations, and private discourses, they declare, that upon information given, their stipends shall be sequestrate, and their persons imprisoned;" as the proclamation more fully bears.

This procedure opened a door to make many offenders for a word, and nobody against whom the present managers had a design could escape. Ministers were attacked for their sermons and other discourses; and many gentlemen, especially such who favoured the remonstrance, were brought to trouble. No small advantage was brought about to the courses now entering upon, by this proclamation. Two things will offer to the reader, almost without my help; the most zealous of the ministers were laid open to a prosecution, and others they hoped to overawe into a sinful silence, in not giving faithful warning to their flocks of the encroachments making upon our civil and sacred rights. And though the protesters, as they were termed, had the storm first falling on them, yet good numbers of the resolutioners, though silent for a little, under hopes given them of a general assembly to set matters right, and being deceived by the letter to the presbytery of Edinburgh, very soon fell under the pains in this proclamation: and all, save the compliers with prelacy, were sent to the furnace together. Another view was, to influence and model to the mind of the court, the elections for the ensuing parliament.

A great body of gentlemen of the best estates and greatest interest in the nation, who had appeared with the greatest vigour for the work of reformation since the (year) 1637, and had likewise given the greatest evidences of concern for the royal family, under the usurpation, several of whom were concerned in the remonstrance, behoved now to be struck at. Their interest in shires was great, they might be troublesome in parliament, being heartily against arbitrary power, and from principle attached to the constitution of this church; and now the managers behoved to be rid of them. Some were cited before the committee, others were confined; and thus their influence upon elections was prevented. And no doubt, threatenings, and fear of danger, in this unsettled time, prevailed with several to lie by, so that the elections went pretty smoothly on, according to the desire of the managers.

Not having seen any full account of the procedure of the committee, with relation to gentlemen, and in prosecution of this severe proclamation, I can give but some hints of what they did, and no doubt much of their work was under ground. At Edinburgh, as we have heard, orders came down to seize some of the most active gentlemen, before the committee sat down. When the commission came to secure Sir Archibald Johnston of Warriston, major-general Morgan was empowered to seize Sir James Stuart, provost of Edinburgh, and Sir John Chiesly of Carswell, two gentlemen of very strict morals, shining piety, considerable influence, and singular for their loyalty to the king under Oliver's government. By a trick, Sir James was trepanned to convoy Sir John to the castle of Edinburgh, and there the major-general left them both the king's prisoners; and for many years they continued either under bond and bail, or confinement, as a reward for their concern and sufferings for the king's interest when at its lowest.*

Mr. John Harper, afterwards Sir John, in Lanarkshire, was in September obliged to sign the bond we shall just now hear of, and to give bail that he should appear before the committee or parliament to answer what should be charged upon him, under the highest pains. And September 26th, I find Ker of Greenhead, and Pringle of Greenknow, are committed by the committee of estates to the castle of Edinburgh, for alleged aiding, assisting, and partaking with the remonstrators and seditious persons. About this time Mr. Pringle of Torwoodlee, as we may afterwards hear, and several others, were brought to no small trouble.

Upon the 10th of October, the committee fugitate Sir Archibald Johnston of Warriston, colonel Gilbert Ker, colonel David

---

* Mr Kirkpatrick Sharpe states that Sir John Chiesly was originally the servant of Mr A. Henderson; he ought in candour to have stated also, that in those days the term "servant" or servitor, meant a clerk or private secretary.—*Ed.*

CHAP. I.] OF THE CHURCH OF SCOTLAND. 79

Barclay, John Hume, Robert Andrew of Little Tarbet, and William Dundas, late supervisor. Their case was indeed peculiar: they had been named trustees in Scotland to Oliver Cromwell; and being at London with William Purves and Mr. Robert Hodge, and pretty much involved in Cromwell's affairs, were all discharged court, save Warriston, who was before this come to Scotland, and ordered to appear before the parliament when it sat. Multitudes of other gentlemen, in many shires upon the south of Tay, were brought before the committee of estates. If they had any tolerable informations against them, as to their compliances under the English, or their warm side to the remonstrance and protestation, then the following bond was offered them, and to several ministers also, to sign; bearing the name and designation of the principal person bound, and a cautioner for each, wherein they were obliged,—" That the principal party shall not in any manner of way, directly or indirectly, plot, contrive, speak, or do any thing tending, or what may tend to the hurt, prejudice, or derogation of his majesty's royal person, or any of that royal family, or of his highness' power and authority; or shall act or do any thing, directly or indirectly, tending, or that may tend to the breach or disturbance of the public peace of his majesty's dominions; nor shall connive, or concur with whatsomever person or persons who shall contrive or do any such thing, as is before mentioned: but shall, to the uttermost of their power, stop and let any such plot or doing; and compear personally before the committee, sub-committee, or parliament, upon a lawful citation. All which he promises to fulfil truly and really. And in case of failie (failure), he and his cautioner, conjunctly and severally, oblige themselves to pay a high fine, by and attour what other censure, personal or pecunial, by law may be imposed upon the principal party his transgression. And considering there was a remonstrance presented to the committee of estates, October 22d, 1650, and thereafter adhered unto by many gentlemen and others, by a bill given in to the said committee in November thereafter; which

1660.

remonstrances being by his majesty and estates of parliament convened at Stirling, June 1651, taken into consideration, his majesty and estates by their act, June 4th, 1651, declare the said remonstrance to be scandalous and injurious to his majesty's person, prejudicial to his authority, dishonourable to the kingdom, and a sowing division among his majesty's subjects: therefore the said principal does acknowledge the justice of the said act, and obliges himself, that he shall not in any time coming, directly or indirectly, own, promote, or abet the said remonstrance, under the highest pains that may follow upon his person and estate." With a clause of registration and execution, in common form.

By threatenings, imprisonments, and other harsh methods, not a few were brought to subscribe this bond, and renounce the remonstrance, in which the most part now harassed had no hand. But this was a good handle to bear down and bring to trouble a great many gentlemen and others who had been most zealous and forward in the work of reformation, and were looked on as most opposite to the projects now on foot, and thus the parliament was also the better modelled for the work they had to do.

A good many worthy ministers were at this time brought before the committee of estates. October 13th, Mr. John Dickson, minister of the gospel at Rutherglen, appeared before them, and was imprisoned in Edinburgh tolbooth. Information had been given by Sir James Hamilton of Elistoun, and some of his parishioners, of some expressions he had used in a sermon, alleged to reflect upon the government and committee, and tending to sedition and division. This good man was kept in prison till the parliament sat, his church vacated, and he was brought to much trouble. We shall afterwards find him prisoner in the Bass, for near seven years; and yet he got through his troubles, returned to his charge at Rutherglen, and for several years after the revolution served his Master there, till his death in a good old age; while the family who pursued him is a good while ago extinct, and their house,

1660. as Mr. Dickson very publicly foretold in the hearing of some yet alive, after it had been a habitation for owls, the foundation-stones of it are digged up. The inhabitants there cannot but observe that the informers, accusers, and witnesses against Mr. Dickson, some of them then magistrates of the town, are brought so low that they are sustained by the charity of the parish.

Mr. James Nasmyth, minister of the gospel at Hamilton, was likewise sisted before the committee, for words alleged to have been spoken by him many years ago. About the year 1650, when Lambert was in the church, it was alleged, he pressed his hearers "to employ their power for God, and not in opposition to the gospel, otherwise they might expect to be brought down by the judgment of God, as those who went before were." Mr. Nasmyth this year was imprisoned for some time, and for several months kept from his charge. Very soon after his liberation, he was, with many others, turned from their flocks. We shall meet with him afterwards.

Mr. James Simpson, minister at Airth, in Stirlingshire, when by an invitation from Ireland he was going thither, to settle in a congregation there, was seized at Port Patrick, without any cause shown him. Mr. Sharp, I know, had a particular pique at him; they had been at London upon different views some years ago; but when once in their hands, he was sisted before the committee, and by them cast in prison, where he continued till the parliament convened, and they saw good, without any trial, to banish this good man out of the king's dominions.

The reader cannot but remark that all those instances of severity, as well as many that follow in this book, before Pentland, yea even to Bothwell Bridge, can never be palliate with the groundless pretences, that those excellent persons were punished for rebellion and treason. All of them owned the king's authority; they had standing law upon their side for much of what they were quarrelled about, yea laws made by their very persecutors: a good many of them had suffered much for his majesty when in exile; and this harsh treatment was all they and hundreds more had in return for their stedfast loyalty from a set of people now in power, many of whom had been deeply involved in compliance with the usurper, and in most of those very things for which those good persons were now harassed. Having thus run through the procedure of the committee of estates to the middle of October, when they adjourned for some days, it is high time to look back a little to the letter from the king, which Mr. Sharp brought with him to the presbytery of Edinburgh; which was produced and timed to soften people's spirits, under the attacks making by the committee upon some of the most zealous promoters of religion and reformation.

In the introduction we have had a pretty large view of Mr. Sharp's procedure at London, where matters were laid so in secret as the constitution of this church was to be overturned, and Mr. Sharp to be at the head of the new frame to be erected. That cunning apostate hastes down to Scotland, and arrived at Edinburgh the last day of August, and brought with him the king's letter, directed to Mr. Robert Douglas, to be communicated to the presbytery of Edinburgh. Upon Saturday, September 1st, some of the brethren of Edinburgh being convened, Mr. Sharp delivered the letter to Mr. Robert Douglas, and made report of his negotiation; for which the brethren gave him thanks, and resolved to convene the presbytery of Edinburgh, upon Monday, September 3d, that from them copies might be transmitted to other presbyteries, and a humble return made to his majesty. Accordingly they met, and the letter was ordered to be communicate to all other presbyteries, as being of public concern; and a committee was ordered to draw up a return to the king and a letter to the secretary, both of which I find approven, September 20th. The king's letter to Mr. Douglas hath been more than once printed, and the reader will no doubt expect it here.

" Charles R. Trusty and well beloved, we greet you well. By the letter you sent to us with this bearer, Mr. James Sharp, and by the account he gave of the state of our church there, we have received full information of your sense of our sufferings, and of your constant affection and loyalty to our person and authority; and therefore we will detain him here no longer (of whose good services we are very sensible), nor will we delay to let you know by him, our gracious acceptance of your address, and how well we are satisfied with your carriages, and with the generality of the ministers of Scotland in this time of trial, whilst some under specious pretences swerved from that duty and allegiance they owed to us. And because such, who by the countenance of usurpers, have disturbed the peace of that our church, may also labour to create jealousies in the minds of well-meaning people, we have thought fit by this to assure you, that, by the grace of God, we resolve to discountenance profanity, and all contemners and opposers of the ordinances of the gospel. We do also resolve to protect and preserve the government of the church of Scotland, as it is settled by law, without violation; and to countenance, in the due exercise of their functions, all such ministers who shall behave themselves dutifully and peaceably as becomes men of their calling. We will also take care that the authority and acts of the general assembly at St. Andrews and Dundee, 1651, be owned and stand in force until we shall call another general assembly (which we purpose to do as soon as our affairs will permit), and we do intend to send for Mr. Robert Douglas, and some other ministers, that we may speak with them in what may further concern the affairs of that church. And as we are very well satisfied with your resolution not to meddle without your sphere, so we do expect that church judicatories in Scotland, and ministers there, will keep within the compass of their station, meddling only with matters ecclesiastic, and promoting our authority and interest with our subjects against all opposers; and that they will take special notice of such, who, by preaching, or private conventicles, or any other way, transgress the limits of their calling,

by endeavouring to corrupt the people, or sow seeds of disaffection to us or our government. This you shall make known to the several presbyteries within that our kingdom: and as we do give assurance of our favour and encouragement to you, and to all honest deserving ministers there, so we earnestly recommend it to you, that you be earnest in your prayers, public and private, to Almighty God, who is our Rock and our Deliverer, both for us, and for our government, that we may have fresh and constant supplies of his grace, and the right improvement of all his mercies and deliverances, to the honour of his great name, and the peace, safety, and benefit of all our kingdoms. And so we bid you heartily farewell. Given at our court at Whitehall, the 10th of August 1660, and of our reign the 12th year.

"By his majesty's special command,
"LAUDERDALE."

Directed, "To our truly and well beloved, Mr. Robert Douglas, minister of the gospel in our city of Edinburgh; to be communicated to the presbytery of Edinburgh."

Reflections upon this letter are in some measure needless, the after management makes the design of it obvious; and the letter discovers itself to be of Mr. Sharp's penning: its expressions are extremely well calculate to lull all asleep till matters were ripe for a thorough change; a very full testimony is given to the loyalty and affection of the presbyterian ministers of this church to the king under his sufferings, which was so glaring that it could not be hid, and yet the declaring of it was as severe a reproach as could be upon the authors of their maltreatment. The innuendo that follows upon those who swerved from their duty and allegiance to the king, is a sensible proof of the confidence and disingenuity of Mr. Sharp, who, though he designed this against the protesters, knew well enough, that not a minister of the church of Scotland, as far as I know, no not Mr. Gillespie, had swerved so far from their allegiance, as to take the tender, or offered to come in to any measures Cromwell would lay down; and yet his own

1660. conscience could not but reproach him as guilty of this. We shall have occasion afterwards to notice the double-faced expression, of protecting and preserving the government of the church, " as it is settled by law." The promise of calling a general assembly was what Mr. Sharp never designed to be performed; Mr. Douglas was never sent for, nor any other ministers: in short, Mr. Sharp took care that none of those things set down here as blinds should ever be done; so that the earl of Middleton's reflection upon it seemeth to have been very just and natural. This nobleman had not seen the draught till the king had agreed to it, and the matter was over. When he read it, he appeared in some concern at its contents, and the promises in it, as thwarting with what he and Mr. Sharp had concerted. And when he was told, that notwithstanding of any thing in the letter, when his lordship went down to Scotland, he might rescind the laws now in force, and then episcopacy remained the church government settled by law: the earl replied, "That might be done, but for his share he did not love that way, which made his majesty's first appearance in Scotland to be in a cheat."

Such was the charity of Mr. Douglas and many other worthy ministers, that they did not suspect a trick here; and really it was so harsh a construction to suppose a man of Mr. Sharp's profession to venture upon so public and gross an imposition upon the king, as to make his majesty superscribe such a letter, and send it down full of such promises and expressions, and meanwhile to be projecting the contrary, that we need scarce wonder the snare was not observed; and therefore the letter was extremely hugged, and a return made to it, agreeable to what might be expected from such who believed Mr. Sharp and the king to have been in earnest. The presbytery of Edinburgh caused print and spread the king's letter through the nation, and found it convenient it should be kept among the public records of the church; and therefore it was delivered by Mr. Douglas to Mr. Andrew Ker, clerk to the general assembly, to be kept by him, as said is; and the presbytery agreed to, and signed the following return to it:

" Most gracious Sovereign,

" We your majesty's faithful subjects and humble servants, the ministers and elders of the presbytery of Edinburgh, did receive your majesty's gracious letter, upon the 3d of this instant (a day which we were formerly made to remember with sorrow), and in obedience to your royal command therein contained, have transmitted copies thereof to all the presbyteries in this your majesty's ancient kingdom, which we hope shall very speedily come to all their hands. And as we are assured it will be most refreshful to them, so we hold it our duty, by this our humble address, to signify to your majesty, how much it hath revived our spirits, and excited us to bless the Lord our God, who hath put and continued such a purpose in your royal heart, to preserve and protect the government of this church without violation. We have been made to groan under the tyranny of usurpers, who did let loose swarms of errors and confusions to invade the comely order of this poor church, (though, we bless God, without that success that was expected and desired by them:) now we are made to say, ' This is our God, we have waited for him;' when we see your sacred majesty, by a supreme and stupendous hand of Providence settled upon your throne, and do find the warm beams of royal authority reaching even to us, in countenancing church order, whereby any disturbances that are among us, may, by the blessing of the Almighty, come to a good issue. We are unwilling to interrupt your majesty in your weighty affairs, seeing by your majesty's secretary, we may represent our humble desires in reference to this church, (and we bless the Lord, who hath directed your majesty to make choice of such a faithful and able person for that weighty employment, and one who is so well acquainted with the affairs of this church:) but we trust that your majesty will pardon, that at this time we could not forbear this immediate address, whereby we might express our loyalty and fidelity to your majesty, our joy in the Lord for your happy restitution, and how much we, and all good people here, are comforted in the expressions of your majesty's moderation, your abhorrence of profanity, and your tender favour to faithful ministers, and the ordinances of the gospel administrate by them, and particularly to the church government settled among us, in the enjoyment whereof this church hath been so happy. And though some may be ready to traduce this government, because in the late times of confusion and usurpation (wherein men made it their interest to break us) the church judicatories have not been able to prevent all disorders, (as no church government, when so discountenanced and borne down, can effectually and universally reach its end in a national church;) yet now your majesty proving so tender a nursing father, we trust it shall appear, that those judicatories are ordinances of Jesus Christ, which will most effectually bear down error, profanity, and schisms, as formerly they have been blessed for that effect. And as heretofore they have given proof of their loyalty and fidelity to your majesty, in a great trial of afflictions, it may certainly be expected that they will still acquit themselves so in their stations, as may witness that the ministers of Christ are taught of him to pay all duty to authority; and that the principles of our church government lead them to be loyal. And for our parts it is our constant resolution, by the grace of God, to behave ourselves as becometh messengers and servants of the Prince of Peace, and to pray that the Lord may preserve and bless your majesty, and lead you forth in his right hand in the exercise of your royal government, for the good and comfort of all your dominions and the lovers of truth and peace therein, as is the duty of

"Your sacred majesty's loyal subjects and humble servants,

"Messrs. J. Reid moderator, Robert Douglas, David Dickson, James Hamilton, John Smith, Robert Lawrie, George Hutcheson, Thomas Garven, Alexander Dickson, James Nairn, Alexander Hutcheson, John Hog, George Kintore, John Knox, Andrew Cant, Robert Bennet, John Charters, John Colvil, David Reedy, Robert Hunter, William Dalgleish, Peter Blair, Charles Lumsden, John Lawder, John Miln, George Lauty, Adam Cuningham, James Windram, James Scot, George Fowlis, Robert Dalgleish, Alexander Elies." 1660.

Jointly with this, another letter was sent to the earl of Lauderdale, then secretary of state, which deserves its own room in this history, and so it follows:

"Right honourable,

"Among other the Lord's great favours to this long distracted church and kingdom, we cannot forbear thankfully to acknowledge his providence, who hath put it in his majesty's heart to make choice of your lordship for that weighty employment, wherein you may have opportunity to employ those talents, wherewith the Supreme Dispenser of all gifts hath endued you, in his majesty's and your country's service; and may also be in a condition to see to the safety and welfare of our mother-church, in the interests whereof you have been pleased so much to concern yourself, as hath been made known to us by your letters to some of our number, to our exceeding satisfaction and refreshment. This doth encourage us to put your lordship to the trouble of presenting the enclosed address to his majesty, wherein we do humbly express our sense of his majesty's gracious letter direct to us, which we had purposed only to signify to your lordship, that you might have acquainted his majesty therewith, but that it lay so much upon our hearts for this once to witness by our immediate address how much we are refreshed by that mercy. We will not doubt of your lordship's pardon for this trouble, and do presume to beg for the continuance of your favour to this poor church, that, as occasion shall offer, you will be pleased to represent to his majesty, what may be found necessary for the promoving of the kingdom of Jesus Christ among us. And since your lordship's goodness hath prompted you to offer your assistance in what may concern the church and the honest ministers thereof, we know you will not take it ill, if from time to time we presume to acquaint you with our desires, in reference to those concernments, as knowing that the service is the Lord's, and that your reward is in heaven, through Jesus

1660. Christ, to whose rich grace we do heartily recommend your lordship, and are in him,

"My lord,

"Your lordship's very humble servants, the presbytery of Edinburgh, and in their name, and at their command,

"Mr. James Reid, Moderator.

"Edinburgh, September 20th, 1660."

Directed, "To the right honourable the earl of Lauderdale, secretary of estate to his majesty, for the kingdom of Scotland."

We shall find afterwards the synod of Lothian made a return to the king's letter in November; but before I come to that, let me take in the rest of the procedure of the committee of estates.

Upon the 16th of October the committee of estates published a proclamation, laying on a month's cess for the paying of the commissioner's charges, who was to represent his majesty in parliament; another for raising three months' cess, to pay and disband the soldiers yet in Scotland; and a third, for searching for, and apprehending the lord Warriston, with a reward of five thousand merks to any who should bring him in. Whatever the necessity might be to have money at this time, not a few questioned the power of this committee to impose taxes upon the subjects, and to act contrary to several standing laws unrepealed, and they alleged several clauses of their proclamations were direct infringements of the laws made since the reformation.

After they had published those proclamations they adjourned till the 1st of November. During this recess, October 17th, the books formerly mentioned, Lex Rex, and the Causes of God's Wrath, were burnt at Edinburgh by the hand of the hangman; no doubt, by order of the committee, though I do not observe any clause for this in the proclamation. It was much easier to burn those books, than to answer the reasonings and facts in them.

November 1st, a proclamation was published with much solemnity, for holding a parliament at Edinburgh, upon the 12th of December: the tenor whereof was,

"Charles, by the grace of God, &c. greeting. The confusions and troubles, by which our good subjects of this our ancient kingdom of Scotland have those many years been deprived of that peace and happiness they might justly have expected in the administration of our royal government among them, being now by the special blessing of Almighty God happily removed, we have thought fit to let you know that we still retain the same tenderness and good affection towards you; and as we will cheerfully interpose our authority in what may be for your good and welfare, and for securing the just privileges and liberties of our people, so we do expect from them those dutiful returns of obedience, and subjection to our person and authority, which are suitable to their obligations, and the duty of loyal subjects. And conceiving that a parliament, in its right constitution, will at this time be a ready mean for establishing a firm peace to our people, and for settling all religious and civil, public and private interests; we have therefore thought fit to call a meeting of our estates of parliament, to be kept at Edinburgh, December 12th, next to come. Our will is herefore, &c. In common form usual in those cases, that shires and burghs choose their members according to law.

"Lauderdale.

"Whitehall, October 10.

"A. Primrose, clerk-register."

The same day another proclamation was published, which deserves a room here. The title of it is:

The king's majesty's proclamation, concerning the carriage of his subjects during the late troubles.

"Charles, &c. We being now, by the special blessing of God Almighty, returned to the exercise of our royal power, and government of our kingdoms; and being desirous to improve this mercy to the best advantage of our people, have thought fit to call a meeting of our estates of parliament of this our ancient kingdom of Scotland, as a ready mean, after so long troubles, for settling a firm and lasting peace, in confirming the just liberties of our subjects, for vindicating our honour, and asserting our ancient royal prerogative, by which alone the liberties of our people can be preserved. And as we do therein rely upon the loyalty, prudence, and care of our parliament, so we do absolutely leave and commit to them, the trying and judging of the carriage of our subjects, during those troubles: concerning which, we will from henceforth receive information and address only from our parliament, or committee of estates, to whom in the meantime we have recommended the preparing and ordering of that affair, and to whom alone, any of our people that are interested, may freely, and can only make their applications; and which we have hereby thought fit to make known to all our public ministers and subjects, whom it doth concern, and who may thereby find, that we have given an undoubted evidence of our affection to, and confidence in our people, by making themselves judges of what may concern both our and their own interests. And hereby we do further assure them, that our own honour, and the honour of that our ancient kingdom, being vindicate, and the ancient prerogative of the crown being asserted, we will grant such a full and free pardon, and act of indemnity, as shall witness there is nothing we are more desirous of, than that our people may be blessed with abundance of happiness, peace, and plenty under our government. And we do hereby command you, our heralds, pursuivants, and messengers at arms, to pass and make publication thereof at the market-cross of Edinburgh, and other places needful, and in our name and authority, to command, charge, and inhibit all and sundry our subjects in Scotland, that none of them presume to go out of the country, without license of the committee of estates, under pain of being esteemed and pursued as contemners of our authority. Given at our court at Whitehall, the 12th day of October, in the 12th year of our reign, 1660. By his majesty's command,

"LAUDERDALE."

This proclamation is most plausibly drawn; and the greatest concern seems to appear for the good of the people, and the maintaining their privileges and liberty. But then, by the paper itself, we are put in mind that it is only such liberty as is consistent with the prerogative; and indeed it is the first time I have observed such an expression, "the king's prerogative, by which alone, the liberties of the people can be preserved." The king's prerogative under the ancient restrictions of it in Scotland, was helpful to preserve liberty; but that ever, especially in the illimited sense here, it was the alone way to preserve liberty, is what I cannot persuade myself of. In a word, we may perceive, that the managers were willing to have all absolutely in their hand, and preclude all access to the king, that they might have the entire disposal of persons and their estates: in order to which, every body is prohibited to leave the kingdom without permission; and the king's indemnity was suspended for a long time, till they had made their market, by the act of fines, which, we shall hear, brought little to the pockets of the first projectors of it, though afterwards the fines were severely exacted, to the oppression of the country, and the raising the first open disturbance of the peace.

1660.

Little more remarkable offers this year. September 13th, the king's brother, the duke of Gloucester, died; and the English parliament, after they had done every thing the court desired, were adjourned; and December 29th, they were dissolved. In September, the English forces left Scotland, having been here since September 1650, and kept this kingdom under subjection for ten years. At this time came on the election of magistrates for the royal burghs; and such were generally chosen, who fell in with the measures of the court. Robert Murray, merchant in Edinburgh, knighted November 1st, following, was provost of Edinburgh; John Campbell, elder, was chosen provost of Glasgow; John Walkinshaw, James Barns, and John Ker, bailies; and generally speaking, all who had been active in the work of reformation, during the former period, were now turned out of all trust.

The 5th day of November was kept this year with great solemnity; and we shall afterward find laws made for the perpetual observation of it. In the beginning of November, the synod of Lothian met at Edinburgh, and sent up an address to the king,

1660. by way of return to his letter above inserted, a copy of which I have not seen: but by an original letter from Mr. Dickson and Mr. Hutcheson to the earl of Lauderdale, writ November 10th, I find them acquainting his lordship, "that their synod had convened that week, and he was shortly to receive their humble return to his majesty from the moderator, wherein they have given a full return to every part of his majesty's gracious letter." They send him a copy of the act of the synod, concerning those in their bounds who have been engaged in schismatical courses, a copy of which I have not seen. They add, "We indeed believe, that the way of clemency and moderation towards the crowd of those who have been misled, and who shall renounce their course (as some in our synod are already doing), will in the issue prove most for the good of his majesty's affairs; and, we doubt not, will be most acceptable to him." They close their letter with some remarks upon a draught of a proclamation, for calling a general assembly, communicate to them privately by Mr. William Sharp, and offer "some alterations fit to be made, to discover his majesty's moderation to such as have made wrong steps." Whether the king, and the nobility now at the helm, really designed to call a general assembly, or if this was another blind of Mr. James Sharp, to keep off applications for an assembly, which would have ruined his ambitious designs, I know not; but nothing was done effectually in it, and the alterations craved, are mostly softenings in relation to the anti-resolutioners, upon whom, it would seem, the plan of the proclamation was very hard. They would have the expression, "turbulent and fanatic spirits," changed, and the phrase, "employing of power for removing rotten members," run thus, "but likewise the power wherewith God hath trusted him, to prevent the further endangering the safety, peace, union, and order of the church." Instead of the restrictions mentioned in the draught, to prevent the election of some pointed at, they propose this general clause, "requiring those, who by the acts and constitutions of this church are allowed to sit in assemblies, to convene in an assembly at the time appointed." And they very earnestly desire the prohibitory clause, of persons so and so qualified in the draught, "their not sitting in any judicatory, till they have renounced," &c. may be reconsidered: and they observe, "That whatever may be the case as to general assemblies, where members are elected out of inferior judicatories, yet in this church, so long as ministers are not deposed or suspended, they are certainly members of sessions, presbyteries, and synods, as being a privilege flowing immediately from the office of the ministry, without any supervenient commission." Another letter I have before me, written by the same persons, November 13th, to the earl of Middleton, which is merely taken up in expressions of their concern for his lordship, and their expectations of kindness from him to the church, and the interests of the gospel, and judicatories of Christ, which his majesty hath resolved to countenance, protect, and preserve without violation; and containing nothing of public concern, I say no more of it.

This month, George Campbell, sheriff-depute of Argyle, was imprisoned, as having been concerned with the marquis of Argyle in several matters, for which he was now called in question. But, upon what views I shall not say, the sheriff was pardoned, and got a remission. Toward the beginning of December the marquis of Argyle was brought down to Edinburgh, the account of which will fall in afterwards. December 10th, our Scots parliament is adjourned till January 1st, because matters were not fully concerted at London, as to church government and other heads. The funerals of king Charles I., January 29th, and the coronation of the king, designed to be February 12th, and some other important matters at London, took the king so up, that our Scots affairs behoved to be delayed.

Upon the 18th of December, the ship which had on board the registers and records of the kingdom of Scotland, which had been taken up to London by Cromwell, as a badge of our subjection, and were now sent down in a ship of Kirkaldy, unhappily perished at sea, to the great loss of the nation: there eighty-five hogsheads of papers, and many original records were lost;

and it was unaccountable such a treasure should have been sent down by sea, and an unlucky thing, not to say omen, to Scotland. The earl of Middleton came down to Holyrood-house upon the last day of this year, commissioner to this new parliament, and was met upon his way with great solemnity. The king allowed him nine hundred merks per day for his table. From a volunteer he was raised to a major, and for his close adherence to the king in his troubles, he made him first lord Fettercairn, and then earl of Middleton, and now high commissioner to the parliament. He continued in favour, till he began to engross the fines and places of trust and power to himself and his friends, and then the earl of Lauderdale got him turned out, and managed all for many years in Scotland. Before this, matters had been prepared, and all was in readiness. The two eastmost kirks of St. Giles were turned into one, and the king's seat put up, and lofts made for the conveniency of the commissioner and members. The crown and sceptre, preserved by the earl marshal in the late troubles, were brought to Edinburgh, and it was resolved to ride the parliament upon the first day of the new year.

CHAP. II.

OF THE STATE AND SUFFERINGS OF PRESBYTERIANS, DURING THE YEAR 1661.

1661. I HAVE not seen any distinct account of the overturning of our reformation establishment by presbyterian government in this church of Scotland, and the vast changes made at this time in religious and civil affairs: therefore I have ventured to give the larger account of this great turn, and drawn it from a good many original papers and authentic accounts, which will let us into the springs of it. The parliament convened the first day of this year, and laid the foundations for all that afterward follows upon presbyterians, till the Lord "turned back their captivity as streams in the south," at the happy and glorious revolution, 1688, and so I have given the fuller accounts of what they did. Besides the general attacks made by them upon our laws and constitution, a good many worthy ministers were brought to very much trouble and hazard, as well as some gentlemen and others. This remarkable year will likewise bring me to the martyrdom of our three first worthies in this church; the truly great and noble marquis of Argyle, the reverend and learned Mr. James Guthrie, and the excellent lord Warriston: the last, though forfeited this year, yet his warfare not being accomplished till some time after, I shall delay the accounts of him to their own place, 1663. There were some efforts made by the ministers of the church of Scotland for the preserving of our valuable constitution; and though one would have wished they had made a greater stand than they could now in their unhappy circumstances, yet really more was done by them than is generally known, though without any success. When the parliament was up, the privy council is erected, and they had the execution of the laws made put in their hands; and we shall find them beginning the work of persecution upon noblemen, ministers, and others this year, and going on with it for about twenty-four years, with less or more severity, as answered the managers' aims; of which I shall essay as distinct an account from their registers and records, as I can gather up. By order from the king, towards the end of the year, prelacy is erected, and the judicatories of the church, which had met under former prelacy, are upon the matter stopped in their meetings, and our bishops consecrate in England. These, with some other incidental things, will furnish matter for seven or eight sections upon this chapter.

SECT. I.

Of the laws and actings of the first session of parliament, in as far as they concern the church, with some obvious remarks.

THIS first parliament after the restoration, beginning with this year, and by their actings paving the way for all the sufferings I am to give the relation of, it will be proper

1661. I begin this chapter with some account of their procedure, from the printed acts of parliament, the registers of that high court, and other narratives come to my hand. We shall find this parliament making a general attack upon the constitution of this national church; and that deserves our consideration before the sufferings of particular persons, noblemen, ministers, and others. Our first martyrs and sufferers were attacked for things done agreeable to standing law; and therefore the first step of our managers was to open a door for a more justifiable, at least legal prosecution of honest people, who stood up for religion, liberty, and property: so they resolved piece by piece to remove the hedges which were about all those, and bring in a new set of laws, which deserve the most serious reflection of the reader, who would understand the true state of the sufferings of the church of Scotland, during this whole period I am describing.

The author pretends to no further knowledge of our laws, than what the bare reading of the acts of parliament, with a little reflection upon them, affords him. He wishes that some person versed in our Scots statutes, and the laws of other kingdoms, would bestow some thoughts upon the laws of this black period: however, the reader is like to have this benefit, that all the observations and remarks offered, will be plain and easy, and the native product of a general view of our records. When once I have made some general remarks upon the disposition and circumstances of this first parliament, I shall go on to offer a few obvious observations upon the acts and procedure of this first session, in as far as they relate to religion, and the sufferings of this church.

That the reader may have some idea of the temper and genius of this parliament, I shall take the liberty, with all truth and freedom, to give a short account of a few matters of fact, abundantly notour in the time I am writing of, but now perhaps not so much known. And there is the greater room for plainness and freedom here, since I abstract from names and persons, that, as soon as the yoke of oppression was off the Scots nation, and they restored to a liberty of thinking and acting, the whole acts I shall have occasion to mention, in as far as they struck at the constitution of this presbyterian church, were most seasonably and unanimously rescinded and annulled, parl. William and Mary, 1690; the very first act of which parliament, than which Scotland never had a more just representation, April 25th, abrogates the act of supremacy in the most extensive manner; and the supremacy was one of the great springs of the iniquitous procedure of this period. Again, the 5th act, June 7th, 1690, ratifying the Confession of Faith, a step of reformation never before attained to in Scotland, whereby the scriptural and pure doctrine of this church, is imbodied with our civil liberties, and settling presbyterian government, does rescind and cass a great number of other iniquitous acts in this interval. I might add act 17th, of the same session, rescinding fines and forfeitures, and act 27th, rescinding the laws for conformity, with many others. Wherefore, since our representatives judged those acts unworthy of any further respect, I hope I may be allowed to say, they were iniquity established by a law; and, in the entry of this work, regret that ever such laws had a being, especially when they were so rigorously execute, and a door opened by other methods, for stretches far beyond the letter of those very laws. And here indeed, as I take it, lies the main spring and stress of that absurd and groundless clamour raised by the episcopal party, of their being persecuted since the revolution, in that those unchristian and wicked laws, upon which their establishment stood, were then rescinded; for a restraint put upon them from persecuting others, is to those complainers a persecution.

The greatest part of the makers of the laws I am entering on, were of such a personal character, as did no way recommend their acts; it was blacker than I am willing to transmit to posterity. If there were any stretches made in the former period, to hold out malignants and anticovenanters, by the act of classes and levies, they are in part vindicated by the door now opened to the greatest wickednesses and grossest im-

CHAP. II.] OF THE CHURCH OF SCOTLAND. 89

moralities in too many of the courtiers. Indeed at this time, a dreadful deluge of iniquity and sins before unknown in Scotland since popery was turned out, brake forth; and atheism and profaneness now growing common, paved the way for slavish principles in civil things, and persecution in matters of conscience. The commissioner, the earl of Middleton, his fierce and violent temper, agreeable enough to a camp, and his education, made him no improper instrument to overawe Scotland, and bring us down from any sense of liberty and privilege, unto a pliant submission to arbitrary designs, absolute supremacy and prerogative. And this was the more easily accomplished, that this nation, now for ten years, had been under the feet of the English army, and very much inured to subjection.

A short account and character of this nobleman, to whom the king intrusted the chief management of affairs at this juncture, may not perhaps be unacceptable to the reader. He was a gentleman in the north of Scotland, who made his first appearance under the earl of Montrose, against the Gordons, who set up against the covenanters, and he had a considerable share in defeating them at the Bridge of Dee. In the years 1644 and 1645, he took service in the army of the parliament of England, against the king, when Montrose changed hands and his men ravaged the country, and among other cruelties killed Middleton's father in cold blood, sitting in his own house. He was called home from England, and was with general Lesly when Montrose was defeat at Philiphaugh. He was major-general under duke Hamilton, and engaged with a handful of countrymen at Mauchlin Muir, in the shire of Ayr, where he was in some hazard. He and his party came upon a company of country people, on a Monday after a communion, who had not the least thought of fighting, and were unprovided for it. Mr. Thomas Wylie, minister of Mauchlin, under whose hand I have an account of that action, and some other ministers travelled betwixt the people and Middleton, and got his promise to permit the people to dismiss peaceably: which when they were doing, his men fell upon the people, and with some slaughter scattered them, and kept the muir. When he came to Mauchlin, the ministers quarrelled his breach of promise and capitulation; and he put it off, with alleging, that some of the people had provoked his men with harsh speeches. We shall afterward hear of his plot to draw the king from the committee of estates to the north; for which he was excommunicate, and Mr. James Guthrie pronounced the sentence. In a little time he professed his repentance with many tears, and was relaxed. With the king he went into Worcester, where he was taken, and imprisoned in the Tower. When he got out, after many difficulties in England, he went over to the king, and was by him sent to Scotland to head the Highlanders, who were on the king's side. This misgiving, he went back to his master, and at the restoration was honoured with the highest post in Scotland.

1661.

Our nobility and gentry were remarkably changed to the worse: it was but few of such, who had been active in the former years, were now alive, and those few were marked out for ruin. A young generation had sprung up under the English government, educate under penury and oppression; their estates were under burden, and many of them had little other prospect of mending their fortunes, but by the king's favour, and so were ready to act that part he was best pleased with. Several of the most leading managers, and members of parliament, had taken up a dislike at the strictness of presbyterian discipline. Middleton had not forgot his excommunication, or the pronouncer of it; and others had been disgusted at their being obliged to satisfy for their lewdness and scandals, and upon this turn, they were willing to enjoy a little more latitude. Add to this, that when the king was pleased to grant a most ample indemnity to his subjects in England and Ireland, for their failures in the late times, his grace did not come so low as his ancient kingdom. Most part of Scotsmen, save the ministers, who received a very ungenerous reward, had been some way or

M

1661. other involved with the English under the usurpation; and now were chargeable with treason, and their lives and estates at the mercy, I say not of the king, but of his hungry courtiers, who laid their measures, so as an indemnity for Scotland was put off, till they got their schemes of oppression and revenge formed. Thus the hopes of timeservers, who had their fortunes to mend, and the fears of many, who perhaps, if left to their own choice, would have inclined to preserve our reformation and liberty, were improven to carry on the designs now on foot.

When the proclamation, October 12th, formerly noticed, was published, calling the parliament, and devolving upon their judgment the behaviour of all under the late troubles, and discharging all petitions and applications to his majesty, this was soon understood to be no act of indemnity; but the plain language was, that every one who would not follow court measures, quit their principles, calmly subject to arbitrary government in church and state, and vote and act as the managers would have them, might expect to be treated as rebels. Indeed it required a greater measure of the old Scots spirit, and more fixedness in principles than many had, to stand out against so heavy an argument. Moreover, great pains was taken upon the elections to this parliament; matters every where in shires and burghs were so carefully managed, that for the most part, persons entirely at the devotion of the court, were chosen: in some places where others were chosen, letters were writ by the courtiers, under some pretext or other, for a second choice. Thus in the shire of Ayr, where a gentleman of one of the first families of the shire, but a firm presbyterian by principle, was elected, a near relation of his own, a courtier, prevailed to get him altered. And some of the most zealous gentlemen in the former times, were *viis et modis* brought under process, and some of them cited before the parliament, that there might be no trouble from them as members. The act of the committee of estates above,*

pointed this way; and the double-faced expressions in the letter to Mr. Douglas, were designed to make all go on as smooth as might be.

After all those previous steps, to dispose for the great things in hand, the parliament convened January 1st, 1661, just that day twelve months, upon which Monk marched up to London, and that day ten years whereupon the king was crowned at Scone. The members rode from the Abbey to the house in great state; the earl of Crawford bore the crown, the earl of Sutherland the sceptre, and the earl of Mar the sword. Duke Hamilton and the marquis of Montrose rode behind the commissioner, covered.

When they had taken their seats in the parliament house, a very good sermon was preached to them by Mr. Robert Douglas, from 2 Chron. xix. 6. "Take heed what you do, for you judge not for man, but for the Lord, who is with you in the judgment." After calling of the rolls, the earl of Glencairn was chosen preses, and the commissioner had a speech, recommending peace and unity. When those forms were over, the commissioner had most of the nobility at dinner with him, where he was served in great state: he sat at a table by himself, and the earl of Athol gave him the cup upon his knee, after he had tasted it, in a cover, before he delivered it.

January 4th, they entered upon business. I have in mine eye a very distinct account of their procedure every day, in manuscript, unto the middle of April, from which I may afterwards give some hints of their actings; but here I shall confine myself very much to the known public acts made in opposition to that work, which had been carried on from the year 1638 to the usurpation, and give the reader as short a view, as the variety of matter will permit, of their procedure, in the vast change made by them in this church and kingdom.

It is very evident, the design on foot, in this parliament, was to make the king absolute, and the laws henceforth only a public signification of the sovereign's pleasure, who after this, is to be above law, and uncontrollable lord of his subjects' property, purse and conscience; and to overturn

---

* See page 20.

what had been formerly established in favours of religion and liberty. This unhappy project was helped forward, at least not a little encouraged, by the fulsome sermons preached by too many before them. The preachers were not now appointed by the assembly or commission, who used formerly to sit in time of parliament; the managers must be their own carvers; the king's advocate's letter was the appointment ministers had to preach, and he was not wanting in pitching on very fit tools for their purpose, who preached smooth things. Some of their sermons yet remain in print, as blots upon their reputation: and though Mr. Douglas, and some few other worthy men were employed now and then, for form's sake, and they preached Christ, and plain duty; yet it was not so with many of their preachers. Their ordinary themes were, the wickedness of rebellion; and in their application, they explained this to be the late work of reformation, and the covenants, even before the parliament had declared against those; the sinfulness of defensive arms, whereby they libelled most part of their hearers, and cast a slur upon the constant practice of this nation; the extensiveness of the king's power, passive obedience, and such like. Those flaming sermons of theirs, bring upon the preachers of them a great share of all the after-guilt of this period, and paved their own way to preferment.

Those corrupt ministers, who had sided themselves with the public resolutioners, and now were carefully serving the courtiers, very much heightened the lamentable breaches betwixt the resolutioners and protesters, who were both against the defection now entering upon: this miserable rent, artfully managed by designing men, so weakened the honest ministry of the church and split the people, who were for our former excellent constitution, that no such seasonable and regular application was made for preventing the change, as was wished for; though somewhat was done, as we shall hear.

Thus every thing concurred in the Lord's holy and righteous providence, for helping forward a dark and black cloud upon this church and kingdom, which began with the acts I am now to give a particular detail of, if once I had further observed, that this parliament when they sat down, so constituted themselves, and acted in such a manner, as made their acts and laws, in the opinion of severals, questionable as to their validity and legality. It is plain they run cross to standing law, before they gave themselves the trouble of any repeal. The reader will find, that by act 5th, parl. 2. Charles I. where his majesty was present, "every member, of succeeding parliaments is to take, and subscribe the national covenant, and give an oath of parliament relative thereunto." This was not now done, as every body knows. Yea, it was expressly provided by our last Scots parliament, where his majesty was present, 1651, "That in all succeeding parliaments, every member, before they entered upon business, should sign and subscribe the covenant; and without this, the constitution of the parliament, and all they do, is declared void and null." The acts of this parliament were not printed, and I have not seen a copy of the act; but from persons yet alive, and papers written at this time, I am assured such an act was made.

1661.

Not to say any thing of the reasonableness or necessity of making such restrictions, it is certain, those were now unrepealed laws, and the last, relative to the very constitution of parliament, made by the king, and many of themselves; and consequently they sat down, and went on in a method directly contrary to the uncontroverted statute law. And though those, with many other excellent laws, made in the former period, were rescinded; it remained doubtful with the persons who objected against the validity of this parliament, how far they could do so, unless, by express instructions from their constituents, they had begun with altering the constitution. But this point I must leave to the gentlemen of the long robe skilled in our laws and the nature of parliamentary power.

Having laid down those general observations, I come to take a more particular view of the acts of this session of parliament; and by a narrow consideration of them, and the order in which they are made, a great

1661. deal of art and cunning will appear, in gradually bringing upon members of parliament, and subjects, the heavy burdens they were under before the (year) 1638, and not a little of the serpentine subtilty of Mr. Sharp, who came lately from England with ample directions concerted with the highfliers there, to bring this church back to its deformed state, about twenty-three years ago.

The first printed act is concerning the president, and oath of parliament.* The civil part of it, their making the chancellor, or any for the time, nominate by the king, president, I do not meddle with; every thing now must be done *antipodes* to the practice of the covenanters, be it ever so reasonable in itself: and it does not appear unreasonable, that a judicatory, such as this, choose their own mouth. But waving this, let me consider a little the oath inserted in this act; the form of which is,

" I,   , for testification of my faithful obedience to my most gracious and redoubted sovereign Charles, king of Great Britain, France, and Ireland, defender of the faith, do affirm, testify, and declare, by this my solemn oath, that I acknowledge my said sovereign, only supreme governor of this kingdom, over all persons, and in all causes; and that no foreign prince, power, or state, nor person civil or ecclesiastic, hath any jurisdiction, power, or superiority over the same: and therefore I utterly renounce and forsake all foreign jurisdictions, powers, and authorities; and shall at my utmost power defend, assist, and maintain his majesty's jurisdiction foresaid, against all deadly, and never decline his majesty's power or jurisdiction, as I shall answer to God."

Members of parliament were to add, " And I shall faithfully give my advice and vote in every thing that shall be propounded in parliament, as I shall answer to God."

Many particulars may be noticed as to this oath. In the title of the act, it is termed " an oath of parliament;" in the body of the act, it is called " an oath of allegiance." There are here two very different oaths; and it was not without a cause why it was huddled over in parliament, under the notion of an oath of parliament, that persons upon whom the first part was to be imposed, might not too soon spy out the design upon them. Yet they must have been very heedless who did not observe, that this oath, in both its views, was calculate to shuffle out our former establishment, and the covenants, and in its nature eversive of them. This new-coined oath might be compared with the English oath of supremacy, which no doubt was its model; every thing now being to be brought as near the English pattern as possible. It appeared to

---

* Act concerning the president, and oath of parliament.

Forasmuch as it hath pleased Almighty God to compassionate the troubles and confusions of this kingdom, by returning the king's most excellent majesty to the exercise of that royal government, under which, and its excellent constitution, this kingdom hath for many ages enjoyed so much happiness, peace, and plenty; and it being, upon good and important considerations, an inviolable practice in this government before these troubles, that the person nominate by his majesty to be his chancellor within this kingdom, did of right, and as due to his place, preside in all meetings of parliament, and other public judicatories of the kingdom, where he was present for the time: and his majesty now considering the great advantages do accresce to the public good of his subjects, by the due observance of such ancient and well grounded customs and constitutions, and the prejudices that do accompany a change thereof: therefore his majesty, with advice and consent of his estates of parliament, doth declare, that the present lord chancellor, and such as hereafter shall be nominate by his majesty, or his royal successors, to succeed in that place, and, in case of their absence, such as shall be nominate by his majesty, are, by virtue and right of the said office, and such nomination respective, to preside in all meetings of his majesty's parliaments, or other public judicatories of the kingdom, where they shall happen to be present, and that they are now and in all time coming to enjoy this privilege. And in discharge of this trust, they are, at the first down-sitting of every parliament, to administer to all the members thereof, the oath of alegiance. (See the oath above.)

Likeas, his majesty, with advice foresaid, doth hereby rescind and annul all acts, statutes, or practices, as to the president or oath of parliament, which are prejudicial unto, or inconsistent with this present act, and declare the same to be void and null in all time coming.

many to have in it the most choking clause of the supremacy; indeed, in so many words, it does not formally assert the king's power in ecclesiastical matters as the other does; but its general and extensive clause, " in all causes and over all persons," takes it in, and appears even somewhat wider than the English phrases themselves.

It seems evident, that this Scots oath of allegiance and parliament, and really of supremacy, is ambiguous in its expressions. The terms of it are artfully enough formed, so as to bear a double face. Presbyterians cheerfully allow the sovereign a civil and sanctional power in ecclesiastical matters and causes, as well as a supreme power over all persons. And there was some shadow of ground for understanding the oath in this safe and favourable sense at this time, when the commissioner and chancellor declared again and again in face of parliament, that they intended not to give his majesty any "ecclesiastical," but only " a civil supreme power." Yet in a little, when ministers offered to take the oath in this sense, they were not allowed. And it would seem those declarations were made from the throne, upon other views than appeared; for when the earl of Cassils and laird of Kilburny demanded those declarations might be insert in the registers, it was peremptorily refused. This demonstrates the ambiguity of the phrases. In themselves, and by reason of this ambiguity, several phrases in the oath were at best dark. To say nothing of the others, that expression, " I renounce all foreign jurisdictions, and shall maintain his majesty's authority foresaid," without explication, may reach further than " foreign prince, power, or person," since " foreign," as it stands here, seems to include " all jurisdiction and power," except the king's, as supreme: and thus it would be an absolute renunciation of all ecclesiastic judicatories. So it proved in the issue, and the whole church power came to be lodged in the bishop, as deriving it from the king. I know this clause relates, in its ordinary sense, to popery, and in so far was safe; but it might, yea actually was further extended, and consequently was dark.

In short, a good many reckoned the last clause of this oath simply unlawful. "Supreme governor," in the first part here, seems explained by " the king's power and jurisdiction," and the swearer obliged " never to decline it." This they thought a step beyond the English supremacy itself; by that, the king is allowed a " limited power" in ecclesiastical matters, but by our Scots oath, the swearer seems bound down to submission to all the instances of the exercise of that power; so that in no case the king must be declined, even though he should take upon him the power of excommunication, for instance. How far this last clause was cast in to prelimit members in the processes to be before them, I do not say; but " the declining the king's jurisdiction" was no small article against Mr. James Guthrie. Several other remarks might be made upon this oath, if I had not already said so much on it. By the act 114 James VI. parl. 12, 1592, now in force, and unrepealed, the jurisdiction of the church is ratified and confirmed, and the allegiance sworn in this oath hath no respect, yea is contrary to the due limitation there contained. Again, every body knew the design of the court at present, to establish a royal supremacy, and put the king in the place of the pope, which, by the way, increased the darkness and ambiguity of the phrases formerly noticed. To be short, this oath came to be the Shibboleth of the state, and in a little it was extended to all subjects of any influence. And after the members of parliament were involved in it, and by credit bound to defend and promote it, it became at first matter of much dispute and strife, and afterwards an occasion of suffering. In the year 1669, when matters were ripe, it came to be explained, cleared, and imposed in its true and extensive meaning; and its sense was made plain, large, and terrible, and an end put to the debates about its meaning.

This oath, though thus involved, as we have heard, was stuck at by very few in the parliament. The earls of Cassils and Melvil, and the laird of Kilburny, refused it; whether there were any more, I have not heard: so well disposed were the members to go in with every thing that came about.

1661.

1661. Having thus inaugurate the king a supreme civil pope, if not some more, by steps they proceed, in the following acts, to assert, explain, and extend the royal prerogative. At this time the parliament's darling design and beloved work seems to have been, the enlargement of his majesty's power, without any great regard to religion, liberty, or property; and they begin with civil offices: and by their 2d act declare it to be "his majesty's prerogative, to choose officers of state, counsellors, and lords of session, as may be seen in the printed acts; and they screw up this branch of the prerogative to a *jus divinum:* perhaps this is the first time that ever the nomination of servants and counsellors is derived from heaven. In the rescissory part of this act, they run pretty high, and pronounce "the contrary laws and practices, and acts since the (year) 1637, to have been undutiful and disloyal," though the king himself was present at some of them.

In their 3d act, as may be seen in the printed acts, they assert the king's prerogative to be, "the calling, holding, proroguing, or dissolving all parliaments, conventions, or meetings of estates; and that all meetings, without his special warrant, are void and null." In the preamble, out of their great loyalty, they declare the "happiness of the people depends upon the maintenance of the prerogative." The presbyterians for many years felt how much their happiness depended upon this, in the parliament's sense, by bonds, imprisonments, hanging, heading, and murders in the field and highways, without any sentence. It is added, they make this law "out of conscience, and from its obligations." Upon how good grounds they assert this, most of them have answered ere this time at a higher tribunal. An odd enough sanction is annexed to this, "that no subject question or impugn any thing in this act, or do any thing contrary thereto, under the pains of treason:" which seems to involve all the members of parliament in a wretched necessity, to vote many of the following acts when proposed, as they would not be guilty of treason; and it is abundantly plain, that piece by piece they prelimited themselves, and gave up the freedom of their acting in a parliamentary capacity.

By their 4th act, they go on, and statute, "that no convocations, leagues, or bonds be made without the sovereign," and declare against all such, made without his consent; and tacitly insinuate, that the work of reformation since the (year) 1638, confirmed by the king and his father, "had well nigh ruined both king and subjects;" and cast a new tash (stain) upon all that was done in that period by his majesty and many of themselves, "as being done on pretext of preserving the king's person, religion, and liberty." They declare "this gloss was false and disloyal," and rescind all done, or to be done, without the king's consent; by which undoubtedly our glorious revolution must come in as black treason.

Further, by their 5th act, they clothe their king with the "sole power of making peace and war." Without any great necessity from the matter they are upon, or connexion with the subject, in the preamble they assert, that "the king holds his crown from God alone;" and statute and declare, "that the raising of subjects in arms, is and was the sovereign's undoubted right; and that it shall be high treason for any subjects, upon any pretext whatsomever, to rise in arms without the king's allowance." It was well they made not this law to look back, as several of their acts did, else the commissioner, and the greatest part of them, had been pronounced traitors.

One would think, by this time, the parliament were near to the plucking up the covenant by the root, and so they were; but an unnecessary step must be taken for the better securing their project, and that is, by act 6th, to declare the convention of estates 1643, who entered into the solemn league and covenant with the parliament of England, void and null. That convention was not called by a king, and therefore all they did must be a nullity; and all acts approving that meeting are rescinded, even the ratification by the parliament, where the king was present. This seems to be a very needless act, since the convention was on the matter rescinded in their 3d and 4th acts; but they must make their game sure, though it be by doing the same things twice or thrice over. Probably the managers were afraid to attack the covenant directly, till once they tried the pulse of the members, who generally had sworn it, and secured themselves by this essay; and if this had misgiven, they would have fallen upon it another way: but all runs smooth, and the courtiers were in no hazard.

Having thus made their approaches with all caution and safety to the fortress of the covenants, it is sapped and overturned by their 7th act; which, because it was occasion of great suffering afterward, and every body who reads this history, may not have our acts of parliament by him, I have insert, * and take the liberty to make some observes upon it. That even after all this previous caution, they do not declare directly that the covenant was treason, for the nation was not yet ripe for this; nor totally rescind the obligation of it; but only, as the title of the act bears, make a declaration concerning it, and discharge the renewing of it, without the king's consent, which was not to be looked for. So sacred and beloved were the covenants in Scotland, that it was not fit as yet to venture further. And even in this declaration, the narrative of the act, and *ratio legis*, is not drawn from any ill thing in the covenant, but the law is founded upon their own new made statutes; all which are sufficiently cassed and overturned, by the king's own consent to the covenant, and his swearing of it. They themselves coin the premises, and then form the conclusion, as best serves their purposes. Indeed, in a very general and dubious manner, they make an innuendo, " that divers things occurred in the late troubles, in making and pursuing of leagues and bonds, that may be occasion of jealousies between his majesty's dominions." How tender do they appear of naming the covenant! Those occasions of jealousy might arise from many other bonds, and the pursuance of them, besides the covenants; and I could instance some of them. However, upon this supposition, they declare, " that there is no obligation, by covenant or other treaties, upon Scotland, to endeavour by arms a reformation in England." It is not asserted in the covenant, that in all cases Scotland was obliged by arms to reform England; to be sure, at this juncture, there was no hazard this way. There follows a very unjust reflection upon the covenanters, " or to meddle with the public government, or administration of that kingdom." This the covenanters never took upon them to do, save when pressed thereto by the English themselves.

1661.

---

* Act concerning the league and covenant, and discharging the renewing thereof, without his majesty's warrant and approbation.

Forasmuch as the power of arms, and entering into, and making of leagues and bonds, is an undoubted privilege of the crown, and a proper part of the royal prerogative of the kings of this kingdom, and that in recognisance of his majesty's just right, the estates of parliament of this his most ancient kingdom of Scotland, have declared it high treason to the subjects thereof, of whatsoever number, less or more, upon any pretext whatsoever, to rise, or continue in arms, or to enter into leagues and bonds, with foreigners, or among themselves, without his majesty's special warrant and approbation had and obtained thereto; and have rescinded and annulled all acts of parliament, conventions of estates, or other deeds whatsoever, contrary to, or inconsistent with the same. And whereas, during these troubles, there have occurred divers things, in the making and pursuance of leagues and bonds, which may be occasion of jealousy in and betwixt his majesty's dominions of Scotland, England, and Ireland; therefore, and for preventing of all scruples, mistakes, or jealousies, that may hereafter arise upon these grounds, the king's majesty, with advice and consent of his estates of parliament, doth hereby declare, that there is no obligation upon this kingdom, by covenant, treaties, or otherwise, to endeavour by arms a reformation of religion in the kingdom of England, or to meddle with the public government and administration of that kingdom. And the king's majesty, with advice and consent foresaid, doth declare, that the league and covenant, and all treaties following thereupon, and acts or deeds that do or may relate thereto, are not obligatory, nor do infer any obligation upon this kingdom, or the subjects thereof, to meddle or interpose by arms, or any seditious way, in any thing concerning the religion and government of the churches of England and Ireland, or in what may concern the administration of his majesty's government there. And further, his majesty, with advice and consent of his estates, doth hereby discharge and inhibit all his majesty's subjects within this kingdom, that none of them presume, upon any pretext of any authority whatsoever, to require the renewing or swearing of the said league and covenant, or of any other covenants, or public oaths, concerning the government of the church or kingdom, without his majesty's special warrant and approbation; and that none of his majesty's subjects offer to renew and swear the same, without his majesty's warrant, as said is, as they will be answerable at their highest peril.

1661. The declaration is again repeated, that there is no obligation upon Scotsmen to meddle with the religion of England by arms, which is now termed a seditious way. It must be owned, that arms in many cases are none of the best ways to propagate a reformation in religion and church government: but it is certain the Scots were invited to England to assist that nation in their own self-defence against popery, and prelates hasting fast back to it; which quite alters the case, and yet is by many overlooked in this matter. In a word, by this act, all the subjects are " discharged to require the renewing of the covenant, or any other oath, or to swear it, without the king's consent." Whether this clause precludes application to the government in a regular way, for renewing those solemn vows against popery and prelacy, I do not know; neither what is included in the other public oaths here spoken of; they may relate to the oath of canonical obedience, for any thing I know, since the prohibition is abundantly wide. Thus far is plain, that the renewing of the covenant itself is not simply discharged, though I must own there was little prospect of getting the condition here required to this, his majesty's consent.

Thus, more softly than one would have expected, the attempt is made upon the solemn league and covenant. Their preparatory acts made it the deed of an unlawful convocation; and they would have it believed, that whatever excellency might be in the matter of it, yet it was no binding law obliging Scotland, being made *a non habente potestatem*. By those blinds, they huddled over the matter, so as some were cheated into the thoughts they might safely renounce the covenant as a law, and stand by it as a private oath. With those colours and distinctions, this act was voted pretty smoothly to the courtiers' wish: yet some of all the states dissented; but the most part, who were against this act, withdrew, and went out of the house, fearing a public judicial vote might render their compliances under the usurpation unpardonable. I find there was one plain honest man, George Gordon, bailiff of Burntisland, whose vote in all the preparatory steps, and this act, was, " he could do nothing against his lawful oath and covenant." Him the managers were pleased to overlook.

In the 8th act, the parliament give in to the old, and yet continued method, of covering their designs against presbyterians with a pretended zeal against popery; and under this view, frame a very good act against priests and Jesuits: but the narrative of it was complained of, as injurious to truth, and every body's experience; that " disobedience to lawful authority, covered with specious pretences," *i. e.* in their meaning, " the work of reformation, and the covenants, had been the occasion of the increase of priests and Jesuits," needs no refutation. The next clause, that " priests and Jesuits abounded more at present, than in the time of the king's father or grandfather," is what I very much doubt of. They were indeed too numerous at present, but they behoved to be many more in king James's time; and what shoals of them were in king Charles I. his reign, the reader will see from the account of the popish government in Scotland at that time, writ by Mr. John Abernethy, a popish priest; which, because it is in the hands of very few, was never printed, and deserves the consideration of all true protestants, I have added.*

---

* Abernethy's (Jesuit) account of the popish government in Scotland.

All governments are either spiritual or temporal, and both require three things. 1. *Rectores*, these that rule and govern. 2. *Rectos*, these that are ruled and governed. 3. *Modum regendi*, the form of their government. All these three things are found in the popish government in Scotland. And 1st, Their governors and rulers are threefold, that is, *remoti, propinqui, et proximi*. Those I call remote, are the pope, and that congregation *de propaganda* (or rather, as I have heard themselves call it, for the politic knavery of it, *de extirpanda) fide*. The nearer, or *propinqui*, are Monsieur Francisco Barberino, a cardinal, protector of our nation, Mr. George Cone, secretary for the Latin tongue to the pope, the generals of the several orders, but especially the Jesuits (they being in great number in the country), and fathers, George Elphinstone in Rome, William Lesley in Douay, John Robe younger in London, and William Henderson in Burghton, beside Edinburgh. Most near, or *proximi*, are some sixteen or eighteen, more or less, as they can find houses in Scotland to place them in. They have all their several places of residence in gentlemen or noblemen's houses, according to William Henderson,

Their 9th act, "approving the engagement 1648," and rescinding the actings of parliaments and committees which ensued thereupon, contains many perversions of matters of fact, and reflections upon the marquis of Argyle, and the ministers who were opposite to the engagement Those last are represented as "a few se-

1661.

superior of the mission, his direction and pleasure: for he has notice of them all before they come into the country, yea, of all their dispositions and qualities, by their superiors or confessors' letters; yet there is no less budding, bribing, envies, malice, and hatred, for obtaining the choice of these houses, than for catching at court a good fat bishopric. And this short relation shall suffice for the notice and knowledge of the rulers and governors of this papistical mission. Concerning the second point, that is, the persons that are ruled and governed by their politic brains, here is little or nothing to be said; although this mass of policy, according to the priests' report, is nothing else but a zealous and pious piece of pains, for the well of the country, and the salvation of poor souls, kept under heretical persecution and bondage. But God knows what Spain means in giving pensions to these zealous men. But this I omit to another place. The number and quality of their poor blindly led folks, is (or should at least be better known to the ordinaries of dioceses) if they be not accessory, and pastors of the particular places of the kingdom, than by me, who lived not two years in the country with them. Yet, if I were stressed, I could set them as well in order as the litanies of the saints are; for I know them both perquire. Therefore, ere I conclude this point, I will only notice, that these priests and Jesuits take care, power, and authority over the papists of this kingdom, as over their own parishioners in other countries, and hear their confessions, say their masses, preach, baptize, marry, give extreme unction to them, as if they were their own subjects and parishioners; whereof they send their relations to the congregation *de propaganda fide*, to the pope and several generals, once in the year at least, and oftener if they please, making mention of all that has been done by them or their followers, good or evil, of the government, both spiritual and temporal, of this kingdom: for this end, one of themselves, the best rhetorician of the younger sort, is chosen secretary thereto. They are called *literæ annuæ*, whereof are drawn out their annals, and of these composed their history. I might likewise speak of their division or distinction they give themselves to their penitents (as they call them), dividing them into church-papists and mass-papists. The first are these who hear the word in protestant churches, subscribe and communicate, or in a word, they are inward papists, and outward protestants. The second are these who do not hear the word. The first were maintained by some of the fathers who gave these persons absolution of their sins, as well as others: the second were governed by the Jesuits, who in end have procured at the pope's hands, that these who participate of the protestant sacraments, shall be excommunicated and debarred from their sacraments; yet, for old acquaintance, they will get leave to be present at their masses and preachings, whereof I know sundry other their benefactors or powerful men. Yet, after all this, *in articulo mortis*, or upon resolution not to return to that sin again, they will obtain remission or absolution. But all this I pass, minding, God willing, to make it more public to the world at another occasion; concluding and ending this point, that this papistry in Scotland may be joined to these old proverbs, and say, *ex illa minore*, Sol. I. de Europa, *pons Polonicus, monachus Bohemus, miles australis, Suevica monialis, Italica dinotio, Ruthenorum religio, Teutonum jejunia, Gallorum constantia, castitas Anglicana, papismata Scoticana, nihil valere omnia*.

The third thing I propounded of their government contains three points, 1mo. The fountain of this government. 2do. Their proceeding in it. 3tio. The sinews of their government, that is, their entertainment and maintenance. For the first, it is to be remembered, that pope Gregory the XIII. (called father of the Jesuits, for his liberality to them,) Paul the V., and Gregory the XV., have built a kinglike house in Rome, called *Congregatio de propaganda fide*. The members of this congregation, is the pope as supreme head of the kirk, and judge of all controversies. His nephew cardinal Francis Barberino is his lieutenant, and immediate governor of the whole church; divers cardinals and generals of all the orders that teach or preach, the great master of the inquisition, and some few doctors, all as judges of equal authority, their officers to have care and charge of the missionaries in foreign kingdoms and countries, where their religion is not professed, or has suffered detriment, throughout all the world: so that there can be no time assigned, day or night, but it is lawful to say, now a Jesuit is saying mass; and yet a mass cannot be said after twelve o'clock, without a dispensation: so great are the limits and extent of their bounds. For this end, they have many colleges or seminaries of divers nations and sundry countries, as in Rome, of Germans, Hungarians, English, Scots, Irish, Greeks, Maronites or Armenians, Nephittes, Copties, &c. Of our nation, out of the country, there be five colleges or seminaries, Rome in Italy, Paris in France, Douay in Flanders, Madrid in Spain, Brunsberg in Prussia. In their colleges, youth are brought up in their discipline, throughout all their humanity, philosophy, and divinity. Their colleges are furnished with scholars by the Jesuits residing in their several countries, some by their popish parents, some under promises of great learning, some seduced by Jesuits and priests in the countries and abroad, some for poverty; all of the quickest and best wits that the Jesuits can find out amongst many that are propounded to them for that use. The Jesuits have the care and guiding of their colleges, although ruled by the popes, cardinals, and bishops, or other benefactors. Their youths, after they have remained three months in any college, they make a vow to take on priesthood, and return for the conversion of their country, after they be found fit, which is always after their studies. The Jesuits having charge of these seminary-youths, put out the best wits

98 THE HISTORY OF THE SUFFERINGS [BOOK I.

1661. ditious ministers," when it is notour that the far greatest number of the ministers of this church were and rarest judgments for their own order. Others become monks and friars, and the shallowest remain secular or seminary priests. Yet, whatsoever order they be of, they are tied to their first oath, by virtue of a bull of this pope's, in favour of the foresaid congregation. So let this suffice as a short relation of their source and fountain.

2dly, Their form of proceeding is, that when they are found fit, after their priesthood received, and studies ended, to be sent to their mission. First, they have approbation of their sound doctrine and godly life, from the Jesuits, under whom they have been brought up. Thereafter, they get their patent letters from their congregation or their general, if they be of any order, to go to their country, furnished with two suits of apparel, all their church apparel, and necessaries thereto, and two, three, four, or five hundred crowns, as they have favour, and are thought worthy for their vocation. Next, to come to Douay, where Mr. William Lesley superior there, gives them some books out of the mission's bibliotheck there, and marks to know and be known of their fellows and country: whence they depart, changing their name always, and sometimes their nations, and come to William Henderson in Burghton, in the Canongate, Paisley, or where he is; for he must visit them all once in the year, in their several residences. By him they are visited, if they have all things fit for their calling; if they have not, he furnishes them; if they have, he gives them a letter to some nobleman or gentleman, where they are received, and kept till they have learned the fashion of the country. Thereafter they go abroad as gentlemen or merchants, thereafter any other dexterity they please to use, or functions for their own ends: and so I was chamberlain and bailie in Caithness, for my lord Berrydale. The reason of this is, because, among the rest of the privileges they receive at their departure from Rome, and kissing the Pope's feet, with his blessing, they get power to dispense with themselves and others in all things, yea, *in articulo mortis et casu necessitatis*, in things reserved to the pope himself, and absolve from all sins, how many soever. Of these fathers, as they call them, there be four already governing in colleges, some agents in great cities for correspondence, whose names are needless, and tedious to rehearse; some who are requisite to be named in Scotland, when I was in it with them, to wit, in Berwick, with Sir James Douglas, and thereabout, one Mr. Brown a Jesuit; in Setton, one Mr. Christison or Campbell, who uses likewise in sundry other places, (excuse me if I know not their names, for we came from several parts at several times) as he is desired, for he is thought of, and sent for in Edinburgh; William Robertson, sometimes in colonel Bruce's, lady Margaret Hamilton's, Riddoch's, John Guthry the taylor's, who for some years bygone brought me to the said William his mass, in the said Margaret's house, with a little Frenchman, where there were some twenty persons, unknown truly to me. The Jesuits frequent lady Margaret Hamilton's, heartily against the engagement, as it was then stated by the party who set up for it. I shall not here enter upon any detail of this Robert Scot's in the Canongate, Burghton, and with my lord Semple, often. For others I know none in Edinburgh, but by report, not having much frequented the town. In Paisley and thereabout, a very subtile Jesuit, and crafty companion, and yet a scholar, one Mr. Smith with the marquis of Douglas, and Mr. David Tyrie a gray friar in Nithsdale, and thereabout: and Mr. Lindsay a gray friar in the west: one Mr. Lesley a capuchin, called by himself the captain, fled out of the north for having a child in Angus. One Mr. Ogilvie a gray friar, and kinsman to my lord Ogilvie; in Ardestie, Pitalpie, Drumkilbo, and thereabout, one Mr. Drummond; but truly all Jesuits. When I came to the country, with my lady Aboyn, and thereabout, were Mr. John Lesley now dead, and his brother Mr. Andrew Lesley, both Jesuits. In Achigore, Lessindrum, Carneo, Arran, and thereabout, one Mr. William Gibson an Augustin friar. In Aberdeen, one Mr. Mortimer; in the earl of Errol's and the laird of Dalgetie's houses, was one Mr. William Lesley, now superior in Douay. In Buchan was Mr. John Seton and Mr. Tobie; now the one is at Madrid, and the other at London, agents for the two missions. In the Bog and Elgin, and thereabout, Mr. Southwel, and Christie, a very timorous but subtile fellow; the first is in Douay, the last in the Bog. In Caithness, and beyond Ardestie in Angus, myself was a certain time, beside one Mr. Cushet a minim, a pensioner of her majesty's, one ready to all travels, and directions of her majesty's command, and two others, one Mr. Duncan a parson, *alias* Macpherson in Scotland, but unknown to me where they reside.

My third point was concerning their entertainment, which is threefold. One from the congregation *de propaganda fide;* above a hundred crowns, or more, as they have his holiness and the cardinals' favour. Another is their own purchase, their confessions, preachings, masses, pardons, &c. and lately from the king of Spain, of whom every one of them that is out of their college, has eighteen shillings Scots a day. Robert Irvine, called Cossopie, brings it in William Hay laird of Fetter-letter, is the treasurer; both receive their pensions therefore. What others receive, the superior with his counsellors, and the treasurer only know, whereby it may be easily seen they lack nothing in *temporalibus*.

Now my counsel for extirpation of them, is only in two ways. 1st. To hold out all appearances, although of indifferent things to come near to them, because they think ye will not come at once, but *gradatim* to them, and this holdeth them fast. 2do. Let them not fail to hear, subscribe, and communicate; for by these means ye shall make the priests idle, having an order to deal, that none be suffered to participate of their and your sacraments. This I have written in sincerity, for the salvation of your souls, and the advancement of the gospel, and not of any malice I have to them, as God shall save my soul at the great day.

THO. ABERNETHY.

affair; any body who writes the history of that period will find matter enough from the very public papers and records, the acts of general assemblies, committees of estates, commissions of assemblies, and not a little in the defences of the marquis of Argyle, to set the matters of fact here, and in other acts of this parliament so much misrepresented, in a just and quite other light. The rescissory part of this act was already made upon the matter, in the preceding acts, and the ratification of what they now make void by the king himself in full parliament, is no hinderance to our levellers in this razing work. I shall likewise leave their 10th act, " against the declaration of the kingdom of Scotland," January 16th, 1647, to the remarks of such who shall give the history of the former period; and I am persuaded they will be easily able to take off the aspersions cast upon such, whom the managers are pleased to term a " few seditious persons, who had then screwed themselves into the government."

When by the preceding steps they have paved their road, they come by the 11th act to require what turned about to be matter of sore suffering afterwards, " the oath of allegiance," and the subscribing " an instrument assertory of the royal prerogative." Such was their spite at the covenant, that though more than once they had already declared it had no authority as a law; yet by this act they must cut off the dead man's head, and, in as far as lay in their power, enervate the obligation of the matter of it. By another act, in a following session of this parliament, the matter of it is declared unlawful, and they order it to be renounced; at length, in Queensberry's parliament, twenty-four years after this, it is declared to be high treason for any to adhere to it. This 11th act being remarkable, and a sort of abbreviate of all they had done, I have insert it. *

The oath of allegiance, or rather supremacy I have considered, upon the first act, and only now add, that when this present act was a framing, some ministers in Edinburgh offered to some of the managers, an amendment only of one word, instead of supreme governor, that it should run supreme civil governor, which would have gone far to have removed the scruples of many: but no alteration would be heard; the members of parliament had taken the oath, and every body who would not follow their example, was reckoned disaffected.

1661.

The oath was now imposed upon all in civil offices; they knew what they had in view shortly to do as to ministers: but lest they should presume upon an exemption, a general clause is added, requiring this oath from " all upon whom the privy council, or any having orders from them, should impose it;" and so it reached most part of the subjects in a little time. The acknowledgment of the king's prerogative, required as a test of loyalty, and condition of enjoying of any public trust, is so remarkable, as it deserves a room in the body of this history, and follows:

" Forasmuch as the estates of parliament of this kingdom, by their several acts of the 11th and 21st of January last, have, from the sense of their humble duty, and 'in recognisance of his majesty's just right, declared, that it is an inherent privilege of the crown, and an undoubted part of the royal prerogative of the kings of this kingdom, to have the sole choice and appointment of the officers of estate, privy counsellors, and lord of session; that the power of calling, holding, and dissolving of parliaments, and all conventions and meetings of the estates doth solely reside in the king's majesty, his heirs and successors; and that, as no parliament can be lawfully kept, without the special warrant or presence of the king's majes-

---

* Act for taking the oath of allegiance, and asserting the royal prerogative.

Our sovereign Lord, being truly sensible of the many sufferings and sad confusions that his dutiful and loyal subjects have been brought under, during these troubles, and desirous, that his royal government, in its due administration, may be refreshing and comfortable unto them, and conceiving it necessary for that end, and for the honour and advancement of his own service, the welfare and happiness of his subjects, and the peace and quiet of this kingdom, that the places of public trust (which be the channels and conduits by which his majesty's government is conveyed unto his people) be supplied and exerced by persons of known integrity, abilities and loyalty, doth therefore declare, that it is and will be his majesty's royal care, that those

1661. ty, or his commissioner, so no acts nor statutes to be passed in any parliament, can be binding on the people, or have the authority and force of laws, without the special approbation of his majesty, or his commissioner, interponed thereto, at the making thereof: that the power of arms, making of peace and war, and making of treaties with foreign princes and states, or at home by subjects among themselves, doth properly reside in the king's majesty, his heirs and successors, and is their undoubted right, and theirs alone; and that it is high treason in the subjects of this kingdom, or any number of them, upon whatsoever ground, to rise or continue in arms, to maintain any forts, garrisons, or strengths, to make peace or war, or to make any treaties or leagues with foreigners, or among themselves, without his majesty's authority first interponed thereto: that it is unlawful for subjects of whatsomever quality or function, to convocate, convene, or assemble themselves, to treat, consult, or determine in any matters of state, civil or ecclesiastic, (except in the ordinary judgments) or to make leagues or bonds upon whatsoever colour or pretence, without his majesty's special consent and approbation had thereto: that the league and covenant, and all treaties following thereupon, and acts or deeds that do or may relate thereunto, are not obligatory, nor do infer any obligation upon this kingdom, or the subjects thereof, to meddle or interpose by arms, or any seditious way, in any thing, concerning the religion and government of the churches in England and Ireland, or in what may concern his majesty's government there: and that none of his majesty's subjects should presume upon any pretext of any authority whatsomever, to require the renewing or swearing of the said league and covenant, or of any other covenants, or public oaths concerning the government of the church or kingdom; and that none offer to renew or swear the same, without his majesty's special warrant and approbation, &c.

" I do, conform to the acts of parliament aforesaid, declare, that I do with all humble duty, acknowledge his majesty's royal prerogative, right and power, in all the particulars, and in the manner aforesaid; and that I do heartily give my consent thereto, by those presents, subscribed by me at ———."

This instrument, assertory of the king's prerogative, which all persons, as above, were to subscribe, comprehends all they had declared in their foregoing acts; and by it, the signers consented to the king's absolute power, owned the unlawfulness of resisting whom (according to the undoubted right of the crown) he hath, or shall think fit to call to his councils, or any public employments, shall be so qualified; and that for the full satisfaction of all his good subjects, and for removing any scruples or jealousies can arise upon this account, they shall, before their admittance to, or exercise of any such trust, give such public testimony of their duty and loyalty, as may evidence to the world, they are such as the kingdom, and all honest men and good subjects may justly confide in. And therefore the king's majesty, with advice and consent of his estates of parliament, doth statute and ordain, that all and whatsoever person or persons, who are or shall be nominate by his majesty, to be his officers of state, of his privy council, session, or exchequer, justice general, admiral, sheriffs, commissar, and their deputes, and clerks, and all magistrates and council of royal burghs, at their admission to their several offices, and before they offer to exerce the same, shall take and swear the oath of allegiance, hereunto subjoined. And also, that all other persons, who shall be required by his majesty's privy council, or any having authority from them, shall be obliged to take and swear the same.

And since all the troubles and miseries that have overspread this kingdom, and almost destroyed all religious and civil, all public and private interests, these twenty years bygone, and upwards, have arisen and sprung from these invasions that have been made upon, and contempts done to the royal authority and prerogative of the crown, his majesty conceives himself obliged, both for his own royal interest, and for the public interest and peace of his people, to be careful to prevent the like for the future. And therefore his majesty, with advice foresaid, statutes and ordains, that all persons who are, or shall be called to any public trust, as said is, shall, beside the taking of the oath of allegiance, be obliged, before they enter to their offices and trusts, to assert under their handwriting, his majesty's royal prerogative, as is expressed in the acts passed in this present parliament, and in the manner hereunto subjoined: certifying all such as, being required, shall refuse or delay to take the oath of allegiance, they shall not only thereby render themselves incapable of any public trust, but be looked upon as persons disaffected to his majesty's authority and government; and such as shall refuse or delay to assert his majesty's prerogative, in manner underwritten, shall from thenceforth be incapable of any public trust within this kingdom.

the vilest tyrant, and materially renounced that work of reformation in Scotland, begun at our secession from popery, and revived and carried on in the year 1638, approven once and again by the king and parliament; and, which is more, signally owned of God. This declaration with the oath of allegiance, became the trying badges of loyalty; and whenever any suspected person was sisted before the council, or other courts, or magistrates, those two were offered him: if he swallowed them, he was dismissed; if he refused, this was turned to a libel, and no mercy for him. In considering the former acts, remarks have been made upon most part of the clauses of this declaration, and I shall not repeat them. In short, by the general imposing of it, the courtiers endeavoured to make the prince absolute, cramp religion, and alter both the frame and principles of the civil and ecclesiastic government here. This declaration must be subscribed, which, as to truth and persuasion, is much the same with its being sworn, under the penalty of being reputed disloyal and disaffected; and the refusal of it made a person incapable of all public trust. And yet not a few assertions are in it, far above the capacities of many upon whom it was imposed; so that they could not make this declaration with knowledge and in truth: thus it became a plain stumblingblock, an occasion of sinning, and a snare to the consciences of many; and the sufferings to be narrated, which followed upon the refusal of this declaration, and the former oath, are purely upon conscience and principle, and can never be alleged to be for rebellion; unless every thing that runs cross to the methods of a corrupt and imposing time, must be so named. I hope the reader will remark it, that till the rising at Pentland, which was the native consequent of this and other impositions, little other reason was pretended or given for the cruelties exercised upon multitudes, save their refusing this involved, ambiguous, complex, and unreasonable oath and subscription.

The three following acts are purely civil, and about the granting of money to the king. But in the 15th act, they come at one dash, to rid themselves of all the parliaments since the year 1633. At first they talked only of rescinding the parliament 1649, because the engagement had then been disapproven: but quickly their design took air, to raze all; and after by their former acts, the king had got in his hands all that was lately called the liberties of the kingdom, and privileges of parliament, it is now boldly enough resolved upon, to rescind all done in parliament since the year 1633, and to remove the civil sanction given to the general assembly at Glasgow, and those which followed; and to abolish all laws made in favour of our church government and covenants.—When this motion was first made, it appeared so choking, that it was laid aside, or rather delayed for some months; but when all the former acts had gone glibly through, the managers, hoping nothing would be stuck at, come briskly to overturn all that had been a building since the year 1638, and they cass and rescind all that was done in former times by king and parliament, with the greatest solemnity and unanimity; and at one stroke, to take away the greatest human securities which could be given to a church or nation.

From their former success, the compilers of those acts grow in boldness. In the narrative of the (present) act, they call all done these twenty-three years, "troubles upon the specious, but common pretext of REFORMATION, the common cloak of all rebellions," and declare his majesty holds the crown "immediately from God Almighty alone;" a proposition which will not hold of any monarch ever upon the earth, unless it be Moses, king in Jeshurun, and a few more under the Old Testament. (And) though in this act they grant, the acts now rescinding were agreed to by king and parliament, yet, in order to bury the covenants under reproach, they add, that the covenanters did most unworthily engage "to subvert his majesty's government, and the public peace of the kingdom of England;" which is notoriously contrary to the very letter of the covenants. Many other things are asserted here as matters of fact, which might easily be disproved; but this would lead me too far into the history of former times.

Upon those perversions of matter of fact, and wrong reasonings, they rescind all the parliaments from the (year) 1640 to 1648, inclusive. A friend may go with a foe, and therefore in this good company, they rescind the act 1648, approving the engagement, which by their own 9th act they had just now ratified; at least that favourite act is not excepted, and therefore, it would seem, is included in the strong and general rescissory terms. To smooth a little so harsh a treatment of our constitution, attained with so great pains, and so much valued lately, an indemnity is promised; and yet much more was to be done, before that favour was granted to Scotland, and it was a long time before it was published. It had not been unusual to rescind particular acts of former parliaments; but I find few instances before this, of voiding and cassing parliaments by the lump and wholesale: none must now be spared, (not even) the parliament 1641, wherein king Charles I. was personally present, nor that 1641, where their beloved engagement was approven; neither does that at Perth, 1651, where his majesty himself was present, escape by this procedure.

When thus the guards, outworks and bulwarks of the church are demolished, they come next to blow up her government itself by their 16th act, " concerning religion and church government." This being one chief foundation of twenty-seven years' melancholy work in Scotland, I have added it. * In it as in the whole of the present procedure, the reader cannot but observe their singular ingratitude, and ungenerous treatment of ministers, and other presbyterians, to whom the king owed his restoration so much, and who had so firmly stood by his interests under the usurpation. What the miracles in this, and other acts, so much talked of in the king's restoration, were, I am yet to learn. A gracious promise follows, " to maintain the doctrine and worship established in the king's father and grandfather's time;" which is a glorious commentary upon the king's letter to the presbytery of Edinburgh. By this a door is opened to bring in books and bishops, at least the articles of Perth. How well the exercises of religion, public and private, were encouraged, will appear by the subsequent acts of parliament and council, and their rigorous execution.

The government of the church is promised to be " secured, as the king finds most consistent with scripture, monarchy, and peace;" and in the mean time, synods, presbyteries and sessions are allowed for a few weeks; and yet, as we shall find, synods are violently abridged in their liberty, and interrupted. Thus in as dark and insensible a manner as might be, presbytery is abolished, prelacy brought in, and the government of the church is left ambulatory, and to be settled, as the king sees good, without an act of parliament; and dying presbyterian government was scarce permitted to live out this year.

I have it from one who lived at this time, and was no stranger to court measures, that before the passing of this act, the commissioner advised the matter with a few of his

---

* Act concerning religion and church government.

Our sovereign lord, being truly sensible of the mercies of Almighty God towards him in his preservation, in the times of greatest trouble and danger, and in his miraculous restitution to his just right and government of his kingdoms, and being desirous to improve these mercies, to the glory of God, and honour of his great name, doth, with advice and consent of his estates of parliament, declare, that it is his full and firm resolution to maintain the true reformed protestant religion, in its purity of doctrine and worship, as it was established within this kingdom, during the reigns of his royal father and grandfather of blessed memory: and that his majesty will be careful to promote the power of godliness, to encourage the exercises of religion, both public and private, and to suppress all profaneness and disorderly walking; and for that end, will give all due countenance and protection to the ministers of the gospel, they containing themselves within the bounds and limits of their ministerial calling, and behaving themselves with that submission and obedience to his majesty's authority and commands, that is suitable to the allegiance and duty of good subjects. And as to the government of the church, his majesty will make it his care, to settle and secure the same, in such a frame as shall be most agreeable to the word of God, most suitable to monarchical government, and most complying with the public peace and quiet of the kingdom. And in the mean time, his majesty, with advice and consent foresaid, doth allow the present administration by sessions, presbyteries and synods, (they keeping within bounds, and behaving themselves as said is) and that notwithstanding of the preceding act, rescissory of all pretended parliaments, since the year one thousand six hundred and thirty-eight.

close friends, the register, Sir John Fletcher, Sir George Mackenzie of Tarbet, and Urquhart of Cromarty, a cousin of Sir George's, who had lately counterfeit the protester, and some time after this ended miserably; whether he should pass this act, which he knew to be the king's darling design, or delay it a while, and go to London first to acquaint the king, how much he had done for his service, and receive the beginnings of his reward. Sir Archibald Primrose advised him to bring in bishops surely, but slowly; for if he were soon through his work, he might come the sooner to lose his power. The commissioner answered, " The parliament was now at his beck, and he loved to serve his master genteelly, and do his business at one stroke." This resolution was applauded, as noble and generous, by the rest of his confidants: so the matter was agreed on in private, and carried stitch-through in public, as it stands in the act. However, afterwards, the first appeared to be the best advice; for in a little time Middleton and his confidants were out of all office in Scotland, the planting of bishops here, being like the building Jericho of old.

Since by the former act prelates are materially brought in, and bishops could never stand alone in Scotland; the parliament's next work is to support them, when the king shall please to name them, with holidays and patrons. Accordingly their 17th act is for keeping the 29th day of May, as a religious anniversary;* it is annexed. It was evidently framed to be a snare unto ministers; and their refusing obedience to it, was one of the first grounds of their sufferings, in a little time.

1661.

Upon reading the narrative (of this act), one will be ready to think the parliament have forgot their design, and are framing the causes of a fast, instead of an act for a thanksgiving; and it was much that any, who retained any respect for the former work of reformation, had freedom to keep the day upon such an introduction. The statutory part will be yet more surprising: they ordain " the 29th day of May to be for ever set apart as an holy day unto the Lord, and to be employed in prayer, preaching, thanksgiving, and praises to God. All servile work is discharged, and the remaining part of the day is to be spent in lawful divertisements suitable to so solemn an occasion." What a pity was it that a book of sports was not framed for Scotland upon this occasion, as was in England in the king's father and grandfather's time, a period set up now so much for a rule? It was certainly unreasonable to set this, or any other day apart "*for ever as a holy day to the Lord*," according to their own principles; and even the favourers of holidays must own it. One may suppose it possible, that upon a 29th day of May, a prince, fully as good and pious as king Charles I. might come to be beheaded by another Cromwell, and a sectarian faction; and then ask those gentlemen, whether it could be *for ever kept* as a holy day of praise

---

* Act for a solemn anniversary thanksgiving for his majesty's restoration to the royal government of his kingdoms.

The estates of parliament of the kingdom of Scotland, taking to their consideration the sad condition, slavery, and bondage, this ancient kingdom hath groaned under, during these twenty-three years' troubles; in which, under the specious pretences of reformation, a public rebellion hath been, by the treachery of some, and mispersuasion of others, violently carried on against sacred authority, to the ruin and destruction, so far as was possible, of religion, the king's majesty, and his royal government, the laws, liberties, and property of the people, and all the public and private interests of the kingdom; so that religion itself, which holds the right of kings to be sacred, hath been prostitute for the warrant of all these treasonable invasions made upon the royal authority, and disloyal limitations put upon the allegiance of the subjects; and hath it not also been pretended unto, for the warrant of all those vile and bloody murders, which, in high contempt of Almighty God, and of his majesty's authority and laws, were, under colour of justice, committed upon his majesty's good subjects, merely for the discharge of their duty to God, and loyalty to the king? Hath not that royal government, under whose protection this nation hath, to the envy of the world, been so famous for many ages, been of late trodden under foot, and new governments and governors established, and kept up without his majesty's authority, and against his express commands? Hath not law, which is the birthright and inheritance of the subject, and the security of their lives and fortunes, been laid in the dust, and new and unjust edicts and orders past and published, for subjecting both life and fortune, and what else was dear unto any of his majesty's good subjects, to the cruel and ambitious lusts of some usurping rulers? Hath not religion and loyalty been the only objects of their rapine and cruelty? And hath not their new and arbitrary exactions and burdens upon the

1661. and thanksgiving to the Lord? and as the institution of this, or any other day, to be a "holy day *for ever*," is what is really beyond the power of creatures, who know not what may fall out, so the following clause is a banter upon what is sacred with themselves. First, the day is set apart "for ever to be kept *holy to the Lord*," and then "*divertisements*" are appointed for the spending the day, after public worship is over: and if their own practices, who were managers, may be allowed to be a just commentary upon their "lawful divertisements," we shall soon see what they were, horrid impieties, revelling, drinking, and excess of riot; and I doubt not but this prostituting of what they professed to believe as sacred, and holy time, was an inlet to that fearful wickedness, debauching of consciences, and corruption in morals, which became so common at this time.

The reader must guess, whether there were any fears in the house, that by those preceding acts, a door might be opened to profaneness. But as if there had been a connexion betwixt keeping the 29th of May, and prostituting the sabbath of the Lord, their 18th act is "for the due observation of the sabbath," and the 19th "against swearing, and excessive drinking;" both of them very good acts, and not unnecessary after the 17th, and those which went before: but the practice of many of the lawgivers, in cursing, swearing, and sabbath-breaking, was a lamentable directory to the lieges, how to keep their laws, and the grossest and most shameless contempt that ever lawmakers put on their own infant laws.

Further, to secure their designed model of church government now coming in, they reintroduced the unreasonable and antichristian burden of "patrons and presentations," upon this church. That heavy grievance had been happily removed by an act of parliament, March 9th, 1649. This reasonable statute not being in every body's hands, I have added it (as under). * It did not satisfy our managers to have this act re-

---

people, exceeded in one month whatever had been formerly in many years paid to any of the kings of this kingdom? And when the best of men, and the most excellent of the kings of the earth, had, in an unusual way of confidence, rendered his person to the trust and loyalty of his native subjects, was not the security of religion pretended unto by some, who then governed in church and state, for the ground of that base (and never enough to be abhorred) transaction, in leaving such a prince, their native and dread sovereign, to the will of these who were in open rebellion, and for the time had their swords in their hands against him? And that when by these and many such like undutiful carriages, the king's majesty was removed from his kingdoms, the foundations of this ancient and well constitute government was overturned, the liberties and property of the people inverted, and this kingdom exposed to be captives and slaves to strangers, and nothing left unto them but the sad meditation of their increasing miseries, and the bitter remembrance of their bypast disloyalties: yet even then it pleased Almighty God to compassionate their low condition, and, by the power of his own right hand, most miraculously to restore the king's most sacred majesty, to the royal government of his kingdoms; and thereby to redeem this kingdom from its former slavery and bondage, and to restore it to its ancient and just privileges and freedom. And the king's majesty acknowledging, with all humility and thankfulness, the goodness, wisdom, and power of God, in this signal act of his mercy to him and his people, doth, with advice and consent of his estates of parliament, statute and ordain, that in all time coming there be a solemn yearly commemoration of the same: and for that end, the twenty-ninth day of May, (which day God Almighty hath specially honoured, and rendered auspicious to this kingdom, both by his majesty's royal birth, and by his blessed restoration to his government) be for ever set apart as an holy day unto the Lord, and that in all the churches of the kingdom it be employed in public prayers, preaching, thanksgiving, and praises to God, for so transcendent mercies: and that all trade, merchandise, work, handy-labour, and other ordinary employments be forborne, and the remaining part of the day spent in such lawful divertisements as are suitable to so solemn an occasion. And it is hereby recommended to all ministers of the gospel, and to all sheriffs, justices of peace, and other public ministers in the several counties, and to all magistrates within burghs, to be careful, that for this present year, and in all time coming, the twenty-ninth day of May be accordingly kept and observed within their several jurisdictions. And for the speedier and more full intimation hereof to all his majesty's subjects, it is appointed these presents be printed, and published at all the market-crosses of the royal burghs.

* Act abolishing Patronages, March 9th, 1649.
The estates of parliament, being sensible of the great obligation that lies upon them by the national covenant, and by the solemn league and covenant, and by many deliverances and mercies from God, and by the late solemn engagement unto duties, to preserve the doctrine, and maintain and vindicate the liberties of the kirk of Scotland, and to advance the work of reformation therein, to the utmost of their power; and considering, that patronages and presentations of kirks is an evil and bondage, under which the Lord's people, and ministers of this land,

scinded in the general, with many other excellent statutes made in that period; and therefore, by their 36th act,* they particularly have long groaned, and that it hath no warrant in God's word, but is founded only on the common law, and is a custom popish, and brought into the kirk in time of ignorance and superstition, and that the same is contrary to the second book of discipline, in which, upon solid and good ground, it is reckoned among abuses that are desired to be reformed, and unto several acts of general assembly, and that it is prejudicial to the liberty of the people, and planting of kirks, and unto the free calling and entry of ministers unto their charge: and the said estates being willing and desirous to promove and advance the reformation foresaid, that every thing in the house of God may be ordered according to his word and commandment; do therefore, from the sense of the former obligations, and upon the former grounds and reasons, discharge for ever hereafter, all patronages and presentations of kirks, whether belonging to the king or to any laick patron, presbyteries, or either, within this kingdom, as being unlawful and unwarrantable by God's word, and contrary to the doctrine and liberties of this kirk; and do repeal, rescind, make void, and annul all gifts and rights granted thereanent, and all former acts made in parliament, or in any inferior judicatory, in favours of any patron or patrons whatsoever, so far as the same doth, or may relate unto the presentation of kirks: and do statute and ordain, that no person or persons whatsomever, shall at any time hereafter, take upon them, under pretext of any title, infeftment, act of parliament, possession, or warrant whatsoever, which are hereby repealed, to give, subscribe, or seal any presentation to any kirk within this kingdom; and discharge the passing of any infeftments hereafter, bearing the right to patronages to be granted in favours of these for whom the infeftments are presented; and that no person or persons shall, either in the behalf of themselves or others, procure, receive, take it away, and directly establish patrons, and presentation of ministers by them, as what they knew had been or make use of any presentation to any kirk within this kingdom. And it is further declared and ordained, that if any presentation shall hereafter be given, procured, or received, that the same is null and of no effect, and that it is lawful for presbyteries to reject the same, and to refuse to admit any to trials thereupon; and notwithstanding thereof, to proceed to the planting of the kirk, upon the suit and calling, or with the consent of the congregation, on whom none is to be obtruded against their will. And it is decerned, statute, and ordained, that whosoever hereafter shall, upon the suit and calling of the congregation, after due examination of their literature and conversation, be admitted by the presbytery unto the exercise and function of the ministry, in any parish within this kingdom; that the said person or persons, without a presentation, by virtue of their mission, hath a sufficient right and title to possess and enjoy the manse and glebe, and the whole rents, profits, and stipends, which the ministers of that church had formerly possessed and enjoyed, or that hereafter shall be modified by the commission for plantation of kirks; and decern all titulars and tacksmen of tithes, heritors, liferenters, or others, subject and liable in payment of ministers' stipends, to make payment of the same, notwithstanding the minister his want of a presentation; and ordain the lords of session, and other judges competent, to give out decreets and sentences, letters conform, horning, inhibition, and all other executorials, upon the said admission of ministers by presbyteries, as they were formerly in use to do, upon collation and institution following upon presentations from patrons: declaring always, that where ministers are already admitted upon presentation, and have obtained decreets conform thereupon, that the said decreets and executorials following thereupon, shall be good and valid rights to the ministers, for suiting and obtaining payment

1661.

---

* Act anent presentation of ministers.
Forasmuch as the king's most excellent majesty, considering how necessary it is, for the right and orderly administration of God's worship, and the exercises of religion, and for keeping of his good subjects within their duties they owe to God, to his majesty, to their native country, and fellow subjects, especially at this time, after so many confusions and distractions, both among churchmen and others, that more than ordinary care be had in presenting of ministers to all such kirks as are or shall be vacant within this kingdom, hath given particular commission under his great seal, as to all presentations to all parsonages, vicarages, and other benefices and kirks at his majesty's presentation. And as to all other benefices and kirks, whereof the presentation belongs to any other patron or patrons whatsoever, his majesty with advice and consent of his estates of parliament, statutes and ordains, that all patrons or persons whatsoever, who hath or pretends any right to the presentations to any patronages, vicarages, or other benefices of cure, kirks, or modified stipends, be careful in all time coming, that presentations to these benefices, kirks, or stipends, be granted by them to such persons only, as shall give sufficient evidence of their piety, loyalty, literature, and peaceable disposition, and shall in presence of the patron or his attorney, and of the sheriff of the shire, steward of the stewartry, or heritable bailie, or commissary of the bounds, if it be in the country, and of the magistrates of the burghs within the burgh, before the granting and their accepting the presentation, take and subscribe the oath of allegiance, the said sheriff, steward, bailie, commissary, and magistrates, having first taken the oath themselves. And it is hereby declared, that if any person who hath not so taken the oath of allegiance, shall be presented by any patron, not only shall the presentation be void and null of itself, but the right of the patronage, as to that vacancy, shall belong to the king's majesty, and the patrons be repute disaffected to his majesty's government, and contemners of his royal authority. And ordains these presents to be printed, and published at the market crosses, that none pretend ignorance.

o

1661. still a dead weight upon, and really inconsistent with the presbyterian establishment. And that in time coming they might have a ministry every way obsequious to their impositions, made and to be made, the act ordains all who shall be presented to "take the oath of allegiance," or supremacy, before set down, and that under very severe penalties, both upon the presenter, and person presented, in case this be neglected: so very soon they got not only the civil government, but the ministry modelled to their wish.

A great many other acts were made by this parliament, which I pass, as not immediately relating to the history I am writing, and some of them very good ones, as that "against cursing, and beating of parents;" that "against blasphemy;" and one against "clandestine marriages." Their 52d act is a pretty singular one, appointing "all vacant stipends" at present, and for seven years to come, to be given "to ministers and others, their wives and bairns, who had been loyal in the late times," *i. e.* against presbytery, and the work of reformation, "and had suffered for their adherence to the king's interests." By this clause, a good many of the protesters might have pleaded a share. Their last act was by some termed, "an act for paying their own debts without money," and alleged to be neither just nor generous; but by others it was reckoned both equitable and good policy, after so general and great calamities. Thus the reader hath some view of the acts of this parliament, as far as they concern the constitution of this church, and our civil liberty. Before I leave this parliament, I shall, from the minutes I spoke of before, give some further account of their procedure, in a few hints, which could not offer themselves from the acts, as they stand in print. What concerns the processes against the marquis of Argyle, lord Warriston, Mr. Guthrie, Mr. Gillespie, and some others, will come in upon the following sections, where I am to give accounts of them by themselves.

January 4th, when they entered upon business, the oath of allegiance was taken by

---

of his stipend, and the presentation and decreet conform, obtained before the date hereof, shall be a valid ground and right for that effect, notwithstanding the annulling presentations by virtue of this present act. And because it is needful that the just and proper interest of congregations and presbyteries, in providing of kirks with ministers, be clearly determined by the general assembly, and what is to be accounted the congregation having that interest; therefore, it is hereby seriously recommended unto the next general assembly, clearly to determine the same, and to condescend upon a certain standing way, for being a settled rule therein, for all time coming. And it is hereby provided, declared, and ordained, that the taking away of patronages and presentations of kirks, shall import nor inforce no hurt nor prejudice unto the title and right that any patron hath unto the tithes of the parish, nor weaken his infeftment wherein the same is contained; but that the said title, right, and infeftment, shall in every respect (so far as doth concern the tithes), be as valid and strong, as when presentations were in use. It is further statute and ordained, that the tithes of these kirks, whereof the presentations are hereby abolished, shall belong heritably unto the said patrons, and be secured unto them, and inserted in their rights and infeftments, in place of the patronage. Likeas, the estates of parliament declare said patrons their right thereunto to be good and lawful, hereby granting full power to them to possess, sell, annalie, and dispone the same in manner after specified, as fully and freely as the minister and patron might have done, before the making these presents: excepting always therefrom, these tithes which the heritors have had and possessed, by virtue of tacks set to them by the ministers, without any deed or consent of the patrons; concerning which it is provided, that the said tithes, at the issue and outrunning of the present tacks, shall belong unto the heritors respective; the said heritors and the patrons abovementioned, each of them for their interest, being always liable to the payment of the present stipends to the ministers, and to such augmentation and provision of new stipends to one or more ministers, such as the parliament or commission for plantation of kirks, shall think fit and appoint: excepting also such tithes as are and have been possessed and uplifted by the ministers, as their proper stipends; concerning which it is hereby declared, that the minister shall enjoy the same without any impediment, as formerly; it being hereby provided also, that this act shall prejudge no person of the right, title, and possession of their tithes, by infeftments, tacks, and other lawful rights acquired by them, and the predecessors and authors, as accords of law. Likeas, the estates of parliament renew the former acts, granted in favours of heritors, for valuing, leading, and buying of their tithes; hereby ordaining any patron, having right to these tithes made to them by this act, and having no right thereunto of before, to accept the value of six years' rents, according to the prices of valued bolls respective, enjoined and set down in the former act thereanent, and that for the heritable right of the said tithes, and for all title, interest or claim that the said patrons can have or pretend thereunto by virtue of this act.

all members present, save the earl of Cassils, who had time given him to advise. If the former account hold, that the earl of Melvil and laird of Kilburny did not qualify, as I have said, from papers writ at this time, it seems they have not been present; and I find that the earl of Cassils is overlooked, till January 11th, where the manuscript, from which I am giving those accounts, takes notice, " that the earl deserted the house, not being satisfied to take the oath agreed to by the parliament." And, April 11th, the earl of Cassils being called to the " house this day, was desired to take the oath of allegiance. He moved by himself, and several of his friends, that he might be remitted to the king, to satisfy his majesty thereanent. But in regard this desire was contrary to an order of parliament, and that he had got many delays formerly for advising the said oath, his desire was refused, and the certification of the parliament passed against him, declaring him incapable of the public trust intended by the king upon him." The earl was a stiff royalist under the usurpation, and the king was very sensible of his services, and he had considerable offers made, and yet quit all, to keep a good conscience towards God; and all the favour he sought, in return to the hardships he had undergone for his loyalty, was a permission to keep a presbyterian minister as his chaplain in his family, after they were turned out of their churches. This the bishops grudged him, yet he was overlooked in it.

I find this parliament had different ministers every day almost, who prayed in the house with them; and unless it be some of the ministers of Edinburgh, there is scarce another employed to pray, but such who conformed to prelacy; so well did the employers know the characters of the corrupt part of the ministry. A good many, who were afterwards bishops, were employed to preach before them, and we heard the nature of their sermons.

By those written minutes of parliament, I observe, that most part of their meetings were in the afternoon, though the day was but short: whether several members were better in case for business, by that time of the day, I determine not; but I knew a peer of the first rank, who had been present in most of the parliaments 1661. during this period, when commissioner to one of the sessions after the revolution, used to declare himself with some warmth against afternoon sederunts of parliament, from what he had observed in this and the next reign.

All the acts of a public nature were formed by " the lords of articles," and presented from them to the parliament, where many of them passed without any great reasoning; sometimes five or six acts of very great consequence would be voted in an afternoon's sederunt. Whether they were debated before the lords of the articles, I know not: but I suppose any little struggle that was made was there; for the parliament met but very seldom, once or twice in a week, or so. This manner of parliamentary procedure was declared against at the revolution, and no more used. Upon the 8th of January, the commissioner proposed this matter to the house, and moved that the parliament might fall to their business, in the ancient road, by the lords of the articles, without devolving their whole power upon them, which he declared was not his meaning. The matter was not a little agitate in the house; at length, " it was resolved, that twelve noblemen, twelve barons, and twelve burgesses, with the officers of state, shall be in the place of the lords of articles; and that other twelve of each of those estates should be a committee for trade and hearing of bills. Those were authorized in their several meetings, to hear all matters presented to them, to receive probation of what they found relevant, and report to the parliament twice a week: but the full power is declared to be reserved to the parliament, to debate and determine all matters, notwithstanding of those meetings, which are declared to be preparatory."

The several estates having withdrawn themselves, brought in the following list for the lords of the articles, which was agreed to:

Nobility—Duke Hamilton, Montrose, Errol, Marshal, Mar, Rothes, Athole, Hume, Haddington, Dumfries, Callendar, Hartfield. *Barons*—Sir John Gilmour, Sir Peter Wed-

1661. derburn, Prestoun, Lie, Polmais, Carden, Dury, Tarbet, Collingtoun, Garff, Ardross, Balmain. *Burghs*—Provost of Edinburgh; Provost of Perth; Dundee, Alexander Wedderburn; Aberdeen, William Gray; Stirling, Duncan Nairn; Linlithgow, Andrew Glame; Glasgow, John Bell; Air, William Cunningham; Haddington, John Beaton; Dumfries, John Irvine; Aberbrothock, John Auchterbos, Hugh Sinclair. To those, with the officers of state, the nation owes the forming and framing of the acts formerly mentioned. The committee for trade and bills I need not insert, since it was mostly private business came before them: the processes indeed against the marquis of Argyle and others began at them; and the lord Cochran was their president.

January 16th, the act discharging all meetings, convocations, leagues, and bonds, without the concurrence of the king, was, after much debate, carried, with a declaration that it looked only forward.

A proclamation by the commissioner and parliament was this day agreed to, " ordaining all persons, who have not actual residence in Edinburgh, and are not obliged to attend the parliament, who had any hand in the remonstrance, or in contriving of, or assenting to the ends thereof, or in that wicked book called ' the Causes of God's Wrath,' to depart the town in forty-eight hours, and not to return, or remain within ten miles thereof, under pain of treason; except those who are already cited to appear for the crimes abovementioned." This was proclaimed at the Cross.

January 22d, the act agreed upon by the lords of the articles, disannulling the convention of estates 1643, was passed, after very much debate. The commissioner declared, " he had no order from his master to encroach upon our national covenant, or upon the consciences of the people: but as to leagues with other nations, he conceived they could not now subsist with the laws of this kingdom." About ten members dissented.

When the act rescissory was brought in by the lords of the articles to the house, February 7th very long reasonings ensued,

and it could not be got through that night. To-morrow, it was again tossed. The earl of Loudon had a long and elegant speech, vindicating himself from the aspersions in the narrative of that act, and setting the affairs in that period in a just light; but it had no weight: that act behoved to be passed, and at length, with a great struggle, it was carried.

Upon the 22d of February, the parliament grant a commission to visit the colleges of Aberdeen, and for removing of such of the masters as had intruded themselves unwarrantably, and reponing those who, without just cause, were put from their offices.

That same day, an act was agreed upon, for discharging the frequent coming of persons of all sorts from Ireland to this kingdom, to the disturbance of the peace of the state and church; and appointing, that none be admitted who bring not passes, bearing their peaceable deportment to the government there established, from the lord chief justices, privy council, or mayors of towns where they reside, under the pain of imprisonment of their persons: and that until they procure such passes, they are to appear before the privy council at Edinburgh, and give surety for their peaceable deportment. This act is ordered to be published at Glasgow, Air, Wigton, and Kirkcudbright. I know no reason of this extraordinary prohibition, unless it was to prevent the retiring of the Scots presbyterians in the north of Ireland, to their native country, now when they are beginning to feel the fury of the prelates there.

February 27th, the commissioner presented a letter directed from his majesty to the parliament, approving all their former proceedings, and declaring that he is ready to give a general remission to all Scotsmen, (except such as the parliament shall except) for their bygone actings, against his royal father, or him. Which was read with great joy, and ordered to be recorded as a glorious testimony of the king's favour; and the commissioner is desired to return the humble acknowledgments and thanks of the house.

The reader may have some view of the procedure of this first session of parliament, from those hints; and for as arbitrary as a good many of the acts now passed will evidently appear, yet much heavier are a coming in the after parliaments. However, by those, one of the best formed civil establishments, and a most glorious ecclesiastical settlement, according to the rules of Christ in his word, were overturned, and a foundation laid for the bringing in of prelacy into the church, and arbitrary government to the state: This vast change in Scotland, was not brought about without some testimony given against it, which may be the subject of

SECT. II.

Of the efforts made by presbyterian ministers, for the preservation of the church during the sitting of the parliament; with some account of the violent treatment of synods, April and May, this year 1661.

ALTHOUGH the miserable rents in the church, the caution and cunning of the parliament's procedure, the fair professions made of a deep concern for those they called the honest ministers, and at length open force and violence upon the judicatories of the church, with some other causes, hindered what ought to have been done at such a critical juncture; yet several essays were made by ministers, to give such a testimony as their present ill circumstances would permit; and because what was then done is very little known, I shall give the larger account of it from well vouched narratives, and some original papers in my hands.

We have already heard that Mr. Robert Douglas, in his sermon before the parliament, dealt fairly with the members at the opening of the session. He was among the eldest ministers of the church, and of the greatest gravity and account; and having plainly warned them to do nothing against the work of reformation in this church, his freedom was not pleasing to the court, and neither he, nor almost any hearty presbyterians, were ever afterwards employed, especially after Mr. Wood and Mr. John Smith, had, in a little time thereafter, laid their duty freely before them. Timeservers and sycophants were afterwards employed, such as Mr. Hugh Blair at Glasgow, Mr. Paterson, and others, whose sermons were carefully printed, and speak for them to this day. Up and down the country, many ministers warned their people fully and faithfully of the evils coming in, and the dangers the church of Scotland was in hazard of, notwithstanding of the severe act, we have seen, was published against ministers' freedom in preaching, by the committee of estates. Mr. M'Ward at Glasgow used very much plainness this way, and was staged before the parliament therefore, as we shall hear.

1661.

Mr. William Guthrie, minister at Fenwick, in the shire of Ayr, used the greatest of freedom and sincerity in his sermons at this time. I am too nearly concerned in this great man, to say much about him, and therefore choose to give this in the words of a worthy minister, his contemporary, in his character of him. " In his doctrine Mr. William Guthrie was as full and free, as any man in Scotland had ever been; which, together with the excellency of his preaching gift, did so recommend him to the affections of people, that they turned the corn field of his glebe to a little town, every one building a house for his family upon it, that they might live under the drop of his ordinances and ministry." Indeed the Lord gave him an opportunity to bear a longer testimony against the defections of this time, than most of his brethren; till at length the malice of the archbishop of Glasgow turned him out in the (year) 1664, as we may hear. A good many ministers kept congregational fasts; and that was all almost they could do, since now there was scarce any opportunities of presbyterial or synodical appointments of this nature: and in some places where there were disaffected persons to delate them, ministers suffered not a little for this practice, and the plainness of their doctrine.

Somewhat likewise was endeavoured in judicatories. The ministers in and about Edinburgh, had the greatest opportunities of observing, and the earliest views of what was a doing, though the managers in parliament did their business as secretly and speedily as might be; and really much of the razing work was over before the minis-

1661. ters at any distance from the parliament had distinct accounts: therefore I choose to insert here the copy of an original paper, I have under Mr. Andrew Ker, clerk to the church, his attestation, formed at this time, as a narrative of the essays of the ministers who lay nearest the parliament, and might be supposed to have the greatest weight with the members at this juncture, for the benefit of the church. The title is,

Proceedings of some brethren, 1661.

" After the parliament was convened, January, 1661, some acts having passed, which occasioned great fears of some purposes to overturn, or weaken our discipline, and the work of reformation; therefore brethren of divers of the next presbyteries, finding it inconvenient to appear in any public way, contented themselves to correspond by some few, with some of the brethren of Edinburgh, who were using all fair means for preventing the evils feared.

" After frequent conference of those brethren of Edinburgh, with the earl of Middleton, his majesty's commissioner, and the earl of Glencairn, chancellor, about matters then in agitation, they being surprised with the passing of some acts, did present the lord commissioner's grace with the following overtures; humbly also desiring, that for security as to the future, there might pass a general ratification of the former acts for religion in doctrine and government."

A few overtures humbly offered for the good of his majesty's affairs, and settling the minds of good people, whose only aim and desire is, that under the shadow of his majesty's government, they may enjoy the ordinances of Christ, as they are established in purity and power.

" I. As to the oath tendered to all the members of parliament, it is humbly offered, that seeing those of the lieges who were in use to take that oath before, and may have it again tendered to them, will want that opportunity of his majesty's high commissioner, and a parliament sitting, to give the interpretation thereof, as was done to the members of parliament; therefore an interpretation thereof may be passed by act of parliament. There is no honest man, but will acknowledge the king's majesty supreme governor, not only in matters civil, but even in ecclesiastical, as to that power formally civil, competent to the christian magistrate about ecclesiastical affairs; and if it be declared by act of parliament, that the sense thereof is none other than what is asserted in the parliament 1592, explaining the act 1584, or in the late Confession of Faith, chap. 23. (which is believed to be the parliament's sense) it will remove fears and stumblings as to that particular.

" II. Whereas acts have passed relative to the constitution and legality of some meetings in this kingdom, in the time of the late troubles, wherein private subjects do not find themselves concerned to pry into the grounds and reasons of those proceedings; yet seeing the people may readily apprehend, that thereby " the solemn league and covenant," (entered into at that time) is annulled, which cannot but be a cause of great perplexity unto them, considering how they stand engaged in an oath of God, concerning a lawful thing, to which they were drawn by the representatives of the kingdom: therefore it is humbly offered, whether it will not much refresh the minds of people, and revive their perplexed spirits, if the parliament be pleased to declare their mind, that they intend not to annul or make void the obligation of the oath of God, under which the people lie?

" III. It is humbly conceived, that an act of parliament approving and ratifying the Confession of Faith, and Catechisms, and the Directory for Worship, approven by the assemblies of this kirk, and the discipline, government, and liberties of this kirk, and acts for suppressing popery and profanity, would remove the fears of sober and honest people, and (it is trusted) will be acceptable to his majesty, and exceedingly satisfy all his good subjects.

" Those overtures his grace and the lord chancellor promised to communicate to his majesty, and thereafter to give an answer to them; and for further security, desired the brethren to draw an act of ratification, as they would have it; and should be considered: which was accordingly done, and given to the lord commissioner, the tenor whereof follows:

Ratification of former acts of parliament, concerning religion, doctrine, worship, discipline, and government.

" Seeing it is a mercy never to be forgotten, that the Lord God, in his infinite goodness, hath been pleased wonderfully and unexpectedly, to bring about the restitution of his majesty to his throne, and the deliverance of this distressed kingdom from all that bondage and misery it was lately under, both as to spirituals and temporals, by the violence and prevailing of usurpers, and to make so universal a restauration, as is to be seen this day: and his majesty, in thankfulness to God for so great mercies, being desirous to employ that royal power and authority, which by divine providence he now enjoyeth, for the service and glory of God, and for countenancing, maintaining, and promoving the gospel of his Son Jesus Christ; therefore his majesty, with consent of the estates of parliament now convened, doth confirm and ratify the true religion professed, received, and practised within this kingdom, in doctrine, worship, discipline, and government, established by general assemblies, approven and ratified by acts of parliaments, particularly those following, viz. act 3. parl. 1. James VI. anno 1567, and act 99. parl. 7. James VI. in 1581, and act 114, parl. 12. James VI. in 1592, and acts 4, 5, 6. parl. 2. of his majesty's royal father of glorious memory, 1640, ratified in act 6. of the parliament held by his majesty's said royal father, in his own person, 1641, which acts, together with all other acts of parliaments made for establishing, maintaining, protecting and preserving the said true religion, in doctrine, worship, discipline, and government, professed, received, approven, and practised in this church; and for restraining and suppressing in this church and kingdom, all impiety, vice, profaneness, and whatsoever is contrary to truth and godliness; his majesty, with consent foresaid, doth approve, ratify, and renew, in all the heads and articles thereof: ordaining the said acts to be in full force, strength, and observance, according to the whole tenor thereof; and declares that no acts of this present parliament, are or shall be held prejudicial to the liberty, profession, exercise, establishment, and entire preservation of the said true religion, doctrine, worship, discipline, and government within this church and kingdom, or any ways derogatory to the authority and strength of the above said acts of parliament, approving and ratifying the same."

1661.

To this was added this brief memorial: " If the parliament 1649, be abrogate, and the acts thereof made void and null, it is humbly desired, that those acts following, which were passed in that year, may be renewed in this parliament, and by their authority enacted."

Session 2.

11th Act, against consulters with devils, and familiar spirits and witches, and consulters with them.

12th Act, against fornication.

16th Act, anent the Confession of Faith, and Catechisms, and ratification thereof.

19th Act, anent several degrees of casual homicide.

20th Act, against swearing, drinking, filthy speaking, &c.

22d Act, against clandestine marriages.

24th Act, against going of mills, kilns, saltpans, and fishing on the Lord's day.

28th Act, against blasphemy.

32d Act, against worshippers of false gods.

33d Act, against beaters and cursers of their parents.

45th Act, concerning manse and glebes.

Renovation of commission for plantation of kirks.

Session 3.

19th Act, for punishing incest.

It hath been remarked, that the parliament, after they had overturned our constitution by their principal acts above narrated, came in to two or three of these acts desired; but the act of ratification drawn at the commissioner's desire, and renovation of the rest, were neglected; and the ministers were kept in hopes, and got fair words, till

1661. matters were past hope. Indeed things were very cunningly managed, and the act rescissory was cast into several shapes, and given out to be a quite other thing, than afterwards it appeared to be, that ministers' appearances against it might be prevented: and by those blinds, and promises to advise with his majesty about the above mentioned reasonable proposals, matters were kept very smooth, until the day the rescissory act was tabled in parliament.

By a narrative under a minister's hand, at that time in Edinburgh, I find that as soon as the nature of the act rescissory came to be known, the presbytery of Edinburgh met, and framed a supplication to the commissioner and parliament, "craving that a new act might be made, for establishing of religion and church government, since they were informed the parliament were about to rescind the civil sanction and statutes in force, for the exercise thereof." The ministers were kept so much in the dark, as to the nature of the rescission projected, that they were necessitate thus to hold in generals, and to desire new laws to be made, when the old hedge was to be removed. I have insert * a copy of a supplication from the presbytery of Edinburgh to the parliament at this time, which I take to be that spoken of above. This supplication was sent to the commissioner, by three of their number they reckoned might be most acceptable, Messrs. John Smith, Robert Lawrie, and Peter Blair Partly by promises, and by threatenings, the commissioner prevailed with them, not to give in their supplication that day; and presently the parliament met, and in haste enough passed the rescissory act, from which a good many members dissented. When the ministers found themselves thus circumvented, to-morrow Mr. David Dickson and some others were sent by the presbytery to the commissioner, to insist in this affair. They were received very roughly, and Middleton told them, they were mistaken if they thought to terrify him with papers, he was no coward. Mr. Dickson replied, he well knew his grace was no coward, since the Bridge of Dee. This was an engagement, June 19th, 1638, when Middleton appeared very gallantly against the king's forces, for the covenanters. To this no answer was given, but frowns. The ministers, knowing there had been so many dissenters in parliament, from yesterday's vote, insisted much

---

* Petition of the Presbytery of Edinburgh.

Unto the king's commissioner, and the honourable high court of parliament, the humble petition of the Presbytery of Edinburgh.

When we reflect upon the sad times that have past over this church and kingdom, during the time of the late usurpers, what grief and affliction of spirit it has been to honest christians, and true countrymen, that their country has been kept in bondage, his sacred majesty driven into a sad disconsolate exile, our nobles and rulers scattered into corners, cast into the far countries, shut up into prisons at home and abroad, and trode upon by base and bloody men, and all our civil and religious concernments left under the feet of violent usurpers, and with what difficulties all honest men have wrestled, (whereof we, with others of the ministry, have had not a little share) which then laboured to keep their garments clean from the defections of the time, and to lament after the Lord, till he should in mercy visit us: we cannot, now when the Lord has returned our captivity, but be as men that dream, and our mouths filled with laughter, and our tongues with singing, the Lord having done great things for us, whereof we are glad; and as we looked upon it as a mercy never to be forgotten, that the Lord in his infinite goodness, has been pleased wonderfully to bring about his majesty's restoration to his throne, and the deliverance of this distressed kingdom, from all that misery and bondage under which it hath groaned; so it is our earnest supplication to God, that this so great a mercy may be improven by all ranks, to the honour of his great name, whose work this deliverance is, and to the good and comfort of this afflicted church and kingdom. We do, with all thankfulness to Almighty God, observe and acknowledge his mercy, who has restored our judges as at the first, and our counsellors as at the beginning, that our nobles are of ourselves, and our governors proceed from the midst of us: and that now your lordships are convened in this high court by his majesty's authority, and with the presence of his high commissioner, that you may be the repairers of the breaches, and may seek the wealth of your people, and may speak peace to all your seed. We have hitherto forborne to make any applications to your lordships, as being unwilling to interrupt you in your weighty and great affairs; yet since there is not a general assembly now sitting which might more freely represent what is of public concernment to the whole kirk, and might remove any grounds of jealousy which might be occasioned by the late actings during our troubles and distractions, being upon the place, and being unwilling to lose the opportunity of your lordships meeting in this present parliament, we do humbly offer unto your lordships, (when now we hope many of your affairs are over) what we conceive may be for the good of the church, as his majesty's gracious letter,

to have their supplication tabled, and read in public, and put the commissioner in mind of the resolutions he had come under, when he was under the prospect of death, and some sharp exercise of mind, at St. Andrews, 1645, to serve the Lord and his interests. It seems he was then in danger from an iliac passion. At this he turned petted, and said, What, do you talk to me of a fit of the colic? and would by no means allow their supplication, and draught of an act for ratification, to come in, and be read in parliament. After this, the presbytery sent their supplication to the king, but it was not regarded. This account leads me back again, to insert what follows in the paper I am inserting; the proceedings of some brethren, 1661.

"After the act rescissory was passed, there was given in to the clerk register a list of some acts of general and public concernment to the church, of new to be enacted; but few of them were taken notice of. Thereafter the brethren hearing more of purposes to alter the government established in this kirk, and that there had been some motion among the lords of the articles, for repealing the act of parliament 1640, ratifying the same, and for calling for the kirk registers; it was thought convenient, that, if it were possible, the whole state of the business were humbly represented to his majesty. To which effect, there was first sent to his secretary the earl of Lauderdale the letter following, and thereafter by another occasion in March, an information." Follows

1661.

Letter to the Earl of Lauderdale.

" My lord,

" It hath been the study of honest men here, to carry so peaceably and modestly, as bearing his resolution to provide and preserve the government of the church of Scotland, as it is settled by law, without violation, hath exceedingly gladdened the hearts of good men, as we understand by letters from the several presbyteries and synods, some directed to his sacred majesty or his secretary, or some directed to us by way of return thereunto, and did secure them against all fears in that particular, or any change; so it was expected that this high court of parliament would confirm and ratify the true religion, in doctrine, worship, discipline, and government, established by general assemblies, approven and ratified by acts of parliament. Yet notwithstanding thereof, your lordships have rescinded the act *anno* 1640 and 1641, whereby our government is to be cast loose, as to the civil sanction thereof, and the church in danger, to be laid open to these snares which formerly were troublesome and grievous to this church; therefore, whatever your lordships have done for the settling and securing the royal power and authority of our dread sovereign, (whose authority and power we do heartily acquiesce, and cordially submit thereto) or for securing the peace of the kingdom, in which we acknowledge none of them ought to oppose one another; yet we are very hopeful, and humbly supplicate, this high court of parliament will, by their civil sanction, establish, maintain, and defend the true religion, in doctrine, worship, discipline and government, presently professed, received, and practised, and restrain and suppress all impiety, vice, and profaneness, and whatsoever is contrary to truth and godliness. And whereas, through the iniquity of the times, and prevalency of the usurpers, the general assembly convened in *anno* 1653, was interrupted, and all meetings of general assemblies declined by us, out of our due respects to his majesty's just right and authority, upon which they would have been ready to have encroached upon such an opportunity, it is humbly desired your lordships would be pleased to move to his majesty, that, with the first conveniency, a free general assembly may be called, which may not only take care to compose and settle these sad and lamentable divisions which have been in the church, but also may recognosce upon these actings, which may be apt to give offence, during the time of the sad and unhappy troubles; and we may assure your lordships, that it is the purpose of honest men, when they shall convene in an assembly, to do what shall be found necessary for rectifying all disorders, and to redress whatsomever has been offensive. We shall not stand to press these our humble desires, by any arguments taken from the lawfulness or warrantableness, or necessity of the things themselves, or from your lordships' obligation to act for him who has so wonderfully restored you to sit in judgment, or from the consideration of ourselves, who with other honest men, have confidence to sympathize with the afflictions of our rulers and country, and have not been wanting, to our power and station, to act for the happy revolution, and are and shall be careful to promote his majesty's interest and authority, of which his people and we do assure your lordships, that, besides the convictions of the things desired, we have not been a little pressed to this humble address, by our tender regard and zeal towards his majesty's affairs; so our desire is, that the minds of God's people may be settled, whose only aim and desire is, that they, under the shadow of his majesty's government, may enjoy the ordinances of Christ in power and purity, as they are established, which will encourage all of us (as in duty we are always bound) to pray for his majesty's long and prosperous reign over us, and for the affluence of divine grace and blessings to be poured out upon his royal person and family, and upon your lordships and your families for ever.

Mr. PETER BLAIR, Moderator.
Mr. ROBERT HUNTER, Cl. *pro tempore*.

1661. might avoid all offence, and therefore they have not at all appeared publicly in matters of their very near concernment, but have contented themselves with some overtures, given in to some in private, which we find have come to your lordship's hands; yet they are not without fears that religion may suffer very much prejudice at this time, there being already some motions for repealing the act 1640, establishing presbyterian government, and abolishing episcopacy. The public registers of the church being called for to be perused by the clerk of register, or his majesty's advocate, (before an assembly be called, to redress by themselves what disorders have been during the ıeat of troubles) of purpose, as would appear, to render the government hateful, upon the account of some actings in times of distraction and animosity; if not also to render the body of honest men (who have been in those judicatories) obnoxious; so that there will be no difference betwixt those who have stood in the gap, for many years of sore trouble, and others.

" Those things lying so sad upon the spirits, not of a few only, but of all honest men, who have occasion to know of them, as they cannot see how that course contributes to the good of his majesty's affairs, more than to their particular satisfaction in conscience, and in pursuance thereof are using all prudent and fit means to prevent those feared dangers, by dealing with those who have power; so we could not omit to acquaint your lordship also with it, that by your prudent and effectual moving, somewhat may come from thence, to stop that course; lest otherwise it overspread, and not only involve them in hazard, who expected no such thing, (yea, are persuaded of his majesty's royal inclination to the contrary) but will bring prejudice to that which is more dear to them than any their particular and personal concernments, and provoke him to displeasure, who is a dreadful party.

" As to what concerns his majesty; honest men's sufferings, and their serious endeavours, by all duties proper to them in their stations, for his restitution, and their cordial rejoicing in the bringing about of so long desired a mercy, and their care to walk modestly when they are under so many fears, may, we hope, speak their loyalty. And as your lordship may perceive, by the overture given in, they are most clear in asserting his majesty's supreme power in all civil causes, and that the power formally civil about ecclesiastical affairs, which is competent to any christian magistrate, doth duly belong to him, and shall be cheerfully submitted unto, and acknowledged by every one of them. And what hath passed in the times of trouble, which hath been offensive, if a general assembly be called, and allowed freedom, (which is humbly and earnestly desired that it may be done with the first) they will be careful so to recognosce those proceedings (the religion established being always preserved) as may satisfy his majesty, and take away all cause of offence. And we think it will be more for his majesty's honour, that an assembly do it by themselves, (which is the real purpose of all honest men) than that others do it for them in a more violent way. Though probably the appearing of some few ministers now, of whom little hath been heard before, and the silence and modesty of others, may give ground to apprehend, that the change of our established government may be brought about, without difficulty or stop; yet your lordship may be assured, that honest men, fixed in their principles concerning religion, and sensible of the obligations that are upon their consciences, cannot but bear testimony against such a current of defection, as would involve us in the hazard of the divine displeasure. And though they have studied to walk modestly (and their resting upon his majesty's gracious letter, assuring them of no violation of the government, did much satisfy and secure them) yet to our knowledge, many presbyteries are ready to bear witness by supplication against the change of government, if it be attempted.

" Your lordship's zeal for the good of his majesty's affairs, your love to your mother church, and the ordinances of Christ in her, and your tender respects to many honest men who will suffer much, if not prevented, do persuade us, that you will interpose with his majesty for some speedy prevention of feared evils, by preventing any prejudice to the established government, and making effectual the desires propounded in the overtures, and the draught of an act sent afterward; by calling a general assembly, according to the animadversions humbly offered to your lordship upon the declaration concerning it; by causing forbear to meddle with the registers of the kirk, till the general assembly in the first instance take some course to set things in order, and by preserving honest men from inconveniences, who mind no other thing, but to get liberty to serve God according to his will, and their engagements, under his majesty's authority. Our confidence that your lordship doth seriously mind this so needful a work, makes us spare to use any motives. The little advantage it will afford to any lawful interest, (and we are sure the grief it will be to your lordship) to see honest and peaceable men, and a work of God in their hands, crushed, will be of weight to persuade you to endeavour to prevent it. And we not only hope, but are confident, that when it shall be considered, how much it will advance his majesty's affairs, that things be thus settled, to the satisfaction and comfort of all good men; it will be accounted special good service to his majesty, to promove so good a design. We are," &c.

Information, March 1661.

" After our manifold distractions, and grievous afflictions under the heavy yoke of usurping oppressors, it pleased the Lord in his free and undeserved goodness, to look upon our low condition, and to visit us with a gracious deliverance, by the wonderful and unexampled restitution of our dear and dread sovereign, the king's majesty, unto the throne of his three kingdoms, which was to us a resurrection from the dead, and a commanding of dry bones to return unto life again. This miracle of mercy the Lord accompanied with a refreshing shower upon his inheritance here, by moving the royal heart of his gracious majesty to make known to the presbyteries of this national kirk, his fixed purpose to preserve inviolable the government of the kirk here settled by law, whereby the hearts of all honest ministers were exceedingly encouraged to lay out themselves, unto the utmost of their power, in their stations, for advancing his majesty's interest in the affections of his people, which they were careful in the darkest times to hold up in their people's hearts.

1661.

" This assurance from so royal a hand, whose heart was inured to constancy through all his unheard of hardships, made all the lovers of the established order of this kirk rejoice in the Lord, and magnify his name for so rich a mercy, and promise unto themselves security from any trouble that might flow from the change of our kirk constitution, which is dearer to them than all their other enjoyments; and though they be somewhat startled by the rumoured noise of a designed change, and yet more by some hints at the removal of the law of the land, that establisheth the same, yet they cannot suffer it to enter into their hearts, that his majesty hath any knowledge of, or giveth any allowance to any change at all in the matters of our doctrine, worship, discipline, and government.

" Our single-hearted confidence upon that his majesty's gracious declaration, and our tenderness to do any thing that might savour of the least degree of distrusting the same, hath prevailed with honest ministers to keep silence, and not to make a noise by public addresses and supplications unto the high and honourable court of parliament, and to content ourselves with presenting private informations to my lord commissioner his grace: yet we would not have this to be interpreted as any diffidence of the cause, or as though we were willing to recede from the established government of this kirk, or were afraid to own the same in an orderly way.

" It is the earnest desire of all honest ministers, that after the parliament, there may be a general assembly called, according to the settled order of this kirk, wherein, they are confident, there will be an effectual course taken for remedying all the evils, and removing all the unsound principles, and irregular practices, which they know, and do acknowledge to have crept in during the late troubles and distractions. They are no less confident, that his majesty shall receive thereby all satisfaction in their hearty and

1661. cheerful attributing to his majesty all that any Christian prince can require in reason of dutiful subjects, reserving only to them the established doctrine, worship, discipline, and government.

"If there happen to be a change made in the settled government, (which the God of heaven forbid, and we are loath to allow ourselves the apprehension thereof, upon the account before mentioned), there is none likelier to taste so soon of trouble and vexation thereby, as some faithful ministers, who have been sufferers upon the king's interest, and have been active instruments in keeping it up in the hearts of people, in the darkest time of its eclipse, and were the main, if not the only men, that most withstood the practices and principles of such as opposed the same: therefore it is confidently expected, that his majesty will be graciously pleased, speedily to interpose himself, and forbid any change of kirk government, since he hath been well pleased to give hopes of a free general assembly, wherein all disorders may be redressed, and his majesty may receive all desirable satisfaction of this kirk's hearty affection to his royal interest and authority.

"It hath been the lot of faithful ministers in all times, to be misrepresented unto authority, and to be wronged by misinformation, under which we ourselves have laboured ere now, and therefore may fear that we are not now altogether free of the same, so long as we abide constant for the government of this kirk, which is our firm resolution in the strength of the Lord: but it is our comfort against this, that his majesty's princely disposition will not permit any such informations to take impression upon his royal heart, before he take due trial what truth is in them, and acquaint those that are concerned, that they may clear themselves.

"It is possible, reports may be going there, as if the plurality of ministers here, were hankering after episcopacy, and looking towards it: but we cannot imagine that such surmises will be believed by understanding men, who have any acquaintance with the state of this kirk, to which that corruption of government, and other corruptions in worship, whereto it made way, have been a burden, whereof they were most desirous to be freed, and which they will never willingly take on again, being now free from it, and engaged to the contrary, by the oath of God: yet lest it should take with any, we know and hear but of a very few, who have appeared to have a look towards that side, and those such as were not of great reputation in this kirk; and whatever they had, it is much diminished in the opinion of all that look indifferently on things, upon the very account of their warping off toward that way; and they are looked upon as men ready to shift their sails, that they may be before the wind, whatsoever way they conceive it is likely to blow. And we can further assuredly affirm, that the generality of the presbyteries of this land, have returned their hearty satisfaction with his majesty's letter, either to his majesty's secretary, or to the presbytery of Edinburgh; and we doubt not but the rest would have done the like, if the distance had not denied them the opportunity.

"It may be supposed by some, that it is good service to his majesty to overturn the government of this kirk, from the very foundations; but we humbly conceive that his majesty will have far other thoughts of the matter, not only on the account of his gracious declaration to the presbyteries of this kirk, but also because he doth undoubtedly esteem that to be the best service can be done to him, which doth most engage the affections of his subjects unto him, and endear his government unto them: for which there can be no more efficacious mean, than that they still enjoy the gospel of the Son of God, the purity of worship, and the simplicity of kirk government, which they do enjoy under the refreshing shadow of their lawful sovereign, and secured to them by his laws.

"There want not strenuous endeavours of some, to rake into all the proceedings of our kirk, in the times of heat and animosities, thereby to render the government hateful, notwithstanding that the judicatories of the kirk, have by their practices, those ten years bygone, witnessed, that whatever was done or declared in times of confusion, yet they were so far from judging those to be their principles, that upon a right understanding betwixt his majesty and his people, they were careful to rectify those things, and so to act for his majesty, and their country's service, as might witness their honest intentions and desires, even in the heat of debates. And when for this their fidelity and honesty, they have been all this while traduced by some among ourselves, as making defection from their principles, and they by their apologies and vindications have cleared their own integrity, it is hoped his majesty will not allow those things to be backtraced, at least till he hear them speak for themselves and their mother-kirk; and they are hopeful to wipe off all the aspersions and calumnies that are frequently and unjustly cast upon the kirk and honest men."

I am apt to think this information, and the papers I have been inserting, are of the reverend Mr. Douglas's drawing; and they savour much of his prudence and solidity. The reader will perceive those proposals are made, and such considerations and arguments used, as probably would have weight at this juncture, and with the persons he is dealing with; and this is all the length they could go in their immediate applications to the government, considering present circumstances. And had not the managers been resolved to please the high-fliers in England, to follow Mr. Sharp's ambitious designs, and carry through their project over all reason, gratitude, and justice, they could not have stood out against such plain and home dealing. Thus the reader hath some view of the efforts of the ministers of Edinburgh at this juncture, with persons mostly engaged.

By the time the synods met in April and May, the parliament were far through their work; now the keys were changed, and every reflecting person began to suspect the house was to be rifled; and so in all the corners of the church, ministers endeavoured to do somewhat, and great was the opposition they met with; which brings me to give some account of what was done by synods at this juncture, and their violent treatment, as far as narratives have come to my hand.

The synod of Glasgow and Ayr 1661. convened April 2d, and when they came to consider the present state of the church, they generally agreed, it was their duty, in this time of the church's danger, to supplicate the parliament; and accordingly a committee was named to form an address and supplication for a new security to religion and this church, when the old fences were fast removing. And Mr. William Guthrie read from the committee, a draft of an address, which was generally satisfying to the members, but the generality were overruled: some worthy men of the resolutioners, but especially such as were gaping after a bishopric, vehemently opposed the supplication, and threatened to dissent, such as Mr. James Hamilton, minister at Cambusnethan, afterward bishop of Galloway, Mr. Robert Wallace at Barnwell, afterward bishop of the Isles, and the correspondent from the synod of Lothian, Mr. James Ramsay, first dean of Hamilton, and afterward bishop of Dumblane. These gentlemen did not so much oppose the draft read, or petitioning in the general, as the seasonableness of supplicating in the present circumstances; and urged the synod's adjourning to a short and new diet. They alleged the west of Scotland was jealoused (suspected), and ill looked on by many in power; that they did not as yet know the practice of other synods, and so it would be much better to delay for a short time, till they saw what other synods did. Such as were for supplicating, could have easily outvoted them; yet considering that without harmony and unanimity, their address would lose much of its weight, they yielded to the adjournment of the synod for a month.

Meanwhile, as a present exoneration of their consciences, they agreed unanimously upon the following declaration, and none were more forward in it, than the members just now named, who in a few months became prelates.

Declaration of the synod of Glasgow concerning the present government of the church of Scotland, April 4th, 1661.

" Whereas there is a scandal, as if some ministers in this church, had made, or were intending to make defection from the govern-

1661. ment of the church of Scotland, to prelatical episcopacy; therefore the whole synod, and every member thereof, do willingly declare, that they are fixed in the doctrine, discipline, worship, and church government, by sessions, presbyteries, synods, and general assemblies, as it is now professed and practised within this church; and that they are resolved, by the grace of God, so to remain. And because divers of the members are absent, therefore the synod recommends it to the several presbyteries to require the same of them."

To this all the members present personally assented. The distinction of prelatical episcopacy, and the omitting of the obligation of the covenants, grieved many; and when this last was urged, Mr. James Hamilton threatened not to concur. Thus the desire of unanimity among themselves, made it pass *pro tanto*, and the synod adjourned unto the second Tuesday of May. At which time the ministers came to Glasgow. But when they were about to convene in the synod-house, they were discharged, in a proclamation from the cross, by orders from his majesty's commissioner, to meet, as being an adjourned meeting, and not warranted by law. Providence is just and righteous, in depriving of opportunities of doing good, when duty is not fallen into in its season. However, the ministers in town convened in Mr. Ralph Roger's house there, to consider what was fit now to be done; and after some deliberation they drew up, and commissioned three of their number to go to Edinburgh, with the following supplication and representation,

'*To his grace his Majesty's High Commissioner.*

"Humbly sheweth,

"That whereas your grace, for reasons best known to yourself, hath been pleased to interdict this adjourned meeting of our synod of Glasgow and Ayr, as illegal and unwarrantable by the laws of this kingdom; we judged it our duty, to testify the due respect we owe to the supreme magistrate, whom the Lord in his good providence hath set over us, to forbear, in obedience to your grace, his majesty's high commissioner, your inhibition, the constituting ourselves into a synod; yet lest we should be found wanting in the discharge of the duty we owe to our Lord and Master Jesus Christ, who hath given power to the ministers of the gospel to meet in their respective judicatories, as the edification of the congregations committed to their oversight doth necessarily require and call for; we also find it incumbent upon us, a considerable number of us, the members of this synod of Glasgow and Ayr, having come to meet in a synod, and being now occasionally in providence cast together, to signify to your grace, that as we are hopeful, whatever may be your grace's apprehensions of the inconveniency of our meeting at this time, it is not the intent of your grace's proclamation to declare that our synod can at no time warrantably meet, whatever be the necessity of the church within our bounds, but twice in the year: so we do humbly, and with all due respect and reverence to our sovereign, the king's majesty, and your grace his high commissioner, seriously testify, that our forbearing to meet in a synod at this time, in obedience to your grace's prohibition, doth not import our yielding that the provincial assemblies of this church have no provincial power to meet, when the edification of the church doth call for it, even oftener than twice a year. All which we have desired our reverend brethren, Mr. Patrick Colvil, moderator in our synod at the last meeting thereof, Mr. Hugh Blair, minister at Glasgow, and Mr. James Stirling, minister at Paisley, humbly to represent to your grace; which we persuade ourselves will not only not be offensive to your grace, but will be constructed a piece of necessarily called for exoneration of ministers of the gospel, who desire to be found faithful." Accordingly those three persons went to Edinburgh, and presented the minister's petition and representation to the commissioner, but had no return. And there were no more synods of presbyterian ministers in Glasgow, till September, 1687.

The provincial synod of Fife met likewise in the beginning of April, at St. Andrews; and the hazard of the church being very evident, they unanimously resolved to petition the parliament for a new act, ratifying religion, and the privileges of the church. The draft agreed upon follows.

To his grace his majesty's high commissioner, and the high and honourable court of parliament, the humble petition of the synod of Fife, convened at St. Andrews, April, 1661.

"That whereas the honourable court of parliament hath judged the parliaments, (thought to have been such) held in the years 1639 and 1640, to be null, and of no authority in themselves, and by this means, all acts ratifying the reformed religion, as it is now received, professed, and practised in this kirk and kingdom, in all the parts and heads thereof, viz. doctrine, worship, church government, and discipline, and rescinding all acts of preceding parliaments, contrary to some parts of the reformed religion, particularly some matters of the worship of God, and government of the church, as all other acts therein made, are become void, and of no force; so those acts of former parliaments, by those acts now made void, are *ipso facto* revived and restored to the authority of standing laws. And albeit it be not competent to us, and is very far from our thoughts to judge of the validity, or invalidity of any parliament, or acts of parliament, this being a thing properly belonging to his majesty and the high court of parliament; yet being, by clear convincing light, persuaded in our consciences, that the reformed religion, in all the parts of it, doctrine, worship, government, and discipline, received, professed, and practised at present within this kirk and kingdom, is grounded upon, and warranted by the word of God revealed in the holy scripture; and knowing how great a mercy and blessing it is to the church of Christ, that true religion, in the profession and practice thereof, be ratified, confirmed and established by the authority and laws of the magistrate, who is the nursing father of the church, and protector of religion; and that there be no laws of his standing against the true religion, in any part thereof: wherefore we find ourselves bound, with all loyal and humble submission of heart to his sacred majesty's authority, and his high and honourable court of parliament, to supplicate and beg, for the Lord's sake, that your grace his majesty's high commissioner, and this high court of parliament, may be pleased to enact now a law, ratifying, confirming, and establishing the reformed religion, at present received, professed, and practised in this kirk and kingdom, in doctrine, worship, government, and discipline, which will not be unacceptable to our dread sovereign, the king's majesty, as we are hopeful, having had by his majesty's letter to the presbytery of Edinburgh, a declaration of his gracious resolution concerning this matter. It will be a refreshing mercy to the people of God in this kingdom, and procure from them abundant praises unto God, and prayers for blessings from heaven upon your lordship, and will exceedingly enlarge the hearts of us who are ministers of Christ, to teach, instruct, and exhort the people of God within our charge, to all loyalty and obedience to his majesty, all submissiveness and subjection to his government, and obedience to all having authority from him; which also we are resolved to exhort them to, and to practise ourselves, by the Lord's grace, however it shall be with us, and whatsoever exercise it shall please the Lord to put us to."

Jointly with this supplication, the synod designed a warning and admonition to the people under their charge; wherein, after a full declaration of their loyalty to the king, and their abhorrence of the English usurpation, they show their resolution of standing by the doctrine, worship, government, and discipline of the church, declare against prelacy, and admonish their people to be constant in God's way, and to be much in repentance. They were not permitted fully to finish this paper; but the draft of it, as it came from the committee, to which, no doubt, the synod would have agreed, with very little alteration, I have inserted below.*

1661.

---

* A seasonable word of necessary exhortation and admonition, by the synod of Fife, convened at St. Andrews, the 2d of April, 1661, to all the people of God within their charge.

Many and divers have been the temptations and trials of the church of God, from the beginning even unto this day, our holy Lord, in his wisdom, ordering all these things for manifesting those that are approved, for clearing of his truth, purging of his house from

1661. Before the synod had formally voted the supplication, and finished the warning, they were interrupted by the earl of Rothes, in the king's name. Him the commissioner had appointed inspector, visitor, or commissioner, I do know what name

dross and corruption, exercising his servants and people in a holy contending for truth and piety, against the speat (flood) of evils that hath been always running in the world, and for the greater advancement of the glory of his power and goodness, in preserving and giving outgate in end to his afflicted people tossed with tempest. And now (right worthy, and dearly beloved in the Lord) the concernments of religion, and the work of God in this land, being under apparent hazard, sad trials likely to ensue, unless the mercy of God, and piety and justice of our dread sovereign, using his authority for God, avert the same, we were most unfaithful, if we should not at such a time (when prelacy, with the dangerous attendants thereof, (of which this church hath had sad experience) is like to be introduced again amongst us) declare our constant resolutions, according to the tie that lies upon us, by the authority of God, and our engagements to him, and give timeous warning to you the people of God, to keep your garments clean, and that ye may not be led away to any measure of accession to these evils, whereunto many may be turning aside. We know perfectly, that in our so doing we shall not escape the common lot of faithful humble contenders for the truth, and be represented as intending reflections on the lawful authority God hath set over us, or as going about to raise jealousies and disaffections in the people towards them, or to move sedition and trouble; and it may fall out that none be more ready to cast black colours upon our actions, than men of our own order and rank. In giving this our faithful admonition and declaration, we have laid our account with all that such persons can load us with, and much more, being confident, that the constant tenor of our deeds hath sufficiently wiped, and shall wipe off all such unjust aspersions. We have our witness in heaven, and a witness every one of us within us, how much our souls did long to have our present sovereign established upon the throne of his kingdom among us, (after the horrible barbarous murder of his royal father, of blessed memory, by the English sectaries) and it is great joy to our hearts, that God blessed us with fidelity to the king's majesty, in a very dark and dangerous time, in the year 1650, when we, with other faithful subjects through the land, followed our duty to his majesty, when our land was half subdued, and the rest under the saddest pressures; and we bless God that at that time, and until this day, we have not been following after the unwarrantable principles and practices of sundry in this land, not a little injurious to his majesty's just right. It is also our joy, that under ten years' bondage, neither the real cruelty, nor seeming civilities of usurpers, have prevailed to debauch our loyalty to our dread sovereign, in whose absence we sat on the ground, as a widow mourning for the loss of her husband. In our darkness we wished for the dawning of that day, when the Lord shall bring back our captivity, and restore our sovereign, that under his shadow we might rest; and how greatly we were affected with that signal work of God, (who is wonderful in counsel, and excellent in working) in that happy restoration of his majesty, what praises were rendered to God with signal cheerfulness, will not soon be forgotten by the Lord's people. But our hearts were more confirmed in loyalty, when, at our last meeting, we received his majesty's gracious letter to the presbytery of Edinburgh, to be communicated : a letter worthy to be engraven in marble or in gold, wherein his majesty declares himself not only well satisfied with the carriage of the generality of the ministers of Scotland, in the time of trial; but also, to prevent jealousies which any might create in the minds of well-meaning people, is pleased to give us assurance, that, by the grace of God, his majesty resolves to discountenance profanity, and all contemners and opposers of the ordinances of the gospel, and to protect and preserve the government of the kirk of Scotland, as it was then settled by law, without violation. Which letter, so graciously sent to us by our sovereign, preventing our desires to express his royal resolution, as to the maintenance of the work of God amongst us, we look upon and esteem as a kind of *magna charta*, given by our gracious king for our church-order and privileges. And as in our letter, directed from us at our last meeting, to his majesty's noble secretary for Scotland, to be humbly presented in our name to his majesty's own hands, we did express our sense of God's mercy to us, in putting such a thing into the king's heart; so shall we be most loath to suffer such thoughts to take place in our hearts, as if so pious and royal a resolution were to be altered upon any instance whatsomever; and we would count it a most undutiful part in us, to be ready to suggest or express to the people of God, the subjects of the king, any fears of that sort: but as our loyalty in former times hath appeared, so we trust that our carriage upon all occasions, shall argue in us indelible evidences of unstained loyalty and love to our sovereign, whom we honour as a man next unto God, inferior to none but God, who is his only judge, invested by God with a peerless supremacy over all persons and ranks of persons, within his majesty's dominions, the chief nurse-father of the church, and keeper of both tables of God's law, the sovereign protector and defender of the worship and ordinances of God, God's vicegerent, sent by him to bear the sword, with imperial power to punish all evil deeds, and evil-doers trespassing against religion and piety, or moral honesty, and duties that man doth owe to man, and to put every one in his dominions to the doing of their duty to God and man, the supreme civil governor of all persons, and in all causes civil and ecclesiastic; though the power of the keys of spiritual government belongs to the officers of the church, appointed by Christ: in a word, we do willingly yield whatsoever that pious and learned divine, Dr. Usher, attributes to the king, in the exposition of the oath of supremacy, for which he was solemnly thanked, in a letter yet extant in print, by that learnedest of princes, king James of blessed memory, who knew the bounds of royal supremacy, as well as any king on earth : no less do we acknowledge to be due to our sovereign lord king Charles, that we

to give to this new and erastian usurpation, to watch over the actings of that synod; and he came in, while they were in the midst of their business, and commanded silence in the king's name, and required them to insist no more upon what

1661.

---

may for ever stop the mouths of these who seek occasion against us in this matter, and may clear our loyalty as with a sunbeam. And we appeal to the great God, in the point of hearty loyalty to our sovereign, though we dare not (and we know he wills us not) in the least thing depart from the known mind of our God, in the matters concerning his house and worship. And having premised this as a guard against mistakes, we aver it to be the true zeal of our hearts, towards the matters of our God, his house and worship, that hath laid a necessity on us thus to declare ourselves, and to admonish the people of God in our charge, without any intention of wronging lawful authority, whom, if in any thing to be enjoined, we cannot please with active obedience, we hope they will be pacified by our passive obedience, which we resolve to yield, as our God calleth us, rather than to sin against him. Therefore, we declare to you the Lord's people in our charge, whom he hath appointed us as ministers to instruct, that we are convinced, that prelacy of any one, with majority of power and jurisdiction over presbyteries and churches, hath no warrant from Christ in his written word, which we are persuaded is a perfect sufficient rule of religion, holding forth all the fundamentals of church government, whereunto belong the offices and officers, by which the Lord's people are to expect his blessing; it being certain and undoubted, that no spiritual efficacy can be in faith expected by any office in the church, or any other religious ordinance, but that which is appointed by God in his word, but is contrary thereto, it being evident that our Lord Jesus Christ hath discharged and inhibited all such majority among the ministers of his church, having committed the whole parts of the spiritual government thereof, to one united company of rulers, and never to one alone; neither did his apostles, when they are purposely mentioning, in their writings, the officers given by Christ to his church, ever make mention of any such prelates over many pastors and churches, nor of his priority and power, or work, as distinct from the presbyters; but do always speak of the presbyter and bishop, as of one office under divers names. And it being so that this office hath no footing in divine scripture, it ought to be refused and rejected by those who know themselves to be bound to follow the rule, not of human but of divine wisdom, in the government of the church of Christ. And although those who stand in opposition to us in this point, do make a great noise (to amaze the simple) about antiquity, and the primitive times of the churches and fathers, as if they all stood on their side, it ought not to stumble the people of God, seeing that (were it so) christian consciences, wanting the warrant of the word to bottom faith upon, can have no consistency nor establishment upon human constitutions; and yet we dare plead with them at the bar of purest antiquity, nearest the times of the apostles, whilst the church remained a chaste virgin, and are confident, that for some hundreds of years after the apostles, there is no evidence of such a bishop as we reject and plead against; and from history we can make appear, that there was no such bishop in our own church, more than three hundred years after receiving of the christian religion among us; but whenever that office did creep in, we are bold to affirm, as our Lord said in another case, it was not so from the beginning.

2. Next, we declare to you our dear people, our own resolutions, by the strength of divine grace, to adhere constantly, all the days of our life, to the doctrine, worship, and present government of the kirk of Scotland, by presbyteries, without the foresaid prelacy in any degree, under the name of a constant moderator, or what else soever, which we have renounced upon the strongest enforcements of scripture authority upon our consciences, and are in that matter under an indispensable tie of a solemn oath to God; and although we cannot, for our conscientious resolutions, expect trouble, being under the protection of so gracious a sovereign, (to whom we would not doubt to justify the sincerity of our hearts, in cleaving to that which is good, had we the opportunity to represent our faithfulness to God, and loyalty to his majesty) yet, however, in this our distance from his majesty, we should meet with extremities in our duty, we shall with quietness commit ourselves and cause to him that judgeth righteously, resolving, in so honourable a cause, to endure, through God's strength, whatsoever trial and hardship it may please the Lord to exercise us with.

3. We do, in the name of the Lord Jesus, exhort you the people of God in our charges, (which we shall also endeavour, through grace, for our parts) speedily to renew our repentance for our unthankfulness under the means of grace, neglect and contempt of the gospel, ungospel-like conversation, for the which the Lord may justly remove all his gospel ordinances from us, and plague us with sundry sorts of judgments, pursuing us as dry stubble, until we were consumed. As also we entreat that ye would stand fast to the profession of the truth of Christ, and to every part of it, and to love the order of the house of Christ, which is so well grounded on his word, and tends so much to the advancement of godliness, and the glory of God, not making light accounts of that which is a part of the truth of the gospel and of the kingdom of Christ, after the lukewarm indifferency of too many, in the holy things of God. We are persuaded better things of you, than that ye should be removed from your steadfastness, after the shining of so much light, after so strong engagements to the Lord: what horrible guiltiness should this draw on us? How great should our infamy be among all the churches of Christ? Whether should we not cause our shame to go for our unsteadfastness in the solemn oath of God which is on our spirits, in a matter not only lawful, but also necessary for us to adhere to, having so much light in it? Remember how dangerous backsliding is; what better fruits can be looked for from that way of government than appeared among us? How loath are we to suffer it to enter in our hearts, that this land

1660. was before them, and immediately to depart. Obedience was given, and they dismissed themselves presently. The case was new, they were perfectly surprised, and in confusion; but it was matter of regret to many of them afterwards, that they had not protested against so plain an invasion of the liberties of Christ's house. *

The synod being thus violently raised, the presbyteries at their first meeting did approve of what they got not finished in synod; and all of them, in a very solemn manner, did record, and declare their adherence to the principles of this church, in their several presbytery books. I have only seen an extract of the declaration to this purpose, by the presbytery of Cupar; probably they were all much of a piece, and so I insert it here.

At Cupar, April 18th, 1661.

" The brethren of this presbytery, after serious consideration of a grievous scandal, raised upon the ministers of Scotland, as if they were falling from their steadfastness in the reformed religion, and inclinable to desire, endeavour, or embrace the introducing again of the renounced, abjured, prelatical government, with its unwarrantable attendants, have thought it our duty to express our sense and judgment thereof, in sincerity of heart, as becomes the servants of God, and in his presence; and accordingly all and every one of the brethren, severally, and with one consent, profess, as in the sight of God, that we are thoroughly persuaded, and fully satisfied in our consciences, by the clear light of the scriptures of God, touching the divine truth of the reformed religion, as it is at present, and hath been for divers years, received, professed, and practised in the church of Scotland, in doctrine, worship, government, and discipline; and that we are convinced in our consciences, that prelacy of any one, with majority of power and jurisdiction over presbyteries and churches, under the name of constant moderator, or any other name or notion whatsomever, hath no warrant from Jesus Christ in his written

---

shall make the fruit of their loosing from ten years' bondage, a shakeloose of the government of Christ? or, that good patriot or people, will embrace that which hath been so bitter to themselves and their antecessors? How sad a thing will it be to lie in chains of our own making, and in end conclude with the simple repentant, *non putaram*? Be exhorted to avoid that evil of prelacy, and all attendants to it, under whatsoever colours, as ye would have the Lord regard you.

4. Finally, we exhort you to all loyalty and obedience in the Lord, to our sovereign the king, not only for wrath, but for conscience' sake, and to due obedience to all who have authority from him, judicatories and persons. We have the Lord to be our witness, that neither the matter of our present administration, nor our purpose, hath any tendency to make trouble; we have done this merely for our own exoneration, and with respect to your good and the honour of Christ. The Lord establish you with us, by his free spirit.

* This pusillanimous conduct on the part of the members of this synod, as well as that of many others, forms a melancholy contrast to what had been the practice of the ministers of the Scotish church, on almost all former occasions of a like kind; and the apology offered for them by our historian, we cannot but regard as ill-timed and not at all corresponding with the fact of the case. It was unhappily no new thing in Scotland, for the government to interfere with ministerial freedom, and the liberties of the church in almost every possible form. James VI. of wisdom-affecting and power-loving memory, left nothing in this respect for any of his successors to achieve, having through a long life, maintained an unceasing struggle with them, from the pulpit up to the council board, and from the general assembly down to the kirk session; but he was grappled with, by the Blacks, the Bruces, the Calderwoods, the Davidsons, the Melvilles, and the Johne Rosses of that day, in a very different manner, than his grandson was now by the synod of Fife. The truth of the matter seems to be, that the Covenanters generally cherished throughout a romantic attachment to Charles II., and were exceedingly reluctant to change their opinion of him; while the greater part of the ministers of the church of Scotland, and the synod of Fife in particular, in their zeal against Cromwell, and the sectaries as they were called [the independents], and the remonstrators, had wrought themselves into a state of phrensy, under which they had so committed themselves that now they dared not utter a word in defence of their own principles, lest it might be interpreted as favouring the notions of these now totally proscribed classes, the tide of prejudice against which they had weakly contributed to swell, and so intemperately united to condemn. This, while it has excited painful regret among all who have been friendly to their cause, has often drawn forth the bitterest sarcasm from their enemies; and it must be confessed gave too good ground for the bitter taunt of the gossipping Burnet, when speaking of their submitting to the managements of the traitor Sharp, after his character was manifested to all the world. "The poor men were so struck, with the ill state of their affairs, that they either trusted him, or at least seemed to do it, for, indeed, they had neither sense nor courage left them."—Burnet's History of his Own Times, Edin. ed. vol. i. p. 171.—*Ed.*

word, to be received in his church : and we do from our hearts the more abhor and detest any motion or purpose of apostatizing to that way; not only because of many sinful errors in doctrine, and corrupt practices in worship, which formerly did, with and by the foresaid prelacy, creep into this church; but also because of the sacred and indispensable ties of the oath of God thereanent, under which we are before the Lord. And further, we all declare, that we are not a little encouraged and strengthened in this our duty, and comfortably borne up against the fear of sinistrous designs, in prejudice of the present government of the church, by that refreshing declaration of our sovereign, the king's majesty, in his letter directed to the presbytery of Edinburgh, and by them to be communicate to the rest of the presbyteries of this church, dated at Whitehall, August 10th, 1660, of his royal resolution, to protect and preserve the government of the church of Scotland, as it was then established by law, without violation, and to countenance, in the due exercise of their functions, all such ministers who shall behave themselves dutifully and peaceably; which also we purpose, in the Lord's strength, carefully to endeavour. All which the brethren present unanimously consented unto, and ordained to be recorded in the presbytery register, *ad futuram rei memoriam*."

In other parts of the church ministers were not idle, when their all was at the stake; but generally they were interrupted by those whom the managers named for commissioners and inspectors ; and it would seem some such were directed to every suspected synod; an office never before used, and I hope shall never more be tried. Upon the north side of Tay, they had no great fears of public appearances against their procedure; but on the south of it, they had their spies in most synods, clothed with, I do not know, whose or what authority. 1 can find no act of parliament constituting them, nor any commission from the king; yea, from the forecited account of the proceedings of parliament, I find, March 28th, " there was likewise presented and agreed unto, a paper, bearing, that ministers shall have power to exerce their ministerial functions in pro-

vincial assemblies, presbyteries and sessions, during the king's pleasure." 1661.
And I cannot guess how they came to be set up, unless it was by the paramount power of the commissioner, exerting his privilege in his commission, by Mr. Sharp's importunity, to do whatever the king might do, if present.

At Dumfries, the synod was upon the same design with that of Fife, and had agreed to an act, censuring all ministers who complied with prelacy, by deposition; but they were interrupted, and summarily dissolved by Queensberry and Hartfield, pretending orders from the commissioner. I find it remarked, that they were both miserably drunk, when they came in to their work.

The synod of Galloway met this same month, and were drawing up a petition to the parliament, against episcopacy, and for the preservation of the liberties of this church, (and under all regular governments, subjects are allowed humbly to supplicate) the copy of which is added. * But when at this, the

---

* Supplication of the Synod of Galloway, against the intended change of government, 1661.
May it please your honours,
We the ministers of Jesus Christ, within the synod of Galloway, laying seriously to heart the wonderful mercies of God, manifested from time to time to this poor nation, first, in the days of our forefathers, many hundred years ago, in which time, a little after the rising of the Sun of righteousness to give light to the gentiles, the Lord was graciously pleased to visit this land with the light of the glorious gospel, and to bless and honour the whole nation, both with purity of doctrine and government, for sundry generations together: During which time, until the incoming of Paladius, ordained bishop by pope Celestine, the Scots knew not such a thing as a prelate-bishop, but had, for the teachers of the faith, administers of the sacraments, and exercisers of discipline, presbyters only, (called culdees, or colidei, because of their piety) of whom some were appointed overseers or superintendents, but had no pre-eminence or rank of dignity above the rest, neither were they of any distinct order from the rest of their brethren. Next, in the days of our fathers, when the nation was involved in the darkness of popish superstition, and idolatry, it graciously pleased the Lord to ransom the land from the bondage of popish tyranny and superstition, and again to bless it with the light and liberty of the gospel, and with discipline and government established according to the pattern showed in the mount: the beautiful lustre of which glorious reformation, remained for many years unstained, until some ambitious and covetous men-pleasing churchmen, imboldened with the smiles of authority, not only marred and eclipsed the beauty and glory of

1661. earl of Galloway came in, and in the king's name dissolved their meeting. The moderator of the synod, Mr. John Park, author of the excellent essay upon patronages, modestly, and yet very pointedly, protested against the encroach-

Christ's government by presbytery, but almost overthrew the government itself, in obtruding upon it, and setting over it a lordly government in the persons of prelates. Which course of defection, to the great grief of the godly, and not without the constant reluctancy, counteracting, protesting, and witnessing of the most learned and faithful pastors in the land to the contrary, was tyrannically carried on for the space of thirty-eight years or thereby. Yet, in the third place, even in our own day, the outgoings of the Lord, in the year 37, and the years following, has appeared so glorious and conspicuous, to the dashing and execrating of that lordly prelacy, and to the replanting and re-establishing of Christ's own government by presbytery, in its integrity, that it were superfluous for us to make mention of these things, which many of your lordships' eyes have seen, wherein many of your lordships have been honoured to be eminent actors, and whereof all our hearts have been joyful and glad. The serious consideration of these things, speaking the Lord's unwillingness to depart, fixes a strong (and we trust) well grounded persuasion on our spirits, that our covenanted Lord has thoughts of peace, and not of evil, towards this poor land, so often, so deliberately, so seriously, and so solemnly, by oath and covenant, engaged to the most high God, and that he will be graciously pleased to fix his tabernacle amongst us, and rest in his love: and though on the contrary, he should, in his righteousness, threaten a departure from us, and denounce also wo unto us when he departeth from us, (the fears whereof, as swelling waves, overwhelm the spirits of the Lord's people at this present time, who, for the most part, are trembling under the sad apprehensions of a change) yet the thoughts of his ancient and late love to this land, should persuade all, in their respective stations, to lay hold on the skirts of his garments, and not to let him go: and therefore, the earnest desire of our hearts is, to plead in secret with the Lord, that he would mercifully preserve his staves of beauty and bands, in their beauty and strength amongst us: so (Christ commanding, necessity urging, and duty calling for it at our hands, to be faithful office-bearers in the house of God) we trust that it will not be offensive to your lordships, that (keeping within our own sphere, and holding ourselves within the bounds of that christian moderation which becomes godliness) we do in all humility exhort your honours, that with all singleness of heart, with all love and zeal to the glory of God, with all tender compassion to this yet panting kirk, faintly lifting up the neck from beneath the yoke of this late exotic tyrant of perfidious men, that with all pious respect to your posterity in the generations to come, whose souls will bless your remembrance, for transmitting a pure reformation to them, and that with all prudent and christian regard to prevent the stumbling, and provoke the holy emulation of the nations round about, whose eyes are upon your lordships, ye would see unto the exact and faithful keeping of the engagements, oaths and vows of the Lord, lying on your lordships and the whole land, to preserve the reformed religion in the church of Scotland, in doctrine, worship, discipline, and government, against all the enemies thereof: and that the Lord's people, his majesty's loyal subjects, may be delivered from the present fears of a change, which they are groaning under, we humbly supplicate your lordships would be pleased to ratify all former acts of parliament, in favours of the reformed religion in this church, in doctrine, worship, discipline, and government: and that, as his majesty has been pleased, in his gracious letter directed to the presbytery of Edinburgh, and by them to be directed to the rest of the presbyteries in this kirk, to declare his resolution to protect and preserve the government of the church of Scotland, as it is settled by law, without violation; so your lordships would be pleased to declare your fixedness to the present settled government, without the least purpose of ever altering the same, or overcharging it with lordly episcopacy: and that (besides the considerations already hinted at) for the reasons following, partly relating to the *terminus a quo* of such a change, which we pray the Lord to avert, partly relating to the *terminus ad quem*, and partly relating to the change itself.

First, If your lordships will consider the *terminus a quo* of this change we supplicate against, to wit, the government of the church of Scotland by presbytery; First, It is the true government of Christ's kirk, who being faithful to him that appointed him, yea, and faithful as a Son over his own house, Heb. iii. 2, 6. has not left his house to confusion, without government, but has appointed the same as to be fed by doctors and pastors, so to be overseen and ruled by seniors or elders, in their lawful assemblies in Christ's name, where he has promised to be in the midst of them; the whole platform of which government, erected in Christ's church in this nation, as to all the essentials, is so clearly warranted in the holy scriptures, that we may confidently say, it is the only government according to that pattern showed in the mount.

Secondly, Albeit in the reformation of religion, whether in doctrine, worship, discipline, or government, the example of the best reformed churches is not to be contemned, but to have its due respect; yet we have good ground to assert, that the present government of the church of Scotland by presbytery, was not inconsiderately borrowed from any other as the pattern, nor headily obtruded on this kirk, (a calumny frequently cast on our government by the adversaries thereof (but that it is the fruit of the many prayers, and the result of the faithful pains and labours of our pious predecessors, who, by the space of six or seven years, did, in free and full assemblies, deliberately debate every point and article of the said government and discipline, and so did in end, by the good hand of God upon them, determine and conclude the same according to the word of God, by the common votes and uniform consents of the whole assembly of this church.

Thirdly, This government, clear in scripture, deliberately closed with by our progenitors, has

CHAP. II.] OF THE CHURCH OF SCOTLAND. 125

ment made upon the judicatory, and took instruments in the hand of their clerk, to which all the members adhered. Mr. Park protested against what was done, as an injury to a court of Jesus Christ, and incompetent to the civil magistrate. And

1661.

now been frequently engaged unto, both, in the days of our forefathers, by the king's majesty, the nobles, and all ranks of people within the land, (whose national oath is no less obliging of us their offspring, than the oath of Joshua and the princes of Israel to the Gibeonites, was obliging of their posterity, who were four hundred years thereafter dreadfully punished for the breach thereof,) and also in our own time we have solemnly engaged ourselves by the sacred oath of God, now thrice, to the said government: and we may be sure, that such a threefold knot and tie will not be easily taken off the conscience upon which it is indispensably and indissolvably fastened by the divine authority of that Almighty God, the searcher of all hearts, whose oath it is.

Fourthly, This government has been ratified and established by many acts of parliament: it were impertinent for us to multiply citations; your honours know how clear and full the 114th act, parl. 12th, of king James VI. is, both for establishing the government and discipline of the church, by assemblies national and provincial, by presbyteries and sessions, and also, for abrogating, cassing, and annulling all former acts of parliament, against the liberty of the true kirk, the jurisdiction and discipline thereof, as the same was used and exercised within the realm at the time, anno 1592. Neither is it needful to mention his late majesty, of worthy memory, his ratifying, anno 1641, the whole progress then made in the work of reformation, which was matter of much joy to all the godly within the land.

Fifthly, This government has been attended with rich spiritual blessings, such as purity of doctrine, the suppressing of popery, error, and heresy, the curbing of licentiousness and profanity, by the prudence and zealous exercise of discipline: so that it has been remarkable, that in all the periods of the flourishing of this government, the pulpits have sounded with pure doctrine, speaking the language of Canaan, and not of Ashdod; gross profanity and mocking of piety retired from the streets, and durst not keep the causey (the generality studying at least, if they attained no more, to walk civilly) and popery, error, and heresy, at such times, durst never adventure to look out of their cells and secret corners; which things are no small mercies to a land.

On the other hand, if your lordships will respect *terminus ad quem* of this feared, threatened, and begun change, to wit, lordly episcopacy: first it is a plant which our heavenly Father never planted, here being no ground nor footing for it in the word of God, even some of the ablest asserters of it themselves being judges. Secondly, After the extirpation of it in the times of reformation, its regress has never been fair, but always through violent intrusion, by the force and fraud of corrupt carnal men, minding their own things, and not the things of Christ, and that contrary to law, reason, equity, conscience, solemn oaths and engagements, and clear scripture light. Thirdly, It is a government that we are solemnly bound, as by the law of God, so by the oath of God upon us, to extir-

pate from the foundation. Fourthly, It is a government that symbolizes with that in popery, and indeed is not different specie from the popish government; yea, and by the erecting of it, the papists will be hardened and heartened, as formerly, in the flourishing of episcopacy, they evidenced themselves to be, by their insulting song, Ye come to us, but we come not to you; and, to speak truth, what difference is there betwixt an archbishop in St. Andrews, pooping it over all Scotland, and an universal bishop at Rome, but a *majus* and *minus, quæ non variant speciem?* Fifthly, It has been always attended in this land with manifold corruptions in doctrine, worship, and manners. How did popery, *Arminianism* and *Socinianism* sound in our pulpits? Was it not in time of lordly episcopacy? Then it was that the pure worship of God was polluted with the mixture of man's muddy inventions, with mimic gesticulations, idolatrous geniculations, superstitious cantings, &c. Then it was that episcopal licenses in the matter of marriage to blank persons, that episcopal connivances at the grossest of scandals, and episcopal simony in selling the ordinances, and satisfactions, made way and opened the door to the slight esteem and profane contempt of the Lord's ordinances, and to bold licentiousness. Let the legend of the bishops, their life and their government, be looked back to with an impartial eye, we are confident it will be acknowledged that the raking them out of the dust, will prove like the breaking up of graves, and opening up of rotten sepulchres. Sixthly, Albeit we lay no weight upon the fallacious arguing, from the accidental corruptions in government, to the eversion of the same, (a calumny most falsely cast upon the instruments of the glorious work of reformation anno 38,) yet, as they having first struck at the root of episcopacy, because not rooted in the word of God, did, in the next place, look upon the sinful and judicial corruptions attending it, as *gravamina intolerabilia*; so we being convinced of the unwarrantableness of the episcopal office, may desire your lordships to call to mind what was the high swelling pride, and the insolent actings of these persons, who in this nation entered in that office, not only in lording it over their brethren and the Lord's inheritance, but also in their presumptuous browbeating the nobles in the land, and in their ambitious, both aspiring unto, and screwing themselves in the highest places of public trust in the state. 'Which things we look upon not only as having been the effects of the men's corrupt hearts, but as having been likewise the effects of the righteous judgment of God upon their spirits, for entering in that office contrary to the oath of God lying on them and the whole nation. Neither need any to think that they may be now better bounded and regulate: caveats will not fetter them, they will soon prove like the princes of Judah, that remove the bound; and we have freedom to assert it, that if they were plagued before with proud, ambitious, presumptuous spirits, they shall be ten times plagued more with these and the like spiritual judgments, who shall succeed the former in their chairs. And if they did formerly act to the great pre-

1661. the ministers would not remove till he had prayed, and regularly concluded their meeting.

In the synod of Lothian things were carried with a very high hand by our statesmen; they were immediately under their eye, and

judice of the nobles in the land, (to whom they became a terror, and whom they began to trample upon and abase) they who enter heir to the former, shall no less, if not to the double, more insolently act in their time, and that in the Lord's righteous judgment, for the punishment of such nobles and statesmen as shall be active for their reintroduction into this kirk. Take good heed therefore unto yourselves, that ye love the Lord your God; else if ye in any wise go back, and cleave unto that abjured generation, know for a certainty that they shall be snares and traps unto you, and scourges in your sides, and pricking thorns in your eyes, Joshua xxiii. 11, 12, 13.

In the last place, we conceive the following reasons, relating to the change itself, will be obvious to any. First, If it be an axiom approved in experience and policy, (as it is) that *omnis mutatio reipublicæ est periculosa, etiamsi in melius*, much more will it be assented to, that *omnis mutatio in ecclesia, quando in deterius*, (such as this is) *est periculosa*; and therefore sound reason will conclude that it should be eschewed. That the feared and threatened change will be in *deterius*, is evident; for it is from such a government, as is conform to the word of God, to the best estate of the primitive church, to good laws and constitutions, to solemn vows and engagements, and conform to the government of the best reformed churches from the coruption of popery, to a government plain contrary to all these; and so it cannot but prove a change most pernicious both to the civil estate of the kingdom (which we leave to the judgment of jurisconsults and politicians,) and likewise to the church of Jesus Christ, which we may confidently conclude, both from former sad experience in the like case, and from the inevitable bitter consequences which naturally spring from such a sad and sinful change. Secondly, It will be palpable, not only to ourselves, who are members of this church, but to all the nations and churches abroad, whether protestant or popish, that are in the least measure acquainted with the affairs of the church of Scotland, and the settlement of government therein, what they have been now these hundred years bygone, since our reformation from popery, that this feared and threatened change will involve persons of all ranks within the land, (who shall in any way have accession to it) in the dreadful and horrid guilt of perjury, which will both expose the land to the wrath of an angry God, who will not hold them guiltless that take his name in vain, but will prove a swift witness against them that swear falsely, and also expose our religion and nation to the insolent blasphemy and derision of our adversaries the papists, who may justly, with all others that hear tell of such a change, change the ignominious proverb, *Punica fides* to *Scotica fides*, and imbolden the papist to give us (ironically) no small thanks, for that by our perjury we have made the Lord angry with us, as did the Grecian Agesilaus to the Persian Tissaphernes, when he broke the league he made with him.

There be none that have the least spark of reason and foresight, who may not say what sad loss and hurt will spring from this feared

change, unto the Lord's people under our ministerial charge. Will not poor souls be in the same case and distraction of thought, the people in Syria, Arabia and Egypt, were in about the 600 year, anent the opinion of Eutyches, when some denying, some affirming, the poor people were so brangled and shaken with contrary doctrines, that in the end they lost all well grounded persuasion of the true religion; so that within short time, they did cast the gates of their hearts open to receive the vile, devilish, and blasphemous doctrine of Mahomet? Even so what can be expected in this land, upon such a change, which will unquestionably occasion not only one to affirm, and another to deny the same position, but one and the same man to affirm what he denied, and deny what he affirmed anent one and the same position, in matter of religion? The forebreathings of which inconstancy are beginning to puff out already. We say, what can be expected in this case through the land, but that the generality of the people shall become so doubtful and indifferent in the matters of religion, that they shall abandon all piety, open their hearts to popery, and what religion, or rather what error and fancy instead of religion, you will? So that the blood of their poor souls will lie heavy on the authors of the change.

1. We are aggrieved that ways are taken to seal up the lips of the most faithful ministers of Jesus Christ within the land, from delivering their Master's message with that freedom and plainness that becomes; while, upon occasion of the proclamation at Edinburgh, September 20th, 1660, men disaffected to, or entertaining grudges and heart-burnings against ministers, may and do take encouragement to delate honest men, using freedom against sin, as unloyal slanderers and trumpeters of treason, sedition, and rebellion, when they are, in the simplicity of their heart, only giving obedience to the Lord's commands. Isa. lviii. 1. "Cry aloud, spare not," &c. We hope it will be acknowledged, that neither private nor public sins, personal nor national sins, sins in the state-members or in church-members, are excepted in the commission of the ministers of the gospel, (if any deny the truth hereof, we are ready to instruct it from the word of truth) and it being so, why should the ministers' faithful discharge of duty, in the discovery of national sins, whether in church or state, be charged with the ignominious aspersions of railing, slandering, &c. or they staged before civil tribunals for the same, seeing that, according to their commission, they are herein only aiming at the upstirring of people to repentance, and to serious deprecating of the wrath of God, that public national sins, and particular faults in rulers ordinarily draw on upon lands? as is clear from Jer. xv. 4. and elsewhere.

2. We are aggrieved that the oath of allegiance does upon the matter carry the oath of supremacy fully in its bosom, and that in such an absolute, general and comprehensive term, without any express limitation or qualification, that in our humble conception, there is conferred upon the king by it a power to do ecclesiastic matters as he pleases; and this is in effect to confer the same, or the like headship over the

were treated most insolently. They were not suffered so much as to speak of any testimony, yea, were forced to do what was very much contrary to the inclinations of many. Some members of the synod, fully ripe for a change, and ready

1661.

church, upon the king, as that which is taken from the pope.

3. We are aggrieved that the civil sanction is taken from the covenant, whereupon the inviolable obligation of the sacred oath of God upon the conscience, is trampled upon with contempt, by very many, which cannot but grievously provoke the Lord, who has declared that he will be a swift witness against them that swear falsely.

4. We are aggrieved that there be such sad breaches made in the walls of our Jerusalem, which once was built a city compact together; we mean, that the church judicatories have not only suffered violent interruption, but also are prohibited and discharged, through which iniquity has more insolently faced the causey these three quarters of a year bygone, than it did for many years before.

5. Looking upon these but as making a wide gap in the walls, the beautiful porches whereof denied an entry, we are most of all aggrieved to see the Trojan horse now a hauling in over the gap, we mean, the reintroduction of lordly prelacy upon this church and kingdom, which being once execrate, and the whole nation solemnly sworn before the Almighty God to its extirpation, it makes our ears to tingle, when we think of what may be the sad tokens of God's displeasure against the lands, for endeavouring to give rooting again to that plant which our heavenly Father never planted. And this being the aggrieving evil which does most sadly afflict our spirits, for exoneration of our own consciences before the Lord, and that it may appear that we are not aggrieved without cause, we do in all humility offer unto your lordships, these few subsequent reasons against the change of our long established government by presbytery, unto that abjured hierarchical government by lordly prelacy.

Besides the foresaid reasons drawn from the *terminus a quo*, the *terminus ad quem* of the change, and from the change itself, we do in all humility beg leave to add two experimental considerations, which we desire to express with that simplicity and singleness of heart, in the sight of God, that becomes the ministers of Jesus Christ, who are looking to give shortly an account of their stewardship unto their Lord and Master. And the first is this: we do find in our experience, that when the Lord at any time is graciously pleased to grant unto any of us more near and familiar access unto himself, and to put our spirits in a more lively, spiritual, and heavenly frame, then are we also filled with more perfect hatred, abhorrency, and detestation of that prelatical dominion we plead against, and in our souls, at such times, we are encouraged and strengthened in the Lord, to set our faces as flint against that course and way, whatever the hazard be we may incur; and when fears of hazard, in opposing that course, do creep upon our spirits, we do ingenuously confess it is but then, when we are at a greater distance from God, and in a more common and natural frame. The next is this: we do find in our experience, that when at any time, any of us are summoned with the messengers of death, or when free of these, we fall upon the serious thoughts and meditations of death, presenting, as in God's sight, to ourselves, what is the course in the profession, avowing, and maintaining whereof we durst venture upon death, upon eternity, and upon the last judgment; and upon the other hand, propose to ourselves what is the course in the profession, avowing, and maintaining whereof we durst not venture upon death, upon eternity, and the last judgment; we do as of sincerity, as of God, in the sight of God, declare, that we durst not, for ten thousand worlds, venture upon eternity, and face the great Judge of the quick and the dead, with the guilt of being instrumental to re-establish, or with the guilt of embracing or conforming unto re-established lordly episcopacy, lying upon our consciences; whereas, upon the other hand, our desires and endeavours to be faithful and constant in the received and established government by presbytery, according to the scripture pattern, is a mean of gladdening and rejoicing our hearts, when we look and hope for the coming of the Lord.

And now, right honourable, having in the simplicity of our hearts, opened up our grievances in part to your lordships, we do in the last place, for remedy, in all humility, prostrate ourselves before your lordships, most humbly and earnestly begging, in the name of Jesus Christ, that your honours would be pleased to intercede with the king's most excellent majesty, First, To take off the restraint laid upon the exercise of the government of the church, in her assemblies, by the late proclamations, without which profanity will abound. Next, That his majesty would be graciously pleased to free and deliver his faithful and loyal subjects of this his ancient kingdom, under our respective charges, and the godly through the whole land, from all fears of innovating and changing the government of the church, by sessions, presbyteries, synods, and general assemblies, which is ratified and approven by king James VI. of blessed memory, as is evident, parl. 114, June, 1592. Thirdly, That his majesty would be pleased to ratify all former acts of parliament in favours of the church and her said government, that she may fully exercise the power granted to her by Jesus Christ, with freedom and liberty. Fourthly, That his majesty would be pleased to ratify all acts both of parliament and the general assemblies, against papists and popery, against prelates and prelacy, that aspiring men get not the church of Christ in this land fetched under bondage again. Fifthly, That his majesty would be graciously pleased to renew the national covenant of this land, first subscribed by king James VI. of worthy memory, and then taken by persons of all ranks and degrees throughout the nation; and also that he would be pleased to revive the solemn league and covenant, subscribed by his majesty's self, and that he would be graciously pleased, by his royal mandate, to ordain that both these covenants would be renewed, sworn to, and subscribed to, by persons of all ranks and degrees, within his majesty's three kingdoms of Scotland, England, and Ireland, and the dominions thereto belonging. Thus will there be a strong bar

1661. to fall in with the manager's designs, proposed that the synod should begin at censuring and sentencing the brethren who had been for the protestation, even though it had been agreed among the resolutioners and protesters in the year 1658, that none of either side should be questioned in their judicatories for their different practices.

This unaccountable proposal, Mr Robert Douglas, Mr. David Dickson, and many others of the best note in the synod, endeavoured to wave, and probably would soon have warded off, had not the two commis-

drawn in the way of popery, and prelacy which ushers the way to popery, that neither of them shall have a regress to a replanting in these lands: thus shall there not an evil beast be left to push in all the mountain of the Lord; and thus may we confidently expect that the Lord shall be one, and the name of the Lord one, in all his majesty's dominions.

Having, in the zeal and fear of God, with all humble and due respect unto your honours, offered these considerations against a change, we humbly beg, that your honours would lay them (with many more that cannot but be obvious to your lordships) seriously to heart, and in the pensitation of them, and the whole matter in hand, sist yourselves as in the sight and presence of the all-seeing God, who standeth in the congregation of the mighty, and judgeth amongst the gods, and will arise to judge the earth; weigh the matter (we beseech you) in the balances of the sanctuary, and not of carnal reason and policy: remember that God has set you up not to be stepfathers, but nursing fathers of his kirk, not to be crossers, but promoters of purity and piety, not to be destroyers of that which many of yourselves have builded, (and so makers of yourselves transgressors) but to be accomplishers and onputters of the cape-stone upon the building of the Lord's house; acquit yourselves zealously and faithfully in this so honourable and reasonable service; and beware, above all things, to strive against God with an open and displayed banner, by building up again the walls of Jericho, (we mean lordly prelacy, the very lair-stone of antichristian hierarchy) which the Lord hath not only casten down, but also laid them under a terrible interdiction and execration, that they be not built up again. These walls in this land, by the power of God, have been once and again demolished: they now lie under the Lord's terrible interdiction and execration, yea, we have all of us, with uplifted hands to the most high God, sentenced ourselves to this dreadful curse, if we re-edify these walls again: assuredly, if there be amongst your lordships, or within the land (which the Lord forbid) an Hiel, one or more, as was in the days of Ahab, to re-edify cursed Jericho, they shall not miss the dreadful execration, and the judgment threatened.

Therefore, we do once again, with all due and reverend respect prostrate at your honours' feet, humbly supplicate, First, That your honours would ratify all former acts of parliament, in favours of the work of reformation, in favours of presbyterial government, in favours of the freedom and privileges of the church, and particularly of the ministers of the gospel, in their faithful and free dispensing of the word; and that your lordships' would cass and annul all acts in the contrary. Next, We humbly supplicate, that your honours, in your wisdoms, would draw such a bar in the way of episcopacy, that this kirk may be fully delivered from the fears and evil thereof, and that corrupt and carnal-minded churchmen, who have the pre-eminence, may be for ever put out of the hopes of lording it hereafter any more over the Lord's inheritance. However it shall please the Lord to incline your honours' hearts to hearken unto these our just and lawful desires, it is the firm resolution of our hearts, to live in all dutiful obedience unto our dread sovereign the king's most excellent majesty, whom we pray the Lord long to preserve under the droppings of his grace, and overloadings of his best benefits, and special blessings. Yet we crave liberty, first, in all humility, to say, that it will tend much to the cheerful quieting of our hearts, and the hearts of the Lord's people we labour among, that your honours favourably grant our foresaid desires, for which the present and succeeding generations shall call you blessed. But next, if your lordships proceed, (which we pray the Lord forbid) to act any thing to the prejudice of the work of reformation, to the prejudice of the government of this church, and to the freedoms and liberties thereof, or to do any thing less or more, directly or indirectly, in favours of episcopacy, or tending towards the change of our present church government, by sessions, presbyteries, synods, and general assemblies; then, and in that case, we crave liberty to except and protest: likeas, by these presents, we do, in the name of the Lord Jesus Christ, who shall hold that great court of parliament, to judge both the quick and the dead, at his glorious manifestation, and in the name of our mother kirk, so richly blessed of God these many years bygone, under the government we plead for, and in the name of the synod and respective presbyteries and sessions we are members of, and in the name of the particular congregations we labour among, for discharging of our necessary duty, and disburdening of our own consciences, except and protest against every thing of the kind aforesaid, done or to be done to the prejudice of reformation, of presbyterial government, and of the liberties of the church, and against all and every thing done or to be done for the advantage of episcopacy, or any way tending to the introduction, erection, confirmation or ratification thereof, at this present parliament; earnestly beseeching the Lord, that your honours, this whole nation, and ourselves, may be kept free of the horrid guilt of such a sinful change of Christ's government, and encroachments upon his royal crown, and free of all the sad inconveniences ensuing inevitably thereupon, both to kirk and state; and most humbly craving, that this our supplication and protestation may be admitted by your honours, and registrated among the acts and statutes of this present parliament, in case (as God forbid) any thing be done to the prejudice of Christ's government, and advantage of episcopacy. Your honours' refreshing answer humbly we expect.

sioners appointed for this synod, the earl of Callendar, and Sir Archibald Stirling of Carden, come in, no doubt by concert with the corrupted members, just when they were reasoning this matter, and required the moderator to purge the synod of rebels, meaning ministers of the protesting judgment: yea, they threatened plainly, that if this was not presently fallen in with they would dissolve them, and stage them before other judges. The synod were so far forced in with the proposal, that they suspended Mr. Alexander Livingstone, minister at Biggar, Mr. John Greig, minister at Skirling, Mr. Archibald Porteous, and Mr. James Donaldson, ministers in Biggar presbytery, and Mr. Gilbert Hall, minister at Kirkliston; all of them ministers of great piety, and some of them persons of great ability in the church, I find that at this synod, Mr. William Weir, minister at Linlithgow, and Mr. William Creighton, minister at Bathgate, were likewise removed from their charges, upon application of some malignant and disaffected persons in their parishes. After this sad work, the commissioners proposed some overtures in favour of prelacy, which the plurality of the synod very briskly opposed, and thereupon were dissolved in the king's name, and obliged to dismiss without prayer.

There seems to have been at this time a formed design to bear down such ministers as had not been for the public resolutions: and therefore in the northern synods I find some harsh dealing with the few there of those sentiments. One instance may suffice, and it is of that extraordinary person we shall meet with frequently afterward, Mr. Thomas Hogg, minister at Kiltearn, in the synod of Ross. The date is not sent me by the reverend minister who gives me the information, which he hath from Mr. Hogg himself, and Mr. Fraser after mentioned; but the fact itself leads us to this synod in the beginning of this year.

Mr. Murdoch Mackenzie was moderator of this synod of Ross, and now gaping after the bishopric of Murray, though he had shown a particular liking to the covenants, and sworn them, some say ten, others fourteen times. Mr. Hogg was one from whom the greatest opposition to prelacy was expected, and therefore a tash must be put on him at this synod; and he, not being to be reached in any point of practice, must be staged for his opinion, and that upon the protestation. When Mr. Hogg appeared before the synod, the moderator interrogate him what he thought of the protestation, and the assemblies of St. Andrews, Dundee, &c.? he modestly replied, that living at a great distance from the places where those things were agitate, he never meddled much in that matter. And being further asked, if he thought the protestation a just and reasonable deed? Mr. Hogg declined to give an answer, knowing what improvement was designed to be made of it, and therefore he would neither own nor disown it judicially.

Mr. Hogg being removed, the moderator had a discourse to the synod, to this effect, that the brother they had before them, was known to be a great man: notwithstanding, the king having espoused the defence of those assemblies against which the protestation was given in, it behoved them to go on in their work. Therefore Mr. Hogg was called in, and required judicially to disown and disclaim the protestation. This he refused to do, and thereupon the synod passed a sentence deposing him from the ministry. Mr. Hogg, in giving account of this, my informer tells me, observed, the sentence was pronounced with a peculiar air of veneration, and looked rather like their consecrating him to a higher office, than a deposition; and that the moderator, in a kind of consolatory discourse after the sentence, spoke very near nonsense. Among other things he was pleased to remind Mr. Hogg, that our Lord Jesus Christ had suffered great wrong from the scribes and Pharisees.

At that same synodical meeting, a motion was made for deposing Mr. James Fraser, of Liny, from his office as ruling elder, for the very same reasons on which they proceeded against Mr. Hogg; but the moderator opposed the proposal, and expressed his regard to him, as an honourable gentleman, and not so far engaged in that way as some others; therefore he moved that they might suspend Mr. Fraser from officiating for some time, and appoint some brethren to confer with him, for reclaiming him from his mis-

1661. takes. A brother rose up and professed himself against that proposal, for this reason, that he was more afraid the gentleman would draw to his side those who should converse with him, than he could entertain hopes of their prevailing on him. What the issue was, my informer does not remember.

This is but a short swatch of the unprecedented force, violence, and heavy oppression of ministers, in their ministerial and judicative capacity; the parallel of which, I doubt, if it can be given, as to any of the reformed churches, or in any well ordered government; especially when laws authorizing their meeting, were yet standing, and they had the king's promised protection. I might name many other aggravations of this surprising procedure, but the naked narrative of facts sufficiently exposeth it. From these the reader will have some view of the oppression, I might say overturning, of our church establishment, the essays used, and testimonies given against this melancholy change, and the attacks made upon church judicatories, while the parliament sat. Those I thought good to give some account of, before the sufferings of particular persons, which I now come to.

SECT. III.

Of the sufferings and martyrdom of the noble Marquis of Argyle, May 27th, 1661.

In giving the narrative of the hardships particular persons underwent this year, we shall find many attacked in their name and reputation, others in their liberty, and others in their estates and lives. I shall begin with the last: and the excellent marquis of Argyle deserves the first room, and after him, the reverend Mr. James Guthrie; each of whose sufferings will fill a section by themselves.

The case of the marquis of Argyle, containing his indictment for high treason, with his large answers, having been several times printed, the less needs be said here concerning this great man. It is pity the whole of this eminent person's management, speeches, and petitions to the lords of articles, and the parliament, cannot now be recovered; some of them I have before me, under his lordship's own hand, and copies of others. From those, and other memoirs of this period, I shall essay as short and distinct an account of this noble peer, his treatment and trial, with what followed upon it, as I can.

When the king came home last year, the marquis was very much solicited to go to court, and some say, he had assurances of welcome. No doubt he was inclinable to wait upon a prince, upon whose head he had set the crown. Indeed several of his best friends were against his going up to court, till matters were come to some settlement; and particularly Mr. Robert Douglas used many arguments to dissuade him: he was forewarned of a change in his majesty's affections towards him, and acquainted that he wanted not enemies at London, who had taken pains to raise calumnies upon his person and conduct. All those prevailed with him to delay his journey for some time: at length he resolved to vindicate himself; and knowing he was able, upon his access to the king, soon to remove whatever dust, a set of people, for their own base ends, had raised against him, he took journey, and arrived at London, July 8th, and with a confidence flowing from the testimony of a good conscience, entered Whitehall, to salute his majesty. I am told that his enemies had so prepossessed the king against him, that even while upon his road to London, orders were given to seize him, and carry him back prisoner to Scotland: if so, he escaped the messengers, and got safe to court. But as soon as the king was told he was come to Whitehall, he ordered Sir William Fleming to go and carry him straight to the Tower of London. The marquis urged much to be allowed to see the king, but our Scots managers took care to prevent that; and he was hurried away in the greatest haste possible. In the Tower he continued under close confinement, until he was sent down to Scotland.

The springs of such surprising treatment of this great man, are either a secret, or not very fit to be propaled.* This much may

---

* The following passage in Kirkton's History of the Church of Scotland, appears to me to throw considerable light upon what are here

be said, he was the head of the covenanters in Scotland, and had been singularly active in the work of reformation there; and of any almost who had engaged in that work, he stuck fastest by it, when most of the nation quit it very much. He had kept his power and influence in Scotland under the various turns of affairs, and stood when many of his rivals fell: and this attack upon him was a stroke at the root of all that had been done in Scotland from the (year) 1638 to the usurpation. It is not improbable, besides the emulation of our Scots noblemen about court, and the peculiar spite of the highfliers in England, against the marquis, for his known principles in church government, and eminent appearances for civil liberty, that general Monk, and others about the king, knowing his great abilities and experience, and how much the king once valued him, might be afraid of his soon coming to have such interest with his majesty, and making such discoveries of affairs, as were not agreeable to their present circumstances and projects. What holy freedom the marquis had used in reproving some vices, and what promises had been made him, which were not now to be performed, I shall not say: but some of those, if not all, concurred to begin and help forward this violent storm now come upon him.

1661.

While in the Tower, he made application for liberty to have the affidavits and declarations of several persons in England, taken upon some matters of fact, when he was concerned in the public administration, before the usurpation; but this piece of justice was flatly refused him. From the Tower he was, toward the beginning of December, sent down to Scotland in a man-of-war, to abide his trial before the parliament. Sir John Swinton came down prisoner with him, and they had a severe storm in their passage, in which the ship before mentioned, with the records of the kingdom, was lost. December 20th, they landed at Leith, and next day, Swinton being a quaker, and excommunicate, was carried up the street of Edinburgh, discovered, and guarded by the town officers; and the marquis walked up the street covered, betwixt two of the bailies of Edinburgh, to the castle, where he continued till his trial came on.

By the minutes of parliament formerly mentioned, I find, January 18th, the lord Cochran, president of the committee for bills, reported to the parliament, that a supplication was presented to them by the laird

---

passed over, as the concealed motives of this prosecution. "This [Charles'] unsuccessfulness in all his other attempts, prevailed with him to close with the Scots more than all the arguments their commissioners could use of ane episcopal man, [a papist he should have said] to become a covenanted presbyterian. And the marquis of Argyle, being all that time almost dictator of Scotland, to make all sure for himself being in great danger from the envy of his enemies, thought good to strike up a match betwixt the king, and his daughter lady Anne, to which the king consented with all assurance, though all that poor family had by the bargain was a disappointment, so grievous to the poor young lady, that of a gallant young gentlewoman, she losed her spirit and turned absolutely distracted. So unfortunately do the back wheels of private design, work in the puppet plays of the public revolutions in the world." After this, no man at all acquainted with human nature, will be in the least surprised when the historian goes on to say that, "the first clap of royal indignation fell upon the marquis of Argyle who, upon the news of his majesty's return, and, as it was believed, upon good encouragement to expect hearty welcome, when he had posted to London with the rest, entering Whitehall with confidence to salute his majesty, had only this for his entertainment, that so soon as ever the king heard he was there, with an angry stamp of the foot, he commanded Sir William Fleming to execute his orders, who, thereupon conveyed the marquis straight to the Tower there to lie, till he was sent down to Scotland to die a sacrifice to royal jealousy and revenge." The above it is probable was one of the reasons, which our historian did not think "very fit to be propaled;" but there was another, which could not surely escape his observation, though he has omitted to record it, Middleton and his associates who had now got into their hands, the administration of Scotish affairs were very poor, and they were equally avaricious; the estate of the marquis of Argyle was a large one; and there appears to be no reason for misdoubting Burnet, when he says, "they had a desire to divide it among themselves." This we may well believe, they supposed, after having cut off the marquis, would not be a matter of much difficulty. Differences among themselves combined with other causes, however, after they had committed the crime, prevented them from reaping those happy results they had anticipated; and Middleton, who unquestionably hoped to have had the whole to himself, was in the issue completely disappointed. *Vide* Kirkton's History of the Church of Scotland, pp. 50, 69, 70. Burnet's History of his Own Times, Edin. Ed. vol. i. pp. 149, 150, 177, 186.—*Ed.*

1661. of Lawmont, craving warrant to a messenger to cite the marquis of Argyle, and some others, to appear before the parliament, to answer to the crimes contained in the bill. Some opposition was made to this; but it was carried, by a vast plurality, to grant warrant. This gentleman was hounded out by the managers, to bring in this charge of severities against the marquis; from which he vindicates himself in his printed defences.

When thus cited, upon the first of February he gives in two petitions to the parliament, the one craving advocates to be allowed him, and the other that the day of his compearance might be delayed. After much debate in the house, both were referred to the lords of articles, where the managers were sure to carry their point as they pleased. What their answer was, I have not seen. February 5th, I find it represented to the house, that the lawyers, given in list by the marquis, being heard before the articles, did prevail to be excused; and a new petition, with a new list, being presented, the parliament granted the desire of it, leaving room for the advocates to plead their excuses before the articles. All this looks like a trick, to deprive him of the benefit of advocates, in a cause which so nearly concerned him; or at least, so to protract the time, that there should be very little room for drawing of answers. The names of his advocates were, judge Ker, Mr. Andrew Birnie, Mr. Robert Birnie, Mr. afterwards Sir George, Mackenzie of Rosehaugh, Mr. afterwards Sir John, Cuningham, and Mr. George Norvel. The day of his compearance was ordered to be February 13th; and till then terrible stories were buzzed about of the marquis's horrid barbarities used against the gentlemen of the name of Lawmont, M'Coul of Lorn, the laird of Appine, the gentlemen of Clanronald, and others, from which there lies a full vindication in his printed defences. But this was necessary, to prepare members of parliament, and the nation, for the barbarous tragedy that was now shortly to be acted.

Upon the 13th of February, the marquis was brought down from the castle in a coach, with three of the magistrates of Edinburgh, attended with the town guards, and presented at the bar, where Sir John Fletcher, the king's advocate, accused him, in common form, of high treason, and presenting an indictment, craved it might be read. The marquis humbly craved, that he might have liberty to speak before the reading of his dittay, (indictment) promising that he should not say any thing to the matter therein contained. When the advocate opposed this with violence, the marquis was removed, and after some debate, the house refused his reasonable desire, and ordered his dittay to be read. When my lord was called in, and this intimate to him, he moved that a bill he had by his advocates given in to the lords of the articles, might be now read in the parliament; the desire of it was, a precognition, with many reasons why this ought to be granted. The lords of articles would not transmit this bill to the parliament, and the marquis had no other method left him, but to move the reading of the petition in the house; this was likewise peremptorily refused. This petition, not being printed in the common copies of his case, and giving considerable light to this trial, I have added in a note. *

---

* Marquis of Argyle's petition, with reasons for a precognition, February 12th, 1661.

That forasmeikle as the petitioner can, with a safe conscience, affirm, and solemnly protest, that whatever his actings or accession hath been, in relation to public business, since the beginning of the troubles, till his majesty's departure hence in the year 1651, though he will not purge himself of errors, failings, and mistakes, both in judgment and practice, incident to human frailty, and common to him, if not with the whole, at least the greatest part of the nation; yet, in one thing, though he were to die, he would still avouch and retain his innocency, that he never intended any thing treasonably, out of any pernicious design against his majesty's late royal father, of ever glorious memory, or his present majesty, (whom God may long preserve) their persons or government, but endeavoured always, to his uttermost, for settling the differences betwixt their majesties and their people. And as to any actings before the year 1641, or since the said year, till his majesty being in the parliament at Perth and Stirling, your petitioner did, with a full assurance, rely upon his gracious majesty, and his royal father, their treaties, approbation, oblivion, and indemnity, for what was past, and firmly believed, that the same should never have risen in judgment, or that the petitioner should have been drawn in question therefore; and during his majesty's absence, and being forced from the exercise of his royal government by the late

CHAP. II.] OF THE CHURCH OF SCOTLAND.

Being overruled thus in every thing, the indictment was read. The reader hath it in his printed case, and I would most willingly insert it in the appendix, were it not very large, and the answers to it necessarily much larger, so that this volume would swell exceedingly were they added. I shall only then point at the heads thereof as briefly as I can, that the reader may have some view of the unaccountable injustice of this procedure. In the general it may be noticed, that this libel was more months in forming, than the marquis had days allowed him to frame his an-

1661.

---

usurpers, and long after that the nation, by their deputies, had accepted of their authority and government, and they in possession, the petitioner was forced to capitulation with them, being in their hands, and under sickness; and the same was, after all endeavours used, according to the duty of a good subject, and, upon the petitioner's part, so innocent, and necessary for self-preservation, without the least intention, action, or effect, to his majesty's prejudice; that albeit, upon misinformation, (as the petitioner humbly conceives) his actings and compliance, both in their designs and quality, have been misrepresented, as particularly singular and personal, stating the petitioner in a degree of guilt beyond others, and incapable of pardon; the same have so far prevailed upon his majesty, as to cloud and damp the propitious and comfortable rays of his royal grace and favour, and have strained his gracious inclination beyond its natural disposition of clemency, expressed to his other subjects, to commit the petitioner's person, and give way to the trial of his carriage and actings: yet, so firmly rooted is the petitioner's persuasion of his majesty's justice and clemency, and that he intends the reclaiming, and not the ruin of the meanest of his subjects, who retain their loyalty, duty, and good affection to his person and government; that, upon true and right representation of the petitioner's carriage and actings, he shall be able to vindicate himself of these aspersions, and shall give his majesty satisfaction, at least so far to extenuate his guilt, as may render him a fit object of that royal clemency, which is of that depth, that having swallowed and past by, not only personal, but national guiltiness, of much more deep die as any the petitioner can be charged with, or made out against him, and so will not strain to pass by and pardon the faults and failings of a person who never acted but in a public joint way, without any sinistrous or treasonable design against his majesty, or his royal father; and against which he can defend himself either by acts of approbation and oblivion, *in verbo principis*, which he conceives to be the supreme, sacred, and inviolable security, or which he was forced to much against his inclination, by an insuperable necessity. And albeit his majesty's grace and favour is strictly tied to no other rule but his will and pleasure, yet his majesty's so innate, essential, and insuperable a quality of his royal nature, that the petitioner is persuaded, in all human certainty, that the leaving and committing to his parliament, (as is expressed in his majesty's declaration, October 12th, last bypast) the trying and judging of the carriage of his subjects, during the late troubles, as indeed it is in its own nature, and ought to be so accepted of all, as an undoubted evidence of his majesty's affection to, and confidence in his people; so no other trial or judging is therein meant, but a fair, just, legal, and usual trial, without any prejudice, passion, or prelimitation, or precipitation. Likeas, by the said declaration, there was a freedom for all the people interested, to make their application to the parliament, or in the meantime to the committee, from whom only his majesty is pleased to declare he would receive address and information; and seeing it was the petitioner's misfortune, during the sitting of the said committee, to be prisoner in England; whereas if he had been prisoner here in Scotland, he would have made application to them, and would have craved, and in justice expected, that precognition might have been taken by them to whom the preparing and ordering of that affair (to wit, anent the subjects' trials during the troubles) was recommended, that the petitioner's absence, which was his punishment, not his fault, may not be prejudicial, seeing the petitioner has lately received two several dittays, wherein there be many crimes grossly false, with all the aspersions and aggravations imaginable laid to his charge, importing no less than the loss of his life, fame, and estate, and the ruin of him and his posterity, which, he is confident, is not intended by his majesty; and that by the law and practice of this kingdom, consonant to all reason and equity, the petitioner ought, upon his desire, to have a precognition, for taking the deposition of certain persons, which being frequently and usually practised in this country, when any person is defamed for any crime, and therefore incarcerate, before he was brought to a trial, at his desire precognition was taken in all business relating thereto; which the petitioner in all humility, conceives ought much more not to be denied to him, not only by reason of respect to his quality, and of the importance and consequence thereof to all his majesty's subjects, of all quality, in all time coming, but also in regard it has been so meaned and intended by his majesty's declaration foresaid. Likeas, the manner of the crimes objected, being actings in times of wars and troubles, the guilt thereof was not personal and particular, but rather national and universal, and vailed and covered with acts of indemnity and oblivion, and so tender and ticklish, that if duly pondered, after a hearing allowed to the petitioner, in prudency and policy, will not be found expedient to be tossed in public, or touched with every hand, but rather to be precognosced upon by some wise, sober, noble, and judicious persons, for these and several other reasons in the paper hereto annexed; nor does the petitioner desire the same *animo protelandi*, nor needs the same breed any longer delay, nor is it sought without an end of zeal to his majesty's power, and vindication of the petitioner's innocency, as to many particulars wherewith he is aspersed; and it would be seriously pondered, that seeing *cunctatio nulla longa, ubi agitur de vita hominis*, far less can this small delay, which is usual, and in this case

swers to it. Besides ordinary form, the indictment consisted of fourteen articles, wherein a heap of slander, perversion of matters of fact, and misrepresentations are gathered up against this good and great man; all which he abundantly takes off in his answers. He is indicted, that he rose in arms in opposition to the king's good subjects, the anticovenanters, and said to Mr. John Stewart, "that it was the opinion of many divines, that kings, in some cases, might be deposed." 2. That he marched with armed men against the house of Airlie, and burned the same. 3. That in the year 1640, he laid siege to his majesty's castle of Dumbarton, and forced it to render to him. 4. That he called, or caused to be called, the convention of estates, 1643, and entered into the solemn league and covenant with England, levied subsidies from the subjects, raised an army, and fought against his majesty's forces. 5. That in 1645, he burned the house of Menstrie. 6. That in 1646, he or those under his command, besieged and took in the house of Towart and Escoge, and killed a great many gentlemen. 7. That he marched to Kintyre, and killed 300 men of the name of M'Donald and M'Coul, in cold blood, and transported 200 men to the uninhabited Isle of Jura, where they perished by famine. 8. That he went up to London, and agreed with a committee there, to deliver up the king to the English army at Newcastle, upon the payment of 200,000*l.* pretended to be due for the arrears of the army, treasonably raised, 1643. 9. That 1648, he protested in parliament against the engagement for relieving his majesty, and convocated an army to oppose the engagers, met with Oliver Cromwell, commander of the English army, and consented to a letter writ to him, October 6th, 1648, and to the instructions given to Sir John Chiesly to the parliament of England, and in May following signed a warrant for a proclamation, declaring the lords Ogilvie and Rae, the marquis of Huntly, John, now earl of Middleton, their wives and families, to be out of the protection of the kingdom. 10. That he clogged his majesty's invitation to his kingdom of Scotland, 1649, with many unjust limitations, and consented to the murder of the marquis of Montrose, to obstruct his majesty's resolution of coming to his kingdom; that he corresponded with Cromwell, without his majesty's knowledge; that he contrived and consented to the act of the West Kirk, August 13th, 1650, and the declaration following thereupon. 11. That in the years 1653 and 1654, he abetted and joined with, or furnished arms to the usurper's forces in the Highlands, against the earls of Glencairn and Middleton, and gave remissions to such as had been in the king's service. 12. That he received a precept from the usurper of 12,000 pounds sterling, and did consent to the proclamation of Richard Cromwell; accepted a commission from the shire of Aberdeen, and sat and voiced in his pretended parliament. 13. That he rebuked the ministers in Argyle, for praying for the king. 14. That he positively gave his advice to Cromwell and Ireton in a conference 1648, that they could not be safe till the king's life were taken away, at least did know and conceal that horrible design.

After reading the indictment, the marquis was allowed to speak, and discoursed at considerable length to the parliament. This extemporary speech was taken from his mouth in shorthand, and is insert in his printed case; and the reader will find it full of close reasoning, and strong sense. "After he had declared his joy at the restoration, and his trust in the king's goodness, and the justice of his judges, he says with Paul in

---

most expedient, if not absolutely necessary, be refused, *ubi agitur, non solum de vita, sed de fama,* and of all worldly interests that can be dear or of value to any man.

Upon consideration of the premises, it is humbly craved that your grace and the honourable estates of parliament, may grant the petitioner's desire, and to give warrant to cite persons to depone before your grace and the estates of parliament, upon such interrogatories as your petitioner shall give in, for clearing of several things concerning his intention and loyalty during the troubles; and for such as are out of the country, and strangers, residenters in England, commissions may be directed to such as your grace and the parliament shall think fit, to take their depositions upon oath, and to return the same: and your petitioner shall ever pray, &c.

another case, the things alleged against him cannot be proven: but this he confesses, that in the way allowed by solemn oaths and covenants, he served his God, his king, and country. He complains he had neither a hearing, nor pen, ink, or paper, allowed him, until this heavy charge was given. He notices in Sir Walter Raleigh's words, that dogs bark at such as they know not, and accompany one another in those clamours: and though he owns he wanted not failings common to all engaged in public business in such a time, yet he blesses God, he is able to make the falsehood of every article of his charge appear. That he had done nothing with a wicked mind; but with many others had the misfortune to do several things, the unforeseen events of which proved bad."

After this he comes to obviate the principal calumnies in his indictment. " As to the king's murder, he declares, that if he had been accessary to the counsel or knowledge of it, he deserved no favour; but he was the first mover of the oath in parliament, 1649, to vindicate the members, and discover the villany. And in a latter will made 1656, he entirely made it appear he was free of that execrable crime, the original copy whereof was ready to be produced. That he never saw, or had the least correspondence with Cromwell, till sent by the committee of estates, 1648, to stop his march to Scotland; and that he declined corresponding with the sectarian army, which he offers instantly to make appear.

" He next asserts his regard to the late duke of Hamilton, and owns that he declined to compliment Cromwell in his behalf; which if he had done, would have been an article of his indictment. He declares he used his utmost endeavours to preserve the marquis of Huntley, and that he never had any thing out of his estate, but what was absolutely necessary for his own relief, and that he was of very great use to that family. As to the marquis of Montrose's death, he appeals to many of the members' knowledge, that he positively refused to meddle, either in the matter or manner of it; and declares, that in the (year) 1645, the marquis and himself had agreed upon a treaty, which would have prevented much hurt afterwards, and it was none of their faults matters were not then compromised.

1661.

" As to his dealings with the English after Worcester, he offers to prove he laid out himself with his vassals to oppose the English; and a strong force being sent into Argyleshire, and he under sickness, he was made prisoner, and at all hazards refused in the least to join with them. This he shows would have been contrary to his interest, as well as duty; and evidences, that all along he did oppose a commonwealth. He complains that the advocate had dealt very ungenerously and unfairly, in forming his libel; and as to other things, refers to his defences."

When the marquis had ended, the advocate subdolously (artfully) endeavoured to bring him to speak upon some heads, which he declined, and referred to his defences; and yet when he came in, after he had been removed, while the house were fixing the time of his next appearance, he spoke to what the advocate had cast up, as to his opposition to the engagers at Stirling, 1648, and made it appear, that he was attacked by Sir George Monro, several of his friends killed, and he himself hardly escaped. The lawyers for the marquis took a protest, " that what should escape them in pleading, either by word or writ, for the life, honour, and estate of their client, might not thereafter be obtruded to them as treasonable;" and took instruments. When the pannel and his advocates were removed, the king's advocate, in order to intimidate and frighten the marquis's lawyers, got the parliament to refuse to record their instrument: yet common rules obliged the house to permit them to speak as freely as is usual in such cases.

The parliament fixed the 26th of February, for the day of the defender his giving in defences in writ. A very short diet indeed, for replying to a charge which contained so many particulars, and related to persons and times at such a distance, and an indictment contrived in so general and captious terms; all which is better represented in the printed defences, than I can pretend to do. When this was signified upon the party's being

1661. called in, the marquis, with his advocates, craved again, that his bill for a precognition might be read, and granted by the house. To which the chancellor replied, " that it had been formerly refused at the articles, and that it would not be granted." Thus we see, whatever the commissioner pretended, in pressing the nomination of the lords of articles, they were an illegal and unreasonable bar to the affairs of the kingdom, their coming under the cognizance of the parliament, and so most justly complained of in our claim of right, and happily taken away at the revolution.

By a petition the marquis applied (to) the parliament, February 26th, that he might have a further time to form his defences, because his advocates were strangers to the process, till put into their hands; and the matter of his indictment was of such extent: and they granted him until the 5th of March; which day, I find him before the lords of articles, desiring the continuation of his affair, till the meeting of parliament to-morrow. This short delay was not allowed him; but by two or three votes he was peremptorily appointed to produce his defences; whereupon he had a most pathetical speech, and when he ended it, gave in a very moving supplication, remitting himself to the king's mercy, and beseeching the parliament may intercede for him. This speech is printed in his case, and he acquaints them, " that this trial nearly concerns him, and is a preparative to the whole nation, themselves, and posterity; and wishes them to take heed what they do; for they judge not for men, but the Lord, who is with them in judgment. He observes, there are many of them young men, who, except by report, know not what was done since the (year) 1638, and are ignorant of the grounds of the procedure of this church and kingdom, in that time: Therefore he desires their charity, till the circumstances be heard and weighed, and proposes several important maxims to their consideration. That circumstances changing sometimes, make what is lawful appear unlawful. That when an invading usurper is in possession, making former laws crimes, the safety of the people is certainly the supreme law. That necessity has no law. That *inter arma silent leges*. That of two evils, the least is to be chosen. That no man's intention must be judged by the event of the action, there being a vast difference betwixt the condition of a work, and the intention of the worker. That it cannot be esteemed virtue to abstain from vice, but where it is in our power to commit the vice, and we have a temptation."

Unto those maxims he subjoins the following considerations: " That subjects' actions are to be differently considered, when their lawful prince is in the exercise of his authority, and when there is no king in Israel; yea, even when the sovereign is in the nation, and when forced to leave his people under the power of a foreign sword. That subjects' actions are likewise mightily altered, when a usurper is submitted unto by the representatives of a nation, and for some years in possession of the government. That submission to a usurping invader, in this case, when after assisting the lawful magistrate to their power, they are made prisoners, and can do no better, softens the case yet more, especially when they continue prisoners upon demand, and are particularly noticed and persecuted for their affection to their sovereign. That a great difference is to be made between a thing done *ad lucrum captandum*, and that done only *ad damnum evitandum*. That all princes have favourably considered such, as in such circumstances voluntarily cast themselves upon their clemency. That his majesty's natural clemency, evidenced to all his English subjects, cannot but be displayed to his subjects in Scotland, who suffered, even by them whom he pardons, for their affection to his majesty.

" Upon the whole, knowing his majesty's good nature, and his declared inclinations in his speech to the English parliament, ' conjuring them to abolish all notes of discord, separations and differences of parties, and to lay aside all animosities, and past provocations;' he hopes their lordships will concur in following so worthy a pattern; and for this end he humbly presents his submission to them."

Accordingly the marquis gave in a signed supplication and submission, which I have insert here.

To my Lord Commissioner his Grace, and High Court of Parliament.

" Forasmuch as I, Archibald, marquis of Argyle, am accused of treason, at the instance of his majesty's advocate, before the high court of parliament; and being altogether unwilling to appear any way in opposition to his sacred majesty, considering also that this is the first parliament called by his majesty, after his happy return to his kingdoms and government, for healing and repairing the distempers and breaches made by the late long troubles; I have therefore resolved that their consultations and debates about the great affairs and concernments of his majesty and this kingdom, shall have no interruption upon occasion of a process against me.

" I will not represent the fatality and contagion of those times, wherein I, with many others in those three kingdoms, have been involved, which have produced many sad effects and consequences, far contrary to our intentions: nor will I insist upon the defence of our actings in this kingdom, before the prevailing of the late usurpers; which (if examined according to the strictest interpretation, and severest censure of law) may be esteemed a trespass of his majesty's royal commands, and a transgression of the law: but notwithstanding thereof, are by his majesty's clemency covered with the vail of oblivion, by divers acts of parliament, and others to that purpose, for the safety and security of his majesty's subjects; and that my actings since, and my compliance with so prevalent a power (which had wholly subdued this, and all his majesty's other dominions, and was universally acknowledged) may be looked upon as acts of mere necessity, which hath no law. And it is known, that during that time, I had no favour from those usurpers; it was inconsistent with, and repugnant to my interest, and cannot be thought (unless I had been demented and void of reason) that I should have had freedom or affection to be for them, who being conspired enemies to monarchy, could never be expected to tolerate nobility.

" And whereas that most horrid and abominable crime of taking away the precious life of the late king, of ever glorious memory, is most maliciously and falsely charged upon me; if I had the least accession to that most vile and heinous crime, I would esteem myself most unworthy to live, and that all highest punishments should be inflicted upon me: 'but my witness is in heaven, and my record on high that no (such) wicked thing, or disloyal thought, ever entered into my heart.'

1661.

" But choosing to shun all debates, rather than to use any words or arguments to reason with his majesty, ' whom, though I were righteous, yet I would not answer, but make supplication;' and therefore (without any excuse or vindication) I do in all humility throw myself down at his majesty's feet and (before his majesty's commissioner, and the honourable estates of parliament) do submit, and betake myself to his majesty's mercy. And though it be the great unhappiness of these times (the distempers and failings of these kingdoms being so epidemic and universal) that his majesty should have so much occasion and subject of his royal clemency; yet it is our great happiness, and his majesty's high honour, that he hath expressed and given so ample testimony thereof, even to those who did invade his majesty, and this nation, for no other cause, than their faithful and loyal adherence to his majesty, and his just royal interests; which rendereth his majesty's goodness incomparable, and without parallel; and giveth me confidence, that his grace, his majesty's commissioner, and the honourable parliament, of their own goodness, and in imitation of so great and excellent a pattern, will compassionate my condition.

" And seeing it is a special part of his majesty's sovereignty and royal prerogative, to dispense with the severity of the laws; and that it is a part of the just liberty of the subjects, that (in cases of great extremity and danger) they may have recourse to his majesty, as to a sanctuary and refuge; it is in all humility supplicated, that the lord commissioner's grace, and the honourable parliament, would be pleased favourably to represent my case to his majesty; and that the door of the royal mercy and bounty, which is so large and patent to many, may not be shut upon one, whose ancestors for

1661. many ages (without the least stain) have had the honour (by many signal proofs of their loyalty) to be reputed serviceable to his majesty's royal progenitors, in defence of the crown, and this his ancient kingdom. And if his majesty shall deign to hold out the golden sceptre of his clemency, as an indelible character of his majesty's royal favour, it will lay a perpetual obligation of all possible gratitude upon me, and my posterity, and will ever engage and devote us entirely to his majesty's service: and the intercession of this honourable parliament in my behalf to his gracious majesty, will be a real evidence of their moderation, and they shall certainly be called a healing parliament; and God, whose mercy is above all his works, shall have the honour and glory which is due to his great name, when mercy triumphs over justice."

Next day, March 6th, the marquis being brought before the parliament, it was reported from the articles, that he had been before them, and offered a submission to his majesty, with a desire the parliament might transmit it to the king. Whereupon, after long reasoning, and much debate, the question was put, if the submission was satisfactory or not? It carried in the negative. When the marquis was called in, he spoke as follows:

" May it please your grace and lordships, my lord chancellor, and this honourable assembly, to consider his majesty's proclamation to Scotland, October 12th, 1660, compared with his gracious declarations and speeches in England, manifesting to his people his inclination to clemency, and commanding, requiring, and conjuring them, to put away all notes of discord and separation, and to lay aside all former animosities, and the memory of bypast provocations, and to return to unity among themselves under his majesty's government; for he never intended to except any from the benefit of his bounty and clemency, but the immediate murderers of his royal father.

" I desire, therefore, your lordships to observe, as all other subjects do, the two conditions only in his majesty's declaration. 1st, The vindication of his majesty's honour, and that of his ancient kingdom. 2dly, The asserting of his ancient royal prerogative. Those two being done, he promiseth a full and free pardon, and act of indemnity to all his subjects in Scotland

" I confess, my lords, it is all subjects' duty to concur in those; and this offer of my submission is all I can contribute to it at this time. It is his majesty's royal honour, not to question what himself and his royal father hath done to his subjects by their former acts, especially such persons who have done and suffered so much for him; and it cannot be misconstructed in me, not to desire to dispute the same, but to fly to that privilege of the subjects in their distress, his majesty's clemency and mercy, whereby I may have share of the benefit of his majesty's prerogative, which, as his royal father saith, ' is best known and exercised, rather by remitting than exercising the rigour of the laws; than which there is nothing worse:' and Solomon, the wisest of kings, saith, ' mercy and truth preserve the king, and his throne is upholden by mercy.' The same way the two most righteous kings (being of God's own choosing) practised, to wit, David and Saul: David, after a most horrid and unnatural rebellion; and Saul, towards the sons of Belial, (which is, wicked men) who refused to admit him for their king.

" So I humbly desire a larger time to consider what I can do more to give your lordships satisfaction; that I may have your lordships' concurrence, that the door of his majesty's mercy may not be shut upon me alone, of all the subjects in his majesty's dominions; for a dead fly will spoil a box of precious ointment."

This affecting discourse had no influence at all; and the chancellor, without so much as removing my lord, and before he had fully ended what he had to say, gave him for answer, that the parliament commanded him next day to give in his defences to the lords of articles. Accordingly, March 7th, being called before the articles, to give in his defences, he told them, " he had seen their lordships' order, that he might forbear his coming, if he would produce his defences: therefore he acquainted their lordships, that if he had them in readiness, he would neither have troubled them, nor himself; but having a petition ready to desire a delay, he thought it his duty to come and propose it himself, hoping their lordships would consider, that his presenting his defences, either wanting somewhat, or blotted, so as they could not be well read, was a very great prejudice to him, and a delay of a few days was no prejudice at all to any thing my lord advocate could say: and therefore he hoped their lordships would not refuse him some competent time to get them ready." When my lord was removed, and, after some debate, called in again, the chancellor told him, in name of the committee, that he was ordained to give in his defences before Monday, April 9th, at ten of the clock, to my lord advocate; otherwise the lords would take the whole business before them, without any regard to what he had to say. The advocate added, that the marquis must give in his whole defences. To which his lordship answered, that was a new form, to give in peremptory defences before the discussing of relevancies. Sir John Gilmor rose up, and said, he was commanded to inform his lordship, that there was a difference betwixt a process in writ, and the ordinary way before the session or justiciary. The marquis answered, he was very ill yoked with so able men, but he behoved to tell them, he had once the honour to sit as chief justice in this city, and he knew the process before them was in writ, and yet the relevancies were always first answered, before any peremptory defences were proposed, since relevancies are most to be considered in criminals. Both of them urged, that it was his lordship's interest to give in his defences as strongly as he could, otherwise the advocate might refer the whole business to the judge, and make no other answer. My lord replied, he would follow the advice of his lawyers, and hoped any order of their lordships at present, was without prejudice to his offering more defences afterwards, since he was so narrowed in time, and commanded to give what was ready. He added, that if their lordships and the parliament had been pleased to grant his desire of a precognition, which, as he humbly conceived, was agreeable both to law and practice, and his majesty's proclamation, which he acquiesced in, it could not but have been the readiest way for trying his carriage during the late troubles; whereas now he must of necessity in the process (which he hopeth will not be refused) crave a way for an exculpation in many particulars; for he both was, and is resolved to deal very ingenuously as to matters of fact. And if that had been first tried, which he was most desirous of, both from the committee and the parliament, he is hopeful there would not remain so much prejudice against him, in most part of things of greatest concernment in the libel. For his own particular, he desired nothing but the truth to have place. They might do with his person as they pleased, for by the course of nature he could not expect a long time to live, and he should not think his life ill bestowed, to be sacrificed for all that had been done in those nations, if that were all.

1661.

The lords, in nothing moved by any thing of this nature, told him, if his defences came not in against Monday, they would take the whole business before them, without any regard to what he should afterwards say. His defences, for any thing I can learn, were given in the day named. They are printed in his case, and in them, at great length, the marquis's management is vindicated from all the falsehoods, calumnies, and misrepresentations maliciously cast upon him; and they contain one of the best accounts of the transactions of those times pointed at in his libel, that I know of. Being thirteen sheets of small print, I cannot take upon me to give an abstract of them: but the most considerable perversions of fact in the indictment being already taken off, by what I have above inserted from the marquis's discourses, little more needs be added; yet, for the setting this affair in its due light, and as the best abstract I can give of the large defences, I shall here insert a paper, drawn up by a very sufficient person at this time, which contains the substance of what is more fully cleared in the defences, which I must still refer the reader to.

Information for my Lord Argyle, against the dittay given in against him by the King's Advocate.

" The deeds alleged done, either before his

1661. majesty left Scotland, 1651, or since, are either deeds of public concernment, or private, relating to private persons.

"As for the public, he never acted without the approbation of parliament, and general assemblies, which were ratified by his majesty's royal father, and his majesty who now reigns. And as for things relating to particular persons, he never had any accession to any thing, but what is warranted by acts of parliament, approven by his majesty, and his royal predecessors.

"As for actings, after his majesty left Scotland, 1651, the marquis was still a prisoner upon demand, and did never capitulate till August 1652, being surprised in his house, lying sick, and that long after the deputies had taken the tender, and gone to London, and all others in arms had capitulated, and the whole kingdom were living peaceably, under the power and government of the usurper.

"1. The first deed is a speech, 1640, at the Ford of Lyon, in Athole, where it is affirmed, that he said it was the opinion both of divines and lawyers, that a king might be deposed for desertion, vendition, or invasion; and said to Mr. John Stuart, that he understood Latin; from whence, treason against the king, and the murder of the said Mr. John is inferred. This is plainly against law, for speeches against the king, by Scots law, go not above the pain of death. 2do, It is not relevant to infer any crime, though those words had been spoken in the abstract terms related, no more than any should speak the tenet of the Sorbonne or Canon law, upon the pope's power. 3tio, To infer the murder of the said Mr. John is absurd, seeing the said Mr. John was, upon his own confession and witnesses' depositions, condemned, having slandered not only my lord Argyle, but the whole committee of estates. 4to, This deed is 1640, and the act of oblivion 1641.

"2. The second deed is the slighting [dismantling] the house of Airlie, and burning of Forthar in Glenyla. It is answered, those houses were kept out in opposition to the committee of estates, and so might be slighted and destroyed; which is clear by acts of parliament yet in force, act 4th, parliament 3d, king Charles, June 24th, 1644, and 35th act, 2d parliament king Charles. By which it is expressly acknowledged, that holding out of houses against the estates, is a crime. And by act 35th, parliament, anno 1640, the same is made a crime. 2do, Oppones the act of oblivion, 1641. 3tio, The said service is ratified and approven in parliament, 1641. *Rege præsente*, unprinted acts, number 70, bearing ratification, exoneration, and approbation, in favours of the marquis of Argyle.

"3. The third deed is, the taking the castle of Dumbarton. It is answered, this was done by order of the committee of estates; and the act of oblivion was after this. As to the taking of cannon, there were only two of them gifted to the marquis by the late duke of Lennox, then lying there.

"4. As to the calling of a convention of estates, and going into England with an army. It is answered, this was done by the conservators of the peace, secret council, and commissioners of common burdens, appointed by the king's majesty for governing the country, and ratified in parliament since; and the general assembly went along in all the steps. 2do, It was allowed by the king, in his agreement at Breda, and by his act of oblivion 1651, at St. Johnston and Stirling.

"5. As to the burning of Menstrie by his command. It is answered, 1mo, he denies any command. 2do, Whereas it bears by men under his command, there is no law to make that treason, nor is it relevant or reasonable, for *noxa caput sequitur, et delicta suos tenent authores*. 3tio, It is remitted by the act of oblivion 1651. 4to, General Bailie had the command, whose service in that expedition, is approven in the parliament 1646, and though he had done this, he had commission from the parliament 1644.

"As to the taking of Towart and Escoge, and murdering a number of men after capitulation. It is answered, the marquis was not in the country, but in England in the time of the said deeds. To the murdering of 200 men, after the taking of Dunavertie, it is answered, that David Leslie had the command there, and what was done, was by a council of war, and Lesly's service was approven by the parliament 1648. And whereas the said article bears, that my lord Argyle caused take 200 persons from Ila to Jura, where they perished: this is false against him; for he knew nothing of it, nor ever heard of it, till he received his dittay. But the truth is, that David Lesly was with his army in Ila, against old Coil M'Gillespick, who held out a fort there, called Dunivaige; and by the continuing of his army there, the isle was spoiled of meat: but Coil being taken, and the fort surrendered, David Lesly came home with his army, and the army left the pestilence in the country. And shortly after the removal of the army, the captain of Clanronald, with Angus M'Donald, son to old Coil, came and destroyed all that was left in the isle, whereupon the sickness being among the inhabitants, and all their food destroyed, it was a joint resolution of the gentlemen in that isle, belonging to the laird of Caddel, that those people should go, some to Ireland, some to Argyle, some to Jura, for their safety, and meat, of which there was abundance in Jura, and if they wanted, it might be had in Lorn and Argyle. But this is a most false and base aspersion on the marquis, who was neither there at that time, or had the least accession to it. The gentlemen of Ila can clear this.

"To the giving up of the king at Newcastle. It is answered, it was a parliament deed, which cannot come upon him; for by law divine and human, a voice in parliament is still free, and cannot be censured. Likeas by act of parliament 1641, *rege præsente*, members of parliament are sworn to give a true judgment to their light: but the truth in fact is, that my lord Argyle was not in Scotland, when the king's majesty came to the Scots army at Newark; and the king's majesty had emitted his declaration to both houses of parliament in England, declaring his resolution to settle matters, by advice of his parliaments. Neither ever did the marquis meddle in that business, but in the parliament 1647.

"As to the protest in parliament 1661, 1648, calling in the sectarian army, writing to Cromwell, that none of those who engaged should be put in places of trust, and emitting a proclamation against certain families. It is answered, that there was no protestation, but a declaration before the vote, that the general assembly ought to be consulted anent the engagement, and that the articles of the large treaty might be kept by previous dealing by all fair means for peace; and that if all fair dealing were refused, that there might be a due warning. As for the letter, no answer can be given, till the letter be seen; and though there were a letter in the terms libelled, yet it is an act of the committee; and as matters went, the army being lost at Preston, and the enemy lying on the border, if they had demanded the strengths of the kingdom, and pledges, or any thing harder, it would scarce have been refused, the Scots army being lost, and a strong one lying on the border. Besides, he never saw Cromwell till 1648, and he was called in by the committee; and the marquis did what he could to stop his career. As to the alleged proclamations, nothing can be said till they be produced, and indeed they were neither proclaimed, neither did any thing follow upon them.

"10. To the clogging of his majesty's proclamation, murdering Montrose, corresponding with Cromwell, and his accession to the act of the West Kirk, and declaration. It is answered, that it was the act of the parliament then sitting, by which the first allegation was done, and the king acknowledged any thing of that kind done good service, by admitting the marquis to places of trust afterwards, accepting the crown from him, and granting a general oblivion. As to Montrose; he had no accession to his death, or the manner of it, but endeavoured to have him brought off, to prevent effusion of blood, 1645, as colonel James Hay can yet witness. His corresponding with Cromwell is scandalously false, and one Hamilton, who was hanged at Stirling, and had said this, declared at his death, that report to be a false calumny. As to the act of the West Kirk; the marquis was at no committee of

1661. the kirk, after his majesty's happy arrival, until they came to Perth, nor did he know of the same: but when the word came to Dumfermline, where the king was, his advice was, to obviate the same, that the king should draw a declaration, and go as great a length as he might safely do; but for all the world would not advise the king to sign the said declaration against his mind, seeing it did reflect, as his majesty thought, against his majesty's father, and was against his majesty's conscience, and desires the duke of Buckingham and the earl of Dumfermline's depositions may be taken herein, and his sacred majesty consulted anent the verity hereof.

" 11. To the opposition to Glencairn and Middleton, when appearing for the king, and his joining with the English, at least giving them counsel. It is answered, that their commission was never intimate to him, either by letter or message; that he sent an express to Middleton to have a conference with him, but received no answer; that indeed the defender did express his dislike with their enterprise, as a business which could not frame, [succeed] and that it had been wisdom to have stayed all moving till the event of the Dutch war had been seen, or that the kings of Spain and France should agree, or the English army divide among themselves: but the rising in the hills made the English stick faster together. As to joining the English in their expedition to the hills; he denies any joining with them, to oppose the Scots forces: but he being a prisoner, and required to be with them, durst not refuse; and denies any kind of acting, either by counsel or deed. The selling of the cannon out of the castle of Dumbarton to Dean; it is false that they were taken out of Dumbarton: but Dean being informed of the cannon, told he would either have them at a price, or take them. As for taking pay from the usurper for a foot company; the practice of all the Highlands in Scotland is, in troubles for safety of their country goods from robbers and limmers, [villains] to keep a watch, which the sheriffdom of Argyle could not do, by reason of the payment of their cesses, and other great burdens and vastations sustained of late by them· and therefore general Monk allowed payment for one hundred soldiers to keep the country, as said is; and because they did not oppose the forces in the hills, the general discharged payment. The keeping of watch was the practice of all the Highlands during the last troubles, and was practised during the usurper's power, in Perth, Inverness, Mearns, Aberdeen, Stirling, and Dumbarton; and all got allowance, less or more.

" 12. As to the assisting at Richard Cromwell's proclamation, his receiving a precept of 12,000*l*. sterling, and sitting in the parliament of England. It is answered, he was not at all at Richard's proclamation, but by command indeed he was at Oliver's, but not at Dumbarton, being in Edinburgh, Monk's prisoner, he was commanded to come to the English council, and assist at the proclamation, and could not refuse, without being made a prey in life and fortune. No law can make this a crime, far less treason; and it cannot be instructed from any history, that a people overcome by an enemy, and commanded to do outward deeds of subjection, were questioned by their lawful prince, when he hath pardoned the invader, or that the subject should be prosecute, for doing what he, being a prisoner, could not refuse, without hazarding life and fortune. The 12,000 pounds is falsely adduced. The parliament of Scotland gave the marquis in payment of just debts half of the excise on wine and strong waters for a time: he having, by his capitulation, his fortune safe, procured a warrant that he might have a yearly duty forth of the said excise, but never received a sixpence of it. And this can no more be censured, than the whole kingdom's taking their just debts one from another, during the usurpation. As for his sitting in the parliament of England, after so long an usurpation; no case or precedent can be shown in any age in this country, whereby this was made a crime, far less treason. The cases adduced in the proposition, relate only to peaceable times, the righteous king being in power.

" 13. To his forbidding to pray for the king, and the rest of the alleged speeches. It is answered, they are false and calumnious, His parish minister and chaplain did always pray for the king in the time libelled, and that in face of the English. The story of what he said at London, is basely false, and he desires gentlemen, without distinction, with whom he conversed, may be asked. And the passage alleged in Masterton's house, it is false, and craves depositions may be taken, by which it will appear, that he has been of a contrary judgment.

" 14. The last head, it is basely false, and oppones thereto the Marquis's oath given in parliament, 1649, and leaves it to all to judge how unlikely and improbable it is, that he would speak any thing contrary to the oath that he had sworn. From this information, some tolerable view may be had of the marquis his defences against the calumnious libel given in. Those and the reasonings before the lords, took up all the time the parliament had to spare to this matter, for some weeks.

April 5th, I find the parliament pass a certification, that the marquis of Argyle shall have liberty to propound no more in his defence after Monday next. Accordingly Tuesday, April 9th, he is brought before the parliament, where he had a very pointed and pretty long speech, wherein he goes through the different periods, from the (year) 1633, to the restoration, and vindicates his conduct; and earnestly desires his supplication and submission to his majesty, may be considered, and recommended to the king. This speech not being in print, I have annexed at the foot of the page.* When his bill was read,

1661.

---

* Marquis of Argyle's Speech, April 9th, 1661.

" My regard to parliaments is well known, and my regard to this cannot be doubted, having his majesty's commissioner upon the throne, and so many worthy members in the same; therefore I hope it will not be mistaken, that I show that parliaments have in them two different inherent powers or qualities, the one *legislative*, the other *executive*, or judicial. The legislative consists in the making and repelling laws; the executive, or judicial, in judging according to law, whether it be betwixt subject and subject, or in relation to any particular person; which I doubt not but your lordships will seriously and wisely consider in all your actions; whereby all parliaments, and this in particular, will be the more acceptable to the people: and for this purpose his majesty indicted the same, that therein all his subjects' carriage during the troubles, might be tried, his honour and the honour of this his ancient kingdom vindicated, and the ancient prerogatives of the crown asserted; which being done, his majesty declareth he will grant such a full and free pardon and act of indemnity, as may witness there is nothing he more desireth, than that his people should be blessed with the abundance of happiness, peace, and plenty, under his government. Your lordships' care and endeavour in these things is not doubted, neither have I been wanting, according to my present condition, to witness my submission and concurrence with the same, by offering myself and all I have, at all occasions, to be disposed of as his majesty should think fit. And although his majesty's proclamation be general, for trying all his subjects' carriage during the troubles, yet (without envy or prejudice to any I speak it) no laick man's carriage is brought in question but mine own, whereby my actions, however public and common, may be the worse liked, when singly looked upon; which if seen otherwise, would appear less censurable: and I am so charitable as to concede the main reasons are these two, which I take from the libel, my alleged being a prime leader and plotter in all the public defences from the beginning, which a short narration of affairs, I hope, will easily clear. The next, my being an enemy to his majesty, and his royal father, which are both most unjustly charged upon me: therefore I am confident, when these are cleared, I shall find more charity and less prejudice from this honourable meeting of parliament. And for satisfying your lordships and all men in these things, I shall say nothing but truth: that in all the transactions of affairs wherein I ever had my hand (I thank God for it) I was never led in them by any private design of advantage to myself, either of honour or benefit, which are the main things that sway the most part of men's actions: so far was I from desiring benefits, that I never had pay as a committee-man or soldier in Scotland, England, or Ireland: few men can say the like who were in employment. And sure if I had aimed at honours, I wanted not opportunities, if I durst have forsaken other things wherein I was engaged by very strict obligations, more binding upon me nor particular ends. Another observation I have from the libel, which is this, that after such an inquisition, the like whereof was never known in Scotland, there is not one particular crime found of my maleadministration in any public trust, though I had the honour to be in public employment since the year 1626, neither any ground for a challenge in my private conversation.

" But to return to the narration of affairs, for vindicating myself from being the prime plotter and leader of affairs during the late troubles; as I forbear to mention the particular grounds and reasons of the kirk and kingdom of Scotland's proceedings, which might readily be mistaken, as many things concerning me have been, and are; neither shall I mention any man's name, because I intend no reflection, some of the prime actors being already with the Lord; I shall, for clearing the more easily to your lord ships, comprehend all my actings during the late troubles, in three periods of time. First, betwixt the years 1633 and 1641; secondly, betwixt that and 1651; thirdly, betwixt that and the year 1660, in which it pleased the Lord, in

1661. and he removed, the chancellor gave him for answer, when called in again, that the parliament, after considering the relevancy and probation, would take his bill to their consideration, and urged him presently to give in his duties, as I shall instruct by their commissions, and ratifications of my service. I shall forbear

his mercy, to restore his majesty to the possession of his just right, to the great comfort of all his people, and of myself in particular.

"Now, in the first period, from 1633 (at which time the differences first appeared) until the year 1638, (though I am not to judge any other man's actions) there are none who then lived, but know that I had no hand during that time, in any of the public differences; neither, after that, did I subscribe the covenant, until I was commanded by his majesty's special authority; and it was in council then declared, that the subscribing of it was with the same meaning which it had when it was first taken, in the years 1580 and 1581. I may add likewise, that I was at that time very earnestly dissuaded by some then called *covenanters*, who are now dead, from subscribing the same by his majesty's command; not that they disliked the covenant, or the king's command for subscribing of it, but fearing a contrary interpretation upon the covenant, because it was thought, that oaths were to be understood according to the meaning of the giver, and not of the taker of them. Notwithstanding whereof, I subscribed, according to the meaning given by the council, which was cleared afterwards in the general assembly of Glasgow, whereupon many supplications were sent to his majesty, for approbation, but without effect: yet thereafter, I did not so much as subscribe any of the national covenants, until the year 1639, when there was an English army upon the border, and the Scottish army at Dunse. And at that time, my endeavours were not wanting to my power, for a settling betwixt the king's majesty and his people, which was then effectuate. And whatsoever I had acted, from my first taking of the covenant, until his majesty being in Scotland, in the year 1641, was not only warranted by public commissions, but all my service is approven by his majesty in his parliament, which, with his majesty's act of oblivion at that time, put a close to that period.

"From that time that his majesty left Scotland, in the year 1641, until the year 1644, what I acted in the fields or counsels was by public commissions, and the service approven by the triennial parliament indicted by his majesty, who met in the year 1644. And though in that interval, betwixt 1641 and the parliament 1644, there was a meeting of the convention of estates, appointed by the council, commissioners for conserving the peace, and these for common burdens: which council had power by themselves to call a convention of estates, in which convention the league and covenant with England was agreed unto, and thereafter approven in the parliament 1644, yet it is very well known, and I can make it very evidently appear, that I was one of the men in Scotland who had least correspondence in England. There are yet some of the commissioners alive who were at that time in England, who may evidence the truth of this: whereby it is manifest I was no prime plotter in such a business.

"And from the year 1644, until his majesty's coming unto Scotland, 1649, I never acted in relation to the late troubles, but by virtue and command of the parliament and their committees, as I shall instruct by their commissions, and ratifications of my service. I shall forbear here to repeat what I spake formerly, concerning my proceedings with Montrose, Mr. Macdonald, and the Irish rebels, and of my agreement with Montrose, which I could not get ratified by the committee of estates, and therefore it broke off again; but one thing I may say, that from the year 1638 until 1648 there was never any considerable difference (in public offices) among all these, of kirk or state, who had once joined together, except a few who went to Montrose after Kilsyth. And any difference which seemed to be in the year 1648, was only anent the form and manner of proceeding, and not in the manner of rescuing his majesty, or relieving the parliament of England from any violence upon them; and the little power that I had either in the parliament 1647 or 1648, showeth that I was no prime leader in affairs.

"And for what was done in the years 1646 and 1647, concerning the disposal of his late royal majesty's person, the return of the Scottish army, and the agreement for the money to be paid for their arrears; it is well known that instructions were sent to and again in these affairs, both from committees and commissioners in Scotland and England: yet it shall never be found, that ever either my hand or presence was at any committees where any thing was debated or resolved concerning the disposal of his late royal majesty's person, or upon any treaties or conclusions for return of the Scots army, or for the money for the satisfaction of their arrears. So that I hope, when it is seriously considered, that I was one of the last in Scotland who subscribed the national covenant, and never did the same till commanded by his majesty, and that I was (of all these who acted in public affairs) one of these who had least accession to those things, though I be most blamed by common report, that your lordships will not find my carriage during the late troubles, to have deserved to have been put in so singular a condition.

"And as for what was acted in the year 1649, it is very well known that what power and interest I then had in the parliament, I did, to my utmost endeavours, employ the same for bringing home his majesty, and possessing him with his crown, and exercise of his royal authority. I shall not mention any difficulty I had in the same, lest I might be thought to reflect upon others: but this I will say, that what I did, I did it really and faithfully for his majesty's service, and by his own command, which was afterward acknowledged by his majesty for good service; and with the like affection I assisted all the time his majesty was in Scotland: for, without vanity and presumption, I may also say, if my counsel had been followed, his majesty's affairs had probably gone better; not that I condemn any other man's different opinion, because of success, which is a very bad rule to judge by; but only to testify mine own sincerity in all my proceedings, during his majesty's being in Scotland.

"As to the last period, after the year '651, it is well known the condition that my nearest relations were in when his majesty went from

plies. The marquis pressed for a short delay, that he might read over his duplies, since he and his lawyers were so straitened in time, that he had not got some sheets of them read over, and there might be treason in them, for any thing he knew; and he asked but till next day to look over his own papers: but this was refused; which made him complain that this was hard measure, and such haste was never made in a par-

1661.

Stirling, and that I did not then stay behind his majesty, without his own particular allowance, and kissing of his hand, though no particular charge or employment was left upon me. I shall here mention nothing that past before the defeat at Worcester, which, I may truly say, was as grievous to myself as any Scotsman; neither shall I trouble this honourable parliament to mention many several meetings which were held by several noblemen and gentlemen in this house, after that time, wherein I was willing and ready to contribute what was in my power; but nothing being found possible to be done, every man was necessitate to retire to his own family. And immediately after that defeat of Worcester, his majesty being driven from his dominions, there were commissioners sent from the pretended parliament of England, unto Scotland, with whom I would never make any agreement, neither did I ever capitulate, till long after all these in arms, by commission from his majesty, had done the same, and the representatives of the nation had accepted the tender of union, to be under one government, and thereafter had jointly met together at Edinburgh, and sent their deputies to London.

"And it is likewise well known, that myself and the gentlemen (my vassals and tenants) within the shire of Argyle, had endeavoured to get a conjunction with our neighbours in the Highlands, for resistance of the English power; which was refused by our neighbours, and the English acquainted therewith: whereupon they resolved upon very hard courses against us. Yet, upon a safe pass, I did meet with major-general Dean, and others, at Dumbarton; but because nothing would satisfy them, except I myself would take the tender, and promise to promote their interest, we parted without any agreement, as a very eminent noble person in this house can testify, who came to Dumbarton at that time: so their prejudice against me did the more increase. And they then fully resolved to invade the Highlands, and the poor shire of Argyle in particular, on all hands, by sending regiments both of horse and foot, by sea, on the east side of it, and general-major Dean himself marching by land to Lochaber, on the west side. But when he came there, missing his ship with his provisions, he returned back very speedily, and shortly thereafter came very unexpectedly to my house of Inveraray, by a frigate from Ayr, and (as it appeared afterwards) he had ordered his whole party to meet him there, and to lie near unto my house. It pleased the Lord that the same time I was in a very great fit of sickness, as Doctor Cunningham's certificate will testify, who was with me when Dean came there; and after himself, and others of his officers, had been a few days in my house, keeping sentry both within and without the same, he presented a paper to me, under his secretary's hand, (which paper I yet have) which I did absolutely refuse; but the next day he presented me with another, which, he told me, I must either yield unto, or he would carry me

with him, and send me to some other prison; whereupon, after some few alterations of it, I did agree, and signed the said paper, which I have likewise ready to be shown. And although I shall say nothing for justifying of it, yet all circumstances, and my condition being seriously considered, I hope it shall be found a fault, though not altogether excusable, yet very pardonable in me to do it, and afterwards, as affairs stood, not to break the same. And for any thing which I did after that, in my compliance with the English, being their prisoner upon demand, I never meddled, but, as I conceived, out of necessity, for the good of my country in general, and preservation of myself and family from ruin, and in nothing to hinder his majesty's happy restoration.

"There are many other things which I might instance, of many aspersions falsely cast upon me by this libel, which I shall pass by at this time, being unwilling to be too troublesome to your grace and this honourable meeting. And because many of them are fully answered and cleared in my defences and duplies, I shall only humbly desire this honourable meeting of parliament, to consider the great difficulty and disadvantage I am put unto, if I shall be forced to debate the grounds and reasons, from the lawfulness of the kirk and kingdom of Scotland's former proceedings, or of the lawfulness (circumstances being considered) of Scotland, or any person in it, their compliance with a prevalent usurping power, which had the full possession which his majesty (in his declaration concerning the treaty with Portugal) acknowledgeth they had. So that I hope, and am confident, that, these things being considered, his majesty will never allow that his father's or his own acts of oblivion and ratification should be called in question, or his subjects pursued for any deed or thing whereby they are indemnified by the same, they having nothing which they hold for a better security. The truth of these things is very well known to the most part of this honourable meeting, that there was an act of oblivion by his late royal majesty, in the year 1641, it is in print; and that his gracious majesty, who now is, did pass an act of approbation, at St. Johnstoun and Stirling, in the years 1650 and 1651, after his majority, there being none at that time kept out of the parliament, nor from his majesty's service in the armies; for all acts of classes were rescinded. And I am also confident, if it were represented to his majesty, by your grace and this honourable parliament, that he would not be less gracious and merciful to these in Scotland (who acted for him so long as they were able, till a prevailing sword had driven him away, and subdued them) when his majesty hath so freely pardoned and indemnified the invaders themselves. And therefore I humbly desire, before I be put to any further necessary dispute in the business, that your grace and this honourable parliament may be pleased to read this my humble supplication and submission, and recommend the same to his majesty."

1661. liament of Scotland. When he gave them in, the advocate took them up to advise, as he said, whether he should give in triplies or not. I have not seen a copy of the marquis his duplies, if they differ from his answers in print, or of the advocate's answers, if there were any; but I suppose we have the substance of both already.

After the advocate had considered the duplies, upon the 16th of April, the marquis is again before the parliament, and his process was read over in the house. Upon the reading of it, he had a very handsome and affecting speech, wherein at considerable length, he removes the reproaches cast upon him, and touches at some things not in his papers, and concludes with renewing his desire, that his supplication and submission may yet be recommended to the king's majesty. This speech tending to clear several matters of fact, and not hitherto, that I know of, published, I have added as a note. *

Whatever the marquis or his lawyers could say, had little weight with the members of parliament; most of them already were resolved what to do. The house had many messages to hasten this process to an end; though by what is above, it appears they lost no time: but the misgiving of many of their designed probations against this good man, embarrassed them mightily for some time. I have it from a very good hand, that upwards of thirty different libels were formed against him, for alleged injuries, oppressions, and the like; and all of them came to nothing, when they began to prove them, as lies use to do. And after they had accomplished their most diligent search, they were forced to betake themselves to his innocent, because necessary, compliance with the English, after every shire and burgh in Scotland had made their submission to their conquerors. Thus, as the sacrifice under the law was washen before it was offered, those

---

* Marquis of Argyle's speech, after reading of his process, April 16th, 1661.

"My Lord Chancellor,

"It is no small disadvantage to me to be standing before this honourable assembly, in this condition, and any, much more so many unjust prejudices against me: but I hope, as my duplies which have been read, have taken off many, as to the libel, I desire to speak to some of them, and others not in the papers; and I shall comprehend the prejudices against me in two. The first against my personal carriage, the second against my public. For the first, of what concerneth my personal, some are in the libel which are answered in the defences and duplies, and they are three. First, Lawmont's business. Secondly, the sending men to starve in Jura. And thirdly, the business in Kintyre. For the first two, I am as free of them as any man; for I was not in Scotland when Towart was taken, and articles broken: and I may say, I never harboured so base a thought as to break articles, neither did I ever allow it in others; yet that can be no excuse to others; for I hold it not lawful in any to do that which they condemn in others; yea, if the one side of a relation fail in their duty, I think it no excuse for the other to do the like. And for the second, the business of Jura, it is so ridiculous, that till I came to Scotland last, I never heard a colourable pretence for the report. For the third, it will be clear it was the act of a council of war, by public authority, approven in parliament, and no deed of mine. I bless God, there is not one deed in the libel against me, for any prejudice done to any man's person, when I was in the fields commanding forces in chief, (as I was several times) neither is there any thing in it for deeds while his majesty was in Scotland, but two great calumnies; the first, my accession to the act of the West Kirk: the second, my corresponding at that time with the English army.

"The prejudices out of this libel are many, which some of the parties say they were pressed to give in; some of them for deeds thirty, some more years ago, being lawful decreets before the session, when such fools as Lauderdale, Haddington, Southesk, and such men, were in employment, where truly I had no more influence nor the justice of my cause procured to me. I hope no man mistaketh my ironical word, in calling these worthy able men fools.

"I confess I thought it strange, when I came from before your lordships on Monday last, I had a summons, by warrant of the lords of articles, at the earl of Airlie's instance, for these things done before the year 1641, so contrary to his majesty's act of approbation of my service, and his own act of oblivion in the same year, 1641, but nothing of that kind is strange to me. One thing not in the libel, which I am informed taketh great impression on some, to my prejudice; it is this: though I told to your lordships formerly, that the marquis of Huntley's debt was a million of merks in the year 1640, yet it is said, his estate being great which I have possessed, I am satisfied of what was due to me, yet I possess all. The very narration of his rent what it is, will show the falsehood of this calumny; for after the death of Lewis, marquis of Huntley, my nephew, now earl Aboyn, and others of his friends, with the chamberlains of the estate, met me and some others who are in this house, at Stirling; and when they had put the least peat or poultry in money, the height of all the rent, as themselves gave it up, is but about fifty thousand merks Scots, which I could never find it to be by a good deal; out of which was to be deduced some ministers' stipends, chamberlains' fees, waste lands, and ill payments, with all public dues. And, (although it be but very small to a person of that quality) the lady Huntley had, by my connivance, six thousand merks in possession, and the earl

attempts were so many absolutions of the marquis, in every body's eye but his pursuers; the more his enemies dived into his conduct, the more innocent he was like to appear; and several of the members of parliament were like to cool in this process, especially after they heard his clear and evident defences in the matter of

1661.

Aboyn, upon the same account, had four thousand, though I acknowledge it is but small to a person of his worth and quality. Yet these things being deduced, I dare confidently say, I came very little above half interest of the sums acknowledged due to me, under the hands of Lewis, marquis of Huntley, and earl of Aboyn. And I did certainly offer to give more ease of the sums than ever I got, if I might either get money, creditors taken off, or land secured to me; and no reasonable man can question the justness of the debts, when they shall but hear them.

"The second prejudice against me, is in my public carriage and constancy in the way wherein I was engaged, which I think a hard case to make my crime. I profess if I had not thought the engagement upon me binding for the time, to such things as I did, I think truly I had been much more guilty in doing as I did; for it is observable in one of the heathen emperors, who, to try his Christian servants, imposed some things contrary to their profession, and such as refused he honoured, others he rejected. And I shall here add an argument, not in my papers, to show clearly to all, I was no prime leader. It hath been told your lordships by a noble lord of this house, that in the year 1647, which is the year and parliament wherein all the business concerning the late king's remaining in England (when the Scots army returned) was ended: in that parliament it is told your lordships, in Montrose's process, that I pressed a ratification of my son's disposition of Muckdock, but could not carry the same; and when I was not able to carry such a particular, was I prime leader? let any rational man judge: so with what is in my papers, this point cannot stick with any to my prejudice. But, on the contrary, I acknowledge my duty to the lawful magistrate to be *jure divino*, and to be contained under the fifth commandment, 'Honour thy father and thy mother.' And as it is well observed by some, they have that style of fathers to procure them all fatherly subjection, reverence, and duty, from their inferiors, and to stir them up to all tenderness and affection toward their subjects.

"I have forborne many things in my papers, of the causes and motives of the church and kingdom of Scotland's proceeding, lest I should have been mistaken : I must do so here likewise, for if I should but mention king James VI. his words, in his own book, concerning a king's duty to his people, and the people's to their king; I might run the same hazard. I shall therefore direct any to his works, and the 155th page, so 157, 195, 200, 174; so 493, 494, 495. I shall here likewise clear that point of compliance, by an observation which divines have from this same fifth command, and the former, the fourth, and it is this; that all the rest of the commands are negative but these two, and therefore they admit of some exceptions: for, as they say, affirmative precepts *semper obligant, sed non ad semper*, bind not at all times; but negative precepts *semper et ad semper obligant*, bind always, and at all times. This is not only the doctrine of divines, but of Christ and his disciples, which they practised;

so did David, and so he instructeth his children on his deathbed; so teach the apostles, and so is every man ready to interpret the fourth command, though the latitude of liberty on that day be not so great as many presume: but doubtless it is much for works of necessity and charity. And the same latitude cannot be well denied to the fifth command, as may be evidenced both by precept and practice of the prophets and apostles. But I will not insist in this, hoping it is clear to any. I shall only at this time, without reflection upon any, regret to your lordships, my own condition, that when his majesty recommendeth the trial of his subjects, I am alone singled out, not to try my carriage, it seemeth, but to find out any crime, which is hard, *nemo sine crimine vivit;* neither am I to justify myself, who am as free as any, of all things which have been worst looked upon in public transactions during the troubles; and was as willing as any to contribute at all times for a settling betwixt his majesty and his people, that his throne might be established in righteousness ; whereof I gave evidence at Dunse, in the year 1639, and by my constant advice and correspondence with that noble person the earl of Rothes, at London, 1640, and no man could do his majesty better service at that time than I did, in refusing some things thereafter in the year 1641, in Scotland, where, in public parliament, I had his majesty's gracious testimony, that I dealt over honestly with him, though I was stiff as to the point in controversy. And as king James saith, many designations are taken in Scotland, from ill hours. Some present know my tenderness of his majesty, to bring that business of the incident to any public trial. After that time, my endeavours in the year 1646 were extended for his majesty's service, in going twice to London by his command and allowance, at which time (though it be otherwise falsely alleged) no mention was ever made of any thing relating to the disposal of his majesty's person, wherein I get the blame; though I may and do say truly, I deserve as little as any. But yet to show the reason of it, I shall mention a few words of a very honest, learned, and godly minister, Mr. Gee, in his book of the Return of Prayer, in his third query concerning the reason of God's hiding himself from his people's prayers, grounded on his promises, and his seeming to answer the contrary by his providences : I hope no man will mistake me in using his words and scripture examples. When he comes to speak of the second way of inquiry for this, he telleth of three indispositions of men, that blear our eyes: first, offence at the thing fallen out ; secondly, men's partiality to themselves; thirdly, their prejudice against others. I intend only the last: for the first he mentioneth the 37th psalm, David's stumbling at the prosperity of the wicked. For the second, partiality to ourselves, he saith, self-indulgence spreads a veil over the eyes, and forestalleth the judgment, that whatsoever cause of the thing be in ourselves, we cannot easily see it. Few will say, 'What have I done?' whereof the prophet complaineth ; fewer, with the dis-

1661. the king's murder, and his pursuers began to fear hazard in a vote of the house. Therefore the parliament was cunningly enough brought in to send a letter to the king, wherein the whole of their past procedure was owned, and no room left for them to go back; and Glencairn and Rothes go post to court with it.* This letter was

ciples, 'Is it I, Lord?' but fewest with David, 'It is I, what have these done?' The third indisposition is, prejudices against others; for we are no less (saith he) hasty and severe in sentencing and faulting other men, than we are well conceited and favourable in judging ourselves; which humour Christ decyphereth, while he saith, 'Why beholdest thou the mote in thy brother's eye, and considerest not the beam in thine own?' And as there is in men a prejudice towards others in general, through which they are disposed to find fault with all but themselves, and to lay that blame, which must rest somewhere, at another man's door rather than their own; so there is a more special and vehement prejudice, when men are banded (as he saith) in parties, each against other, when usually men, without standing to inquire or reflect on any other way, they cast all the charge and procurement of calamitous events, upon their contrary way or party: and for this he instanceth that of Korah, which, after the Lord had cut them off by his own immediate hand, the conspirators said, it was Moses and Aaron had killed the people of the Lord. So did the Jews cast all the blame of their hard usage from the Romans, on Christ and his apostles: so did the Romans, the destruction of Rome by the Goths and Vandals, on Christians and Christianity, which occasioned Augustine to write that book, *De Civitate Dei*. All this may evidently show the ill of these three indispositions of mind, and particularly this of prejudice against others, especially to all who are concerned in it.

"I have but only a few words to say, in remembering your lordships of three things observable in my carriage during the late troubles. First, my never joining in the national covenant, till commanded by his late royal majesty. Secondly, my never receiving any pay during all the troubles, either as committee-man, commander-in-chief, colonel, or captain, in all the services of England, Scotland, or Ireland, in a parliament of the year 1646, which was after all I had was destroyed by the Irish rebels and their associates: and what I got from the parliament 1647, was after my estates and lands were ruined, and was only for my family's subsistence, and paying some necessitous creditors some annual rents; as the act of parliament 1647, and order to the Scots commissioners at London, the same year can show. And for the first negative part, Sir William Thomson's hand will prove it, who was either depute or principal receiver and layer out of all public monies all that time. Thirdly, my being free of any actings in the years 1646 and 1647, anent the disposing of his majesty's royal father's person, never having concurred in committees in Scotland or England, nor as a commissioner at London, anent the same, nor in any resolutions concerning the return of the Scots army, nor the money for their arrears agreed to in these times; except that I was present in the parliament 1647, which I do not well know. By all which it is evident, how clearly and freely I may say, that I do not deserve to be the single sufferer in all his majesty's dominions, for my carriage during the late troubles, his majesty having (to his eternal praise) pardoned all but some of the murderers of his late royal father.

"Therefore I take the boldness, now that all the papers are read, to show your lordships, that so much pains needed not to have been taken in summoning witnesses, and otherwise, in this business; for I ever offered, and do offer to acknowledge all matters of fact which any man can justly prove, (much of the libel being matter of fact) except some alleged words which are notoriously false and irrelevant, and even so libelled. And as I did formerly, so I do still entreat, before any further procedure, my humble submission, with your grace and this honourable parliament's recommendation, may be sent to his majesty, which I hope none of your lordships will ever have cause to repent you of, having now heard and seen the favourableness of my cause, and desire in this."

* The following is Sir George M'Kenzie's account of this affair; it is a little different, and contains, besides a testimony to the fact of the marquis being a martyr for religion, some circumstances which Wodrow, full and circumstantial as he is, has omitted : " Lauderdale had passionately opposed the intended marriage betwixt the king and Argyle's daughter; yet Lauderdale being now raised above all hazard of his opposition, and being desirous to lessen Middleton, and to oppose whatever he owned, did many good offices to the marquis; and some ascribed this assistance to the respect he had still to the good old cause, for which the marquis mainly suffered, and to the intercession of the lord Lorn, who had married the countess of Lauderdale's niece, and who stayed at court to manage his father's business. To balance all which, the commissioner did send the earls of Glencairn and Rothes, commissionated, as was pretended, by the parliament, to represent what they had done in his service, but the true design was, that they might oppose all applications that should be made in favours of the marquis of Argyle: and I remember, that the marquis hearing of the commission, did immediately conclude himself destroyed, and his conjecture was very well founded; for Glencairn did daily incense the duke of Albemarle [Monk], and the chancellor of England [Clarendon], and Rothes, who was very intimate with Lauderdale, and knew very well how to manage his humour, did much lessen Lauderdale's kindness to the marquis, by representing to him how violently Argyle had persecuted him formerly; what new trouble he might bring to his lordship's affairs, if he escaped; and that all his endeavours would at last prove ineffectual, and so it was not prudence to engage too far in a desperate quarrel." What follows is particularly worthy of the reader's attention, as exhibiting on the part of the parliament, one of the most perfect specimens of legal tyranny, and on the part of lord Albemarle, of personal depravity, that has yet been put on record.—" The rele-

signed by almost all the members, and the pretext was, that some misinformations had been given at London of their procedure; and that their actings might be the better cleared, the parliament desire Mr. James Sharp, late minister of Crail, and now divinity professor at St. Andrews, may go up in company with them as one of the churchmen best acquaint with his majesty. The event showed the mystery of this. The two statesmen were to push the marquis's business, regulate the act of fines, and other matters, and Mr. Sharp was to join the highfliers in England, and take off any impressions left by the representation made by the ministers of Edinburgh, of which before, and model matters as to the church. They set out for London, April 29th. A little before this, the marquis's son, lord Neil Campbell, had gone up to court, and represented his father's defences, with all the advantage he could; and had done this, as was then said, not without some consider- able influence upon a good many there.

1661.

In the beginning of May, witnesses were examined against the marquis. I have not seen their examination and depositions, and can only set down the list of witnesses given in to him, with diets of their examination. May 3d, anent my lord's being in arms with the English, and exchanging prisoners with the Scots, "William, duke of Hamilton, John, earl of Athole, James lord Forrester, Sir Norman M'Leod, John M'Naughtan, John Semple, younger, of Fulwood, Gavin Walkinshaw, of that ilk, Walter Watson,

---

vancy of the articles being discussed, probation was led for proving the late compliance after the year 1651, and his accession to the king's murther which was excepted out of the letter; and though very many witnesses were adduced, yet some thought the probation not full enough. But after the debate and probation were all closed, and the parliament ready to consider the whole matter, one who came post from London knockt most rudely at the parliament door; and upon his entry with a packet, which he presented to the commissioner, made him conclude that he had brought a remission, or some other warrant, in favours of the marquis, and the rather because the bearer was a Campbell. But the packet being opened, it was found to have in it a great many letters which had been directed by the marquis to the duke of Albemarle, when he was governor of Scotland, and which he reserved to see if they were absolutely necessary: and being by these diligent envoys advertised of the scantiness of the probatim, he had sent them post by M'Naughtan's servant. No sooner were these produced, but the parliament was fully satisfied as to the proof of the compliance; and the next day he was forefaulted, and the manner of his execution was put to the vote; and being stated 'hang, or behead,' it was concluded that he should be beheaded, and that his head should be placed on the tolbooth, by where Montrose's head had formerly stood."—M'Kenzie's History of Scotland, pp. 38, 40.

As a conclusion to this note, we shall give one paragraph on the state of the nation that issued in such monstrous proceedings, and the character of the man who thus frankly lent his honour and sold his integrity to promote them, from the pen of certainly one of the first of orators, as well as the most experienced of statesmen: "The short interval between Cromwell's death and the Restoration, exhibits the picture of a nation either so wearied with changes as not to feel, or so subdued by military power as not to dare to show any care or even preference with regard to the form of their government. All was in the army; and that army, by such a concurrence of fortuitous circumstances as history teaches us not to be surprised at, had fallen into the hands of one, than whom a baser could not be found in its lowest ranks. Personal courage appears to have been Monk's only virtue; reserve and dissimulation made up the whole stock of his wisdom. But to this man did the nation look up, ready to receive from his orders the form of government he should choose to prescribe. There is reason to believe, that, from the general bias of the presbyterians, as well as of the cavaliers, monarchy was the prevalent wish; but it is observable, that although the parliament was, contrary to the principle upon which it was pretended to be called, composed of many avowed royalists, yet none dared to hint at the restoration of the king, till they had Monk's permission, or rather command, to receive and consider his letters. It is impossible, in reviewing the whole of this transaction, not to remark that a general, who had gained his rank, reputation, and station, in the service of a republic, and of what he, as well as others, called, however falsely, the cause of liberty, made no scruple to lay the nation prostrate at the feet of a monarch, without a single provision in favour of that cause; and, if the promise of indemnity may seem to argue that there was some attention, at least, paid to the safety of his associates in arms, his subsequent conduct gives reason to suppose that even this provision was owing to any other cause rather than to any generous feeling in his breast. For he afterwards not only acquiesced in the insults so meanly put upon the illustrious corpse of Blake, under whose auspices and command he had performed the most creditable services of his life, but in the trial of Argyle, produced letters of friendship and confidence to take away the life of a nobleman, the zeal and cordiality of whose co-operation with him, proved by such documents, was the chief ground of his execution; thus gratuitously surpassing in infamy those miserable wretches, who, to save their own lives, are sometimes persuaded to impeach, and swear away the lives of their accomplices."—History of the Early Part of the Reign of James II. by Charles James Fox, pp. 19, 20.

1661. provost of Dumbarton, John Cunningham, bailie there, John White, trumpeter, Alexander Ramsay, servant to the earl of Glencairn, John Carswel, one of his majesty's lifeguard, Hugh M'Dougal, in Lorn, Duncan M'Culloch there, Halbert Glaidstains, in Edinburgh, commissary Beans, at Leith. May 7th, anent my lord's joining in arms with the English, Donald M'Clean, of Borlas, Major David Ramsay, captain James Thomson, in Leith citadel, Daniel O'Neil there, Jonathan Moisly there, James Savel there, Robert Darkems, James Hersky, John Moisly there. And for proving the words spoken in parliament, 1649, John lord Kirkcudbright, James lord Cowpar, Robert lord Burleigh, John Corslate, provost of Kirkcudbright, William Grierson, of Bargatton. May 8th, anent his joining in arms, Henry O'Neil, of the lifeguard, Archibald M'Clean, servant to the tutor of M'Clean, Angus M'Claughson, son to the captain of Inchconnel, Donald M'Clean, of Calzeach, John Campbell, of Dunstafnish, Mr. James M'Clean, of Kilmaloag. Words spoken at London, and James Masterton's house in Edinburgh; George, earl of Linlithgow, earls of Callendar, Hume, and Aboyn, Sir James Fowlis, of Collingtoun. There were a great many other witnesses, but I have not seen either their names or declarations, and the reader will find the plain facts, as indeed they were, in the marquis's defences.

How those who went up to court, managed matters there, I shall not say; but from their arrival, to the day of the parliament's sentence, the parliament had, almost every day, renewed messages to haste through his trial. These were obeyed as much as might be. Accordingly upon Saturday, May 25th, he was brought to the bar, and received his sentence in face of parliament, " That he was found guilty of high treason, and adjudged to be execute to the death as a traitor, his head to be severed from his body at the cross of Edinburgh, upon Monday, the 27th instant; and affixed in the same place where the marquis of Montrose's head was formerly, and his arms torn before the parliament, and at the cross." And from the bar he was sent to the common prison of Edinburgh. That day the parliament was extremely thin, and all withdrew, but such who were determined entirely to follow the course of the times. When he was brought to the bar to receive his sentence, he put the parliament in mind of the practice of Theodosius the emperor, who enacted, that the sentence of death should not be execute till thirty days after it was passed; and added, " I crave but ten, that the king may be acquainted with it." This was refused, and he was told, that now he behoved to receive the parliament's sentence upon his knees; he immediately kneeled, and said, " I will, in all humility." The sentence being pronounced, he offered to speak : but the trumpets sounding, he stopped till they ended, and then said, " I had the honour to set the crown upon the king's head, (and indeed the marquis brought him to the crown) and now he hastens me to a better crown than his own." And directing himself to the commissioner and parliament, he said, " You have the indemnity of an earthly king among your hands, and have denied me a share in that, but you cannot hinder me from the indemnity of the King of kings, and shortly you must be before his tribunal, I pray he mete not out such measure to you, as you have done to me, when you are called to account for all your actings, and this among the rest."

Without doors it was said, the marquis of Argyle had done nothing, but what was necessary by the natural law of self-preservation, and just, since conquest and consent make a good title in the conqueror; and April 2d, 1652, all Scotland had in a very solemn manner consented to Oliver's government at Dalkeith, and his solitary resistance could never have restored the king. And though the marquis had not been the last man who stood out, but had done as all the rest of the nation did, and submitted to the usurper, it was observed, that not a man in England or Ireland had suffered merely for owning Cromwell, though he was there a rebel, and in Scotland a conqueror. It was further asked, Where was the justice to punish one man for a guilty nation? or the mercy to forgive many, and not take in so good and great a man with others? and every body saw that the marquis was sentenced by his *socii criminis*, his complices, as he himself told Sir John Fletcher in the house, and those who were in the transgression, if it must be made one, long before he was in it. But who can stand before envy, revenge, and jealousy! The tree of prelacy and arbitrary measures behoved to be soaked when a planting, with the noble blood of this excellent patriot, staunch presbyterian, and vigorous asserter of Scotland's liberty: and much bitter and bloody fruit did it bear in the following twenty-six years, as will appear in the sequel of this history.

The sentence against this noble person was, not only, in the eyes of onlookers, iniquitous and unrighteous in itself, but really contrary to their own new made law, and an act made by this very parliament, no longer since than March 30th, act 15, parliament 1, session 1, Charles II., where in express terms, " his majesty, by advice of the estates of parliament, grants his indemnity and full assurance, to all persons that acted in, and by virtue of the said pretended parliaments, (viz. those from 1640 to 1650,) and other meetings flowing from them, to be unquestioned in their lives and fortunes, for any deed or deeds done by them in their said usurpation." By a proclamation, June 10th, this year, concerning ecclesiastical affairs, which the reader will find at the bottom of the page, * I find the fore-

said date of this act, and the king approves it. And it is very plain the marquis's indictment and sentence runs upon deeds done in those parliaments, and during that alleged usurpation in them, save what relates to his joining with the English, as to which enough has been set down for his vindication: so that I cannot but be of opinion, that the parliament, in condemning the marquis for these deeds, contradict themselves. There is indeed a reservation 'n the act, as to such as shall be excepted in the general indemnity to be passed by his majesty, and such who were guilty of the king's murder: but that exception only concerned the persons who afterwards were fined, and neither that nor the other concern the marquis. Thus in this sentence the parliament must be reckoned *felo's de se*.

1661.

As through the whole of his trial, this noble person gave the brightest example of meekness and patience, when most unaccountably abused by the king's advocate and others; so he received his sentence with that composure which became so innocent a man, and excellent christian; and would by no means depart from the honourable testimony for religion and liberty he was engaged in. When his case was beyond all hope in his friends' eyes, and no prospect of any justice appeared, some gallant gentle-

---

* The King's Majesty's Proclamation concerning Church affairs, June 10th, 1661.
Charles R.
Charles, by the grace of God, king of Scotland, England, France, and Ireland, defender of the faith, to our lovits, lyon king at arms, and his brethren heralds, messengers, our sheriffs in that part, conjunctly and severally, specially constitute, greeting. As soon as it pleased Almighty God, by his own outstretched arm, wonderfully to bring us back in peace, to the exercise of our royal government, we did apply ourself to the restoring of our kingdoms to that liberty and happiness which they enjoyed under the government of our royal ancestors; and in order thereunto, we called a parliament in that our ancient kingdom of Scotland, as the most proper mean to settle the same, after so many years' troubles, and to restore its ancient liberty, after those grievous sufferings, and that heavy bondage imposed of late by bloody usurpers, because of their loyalty expressed to us. And whereas the estates of parliament of that our ancient kingdom, have so fully, freely, and unanimously vindicated their own honour, in asserting our royal power, prerogative, the privileges of our crown, and our supremacy over all persons in all causes, as absolutely as ever any of our royal progenitors, kings of Scotland, at any time possessed, used and exerced the same, not only by taking away of these invasions, brought on by the iniquity of the times, during the late troubles; but also by their rescinding all those pretended parliaments, wherein any force might have appeared to have been put on our royal father, since the year 1688, reserving private rights, and indemnifying our subjects, for what was done during that time: and whereas our parliament, by their act the twenty-ninth of March, hath declared, that it is our full and firm resolution, to maintain the true protestant religion, in its purity of doctrine and worship, as it was established within that our kingdom, during the reigns of our royal father and grandfather of blessed memory, and that we will be careful to promote the power of godliness, to encourage the exercises of religion, both public and private, and to suppress all profaneness and disorderly walking; and for that end, will give all due countenance and protection to the ministers of the gospel, they containing themselves within the bounds and limits of their ministerial calling, and behaving themselves with that submission and obedience to our authority and commands, that is suitable to the allegiance and duty of good subjects.

1661. men undertook to bring him out of the castle, partly by force, and partly by a stratagem. The project was so far gone into, that I am told, the marquis was once in a complete disguise; but on a sudden he altered his mind, thanked his friends, and told them, he would not disown the good cause he had so publicly espoused, and threw aside his borrowed habit, and resolved to suffer the utmost.* When after the sentence he entered the tolbooth, his excellent lady was waiting for him there. Upon seeing her, he said, "they have given me till Monday to be with you, my dear, therefore let us make for it." She embracing him, wept bitterly, and said, "the Lord will require it, the Lord will require it." The bailie who accompanied his lordship, though no great friend to him, was deeply affected, yea none in the room could refrain from tears. The marquis himself was perfectly composed, and said, "forbear, forbear: truly I pity them, they know not what they are doing: they may shut me in where they please, but they cannot shut out God from me: for my part I am as content to be here as in the castle, and as content in the castle as in the Tower of London, and as content there as when at liberty; and I hope to be as content upon the scaffold as any of them all." He added, "that he remembered a scripture cited to him by an honest minister lately in the Castle, and endeavoured to put it in practice, when Ziklag was taken and burnt, and the people spoke of stoning David, he encouraged himself in the Lord." This account, and much of what follows, I have under a worthy minister's hand, who was present with the marquis, and took notes of what he spoke at the time.

All his short time till Monday, the marquis spent with the greatest serenity and cheerfulness, and in the proper exercises of a dying christian. He said to some ministers allowed to be with him in the prison, "that shortly they would envy him who was got before them," and added, "mind that I tell it you, my skill fails me, if you who are

---

And as to the government of the church, that we will make it our care to settle and secure the same in such a frame as shall be most agreeable to the word of God, most suitable to monarchical government, and most complying with the public peace and quiet of the kingdom: and in the meantime, that we do allow the present administration by sessions, presbyteries and synods (they keeping within bounds, and behaving themselves as said is) and that notwithstanding of the act passed that day, rescissory of all pretended parliaments since the year 1633. Therefore we have thought fit, by this our proclamation, not only to declare our gracious acceptance of these ample testimonies of the duty and affection of that our parliament, by which the world may take notice, how unanimously loyal that kingdom is, and how hearty in our service, of which we ourself was ever confident: but also to make known our firm resolution, to maintain and preserve that our kingdom in their just liberties: and likewise to make good what our parliament have declared in our name, as to matters of religion. And considering how much our interest and the quiet of that kingdom is concerned, in the right settlement and peace of that our church, which through the confusions of these latter times, hath been much discomposed, we do purpose, after mature deliberation, with such as we shall call, to employ our royal authority, for settling and securing the government and the administration thereof, in such a way as may best conduce to the glory of God, to the good of religion, to unity, order, and to the public peace and satisfaction of our kingdom: and in the meantime, we will and command all our loving subjects, ministers and others, as they will answer at their peril, to abstain from meddling with what may concern the public government of that our church, either by preaching, remonstrances, warnings, declarations, acts, or petitions of church judicatories, or any other way; and to compose themselves to that quietness and inoffensive deportment, which their duty to us, and the peace of the church doth require. Our will is herefore, and we charge you straitly and command, that, incontinent these our letters seen, ye pass to the market-cross of our burgh of Edinburgh, and to the remanent market-crosses of the head burghs of that our kingdom, and there, by open proclamation, in our name and authority, make publication hereof to all our lieges and subjects, wherethrough none pretend ignorance of the same, as you will answer to us. The which to do we commit to you conjunctly and severally, our full power by these our letters, delivering the same by you duly execute and indorsed, again to the bearer. Given under our hand at Whitehall, the tenth day of June, 1661, and of our reign the thirteenth year.

By his majesty's command,
LAUDERDALE.

---

* Burnet says, "For some time there was a stop to the proceedings in which lord Argyle was contriving an escape out of the castle. He kept his bed for some days, and his lady being of the same stature with himself, and coming to him in a chair, he had put on her clothes and was going into the chair, but he apprehended he should be discovered, and his execution hastened, and so his heart failed him."—Vol. i. p. 177.

ministers will not either suffer much, or sin much; for though you go along with those men in part, if you do it not in all things, you are but where you were, and so must suffer; and if you go not at all with them, you shall but suffer." During his life the marquis was reckoned rather timorous than bold to any excess; and in prison he said, he was naturally inclined to fear in his temper, but desired those about him to observe, as he could not but do, that the Lord had heard his prayers, and removed all fear from him. Indeed his friends' work was to restrain and qualify his fervent longings after his dissolution, and not to support him under the near views of it. At his own desire his lady took her leave of him upon the Sabbath night. Mr. Robert Douglas, and Mr. George Hutcheson preached to him in the tolbooth on the Lord's day, and his dear and much valued friend Mr. David Dickson, and others, prayed with him at night, and I have been told, Mr. Dickson was his bedfellow the last night he had in time.

Upon Monday, when very much thronged in subscribing papers, making conveyances, and with other necessary things relating to his business and estate, of a sudden, about seven of the clock in the morning, when in the midst of company, he was so overpowered with the sensible effusion of the joy of the Holy Ghost, that he could not contain, but brake out in the greatest affection and rapture, and said, " I thought to have concealed the Lord's goodness, but it will not do, I am now ordering my affairs, and God is sealing my charter to a better inheritance, and just now saying to me, ' son, be of good cheer, thy sins are forgiven thee.'" Such expressions I know will be reckoned the effects of enthusiasm, and reproached under the name of cant, and I doubt not but it will be construed weakness in me to regard or relate them in so degenerate an age as we are fallen into: but I have this passage confirmed by so many and indubitable hands, some of them alive when I write this, that I cannot only assert it for truth, but likewise record a remarkable harmony betwixt this and the wrestlings and prayers of many, before, and at that very moment, on the marquis's behalf. And if any mock at such instances of the divine condescension, I wish their bands be not made strong; he who is ignorant is like to be so still.

1661.

Either upon Monday or some other time after his sentence, the marquis received the following letter from a minister, who with others was much concerned for the Lord's presence with him: it was sweet to this godly martyr, and contains some things in it, which clear up the marquis's circumstances, and I reckon it will not be unacceptable to the serious reader, being short but substantial.

" My Lord,

" I hope by this time you know that God sendeth no man a warfare upon his own charges; the report of your seasonable and suitable support, and of what the Lord doth to your soul, with your rising integrity before the world, as it was clear to others before, so it doth much comfort us over many things, so that we can speak with the adversary in the gate. We reckon it was a mercy to the cause, (if I may speak so) and to many friends of it, that God has brought your lordship upon the stage: he hath vindicated his reproached work in spite of reproach, so that it will be advantageous for the nation; neither do I doubt but it was a singular mercy to yourself, and shall be a relief to your oppressed name, which this day is visibly come above water. If you had been in favour with the greatest of men, and had the world smiling upon you, I much question if it had been so well with your soul and conscience, and if you had had that room in gracious hearts, which I can confidently say now you have. We enjoy the sweet fruits of what you now sweat for; and your lordship may reckon your labours and sufferings sold at a good rate, when you consider how many souls have been refreshed these twenty-three years bygone; the reward of which we wish may now richly return to your bosom: so are many wishing this day who never saw your face, to whom your name and chain are savoury. Be of good courage, and God shall strengthen your heart, and be your

1661. guide even unto death. O death! where is thy sting? Thou art now a smiling bridge to eternal serenity, where no inbreaking, no sin shall be, but sweet breathings of the Holy Ghost, and songs of victory; no dreadful sentence, where the Accuser of the brethren has no place: a little bit of time might have sent you thither with less credit, and not capable of so large a crown; for great is the reward of some there! My lord, keep the kindly sense of your failings upon your heart, that Christ may be as precious to you as to the beggar that never was honoured to suffer for him. The Lord Jehovah be your shield and exceeding great reward; to him we commit you, and do submit; and we hope he shall give a good account of all we have in dependance before him. I am," &c.

This same day, a little before his going out to the place of execution, the marquis wrote and subscribed a letter to the king, which, I persuade myself, the curious reader will desire to have inserted here, and it is as follows.

" Most sacred Sovereign,

" I doubt not but your majesty hath an account given you from others, of the issue of that strange process and indictment laid against me, before this can come to your royal hands; of which if I had been guilty according to the charge, I should have esteemed myself unworthy to breathe upon the earth, much less would I have presumed to make any application to your majesty. But of all those great crimes which have been charged upon me, there hath nothing been proven, except a compliance with the prevalent usurping rebels, after they had subdued all your majesty's dominions, whereby I was forced, with many others, to submit unto their unlawful power and government, which was an epidemic disease, and fault of the time.

" What measure soever I have met with, and whatever malice or calumny hath been cast upon me, yet it is my inexpressible joy and comfort under all these sufferings, that I am found free, and acquit of any accession to that execrable murder committed against the life of your royal father, which (as I desire a comfortable appearance before the Judge both of the quick and the dead) my soul did ever abominate; for death, with the inward peace of my innocency is much more acceptable to me, than life itself, with the least stain of treachery.

" And now I am confident that your majesty's displeasure will be satisfied, and you will suffer my failings to be expiate with my life, which with all humility and submission I have yielded up; and in this small period that remains of my life, no earthly thing shall be more cordially desired by me, than your happiness; and that your majesty and your successors to all generations, may sway the sceptre of these nations, and that they may be a blessed people under your government.

" And now hoping that the humble supplication of your majesty's dying subject, may find some place within the large extent of your princely goodness and clemency, I have taken the boldness to cast the desolate condition of my poor wife and family upon your royal favour; for whatever may be your majesty's displeasure against myself, these, I hope, have not done any thing to procure your majesty's indignation. And since that family have had the honour to be faithful subjects, and serviceable to your royal progenitors, I humbly beg my faults may not extinguish the lasting merit and memory of those who have given so many signal proofs of constant loyalty for many generations. Orphans and widow, by special prerogative and command from God, are put under your protection and defence, that you suffer them not to be wronged: they will owe their preservation so entirely to your majesty's bounty and favour, that your countenance, and nothing else that is human, can be a shield against their ruin.

" I shall add no more, only being addebted to severals of your majesty's good subjects, and your royal justice being the source and fountain of all equity, whereby all your people are preserved in their just rights and interests, I humbly beg, that none of them may suffer for my fault, but that you would allow them satisfaction and payment of what is justly owing unto them, of those sums and debts which are truly resting to

CHAP. II.] OF THE CHURCH OF SCOTLAND. 155

my son and me. And as it is my serious and last desire to my children and posterity, next to their duty to Almighty God, that they may be faithful and serviceable to your majesty; so, were I to enjoy this frail life any longer, I would endeavour before all the world, to evidence myself to be

"Your majesty's most humble, devoted, and obedient subject and servant,
" ARGYLE."
" From your prison, Edinburgh,
May 27th, 1661."

The marquis had a sweet time, as to his soul, when he was in the tolbooth, and this increased still, the nearer he was to his end. As he had slept most calmly and pleasantly his last night, so in the intervals of his necessary business, he had much spiritual conversation with Mr. Hutcheson and other ministers upon Monday before dinner. He dined with his friends precisely at twelve of the clock, with the utmost cheerfulness: and after he had retired some time alone, when he opened the door, Mr. Hutcheson said, "what cheer, my lord?" He answered, "good cheer, Sir, the Lord hath again confirmed, and said to me from heaven, 'Son, be of good cheer, thy sins are forgiven thee,'" and he gushed out in abundance of tears of joy, so that he drew back to the window and wept there; from that he came to the fire, and made as if he would stir it a little to cover his concern, but all would not do, his tears ran down his face; so coming to Mr. Hutcheson, he said in a perfect rapture, I think his kindness overcomes me, but God is good to me, that he lets not out too much of it here, for he knows I could not bear it: get me my cloak, and let us go. Then they told him the clock was kept back since one, till the bailies should come. He answered, they are far in the wrong; and presently kneeled down and prayed before all present, in a most sweet and heavenly manner, to the ravishment of all there. As he ended prayer, the bailie sent up notice to him to come down. Upon which he called for a glass of wine, and asked a blessing upon it standing, and continuing in the same frame; and said, " Now let us go, and God go with us."

After he had taken his leave of such in the room, as were not to go to the scaffold with him, when going towards the door he said, " I could die like a Roman, but choose rather to die as a christian. Come away, gentlemen, he that goes first goes cleanliest." When going down, he called Mr. James Guthrie to him, and embracing him in the most endearing way, took his farewell of him. Mr. Guthrie at parting addressed the marquis thus, " My lord, God hath been with you, he is with you, and God will be with you; and such is my respect for your lordship, that if I were not under the sentence of death myself, I could cheerfully die for your lordship." So they parted for a very short season, in two or three days to meet in a better place.

1661.

The marquis was accompanied to the scaffold by divers noblemen and gentlemen; he was, and all with him, in black, had his cloak and hat on as he went down the street. He mounted the scaffold with the greatest serenity and gravity, as one going to his Father's house, saluted all who were on it: and then Mr. Hutcheson prayed; and next the marquis delivered his speech, which hath been many times printed, but deserves a room in this collection; and so it is added below. *

---

* Marquis of Argyle's Speech upon the scaffold, May 27th, 1661.
" Gentlemen,
" Many will expect that I will speak many things; and according to their several opinions and dispositions, so will their expectations be from me, and constructions of me: but I resolve to disappoint many; for I came not either to justify myself, but the Lord, who is holy in all his ways, and righteous in all his works, holy and blessed is his name; neither come I to condemn others. I know many will expect that I should speak against the hardness of the sentence pronounced against me, but I will say nothing to it. I bless the Lord I pardon all men, as I desire to be pardoned of the Lord myself: let the will of the Lord be done, that is all that I desire. I hope that you will have more charity to me now, than you would have had at another time, since I speak before the Lord, to whom I must give account shortly. I know very well that my words have had but little weight with many, and that many have mistaken my words; many have thought me a great enemy to those great works that have of late been brought to pass; but do not mistake me, people, I speak it in the presence of the Lord, I entered not upon the work of Reformation with any design of advantage to myself, or prejudice to the king or his government, as my will (which was written in

1661. After this pertinent, pathetic, seasonable and affecting speech, Mr. James Hamilton prayed. After him, my lord prayed most sweetly himself, then he took his leave of all his friends on the scaffold. He gave first to the executioner a napkin, and some money in it. To his sons-in-law, Cathness [Caitness] and Ker, his silver watch, and the year 1655, and then delivered to a friend, in whose hands it still remains) can show. As for these calumnies which have gone abroad of me, I bless God I know them to be no more but calumnies; and as I go to make a reckoning to my God, I am free as to any of them, concerning the king's person or government. I was real and cordial in my desires to bring the king home, and in my endeavours for him when he was at home; and I had no correspondence with his adversaries' army, or any of them, in the time his majesty was in Scotland; nor had I any accession to his late majesty's murder, by counsel or knowledge of it, or any other manner of way. This is a truth, as I shall answer to my Judge: and all the time his majesty was in Scotland, I was still endeavouring his advantage: my conscience beareth me witness in it. That is for that. (At this he turned about, and said, 'I hope, gentlemen, you will all remember this.')

"I confess many look on my condition as a suffering condition, but I bless the Lord, that he hath gone before me, hath trod the wine-press of his Father's wrath, by whose sufferings I hope that my sufferings shall not be eternal. I bless him that hath taken away the sting of my sufferings. I may say my charter was sealed this day; for the Lord hath said to me, 'Son, be of good cheer, thy sins be forgiven thee:' and so I hope my sufferings shall be easy; and ye know the scripture saith, 'That the Captain of our salvation was made perfect through sufferings.' I shall not speak much to these things that I am condemned for, lest I seem to condemn others: it is well known, it is only for compliance, which is the epidemical fault of this nation; I wish the Lord may pardon them, I say no more. There was an expression in my submission, presented to the parliament, of the contagion of the times, which may be misconstrued, as if I had intended thereby to lay imputation upon the work of Reformation; but I declare I intended no such thing, but it was only in relation to the corruptions and failings of men, occasioned by the prevalency of the usurping power.

"Now, gentlemen, I think there are three sorts of people that take up much of the world, and this nation: there are, first, the openly profane: and truly, I may say, though I have been a prisoner, yet I have not had mine ears shut; I hear assuredly that whoring, swearing, and drinking were never more common, and never more countenanced than now; and truly if magistrates were here, I would say to them, 'If they lay forth their power, for the glorifying of God by the restraining of this, they would fare better; if they continue in not restraining of it, they will fare the worse.' I say no more, but let either people shun profanity, or magistrates restrain it, or assuredly the wrath of God will follow on it.

"Secondly. Others they are not openly profane, every one will not allow that, but yet they are *Gallios* in these matters; if things go well as to their private interests, they care not whether religion and the church of God sink or swim: but whatever they think, God hath laid engagements upon Scotland, we are tied by covenant to religion and Reformation; those that were then unborn are engaged to it, and in our baptism we are engaged to it, and it passes the power of any under heaven to absolve a man from the oath of God, they deceive themselves, and it may be will deceive others that think otherwise; but I would caveat this. People would be ready to take this as a kind of instigation to rebellion, but they are very far in the wrong that think so, and that religion and loyalty are not consistent; if any man separate them, religion is not to be blamed, but they: it is the duty of every christian to be loyal, yet I think the order of things is to be observed, as well as their nature, the order of religion as well as the nature of it: religion must not be the cockboat, but the ship; God must have what is his, as well as Cæsar what is his; and those are the best subjects that are the best christians: and that I am looked upon as a friend to reformation, is my glory.

"Thirdly. There is another sort that are truly godly, and to speak to them I must say what I fear, and every one hath reason to fear, (it is good to fear evil.) It is true that the Lord may prevent it, but if so, I do not, and truly I cannot see any possibility of it. These times are like to be very sinning times, or very suffering times; and let christians make choice; there is a sad dilemma in the business, sin or suffer: and truly he that will choose the better part will choose to suffer; others that will choose to sin, shall not escape suffering; they shall suffer, but it may be not as I do here, (turning him to the maiden when he spake it) but worse; mine is but temporal, but theirs shall be eternal; when I shall be singing they shall be howling: beware therefore of sin, whatever ye beware of, especially in such times. Yet I cannot say of my own condition, but the Lord in his providence hath minded mercy to me, even in this world; for if I had been more favourably dealt with, I fear I might have been overcome with temptations, as many others are, and I fear many more will be, and so should have gone out of the world with a more polluted conscience than, through the mercy of God, now I have: and hence my condition is such now, as when I am gone, will be seen not to have been such as many imagined. It is fit God take me away before I fall into these temptations that I see others are fallen into, and I fear many others will fall: I wish the Lord may prevent it. Yet blessed be his name that I am kept both from present evils and evils to come.

"Some will expect that I will regret my own condition; but truly I neither grudge nor repine, nor desire I any revenge. And I declare I do not repent my going to London; for I had always rather have suffered any thing than lie under such reproaches as I did. I desire not that the Lord should judge any man, nor do I judge any but myself: I wish, that as the Lord hath pardoned me, so may he pardon them for this and other things, and that what they have

some other things in his pocket. He gave to Loudon his silver penner, to Lothian a double ducat; and bowed round, and then threw off his coat. When going to the maiden, Mr Hutcheson said, " My lord, hold now your grip sicker." [fast] He answered, " Mr. Hutcheson, you know what I said to you in the chamber, I am not afraid to be surprised with fear." The laird of Skelmorlie took him by the hand when near the maiden, and found him most composed. His last words before his kneeling are added to his speech. He kneeled down most cheerfully, and after he had prayed a little, he gave the signal, which was the lifting up of his hand, and the instrument called the maiden struck off his head, which was affixed upon the west end of the tolbooth, as a monument of the parliament's injustice, and the land's misery.* His body was received by his friends, and put into a coffin, and carried away with a good many attendants, through Linlithgow and Falkirk, to Glasgow, and thence with a numerous company to Kilpatrick, where it was put in a boat, and carried to Denune, and buried in Kilmun church.

It is scarce worth while here to take notice of the ill natured account Mr. archdeacon Eachard gives of the marquis's trial and death in his history, vol. iii. p. 63. He is pleased to bespatter the marquis's defences, with the character of long and subtle. How they could have been any shorter, and yet go through so great a heap of scandal as lies charged against him in his tedious indictment, I cannot see. Where the subtilty of his defences lies, needs to be explained, since in every point that noble person is most plain and home in his answers, and insists upon evident facts and reasonings. This writer seems to have glanced over the marquis's case, to pick out some of his expressions, in order to expose him; had he duly pondered what he advances in his defences, petitions, and speeches in print, and inclined to represent this great man fairly, we should have had quite another state of this affair than Mr. Eachard gives, from detached sentences here and there culled out. How unjust will it appear to any unprejudiced person to land the whole stress of the marquis's defences upon the indemnity, 1641. When, if he had considered his defences, he might have observed a multitude of other things after that time advanced? he ought in justice to have condescended upon the treasonable actings, not fairly accounted for in the defences, proven against him, and brought proofs of the aggravating expressions he talks of, had he acted the part of an impartial historian. Of a piece with all this are the lame and unfair hints from the marquis's last speech, which Mr. Archdeacon concludes with an idle story, one at first sight may observe to be childish and evidently false, that the marquis tore his written speech into six parts, and gave to six of his friends. Nobody of sense can give credit to so foolish a representation. Where Mr. Eachard has raked it up I cannot imagine, unless it be from some of the scandalous diurnals writ about this time. Undoubtedly such an account as he has patched up of this great man, must very much weaken his reputation as a historian in Scots affairs. However, Mr. Archdeacon, in his Appendix to the three volumes of his history, printed after I had wrote what is above, does the marquis's memory the justice, as to insert

1661.

---

done to me may never meet them in their accounts. I have no more to say, but beg the Lord, that since I go away, he may bless them that stay behind."

His last words, immediately before he laid his head upon the block, were the vindication of his innocency from that horrid crime of the king's murder, in these words:

"I desire you, gentlemen, and all that hear me, again to take notice, and remember, that now when I am entering on eternity, and am to appear before my Judge, and as I desire salvation, and expect eternal happiness from him, I am free from any accession, by knowledge, contriving, counsel, or any other way, to his late majesty's death; and I pray the Lord to preserve the present king his majesty, and to pour his best blessings upon his person and government, and the Lord give him good and faithful counsellors."

* As in a previous note we have given a passage from Burnet, which looks like an attempt to detract from the courage of the marquis, justice requires that we should give the following relating to his appearance on the scaffold. " He came to the scaffold in a very solemn but undaunted manner, accompanied with many of the nobility and some ministers. He spoke for half an hour with a great appearance of serenity. Cunningham, his physician, told me, he touched his pulse, and it did then beat at the usual rate, calm and strong."—Burnet's Hist. of his Own Times, Edin. edit. vol. i. p. 179.—*Ed.*

1661. the following letter or declaration, written by the hand of king Charles II. and signed with his seal manual, communicated to him by his grace the present duke of Argyle.

"Having taken into my consideration the faithful endeavours of the marquis of Argyle for restoring me to my just rights, and the happy settling of my dominions, I am desirous to let the world see, how sensible I am of his real respect to me, by some particular marks of my favour to him, by which they may see the trust and confidence which I repose in him: and particularly I do promise, that I will make him duke of Argyle, and knight of the garter, and one of the gentlemen of my bedchamber; and this to be performed when he shall think it fit. And I do farther promise him, to hearken to his counsels ——————— (worn out) ——————— whenever it shall please God to restore me to my just rights in England, I shall see him paid the forty thousand pounds sterling, which is due to him. All which I do promise to make good upon the word of a king.

"CHARLES R."

"St. Johnston, Sept. 24th, 1650."

I have given the narrative of this protomartyr for religion, since the reformation from popery, at greater length than at once I designed, having the fullest assurance of these facts, and my accounts of them from unquestionable vouchers; and it is pity they should not be known. His character I dare not adventure to draw: enemies themselves must allow the marquis to have been a person of extraordinary piety, remarkable wisdom and prudence, great gravity and authority, and singular usefulness. Though he had been much reproached, his trial and death did abundantly vindicate him. And as he was the great promoter and support of the covenanted work of reformation during his life, and steadfast in witnessing to it at his death, so it was much buried with him in the grave for many years.

After the revolution, when the most accurate search was made into the procedure against the marquis, I am well assured, that though indeed his sentence was passed in parliament, yet there was no warrant given or signed for his execution, commonly called the dead warrant, so great a haste were the managers of this bloody design in: and as his sentence was against many former laws and statutes in Scotland, as well as against their laws just now made; so the execution was directly illegal and without warrant, and consequently *a non habente potestatem*. And this excellent person's death, by the very letter of our Scots law, is murder: so infatuate in their thirst after blood have some people been. But I shall have done with this, when once I have observed, that so utterly unaccountable was this procedure against the marquis, that Sir George M'Kenzie, who, among the last things he did while in this world, wrote a vindication of the government in Scotland during king Charles's reign; though he was every way the ablest advocate ever that party had, yet is so far from adventuring to justify the conduct against this noble person, that he does not so much as name the marquis or his process. And though he was one of the lawyers allowed to my lord Argyle, this would not have hindered him afterwards to have advanced what would have softened that matter, if he had had any thing to produce upon this subject. Must not then the party own that his vindication, whereof they boast so much, is lame? but indeed that is not its worst fault; I am well assured I shall, ere I have done, prove it false, as well as lame. In short, upon searching the parliament registers, I find there is not one word of this great man's process or sentence in them: though those took up a good many sederunts, there is nothing in record, when many things of far less import are there, as to the marquis, Mr. James Guthrie, or the lord Warristoun's trial. The reasons of this may be easily guessed, indeed it was for the reputation of this parliament, that so foul steps and black processes should not be in their books.

SECT. IV.

Of the sufferings and martyrdom of the Rev. Mr. James Guthrie, minister of the gospel at Stirling, June 1st, 1661.

Some account of the beginnings of the trouble this excellent and singular person met with last year, is already given in the first chapter, where we left him in prison at Stirling; and there he was, and at Dundee, till by order of parliament he came in prisoner to Edinburgh. From first to last he was near ten months close prisoner.

Mr. James Guthrie was son to the laird of Guthrie, a very ancient and honourable family. He had taught philosophy in the university of St. Andrews, where, for a good many years, he gave abundant proof that he was an excellent philosopher, and exact scholar. His temper was very stayed and composed, he would reason upon the most eristical points with great solidity, and when every one about him was warm, his temper was never ruffled. At any time, when indecent heat or wrangling happened to fall in in reasoning, it was his ordinary to say, "Enough of this, let us go to some other subject, we are warm, and can dispute no longer with advantage." Perhaps he had the greatest mixture of fervent zeal and sweet calmness in his temper, as any man in his time.

I am well assured he was educate in opposition to presbyterian government; perhaps it was this made the writer of the diurnal, no friend of his, say, about the time of his trial, "That if Mr. James Guthrie had continued fixed to his first principles, he had been a star of the first magnitude in Scotland." When he came to judge for himself, Mr. Guthrie happily departed from his first principles, and upon examination of the way he had been educated in, left it, and was indeed a star of the first magnitude. He was, I am told, highly prelatical in his judgment when he came at first to St. Andrews; but by conversation with Mr. Samuel Rutherford and others, and especially through his joining with the weekly societies there, for prayer and conference, he was entirely brought off from that way.

1661.

Even while at that university he wanted not some fore notices of his after sufferings for the cause of reformation, now heartily espoused by him. And the year before the king's return, when minister at Stirling, he had very plain, and some way public warnings of what afterwards befell him: those were carefully observed by him, and closely reflected upon. But I am not writing the history of this great man's life, otherwise I might narrate a good many very remarkable providences concerning him, and say much as to many steps of his carriage, from his entry into the holy office of the ministry, until this time: therefore I shall only take notice of two pretty singular passages which may help us a little into the springs, original, and occasion of his sufferings.

When the commission of the general assembly at Perth, came into the public resolutions we have heard of, December 14th, 1650, Mr. Guthrie and Mr. David Bennet were ministers of Stirling, and jointly with the rest of that presbytery wrote a letter to the commission at their next meeting, showing their dissatisfaction with the resolutions; which was done likewise by many other presbyteries. But it seems the two ministers of Stirling went some further, and preached against the public resolutions, as involving the land in a conjunction with the malignant party.

In February, 1651, by a letter to Messrs. Guthrie and Bennet, the chancellor ordered them to repair to Perth, and answer before the king and committee of estates for their letter to the commission, and their doctrine. The two ministers sent an answer to his lordship, excusing their not coming to Perth that week, and promising to come the next. The curious reader will desire probably to see it, and it follows:

"Right Honourable,

"We did this afternoon receive from the king's majesty, and committee of estates, a letter desiring and requiring us to repair to Perth, against the 19th of this instant, for the effect therein specified; and albeit the

1661. diet assigned to us be very short, yet should we have striven to keep that day, if one of us had not been under so great weakness of body at this time, as that he hath come little abroad in the congregation where we serve, these ten days past: therefore we entreat so much favour of your lordship, as to signify to the king's majesty, and the committee of estates, that it is not from any disrespect to their letter, or from any purpose to disobey their commands, that we did not immediately, upon the receipt of their advertisement, hasten to wait upon whatsomever they had to signify to us, but merely upon the ground we have already represented unto your lordship; and you will be pleased withal to show them, that if the Lord shall please to give any probable measure of strength to him who hath been infirm those days past, that both of us shall attend at Perth towards the end of this week; or if he shall not be able to travel, that the other of us shall come with the mind of both. We commend your lordship to God, and continue,

"Your affectionate servants,

"Mr. JAMES GUTHRIE.
"Mr. DAVID BENNET."

Accordingly, February 22d, I find the ministers of Stirling appearing at Perth, where they gave in the following paper signed, to the committee, which, with what followed upon it, being much insisted upon in Mr. Guthrie's trial, I shall here insert:

Protestation of the ministers of Stirling, February 22d, 1651.

"Whereas the king's majesty and your lordships have been pleased, upon a narrative relating to our doctrine and ministerial duties, to desire and require us to repair to this place against the 19th of this instant, that, after hearing of us, such a course might be taken as shall be found most necessary for the good and safety of the place where we serve in the ministry: therefore conceiving the judicatories of the church to be the only proper judges of our doctrine, and carriage in those things that concern our ministerial calling, as we do, from the respect we owe to the king's majesty and your lordships' authority, compear before you, being desirous to hear what is to be said to us, and ready to answer thereunto; so we humbly protest, that it is with preservation of the liberties and privileges of the church of Scotland, and of the servants of Jesus Christ, in those things that do relate to their doctrine, and the duties of their ministerial function. And though we be most willing in all things to render a reason to those who ask us of our faith; and in a more special way to the king's majesty, and your lordships, a reason of our writing to the commission of the general assembly, a letter containing the grounds of our stumbling at the present resolutions of kirk and state, in order to a levy, and of our preaching against these resolutions, as involving a conjunction with the malignant party in the land, which we hold to be contrary to the word of God, and the solemn league and covenant, and to our solemn vows and engagements, and to the constant tenor of the declarations, warnings, remonstrances, causes of humiliations, and resolutions of this kirk these years past, and to be destructive to the covenant and cause of God, and scandalous and offensive to the godly, and a high provoking of the eyes of the Lord's glory, and of our protesting against and appealing from the desire and charge of the commission of the general assembly in this particular, and of our persisting to preach the same doctrine still; yet that our compearing before the king's majesty and your lordships, doth not at all import any acknowledgment in us, that his majesty and your lordships are the proper judges of those things. And this our protestation we make, not from any disrespect to the king's majesty or your lordships' authority, nor from any purpose to decline or disobey the same in any thing civil, but from the tender regard which we have and owe unto the liberties and privileges of the church of Jesus Christ, which both the king's majesty, and your lordships, and we, are in so solemn way bound to maintain and preserve inviolable. We do acknowledge the king's majesty and your lordships are the lawful civil power and authority in the land, to whom we owe, and shall be most willing and ready to yield obedience in all things, which the king and your lordships shall command, according to the will of God; or if in any thing his or your commands to us shall fall out to be contrary to that rule, we shall patiently, in the Lord's strength, submit ourselves to any civil censure and punishment inflicted upon us because of our denying obedience to the same.

"James Guthrie,
"David Bennet."
"Perth, February 22d, 1651."

What passed in the committee, upon their giving in this paper, I have seen no particular accounts of, and only from the ministers' following paper observe, that by a second letter the matter was delayed for some days, and put off till the king's return from Aberdeen; and in the meantime the two ministers were confined to Perth and Dundee, whereupon they offered a second paper, February 28th, which was read, and the tenor of it follows.

Ministers of Stirling, their second Protestation.

"Whereas the king's majesty and your lordships have been pleased, upon a narrative relating to our doctrine and ministerial duties, to desire and require us to repair to this place, against a certain day contained in your letter, viz. the 19th of February; in answer whereunto we excused ourselves, that we could not so precisely come hither, because of bodily indisposition of the one of us, known to be of verity, promising withal to wait on his majesty and your lordships so soon as the Lord shall remove the necessity of our delay; and in case of the not removal thereof, the other should come towards the end of that week, with the mind of both: and we accordingly appearing before your lordships, did show how willing we were to hear what was to be said unto us, and to answer thereunto, as is contained in our protestation and declaration, formerly given in to your lordships thereanent: yet, nevertheless in the interval of time betwixt his majesty's and your lordships' receipt and reading of our humble excuse, and appearance before your lordships, it hath pleased his majesty and the committee of estates, not only to require us to come again to this place, which upon the first letter we have been careful to do with all possible diligence; but also to ordain that we should stay here, or at Dundee, till his majesty's return from Aberdeen, that, in a full meeting of the committee, such course might be taken as might be found most conducing for the safety of that place where we serve in the ministry, as his majesty and your lordships' second letter, of the date February 20th, 1651, bears. Which letter, albeit it came not to our hands before the time of our appearing before your lordships, and was then delivered and communicated to us; yet in relation thereunto, we have likewise offered to your lordships' assurance that we should return hither against his majesty's coming back from Aberdeen; until which time his majesty and your lordships' letter did continue and delay the business; as also was declared by your lordships at our appearance before you: notwithstanding whereof your lordships have not been pleased to accept of any such assurance, nor to allow us your liberty to repair to our charges till that time. And albeit this seems strange to us, especially in a matter of our ministerial function, and yet in dependance, between the church judicatories and us, undecided; nevertheless, that we even should not so much as seem in any wise to irritate, yea, that offence be not in any wise taken by any, especially by the civil magistrate, do resolve, for preventing of mistakes, and testifying our respect to civil authority, to endeavour to satisfy such an appointment so far as we can, without prejudice to our conscience, and the liberties of our ministry, and the solemn bonds and obligations that lie upon us to preach the gospel in the stations where God set us, adhering always to our former declaration and protestation. Likeas, we do now protest, that we do not hereby acknowledge his majesty and your lordships to be competent judges to presbyterial acts and letters, or our ministerial function, or preaching, or any part thereof, which are the subject

x

1661. matter of your lordships' letter, requisition, and ordinance; because that they are ecclesiastical, and belong to ecclesiastical assemblies, as the only proper judges thereof; and because neither the presbytery of Stirling, who are the proper authors of the foresaid letter, which is the first ground of the foresaid requisition and ordinance, nor have we been convened therefore before any ecclesiastic judicatory, neither were ever convened or convinced for breach of any ecclesiastical act in the premises; and so there has proceeded no antecedent sentence of the said judicatories, finding that we have violated any act of the church, in preaching against the present way of levy, or that we have ill or unwarrantably appealed from the commission of the general assembly their desire and charge to us in that particular. And also we humbly protest, that there be reserved to us all remedy competent of the law, against the injury we suffer by being thus convened and confined by a civil judicatory, and having your liberty refused to us to return to our charges, notwithstanding of assurance offered to attend at the time to which our business is continued; seeing this procedure is contrary not only to divine law, the word of God, the covenant, and solemn engagements unto the acts of our church; but also to the acts of parliament, and laws of this kingdom, and established rights, privileges, and liberties of the judicatories of the kirk. And upon supposal that his majesty and your lordships were competent judges of these things, which we do not acknowledge, but protest against, for the reasons contained in this and our former protestation, and for many other reasons of that kind; yet the hearing of parties before judgment passed upon them, being a part of that native liberty, that is due to all men, who do not by their wilful absence from, and contempt of the judicatory, forfault the same, as being founded on the light of nature, common equity, and reason, and agreeable to the word of God, and laws of all nations; and the king's majesty and your lordships having, in your first letter to us, propounded that method of proceeding with us: notwithstanding thereof, and our undertaking to compear in competent time, his majesty and your lordships have, without hearing us, passed such a judgment in reference to us; therefore we also protest against such method of procedure, as being contrary to that liberty which is due to us, and which we may justly challenge as subjects, and which his majesty and your lordships are bound by the light of nature, law of God, the covenant, and laws of the land, to maintain and preserve inviolable. And albeit we do not resolve, upon any light consideration, to depart from this place, or from Dundee, where his majesty and your lordships have commanded us to stay till his majesty's return from Aberdeen, but for preventing of mistakes, and testifying our respects to civil authority, to endeavour, as we have already declared, to satisfy such an appointment, so far as we can, without prejudice to our consciences, the liberty of our ministry, and the solemn bonds and obligations upon us to preach the gospel in the stations wherein God hath set us: yet do we protest, that our staying here, or at Dundee, may not be esteemed or interpreted an acknowledgment of the ordinance in reference to our stay; but that notwithstanding thereof, it is still free for us to make use of all these privileges and liberties which are due to us as ministers of Jesus Christ, in as free a way in time coming, as we might have done before our compearing before your lordships, or having any such ordinance intimate to us.

"JAMES GUTHRIE.
"DAVID BENNET."

"Perth, February 28th, 1651."

Those protestations are so fully spoken to, and the arguments the authors of them had in their defence, set down in Mr. Guthrie's first speech before the parliament, afterwards to be insert, that I shall say nothing of them here. I can give no further account of the procedure of the committee of estates in this affair, save that the king and they thought fit to dismiss the two ministers, and to go no further on in this matter. Yet now ten years after, this is trumped up, and made a principal article of Mr. Guthrie's indictment, after

CHAP. II.] OF THE CHURCH OF SCOTLAND. 163

he had suffered not a little for his loyalty to the king. I have it from good hands, that Mr. Guthrie defended the king's right in a public debate with Hugh Peters, Oliver's chaplain, and from the pulpit he asserted the king's title, in the hearing of the English officers: but now all this must be forgot, and give way to a personal pique Middleton had against him; which brings me to the other passage relative to Mr. Guthrie, which I promised, and it lets us into the real spring of the hard measure this excellent man met with.

By improving of an affront the king met with in the year 1650, some malignants, as then they were termed, prevailed so to heighten his majesty's fears of evil designs against him by some about him, that a correspondence with the malignants, papists, and such who were disaffected to the covenant in the north, was set on foot. Matters were brought in a little time to such a pass, as a considerable number of noblemen, gentlemen, and others, were to rise and form themselves into an army, under Middleton's command; and the king was to cast himself to their arms and management. Accordingly the king, upon a sudden, with a few in his company, as if he had been going to the hunting, left his fastest friends, crossed Tay, and came into Angus, where he was to have met with those people. The circumstances of this story are to be had in the historians of that time. But the king soon found himself disappointed, and came back to the committee of estates, where indeed his strength and safety lay. Meanwhile several, who had been upon the plot of engaging his majesty to go and head the north, fearing punishment, got together under Middleton's command. General Lesly marched against them, and the king wrote to them most earnestly to lay down their arms, and the committee of estates send an indemnity to such as should submit.

While the state are thus dealing with them, the commission of the assembly were not wanting to show their zeal for the king, against such who ventured to disturb the public peace. And it is said, Mr. James Guthrie there proposed summar excommunication, as a censure Middleton deserved, and as what he took to be a seasonable testimony from the church at this juncture. This highest sentence was carried in the commission by a plurality of votes, and Mr. Guthrie is appointed the very next sabbath, and accordingly did pronounce that censure upon Middleton in the church of Stirling.

1661.

When the committee of estates had agreed, not without some debate, to an indemnity to Middleton, and had hope to get matters some way compromised in the north, there was one sent express to Stirling, with accounts how things stood, and a letter desiring Mr. Guthrie to forbear the intimation of the commission's sentence. I am told, this letter came to Mr. Guthrie, just when going into the pulpit, and he did not open it till the work was over; and though he had opened it, it may be doubted, if he would have ventured to delay the execution of the sentence of the commission, which he was obliged to pronounce, and could not cut and carve in, upon a private missive to himself. Thus the sentence was inflicted, and it was believed Middleton never forgot nor forgave what Mr. Guthrie did that day; though I find the commission of the church, January 3d, 1651, at their next meeting, did relax Middleton from that censure, and laid it upon a far better man, colonel Strachan. However after this, Middleton conceived such prejudice against Mr. Guthrie, as abundantly discovered itself in his trial before the session of parliament. So, January, or February 1661, Mr. Guthrie was brought to Edinburgh, and had his indictment given him by the king's advocate for high treason.

It is pity we have not this case in print, as well as that of his fellow-martyr the marquis. I have not seen his indictment at large, nor the answers formed by his lawyers, among whom Sir John Nisbet was one: had we those, I doubt not but the iniquity and injustice of his severe sentence would fully appear. To retrieve the want of those, I shall put together what hints I have met with as to his trial, and give his own excellent speeches before the parlia-

1661. ment, hitherto not published for what I know; and from those the state of his process will pretty clearly appear. February 20th, he was first before the parliament. The chancellor told him he was called before them, to answer to the charge of high treason, a copy whereof he had received; and the lord advocate proposed his indictment might be read, which the house went into. The heads of his dittay were, " 1. His contriving, consenting to, and exhibiting before the committee of estates, the paper called, The Western Remonstrance. 2. His contriving, writing and publishing that abominable pamphlet called, The Causes of God's Wrath. 3. His contriving, writing, and subscribing to the paper called, The humble Petition, of the 23d of August last, when he was apprehended. 4. His convocating of the king's lieges at several times, without warrant or authority, to the disturbance of the peace of the state and of the church. 5. His declaring his majesty, by his appeal and protestation, incapable to be judge over him, which he presented at Perth: 6. And some treasonable expressions he was alleged to have uttered in a meeting, 1650 or 1651."

His indictment being read, he had an excellent speech to the parliament. It is considerably long; but containing the best and almost the only account I can give of his case, I have chosen rather to put it here than in the appendix.

" My Lord Chancellor,

" I being indicted at the instance of Sir John Fletcher, his majesty's advocate, for his majesty's interest, upon things alleged to be seditious and treasonable, I humbly desire, and from your equity expect, that my lord commissioner his grace will patiently and without interruption hear me, as to a few things which I have to say for myself, in answer to that indictment: and that I may proceed therein distinctly, following the order of the indictment itself, I shall speak first a word to the laws that are mentioned and acted, whereby I am to be judged; then to the things whereof I am accused concerning those laws.

" I am glad that the law of God is named in the first place; it being indeed the supreme law, not only of religion, but also of righteousness, to which all other laws ought to be squared and subordinate; and there being an act of the 1st parl. king James VI. whereby all clauses of laws or acts of parliament, repugnant to the word of God, are repealed, an act most worthy of a christian king and kingdom, I hope your lordships, in all your proceedings, will give most respect to this, that I may be judged by the law of God especially, and by other laws in subordination thereunto.

" As to those laws and acts of parliament, mentioned in the indictment, concerning his majesty's royal prerogative, and declining his majesty's judgment and authority, and keeping of conventions; I hope it will not be denied that they are to be understood according to the sense and meaning that is given thereof by posterior acts of parliament, it being a maxim in law, no less true than equitable, that when there is any seeming or real contradiction betwixt laws, *posteriora derogant prioribus;* otherwise laws, instead of being preservatives to states and commonwealths, might prove nets to entangle the lives, reputations, and estates of the subjects: and it must also be granted, that laws and acts of parliament are to be understood and expounded by our solemn public vows and covenants, contracted with God by his majesty and subjects, which are not only declared by the laws of the land, to have the strength of acts of parliament, but both by the law of God, and common law, and light of all the nations in the world, are more binding and indispensable than any municipal law and statute whatsomever.

" As to those acts of parliament that are cited against scandalous, slanderous, and untrue speeches, to the disdain, contempt, and reproach of his majesty's authority; I think I need not say, that none, much less his majesty's commissioner, and this honourable court of parliament, does understand them of truths pronounced in sobriety, by those who have a lawful call thereunto; and that those acts which speak against the meddling in the affairs of his majesty and state, are not to be understood of such meddling as men are bound unto by virtue of their calling, and wherein they do not transgress the bounds of it.

"The next thing I shall speak to, are the particulars wherewith I am charged, concerning which I shall give your lordships a true and ingenuous account of my accession thereunto, knowing that I stand in the sight of him who sits in the assembly of the gods. Next, I shall be bold to offer to your lordships some defences for vindicating my carriage from the breach of his majesty's laws, and exempting me from the punishment appointed thereby.

"As to the matters of fact I am charged with in the indictment, I am first charged in general, of being culpable of sundry seditious and treasonable remonstrances, declarations, positions, instructions, letters, preachings, declamations. To which I say, that *generalia non pungunt*, they can have no strength in the inferring of a crime or guilt, except in so far as they are instanced in particulars; but are like to those *universalia* which have no foundation *in re*, mere chimeras or notions.

"Only one thing there is in that general charge, that I cannot, and ought not to pass, to wit, that I have seditiously and traitorously purposed the eradicating and subverting of the fundamental government of this his majesty's ancient kingdom, at least the enervating, or violating, or impairing of his authority, &c. concerning which I am bold to say, it is an unjust charge; there was never any such purpose or design in my heart: and since I am thus charged, I may without vanity, or breach of the law of sobriety, affirm, that as I had never any compliance with the counsels or designs of the late usurping powers, against his majesty's royal father, or himself, or against his kingdom, or the ancient government thereof, or of the kingdoms of England or Ireland; so was there no part of their ungodly or unjust actings, but I did, in my station and calling, bear open and public testimony against the same, both by word and writ; which is a thing better known and manifest than that I can be liable to suspicion therein, many of these testimonies being given before many, and many of them being extant to the world, and such as will be extant to posterity.

1661.

"My lord, albeit it does become me to adore God in the holiness and wisdom of his dispensations, yet I can hardly refrain from expressing some grief of spirit, that my house and family should not only be so many months together cessed by a number of English soldiers, and myself kept from the pulpit for preaching and speaking against the tender, and incorporating this nation in one commonwealth with England; and that I should thereafter, in time of Oliver Cromwell his usurping the government to himself under the name of protector, being delated by some, and challenged by sundry of his counsel in this nation, for a paper published by me, wherein he was declared to be an usurper, and his government to be usurpation; that I should have been threatened to have been sent to the court for writing a paper against Oliver Cromwell his usurping the crown of these kingdoms; that I should have been threatened with banishment for concurring in offering a large testimony against the evil of the times, to Richard Cromwell his council immediately after his usurping the government; I say, my lord, it grieves me, that, notwithstanding of all those things, I should now stand indicted before your lordships, as intending the eradicating and subverting of the ancient civil government of this nation, and being subservient to that usurper in his designs. The God of heaven knows that I am free of this charge; and I do defy all the world, allowing me justice and fair proceeding, which I hope your lordships will, to make out the same against me.

"The first particular wherewith I am charged in the indictment, is, that I did compile and draw up a paper, commonly called The Remonstrance, and presented it, or caused it to be presented to his majesty and committee of estates, October 22d, 1650. To which I answer, by denying that part of the indictment. I never did compile or contrive that Remonstrance, nor did I present it, or cause it to be presented to the committee of estates, then, or at any other time. I indeed being a member of the commission

1661. of the general assembly, when they gave their judgment upon it, did dissent from the sentence which they passed upon it, which cannot be reckoned any culpable accession thereunto, every man being free, without hazard or punishment, and bound in conscience, as before God, to give his judgment freely in the judicatory whereof he is a member. If it be alleged that I did afterwards abet the same in the book of The Causes of God's Wrath, in the 6th Book, in the 9th Article thereof, by asserting the rejecting of the discovery of the guiltiness contained therein to have been a sin. It is answered, 1st, That it was no more than the asserting of my former dissent. 2dly, That it was no more upon the matter, than was acknowledged and asserted by the whole commission of the general assembly, when they passed sentence upon it; in which sentence it is acknowledged, that it did contain many sad truths which yet were not received, nor any effectual remedy endeavoured for the helping the evils represented thereby. 3dly, It cannot be accounted culpable in a minister of the gospel, who is thereunto bound by virtue of his calling, to assert the rejecting of the discovery of guiltiness to be a sin.

"The next particular I am charged with, is the book of The Causes of God's Wrath, especially the fifth and sixth articles thereof, which are particulars, I believe, upon the looking thereof, will not be found to contain any just matter of accusation, much less matter of sedition and treason; there being nothing mentioned therein, but the discovery of the sin of covetousness, and abuse of the public faith of the land in borrowing money. But because I did apprehend it was the fifth or sixth step of the 9th article was intended by my lord advocate, I humbly profess to your lordships and this honourable court of parliament, that I am very unwillingly drawn forth to speak of those things, and shall only say, 1st, That the God of heaven is witness, my accession thereunto did not flow from any disrespect unto, or dissatisfaction with his majesty's person or government, much less from any malicious purpose to render him odious to the world or to his subjects, or to give advantage to his enemies and the enemies of these kingdoms, or from any purpose in any thing to be subservient to the designs or actings of the late usurping powers; but merely and singly from a constraining power of conscience, to be found faithful, as a minister of the gospel, in the discovering of sin and guiltiness, that it being taken with and repented of, wrath might be taken away from the house of the king, and from these kingdoms. Your lordship knows what charge is laid upon the ministers of the gospel to give faithful warning to all sorts of persons, and how they expose their own souls to the hazard of eternal damnation, and the guilt of the blood of those with whom they have to do, if they do not this; and you do also know that the prophets and apostles of our Lord Jesus Christ himself, did faithfully warn all men, though it was their lot, because of the same, to be reckoned traitors and seditious persons, and to suffer as evildoers on the account thereof. Next, my lord, I wish it may be seriously pondered, that nothing is asserted in these causes as matter of sin and duty, but what hath been the common received doctrine of the church of Scotland, as may appear from the records of the work of reformation from popery, from the national covenant, and solemn league and covenant, and the public declarations and acts of this church and kingdom, concerning the necessary security of religion; the truth of which doctrine is confirmed from the word of God, and divine reason, in those public papers themselves; and as to matters of fact, they are no other than are mentioned in the solemn public causes ot humiliation condescended upon, and kept by the whole church jointly, and his majesty and family, with the commission of the general assembly, and committee of estates, before his coronation at Perth. As to the sixth step, there is nothing therein mentioned but what is truth; all the particulars therein mentioned, even the Remonstrance itself, containing some discovery of known and undeniable sins and guiltiness, the rejecting whereof behoved to be a sin, and therefore the asserting of it cannot be sedition and treason.

"The third particular wherewith I am

charged, is the supplication at Edinburgh, August 23d, to which I acknowledge my accession, but deny it to be treasonable or seditious; because, besides the former vindication of my former carriage and actings from the compliances with the late usurping powers, and a humble profession of the subjection, loyalty, and obedience which I owe to his majesty, of my resolutions to render the same unto him as the supreme and rightful magistrate over these kingdoms, and some serious prayers and supplications for his majesty, it doth contain nothing but a humble petition concerning those things, to which his majesty, and all the subjects of this kingdom, are engaged by the solemn and indispensable oath of the covenant, with a sober and serious representation of the danger that threatens religion, and of those things that are destructive unto the duties contained in those articles of the covenant; and being established by law, and confirmed by the public oath of God, which is more than a law, a humble petition and representation, concerning those things, cannot be accounted sedition, or treasonable. The indictment is pleased to say, that I charged his majesty with dissimulation and perjury; but there is no such thing in the supplication, which doth only put him in remembrance of holding fast the oaths of the covenant.

"As to what is alleged against the lawfulness of our meeting: it was presbyterially resolved that I should keep that meeting; and suppose that had not been, yet that meeting cannot fall within those acts of parliament that strike against unlawful conventions; because every meeting for business, in itself lawful, is agreeable to the word of God and laws of the land, and when kept without tumult and multitude, such as that was, needs no particular warrant from authority; as may be instructed from several other meetings up and down the land every day, for several sorts of business. Are there not some meetings kept by persons of all sorts in all the parts of the country, in reference to application to judicatories, and the supreme magistrate, for civil interest and right? and if so, how much more may ministers meet for the supplicating his majesty for the interest and rights of Jesus Christ, keeping themselves for the matter of their supplication within the bounds of the covenant, and of those things which are established by law? yea, such meetings are clearly exempted from the breach of those acts of parliament by a posterior act of parliament, viz. act 29, parl. 2, Charles I.

1661

"As to the last particular of the indictment, to wit, my declining of his majesty's authority, I acknowledge I did decline the civil magistrate as a competent judge of ministers' doctrine in the first instance. His authority in all things civil, I do with all my heart acknowledge, and that according to the Confession of Faith in this church; and that the conservation and purgation of religion belongs to him as civil magistrate, and that ecclesiastical persons are not exempted from obedience to civil authority and the commands thereof, nor from punishment in case of their transgression: but that the declining of the civil magistrate his being judge of ministers' doctrine in the first instant, may appear not treason and sedition, but lawful and warrantable, I do humbly offer,

"1st, That such declinatures are agreeable to the rule of God's word, and to the Confession of Faith, and doctrine of this church, confirmed and ratified in parliament by many several acts, and therefore have the strength both of divine and human laws. That they are agreeable to God's word is evident from this, that the Scriptures do clearly hold forth that Christ hath a visible kingdom which he exerces in or over his visible members by his spiritual officers, which is wholly distinct from the civil power and government of the world, and not depending upon, or subordinate to those governments and the acts thereof, John xviii. 36, 37. Matth. xvi. 19. John xx. 23. That they are agreeable to the Confession of Faith and doctrine of this church is evident, because those do acknowledge no head over the visible church of Christ but himself, nor any judgment or power in or over his church, but that which he hath committed to the spiritual office-bearers thereof under himself: and therefore it hath been the ordinary practice of this kirk, in such cases, to use such declinatures, since the time of the reformation from popery; as may appear from many clear,

1661. undeniable and approven instances, extant in the acts of the general assembly, and records of this church, particularly those of Mr. David Black, 1596, which was owned and subscribed by three or four hundred ministers, besides sundry others which are well known. And I believe, my lord, this is not only the doctrine of the church of Scotland, but of many sound protestant divines, who give unto Cæsar the things that are Cæsar's, and to God the things that are God's.

"2d. Such declinatures are agreeable to, and founded upon the national covenant, and solemn league and covenant, by which the king's majesty himself, and all the subjects of this kingdom, are bound to maintain the doctrine, worship, discipline, and government of this church, with solemn vows and public oaths of God; which hath always in all kingdoms, states, and republics, been accounted more sacred and binding than any municipal law or statute whatsomever; and being posterior to the act of parliament 1584, do necessarily include a repealing of it.

"Upon these grounds it is that I gave in, and do assert that declinature for vindicating the crown, dignity, and royal prerogative of Jesus Christ, who is King of kings, and Lord of lords; but with all due respect to his majesty, his greatness and authority.

"As to that act of parliament, 1584, it was made in a time wherein the settled government of this church by presbyteries and synods was wholly overturned, and their actings utterly discharged, and the depositions of ministers, and things properly spiritual and ecclesiastical, put into the hand of the civil magistrate. Further I do assert, that that act, in so far as concerns decliners, hath, since the making thereof, been often repealed and rescinded, and stands repealed and rescinded now at the downsitting of this parliament.

"It was reversed and annulled by a posterior act, 1592, viz. 1st act, 12th parl. James VI. in the last section of which it is expressly declared, ' that that act, 1584, shall noways be prejudicial, nor derogate any thing from the privilege God hath given the spiritual officers in the church, concerning heads of religion, matters of heresy, collation, or deprivation of ministers, or any such like essential censure, especially grounded upon, and having warrant from the word of God.' But so it is, that the freedom and independency of the spiritual officebearers of the church of God, in things ecclesiastic that concerned their calling, is a special privilege, and a special head of religion; and that the free discovery of the sins of all persons, by ministers, in their doctrine from the word of God, is an essential censure, grounded upon, and having warrant from the word of God.

"And accordingly, king James VI., anno 1585, considering the great offence given and taken by that act, 1584, did, for removing thereof, send a declaration penned and signed with his own hand, to the commissioners of the kirk of Scotland at Linlithgow, December 7th, which, he saith, shall be as good and valid as any act of parliament whatsomever; in which declaration he hath these words: ' I for my part shall never, neither ought my posterity, ever summon or apprehend any pastor or teacher, for matters of doctrine, religion, salvation, heresy, or true interpretation of the Scripture: but according to my first act, which occasions the liberty of the preaching the word, administration of the sacrament, I avow the same to be a matter merely ecclesiastical, and altogether inexpedient to my calling; and therefore shall not, nor ever ought they, I mean my posterity, claim any power or jurisdiction in the foresaids.'

"It is also to be considered, that that act, 1584, is also repealed by the 4th act, parl. 2, Charles I. which reckons it among the evils that had sore troubled the peace of kirk and kingdom, that the power of the keys and kirk censures was given to persons merely civil; and therefore doth provide, that for preservation of religion, and preventing of such evils in time coming, general assemblies rightly constitute, as the proper and competent judge of all matters ecclesiastical, hereafter be kept yearly, and oftener *pro re nata*, as occasion and necessity shall require.

"The same act, 1584, is also repealed by the 6th act, parl. 2, Charles I. called 'the Act Rescissory,' which expressly provides and declares, ' that the sole and only power of jurisdiction within this church, stands in the church of God, as it is now reformed, and in the general, provincial, and presbyterial assemblies, with kirk sessions established by that act of parliament, June, 1592.' Which act is expressly revived and renewed in the whole heads, points, and articles thereof, in the foresaid Act Rescissory, and is appointed to stand in full strength, as a perpetual law in all times coming, notwithstanding of whatsomever acts and statutes made in contrar thereof, in whole or in part, which the estates by that Act Rescissory, casses and annuls all and whatsomever acts of parliament, laws, or constitutions, in so far as they derogate, and are prejudicial to the nature, jurisdiction, discipline, and privileges of this kirk.

" By all which it is evident, that not only that act, 1584, but also the 1st act, parl. 18, James VI. and the 3d act, parl. 1, Charles I. which ratify and establish the royal prerogative over all estates, persons, and causes within this kingdom, is declared to be of no force, in so far as the same may be extended, to make the supreme magistrate the competent and proper judge of matters spiritual and ecclesiastical.

" It is to be observed further, that it hath been lawful, and in continual practice, that his majesty's secret council hath been declined in sundry causes, and the cause drawn to the ordinary and competent judge; as matters civil to the lords of session, matters criminal to the chief justice, matters of divorce to the commissaries; yea, the meanest regality in the country hath power to decline the supreme judicatory.

" As to what is alleged in the close of the indictment, of protesting for remeed of law against his majesty, the protestation was but an appendix and consequent of the other, made only in reference thereunto; and a protestation against any particular act for remedy, according to his majesty's law, cannot be treason against his majesty, there being no act of parliament declaring it to be so; and it being not authority in itself that is protested against, but only a particular act of the authority, against which protestations in many cases are ordinary. Lastly, It is to be observed, that this declinature was buried in silence by his majesty, and committee of estates, after the ingiving thereof, and Mr. Guthrie sent home without ever challenging him for the same, and permitted to exercise his ministry in Stirling.

1661.

" Those few things, my lord, I thought fit at present to say in vindication and defence of my own innocence, notwithstanding of any thing contained in the indictment now read against me. The sum of what I have said I comprise in these two: 1st, That I did never purpose or intend to speak or act any thing disloyal, seditious, or treasonable against his majesty's person, authority, or government, God is my witness, and that what I have spoken, written, or acted in any of those things wherewith I am charged, hath been merely and singly from a principle of conscience, that according to the weak measure of light given me of God, I might do my duty in my station and calling as a minister of the gospel. Next, because conscience barely taken is not a sufficient plea, though it may extenuate, yet cannot wholly excuse, I do assert, that I have founded my speeches, and writings, and actings, in those matters, on the word of God, and on the doctrine, confessions of faith, and laws of this church and kingdom, upon the national covenant of Scotland, and the solemn league and covenant, betwixt the three kingdoms of Scotland, England, and Ireland: if those foundations fall, I must fall with them; but if they sustain and stand in judgment, as I hope they will, I cannot acknowledge myself, neither I hope will his majesty's commissioner, and the honourable court of parliament, judge me guilty of sedition and treason, notwithstanding of any thing contained in the indictment."

This pointed and pathetic speech wanted not some influence upon the house; but his death was designed, and the process behoved to go on. When he was ordered to remove, he humbly craved that some time might be given him to consult and advise with his lawyers. This was granted, and he allowed till the 29th to give in his peremptory defences.

I shall only further take notice, that the article in his indictment with most shadow of reason insisted upon, was, his declining the king's authority to judge in matters of doctrine *prima instantia*, and the protestation

1661. and declinature he gave in upon this, above set down. This we have already seen he fully takes off, as what was reasonable in itself, and every way legal, and according to the common practice of that time. To clear this matter of fact, I have cast it in at the foot of the page,* a protestation and declinature, August 22d, 1655, with the summons whereupon it was given in to the sheriff principal of Mid Lothian, by the ministers of Edinburgh, when called before that civil court, for their praying for the king contrary to the order given by the usurpers. And the reader will find it comes close up to Mr. Guthrie's declinature, and is signed by Mr. David Dickson and Mr. Robert Douglas. And the reader will find

Mr. James Hamilton, minister at Edinburgh, his declinature at the same time:* from which it is plain, that as Mr. Guthrie takes notice, "there were many instances of this procedure at that time well known." And great numbers, as well as he, might have been staged upon this score of declining civil courts, as judges of doctrine, and ministerial actings. Indeed those declinatures in the reasoning and very phrases, agree so much with Mr. Guthrie's, that one would think they had his in their eye, when they formed theirs.

I have it from very good hands, that when Mr. Guthrie met with his lawyers to form his defences, he very much surprised them by his exactness in our Scots law, and suggested several things to be added, which had escaped his advocates. Sir John Nisbet expressed himself upon this head to those I have it from, to this purpose. " If it had been in the reasoning part, or in consequences from scripture and divinity, I would have won-

---

* Summons to the Ministers of Edinburgh, before the Sheriff, for praying for the King, August 20th, 1655, with their declinature.
I, John Cockburn, summon you, Mr. James Hamilton, (and so the rest of the ministers aftermentioned) minister within the old kirk of Edinburgh, to compear before the sheriff-principal of Mid Lothian and Linlithgow, in the old Exchequer-house at Edinburgh, upon the 22d day of August, at two hours in the afternoon, to hear and see witnesses led and deponed against you, for not observing and obeying the order and inhibition lately emitted by the honourable commissioners for visiting universities, against the praying for the late king, and that under the highest pain and charge that may follow thereupon, conform unto the principal warrant direct thereanent. Dated at Edinburgh, the 20th day of August, 1655.

The Ministers' Declinature.
We, undersubscribing, ministers of Edinburgh, having received summons to compear at this diet, before the sheriff of Lothian, about a matter that directly concerns our ministerial function, and being unacquainted in this land with summons of this nature, thought it incumbent on us to declare, likeas, by thir presents we do declare, that by this our compearance we do not subject the liberties of the kingdom of Christ, or the immediate acts of our ministry, to the judgment and determination of a civil judicatory; and declare in all humility, according to the duty we owe to our Lord and Master Jesus Christ, that his ministers are not convenable for the immediate acts of their ministry, before any civil judicatory; and that we do compear only to make our Master's interest known, and lest our not compearing should be reckoned contempt. And since, by the providence of our God, we are brought here, we do earnestly desire and obtest, in the name of our Lord Jesus Christ, whose servants we are, that nothing be done prejudicial to the liberties of this kirk, and to the standing ministry settled therein. Subscribed at Edinburgh, August 22, 1655.
DAVID DICKSON.
MR. ROBERT DOUGLAS.
MR. THO. GARVAN.

* Mr. James Hamilton's Declinature at the same time.
Forasmuch as I am brought before you, the sheriff of Mid Lothian, to answer in matter of the discharge of my ministerial function, the judging whereof, in the first instance, is only competent to the officers and judicatories of the kirk of Christ, our Lord and Master, according to the order and government of this kirk, warranted by the word of God, acknowledged and established by many civil and ecclesiastical laws, and peaceably possessed and enjoyed these many years, to the preservation whereof this nation is bound, as by many obligations, so by the national covenant, and both nations are obliged thereto by the first article of the league and covenant: I therefore, being in this case called to give testimony for that interest, not out of any worldly design or wilful obstinacy, but (my witness being on high) out of zeal to the glory of God, conscience of the oaths of God, love to the precious liberties of the kirk of Christ within this kingdom, which are dearer to me than my life, fear of being found accessory to the betraying the interests of Christ to the power of men, and desire to be found faithful in the day of my accounts to the great Shepherd of souls, according to the laudable examples of our worthy predecessors, and of other reformed kirks, in the like case, am necessitate to give this testimony, against the subordinating the privileges given to the officers and government of the kirk of Jesus Christ, on whose shoulders the government of his house lieth, unto the will and power of men; and do hereby decline your judgment, as no ways competent in these matters, my appearance before you being only to give a reason of my actions, for clearing and vindicating them, my ministry, and myself from all unjust aspersions.
JAS. HAMILTON.

CHAP. II.] OF THE CHURCH OF SCOTLAND. 171

dered the less he had given us some help; but even in the matter of our own profession, our statutes and acts of parliament, he pointed several things which had escaped us." I am likewise told, that the day before his first appearing in parliament, he sent a copy of his speech just now inserted, to Sir John and the rest of his lawyers, at least of the reasoning and law part of it, and they could mend nothing in it.

The giving in his defences, and the advocate's considering of them, took up some weeks, until the 11th of April, when I find him again before the parliament, and his process is read over the first time. Whereupon he had a most moving speech, which likewise deserves a room here.

Mr. Guthrie's speech in parliament, immediately after the reading of his process, April 11th, 1661.

" My Lord Chancellor,

" I did, at my first appearance before his majesty's commissioner, and this honourable court of parliament, give an account of my accession to the particulars contained in the indictment, and of the grounds and reasons thereof; I have now done it more fully in my defences and duplies to the replies given by my lord advocate; in all which I have dealt ingenuously and without shifting, holding it the duty of a christian, especially of a minister of the gospel, in the matter of his duty and calling, so to do. I have now only to add these few words.

" I hope I have made it sufficiently to appear, that what I have spoken, written, or acted in this matter, was from no malicious or sinistrous end or intention against his majesty's person or government, but from a principle of true piety towards God, and true loyalty towards his majesty: as I have demonstrated those from the tenor of my carriage and actings, so have I herein confidence towards God, and, in the persuasion of the integrity of my soul in this particular, may, with a good conscience, not only make this declaration before your lordships, but also hazard to step into eternity.

" Next, my lord, I hope I have made it appear that besides the conformity my ac-cession to these things hath with 1661. the word of God, so they have a foundation in the national covenant, and in the solemn league and covenant, the obligation whereof I dare not but profess to own as binding and standing on those kingdoms; and that they are agreeable to the actings of public authority before the English their invading of this nation, to the canons of the church, laws of the kingdom, and the public declared judgment both of church and state before those times. And, my lord, if this will not plead an oblivion and indemnity for me, but that, notwithstanding of all this, I shall be judged a seditious person and traitor, not only shall the whole church and kingdom of Scotland be involved in the guilt of sedition and treason, and few or none have any security for their lives, honours, and estates, further than the king's mercy doth give, but also a very dangerous foundation shall be laid in time to come, for men of differing judgments, upon every emerging revolution, to prosecute the worsted party unto death, notwithstanding they have the public authority, and the laws then standing, to plead in defence of their actings.

" I know, my lord, it lieth on the spirits of some as a prejudice against me, that I am supposed to have been a chief instrument and ringleader in those declarations, laws, canons, and public actings of the kirk and kingdom, which I do now plead in my own defence. I shall not say that this hath any rise from any, who, to lighten their own burden, would increase mine, holding that unworthy of any man of an ingenuous spirit, and most unworthy of a Christian. As I charge no man in particular, with accession to any of those things, so, as for myself, I do for the truth's sake ingenuously acknowledge, that throughout the whole course of my life, I have studied to be serious, and not to deal with a slack hand in what I did look upon as my duty; and yet, my lord, lest I should attribute to myself what is not due to me, I must, for staining of pride and vain glory, say, I was not honoured to be o those who laid the foundation in this kir¹ and kingdom. I am not ashamed to give glory to God, in acknowledging that until the year 1638, I was treading other steps, and

1661. the Lord did then graciously recover me out of the snare of prelacy, ceremonies, and the service book, and a little thereafter put me into the ministry. Yet I never judge myself worthy to be accounted a ringleader in any of these superstructures of that blessed work, there being a great many elder for years, and more eminent for piety, parts, prudence, faithfulness, and zeal, whom I did reverence and give precedency to in those things.

" It may also, my lord, haply be, and a little I have been informed of it, that besides any thing contained in the indictment, there be some other things that bear weight upon the spirits of some of the members of this house, from some reports that have passed of my carriage towards his majesty's royal father, towards himself, and some others. As to those things, my lord, if there be any thing of that kind, I do most humbly and seriously beg, and I think I may most justly expect, both in order to justice, and to the peace of their own consciences, that seeing they have no proof of it, but at least have taken it upon information, that they would altogether lay it aside, and lay no weight upon it; or else, before they give judgment of me, they would let me know of it, and allow me a fair hearing upon it; and if I cannot vindicate myself, let me bear the weight of it.

" In the next place, my lord, knowing that it is wondered at by not a few of the members of this parliament, that I should stand to my own justification in those things whereof I am challenged, and that this is looked upon as a piece of peremptory and wilful humour, which if I pleased I might easily lay aside: my lord, I humbly beg so much charity of all that hear me, as to think that I have not so far left the exercise of all conscience towards God, and of all reason towards myself and my dearest relations in the world, as upon deliberation to hazard, if not cast away both my life and soul at once. God knows, it is not my humour, but conscience that sticks with me; and could I lay it aside, and not sin against God, and dissemble with men, by professing or confessing what I think not, I should not stand in the defence of one of those things for the minute of an hour: but, my lord, having, with prayer and supplications to the God of truth, searched the word of God, and consulted the judgment and practice of the reformed churches, especially our own since the reformation from popery, and the writings of many sound and orthodox divines, and having frequently conversed with the godly ministry, and praying people of this nation, and tried the pulse of their spirits anent the national covenant, and solemn league and covenant, the particulars contained in them, and the superstructures that have been builded upon them, and anent sin and duty, and the power of the civil magistrate in matters ecclesiastical; I find my practice and profession anent these, agreeable to all those, and therefore cannot reckon my light for humour and delusion, but must hold it fast, till better guides be given me to follow.

" My lord, in the last place I shall humbly beg, that, having brought so pregnant and clear evidence from the word of God, so much divine reason and human laws, and so much of the common practice of kirk and kingdom in my own defence, and being already cast out of my ministry, out from my dwelling and maintenance, myself and family put to live on the charity of others, having now suffered eight months' imprisonment, your lordships would put no further burden upon me. I shall conclude with the words of the prophet Jeremiah, ' Behold, I am in your hands,' saith he, ' do to me what seemeth good to you: I know for certain that the Lord hath commanded me to speak all those things, and that if you put me to death, you shall bring innocent blood on yourself, and upon the inhabitants of this city.'

" My lord, my conscience I cannot submit, but this old crazy body and mortal flesh I do submit, to do with it whatsoever you will, whether by death, or banishment, or imprisonment, or any thing else; only I beseech you to ponder well what profit there is in my blood: it is not the extinguishing me or many others, that will extinguish the covenant and work of reformation since the year 1638. My blood, bondage, or banishment will contribute more for the propagation of those things, than my life or liberty could do, though I should live many years.

OF THE CHURCH OF SCOTLAND.

I wish to my lord commissioner his grace, and to all your lordships, the spirit of judgment, wisdom, and understanding, and the fear of the Lord, that you may judge righteous judgment, in which you may have glory, the king honour and happiness, and yourselves peace in the day of your accounts."

This singular and most affecting speech had very little weight in the house, by what might have been expected from the native eloquence, close dealing with their reason and consciences, and the full removal of all that could be even insinuate against this holy man, contained in it; yet it had influence upon a good many of the members, who retired after he had ended, and declared one to another at their coming out of the house, they would have nothing to do with the blood of this righteous man. I could name noblemen, and no presbyterians either, who, after hearing Mr. Guthrie till he ended, not only came out themselves, but prevailed with some of their friends to go with them, from the strong convictions raised in them of his innocency, by this melting speech; than which I have seen little in our modern martyrologies, that comes so fully up to the apologies of the primitive martyrs and confessors, for themselves and the cause they suffered for.

But his judges were determined to go on, and in a very little time, that same diet, though in a thin house, the relevancy of the indictment was sustained, and he found liable to incur the pains and penalties in the acts of parliament, specified in the several articles of his dittay. I do not find the day of his execution named, till the 28th of May, when the parliament, after the marquis of Argyle's execution, ordain, " Mr. James Guthrie and William Giffan, or Govan, to be hanged at the cross of Edinburgh, Saturday June 1st, and the head of the first to be affixed on the Nether Bow, his estate to be confiscate, and his arms torn, and the head of the second upon the West Port in the city of Edinburgh."

It was resolved that this excellent minister should fall a sacrifice to private personal pique, as the marquis of Argyle was said to be to a more exalted revenge. I am told the managers had no small debates what his sentence should be. Mr. Guthrie was dealt with, by some (sent) from some of them, to retract what he had done and written, and to join in with the present measures; and he was even offered a bishopric. The other side were in no hazard in making the experiment, for they might be assured of his firmness in his principles. A bishopric was a very small temptation to him, and the commissioner improved his inflexibleness, and insisted to have his life taken, to be a terror to others, and that they might have the less opposition in erecting of prelacy. Thus a sentence of death was passed upon him, for his accession to the Causes of God's Wrath, his writing the Petition last year, and the Protestations above mentioned; matters done a good many years ago, and when done, not at all insisted on by the king himself, and every way agreeable to the word of God, and principles and practice of this and other churches, and the laws of the kingdom. *

1661.

Since the writing of what is above, I have lately had access to all the original papers

---

* Burnet says, " his declining the king's authority to judge of his sermons, and his protesting for remedy of law against him, and the late seditious paper, [as he is pleased to style the petition of the preceding year] were the matters objected to him. He was a resolute and stiff man; so when his lawyers offered him legal defences, he would not be advised by them, but resolved to take his own way. He confessed and justified all that he had done as agreeing to the principles and practices of the kirk, who had asserted all along, that the doctrine delivered in their sermons did not fall under the cognizance of the temporal courts till it was first judged by the church, for which he brought much tedious proof." The bishop, however, is candid enough to add, though contrary to the assertions of some of his episcopal friends, that " he gave no advantage to those who wished to have saved him by the least step towards any submission, but much to the contrary. I saw him suffer. He was so far from showing any fear, that he rather expressed a contempt of death. He spoke an hour upon the ladder with the composedness of one that was delivering a sermon rather than his last words. He justified all he had done, and exhorted all people to adhere to the covenant, which he magnified highly." Hist. of his Own Times, vol. i. pp. 180, 181.

M'Kenzie, though he repeats the foolish story of his being willing to have saved his life by submission, from which he was driven by the upbraiding of ladies, &c. &c. says, " It was to be regretted, that a more tractable and quiet person had not the keeping of his great parts and carriage, for he was both the secretary and champion of his party." Hist. of Scotland, pp. 50, 51. —*Ed.*

1661. relative to Mr. Guthrie's process, yet remaining at Edinburgh among the warrants in the parliament house, and have for the reader's satisfaction, added in a note, Mr. Guthrie's indictment, his defences, and the minutes of the criminal process. The advocates' replies, and Mr. Guthrie's duplies are likewise before me, but they are so large that I have not insert them, since, as far as I can judge, the state of this process is fully and at length enough contained in the indictment and defences, given below.*

One who attended Mr. Guthrie in the prison, and during the whole of his trial, tells me, that day he received his sentence, he was removed from the bar to the outer house, and in a hurry of soldiers, pursuivants, servants, and such like, until the clerk wrote his sentence, and he well enough knew the house were debating about the disposal of his body; yet this extraordinary person, as afterwards he owned, never felt more of the sensible presence of God, sweet intimations of peace, and real manifestations of the

---

* Indictment against Mr. James Guthrie, February 7th, 1661.

Mr. James Guthrie, sometime minister at Stirling, you are indicted and accused, and are to answer at the instance of Sir John Fletcher, knight, his majesty's advocate, for his majesty's interest, that whereas by the laws of God, of nations, and of all well governed realms, the common law, municipal law, acts of parliament, and practick of this his majesty's ancient kingdom, especially by the first act, 18th parliament of king James VI. of blessed memory, and by several other acts of parliament, holden by his majesty's royal predecessors, all his majesty's good and loyal subjects are bound and obliged perpetually to acknowledge, obey, maintain, and defend, and advance the life, honour, safety, dignity, sovereign authority and prerogative royal of their sovereign lord and king's majesty, their heirs and successors, and privileges of their throne, with their lives, lands, and goods, to the utmost of their power, constantly and faithfully to withstand all and whatsomever persons, powers, or estates, who shall presume, press, or intend any ways to impugn, prejudge, hurt, or impair the same, and shall no ways intend, attempt, enact, or do any thing to the violation, hurt, derogation, impairing, prejudice of his majesty's sovereign authority, prerogative, or privilege of his crown, in any point or part, and whoever does in the contrary, to be punished as traitors, and forfeit their honours, lives, lands, and goods: likeas, by the 129th act of king James VI. parliament 8th, upon some treasonable, seditious, and contumelious speeches uttered in pulpits, schools, and otherwise, to the disdain and reproach of his majesty's progenitors and council, some persons being called before his majesty and his council, did contemptuously decline his and their judgment in that behalf; his majesty and his three estates in parliament did ratify, approve, and perpetually confirm the royal power and authority over all states, as well spiritual as temporal, within this realm, in the person of the king's majesty, their sovereign lord, his heirs and successors, and did, statute and ordain, that his majesty, his said heirs and successors, by themselves and their council, were, and in time to come should be judges competent to all persons his majesty's subjects of whatsoever estate, degree, function, or condition that ever they may be of, spiritual or temporal, in all matters wherein they or any of them shall be apprehended, summoned, or charged to answer to such things as shall be inquired of them by his majesty and his said council, and that none of them who shall happen to be apprehended, called, or summoned to the effect aforesaid, presume, or take upon hand to decline the judgment of his majesty, his heirs or successors, or their council, in the premises, under the pain of treason. As also by the 134th act, parliament 8th, the 10th act of the 10th parliament, the 205th act, parliament 14th, king James VI. of blessed memory, it is statute and ordained by his said majesty and three estates in parliament, that none of his majesty's subjects (of whatsoever degree, function, or quality,) in time coming, shall presume or take upon hand, privately or publicly, in sermons, declamations, or familiar conferences, to utter any false, slanderous, or untrue speeches, to the disdain, reproach, contempt of his majesty, his council, and proceedings, or to the dishonour, hurt, and prejudice of his majesty, his parents and progenitors, or to meddle in the affairs of his majesty and his estates, present, bygone, and in time coming, under the pains contained in the acts of parliament made against makers and tellers of leasings: and that whosoever hears any such slanders, and reports not the same with diligence, the like pains should be executed against them with all rigour, as at more length is contained in the said acts. And also, by the act of the 25th day of November, 1650 years, passed by his majesty and his committee of estates, thereafter ratified upon the 4th day of June, 1651 years, by his majesty and his estates of parliament, a paper called a remonstrance, presented to the said committee upon the 22d day of October, and insisted upon thereafter upon the 19th day of November, 1650, was declared to be scandalous and injurious to his majesty's person, prejudicial to his authority, dishonourable to his kingdom, holding forth the seeds of division, strengthening the hands of the enemy, and weakening the hands of many honest men: and also by the 131st act of the 8th parliament of king James VI. it is statute and ordained by his said majesty and his three estates, that none of his majesty's subjects, of whatsomever quality, estate, or function they be of, spiritual or temporal, presume or take upon hand, to convocate, convene, or assemble themselves together, for holding of councils, conventions, or assemblies, to treat, consult, or determinate in any matter of estate, civil or ecclesiastical, (except in the ordinary judicatories) without his majesty's special commandment, or express license had and obtained to that effect, under the pains ordained by the laws and acts

divine love and favour, than at this very time, when in that outward confusion: and when called in, received his sentence with the greatest composure and cheerfulness.

1661.

The iniquity of this sentence appears fully of parliament, against such as unlawfully convocate his majesty's free lieges. Nevertheless it is of verity, that you the said Mr. James Guthrie, having laid aside all fear of God, loyalty to his majesty your sovereign lord and king, natural duty and affection to your country and countrymen, respect and obedience to the laws of all well governed realms, the common law, and the laws, statutes, acts of parliament, and practick of this his majesty's ancient kingdom, and having seditiously and traitorously intended and purposed the eradicating and subverting the fundamental government of this his majesty's ancient kingdom, at least the enervating, violating, derogating, or impairing the sovereign authority, royal prerogative, and privilege of his majesty's crown, did, for raising division amongst his subjects, and sedition against his majesty's person, dignity, authority, and privilege of his crown, and, so far as in you lay, the alienating of the affections, and brangling the loyalty and allegiance of his majesty's people, to the great encouragement and advancement of the designs and attempts of that bloody usurper, Oliver Cromwell, and bringing of his majesty, and his ancient and your native country in subjection and bondage under him, contrive, complot, counsel, consult, draw up, frame, invent, spread abroad, or disperse, speak, preach, declaim, or utter divers and sundry vile, seditious, and treasonable remonstrances, declarations, petitions, instructions, letters, speeches, preachings, declamations, and other expressions tending to the vilifying and contemning, slander and reproach of his majesty, his progenitors, his person, majesty, dignity, authority, prerogative royal, and government, not only within this his ancient kingdom of Scotland, but also in his majesty's kingdoms of England and Ireland; at least did hear and conceal, and not reveal the same to his majesty, nor to any of his judges or officers, mentioned in the said acts of parliament; at least did aid and abet, or was art and part thereof, or of one or other of them, in so far as, after the cruel bloody usurper, Oliver Cromwell, and his accomplices, had most barbarously and cruelly murdered his majesty's royal father, of ever blessed memory, their dread sovereign and lord, and his majesty's arrival to this his ancient kingdom from foreign parts, after a most tedious and dangerous voyage at sea, and after that treacherous usurper, in pursuance of his horrid and treasonable designs, for hindering his majesty to inherit that his just and lawful right to the crown of the said kingdom, had, with an army of sectaries, invaded the same; and that God Almighty had been pleased to blast and frustrate his majesty's first endeavours for opposing his said treasonable invasion, by suffering his majesty's armies to fall and flee before him at Dunbar, upon the 3d day of September, 1650 years. First, you immediately thereafter did compile and draw up a paper, commonly called the "Remonstrance," and presented, or caused present the same to his majesty's committee of estates at Perth, upon the 22d day of October, wherein most treasonably you utter and belch forth a great many damnable and execrable leasings, slanders, and reproaches against his majesty's dearest father, of eternal memory, and others his majesty's noble progenitors, their persons, majesty, dignity, authority, and government: and also, you not only disclaim his majesty's authority over you, and disown him in the exercise of his royal power and government, in the right whereof his majesty and his predecessors were invested by God, and in possession by a series of one hundred and eight progenitors; but also most treasonably reproach others, his majesty's good subjects, for doing the same, and most impiously held forth, that the main and great cause of the sufferings of his majesty's people, under the tyranny and oppression of the bloody usurper, is the owning of his majesty's interest in this his ancient kingdom, and the purpose of restoring his majesty to his throne and government of his kingdom of England, from which most wretchedly and godlessly you aver, that his majesty was most justly removed; wherein also are many more bitter and ignominious reflections, seditious, treacherous, and treasonable expressions, tending to the contempt and disdain, slander and reproach of his majesty, his progenitors in his person, majesty, dignity, authority, and government, as at more length is contained in the said malicious paper, and which is here repeated, as a part of the libel, *brevitatis causa.* Secondly, After it had pleased God to suffer the said bloody enemies and murderers of his majesty's royal father so far to prevail as to avoid their fury and cruelty, his majesty was necessitate to withdraw himself from his dominions, and live in foreign parts, under great difficulty and hardships, (which low condition of his majesty's, might have calmed and quieted the wicked and malicious spirits of his majesty's rebellious subjects, at least their venomous and viperous tongues and pens) not the less the bitterness and insatiable malice of you the said Mr. James Guthrie, was such, that not satisfied with the injuries committed by you against his majesty's person, dignity and authority, expressed in the foresaid paper of remonstrance, you did contrive, write, compile, and that it might be the more public, and follow his majesty beyond seas, and defame and bring him in contempt with foreign princes and states, caused print, *in anno* 1653 years, a seditious pamphlet, called "The Causes of God's Wrath," not only containing all the former injurious, wicked, and seditious reflections and expressions, fully set down in the foresaid papers, formerly condemned by act of parliament, and expressly relative thereto, but also many more malicious, ignominious, dishonourable, and treasonable passages, at length set down in the said pamphlet, and specially in the fifth and sixth articles thereof, and enlargements in the said articles, which is repeated as a part of the libel, and which being considered by the said committee of estates, they have found the same, by their act of the date the 19th day of September, 1660 years, of so high and treasonable a nature, and that it deserves publicly to be burned with the hand of the hangman, and the havers and users thereof hereafter to be punished, in manner as at more length is expressed in the said act. Thirdly, God, in his great mercy to his majesty and his

1661. from Mr. Guthrie's own speeches already inserted, and is very well discovered by a fellow-sufferer of his at this time, though not unto blood, the author of the Apologetical Narration, in his fifth section. Mr. Guthrie was undoubtedly one of

oppressed kingdoms, having wonderfully, contrary, and in despite of all the wicked, damnable, and treasonable practices and machinations of you and your accomplices, restored his majesty again to his just and lawful inheritance, as to the exercise of his regal power and authority in all his dominions, in peaceable manner, which so wonderful and immediate acting of divine providence might have justly quieted the spirits of all his majesty's enemies, and have made them acknowledge the sinfulness of their former ways and courses, and that God was displeased therewith, and that they had highly provoked him thereby, and have made them walk more answerable to such deliverances and mercies, and have behaved themselves more dutifully and obediently to his majesty: yet the evil spirit wherewith they are possessed, prevails so in them, that the more they see of the Lord's appearances, the more they are hardened in their former wicked, malicious, and treasonable designs and attempts; and therefore knowing, that without great hazard to themselves, (now when the Lord has returned the hearts and affections of his majesty's good subjects to him) they durst not so openly and avowedly act, speak, or write against his majesty, his authority or government, or any ways meddle in the government, affairs, or estate of either his majesty's kingdoms, as formerly they have done, and as is more fully expressed in the above written article; you, in a most subtile and covered manner, under the pretext and cover of piety, loyalty, and zeal for religion, with many insinuating expressions of your joy and gladness for his majesty's restoration, and your good wishes for him in time coming, did, by way and in the dress and garb of an humble petition to his majesty, not only most wickedly calumniate, traduce, and asperse his majesty with dissimulation and perjury, but also most unwarrantably, seditiously, and treasonably reflect upon his majesty, and the lawful government and order of his church and estate of England and Ireland, and of his majesty's chapel and family, and calling him to alter and invert the same, and most grossly encroach upon his majesty, his authority and prerogative, in meddling with his majesty's affairs, and filling of all places of power and trust under his majesty, contrary to the foresaid laws and acts of parliament, as is more fully expressed in the said pretended petition, which is here repeated, *brevitatis causa*, as a part of the libel. Fourthly, Not only did you and your accomplices convocate yourselves, but also by missive letters, commissions, and instructions drawn up by you at the same time, you did frame the foresaid pretended petition, did presume and take upon you to convocate and convene his majesty's subjects and lieges, whereby it is evident that you have not only contravened his majesty's foresaid acts of parliament, made against unlawful convocations of his majesty's lieges, but that your only purpose and intent in contriving the slanderous and infamous pretended petition, was to publish and disperse the same, thereby to sow sedition amongst his majesty's subjects, and, as for as in you lay, to render his majesty and government hateful and contemptible to them, as if his majesty intended to subvert the true Protestant religion, and bring in popery and idolatry amongst them. Fifthly, You, the said Mr. James Guthrie, being convened before his majesty and committee of estates at Perth, to answer for some seditious and unwarrantable speeches uttered by you in your sermons, at Stirling, and otherways, against his majesty, his authority and laws, and having appeared, you most contemptuously, disobediently, and treacherously did disclaim and decline his majesty and his authority, and did protest for remede of law against his majesty, for a pretended *gravamen*, as you term it, in convening you before his majesty, and confining you, as the same had been contrary to the laws of God, of nature, and the laws of the land, the right and privilege of his majesty's subjects, as is more fully contained in two protestations given in and subscribed by you, dated in February, 1651 years, which are here also repeated as a part of the libel, *brevitatis causa*. And further, you, the said Mr. James, are indicted and accused for having, in Stirling, at a meeting with certain ministers and ruling elders, *in anno* 1650, or 1651, most treasonably moved, and offered as your judgment, that his majesty should not only be debarred the exercise of his royal power, but that his person might be secured and imprisoned within the castle of Stirling; and in answer was made thereto by some of the said number, "that they might as well proceed to the taking of his life as the imprisoning of his person:" you did reply, "it was not yet seasonable, nor time to speak to that, but that it was necessary to do the one before the other."

By all which particulars respective above expressed, it is clearly evinced, that you were author, contriver, deviser, consulter, adviser, or art and part of the foresaid crimes of treason, and others respective above libelled, or one or other of them, in manner above declared, and thereby has incurred the pains and punishment of high treason, and others contained in the laws and acts of parliament, which might and should be inflicted upon you with all rigour, in example to others in all time coming.

Edinburgh, 7th February, 1661.

The lords of the articles having heard, seen, and considered the above written indictment of treason, do appoint the same to be given up to Mr. James Guthrie, to be seen by him, and to answer against Tuesday, the 19th of this instant.

GLENCAIRN,
Cancellarius, I. P. D. Art.

Mr. James Guthrie's Defences.

Whereas Mr. James Guthrie is indicted before my lord commissioner his grace, and the three estates of parliament, upon sundry particulars alleged to be seditious and treasonable; he is glad, that through the holy and good providence of God, it is his lot to plead his cause not before strangers, usurpers, who, as they were not acquainted with the doctrine and laws, and the estate of the affairs of this church and kingdom, so have they not just title or claim to exercise any power or jurisdiction in or over the same, but

CHAP. II.] OF THE CHURCH OF SCOTLAND. 177

the most eminent of the ministers of the church at this time, and of the protesting way; and all of that set were now hated and persecuted to satisfy Mr. Sharp's malicious and ambitious designs. He had likewise been a steady opposer of the

1661.

---

before an honourable court of parliament of his own nation, well acquainted with the laws of this kingdom, and bred up in the doctrine and profession of the church, and called and countenanced by his majesty, whose native and just title to the crown of these kingdoms, as he did ever acknowledge, so doth he bless God for the preservation of his person, and for removing out of the way these usurping powers that hindered the exercise of his government, and prays that his throne may be established in righteousness over these nations, that the Lord's people under him may live a quiet and peaceable life, in all godliness and honesty. The defender is glad also, that among the laws mentioned in the proposition of his indictment, the law of God is set in the first room, that being the sovereign and supreme law which is the fountain and source of all other laws, according to which they are to be squared, and there being an express act of parliament, James VI. parliament 1st, cap. 3d, whereby all laws and statutes made against God's holy word, are declared to be void and null in themselves; a law well beseeming, and most worthy of a christian king and kingdom: therefore, the defender doth humbly expect that judgment shall be given of him, and of his proceedings by this law, especially as by that which is most perfect and absolute, and, in confidence hereof, comes to his defences.

And alleges, first, that there can be no process upon this libel, till the act of the committee of estates, of the date 25th of November, 1650, and the act of parliament whilk is libelled upon, as ratifying the same, dated 24th of June, 1651, anent the paper called the "Remonstrance," be produced and given up to the defender to see; because albeit printed laws *allegari debent non probari;* yet whatever is not a written law, whether acts, decreets, and writings, whereupon processes are founded as they must be produced to the judge, and not alleged only; so for the same reason they must be given up to the party to see, which is both our law and practick, and consonant to common law, *l.* 1, § 3, *ff. de edendo; ubi edenda sunt omnia quæ quis apud judicem editurus est;* that is, whatever the party pursuer is to produce before the judge, that ought to be given up to see to the defender, and the reason is given there, and *l.* 3, *cod. eod.* to wit, that the defender may come prepared to make his defence. This is so uncontroverted that it needs be confirmed by no more law. But so it is, the foresaid acts of committee of estates and parliament, anent that remonstrance were never printed, and therefore *ante omnia* they ought to be produced, and, before they be produced, no process.

Secundo. Every libel ought to be clear, and criminal dittays ought to be most clear. *Damhond. T.* 3, *N.* 4, and should contain no ambiguity nor obscurity, *chap. constitutis* 6. *Extra de Relig. Dom.* and therefore, *Libellus criminalis obscurus, parte etiam non excipiente, extenditur favore rei;* that is, a criminal libel that is obscure, is extended in favours of the defender, though he should propound no defence against it, *Bald. in L. edita N.* 10, *C. de Edend.* and other doctors.

But so it is, this libel is indistinct and obscure, in so far as in the proposition there are several different acts of parliament libelled upon, made upon facts of divers natures, and containing divers pains; and in the subsumption different facts and alleged crimes falling under the compass of one and the same law, ought, as the defender humbly conceives, to have been libelled and subsumed immediately after the same, whereby the defender might have known for contravention of what law by every fact he was convened, whereanent he is left now in an uncertainty, and therefore the libel herein is uncertain and obscure, and there can be no process thereupon.

Tertio. As to the first part of the proposition of the libel, founded upon the act 1, parliament 18, James VI. there is no such act as is libelled, for it is libelled otherwise than it bears, against act 107, parliament 7, James I. whereby it is forbidden that any man interpret his majesty's statutes otherwise than the statutes bear; but so it is, that statute, act 1, parliament 18, aforesaid, bears no pain at all, let be the pain of treason, and forfeiture of honour, life, lands, and goods, and therefore there can be no process of treason thereupon founded to infer any pain, far less the pain of treason, seeing it bears no pain, as said is, which is confirmed. 2do. Because there can be no process of treason, but upon particular acts of parliament, made under the pain of treason against disobeyers and contraveners, by the express act of parliament, act 28, parliament 2, Charles I. *anno* 1640. But so it is, the act libelled on, as said is, bears no such pain; therefore it can found no process of treason. And Stio. Every pain ought to be irrogate and established by a law, *Doct. ad L. At si quis § divus ff. de relig. et sumpt. fun.* For it is by a sanction of law that punishments are established, *legis* 11. *Virtus est imperare, vetare, permittere, punire L.* 7. *de leg.* that it is the virtue of law to command, forbid, permit, and punish. Now there is nothing in the said law and act of parliament, but a declarature of the king's royal prerogative, and of an obligation of the three estates to maintain the same; and therefore seeing that law hath made no sanction, neither of treason nor any other, this part of the proposition of the dittay founded thereupon, is altogether without ground, and there can be no process thereupon.

Quarto. No process upon the act of the committee of estates, libelled to be of the date 25th November, 1650, and act of ratification in parliament, libelled of the date 24th of June, 1651, anent the paper called the "Remonstrance," because these are not printed acts, and are not produced, as said is.

The next thing in the indictment is the subsumption, in which there is first a general charge upon the defender, of his being culpable of sundry seditious and treasonable remonstrances, declarations, petitions, instructions, letters, speeches, declamations, &c. To all which he saith, that *generalia non pungunt,* they can have no strength as to the inferring one crime or guilt upon the defender, except in so far as they

z

1661. malignant party, and prelacy now fast hasting in, and a vigorous enemy to scandalous ministers; and the commissioner could never forgive his excommunicating him. The king himself was so sensible of his good services to him, and his in-

are instanced and verified in particulars, and therefore doth he not judge himself bound to make any answer thereunto, were it not that he is therein charged, to have seditiously and traitorously intended and proposed the eradicating and subverting the fundamental government of this his majesty's ancient kingdom, at least the enervating, violating, and impairing his majesty's authority, by complying with, and being subservient unto the designs and purposes of that usurper, Oliver Cromwell, and his complices; concerning which he is bold to say, that it is an unjust charge, and mere forgery, there was never any such intention or purpose in his heart, nor can it be proven from any of his speeches, or writings, or actions. He dare and doth truly affirm, that as he never had any compliances with the designs and counsels, or actings of the late usurping powers, against his majesty's royal father, or himself, or against the kingdom, or the ancient government thereof, or of the kingdom of England or Ireland, so there was no part of their ungodly courses, and unjust attempts, and violent usurpations and actings, but he did, in his station and calling, doth by word and writ, bear testimony against the same, which is a thing better known and more manifest than that he can be liable in the least to suspicion therein, many of these testimonies being given before many living witnesses, and many of them being yet extant, and such as will be extant to posterity for his vindication in this particular; besides two or three common solemn public testimonies, in which he joined with many of his brethren against these things, one of which was condescended upon and directed to these usurping powers, at the very time the causes of the Lord's controversy were condescended upon, which may sufficiently clear the honesty of his intentions and actings as to these causes: besides these common public testimonies, he was violently thrust from the pulpit, and quartered upon for six months together, for preaching against the tender, and giving warning to his congregation not to take the same, as being destructive to religion, and the liberties of the nation, and the ancient civil government of this kingdom in his majesty's person and family. He was called before the president and some others of Oliver Cromwell his council in Scotland, for writing and spreading a paper, holding him forth in express words to be an usurper, and his government to be usurpation; he was threatened with imprisonment for writing and communicating a paper against Oliver Cromwell his usurping of the crown of these kingdoms; he was threatened with banishment for being accessory to the offering of a public subscribed testimony against the actings of the late usurping powers, unto Richard Cromwell his council in Scotland, immediately after his usurping of the government of these kingdoms: which things he should not mention, knowing that he hath nothing wherein to boast in himself, were it not that he is thereunto constrained, for vindicating himself from the unjust aspersions that are cast upon him, and that by telling of known and manifest truths, concerning his faithfulness and zeal against the king's enemies, he may make it appear, that not only is he innocent of these aspersions, but also in his accession to "The Causes of God's Wrath," and to the "Supplication," and "Declinator," mentioned in the indictment, he had no dole, or fraud, or intention to defame or reproach the king, but in these things he walked in the simplicity of his heart, with an eye upon his duty both to God and to his majesty, and acted in these things from a true principle of piety towards God, and loyalty towards his majesty, and therefore cannot, because of his accession to any of these things, be judged guilty of treason and sedition.

The first particular deed subsumed in the indictment against the defender, is, that he did compile and draw up a paper, commonly called "the Remonstrance," and presented it, or caused it to be presented to his majesty, or the committee of estates, upon the 22d October, 1650. To which he answers, 1mo, By denying what is alleged. He did not compile or draw up that remonstrance, neither had he any hand in the compiling or drawing up thereof, nor did he present it, nor caused it to be presented to his majesty and the committee of estates; and it is notour, and the defender could prove by many hundreds of witnesses, if need were, that he was so far alibi in the time of the drawing up thereof, that he was at Stirling that time, many miles distant: and that he did not present the same, nor caused it to be presented, is also notour. And as to what may be alleged of his abetting the same in the "Causes of Wrath," he shall answer in its own place.

The second particular head, or article of the indictment, is anent the defender's contriving, compiling, causing print, in anno 1653 years, that seditious pamphlet (as it is libelled) called, "The Causes of God's Wrath," containing many malicious, ignominious, and treasonable passages, as is alleged therein, and specially in the 5th and 6th articles thereof, and which is declared against by an act of the committee of estates, of the date the 19th day of September 1660. To this article the defender answers as follows: 1mo. That act of committee, if any thing be intended to be founded thereon, ought to have been produced, and given up to see, and till then no process, for the reasons above alleged. Secundo, If it were produced, no act can be a ground to found a dittay of treason, and to infer the same, but an act of parliament, by the express act of parliament before cited, act 28, parl. 1640 years, and that must be an act made under the pain of treason against the contraveners. But, Tertio, It seems, from the place wherein this is libelled, being in the subsumption, it is only intended for an argument of the alleged guilt of that paper, and the defender doubts nothing, but whatever it pleased the committee to do anent that paper, there being none concerned therein called and heard before them at that time or before, yet the commissioner's grace and the estates of parliament will be very far from condemning the defender unheard, and therefore he shall shortly premise the true case of his accession to that

CHAP. II.] OF THE CHURCH OF SCOTLAND.

terest when at its lowest, and the severity of this sentence, that when he got notice of it, he asked with some warmth, " And what have you done with Mr. Patrick Gillespie?" It was answered, that Mr. Gillespie had so many friends in the

1661.

paper, and motives, and ends therein; and thereafter shall proceed to his further defences. The case is truly thus: The Lord, by the sad defeats of our armies at Dunbar, Inverkeithing, and Worcester, and rendering our whole nation captives in all their precious interests, unto the cruelty and lusts of usurping strangers, having declared from heaven much of his wrath and indignation against this whole land, and all ranks of persons therein, from the highest to the lowest, especially against the ministry of this church; the defender, with many of these ministers and elders who had been dissatisfied in their consciences with the public proceedings of the former year, did come together after Worcester, not to comply with or strengthen in any thing the hands of adversaries, or to cast any reproaches upon the person of the king's majesty, or do any injury to the ancient civil government of the kingdom in his majesty's person and family, but in singleness of heart to search into the causes of all this great wrath, both as to their own sins, and the sins of all sorts of persons in the land, so far as God should be pleased, from the light of his word, to discover the same to them. Therefore, having first searched into and acknowledged their own sins, they did, in the next place, search into the sins of the land; and after conference and prayer, to the best of their light and apprehension, win at some discoveries thereof, they did draw the same first into some short heads and articles, which they did afterwards enlarge, merely in order to a more clear discovery of sin and guilt to such of the land, especially of their own congregations, whom God should be pleased by his word and Spirit to convince thereof.

The case being thus truly, the defender alleges, *Quarto*, Whatever may be in the matter of that paper, yet this article of the dittay is no ways relevantly libelled, nor subsumed under the acts of the proposition to infer the crime and pain of treason, because this article can only be subsumed on that part of the proposition founded upon the acts of James VI. parl. 8th, 10th, and 14th, mentioned therein against authors of slanderous speeches or writs against his majesty, the pain whereof is not the pain of treason in none of those, nor no other acts of parliament whereunto they may relate; for in the foresaid 134th act, parl. 8th, James VI., relation is made to the pains statuted against leasingmakers, which is not the pain of treason, but of tinsel of life and goods, as is clear by the 43d act, parl. 2. James I. anent leasingmakers, wherein, by goods is only understood goods moveable, and that pain is no ways the pain of *treason*, nor is that crime ordained to be treason by any of our acts of parliament, as is clear by the style and tenor of the same by Skene in his Tract of Crimes in the end of the Majesty, and by his Index of the Acts of Parliament on the word *treason*: and therefore, in so far as the passages of that paper are libelled here to be treasonable, the article cannot be reasonably subsumed under the aforesaid acts, nor no other acts of parliament, and the defender ought to be assoilied therefrom.

Quinto, This article, as it is subsumed upon the acts of parliament, false and scandalous speeches and writs against his majesty, &c. is no ways relevantly libelled, because as all crimes require as well malice in the person as evil in the thing done, that is, dole *et malitia subjectiva* as well as *objectiva, d. d. ad l. i. ff. de sua,* so specially in injuries, whether by word, writ, or otherwise, dole and an intention to injure and reproach, is essentially requisite, so that without there can be no action of injury; *nam ad hoc debitum, requiritur animus injuriandi,* say the doctors, and the law is express, *lib.* iii. § 1. *ff. de injuriis et famosis libellis.* In that title of the law anent injuries and infamous libels, the words are, *injuria ex affectu consistit,* that is, an injury depends all upon the intention of him who does it, thereby to injure; and the doctors, following the words, express that law and principle, *instit. de injuriis;* and specially *Craveta Concilio* 419, No. 1, and *Concil.* 9, No. 36, says, That *agens actione injuriarum debet allegare dolum,* that is, he that pursues an action of injury should allege dole. And Menoch. says in *Concil.* 197. lib. 12. that the words must be injurious, and must be *prolata animo injuriandi,* that is, they must be also spoken and written with intention to injure; and many others, whom it were tedious to allege. But so it is that there is nothing libelled to infer that the defender had an evil, seditious, ignominious, dishonourable, or any ways sinister intention, in order to his majesty, in what hand he had in that paper, without which, the dittay in this part is not relevant; but that neither is nor can be libelled: but on the contrar, to clear that the defender had no dole or intention of injury against his sacred majesty, it is evident, 1mo, because Menoch. in the forcited place, *Concil.* 197. lib. 12. disputing the case of words of a subject that may seem to reflect against his prince, says, *animus injuriandi non praesumitur in bono subdito adversus principem,* but rather *prolata esse bono animo et zelo versus principem,* that is, in a good subject it is not presumed that he intended to injure his prince, but rather that his words (whether spoken or written, for both are but words) was from a good zeal towards his prince. Now what a good subject the defender hath been, and what zeal he has had for his prince and against his enemies, and how much he did suffer therefore, he is confident has been evident from the true information thereanent abovewritten, and which is notour, as has been said: whence law and reason will presume, that he intended no injury against his majesty by that paper, especially seeing, 2*do.* (which if need be, he propones jointly) That the nature and quality of the act, being that by which the intention of the agent is best known, as lawyers observe well from *d. L. i. ff. ad L. Cornel. de Sicar.* it is clear from the nature of the act whereabout the defender was in that paper, that he intended no injury to his majesty, nor was there any dole or malice in it; for it is an act directory of acknowledgment of sins and repentance, which consists of two parts, conviction and sorrow for sin, which

1661. house his life could not be taken. "Well," said the king, "if I had known you would have spared Mr. Gillespie, I would have spared Mr. Guthrie." And indeed there was reason for it, as to one who had been so firm and zealous an assertor of

is no ways dole or malice against the supposed sinner, and without which dole and malice there is no crime or injury; but on the contrar the very end of it is the recovery of the supposed sinner, and appeasing of divine wrath against him: whereunto adding 3tio, That repentance is πρὸς τὸν Θεὸν, *that is*, towards God, and so has no tendence toward, and cannot be a crime against any creature. And 4to, Though there were even a mistake upon the matter, in acknowledging and repenting of what were duty, (or at least what were not sinful) for sin, yet a naked error in opinion, without dole or malice is no crime, as has been said, though the error were even *latæ culpæ*, that is, not to understand that that all understand, as it is defined in *L. lata culpa, ff. de Verb. Signif.* For where even a law or statute irrogates corporal punishment or death, there that *lata culpa*, or gross mistake, is not sufficient to infer it *D. D. in Lib.* i. *ff. de Sicar*, and *Godseid*, super *L. pen. Cod. de custod. reor. et L. pen. ff. de in litem jurand. Buttand. Reg.* 8. *prox. crim. in primo*, citing many doctors for it, and *Damhond. cap.* 85. *N.* 11. Yea, it is not sufficient and relevant to infer but infamy per *Gloss. in L. in actionibus, ff. de in lit. jurand. Bastol. in L. Cod. nec Num.* 20. *cum seqq. ff. de possit.* But as to *levis culpa*, which is not giving that diligence to do or to know, which other exact persons may give, as it is commonly defined, was never made equivalent to dole, or made the ground of a crime by no lawyer, and yet the defender subsumes, that if there were any mistake upon the matter in that paper, specially the 5th step (called) of defection, it was an opinion common to him and the church, and states of the kingdom, as by many of the declarations may appear; and therefore in him had neither *latam* nor *levem culpam* in it, far less *dolum*, and so he is, as not culpable, so not criminal therein. 5to. *Quævis causa, injasta etiam et fatua, excusata dolo*, and so from injury, *Clarus, lib.* v. *Sent. § fin. et alii per L. igitur, Gloss. in L. Num. ff. Si quis jus dicenti non obtemp. et Jason, ibid.* How much more ought the defender to be excused, who had for the cause and motive of his and others' acknowledgments in that paper, the declarations, warnings and other papers, both of church and state, particularly aftermentioned, and had a far other end than malice, imported in the very nature of the action, as said is, to wit, deprecating and appeasing divine wrath, which had gone out against the whole land, reconciling him by repentance, as well to the defender as others, from love to all, eminently to his majesty, as having eminently suffered by that displeasure, under the chastisement whereof all of us then were: in respect whereof the defender ought to be assoiled from any dole or *culpa*, and so from any action of injury, and from all crime and pains libelled in or upon that article. As for the two articles specially condescended on of the said paper, viz. the 5th and 6th articles, as they are designed in the libel, it is answered, 1mo, That these articles are anent the sin of covetousness of the people, and ministers and others who had been in the army, and other places military and civil over them, and their abusing of public faith; and as to these they are both incontroverted sins, and clearly meant no ways of his majesty, but of the people and other inferior rulers, who, before his majesty's return, had been in places of power over them; but it seems, it is not meant of the 5th and 6th steps (called) of defection and therefore the defender, adhering to his general answer made against all this article, upon this paper in general, alleges specially to the 5th step. 1mo, That for what is contained therein, has proceeded according to the proper rules of acknowledgment of sins, and of repentance, viz. church canons in their declarations, and therefore *culpa vacabat*; the defender was not culpable, and so not criminal therein, having therein walked according to ecclesiastic rules and declarations then standing. 2do, It is alleged that there is nothing in these acts of parliament cited in the indictment, that concerns lies, and slanders, and reproaches, &c. of his majesty, that can infer or include the crime of treason and sedition against the defender, because any thing asserted in that part of the book of Causes of Wrath. For, first, Mr. Coke, in his Reports of the English Law, tells, that all the judges certified his majesty, that the speaking of any words, whereby a personal vice is charged upon the king, cannot be treason, and this he said, judge Zelvertoun said, was held by the judges in debate, about Mr. Pothin's case, who was judged for divers treasonable speeches in his sermon. And the same Mr. Coke in his Treatise of Treason, tells us, that words may make an heretic but not a traitor. And for this there is an excellent law. *Cod. Si quis imperatori maledixerit, si quis modestiæ nescius, et pudoris ignarus, improbo petulantique maledicto nomina vestra tradiderit lacessenda, ac temulentia turbulentus obtrectator temporum nostrorum fuerit, eum pœna nolumus subjugari, neque durum aliquid nec asperum volumus sustinere; quoniam si id ex levitate processerit, contemnendum est, si ex insania, miseratione dignissimus, si ab injuria, remittendum seu condonandum.* That is to say, if any man ignorant either of modesty or shame, thinks to provoke our majesty or name, by wicked or reproachful speeches, and being troublesome through drunkenness, become a reproach of our times, we will not have him punished, nor suffer any hard thing therefore; because if it has proceeded of levity it is to be despised, if of madness, it is worthy of pity, if of intention to injure it is to be forgiven. And in France, as Coke well observes, it is no treason for a Hugonote to call the king an heretic, for says he, it is no treason to say, the king is a catholic, neither is treason to say, that a catholic is an heretic, which seems very agreeable to that of the prophet Isaiah, wherein he reproves it as one of the sins in his time, that a man was made an offender for a word. But, secondly, If it be true that it was a sin, to close a treaty with the king for investing him with the exercise of his royal power, he still continuing in his former known opposition of

his majesty's title and interest, and had suffered so much for his continued opposition to, and disowning of the English usurpation.

the work of reformation, as is asserted in the 5th step of the article, then cannot the defender fall within the compass of the breach, or pains of any of these acts of parliament relating to slanders, lyings, &c. But that it is true, that this was a sin, is, as the defender humbly conceives, holden forth and proven in the common received doctrine of this church, and public declared judgment of this kingdom, both before the treaty, and in the time of the treaty, and after the close of the treaty with the king at Breda. Therefore, for making out of the subsumption, he doth humbly offer unto your lordships, the serious perusal of the following paper herewith presented, in which are mentioned many clear testimonies, out of the public papers of kirk and state, confirming the same to have been their judgment likewise; and craves it might be read, and as the papers therein mentioned are notour, so your lordships will find them conform to the registers and records, both of kirk and state; and humbly craves, that your lordships would hold these testimonies sufficiently verified *notorietate juris*, most of them being printed; or if any thing further be needful for the verifying thereof, that your lordships would search the registers, and allow him extracts out of the registers themselves, in which these testimonies are contained, and, as a part of the public proceedings of this kirk and kingdom, are ratified by his majesty's treaty at Breda, and act of ratification at St. Johnston, or Stirling, or is conform to that which was ratified. From all which, *Stio*, The defender alleges, that seeing what is asserted in the 5th step was warranted by the acts of church and state, and ratified in manner foresaid, it cannot be libelled to infer a crime against him, and he ought to be assoilied from that part of the dittay; neither can these acts of parliament cited in the indictment, against meddling with his majesty's affairs, conclude the defender culpable in this matter, because the crime condemned by these acts, is only extravagant and unwarrantable meddling, or such as do not fall within the compass of, or is not confined within the bounds of a man's station and calling; otherwise it should be culpable for any of his majesty's officers, or for any subordinate magistrate, or any person whatsoever, to meddle in his majesty's affairs: but so it is, that the defender his meddling in this business was not extravagant or unwarrantable, but that whereunto he was called, and to which he was bound *virtute* or *necessitate officii*, as a minister of the gospel. It is competent and incumbent to the ministers of the gospel, to cry aloud, and not to spare in showing the Lord's people their transgressions and sins, to warn persons of all sorts concerning sin and duties, and to declare the whole counsel of God, the whole book of God, which contains the whole counsel of God, without exception of any part thereof; being the subject matter of that commission, which ministers do receive from Jesus Christ their Lord and Master, and therefore, there be many instances in the book of God, the practices of the prophets and apostles, and of Jesus Christ himself, discovering and reproving sin in persons of all ranks, though it was their lot often to be misconstructed or mistaken in their doing thereof, as though they had been no friends to civil authority.

After the sentence, and a little before his death, Mr. Guthrie received the following letter from a dear friend of his, 1661.

In defence of the 6th step of the 9th article of the Causes of Wrath, the defender doth offer to your lordships' consideration, that there is nothing therein that can be accounted treasonable, because there is nothing asserted therein but what is true, even that which relates to the Remonstrance itself, to wit, that it doth contain a testimony concerning sin and duty, the discovery whereof was rejected, as may appear from the public judgment at the commissioners of the general assembly at Perth, the 29th of December, 1650, in their Remonstrance to the honourable estates of parliament, concerning this business. The words be these: "Whatever has been your lordships' sense of that paper, presented to you by the gentlemen, officers and ministers attending the forces in the west, yet we wish you seriously to lay to heart the many sad truths contained therein; we will not here mention the sins relating to the king and the royal family, having particularly represented these to his majesty's self, and appointed a day of solemn humiliation therefore; but we do with all earnestness exhort your lordships to take to consideration, the sins herein held forth relating to yourselves, and to mourn before the Lord for them: and particularly, and in the first place, that your lordships may impartially, and in a self-denying way, as in the sight of the Lord, seriously ponder if there has not been, at least in some of you, sinful precipitance, unstraight designs and carnal policy in appointing addresses for treating with the king, and in a way of carrying on and closing of the same."

As to what is asserted in the close of this step, concerning the rejecting of the means of peace, it doth not strike against any act of parliament whatsoever, nor can be judged culpable, seeing robbers and pirates, and brigandines, and usurpers, and unjust invaders may, yea, sometimes ought, in some cases, be communed or treated with, upon conditions that are sinless, and there may be pride and presumption of spirit in not doing so.

To the third article of the dittay, bearing, that the defender under colour of piety, loyalty, and zeal for religion, and in the address and garb of a humble petition, did calumniate his majesty with dissimulation and perjury, reflected upon his majesty, and the lawful government of the church and state of England and Ireland, and of his chapel and family, and challenged him to alter and invert the same, encroached upon his authority and prerogative, in meddling with his majesty's affairs, and filling all places of power and trust under his majesty. It is answered, 1mo, It is not relevantly libelled, except it had been libelled that the said petition had been publicly presented, divulged and exhibited, being otherwise but *nudus conatus*, especially, seeing though the same had been, and of the contents and tenor libelled, yet could it not, upon any act of the proposition, infer the crime and punishment of

1661. if I am not mistaken, a very eminent minister, which as it was supporting to him, so it shows the sense, that not only the writer of it, but many others had of the present procedure of the managers, and of the dark cloud coming upon this church.

treason, seeing the acts made against slanderous speeches and writs and slanderers, under the which only it can be subsumed, are not made under the pain of treason, as has been abundantly evinced in the answer to the former article anent the paper, called "The Causes of God's Wrath." In which crime of lese majesty allenarly *affectus sine effectu* is *humilis*. 2do, Although the same had been printed, yet as to the calumniating his majesty thereby, as the defender denies any intent or purpose he had for that effect, so, with confidence, thereto he doth oppone the petition itself, bearing no such thing. 3tio, As to his reflecting upon, and meddling with his majesty's affairs, and the government of his church in England and Ireland, his majesty's chapel and family, and filling of places of trust, &c. *non relevat*, except it had been libelled, and made appear by the petition, that the same was to the disdain, reproach, and contempt of his majesty or his government, as he is hopeful, no word in that petition can genuinely infer. Next for any expressions relating therein to the government of the church of England and his majesty's chapel, as there is no mention made thereof in any of the acts of the proposition, wherein his majesty's lawful government is only expressed and forbidden, so he humbly conceives that prelacy and the chapel is no such lawful government and form, but that a minister of the church of Scotland, sworn against the same by the oath of the national covenant, and solemn league and covenant, both which are approven, authorized, and enjoined by the canons of this church and law of this land, and declared to have the strength of acts of parliament, may in all humility petition his majesty, who is in the same covenant with him, that the same be not established nor received in any part of his dominions, because of the oath of God foresaid, and that he may, according to the received doctrine of the church of Scotland, and Confession of Faith of both kingdoms, ratified by parliament, publicly preach, that prelacy is no lawful government, and that the order of the chapel is no warrantable worship, without incurring the pains of sedition and treason, which yet is more than a private petition; and without being thought a meddler, or busybody *in re aliena*: in respect whereof he humbly conceives, he cannot be convict of any crime, much less high treason, upon this article of the dittay: and the whole subjects of this nation, being obliged by the solemn public oath of God in the 4th article of the solemn league and covenant, to endeavour the discovery of malignants, which is approven not only by an act of the committee of estates in the year 1648, but also by an act of parliament 1649, that all places of power and trust might be filled with men of unquestionable integrity and affection to the cause of God, and of a blameless and Christian conversation; he doth humbly conceive that his petitioning his majesty to this effect, is so far from being treasonable, or seditious, or any ways culpable by the laws of God, or of the land, that he was thereunto engaged by the indispensable oath of God in the covenant, and in the solemn public engagement unto duties.

The next part of this article bearing, that the defender and his complices did not only convocate themselves, but also by their missive letters, commissions, and instructions drawn, they did presume to convocate his majesty's lieges, &c. It is answered, 1mo, It is not relevantly subsumed under the act of parliament 131, parliament 8th, James VI. in the proposition. For first, in that act meetings only that take upon them jurisdiction, lead process, give forth sentence, and put the same to execution, are prohibit, as is clear from the occasion, ground, and rise of that law in the beginning thereof, seeing that during twenty-four years preceding the making of that act, sundry forms of judgments and jurisdictions, as well in spiritual as temporal causes, are entered in the practice and custom, whereby the king's majesty's subjects are often convocated, and assembled together, and pains as well civil and pecunial as ecclesiastical enjoined to them, process led and deduced, sentence and decreets given, and the same put to execution. It is, secondly, clear from the dispositive reason of the act, which is, that there was no such order, that is aforesaid, of jurisdiction established by his majesty and three estates, which is contrary to the common custom observed in any well governed commonwealth. Thirdly, From the statutory words, which prohibit jurisdictions, spiritual and temporal, not approven by his majesty and three estates of parliament, and convocating for holding of council, conventions, or assemblies, to treat, consult and determine (not alternative, or determine, as it is libelled) in matters of state: but so it is, the meeting or convocation libelled was not taking upon them any jurisdiction, nor to determine as having power in any matter to either, of state or others: and therefore comes not under the compass of that act, and cannot be relevantly subsumed thereupon. 2do, *Non relevat* drawn up except subscribed, nor subscribed except sent, nor sent except thereupon some convocation had happened, nor convocation except the same had been tumultuary and seditious; and the defender oppones the common unquestioned and proven custom of the nation, by which persons of all ranks, according to their several occasions, bring together many of his majesty's lieges, and were never quarrelled therefore, except it manifestly appear, that they had been brought together of purpose to disturb the peace, the contrary whereof was manifest in the convocation, wherein the petition was drawn up, they being assembled neither with multitude nor tumult, but in a very small number, and for business in itself lawful, to wit, humble petitioning of his majesty for preserving and carrying on the work of Reformation and uniformity in religion, according to the covenant, which obliges them to do the same sincerely, really, and constantly, all the days of their life. Next, 3tio, *Absolvitor*, because by the act 29, parliament 40, it is found and declared, that councils, conventions, and assemblies, intended for the defence and preservation of religion, are not prohibit by any preceding laws, such as the acts of the proposition are, and for this purpose the meeting was clearly intended of them: therefore,

"Dear Sir,

"I am now past hopes of seeing your face any more in the flesh; to tell you the wrestlings of my poor soul on your behalf were not worth your time, but that affection constraineth me to say, I am both in

1661.

The fifth article bears, that the defender being convened before his majesty and the committee of estates at Perth, to answer for some seditious and unwarrantable speeches uttered by him in sermons, in Stirling, and otherways, against his majesty's authority, and having compeared, that the defender did treasonably disclaim and decline his majesty and his authority, and that he did protest for remeed of law for his confinement, which at more length is contained in the declinator and protestation, repeated as a part of the libel *brevitatis causa*. It seems that this article is specially founded on the 129th act, parliament 8, James VI. *anno* 1584, confirming his majesty's royal power over all estates and subjects within this realm; to which the defender says, 1mo, *Non relevant* as to the inferring the crime and punishment of treason. First, that act confirms no power and authority to his majesty, but his royal power and authority. And albeit the defender doth most readily acknowledge his majesty's royal power and authority to extend to all things civil, and that as civil magistrate, the conservation and purgation of religion, as is asserted in the Confession of Faith of this church, doth belong unto him, or that as it was said of the christian emperor, that he is *episcopus ad extra*; yet he humbly conceives, that the power and authority to judge of ministers' doctrine in the first instant, especially in an orthodox and rightly constituted church, whose judicatories are acknowledged and established by his majesty's own authority and laws, is not a power and authority that belongs to him as civil magistrate; but being a power and authority in its own nature spiritual and ecclesiastical, which properly belongs to the spiritual officebearers of the house of God under Jesus Christ, who is Lord and Master over his own house, and Head of his church, whose kingdom is not of this world, and hath appointed that the spirit of the prophets should be subject to the prophets; and the magistrate's power is not spiritual and ecclesiastic, but civil only, and what is most consistent with, and consonant to his majesty's royal prerogative, as it is established by the 1st act, parliament 18, James VI. aforesaid, can never contravene, as not that act itself libelled on, so neither the other act 129, parliament 8, James VI. also libelled on. That establishes that same royal power in his majesty's person over all estates, in respect whereof he is judge competent to all his subjects of whatsoever estate, and his judgment to prohibit to be declined, because prior laws are drawn to posterior laws, *non est novum, et l. ideo. ff. de leg.* and this posterior act 1, parliament 18, is declaratory of that prerogative confirmed in that first act, in respect whereof his majesty is judge competent to persons of all estates in manner therein contained : but so it is, the declinator and protestation mentioned in this article does contravene that act parl. 18, in so far as all that is declared there, is that his majesty has the sovereign authority over all estates, persons, and causes, which does no way take away nor exclude the proper jurisdictions of the several judicatories established by the laws of the kingdom, otherwise it should evacuate all the jurisdictions of the same, and presently might bring all causes immediately before his majesty and council; which will not be affirmed.

2do, *Non relevat*, because of the transferring the judgment of a minister's doctrine from his majesty's immediate decision in a civil court, to the decision of the judicatories of the kirk, is not a declining, but an acknowledging and maintaining and confirming his majesty's power and authority in an orderly way, or in such a manner as his power and authority is asserted and established by himself, and his own authority, in his laws; because he hath by many laws and acts of parliament, ratified and established the judicatories of the kirk, as the proper and competent judges of ministers' doctrine, particularly in his 114th act, parl. 12, anno 1592, in which the haill jurisdiction and discipline of the kirk over judicatories is ratified and confirmed; and the 6th act of the 12th parl. Charles I. And therefore, though there may be reason to condemn these declinators of his majesty's royal power and authority, that are made upon respect to powers, foreign and exotic, which are not acknowledged by his majesty, nor established by his laws; yet there can be no reason to condemn this, because the avocating of a cause from one court, or his majesty's jurisdiction and authority in one court, to another court established by the same authority, in and by the laws of the kingdom; it is but a taking of it *a Cæsare ad Cæsarem*, and from that authority in one court to the same, as approving the other, and that the doctrine contained in the protestation libelled on, belonged to the spiritual jurisdiction of the kirk doth yet more appear, because it was, as is clear by the protestation itself, upon a question merely spiritual, to wit, whether the resolutions were contrary to the word of God, to the oaths of the covenant, and league and covenant, to the solemn engagement, to the declarations, remonstrances, warnings, causes of humiliation, and resolutions of the kirk, offensive and scandalous, which are all mere spiritual considerations, and no ways civil and politic.

3tio, *Non relevat*, because declinators that are not made upon the account of foreign and exotic jurisdictions, are lawful in all the judicatories of the kingdom from the highest to the lowest. It is usual to propone a declinator or exception of incompetency, against any judge or judicatory within the nation, when in the exercise of their jurisdiction, they do exceed the bounds prescribed by the law, which could not be said, if it were treasonable to decline the king and the council as incompetent judges in some cases, because the king's majesty may be personally present, and is always virtually and by his authority present in all the judicatories of this nation, as effectually *quoad omnes effectus juris*, as in the committee of estates; and is it not daily ordinary that when parties trouble his majesty's commissioner's grace, and three estates of parliament, with causes and business proper to the lords of session, that they refer it to the judge ordinary, and will not meddle therewith?

4to, Absolvitor, because that act, since the

bonds and in the body with you, and will travail till you be delivered, and I may well do it, for it draweth near, and you may lift up your head, when ours as yet must hang down. God hath provided a sacrifice for himself, not an Isaac, but your-

---

making thereof, hath been often repealed, first materially in the year immediately thereafter, by a declaration under king James his own hand, sent to the commissioners of the general assembly of the kirk of Scotland at Linlithgow, December 7th, 1585, which, he says, shall be as good and valid as any act of parliament whatsoever, insert in the register of the kirk; in which declaration he hath these words: " I for my part shall never, neither my posterity ought ever cite, summon, apprehend any pastor or preacher for matter of doctrine in religion, salvation, heresies, or true interpretation of the scripture, but, according to my first act, which confirmeth the liberty of preaching, ministration of the sacraments, I avouch the same to be a matter mere ecclesiastic, and altogether impertinent to my calling; therefore neither shall I, nor ever ought they, I mean my posterity, acclaim any power or jurisdiction in the foresaids." Which declaration we cannot but look upon as a material repealing of that act, because it was directly and of purpose penned and subscribed, and sent by the king to the commissioner of the general assembly, for removing the stumbling offence, and easing of the grievance and complaint, which was made by the whole kirk of Scotland, because of the making of that act. *Secondly,* That act is formally and expressly repealed in the 12th parl. James VI. act 114, in which the government and jurisdiction is established by assemblies, presbyteries, &c. . And the act libelled upon, in so far as concerns or is prejudicial to the privilege of spiritual office-bearers, concerning heads of religion, heresy, excommunication, or any censure, specially grounded, and having warrant from the word of God: but so it is, that the act of parliament propounded upon by the pursuer, doth in nothing concern the jurisdiction of the kirk, or the privileges of the spiritual officers thereof, but in so far as the same does establish his majesty's jurisdiction in spiritual causes, and prohibits all declinators of that judgment, which, as in this derogatory and prejudicial clause to the privilege of the kirk, is in this rescissory act expressly cast and made void: likeas, the 1st act, parl. 18, James VI. proponed upon, with the 3d act of 1st parl. Charles I., whereby the king's authority and prerogative is established over all estates, persons and causes, is repealed, in so far as the same are prejudicial and derogatory to the privilege of the kirk of God, the discipline and government of her officebearers and church judicatories, in the 4th act, parl. 2d, Charles I., and act 5, of the same parliament, wherein amongst the causes of bygone evils, the jurisdiction of secular powers in matters spiritual is complained upon, and the committing of the power of both swords to persons merely ecclesiastical, and the giving the keys to persons merely civil against the privilege of the church, her officers and judicatories, and remedy provided against the same for the time to come; and likewise by the 6th act, 2d parl. Charles I., jurisdiction and power of the kirk is solely and only in the general assembly, provincial synods, presbyteries, as was established by the act 1592. If therefore the act 1592, did rescind that act 1584, anent the jurisdiction of the king in all causes spiritual, and since by this act of Charles I. the act 1592 is confirmed, it must rescind and repeal the act 1584, and doth in express words rescind and annul all and whatsomever acts of parliament and constitutions, in so far as they derogate and are prejudicial to the spiritual nature, jurisdiction, discipline, and privileges of this kirk in her general, provincial, presbyterial assemblies and kirk sessions. *Lastly,* That act anno 1584, and all other acts of that nature, are rescinded and annulled both by the national covenant, and by the solemn league and covenant, which were not only posterior in time, and are ratified in parliament, and declared to have the strength of laws and acts of parliament; but also in the nature of them are of more strength than any municipal law or statute, as being confirmed by the solemn public oath of God taken by his majesty and all the subjects of this kingdom, which binds to maintain and defend the doctrine, worship, discipline and government of this kirk; which covenant is confirmed by the treaty at Breda, and ratifications at St. Johnston and Stirling, ratifying the said treaty, and acts of parliament that ratify these covenants.

That it may further appear how good reason there was for repealing and rescinding that law, and for declining the civil magistrate, as competent judge of ministers' doctrine in the first instance, the defender doth humbly propone, that such declinators are warrantable, *First,* By the word of God, which is the sovereign and supreme law by which all other laws are to be regulated and squared. *Secondly,* By the confessions of faith, and doctrine of this church, which doubtless ought to be acknowledged by all the members thereof, to be binding and obligatory, and by all the subjects of this kingdom, seeing they are ratified and confirmed in parliament. *Thirdly,* By the practice of this church, not only before, but also since that act of parliament, anno 1684, was made. And *Fourthly,* By the judgment of sound orthodox divines, and the strength of divine reason.

The word of God doth clearly hold forth, that Jesus Christ hath a visible kingdom, which he exercises in or over his visible church, which is wholly distinct from the civil powers and governments of the world, and not depending upon nor subordinate unto these governments in the administrations thereof, which are spiritual, and are to be regulated not by the laws of men, but by his own laws set down in his word, who is King and Lawgiver of his house, and hath committed the ministry to his own office-bearers under himself, John xviii. 36, 37. Matth. xvi. 19. John xx. 28. Ezek. xliii. 10, 11, 12. Heb. iii. 5, 6. The Confessions of Faith and doctrines of this church do also affirm the same thing; these do acknowledge no head or lawgiver over the visible church of Christ, but Jesus Christ himself, and do assert the government of the church to be distinct from that of the civil magistrate, and such as ought to be squared by Christ's own laws, and exercised by the office-bearers of his own house, and may

self. That eminent peer of the land, highly honoured of the Lord, and yourself, are the first-fruits, and the first blood in this kind after an hundred years' interruption and indulgence: who may or shall follow God knoweth; every one can-

be seen in the Confessions of Faith and Books of Discipline of this church: for the practice of this church there, there be many instances of such declinators extant in the registers and story thereof, particularly that of Mr. David Black in the year 1596, which was first subscribed and given in by himself to the king's majesty and his council, then sitting at Edinburgh, upon occasion of his being cited to compear before them to answer for some doctrine which he had preached at St. Andrews, where he was then minister, which was alleged by the king's majesty and his council to be treasonable and seditious; which declinator was owned by the assemblies of this kirk; and a little after his giving in thereof, was subscribed by three or four hundred ministers, who yet were not, because of so doing, judged nor proceeded against as guilty of treason and sedition. It would be tedious to cite the testimonies of orthodox and sound divines, who have written on this subject, both ancient and modern. It is known what was said to the emperors who were Arian, and took upon them to judge of the doctrine of the orthodox. *Tibi Deus imperium commisit, nobis quæ sunt ecclesiæ concredit; date, scriptum est, quæ sunt Cæsaris Cæsari, quæ sunt Dei Deo, neque fas est nobis imperium in terra tenere, neque cum imperator thyaniameton, et sacrorum, aut clavium ecclesiæ potestatem habes.* The treatises and books of Scots, English, Belgic, and French, and other divines, written for the defence and clearing of the divine right of church government, and of the power of the magistrate about holy things, and that appeals from the church in church matters to the civil magistrate are not lawful, do contain many assertions and testimonies to this purpose. As for divine reason, the defender doth only say, that if the function of the magistrate be distinct from the ministerial function in all the causes thereof, then must needs the jurisdictions and exercises thereof be also distinct, and not depending one upon another; as the church cannot lay hold upon the sword of the magistrate, so neither can the magistrate take the keys of the church. The confounding of these, and the clashings and encroachments of the civil and ecclesiastical powers, have been the cause of much trouble and confusion in the world, and the preserving of them distinct, and giving to "God the things that are God's, and to Cæsar the things that are Cæsar's, is the best foundation of order, union and peace, both in church and state.

For the other branch of this article, viz. for protesting for remeed of law, *non relevat*, because there is no act of parliament contained in the proposition, which doth prohibit the same, neither doth the act anent declining his majesty's authority, concern the protestation, seeing the same is consistent and compatible with his majesty's authority, and *in criminalibus*, especially in *atrocibus delictis*, as that of treason, there can be no extension of an act of parliament from the genuine native sense of the words of the act itself, specially seeing by the 28th act, parl. 2, Charles I. it is expressly provided, that nothing shall be counted treason, but that which is declared and statute to be such by an act of parliament. Secondly, such a protestation for remeed, against a particular law for remeed, against a particular grievance according to law, is so far from importing any declamation of his majesty's authority, that it doth import an acknowledging and establishing of the same, because it imports an establishing of his majesty's authority in his laws, according to which, and no otherwise, remeed is desired.

The last article wherein the defender is accused, for giving advice in a certain meeting of ministers and elders at Stirling, not only to suspend his majesty from the exercise of his royal power, but also to imprison him in the castle of Stirling, and when it was answered by one of the number, they might as well proceed against his life, that the defender replied, that it was not yet seasonable to speak of that, but that it was fit he should first be secured. To which the defender answers, 1mo, That the same is an unjust and false aspersion; he had never such a purpose in his heart, much less did he utter any such words. 2do, The article, as it is conceived, is not relevant in so far as it doth condescend upon such a lax and wide space of time, viz. 1650 or 1651, whereas in law the pursuer ought to condescend upon the year, month, and day of the crime alleged, especially in *delictis momentaneis*, which are not reiterated nor repeated *ex sua natura*, but once only committed, *L. 3. ff. de Accus. L. si quando*, and if the day were condescended upon, the defender might have good ground thereby given him to prove that he was *alibi* that day. *Lastly*, The said article is no ways relevant, in respect it doth not condescend upon the names of the ministers, and ruling elders in the meeting, to whom these words were alleged to have been spoken, neither upon the name of that person who did answer the defender his alleged overture, nor upon the circumstance of the place, in Stirling, in which these speeches are alleged to have been spoken, by which general libelling the defender is deprived of his lawful defences, viz. that those persons were *alibi*, or were dead: in respect whereof the libel is irrelevant, and ought not to be sustained by your lordships.

The defender having now answered the whole indictment, concludes thus, 1mo, That he did never purpose or intend to speak, write, or act any thing disloyal, or seditious, or treasonable against his majesty's person, or government, God is witness. And what he has spoken, written, or acted, in any of these things wherewith he is charged, hath been merely and singly from a principle of conscience; that according to the weak measure of light given him of God, he might do his duty in his station and calling, as a minister of the gospel, upon which account only, and no other, he hath meddled in these matters, keeping himself within the bounds of what was competent to a minister of the gospel. 2do, Because conscience taken *quovis modo*, is not a sufficient plea, though it may in a good measure extenuate, it cannot wholly excuse; he doth humbly say, that he hath foun led his speeches, and writings, and actions in these things, so far as he was accessary thereunto, upon the word of

1661. not receive this dignity, save they to whom it is given. The buried cause of Christ shall live in your death, and what all your contendings for it while you were alive could not do, your blood shall do when you are gone. The Lord seemeth

God, and the Confessions of Faith, and doctrine of this church, and upon the national covenant, and solemn league and covenant, and solemn public acknowledgment of sins, and engagement unto duties, and upon the laws of the land, and public declared judgment of the kingdom: and therefore humbly prays and expects, that your lordships will not look upon him as a person guilty of any disloyalty, or sedition, or treason against his majesty and his laws, but that ye will absolve him from the charge thereof libelled against him in the Indictment.

Addition to the defence of the 5th step, of the 9th article of the Causes of Wrath.

Testimonies out of the Declarations and public Papers of the kirk and kingdom of Scotland.

First, the commissioners of the general assembly, in their " Solemn and Seasonable Warning," December 19th, 1646, printed at Edinburgh, page 4th, have these words: " So long as his majesty doth not approve in his heart, and seal with his hand, the league and covenant, we cannot but apprehend that, according to his former principles, he will walk in opposition to the same, and study to draw us in to the violating thereof."

Secondly, The kirk of Scotland did, before the treaty with the king, in many of their public declarations and papers, hold forth, that the king's interest was subordinate to the interest of God, and of religion ; and therefore we find this subordination holden forth, and engaged unto both in the national covenant, and in the solemn league and covenant, which doth oblige us to maintain and defend the king's person, and authority, in the defence and preservation of true religion, and liberties of the kingdom, upon which consideration the commissioners of the general assembly, in their humble representation to the honourable estates of parliament, the 28th of April 1648, printed, do take notice of a new interpretation, which the declaration of the parliament puts upon this article of the solemn league and covenant, and tells their lordships, that no such interpretation hath been made by the assembly of the kirk, of the solemn league and covenant, as their lordships are pleased there to make of it.

The commissioners of the general assembly, in their declaration at Edinburgh, 1st March, 1648, printed, do declare, " that although in the covenant, the duty of defending and preserving the king's majesty's person and authority be joined with, and subordinate unto the duty of preserving and defending the true religion and liberties of the kingdom; and that although from the beginning of the cause, the good, safety, and security of religion have been principally sought after, and insisted upon, yet solicitations, persuasions, and endeavours have not been, nor are wanting for his majesty's restitution to the exercise of his royal power, and for espousing his majesty's quarrel, notwithstanding his not granting the public desires, concerning the covenant and religion ; and this course is clearly contrary to the declared resolution of the parliament of this kingdom, after advice desired from us, upon the case concerning the king then propounded to us; and it is no less contrary (say they) to the principles and professions of the convention and of the committee of estates, before any such advice was desired or had from us."

The commissioners of the general assembly, in the year 1650, in their answer to the estates' observations upon the assembly's declaration, printed, speak thus, page 23d, concerning the subordination of civil power, to the good of religion : " It is granted by your lordships, and that it is a great sin in kings to do otherwise, but that, if kings fail in religion, the subjects are notwithstanding tied to obedience in things civil. We conceive that it will not be denied, (say the commissioners) that subjects are as straitly tied to a subordination of all to God as the king is. Doth not the word oblige all men, whether king or subjects, to prefer the glory of God, and the good of religion to all things, to seek it in the first place, to postpone it to nothing whatsoever ? And again, page 28th, of the same answer, We are sorry (say they) to see their interests still so carefully provided for, and so little security for religion, which indeed was the main and principal cause of our engagement in the late wars. The declaration also of the general assembly in the year 1648, printed, speaketh thus : " Whereas the duty of defending his majesty's person and authority, is, by the 3d article of the covenant, qualified with a subordination unto the preservation and defence of the true religion and liberties, there is no such qualification nor subordination asserted in the present engagement, but is so carried on, as to make duties to God, and for religion, conditional, qualified, limited, and duties to the king absolute and unlimited:" And again, in the same declaration, malignancy is revived, in spreading of specious pretences, vindicating wrongs done to his majesty. We desire not to be mistaken, as if respect and love to his majesty were to be branded with the infamous mark of malignancy; but we warn all who would not come under this foul stain, not only in their speech and profession, but really in their whole carriage, not to own nor prefer their own nor the interest of any creature whatsoever, before the interest of Christ and religion."

The representation also of the commissioners of the general assembly, 1648, April 28th, page 4th, printed, speaketh thus : " Your lordships are obliged by the 3d article of the covenant, to defend his majesty's person and authority, in the defence and preservation of the true religion and liberties of the kingdom; we suppose your lordships should not demand from, nor press upon the kingdom of England, his majesty's restitution, except with that qualification in the covenant, and with subordination to religion, and the liberties of the kingdoms ; and how can this subordination according to the covenant, be said to be observed in your lordships' demand as it stands, if his majesty be brought with honour, freedom and safety, and without security for establishing religion and peace ? we then leave it to your lordships' consciences, whether his majesty shall be restored to his honour, before Jesus Christ be restored to his honour, and set upon his throne of government, before Jesus Christ be set upon his throne of government of his church, and his majesty put in a condition of liberty, be-

now to be about to set and fix his standard for a while in the blood and sufferings of his servants and people, it may be of all ranks and sorts of persons within the land, ere all be done: and whether many or few, or none at all, (which is not likely) 1661.

fore the ordinances of Christ have a free course; and whether his majesty's safety shall not be provided for, and secured, before either church or kingdom can say, that they are in a condition of safety. And is this to endeavour the settling of religion, before all worldly interests, or rather it come after the king's interest?" The same representation in the 26th page, speaketh thus: " We only put your lordships in mind, that the national covenant doth join with his majesty's safety, his good behaviour in his office, saying, that the quietness and stability of religion and kirk, doth depend upon the safety and good behaviour of his majesty, as upon a comfortable instrument of God's mercy, granted to this country for the maintenance of this kirk, and ministration of justice: otherwise, if a king do not his duty for the maintenance of true religion, and ministration of justice, it is not his safety alone that makes the people to be in quietness and happiness withal, as our quietness and happiness dependeth on his majesty, and his doing of his duty, as an instrument and minister of God for good, so the honour, greatness, and happiness of the king's royal majesty, and the welfare of his subjects, doth depend upon the purity of religion, as is well expressed in your lordships' oath of parliament. In the printed answer of the commission to the estates' observations on the assembly's declaration, August 1648, p. 19th, be these words: Their lordships press doing duties to his majesty, viz. his restoring to honour, freedom and safety, notwithstanding of the fear of any bad consequence, how much more ought we to do duties to God, viz. to see the security of religion before his majesty's restitution, whatever danger or bad consequence come? In the declaration of the general assembly to England, in the year 1648, printed, be these words: " We are not against the restoring of his majesty to the exercise of his power in a right and orderly way, yet considering the great expense of blood, and pains this kingdom hath been at, for maintaining their just liberties, and bringing the work of reformation this length, and considering his majesty's averseness from the reformation, and his adhering to episcopacy, we trust, that security shall yet be demanded for religion," &c. And which is yet more considerable, not only is it acknowledged to be a sin, in the solemn acknowledgment of public sins, and breach of the covenant, condescended by the commissioners of the general assembly, and approven by the committee of estates, October 1648, and afterwards by the parliament, and solemnly kept with a day or two of solemn public humiliation, by all the ministers and congregations of the land: " That some among ourselves have laboured to put into the hands of our king, an arbitrary and unlimited power, and that under the pretence of relieving and doing for the king, whilst he refuses to do what is necessary for the house of God, some have ranversed and violated most of all the articles of the covenant." But also in the solemn engagement to duties, condescended upon by the commissioners of the general assembly, and approven by the committee of estates and parliament, and solemnly sworn by the whole land at the time of the renewing of the covenant, we are all of us solemnly obliged in the first article of that engagement, " That because religion is of all things the most excellent and precious, the advancing and promoving the power thereof against all ungodliness and profanity, the securing and preserving the purity thereof against error, heresy, and schism, and carrying on the work of uniformity, shall be studied and endeavoured by us before all worldly interests, whether concerning the king, ourselves, or any other whatsoever."

Secondly, There be many things to be found in the public papers of the kirk of Scotland, arguing the sinfulness of restoring the king to the exercise of his royal power, whilst continuing in known opposition to the work of reformation, or before necessary security given for religion, from the great end and duty of magistracy itself, from the mutual covenants and contracts betwixt the king and his people, from the oath of coronation, which is ratified by act of parliament, and is to be taken by all the kings that reign over the realm, at the time of their coronation, and receipt of their princely authority, whereby they are obliged to be of one perfect religion, or to serve the same eternal God to the utmost of their power, according as he hath required in his most holy word, and to maintain the true religion of Christ Jesus, the preaching of his holy word, and the due and right administration of the sacraments, now received and preached within this realm, and that they shall abolish and gainstand all false religion contrary to the same, and from the danger of arbitrary and unlimited power; and sundry other grounds and reasons of that kind, which would be tedious to repeat, with the passages of the public papers wherein they are mentioned. Therefore, passing other papers emitted by the kirk concerning those things, we do only refer unto the printed declaration of the general assembly, 1649, in which we will find a brief sum of the arguments and reasons that are more largely scattered in former papers to this purpose, with a conclusion drawn therefrom concerning the sinfulness of admitting the king to the exercise of his royal power, before the obtaining real security for religion, which security could not be obtained, he continuing in his former known opposition to the work of reformation; which declaration, in so far as concerns this business, is repeated in the book of " the Causes of Wrath," in the enlargement of the 5th step of the 9th article.

In the third place it is to be remembered, that the commissioners of the general assembly, in the years 1649 and 1650, do hold forth in their instructions and letters relating to the treaty with the king, concerning this purpose. First, in their instructions 1649, they do require their commissioners effectually and seriously to represent unto the king's majesty, the evil of the popish, prelatical and malignant party, and to labour to persuade him to forsake their counsels and courses, and to cleave to those who would be faithful to God and to his majesty. And in their instructions 1650 they are in-

1661. shall be added unto you, I believe to it shall be the gathering of his people; and then I am sure your sufferings are well rewarded, and not only yours, but all the blood that shall be shed, well bestowed in the gathering of his scattered

structed to desire him to take course, that his council and family may consist only of such as are of known integrity and affection to the cause of God, and of a blameless and Christian conversation; which, they say, there is the more reason to urge, because most of the evils that have afflicted the king's house and his people, have issued in a special manner from the king's council and family, their disaffection and looseness.

The commissioners of the general assembly, upon report of closing of the treaty with the king at Breda, in the year 1650, by an express sent from them for that effect, they do in a large letter written to their commissioners, of the date 20th of May 1650, profess their disaffection therewith, in which letter are these passages. "We cannot," say they, "but profess ourselves to be exceedingly unsatisfied with his majesty's concessions, as coming short of many of the material and important desires of this kirk and kingdom, concerning the security of religion, and the peace of the kingdom." And in another place of that letter: "Albeit," say they, "we conceive ourselves bound with all cordial affection, heartily to invite and welcome his majesty upon complete satisfaction to the desires of kirk and kingdom; yet it is matter of stumbling to us, that he should, not only without such satisfaction so far as we could discern, but that assurances are also given to him in matters of great importance, not yet determined by the parliament of this kingdom, or general assembly, or commissioners of the kirk." And again in the same letter: "As we earnestly pray for, and desire to endeavour a sound agreement with his majesty, so we conceive ourselves bound to discover and avoid the evil of such an agreement as will prove dangerous and destructive to the kirk of God in our hands; and therefore, as we are confident that ye will be short in no duty that ye owe to the king, or that may procure a right understanding or happy settling betwixt his majesty and this kirk and kingdom, so we also persuade ourselves that ye will take heed of snares, and discern well of the counsels of all these who have been involved in the late defection, and are not yet convinced of, nor humbled for the offence given thereby." The commissioners of the general assembly, did at the same time send this particular instruction to their commissioners at Breda. "You shall not fail, for preventing and removing of all questions and debates anent the king's oath, to declare by a paper to his majesty, that it doth not only import his allowance and approbation of the national covenant and solemn league and covenant, to his subjects, but also that his own swearing and subscribing the same, and in the words subjoined thereto, imports his allowance and approbation of all the heads and articles thereof, in his own particular judgment, and his engagement to every one of them, as much as the oath of any of the subjects thereto, imports their approbation and engagement."

By these things we hope it is manifest and clear, that the kirk of Scotland did require in the king, a discontinuing from his former op-

position to the work of reformation, before admitting him to the exercise of his royal power, as a thing necessary for the security of religion, and that they judged it not duty, but sin to do otherwise.

Fourthly, We shall show this to have been the common received doctrine, and public judgment of the kirk of Scotland, after the treaty with the king, or after the king's homecoming into Scotland; which appears first from the printed declaration of the commissioners of the general assembly, the 13th August, 1650, which speaks in this manner: "The commission of the general assembly considering, that there may be just ground of stumbling, from the king's majesty's refusing to subscribe and emit the declaration offered to him by the committee of estates, and commissioners of the general assembly, concerning his former carriage, and his resolution for the future, in reference to the cause of God, and the enemies and friends thereof, do herefore declare, that this kirk and kingdom do not own nor espouse any malignant quarrel or interest, but that they fight merely upon their former grounds and principles, and in defence of the cause of God, and of the kingdom, as they have done these twelve years past, and therefore, as they disclaim all the sin and guilt of his house, so they would not own him nor his interest, otherways than with subordination to God, and so far as he owns and prosecutes the cause of God and the covenant, and likewise all the enemies and friends thereof." Secondly, It appears from the cause of the fast at Stirling condescended upon, first, by the presbytery with the army, and afterwards approven by the commissioners of the general assembly at Stirling, a little after the defeat at Dunbar, in which it is offered, that we ought to mourn for the manifold provocations of the king's house, which we fear are not truly repented of, nor forsaken by him to this day, together with the crooked and precipitant ways that were taken by sundry of our statesmen for carrying on the treaty with the king. Secondly, The commissioners of the general assembly, in a remonstrance of theirs to the states, of the date at Perth, 29th of November, 1650, do exhort, "That they would seriously lay to heart any sin or guiltiness through sinful precipitancy, and unstraight designs and carnal policy, in appointing addresses for treating with the king, and in the way of carrying on and closing the same, and what, upon serious search, your lordships shall find may give glory to God, in an ingenuous confession and acknowledgment thereof, and sincere humiliation before him for the same." Thirdly, The causes of the fast at Perth, condescended upon by the commissioners of the general assembly, for the king and his family, 26th of December, 1650. In which causes, besides what relates to the king, his royal father, and his royal grandfather, are these things relating to the king himself, the present king, "His entering to tread the same step, by closing a treaty with the popish Irish rebels, who had shed so much blood, and granting them not only their personal liberty, but also the free exercise of the popish religion, so that he might use

CHAP. II.] OF THE CHURCH OF SCOTLAND. 189

people. The healing and reparation of all their breaches shall begin at your ashes, who in your days have been esteemed a man of strife and contention. God hath much to do for you and yours, when you are gone; but alas! I fear a dark

1661.

them against his protestant subjects. 2dly, By commissionating ——— James Graham again to invade the kingdom, who were striving to be faithful to the cause and to his majesty, and to give commissions for sundry at sea and land for that end. 3dly, By his refusing for a time the just satisfaction which was desired by the kirk and kingdom. 4thly, His entertaining private correspondences with malignants and enemies to the cause, contrary to the covenant, whereupon he was drawn at last to a public and scandalous deserting of the public judicatories of this kingdom, so contrary to the treaty, his oath, declarations, and confessions; whereupon followed many offences and inconveniences, and to join with malignants and perverse men, who were by his warrant encouraged to take arms at such a time, to the hazarding of the cause, fostering of jealousies, and the disturbing the peace of this kingdom. These things, say the commissioners of the general assembly, in the causes of humiliation, being sensibly laid out before the Lord, he is with fervent prayers to be entreated to do away the controversies he has against the king or his house for these transgressions, and that he may be graciously pleased to bless the king's person and government." These causes of fast at Stirling and Perth, and the remonstrance cited, are to be found in the registers of the kirk.

In the last place, we shall bring some things which may also prove the same to have been the public judgment of this state or kingdom of Scotland. First, The parliament 1648, in their declaration concerning their resolutions for religion, king, and kingdoms, in pursuance of the ends of the covenant; as they do all along acknowledge the first motive of these kingdoms engaging in a solemn league and covenant, to have been for reformation and defence of religion; so in the 6th page of that declaration, as it stands printed in the acts of parliament, they do expressly declare, "that they resolved not to put in his majesty's hands, or any other whatsomever, any such power, whereby the ends of the covenant, or any one of them may be obstructed or opposed, religion or presbyterian government endangered; but on the contrar, before an agreement or condition to be made with his majesty, having found his majesty's late concessions and offers concerning religion not satisfactory, that he give assurance by his solemn oath under his hand and seal, that he shall for himself and his successors give his royal assent, and agree to such act or acts of parliament, and bills, as shall be presented to him by his parliaments of both or either kingdoms respective, by enjoining the league and covenant, and fully establishing presbyterial government, Directory of Worship, and Confession of Faith, in all his dominions, and that his majesty shall never make any opposition to any of these, nor endeavour any change thereof." 2dly, The parliament 1649, as they do in their second act, January 5th, approve of the solemn public confession of sins, and engagement unto duties; so do they in the 4th act, of the date 16th of January, 1649, approve of the desires, supplications, remonstrances, declarations of the kirk, and representation of the commissioners of the general assembly, against the restoring the king without sufficient security first had from him concerning religion, and do condemn the unsound gloss that is put upon the covenant and acts of the general assembly, in the close of the declaration of the parliament 1648, in these things that concern our duty to the king. 3dly, The parliament 1549 in the act of the 7th of February, anent the securing the covenant, religion, and peace of the kingdom, doth provide, "that before the king's majesty who now is, or any of his successors, shall be admitted to the exercise of his royal power, they shall not only swear the oath of coronation, and his allowance of the national covenant, and obligation to prosecute the ends thereof in his station and calling, and that he shall for himself and his successors, consent and agree to acts of parliament enjoining the same, and fully establish presbyterian government, Confessions of Faith, and catechisms of this church, and parliament of this kingdom, in all his majesty's dominions, and that he shall observe these in his own practice and family; and that he shall never make opposition to any of these nor endeavour any change thereof: but it is also declared and ordained in the same act, that before the king, who now is to be admitted to the exercise of his royal power, he shall leave all counsel and counsellors prejudicial to religion and to the national covenant, and to the solemn league and covenant." 4thly, The parliament at Edinburgh, 18th May, 1650, taking to consideration the invitation that was given to his majesty by their commissioners at Breda, in their explanation of the invitation do declare, "that the assurance given to his majesty therein, doth include the condition of his majesty's performing satisfaction to the desires of the kingdom, according to the four demands which they sent with that explanation: and in their instructions sent at that time to the commissioners, they do expressly instruct them, that they shall not fail, for removing all questions and doubts about the king's oath, to declare by a paper to his majesty, that it doth not only import, that the national covenant, and the solemn league and covenant be taken by the subjects, but also that his own swearing and subscribing the same, and the words subjoined thereto, imports his approbation of all the heads and articles thereof in his own particular judgment, and his engagement to every one of them, as much as the oath of any of the subjects imports their approbation and engagement thereto." And it is considerable, that in these instructions they do require clear satisfaction from his majesty to their necessary desires, and that they do declare, that without such satisfaction not only will that joy and cheerfulness, wherewith all his majesty's good subjects desire to receive him, be impeded, but also his coronation be delayed, and this kirk and kingdom be necessitate to declarations, which will be inconvenient both for his majesty and them. For instructing these things we refer to the registers of the kingdom.

1661. and woful day on these nations, ere these things be. As for myself I have been kept off from public appearance hitherto; I know no more than some in my name have communicate to you. Whereto or wherein any forbearance I have, shall re-

Lastly, As the parliament and committee of estates of this kingdom did not for a good while after his majesty's coming into Scotland, admit the king to the exercise of his royal power; so the committee of estates, in order to the necessary security of religion, did, with advice of the general assembly, judge it necessary to desire him to subscribe a declaration, concerning his former carriage, and resolutions for the future in reference to the cause of God, and the enemies and friends thereof; and upon his majesty's refusing to subscribe that declaration of the commissioners of the general assembly, of the 13th of August, 1650, did approve of the declaration, and heartily concur therein, as is evident from their own act subjoined thereto, and published therewith.

From these things, we hope, it is manifest, that it was the common received doctrine of the church, and the public judgment of this kingdom, concerning the necessary security of religion, that it was not our duty, but our sin, to close a treaty with the king for investing him with the exercise of his royal power, he still continuing in his former known opposition to the work of reformation.

Minutes of the Process against Mr. James Guthrie.

At Edinburgh, 11th April, 1661.—In the criminal pursuit and indictment of sedition and treason, at the instance of Sir John Fletcher, his majesty's advocate for his majesty's interest, against Mr. James Guthrie, sometime minister at Stirling, before the lord commissioner the earl of Middleton, and the three estates of parliament, compared for the king's majesty's interest, the said Sir John Fletcher; and for and with the pannel at the bar, Mr. Robert Burnet, Mr. John Cunningham, Mr. Andrew Birnie, and Mr. George Mackenzie, advocates. After reading of the libel, defences, replies, and duplies, in open parliament, his majesty's advocate declared he insisted against the pannel upon the first article, concerning the "Remonstrance," without prejudice to the rest, so far allenarly as he did own and homologate the same, by framing the 5th and 6th steps of the 9th article of " the Causes of God's Wrath," and explanation thereof; and declared he did not insist upon the act of the committee of estates, in anno 1650, condemning the "Remonstrance," nor upon the act of parliament in anno 1651, ratifying the said act of the committee of estates, because they have not been, nor are produced for instructing that part of the libel. The pannel at the bar, being inquired concerning his accession to "the Causes of Wrath," acknowledges, that he was one that framed the same.

Edinburgh, 12th April, 1661.

The estates of parliament, after advising the relevancy of the whole process, do repel the allegances against the first two articles of the dittay, concerning the "Remonstrance" and "Causes of Wrath;" and notwithstanding thereof, find the libel, as to those two articles thereof, relevant to bring the pannel under the compass of the acts of parliament made against slanderers, viz. 134th act, parl. 8, James VI., the 205th act, 14th parl. James VI., and other acts mentioned in this last act. As likewise the said estates of parliament repel the allegances against the third and fourth articles of the dittay, concerning the meeting libelled, and the petition and instructions, and others done therein; and notwithstanding thereof, find the meeting, with the petition, instructions, and what else was in that meeting, to have been unlawful and seditious: and also the said estates of parliament repel the allegance against the fifth article of the dittay, concerning the declining his majesty's authority, and protesting for remeed of law against his majesty and committee of estates, for a pretended gravamen ; and notwithstanding thereof, find the declinator containing the protestation falls under the 129th act of the parliament 1584, made anent the king's majesty's royal power over all estates.

Edinburgh, 15th April, 1661.

The lord advocate declares, for proving the articles of the dittay, he repeats the pannel's confession at the bar, and throughout the whole defences, with the Remonstrance, Causes of Wrath, Petition, Instructions, Declinators, and others produced, all acknowledged, written, or subscribed by the petitioner's own hand, and renounces further probation. Thereafter, the estates of parliament having this day again considered the former interlocutors, as also having considered the pannel's confession at the bar, and extant throughout his whole defences, anent his accession to the pamphlet, entitled, "the Causes of God's Wrath," wherein one of the causes is mentioned to be the rejecting of the "Remonstrance," and having considered the said two pamphlets themselves, they find the libel sufficiently proven thereby, in so far as relates to the first and second articles; as also having considered the petition, instructions, and others done in that meeting, mentioned in the third and fourth article, and his judicial acknowledgment, that he was at the meeting, and subscriber of the petition, and writer of the instructions ; they find these articles also proven: and having considered also the declinator containing the protestation, with the other protestation, both acknowledged by the pannel, and subscribed with his hand; the estates of parliament find the fifth article thereby proven. The lord advocate takes instruments upon the dittay being found relevant and proven, and protests, that the pains contained in the acts of parliament may be inflicted upon the pannel.

GLENCAIRN, Cancel. I. P. D. Parl.

At Edinburgh, 25th May, 1661.

The estates of parliament find, that Mr. James Guthrie, sometime minister at Stirling, has committed the crime of treason against the king's majesty, his sovereign authority and royal government, and has slandered his majesty's person, state, and government, in so far as the said Mr. James had accession to the framing of a pamphlet called, "the Causes of God's Wrath," wherein one of the causes is mentioned to be the rejecting of the "Remonstrance," and that thereby he has contravened the 205th act, 14th parl. James VI., and the 10th act of the 10th parl. James

solve, God knoweth; I can say in the apostle's words, not unapplicable in this case, I think, if my heart deceive me not, to will and to resolve is present with me in my best times, but how to perform I find not; which makes me ofttimes to doubt of the very truth of my resoluteness, yet he knoweth that I desire to be sincere before him; and whatever may become of me, it is the present impression and persuasion of my heart, that whoever they be that through their shrinking shall put a stain upon the cause of your suffering now to be sealed with your blood, shall have and draw upon themselves a guilt of a double dye.

"Dear Sir, forgive me for such a trouble at such a nick; but it is the last expression of my affection which can reach you, to whom my soul hath been ever knit since my first acquaintance with you: I shall say no more, but that I cannot pass the mentioning of that scripture which hath been often in my mind concerning you, and which I remember you once told me was borne in upon your mind, amidst some of these former conflicts you have been essayed with before it came to this. You know the place; 'I have made thee this day a defenced city and a brazen wall, &c. and they shall fight against thee, but they shall not prevail against thee, for I am with thee to deliver thee, saith the Lord.' I confess I would have fain drawn forth the performance of that promise to a longer life to you, and more work therein; but God hath performed it well, you have had very great and undeniable performances of it already, and now the best is at hand. Within a little it shall be said, they have got the foil, and you the victory; and no wonder, for ' he is still with you to deliver you.'

1661.

"Now that the Lord may send down upon your soul liberal showers of divine influences, and his plentiful rain to confirm you against all weariness; that the tongue of the learned may be given to you for your last words, and that all the communicable blessings of the cross of Christ may run over yours, till that word be made out in your sufferings, ' except a corn of wheat fall into the ground and die, it abideth alone, but if it die, it bringeth forth much fruit.' The words following, John xii. 25, &c. are well worth your reading. God can, and I trust will make you that corn of wheat, that the brethren in the Lord may wax bold through resisting unto blood; and that the Lord may recompense your work, and a full reward be given you of the Lord God of Israel, under whose wings you trust. These are the requests and supplications of his soul to the Lord for you, who earnestly desires your blessing and best wishes to be left behind

---

VI., and incurred the pain of death therein contained: and likewise, the said Mr. James did contrive and petition at a meeting of some ministers in the month of 1660, last bypast, which meeting, petition and instructions, and what else was done at the said meeting, the estates of parliament find unlawful and scandalous; and in so far as the said Mr. James did decline his majesty's authority, and protested for remeed of law against his majesty and committee of estates, for a pretended gravamen, and that thereby he has contravened the 1st act, 8th parl. James VI., in anno 1584, and incurred the pain of treason therein contained: and therefore, upon the ground of the foresaid treasonable crimes and acts of parliament abovementioned, thereby contravened, the king's majesty, with advice and consent of the estates of parliament, finds and declares, that the said Mr. James Guthrie has incurred the pain of high treason, and other pains contained in the said acts, and decerns and ordains him to underly the punishment due to traitors, viz. the tinsel and confiscation of his life, and of all his lands, goods, moveable and immoveable, offices, dignities, sums of money, and all rights and others whatsomever belonging to him, or which may any way pertain or belong to him, and ordains the same to be confiscate and appertain to the king's majesty, and to remain for ever with his majesty in property; and that he be hanged to death at the cross of Edinburgh, upon Saturday next, the 1st day of June, at two of the clock in the afternoon, as a traitor against his majesty; and thereafter his head be cutted off, and affixed on the Nether Bow of Edinburgh, and that presently his arms be delete out of the books of heraldry, and torn in pieces by the lion-herald, at the market cross of Edinburgh, and there to be left torn and ranversed, as a testimony of the vile and abominable treason; and declares his children and posterity incapable in all time coming, to bruik, possess, or enjoy any office, dignities, successions, possessions, lands, goods, moveable and immoveable, or any other thing within this kingdom.

At Edinburgh, 28th May, 1661.

This decreet read and voted in parliament, approven and pronounced, touched with the royal sceptre, and appointed to be recorded, published, and put in execution accordingly.

CRAWFORD I. P. D. parl.

1661. you in his behalf. 'Even so come Lord Jesus, he saith, I come quickly.' Amen, amen."

Betwixt Mr. Guthrie's sentence and the execution of it, he was in a perfect composure and serenity of spirit, and wrote a great many excellent letters to his friends and acquaintances, which, could they be recovered, might be of great use. In this interval he had not a few prophetical expressions, some of which I have well attested, but I shall not insert them here. I wish this great man's life were published by some good hand.

The day he was execute, June 1st, upon some reports spread most groundlessly, that he was to buy his life at the expense of retracting some things he had formerly said, owned, and done, Mr. Guthrie wrote, and before the underwritten witnesses subscribed the following declaration.

"These are to declare, that I do own 'The Causes of God's Wrath,' the 'Supplication at Edinburgh,' August last, and any accession I had to the 'Remonstrance;' and if any do think, or have reported that I was willing to recede from any of these, they have wronged me, as never having any ground from me so to think, or so to report. This I attest under my hand, at Edinburgh, about eleven of the clock in the forenoon, before these witnesses,

"JAMES GUTHRIE."

" Mr. ARTHUR FORBES,
" Mr. HUGH WALKER,
" Mr. JOHN GUTHRIE, and
" JAMES COWIE."

That day he dined with his friends in the greatest cheerfulness. After dinner he called for a little cheese, which he had been dissuaded from eating for some time, as not good for the gravel he was troubled with, and yet had a great liking to it, and said, I hope I am now beyond the hazard of the gravel. When he had been in secret some time, he came forth in the greatest serenity and composure, and was carried down under a guard from the tolbooth to the cross of Edinburgh, where a scaffold was erected, and there the sentence was executed in all its branches. He gave to his friends a copy of what he designed for his speech, if he should be allowed to deliver it on the scaffold, subscribed and sealed, to be delivered to his son, and, he being a child, to be kept for him till he came to years. The copy of it is in "Naphtali," and hath been many times printed, yet I add it at the bottom of the page.*

---

* Mr. James Guthrie his last speech, June 1st, 1661.

Men and brethren, I fear many of you are come hither to gaze rather than to be edified by the carriage and last words of a dying man: but if any have an ear to hear, as I hope some of this great confluence have, I desire your audience to a few words. I am come hither to lay down this earthly tabernacle and mortal flesh of mine, and, I bless God, through his grace, I do it willingly, and not by constraint. I say, I suffer willingly: if I had been so minded, I might have made a diversion, and not been a prisoner; but being conscious to myself of nothing worthy of death, or of bonds, I would not stain my innocency with the suspicion of guiltiness, by my withdrawing: neither have I wanted opportunities and advantages to escape since I was prisoner, not by the fault of my keepers (God knoweth) but otherwise; but neither for this had I light or liberty, lest I should reflect upon the Lord's name, and offend the generation of the righteous: and if some men have not been mistaken, or dealt deceitfully in telling me so, I might have avoided not only the severity of the sentence, but also had much favour and countenance by complying with the courses of the time. But I durst not redeem my life with the loss of my integrity, God knoweth, I durst not; and that since I was prisoner he hath so holden me by the hand, that he never suffered me to bring it in debate in my inward thoughts, much less to propone or hearken to any overture of that kind. I did judge it better to suffer than to sin; and therefore I am come hither to lay down my life this day, and I bless God I die not as a fool; not that I have any thing wherein to glory in myself: I acknowledge that I am a sinner, yea, one of the greatest and vilest that has owned a profession of religion, and one of the most unworthy that has preached the gospel. My corruptions have been strong and many, and have made me a sinner in all things, yea, even in following my duty; and therefore righteousness have I none of my own, all is vile. But I do believe that Jesus Christ came into the world to save sinners, whereof I am chief: through faith in his righteousness and blood have I obtained mercy; and through him, and him alone, have I the hope of a blessed conquest and victory over sin and Satan, and hell and death, and that I shall attain unto the resurrection of the just, and be made partaker of eternal life. I know in whom I have believed, and that he is able to keep that which I have committed unto him against that day. I have preached salvation through his name, and as I have preached so do I believe, and do commend the riches of his free grace and faith in his name unto you all, as the only way whereby ye can be saved.

And as I bless the Lord that I die not as a fool, so also that I die not for evil-doing. Not a few of you may haply judge, that I suffer as a

OF THE CHURCH OF SCOTLAND. 193

We have seen that the parliament ordered William Govan, in some papers I find him termed captain Govan, to be hanged with Mr. James Guthrie. There were different accounts of the reason why the parliament sentenced him: 1661.

hief, or as a murderer, or as an evil-doer, or as a nusybody in other men's matters. It was the ot of the Lord Jesus Christ himself, and hath een of many of his precious servants and people, o suffer by the world as evil-doers; and as my oul scareth not at it, but desireth to rejoice in eing brought into conformity with my blessed Head, and so blessed a company, in this thing; nd so I desire and pray that I may be to none f you to-day upon this account a stone of tumbling and a rock of offence. Blessed is he hat shall not be offended at Jesus Christ, and is poor servants and members, because of their eing condemned as evil-doers by the world. God is my record, that in these things for which entence of death hath passed against me, I have good conscience. I bless God they are not natters of compliance with sectaries, or designs r practices against his majesty's person or government, or the person or government of his oyal father: my heart (I bless God) is concious unto no disloyalty; nay, loyal I have een, and I commend it unto you to be loyal and bedient to the Lord. True piety is the foundation of true loyalty: a wicked man may be a latterer and a timeserver, but he will never be loyal subject. But to return to my purpose; he matters for which I am condemned are matters belonging to my calling and function, as a ninister of the gospel, such as the discovery and eproving of sin, the pressing and the holding ast of the oath of God in the covenant, and preerving and carrying on the work of religion nd reformation according thereto, and denying o acknowledge the civil magistrate, as the proer competent immediate judge in causes ecclesiastical: that in all these things (which a God so ordering by his gracious providence) are he grounds of my indictment and death, I have good conscience, as having walked therein acording to the light and rule of God's word, and s did become a minister of the gospel. I do also bless the Lord, that I do not die as 'one not desired." I know that by not a few, neither have been nor am desired. It hath een my lot to have been a man of contention nd sorrow; but it is my comfort, that for my wn things I have not contended, but for the hings of Jesus Christ, for what relateth to his nterest and work, and the wellbeing of his peoile. In order to the preserving and promoting f these, I did protest against, and stood in opiosition unto these late assemblies at St. Anlrews, Dundee, and Edinburgh, and the public esolution for bringing the malignant party into he judicatories and armies of this kingdom, onceiving the same contrary to the word of God, and to our solemn covenants and engagenents; and to be an inlet to the defection, and o the ruin and destruction of the work of God. And it is now manifest to many consciences, hat I have not been therein mistaken, nor was lot fighting against a man of straw: I was also lesirous, and did use some poor endeavours, to ave the church of God purged of insufficient nd scandalous and corrupt ministers and elders; or these things I have been mistaken by some, nd hated by others: but I bless the Lord, as I ad the testimony of my own conscience, so I

was and am therein approven in the consciences of many of the Lord's precious servants and people; and however so little I may die desired by some, yet by these I know I do die desired, and their approbation and prayers, and affection is of more value with me, than the contradiction, or reproach, or hatred of many others; the love of the one I cannot recompense, and the mistake, or hatred, or reproach of the other I do with all my heart forgive; and wherein I have offended any of them, do beg their mercy and forgiveness. I do from my soul wish that my death may be profitable unto both, that the one may be confirmed and established in the straight ways of the Lord; and that the other, if the Lord so will, may be convinced, and cease from these things that are not good, and do not edify, but destroy.

One thing I would warn you all of, that God is wroth, yea, very wroth with Scotland, and threateneth to depart and remove his candlestick. The causes of his wrath are many, and would to God it were not one great cause, that causes of wrath are despised and rejected of men: consider the cause that is recorded, Jer. xxxvi. and the consequences of it, and tremble and fear. I cannot but also say, that there is a great addition and increase of wrath. 1st, By that deluge of profanity that overfloweth all the land, and hath reins loosed unto it everywhere, in so far that many have lost, not only all use and exercise of religion, but even of morality, and that common civility that is to be found amongst the heathen. 2d, By that horrible treachery and perjury that is in the matter of the covenant, and cause of God, and work of reformation: " Be astonished, O ye heavens, at this, and be ye horribly afraid, and be ye very desolate, saith the Lord; for my people have committed two great evils, they have forsaken me the Fountain of Waters, and hewed them out cisterns, broken cisterns that can hold no water: Shall he break the covenant and prosper? shall the throne of iniquity have fellowship with God, which frameth mischief by a law?" I fear the Lord be about to bring a sword on these lands, which shall avenge the quarrel of his covenant. 3d, Horrible ingratitude; the Lord, after ten years' oppression and bondage, hath broken the yoke of strangers from off our necks: but what do we render unto him for this goodness? Most of the fruit of our delivery is, to work wickedness, and to strengthen ourselves to do evil. 4th, A most dreadful idolatry and sacrificing to the creature; we have changed the glory of the incorruptible God, into the image of a corruptible man, in whom many have placed almost all their salvation and desire, and have turned that which might have been a blessing unto us (being kept in a due line of subordination under God) into an idol of jealousy, by preferring it before him. God is also wroth with a generation of carnal, corrupt, timeserving ministers; I know and bear testimony, that in the church of Scotland there is a true and faithful ministry: blessed be God, we have yet many who study their duty, and desire to be found faithful to their Lord and Master; and I pray you to honour,

2 B

1661. in his own speech he says, it was for laying down his arms at Hamilton, as all the company did, and takes notice, that he carried up Montrose's standard through the streets of Edinburgh. It was alleged he was present upon the scaf-

and reverence, and esteem much of these for their work's sake; and I pray them to be encouraged in their Lord and Master, who is with them, to make them as iron pillars and brazen walls, and as a strong defenced city in the faithful following of their duty. But oh! that there were not too many who mind earthly things, and are enemies to the cross of Jesus Christ, who push with the side and shoulder, who strengthen the hands of evil-doers, who make themselves transgressors, by studying to build again what they did formerly, warrantably destroy; I mean prelacy, and the ceremonies, and the Service-book, a mystery of iniquity that works amongst us, whose steps lead unto the house of the great whore Babylon, the mother of fornication; or whosoever else he be that buildeth this Jericho again, let him take heed of the curse of Hiel the Bethelite, and of that flying roll threatened, Zech. v. And let all ministers take heed that they watch, and be steadfast in the faith, and quit themselves like men, and be strong; and give faithful and seasonable warning, concerning sin and duty. Many of the Lord's people do sadly complain of the fainting and silence of many watchmen, and it concerneth them to consider what God calleth for at their hands in such a day: silence now in a watchman, when he is so much called to speak, and give his testimony upon the peril of his life, is doubtless a great sin. The Lord open the mouths of his servants, to speak his word with all boldness, that covenant-breaking may be discovered and reproved, and that the kingdom of Jesus Christ may not be supplanted, nor the souls of his people be destroyed without a witness. I have but a few words more to add: all that are profane amongst you, I exhort them to repentance, for the day of the Lord's vengeance hasteneth, and is near; but there is yet a door of mercy open for you, if ye will not despise the day of salvation. All that are maligners, and reproachers, and persecutors of godliness, and of such as live godly, take heed what ye do; it will be hard for you to kick against the pricks; you make yourselves the butt of the Lord's fury, and his flaming indignation, if you do not cease from, and repent of all your hard speeches and ungodly deeds. All that are natural, and indifferent, and lukewarm professors, be zealous and repent, lest the Lord spue you out of his mouth. You that lament after the Lord, and mourn for all the abominations that are done in this city and in the land, and take pleasure in the stones and dust of Sion, cast not away your confidence, but be comforted and encouraged in the Lord; he will yet appear to your joy: God hath not cast away his people nor work in Britain and Ireland, I hope it shall once more revive by the power of his Spirit, and take root downward, and bear fruit upward, and of this I am now confident. There is yet a holy seed and precious remnant, whom God will preserve and bring forth: but how long or dark our night may be, I do not know, the Lord shorten it for the sake of his chosen. In the meanwhile be ye patient and steadfast, immoveable, always abounding in the work of the Lord, and in love one to another; beware of snares which are strewed thick; cleave to the covenant and work of reformation; do not decline the cross of Jesus Christ, choose rather to suffer affliction with the people of God, than to enjoy the pleasures of sin for a season, and account the reproach of Christ greater riches than all the treasure of the world. Let my death grieve none of you, it will be more profitable and advantageous, both for me and for you, and for the church of God, and for Christ's interest and honour, than my life could have been. I forgive all men the guilt of it, and I desire you to do so also: pray for them that persecute you, and bless them that curse you, bless, I say, and curse not. I die in the faith of the apostles and primitive Christians, and protestant reformed churches, particularly of the church of Scotland, whereof I am a member and minister. I do bear my witness and testimony to the doctrine, worship, discipline, and government of the church of Scotland, by kirk sessions, presbyteries, synods, and general assemblies; popery and prelacy, and all the trumpery of service and ceremonies, that wait upon them, I do abhor. I do bear my witness unto the national covenant of Scotland, and solemn league and covenant betwixt the three kingdoms of Scotland, England, and Ireland: these sacred, solemn, public oaths of God, I believe can be loosed nor dispensed with, by no person or party or power upon earth; but are still binding upon these kingdoms, and will be for ever hereafter; and are ratified and sealed by the conversion of many thousand souls, since our entering thereinto. I bear my witness to the protestation against the controverted assemblies, and the public resolutions, to the testimonies given against the sectaries, against the course of backsliding and defection that is now on foot in the land, and all the branches and parts thereof, under whatsoever name or notion, or acted by whatsoever party or person. And in the last place, I bear my witness to the cross of Jesus Christ, and that I never had cause, nor have cause this day to repent, because of any thing I have suffered, or can now suffer for his name: I take God to record upon my soul, I would not exchange this scaffold with the palace or mitre of the greatest prelate in Britain. Blessed be God who hath showed mercy to such a wretch, and hath revealed his Son in me, and made me a minister of the everlasting gospel, and that he hath deigned, in the midst of much contradiction from Satan and the world, to seal my ministry upon the hearts of not a few of his people, and especially in the station wherein I was last, I mean the congregation and presbytery of Stirling; and I hope the Lord will visit that congregation and presbytery once more, with faithful pastors. God forgive the poor empty man that did there intrude upon my labours, and hath made a prey of many poor souls, and exposed others to reproach and oppression, and a famine of the word of the Lord. God forgive the misleaders of that part of the poor people, who tempted them to reject their own pastor, and to admit of intruders: and the

fold when king Charles was beheaded, but, to the conviction of all, he proved himself *alibi.** The commissioner had no orders from court about him, and many were of opinion he was cast in among so good company as the Marquis and Mr. Guthrie, both executed this week, that so unknown an attendant might obscure and cloud, if possible, such remarkable and eminent sufferers. He was reckoned a pious good man, and had been a soldier under colonel Strachan. His speech is the largest and best account I can give of him; and therefore I have insert it below.† After he had

---

Father of mercies pity that poor misled people, and the Lord visit the congregation and presbytery of Stirling once more with faithful pastors, and grant that the work and people of God, may be revived through all Britain, and over all the world. Jesus Christ is my light and my life, my righteousness, my strength, and my salvation, and all my desire: him, O him I do with all the strength of my soul commend unto you: "blessed are they that are not offended in him; blessed are they that trust in him. Bless him, O my soul, from henceforth even for ever." Rejoice, rejoice all ye that love him, be patient and rejoice in tribulation: blessed are you, and blessed shall you be for ever and ever; everlasting righteousness and eternal salvation is yours; all are yours, and ye are Christ's, and Christ is God's. "Remember me, O Lord, with the favour thou bearest to thy people; O visit me with thy salvation, that I may see the good of thy chosen, that I may rejoice in the gladness of thy nation, that I may glory with thine inheritance. Now let thy servant depart in peace, since mine eyes have seen thy salvation.

* It is evident from Baillie's letters, that Govan's crime, like that of the illustrious confessor whom he thus nobly and honourably accompanied, was his accession to the Western Remonstrance, &c. &c.; and from the peculiar bitterness with which that very partial writer speaks of him, he must have been a man of more consequence than either from his own speech, or Mr. Wodrow's account of him, the reader would be led to believe. Speaking of colonel Strachan, when, by the favour of the church for his services against that infamous ruffian, but eminent loyalist, James Graham, marquis of Montrose, he had obtained a regiment "stronger than any two regiments in the kingdom." Baillie says, "many of his old doubts revive upon him, which, by the knavery of his captain, lieutenant Govan, and frequent messages of his late friends, Cromwell, and those about him, became so high, that though extraordinary pains were taken upon him, yet he would receive no satisfaction so far as to act any thing against the enemy, except there might be a treaty;" and when upon giving in the Remonstrance from the army, Strachan was, by the committee of estates, under the influence of the public resolutions, forbid to again join his regiment; "Govan," he tells us, "was at the same time cashiered!" Relating the defeat of colonel Ker at Hamilton by general Lambert too, he adds, "Some speak of treachery, for Govan, for all his cashiering, was admitted by Ker upon fair promises." There is not the smallest evidence of treachery in the case; yet it would appear, that in some of those frantic fits of loyalty to which the judicatures of the church were at this period too liable, captain Govan had, under some surmise of the kind, been excommunicated; for the last notice taken of him by Baillie is, when he is lamenting the relaxing of lord Swinton from that sentence by the Resolutioners, when he remarks that, "our brethren [the protesters] would not long be behind with us, for at once the presbytery of Ayr relaxed good William Govan, who was at least on the scaffold at the king's execution if no more." Baillie's Letters, vol. ii. pp. 352, 362, 364, 409.

"So inconsiderable a person," says Mackenzie, "had not died if he had not been suspected of being upon the scaffold when king Charles the first was murthered, though he purged himself of this when he died, and his guilt was, that he brought the first news of it, and seemed to be well satisfied with it." Mackenzie's History of Scotland, p. 51.—*Ed.*

† Captain Govan's speech upon the scaffold at his death, June 1st, 1661.

Gentlemen and countrymen,

I am here to suffer this day; and that I may declare to you the cause, it is for laying down my arms at Hamilton, as did all the rest of the company that was there. What was I, that king and parliament should have taken notice of me, being a private boy thrust forth into the fields, who was not worthy to be noticed by any? for as I was obscure in myself, so were my actions not conspicuous: yet it pleased the Lord to employ me as a mean and instrument (unworthy as I was) for carrying on a part of the late reformation; which I did faithfully endeavour in my station, not going beyond it; for which I am to suffer here this day. Licentious people have taken occasion to calumniate me this time past, in saying I was an instrument of his late majesty's death, and that I should have said, I was on the scaffold in the time of his execution; all which I do here deny in the presence of Almighty God, to whom I must shortly answer: and before you all, I do here protest, as I hope for salvation, that I was not instrumental in that, either in word or deed; but, on the contrary, it was sore against my heart, who was still a wellwisher to his majesty, and even wished he might be unto these lands as David, Solomon, and Josiah: but what could a simple protestation of one who is the least among men do? I do indeed remember, I was honoured to bring up Montrose his standard through these streets, and deliver it to the parliament, in which I glory, as thousands more than I did at that time, for I was but an executioner, but now I am a sufferer for those things. Let me now speak a word to some sorts of people. First of all, you that are profane, leave off your profanity, forbear sin and seek mercy, otherwise you will undoubtedly repent it when too late; for ere long you must answer, as I am shortly to do, before a just God. Again, to you civilians and indifferent folks, who if your own private earthly interest prosper, do not care how the affairs of Christ and his church go; know that that will not do

1661. ended it, he took off a ring from his finger and gave to a friend of his upon the scaffold, desiring him to take it to his wife, and tell her, "He died in humble confidence, and found the cross of Christ sweet." He said, "Christ had done all for him, and it was by him alone he was justified;" and being desired to look up to that Christ, he answered, "He looketh down and smileth upon me." Then cheerfully mounting up some steps of the ladder to the cord, he said, "Dear friends, pledge this cup of suffering before you sin, as I have now done; for sin and suffering have been presented to me, and I have chosen the suffering part." Then the cord being about his neck, he said, "Now I am near my last, and I desire to reflect on no man, I would only acquaint you of one thing, the commissioner and I went out to the fields together for one cause, I have now the cord about my neck, and he is promoted to be his majesty's commissioner, yet for a thousand worlds I would not change lots with him, praise and glory be to Christ for ever." After he had prayed again a little, and given the sign, he was turned over.

It was very confidently asserted at this time, that some weeks after Mr. Guthrie's head had been set up on the Nether Bow Port in Edinburgh, the commissioner's coach coming down that way, several drops of blood fell from the head upon the coach, which all their art and diligence could not wipe off. I have it very confidently affirmed, that physicians were called and inquired, if any natural cause could be assigned for the blood's dropping so long after the head was put up, and especially for its not washing out of the leather; and they could give none. This odd incident beginning to be talked of, and all other methods being tried, at length the leather was removed, and a new cover put on: this was much sooner done than the wiping off the guilt of this great and good man's blood from the shedders of it, and this poor nation. The above report I shall say no more of. It was generally spoken of at the time, and is yet firmly believed by many; at this distance I cannot fully vouch it as certain, perhaps it may be thought too miraculous for this age we are now in: but this I will affirm, that Mr. Guthrie's blood was of so crying a nature, that even Sir George Mackenzie was sensible, that all his rhetoric, though he was a great master in that art, had not been sufficient to drown it; for which cause he very wisely passed it over in silence. This is another instance of the lameness of his vindication.

SECT. V.

Of the sufferings of Mr. Alexander Moncrief, Mr. Robert M'Vaird, and some other ministers, not unto death; as likewise of several gentlemen, during this session of parliament, 1661.

THE sufferings to be narrated in the after books of this history, were alleged to be for crimes and misdemeanors contrary to the then laws: but it is plain the things alleged

---

your turn, you must bear testimony for God, be zealous for his cause, and repent now of your sins; so shall you avoid that curse pronounced against the lukewarm Laodiceans, "I will spue you out of my mouth." As to the really godly, I would say this, be not afraid nor astonished to bear testimony, and suffer for his truth. As for myself, it pleased the Lord, in the fourteenth year of my age, to manifest his love to me, and now it is about twenty-four years since, all which time I professed the truth, which I suffer for, and bear testimony to at this day; and I am not afraid of the cross upon that account: it is sweet, it is sweet, otherwise how durst I look upon the corpse of him who hangs there, with courage, and smile upon those sticks and that gibbet, as the gates of heaven. I die confident in the faith of the prophets and apostles, bearing my testimony to the gospel, as it is now preached by an honest ministry in this city; though alas! there be a corrupt generation among the ministry. I bear witness with my blood to the persecuted government of this church, in general assemblies, synods, and presbyteries, and also to the protestation against the public resolutions. I bear witness to the covenants, national and solemn league, and now am to seal these with my blood. I likewise testify against all popery, prelacy, idolatry, superstition, and the Service-book, for I have not taken a little pains in searching out those things, and have found them to be but the relics of the Romish superstition and idolatry, left in king Henry VIII. his time, who, though it pleased the Lord to make use of him for beginning the work of reformation, yet he was no good man.

against the two martyrs we have been hearing of, were evidently according to standing law and equity, our constitution and statutes, overturned by this parliament, and those which followed.

After the reader hath had the vouched narrative of the managers' proceedings against the two first worthies in Scotland's wrestlings and battles, he cannot but stand amazed at the impudence of some episcopal writers, who assert, that no presbyterians in the reign of king Charles II. suffered for their principles, and upon matters of conscience. Though it should be pretended, that my lord Argyle and Warriston suffered for their compliances with the English, after they had conquered the nation, and this be made treason against all sense and reason, yet what can be said of Mr. Guthrie, whom the king himself vindicates, and all the world knew had opposed Cromwell, and several other ministers and gentlemen in this section, and the after part of this book? To those then I come forward, and shall give some account of a good many ministers and gentlemen, who, during the meeting of parliament, suffered very much, though by the good providence of God, their lives were spared for a season. I begin with the ministers.

I have little more to record of the ten ministers who were seized with Mr. Guthrie, than what has been pointed at upon the former chapter. Their paper, designed for a testimony, was, when sent to court, entertained with threatenings and ridicule. This, with the restless endeavours of the managers at Edinburgh, in this hour and power of darkness, prevailed so far, that one or two concerned in it, fainted, and, after some verbal acknowledgments, of which I have not heard the tenor, got off, and were permitted to retire to their houses.

None, I have heard of, was dealt more severely with by this session of parliament, than Mr. James Simpson, minister at Airth, of whom some account hath been given upon the first chapter. He was a person of singular piety, considerable learning, and a most affectionate and melting preacher. I am told he came a great length in writing a critical and very exact commentary upon the whole Bible, which was once in his friends' hands; but now, with many other valuable remains of this excellent sufferer, it is lost.

1661.

Mr. Simpson was not at the meeting in Edinburgh, August last, though I find he is charged with this in his indictment, which, with his answers, falling much in with Mr. Guthrie's process, above insert, I do not insert here. Towards the beginning of June, after he had been accused in parliament by the king's advocate, of seditious practices, and the copy of a libel sent him to answer in prison; such was the justice of this period, that the parliament, without allowing him to be heard, or, as far as I can find, so much as once sisting him before them, banished him the king's dominions; which some questioned whether a Scots parliament could do.* He was cast in with Mr. M'Vaird, and underwent the same fate, both of them dying in Holland.

The reverend Mr. Alexander Moncrief, minister of the gospel at Scoonie in Fife, was another of those ministers, and was indeed very hardly dealt with. I shall give a distinct account of this singularly pious and useful minister, from some hints I have from very good hands, and the parliament records: his papers were burnt some time before his death, and his contemporaries much gone;

---

* The editor of Kirkton's History of the Church of Scotland informs us, that Mr. Simpson's life was spared at the intercession of Sharpe; and in support of this opinion, quotes from the Wodrow MSS. the following letter from that prelate to Primrose, lord register: "That your parliamentary acts of justice have been tempered with mercy, I think, should not be displeasing, especially since the object of that mercy hath made a confession, which I wish may have as binding an influence for converting those of his way as his former actings had in perverting them. I did, at my first access to the king, beg that the lives of Mr. Gillespie and Mr. Guthrie might be spared, which his majesty denied me, but now the recommendation of the parliament, upon a ground which I could not bring, I hope will prevail with so generous a prince, more merciful than the kings of Israel. Upon an earnest letter from Mr. James Simpson to me, to whom I did owe no great kindness, I begged of the king that he might not be proceeded against for his life and corporal punishment, which his majesty was pleased generously to grant to me by a letter for that purpose, directed to my lord commissioner. When your lordship shall hear my inducements, I hope you will not condemn me." Kirkton's History of the Church of Scotland, p. 113, *Note.—Ed*.

1661. and it is to be regretted so lame an account can be given of this man of God. I shall put all I have to say of this good man in this place; and indeed much of it concerns this period.

During the usurpation, Mr. Alexander Moncrief was persecuted by the English for his loyalty to the king, and his constant praying for him. His house was many times searched and rifled by the English, and he obliged to hide. Upon the Sabbath he had spies set upon him, and was closely watched where he went after preaching. Frequently he was hotly pursued; and one time a party of horse came after him when fleeing, and by a special providence, though attacked once and again by them, by his own fortitude and resolution he got clear of them, and escaped at that time. Thereafter in a neighbouring congregation he was seized, and imprisoned some time, merely for praying for the king.

Being shortly after liberate, he was pitched upon, as a person of great courage and boldness, to present the protestation and petition against the toleration, and other encroachments upon the church and state, October, 1658, signed by himself and several other ministers of Fife, to general Monk. This he did with the greatest firmness, and it exposed him further to the extremities of that time. All the return he had to those sufferings for his loyalty, was, as we heard, August 23d last, to be seized when petitioning according to law. For any thing I can find, he continued under confinement till July 12th this year; and every body, and he himself expected he should never have been liberate till he came to a scaffold.

Much about the time with Mr. James Guthrie, he had his indictment and charge sent him, which I have not seen, but find it run upon his having a share in the "Remonstrance," and in forming the "Causes of God's Wrath;" and he refused to retract any thing in them. He was several times brought before the parliament, and his prosecution for his life was so hot, that the earl of Athole and others in parliament, particularly interested and concerned in Mr. Moncrief and his wife, being importuned by her to appear for him in parliament, dealt with her to endeavour to prevail with him to recede from some of his principles, otherwise, they told her, it was impossible to save his life. This excellent woman answered, "That they all knew she was happy in a good husband, that she had great affection to him, and many children; yet she knew him to be so steadfast to his principles where his conscience was concerned, that nobody needed deal with him upon that head; for her part, before she would contribute any thing that would break his peace with his Master, she would rather choose to receive his head at the Cross." About this time likewise, two ladies of the first quality were pleased to concern themselves so far in Mr. Moncrief, as to provide a handsome compliment in plate, (which was not unusual at this time) and send it to the advocate's lady. Afterwards they went and visited her, and addressed her in his behalf, but were told, it was impossible to save his life; and the compliment was returned. Yet providence so over-ruled this matter, that Mr. Moncrief being much respected, and his hardships almost universally regretted upon account of his eminent piety, integrity, and uprightness, severals of all ranks and different persuasions, and unknown to him, did zealously, and without any application, interpose for him; so that the spirits of some of his hottest and most violent persecutors, who had resolved upon his death, began to soften and become more friendly. His process lingered till, after a tedious imprisonment, he fell sick, and obtained the favour of confinement to a chamber in Edinburgh. By the records of parliament, I find they passed the following sentence upon him, July 12th, " The king's majesty and estates of parliament, having considered the report of the lords of articles anent the process against Mr. Alexander Moncrief, minister of Scoonie, and his own carriage before them, in owning his accession to the " Remonstrance" and " Causes of God's Wrath," do accordingly declare the said Mr. Alexander to be for ever incapable of exercising any public trust, civil or ecclesiastic, and also discharge him of all public trust, civil or ecclesiastic within this kingdom, until, in the next session of parliament, further order be taken concerning him, and discharge him in the meantime to go to the said parish."

And to give the reader all I have of this worthy person together. After this sentence, when living peaceably some eight or nine miles from his parish, people began to resort to him, and hear him preach in his own family; whereupon, under a most severe storm in the middle of winter, by virtue of an act we shall afterwards meet with, he was charged to remove from his house, and required to live twenty miles from his charge, and seven or eight miles from a bishop's seat or royal burgh, and was with his family forced from his house, and obliged to wander in that great storm. And when he had transported his furniture to a place at a competent distance, even there he got a second charge to remove to a further distance, till he was obliged to transport his family to a remote place in the Highlands, where his good God, who had all along countenanced and supported him wonderfully in his troubles, honoured him to be instrumental in the conversion of many.

Thereafter, the persecution somewhat abating, he brought his family to Perth for the education of his children, where he continued preaching the gospel; a few at first, but afterwards a great many attended his ministry. Being informed against, we may easily guess by whom, a party of the horse guards were sent to apprehend him, but he escaped, though his house was narrowly and rudely searched: this forced him from his family, and he was obliged to lurk a good while. At length he came in with his family to Edinburgh, where he preached the gospel many years in private, under a series of trouble and persecution. He was intercommuned, as we shall hear, and his house and many other places in and about the city narrowly searched for him, yet he was always marvellously hid. Many instances might be given when he went to the country. Many times parties of the guards were sent in quest of him, and sometimes he would meet them in his return, and pass through them unknown. When he was lodged in a remote part of the suburbs of Edinburgh, a captain with a party of the regular troops, searched every house and chamber of the close, save the house where he lodged, into which they never entered, though the door was open. At another time when he was lurking in a private family without the wall of Edinburgh, a party was sent to apprehend him; providentially he had gone out to walk near by the house where he was: the party observing him, and by his gravity suspecting him a minister, one of them said, " That may be the man we are seeking :" " Nay," said another, " he would not be walking there ;" thus they entered into the house and searched it narrowly for him. Again, when advertised that the soldiers were coming to search for him in his own house, he lingered till another minister came in to him, and said, " Sir, you must surely have a protection from heaven, that you are so secure here, when the town is in a disorder, and a general search to be made ;" and immediately he went off. In a little Mr. Moncrief went out, and he was not well down stairs, when the guard came up and searched his house. He took a little turn in the street, and came back to his house again, just as the guards went off.

1661.

Those and many other preservations he could not but remark. But the persecution still continuing, and turning hotter, he was obliged to dismiss, and scatter his family for some time. He was solicited, when in those circumstances, to leave the kingdom, and had an ample call to Londonderry in Ireland; yet he always declined to leave his native country, and in his pleasant way used to say, " He would suffer where he had sinned, and essay to keep possession of his Master's house, till he should come again." He had a sore sickness about the beginning of June, 1680. I have in mine eye a large collection of heavenly expressions he then had, too long to be here inserted.

Mr. Moncrief's memory is yet savoury to many; and there are several alive who can bear witness that God was with him and in him of a truth. He left many seals of his ministry in Fife, and was a most faithful and painful minister. His sufferings are a little hinted at in " The Fulfilling of the Scriptures," p. 343. But such was his self-denial, that though he be not named nor his persecutors, as long as he lived he would not

1661. suffer that book to be in his family.

He lived till harvest, 1688, and so may be said indeed to "have kept possession of his Master's house till he came back;" as he frequently used to express his own hopes under this dark period of sufferings. He was mighty in prayer, and a singular prevailer; and I have some remarkable and strange returns of his prayers well vouched before me, not so needful to be insert here. I wish his worthy son, at present a reverend and useful minister in this church, could be prevailed with to give us the life of this holy person.

I find Mr. Robert Trail, Mr. John Stirling, and some other of the ministers who were seized, August last, toward the beginning of March this year before the lords of the articles; where it is observed by one who appears no great friend of theirs, that they had very handsome speeches in their own vindication. None of them I have heard of were brought before the parliament, save Mr. Trail, a copy of whose speech to the parliament deserves a room here, being all I have to give the reader of this worthy person, and from it he may easily gather both his indictment and defences; and it follows.

" My Lord,

" I do rejoice to see my lord commissioner his grace, your lordships, and this honourable company upon this bench, and shall, in the beginning, humbly beg, that I may be allowed to answer my libel as becomes a minister of the gospel, and as one who desires to remember that I have an higher Judge to answer, even one who is higher than the kings of the earth, before whose tribunal all of us must ere long be sisted, there to be judged, and receive according to what we have done in the body, whether good or evil. Knowing therefore the terror of the Lord, and the certain and speedy coming of that day, I dare not use flatteries to men, nor dissimulation, but speak the truth in sincerity and singleness of heart, as before him who tries and searches the reins.

" My whole libel drives at this, to prove me guilty of high treason, as having been disloyal to my king, and his authority and government, grievous crimes, and iniquity to be indeed punished by the judges, if it could be proven against me, and would contradict the doctrine which I have at that time preached before many witnesses, yea, in the face of unjust usurpers, for which I was challenged, when I was preaching to my own people, in hearing of some of their commanders upon my ordinary text, which therefore I would not balk, [alter] John xvi. 2. ' The time shall come, when they who kill you, shall think that they do God service:' but I bless the Lord, I came fair off in that debate, without any advantage to them, or shame to myself, or the word I preached.

" I did often, both in private and public, witness and declare against that base and treasonable tender, when it was pressed upon the land. I have always laboured, and do still, to keep in mind that divine precept given by a great king, even Solomon; ' Fear God and the king, and follow not them that are given to changes:' and of a greater than Solomon, ' Give unto Cæsar the things that are Cæsar's, and to God the things that are God's.' I willingly subscribe to that which is in the imperial law, where it is said to be a great sacrilege, *eripere Cæsari quod ejus est;* how much more must it be the greater sacrilege, *eripere Christo quod ejus est?*

" In answering the particulars of my libel, I cannot altogether keep silence as to the many bitter and injurious words wherewith it is stuffed, as that I have laid aside all loyalty to my prince, all natural affection to my country and countrymen, and all respect to law: those of your lordships who know me, will allow me more charity than to think me such an one; and such as know me not, I hope, will suspend their judgment till they know me: yea, I durst appeal to my lord advocate's own conscience, if he thinks me to be such a man. But I have not so learned Christ, yea, I have learned of him not to render evil for evil, or railing for railing, but contrariwise, blessing; and therefore I do from my heart pray for the honoured drawer up of the libel, as I would do for myself, that the Lord would bless him with his best blessings, and would give him to find mercy in the day of the Lord Jesus.

"The particulars of my libel are four, and I shall answer to them shortly and ingenuously as they lie there.

" The first is, that Remonstrance which was presented to the committee of estates in the end of the year 1650. Whatever be said against that paper in my libel, or whatever be said for it by the presenters and compilers of it, I shall need say nothing of it at present, but that I was neither at the contriving or presenting of it. It is well known that I was then in the castle of Edinburgh, besieged there by the unjust invaders of this land; and what my carriage was there in exhorting and encouraging that garrison to be faithful to the great trust committed to them, having the chief strength of the land in their custody, and the registers embarked with them; what, I say, my carriage was there, my brethren who were there with me, Messrs. Hamilton, Smith, and Garvan can testify. I did resolve to lay down my life in the defence of that place for his majesty and my country's service, if the Lord should please to call me to it; yea, I did run a very great hazard by a dangerous wound which I received; and shall I be no otherwise rewarded than by having such a libel drawn up against me! which, I may say, hath been more sad to read and think upon, than all the pain and danger I was at that time under; yet I hope your lordships, especially my lord commissioner, know better how to reward soldiers who have hazarded life in their service.

" The second point of my libel is, the book of ' The Causes of God's Wrath,' which, I grant, is more ticklish to answer, and therefore I shall speak the more warily to it. I do not deny that I was present at that meeting, when those things were spoken of and confessed, when some brethren did meet to mourn before the Lord, who hid his face from us, and whose hand had gone forth against us with much wrath and sore judgments, and had brought kirk and state under the feet of proud usurpers: I believe your lordships will judge it no treason at such times, for ministers of the gospel, who, by virtue of their office, are called to be among the wise men, to whom the mouth of the Lord hath spoken, to declare wherefore the land does mourn; for these, I say, to meet for prayer, and confessing their own sins, and of their rulers, according to the commanded practice of the servants of God in former times, in the like case. Neither can it be accounted treason in such a case to seek the Lord's face, and to inquire into the provoking and procuring causes of so much wrath as had come upon us. I am persuaded there are many things in that book which none here will deny to be the uncontroverted guilt of this land, such as atheism and ignorance in many, despising of the Lord Jesus Christ offered in the gospel, neglect of the exercises of religion and godliness in families, greater and smaller; those have been great sins in the land, yea, continue to be so, and receive a great aggravation from the great and wonderful deliverance which the Lord hath wrought for us, as if we had been delivered to continue in all those abominations; and when the Lord hath bound up and strengthened our arm, we rebel against him.

" But I know it is not those things I am challenged for, neither is it the two articles cited in the libel, but the 5th and 6th step of defection, under the 9th article, to which I shall answer.

" The first of them, ' The closing a treaty with the king, after he had given such evidences of his disaffection and enmity to the work of God,' as it is in the book. To this I say two things, 1st, That I never did deny his majesty's just right and title to the government of these kingdoms, and did always acknowledge him the only righteous heir of those crowns; and I do now from my heart bless the Lord, who hath in so wonderful and peaceable a way brought him to the full possession of them, purposing to live in all true and due loyalty under his government, and praying, that he who is set over men, may be just, ruling in the fear of God, that his reign may be long and prosperous, and a blessing to these lands, that when he shall have fulfilled his days, and laid by his earthly crown, he may receive a greater and better, which fadeth not away, but is eternal in the heavens. But in the 2d place, I cannot deny, unless I should lie against my own conscience, that I was at that time con-

1661. vinced, there was not care enough to get him brought off from his prejudices against the work of reformation, and from some contrary principles which he had drunk in from his tender years, that so when he came to be invested with the royal power, he might improve the same the more for the Lord, and for his work in his dominions, according to the oath to be taken by the king who shall reign in Scotland; the which oath his majesty did take at the coronation at Scone. Neither is my meaning in that article, as if his majesty, not giving full satisfaction to the just desires of church and state, should never have been invested into his power, but that more care should have been taken, previously thereunto, to have brought him to a cordial owning of the work of God in these lands, which, as I believe, would have been acceptable service to God, and much conducing to the peace and happiness of his majesty in his dominions. In a word, my meaning in that article is, that security for religion, and the work of reformation, should be endeavoured in the first place, that so we, according to our Lord's direction, seeking first the kingdom of heaven, and the righteousness thereof, other things may succeed the better with us.

" The next article is, concerning ' taking of malignants into the army and judicatories,' as it is set down in ' The Causes of God's Wrath.' To this I say, there is nothing asserted there, but what is clearly consonant to the word of God, and to the received doctrine of this church according to the word, as may be seen in the many ' declarations, remonstrances, warnings, and causes of fasts,' emitted and printed by the supreme judicatories of this church: for if it be a commanded duty to put into places of trust and power, men fearing God, men of truth, and hating covetousness; then must the neglect of that be a sin, and so a cause of wrath.

" The third point of my libel is, that supplication which was drawn up and subscribed by some few ministers here at Edinburgh, in August last, for which we were imprisoned by the honourable committee of estates, and upon which I am cited this day to answer before your lordships. That petition is misrepresented in the libel, as if I had therein been injurious to his majesty; whereas, I can say, I had not in that the least thought of disloyalty against his majesty, but on the contrary, I did most willingly and cheerfully subscribe that supplication, as a testimony of my loyalty to my king, and of my ardent desire to have wrath holden off his throne and dominions, by a humble minding him of the sacred ties of the covenant which he had taken on, and by earnestly supplicating him, that he would walk according to those, both in his court and family, and in the government of his kingdoms; and I do desire, in the Lord's strength, and through his grace, to adhere to that supplication as long as I live, as a real evidence of my loyalty, and as a testimony to those blessed covenants, which are now so much spoken against.

" The last point of my libel is, ' The imperfect scroll of a letter and instructions,' which were found with us at our meeting. Though I might say I need not own these, they never being fully written out, or once read among us, yet I will ingenuously acknowledge, they were intended to have been sent to some of our brethren in another part of the country, for procuring their subscription to our petition, and for advising anent a way for charges to be furnished for sending of it up to his majesty, by one of our number. But the honourable committee did soon free us of that trouble, and of those charges, by sending it up their own way, and by putting us to another sort of trouble, and other charges, by seven months' imprisonment. I may confidently say, there was not the least thought of stirring up any to rise in arms, yea we would have accounted such a thought not only disloyalty, but dementation and madness.

" Now, my lord, having shortly and ingenuously answered my long libel, I must in all humility beg leave to entreat your lordships, that you would seriously consider what ye do with poor ministers, who have been so long kept, not only from their liberty of preaching the gospel, but of hearing it, that so many congregations are laid desolate for so long a time, and many poor souls have put up their regrets on their deathbed for their being deprived of a word of comfort from their ministers in the hour of their greatest need. "The Lord give you wisdom in all things, and pour out upon you the spirit of your high and weighty employment, of understanding, and of the fear of the Lord; that your government may be blessed for this land and kirk; that you may live long and happily; that your memory may be sweet and fragrant when you are gone; that you may leave your name for a blessing to the Lord's people; that your houses and families may stand long, and flourish to the years of many generations; that you have solid peace and heart-joy in the hour of the breaking of your heart-strings, when pale death will sit on your eyelids, and when man must go to his long home, and the mourners go about the streets; for what man is he that liveth and shall not see death? or can he deliver himself from the power of the grave? No assuredly, for even those to whom he saith, ye are gods, must die as men, seeing it is appointed for all men once to die, and after death is the judgment, and after judgment endless eternity. Let me therefore exhort your lordships in the words of a great king, a great warrior also, and a holy prophet, 'Be wise, and be ye instructed, ye judges of the earth, serve the Lord with fear, and rejoice before him with trembling: kiss the Son, lest he be angry, and ye perish from the way; when his wrath is kindled but for a little, then blessed will all those, and those only be, who put their trust in him.' Now the Lord give you in this your day to consider the things that belong to your eternal peace, and to remember your latter end, that it may be well with you, world without end."

From the seven months' imprisonment Mr. Trail speaks of, we may guess this speech was delivered towards the end of March. I find this good man with the rest, continuing in prison, June 13th, when in an original letter of his to Mr. Thomas Wylie, minister at Kirkcudbright, I find him giving this account. "I need not write to you how matters go here, this I must say, your imprisoned and confined brethren are kindly dealt with by our kind Lord, for whose cause and interest we suffer; and if any of us be straitened, it is not in him, for we have large allowance from him, could we take it. We know it fares the better with us, that you and such as you mind us at the throne. We are waiting from day to day what men will do with us; we are expecting banishment at the best, but our sentence must proceed from the Lord; and whatsoever it be, it shall be good as from him, and whithersoever he shall send us, he will be with us, and shall let us know that the earth is his, and the fulness thereof." This was the resigned Christian temper of those worthies.

1661.

I have before me the original summons of high treason, against Mr. John Murray, minister at Methven, who was at the meeting in Edinburgh August last, with his answers to the charge contained in the summons. By the first I find, that a general form has been used in the citations given to all these ministers, and, *mutatis mutandis,* it falls in with Mr. Guthrie's indictment; therefore I do not swell this work with it, nor with Mr. Murray's answers, which agree with Mr. Guthrie's and Mr. Trail's, save that Mr. Murray was neither at the framing "the Remonstrance," or "Causes of God's Wrath." What issue the parliament came to as to Mr. Murray, I know not; it would seem he was turned over with others to the council. We shall find, that the parliament some way remitted those imprisoned and confined ministers to the council; and from their registers this year, I shall be in case to give some further hints about them. The two ministers of Edinburgh were soon turned out, and all the rest of their brethren there save one, who was termed the nest egg.

This is all come to my hand, as to the sufferings of those worthy and excellent persons, who were in the meeting August last; unless it be those of Mr. James Kirko of Sunday-well, which I shall likewise give a hint of in this place. This religious and zealous gentleman was detained prisoner near four months after he was seized: thereafter he was not forgot in the act of fines, and paid 600 merks of fines, and 300 by way of cess to the soldiers who uplifted it. In a little time after one Paterson, by an

1661. order from the council, got his bond for a considerable sum, which afterward he compounded for 200 merks. In the year 1666, for mere not hearing, he was fined by Sir James Turner in 500 merks, and paid 300 to him, after eight soldiers had continued in his house a long time. Before the rising at Pentland, because of his nonconformity, he was so oppressed with parties of horse and foot soldiers every day, that he was obliged to dismiss his family in the month of October, and leave his house and all he had in it, to be disposed of as they saw good. And after Pentland, upon allegance that he had been there, though it could never be proven, he was obliged to leave the kingdom for three years. And when he returned, he was put to a prodigious charge by a process of forfeiture, raised against him by the lord Lyon, which continued till his death. He was succeeded in his estate by James M'Cleland, whom we shall afterwards meet with under very grievous sufferings.

The next minister I name is Mr. Patrick Gillespie, first minister in the town, and then principal of the college of Glasgow. His works speak for him, and evidence him a person of great learning, solidity, and piety, particularly what remains we have of his excellent treatises upon "the Covenants of Grace and Redemption;" and it is pity we want the three other parts upon those subjects, which he wrote and finished for the press.

By some he was said to be a person of a considerable height of spirit, and was blamed by many for his compliances with the usurper, and there is no doubt he was the minister in Scotland who had the greatest sway with the English when they ruled here, yea, almost the only presbyterian minister that was in with them. This laid him open to many heavy reflections, and we need not wonder he was attacked by the managers at this time, when so many who had stood firm to the king's interest, were so ungenerously treated: besides, he was on the protesting side, and had no small share in the "Western Remonstrance," and probably it fared the worst with all the ministers of that judgment, because of the reproaches cast on him, and the compliances made by him. The king had a particular design against him for his open dealings with the usurpers, and we have heard, it was with some difficulty the managers were excused for sparing him. We left him last year imprisoned in Stirling castle, and he was brought in to Edinburgh, and March 6th, staged before the parliament, where his indictment was read: I have not seen a full copy of it, but find the following abstract in the papers of this time.

"That he contrived, compiled, consented to, and subscribed the paper called 'the Western Remonstrance,' which he also produced in several judicatories, when it was declared treasonable, and condemned by the parliament or committee of estates. That he consented to, or approved that abominable pamphlet, called 'the Causes of God's Wrath,' containing many treasonable wicked lies and expressions against the king and his royal father, and which by the late committee of estates was appointed to be burnt by the hand of the hangman. That he kept constant correspondence with Cromwell the usurper That at Westminster, and in and about London, he preached in his presence seditious sermons; that he prayed for him as supreme magistrate; that for his so doing he received from him several gifts, and great sums of money."

After his indictment was read, he had a long and pertinent speech, which I have not seen, but am told that therein he gave his sense of "the Western Remonstrance," and of "the Causes of God's Wrath:" and as to his receiving money from Cromwell, he confessed it; but said, he never put a farthing in his own pocket; that he sought it and got it for the university, and if that was blameworthy, he acknowledged his crime: but it was his opinion, if he could have drained the usurper's coffers for so good an end as the service of the college, it could have been no disservice to the king. He ended with a desire that he might be allowed to give in a paper containing his sense of the "Remonstrance," and other things in the late times. The parliament ordained him to give in his defences in writ, to the lords of articles, the 13th instant; and if he should offer any paper to them, that they should hear it.

Nothing further as to his process hath come to my hand. He had friends in the house, and favour was shown him; an aggravation certainly of the managers' severity against such who had never gone his lengths. Towards the end of May I find him before the parliament, confessing civil guilt, and asking pardon of the house, submitting himself to his majesty's mercy and favour; and the parliament transmitted his supplication to the king. I have not seen a copy either of his sense of the "Remonstrance," or this supplication; but have heard that he renounced the "Protestation," and some expressions in "the Causes of God's Wrath," and "Lex Rex," and declared his grief for his compliance with the English. And his supplication bears, that, " he acknowledged he had given offence to his majesty by the ' Remonstrance,' and otherwise, which he now was sorry for, and did disclaim, and therefore cast himself upon the king's mercy, and humbly desired the commissioner his grace, and the parliament, to proffer his petition to his majesty;" or to this effect. This was interpreted by the parliament an acknowledgment of guilt; and some words in his declaration and supplication were indeed strained further than he intended: and they interceded for him, and in a little time he was liberate, and confined to Ormiston, and six miles round it, as we may afterwards hear.*

Mr. Gillespie's going this length was much condemned at this time, as a step of great fainting in a person of his forwardness, zeal, and activity, during the preceding years. The beginnings of his yielding, when signified to Mr. Rutherford, were distressing to him on his deathbed; and Mr. James Guthrie, who lived to see his paper, said, " And hath he suffered so much in vain, if it be in vain?" In an original letter of Mr. M'Vaird's, dated June 5th, this year, he expresses himself thus, " Mr. Gillespie's submission in quitting the ' Remonstrance,' with some other expressions in the submission, that are strained beyond his meaning, have sadly stumbled many, and are like to be the *minimum quod sic* of satisfaction that shall be accepted from any that follow."

1661.

That bright shining light of this time Mr Samuel Rutherford, may very justly come in among the sufferers, during this session of parliament. To be sure he was a martyr both in his own resolution, and in men's designs and determination. He is so well known to the learned and pious world, that I need say very little of him. Such who knew him best, were in a strait whether to admire him most for his sublime genius in the school, and peculiar exactness in matter of dispute and controversy, or his familiar condescensions in the pulpit, where he was one of the most moving and affectionate preachers in his time, or perhaps in any age of the church. He seems even to have outdone himself as well as every body else, in his admirable, and every way singular letters; which, though jested upon by profane wits, because of some familiar expressions, yet will be owned of all who have any relish of piety, to contain such sublime flights of devotion, and to be fraughted with such massy thoughts, as loudly speak a soul united to Jesus Christ in the closest embraces, and must needs at once ravish and edify every serious reader.

The parliament were to have had an indictment laid before them, against this holy man, if his death had not prevented it. After his book " Lex Rex," had been ordered to be burnt at the Cross of Edinburgh, and the gate of the new college of St. Andrews, where he was divinity professor; in their great humanity they were

---

* " Mr. Patrick Gillespie," says Mackenzie, speaking of Mr. Guthrie, " was guilty of the same and greater crimes, having courted the Protector, whom Guthrie really hated; nor had his majesty so great aversion for any minister as for him, because he behaved himself so insolently in his own presence, and toward his own person; yet upon a humble submission, (which was the more regarded, because it was refused by Guthrie, and might be exemplary to others,) he was brought off by the lord Sinclair and others, with whom he had behaved himself as a gentleman when he was young; and in his case the courtier served the minister: yet his majesty retained so far his former resentments, that he would never allow him to be brought into the ministry, notwithstanding of many intercessions."—History of Scotland, p. 51.—*Ed.*

1661. pleased, when every body knew Mr. Rutherford to be in a dying condition, to cause cite him to appear before them at Edinburgh, to answer to a charge of high treason. But he had a higher tribunal to appear before, where his Judge was his friend. Mr. Rutherford died in March this year, the very day before the act rescissory was passed in the parliament. This eminent saint and faithful servant of Jesus Christ, lamented, when near his end, that he was witheld from bearing witness to the work of reformation since the year 1638, and giving his public testimony against the evil courses of the present time; otherwise he was full of peace and joy in believing. I have a copy before me of what could be gathered up of his dying words, and the expressions this great man had during his sickness, too large to be insert here.

The reverend Mr. Robert M'Vaird deserves the next room in this section. He was minister of the gospel at Glasgow, and a person of great knowledge, zeal, learning, and remarkable ministerial abilities. This good man, and fervent affectionate preacher, in February this year, when the designs of the managers in parliament began to appear, and that nothing less was resolved upon than the overturning the whole covenanted work of reformation, had a sermon in the Tron church at Glasgow, upon a week-day, wherein he gave his testimony against the courses now entered upon, which was the foundation of a severe prosecution. A copy of this excellent sermon lies before me: the text was, Amos iii. 2. " You only have I known of all the families of the earth; therefore I will punish you for all your iniquities." He had preached upon it for some time upon the week days, and in this discourse goes through the sins and iniquities now abounding, which were drawing down the punishment threatened in the text, in a most serious, close, and pathetical manner; and after he has in a fluent oratory, of which he was peculiarly a master, run through abounding personal sins, and those of the city he preached to, he comes to the general and national sins at present abounding. Some few hints may not be unacceptable; he begins with national backsliding from God.

" Alas," says he, " may not God expostulate with us, and say, we are backslidden with a perpetual backsliding, and what iniquity have you found in him? We make ourselves transgressors by building the things we lawfully and laudably destroyed: and if a word in sobriety be dropt against such a course, one presently forfaults his reputation, and passes for a hotheaded and turbulent person—this leaven hath leavened the whole lump; we are backslidden in zeal and love—the glory of a begun reformation in manners is eclipsed, and an inundation of profanity come in—those who once cried, ' Grace, grace,' to the building, are now crying, ' Raze, raze it'—many who once loved to walk abroad in the garment of godliness, now persecute it—the faithful servants of Christ are become enemies, because they tell the truth—the upright seekers of God, are the marks of great men's malice—he that in this general backsliding departs from iniquity makes himself a prey; and may become so to councils and synagogues. May it never be said of faithful ministers and Christians in Scotland, ' We have a law, and by this law they must die!' Backsliding is got up to the very head, and corrupts the fountains, and wickedness goeth forth already from some of the prophets, through the whole land. The whole head is sick, the whole heart is faint, and many of his disciples are like to go back. What would our fathers, who laid the foundation of our reformation, think, if they saw our state? Would they not say, is this the church of Scotland? How is thy gold become dim?—The foundations are out of course, the noble vine is degenerate to the plant of a strange vine—Is this the land that joined in covenant with the Lord? Are those the pastors and rulers that bound themselves so solemnly, and acknowledged their former breaches?—How hath the faithful city turned an harlot! What shall the end of those things be?—We are in a forlorn condition; sin is become national by precept and practice; sins nationally condemned are become national by precept, and evil is called good, and good evil—We walk willingly after the commandment, and there is not a party so much as to offer a dissent."

After he has enlarged upon these things, in scripture eloquence, and a most moving way, he gives a good many pertinent directions to mourn, consider, repent, and return, to wrestle and pray, and pour out their souls before the Lord; and encourages them to those from this, "that God will look upon those duties, as their dissent from what is done prejudicial to his work and interest, and mark them among the mourners in Zion." But the passage most noticed was that, with which he closes the sermon, after what I have just now set down. "As for my own part, as a poor member of this church of Scotland, and an unworthy minister in it, I do this day call you, who are the people of God, to witness, that I humbly offer my dissent to all acts which are or shall be passed against the covenants, and work of reformation in Scotland: and 2dly, protest, that I am desirous to be free of the guilt thereof, and pray, that God may put it upon record in heaven." Thus he ends his sermon, as my copy, taken from his mouth bears.

The noise of this sermon quickly flew abroad, and Mr. M'Vaird was brought in to Edinburgh under a guard, and imprisoned: very soon he had an indictment given him by the king's advocate, for sedition and treasonable preaching. I have not seen the copy of it, but we may easily guess its nature from what I have extracted from the sermon; and Sir John Fletcher could easily flourish his pen on such a subject. He was allowed lawyers, and his process was pretty long and tedious. I know no further of it, than by his own papers following, and the original letter above cited, to Mr. Wylie, June 5th.

Where he says, "I know you have heard of the sad, and yet, in many respects, sweet and comfortable news of steadfast and faithful Mr. Guthrie's death, Saturday last. Upon Thursday I was called in before the parliament, and expected to have accompanied him, but the president, my lord Crawford, shifted it off that day. I was sent back again to prison, to be in a readiness against the next diet. That night they adjourned to this Tuesday, when I expected to be called, but was not. It is thought they were expecting Mr. Sharp's brother with some new orders, which made them sist. I expect to be called in to-morrow, the 6th. Dear brother, there is no way for us to stand upon our feet before such fury and force, but by your and our falling upon our knees, praying with all manner of prayer and supplication, to be strengthened with all might, according to his glorious power unto all long-suffering and patience with joyfulness. What will be the issue of my process, whether death or banishment, I know not; and he can put me in case to say, I care not. Pray for nothing to us but steadfastness." Mr. Gillespie's submission, &c., as I have already set down above. And then he tells him, he has sent Argyle and Mr. Guthrie's speeches. And adds, "before this come to your hands, my business will be at some close. God may restrain them, but I expect the sentence of death. O! for a heart to give him this head. I desire not this to be much noised till you hear further, lest my friends hear of it; only pray for strength to us to endure to the end. Time will permit me to say no further, save that I am,

"Your unworthy brother in bonds,
"R. M."

Accordingly, June 6th, he was brought before the parliament, where he had a very public opportunity to give a proof of his eminent parts and solid judgment. His charming eloquence was owned even by his adversaries, and he defended, by scripture and reason, his expressions in his sermon. I have no more of this great man's case than his speech at the bar of the house; and therefore I insert it here.

Mr. Robert M'Vaird, Minister of the East quarter in Glasgow, his Speech before the Parliament, Thursday, June 6th.

" My Lord President,

" Since it is permitted, that I may speak before my lord commissioner his grace, and this honourable court of parliament, I must in the entry confess, that I am neither so far below nor above all passion and perturbation of mind, as not to be somewhat troubled, yea sensibly touched, to see and

1661. feel myself thus loaded with the crime, and lashed with the reproach of a traitorous and seditious person: but with all I must say this also, that *nil conscire sibi, nulla pallescere culpa,* doth exceedingly sweeten the bitterness of this lot, and mitigate the asperity of my present trouble. It is to me *murus aheneus* indeed, a brazen wall and bulwark against the storm, tempest, and impetuosity of calumny and reproach, that herein, according to my weak measure, I have endeavoured to exercise myself, to have and keep a conscience void of offence, as to that particular guilt, wherewith I am charged in my indictment: this, I say, is sufficient to make me digest those hard and heavy things, without grieving or grudging, and to guard me against an unprofitable overplus of cutting and disquieting anxiety, even when I am so odiously represented to the world; so that my enemies are not those of mine own house, because not within me."

" And now, my lord, I hope I may, without vanity or offence, say, what in part is known to be no fiction or falsehood, that my carriage, since my first appearance before my lord commissioner his grace, and the honourable parliament, (whatever else was wanting in it, which were to be wished, as much was, I grant, and yet is) hath, to conviction, spoke forth so much ingenuity and candour, as I may some way suppose myself above the just suspicion of having chosen the tongue of the crafty, or used deceit or dissimulation in any thing about which I was questioned; since I have, with so much simplicity, and in so much singleness of heart, declared, either without alteration or addition, what I spoke, notwithstanding I easily foresaw how I might, and probably would be supposed by many to have lost, at least laid aside the greatest part of my little reason, while I plainly spoke my knowledge and conscience: but, my lord, it neither was nor is my desire to covet or court the reputation of wise and prudent, especially of being wise above what is written. I am satisfied to be looked upon as an ingenuous man, who dare not venture to unsay or gainsay what, with some clearness and conviction of truth, I have said, either for fear of prejudice and hurt, or hope of favour and gain; knowing that it is a very cold and vanishing advantage which is the price of, and purchased with the loss of a man's peace with God and himself; nay, what gain can be in such a case, when the gainer himself is lost?

" The consideration hereof moved me, when challenged for some alleged notes of a sermon, readily to condescend upon, and without reluctancy to give in, for information in point of fact, all these passages in that sermon which were hinted at, but misrepresented by the informer; which paper I did and do own, according to which I was and am willing to be judged. If it had been a matter of mere humour or indifference, I would, in order to the satisfaction of any who might have offended at what was said, much more in order to the satisfaction of my superiors, whom I honour and obey in the Lord, without any hesitation, have relinquished and retracted it, though in so doing I had crossed my own inclination, judging it below a man and a Christian to adhere to those things peevishly and petulantly, which he may let go without shipwreck of a good conscience; much more unworthy of a minister of the gospel, who should not have an humour of his own, being obliged to become all things to all men, in order to the gaining and engaging them to be Christians.

" But, my lord, I cannot, I dare not dissemble, that having spoken nothing in those, but what I hope will be the truth of God, when brought to the touchstone, and such a truth, as without being guilty of lesemajesty against God, I durst not conceal while I spoke to the text. I conceive myself obliged to own and adhere to it; and being persuaded also as to what was said in *hypothesi,* I was so far from doing or designing what is charged upon me in the indictment, that it was the highest part of loyalty toward my prince, the greatest note of respect I could put upon my superiors, the most real and unquestionable evidence of a true and tender affection to my countrymen, and the congregation over whom the Holy Ghost made me, though most unworthy an overseer to give seasonable warning of the heavy judgment which the sin of Scotland's backsliding will bring on, that so we may be instructed at length to search and try our ways, and turn to the Lord, lest his soul be separated from us, for wo will be to us if our glory depart. No man will or ought to doubt, whether it be a minister's duty to preach this doctrine in season, and out of season, which is yet never unseasonable, and to avow, 'that the backslider in heart shall be filled with his own ways,' and, 'if any man draw back, his soul shall have no pleasure in him:' and if so, what evil have I done, or whose enemy am I become for telling the truth?

"This, my lord, being the sum of what I said, and the scope of my discourse, as also of the paper I gave in to his grace, and the honourable lords of articles, and which, together with my defences which I have reproduced, I cannot disown or retract, without making myself a transgressor, by destroying what I have builded, and building what I have destroyed, and so bring on myself the guilt and punishment of unfaithfulness to my God, my prince, to the high and honourable court of parliament, to the whole nation, and souls committed to my oversight; which I hope God will not suffer me to do, and whereof I desire to be free in the day when I must give an account of my stewardship. But, my lord, if these things should seem hard, or sound harsh to any at first hearing, which I shall not suppose, then, besides the tranquillity and calm in mine own conscience for the present, which is the very rest of the soul in motion, and affords a strict inward peace and serenity of mind, in the deepest distress, and greatest extremity of outward trouble; besides this, I say, my lord, I want not a confidence, (at least a rational ground for it) that I shall find more favour afterward both of God and men, than if I had flattered with my lips, and, by daubing with untempered mortar, had essayed to heal the wound of this nation slightly.

"This is all, my lord, I intend by way of apology: and as to the indictment itself, I hope it shall be found, when things are weighed in an even balance, that my advocates have so abundantly, to the conviction of all, both in law and reason, demonstrated the irrelevancy in the whole, and each article thereof, that it would be judged a needless undertaking, and a superfluous waste of words, to offer any addition to what, with so much evidence and strength of reason, is by them adduced to invalidate the same; only I judge it incumbent and necessary for me, as a minister of the gospel, to offer a word for explication and vindication, (not of the whole, for that were needless) but of what I have said, and do own in the 6th article, (which yet I do not own as it is libelled) because I hear this is most struck upon, and stumbled at, and may possibly be most liable to mistake and misconstruction: therefore, in order to the removing of any thing that may seem to stumble, or give offence in my practice, as either rash and irrational, or ridiculous and unwarrantable, I humbly desire it may be considered.

"That a ministerial protestation against, or a dissent from any acts or act which a minister knows, and is convinced to be contrary to the word of God, is not a legal impugnation of that or those acts, much less of the authority enacting them, which it doth rather presuppose than deny or impugn; but it is a solemn and serious attested declaration or witness and testimony against the evil and iniquity of these things, which, by the word of God, is a warrantable practice; and here and at this time a necessary duty: and for which way of protesting, or testifying, or witnessing, a minister hath the prophets a pattern for his imitation; as is clear, 1 Sam. viii. 9. "Howbeit, yet protest solemnly unto them, and show them the manner of the king that shall reign over them. Where the Lord, to signify his great resentment and dislike at the people's course and carriage towards him, commands the prophet in his name to protest against their procedure; 'Howbeit, yet protest solemnly unto them,' (saith he) or, as the words are rendered on the margin of our Bible, and spoke to by interpreters, 'notwithstanding, when thou hast solemnly protested against them,' &c. Which reading seems best to agree both with the scope, and what is said ver. 19. It is clear also, Jer. xi. 7. when

1661. the Lord sums up all his serious exhortations to obey his voice, and all his sharp expostulations for not obeying his voice, and keeping his covenant, in this very term 'of protesting earnestly:' 'for I earnestly protested unto your fathers, in the day,' &c. 'rising up early, and protesting, saying, obey my voice.' So that my protestation, testimony, and dissent not being without a precedent practice in the prophets, and so not without divine precept, cannot be called, nor ought to be accounted a contravention of the acts libelled in the indictment; neither can I for this come under the lash of the law, unless it be said and asserted, which I know will be denied with abhorrency and detestation, that these acts do discharge, under pain of treason, what God the supreme Lawgiver commands his servants to do under pain of his displeasure, as they would not, by their unfaithful silence, lose their own, and betray the souls of others. So that take the word 'protesting' in the scripture sense, for solemn declaring and witnessing against sin, and for duty, in which sense alone I take it, it will not be liable to any just exception, nor is it quarrellable, there being nothing more frequent in the word, than such protesting, declaring, and witnessing against sin, and for duty."

"And it is observable to this purpose, that the word in the original, which is rendered 'testify against,' Deut. viii. 19. and xxxi. 22. 2 Kings xvii. 13. 2 Chron. xxiv. 19. Nehem. xiii. 15—21. Psalms l. 7. and elsewhere, is the same word which Jeremiah xi. 7. is rendered to 'protest,' and 'protest earnestly,' and it is so rendered often in the old translation: Junius and Tremellius expound it 'contestor.' And besides, I hope it will not a little contribute to remove what matter of offence is taken at the manner of my testimony, because in the term of 'dissenting' and 'protesting,' if it be considered that all the reformed churches of Christ this day have their denomination and distinction from the church of Rome, from a solemn public protestation against the decree which was made by Charles V., and the estates of the empire, at [Spires in Germany], anno [1529], in prejudice to religion and reformation, though I do not plead a perfect parallel betwixt this and that.

"As to the matter of my protestation, I hope it will be found no less justifiable than the manner, which, I humbly conceive, the word of God doth put beyond exception. I do not presume to play the *jurisconsult*, nor do I pretend to any knowledge in the formalities and subtilties of law, neither am I holden to know them; neither is it a secret to any seen in the municipal law of the nation, how that nothing is, or ought to be accounted for treason, which is not a formal, direct, and downright contravention of some act of parliament made thereanent, with this express certification, 'that the contravention thereof shall be treason.' But there is nothing spoken of by me in the 6th article, which is a direct contravention of any such act, there being no act of parliament which saith, either *recto* or *obliquo*, (directly or indirectly) that it shall be treason in a minister to protest, that is, in the scripture sense already given, to testify, declare, and witness against such acts as are contrary to the covenant, and prejudicial to the work of reformation: therefore I humbly conceive it cannot be said, that I fall under the compass of any such acts, nor am I punishable by them, *cum non entis nulla sunt accidentia, non causæ nullus affectus*.

"But, my lord, besides, my practice seems neither contrary to reason nor religion, and consonant to both, it being commonly taken as a principle, rather than tossed as a problem, that where there is a *jus quæsitum domino*, it is competent, incumbent, and necessary for the servant and ambassador in the behalf and interest of his Lord and Master, to dissent from, and protest against all acts made to the prejudice of that right: but so it is, and there was a right acquired to the Lord my Master, whose servant and ambassador I am, though most unworthy, to wit, the confirmation civil of those covenants and vows made to and with him, for reformation in this church, according to his will revealed in his word, and the obligation civil of the lieges thereunto by the interposition of civil authority; therefore I humbly conceive, that as a right cannot, at least ought not to be taken away in prejudice of a third party, so far less in things concerning the Lord and his interests, the public faith of the kingdom being engaged to God to promote and secure that: so that in this case, for me to have protested for my Master's interests, to whom there was a civil right made, and to dissent from all acts prejudicial to the same, will, I hope, be thought to be the duty of the man who desires to approve himself to God, and who expects in the day of his accounts, the approbation of 'well done, good and faithful servant.'

"These, my lord, with many other obvious and weighty reasons, did at first preponderate with me, and presented themselves with such evidence and conviction of truth and duty, that they were in my weak judgment sufficient enough to persuade and press me to give this testimony against whatsomever is prejudicial to the covenant and work of reformation: and those, I hope, when weighed in the balance of the sanctuary, which is absolutely the evenest one, or in the scales of rectified reason, will still be found to have so much weight in them, as to acquit me of any guilt, and warranting adherence to what I have done.

"Neither can I conceal this, my lord, which is the *primum* and *principale movens*, that when I reflect upon, and remember what I have said and sworn to God, in the day when, with an uplifted hand to the most High, I bound my soul with the bond of the covenant, and engaged solemnly as I should answer to the great God the searcher of hearts, in that day when the secrets of all hearts shall be disclosed, never to break these bonds, nor cast away these cords from me, nor suffer myself directly nor indirectly, neither by terror nor persuasion, to be withdrawn from owning the same.

"And when withal I have some clearness in my conscience, that the matter of the covenant is not indifferent, which if it were, yet in regard of the oath and vows of God which are upon me, it is no more indifferent to me, but puts a subjective obligation upon me, never to be shifted or shaken off at pleasure: the matter, I say, is not indifferent, but necessary, and so hath an objective obligation in it, and did morally oblige antecedaneously to all oaths taken, and acts made thereanent, and unalterably also: I cannot conceive it, I say, my lord, when I think upon the matter thus, that in reflection, whether I consider myself as a Christian, who, when swearing to his own hurt, ought not to change, or in the capacity of a minister of the gospel, and watchman, whose office it is to give warning of sins and snares, in order to the preventing of wrath that follows upon a resolved and deliberate violation of the sacred bonds and engagements to God, or silence at the matter, in others, when called to declare, testify, and bear witness against it, and banishment from the presence of the Lord, and the glory of his power, do never present themselves apart to my judgment; that ever holding true, 'he will not hold him guiltless,' (however men may plead innocent, and palliate the matter) 'who takes his name in vain;' nay, he holds him for his enemy, and will handle him so: and therefore I humbly conceive it ought not to stumble, and I hope it will not seem strange to any, that I cannot make light of so weighty a matter as a covenant made with God, for reformation in his church, according to his will revealed in his word, and righteousness in the land, so long as I believe the obligation to be permanent and perpetual, because of divine imposition: nay, when I lay all temporal disadvantages, which can only affect the outward man, that may be supposed to wait upon the keeping of that covenant, and witnessing for it, in the balance with the hazard of incurring present misery, and future destruction by breaking thereof, (if it be persisted in) the loss appears gain, and the one is downweight by so far, that it seems sufficient to anticipate all deliberation and consultation, as to what is to be done in my case, seeing there needs but small deliberation where there is no choice. My lord, if the cogency of that obligation on my conscience had not been such as it is, and if matters had not stood thus with me, I have not so great a desire to speak at any

1661.

1661. time, but I could have laid my hand upon my mouth at that time when I spoke, and at this time also, and carried as one not concerned in the present affairs.

"I have, my lord, only a desire or two to add to what I have said, and so shall shut up all I intend further to say at present. And, first, I humbly beseech my lord commissioner his grace, and this honourable and high court of parliament, that I may not be looked upon as a disloyal person, either as to my principles or practice: I shall without debate both give and grant, that I was never in case to do his majesty any service which deserves to be publicly mentioned; nor could I have showed myself so void of discretion, as to have spoken any thing to that purpose at this time, if, being charged with disloyalty and treason, the credit of my ministry had not imposed the necessity, and extorted it from me; so that I ought, and do mention it rather for the vindication of my function, than for preventing and removing prejudice against my person. And therefore I humbly crave liberty to say, that though I have not been in case to make my loyalty remarkable by any signal or singular action, yet I have sufficient matter to clear me of disloyalty; and if pure negatives will not prove it, never having acted, or consented to act any thing prejudicial to his majesty, I hope it will be sufficient in a minister of the gospel to bring his loyalty to the quality and consistency of a positive. If in his station he preached against those who usurped his majesty's right, and prayed, they themselves being present, that God would give us governors of our own: if this, I say, be sufficient, either to prove a minister loyal, or to clear him of the stain and imputation of disloyalty; then I want not a cloud of witnesses who can testify my integrity in this matter. And I hope, through the grace of God, never to be tempted, or if tempted, never to yield to such a temptation, whatever measure I meet with to repent or regret that I desired this as a mercy of the Lord, to these much tossed and long troubled kingdoms, 'that he would overturn, overturn, overturn, till he come whose right it was;' and that I rejoiced in the day when he broke the yoke of the oppressors, who kept us captive in our own land, and made the foot of pride who came against us, to slip. Now, my lord, my conscience is so clear, that there was neither iniquity in my heart, nor wickedness in my hands against his majesty, that I have confidence to wish, that the issue and decision of my business were put upon this, whether the informer's carriage, (be who he will, in the place where I live) or mine, during the prevalency and usurpation of the enemy, hath had most loyalty in it? But I do not suspect him to be of so little prudence, as to wish to come to this reckoning.

"The next and last desire which I have at present humbly to propose to my lord commissioner his grace, and the high and honourable court of parliament, before whom I now stand to be judged, and from whom I am holden to expect all equity and justice, is, since your grace and honours have heard my indictment and defences, and are to proceed towards a sentence, that there may be some caution and tenderness as to what shall be determined in this matter: nay, I am obliged to hope and expect, that his grace and the honourable parliament, overlooking the despicableness and worthlessness of the person to be judged, who is really below the indignation of any whom God hath set so high, will carry so in reference to this cause and conclusion, as it may appear, that he who is higher than the highest, who regardeth, and will bring all causes and sentences under a final recognition, is regarded and eyed as standing among the gods in this decision. But as for me, my lord, while I wait for the coming forth of my sentence from his presence, whose eyes behold the things that are equal; I declare, that however I cannot submit my conscience to men, yet I humbly, and as becometh, submit my person. Behold, I am in your hands, do to me whatsoever seemeth good in your eyes.

Mr. M'Vaird's former speech and defences, he here refers to, I have not seen; but from this, and the strong and pathetical reasonings in it, we may have a tolerable view of his case; and though it had not the influ-

CHAP. II.] OF THE CHURCH OF SCOTLAND. 213

ence might have been expected, yet it had some, and the house delayed coming to an issue at this time. He indeed expected a sentence of death, which no way damped him; but his Master had more and very considerable work for him elsewhere. Whether it was from orders from court to shed no more blood, or what was the reason, I know not, but his affair was delayed some time; and upon some encouragement given him of success, upon Monday thereafter, he gave in the following supplication.

To my Lord Commissioner his grace, and the honourable and high court of Parliament, the humble supplication of Mr. Robert M'Vaird, minister of the gospel.

" Sheweth,

" That whereas your grace, and honourable estates of parliament, out of much clemency and tenderness towards me, have sisted your procedure as to final determination, and forborne to draw forth a censure, or pronounce a sentence against me, (which favour I hope shall not be forgotten so long as I can remember any thing, and whereof I resolve I shall not cease to be sensible) until my mind should be further and more fully known, in reference to some particulars in my process; I conceive myself obliged not only in order to my own preservation, but to his grace and your lordships' satisfaction, to declare positively and plainly my mind in these things, which my want of dexterity in expressing myself, hath made more dark, or liable to mistake or misconstruction.

" And whereas I myself have perceived, and am further informed by others, that the main and principal, if not the very thing in my indictment, and all along my defences, and throughout my discourse, which hath been offended at, is, my making use of the words, 'protest' and 'dissent,' as if I had intended thereby a legal impugnation of the acts or authority of parliament; wherein, though I did, in my last discourse, in sobriety, and according to my measure, endeavour at some length to clear my meaning, asserting that I did intend a mere ministerial testimony, against what I conceived to be sin; yet that it may appear that I desire not to contend about words and formalities, since the words 'protest' and 'dissent' are forensic, and for the most part made use of as legal salvos and impugnations, (however the word 'protest' be used several times in scripture by the prophets, as a ministerial testimony and solemn declaration against sin, as I have already hinted and held forth in some particular instances) I am satisfied to change and pass from the expressions of 'protesting' and 'dissenting,' and only to use those of 'testifying' solemn 'declaring,' and 'bearing witness,' by which I still hold the matter of my testimony, the great and only thing first and last intended by me, from which to pass, now especially when the hazard is great, I assure myself, your grace and lordships would not only not allow me, but would count me, in doing so, void of a principle, and unfaithful.

1661.

" I beg leave therefore in all humility to signify to your grace, and this honourable and high court, that I am brought to offer this alteration, not so much, if my heart deceive me not, for the fear of prejudice to my person, (though being but a weak man, I am easily reached by such discomposing passions) as from an earnest desire to remove out of the way any the least or remotest occasion of stumbling, that there may be the more ready and easy access, without prejudice of words, to ponder and give judgment of the matter; and that likewise, if the Lord shall think fit to call me forth to suffer hard things on this account, it may not be said or thought by any, that it was for wilful and peremptory sticking to such expressions, whereas I might, by using others, without prejudice to the matter, and no less significant, have escaped the danger; and lest withal I should seem to insinuate, which is far from my thoughts, and would be a rash judgment, and harsh censuring of others, that a minister of the gospel could not have sufficiently exonered his own conscience as to that matter, without such formal and legal terms and expressions.

" I shall presume to add, that if your grace and the honourable court of parliament shall be graciously pleased to show me favour, then, as I have designed and desired to carry hitherto as a loyal subject,

1661. abstaining from all things that might look like a shadow of reflection upon his majesty's person or government, so I still purpose through grace to continue, as knowing, that giving to God the things that are God's, and to Cesar the things that are Cesar's, and the fearing of God, and honouring the king, are inseparably joined of the Lord together. And however, I do humbly, as becometh, prostrate my person at your grace and honours' feet, to be disposed upon as shall seem good in your eyes. Your grace and the honourable parliament's answer is expected by your truly loyal supplicant.

"Mr. ROBERT M'VAIRD."

This supplication was given in, and though one would think, with what went before, it might have softened the persecutors, yet it had no great effect. Mr. Sharp and his friends resolved now to be rid, as much as they could, of the most eminent of the presbyterian ministers; and therefore he behoved to be banished, which was the highest they could go to, unless they had taken his life. And so, July 5th or 6th, I find the parliament give him for answer, "That they pass sentence of banishment upon the supplicant, allowing him six months to tarry in the nation, one of which only in Glasgow, with power to him to receive the following year's stipend at departure." His master had work for him elsewhere, and that very considerable work too; and he submitted to the sentence, and transported himself and family to Rotterdam, where, for a while, (after the reverend and worthy Mr. Alexander Petrie) he was employed as minister of the Scots congregation at Rotterdam, and edified many. Even thither his persecutors' rage followed him, as we may afterwards hear; and he with some others were again forced to wander further off from their native land. This worthy person died at Rotterdam about twenty years after this.

Thus the acts of this parliament were sealed with blood, and many tears of people who had their beloved pastors torn from them, and scattered into strange lands. The episcopal party will oblige us, if they can show what part of Sir George Mackenzie's vindication accounts for the banishment of Mr. M'Vaird and Mr. Simpson; if they cannot, I hope this will be another instance of its lameness, and an argument of its falseness too: for, if to be banished from one's country, for dissenting from acts against the covenanted work of reformation, was not suffering upon principle and persecution for conscience' sake, pray what can be such? If exhorting people to mourn for the defection of the land, be rebellion, then indeed Mr. M'Vaird was guilty; but I hope every body will allow, that mourning and fighting are two things, unless *preces et lachrymæ sunt arma ecclesiæ*, be judged a rebellious maxim.

Besides those sufferings of ministers to blood and banishment, bonds and bondage, I might insist upon other branches of their sufferings; but they will come in afterwards when they turn more conspicuous in the following years. I have already noticed the attacks made upon synods during this session of parliament, which, as it was a contrivance of Mr. Sharp's, so in itself was an high invasion of the prerogative of the Redeemer, and the exerting the Erastian supremacy before it was an iniquity established by a law. I shall shut up the sufferings of ministers with a hint at the persecution of the tongue, liberally enough bestowed upon them at this time.

Mr. James Sharp, and the noblemen who joined him about the king, under the patronage of chancellor Hyde, and the English highfliers began their designs of overturning the government and discipline of the church of Scotland, by buzzing into the king's ear that wicked lie, and scandalous misrepresentation, that the generality of the old, wise, and learned ministers of the church of Scotland, were for prelacy, at least a moderate episcopacy. This I find some of the ministers, then living, complaining heavily of in their letters; and Mr. Douglas takes off this calumny, as we have heard in the introduction. I have formerly regretted the unhappy difference betwixt the resolutioners and protesters. The woful heats betwixt them effectually stopped any joint application to the king from presbyterian ministers, or general declaration of their principles and adherence to presbyterian government, save what we heard of at some length, section 2d. This silence, and these heats, cunning Mr. Sharp did not fail to improve into this gross untruth, that the bulk of Scots ministers were not against prelacy. Nothing was stuck at by this unhappy man, now entirely corrupted by Hyde's party at London, and bribed by and gaping after what in a little now he got, the archbishopric of St. Andrews. Whereas indeed, excepting a few lax men in the north, under Mr. Sharp's conduct, and promises of bishoprics, who influenced the synod of Aberdeen, to send up to court a flattering address in favour of episcopacy; which, by the way, came afterwards to lie very heavy on the consciences of some of the best of the ministers who signed it; there was indeed nothing could be more disagreeable to the whole of the presbyterian ministers through the kingdom: how far soever they differed in some other things, yet all honest ministers centred in this.

At great length I could make this out by particular instances of Mr. Robert Douglas, Mr. Robert Bailie, Mr. James Wood, Mr. David Dickson, Mr. James Ferguson, and other great men, public resolutioners, with whom the courtiers dealt in the greatest earnestness to accept of bishoprics; but they firmly refused, and used no small freedom with Mr. Sharp, and the noblemen in this matter: Mr. Douglas told the first, that the curse of God would come to him with his bishopric;* and the last, particularly the chancellor, that by putting his hand to the ark of God with others, their families and their own peace at death would be ruined. This was evidently enough made out in several instances. Yet for all this plain dealing, of which afterwards we shall have several instances, these worthy men were laid under this hellish obloquy, and the scourge of tongues. And Thomas Sideserf, son to the bishop of that name, the Diurnaller, made it his daily trade to bespatter the greatest men of this time, without the least provocation or foundation, such as Mr. David Dickson, Mr. Robert Blair, Mr. George Hutcheson, and many others, to that pitch of insolence, that the king was pleased to order that libeller to be silenced.

1661.

I promised in this section to take notice next of the trouble and sufferings several worthy gentlemen were brought to during this session of parliament, and shall be but short upon it, because most of them will come in afterward, in the progress of this history. We shall just now meet with some gentlemen harassed before the council, but it is the processes before the parliament come in here. All could be objected against most of them, was, the ordinary compliance with the English, which every body was necessitate to give. This English guilt was a good handle for prosecuting such who had been active in the work of reformation, and had estates, which our indigent courtiers had their eye upon, and by the act of fines, and otherwise, they reached a good many: though England was indemnified, yet the ancient kingdom must not enjoy that favour for some time.

In January, towards the beginning of this parliament, I find the lairds Arkinglass, and M'Condochy, the first a very considerable family we shall afterward meet with, were forfeited by parliament. They had been cited to appear, and did not come, not being in safety as to their lives, because friends of the family of Argyle: for any thing I know of, nothing further was to be charged on them; and yet they found it not safe to appear. In the unprinted acts I find a decreet D. Ham. against Arkinglass; but whether it referreth to this, I know not.

---

* "In the meantime Mr. Sharp makes for the fashion, a visit to Mr. Robert Douglas at his own house, where after his preface, he informs him it was the king's purpose to settle the church under bishops, and that, for respect to him, his majesty was very desirous Mr. Douglas would accept the archbishopric of St. Andrews. Mr. Douglas answered he would have nothing to do with it (for in his private conversation he used neither to harangue nor to dispute;) Sharp insisted and urged him; Mr. Douglas answered as formerly; whereupon Sharp arose and took leave. Mr. Douglas convoyed him to his gallery door, and after he had passed the door, Mr. Douglas called him back and told him, 'James,' said he, 'I see you will engadge. I perceive you are clear, you will be bishop of St. Andrews, take it, and the curse of God with it.' So clapping him upon the shoulder, he shut his door upon him."—Kirkton's History of the Church of Scotland, p. 135.—*Ed.*

1661. February 1st, the summons of, and indictment against the lord Warriston, William Dundas, and John Hume of Kello, were this day read in parliament; none of them were present: the first we shall again meet with. Whether they were separately indicted, or a general charge given against them all, I know not; all I have seen is the following abstract of the charge against them; that they have contravened many acts of parliament in the following particulars, and therefore are guilty of sedition and treason. The particulars are, " 1st, The protestation at the Cross of Edinburgh against the late king his proclamation. 2d, The convention of estates, 1643, their calling, convening, and assisting thereuntil. 3d, Obstructing the engagement in the year 1648, for the late king's delivery, dissenting therefrom, and voting against the same. 4th, Unlawful convocating the king's lieges, the same year, in opposition to his majesty's forces under the command of duke Hamilton, Monro, &c. 5th, Calling in of the sectarian rebels, in opposition to his majesty's good subjects. 6th, The writing, dictating, and contriving a letter directed to the perfidious Oliver Cromwell, and trysting with him and his officers at the lady Hume's lodgings, tending to the ruin of the late king, and these kingdoms. 7th, The drawing up, consulting, advising, and consenting to the instructions then given in to Sir John Chiesly, to be communicated to the parliament of England, or their committee, for the ends foresaid. 8th, The said Warriston his pleading against Newton Gordon, who was executed, though he had the king's express orders to plead for him. 9th, Their crossing the freedom of the parliament, and people, in their invitation offered to be sent to the king, without limitations, to come to this kingdom. 10th, Their contriving and assisting in the murder of the marquis of Montrose. 11th, Their constant correspondence with Oliver Cromwell in the year 1649, instanced in several particulars. 12th, Their contriving or assisting to the act, called ' the Act of the West-kirk,' and the declaration of the officers of the army then de. 13th, Their drawing, contriving, or senting to the paper called 'the Western Remonstrance,' and the book called ' the Causes of God's Wrath.' Withdrawing themselves from the king's service and army at Stirling, in the time of his greatest necessity. 14th, The said Warriston his sitting in parliament as a peer in England, contrary to his oath, and accepting the office of clerk-register from the usurper Oliver Cromwell, and being president of the pretended committee of safety, when Richard was laid aside."

By the unprinted acts of this session, I find decreets of forfeiture are passed against Sir Archibald Johnstoun of Warriston, and William Dundas of Magdallans, and John Hume of Kello. They did not appear, and consequently had no answers to the above articles; and I may safely enough refer the reader to what hath been said upon most of them, and all of them upon the matter, in the marquis of Argyle's case, and Mr. Guthrie's.

February 22d, I find the laird of Swinton also brought before this parliament. We have seen he was sent down prisoner with Argyle; being a professed quaker, his hat was taken off for him when he came in to the bar. The heads of his indictment were; " 1st, That being a member of parliament, he contrived and voted to the acts made 1648, relative to the king's delivery; and being a member of parliament, contrived and voted to the murder of the marquis of Montrose, lord Huntley, Hary Spotiswood, and others, the king's friends and servants, and to the displacing of the king's officers of estate, and to the deposition of many who suffered for the king's cause. 2d, That being one of the officers of the king's army at Stirling, after the defeat at Dunbar, he kept constant correspondence with the English and Cromwell, and deserted his trust in the king's army, by joining himself with the usurping party. 3d, His going along with Cromwell to Worcester, and there fighting against the king in proper person, against his duty and allegiance. 4th, His sitting and voicing in the pretended parliament of England, for extirpating the king and his family from their due right of government; and exercising those offices and places which Cromwell had bestowed on him for that service."

When his indictment was read, he had a

very accurate and pointed speech in his own vindication, and being interrogate by the chancellor, if he had any more to say for himself? He answered "not positively," but said, " he knew not whether he would make use of any lawyers or not, seeing he walked not now by his own will." The parliament assigned him till the 13th day of March, to give in peremptory defences. By the table of unprinted acts I find, that the parliament forfeited him; but the papists at court interposed in the quaker's behalf, and he had favour shown, though he had as great a share in joining with the usurper as any in the kingdom. After the revolution Swinton's son published his case in print, wherein it seems pretty evident, that no direct forfeiture was passed against his father by this parliament: but, upon a paper formed many years afterwards, Lauderdale possessed the estate of Swinton until his death. By the passages there cited from Swinton's defences at this time, it appears that he went with Cromwell to England about the time of Worcester engagement, as a prisoner. However, it is undeniable this gentleman did openly enough join in with the usurper, and had no small management of our Scots affairs under him.

I find by some papers of this time, that Sir John Chiesly was before the lords of articles, March this year, and it is probable received an indictment, since he was singularly active in the work of reformation: but I have not seen the articles. We shall find him under confinement after this, for many years. Several other worthy gentlemen and ministers were brought to much suffering during the after-part of this year, before the privy council, who after this have much of the persecution I am to describe among their hands. This brings me to

SECT. VI.

Of the establishment and erection of the privy council, their first meeting July 13th, and procedure against particular noblemen, gentlemen, and ministers of the presbyterian persuasion, this year 1661.

WE have seen the civil government of Scotland last year in the hands of the committee of estates, and this year the high court of parliament continued sitting till the 12th of July; and the last day of that month, their acts were in great solemnity proclaimed at the Cross of Edinburgh, and it took from eleven of the clock forenoon, till six at night, to publish those of a public nature. As soon as the parliament was up, next day the privy council met, and a vast power was in their hands.

In this kingdom there had been a long interruption of all our civil courts; and it may not be unacceptable to the reader to give the list of the members of the different courts at this juncture, and the time of their meeting; though it has no great relation to the general subject of this history, it will take up no great room, and may be of some use. Some good time was taken up before persons could be fallen upon to fill up the total vacancies; and in the beginning of April the lists came down from court.

April 5th, as many as were in town of the lords of the session took the oath of supremacy, and *de fideli administratione*, before the parliament; and the parliament ordered them to sit down June 4th, they were as follows. " Sir John Gilmour president, lord Cranstoun, *alias* Oxenford, Sir Archibald Primrose clerk-register, Ley, Halkertoun, Collingtoun, Carden, Tarbet, Mr. James Robertoun, Mr. John Scougal, Mr. Robert Nairn of Strathurd, Mr. Robert Burnet elder, Mr. Andrew Aiton of Kinglassie, Mr. James Dalrymple of Stairs, and Sir Robert Murray." The extraordinary were Rothes, Crawford, Cassils, and Lauderdale. My lord Cranstoun did not accept, and Mr. David Nevoy was put in his place; and when my lord Cassils, upon refusing the supremacy, was declared incapable of public trust, Middleton was put in his room.

June 10th, the exchequer sat down, and the lords of that were, William earl of Glencairn chancellor, Rothes, Marishal lord privy-seal, Lauderdale, Middleton, Halkertoun president of the session, clerk-register, Sir John Fletcher advocate, Sir Robert Murray justice-clerk, Sir James M'Gill of Crawstoun, Sir James Lockhart of Ley, Sir William Fletcher, Sir John Wauchop, Mr.

1661. Robert Burnet elder, Mr. James Robertoun, William Scot of Airdrie, with the treasurer earl of Crawford, or treasurer depute Sir William Bannantyne, one of the quorum.

But the court which the sufferers I am to account for, at least for many years, were mostly before, was the privy council; and in the intervals of parliaments, they had all the executory power in their hand, and assumed little less than a parliamentary power. They were indeed a very sovereign court, and therefore I shall here give the list of them. The earl of Glencairn chancellor, earl of Crawford treasurer, earl of Rothes president of the council, dukes of Lennox and Hamilton, marquis of Montrose; earls, Lauderdale secretary, Errol, Marishal, Mar, Athole, Morton, Eglinton, Cassils, Caithness, Murray, Linlithgow, Hume, Perth, Dunfermline, Wigton, Kellie, Roxburgh, Haddington, Tullibardin, Weems, Southesk, Hartfield, (now Annandale) Callander, Tweeddale, Middleton, Dundee, Newburgh; lords, Sinclair, Halkerton, Duffus; Sir Archibald Primrose, Sir John Fletcher, Sir William Bannantyne, Sir Robert Murray, Sir John Gilmour of Craigmillar, Sir William Fleming, laird of Ley, laird of Blackhall, Sir John Wauchop of Niddry, knight, Gibson of Durie, Sir George Kinnaird of Rossie, Alexander Bruce, brother to the earl of Kincardine, Sir William Scot of Airdrie. The English counsellors added, were, chancellor Hyde, duke of Albemarle, marquis of Ormond, earl of Manchester,* and the principal secretary of state for England. Their quorum is declared to be nine; the chancellor or president, or in their absence, the eldest counsellor to be one of the quorum.

I come now to give some account of the procedure of the privy council, from their registers; and in this section I shall confine myself to the hardships and sufferings particular persons of all ranks were brought under by this arbitrary court, during what is before us of this year. I shall leave their general acts, with relation to the introduction of prelacy, to the following section, where I am to essay some account of this great turn in this church.

July 13th, the council met at Holyroodhouse, and after the public reading of their commission, with their powers, all who were present took the oath of allegiance, which hath been above insert; and then they took the oath of council, a copy of which the curious reader will perhaps desire to see, therefore I insert it.

Oath of the privy counsellors.

"I swear to be a true faithful servant to the king's majesty, as one of his privy counsel; I shall not know nor understand of any manner of thing to be attempted, done or spoken against his majesty's person, crown, or dignity royal, but I shall let and withstand the same to the utmost of my power, and either cause it to be revealed to his majesty himself, or such of his privy council as shall advertise his highness of the same. I shall, in all things to

---

* These English counsellors were not very well calculated for giving advice upon Scottish affairs. Hyde, earl of Clarendon, was unquestionably the man who had most strongly and most successfully impressed upon Charles the propriety of restoring episcopacy in Scotland, an attempt which imbittered his whole reign, and persisted in by his successor, was a principal mean of driving his family into an exile from which they were never recalled. Burnet remarks of Clarendon, " that he was a good chancellor, only a little too rough, but very impartial in the administration of justice. He never seemed to understand foreign affairs well, and yet he meddled too much with them. He had too much levity in his wit, and did not always observe the decorum of his post. He was high; and was apt to reject with too much contempt, those who addressed themselves to him. He had such a regard to the king, that when places were disposed of, even otherwise than as he advised, yet he would justify what the king did, and disparage the pretensions of others, not without much scorn, which created him many enemies. He was indefatigable in business, though the gout did often disable him from waiting on the king, yet during his credit, the king came constantly to him when he was laid up by it." Lord Clarendon's character has been in latter times much less favourably treated. From the light thrown upon it in a later treatise by the Hon. Agar Ellis, there can be no doubt that he was a bigot in religion and a sycophant in politics. As a man, proud and imperious; as a judge, covetous, partial, and unjust; and finally, as a historian, an advocate for tyranny, an apologist for duplicity, and an artful perverter of truth. The following character of Albemarle from the pen of Burnet, is graphic, and we believe perfectly just. " Monk

be moved, craved, and debated in council, faithfully and truly declare my mind and opinion, according to my heart and conscience, and shall keep secret all matters committed and revealed unto me, or that shall be treated of secretly in council; and if any of the same treaties and counsels shall touch any of the counsellers, I shall not reveal it unto him, but shall keep the same until such time, as, by the consent of his majesty or the council, publication shall be made thereof. And generally, and in all things, I shall do as a faithful and true servant and subject ought to do to his majesty. So help me God, and the contents of this book."

When all present had taken this oath, the commission of Sir Peter Wedderburn, to be clerk, was read, and he admitted. The earl of Crawford is president, and the earl of Callender to preside in his absence. They have little before them till the return of the chancellor and Rothes, who came down on the last of August, with what was concerted at court about the change of church government, of which afterwards.

In September, they have a very remarkable process before them, with relation to the earl of Tweeddale. Information had been sent up, it seems, to court, of his speaking in favours of Mr. James Guthrie, when his process was in dependance before the parliament; and it seems this was reckoned a high crime for this nobleman to speak his light in his judicative capacity: therefore he is ordered to be imprisoned; and the execution of this arbitrary step is put in the hands of the council, as one of their first works. This is so odd a management, and forebodes so much oppression and severity in this reign, that I shall venture to say nothing upon it, but give the progress of it from the original records.

Upon the 13th of September, the following letter from the king is read, ordering the earl of Tweeddale to be made a prisoner.

" Right Trusty, &c. Having received information of some speeches uttered by the earl of Tweeddale, in the trial of Mr. James Guthrie attainted and executed, which, as we are informed, did tend much to the prejudice of our authority, we require you to commit the said earl to the castle of Edinburgh, there to remain till we have examined the business, and declare our further pleasure; and that he be kept in durance, but not as close prisoner. Given at our court at Whitehall, September 7th, 1661.

" LAUDERDALE."

These orders were immediately executed, and the earl entered prisoner in the Castle; and September 17th, he sent the following petition to the council.

" *To the Right Honourable, the Lords of his Majesty's Privy Council, John earl of Tweeddale*

" Humbly sheweth,

" Whereas your lordships have been pleased, upon a command from his majesty, to commit me to the Castle, and being exceedingly affected with his majesty's displeasure, I desire to express to your lordships the grief of my heart, for whatsoever has been the occasion of procuring such resentment from so gracious a prince, of whose favour I have so largely shared, and to whose commands I account a perfect submission acceptable service to God, and suitable to the duty of every subject. How observant of them I have been, and what ready submission I have given, your lordships can witness: being filled with the sense of

---

was ravenous as well as his wife, who was a mean contemptible creature. They both asked and sold all that was within their reach, nothing being denied them for some time, till he became so useless, that little personal regard could be paid him. But the king maintained still the appearances of it; for the appearance of the service he did him, was such that the king thought it fit to treat him with great distinction even after he saw into him, and despised him.' " Ormond," we are told by the same authority, was " a man of a graceful appearance, a lively wit, and a cheerful temper, a man of great experience, decent even in his vices, for he always kept up the form of religion. He was firm to the protestant religion, and so firm to the laws, that he always gave good advices, but when bad ones were followed he was not for complaining too much of them."—" The earl of Manchester was of a soft and obliging temper, of no great depth, but universally beloved, being both a virtuous and a generous man."—Burnet's History of his Own Times, Edin. Ed. vol. i. pp. 133, 138, 139.—*Ed.*

1661. my obligations, and engaged in duty, to be thus clouded with his majesty's displeasure, is a burden I am unable to bear. May it therefore please your lordships to give such an account of mine actings, as I may be restored to his majesty's favour, and to interpose for my enlargement, that at least my imprisonment may be changed to a confinement, at my house at Bothams, in regard of my wife's condition, now near the time of her delivery.

" TWEEDDALE."

The clerk is ordered to have a draught of a letter ready against to-morrow. Accordingly, September 18th, a letter is signed by the council to the secretary, the tenor of which is subjoined.

" My Lord,

" At our last meeting, which was occasioned by his majesty's letter, for committing the earl of Tweeddale prisoner to the castle of Edinburgh, we issued orders for it; which were no sooner intimate to him, but he immediately obeyed, and entered prisoner. From him we have since received a petition, which we send enclosed, to be presented by your lordship to his majesty; and find ourselves obliged to give this testimony in his behalf, that, in the late meeting of council, when the matter of church government was under deliberation, he did heartily comply with his majesty's commands, and carry himself as a faithful counsellor, and loyal subject. When his majesty's further pleasure shall be signified as to this particular, we shall be ready to prosecute the same; and are, my lord, your lordship's affectionate friends."

As in Sederunt.

Matters stood thus till next council-day, October 1st, when was read the following letter from the king.

" Right trusty, &c. We received yours of e 7th of this instant, and have seen the proclamation you have published, in obedience to what we recommended by our letter of the 14th of August; with which we are so well satisfied, that we thought fit to give you hearty thanks. We got notice of the commitment of the earl of Tweeddale, by our order: you shall examine what his carriage was at the late vote in parliament, which condemned Guthrie, and report the same speedily to us, to the end that we may declare our further pleasure. And so we bid you heartily farewell.

" LAUDERDALE."
" Whitehall, September 23, 1661."

Jointly with this, there came a letter from the earl of Lauderdale to the council, whereof the tenor is :

" May it please your lordships,

" In obedience to your lordships' commands, I did yesterday present the earl of Tweeddale's petition. After reading of it, his majesty was graciously pleased to order the change of his prison in the castle, to a confinement at his house: and his majesty hath commanded me to signify his pleasure to your lordships, that he be confined to the Bothams, and three miles about it, until, upon report from your lordships, the king shall declare his further pleasure. This is all I have in command, who am, may it please your lordships,

" Your lordships' most humble servant,
" LAUDERDALE."
"Whitehall, September 26, 1661."

After the reading of those letters, the council came to the following resolve, " Ordered, that in pursuance of his majesty's orders, the earls of Haddington, Annandale, and Callender, the lord president of the session, the lord register, lord advocate, and lord Lee, do examine the earl of Tweeddale, in the castle of Edinburgh, the morn (to-morrow) at nine of the clock, anent his carriage at the late vote in parliament, which condemned James Guthrie, and to take his own declaration under his hand, upon the several votes which passed upon that process whereupon he is to be interrogate, and report the same next morning."

This was accordingly done, and to-morrow, October 2d, the lords appointed to examine the earl, gave in his declaration, signed by himself and the lord president; the tenor whereof follows:

At the Castle of Edinburgh, October 2, 1661.

" The earl of Tweeddale being interrogate, what his carriage and expressions were at the vote in parliament, in Mr. Guthrie's process, dated 12th of April, 1661, and being first interrogate upon the first member of the vote, concerning the first two articles of Guthrie's dittay, wherein he was charged with the Remonstrance and Causes of God's Wrath, which were found relevant to bring the pannel under the compass of the acts of parliament mentioned in the said vote made against slanderous speeches against his majesty's person and authority: the said earl of Tweeddale doth declare, that though he was clear in his judgment, and did express so much, that the first two articles brought the pannel under the compass of the law, and that the law made him liable to the sentence of death; yet some circumstances, as the distraction and disorder men were then under, and the epidemic distemper of those times, and the restraining power of the law having been of a long time sadly abated, and upon the consideration of his majesty's compassionate clemency, and construction of the failings of those times, which inclined him to some other punishment than death, he conceived and voted that article not relevant as to death. As to the 2d member, concerning the petition and instructions mentioned in the vote, he declares, that, to the best of his memory, he had no discourse thereupon, and doth not remember what was his vote. As to the 3d, concerning the declinature, he declares, that, having heard the process only once read, and not having heard distinctly the debate upon that article, and being the first criminal process he was ever at, he thought himself unfit to judge in a particular of so large a debate upon once reading, and so could not be clear to give a positive vote at that time, and therefore was *non liquet*."

"TWEEDDALE,

"JO. GILMOUR, P."

Upon the producing of this, the council order the earl, "to be put to liberty from his confinement, and to repair to his house, and confine himself within the same, and three miles about, till his majesty's pleasure shall be further known; he always finding sufficient caution, under the pain of one hundred thousand merks, to appear, or return to the castle, whensoever his majesty or the council shall order the same, and in the meanwhile keep his confinement." And further, October 3d, they declare, "that all of their number who were members of parliament, and present when the said votes passed, as to all the articles of the declaration they remember, he went not alongst with them in the affirmative which passed in the parliament." That same day, the council send a letter to the king, narrating all the steps (above) they had taken, with the declaration. This is all I meet with in the registers, about this odd treatment of a nobleman. Towards the beginning of May next, the confinement was taken off, and the earl was in very much favour. What were the springs of this prosecution, I cannot say: perhaps it was not so much from any special design against the earl, as to fright people afterwards into their measures, by those terrible inquiries into votes and speeches in parliament. I have scarce ever met with a parallel in history. We see this noble lord's reasons for what he did in his own declaration. His imprisonment about three weeks, for his vote in parliament, and the exorbitant bail demanded of him, are what cannot be defended, and will not endure reasoning; and I have seen none of the advocates of this period, who set up for vindicating this unaccountable procedure against the earl of Tweeddale.

I come now forward, to hint at some begun sufferings of ministers this year, before the council. September 17th, "a letter is ordered to be writ to the sheriff of Clydesdale, or his depute, to apprehend two ministers come from Ireland, whose names the chancellor is to condescend on; and they are to be convoyed from sheriff to sheriff till they come to the magistrates of Edinburgh." I know no more about them than is in this article of the council registers: it seems plain they were two presbyterian ministers, who had fled over from the persecution of the prelates in Ireland, and probably did not know of the parliament's proclamation above narrated, discharging all Scotsmen to come over thence without passes.

1661. The reverend Mr. Robert Blair, minister of the gospel at St. Andrews, was one whom Mr. Sharp could not bear to be any longer at his work there, though he was under particular obligations to Mr. Blair; and therefore matters are so ordered as the council must attack him, October 1st, this year. He was a minister of known piety, gravity, prudence, and great loyalty to the king; and nothing could be laid to his charge, save that he was a presbyterian minister, and now stood in Mr. Sharp's way. Thus, upon some information or other, wherein Mr. Sharp took care not to be seen, the council the foresaid day order the clerk to write to the magistrates of St. Andrews, upon the sight of his letter, to go to their minister Mr. Robert Blair, and in name of the council to demand him to present himself before my lord chancellor at Edinburgh, betwixt and the 9th instant, that by his lordship he might know the council's pleasure. I find no more about Mr. Blair till November 5th, where the registers bear, "information being given of some particulars against Mr. Robert Blair, ordered, that the earls of Linlithgow, Hume, Haddington, lord advocate, and Sir George Kinnaird, examine the said Mr. Robert upon these particulars, and report to the next meeting of the council." The next meeting is November 7th, and that day I find a blank in the records of near half of the page, and upon the margin, act, Mr. Robert Blair. Whether they were ashamed to insert what they went into against so great and good a man, whom every body almost had a regard to, or what was the reason, I cannot say. We shall meet with him again next year, when, in September, the council declare his church vacant.

Last year we heard of the reverend Mr. William Wiseheart, minister at Kinneil, his confinement: and now I find an application by the presbytery of Linlithgow, to the council, November 7th, which is all I know in this matter, and set it down, with the council's answer.

"Anent a supplication presented by Mr. James Ramsay, Mr. Patrick Schaw, and Mr. John Wauch, commissioners, for themselves, and in name and behalf of the remanent brethren of the presbytery of Linlithgow, showing, that whereas the parish of Kinneil, within the bounds of the said presbytery, has long lien destitute of the free exercise of the ordinances, except what the presbytery was able to provide for them, which was but little, having eight kirks besides that to provide with preaching· and this the presbytery's burden of the said parish of Kinneil doth lie upon them, through the imprisonment and confinement of Mr. William Wiseheart minister there, now these thirteen months bypast. The presbytery did consider of the condition of the said kirk, and minister thereof; and having conferred with himself, have proceeded that length, that if his imprisonment and confinement were taken off, access will be had for the present planting of the said kirk with some other, whom the patron shall be pleased to name: desiring therefore that such course may be taken, for taking off the imprisonment and confinement of the said Mr. William Wiseheart, as may give access to the presbytery to proceed in the plantation of the said church; as the petition bears. Which being at length read, heard, and considered, the lords of council do take off the said Mr. William Wiseheart his confinement, and declare him to be free thereof, and of his band of caution given in by him for that effect."

What were the particular occasions of the favour shown to the two following ministers, confined August, 1660, I have not learned at this distance: but November 21st, the council gives warrant to the lord chancellor, to grant liberty to Mr. John Scot minister at Oxenam, to exercise the function of the ministry within his own parish, notwithstanding the restraint put upon him. And December 10th, "the council, upon good considerations, take off the restraint laid upon Mr. Gilbert Hall minister at Kirkliston, discharging him from preaching; and grant him warrant to exercise the ministerial function as formerly before the restraint was put on him, he behaving himself peaceably, as becometh a faithful minister." Both these were very worthy ministers, and, it seems, got some interest made

CHAP. II.] OF THE CHURCH OF SCOTLAND. 223

with the counsellors. This is all I meet with before the council, as to particular ministers this year.

November this year, I find a great many west country gentlemen brought to a vast deal of trouble, for their joining with colonel Strachan, and going in with the forces to Nithsdale, 1650: and a fine of 2000 pounds sterling is laid on the lairds of Rowallan, Cunninghamhead, Nether Pollock, Earlston, Aikenhead, Halcraig, and others, who had appeared firm presbyterians, and active in the work of reformation. But this process not coming to a close this year, I shall delay it till I bring it in altogether afterwards. A good many other gentlemen in other parts were brought to trouble this year, as we may hear when I come to the detail of their severer sufferings, in the succeeding years: and therefore I come now forward to the proceedings of the council, as to church government, and the regal introduction of episcopacy.

SECT. VII.

Of the regal erection of bishops, with some new attacks made upon the judicatories of the church.

As soon as this pliant session of parliament rose, and the council was constitute to manage all in the intervals of parliament, Middleton and the courtiers haste up to London, where, no doubt, they were most graciously received. The subjects of Scotland were now made as obsequious as ever the former set had been reckoned rebellious. The bishops of England in a very particular manner caressed our Scots peers, for procuring them another national church among all the reformed, to bear them company in their prelatical way.

When their report is made, and the plan laid at London, formerly concerted by Mr. Sharp, and the other two who went up, for modelling this church *a la mode d'Angleterre*, Mr. Sharp comes down again, and the council fall to execute the orders and letters sent down from London, and overturn one of the best established churches since the re-

formation, by their proclamations. 1661.
Mr. Sharp carries up with him three of his brethren, whom he thought good, and who were as he, thirsting after "dominion over their brethren." Them we have sent down, consecrated, and empowered to make the rest of their order. These, with such as they adopted, were the great authors of all the troubles which followed for many years upon the presbyterians in Scotland. This unscriptural office imposed by the king, and set up by the council, is next year confirmed in parliament; and the consequence is the laying desolate many hundreds of congregations in one day, as we shall hear.

The estates of the kingdom of Scotland, as soon as they convened after the revolution, among other things declare, "that prelacy, and the superiority of any office in the church above presbyters, is, and hath been a great and insupportable grievance to this nation, and contrary to the inclinations of the generality of the people, ever since the reformation, we having been reformed by presbyters from popery." This being the sense of the representatives of this nation, when at their full freedom, and really themselves, and under the nearest views, and most intimate knowledge of prelacy that had been rampant for twenty-seven years, I may well represent the introduction of prelates by the king, without the parliament, who had indeed put a blank in his hand, as a great hardship, and one of the first branches of the sufferings of this church. It was contrary to the most solemn establishments, ratified by the king himself, sealed with an oath, and contrary to the inclinations of the people. And from this plain invasion upon the right of Scotsmen, proceeded much of the bloody persecution which followed. Indeed the whole of the severity, hardships, and bloodshed, from this year until the revolution, was either actually brought on by the bishops, procured by them, or done for their support.

Prelacy was never popular in Scotland, no not in the days of ancient ignorance: our reformation from popery, and reformers were quite upon another bottom. Abstracting from the arguments from antiquity and

1661. history, the common people in Scotland used to advance unanswerable arguments, and exceptions of a more convincing nature to them, against episcopacy. They had observed almost all the bishops of Scotland to have been either patrons or patterns of profaneness; and these few among them who had any reputation formerly, as soon as they became prelates, changed remarkably to the worse; and, as Beza had foretold, in his letter to Knox, bishops first brought in epicurism, and then atheism; religion and piety first withered under their shadow, and wickedness grew prodigiously. They used to say, those changelings being perjured themselves, like the fallen angels, they endeavoured to involve as many as they could in their guilt. They noticed likewise visible disasters and curses falling upon their persons and families, yea, upon all such who were active in bringing in prelates to this church. They believed firmly, that as the branch leads to the root, so episcopacy brought in popery; and therefore bishops, by Scotsmen, generally speaking, were looked upon as the pope's harbingers. Upon all those accounts, founded upon feeling and experience, the body of the people in Scotland were very much against their re-introduction.

Upon the other hand, some of our noblemen were as heartily for them. When our noblemen and Mr. Sharp were at court, and had the church government in Scotland under their consideration, the commissioner and chancellor were resolute for bishops, as what would please the king, or at least some people about him, whose favour they needed. Lauderdale secretary, Crawford treasurer, and duke Hamilton for some time opposed them. The secretary with some warmth urged, that the introduction of bishops will evidently lose to the king, the affections of the best of his subjects in Scotland; and bishops would be so far from enlarging the king's power, that they would prove a burden upon it. Both which accordingly came to pass. Those debates, I am told, continued some days, and it was here the foundation of discord was laid betwixt Middleton and Lauderdale, which issued in the ruin of the first. At length Lauderdale yielded to the current that was against him, and his master's alleged inclinations. A little thereafter, the chancellor, in a conversation with Lauderdale, desired him not to mistake his conduct in that affair, for indeed he was not for lordly prelates, such as had been in Scotland formerly, but only for a limited, sober, moderate episcopacy. The secretary, it is said, replied, " My lord, since you are for bishops, and must have them, bishops you shall have, and higher than ever they were in Scotland, and that you will find." And indeed he felt it more than once in a few years.

The reasons inducing the courtiers to be so much for episcopacy, after their declarations and engagements against it, were many. They found it necessary to gratify the prevailing party at this time in England, who were highfliers in this matter; and since the union of the two crowns, the prevailing party in England had a vast influence upon our managers in Scotland. It was well known, that prelates in Scotland had never been reprovers of great men, do what they would; their only sting was against presbyterians, and they had the discretion to overlook courtiers' faults, and were no way so strict as presbyterians. The first article of their creed was nonresistance, and their constant doctrine, that kings could do no wrong; ignorantly or wilfully mistaking that brocard of the law, as if the meaning were, that nothing a king does is to be reckoned wrong; whereas the true sense of it is, that *jure* he can do no wrong, that is, even the prerogative does not impower him to do wrong, nor can excuse him when he hath done it, and much less justify him. They were the best tools that could be for arbitrary government; the king was still sure of the bishops' vote in parliament in all ordinary cases: and it was well known they would quickly plant the church with a set of ministers, who would instil principles of unbounded loyalty into their people, till they were first made slaves, and then beggars. All of them were for the king's absolute illimitable power, and some for his universal property, and making him master of the people's purse, without the trouble of calling parliaments.*

When I am giving some account of the springs of this dismal alteration made in the

---

* These observations seem to have been copied almost verbatim from Kirkton, though they are a little softened, especially when the king is mentioned, Wodrow, though he was exceedingly loyal himself, being probably ashamed of the senseless servility of the presbyterians of this period. "The king," says Kirkton, "even as his father, was resolute for bishops, notwithstanding his oath to the contrary, he knew well bishops would never be reprovers of the court, and the first article of their catechism was nonresistance. They were men of that discretion as to dissemble great men's faults, and not so severe as the presbyterians. They were the best tools for tyranny in the world; for doe a king what he would, their daily instruction was kings could doe no wrong, and that none might put forth a hand against the Lord's anointed and be innocent. The king knew also he could be sure of their vote in parliament, desire what he would, and that they would plant a set of ministers which might instil principles of loyalty into the people, till they turned them first slaves, then beggars. They were all for the king's absolute power, and most of them for the universal propriety, and to make the people believe the king was lord of all their goods, without consent of parliament; and for these reasons, and such as these, they were so much the darlings of our kings, that king James was wont to say, 'no bishop no king,' so bishops the king would have at any rate. Meantime the king's character stood so high in the opinion and idolatrous affections of the miserable people of Scotland, that a man might more safely have blasphemed Jesus Christ, than derogate in the least from the glory of his perfections. People would never believe he was to introduce bishops till they were settled in their seats; and there was a certain man had his tongue bored for saying the duke of York was a papist, which the priests at London would not believe upon his coronation day; and that day he went first to mass, fourteen of them choosed for their text Psalm cxviii. 22. making him the corner-stone of the protestant religion. As for Charles, many a time did the ministers of Scotland, and even many godly men among them, give the Lord hearty thanks that wee had a gracious protestant king, though within a few years he published it to the world that he lived a secret papist all his life, and died a professed one with the hostie in his mouth. Alace that the world should be so ignorant of that which concerns them so much!"—Kirkton's History of the Church of Scotland, p. 132.

The illustrations which these passages afford of the loyalty of the presbyterians, should go far to shut the mouths of those who perpetually rail against the covenanters, on account of their rebellious and democratical spirit. The facts of the case are precisely the reverse; the presbyterians entertained the justest sentiments on the subject of civil obedience; and if they are to be blamed at all on this head, it is because they carried their attachment to monarchy and to Charles, to a questionable excess.—*Ed.*

church of Scotland, I think it proper to insert here the sentiments of that truly great man Mr. Robert Douglas, who, for his prudence, solidity, and reach, was equalled by very few in his time; and he had occasion to know the inmost springs of this great turn, and therefore I will give the reader a pretty large extract from an original paper of his, entitled, "A brief Narration of the coming in of Prelacy to this Kirk," communicated to me by his worthy son; and that in his own words. I choose rather to insert it here than in the appendix, because it contains several particulars relating to the history of this turn, which I might have insert in their own places before, but thought it better to leave them altogether to this place.

"By the mercy of God prelacy was rejected by our kirk, yea, all ranks of persons, from the highest to the lowest, were solemnly bound to extirpate it, and never to assume it again; all judicatories civil and ecclesiastic were bound, and every person engaged by oath; and this kirk was free of it by the space of twenty-two years and more. We were certain years indeed under the tyranny of usurpers; yet at that time we had the liberty of preaching, and meeting in our kirk judicatories without interruption, save in so far as interruption was made to the assembly, occasioned by our ownselves, upon design to have power in their hands.

"During this time of our bondage, the whole nation lying under their feet, yea, a great many taking the tender, renouncing the king and his family, and all the rest under the power of the enemy's sword, our king in a banished condition, none to act for him, or serve him, only not joining with the usurper, yet not able to do any thing for the king, but to pray, and hold up his condition to God.

"It was maliciously asserted, that we left off praying for him: the truth of this is, the ministers who all stood for the king and his government, did never leave off praying for him, till they acquainted him by letters, and had advice what to do. The return of our letter came, showing that it was meet to forbear for a time, that we might be the

1661. better in case to keep up his interest in the hearts of his people. After this it was resolved among us to forbear naming him publicly in our prayers; yet, notwithstanding of that, the prayers of ministers were so plain for the king's interest, that the usurpers themselves confessed it had been better to suffer us to name him, than pray as we did, for it kept up affection for him in the hearts of the people. Yea, we prayed longer for the king by name, than any did appear to fight for him; all arms were laid aside, and no visible opposition in all the three kingdoms; and as long as any party appeared for him in Ireland, we prayed and named him king.

" When all had left the king, we never complied with the usurper against his interests, as many did, who nevertheless are counted very loyal, because they can comply with all times and changes.

" Thus matters continued, till God suffered divisions to fall in among the chief captains of the usurpation, Monk and Lambert. The last brought his forces towards Newcastle, and Monk marched from Edinburgh to meet him, but was hindered by some articles offered him by those in power, which made him retire, having a purpose to subscribe. At this time no man appeared: divers noblemen dealt with me to go and speak with Monk, which I did early in the morning, before his officers met to agree upon the articles. By the blessing of God, speaking with him succeeded, and he resolved to march, and not return. It is true, I knew he had no great inclination to bring home the king; but I was persuaded, that if they were divided, it would occasion at last the king's bringing home.

" Monk went to London, and Lambert's forces evanished. When he came to London he discovered his averseness to bring home the king; only the people desired it, and a letter was writ to him from Scotland, pressing him to fall in with every body's desires, which were so earnest, that it was thought a call from God. The return to this letter declared his averseness from the thing.

" At that time, the best affected in Ireland had sent letters, requiring us to be stedfast to the king, and promising all assistance. These I showed to the chief in this land, and wrote another letter to Monk, requesting him to undertake for the king, and if he did it not that it would be done to his hand; but I did not write by whom. Whatever was his averseness, God overruled him and others there, so that, upon some discontentment general Monk met with, he inclined to be for the king.

" The parliament of England meeting, when Scotland might call neither parliament nor meeting, being under the feet of the usurpers, some king's men from Scotland did write to that parliament, before they had resolved to call the king, dealing earnestly for king and covenant; and a paper, entitled, The Judgment of sober-minded men in Scotland, was sent up, (as hath been noticed in the Introduction; and the paper is inserted there.)

" Now all being ready to call in the king, all the wellwishers to the king and kirk wished that he might come in upon the terms of the covenant; but the English who had a hand in his coming home, would have him brought in without conditions and limitations, giving out that he would satisfy all his subjects in their desires.

" Our Scotsmen, not being a free nation at this time, did not much meddle in any messages to the king. Mr. Sharp, at this time at London, is pitched upon, at the charges of honest men, to go to the king with letters from presbyterian ministers here; and Monk was writ to, that he might have liberty and a free passage to the king. He went, delivered our letters, and wrote back the king's gracious reception of our letters, assuring us of a satisfactory answer.

" Upon this we wrote a letter to our brethren in London, that we were assured of their stedfastness, and gave them our advice then to care for the presbyterian interest, when the king came to London; which was delivered by a person of quality, Sharp not being returned. From time to time he wrote, that we needed not doubt of the king's favour to our presbyterian government.

CHAP. II.] OF THE CHURCH OF SCOTLAND. 227

" The king was brought home with joy, and if his majesty had kept his covenant engagements, he had been the happiest king that ever reigned since the days of Christ: but this was marred by the liberty episcopal men took, and the parliament's inclination to bring in bishops or prelates, which saddened the hearts of many, and prelatical government was established in England.

" Meanwhile, we wrote exhortations to our brethren in England to stedfastness; and Mr. Sharp wrote to us, that bishops would be set up in England, but we needed not fear episcopal government in Scotland, since the king had given assurances to the contrary; and he did earnestly entreat, that we would not meddle with England, for it would be provoking, and it were enough to have our own government settled: but we did not believe, if episcopal government were settled in England, we could be free of the temptation of it now, more than in former times.

" The king, to give us assurance, wrote a letter to the presbytery of Edinburgh, which was communicated to other presbyteries: and the most part of presbyteries and synods made a return, expressing their thankfulness for his majesty's favour to the established government of presbytery. It was said, that Sharp alleged the letter spoke of the government settled by law, which was episcopal. Indeed this was objected to some of us ministers of Edinburgh; but it was clearly shown, that the king's letter could have no other meaning than the present presbyterial government, because it mentions good services done by presbyterians, and the general assembly at St. Andrews countenanced by his majesty's commissioner, and afterward by himself. And it was told them, to give another meaning, was an intolerable reflection upon his majesty's honour and reputation.

" Besides those letters from Sharp, giving assurance of no change with us, when he came down, he dealt with all not to meddle with the government in England, seeing our own was made sure.

" When the parliament met, Middleton sent for me at his coming, telling me the king had commanded him to do so. We spoke at large about the condition of our kirk; and I told him my mind freely, if the king would not break the covenant, nor alter our government, I could assure him his majesty would get as much as his heart could wish, with the affections and love of all the people; but many inconveniences would follow, if there were a change of government; for prelates never yet proved profitable to kirk or commonwealth. He assured me, and I think it was true, he had no instructions for the change of the government, and we were still borne in hand that there would be no change.

1661.

" In the meantime Sharp fearing supplications, dealt earnestly there should be none; but finding himself disappointed, he caused the commissioner send for some of us. The commissioner, chancellor, and some others present, did allege, that the king's letter did not bear any thing of presbyterian government settled, but the government settled by law, which was episcopal. The answer to this was what I told already, that it could have no other meaning; and most part of the church had returned answer according to that meaning. Always we were still borne in hand, that there was no warrant from the king for this change.

" And upon this the presbytery of Edinburgh was dissolved without doing any thing. Yet in the afternoon, hearing they were upon a rescissory act in the articles, the presbytery were convened, and that same day the supplication was read, and approven by all present, ministers and ruling elders, for keeping the covenant and presbyterial government. This was sent to the commissioner by Mr. John Smith, and Mr. Robert Lawrie ministers of Edinburgh, and Mr. Peter Blair minister of the West Kirk. They went to the commissioner and delivered it, but he in wrath rejected it. And after that, the parliament passed the act rescissory of all that was in favours of the covenant, or presbyterial government. So here was a deed wherein a covenant kirk government, solemnly settled in the land, is solemnly broken; a covenant taken before God, men, and angels, broken before God,

1661. men and angels: this was the day of the beginning of our sorrow, by breaking covenant, and dissolving government; and it was known that the king's consent was given after that act was passed.

"A little after bishops were brought in, and Sharp and others sent for to receive new ordination, that the presbyterian stamp might be abolished, and a new prelatical stamp taken on. Our kingdom lately held of usurpers, now our kirk must hold of an usurping kirk. Those are the men, Sharp, Fairfowl, Lightoun, and Hamilton, that betrayed the liberties of the kirk of Christ in Scotland.

"Sharp came to me before he went to London, and I told him, the curse of God would be on him for his treacherous dealing. And that I may speak my heart of this Sharp, I profess I did no more suspect him in reference to prelacy, than I did myself." What follows I have formerly given in the Introduction, p. 24th, and then Mr. Douglas goes on.

"I profess I blame not the king, for he was not well acquainted with our government; and for any acquaintance he had, he met with some hasty dealing: but our evil proceeded from ourselves; some noblemen thinking to make themselves great by that way, were very instrumental in the change, and being wearied of Christ's yoke, they promised unto themselves liberty, they themselves becoming servants of corruption. They thought they would have more liberty under that loose government, than under presbytery, which put too great a restraint upon their vices. And with them were ministers who loved the world, especially that Sharp, who, as Peter speaks, 2 Epistle ii. 15. 'He went astray, following the ways of Balaam who loved the wages of unrighteousness.' Yea, he was in a worse state than Balaam, for God restrained Balaam, so that he confessed he durst not, for a house full of gold, wrong God's people: but God put no restraint on that covetous person; but he cursed whom God blesseth, and he betrayed the people of God for promotion and gain. That of the apostle is verified in him. 'The love of money is the root of all evil, which some having coveted after, have fallen from the faith, and pierced themselves through with many sorrows.'

"Yet we must not look on this man as alone guilty; he was the chief apostate and prime leader to this wicked course, but others are guilty, even all who followed his vices, making the truth of God to be evil spoken of. God himself will be avenged upon them, for they dealt treacherously in his covenant.

"And that I may further free the king's majesty of this thing, whatever his opinion might be of episcopal government, and his wish and ardent desires to have it, yet he was sparing to impose it in this kingdom, as is evident by this one thing.

"When we heard the king was dealt with to set up bishops in Scotland, we did write a letter to the secretary to be communicate to his majesty, signed by five of our hands, persuading him that they were very considerable who were against prelacy, if he would take the trial of it by a general assembly; and told him, if he made a change in the government, his majesty would be forced to trouble the best men, who were his best friends in his low estate, men who had all due respects towards him, and were most loyal, only they could not in conscience admit of the prelatical government, as being against the mind of Christ, and their own engagements. I know that when this letter was read in the Scots council, his majesty was at a stand: but those noblemen, with Sharp, did bear in upon him, that it was the desire of his nobles, and the generality of the kingdom, and only a few inconsiderable persons against it.

"All this being done, we must have episcopacy; and prelates are set up by the ordination of bishops of another nation. Thus I have brought those men to the chair of worldly estate. I must in the next place show you what means were used to keep them in the chair." Mr. Douglas goes on to narrate the several acts of council made this and the next year, and to make reflections upon their unaccountableness. In our progress we will meet with those acts of council, and I shall take notice of any thing needful from his remarks, as I go through them.

We have seen the parliament putting the whole power, as to church affairs, into the king's hands, by their 16th act, which was passed March 29th. I have formerly made remarks upon that act, and it is really of an odd tenor, for it is only declaratory, that the king resolves, and will do, as in the act and particularly settle the government as he finds most agreeable to scripture and monarchy. The parliament does not desire or empower the king to do so, but only consent to his declarations, that he will do so: so that I really know not what foot the introduction of episcopacy stands upon by this act. The king declares what he is to do, declares so with advice and consent of parliament; but I do not see that the parliament can be said either to empower him to make this change, or do it themselves. Indeed next session they actually put all church power in his hand, after episcopacy is settled by the council, in pursuance of the king's letters to them: but still prelacy does not appear a proper parliamentary settlement in Scotland, but a mere act of the king's assumed power. But I shall leave this to the gentlemen skilled in law.

The king, by this power which he is pleased in parliament to declare he hath, emits a proclamation concerning church affairs, June 10th, even when the parliament is sitting, which I have annexed in a former part of the work.* And there, after narrating the foresaid act, is graciously pleased to declare his acceptance of the parliament's duty and affection, in consenting, as I take it, to his own declaration of his power; and that he purposes to settle the government of the church, as he sees good; and discharges all petitions to him with relation to this.

To me there appears a very remarkable inconsistency in this proclamation. It is promised, the government of the church shall be settled to the satisfaction of the kingdom: and yet a few lines after, all subjects, ministers, or others are discharged to meddle with the government of the church, or address him thereanent. One must think the king had no great mind to know what was satisfying to his subjects, when he so peremptorily discharges all application to him; certainly he was already determined what to do, to whatever side his subjects' inclination ran. There is another piece of the proclamation I cannot easily knit together. The king allows synods, presbyteries, and sessions to meet for the present, and yet peremptorily discharges them to meddle with the public government of the church any way, particularly by petitioning. Here Mr. Douglas remarks, " that the like has not been heard, that subjects should be debarred from showing their grievances to competent judicatories, to be redressed. This way the king was to be kept from information, and the managers were without control, and honest men were borne down without remedy." It is plain, that the freedom of addressing and petitioning the sovereign is never discharged, but when some scandalous and unhappy measures are concerting to enslave them, in which no interruption is desired.

1661.

The allowance in the proclamation for synods, &c., to meet and act, was a mere jest. It was well enough known synods did not now meet, and before their ordinary time of meeting in October, care was taken about them. By this proclamation the church government is brought entirely to depend upon the royal supremacy, by virtue of which the king is pleased to allow judicatories to meet. However, ministers did not reckon themselves bound to regard this procedure, but went on in their ordinary work; this being a plain force put upon them, which, as they did not approve, so they could not help.

Thus matters stood till the parliament was up. We have heard of the debates at London, about a new settlement in this church. I am told they were not like to have ended peaceably, had not the king, pushed forward by Mr. Sharp and his supporters in England, interposed, and signified, he would not reckon them his friends who were not for establishing prelacy in Scotland. After this there was no more reasoning; the king's friends, they all resolved to be at all hazards.

---

* See page 151.

1661. Upon the last of August, the earls of Glencairn and Rothes, with Mr. Sharp, returned from court, and the next council day, September 5th, after the earl of Dumfries and Sir Robert Murray had been admitted counsellors, the lord chancellor presented a letter from his majesty, for establishing of the church government in Scotland; which was read, the tenor whereof follows.

" Charles R.

" Right trusty and well beloved cousins and counsellors, we greet you well. Whereas in the month of August, 1660, we did, by our letter to the presbytery of Edinburgh, declare our purpose to maintain the government of the church of Scotland settled by law; and our parliament having since that time, not only rescinded all the acts since the troubles began, referring to that government, but also declared all those pretended parliaments null and void, and left to us the settling and securing of church government: therefore, in compliance with that act rescissory, according to our late proclamation dated at Whitehall the 10th of June, and in contemplation of the inconveniences from the church government as it hath been exercised these 23 years past, of the unsuitableness thereof to our monarchical estate, of the sadly experienced confusions which have been caused during the late troubles by the violences done to our royal prerogative, and to the government civil and ecclesiastical, settled by unquestionable authority, we, from our respect to the glory of God, and the good and interest of the protestant religion, from our pious care and princely zeal for the order, unity, peace, and stability of that church, and its better harmony with the government of the churches of England and Ireland, have, after mature deliberation, declared to those of our council here, our firm resolution to interpose our royal authority for restoring of that church to its right government by bishops, as it was by law before the late troubles, during the reigns of our royal father and grandfather of blessed memory, and as it now stands settled by law. Of this our royal pleasure concerning church government you are to take notice, and to make intimation thereof in such a way and manner as you shall judge most expedient and effectual. And we require you, and every one of you, and do expect, according to the trust and confidence we have in your affections and duty to our service, that you will be careful to use your best endeavours for curing the distempers contracted during those late evil times, for uniting our good subjects among themselves, and bringing them all to a cheerful acquiescing and obedience to our sovereign authority, which we will employ by the help of God for the maintaining and defending the true reformed religion, increase of piety, and the settlement and security of that church in her rights and liberties, according to law and ancient custom. And in order thereunto, our will is, that you forthwith take such course with the rents belonging to the several bishoprics and deaneries, that they may be restored and made useful to the church, and that according to justice and the standing law. And moreover you are to inhibit the assembling of ministers in their several synodical meetings through the kingdom, until our further pleasure, and to keep a watchful eye over all who, upon any pretext whatsoever, shall, by discoursing, preaching, reviling, or any irregular or unlawful way, endeavour to alienate the affections of our people, or dispose them to an ill opinion of us and our government, to the disturbance of the peace of the kingdom. So expecting your cheerful obedience, and a speedy account of your proceedings herein, we bid you heartily farewell. Given at our court at Whitehall, August 14th, 1661, and of our reign the 13th year. By his majesty's command.

" LAUDERDALE."

To this diet of the council, all the counsellors had been called by letters from the clerk: and they were pretty well convened. After reading the king's letter, the clerk is ordered to draw up an act in obedience thereunto, to be proclaimed and made known to all his majesty's lieges, that none pretend ignorance. Accordingly the clerk presents the draught next day, September 6th, and the council approve it, and order it to be printed and published; and it was proclaimed over the Cross with great solemnity, by the lyon king at arms, with all the trumpets, and the magistrates of Edinburgh in their robes. The proclamation I have insert below.* It is very near a resuming of the letter just now insert, with some little alterations in form, and the addition of the penalty of present imprisonment, in case of failzie. And in making remarks upon the proclamation I will have occasion to set all the parts of the letter in their due light.

This letter, act, and proclamation, being the foundation of the setting up of episcopacy in Scotland at this time, 1661. and presbytery having only lived about two months under the shadow of the royal supremacy; and what is contained in the king's letter and this act being so singular, and of such importance, the reader will bear with me in making some observes upon them, and this great turn in church affairs. It will have been already observed, that the parliament for as far as they went, yet would not venture upon the direct introduction of prelates; this might have had inconveniencies. And till once matters were prepared by the interposition of the king's credit and authority,

---

* Act of council at Edinburgh, the 6th day of September, 1661.

The lords of his majesty's privy council, having considered his majesty's letter, of the date, at Whitehall the fourteenth day of August last, bearing, that whereas his majesty by his letter to the presbytery of Edinburgh, in the month of August, one thousand six hundred and sixty years, declared his royal purpose, to maintain the government of the church of Scotland settled by law. And the estates of parliament of this kingdom, having since that time, not only rescinded all the acts since the troubles began, relating to that government, but also declared all those parliaments null and void, leaving to his majesty the settling of church government: therefore, in compliance with that act rescissory, and in pursuance of his majesty's proclamation of the tenth of June last, and in contemplation of the inconveniencies that accompanied and issued from the church government, as it hath been exercised these twenty-three years past, and of the unsuitableness thereof to his majesty's monarchical estate, and of the sadly experienced confusions, which during these late troubles, have been caused by the violences done to his majesty's royal prerogative, and to the government civil and ecclesiastical, established by unquestionable authority: his majesty, having respect to the glory of God, and the good and interest of the protestant religion, and being zealous of, the order, unity, peace, and stability of the church within this kingdom, and of its better harmony with the government of the churches of England and Ireland, hath been pleased, after mature deliberation, to declare unto his council, his firm resolution to interpose his royal authority, for restoring of this church to its right government by bishops, as it was by law before the late troubles, during the reigns of his majesty's royal father and grandfather of blessed memory, and as it now stands settled by law, and that the rents belonging to the several bishoprics and deaneries, be restored and made useful to the church, according to justice and the standing law, have therefore, in obedience of, and conform to his majesty's royal pleasure aforesaid, ordained, and by these presents ordain the lyon king at arms, and his brethren, heralds, pursuivants, and messengers of arms, to pass to the market-cross of Edinburgh and other royal boroughs of the kingdom, and there by open proclamation, to make publication of this his majesty's royal pleasure, for restoring the church of this kingdom to its right government by bishops; and in his majesty's name, to require all his good subjects, to compose themselves to a cheerful acquiescence and obedience to the same, and to his majesty's sovereign authority now exercised within this kingdom. And that none of them presume, upon any pretence whatsomever, by discoursing, preaching, reviling, or any irregular and unlawful way, the endeavouring to alienate the affections of his majesty's good subjects, or dispose them to an evil opinion of his majesty or his government, or to the disturbance of the peace of the kingdom, and to inhibit and discharge the assembling of ministers in their several synodical meetings, until his majesty's further pleasure therein be known: commanding hereby, all sheriffs, bailies of bailiaries, stewards of stewartries and their deputes, all justices of peace, and magistrates and council of boroughs, and all other public ministers, to be careful within their several bounds and jurisdictions to see this act punctually obeyed: and if they shall find any person or persons, upon any pretexts whatsomever, by discoursing, preaching, reviling, or otherwise, as aforesaid, failing in their due obedience hereunto, or doing any thing in the contrary thereof, that they forthwith commit them to prison, till his majesty's privy council, after information of the offence, give further order therein. And hereof, the sheriffs, and others aforementioned, are to have a special care, as they will answer upon their duty and allegiance to his majesty. And further, the lords of his majesty's privy council do hereby inhibit and discharge all persons liable in payment of any of the rents formerly belonging to the bishoprics and deaneries, from paying of the rents of this present year, one thousand six hundred and sixty-one years, or in time coming, or any part thereof, to any person whatsomever, until they receive new order thereanent from his majesty or his council: and ordain these presents to be printed and published, as said is, that none may pretend ignorance of the same.

Extract. per me,

PET. WEDDERBURN, Cl. Sec. Concilii.

God save the king.

1661. I question if it would have carried in the house.

Now we have a plain gloss upon the etter to the presbytery of Edinburgh, which indeed the text cannot bear from which it appears that many ministers and others were shamefully bubbled by that trick of Mr. Sharp. However it deserves our notice, that in the resumption of that letter at this time, the little mighty word *as*, upon which so much weight was laid, is left out, that there might be the fairer room to bring in bishops upon that very ground, which so many took to be an assurance given against them.

We have next a clear view here of the real design of the act rescissory, passed by the parliament, as we have seen, to unhinge presbytery, and take away the hedge from about it, and leave it to Mr. Sharp and his associates, their will. And by Mr. Sharp's spite against presbyterian government of Christ's institution, and his ambition, Scotsmen must be deprived of many excellent laws about civil things, as well as religious, made from the (year) 1640 to the (year) 1651. Indeed religion and civil liberty stand and fall together.

It appears further from this letter and proclamation, that the settlement of episcopacy in Scotland is the child of the regal supremacy, one of the first-fruits of absolute and arbitrary power, and the mere effect of royal pleasure. The king is so tender of this, that he neither advises with his council in this matter, nor seeks their consent, but requires their publishing of his pleasure in this point; and the council themselves put it upon this foot, and lay the burden off themselves upon the king's letter. Episcopacy was still thus brought in upon us in this church, and crammed down our throat in Scotland, not from convincing reasons, or pretext of divine right, but merely as the sovereign's will; yea, it never had the shadow of parliamentary authority, till the king's honour was once pledged and engaged; which, we may easily believe, went very far afterwards in parliament, with such who had no principle, and as little concern about church government: and our episcopalians have the less ground to object against the throwing out of prelacy at the revolution, by a king and parliament jointly acting, and in the fullest freedom.

A heap indeed of alleged grounds for bringing in of bishops are cast into the letter and act, which might be at much length exposed, were not this a little foreign and wearisome in a history. The inconveniencies accompanying and issuing from the exercise of church government these twenty-three years past, are put in the front. Inconveniencies, I own, is a softer term than I expected at this time; those may, and do accompany the best constitutions, the exercise of just power, and the execution of the most excellent laws; what they were I shall not affirm: but this I am sure of, much real piety, conversion of multitudes, a signal bearing down of profaneness, and a great reformation of manners accompanied presbytery in the interval spoken of, to the observation of all the reformed churches. Perhaps some people now might reckon these inconveniencies, at least their practice seemed to speak out this.

Presbytery, though never named, is next supposed contrary to monarchy: the reasons of this cry have in part been already noticed. King James VI., whose apophthegm seems here pointed at, was of another opinion, till he had the gaining and gratifying the English prelates in his eye; and if the two crowns had not been to be united, I cannot help thinking he would have continued in his first and justest sentiments: yea, king Charles I. did not stifle the conviction he had, "that the covenanters were his best friends," when he wrote his sentiments to his queen, without any bias, and for the benefit of his children: and since the revolution, as the presbyterians, by their unshaken loyalty, have demonstrate the falseness of this calumny, so the repeated acknowledgments of the consistency of their carriage to their principles, and of their real regard to our limited monarchy, now during four reigns, from our sovereigns themselves, almost every year to our assemblies, do abundantly prove the same.

The confusions of the late times, and other things in the letter, can never be charged upon presbyterian ministers, without the greatest impudence, since they were the only body in the three kingdoms, who stood out against the usurper; and their loyalty since the reformation, and in the period here spoken of, hath been lately made evident in more books than one, and fully vouched.

I do not enter upon the motives made up by somebody for the king, and in the letter alleged to sway him in this change. How far there was regard to the glory of God, in acting contrary to the solemn oath, wherein God's name was called in, when presbytery was overturned, the world must judge. In the next clause, the religion of England and Ireland ought to have been put instead of the reformed religion, and then the sentence would have run agreeably to truth; since no other reformed church save these two, ever thought their good or interest consisted in having bishops. Whether unity, order, or peace followed upon this prelatical establishment, the reader will be in case to form some judgment, after he has perused this history: indeed confusion, division, and cruelty were still the produce of prelacy in Scotland. The true and real reason, though but a partial one, of this change, comes last, that there may be a harmony betwixt the government of England, Ireland, and Scotland. The altar at Damascus was a model of old, and now the English constitution in church must be Scotland's model. Our civil affairs were very much henceforth to be under English influence, and as a step to this, and to gratify the highflying party in England, and bishops there, our excellent church government, legally and solemnly settled, must be overturned. The days have been when this would not have gone so well down in Scotland, as it did at this juncture.

These are the reasons, such as they are, given in the letter, for this vast alteration in the church of Scotland. It is good in so far, that neither a *jus divinum*, first the Tridentine, and then the Laudean scheme of episcopacy, neither scripture, nor uninterrupted lineal succession from the apostles, nor boasted antiquity, are so much as pretended. Our noblemen, through whose hands this letter was to come, were of better sense than to insist on those; and if they were in Mr. Sharp's first draught, they found it proper to drop them.

Perhaps I have been too long in my remarks on this letter, and therefore I only further take notice, that episcopacy, as in the reign of the king's father and grandfather, is set up; and so Perth articles are brought in, and the encroachments upon religion and liberty begun again, which were the true inlets to what is so much talked of now, the troubles of the late times. The solemn charge given unto all subjects, to compose themselves to a cheerful acquiescence and obedience to the king's will, in this imposition, says, that it was scarce expected this change of government would be acceptable, yea, that it was against the inclinations of the most part. The positive requisition of obedience to the king's sovereign authority, in this very thing exercised now in Scotland, lets us see again, that bishops came in here from the sole exercise of the prerogative, and all who subjected to them homologated the supremacy. To support this establishment persecution is begun, and iniquity established by a law. Imprisonment is ordered for all who speak according to their conscience, known principles, and solemn engagements, or preach against episcopacy, or any thing now enacted. Men must either be silent and dumb; or, if they have any principles and conscience, lie and dissemble. The contraveners are to be punished by the privy council; and we shall find this court very much under the management of the bishops, and most arbitrary. And all in civil offices are required to begin this persecution upon their allegiance to his majesty. This was the first remarkable act of our new constitute council, and the preface to many severe processes and oppressions, as we may hear.

That same day, September 6th, the council order a just double of the above act and proclamation to be forthwith transmitted to his majesty, with the following letter.

" Most Sacred Sovereign,

" We no sooner perused your majesty's letter, of the date the 14th of August last, but in the acknowledgment of your majesty's piety and care for the preservation of the protestant religion, the establishment of

1661 the right government of the church, and peace and happiness of all your subjects, we did immediately issue a proclamation, to be printed and published, fully relating to all your royal commands; whereof we have sent a copy herewith enclosed We hope all your majesty's good subjects will acquiesce and give due obedience to them, and thereby testify their faithfulness and affection to your majesty's government and authority. We shall endeavour to have a watchful eye over all persons, and be ready to prosecute your majesty's commands, in order to what is enjoined, as becomes,

"Most sacred Sovereign,
"Your Majesty's most humble, dutiful, and obedient subjects and servants,
"Tweeddale, Sinclair, Dundee, Duffus, President of the Session, Register, Advocate, Ley, Blackhall, Niddrey, Alexander Bruce, Sir George Kinnaird, Sir Robert Murray, Glencairn chancellor, Rothes, Montrose, Morton, Hume, Eglinton, Murray, Linlithgow, Roxburgh, Haddington, Southesk, Weemyss, Callender."

The king, as we have seen above in his letter about the earl of Tweeddale, approves of, and returns his thanks for this proclamation, September 23d. Thus episcopacy is brought in again to Scotland, and every thing now must be done for supporting the prelates, and taking away any power presbyteries yet essayed to exercise. Accordingly, December 10, the council desire the chancellor to send the following letter to the presbytery of Peebles, upon information they were about to ordain a minister.

" R. R.
" The lords of his majesty's privy council, being informed, that you are about to proceed to the admission of Mr. John Hay, student of divinity, to the kirk of Manner, which is within the diocese of the archbishop of Glasgow, and so cannot be admitted by you, since the archbishop is restored to all the rights and privileges belonging to any of his predecessors since the reformation, have therefore desired me to intimate to you, in their name, that you do not proceed to the admission of the said Mr. John, but continue the same until the return of the archbishop, which will be in a very short time. I doubt not but you will obey this command, signified to you from

" Your affectionate friend,
" GLENCAIRN, Chancellor."

At their next sederunt, they go on to make a general act to reach all presbyteries and patrons, that no ministers be ordained unless their presentation be directed to the bishop. This act I have not seen in print and therefore insert it here.

" Apud Edinburgh, Dec. 12th, 1661.
" Forasmuch as by an act of privy council, dated September 6th, last, his majesty's royal pleasure, to restore the church of this kingdom to its government by bishops, as it was by law before the late troubles, during the reigns of his majesty's royal father and grandfather of blessed memory, and as it now stands settled by law, was made known to all the subjects of this kingdom, by open proclamation at the market-cross of all royal burghs: and that it is statute by the act 1. parl. 21. James VI. that all presentations to benefices should be directed thereafter to the archbishop or bishop of the diocese, within the bounds whereof any vacant church lieth; so that since their restitution to their former dignities, and privileges, and powers settled upon them by law and acts of parliament, no minister within this kingdom should be admitted to any benefice, but upon presentations directed as said is. And yet notwithstanding hereof, it is informed, that, upon presentations directed to presbyteries, they do proceed to admit ministers to kirks and benefices, albeit the bishops be restored to their dignities, some of them already consecrated, and all of them in a very short time will be invested in their rights and benefices, and empowered to receive presentations, and grant admissions thereupon. Therefore the council prohibits, and by these presents discharges all patrons to direct any presentations to any presbytery: and also discharges all and sundry presbyteries within this kingdom to proceed to the admission of any minister to any benefice or kirk within their respective bounds, upon any such presentations, as they will be answerable. With certification, if

they do otherwise, the said presentation and admission shall be void and null, as if they never had been granted. And ordains these presents to be printed, and published at the market-crosses of the head burghs of the several shires within this kingdom, that none pretend ignorance."

That same day the council make the following act concerning the presbytery of Peebles, who, it seems, either had not received the chancellor's letter to them, of the 10th, or could not stop the ordination, having all necessary to the gospel settlement of a minister.

"Apud Edinburgh, Dec. 12th, 1661.

"Forasmuch as the presbytery of Peebles have proceeded to the admission of one Mr John Hay to the kirk of Manner, notwithstanding of the letter and command to the contrary from the lords of council, of the 10th instant; the council do therefore ordain letters to be directed against the haill members of the said presbytery, who were present at the said admission, viz. Messrs Richard Brown minister at Drumelzier, Robert Brown of Lyne, Robert Eliot at Linton, Hew Craig at Railey, David Thomson at Dask, Patrick Purdie at Newlands, and Patrick Fleming at Stobo, to compear and answer to the premises, under pain of rebellion."

I have nothing further of this matter, but what is now insert from the registers, where I do not find any more concerning this presbytery: but next year we shall find some other presbyteries writ to by the council; and in a little time all presbyteries were suppressed, save such as came and subjected to the bishops. This procedure against presbyteries was a stretch beyond the king's letter in August, and the council's own act, September 6th, which only discharged synods. They might have as well prohibited presbyteries to cognosce upon scandal, and have abrogate all discipline, to which indeed many were obnoxious, as limit them in point of ordination, which is one great part of their ministerial function, yet reserved to them by the king's last letter; and in this the council, without any warrant from the king or parliament, turn lawmakers, and go beyond their power, which was only to execute the laws made; but of this we shall have more flaming instances afterwards. Perhaps they thought nothing beyond their sphere, which might be a service to the prelates, and they would rather suffer many congregations to lie vacant, than hazard the admission of one who might happen to be averse from episcopacy. Thus I have gone through what I find done by the council this year, for the erection of episcopacy, by the king's orders, and their abridging church judicatories in their liberties; I shall now shut up this section, with some account of the bishops themselves now set up, their character and reordination in England.

1661.

When law, such as it was, had made way for the prelates, solicitations begin apace for bishoprics. No great disliker of prelacy observes, "In September and October this year, many of the ministry were seeking after the episcopal dignity, while in the mean time a great many others spoke and taught against it as unlawful." Such apostate, ambitious, and aspiring ministers as had most friends in court, carried them. Mr James Sharp had secured the primacy and archbishopric of St Andrews to himself: though he wanted not the impudence and dissimulation to make offers of it to some eminent presbyterian ministers, one of which told him, he doubted not but he designed that for himself, and he would receive the curse of God with it.

Our bishoprics in Scotland are far from the fatness and opulency of those in England. An account before me bears, that in bulk they came but to £4000 or £5000 sterling a year, in ordinary years, much of their rent being in victual. I suppose I will not be much out, when I say the bishopric of Winchester is better than all our Scots bishoprics put together. Some of them are very mean; the revenue of that of Argyle is but about £130 a year. That of Dumblane is about £120. But a weak temptation goes far, where there is a strong corruption. Surely it was

1661. violent avarice and ambition, which could persuade them to accept an office so odious, and of so inconsiderable incomes.

For the honour of the first and great authors of all the ensuing sufferings of presbyterians, I thought it not improper to give here a short hint of the persons the king was pleased to pitch upon for the first set of our bishops; aud as they were persons abundantly obsequious to the designs now on foot, so it will easily appear that none of them were any great ornaments to their office, which was so much hated in Scotland, neither any great credit to their brethren in England.

Mr. James Sharp was metropolitan, and placed as primate at St. Andrews. I shall not offer any large character of him; somewhat has been narrated, and more is yet before us. His life, until his arriving at the top of his ambition, I have read, written by one of the after-sufferers, a worthy gentleman; and should I give an abstract of it, the portrait would be very black and surprising. His dream, when at the university; his taking the tender; his proposal to Oliver Cromwell, which made the usurper to assert him very publicly to be an atheist; his betraying presbyterian ministers when at court, and afterwards pursuing them for his charges; his baseness with Isobel Lindsay, as she declared in his face openly enough, and share in the murder of the poor infant; his perjury in Mr. James Mitchel's case; his cruel life and strange death, would make up a very black history; and as they were commonly talked of, so I find they were generally believed by those who lived with, and had access to know him. But this is not a place to insist on them. His great talents were caution, cunning, and dissimulation, with unwearied diligence; these very much qualified him for his terrible undertakings. He got himself into the archbishopric of St. Andrews, as a reward for betraying this church. Indeed when he first came down, August 1660, as we have heard, with the double faced letter to the presbytery of Edinburgh, and gave a narrative of his pains at London, the cheat was not perceived, and the suspicions the protesting ministers had about him, were not regarded: but very soon he opened out, and at length appeared in his true colours; and none were more grieved at his base dealing than the reverend Mr. Douglas, and the ministers of Edinburgh, who had formerly so much confided in him; and we have seen Mr. Douglas's thoughts of him. However, he got his ambition satisfied, and his patent and gift under the great seal in November this year, of which some notice may be taken afterwards.

Mr. Andrew Fairfoul got the archbishopric of Glasgow; a man of some learning and neat expression, but never taken to be either serious or sincere. He had been minister first at Leith, and at this time was at Dunse, and in that country there was no small talking of his intrigues with a lady, who shall be nameless; but death cut him off in little more than a year after his promotion, as will be noticed afterwards.

Mr. George Wiseheart is placed at the see of Edinburgh. He had been laid under church censure by the old covenanters, about the time of the encampment at Dunselaw, in the year 1639, and this probably recommended him now. This man could not refrain from profane swearing, even upon the street of Edinburgh; and he was a known drunkard. He published somewhat in divinity; but then, as I find it remarked by a very good hand, his lascivious poems, which, compared with the most luscious parts of Ovid, *de Arte Amandi*, are modest, gave scandal to all the world.

Mr. Thomas Sideserf is fixed at Orkney. He had been bishop of Galloway, and deposed in the year 1638, for the common faults of the prelates at that time, and in particular for erroneous doctrine; and now he is translated to a better benefice.

Mr. David Mitchel, once minister of Edinburgh, but deposed by the general assembly for heresy, and thereupon going to England, was made one of the prebendaries of Westminster, is named for Aberdeen, but enjoyed it not a full year.

Mr. James Hamilton, brother to the lord

Belhaven, minister at Cambusnethan, is placed at Galloway. His gifts were reckoned every way ordinary; but he was remarkable for his cunning timeserving temper.

Mr. Robert Wallace, minister at Barnwell in the shire of Ayr, famous for his large stomach, got the bishopric of the Isles, though he understood not one word of the language of the natives. He was a relation of the chancellor's, and that was enough.

Mr. David Fletcher, minister at Melross, a remarkable worldling, was named for the bishopric of Argyle: I doubt if he understood the Irish language either. Melross was a good stipend, and he continued a while preaching there, and because of his preaching there, he boasted of his diligence beyond the rest of his brethren, who, it must be owned, for the most part preached little or none; meanwhile I do not hear any of them, save he, took two stipends.

Mr. George Haliburton, minister at Perth, had the see of Dunkeld. His character at that time was, a man who had made many changes, and was sincere in none of them.

Mr. Patrick Forbes, the degenerate plant of the excellent Mr. John Forbes, who kept the assembly at Aberdeen, 1605, was fixed at Caithness.

Mr. David Strachan, minister at Fettercairn, the commissioner's minister, got the small bishopric of Brechin.

Mr. John Paterson, minister at Aberdeen, got the bishopric of Ross, his son made a greater figure than he did.

Mr. Murdoch Mackenzie, minister at Elgin, was placed at Murray. While a minister, he was famous for searching people's kitchens on Christmas day for the superstitious goose, telling them, that the feathers of them would rise up in judgment against them one day; and when a bishop, as famous for affecting always to fall a preaching upon the deceitfulness of riches, while he was drawing the money over the board to him.

Mr. Robert Leighton, once minister of Newbottle, and at this time principal of the college of Edinburgh, son to Mr. Leighton in England, * the author of " Zion's Plea against Prelacy," who was so severely handled by the prelates there,

1661.

---

* Alexander Leighton, father to the bishop, had an information exhibited against him in the starchamber, in the year 1630, for writing a book, entitled, " An Appeal to the Parliament, or a Plea against Prelacy," wherein he was charged with having set forth, " 1st, That we read not of greater persecution of God's people in any Christian nation than in this island, especially since the death of queen Elizabeth. 2d, That the prelates were men of blood, and enemies to God and the state, and that the establishing bishops by law is a master sin, and ministers should have no voices in council, deliberative or decisive. 3d, That prelacy is antichristian and Satanical; the bishops, ravens and magpies. 4th, That the canons of 1603 are nonsense. 5th, He condemns that spawn of the beast, kneeling at the sacraments. 6th, That prelates corrupted the king, and the queen was a daughter of Heth. 7th, He commends him that murdered the duke of Buckingham, and encourages others in the like attempts. 8th, He saith all that pass by spoil us, and we spoil all that rely upon us, and instances in the black pining death of the Rochellers to the number of fifteen thousand in four months. 9th, Saith, that the church has her laws from the scriptures, and no king may make laws in the house of God, for if they might, the scripture would be imperfect. 10th, He saith it is pity, and will be an indelible dishonour to the state's reputation, that so ingenuous and tractable a king should be so monstrously abused to the undoing of himself and his subjects."

The defendant did not deny the book, but refused to acknowledge any evil intention, his end being only to "remonstrate certain grievances in church and state, that the parliament might take them into consideration and redress them." He was, however, sentenced to be committed to the Fleet, during life; to pay a fine of £10,000; to be carried to the pillory at Westminster, and there whipped, and after whipping to be set in the pillory, have one of his ears cut off, one side of his nose slit, and be branded on the one cheek with the letters S. S. for a sower of sedition: and on another day to be carried to the pillory in Cheapside, to be there again whipped, have his other ear cut off, the other side of his nose slit, and his other cheek branded with the double S. Mr. Leighton made his escape out of prison the night before his sentence was to have been in part executed, but he was soon retaken, and on the sixteenth of November, underwent the one half of his sentence in Palace Yard, Westminster. On that day sevennight, his sores on his back, ear, nose, and face, not being cured, he was again whipped at the pillory in Cheapside. The hangman on this occasion was purposely half intoxicated, and performed his duty with the most savage ferocity. After being thus unmercifully whipped, the poor culprit was exposed nearly two hours on the pillory in a severe frost, and heavy fall of snow, at the end of which he underwent to the full extent thereof, the remainder of his brutal sentence, and being unable to walk, he

1661. made choice of the small bishopric of Dunblane, to evidence his abstractedness from the world. His character was by far the best of any of the bishops now set up: and to give him his due, he was a man of very considerable learning, an excellent utterance, and of a grave and abstracted conversation. He was reckoned devout, and an enemy to persecution, and professed a great deal of meekness and humility. By many he was judged void of any doctrinal principle, and his close correspondence with some of his relations at Doway in popish orders, made him suspected as very much indifferent as to all professions, which bear the name of Christian. He was much taken with some of the popish mystic writers, and indeed a latitudinarian, and of an over extensive charity. His writings published since the revolution, evidence his abilities, and that he was very much superior to his fellows.

This is the set of men pitched upon to lord it over the church of Scotland. They were, it must be owned, very well chosen for their work, and agreeable enough to the design of setting them up; unless it was,

---

was carried back by water to his confinement, where he remained till he was liberated by the long parliament.—Rushworth's Col. vol. ii. p. 55 —57. Neal's Hist. of the Puritans, vol. ii. p. 188. Leighton had the degree of D. D. from two celebrated universities, Leyden and St. Andrews; and we may rest assured, that this honour, *then* so rare, would not have been conferred on an ordinary man.

That the covenanters generally should have a suspicion of the archbishop, his son, is quite natural, when it is considered, that he was bred a presbyterian—had taken the covenant himself and enforced it on others—renounced his former solemn vows—received re-ordination from the bishops—and became successively bishop of Dumblane and archbishop of Glasgow. But no man will say that presbyterians *of the last* 100 *years* have been *severe* upon the character of Leighton. Principal Fall, indeed, was the first who published a portion of his writings, but it is to the Wilsons of Scottish presbytery, and the Doddridges of English non-conformity, that the public are mainly indebted for bringing the works of that singular man under the notice of the British public. And if we wish to find admirers and vindicators of Leighton, we must not look to the high church party in England: they never relished the moderation of his views, or the spiritual unction of his sentiments. Bishop Burnet is one of the few dignitaries of the church who have thought it worth while to ponder his works, and to imbibe his spirit.—*Ed.*

---

that the primate turned too heavy for several of our nobility, who would have only had a moderate prelacy brought in: but when considered as to their personal character, they made good the countryman's remark, " that the bishops of England were like the kings of Judah, some good, some bad; but the prelates in Scotland were like the kings of Israel, not one of them good, but all of them followers of Jeroboam, the son of Nebat, who made Israel to sin."

There were no bishops, before the year 1638, alive in Scotland, save Sydeserf; and so it was necessary these persons receive their orders somewhere else: none of the reformed churches, except England or Ireland, could help them in this matter. It was not so fit, and perhaps not practicable, that the whole fourteen should be brought up to England, therefore the court pitched upon Messrs. Sharp, Fairfoul, and Hamilton to come up to London, and learn the service of that land, and receive episcopal ordination. Mr. Leighton, I think, was in England this summer and harvest, and October 18th, the other three go up.

At this time the unchurching of all the protestant churches who had not prelatic ordination, the cassing and voiding their ministry, and consequently their sacraments, with the *jus divinum*, and absolute necessity of episcopal ordination, were doctrines mightily coming in request. From those abominable principles came the application about this time made by some great names in the English church to the king, that his ambassador in France might be discharged to hold communion with the protestants there, because they wanted prelatic ordination, and that he might no more go to the seat he had appointed for him in the protestant church at Charenton, and that he might have a chapel of his own. Hence it was insisted upon, that our Scots bishops must be re-ordained, having only formerly had presbyterian ordination. This was a proper juncture for highfliers to insist in this matter; and a commission under the great seal of England was directed to Doctor Sheldon bishop of London, the bishop of Worcester, and some other suffragans of the diocese of

Canterbury. The two archbishops in England declined to be put in, upon what views I shall not say: but one would have thought, that our old prelate Sydeserf might have been joined in commission with them. The royal prerogative from which all their power came in this consecration, might have sufficiently authorized a Scots bishop to have acted in this matter in England; but this was not done: whether the English prelates refused to act in a concert with a deposed and excommunicate bishop, though restored by the king, or what the reason was, I cannot say.

When Doctor Sheldon made the proposal, that they must be first ordained deacons, and then presbyters, before they could be consecrate bishops; Mr. Sharp made some bustle, and urged the sustaining of Spotiswood's presbyterian ordination, 1610, by the English bishops, when he was consecrate; with some other arguments. But the Doctor was peremptory, and abundantly fixed on this point. The others very soon yielded, when they found this would be insisted upon; which made the bishop of London to tell Mr. Sharp, when he came to acquaint him with their consent to re-ordination, "that it was the Scots fashion to scruple at every thing, and to swallow any thing." Thus they were justly reproved, but they resolved to boggle at nothing in their way to the prelacy; and one of them frankly declared, he would be ordained, re-ordained, and re-ordained again, if it was insisted upon. So our first prelates cast a slur upon, yea, on the matter nullify all they had done as gospel bishops; they must become the king's creatures, and renounce their presbyterian ordination, before they can receive the episcopal dignity and consecration.

In December, these four with a great parade at Westminster, before a great confluence of Scots and English nobility, were dubbed, first preaching deacons, then presbyters, and then consecrated bishops in one day, by Doctor Sheldon and a few others. The ceremony was performed in all the modes of the English church, with vestments, and all their cringes and bows; at which it is said, some indecencies fell out, and after they had received the sacrament kneeling, in all points they were ordained according to the office and form there. After 1661. the consecration, the bishops and peers were feasted at Westminster, and then went again to church, and heard another sermon. Being thus empowered, early next year they came down, and lay on their episcopal hands upon their brethren in Scotland, named by the court for the different sees, as we may afterwards hear. Thus our Scots prelates are set up; and some obvious reflections rise from this, with which I shall end this section.

Our Scots bishops, by submitting to be re-ordained as presbyters, declared to all the world, that they did not believe their presbyterian ordination to be valid; and yet when they came down to Scotland, and entered upon the exercise of their episcopal office, they did not re-ordain such of the ministers as complied with them. The natural question upon this, which offers to the episcopal party, is, whether such compliers, not having episcopal ordination, were true gospel ministers? If they were not, as is certain by the episcopal principles they could not be; was it not the most barbarous thing in the world, to persecute people for not owning them as ministers, who by their own principles were indeed no ministers? It is in vain to say, that the bishop's allowance of them was equivalent to ordination, by the imposition of his hands: for if so, why were they themselves re-ordained by imposition of hands; and thereby gave scandal to all the reformed churches? I must leave the party to answer this at their leisure, the best way they can; I am sure they have reason to find a good answer to it if possible, upon more accounts than one; for I do not see how the sacraments dispensed by them could be valid, any more than how their harassing the presbyterians can be justified.

Perhaps the curious reader may be willing to have the tenor of the letters patent, and royal gift, establishing those first prelates after the restoration; and therefore I subjoin here an abstract of these for Mr. Sharp, of the date November this year, from which we will easily guess at the form of the rest; and they run,

" That during the tumults in the kingdom

1661. for twenty-three years preceding, laws were made for the extirpation of the church government by the archbishops and bishops, against the established law and government of the church of this kingdom, in prejudice of his majesty's power and prerogative, which are rescinded by the current parliament; so that the authority civil and ecclesiastic is redintegrate, according to the laws in force before the rebellion.

"And because at this time the deans and members of chapters are for the most part dead, and their offices vacant; so that archbishops and bishops cannot be nominated, presented, and elected according to the order prescribed by act of parliament, 1617.

"And that his majesty considereth, that the offices of the bishops and archbishops in this kingdom do vaik in his majesty's hands, by the death and demission of the last incumbents, particularly the archbishopric of St. Andrews, by the decease of the last bishop thereof, to wit, Mr. John Spotiswood.

"And his majesty being informed of the piety, prudence, &c. of Mr. James Sharp, Doctor in divinity, therefore his majesty, *ex authoritate regali, et potestate regia, certa scientia, proprioque motu*, makes, creates, and ordains the said Doctor James Sharp archbishop of the said archbishopric of St. Andrews, and primate and metropolitan of all Scotland."

Before I end this section, let me take some notice of the mistakes, not to say designed misrepresentations of some of the most celebrated English historians, when they give the account of the re-introduction of prelacy to Scotland. More than once I shall have occasion to observe their gross blunders in plain facts, for which the best excuse I know of, is, our own unaccountable negligence in giving the world and our neighbours just accounts of Scots affairs. I hope after this they shall do us more justice. The author of the "Complete History of England," generally reckoned to be bishop Kennet, vol. iii. p. 253, first edition, sets this affair in a quite wrong light. He would have us believe, that in Scotland "presbytery began to vanish upon the first appearance of monarchy." Some few sheets before, he had done the English presbyterians the justice to own they were heartily for monarchy, while the independents, according to him, were for a commonwealth. The Scots presbyterians were not a whit behind them; so that if presbytery vanished upon the return of the king, the reproach of ingratitude must fall, where perhaps the author did not design it; and how agreeable this was to promises and engagements the king and his party were under, he cannot be ignorant. I am sorry there is such ground given from the unfair narrative of the act of parliament he cites, and other acts of parliament after the restoration, to say that the miseries of Scotland in the former period, came from the kirk party. But as a historian, he might have known and observed, that those narratives were not agreeable to truth, and nothing else but partial and unjust representations, to serve the designs of a prevailing party, vampt up by the earl of Middleton and Mr. Sharp, as a pretext for introducing prelacy and arbitrary power in Scotland. Indeed I suspect these unhappy narratives have misled many of the English writers into much of their foolish satire against the presbyterian establishment; but had they been so equal as to have considered the public papers of the kingdom, and church of Scotland from the (year) 1638, to the usurpation, and the fair accounts of that period in the marquis of Argyle's case and other papers, much of this might have been prevented, and the world would not have been so much imposed upon in this matter.

He adds, "the kirk had an establishment by law;" which is an evidence of the author's candour, and more than our episcopal writers will allow, and confirms the remarks before made upon the base treatment of this church, in the double-faced letter to the presbytery of Edinburgh. A writer who is heartily upon the revolution bottom, cannot in any consistency with himself, treat the procedure of the Scots nation after the (year) 1637, as illegal. What follows, "but weak in the hearts of the people," is apparently a most groundless innuendo; witness the insuperable backwardness of the body of the people for twenty-seven years to prelacy; which could not be rooted out from such who were not either indifferent about every thing of this nature, or plainly under the influence of the nobility and gentry, who set up for prelacy, especially in the northern shires. He adds, " especially the nobles and lairds." That great numbers of those fell in with Middleton's projects, in his two sessions of parliament, I do not deny: but then as to the lairds, no small care had been taken to keep out of the parliament the most substantial and sensible gentlemen, at least in the east, south, and west, as much disaffected to prelacy. And our nobility in Scotland were generally against episcopacy, save such who were in places of power, and some of their relations whom they influenced, and those who were of broken fortunes, and inclined to mend them. Some few, indeed, once of other sentiments, when grated by the faithful exercise of discipline under presbytery, turned favourers of prelacy, and with those joined many of our younger noblemen, who knew little but slavery and oppression under the usurpation, and were taught to speak against the presbyterian establishment.

" Thus," concludes he, " presbytery was to fall without the honour of a dissolution." I imagine the author did not know, that the commissioner, Middleton, notwithstanding all his numbers, durst not venture upon a direct dissolution of presbytery: it was thought safest to make a change, so contrary to the inclinations of the best part of the nation, as gradual and insensible as might be; and when different measures were taken in the act at Glasgow, they soon felt the mistake, and with some difficulty Mr. Sharp retrieved it. The falling of presbytery then, without what the author calls the " honour of a dissolution," was from necessity and fear, and not choice. In short, according to this author's expressing himself, one would think that presbytery remained the legal establishment during the two brothers' reigns. He owns it was established by law, and that these laws were not dissolved and repealed; and in some respect this was indeed the state of the case, as may afterwards be observed.

" Upon the prospect of this favourable turn," adds the Doctor, 1661 " some of the most worthy of the Scots presbyters, Mr. James Sharp, Mr. Hamilton, Mr. Farewel, and Mr. Logtoun, were consecrated by the bishop of Winchester." His mistake of Farewel for Mr. Fairfoul, and Logtoun for Leightoun, may be an error of the press; and yet the following historians, Mr. Collier, and Mr. Eachard, and other English writers have copied after him. The worth of those presbyters is well enough known in Scotland, and their character hath been already given. He further observes very justly, that those four obtained the proclamation, September 6th, for restoring archbishops and bishops. This indeed was not the deed of Scotland, but impetrate at London, by the influence of the highfliers there, and chimed in with next year by our obsequious parliament. His remark in the same place, of the inconsistency of patronages with presbytery, is also very just.

This great change in Scotland the author attributes to the earl of Middleton, and so he well might; but what follows is such a blunder as gives us a full proof how little acquaintance the best of our English writers have with our Scots affairs: " But, 1663, Middleton was removed, and the earl of Rothes appointed high commissioner of Scotland, a ringleader of the presbyterians under king Charles I. and even the principal of the conspirators who subscribed a letter *au Roy*, to aid the kirk and covenant. And now the presbyterians lost ground more and more." The letter here pointed at, to the French king, I hope will be set in its due light by those who write the history of that period; and the memory of that extraordinary person the earl of Rothes, and others upon whom it is charged, may be easily vindicated from the conspiracy this author talks of. Since he wrote the history of the former reign, he ought to have known, that that excellent person, the earl of Rothes, was got to heaven many years before the restoration; and the earl who was commissioner at this time, was never so unlike his father and himself, as when serving the in-

2 H

1661. terests of prelacy, and under bishop Sharp's management, at the top of the high commission.

What this author incidentally drops afterwards, p. 405, comes in the last room to be considered here. In giving the duke of Lauderdale's character, among other things, he makes him " the underminer of episcopacy in Scotland, by laying it upon a new foundation, THE PLEASURE OF THE KING." This is not a place to inquire how far the establishment of prelacy in the Christian church was still from the pleasure of the civil magistrate, and was brought in to model the church government, and governors, in a dependance upon the state: at least this seems plain enough, that the continuance of the hierarchy in protestant churches since the reformation, is very much owing to this spring. But the Doctor is certainly mistaken, when he calls this a " new foundation in Scotland," since it must be owned, by all who know any thing of our Scots affairs since our reformation from popery, that prelacy here had never any other foundation save the " pleasure of the king." What hath been said upon this historian, may serve upon the matter, as remarks upon the other English writers, who have very much copied after " The Complete History of England," in our Scots affairs, and frequently keep by this author's words.

Mr. Collier, in his account of this turn, has nothing different from the former, unless it be an insinuation, " that the presbyterians had seized patronages :" what he means by seizing them, needs to be explained. Presbyterian ministers still complained of them since the reformation, and a presbyterian parliament abolished them, but presbyterians never made use of them themselves. Mr. Eachard very faithfully copies the two former, without observing that distinctness, as to the years, he might have done. His reader will very readily imagine from his account of this, that the act of parliament, restoring bishops, was May 8th, 1661, especially since it stands so upon the head of his page; and several acts he mentions, as well as the proceedings against the marquis of Argyle, were during that year.

SECT. VIII

Of several other remarkables, which come not in upon the former Sections, during this year, 1661.

HAVING thus gone through the great turn of affairs in Scotland this year, under such general heads as appeared to me most proper, I have, in holding close by them, overlooked several things remarkable enough, and not altogether alien from the design of this history, which I am now to gather up here, and so end what I have upon this year. And I take the greater liberty to notice these incidental matters, in this and the following years, that we have yet almost nothing of a history of this period I am upon.

Last year, this kingdom was delivered from the English army, under the fear of which, and an absolute subjection, Scotland had been for a good many years; and I find some remarkables which were applied, perhaps without any ground, to this turn, in several papers come to my hands. I only hint at two, which seem most observable. When the English subdued Scotland, the swans which were in the loch on the north side of Linlithgow, left it, and, as it was then termed, took banishment on them; but last year, or the beginning of this, they came back upon the king's return; and upon the citadel of Perth, where the arms of the commonwealth had been put up, in May last year, a thistle grew out of the wall near the place, and quite overspread them, which was much observed, and our old Scots motto, *nemo me impunè lacesset.* Both these may be, without any thing extraordinary, accounted for; but they were matter of remark and talk, it may be, more than they deserved.

At the first session of parliament this year, when the forms were over, January 4th, the commissioner signified to the house, that it was his majesty's pleasure, that the bones of the marquis of Montrose should be gathered together to one place, to be interred with the funeral honours due to one

CHAP. II.]   OF THE CHURCH OF SCOTLAND.   243

who had died in his majesty's service. Accordingly, January 7th, all the remains of his body were gathered from the places where they were placed, May, 1650. His corpse was raised from the Burrow Muir, put in a fine coffin, and carried up under a rich canopy to the tolbooth; where all being ready before, his head was taken down, and put into the coffin, with colours flying, cannons shooting, and trumpets sounding, and carried down to Holyrood-house, and depositate in the aisle, till afterwards what of his members had been at Glasgow, Stirling, Perth, and Aberdeen, had been taken down, and brought to Edinburgh beforehand: and May 11th, the solemnity of the funeral was performed in a vast deal of state, and the coffin was brought up to St. Giles's church, with mourners, led horse, the lyon, heralds, and all the members of parliament attending, and the commissioner in a mourning coach.

Upon the 2d of April, the king's life-guard was formed. By their constitution they were to consist of noblemen and gentlemen's sons, and they were to be one hundred and twenty in number, under the command of the lord Newburgh. After their taking an oath to be loyal to his majesty, they made a parade through the town of Edinburgh with carabines at their saddles, and their swords drawn. Whatever was their first settlement, the scum of the nation was taken into them; and we shall afterwards meet with them as ready instruments in the persecution which followed.

April 23d was the day of the king's coronation at London; and it was solemnized at Edinburgh, by preaching in all the kirks; and care was taken to have it kept with great state through all the remarkable places in the kingdom. There was sermon in the parliament house, and great rejoicings at the Cross, a sumptuous feast at the Abbey, ringing of bells, bonfires, and all other demonstrations of joy.

May 13th, by order of parliament, my lord Warriston's forfeiture was publicly intimate at the Cross by the heralds, his arms torn, and set up most contemptuously upon all the public places in Edinburgh. May 15th, the proclamation for keeping the 29th of May was intimate by the lyon with great solemnity.

1661.

May 22d, the covenant was burnt with great solemnity at London, by the hand of the common hangman, with all the spite and contempt that could be devised, and several senseless roundels and ballads were printed and spread, particularly one, entitled, " The execution of the covenant burnt by the common hangman, London, May 22d, 1661." One needs not be so much surprised at this by the highfliers in England, since we shall just now meet with little less contempt poured upon it in Scotland.

According to the act of parliament lately made and published, the 29th of May this year was observed with the greatest solemnity at Edinburgh. Sermons suitable to the occasion were preached by timeserving ministers, in all the kirks there. After sermons a great feast was prepared by the town, in the great college-hall, at which the commissioner, the whole nobility, and principal members of parliament were present: the bells were rung, the cannons discharged, and every thing else that could be contrived to grace that solemnity. Some observations have been already made upon the act of parliament for keeping this day. The church of Scotland, since the reformation, had still vigorously opposed the observation of anniversary holidays. They kept the holy Christian Sabbath with the most religious strictness, and from principle refused to keep any other stated holidays: and when upon very good reasons they could not observe Christmas and Pasch, they could never think of doing that for their king, which their Saviour had not required to be done for himself. Certainly many who kept this day, kept it not to the Lord, but it was solemnized with almost as much riot, revelling, and madness, as if it had been one of the heathen holidays. For all these reasons, the true children of this reformed church refused this imposition, as what by their reformation rights and principles, as well as their solemn vows, they were bound up from. However this was a most melancholy day to Scotland, being the triumph of the wicked, betwixt the days of the execution of the noble marquis of Argyle, and Mr. James Guthrie;

1661. which made a very eminent minister in the west of Scotland, yet in his church, choose that text to preach upon this day, it being his stated week day for sermon, Esth. iii. 15. " And the king and Haman sat down to drink, but the city Shushan was perplexed."

July 10th, Sir Alexander Durham, lord lyon, was, with a great deal of solemnity, crowned lyon king at arms. In the face of parliament there was a gold crown put upon his head, and the commissioner had a speech to him, and the lord register another. Before the solemnity, Mr. Robert Lawrie had a sermon in the house, from that text, Esth. vi. 6. " What shall be done to the man whom the king delights to honour?"

When the parliament arose, and the council sat down, with the whole executive power in their hands, at their first meeting, July 13th, they order the citadels built by the English, to be demolished: and the earl of Murray is appointed to slight and demolish that of Inverness; the earl of Eglinton, that of Ayr; the lord Bellenden, that at Leith; and the magistrates of Perth, with Sir George Kinnaird, that at Perth.

July 25th, Mr. David Dickson applies (to) the council for their license and privilege to print his " Therapeutica Sacra," now translated into English by himself. The council appoint Mr. Andrew Fairfoul to revise it, and report to the council, whether it is fit to be reprinted. Now indeed the world was changed in Scotland, when Mr. Fairfoul is pitched upon to revise Mr. David Dickson, professor of divinity, his books.

This year and the next, there are vast numbers of commissions granted by the council to gentlemen in every shire, and almost in every parish, especially in the north and east country, to try persons for witchcraft: and great numbers of these wretches confess; clear probation is found against others, and they are executed. The numbers of these commissions for trial of witches for several years, surprised me when I met with them in the registers.

August 1st, the council order that day to be kept with such solemnities as were formerly used before the late usurpation, in commemoration of. the deliverance of his majesty's grandfather, James VI., of ever blessed memory, from the conspiracy intended by the earl of Gowrie, conform to the late act of parliament made thereanent; and direct their orders to the magistrates of Edinburgh, and governor of the castle, to see to this. And, October 3d, the like orders are given, but more timeously, for the keeping of the 5th of November.

September 17th, the clerk is ordered to draw up a proclamation, discharging the electing of any person to be magistrate or counsellor within burgh, but such as are of known loyalty and affection to his majesty To-morrow, September 18, it was approven, and the tenor of it follows. ·

"Whereas, during the late unhappy troubles, some persons who were of fanatical principles, and enemies to monarchical government and his majesty's lawful authority, to attain their ambitious designs, did so comply with the usurpers of the government for the time, and join with them, to secure their tyranny and usurpation, that by their assistance and countenance they did screw into their own hands the sole administration of affairs and jurisdiction within the most part of the burghs royal in this kingdom, and in time did so settle their interest, that none were chosen to be magistrates, or of the council, but such as adhered to them; and lest those practices may be endeavoured to be set on foot again, and attempts made to have such persons elected, and the power and government continued as of late; which if not remedied, may be of dangerous consequence, and prejudicial to his majesty's service and authority, by obstructing these who are of known integrity and loyalty, to exercise his majesty's laws and commands, in order to the securing his royal interest, and the peace of the kingdom, which is now necessary to be taken notice of, when the time of election of magistrates for royal burghs is approaching. Therefore the .lords of his majesty's privy council, inhibit and discharge the electing of any person to be magistrate or counsellor within burgh, but such as are of known loyalty and affection to his majesty's government, qualified as is expressed in the late acts of parliament, and others

CHAP. II.] OF THE CHURCH OF SCOTLAND. 245

made for that effect, and whose carriage, during the late troubles, has been no evidence to the contrary: with certification, if any elections be otherwise made, the said elections shall be declared null and void, and the persons elected, and these who shall elect them, shall be censured with all rigour as persons disaffected. These presents to be forthwith published at the Market-cross of Edinburgh, and all other royal burghs."

I will have frequent occasion, in this history, to observe the strict chain betwixt religious and civil privileges and liberty; when the one is attacked, the other readily sinks. Last year, in September, matters were a little more smoothly managed. The chancellor wrote to the meeting of the royal burghs, and that convention wrote to each of their number, giving them what they call caveats in their elections, that none be chosen but well affected persons to his majesty and his government, whether on the council or magistracy. They forbid likewise the choosing any who had subscribed the " Remonstrance," " Association," or who concurred in any course for promoting the ends thereof, or who protested against any public judicatories or their determinations, since the year 1650. But now the managers grow in these attacks, and, beyond what the act of parliament ordains, declare the elections void, if they be not of such persons who showed their loyalty during the troubles, and other conditions spoken of in the proclamation. I need make but few remarks on it; several new ways of speaking are in it, " the king's laws," and the like. In short, the design of this proclamation was to exclude all from any management of burghs, who were any ways favourers of presbytery, or were not fully and heartily for the bishops, and the king's arbitrary power, and to bring the royal burghs entirely under yoke to the courtiers: and they begin with Edinburgh, as a pattern to all the rest; and when they were thus treated, none of the rest could think to stand out. Thus, October 3d, " the council understanding, that since their last proclamation anent the elections of magistrates, these of Edinburgh are chosen, do ordain one of their macers

to warn the haill magistrates, counsellors, and deacons of crafts who are elected, as also these who did vote, or should have voted at the said election, to compear before the council November 1st, and give an account of their carriage as they will be answerable. Accordingly, November 1st, the council find the election good, and the present magistrates of Edinburgh, Canongate, and Portsburgh, lawfully elected, and authorize the same. They declare against some protestations made by the crafts. Thus we see the liberty of the royal burghs overturned; and if the council please, they may, by citations and otherwise, harass all the electors, and elected, if not according to their scheme; and we shall find other attacks made upon them afterwards.

1661

At that same diet, September 18th, the council order that such suffering ministers as petition for redress, and are recommended, by his grace the lord commissioner and parliament, to the council, shall have precepts on Mr. John Wilkie, collector of the vacant stipends, for such sums as shall be modified and allowed by the council, notwithstanding any former act. This was only meant of episcopal ministers; if presbyterians had been allowed a share, the fund would have soon been exhausted: and a provision is not only made for ministers, but others reckoned sufferers for the king's interest. Accordingly, November 7th, I find Andrew Glen late provost of Linlithgow, and James Glen, represent their losses for adherence to his majesty's interests, and constant affection to his service. Last council day a committee had been appointed to examine their losses, and upon report, the council find their losses extend to £7,834 : 5 : 8d. and recommend them to his majesty's favour. I could name presbyterian ministers who lost as much as any of them, by standing up for the king, and yet now they are harassed, turned out, and persecuted: whereupon I may safely enough apply the learned and great Doctor Barrow his distich he wrote on such treatment in England, common to him and many good men.

" Te magis optavit rediturum, Carole, nemo;
Et nemo sensit te rediisse minus."

October 3d, the council ordain the presi-

1661. dent of the session, lord register, and lord Ley, and such of the counsellors as shall be present, to be auditors for taking away and composing the differences betwixt the moderators of the university of Glasgow, and Mr Patrick Gillespie: and in case of variance betwixt the said auditors, the lord chancellor is to be oversman; and give power to the lord chancellor to grant warrant to the said Mr Gillespie to repair to Edinburgh for that effect, notwithstanding of his confinement.

November 7th, information being given, " that George Swinton, and James Glen, booksellers in Edinburgh, have caused print several seditious and scandalous books and papers, such as ' Archibald Campbell's Speech,' ' Guthrie's Speech,' ' the Covenanters' Plea,' &c. Ordered, that the lord advocate and provost of Edinburgh seize upon these books and papers, and discharge them and the rest of the printers to print any more books or papers, till they have warrant from the king, parliament, or council." And, December 5th, they grant liberty to Robert Meiń, keeper of the letter office at Edinburgh, to publish the Diurnal weekly, for preventing of false news.

When at this time the council are prosecuting the worthy Mr Robert Blair, and other presbyterians, for shame they could not but do somewhat against trafficking papists now mightily increasing;[*] and indeed for some years, as we shall see, the council show pretty much zeal against papists, but are retarded by the backwardness of the prelates in this affair. Therefore, November 7th, the chancellor reports that, upon information that several trafficking papists were come into this kingdom, and that John Inglis was one of them, he had caused seize him, and found two letters upon him, which were read in council, and had caused commit him to prison. The council, finding that the said Inglis and William Brown had brought into this kingdom several books and papers, order the provost of Edinburgh to secure their persons in the tolbooth, till further order, and cause seize all their books and papers, which are to be revised by the earl of Linlithgow, lord president, Mr. Bruce, and the said provost of Edinburgn, who are to report; and that the president, advocate, and clerk draw up a proclamation against trafficking papists. November 14th, the lords above named report, that William Brown was content to take voluntary banishment upon him; that Inglis acknowledged himself a trafficking papist, and that he had brought in popish books, and refused to give any account of popish priests lately come into the kingdom, or to relinquish his profession. Both of them are banished, and ordered to remove in three weeks, and never return, under the pains in the acts of parliament.

November 19th, The council issue out the following proclamation against papists, Jesuits, and trafficking priests.

" The lords of his majesty's council, considering that since the reformation and establishment of the protestant religion within this kingdom, many desperate plots and conspiracies have been hatched, and incessantly prosecuted by the emissaries of the pope and his counsels, to the hazard of the undermining of that glorious and blessed structure; wherethrough not only many simple and ignorant people have been deluded and withdrawn from their holy profession, and those principles of truth wherein they were bred and educated; but the pillars and foundations of allegiance and obedience to supreme authority and laws have been sore shaken, by saying and hearing of mass, resetting of Jesuits, and seminary priests, trafficking, and perverting unstable souls, and settling of superiors and other officers depending upon the Romish hierarchy, by whose council and conduct they may propagate the rebellious principles, and erroneous doctrines, which in all probability had prevailed to the great hazard of religion, monarchical government, and the peace of the kingdom, if by the wholesome laws and statutes, and pious care and endeavours of

---

[*] " It was observable in these times, that whenever any thing was done in favours of episcopacy, there was, at the same time also, somewhat done against popery, for allaying the humour of the people, who were bred to believe, that episcopacy was a limb of antichrist."— Mackenzie's History of Scotland, p. 62.—*Ed.*

his majesty, and his royal ancestors, the same had not been prevented: and being informed, that, notwithstanding of the late act of this current parliament, solemnly published against popish priests and Jesuits, whereby his majesty, to witness his royal care of, and zeal for the protestant religion, with consent of the estates of parliament, did command and charge all and sundry Jesuits, priests, and trafficking papists, to depart this kingdom within a month after the publication thereof, and discharged all his subjects to reset, supply, entertain, furnish meat or drink, or keep correspondence with any of the foresaids, under the pains contained in that and former acts of parliament, which, during the late troubles, have not been put in execution against the contraveners: yet divers persons are come into this kingdom, with instructions, popish books, and writings, and priests' vestments, for prosecution of these abominable practices; who, finding themselves now mightily disappointed of that great increase of their numbers, and advancement of their designs, whereof they had great hopes from the late horrid confusions, introduced into church and state by sectaries, do again adventure to trace their old steps, and embroil that order and government restored to us by Almighty God. Therefore they command and charge all his majesty's subjects, of whatsoever quality and degree, to observe and obey the foresaid act, and all other acts of parliament made against priests, Jesuits, and trafficking papists: with certification, if they do otherwise, the whole pains there contained, shall be inflicted without mercy. And ordains all sheriffs of shires and their deputes, magistrates of burghs, and other judges, and all ministers of the gospel, within their respective bounds and jurisdictions, to make exact inquiry after the offenders, and to apprehend their persons, and secure them in the next prison, and immediately to give notice thereof to the privy council: as also to send in yearly to the lords of the privy council, a list of such persons as are known or suspected to be papists, and to seize on all popish books, writings, commissions, instructions, and others belonging to them, which they can apprehend, conform to 194th act, parl. 13th, James VI. and other acts and statutes, as they will be answerable, under all highest pains. And ordains these forthwith to be printed and published."

1661.

That same diet of council, the following letter from the king is read. "Right trusty, &c. Having given orders to our archbishops here, that in all the churches and chapels of this our kingdom, our royal consort queen Katharine be prayed for; we have resolved also, that in our ancient kingdom she be prayed for: and seeing our bishops of that kingdom are not yet consecrated, we have thought fit to require you to issue commands to all the presbyteries of Scotland, that in all the several churches, immediately after their prayer for me, they pray for queen Katharine, and for Mary queen mother, James duke of York, and the rest of the royal family." In the close of the letter, he orders them to raise the value of gold to the same proportion which it is in England. The council order a proclamation to be drawn, and it is published in the above terms, November 21st. Thus the reader hath a pretty large account of this remarkable year, 1661.

CHAP. III.

OF THE SUFFERINGS OF PRESBYTERIANS, AND STATE OF AFFAIRS IN SCOTLAND, DURING THE YEAR 1662.

This year, and the second session of parliament, affords the reader a new scene of persecution. Though none suffered death this year, yet a good many were imprisoned, and not a few ministers banished into foreign countries; several of whom never returned.

1662.

Till the parliament sit down, the council have but little before them; the bishops who were consecrated at London, not coming down till April, and the rest were not consecrated till four days before the parliament sat down. And indeed it was our prelates who pushed the council to most of their severities: however, that arbitrary court, in the beginning of the year, perfect what they

1662. had begun last year, and discharge all ecclesiastical meetings, and prepare matters for the parliament, who sit down May 8th. The parliament set up the prelates, and receive them with solemnity enough into their meeting; they persecute some of the most noted of the presbyterian ministers in the west country, and attack the ministers of Edinburgh: a new set of acts, for the establishment of bishops, and the further harassing of presbyterians, are made; they also pass the sentence of death upon the lord Lorn, afterwards earl of Argyle, and spend much time upon the fining of presbyterians.

But the chief part of the persecution is managed by the council, after the parliament rises; and when some things are done at Edinburgh, they come west to Glasgow, and there turn out some hundreds of presbyterian ministers: and upon the commissioner's return from his progress, the council, in the end of the year, attack a great number of presbyterian ministers, in all the corners of the country, and banish some of them, and confine others. Those things, with some other incidental matters, will afford matter for four or five sections upon this chapter.

SECT. I.

Of the proceedings against presbyterians, before the down-sitting of the parliament, with some essays made to bear testimony against those, and some account of the consecration of the rest of the bishops in Scotland, this year 1662.

MOST part of the proper matter for the history of the sufferings of this church, during this year, falls in during the sitting of the parliament, and towards the end of the year. The council had little before them till the consecrated bishops came down; and yet in January they perfect the work they had entered upon at the close of the last year, the overturning the judicatories of this church, to pave the way for prelates: and therefore I am to give some account of this, with some hints at the testimony essayed against it by some few ministers; and shall shut up this section with an account of the ordination of the rest of our prelates, which will hand us into the 2d session of this current parliament, held by Middleton.

Our Scots council receive their orders from England, where things were now concerted by Mr. Sharp, and the rest of our bishops at this time there; and these are carefully executed at Edinburgh, and proclamations accordingly issued out. Thus, January 2d, the council receive a letter from the king, discharging all ecclesiastical meetings in synods, presbyteries, and sessions, until they be authorized by the prelates: the tenor whereof follows.

" Charles R.

" Right trusty, &c. Whereas, by the advice and consent of our parliament, we did allow the administration of the church government of Scotland, by sessions, presbyteries, and synods, notwithstanding of the act rescissory, until we should take care for the better settlement of the government of that church: and we having, by our late proclamation, declared our royal pleasure for restoring the ancient and legal government of that church, by archbishops and bishops, as it were exercised in the reign of our royal father, before the year 1637, and, in pursuance of that our resolution, have nominated and presented persons to the several bishoprics of Scotland, of whom there has been lately four consecrated, and invested with the same dignities, church power, and authority, which was formerly competent to the bishops and archbishops of that church, in the reigns of our royal grandfather and father.

" Therefore our allowance of the administration of the government of that church, in the way it hath been since the violent interruption of episcopal government, being inconsistent with the same now established, and being now of itself void and expired, seeing it was only for a time, till we should settle and secure church government in a frame most suitable to monarchy, and complying with the peace of the kingdom.

" Our will is, that the said allowance be, of no further force or continuance; but that the jurisdiction and exercise of church government shall be ordered in the respective synods, presbyteries, and sessions of the church of Scotland, by the appointment and authority of the archbishops and bishops thereof, according to the standing laws, and their known privileges and practice conform thereunto.

" This our will and pleasure, you are required forthwith to publish by proclamation, discharging all ecclesiastical meetings in synods, presbyteries, and sessions, until they be authorized and ordered by our archbishops and bishops, upon their entering into the government of their respective sees; which is to be done speedily.

" We do further require, that you take special care, that all due deference and respect be given by all our subjects, to the archbishops and bishops of that church; and that they have all countenance, assistance, and encouragement from our nobility, gentry, and burghs, in the discharge of their office, and service to us in the church; and that severe and exemplary notice be taken of all and every one who shall presume to reflect, or express any disrespect to their persons, or authority with which they are intrusted. And so we bid you heartily farewell. Given at our court at Whitehall, December 28th, 1661. By his majesty's command,

" LAUDERDALE."

The clerk is ordered to draw up a proclamation conform to this letter and the commands therein contained, and have it ready next council day. Accordingly, January 9th, it is read, agreed to, and ordered to be printed and published. It agrees very much with the above letter; however, because of the importance of it, I have insert likewise the proclamation, in a note,* and it

is signed by Glencairn, Rothes, Morton, Roxburgh, Southesk, Weemyss, Annandale, Dundee, Sinclair, Bellenden, John Fletcher, Robert Murray. 1662.

At the same time the council recommend it to the lord chancellor, to sign the following letter to the sheriffs and their deputes, through the kingdom, to be communicated to each minister.

" Right Honourable,

" There is a proclamation emitted by the lords of privy council, intimating his majesty's pleasure for discharging all meetings of synods, presbyteries, and kirk sessions, until they be ordered by the archbishops and bishops of the church of this kingdom: and lest the contributions for the poor, and the distribution thereof within the several parishes in the meantime be interrupted, the council has recommended it to me, to write to you in their name, to acquaint the several ministers of all the parishes within your shire and jurisdiction, that notwithstanding of the said proclamation, they may appoint some of their parish for contribution of the collection, and distributing the same to the poor thereof, for which these presents shall be your warrant, from

" Your affectionate friend,

" GLENCAIRN, Chancellor."

What hath been said upon the former public papers, may supersede reflections on this letter and proclamation. We see that gradually, yet pretty quickly, the presbyterian constitution of this church was overturned. Synods were first interrupted, and then discharged; presbyteries were inhibit to ordain any to their vacancies, and now

---

* At Edinburgh, 9th of January, 1662. The lords of his majesty's privy council having considered his majesty's letter, of the date, at Whitehall the 28th of December last, 1661, bearing, that whereas by the advice and consent of the parliament, his majesty did allow the administration of the church government of this kingdom, by sessions, presbyteries, and synods, notwithstanding of the act rescissory, until his majesty should take care for the better settling of the government thereof: and that having, by a late proclamation, of the date the 6th of September, 1661, declared his royal pleasure for restoring the ancient and legal government of the church, by archbishops and bishops, as it was exercised in the year 1637, and that in pursuance of that resolution, his majesty hath nominated and presented persons to the several bishoprics of this kingdom, of whom some have been lately consecrated, and invested with the same dignities, church power, and authority, which was formerly competent to the archbishops and bishops of this church, in the reigns of his royal grandfather and father, of blessed memory; and that the allowance of the administration of this church, in the way it hath been, since the violent interruption of episcopal government, being inconsistent with the same now established, is now of itself void and expired, as being only for a time, till his majesty should

1662. to meet; and sessions likewise must die with the expiring government of this church. This proclamation razed presbyterian government quite. And we may observe a considerable difference betwixt prelacy now obtruded, and the old Scots episcopacy. Presbyteries and sessions remained under the bishops, during king James VI. his reign, almost in the full exercise of their power, saving that presbyteries were cramped with constant moderators: but now presbyteries and sessions are made entirely to depend upon the bishop, and indeed materially abrogated, as may afterwards be noticed.

The same day this proclamation is published, the council having considered a letter from the earl of Lothian, desiring that the presbytery of Kelso may be discharged to plant the kirk of Yetholm, ordered the clerk to sign the following letter to their moderator.

" Right Reverend,

" The lords of privy council are informed that the kirk of Yetholm being vacant, the earl of Lothian did give in a presentation, as likewise some other persons pretending to have right to the same; and that notwithstanding of the late act, discharging the presentations to presbyteries, you are proceeding in order to the admission of some person to be minister at the said kirk; and therefore have commanded me to acquaint you of the foresaid proclamation, that you do not proceed to admit any person to be minister at the said church, as you will be answerable, which you are to communicate to your brethren, I am, sir,

" Your humble servant,

PETER WEDDERBURN."

Little more offers from the council registers till the parliament rises, and then we shall meet with enough of matter for this history.

Those invasions upon judicatories, but especially the letter and proclamation, quite overturning them, raised an universal sorrow and concern through the kingdom, Presbyterians, formerly broken among themselves, could not easily make any concert, and the ministers were of different sentiments what course was best to take. Now indeed they came to understand one another much better than formerly, when going to a joint furnace. Mr. Douglas, I am told, said, when he saw matters came to this pass, " our

---

settle and secure church government in a frame most suitable to monarchy, and complying with the peace of the kingdom; and so the said allowance should be of no further force and continuance, but the jurisdiction and exercise of church government should be ordered in the respective synods, presbyteries and sessions of this church, by the appointment and authority of the archbishops and bishops thereof, according to the standing laws and their known privilege, and practice conform thereto: and that special care be taken that all due reverence and respect be given by all the subjects, to the archbishops and bishops of the church, and that they have all countenance, assistance, and encouragement, from the nobility, gentry, and others, in the discharge of their office and service to his majesty in the church: and that strict notice be taken of all and every one who shall presume to reflect or express any disrespect to their persons, function or authority, with which they are invested; which his majesty requires to be intimate to the whole lieges by proclamation, discharging all ecclesiastical meetings in synods, presbyteries or sessions, until they be authorized and ordered by the archbishops and bishops, upon their entry unto the government of their respective sees, which is to be done speedily: therefore, in obedience of, and conform to his majesty's royal pleasure and command, have ordained, and by these presents ordain the lyon king at arms, and his brethren heralds, pursuivants, and messengers at arms, to pass to the market-cross of Edinburgh, and there, by open proclamation, to make publication of his majesty's royal pleasure foresaid; discharging all ecclesiastical meetings in synods, presbyteries, and sessions, until they be authorized and ordered by the archbishops and bishops, upon their entering unto the government of their respective sees, as said is; and to require all his majesty's subjects of whatsoever rank, quality, or degree they be, to give all due reverence and respect unto the archbishops and bishops; and that all the nobility, gentry, and boroughs, sheriffs of shires, stewards of stewartries, baillies of regalities, magistrates of burghs, justices of peace, and other public ministers, within their respective bounds and jurisdictions, at all times, give all countenance, assistance, and encouragement to them, in the discharge of their office and service to his majesty in the church: with certification, that if any shall presume to reflect or express any disrespect to their persons, function, or authority with which they are invested, they shall be severely and exemplarily punished, according to the nature and quality of their offence. And ordain these presents to be printed, and published at the market-cross of Edinburgh, as said is, and other places needful, that none may pretend ignorance.

PET. WEDDERBURN, Cl. Sec. Concilii.

God save the king.

brethren the protesters have had their eyes open, and we have been blind." Mr. Dickson used to say, " The protesters have been much truer prophets than they." And Mr. Wood acknowledged to several of his brethren who differed in judgment from him, " That they had been mistaken in their views they took of matters." And till the ashes of those burnings were raised to add fuel to the flame about the indulgence, and after separation for a good many years, the resolutions and protestation were quite buried. Nevertheless, this was a juncture of very much difficulty; and ministers and honest people had their thoughts perhaps as much spent in the melancholy forecastings of approaching sufferings, as upon due methods of a joint opposition to the encroachments so fast making upon them. And it is with regret I observe it, that too little of a spirit for this appeared either with ministers or people. At the first defection to episcopacy in this church, after our reformation from popery, a considerable stand was made by ministers then perfectly united: but now the most part of presbyteries silently obtemperated this proclamation. In some places when they did meet, they found they could do nothing; and the essays of some presbyteries to keep themselves in *possessorio* by meeting, were useless, and reckoned singular by others; and by piece and piece all the presbyteries of the church were deserted, save some few, very few, who subjected to the prelates' orders.

Those heartbreaking encroachments upon the liberties of this church, brought many worthy gray hairs to the grave with sorrow: now indeed the prelatic and old malignant party " saw Zion defiled, and their eyes looked upon her" with pleasure, when many better men mourned and wept to their graves. Those may well be reckoned sufferers; and though they were not martyrs by men's hands, because death prevented that, yet they were confessors and martyrs in resolution, and their death is justly chargeable upon the contrivers and carriers on of the iniquity of this time. Among those I shall afterwards, when I come to the sufferings of particular persons, take notice of the earl of Loudon and Mr. Robert Bailie, who both died, I think, before the parliament sat down.

1662.

Yet some testimony was given by presbyteries in some places; besides others recorded in their registers, declarations against prelacy, and the present encroachments. In Edinburgh, Glasgow, and other chief places, care was taken by the magistrates, there should be no more meetings of presbyteries; so that indeed we can expect little or nothing from them. I shall take notice only of what the presbytery of Kirkcudbright essayed to do at this time, from some original papers come to my hand, preserved among others belonging to that truly great man Mr. Thomas Wylie, minister at Kirkcudbright, whom we shall meet with this year as a sufferer. When the council proclamations against supplicating, taken notice of last year, and those discharging synods, and restricting presbyteries, came to their knowledge, they send two of their number to Edinburgh, with the following commission, which I give from the original before me.

" At Kirkcudbright, January, 1662.

" The presbytery taking to their serious consideration the condition of the work of God in the land at this time, upon mature deliberation do judge it expedient to supplicate the right honourable the lords of his majesty's privy council for removing the bar that lieth in the way of address; and therefore do appoint their reverend brethren, Mr. John Duncan, minister at Rerick, and Mr. James Buglos, minister at Crossmichael, to repair to Edinburgh, or where it shall happen their lordships to be for the time, and present unto their lordships our humble desires, and return their diligence.

" M. W. CANT, Clerk."

I do not question but the two came in to Edinburgh accordingly; and though there be no account of this in the council records, and scarce can be expected there, I as little doubt they essayed to present the following supplication.

1662. "*Unto the right honourable the lords of his majesty's privy council, the humble supplication of the presbytery of Kirkcudbright.*

"May it please your Lordships,

"At our synodical meeting in April last, we were fully resolved in all humility to have presented our earnest petition in Zion's behalf, unto the high and honourable court of parliament, if we had not then been interrupted; and in October last the same resolutions did revive in our breasts, and would have vented themselves, if our meeting had not been prohibited. And truly at this time we do ingenuously confess, if we could obtain it of ourselves and our consciences before God, (when in his presence we are most serious upon the search, what Israel ought to do) we say, if we could obtain it of ourselves to be silent, we should contentedly thrust our mouths in the dust, and not so much as presume once to move a lip.

"But when we consider the work of the Lord, at what height of perfection it was, in the purity of doctrine, worship, discipline, and government in this land; and when we look upon the sad breaches already made upon the wonted integrity of the discipline and government, without which the purity of worship and doctrine cannot long continue; and upon the present actings and preachings of some, which sadly threaten the utter aversion and overturning of the established discipline and government; and when withal we lay to heart, that the Lord requireth of us, 'that for Zion's sake we should not hold our peace, and that for Jerusalem's sake we should not rest, that we should earnestly contend for the faith, and be valiant for the truth upon the earth,' and that we should plead with the powers of the earth in behalf of Zion: when we consider and lay to heart those things, we cannot, we dare not any longer lay the hand upon the mouth, lest by sinful silence, and truth prejudising modesty, we betray a good cause, and fetch a cutting lash upon our own consciences, and provoke the holy One to be offended with us.

"Wherefore, right honourable, we do in all humility prostrate ourselves before your lordships, most humbly and earnestly begging in the name of Jesus Christ, that your honours would be pleased to grant unto us freedom and liberty to unfold our bosoms unto your honours in those things that, relating to the work of God in the land, do sadly aggrieve our spirits; or, if your honours do not of yourselves grant this liberty, we humbly beg that your lordships would be pleased to intercede with the king's most excellent majesty, that he would be graciously pleased to remove the bars that are drawn in the way of address, that so we may have free and safe access unto your lordships, and the ensuing high and honourable court of parliament, to represent our sad grievances arising from the undeniable evils and dangers that the work of reformation in this land is now more than ever threatened with, and to supplicate your and their honours for remedy and redress.

"And particularly we humbly beg, that we may have liberty, with freedom and safety, to express our minds, against the reintroduction of prelacy upon this church and kingdom; in doing whereof we resolve in the Lord to walk (according to the measure we have received) close by the rules of scripture, of Christian prudence, sobriety, and moderation; in all our actings testifying our real affection, faithfulness, and loyalty to the king's most excellent majesty; the preservation of whose royal, person, and whose long flourishing reign in righteousness, is the thing in this world that is and ever shall be dearest unto us, next unto the flourishing of the kingdom of Jesus Christ.

"His majesty's gracious condescending unto those our just and humble desires, will yet more engage our already most deeply engaged hearts and affections unto his majesty's person and government, under whom it is the firm resolution of our hearts, to live in all dutiful obedience, praying that the Lord may long preserve his royal person under the droppings of his grace, and abundant loadenings of his best blessings, and special mercies: and your honours' favourable acceptance of this our humble petition off our hands, and transmitting of the same to his sacred majesty, seconded with your lordships' intercessions for his majesty's grant of these our just desires, will make the present generation bless you, and the generation to come call you happy, and shall add to our former obligations to supplicate at the throne of grace for the Spirit of counsel and government, in the fear of the Lord, unto your lordships, and that your persons and government may be richly blessed of the Lord. Thus we rest, expecting your honours' favourable answer."

When so modest and well drawn a petition could not be heard, we may see what a low pass matters were at in Scotland. All they ask is a fair hearing; and instead of this we shall find afterwards the reverend Mr. Wylie, and a good many others in this presbytery, where I think there was not one conformed to prelacy, were attacked by the council this year and the following. This unreasonable and unmanly method of discharging addresses and applications to a government, and peremptory refusing the most humble applications for the liberty of them, as it cannot be defended, so it was the occasion of all that can be, with the least show of reason, objected against the loyalty of presbyterians: and who can justly blame them for seeking a hearing to their grievances in an armed posture, when the oppression of their enemies had forced them to this? Yet they even came not this length, but after several years' patient suffering of the greatest hardships; as we shall see in the progress of this history.

It was expected the parliament would have sit down early this year; and the presbytery of Kirkcudbright had under their consideration the form of an address to the parliament, a copy whereof is before me, under the reverend Mr. Wylie's hand: it is but the first draft, and no doubt would have been smoothed and altered to the better, had any door been opened for presenting it. Imperfect as it is, in my opinion it deserves a room in this work, as the designed testimony of those worthy persons at this juncture; and I persuade myself they did well that they had this in their hearts. The rude draft, with some clauses added on the margin of it, which seem to relate to the following years, I have added at the bottom of the page.*

---

* Address to parliament from the presbytery of Kirkcudbright.

"Although we have no desire to appear in public view, but incline rather to weep in secret, and pour out our complaints and supplications in Zion's behalf, before the Lord, who sees the afflictions of his people, and hears their cry; yet having this happy opportunity of your honours being assembled in this present parliament, under his most excellent majesty our dear and dread sovereign, (the fruits of whose fatherly care and gracious inclination to relieve the oppressed, and refresh the wearied, conveyed to us by your honours' endeavours, we hopefully expect to taste of) we should be unfaithful to God and his cause, undutiful to our sovereign, cruel to ourselves, and to the present and following generations, if we should let the present occasion slip by in deep silence, not making so much as a mint to groan out our grievances before your honours, who in the Lord's providence seem to be brought together for such a time as this, that enlargement may arise by you, as noble and worthy instruments, unto the people and work of God. We shall forbear to mention the height that the glorious work of reformation had attained to in this kirk, both in our forefathers' time, and especially in our own, in this land. All monuments of idolatry, all superfluity of pompous ceremony, all superiority of lordly prelacy, root and branch, being cut off and removed; the pure worship of God in word and sacraments, the pure government of his house was restored, according to the pattern showed in the mount, and solemnly engaged unto: then were we a crown of glory in the hand of the Lord, and a royal diadem in the hand of our God; then the Lord accompanied his word in the mouth of his faithful servants, with such power and life in converting, comforting, and confirming souls, that it was indeed the power of God unto salvation, and backed it with such power and authority against sin, that by it the works of the devil were destroyed, and Satan fell like lightning, profanity was dashed, and atheists changed either in heart, or at least in countenance; popery, with all error and heresy, so curbed, that it durst not set up its head. Those are so notour that to insist upon them were to trouble your honours by a recital of things, which are so manifestly known that our adversaries themselves cannot deny them; or if they should, many of your honours, being eminently instrumental in the late glorious reformation, and eye-witnesses of the blessed effects thereof, which increased daily until obstructed by the unlawful invasion of the perfidious usurper, whose feet the Lord made to slide in due time, could put them to shame and silence. And though we did give real demonstrations of our loyal affections to his majesty, during that unjust and rebellious usurpation, and may, as to this, without vanity compare and reckon in the gate with several, who now, pretending much to loyalty, do restlessly endeavour to fetch, and keep us, with many others of his majesty's faithful subjects, under the lash of the law, and discountenance of sacred authority,

1662.

1662. Little more offers before the sitting down of the parliament, save the consecration of the rest of the bishops; of which, with their admission into that assembly, I shall here give some account. April 8th, the primate and the other three

---

as if we were the most disloyal persons on the face of the earth, which, the Lord knows is far from our thoughts; neither can any justly or rationally gather any such charge against us from our actions, we having obtained mercy, to carry so under the greatest difficulties, and darkest of times, as our heart doth not reproach us, and, we hope, are approved of God who is greater than our heart; so we are able sufficiently to stop the mouth of calumny itself in speaking against us in this matter. But the vindication of ourselves, however necessary in its own place, not being our main intendment, we can easily command ourselves silence, as willing to be repute any thing, or nothing, for God. We spare to speak upon this subject; if it were our things we were to speak for, we should choose to put our mouths in the dust, and be altogether silent rather than move a lip: but considering the cause we plead for, is the Lord Jesus Christ's, which nearly concerns the souls of his people, and knowing that sinful silence of the mouth in such matters, will make the conscience within to cry, we crave your honours' leave and pardon to pour out our complaints and humble desires before you.

"After our patient enduring of trouble, and our faithful and loyal deportment in relation to his majesty and his interest, during the time of the usurper's prevailing, and of his majesty's sad suffering, we expected, upon his majesty's restoration, not only a reviving from our bondage, but also the promoving and supporting of the covenanted work of reformation; and now that it is fallen out otherwise, is the matter of our grief, and has been the occasion of sad sufferings to many of his majesty's most faithful and loyal subjects, in their consciences, persons, names, and estates, while they refused to give active compliance in such things as they cannot obtain of their consciences to come up to: instead of promoving the reformation, we have lost all that we formerly attained unto; and the glory of our kirk, once beautiful in the eyes of the nations, is now turned into shame, and we are become a reproach unto our neighbours round about: the word was purely and powerfully preached, and followed with a blessing from the Lord, discipline was impartially exercised, then the government of his house did run in the right channel, and was execute by those to whom God had given that charge, in opposition both to episcopacy, independency and erastianism, and the Lord thus feeding his flock, both with the staves of beauty and bands, the staves being in right hands, the church of Christ in the land was edified, holiness was countenanced, profanity decried, and the Lord rested in his love among us. But now the poor of the flock that wait upon the Lord, cry out of soul-starving, and that they are destroyed for lack of knowledge. Now profanity and dissoluteness lift up the head, without shame, without reproof, and keep the crown of the causey. Now popery spreads in all the corners of the land, and papists not only avow themselves, but talk insolently. Now irrational quakers traffic from place to place, and make their proselytes among the simple and unstable.

Now the wicked are hardened and imboldened in their sins, and the tender godly, who will not run with them into the same excess of riot, reproached, discountenanced and persecuted. Now atheism abounds, and the generality are become so ignorant of, and indifferent about the matters of God, and their soul-concernments, that they are apt to receive the impress of any religion, how corrupt soever. And all these wrath-provoking evils do flow, as may be evident to all who do not shut their eyes, from reintroduced prelacy; for the prelates having abandoned discipline, and thrust in and kept in useless, insufficient and scandalous persons upon the Lord's people, several of whom are not worthy to be members of a civil commonwealth, much less to officiate in the house of God; from hence it is that profanity, as from a foul puddle, does flow through the whole land.

"For those things our souls mourn, and for remedy thereof we make this application to your honours, humbly beseeching your lordships, that as you respect the glory of God, the flourishing of Christ's kingdom in the land, the safety of immortal souls, the adorning of his majesty's crown, the quiet of the persons of his majesty's loving and loyal subjects, your own endless praise, and flourishing of your honourable families, the comfort of many oppressed ministers and groaning congregations within the kingdom; and that as you respect your own comfort and peace in the great day of your accounts, you would grant a favourable answer to our most just, reasonable, and in order to the remedying of the forementioned evils, necessary desires. And, 1st, We humbly beg, that by your honours' timous intercession at his majesty's hands (and the Lord grant you favour in the presence of the king) and by your own authority and power, this poor kirk and kingdom, lying in her tears, grief, and fear, may be delivered from the burdensome yoke of prelacy, a yoke which neither we nor our fathers were able to bear, a plant which our heavenly Father hath not planted, and which never took, even from the reformation hitherto, with this kirk and kingdom as its kindly soil, but has still been the occasion and cause of many grievous evils, as experience of old, of late, and at this present, does abundantly witness. 2dly, We humbly beg, that the pure government of the church, by sessions, presbyteries, synods, and general assemblies, may be restored, and suffered without all encroachments to reside in right hands, and all former acts of parliament in favours of the same be revived and ratified for its establishment; that the courts of Christ, thus countenanced by the civil authority, may be in case to purge this church from scandalous ministers and members. 3dly, That all ministers removed from their charges, be restored to their places and functions, to feed the flock of Christ, purchased by his own blood, that the banished be called home, and that his gracious majesty would lay aside his displeasure conceived against others of his majesty's faithful and loving subjects. 4thly, That your lordships would take an effectual way for removing the useless, insufficient, and scandalous persons, that have been thrust

consecrated at London came to Berwick, and were met by considerable numbers of noblemen, gentlemen, and others, upon the road to Edinburgh: some gave themselves the trouble to go as far as Cockburns-path, others to Haddington, and many met them at Musselburgh; and under pretext of obedience to his majesty's commands to put all respect on them, they were received at their coming in with all pomp and solemnity, and trumpets sounding, which was not a little pleasing to Mr. Sharp's ambitious temper.

The commissioner Middleton came down from court to Holyrood-house upon Sunday, May 4th, and the consecration of the rest of our prelates was put off till he should be present to countenance this solemnity, which was indeed a new thing in Scotland. Accordingly, May 7th was fixed for their consecration, in the church of Holyroodhouse. The nobility and gentry in town, with the magistrates and town council of Edinburgh, contributed their best endeavours to put respect upon this work. The church doors were strictly kept, and none had access but those who had warrants. The two archbishops went to the church in great parade in their pontifical habits, black gowns, surplices, lawn sleeves, copes, and all other things in due form. Before the consecration, a sermon was preached by Mr. James Gordon, minister at Drumblait, in the north of Scotland: his text was, 1 Cor. iv. 1. " Let a man so account of us as ministers of Christ, and stewards of the mysteries of God." And in his sermon he insisted upon the faults and escapes of the former prelates, which made them fall, and exhorted the bishops not to encroach upon the nobility, but to keep themselves sober, and not exceed the bounds of their function. The consecrators were the two archbishops. The primate made use of the English forms, and read all from the book, the Lord's Prayer, Creed, and Ten Commandments, and consecration and exhortation after it. I do not find that the bishops were re-ordained presbyters and deacons before their consecration, as the four had been at London; neither that ever it was once proposed. Three of the bishops nominated were not present, but hasting up as soon as possible, the bishop of Aberdeen, and other two who were out of the kingdom: and those three were consecrate afterwards at St. Andrews, in June this year.

1662.

This ceremony paved the way for their admission as members in the parliament, to-morrow, May 8th; where, after the voting of the 1st act, for "restitution of bishops," of which in the next section, they were brought up to the house, and convoyed from it with much pomp. All the bishops were together in the archbishop of St. Andrews' lodgings, near the Nether Bow, waiting for the honour to be done them. Six members of parliament, two noblemen, the earls of Kelly and Weemys, and two barons, and two burgesses were sent to invite them to come and take their seats in the house. From the Nether Bow they came up in state: the two archbishops in the midst of the first rank; the gentlemen, baillies, and the town council of Edinburgh, mixed in with the rest of the bishops, who had all their black gowns and robes. When they came to the house, a speech was made

---

in, and kept in upon the Lord's people, to their great grief, and the starving of their souls. 5thly, That a sufficient defence be provided by your lordships, against all novations in doctrine, sacraments, worship and discipline, and that no acts pass in prejudice of our religion, as reformed in all these, or in corroboration of new opinions against the same, whether episcopacy, ceremonies, or any thing else which should be rejected and not ratified. 6thly, That all former acts of parliament, against cursing, swearing, and fearful blasphemy of God's name, profaning the Lord's day, drinking, whoring, and other abominable sins, universally abounding in the land, and against popery and popish emissaries, by whose means it so much spreadeth every where, be revived, and put in due and ready execution. Thus, earnestly praying God to bless your honours, with the spirit of righteous judgment in the fear of the Lord, and to direct and enable you to do that which may be right in his sight, profitable and refreshing to this poor languishing kirk, comfortable to your own souls in the day of your appearance before the judgment-seat of our Lord Jesus Christ, and to bless and preserve his majesty's royal person, and to establish his throne in righteousness, to endure as long as sun and moon run in their courses, and to bless your honours with sincere zeal for God, true loyalty to his majesty, and endless glory with Christ for ever, we expect your lordships' favourable and refreshing answer.

1662. to them, and the parliament's act restoring them, read, and the house dismissed that day. They were all invited to dine with the commissioner; and he did them the honour to walk down the street with them on foot. Six macers went first, with their maces elevated: next, three gentlemen ushers, one for the commissioner, another for the chancellor, and the third for the archbishop of St. Andrews; and then the pursebearer discovered. The commissioner and chancellor came next, with two noblemen upon their right hand, and the archbishops upon their left hand, in their gowns: and the other noblemen and members of parliament invited, and the rest of the bishops, followed, making up the cavalcade.

When I come to consider the act for their restitution, some general remarks upon the re-introduction of prelacy will offer themselves: only here it may be matter of wonder, that bishops are thus brought in upon this church, without the least shadow of the church's consent or authority. In king James VI. his time, another method was judged better. The corrupted and overawed assembly at Montrose, 1600, after a great struggle, agreed to the caveats, and paved the way for their coming in under another name than that of bishops: and this was found necessary by the court, to prepare matters for the king's succession to England, and the union of the two crowns. The yet more corrupted assembly at Glasgow, 1610, which was so scandalously and openly bribed, did more directly countenance, and some way ratify prelacy. But now they come in without the least consent of the church; yea, contrary to many unrescinded church canons, which made many in Scotland look upon them, and such as they authorized and hatched, as real intruders, not only without consent, but *renitente et contradicente ecclesia*. The reasons of such procedure in this obtrusion were various: the bishops and managers durst not hazard any considerable meeting of ministers in Scotland upon this point. Things were not so ripe for this as in the year 1610, nor so gradually prepared for their giving consent. And now when absolute and arbitrary government was to be set up in the state, and the prerogative stretched to its utmost, it was not unfit to have the ministry and the government of the church entirely depending upon, and set up by the royal prerogative and pleasure: so a church concurrence was not so much as endeavoured, but prelates and prelacy brought in entirely by the supremacy. And upon this foot the parliament give their consent to, and settle episcopacy in their second session; to which I now come, if once I had remarked, that

May 7th, the commissioner in council declares, that it is his majesty's royal will and pleasure, that the earl of Tweeddale's restraint be taken off, and he restored to all his former rights and privileges, and his bond be delivered up to him. Which the council orders to be done; and he had opportunity to sit in parliament to-morrow: but he and others must be taught, by his eight months' imprisonment and confinement, how dangerous it would be to speak their light, and cross the court in any of their votes in the ensuing parliaments.

SECT. II.

Of the acts of the second session of parliament, with reflections upon them, in so far as they concern church affairs this year, 1662.

IN my account of the sufferings of presbyterians this year, I shall begin with the laws made by this session of parliament, which were the foundation of much after-persecution, and then consider the procedure of the council, and their acts, during the rest of the year. The particular sufferings of ministers, gentlemen, and others, I shall leave to a section or two by themselves, though several of them were during the sitting of parliament. I begin now with the acts of this session of parliament under Middleton.

The parliament had been adjourned to March; but it being resolved, that the prelates should have their places in it, and matters not being concerted as to their consecration, it was put off till that could be completed: besides, our nobility at London

CHAP. III.] OF THE CHURCH OF SCOTLAND. 257

were fond of being there at the solemnity of the queen's reception. When she arrived, her majesty was received with the utmost pomp and expectation: and when, in some years, people's expectations of a successor from her failed, it began to be alleged, that chancellor Hyde pitched upon a barren woman for the king, that his grandchildren, by the duke of York, might succeed: but Providence had a further view in it, and both made way for the wonderful revolution, 1688, and deliverance of those kingdoms, when well nigh ruined by the wide steps taken towards popery, during the two brothers' reigns, and the seasonable establishment of the protestant succession, so happily now taken effect, upon the extinction of that line.

Accordingly, May 8th, the parliament sat down. After the old fashion, this session was, if I might speak so, opened by a sermon, preached by Mr. George Haliburton, now bishop of Dunkeld. What his subject was, I do not know, but find he was prolix enough, and exceeded two hours considerably. But leaving this, I come to their acts and proceedings, in as far as they concern ecclesiastic matters. The length of my remarks upon the acts of the former session, will help to shorten any observations I have to make upon this session. The same persons were prosecuting the same design, and much by the same methods, only a little more openly and roundly.

The prelates, already brought in by the king, must now be confirmed by act of parliament; and that is all the warrant they had in Scotland. They were already set up by his majesty's sole authority, and it was very fit they should lean entirely upon his supremacy: however, the representatives of the nation, his majesty's and his bishops' obedient servants, must give their assent; yet not until they could not refuse it, without blaming themselves in giving an absolute power to the king, or casting a blur upon what his majesty had done. Therefore they fall to work; and their very first act is, "For the restitution and re-establishment of the ancient government of the church, by archbishops and bishops;" which I have added below.* It was the prelates' fault if this act was not ample enough, for it was drawn at the sight, and

1662.

---

* Act for the restitution and re-establishment of the ancient government of the church, by archbishops and bishops.

Forasmuch as the ordering and disposal of the external government and policy of the church, doth properly belong unto his majesty, as an inherent right of the crown, by virtue of his royal prerogative and supremacy in causes ecclesiastical; and in discharge of this trust, his majesty, and his estates of parliament, taking to their serious consideration, that in the beginning of, and by the late rebellion within this kingdom, in the year 1637, the ancient and sacred order of bishops was cast off, their persons and rights were injured and overturned, and a seeming parity among the clergy factiously and violently brought in, to the great disturbance of the public peace, the reproach of the reformed religion, and violation of the excellent laws of the realm, for preserving an orderly subordination in the church: and therewithal considering, what disorders and exorbitances have been in the church what encroachments upon the prerogative and rights of the crown, what usurpations upon the authority of parliaments, and what prejudice the liberty of the subject hath suffered, by the invasions made upon the bishops and episcopal government, which they find to be the church government most agreeable to the word of God, most convenient and effectual for the preservation of truth, order and unity, and most suitable to monarchy, and the peace and quiet of the state: therefore his majesty, with advice and consent of his estates of parliament, hath thought it necessary, and accordingly doth hereby redintegrate the state of bishops to their ancient places and undoubted privileges in parliament, and to all their other accustomed dignities, privileges and jurisdictions, and doth hereby restore them to the exercise of their episcopal function, presidence in the church, power of ordination, inflicting of censures, and all other acts of church discipline, which they are to perform with advice and assistance of such of the clergy as they shall find to be of known loyalty and prudence. And his majesty, with advice foresaid, doth revive, ratify, and renew all acts of any former parliaments, made for the establishment, and in favours of this ancient government, and doth ratify and approve all acts and proclamations emitted by his majesty or his privy council, since the first day of June last, in order to the restitution of bishops. And further, it is hereby declared that whatever shall be determined by his majesty, with advice of the archbishops and bishops, and such of the clergy as shall be nominated by his majesty, in the external government and policy of the church (the same consisting with the standing laws of the kingdom) shall be valid and effectual. And his majesty, considering how necessary it is, that all doubts or scruples, which from former acts or practices may occur to any concerning this sacred order, be cleared and removed, doth therefore, of certain knowledge, and with advice foresaid, rescind, cass, and annul all acts of parliament, by which the sole and only power

2 K

1662. by the direction of the primate: and yet, it was said, some of our bishops grumbled that they were not reponed to all that the popish bishops enjoyed. This act, I find, passed in the house with very little opposition: some objections were

and jurisdiction within this church, doth stand in the church, and in the general, provincial, and presbyterial assemblies, and kirk sessions, and all acts of parliament or council which may be interpreted to have given any church power, jurisdiction or government, to the office-bearers of the church, their respective meetings, other than that which acknowledgeth a dependance upon, and subordination to the sovereign power of the king, as supreme, and which is to be regulated and authorized, in the exercise thereof, by the archbishops and bishops who are to put order to all ecclesiastical matters and causes, and to be accountable to his majesty for their administrations. And particularly, his majesty, with advice foresaid, doth rescind and annul the first act of the twelfth parliament of king James VI. holden in the year 1592, and declares the same, and all the heads, clauses, and articles thereof, void and null, in all time coming. And his majesty considering, that the jurisdiction of the commissariots is a proper part of the rights and privileges belonging to the bishops, doth therefore, with advice foresaid, restore the archbishops and bishops to their said jurisdiction of commissariots, according to the sixth act of the parliament 1609, which is hereby ratified and renewed: and accordingly ordains, that in all time coming the quotes of testaments be paid in to the archbishops and bishops in their respective dioceses, as formerly; and rescinds and annuls the twenty-eighth act of the last session of this present parliament, anent the quotes of testaments, and declares the same void in all time coming. It is always hereby declared, that this act is without prejudice of the present commissaries, their clerks and fiscals, their enjoying their places and benefits thereof, conform to their gifts and laws of this kingdom; unless, for their insufficiency or misdemeanours they be found incapable of the same. Further, his majesty, with advice and consent foresaid, statutes and ordains, that no act, gift, tack, or deed, passed by whatsoever authority, since the interruption of the government by archbishops and bishops, in the year 1637, to the prejudice of their rights, patronages, admiralties, superiorities, rents, possessions, and jurisdictions pertaining to the several bishoprics, stand valid or be in force: but that the said archbishops and bishops may have their claim, right and possession for the year 1661, and all years following, to whatsoever was possessed by, or by the laws of the kingdom was due to their predecessors in anno 1637, and that notwithstanding of any donation or rights made to colleges, churches, corporations, ministers, or any other persons, since the year 1637, by whatsoever order, deed, or warrant, excepting as is aforesaid, in favours of commissaries, clerks, and fiscals. And whereas, divers persons having right to lands, annualrents, or some other estate holden formerly of bishops, or who had succeeded, or acquired rights to the said lands, and others of the nature and holding foresaid, have been forced, during the late troubles, there being no other way or superior for the time, to obtain themselves infeft

therein, holden of his majesty or his royal father, or of their donators having right for the time; and to that effect did take precepts out of the chancery, and to pass infeftments under the great seal, and to obtain precepts and charters from the said other persons who had right to their superiorities for the time; and his majesty being graciously pleased, that such rights and infeftments as, for the time, were necessary and of course taken and passed in manner foresaid, should not be prejudised: therefore it is statute and declared, that all persons, who, since the beginning of the troubles in the year 1635, are entered or infeft by his majesty or his royal father, by the pretended authority for the time, or any other person having right from them in any land or estate holden immediately of the bishops before the said troubles, shall now hold the same of the respective archbishops and bishops, their lawful superiors, in the same manner as they, their predecessors and authors, held the same before the late troubles. And it is declared, that neither this nor any other act of the last or present session of this parliament, shall prejudge any retours, signatures, charters, precepts, infeftments, sasines of lands, annual rents, or any other estate holden immediately of bishops, whereby the same are retoured, or infeftments of the same are taken, to be holden of the king or his donators, since the time foresaid, upon retours, resignations, comprisings, adjudications, or by way of confirmation, or precepts of *clare constat*, or otherways: which infeftments being orderly passed, as they ought to have been for the time, with the retours, signatures and other warrants of the same, his majesty, with consent foresaid, doth ratify and approve, and declares to be valid rights, as if the same had been granted or renewed by the said archbishops or bishops. It is always declared, that the declaration and ratification foresaid, shall not be extended to any new gift or grant, or any other clause or right contained in the said infeftments or signatures, or other warrants of the same, whereby any new gift or original right of the said lands and others are given, or the right of the same is granted or conveyed otherways than conform to the rights and infeftments thereof, before the time aforesaid. Likeas it is declared, that the said ratification and declaration foresaid, shall not corroborate or import any ratification to the said vassals, their former rights, which are to be in the same case as they were in the beginning of the said troubles, in the year foresaid; in regard it is his majesty's intention: likeas it is declared by his majesty, with consent foresaid, that the archbishops and bishops shall be, as to their patrimony and rents, in the same case and condition as they were in the year foresaid, notwithstanding of whatsoever acts of the pretended parliaments since the time foresaid, to the contrary: and notwithstanding of whatsoever rights, grants, or deeds flowing from, or depending upon, or done or granted by virtue of any act or acts of the said pretended parliaments, which his majesty, with consent foresaid, doth declare, decern, and determine to be void and null,

made, as to some clauses, by some of the lords of erection. David Lesly, this day admitted to the house as a temporal lord, dissented from the act; and when he did so, and some near him began to smile, he roundly told them, "the day was, when none of them durst have mocked him." The reader will bear with me in making a few remarks upon this "act restoring bishops."

The title of the act would not be at all disagreeable to popery, had they been re-introducing it. The ancient government of the church under antichrist, was by the pope, archbishops, and bishops. In the body of the act, indeed they find that government to be most agreeable to the word of God. Had they been as freely chosen representatives, as those after the revolution, and had declared prelacy agreeable to the inclinations of the people in Scotland, as then, upon just grounds, prelacy was declared an insupportable grievance, and contrary to the inclinations of the people, it had been a declaration very competent for them, providing it had agreed with truth. But, without any breach of charity, we may suppose, that few who voted this act, had been at any great pains to search into the word of God; it was enough to many, that it was the king's word, and what he was for. For my share, I cannot well see the consistency of their finding this government agreeable to the word of God, with the very first clause of the act, "forasmuch as the ordering and disposal of the external government, and policy of the church, doth properly belong to his majesty, as an inherent right of the crown."

1662.

This leads me to observe, that the parliament bottom their bishops upon the king's prerogative, and the ecclesiastical supremacy; which abundantly seems to explain the oath of allegiance, really of supremacy, formerly spoken of. I have said so much already upon that oath, that I need only observe, that presbyterians allow heartily all the prerogatives to their sovereign which scripture and sound reason can allow of; yet the people of that persuasion have still stood up in asserting liberty and property, in conjunction with the prerogative bounded by the laws of the land. And it is worth our notice, that so soon as our princes set up for an unbounded prerogative and absolute power, they continually attacked presbyterian government, as most agreeable to law and liberty. Indeed the cause and interest of liberty and presbytery have still stood and fallen together in Scotland.

By this act, the bishops are "restored to their ancient prerogatives, privileges, and functions, which they are to exercise with advice of such of the clergy, as they shall find to be of known loyalty and prudence." Hereby it is left to their choice to pitch upon whom they please, among the underlings, to join with them in the management: and, for what I can see, they may act entirely without taking any of them in at all. Thus indeed they generally did in fact.

The parliament, in the next room, approve all the acts of council, since they were erected; and so, by their own deed, discharge all petitioning of the king by his subjects, in the matters of the church, and prohibit all synods, presbyteries, or sessions, to meet, except as the bishops shall allow them, and all subjects to countenance or submit to these judicatories of Christ's institution. We shall afterwards find, that it is very customary for our parliaments to make their acts to look backwards. Yea, they for ever put the power out of their own hand, and from their entire confidence of the infallibility of the civil pope, and his council, the archbishops and bishops, the parliament beforehand ratify, make valid and effectual "all

---

except in so far as is reserved and ratified in manner above written. It is hereby declared, that this act of restitution shall give no right to any of the said archbishops or bishops, or their successors, nor to the heirs or executors of the deceased bishops, of any rents belonging to the archbishoprics or bishoprics, preceding the year 1661, after the said year 1638, but that all the said rents intromitted with by, and pertaining to such persons as had right thereto for the time. As also, all such persons who, *bona fide*, have made payment of their feu duties, tiends, and tiend duties, and others, rents of their bishoprics, are and shall be also secured for bygones allenarly, free of any action or question, notwithstanding of this present act, or any thing therein contained.

1662. that shall be determined by his majesty, with the advice of his bishops and archbishops, and such of the clergy as he shall call, as to the external policy and government of the church;" and frankly give them liberty to do every thing, but establish presbytery, which was against the (then) standing laws.

They go on to cass and annul all acts and laws, which gave any jurisdiction to churchmen, or judicatories independent of the king's supremacy. One must in charity hope, they mean this only of human laws, and they take not upon them to abrogate the divine law establishing a jurisdiction and ministerial power in the officers of Christ's house, as a spiritual society independent, to be sure, upon the regal supremacy, and some hundreds of years in exercise of those powers, before a regal supremacy was thought upon. However, in as far as in them lies, this is a home-thrust at all ecclesiastical power, and a putting the king, as far as their law could put him, in Christ's room, and making him somewhat above the pope himself, in the eyes of a great many papists. And the act of parliament, 1592, which because not in every body's hands who may read this history, I have annexed, in a note,*

is particularly rescinded *in all its heads and clauses.* This act relates to the doctrine as well as the government of this church, and was one of the greatest bulwarks against popery we had, being the act about religion, framed with the greatest deliberation and care, when James VI. was come to his majority, and about the time when our excellent national covenant was formed: so that the introduction of prelacy was attended with the sapping the very foundations of our reformation in Scotland; and this act restoring bishops, makes not only the government of the church, but also the profession of the protestant religion, in its doctrine, depend entirely upon the king's pleasure. Thus king James VII. had a short and easy game to play in Scotland, had not the happy revolution prevented him. Any church power remaining, is to be exercised in a line of subordination to the king, by the archbishops and bishops, who are to put order to all ecclesiastical matters and causes, and to be accountable to the king only, for their administration, no, not to the parliament itself; though, in the beginning of the act, they seem copartners with his majesty in the administration. Certainly the management of all ecclesiastical matters and causes, was

---

* Act 114, Parl. 12.—James VI., 1592. Ratifying the liberty of the true kirk, &c.

Our sovereign lord, and estates of this present parliament, following the loveable and good example of their predecessors, has ratified and approved, and by the tenor of this present act ratifies and approves all liberties, privileges, and immunities, and freedoms whatsomever, given and granted by his highness, his regents in his name, or any of his predecessors, to the true and holy kirk, presently established within this realm, and declared in the first act of his highness's parliament, the twentieth day of October, the year of God, 1579, and all and whatsomever acts of parliament, and statutes made of before by his highness and his regents, anent the liberty and freedom of the said kirk: and specially, the first act of the parliament holden at Edinburgh, the twenty-fourth day of October, the year of God, 1581, with the haill particular acts there mentioned: which shall be as sufficient as if the same were here expressed, and all other acts of parliament made sensine in favour of the true kirk: and siklike ratifies and approves the general assemblies appointed by the said kirk, and declares that it shall be lawful to the kirk and ministers, every year at the least, and oftener *pro re nata,* as occasion and necessity shall require, to hold and keep general assemblies, providing that the king's majesty, or his commissioners with them to be appointed by his highness, be present at ilk general assembly before the dissolving thereof, nominate and appoint time and place when and where the next general assembly shall be holden; and in case neither his majesty nor his said commissioners be present for the time in that town where the said general assembly beis holden; then and in that case it shall be leisom to the said general assembly by themselves to nominate and appoint time and place where the next general assembly of the kirk shall be kept and holden, as they have been in use to do thir times past. And also ratifies and approves the synodal and provincial assemblies to be holden by the said kirk and ministers twice ilk year, as they have been and are presently in use to do, within every province in this realm: and ratifies and approves the presbyteries and particular sessions appointed by the said kirk, with the haill jurisdiction and discipline of the same kirk, agreed upon by his majesty, in conference had by his highness, with certain of the ministers convened to that effect: of the which articles the tenor follows. Matters to be entreated in provincial assemblies. Thir assemblies are constitute for weighty matters, necessary to be entreated by mutual consent and assistance of brethren within the province, as need requires. This assembly has power to handle, order, and redress all things omitted or done amiss in the particular assemblies: it has power to depose the office-

a trust too great for any fourteen men upon earth, with the best king at their head. In former times, the bishops, when first palmed upon this church, were accountable to general assemblies, and the ministry had some share in the government; but now they have none, except the bishops please to call for them.

To complete the power of the prelates, they are restored to all the commissariats in Scotland. Our Lord would not be judge about inheritances, nor the Apostles serve tables, nay, not so much as take up their time in ordering the money collected for the poor: yet our pretended successors to them, take willingly upon themselves the whole burden of the testamentary causes in Scotland, those of divorces, and many others: and rather than the bishops want this branch of their dignity, this loyal parliament will rescind their own 28th act made last year. In short, by this act, Erastianism is set up in its greatest vigour and extent. The actings approven by the king and his father, in many parliaments and treaties, are branded with rebellion, and all the evils which fell out in the former times, are charged upon the presbyterians; whereas indeed, it was the bishops themselves, now brought in contrary to the acts of assembly,

1662.

---

bearers of that province, for good and just cause deserving deprivation: and generally thir assemblies have the haill power of the particular elderships whereof they are collected. Matters to be entreated in the presbyteries. The power of the presbyteries is to give diligent labours in the bounds committed to their charge: that the kirks be kept in good order; to inquire diligently of naughty ungodly persons, and to travel to bring them in the way again by admonition, or threatening of God's judgments, or by correction. It appertains to the eldership, to take heed that the word of God be purely preached within their bounds; the sacraments richly ministered, the discipline entertained, and ecclesiastical goods uncorruptly distributed. It belongs to this kind of assemblies, to cause the ordinances made by the assemblies, provincials, nationals, and generals, to be kept and put in execution; to make constitutions which concern τὸ πρέπον in the kirk, for decent order in the particular kirk where they govern, providing that they alter no rules made by the provincial or general assemblies; and that they make the provincial assemblies foresaid privy of the rules that they shall make; and to abolish constitutions tending to the hurt of the same. It has power to excommunicate the obstinate, formal process being led, and due interval of times observed. Anent particular kirks, if they be lawfully ruled by sufficient ministry and session, they have power and jurisdiction in their own congregation in matters ecclesiastical. And decerns and declares the said assemblies, presbyteries, and sessions, jurisdiction, and discipline thereof foresaid, to be in all times coming most just, good, and godly in the self, notwithstanding of whatsomever statutes, acts, canon, civil, or municipal laws made in the contrar; to the which and every one of them thir presents shall make express derogation. And because there are divers acts of parliament made in favour of the papistical kirk, tending to the prejudice of the liberty of the true kirk of God, presently professed within this realm, jurisdiction, and discipline thereof, which stand yet in the books of the acts of parliament not abrogated nor annulled, therefore his highness, and estates foresaid, has abrogated, cassed, and annulled, and by the tenor hereof abrogates, casses, and annuls all acts of parliament made by any of his highness's predecessors for maintenance of superstition and idolatry, with all and whatsoever acts, laws, and statutes, made at any time before the day and date hereof, against the liberty of the true kirk, jurisdiction, and discipline thereof, as the same is used and exercised within this realm. And in special, that part of the act of parliament holden at Stirling, the fourth day of November, the year of God 1443, commanding obedience to be given to Eugenius, the pope for the time; the act made by king James III. in his parliament, holden at Edinburgh, the 24th day of February, the year of God 1480, and all other acts whereby the pope's authority is established: the act of king James III. in his parliament, holden at Edinburgh, the 20th day of November, the year of God 1469, anent the Saturday and other vigils to be holidays, from evensong to evensong. Item, That part of the act, made by the queen regent, in the parliament holden at Edinburgh, the 1st day of February, the year of God 1551, giving special license for holding the Pasch and Yule. Item, The king's majesty and estates foresaid declare, that the 129th act of the parliament, holden at Edinburgh, the 22d day of May, 1584, shall no ways be prejudicial, nor derogate any thing to the privilege that God has given to the spiritual office-bearers in the kirk, concerning heads of religion, matters of heresy, excommunication, collation, or deprivation of ministers, or any siklike essential censures, specially grounded and having warrant of the word of God. Item, Our sovereign lord and estates of parliament foresaid, abrogate, cass, and annul the act of the same parliament, holden at Edinburgh the said year, 1584, granting commission to bishops and other judges, constitute in ecclesiastical causes, to receive his highness's presentations to benefices, to give collation thereupon, and to put order in all causes ecclesiastical, which his majesty and estates foresaid declare to be expired in the self, and to be null in time coming, and of none avail, force, nor effect: and therefore, ordain all presentations to benefices, to be direct to the particular presbyteries in all time coming, with full power to give collation thereupon; and to put order to all matters and causes ecclesiastical within their bounds, according to the discipline of the kirk: providing the aforesaid presbyteries be bound and astricted to receive and admit whatsomever qualified minister, presented by his majesty, or laick patrons.

1662. ratified in the parliaments held by the king's father and himself in person, who, by their innovations, and imposing the service book and canons, occasioned any confusion or disorder which was in that period.

Upon the whole, any body who is acquaint with the history of this church, must observe, that the old set of bishops made by the parliament, 1612, were but pigmies to the present high and mighty lords. A large account might be given of the differences betwixt the former establishment of prelacy in Scotland, and this; some of them have been pointed at, and I shall notice a few more, and mix in some remarks of the reverend Mr. Douglas, from his paper formerly spoken of. Our first prelates were not against the meetings of presbyteries in their several jurisdictions, but they continued to meet regularly, and had almost the whole of church discipline in their hands: but now there is no church power save in the person of the bishop, and what he pleases to measure graciously out to whom he pleases. All church judicatories, as we have seen, are pulled down, to make way for the episcopal throne. It was some years after this, before the curates and inferior clergy in most places were allowed to meet for the exercise of their gifts together; and when at length this was permitted, they were constituted only for such and such ends, by a commission from the bishop, allowing the ministers in such and such a precinct to meet, with a clause excluding ruling elders. Mr. Douglas remarks here, " that he dealt with the statesmen not to discharge presbyteries, but allow them to stand as under the former bishops; and suggested, that several ministers would keep those meetings, if permitted to continue as before, notwithstanding bishops were set up; but, if pulled down, and set up in subordination to the prelates, no honest minister could keep them. But, says he, our prelates would have them discharged, fearing that their lordly and absolute power would be diminished by them; and in this they discovered their folly and vanity. The former bishops advanced not without presbyteries, synods, and assemblies. Those indeed were corrupt meetings, yet this way they came to have their power and jurisdiction by a sort of consent: but these men want all consent, which shows their usurpation and lordly dominion the more. God, in his providence, infatuated them so, as they waited not for any consent: I am afraid they might have met with too many corrupt men to give consent, but they would not hazard this; and our suffering is the more clear, that they are plain usurpers without consent of the kirk; and whatever hath been the carriage, or rather miscarriage of particular persons, I am glad the kirk in her courts is free of that usurpation, and only those who joined are guilty of it.

" When I compare the former prelates with the present, whose little finger is bigger than their predecessors' loins, I would not be thought to approve the former bishops; for they are both evil, but the last exceed. The former bishops removed very few, but suffered many eminent godly men to live at their charges; but the present have cast out heaps, and scarce a nonconformist is at his charge. Those who were removed formerly, were suffered to live where they pleased, and even to converse with their people; but now they must remove at such and such distances from their flock.

" Formerly, when nonconformists were removed, no restrictions were laid upon them; they might preach any where save in their own charges; and I know some of them who did preach even in the next congregation; but now it is made a crime to preach in the kingdom. Now ministers are discharged to come near cathedrals or burghs: the former prelates did not think their cathedrals so holy as to be defiled by the nearness of nonconformists; yea, some of them continued in their charges very near them, and were never before prohibited to live in burghs for their own conveniency, and the education of their children. The former bishops never cared how many ministers lived in one place; and they knew it was better to have the nonconformists together, than scattered abroad: but now none but one must be in one congregation, and that will the more scatter them. The former bishops never thought of such an impossible division of confinements, as twenty miles from a minister's former charge, six from a cathedral, and three from a burgh, with one only in one parish; neither of prohibiting ministers from coming to Edinburgh, without the bishops or council's license, which is against law and reason; far less did the former prelates ever think of discharging charity to suffering ministers." Thus far Mr. Douglas. We shall meet with those acts afterward in their place.

Those were peculiarities of this prelacy, unknown almost any where save in Scotland. In short, the first prelates claimed only a sort of negative over the brethren of the exercise or presbytery, and great were the struggles before even this was yielded in several places: but now the bishop has not only a negative, but a positive; and all church power and government is lodged in his sole person, his assistants being only his own choice, and mere shadows as to power of deciding in any case. I have run out at so great a length upon this act restoring prelacy, that I shall be the shorter upon the following.

Their second act, " For the preservation of his majesty's person, authority, and government," is every way so singular an establishing iniquity by law, a foundation for much persecution, and an opening the door to popery, since the national covenant, and acts relating to it, pointed most against popery, that I could not omit inserting it below. * Reflections are now obvious,

things are no longer disguised, or 1662. softly and ambiguously expressed, but the carved work pulled down at once; yea, all petitioning for a redress of grievances, upon the matter is discharged by this odd act, when the prelates have taken their seats in the house. The very title of the act supposes the king's authority and government could not be preserved without overturning all that work in the late times, so signally owned of God; which sober people must reckon a lasting blot upon the king by this loyal parliament.

They thank the king for " passing by the miscarriages of his subjects;" witness his unparalleled grace and goodness to the marquis of Argyle, whose son they are just now about to try and condemn! Next, they thank him for " restoring of bishops," which being really his proper deed, and never the desire of Scotland, had it been worth thanks, they belonged to his majesty. Then they declare it a treasonable position and seditious, " that it is lawful for subjects to enter into leagues and covenants for reformation." This declaration runs so flatly in the face of scripture, reason, and the approven practice of many, that it is a shame and reproach that it stands in the body of our Scots laws, and casts a slur upon our excellent reformation from popery, which upon the matter is here declared to have been seditious and treasonable. And we need not be surprised to find them declaring all done since the

---

* Act for preservation of his majesty's person, authority, and government.

The estates of parliament, taking into their consideration the miseries, confusions, bondage, and oppressions this kingdom hath groaned under, since the year 1637, with the causes and occasions thereof, do with all humble duty and thankfulness acknowledge his majesty's unparalleled grace and goodness, in passing by the many miscarriages of his subjects, and restoring the church and state to their ancient liberties, freedom, rights, and possessions; and the great obligations thereby lying upon them to express all possible care and zeal in the preservation of his majesty's person, (in whose honour and happiness consisteth the good and welfare of his people) and in the security and establishment of his royal authority and government, against all such wicked attempts and practices for the time to come. And since the rise and progress of the late troubles, did, in a great measure, proceed from some treasonable and seditious positions infused into the people, " that it was lawful to subjects, for reformation, to enter into covenants and leagues, or to take up arms against the king, or those commissionated by him, and such like:" and that many wild and rebellious courses were taken and practised in pursuance thereof, by unlawful meetings and gatherings of the people by mutinous and tumultuary petitions, by insolent and seditious protestations against his majesty's royal and just commands, by entering into unlawful oaths and covenants, by usurping the name and power of council tables and church judicatories, after they were by his majesty discharged, by treasonable declarations, that his majesty was not to be admitted to the exercise of his royal power, until he should grant their unjust desires, and approve their wicked practices, by rebellious rising in arms against his majesty, and such as had commission from him; and by the great countenance, allowance, and encouragement given to these pernicious courses by the multitude of seditious sermons, libels, and discourses, preached, printed, and published, in defence

1662. year 1637, in meetings, petitions, protestations, &c. to be unlawful and seditious.

Then they declare, " those oaths, the national covenant, as sworn and explained 1638, and afterward, and the solemn league and covenant were, and are in themselves unlawful oaths, and imposed against the fundamental laws of the kingdom." *O tempora! O mores!* Will nothing satisfy them, and the prelates now among them, save the making themselves and the king guilty of taking the Lord's name in vain; and to arraign his majesty as an invader of the fundamental laws of the kingdom: then they assume the pope's power, and declare the consciences of all who had taken those oaths free from the obligation of them. The motive whence all this eccentrical and wild work flows, is plain from what follows: those solemn oaths had barred out prelates, so they must as far as they can disengage themselves and the nation from them, that no alteration be now made in the church;

---

thereof. And considering, that as the present age is not fully freed of those distempers, so posterity may be apt to relapse therein, if timous remeed be not provided: therefore the king's majesty and estates of parliament do declare, that these positions, " that it is lawful to subjects, upon pretence of reformation, or other pretence whatsoever, to enter into leagues and covenants, or to take up arms against the king; or that it is lawful to subjects, pretending his majesty's authority, to take up arms against his person or those commissionated by him, or to suspend him from the exercise of his royal government, or to put limitations upon their due obedience and allegiance," are rebellious and treasonable; and that all these gatherings, convocations, petitions, protestations, and erecting, and keeping of council tables, that were used in the beginning, and for carrying on of the late troubles, were unlawful and seditious: and particularly, that these oaths, whereof the one was commonly called " the National Covenant," (as it was sworn and explained in the year 1638, and thereafter) and the other entitled, " a Solemn League and Covenant," were and are in themselves unlawful oaths, and were taken by, and imposed upon the subjects of this kingdom, against the fundamental laws and liberties of the same; and that there lieth no obligation upon any of the subjects from the said oaths, or either of them, to endeavour any change or alteration of government either in church or state; and therefore annul all acts and constitutions, ecclesiastical or civil, approving the said pretended national covenant, or league and covenant, or making any interpretations of the same or either of them. And also it is hereby declared by his majesty and estates of parliament, that the pretended assembly, kept at Glasgow in the year 1638, was in itself (after the same was by his majesty discharged, under the pain of treason) an unlawful and seditious meeting; and that all acts, deeds, sentences, orders or decreets passed therein, or by virtue of any pretended authority from the same, were in themselves from the beginning, are now, and in all time coming, to be reputed unlawful, void and null: and that all ratifications or confirmations of the same, passed by whatsoever authority, or in whatsoever meetings, shall from henceforth be void and null. Likeas, his majesty and estates of parliament, reflecting on the sad consequences of these rebellious courses, and being careful to prevent the like for the future, have therefore statute and ordained, and by these presents statute and ordain, that if any person or persons shall hereafter plot, contrive, or intend death or destruction to the king's majesty, or any bodily harm tending to death or destruction, or any restraint upon his royal person, or to deprive, depose or suspend him from the style, honour, and kingly name of the imperial crown of this realm, or any others his majesty's dominions, or to suspend him from the exercise of his royal government, or to levy war or take up arms against his majesty or any commissionated by him, or shall entice any strangers or others, to invade any of his majesty's dominions, and shall, by writing, printing, preaching, or other malicious and advised speaking, express or declare such their treasonable intentions, every such person or persons, being upon sufficient probation legally convicted thereof, shall be deemed, declared, and adjudged traitors, and shall suffer forfeiture of life, honour, lands, and goods, as in cases of high treason. And further, it is by his majesty and estates of parliament declared, statute and enacted, that if any person or persons shall, by writing, printing, praying, preaching, libelling, remonstrating, or by any malicious and advised speaking, express, publish, or declare any words or sentences to stir up the people to the hatred or dislike of his majesty's royal prerogative and supremacy in causes ecclesiastic, or of the government of the church by archbishops and bishops, as it is now settled by law, or to justify any of the deeds, actings, practices, or things above mentioned, and declared against by this present act, that every such person or persons so offending, and being, as said is, legally convicted thereof, are hereby declared incapable to enjoy or exercise any place or employment, civil, ecclesiastical, or military, within this church and kingdom, and shall be liable to such further pains as are due by the law in such cases: provided always, that no person be processed for any of the offences aforesaid, contained in this act, (other than these that are declared to be high treason) unless it be by order from his majesty, or by order of his privy council for the time; neither shall they incur any of the penalties above mentioned, unless they be pursued within eight months after the offence committed, and sentenced thereupon within four months after the intenting of the process. And it is also declared, that if his majesty grant his pardon to any person convicted for any of the offences contained in this present act, after such pardon, the party pardoned shall be restored to all intents and purposes, as if he had never been pursued nor convicted; any thing in this act to the contrary notwithstanding.

and to complete all, further they rescind all acts, ecclesiastical or civil, approving those covenants, particularly the acts of the assembly at Glasgow, 1638. It is a wonder they spared the succeeding assemblies. Next it is made treason, "to take up arms against any commissioned by his majesty, or to invite strangers to come into any of his majesty's dominions." By this our revolution, had matters ripened far enough, as they were pretty fast hastening some years ago, would have been found to be treason.

There follows a hedge about the supremacy and prelacy, which appears odd enough, and became a foundation of a most extensive persecution for conscience' sake, if any thing can be so called; "all writing, speaking, printing, preaching, praying, &c., tending to stir up a dislike of his majesty's royal prerogative and supremacy in causes ecclesiastical, or the government by archbishops and bishops now settled." Which takes in not only presbyterians, but many prelatists, and all who were upon any other lay in this matter, but that of absolute supremacy; "or tending to justify any thing done since the year 1638." Such as were guilty, upon conviction, are declared incapable to enjoy any public trust, civil, ecclesiastical, or military, yea further, made liable to all the pains appointed by law for sedition. The very naming of these clauses of those acts, does abundantly justify the happy revolution; and cannot but expose our prelates, to whom we owe all those iniquitous clauses, and plainly evince that prelacy in the church of Scotland was still the road to tyranny in the state, persecution in the church, horrid invasions upon the liberty of the subjects, and dreadful oppression in the matters of conscience.

Their third act, concerning benefices, stipends, and patrons, which is added below,* gives us a new proof that patronages were one of the great pillars of 1662. prelacy. The parliament find, that patrons' rights were unjustly taken away in the year 1649. Whereas, as we have seen, nothing was removed by that act, save the unreasonable as well as unchristian burden of the patron's presentation of ministers, so obstructive to the planting of congregations according to Christ's rule, the interests of the gospel, and good of souls; and the civil interest and benefit of patrons was preserved and enlarged.

By this act, all ministers entered since the year 1649, are to take presentations from their respective patrons. The reason given in the act, "at and before which patrons were injuriously dispossessed," seems to lead them higher than that year. Jointly with this, ministers must receive collation from the bishop, before the 20th of September this year. One of the ordinary clauses of collations was, "I do hereby receive him into the function of the holy ministry:" and one may easily see what a strait this would be to a minister who reckoned his former actings in that holy office good and valid. If ministers neglect this, and the patron present not another before March next year, the right of presentation is declared to fall *jure devoluto* to the bishop, and he is ordained to settle a minister in the place, yea, the bishops are appointed to plant the kirks which have vaiked since the year 1637. I imagine they had but few of these, if any; and to be careful to provide all the kirks of their diocese, according to this act.

It will be remembered, that last year the parliament had ordained, that both presenters and presented should take the oath of allegiance or supremacy, now pretty fully explained; and by this act the presented must own the prelates: thus a great part of the ministry of the church of Scotland,

---

* Act concerning such benefices and stipends as have been possessed without presentations from the lawful patrons. 1662.
The king's most excellent majesty being desirous, that all his good subjects may be sensible of the happy effects and fruits of the royal government, by a free, peaceable, and safe enjoyment of their due interests and properties under his protection; and that in his restitution they may find themselves restored to these rights which by law were secured unto them, and by the violence and injustice of these late troubles and confusions have been wrested from them: and considering, that notwithstanding the right of patronages be duly settled and established by the ancient and fundamental laws

1662. must either quit their principles or their charges. Certainly it was very hard upon the ministers, who had been admitted since the year 1649, according to standing law, that they are declared intruders, and to have no right to their stipends since their admission, merely because a new law was made for the support of prelates. Such, who in that same period had purchased an estate, or possessed a rent, are by this same parliament declared lawful possessors: but nothing now can be seen unreasonable, which may strike at presbyterian ministers, the bishops' great eyesore. Thus a great number of worthy pastors, who had suffered sensibly for noncompliance with the English, and their staunchness to the royal family, who had been admitted to their charges in the scripture manner, where patrons are not to be found, according to law and acts of parliament approven by the king himself,

are declared, if they will not alter their principles, and cast a reproach on their former administration, robbers and intruders. The plain view of this act seems to have been, to tempt the younger ministers gradually to conform, and, if they had the courage to stand out, to ruin them and their families. The elder sort were but few, and it might be expected they would soon wear out, and less compliance was to be looked for from them, who had been so active in the covenants, and late work of reformation: but our managers were disappointed as to the younger entrants, and they did with great firmness and resolution stand to their principles, and suffer rather than sin.

To secure the hierarchy now established, to entail it upon the nation, and to corrupt and bias the youth, the parliament by their fourth act, concerning masters of universities, inserted at the bottom of the page,* turn out "all masters of colleges who do

---

and constitutions of this kingdom, yet divers ministers in this church have, and do possess benefices and stipends in their respective cures, without any right or presentation to the same from the patrons: and it being therefore most just, that the lawful and undoubted patrons of kirks be restored to the possession of the rights of their respective advocations, donations, and patronages; therefore, his majesty, with advice and consent of his estates of parliament, doth statute and ordain, that all these ministers who entered to the cure of any parish in burgh or land within this kingdom, in or since the year 1649, (at and before which time the patrons were most injuriously dispossessed of their patronages) have no right unto, nor shall receive, uplift nor possess the rents of any benefice, modified stipend, manse or glebe for this present crop, 1662, nor any year following, but their places, benefices, and kirks are, *ipso jure*, vacant. Yet, his majesty, to evidence his willingness to pass by and cover the miscarriages of his people, doth, with advice foresaid, declare, that this act shall not be prejudicial to any of these ministers in what they have possessed, or is due to them, since their admission: and that every such minister who shall obtain a presentation from the lawful patron, and have collation from the bishop of the diocese where he liveth, betwixt and the 20th of September next to come, shall from thenceforth have right to, and enjoy his church, benefice, manse and glebe, as fully and freely as if he had been lawfully presented and admitted thereto at his first entry, or as any other minister within the kingdom doth or may do. And for that end, it is hereby ordained, that the respective patrons shall give presentations to all the present incumbents, who in due time shall make application to them for the same. And in case any of these churches shall not be thus duly provided before the said 20th of September, then the patron shall have freedom to present another betwixt and the 20th day of March, 1663. Which if he shall refuse or neglect, the presentation shall then fall to the bishop, *jure devoluto*, according to former laws. And such like his majesty, with advice foresaid, doth statute and ordain the archbishops and bishops, to have the power of new admission and collation, to all such churches and benefices as belong to their respective sees, and which have vaiked since the year 1637, and to be careful to plant and provide these their own kirks conform to this act.

* Act concerning masters of universities, ministers, &c. 1662.

The king's most excellent majesty, according to the laudable example of his royal progenitors in former parliaments, doth, with advice and consent of his estates convened in this present parliament, ratify and approve all and whatsoever acts and statutes, heretofore made, concerning the liberty and freedom of the true church of God, and the religion now professed and established within this kingdom; and considering how necessary it is for the advancement of religion and learning, for the good of the church, and peace of the kingdom, that the universities and colleges be provided and served with professors, principal, regents, and masters, well affected to his majesty, and the established government in church and state; his majesty, with advice foresaid, doth statute, ordain, and enact, that from this time forth, no masters, principal, regents, nor other professors in universities or colleges within this kingdom, be admitted, nor allowed to continue in the exercise of any function within the same, but such as are of a pious loyal and peaceable conversation, submitting to, and owning the government of the church by archbishops and bishops, now settled by law;

not submit to, and own the government by archbishops and bishops, and who take not the oath of allegiance." The cunning of Julian the apostate, in suppressing and poisoning Christian schools, as the most effectual way for ruining of Christianity, was now much spoken of, and some did not scruple to compare primate Sharp to him in more respects than one. This act further obliges all ministers to wait upon the bishops' visitations and diocesan meetings, or synods, which were but seldom kept in many dioceses; and further, ministers are required " to give their assistance in all things, as they shall be required by the bishops :" which certainly was hard enough, and next door to. implicit obedience. And this is to be done as a token of their complying with the present church government, and under the penalty of suspension, for the first fault, from benefice and office, until the next diocesan meeting, which, for any constitution I can find, might be long enough; and deprivation for the next. This act strikes at the elder ministers not thrown out by the former act about patronages.

1662.

Further they discharge all private meetings, or conventicles in houses under pretext of religious exercises. How far this agrees with the 16th act of the former session of this parliament, wherein the king promises to promote the power of godliness and encourage the exercises of religion both public and private, the advocates for this present management may explain. And, to make thorough work, none are allowed " to preach, or keep school, or to be pedagogues to persons of quality, without the bishop's license."

By their fifth act, the parliament put the copestone upon the building of prelacy, and, in as much as is in their power, the gravestone upon the covenants and presbytery; and ordain all persons in public trust, to sign and subscribe a declaration. The act itself the reader hath below.* The declaration being the foundation of a

and who having given satisfaction therein to the bishops of the respective dioceses, and patrons, and having in their presence, taken the oath of allegiance, shall procure their attestation of the same; that is to say, the professors and other masters of the universities of St. Andrews, Glasgow, and Aberdeen, to have the approbation and attestation of the archbishops and bishops, who are the respective chancellors of the said universities; and the professors and other masters of the New-town College in Aberdeen, and College of Edinburgh, to have the approbation of the respective patrons, the earl of Marshal, and magistrates of Edinburgh and Aberdeen, and an attestation and certificate under the hand of the bishops of Edinburgh and Aberdeen, respective, that they have taken the oath of allegiance, and that they are persons who submit to, and own the church government as now settled by law. Likeas, his majesty, finding it necessary for the peace and quiet of the church, that the ministers be such as will acknowledge and comply with the present government of the same, doth therefore, with advice foresaid, statute and enact, that whatsoever minister shall, without a lawful excuse, to be admitted by his ordinary, absent himself from the visitations of the diocese, which are to be performed by the bishop, or some of the ministers to be appointed by him, or from the diocesan assembly; or who shall not, according to his duty concur therein, or who shall not give their assistance in all the acts of church discipline, as they shall be required thereunto by the archbishop or bishop of the diocese, every such minister so offending shall, for the first fault, be suspended from his office and benefice till the next diocesan meeting; and if he amend not, shall be deprived, and the church and benefice to be provided as the law alloweth in other cases of vacancies. And his majesty considering, that under the pretext of religious exercises, divers unlawful meetings and conventicles (the nurseries of sedition) have been kept in private families, hath thought fit, with advice foresaid, hereby to declare, that as he doth and will give all due encouragement to the worship of God in families, amongst the persons of the family, and others who shall be occasionally there for the time, so he doth hereby discharge all private meetings or conventicles in houses, which under the pretence of, or for religious exercises, may tend to the prejudice of the public worship of God in the churches, or to the alienating of the people from their lawful pastors, and that duty and obedience they owe to church and state. And it is hereby ordained, that none be hereafter permitted to preach in public, or in families, within any diocese, or teach any public school, or to be pedagogues to the children of persons of quality, without the license of the ordinary of the diocese.

* Act concerning the declaration to be signed by all persons in public trust.

Forasmuch as it hath pleased Almighty God, in his majesty's restitution to his royal government, to restore this kingdom to its ancient liberties and peace, and to deliver his majesty's good subjects from these miseries and bondage whereby they have been oppressed during these troubles; and the estates of parliament, finding themselves obliged, in a due resentment of this mercy, and in discharge of that duty they owe to God, to the king's majesty, to the public peace of the kingdom, and the good of his subjects, to use all means for the due preservation of that peace and happiness they now enjoy under his royal government; and to pre-

1662. great part of the following sufferings, deserves a room in the body of the history, and is as follows.

"I do sincerely affirm and declare, that I judge it unlawful to subjects upon pretext of reformation, or any other pretext whatsomever, to enter into leagues and covenants, or to take up arms against the king, or those commissioned by him; and that all those gatherings, convocations, petitions, protestations, and erecting or keeping of council tables that were used in the beginning, and for the carrying on of the late troubles, were unlawful and seditious: and particularly, that these oaths, whereof the one was commonly called the 'National Covenant,' (as it was sworn and explained in the year 1638, and thereafter) and the other, entitled, 'A Solemn League and Covenant,' were and are in themselves unlawful oaths, and were taken by, and imposed upon the subjects of this kingdom, against the fundamental laws and liberties of the same; and that there lieth no obligation upon me or any of the subjects, from the said oaths, or either of them, to endeavour any change or alteration of the government either in church or state, as it is now established by the laws of the kingdom."

Some remarks have been made on several clauses of this declaration, upon the acts of this and the former session of parliament. Such who had taken the covenants, and thought them obligatory upon posterity, and their ties indissoluble by human authority, could not but reckon, that perjury was, by this act and declaration, made a chief qualification and necessary condition required of all to be admitted to places and offices in church and state. The reader cannot but observe, that under this period, and during the establishment of prelacy, there were more ensnaring and conscience-debauching declarations, bonds, and oaths, invented and imposed through the contrivance and influence of the bishops in

---

vent and suppress every thing that may tend to the renewing or favouring of these courses, by which the late rebellion hath been fomented and carried on; and conceiving that the employing of persons of sound principles and entire loyalty, in all offices of trust, and places of public administration, will conduce much to these ends: therefore, and for quieting the spirits of his majesty's good subjects, and begetting a confidence in them of their security for the future, his majesty hath thought fit, with advice and consent of his estates of parliament, to statute, ordain and enact; likeas his majesty by these presents, doth, with advice foresaid, statute, ordain, and enact, that all such persons as shall hereafter be called or admitted to any public trust or office, under his majesty's government within this kingdom; that is to say, to be officers of state, members of parliament, privy counsellors, lords of session, commissioners in exchequer, members of the college of justice, sheriffs, stewards or commissaries, their deputes and clerks, magistrates and council of boroughs, justices of peace and their clerks, or any other public charge, office and trust within this kingdom; shall, at and before their admission to the exercise of such places or offices, publicly, in face of the respective courts they relate to, subscribe the declaration underwritten: and that they shall have no right to their said offices or benefits thereof, until they subscribe the same, as said is; but that every such person who shall offer to enter and exerce any such office, before he subscribe the declaration, is to be reputed and punished as an usurper of his majesty's authority, and the place to be disposed to another. Likeas his majesty doth, with advice foresaid, remit to his commissioner, to take such course as he shall think fit, how these who are presently in office may subscribe the said declaration. And it is hereby declared, that this act is without prejudice of any former acts, for taking the oath of allegiance, and asserting the royal prerogative.

"I do sincerely affirm and declare, that I judge it unlawful to subjects, upon pretence of reformation or other pretence whatsoever, to enter into leagues and covenants, or to take up arms against the king, or those commissioned by him; and that all these gatherings, convocations, petitions, protestations, and erecting and keeping of council tables, that were used in the beginning, and for carrying on of the late troubles, were unlawful and seditious: and particularly, that these oaths, whereof the one was commonly called, "The National Covenant," (as it was sworn and explained in the year 1638, and thereafter,) and the other entitled, "A Solemn League and Covenant," were and are in themselves unlawful oaths, and were taken by, and imposed upon the subjects of this kingdom, against the fundamental laws and liberties of the same. And that there lieth no obligation upon me, or any of the subjects, from the said oaths, or either of them, to endeavour any change or alteration of the government, either in church or state, as it is now established by the laws of the kingdom."

this kingdom, than ever were in so short a space upon any part of the world. We shall see that scarce a year passes but some new declaration, bond, or oath, was brought upon the subjects in Scotland; all of them dubious, many of them impossible to keep, and some of them evidently self-contradictory. This dreadfully corrupted people's morals, and was a sad inlet to the atheism, profaneness, and unrighteousness, which now abounded.

Some compared this declaration to the receiving the mark of the beast in the right hand. The very matter of the declaration cannot but stun such as seriously reflect upon it. The declaring "all leagues and covenants among subjects, upon any pretext whatsoever, unlawful," is unreasonable and foolish. All resistance upon any pretext, even against the least person who hath a commission from the king, is what will now be laughed at. The covenants are declared to be unlawful in themselves; and the declaration goes further, and affirms, " they can have no obligation upon others." Every where but in Scotland, it would have sufficed to declare an oath unlawful, and for a man not to take it himself, or renounce it, without any declaration as to others; but our prelates can never be secure enough against the covenants. Last session they procure them to be declared illegal; this session, by act 2d, they are cassed and annulled, and now all in public trust declare so much in a separate instrument; and in a few years the covenants must be forsworn and renounced by the test, that one oath may expel another. In short this declaration is but prejudice of the oath of allegiance, that is, both must be taken. The allegiance, this declaration, and in some years afterward the test, were the great snares of this time. And as upon the one hand the unaccountable and violent pressing of them, run some poor people to extremities, and some measure of wildness; so upon the other, such methods turned severals of greater knowledge to irreligion, atheism, and rejecting every thing serious, when they observed the bishops and their time-serving ministers fall in with this declaration; though a little time ago they had pressed the covenant, as the great duty of the times, a mode 1662. of the covenant of grace, * and what not; yet now it is to them rebellion and sin.

---

* If this was really the view which the bishops and their underlings originally entertained of the covenants, their unsteadiness in them ceases to be a matter of surprise, for men whose conceptions were of such a shapeless character, could not reasonably be expected to be steady to any thing. Such an idea of our covenants, I cannot help regarding as most ridiculous, and nearly, if not altogether, as incomprehensible as the doctrine of transubstantiation. It has not, however, wanted advocates even in modern times, and among those who profess the highest attachment to the covenants. I have just now before me a sermon preached by the late Dr. John Young of Hawick, at what was called the renovation of these covenants by a congregation of Seceders, in which I find the following assertions: " All acceptable covenants are neither more nor less than our acceptance of God's covenant of grace! We neither consider our covenant of duties as a distinct covenant by itself, nor is it properly the same thing with the covenant of grace! what we say is, our covenanting is the same thing with our acceptance of the covenant of grace! We enter into no covenant but the covenant of grace! Cursed be all that religious covenanting that amounts to any thing more than an explicit acceptance of God's covenant." If the views of the congregation, on the subject of the solemn services they were on this occasion assembled to perform, were equally indistinct with those of their preacher, to the question, Who hath required this at your hand? they must certainly have found it no easy matter to give a satisfactory answer. Held up in this absurd point of view, is it any wonder that our covenants should have been derided, their propriety called in question, and their utility denied? No genuine covenanter, however, ever did, or ever can so represent them. " The oath of God," said an eminent defender of these covenants, " which we enter into, is not the covenant of grace, but a covenant of duty and gratitude. It is not the covenant of grace, but a covenant of duty which is consequential of our taking hold, or accepting of the covenant of grace." [Vide Sermons on Covenanting, by Alexander Moncrief of Calfergie.] " The Solemn League and Covenant," says a modern author of singular ability, " was a national covenant and oath in every point of view—in its matter, its form, the authority by which it was enjoined, the capacities in which it was sworn, and the manner in which it was ratified. It was a sacred league between kingdom and kingdom, with respect to their religious as well as their secular interests, and, at the same time, a covenant in which they jointly swore to God to perform all the articles contained in it. National religion, national safety, liberty and peace, were the great objects which it embraced. It was not a mere agreement or confederation, however solemn, of individuals or private persons, however numerous, entering spontaneously, and of their own accord, into a common engagement. It was formed and concluded by the representatives of kingdoms, in concurrence with those of the church, it was sworn by them in their public

1662. Some acts in this session about civil affairs, seem designed for the further establishment of episcopacy: but I do not enter upon them. Towards the end of the session they came at length to the much longed for indemnity, which had been granted

capacity; at their call and by their authority it was afterwards sworn by the body of the people, in their different ranks and orders; and finally, it was ratified and pronounced valid by laws both civil and ecclesiastical. The public faith was thus plighted by all the organs through which a nation is accustomed to express its mind and will. Nothing was wanting to complete the national tie, and to render it permanent; unless it should be maintained that absolute unanimity is necessary, and that a society cannot contract lawful engagements to God or man, as long as there are individuals who oppose and are dissentient. Sanctions less sacred, and pledges less numerous, would have given another nation, or even an individual, a perfect right to demand from Britain the fulfilment of any treaty or contract; and shall not God, who was not only a witness, but the principal party, and whose honour and interests were immediately concerned in this transaction, have a like claim, or shall we "break the covenant and escape?" [Vide Dr. M'Crie's Unity of the Church, p. 165.] Thus stated, our covenants assume tangibility; they may be approached and examined, and indeed seem highly worthy of being inquired into. Thus stated, multiplied circumstances present themselves in which they may be interposed, obviously with the greatest propriety, while most of the sophisms wherewith they have been assailed fall to the ground. Thus stated, there is scarcely room for the ridiculous inquiry which has so often been instituted, and not unfrequently settled, in opposition both to revelation and the common sense of mankind, Whether covenants, oaths or vows, bring along with them any superadded obligations, when the persons employing them are already bound by the divine law? for they may in this way be extensively employed, and constitute a bond of duty where there was no previously existing obligation. Thus stated, there is no room for disputation on the character which a man sustains in entering into these solemn covenants, which has often been confidently stated to be simply and solely that of a church member. Covenants, oaths and vows, as above explained, have their foundation, not in positive institution, but in the moral law or law of nature; consequently men enter into them as subjects of God's moral government. To do so acceptably, we admit they must do it as Christians, but this is something very different from doing so merely as church members. The subject of the covenant, the oath, or the vow to be taken, may require the person to take or to enter into it as a Christian magistrate, a Christian minister, a Christian soldier, or a Christian citizen, as well as a Christian church member. It was in these characters, and on this broad basis, that our covenants were originally sworn and subscribed. Their foundation is laid as deep as the pillars that support human society; and till these pillars be removed, or to speak without a figure, till federal representation be no longer necessary to the existence of human society, so long must they be respected by the good, and so long by the wise their tie must be regarded as indissoluble.

The following paragraph on the restricting of religious covenants, oaths and vows, to men merely in their character of church members, which seems a prevailing idea among covenanters of the present day, is so admirable, that I cannot resist adding it to this note, though considering the subject, I am afraid of having already borne hard upon the patience of my reader:—" By church members may be meant either those who are in actual communion with a particular organized church, or those who stand in a general relation to the church universal; but in neither of these senses can it be said that religious covenants or bonds are incompetent, or non-obligatory in every other character. This is to restrict the authority of the divine law in reference to moral duties, and to limit the obligations which result from it in a way that is not warranted either by scripture or reason. How can that which is founded on the moral law, and which is moral-natural not positive, be confined to church members, or to Christians in the character of church members only? The doctrine in question is also highly objectionable, as it unduly restricts the religious character of men and the sphere of their actions about religious matters, whether viewed as individuals or as formed into societies and communities. They are bound to act for the honour of God, and are capable of contracting sacred obligations, sacred both in their nature and their objects, in all the characters and capacities which they sustain. I know no good reason for holding that, when a company of men or a society act about religion, or engage in religious exercises, they are thereby converted into a church, or act merely and properly as church members. Families are not churches, nor are they constituted properly for a religious purpose, yet they have a religious character, and are bound to act according to it in honouring and serving God, and are capable of contracting religious obligations. Nations also have a religious character, and may act about the affairs of religion. They may make their profession of Christianity and legally authorize its institutions, without being turned into a church; and why may they not also come under an oath and covenant, with reference to it, which shall be nationally binding. Covenanting may be said to be by a nation as brought into a church state, acting in this religious capacity; the oath may be dispensed by ministers of the gospel, and accompanied by the usual exercises of religion in the church, and yet it may not be an ecclesiastical deed. The marriage covenant and vow is founded on the original law, and its duties, as well as the relation which it establishes, are common to men, and of a civil kind. Yet among Christians it is mixed with religious engagements, and celebrated religiously in the church. Ministers of the gospel officiate in dispensing the vow, and accompany it with the word and prayer. The parties are bound to marry in the Lord, and to live together as Christians. But is the marriage vow on that account ecclesiastical, or do the parties engage as church members only? The Christian character is, in such cases, combined with the natural, domestic, civil, political,

in England, almost as soon as the king came home: but his ancient kingdom must not enjoy such a favour till the prelates had their main interests settled and secured; though they were the Scots who crowned him, fought for him, suffered most for him under the usurpation, and moved first his restoration. This act of indemnity and oblivion was clogged with some exceptions in the body of it: besides the ordinary crimes still excepted in such acts, and the murderers of the king's father, if any such were in Scotland, the parliament except out of the indemnity, all who had been declared fugitive by the committees of estates or parliament, since August 1660, and in particular, " the marquis of Argyle, Warriston, Swinton, Mr. James Guthrie, William Govan, John Hume, William Dundas, and the Campbells of Ardkinglas, and Ormsay."

This act of favour was further clogged with an unprinted act, secluding twelve persons from places of trust, who were to be named in parliament by ballots: which act, commonly called the balloting act, was a contrivance of Middleton's, to turn out Lauderdale, Crawford, and Sir Robert Murray, from all their offices and posts. However, this turned about to Middleton's ruin, and occasioned an odd reckoning betwixt the king and parliament, as may be seen at the end of the printed acts of parliament, 1663, when the parliament, after a flaunting letter to the king, wherein they, I had almost said blasphemously, declare the king's royal judgment is the rule of their actions, rescinded this balloting act. Some of the members of parliament, when giving in their lists or ballots, were so merry as to put down any twelve of the bishops the parliament pleased.

The last clog upon this indemnity 1662. is, "the act containing exceptions from the act of indemnity;" the tenor of which will fall in afterwards in the act, September 9th, 1663, rescinding the balloting act. I find the reason alleged for this act of fines, or the exceptions from this indemnity is, " that the fines therein imposed, may be given for the relief of the king's good subjects, who had suffered in the late troubles," as now it is fashionable to term the work of reformation since the year 1638. The parliament appointed a committee for pitching upon the persons to be fined, with the quota of their fines, the members whereof were solemnly bound to discover none whom they pitched upon, till once the act was passed in the house. This committee most arbitrarily formed a list, which the parliament, I may say, implicitly approved, of seven or eight hundred noblemen, gentlemen, burgesses, and others, mostly in the western shires, to be arbitrarily fined in the sums they named, without any libel, probation, or pretended crime, but what was common to the whole nation during the usurpation, and now was indemnified to the rest of the subjects. I have heard of nothing of this nature imposed upon the compliers with Cromwell, in England or Ireland. The persons they name are fined in the sum of one million seventeen thousand, three hundred, fifty-three pounds, six shillings and eight penies, Scots money, as will appear by the list of them, annexed at the bottom of the page.* This list may be faulty in the syllabication of some persons' names and styles, but as to the sums and the bulk of persons named it is exact. The persons contained in this act of fines, as far as I can

---

Much confusion also arises on this subject, from not attending to the specific object of our national covenants and the nature of their stipulations, by which they are distinguished from mere church covenants. I shall only add, that several objections usually adduced on this head, may be obviated by keeping in mind that the obligation in question is of a moral kind, and that God is the principal party who exacts the fulfilment of the bond." M'Crie's Unity of the Church, pp. 167, 168. The reader may consult on this subject, with advantage, The Covenanters' Plea, Crofton's Fastening of St. Peter's Fetters, &c. &c.—Ed.

* List of fines imposed by Middleton, in parliament, 1662.

EDINBURGHSHIRE.

Earl of Lothian fined in	L.6,000
Lord Borthwick	2,400
Lord Balmerinoch	6,000
Mr. John Inglis of Cramond	6,000
Mr. James Scot of Bonnyton	1,200
Mr. Laurence Scot of Paisley	2,400
Thomas Craig of Rickarton	2,400
Sir John Scot of Scotstarbet	6,000
Walter Young, merchant in Edinburgh	1,200
Robert Hamilton, elder, merchant there	1,000

1662. now learn about them, were, generally speaking, of the best morals, and most shining piety in the places where they lived, and chargeable with nothing but being presbyterians, and submitting to their conquerors when they could do no better

James Mason, merchant there	L.800
Alexander Brand, merchant there	6,000
Mr. John Harper, advocate	2,400
Henry Hope, merchant in Edinburgh	3,600
Mr. James Ritchie there	1,200
Hugh Watt in Leith	1,600
James Dalgleish, late collector of vacant stipends	1,200
Mr. Robert Dalgleish of Lauriston	3,600
Robert Campbell, apothecary	600
William Blackwood, merchant in Edinburgh	1,200
Sir James Stuart of Kirkfield	6,000
George Graham, merchant in Edinburgh	600
Thomas Lawrie, merchant there	600
James Melvile, there	1,800
William Melvile, merchant there	3,600
Adam Mushet there	1,200
Mr. John Elles, advocate there	2,400
Mr. William Hogg, advocate there	1,800
John Macklary, there	360
James Bruce, merchant there	600
James Melross, there	600
George Blackwood, there	360
William Hamilton, writer in Edinburgh	1,200
James Graham, merchant there	600
William Rae, vintner there	600
John Lamb, merchant there	720
John Bonnar of Bonnarton	1,200
James Wilson, vintner in Edinburgh	360
Laird Dodds	2,400
John Lawrie, in Loganhouse	360
Robert Selkirk, merchant in Edinburgh	360
William Anderson, merchant there	600
Robert Jack, merchant there	360
Robert Fowlis, merchant there	1,200
Robert Simpson, vintner there	600
Robert Lockhart, merchant there	2,400
Patrick Crichton, merchant there	1,200
John Crawford, merchant there	600
Alexander Henderson, merchant there	500
Joseph Brodie, brother to the lord Brodie	600
Captain William Bannatyne	600

HADDINGTONSHIRE.

Patrick Temple, in Lintonbridges	300
—— Hepburn of Bennistoun	1,200
Robert Atchison of Saintserf	3,000
Mr. Robert Hodge of Glaidsmuir	600

PEEBLES-SHIRE.

The laird of Palnin	600
William Russel of Slipperfield	600
—— Douglas of Linton	360
—— Cranston of Glen	800
John Horseburgh, bailie of Peebles	360
Mr. Andrew Hay, brother to Mr. John Hay of Hayston	600
Joseph Learmont	1,200

BERWICKSHIRE.

Sir William Scot of Hardin	18,000
John Home in the Law	600
John Ker of Westnisbet	3,000
Walter Pringle of Greenknow	3,000
John Erskine, portioner of Dryburgh	600
Thomas Haliburton of Newmains	600
Robert Brown of Blackburn	600
William Craw of Heughead	600

Mr. Mark Ker of Morningston	L.5,000
Andrew Gray, portioner of Swinewood	600
Patrick Wardlaw, portioner of Westereaster	600
John Hunter of Colingslie	1,200
Abraham Home of Kennetsidehead	600
William Somerwel in Hilton	360
Robert Brownfield of Todrig	600
Patrick Gillespie in Stempreneze	360

SELKIRKSHIRE.

George Currier of Fondoun	000
—— Pringle of Torwoodlie	1,800
Laird of Whytebank younger	3,000
—— Pringle of Newhal	600
James Eliot in Sutherlandhall	600
William Scot of Tushelaw	600
Robert Scot of Brownhall	600
Andrew Scot of Broadmeadows	1,800
John Scot of Gilmensleugh	1,800
Andrew Eliot of Phillip	1,000
Thomas Scot of Todrig	1,200
Thomas Scot, bailie of Selkirk	360
Archibald Eliot of Middlesteed	600
James Scot of Gallowshiels	2,400

LANARKSHIRE.

Sir Daniel Carmichael	2,400
Sir James Carmichael	1,200
—— Hamilton of Halcraig	1,200
William Lawrie of Blackwood	600
—— Moor of Arniston	1,200
William Hamilton of Netherfield	600
James Cunningham of Bonniton	360
John Weir of Newton	360
John Weir of Clowburn	600
William Brown of Dolphinston	1,200
John Hamilton, chamberlain of Hamilton	360
George Weir of Harwood	360
James Hamilton of Neisland	1,000
Mr. John Spreul, late clerk of Glasgow	1,200
John Graham, late provost of Glasgow	1,000
Mr. William Brown of Milridge	360
Andrew Hamilton of Overton	600
James Alexander, in Overhill of Drips	360
Thomas Petticrew in the barony of Glasgow	360
—— Bailie of Walston	9,600
Matthew Wilson, tanner in Glasgow, Thomas Paterson there	360
John Johnston there	600
Laird of Auchterfardel	1,800
William Chiesly in Douglas	600
Andrew Brown, brother to the laird of Dolphinston	600
Michael Somerwel, bailie of Lanark	600
—— Ellon, there	360
Alexander Tennent, in Lanark	360
Gabriel Hamilton there	360
Mr. Andrew Ker	1,800
Gabriel Hamilton of Westburn	1,000
Alexander Wilson in Lanark	360
John Nimmo, in the Westport of Glasgow	360
James Elphinston, glasswright there	360
Sir John Chiesly	2,400
John Small, in Kilbride	360
Mr. Cumming in Glasgow	600
William Cortes, merchant there	360
John Kirkland of Kardonar	600

CHAP. III.] OF THE CHURCH OF SCOTLAND. 273

Middleton thought to have got all this money to himself and his dependants, as well as the estate of the marquis of Argyle, with the addition of the title of duke; but he was balked in both; and neither he nor his friends fingered those 1662.

Matthew Fleming in Kilbride	L.360
Captain Hutcheson in Carstairs	600
John Powder in Stobberlie	330
James Gray, merchant in Glasgow	360
—— Telfer of Harecleugh	2,400
David Gardener of Bonsmat	480
David Somerwel of Grange	600
John Menzies of Harperfield	1,000
—— Cleland of Honhoblin or Hinnoble	600
James Bailie of Todholes	360
John Pirry, chamberlain of Mansley	360
Claud Hamilton of Barin	1,200
Richard Maitland in Park of Mansley	300
—— Prentice of Thorn	300
James Paterson in Inditshire	300
Archibald Ing	240
James Hastie in Sandyford	360
John Kid in Overton	300
John Forest in Thriepwood	300
John Scouler in Law of Mansley	240
George Gilbertson in Broadwood	240
Hugh Roxburgh in Muirhouse of Libberton	240
—— Gladstanes of Overshiels	360
William Bartram, portioner of Nisbet	480
Walter Carmichael in Grangehall	600
Patrick Nimmo, portioner of Quathiel	480
—— Johnston of Newbigging	240
James Brown in Carstairs	240
James Logan in Strafrank	240
James Murray in Hartiham	240
John Whyte of Caldyke	360
James Bailie in Thankerton	240
George Whyte, brother to the said John of Caldyke	240
George Porterfield, late provost of Glasgow	3,000
Gideon Jack in Lanark	1,000
—— Hamilton of Southfield	360
—— Hamilton of Hisson	240
John Brown, younger of Draphan	360
—— Hamilton of Aikenhead	600
Thomas Stevens in Lesmahago	240
John Stevens there	240
Thomas Macquary there	360
David Hamilton, younger in South Cumberlaid	360
David Hamilton in Calderwater	300
—— Hamilton in Bothwell-bridge	360
Archibald Hamilton in Causeyhead of Netherton	240
John Hamilton in Stonehal	360
David Somerwel in the Green of Balveth	360
Thomas Carmichael in Newbigging	240
Thomas Gibson in Cothquhan	360
John Kello there	240
John Braid in Kilhead of Covington	600
Robert Logan of Hintshilnood of Carnwath	240
William Bruce of Skellieton, elder and younger, betwixt them equally	600
James Bruce of Kilback of Lesmahago	240
John Pillan in Lanark	240
James Gray in Jerviswood	600
—— Simpson in Lanark	240
John Fisher in Lanark	240
Thomas Hutton in Hamilton	1,000
George Tain in the parish of Monkland	240
John Hamilton of Lesmahago	240
John Hamilton of Priorhil	300

Thomas Steel in Skelliehill	L.300
Lieutenant Lindsay	600
—— Wardrop of Daldowie	600
Mr. William Somerwel in Douglas	1,800
—— Robin in Sheeney	400
DUMFRIES-SHIRE.	
Mr. William Ferguson of Killoch	1,000
William Wilson of Lard	300
John Douglas of Stonehouse	1,000
John Welsh of Colliestoun	300
John Scot younger in Katshaw	1,000
John Macburney, portioner of Leggat	240
John Maitland, glover there	240
John Short, glover in Dumfries	240
James Moffat, merchant there	300
James Kalling, glover there	300
Robert Wallace, merchant there	600
James Muirhead, merchant there	1,000
John Williamson, merchant there	240
Abraham Dickson, merchant there	240
James Grierson of Dogmare	360
John Kirkwell of Bogrie	360
John Kirkwell of Sandewal	360
James Hunter in Townhead	600
William Bell in Albey	1,000
George Bell in Gotsbridge	1,000
James Clark of Tilloch	600
John Clerk of Killymie	480
John Craig in Dumfries	240
Andrew Johnston of Lockarbie	1,200
Patrick Murray of Brockhulrig	600
—— Taggit in Dumfries-shire	600
William Macmarran in Kilbin	240
John Ewet in Dumfries	360
John Gilchrist there	360
John Copland there	360
John Lawrie of Maxwelston	3,600
John Kennedy of Hellies	720
John Osclencroch	600
William Eliot of Birks	1,200
Robert Eliot his brother	1,200
Adam Eliot of Efgel	1,800
William Eliot, called of Unthank	1,800
Gavin Eliot of Waterside	600
John Bell of Crowtliknow	600
—— Murray of Murrayslat	360
Thomas Glaidstanes	1,000
ROXBURGHSHIRE.	
The Sheriff depute	1,200
John Turnbull of Know	2,000
Robert Flennit of Chesters	1,200
The Laird of Langhouse	1,800
Robert Pringle of Elieston	1,200
William Kerr of Swinside	1,200
Mr. Gilbert Eliot of Craigen	1,200
Andrew Bell of Mow	360
John Fasnel, collector	360
Robert Handyside, merchant in Kelso	360
—— Scot of Clashell	1,200
William Scot of Husleyhil	1,200
Sir Walter Riddel of that ilk	6,600
William Kerr of Newtown	600
Sir Gideon Scot of Heychester	4,800
—— Scot of Gandilands	600
Robert Scot of Broadhaugh	300
Gideon Wauchop, brother to the laird of	2,400
Robert Ker of Middlemaswal	600

2 M

1662. fines. They were indeed uplifted, and much more, as shall be observed in its own room, by military force; but the money came to other hands.

Many observations were made upon this act of fines at this time: that some named in it were in their grave, some upon the nurse's breast, some, never had a being:

John Ker of Chester	L.360
Thomas Ker, portioner of Home	360
Sir Thomas Ker of Cavers	6,000
Patrick Scot of Thirlestone	3,000
Samuel Morison of Massendien	1,200
Sir Archibald Douglas of Cavers	3,600

FIFESHIRE.

George Gairns in Burntisland	600
Lord Burleigh	L.13,333 6s. 8d.
—— Weems of Belfarge	1,000
Sir Thomas Nairn of Samford	1,800
Thomas Oliphant of Kirkbarn	1,200
John Moncrief of Crossel	12,00
John Brown of Burntisland	600
Thomas Glover, late collector in Fife	600
Colonel Brymer	1,200
—— Macgill of Rankeilor	3,000
The laird of Ayton in Fife	2,400
Robert Bailie, late chamberlain in Falkland	1,200
Robert Whyte in Kirkaldy	1,200
—— Weems of Fenzies	600
—— Hamilton of Grangemuir	1,200
John Lindsay, in Anstruther	240
Thomas Mitchel of Kondan	1,200
Laird of Leuchart	1,200
William Hamilton of Anstruther	360
John White in Burntisland	1,200
Robert Andrew, late collector in Perthshire	2,400
Mr. Robert Pittulloch	1,800
Mr. Robert Preston of Preston	1,200
Robert Dempster in Balbongie	1,800

DUMBARTONSHIRE.

Colin Campbell of Ardentenny	1,200
Patrick Ewing in Dumbarton	600
—— Brown of Bancleugh	1,200

INVERNESS, ROSS, AND CROMARTY.

—— Monro of Fowlis	3,600
Ross of Innercharran	1,200
John Forbes of Culloden	1,200
Andrew M'Culloch, burgess of Tain	1,200
Laird of Strue	1,200
—— Belledrum	600
Donald Fowler of Allen	2,400
Malcom Ross of Kindies	600
Gilbert Robston in Inverness	2,400
Hugh Monro, collector there	1,200
David Ross of Pitcannay	720
Hector Douglas of Mildarg	2,400
—— Monro of Culcairn	360
Malcom Tosh of Kylachie	360
Thomas Chevis of Muirtoun	1,800
Alexander Dunbar, burgess of Inverness	3,600
James Fowler, burgess there	600
George Lesley, clerk of Inverness	600
Mr. William Ross of Sandwick	600
Duncan Forbes, merchant there	1,200
Walter Innes of Innerbrachy	2,400
Macpherson, tutor of Clunie	600
Macpherson, tutor of Inverness	600
—— Cumming of Kinhardie	360
—— Macintosh of Connage	3,600
—— Mackenzie of Killcourie	6,000
William Duff, collector of the excise of Inverness	L.1,800

ELGIN AND NAIRN.

Sir Lodowick Gordon of that ilk	3,600
Alexander Brodie of that ilk	4,800
Patrick Campbell of Buth	600
—— Brodie of Lethem	6,000
—— Brodie of Lethem younger	1,200
—— Hay, tutor of Knockudie	360
Hugh Hay, tutor of Park	1,200
Francis Broddies elder and younger of Belnoat	3,000
Laird of Grant	18,000
—— Campbell of Calder	12,000
Colonel Innes of Bog	1,200
Mr. John Campbell of Mey	600
Patrick Nairn of Alchrose	1,200
Park Hay, in the North	2,400
John Innes of Culraick	1,000
Robert Stuart of Letherin	360
Alexander Anderson of Garmoch	1,200
John Tulloch in Nairn	600
John Falconer of Tulloch	1,200
Alexander Dunbar, commissar of Murray	1,200
David Brodie of Pitgairn	1,200

SHERIFFDOM OF AYR.

Mr. Robert Barclay, burgess of Irvine	1,200
Laird of Cunninghamhead	4,800
—— Fullarton of Corsbie	2,000
Sir Hugh Campbell of Cesnock	8,000
The laird of Rowallan	4,000
The laird of Crawfordlane	1,200
—— Hunter of Hunterston	600
John Reid, late provost of Irvine	600
James Campbell of Newmills	600
John Shaw of Sornbeg	1,200
John Haldane of Entrekin	1,800
Alexander Crawford of Skeldoun	1,000
William Hamilton of Garrive	360
John Fergushil, bailie of Ayr	1,200
The laird of Pinkel elder	4,800
The laird of Pinkel younger	1,200
—— Gruntishaw	240
The laird of Kirkmichael	4,000
—— Eccles of Kildonnan	400
—— Kennedy of Dannare	600
Gilbert Rickart of Barskiming	1,800
Robert Kelso of Kelsoland	800
Thomas Blair, merchant in Ayr	800
—— Kennedy of Kirkhill	360
—— Caldwell of that ilk	600
Mr. Cuthbert Cunningham	1,200
Patrick Crawford of Cumnock	2,000
—— Whytford of Balloch	4,000
Allan Dunlop, provost of Irvine	360
Charles Hall in Newmills	360
—— Crawford of Smiddieshaw	600
—— Reid younger of Ballochmyle	600
—— Boyd of Pitton	600
—— Campbell of Shaw	1,200
—— Kennedy of Bellimuir	600
William Pedin in Ayr	360
James Wallace of Drummalloch	600
George Crawford in Broch	600
John Frow in Newmills	360

OF THE CHURCH OF SCOTLAND.

several were in the act who were subsisted upon the weekly collections for the poor of the parish where they lived; and a good many were put in, as much from little private pique, as for any activity in the late times. Generally speaking, these fines were inflicted upon such whom they reckoned presbyterians, and averse from the

Robert Nisbet in little Cesnock	L.360
—— Reid of Dandilling	600
—— Mitchel of Dalgen	600
—— Nisbet of Greidholm	600
John M'Culloch, in Rue	360
John M'Hutchison, there	360
—— of Drochallan	360
—— of Dalreoch	600
—— Brown of Walwood	360
—— Campbell of Harecleugh	480
—— Campbell of Glasnock elder	480
—— Campbell younger of Auchmannoch	600
—— Aird of Milton	360
—— Brown of Gordons	600
—— Campbell of middle Walwood	360
Robert Wallace of Carnhill	1,200
Campbell of Shaw	1,000
—— Kennedy of Bellimuir	480
James Gordon, chamberlain to the earl of Cassils	360
—— Douglas of Carrallow	600
Alexander Kennedy of Mynybole	360
—— Kennedy of Knockdoon	600
John Kennedy his brother	300
John Fergusson of Millander	1,000
Thomas Fergusson of Finage	600
Hugh Fergusson of Mains	600
Andrew Ross of Travier	600
James Hunter in Carbton	600
—— Kennedy of Glenmuir	600
Adam Wright in Dalmelington	200
John Shaw in Belloch	360
Robert Wallace in Holmston	360
David Kennedy of Barchlanachan	360
Thomas Kennedy of Grange	360
John Shaw of Niminshoun	600
John Macmirry	600
—— Shaw of Keir	360
Mr. Robert Auld of Hill	1,200
—— of Knockdall	1,200
Earl of Loudon	1,200
BUTESHIRE.	
Donald Macneil of Kilmorie	360
Neil Macneil of Kilmorie	360
Ninian Spence of Wester Kames	1,200
James Stewart of Kilwhinleck	360
ABERDEENSHIRE.	
The laird of Echt	3,600
Master of Forbes	3,600
William Forbes of Corsendey	1,200
—— Forbes of Knockquharry	300
—— Arbuthnot of Cairngall	1,000
Thomas Forbes of Auchortes	600
Arthur Forbes of Innernochty	1,000
Gilbert Skene of Dyte	2,400
Sir John Baird, advocate	2,400
Walter Cochran, in Aberdeen	3,600
Alexander Harper there	600
Mr. Alexander Burnet in Craigniel	2,400
—— Forbes of Culquharry	600
Robert Ker of Meny	3,600
David Tyrie in Strathbogie	600
John Innes of Culrain	1,200
Henry Paton	600
—— Sangster, in Aberdeen	600
Charles Din, litster there	L.600
Mr. Robert Burnet of Alberedge	600
—— Forbes of Baslayd	1,800
—— Forbes of Gask	1,800
David Rickart of Auchnacant	3,600
George Cruikshank of Barrihil	1,800
Patrick Muir, bailie of Aberdeen	1,800
—— Burnet of Adors	1,800
William Allardice in Aberdeen	1,000
Thomas Cushny, glasswright there	1,800
Robert Cruikshank of Elrick	1,000
Andrew Goodale	300
Mr. Alexander Farquhar of Tonley	1,200
John Ross, merchant in Aberdeen	1,200
George Piper there	600
—— Tutor of Pitsligo	6,000
Alexander Jeffray of Kingswells	2,400
Mr. William Moir, late principal of the earl Marshal's college, in Aberdeen	2,400
KINCARDINESHIRE.	
Mr. William Beaton	1,200
—— of Halgreen, elder	2,400
Andrew Arbuthnot of Fiddes	1,800
CAITHNESS-SHIRE.	
Robert Innes of Thurston	600
James Sinclair of Assery	600
William Bailie	600
SUTHERLANDSHIRE.	
Robert Gray of Skibo	1,200
Robert Murray of Pulross	1,000
Patrick Dunbar of Siddery	1,000
Robert Gray of Arbo	4,800
—— Gray of Creigh	2,400
John Sutherland in Clyne	1,000
LINLITHGOWSHIRE.	
—— Sandilands, tutor of Calder	1,200
—— Dundas of Duddiston	2,000
Major Whythead	600
John Gillen	600
John Clexam of Cousland	1,200
Robert Cuthbertson in Linlithgow	360
—— Galloway of Todhaugh	600
Patrick Liston	600
John Mill in Queensferry	300
John Wardrop in Livingston	300
Gavin Marshal in Linlithgow	600
—— Muirhead of Lennox	4,000
Patrick Young in Killiekanty	1,200
George Drummond of Kartenry	3,600
Walter Stuart in Linlithgow	1,200
John Crawford, son to umquhile William Crawford in Kinneil	2,400
—— Bailie of Bothkenner	1,200
John Hill in Queensferry	600
John Robertson, merchant there	600
George Logie there	600
PERTH.	
Lord Cowpar	4,800
Lord Ruthven	4,800
Major-general James Holburn	9,600
Archibald Stirling of Coldoch	600
James Campbell of Cathwick	1,800

1662. present establishment in the church; and we shall meet with a good many of them suffering greater hardships in the after part of this history. I am told, that a good many presbyterian ministers were at first named in the list, but it seems upon re-

William Hutton of Belnusk	L.600
Robert Stuart of Morloch	6,000
—— Blair of Kinfawns	2,400
—— Oliphant of Gask	6,000
Sir David Carmichael of Kilnedie	2,400
Major John Moncrief	1,200
—— Hay Leys, elder	600
John Campbell of Aberledin	1,000
Patrick and John Campbells, equally betwixt them	1,000
Mr. Henry Stuart, brother to Sir Thomas Stuart of Grantully	600
Hugh Craig of Dumberny	1,000
Alexander Robertson of Downie	600
Alexander Robertson of Easter Stralloch	1,000
Sir Thomas Stuart of Grantully	18,000
Colonel Menzies	1,800
James Campbell of Glenwhigh of Tollerie	1,200
—— Campbell of Mackaster	1,200
James Stirling in the Mill of Keir	300
—— Mackallan of Kilmadock	300
William Oliphant of Forgan	1,200
The Baron Schell	600
Mr. William Blackburn in Middleton	1,200
Henry Chrystie, chamberlain to the laird of Glenorchie	1,200
James Crichton in Cowpergrange	1,200
Andrew Sutor in Newtyle	1,200
Mr. Robert Macgill of Fenzies	1,200
John M'Callum of Forther	1,800
Mr. George Blair of ——	2,400
William Main of Pollockmill	1,200

FORFAR.

The laird of Edzel	3,000
—— of Balzordie	600
The laird of Findowrie, elder and younger, equally betwixt them	2,400
—— Ogilvie of Balfour	2,400
—— Guthrie of Pitforthie	600
—— Rait of Cunningsyth	600
James Mill in Mendose	360
John Hunter in Glamis	600

BAMFF.

James Hay in Mildavid	1,000
William Innes of Killermenie	360
Park Gordon, elder	3,600
Park Gordon, younger	1,200
John Lyon of Muiresk	3,600
John Innes of Knockorth	300

RENFREW.

Sir George Maxwell of Nether Pollock	4,000
Mr. James Montgomerie of Wetlands	360
—— of Walkinshaw, younger	360
John Kelso, bailie in Paisley	500
John Spreul, bailie there	360
John Park, bailie there	480
Mr. Hugh Forbes, sheriff-clerk of Renfrew	1,000
Gabriel Thomson in Corshill	300
Robert Pollock of Milburn	300
John Govan in Main	300
John Fawns, portioner in Neilstounside	360
John Norris, elder and younger, equally betwixt them	360
John Semple of Balgreen	300
John Orr of Jeffraystock	300

John Adam in Bonnyfield	L.300
—— Barber of Rushiefield	300
Robert Low of Bavan	300
—— Caldwell of Risk	300
—— Caldwell, portioner of Beltrees	300
—— Barber of Risk	300
John How in Damtoun	300
James Orr in Longyard	300
John Fulton of Spreulston	600
—— Fulton of Boydston	360
Nicol Craig in Eastmayes	300
James Campbell of Rivoe	300
John Roger of Park	360
Andrew Gaw of Brink	360
Matthew Harvison in Titwood	300
Robert Rankin of Broadlees	300
George Craig of Brome	200
John Rankin of Newton	600
John Spreul in Renfrew	400
—— Pollock of Flender	200
George Pollock of Falside	480
James —— of Cartbridge	200
Andrew Gilmour in Newton	200
John Rankin of Mallasheugh	300
John Smith there	300

STIRLING AND CLACKMANNAN SHIRES.

Sir Charles Erskine of Alva	6,000
Sir William Bruce of Stenhouse	1,200
—— of Leckie	600
Captain William Monteith, son to umquhile James Monteith	1,200
Sir Thomas Nicholson of Carnock	6,000
William and David Tennents in Slamaima-muir, equally betwixt them	300
Robert and John Foresters equally betwixt them	300
Thomas Fleming there	300
William Young there	300
David and Patrick Youngs, there, equally betwixt them	240
Robert Arthur in Balcastle	240
Alexander Waddel there	240
Alexander Arthur there	240
John Gibson there	240
John Boyd	240
John Boyd in Lerghous	240
Allan Taylor in Middlerigg	240
James Boyd in Balmitchel	240
John Cardwirhothgus	240
William Tender of Burn	240
James Mochrie of Strandrigg	240
William Row in Bendath	240
—— of Milhaugh	240
James Guidlet of Abbotheugh	600
Archibald Row of Innerallen	600
William Marshall, portioner of Bogston	240
Allan Bog, portioner there	240
William Dick of Bankhead	240
Thomas Robertson, portioner there	240
David Robertson, portioner there	240
Patrick Eadie, portioner of Bogow	240
John Hastie, portioner there	240
James Shaw of Dochquhan	240
James Binning of Bridge-end	240
James Black of Hillend	240
James Eadie of Ballinbriech	240
John Robertson, portioner of Blackston	240
Alexander Lightbody, portioner there	240

CHAP. III.]   OF THE CHURCH OF SCOTLAND.   277

flection the most part of the managers themselves were ashamed of this: and indeed it would have looked odd enough, to levy fines from such as they were turning out of their houses and livings as fast as might be. But enough of

1662.

Peter Bryce, portioner of Belbrick	L.240	Sir Andrew Agnew, sheriff of Galloway	L.660
Archibald Bryce, portioner there	240	—— Gordon of Grange	1,800
James Marshal, portioner of Kinower	240	—— M'Culloch, younger of Ardwall	1,200
John Glen of Candiend	240	John Cathcart of Gennock	2,000
—— Calder of Hill	240	Francis Hay of Hareholm	1,000
James Dick of Millersplace	240	Patrick Agnew of Sewchan	1,200
John Arthur of Quarter	240	Patrick Agnew of Whig	2,000
—— Brown, portioner in Woodside	240	Gilbert Neilson of Catchcathie	1,300
—— Taylor, portioner there	240	Patrick M'Ghie of Largie	260
John Wardlaw of Hungriehill	240	William M'Kieffock, collector of Wigtonshire	3,600
Patrick Calder of Campston	240		
John Higgen of Bowes	240	George Campbell, captain-lieutenant to Sir Robert Adair	600
John Jap, portioner of Crownerland	240		
James Gray, portioner of Gilmudie	240	Alexander Kennedy of Gillespie	480
Alexander Marshal of Masterston	240	James Johnston in Strawrawnard	600
Andrew Baird, late bailie of Stirling	600	John Bailie of Litledoneraclet	360
Gilbert Robertson, there	600	Alexander Bailie of Meikleton	360
Robert Gib, merchant there	360	—— M'Donald of Crachen	360
Thomas Scotland of Dallarbyge	360	John M'Dougal of Creesein	600
John Scotland, there	360	Alexander Agnew of Crach	600
Alexander Fergusson, there	600	Martin M'Ghie of Penningham	600
James Stirling of Badirnoch	1,200	William M'Kuffock	3,600
James Boyd of Balmitchel	600	—— Stuart, bailie of Wigton	360
—— Rollock of Bannockburn	600	—— Cantrair, late provost of Wigton	1,200
—— Monteith of Insholm, younger	600	William M'Ghie of Magdallen	360
David Bruce in Alva	360	—— Ramsay of Boghouse	400
James Forest of Bankhead	480	John M'Culloch in Glen	400
Thomas Buchanan of Boquhan	360	Patrick Agnew of Caldnoth	1,000
Robert Forest of Queenshaugh	360	Thomas Boyd of Kirkland	360
Robert Forest of Rushiehill	600	Alexander Martin in Stramavart	600
Mr. Robert Bruce of Kennet	1,800	Patrick Kennedy there	360
John Mitchel in Larber	360	John Machans, tanner there	600
David Guidbet of Langlewin	480	Gilbert Adair there	360
James Callendar in Falkirk	300	David Dunbar of Calden	4,800
David Campbell there	300	John Gordon merchant in Stranrawart	240
John Simpson there	240	John M'Dougal there	240
John Edet in Dalwhatston	200	William M'Culling there	240
James Tennent in Dykehead	240	John Adair of Littlegennock	600
John Auld there	210	Alexander Crawford tutor of Herymen	360
John Wauch there	240	William Gordon of Barnfallie	360
John Shaw in Greenhill	240	John Hannah in Granane	480
James Easton there	240	William M'Dougal in Kilroe	1,000
John Mounghill in Lennox	240	—— Trissel, burgess of Wigton	360
John Lightbody there	240	Adam M'Kie, late provost of Wigton	1,000
James Pender in Limemill	240	—— Stuart of Fintilloch	1,000
Peter Russel in Cowholm	240	James Mackitrick in Kirkmaiden	960
William Tennent in Burnhead	240	Michael Malrae in Stonykirk	600
Thomas Fleming in Rushiehill	240	James Macnaught in Portpatrick	360
George Neil there	240	Nevin Agnew in Clod-house	240
Thomas Russel in Middleridge	600	—— Agnew in Kilconquhar	240
John Russel in Balcastle	300	John Macmaister in Kirkcum	360
Thomas Taylor in Newhouse	300	John Macguieston in the Inch	360
Andrew Clerkiston	300	Andrew Agnew of Park	360
John Weston in Craigend	400	Patrick Hannah in Gask	360
Alexander Crawford in Mannellingle	600	—— Mackinlenie in Darmenew	300
James Granton in Morwimside	240	Gilbert Macricker in Knockedbany	360
John Andrew there	240	John Macilvain in Milboch	360
Thomas Baird in Balinbreich, William Black, John, Robert, and James Eastons, William Andrew, Patrick Baird, and William Baird, each of them L.15 Sterling, inde is	1,260	—— Mackinnen of Glenhill	360
		—— Mackinnen of Glenbitten	360
		—— Kennedy of Barthangan	240
		Edward Lawrie in Derward	240
		Mr. William Cleland in Sheland	240
Alexander Mill of Skene	1,000	Thomas Macmoran there	360
William Row in Bawheich	600	John Paterson there	360
Lord Rollock	6,000	—— Mackinnen in Polpindoir	240
Thomas Mitchel of Cowdon	600		
WIGTONSHIRE.		KIRKCUDBRIGHTSHIRE.	
Colonel William Stuart	600	Major Maculloch of Balhome	500
		Robert Kirk of Kildane	300

1622. the indemnity: it was no wonder it was so slow a coming, when it had so many clogs hanging upon it. I remember Sir George Mackenzie, in his "Vindication," affirms, "that more indemnities were granted by this king than by any

Robert Howison, subcollector	L.240
Alexander Gordon of Knockgray, elder and younger	120
William Whitehead of Mibhouse	360
John Corcadi of Senwick	1,200
David Arnot in Barnkapel	360
Mr. William Gordon of Earlston	3,500
John Gordon of Rusco	2,400
John Turner in Adwell	360
—— Gordon of Traquair	2,400
John Fullarton of Carleton	1,000
John Macart in Blaikit	800
John Gordon in Waterside	600
—— Gordon of Ballechston	800
James Logan of Hills	1,000
—— Logan of Bogrie	480
Patrick Ewing of Anchescioch	1,000
John Maxwell of Milton	800
—— of Dendeoch	600
William Gordon of Midton	240
Robert Stuart of Mungohill	1,000
Archibald Stuart of Killyreuse	1,000
John Thomson of Harriedholm	240
John Brown of Muirheadston	360
—— Brown of Lochill	360
Alexander Gordon of Culwening	600
John Lindsay of Fadpirth	600
John Aitken of Auchinlaw	360
William Gordon of Chirmers	600
James Chalmers of Waterside	600
—— Heron of Kerrochiltree	600
William Gordon of Robertson	360
William Corsan, there	240
John Logan in Edrick	240
William Glendoning of Curroch	360
William M'Culloch of Ardnall	600
Robert M'Lellan of Bargatan	360
Alexander Mackie, merchant in Kirkcudbright	200
Alexander M'Lellan, merchant there	200
Alexander M'Lellan, maltman there	280
William Telfer, in Dunroe	300
—— Gibson of Brocklelo	360
John Stuart, of Shambellie	600
David Gordon of Glenladie	600
Alexander Gordon of Auchincairn	200
Laird Mertine	240
William Gordon of Meniboe	280
John Wilson of Corsock	600
Robert M'Culloch of Auchillarie	240
Cornet Alexander M'Ghie of Balgown	480
Edward Cairns of Tore	240
—— Corsan in Dundrenan	200
James Logan of Boge	600
John M'Michan of Airds	360
John M'Millan of Brackloch	360
John Cannor of Murdochwood	360
Robert Gordon of Grange	2,400
John Grierson, there	600
Robert Gibson in the parish of Kells	360
Edward Gordon of Barmart	480
Alexander Cairns of Dulliparish	480
James Glendonning of Mochrum	480
James Neilson of Ervie	360
—— Grierson, son of Bargatan	600
—— Martin in Dullard	360
William Glendonning of Logan	360
Robert Ga, there	360
James Wilson in Creirbrane	240

Alexander Livingstone of Countinspie	L.360	0	0
Robert Corsan in Nether-rerick	360	0	0
James —— of Parberest	240	0	0
Patrick Corsan of Cudoe	600	0	0
John Harris of Logan	360	0	0
—— Telfer of Harecleugh	1,800	0	0
James Thomson of Inglistoun	1,000	0	0
John M'Lellan of Balnagoun	240	0	0
Captain Robert Gordon of Barharro	240	0	0
—— Gordon of Gedgill	300	0	0
—— Bugble in Comrle	240	0	0
Edward Clauchane in Casselzowere	240	0	0
John M'Gill in Gall	240	0	0
John Cannan in Guffartlaid	240	0	0
John Hamilton in the Muir of Kirkpatrick	240	0	0
Thomas Neilson of Knockwhawock	240	0	0
William Gordon of Mackartnie	240	0	0
James Gordon of Killnelnarie	240	0	0
John Welsh of Skair	240	0	0
James Smith of Drumlaw	240	0	0
Robert Greill in Kinharvie	240	0	0
William Maxwell in Norther-rait	600	0	0

ARGYLESHIRE.

George Campbell, tutor of Caddel	5,000	0	0
Donald Campbell of Skamadel	600	0	0
Alexander Campbell of Auchinverum	400	0	0
Mr. Donald Campbell of Auchaird	500	0	0
Alexander Campbell of Glenverie	200	0	0
Malcom M'Compter of Letters	500	0	0
James Campbell	1,000	0	0
Donald M'Allaster, alias Campbell	3,000	0	0
John Campbell his son	1,500	0	0
John Campbell of Kirkton	200	0	0
Archibald Campbell brother to Dunstafing	200	0	0
Donald Campbell his brother	400	0	0
Campbell of Ardorane	300	0	0
John Campbell of Largs	500	0	0
—— Campbell of Breghumore	300	0	0
—— Campbell of Breghubec	200	0	0
John Campbell of Auchinrach	600	0	0
Hector M'Lean of Torloisk	4,000	0	0
Neil oy M'Neil of Drumnammickloch	1,000	0	0
Duncan M'Arther of Drumack	500	0	0
Duncan M'Arthur of Inchstrenick	1,000	0	0
James Campbell, brother to the tutor of Calder	400	0	0
Colin Campbell, brother to Dunstaffnage	400	0	0
Donald Campbell of Sonnachan	300	0	0
Alexander Campbell, captain of Craigneish	4,000	0	0
Donald Campbell of Barbraick	2,666	13	4
Laird of Duntroon	2,666	13	4
John Campbell of Kilmartin	200	0	0
Neil M'Kellar of Letter	300	0	0
John Campbell of Strondour	600	0	8
Malcom M'Kellar of Deal	400	0	0
The Captain of Skipnish	1,500	0	0
Archibald Campbell of Glencaridale	2,666	13	4
Duncan Campbell, bailie of Kiltyre	800	0	0
John M'Neil of Ross	800	0	0
Neil M'Neil, tutor of	200	0	0
Lauchlan M'Neil of Ferargoes	280	0	0
Patrick Campbell of Kilmoir	3,000	0	0

who ever reigned." And indeed had they come seasonably and freely from him, they would probably have endeared him to the subjects; but to grant an indemnity after the nation had been overawed into so many ill things by the delay of it; to grant it so encumbered with fines and exceptions; in a word, to grant it after some of the best blood in the nation was spilt, and more designed, was, I must needs say, but an indifferent compliment, and very near the common proverb, "when I am dead make caudle." *Gratia quæ tarda est, ingrata est gratia.* It is the lovely character of God Almighty, that he is ready to forgive, and which therefore would have well become him who was called his vicegerent. But when a favour sticks to the fingers of the giver, it is the less obliging. As for the number of indemnities Sir George boasts of, I believe it will, I am sure it ought to be granted, that they were much fewer than ensnaring and oppressive laws, which made people stand in need of them.

Those are the printed acts that chiefly relate to the subject of this history, during this second session of parliament. Among the unprinted acts I find one concerning the ministers of Edinburgh, of which I may afterwards take notice, when I come to the sufferings of particular persons this year. Those worthy persons, without any citation, libel, or reason given them, are discharged from the ministry, and ordained to remove themselves and families out of the city, some time in September. In the same place I find the title of a proclamation of parliament for keeping the anniversary of the 29th of May, the month and day which they had devised of their own heart for a feast unto the people. Unto it the parliament saw good to add a certification of the deprivation of benefice, upon such ministers as did not keep it. Whereupon a good many were, without citation, or being heard, deprived of their stipends that year, though they had served the cure; and their just incomes were uplifted by a common collector, and disposed of otherwise.

This session of parliament continued long, and did very little, save what we have heard in favours of the prelates. In June, Sir George Mackenzie of Tarbet, was sent up to the king by the commissioner, with some things to be advised with his majesty. He was not well received, but from time to time delayed; and he was told the king's other weighty affairs hindered him from minding those matters. But Lauderdale was averse to several things proposed by Middleton, and the differences betwixt them were drawing now to some head, and this was the true spring of this delay. They had my lord Lorn's affair before them, and several west country ministers were called in to Edinburgh during this session of parliament, the accounts whereof may come in as well under the succeeding sections. The matter of the forming the list of persons to be fined, took them up likewise for a considerable time, and it was the 9th of September, before they dismissed, and adjourned till May, next year.

So much for this second and last session of parliament, held by the earl of Middleton, wherein he reckoned he had merited very much at his master's hands, by screwing up the prerogative, and establishing the bishops, to support it, and flatter the king. And yet after he had made a circuit through the west and south, and in council passed many iniquitous acts against presbyterians, when he went up to court, his reception was but indifferent, and his rival in a short time prevailed against him; and he never sat in another parliament, and, for any thing I know, never saw Scotland again.* I come now to the procedure of the council.

Evan M'Ivernock of Obb	L.500	0 0
Donald Campbell of Obb	1,200	0 0
Alexander Campbell, late commissar of Argyle	600	0 0
John Campbell of Dana	600	0 0
—— Campbell of Knab	2,000	0 0
Colin Campbell of Glentibbart	500	0 0
The laird of Otter	2,000	0 0
Duncan Campbell of Enlane	1,200	0 0
Colin Campbell of Arteneish	800	0 0
John Campbell, bailie of Glenderule	300	0 0
John Ger-Campbell of Glenderule	240	0 0
John Mackermaise of Ishanzelaw	400	0 0
—— Campbell of Gargathie	500	0 0
—— Campbell of Lochzel	3,000	0 0
John M'Arthur of Dullosken	400	0 0
Summa totalis, £1,017,353	6	8

* See a succeeding Note.

SECT. III.

Of the acts and proceedings of the council after the parliament rose, and particularly of the act at Glasgow, October 1st, this year 1662.

662. Having thus seen the procedure of this second session of parliament, it may be fit to take a view of the acts of council, who begin where they left, and go on vigorously against presbyterians, especially ministers; and we shall understand the sufferings of particular persons the more distinctly, after we have seen the train of the more public actings this year.

Now prelacy, that tree of sorrow and death in Scotland, is planted, the fruits it bears will be best gathered from the records of the council, who were for many years the bishops' executioners, and spent much of their time to serve them and harass the presbyterians. There we shall meet with a large harvest of " imprisonments, finings, confinings, scourging, tortures, banishments, selling as slaves, scattering of many poor but religious families, night searchings, heading, hanging." Yet just as Pharaoh's policy to extirpate the children of Israel succeeded of old, so now it did in its copy; the more presbyterians were oppressed, the more they multiplied.

The very next day after the parliament rose, the council begin their iniquitous acts; and in prosecution of what they left at January last, they publish their act anent diocesan meetings, September 10th, which I have added in a note.* The council begin with remarking, that the bishops and archbishops had been taken up since their consecration, in attending the service of the parliament, and thereby kept from the exercise of the government, and ordering the affairs of the church: which may sufficiently convince even the abettors of prelacy, of the unreasonableness of the civil places and powers of churchmen, and how much their seats in parliament abstract them from what ought to be their proper work. Now they are to go to their respective dioceses, to exercise the authority and jurisdiction established upon them by the laws: and to be sure they had no other establishment; and it had been dangerous, for what I can observe, for them to claim any other but what flowed from the regal supremacy. The second Tuesday of October, is to be the diet for the dioceses of St. Andrews, Glasgow, Edinburgh, Dunkeld, Brechin, and Dumblane, whereupon their diocesan assemblies are to be held; and the third Tuesday, for those in the dioceses of Galloway, Aberdeen, Murray, Ross, Caithness, Isles, Argyle, and Orkney. All parsons, vicars, and ministers, are required to be present, and give their concurrence in their stations, for the exercise of ministerial duties, and that under the penalties of contemners of his majesty's authority: and all other meetings of ministers are henceforth to be held as seditious. This proclamation put it out of the power of presbyterian ministers to attend those meetings, if they were not resolved to quit their principles, since all their power is derived from the prelates, and theirs from the king. Accordingly they came under a course of sore sufferings.

Those diocesan meetings were very ill kept

---

* Act of council anent Diocesan Meetings. At Holyrood-house, the 10th day of September, 1662.
The lords of his majesty's privy council, having, in pursuance of his majesty's royal pleasure and commands, by the proclamation, dated at Edinburgh, the 9th day of January last bypast, discharged all ecclesiastical meetings in synods, presbyteries, and church sessions, until they be authorized and ordered by the archbishops and bishops in their respective sees. And considering, that the lords, archbishops, and bishops, have, all this session of parliament, been engaged to attend the service thereof, and now are to repair to their respective sees, for exercising of the government, and ordering the affairs of the church, according to that authority and jurisdiction which is settled and established upon them by the laws; and for that effect, have resolved to hold their diocesan assemblies in the dioceses of St. Andrews, Glasgow, Edinburgh, Dunkeld, Brechin, and Dumblane, upon the second Tuesday of October next, and to hold the assemblies in the dioceses of Galloway, Aberdeen, Murray, Ross, Caithness, Isles, Argyle, and Orkney, upon the third Tuesday of the said month. Therefore, the lord commissioner his grace, and the lords of his majesty's privy council, do think fit, by open proclamation, to make publication hereof to all persons concerned, and to command and require, that all parsons, vicars, ministers in burgh or land, within these respective dioceses, do repair to the said diocesan meetings, upon the foresaid days, and in time

save in the north. Synods and presbyteries were now discharged, and those meetings did entirely depend on the bishop, and attendance upon them was reckoned a subjection to prelacy. In the diocese of Glasgow, consisting of the presbyteries of Ayr, Irvine, Paisley, Dumbarton, Glasgow, Hamilton, and Lanark, the largest body of ministers, next to the assembly, in this church, together with the shires of Nithsdale, Tweeddale, and Teviotdale, the bishop had only twenty-seven present with him.

At Edinburgh, the bishop had double their number with him, and great pains was taken by the noblemen and courtiers, to get ministers to be present. October 14th, the bishop and his chapter held the diocesan meeting, which consisted of fifty-eight members present. To put honour upon this first prelatical synod, the king's advocate, some of the lords of council and session, with the magistrates of Edinburgh, were present. The bishop opened the meeting with a sermon from Phil. iv. 5. " Let your moderation be known unto all men." Two out of every presbytery were pitched upon by the bishop, as a committee, which was named " the brethren of the conference," to prepare business for the synod. They proposed, and the synod went into it, that there should be morning and evening prayers in the church, in every burgh, and every other place where any confluence of people could be had. I do not find that this was continued during prelacy. That the Lord's Prayer should be repeated by every minister once at every sermon, or twice as he saw good. That the " Doxology," or " Glory to the Father," being a song composed and sung in the church, when Arians and other sects denied the Deity of our Saviour, should be again revived and sung, this being a time when many sectaries deny the Godhead of Christ. That the " Creed," or " Belief," be repeated at the administration of the sacrament of baptism, by the father of the child, or the minister, at his discretion. Probably those things were concerted beforehand among the bishops, and proposed to every meeting, and agreed to. It had been good for them and this church, if they had rested here.

1662.

This meeting likewise agreed, that all ministers within their diocese, who had not conformed to the act of council made at Glasgow, of which more just now, should be indulged to come in and accept of collation from the bishop, betwixt and the 25th day of November next to come, otherwise the bishop is to proceed against them, and fill their kirks with other ministers. The meeting continued part of two days, and were appointed to meet after Pasch next. The writer of the papers, from which I take this, no disliker of prelates, observes, " That all this did not please the people, who much hated the bishops, and favoured the doctrine of their own ministers, and loathed episcopacy: however, some ministers in the diocese came for and accepted collation." But to return to the proceedings of the council.

To put this act the better in execution, and put the more honour upon the prelates in the western and southern shires, where they were generally disliked, towards the end of September, the commissioner resolves upon a tour through that part of the country, where he expected most coldrifeness to the bishops, and makes his best efforts to bring all to a subjection to them. He had a full quorum of the council with him, ready to meet as occasion offered, not only for the executing of what the parliament had enacted, but even to go beyond them. Accordingly,

---

coming, as they shall be required to give their concurrence in their stations, for the exercise of ministerial duties, for the order and peace of the church: with certification, that whosoever shall presume not to give their presence and dutiful attendance upon these diocesan assemblies, and shall not concur in other church meetings, as they shall be appointed and authorized by the respective archbishops and bishops, shall be holden as contemners of his majesty's authority, and incur the censures provided in such cases. And it is hereby always provided, that no minister or ministers, upon whatsoever cause or pretence, shall presume to keep any ecclesiastic meetings, who shall not submit to, and own the ecclesiastic government by archbishops and bishops; with certification, that all such meetings shall be holden henceforth as seditious. And ordain these presents to be printed, and published at the market-crosses of the head burghs of the shires, that none pretend ignorance.

Pet. Wedderburn, Cl. Secr. Concilii.

1662. his grace the commissioner, the chancellor, the earls of Morton, Linlithgow, Callender, and the lord Newburgh captain of the king's lifeguards, with the clerk to the council, and a great many attendants, came to the west country with much solemnity, macers, trumpeters, and kettle-drums. They came to Glasgow, September 26th, and were regaled and royally treated at Hamilton, Paisley, Dumbarton, Rosedoe, and Mugdock, and, some other places about, by the noblemen and burghs concerned.

Many remarks upon the prodigality, profaneness, and terrible revelling at this progress, were made at this time. Such who entertained the commissioner best, had their dining-room, their drinking-room, their vomiting-room, and sleeping-rooms, when the company had lost their senses. I find it regretted, that while they were at Ayr, the devil's health was drunk at the cross there, in one of their debauches, about the middle of the night; indeed it was a work of darkness; but I leave those things to such as shall write a history of the morals of this time, which will be black enough, and ungrateful to Christian ears, but a proof that profaneness and prelacy in Scotland go hand in hand.

It was given out, that Middleton went west to press the declaration imposed by parliament upon the presbyterians in that country. Whether the kindness and good company he met with at Glasgow, and the neighbourhood, where every body almost waited on him, softened his spirit, or what was the reason I know not, but I do not find he pressed it.

When he came to Glasgow, the commissioner was entertained with a very heavy complaint from the archbishop, that notwithstanding of the act of parliament, and that the time was elapsed, there was not one of the young ministers, entered since 1649, had owned him as a bishop; that he had only the hatred which attends that office in Scotland, and nothing of the power; that his grace behoved to fall upon some other and more effectual methods, otherwise the new made bishops would be mere ciphers. Middleton desired to know what the archbishop had to propose, and he should heartily fall in with it. Fairfoul moved, that the council might agree upon an act and proclamation, peremptorily banishing all the ministers who had entered since the year 1649, from their houses, parishes, and respective presbyteries, betwixt and the 1st of November next to come, if they come not in to receive collation and admission from the bishop; assuring the commissioner, there would not be ten in his diocese who would stand out, and lose their stipend in this cause.

Every desire of the prelates was now next to a law: and so a meeting of council was agreed upon, and convened at Glasgow, in the college fore-hall, towards the street. At this time it was termed the drunken meeting at Glasgow, and it was affirmed, that all present were flustered with drink, save Sir James Lockhart of Lee. When the council met, the commissioner laid before them the archbishop's desire and overture, and the necessity of supporting the bishops the king and parliament had brought in. There was no debate upon it, save by the lord Lee above named. He reasoned some time against it, and assured them such an act would not only lay the country desolate, but cast it in disorder, yea, increase their dislike to the bishops, and at length bring the common people into confusions and risings; he peremptorily asserted, that the younger ministers, admitted since the (year) 1649, would go further than the loss of their stipends, before they would acknowledge and submit to bishops: but reasoning, though never so just, could not have any great weight in the present circumstances. Thus the act was formed in the terms of the archbishop's demand, though some say it was with difficulty, whether for want of a fresh man to dictate or write, I know not. The tenor of it follows.

" *At Glasgow, October 1st,* 1662.

" The lords of his majesty's privy council taking to consideration, that notwithstanding it is statute and ordained, by an act of the last session of the current parliament, entitled, ' act concerning such benefices and stipends as have been possessed without

CHAP. III.] OF THE CHURCH OF SCOTLAND. 283

presentation from the lawful patron;' that all ministers who have entered upon the care of any parish in burgh or landward, in or since the year of God 1649, (at and before which time the patrons were most injuriously dispossessed of their patronages) have no right unto, or shall uplift the rents of their respective benefices, modified stipends, manse or glebe, for this instant year 1662, nor for any year following, unless they should obtain presentation from the lawful patron, and have collation from the bishop of the diocese where they live, before the twentieth day of September last: as likewise, that it is statute and ordained, that the twenty-ninth of May be yearly kept as a holyday unto the Lord, for a solemn anniversary thanksgiving for his majesty's restoration to his royal government, and that all ministers should observe the same in their respective parishes, under the pains therein contained: yet several ministers have not only contravened the foresaid acts of parliament, but, in manifest contempt of his majesty's royal authority, albeit they have justly forfeited their right to the benefices, modified stipends, and others, continue to exercise the function of the ministry at their respective churches as of before; therefore they prohibit and discharge all ministers who have contravened the foresaid act of parliament concerning the benefices and stipends, to exerce any part of the function of the ministry, at their respective churches in time coming, which are hereby declared to be vacant: and that none of their parishioners who are liable in any part of their stipends, make payment to them of this instant crop and year of God 1662, or in time coming, as having no right thereunto: and that they do not acknowledge them for their lawful pastor, in repairing to their sermons, under the pain of being punished as frequenters of private conventicles and meetings. And command and charge the said ministers to remove themselves and their families out of their parishes, betwixt and the first day of November next to come, and not to reside within the bounds of their respective presbyteries. As likewise, that no heritor or other, liable in payment of any part of the ministers' stipend, make payment to any minister who hath contravened the foresaid act of parliament, for keeping the anniversary thanksgiving, of any part of this year's stipend; and declare, that the ministers who have contravened the said act, shall be liable to the whole pains therein contained. And ordain those presents to be forthwith printed, and published by the sheriffs of shires, and magistrates of burghs, that none may pretend ignorance."

1662.

In the registers, this act stands signed by Glencairn chancellor, duke Hamilton, Montrose, Morton, Eglintoun, Linlithgow, Callender, Newburgh, Sinclair. There are in the sederunt this day, besides the commissioner, the lairds of Lee and Blackhall, who do not sign the act.

This act appears to be beyond the council's power, which was only to execute the acts of parliament, and not to make new laws; and they evidently go beyond what the parliament had statuted. But a little time convinced them that they had taken a false step. The most part of the west and south of Scotland was laid waste of ministers, and people turned discontent, and almost desperate: and what they did at Glasgow, was disliked by some of their best friends; particularly the primate was mightily dissatisfied, and complained, that Fairfoul's folly had well nigh ruined them. His scheme was to have presbyterian ministers more insensibly turned out at first; and therefore another proclamation was shaped at Edinburgh, in December, partly rescissory of this, and a little more soft, as we shall hear.

By this act of Glasgow, near a third part of the ministers of this church were cast out of their charges, and, by the following acts some more, merely for conscience' sake, being free of the least degree of disloyalty or rebellion. They could not keep holydays, they could not take the oath of allegiance or supremacy, they could not own patrons, nor subject themselves to bishops; and therefore must be turned out.

1662. I shall afterwards have occasion to observe the lamentable consequences of this act; and only here remark, that, at Glasgow, the council proceeded to severe enough measures with some particular gentlemen and ministers, of which in its own place.

After this heavy work at Glasgow, the commissioner went forward in his circuit, through Renfrew, Cuningham, Kyle, and Carrick: he was some time at Ayr, and from thence went to Wigton and Dumfries; and upon the last of October, he returned to Holyrood-house. When the accounts came in to Edinburgh of the rueful circumstances of the west and south, by the silencing their ministers, Middleton, who had depended upon the accounts given him by the archbishop of Glasgow, that few or none would lose their stipends for nonconformity, raged and stormed exceedingly. He knew many of the ministers had little to sustain themselves and their numerous families; and cursing and swearing, asked, "What will these mad fellows do?" knowing nothing of their living by faith, as sufferers for conscience and a good cause use to do.

During the month of November, the council are taken up in retrieving, as much as possible, this hasty act at Glasgow. Their prosecutions of particular ministers and gentlemen shall be noticed in the following sections. Accordingly, the very first meeting at Edinburgh, November 4th, they appoint the following letter to be writ to the archbishops of St. Andrews and Glasgow.

" My Lord,

" Having considered, that by the execution of the late acts of parliament and council, against several ministers who have contravened the same in many places of the kingdom, the condition of the parishioners will be rendered very hard, through the want of the ministry, and the benefit of the ordinances. We have thought fit your lordship come here with your first convenience, that by your advice we may redress those disorders, and provide for the good of the people, which shall be seriously looked to by

" Your lordship's friends,

" Glencairn chancellor, Hamilton, Morton, Linlithgow, Haddington, Roxburgh, Tweeddale, Sinclair, Halkerton, J. Lockhart, George Mackenzie, Sir Robert Murray."

How much better had it been to have considered those fatal consequences, before they had made such laws and acts, than after they were made to provide remedies? Had they seriously looked to the good of the people, certainly they had never been made. However, this was the next best: the archbishop of Glasgow seems to have been backward to come to discourse with the lords, as perhaps knowing he was to blame. November 6th, under expectation of the upcoming of the archbishops, the duke of Hamilton, lord register, Tarbet, advocate, and any other the commissioner pleases to name from the council, are appointed to meet with his grace, the chancellor, and the two archbishops, anent such matters and business as do concern the affairs of the church. But it seems the archbishop of Glasgow still hangs off; for, November 18th, the following letter is writ to him.

" Most reverend,

" It is now a fortnight since we did write to your lordship to come here, in order to some affairs that concern the church: and seeing we have had no return, we thought fit to renew our desires; and the matter being of such importance, your lordship is expected as soon as he can be, by

" Your assured friends,

" GLENCAIRN, Chancellor, &c,
ut in sederunt."

That same day, the members of council are writ to, to attend on the 21st; and on the 21st, duke Hamilton, Montrose, and other members are again writ to, to attend upon the 27th. Whether the archbishop of Glasgow came up or not, I cannot tell, but, November 27th, the chancellor, Roxburgh, Haddington, Callender, the register,

CHAP. III.] OF THE CHURCH OF SCOTLAND. 285

and Lee, are appointed to meet in the afternoon with the commissioner, about such business as his grace shall propose: but I find no account of the archbishop's coming up. Meanwhile, the council go on to the banishment and confinement of a good many particular ministers, as we shall hear. It seems they could not concert their general act till December 23d, which was the last meeting of council Middleton was ever present at. That day the council publish their act and proclamation, which being pretty long, I have annexed it as a note.*

The council, under the sense of the wrong step taken at Glasgow, 1662. and how hard it was to leave so vast a number of congregations desolate, as had their ministers ejected by that act, and the bishops having but few ready to fill them, extend the day, and allow ministers to obtain presentation and collation before the 1st of February next: but if betwixt and that time they neglect, they are ordained to remove out of their parishes, presbyteries, and the dioceses of St. Andrews and Edinburgh; and such

---

* Act of Council.

At Edinburgh, the 23d day of December, 1662.

The lords of his majesty's privy council, taking to consideration the great happiness this kingdom doth now enjoy in his majesty's restitution, the church being thereby restored to its ancient and right government, the laws to their due course and splendour, and the subjects to the peaceable possession of their rights and properties; and the administration of all these, tempered with that moderation, which should justly endear them to all honest and loyal subjects, but especially to these of the ministry, who have so largely shared in his majesty's grace and pardon, both as to their public actings and their undue possessing of benefices, many of them having, during these late troubles, intruded themselves into churches, stipends and benefices, without any right from the lawful patrons, and so being liable in law for their intromission; yet were, by his majesty's favour, indemnified for what they had possessed, and the patrons ordained to give to them new presentations, and a competent time allowed for obtaining the same, with collation from the bishop of the dioceses thereupon; which being done, they were from thenceforth to enjoy their churches as freely as any other ministers within the kingdom. And albeit such favourable dealing might have challenged a most cheerful submission and obedience from all concerned therein; yet, such was the froward disposition of some, in slighting of his majesty's favour, by not accepting of presentations, and in contemning his majesty's authority, by continuing in the exercise of their ministry, that the council was necessitate by their act at Glasgow, upon the first of October last, to discharge all such ministers from exercising any part of their ministry, and to charge them to remove themselves and their families out of their parishes; and though in order thereunto, the carriage of divers ministers hath not been suitable to their duty, yet, the council being desirous to exercise further indulgence towards these men, if possibly they may be reclaimed, have therefore thought fit (being also thereunto solicited by such of the lords of the clergy as were upon the place) to allow a further time until the first day of February next, 1663, betwixt and which they may yet obtain presentations and collations, as said is, provided, that such who since the first of October are already placed, or may be judged fit to be placed in these places declared vacant, by

act aforesaid, shall enjoy their churches and benefices, any thing in this act to the contrary notwithstanding: certifying always, such as shall fail in obtaining their presentations and collations, they are from thenceforth to be esteemed and holden as persons disaffected to his majesty's government: and such of them as are within the dioceses of Glasgow, Argyle, and Galloway, are, conform to the former act of council, to remove themselves and their families forth of the bounds of their respective presbyteries, but that they do not offer to stay nor reside within the bounds either of the dioceses of St. Andrews or Edinburgh; and wherever else they shall happen to reside, they are hereby discharged two of them to reside in one parish: and such within the dioceses of St Andrews and Edinburgh as shall not obtain presentation and collation betwixt and the said first day of February next to come, they are from thenceforth to retire themselves, and stay and reside benorth the river of Tay; and all of them who shall not give satisfaction as aforesaid, are hereby discharged from exercising any part of their ministry in public or in private, and from keeping any meetings in families, upon pretence of religious exercises, except in and with their own families; with certification, to such as shall contravene any part of this act, they are to be punished as seditious persons. And forasmuch, as besides these persons above designed, there be divers ministers, who, in contempt of his majesty's authority and command, did absent themselves from the meetings of the synods whereto they were called by his majesty's authority; and the lords of his majesty's privy council, being desirous to reclaim all of them, have therefore at this time thought fit, only to confine them within their several parishes, until the next meeting of the synod, discharging them hereby to transgress the bounds of their confinement, unless, upon application to the bishop of the diocese, they obtain a warrant under his hand for the same. And since the disorderly carriage of some ministers hath occasioned, that divers of the people, with whom they have interest, do withdraw from the worship of God in their own parish churches, to the dishonour of God, the contempt of his ordinances, and the scandal of the protestant religion, for making way for atheism, schism, and separation in this reformed church, and for alienating of people from their duty and obedience to the authority established therein: therefore the council do

1662. ministers as were in those dioceses are ordained to remove beyond Tay before the first of March, as the proclamation itself more fully bears.

This act some looked upon as a permission to return to their parishes, at least until the first of February; and so a good many up and down the country did come back and preach. But very soon they found no favour was designed for presbyterian ministers by that act, save what was absolutely necessary for a present conveniency; and ministers' return and removal so quickly after, at the diets named by the council, was one of the first handles to the common people to censure them. Ignorance, scrupulosity, and censure, ordinarily go together, especially in so dark an hour as this. In reality this act was a cunning fetch of the primate, and an insidious lengthening out of the time, which it now appeared had been too much shortened at Glasgow, for ministers coming in; and in the event it turned to the disadvantage of the persecuted ministers. Cunningly enough, in the proclamation, ministers are blamed for "refusing to ask a presentation from patrons," and no notice is taken of the clause enjoined with this in the act of parliament, "their receiving collation from a bishop," which was a plain renunciation of presbyterian principles. And no doubt this was designed to exasperate the nobility and gentry at ministers, though out of principle and conscience they refused both; and beside what hath been observed upon those heads, the remarks of Mr. Douglas on this act, deserve a room here. He says, " The receiving a presentation and collation may be accounted a small matter, but who considers it well, will find it very weighty. Taking of presentations condemns the removal of laick patrons, and which is more, condemns the call from the people: and presentations directed to bishops, condemn the call from the presbytery; and it vacates the right to the beneficе, and says, they had no right to it; and yet in law *beneficium sequiter officium.* Besides, the collation is not a simple collation, and giving a right to the benefice, which is tolerable; but the right is given upon the account of their acknowledging their ordinary, and submission to the present episcopal government, which is a real acknowledging their power. This honest ministers could not do; therefore by the act they are removed from their charges; and more ministers were removed in one month, than ever were removed in Scotland since the reformation. It is no wonder then the complaint against their bishops be, that their little finger is thicker than the loins of the former."

The king's goodness is magnified in not making ministers pay back all their stipend since the year 1649, in which period they had as good a title to them as the law of the land and the king's consent to it could give. It is noticed, that this prolongation of the time was at the request of the bishops present, which might be matter of fact, since the act of Glasgow was reckoned by the primate and the wiser part of them, to be of ill consequents to their interests; and they

---

hereby appoint all his majesty's subjects, to frequent the ordinary meetings of public worship in their own parish churches; and in case there be no sermon there, that they go to the next church where sermon is, and that otherways they presume not, without lawful excuse, to stay from their own parish church, or go out of their own parishes on the Sabbath day: commanding hereby, all magistrates within burgh, and justices of peace, to take trial of the contraveners, and to punish them as Sabbath-breakers, and to exact twenty shillings Scots from each of them, *toties quoties*, to be applied for relief of the poor of the parish. And whereas the sacrament of the Lord's supper (which was instituted as a special mean and bond of love and unity, duty and obedience amongst Christians) is, at the administration thereof in some places, abused and perverted, by the unlicentiate confluence of some people, and extravagant sermons of some ministers of unquiet and factious spirits, and made a special engine to debauch people from their duty, and lead them to disobedience, schism, and rebellion: therefore the lords of his majesty's privy council, in pursuance of the trust reposed in them, and for preventing of disorder and disturbance, do prohibit and discharge every minister of a parish, to use or employ the assistance of any more ministers, by preaching or administrating the holy communion, save one or two neighbouring ministers, unless they be licentiate thereunto by the bishop of the diocese; and that no person of another parish be admitted to the participation of that sacrament, without a certificate under the hand of the minister of the parish where the said person doth reside. And ordain these presents to be forthwith printed, and published at the market-cross of Edinburgh and other places needful, that none may pretend ignorance.

Pat. Wedderburn, Cl. Secr. Concilii.

were glad to amuse, and give a little quiet to the country, who now hated the bishops more than ever. Their banishing ministers from such and such precincts, and tossing them up and down, as in the proclamation, was both cruel and beyond the acts of parliament, of which they were only executors, and contrived and calculated to hold off applications to persons of influence at Edinburgh, and to deliver bishop Sharp's diocese of the trouble of presbyterian ministers. It was hard enough measure to oblige the ministers who lived upon the border of England, to which the diocese of Edinburgh reacheth, to remove themselves and families be north Tay, for no other fault save noncompliance with prelates, for which they had already lost their benefices. In the next room, the elder ministers, who were not reached by the act of Glasgow, are imprisoned in their own parishes for their not being present at the diocesan meeting. This is plainly illegal; but harder things come upon them afterward. Neither does this proclamation spare the people, but after, most groundlessly, the blame of their not hearing the curates is laid upon presbyterian ministers, their not keeping their parish churches, while in the meantime they were banished, I know not at what distance, from them, the council orders twenty shillings Scots, to be uplifted by magistrates and justices of the peace, from every one who is absent from his parish church; which would have been a goodly sum, had it been uplifted; as indeed it was in a little time upon presbyterians, most severely. In the end of the act the council come to regulate communions, and restrict ministers as to their helpers at them; being grated lately with that which Mr. John Livingstone kept at Ancrum, with sensible measures of the Divine presence. Truly they were a very unfit company to make ecclesiastical canons and regulations.

Under all those acts against presbyterian ministers and people, Middleton is daily losing ground at court, and Lauderdale gaining; and after this proclamation he never sat in a court in Scotland. He was, in the end of December, called up to London, and charged with high treason, and reduced to no small difficulties, as shall be afterward noticed. The king being informed of the partial manner of imposing, and unreasonableness of the act of fines the commissioner had brought the parliament to, prorogated the time of paying the first moiety. Middleton for some time kept up the order for this, being fond of a share in the payment of them, and forbare publishing a proclamation for this effect. This irritated the king exceedingly, and Lauderdale was not wanting to improve such a step to his own advantage. Thus we have some view of the more general procedure of the council this year.

1662.

SECT. IV.

Of the particular sufferings of ministers and gentlemen, from the beginning of this year to the rising of the parliament.

THE sufferings of particular persons, noblemen, considerable numbers of gentlemen, ministers, and others, this year, grow so much upon my hand, that I am obliged to give them in two sections, the one before, and during this second session of parliament, and the other after it was up; and we shall find great numbers attacked by the council towards the end of the year. I might begin with such whose heart was indeed broke with the change made upon this church last year, and the dismal alteration this year, by the introduction of prelacy: those were certainly confessors and martyrs in resolution. Their death is some way chargeable upon the present managers, and it is probable, had not death prevented, they would have been attacked in this evil time. Among this kind of sufferers I only instance two, both very eminent in their stations, and singular ornaments to Scotland; the right honourable the earl of Loudon, and the reverend and learned Mr. Robert Bailie professor of divinity, and for a little space principal of the college of Glasgow. The first died in the beginning of the year, and the other in a little time afterward, and both of them of grief in some measure.

John, earl of Loudon, late chancellor of Scotland, was a prime instrument in the late work of reformation begun 1637, and such

1662. who write the history of that period will do him the justice his memory deserves. He was a nobleman of excellent endowments, great learning, singular wisdom and conduct, bewitching eloquence, as the impartial pen terms it, joined with remarkable resolution and courage. Next to the marquis of Argyle, he was the great butt of the spite and malice of the party now in power, as well as their envy. He knew his life was at the king's mercy for the political guilt all the nation lay under: he had frequently applied for his majesty's grace, and was as often refused. The courses now so violently carrying on, and the plain invasions upon the liberty and religion of Scotland, made this great man weary of his life. He often exhorted his excellent lady to pray fast, he might never see the next session of parliament, else he might follow his noble friend the marquis of Argyle. The Lord was pleased to grant the request, and he died in a most Christian manner, at Edinburgh, March 15th, this year, and his corpse was carried to the west country, and interred with his noble ancestors.*

Mr. Robert Bailie may most justly be reckoned among the great men of this time, and was an honour to his country, for his profound and universal learning, his exact and solid judgment, that vast variety of languages he understood, to the number of twelve or thirteen, and his writing a Latin style which might become the Augustan age: but I need not enlarge on his character, his works do praise him in the gates. He had been employed in much of the public business of this church since the year 1637, and was a worthy member of the venerable assembly at Westminster, and at London almost all the time of it; and hath left behind him very large accounts of matters both of church and state, which passed in his time. He was of a most peaceable and healing temper, and always a vigorous assertor of the king's interest. And although at the first he wanted not his own difficulties from his education, and tenderness of the king's authority; yet after reasoning, reading, and prayer, as he himself expresseth it, he came heartily in to the measures of the covenanters. I have it from an unquestionable hand, one of his scholars, who afterwards was his successor, and waited on him a few weeks before his death this year, that he died under a rooted aversion to prelacy in this church. My author desired Mr. Bailie's judgment of the courses this church was so fast running into. His words to him were, " Prelacy is now coming in like a land-flood; for my share I have considered that controversy as far as I was able, and after all my inquiry I find it, and am persuaded it is inconsistent with scripture, contrary to pure and primitive antiquity, and diametrically opposite to the true interest of those lands." The incoming of this land-flood, which lasted twenty-seven years, indeed shortened his days, and broke his heart. And that the reader may not take this upon my word, it is worth while to insert here this excellent person's sense of things, from two original letters under his own hand, to the earl of Lauderdale; and they may serve as his testimony against the courses of this time.

His first letter is dated June 16th, 1660, and therein he says, " I was one of those, who in my heart, and all needful expressions, adhered to the king in all his distresses; he had my continual prayers to God for his restitution, any way God pleased, even the most hard. Divers know my readiness to have furthered his return to his throne, by laying down my head on the block for it, and the utter ruin of all my worldly fortune. When the Lord lately, at a very cheap rate, brought all my prayers, and much more, to pass, there were few had a more hearty joy for it than I. While I am going on in my daily renewed joy, behold, your unhappy diurnals and letters from London have wounded me to the heart! Is the service-book read in the king's chapel? Has the bishop of Ely (I still feared Wren) the worst bishop of our age after D. Laud, preached there? Has the house of lords

---

* Kirkton says, " He was a man of excellent endowments, learning, wisdom, judgment, and courage; he died a very godly death, and purged himself of his sins by ingenuous confession, and hearty application of the blood of Jesus."—History of the Church of Scotland, p. 138.—*Ed.*

passed an order for the service-book? Ah, where are we so soon? The granting us in Scotland the confirmation of what we have, brings us just back to James Graham's time. Is our covenant with England turned to Hary Martin's Almanack? Is the solemn oath of the lords and commons assembled in parliament, subscribed so oft by their hands, to eradicate bishops, turned all to wind? Why did the parliament a few months since appoint the covenant to be hung up in every church in England, and every year to be publicly read? Is Cromwell the great enemy of our covenant so soon risen out of his grave? Can our gracious prince ever forget his solemn oath and subscription? He is a better man than to do it, if those about him be not very unfaithful servants.

"For myself, such are my rooted respects both to his person and place, that do what he will, and tolerate what he will, I purpose while I live to be his most loving and loyal subject. But, believe me, if I were beside him I would tell him sadly and with tears, that oaths to the Almighty are not to be broken, and least of all by him for whom the Lord has wrought, at this very time, a more marvellous mercy than he hath done for any, yea for all the princes in Europe those three hundred years.

"Bishops were the very fountains of all our mischiefs. Will they ever change their nature? Will God ever bless that plant which himself hath not planted? 'Tis a scorn to tell us of moderate episcopacy, a moderate papacy! The world knows that bishops and popes could never keep caveats. The episcopal faction there, were never more immoderate than at this day. You know how far Pierce, Heylin, and Taylor justify all the challenges against episcopacy in their late writs, and go beyond them to all the tridentine popery of Grotius. T. G. Thomas Gallovidianus, for his printing doctor Forbes bishop of Edinburgh his wicked dictates, is now in his way for London, being sent for by the English bishops who scoff at our church's excommunication.

"Your lordship was the man who procured and brought down to us the ordinance for abolishing of episcopacy; I doubt not but you and Mr. Sharp have done your endeavours; but could I ever have dreamed that bishops and books should have been so soon restored with so great ease, and silence of the presbyterian covenanters in both houses, the city, and assembly at London, of Lancashire and other shires?

1662.

"Be assured that whatever surprise it be for the time, this so hideous a breach to God and man, cannot fail to produce the wrath of God in the end. Shall all our blood and labour for that covenant be so easily buried? Though all flesh, English and Scots, for their own designs, were silent at so needful a time, I doubt not but the Lord himself will hear our cries against the beast which hath got so deadly a wound, that all the kings and parliaments of the earth will never be able to cure. I and many more, who have and will rejoice in the restitution of our king, resolve to complain to God and man, while we live, for the return of books and bishops. Thus far I have poured out my heart to you at this time."

The reader will not grudge to have this honest and great man's sentiments, when our parliament last year were overturning the work of Reformation very fast, in another letter to the same noble lord, dated April 18th, 1661.

" My lord,

"Having the occasion of this bearer, I tell you my heart is broken with grief, and I find the burden of the public weighty, and hastening me to my grave. My prayers daily, when my heart is loosed, are for the king and you, and his blessing on you both. I have no private desires nor fears, but I think we are very ill guided, and very needlessly so. What needed you do that disservice to the king, which all of you cannot recompense; to grieve the hearts of all your gracious friends in Scotland, to whom the king's majesty was, is, and will be, I hope, after God, most dear, with pulling down all our laws at once, which concerned our church since the (year) 1633? Was this good advice, or will it thrive? Is it wisdom to bring back upon us the Canterburian times? The same designs, the same practices, will they not bring on the same horrible effects,

1662. whatever fools dream? That old maxim of the state of England is wise and good, That the king can do no fault: but the highest ministers of state ought in all reason to answer on their highest pain for all miscarriages. It was one of king James VI. his wisest practices, to permit his greatest favourites to sink, before that by protecting them, the grief of his people should fall on his back. Ye have seen the contrary principle destructive, and it will be still so.

" My lord, you are the nobleman in all the world I love best, and esteem most; I think I may say and write to you what I like: if you have gone with your heart, to forsake your covenants, to countenance the re-introduction of bishops and books, and strengthened the king by your advice in those things, I think you a prime transgressor, and liable among the first to answer to God for that great sin; and the opening a door, which in haste will not be closed, for the persecution of a multitude of the best persons, and most loyal subjects that are in all the three kingdoms. And if otherwise your heart be where it was, as I hope it is, and that in your own way you are doing what you can for the truth of God, yet daily I have my fears for you. I think you stand in a ticklish place: remember your cousin Hamilton's poisoning before king James's eyes, without search. My heart whiles trembles for you; I will continue to pray for you, do what you will. I ever opposed Mr. James Guthrie his way; but see none get the king persuaded to take ministers' heads. Send them to some place where they may preach and live; you may obtain this if you will." Then he goes to college affairs, and adds, " I will beg for it while I live, which I think shall not be long; for presbyterians at London, their misguiding has slain me. There are some of my twenty year old pamphlets reprinted at London; it is totally without my knowledge, though indeed I remain fully in the mind I was then in. If you and Mr. Sharp, whom we trusted as our own souls, have swerved towards chancellor Hyde's principles, as now we see many do, you have much to answer for. This may possibly be my last to you, therefore I crave no pardon for its length. I am

" Your lordship's old friend,
" ROBERT BAILIE."

By another original letter of his to Mr. George Hutcheson, June 24th, this same year, I find Mr. Bailie acquainting him, " What you desire me to write to L. I have done it already, as my testament to him, fully and sharply to obviate the chancellor, &c. at their last going up: I think verily if that wicked change come, it will hasten me to my grave." And in the last letter I have seen of this good man's, dated May 12th, 1662, which I take to have been a few weeks before his death, he tells his cousin, Mr. Spang, after some account of the west country ministers being called in to Edinburgh, " The guise is now, the bishop will trouble no man, but the state will punish seditious ministers. This poor church is in the most hard taking we have ever seen: this is my daily grief—this has brought all my bodily trouble on me, and is like to do me more harm."* And very quickly he got

---

* It has been fashionable of late, to talk of the covenanters of the seventeenth century, as 'illiterate' and 'illiberal;' (See Critique of M'Crie's Life of Knox, Quarterly Review, 1813.) and *Baillie* has been sometimes quoted as an instance! Baillie's learning, however, has been rarely equalled; and it was certainly not surpassed by any of his cotemporaries. He was born in Glasgow, in the year 1599. His father, Mr. Thomas Bailie, was a citizen of that place, and son to Baillie of Jerviston, and allied to some of the first families in Scotland. He received his education in the university of Glasgow; and when there, he was much distinguished for the superiority of his talents, and furnished a remarkable example of great literary diligence. Having, about the year 1622, taken orders from archbishop Law, he was chosen a regent of philosophy in the university. He was afterwards presented to the parish of Kilwinning. In the year 1633, he declined on a principle of modesty, an offer which was made to him of one of the churches of Edinburgh. In 1637 he was asked by the archbishop of Glasgow to preach before the general assembly, and to recommend the book of Common Prayer and Canons, then attempted to be thrust upon the church; but this he steadily refused to do. Hitherto his mind seems to have wavered between the two systems, but from this period he became decided in favour of presbytery; and his reputation rose higher and higher among the covenanters. In the assembly at Glasgow, 1638, he displayed great wisdom, zeal, and learning; and was particularly distinguished by his strong opposition to prelacy and Arminian-

to his rest and glorious reward. This was the case, and those were the sentiments of many ministers and others at this time.

But I go on to the direct sufferers of this period. In the end of the last year, and beginning of this, many worthy gentlemen in the west country were brought to much trouble, upon the pretext they had done prejudice to the earl of Queensberry's lands, and were with the forces under colonels Strachan and Ker, in the year 1650. But the real reason was, because most part of them had appeared for the remonstrance, and were heartily against prelacy; and therefore some money must be raised from them, and given to Queensberry and his son. All of them are likewise in the act of fines, and we shall meet with a good many of them under other branches of suffering, as we proceed in this history. I shall then give as short an account of this affair as I can, from the council registers.

The parliament, last year, upon a complaint of losses sustained by the said earl, and some agreement among parties, by their act of the 29th of March, did state the losses at two thousand pounds sterling, and appointed a committee to meet at Cumnock, to inquire into the persons who were with the army under the foresaid colonels, and to proportion the said sum upon the guilty persons. Accordingly the committee, the

---

ism. He was also a member of all the following general assemblies of the church of Scotland, until the year 1653, excepting when he attended the assembly of divines at Westminster. By his brethren he was promoted first to the professorship of oriental languages, and next, to that of divinity, in the university of Glasgow. At the restoration he was advanced by the episcopalians to the principality. They who wish to see his talent for controversy, may read what he published on the subjects of Episcopacy and Arminianism, which formed the chief topics of theological dispute in his day. He wrote also a variety of histories on matters connected with church-government. But the work which establishes his learning beyond all question, is his 'Opus Historicum et Chronologicum'—a book of immense research, and written in a style that would not discredit Eton or Cambridge. He was held in high esteem by the greatest men of the continent, particularly, Spanheim, Salmasius, Rivet, Leusden, and Constantine l'Empereur. With many learned men of Europe he held frequent intercourse; and his printed "Letters," (although a small specimen only) exhibit a mind, alive to the best interests of literature and religion, not in his own church, only, but in the church universal. When the Westminster assembly of divines had finished their labours, the English parliament, to testify their high sense of Baillie's merits, made him a handsome present of silver plate, with an inscription, intimating, that it was a token of their great respect to him, and as an acknowledgment of his valuable services. And yet so attached was he in common with his brethren, to the house of Stuart, that after the execution of Charles I. in 1649, the general assembly appointed him one of the embassy from their body, to Charles II. at the Hague, after he was proclaimed in Scotland. On that occasion he addressed the king in a most loyal speech, expressing in the strongest terms his joy and that of his brethren in his succession to the throne, and their abhorrence of the murder of his royal father. In Baillie's sentiments on this subject, it appears, that the presbyterian divines of that period, both at home and abroad, very generally agreed. (Life of Baillie by Reid, see his History of the Assembly of Divines at Westminster, vol. ii. p. 275. See also an able and eloquent vindication of Baillie and the other covenanters, in the Edinburgh Christian Instructor, for November and December, 1813, in reply to the Quarterly.) Although he sided with the *resolutioners* he nevertheless remained steady to the presbyterian interest, and it is said, refused a bishopric when bribed by the offer of one from the king. Scots Worthies, p. 261, 4th edition. Candour requires us, nevertheless, to say, that amiable and learned as Baillie was, he did imbibe certain causeless prejudices against his more zealous brethren of the *protesting* side; and this accounts for the contemptuous manner in which he speaks of some of those noblemen and ministers, with whom he once walked in the bonds of unity and love. He supposed that all the evils which befell the church and the state, flowed from the protestors refusing to join with the resolutioners; whereas it seems to have been rather the reverse. " Several hundreds of the resolutioners, on the very first blast of temptation, involved themselves in fearful apostasy and perjury. Some of them became violent persecutors of their more faithful brethren, and not a few of them absolute monsters of iniquity. The dreadful effects of this have almost ruined both church and state in these lands." Scots Worthies, p. 263, 4th edition. Nevertheless, we may remark, that no candid man will be surprised at the conduct of Baillie in regard to the protestors; who recollects the unfortunate quarrels on the same head, between Rutherford and his colleagues Wood and Blair, at St. Andrews; and the differences, even on slighter grounds, which alienated such congenial spirits as those of Peden and Renwick. The truth is; among the friends of the good cause, there had been industriously sown the seeds of division; and we have in those painful schisms, a striking illustration of the well known adage—*divide et impera*. With the causes of disunion, which were constantly multiplying, men's minds were more and more heated; and what with the violent contests about the resolutions, the indulgences, the payment of cess, and the toleration of conventicles, our wonder rather is, that amid the collision of parties, and the tearing asunder of the bonds of Christian fellowship, spiritual religion was not utterly extinguished. —*Ed.*

1662. earl of Eglinton, lord Cochran, the sheriff-depute of Nithsdale, Gilbert Richard of Barskimming, and some others, meet, and make their report to the council, who had this affair committed to them by the parliament, December 3d, last. By their report, it appears they found the underwritten persons present in Nithsdale, at the time complained, with the said colonels, when Queensberry sustained his losses, and therefore, that they ought to bear the proportion of the two thousand pounds sterling. A good many of them are absent, and some off the country; but all are found guilty of being present with the forces aforesaid, and that many of them were instrumental of the losses sustained. And having taken the most exact trial of the estates real and personal, they rated them at the valuations aftermentioned, as their part of the two thousand pounds.

The Laird of Rowallan	L.940	0 0
Sir George Maxwell of Nether Pollock	1,044	9 0
Sir John Kennedy of Cullen	814	13 4
Thomas Hay of Park	940	0 0
Mr. William Gordon of Earlstoun	1,444	9 0
Sir Hugh Campbell of Cesnock	1,566	13 4
James Fullarton of Corsby	626	13 4
Thomas Boyd of Pinkel	495	0 0
John Shaw of Sornbeg	313	0 0
The heirs of the laird of Glanderston	313	0 0
The heirs of Gilmerscroft	325	18 8
James Hamilton of Aikenhead	295	6 8
John Boyd of Trochridge	438	13 4
Gavin Walkinshaw of that ilk	112	15 8
John Gordon of Boghall	41	16 0
Hugh Wallace of Underwood	156	13 8
Robert Wallace of Cairnhill	82	17 8
William Wallace of Garrick	20	17 0
Captain Andrew Arnot	41	16 0
Thomas Kennedy of Grange	188	0 0
Alexander Brodie of Letham	1,044	9 0
James Nisbet of Greenholm	165	0 0
John Crawford of Crawfordland	626	13 4
Sir William Cunningham of Cunninghamhead	2,401	6 8
Robert Andro of Little Tarbit	652	0 0
John Kennedy of Kirkmichael	999	13 4
Robert Barclay of Perstoun	438	10 4
Alexander Cunningham of Craigends	908	0 0
Sir John Chiesly	336	6 8
John Cunningham of Hill of Beeth	206	4 4
Robert Simpson in Edinburgh	125	13 4
Robert Hamilton in Halcraig	180	0 0
Captain George Campbell	62	13 4
Mr. Cuthbert Cunningham of Cochilbee	626	13 4
Mr. Lindsay of Belstane	250	1 4
Bruce of Stainhouse	626	13 4
Robert Atcheson of Sydeserf	1,141	6 8
Colonel Gilbert Ker	626	13 4
Hunter younger of Hunterstoun	83	10 8
John Aird of Miltoun	62	13 4
Captain Hutcheson	83	11 0
Mr. Alexander Neilson	86	7 0
Colonel Halbert	376	0 0
John Shaw of Greenhill	41	16 0
Ralston of that ilk	567	0 0
William Adair of Kinhilt	504	13 4
John Johnston in Glasgow	250	13 4
James Hamilton there	188	0 0

There are a good many objections given in to the council against several of those quotas. Cunninghamhead, Craigends, Glanderston, and some others are declared by the council to be free, and their defences sustained. And the council approve of the rest, and renew their appointment upon the committee to meet, and adjust the proportions of the others, take further trial of some not cited, and report to the council against the 1st of March next. I do not observe any further report in the registers, but find those sums were increased upon some, and a few added to make up the quota. I need not insist upon the unreasonableness of attacking so many gentlemen, a good many of them of the first rank, and singular for probity and religion, for an alleged fault, committed upwards of ten years ago, and merely because they were hearty presbyterians, and suspected to be averse from the courses entering upon; and in a little time to fine most, if not all of them, in the act of fines: those were steps peculiar to this time.

As the fury of this period ran much against gentlemen who had been active in the work of reformation, so, in a particular manner, some of the most eminent ministers of this church must be attacked. The reverend Mr. Robert Blair is among the first. And when our new consecrated bishops came down, a new and more general storm comes, and persecution upon presbyterians turns very sharp: and the prelates resolve to be as sovereign in the church, as the king, their creator, was over the state and them; and therefore they must be rid of all presbyterian ministers, especially of such as were too hard for them. Accordingly, I find Mr. Robert Blair before the council, towards the beginning of the year. January 9th, the lord Bellendon, the advocate, and provost of Edinburgh, are appointed to examine all the witnesses cited in Mr. Robert Blair's case, and report. I find no more about him till September 4th, when, " the macers, or any of them, are ordained to bring the person of Mr. Robert Blair, late minister at St. Andrews, to Edinburgh, betwixt and Saturday next, and secure his person in the tolbooth till further orders. September 10th, information being given to the council, and testificates produced from sure hands, that Mr. Robert Blair is under great sickness for the present, so that at this time he cannot travel nor be transported to Edinburgh, without the manifest hazard of his life: and it being represented, that he is content to quit the charge of the ministry at St. Andrews, and for that end he had sent in his presentation, to be disposed of at the council's pleasure; which was produced in council: for all which causes, the lords dispense with his imprisonment, and declare his place vacant."

This is all I meet with in the council registers about Mr. Blair. From other papers I find, that after their most diligent search, nothing could be fixed upon against this great man.* His life is writ by himself to the year 1638, and had Mr. Blair gone through with it, I persuade myself it would have been one of the best accounts of that time we could have had: but there remain only some short hints by another hand, as to the last part of this great man's life.

From those and other accounts come to my hand, I find, that Mr. Blair, after the imprisonment of the ministers, August 1660, and the appearance of re-introducing prelacy by the rescinding of our former excellent laws, had a free and yet cautious sermon upon 1 Peter iii. 14. This was most unfairly represented to the council last year, and he was cited over to Edinburgh. The citation came to him on Saturday night late, and resolving to obey it, and foreseeing he should not return to his people, to-morrow, being the last sabbath of September, 1661, he preached upon these words, " Finally brethren, farewell," &c. when there was an extraordinary concern among his hearers. When he came to town, after some days, he was examined by a committee of the council upon the matter of his sermon, of which he gave a most distinct account. All they did was to confine him to his chamber at Edinburgh, where falling ill for want of the free air, he had his confinement altered to the town of Musselburgh. There he continued till September this year, when bishop Sharp, having a mind to have Mr. Andrew Honeyman planted in his room, procured a new order from the council, and a macer was sent to bring him in prisoner. But the Lord ordered another messenger to seize him, and he fell very ill of a fit of the gravel, and could not come. And the next council day he was under a very severe sickness, which was attested by his physicians. Mr. Blair, hearing that his charge had been declared vacant the former sederunt of council, and the order which the macer brought designing him late minister at St. Andrews, did, with the attestation of his illness, send in his presentation, which allayed their fury against him. In some time thereafter he procured liberty to reside in Kirkaldy, where he continued in very much respect for a considerable time. Meanwhile his back friend the primate, vowed he would harry that nest. And soon after, the order came out discharging all presbyterian ministers to live in burghs; and he removed to Couston. In short, the true ground of all this trouble this excellent person met with, was, the archbishop could not be easy when so good a man was near him. And

1662.

---

* Mr. Blair was not a protestor, neither was he a resolutioner, but attempted to hold himself neuter, and to be a mediator between these parties. Of course he was not so liable to be caught as those who had explicitly declared themselves by joining in the remonstrance, which, in the estimation of the court, was the great political crime of that day, and a crime into which no one who had fallen was allowed to escape with impunity. On the other hand, he who was known to have been a resolutioner, if he was not very obstinate, or altogether destitute of friends, generally found means of getting off with a more lenient punishment.—*Ed.*

1662. the primate had a particular quarrel against Mr. Blair, because of a free and faithful admonition given him by order of the presbytery, by Mr. Blair and Mr. David Forret.

But the most remarkable prosecution of ministers, in the period I am now upon, was that before the parliament, of Mr. John Carstairs minister at Glasgow, Mr. James Naismith minister at Hamilton, Mr. Matthew Mowat, and Mr. James Rowat, ministers at Kilmarnock, Mr. Alexander Blair minister at Galston, Mr. James Veitch minister at Mauchline, Mr. William Adair minister at Ayr, and Mr. William Fullarton minister at St. Quivox.

When the bishops came down from England, it was found necessary to endeavour to bring some of the most eminent presbyterian ministers in the west country, where the greatest aversion to prelates was, either to subject to the government now set up, or to suffer. Besides this general view in this prosecution, several others concurred. Some say that a difference betwixt the chancellor and the primate had fallen in, very soon after the latter his coming down from court; and the first designed, by this act of zeal for the bishops, to make up the breach. It was further pretended, that this treatment of so many noted ministers, would be a good way to keep the west country in awe, and prevent what they termed sedition and disorder, upon the intended parliamentary establishment of bishops; and this was their ordinary colour and pretext for many of their severities. In short Mr. Carstairs behoved to preach no more in so eminent a place as Glasgow, with that freedom and plainness, as well as caution, he used to do; and Mr. Naismith behoved to give way to Mr. James Ramsay, who was designed to be dean of Hamilton, and assistant to the archbishop. Thus the chancellor was empowered by the council to send letters to such ministers in the west country, as he thought fit; and by the advice of the prelates, and particularly the bishop of the Isles, he pitched on the above named. Mr. Fullarton had been pretty forward for the public resolutions, and had some friends at Edinburgh, through whose interest he got favour, and was dismissed. Mr. Adair took a different course from his brethren, as we shall hear, which grieved them and many others. All of them obey the chancellor's letters, and came to Edinburgh. When they appeared before him, he threatened them severely for their alleged disloyal principles, and particularly for some expressions, he said, they had in their sermons. They fully vindicated themselves in point of loyalty, and desired particular condescensions might be made, as to any thing blameworthy in their sermons; but no condescensions could be made. The interview was concluded with insinuations, that their only way of escape would be by complying with the bishops the king had set up. And when no ground could be gained that way, the chancellor commanded them to stay at Edinburgh, till the parliament should meet; which accordingly they did.

When the parliament sat down, the ministers were dealt with in private, and all methods were used to bring them to a subjection to prelacy, but in vain. The managers, finding them fixed in their principles, resolved to put the oath of allegiance to them; and here they imagined they had them under a dilemma: if they sware, they reckoned they were obliged to submit to the bishops now set up, by virtue of the supremacy contained in the oath; and if they refused, they lay open to the penalties appointed by law, against disloyal and seditious persons. All of them, save Mr. Fullarton, were cited before the parliament, for a terror to the rest of presbyterian ministers who stood firm to their principles, and to fright them into a submission to the bishops. Nothing of a libel could be formed from their carriage, or any thing in their sermons; and therefore, to catch them, they are brought before the lords of the articles, and, as a test of their loyalty, they are required to take and subscribe the oath of allegiance, as it stood in the act of parliament. The ministers desired time to advise, and with difficulty obtained a few days. Now they were upon the stage, in a matter which very nearly concerned the crown and kingdom of Jesus Christ; and being the first presbyterian ministers to whom this oath was tendered, they conceived their carriage and practice was a matter of no small consequence. And, after they had set some time apart, for asking of the Lord light, direction, and conduct in this important matter, they came to this issue: That if they sware the oath as it stood, without any explication, especially in this juncture, they might be reckoned thereby obliged to comply with episcopacy, seeing the act of parliament just now made for the restitution of bishops runs, " Forasmuch as the ordering and disposal of the external government and policy of the church, doth properly belong to his majesty, as an inherent right of the crown, by virtue of his royal prerogative and supremacy in causes ecclesiastical." Upon the other hand, if they altogether refused the oath of allegiance, they feared they might be reckoned refusers of lawful subjection in civil things, to him whom they heartily owned their lawful sovereign.—Upon the whole, they resolved to offer an explication of their sense in this matter to the legislature, and if it was received, then to take the oath in that declared sense; if not, cheerfully to suffer, which, in that case, they hoped would not be as evil-doers, or disloyal persons, but merely for conscience' sake. Next, it came to be considered, whether it was most proper to give in their sense in writ, or verbally, and found it safest to give it in in writing; and accordingly, six of them agreed to the underwritten draft, and signed it. Mr. Adair would not sign it, till once the chancellor had seen it, as it seems, he had promised to his lordship. The rest judged this inconvenient, that any of the managers should see it, till it was tabled before the parliament. The tenor of the paper follows.

" We underscribers, ministers of the gospel, being commanded on Monday last, by the lord commissioner his grace, and the honourable lords of articles, to take the oath of allegiance, do, from the sense we have of that duty which lieth upon all his majesty's subjects, and more eminently and exemplarily upon ministers of the gospel, in ingenuity and plainness, upon every occasion, to declare their loyalty to his majesty our dread sovereign, and in obedience to your lordship's commands, heartily and cheerfully acknowledge, that his majesty is the only lawful supreme governor, under God, within this kingdom; and that his sovereignty reacheth all persons, and all causes, as well ecclesiastic as civil, having them both for its object, albeit it be in its own nature only civil and extrinsic as to causes ecclesiastical: all which we are most willing, in testimony of our loyalty, to declare upon our most solemn oath. And accordingly, upon that same oath, in the foresaid sense, we declare, that, in testification of our faithful obedience to our most gracious and undoubted sovereign, Charles king of Great Britain, France, and Ireland, defender of the faith, we do acknowledge his majesty our said sovereign, the only supreme civil governor of this kingdom, over all persons, and in all causes; and that no foreign prince, power, state or person, civil or ecclesiastic, hath any jurisdiction, power or superiority, over the same. And therefore, we do utterly renounce and forsake all foreign jurisdictions, powers, and authorities, and shall, at our utmost power, defend, assist, and maintain his majesty's jurisdiction foresaid, as we shall answer to God. Subscribed at Edinburgh, May 28th, 1662, by

" Messrs. JAMES NASMITH,
MATTHEW MOWAT,
ALEXANDER BLAIR,
JOHN CARSTAIRS,
JAMES ROWAT,
JAMES VEITCH."

1662.

Here the ministers explain the most dark and dangerous part of this oath. Their explication was reckoned a refusal; but their very enemies must grant it was a respectful and conscientious refusal, if it must be one; and that they went as far as their light would allow them, to satisfy the imposers. But it was resolved by our prelates, that those six ministers shall be either examples of obedience, or suffering. So, May 28th, when they are called upon, and present the above written paper, it was reckoned a

1662. high crime. When the ministers appeared before the house, and the chancellor received the paper, he observed that Mr. Adair, who was present with the rest, had not signed it; ordered him presently to remove, and I have no more about him. As soon as the declaration was read, there were many warm speeches on it. It was arraigned as presumption, and a putting a restriction on the oath framed by the parliament, with many other hard names: and the six ministers straight committed to close prison, three and three of them to one chamber, to the great prejudice of their health; and nobody was permitted to have access to them. Thus they continued several weeks. Great pains were taken to prevail with them to take up their paper, and swear the oath absolutely, and as it stood; but they remained unshaken. Among others, bishop Leighton was sent in to them: he used all his eloquence and art, but was entertained with solid arguments against the oath, and very free checks, and a charge of apostasy and desertion, and laying stumbling-blocks before his brethren. At length their case came to this vote, " Whether process them criminally, or banish them?" and the last carried; and, by vote of parliament, they were banished out of the king's dominions, to bear company with their worthy brethren sent off last year. And the time was left to the commissioner and council to name, and they continued in close confinement.

In some time, when the commissioner's rage was a little cooled, and he and the prelates began to reflect upon the consequents of this warm procedure, some more sober measures came to be entertained. Mr. Robert Douglas, and some others, plainly told the managers, that the ministers' paper was sound and orthodox, and what the whole reformed churches would heartily approve of as their common doctrine; and the ministers' banishment, upon such a declaration, would expose them every where. Upon this, they began to allow them some more liberty; their friends were permitted to see them, and some of them permitted to go out of town for their health. Indeed their confinement was so close, and treatment so severe, that during their confinement, and before the sentence, Mr. John Carstairs fell so dangerously ill, that, upon the testimony of physicians, he was allowed to go to Dalkeith for his health; and accordingly he escaped the sentence. The rest continued in prison till the parliament was up, and then the commissioner and council were much solicited by the prelates, to pronounce the sentence. It was put off till the 16th of September, when, I find, the council's act runs as follows.

" Forasmuch as the king's majesty, with advice and consent of the estates of parliament, have pronounced sentence against Mr. James Nasmith, minister at Hamilton, Mr. Matthew Mowat, and Mr. James Rowat, ministers at Kilmarnock, Mr. Alexander Blair, minister at Galston, and Mr. James Veitch, minister at Mauchline, for refusing to take the oath of allegiance, leaving the time thereof to his majesty's commissioner, and have remitted to the lords of his majesty's privy council, the course to be taken with them in the interim: and the said lords having taken the same to their consideration, have thought fit to discharge, likeas, they hereby do discharge the forenamed persons, all further exercise of their ministry at the former churches above mentioned respective; and declare the said churches and cures at the said time to be vacant, and ordain the said persons to remove their families, and to leave the possession of their manses and glebes, at Martinmas next to come; withal, discharging them all residence within the presbyteries where the said churches lie, or within the city of Glasgow or Edinburgh: as also declare they have no right to the stipends of the said kirks for this instant year, 1662, and ordain the macers of the council, or any of them, to make intimation hereof to the said persons, that none of them pretend ignorance."—Thus the ministers got off for a season: we shall afterwards meet with several of them under new sufferings; and their churches were vacated to be filled with the creatures of the bishops, and this persecution did but confirm the disciples, whom the prelates would have taught with briers and thorns. This persecution I hope, will be owned to have been upon conscience and principle, and so much the rather that Sir George Mackenzie durst not attempt to vindicate it. During this session of parliament, there were letters writ to several other ministers in the south and west, to come in to Edinburgh, as we shall hear afterwards in Mr. Thomas Wylie's case, when it comes in before the council at Glasgow, in October. But finding the constancy of these just now spoken of, the prosecution was put off, and this matter left to the council to manage after the parliament was up.

I find likewise the lord Lorn, eldest son to the late marquis of Argyle, whom we shall afterwards meet with more than once, was sisted before this session of parliament. The pretended reason of this was some letters he wrote down to his friends from London, which were intercepted, or some way or other came to Middleton's hands; but the real design was to make way for Middleton's access to the estate, titles, and jurisdictions of that family, wherein, as in many other of his projects, he was baulked by Lauderdale.

In June the commissioner informed the parliament, that the lord Lorn, now at London, had both spoken and written against the proceedings of this supreme meeting. The most, as far as I can learn, that was in his letter, was some free expressions about the procedure last year against his excellent father, and some tacit insinuations of private views in the designed act of fines. However, the parliament, at the pressing instances of the commissioner, find his speech and actions treasonable. Accordingly, June 24th, they sent up an information upon this affair to the king, which I have not seen, with their desire that the said lord Lorn may be immediately secured and sent down to them, to abide his trial. The king was pleased to grant their desire, and caused him find my lord Lauderdale bail for him, that he should compear before the parliament in July. Probably the king scarce expected they would push matters so far as they did, or if they did, he knew how to stop the execution of the sentence. My lord came down to Edinburgh, July 17th: and such was their haste, that he was immediately charged to appear that afternoon at the bar; which he did, and after a handsome speech, he was committed close prisoner to the castle. I know no more of his process, but that, August 26th, he received sentence of death for his treasonable speeches and writings against the parliament, to have his head severed from his body, and his lands, goods, and estate to be forfeited The time of execution is remitted to the king; and he was sent back to the castle close prisoner. We shall afterwards find a remission granted him. And the parliament go on against some of the friends of that noble family, and September 3d, Campbell of Ardkinglas, and Campbell of Ormsay, fugitives from the last session of parliament, are now forfeited in absence, and declared traitors for some alleged crimes against gentlemen of the name of Lamont, I know not how long ago. Their forfeiture was intimated at the Cross of Edinburgh; and George Campbell, sheriff-depute of Argyle, was about the same time declared fugitive. I only name these, that the reader may have some view of the temper of this period I am giving the history of.

1662.

I shall conclude this section by observing that Mr. James Hamilton, Mr. George Hutcheson, and Mr. John Smith, ministers of Edinburgh, were silenced, and deposed by the parliament for not giving obedience to their bishop; and it was intimate to the rest of the ministers of Edinburgh, that they were to meet with the same punishment and censure, if they did not without delay submit to their ordinary: but not having seen the unprinted act, I shall say no more of it till we find them before the council in the following section.

SECT. V.

Of the sufferings of presbyterian ministers, gentlemen, and others, after the parliament rose, to the end of this year, 1662.

IN this period now before me, the severities against presbyterian ministers and others grow very much, and a good many particular ministers from all the corners of the church are sisted before the council, and hardly enough dealt by, to gratify the new made

1662. prelates. We have already had the more general proceedings of the council towards the close of this year, and now I come to the detail of the particular processes against ministers and others, much in the order they lie in the council books.

When the parliament is up, the council fall about their work of harassing presbyterians; and because people, when persecute in the country, sometimes came into Edinburgh, where they lurked more easily, to prevent this they make the following order.—September 16th, " Information being given, that many disaffected persons to his majesty do daily and continually resort and haunt to the burgh of Edinburgh, the lords of his majesty's privy council do order and command the magistrates of the said burgh, to cause all their burgesses, vintners, innkeepers, and all other inhabitants thereof, to give notice to them, or such as they shall appoint, of all such persons as are lodged or harboured by them every evening, and that under such pains and penalties as the said magistrates shall think fit to inflict."

That same day they attack the ministers of Edinburgh, and pass the following act with relation to them. " Consideration being taken, that by an act of the last session of parliament, Mr. James Hamilton, Mr. John Smith, and Mr. George Hutcheson, are discharged from any further exercise of their ministry within the town of Edinburgh, and their places declared vacant; and that all the other ministers within the town, who shall not, betwixt and the first of October next to come, own and acknowledge the present government of the church, and concur in the discipline thereof, are also discharged from any further exercise of the ministry within the said town, after the said day. And finding it not fit that those, who upon such an account are removed from the ministry, shall reside in the town; therefore the lords of council ordain the magistrates of Edinburgh to make intimation to the said Messrs. Hamilton, Smith, and Hutcheson, and to all such others of their ministers, as shall not betwixt and the first day of October next, give satisfaction thereanent that they remove themselves forth of the said town, and make their residence elsewhere at Martinmas next."

This act of parliament, with relation to the ministers of Edinburgh, I have not seen: but it is plain from the fourth printed act of this parliament, that ministers were permitted to continue in their charges till their nonattendance on the bishops' diocesan meeting; yet a singular method is taken with the ministers of Edinburgh before the time of that; and the council banish them from the city and place where they had exercised their ministry, and deprive them not only of their legal maintenance, but, as far as they can, of the company, comfort, and compassion of their flocks, when destitute of all other support. This appears both illegal, and beyond the act of parliament, and cruel, and is a prelude to the Mile acts a coming. We shall have frequent occasion to notice, that the council in this period assume a parliamentary power, and either enlarge or go beyond the penalties inflicted by the parliament, or anticipate most of the acts to be made, and make an experiment how they will take, before they are enacted by the parliament. Not only are the ministers turned out from their office and benefice, but tossed up and down with their innocent families, at this season of the year: and all this upon no other crime save their nonsubjection to prelates, which office in conscience they judged unscriptural and so unlawful. Sure our prelatical writers cannot say, those excellent persons and their good families were thus treated for rebellion and resistance. What impudence then was it for Sir George Mackenzie to say in his " Vindication," " that the governors of that time might truly and boldly say, that no man in Scotland ever suffered for his religion!" Accordingly, the ministers of Edinburgh had this act intimate to them, and submitted. Mr. Robert Trail had withdrawn some little time before, and we shall meet with him before the council just now; only Mr. Robert Lawrie by the common people called " the Nestegg," conformed, and as a reward got first the deanery of Edinburgh, and then the small bishopric of Brechin, which he possessed but a short time, and died under that remorse, so bitter a morsel was a bishopric to many of them, that, a little before his death at Edinburgh, he discharged the bellman to cry him by the designation of bishop, but ordered himself to be cried late minister of Edinburgh.

Before I leave this melancholy ejection of so many worthy men, and bright lights in the city of Edinburgh, let me add the reverend Mr. Robert Douglas's reflections upon and account of this step of the managers.—
" Seeing ministers are in the prelates' way, they must be laid aside. Some are banished, some sentenced to be banished, but the act not put in execution; and some are confined. Because the ministers of Edinburgh are in the great city, they must be first dealt with to give obedience to the acts made for bishops.

" The commissioner sent for me; and he and the chancellor being alone in a room, I was told we must speak with the bishop. I desired to know their meaning; for wise men had an end in all their actings and commands. Then it was told me, the end was not merely to speak to the bishop, but to own and acknowledge him. I answered, I was clear I could not do that, and since they had called me, I took it to be my duty to use freedom. I wished they might be more sparing in what they did; they were setting up men who would tread upon them, as they had done in former times. After a little silence the chancellor said, We will take care to keep them from that. I answered, It is impossible to keep those men down, they will domineer over noblemen as well as ministers; and they both found it so. The chancellor, before he fell sick, desired a worthy gentleman to tell me that I was a true prophet, and Middleton said the like. I might tell that without prophecy, for the nature of the preferment leads to it.

" In a little time three of the ministers of Edinburgh, Messrs. James Hamilton, John Smith, and George Hutcheson, are required to acknowledge the bishop, or remove from their charges; and they choosed rather to suffer than sin. After their removal, Mr. Thomas Garvan, Mr. John Stirling, and myself, sat still for a short time: their removal was in August, we preached 1662. not long after; but are charged to acknowledge the bishop, and confer with him, before the first of October, or else to remove out of Edinburgh with our families. What was acted in parliament is followed out by the secret council, for they charge us beforehand to remove upon that day; and upon the very first of October, a macer came to every one of us, and charged us and our families out of the town."

Mr. Douglas subjoins a short vindication of the ministers, as to their doing so little in opposition to episcopacy, and observes, " They dealt with the king, supplicated the parliament; that to show their detestation of it, they preached against it, and, when called, suffered for not submitting to it; and that is all that is in the examples of the prophets. James v. 10. " Take, my brethren, the prophets who have spoken in the name of the Lord, for an example of suffering and of patience." We have spoken and suffered; and if any say we should have stayed, notwithstanding of the parliament's inhibition, and preached, I understand it not. The Apostles were persecuted from city to city; and in the primitive times godly men, when obliged to it, removed from one place to another. I look upon the commands of the parliament as a physical impediment and restraint, and such who speak otherways reflect upon the banished."

To return to the subject of this chapter, I find no particular persons before the council till their meeting at Glasgow, October 1st, where they grant a commission to some persons to be nominate by the commissioner to take James Campbell, sometime of Ardkinglas, and James Campbell, sometime of Ormsay, declared traitors, to pursue them and their complices, take in forts, raze houses, &c. in the common form of commissions of fire and sword, as they are ordinarily called. And further, they order letters of intercommuning against them.

After they have passed the forementioned act, they come to make two acts, one against Mr. Donald Cargill, and the other against Mr. Thomas Wylie, and they did not more at Glasgow. I transcribe them as they stand in the registers.

1662. "Information being given, that Mr. Donald Cargill, minister of the barony church at Glasgow, has not only disobeyed the acts of parliament for keeping an anniversary day of thanksgiving for his majesty's happy restoration, and for obtaining a lawful presentation and collation from the archbishop of Glasgow, before the 20th of September last, but that also his carriage hath been seditious, and that he hath deserted the flock, to their great prejudice by want of the ordinances: therefore the lords of council declare the foresaid church to be vacant, and at the disposal of the lawful patron. And, for avoiding the inconveniences that may follow by his residing at Glasgow, or places near adjacent, they command and charge the said Mr. Donald Cargill not to reside in any place on the south side of the river of Tay, and to cause transport his family and what belongs to him out of the town of Glasgow, before the first of November next to come: with certification, that if he be found to contravene, and be seen on this side of Tay, he shall be apprehended, imprisoned, and proceeded against as a seditious person. And ordain these presents to be intimate to him personally, or at his dwelling place, or at the market cross of Glasgow, and parish kirk where he lives, that he pretend not ignorance."

We shall afterward meet with this pious and zealous minister, in the progress of this history, a martyr for the truth. And shortly a good many of his fellow servants are sent to north side of Tay, as well as he, where they did service by their preaching and conversation. The deserting of his flock, here spoken of, is his withdrawing from a party of soldiers who were about to take him into Edinburgh, and his sedition is to be understood of his faithful preaching against the sins of this time.

Mr. Thomas Wylie follows next; and I shall first give his case as it stands in the registers, and then his sufferings this year, from an account before me under his own hand. In the council books follows, "The like act made against Mr. Thomas Wylie, minister at Kirkcudbright, who hath deserted his flock, and contravened the foresaid acts of parliament, which is to be intimated to him personally, or at his dwelling-house, or at the market cross of Kirkcudbright, or parish church where he lives."

I come now to give some account of this excellent person's hardships since the end of May this year, from his own papers, wherein he records some very remarkable providences, and answers of prayer he met with when under his hiding and wanderings, too long to be here insert. Mr. Wylie and the whole brethren of that presbytery continued preaching, and to keep their presbyteries, notwithstanding of the acts made against their meeting, and Mr. Wylie was the person the managers had their eye chiefly upon in that country. He laid his account with troubles a coming, and was earnestly desirous to have the sacrament of the supper dispensed to his people before the cloud came on. The Lord granted his and the people's earnest prayer: and June 8th, he had his first day of distribution of the sacrament; for he had so many communicants, and such numbers joined with him, that they could not all communicate in one day. After sermon on Monday he had a letter signifying that the whole presbytery of Kirkcudbright was to be cited in to Edinburgh, for keeping presbyterial meetings, which much troubled him: yet he went on in his design to give next Lord's day the Supper to his people who had not participate. On the Friday he received certain accounts, that only himself, Mr. Robert Fergusson, Mr. Adam Kae, Mr. John M'Michan, and Mr. John Wilkie, were to be sent for by a party, and they were very soon to be at them. However, with an eye to Providence, he resolved to go on in the designed solemnity, and they had Saturday, Sunday, and Monday, quiet and free of distraction. But on Monday, when at dinner, they were alarmed with accounts that the party were to be in town that night: the ministers, Mr. Wylie's helpers, advised him to remove; which he did after the gentleman who brought the account told him, the party had letters to the other four, but orders to apprehend him, and bring him in. Tuesday at twelve of the clock, the party came straight to his house, and searched it with the utmost exactness for him. Mr.

Wylie thought it convenient to move the most secret way he could into Edinburgh, and met with many remarkable providences and answers of prayer by the way; and when he came there, he found that ill impressions had been given of him to the managers; and there was no getting out of their hands without taking the oath, and therefore was resolved to retire from the storm, till he should see if their rage against him calmed. He left Edinburgh on Saturday undiscovered; and, after some stay in a friend's house, he drew up a vindication and supplication to be presented, if need were, to the commissioner. He wandered up and down drawing toward home, near to which he came, Saturday, June 28, and heard that orders were left by the party to the magistrates of Kirkcudbright to seize him as soon as he was returned.

He continued under his hiding the whole month of July, when he had new and wonderful experiences of God's special interposition, in his providence, in his behalf, and that even as to his outward worldly affairs. He heard from the rest of the brethren, who went into Edinburgh upon the letters received, and waited upon the commissioner at Holyrood-house, which was the purport of their letters; that the commissioner was civil to them, and wondered Mr. Wylie came not in, and promised him free access to him when he came. Whereupon, towards the end of July, his wife Mrs. Wylie went into Edinburgh with letters from her husband, a new supplication, and instructions how to present it, with a vindication of his procedure, for the former had not been made use of. In some weeks his wife returned from Edinburgh, and acquainted him that she had been three times with the commissioner; that his grace assured her, his life should not be in hazard, and offered this under his hand if she pleased; that he had given liberty to the other four ministers to return home, and visit their families, and continue a month, with an express charge not to preach, and after that required them to return to Edinburgh; that he allowed Mr. Wylie the same liberty, with express condition that he should not come near the town of Kirkcudbright; but my lord Ken-mure prevailed to get that taken off: and so he returned home till the 20th of September.

1662.

When he with the other four ministers went into Edinburgh, the commissioner being on his progress to the west, they had not access to him, and returned to Galloway. We have heard of the act of council at Glasgow; and it was hard enough to send him and his family to the north side of Tay by the first of November, without ever hearing him, and when he had come in to Edinburgh to be heard according to concert. However his wife, being in the west country through the interposition of my lady Cochran, obtained a mitigation of the sentence from the commissioner, the account of which came to him before the act at Glasgow was intimate to him, which was not till October 20th. October 21st, the commissioner came to Kirkcudbright, and Mr. Wylie waited on him, and found his anger much abated. The commissioner discoursed him upon the covenant, church government, and several matters of fact, and professed his regard to him, but as a friend advised him to remove with his family as soon as possible; told him that he was loaded with reports, and would be so as long as he stayed in Kirkcudbright, or was in the west country. He promised to do his best to get him allowance to stay on this side of Forth; and desired him to wait on the council Tuesday come a fortnight; which Mr. Wylie did, but got nothing done. At that time the commissioner told him, that the council were yet averse; but desired him to bring his family to Lothian, and he would see what might be done for him.

In the end of November, Mr. Wylie brought his family to Leith in a great storm of frost. When he came to Edinburgh, he found that his name was in a list with Messrs. Livingstone, Trail, Carstairs, Dunlop, and a good many others, who were to have the oath tendered to them; and upon their refusal to be banished. Upon the 1st of December, he waited on the commissioner, who stopt his citation at that time, and in some days thereafter had a long conversation with Mr. Wylie, and pressed him to declare himself against defensive arms; but especially insisted upon his taking the oath,

1662. which Mr. Wylie offered to take with an explication. This the commissioner peremptorily refused, and yet expressed his great kindness for him, and dismissed him by saying, well, Mr. Wylie, I shall give you time enough to think upon it. Thus far I have given this excellent man's case this year from his own papers, and from it we may understand the case of many ministers at this time.

I find subjoined to this account some grievances under Mr. Wylie's hand, written at this time; and they contain several matters of fact, which tend to set the present state of things in this church in their due light: and I apprehend they were designed to be put in some paper he was to have presented to the king, or some who were most favourable about him; and therefore, though they are but the first draught, and would no doubt have been put in better form if presented, I have added them here.

Grievances, 1662-3.

" 1. That free access should be debarred to present our grievances to his majesty, except in a way that is unfeasible, and scars men from expressing them.

" 2. That the government of the church should be changed from that form which the generality, both of ministers and people within the kingdom, judge to be of divine institution, which has been established by many wholesome laws, which the land has been in an universal enjoyment and exercise of and under which error, heresy, superstition, and profanity has been discountenanced, timously discovered, censured, and suppressed, unto a new form, which the generality look upon as merely of human institution, imposed upon political considerations, under which error, superstition, and profanity in former times abounded, and with which, at this present time, profanity is springing up to so great a height already; so that the generality in the land are as barbarous in inhumanity, and brutish in impiety, as were once our forefathers in their heathenish paganism, and darkness.

" 3. That this change should be carried on, and closed in an arbitrary way, and imposed upon the church, without any previous consultation, not to speak of a conclusion, had by her in church-judicatories, and especially in her general assemblies; whereby the affection or disaffection to the change, would have been more clearly evident.

" 4. That general acts relating to ministers should be emitted by parliament, not clear and full, but ambiguous and dark, and that without any penal statute or certification; and that the council, without any known warrant, should, by their after-acts, enlarge the meaning of parliamentary acts, statute the penalty, and instantly apply it to hundreds of ministers through the kingdom, ere ever they have known whether they have been in *culpa*, or transgressors of any law or not: whereby it comes to pass, that with one unexpected blow, hundreds of congregations are laid waste, to the great grief and prejudice of thousands of souls.

" 5. That letters should be sent by persons in highest trust under his majesty, requiring worthy ministers of the gospel to repair to the said persons at Edinburgh, or where they are at the time, and to speak with them of business of importance, to be communicate at meeting: which letters seem to import, to candid and well-meaning men, that nothing is intended but a friendly craving of counsel and advice in those businesses of importance; whereupon the ministers, in dutiful obedience to the magistrate, have, without regard to pains or expense, repaired to the said honourable persons; and yet, upon their appearance, have found nothing of what the letters, sent to them, seemed to import; but are posed with ensnaring and entangling questions, and put under restraint not to pass off the town, and delayed from time to time, until they have been wearied and outspent in attendance; yea, though offering just satisfaction, imprisoned, or otherwise sentenced. And some so called upon, though liberate to return to their families, yet discharged, by particular persons in civil trust, to preach, without any sentence of a judicatory: so that be this practique, several ministers with their families have been put to hard suffering, and their congregations robbed of ordinances.

" 6. That there should be a citation of several most faithful and loyal ministers, *indicta causa particulari,* to appear before the council, charged as persons suspected of disloyalty, without giving the least presumption as a ground of suspicion, and then the oath presented, as a test and touchstone; upon the 'refusal of which, in the general comprehensive terms, (though subscriptions be heartily offered, with an explication of the meaning, according to what the council themselves profess to be the only sense of the oath) yet is all such explanation refused, and honest men, most loyal to their prince, banished.

" 7. That when sentences are thus passed against honest men, they should press them, under pain of imprisonment, to subscribe, that betwixt and such a day, they shall pass off the country, and never return on pain of death: a practice, as it is unusual, so it may be involving to honest men in inextricable difficulties.

" 8. That some should be discharged preaching, and charged to leave their congregations, at the commissioner his pleasure, and without the sentence of any judicatory, and, for any thing known to the party or others, without any alleged, let be just, cause.

" 9. That some are sentenced by the council upon mere information, without citation, without process, for trial of the verity and truth of the information, to remove with their whole family, in the winter season, above 100 miles from their congregation and place of residence, with peremptory certification of imprisonment, and indictment upon sedition, in case of contravening; which necessitates the party, to his great loss, and hazard of his young children, to take upon him a long journey in the stormy winter.

" 10. That letters should be sent to ministers, with a party of soldiers under command, requiring the ministers to repair unto Edinburgh, and immediately after to Holyrood-house, to speak with the commissioner of business of importance; and yet the leader of the party to be expressly instructed, personally to apprehend one of them to whom the letters were directed, and instantly to carry him as a prisoner to Edinburgh. The verity of which, though there were no more to make it out, appears

from the practice of the party, who diligently searched all the corners of beds, chests, &c. in the minister's house, for his person, as if he had been a most notorious malefactor, and commanded one of the bailies of the town to be assisting to them herein. 1662.

" 11. That after passing of acts, discharging ministers to preach, acts of indulgence should be emitted, permitting ministers, at least consequentially, to preach again for some time; and yet when they, out of zeal to benefit the people of their charges, have preached, letters of horning, and citation before the council, are used against them, to their great molestation and trouble.

" 12. That the council should punish ministers, though fully called and ordained, with deprivation, not only of the benefice, but of their ministerial office amongst the Lord's people, to whom they were lawfully sent, and amongst whom they have laboured to the great benefit of their souls, and that only for the want of the bishop's collation. If the collation be merely a civil thing, giving the incumbent right to plead in law (in case of necessity) the payment of his stipend, as is pretended, it is the minister's own loss and disadvantage that he wants it: but what reason is there that both he and the people of his charge, should be so severely punished by the secular power, with an ecclesiastical stroke, which robs them both of that which is dearer to them than all their civil liberties, and that only for the minister's voluntary want of an alleged civil benefit?" *

From those matters of fact, which in the former part of this chapter are all plain, the severity and unreasonableness of the procedure of the managers appears in its due light; but it is time to return to the further particular attacks on gentlemen and ministers, which turn throng when the council meet at Edinburgh in November. Though the act at Glasgow by that time was per-

---

* The above statement of grievances, which is proved to be a true statement from the united testimony of historians of all parties, sets the government of this period in a most odious light, and the people who suffered it to exist for seven and twenty years, deserve every character but that of being turbulent and unruly.—*Ed.*

1662. ceived to have been rash and impolitic, yet the prelates and their supporters were fretted with the noble stand made by so many ministers, and the general dissatisfaction of the country at the loss of their ministers; and it is resolved to go further, and destroy those they cannot terrify. I give the procedure just as it lies in order of time, and each person's sufferings together, as much as may be.

November 6th, the council begin a process against Sir James Stuart, late provost of Edinburgh, and his son, upon a most groundless and malicious information, which when dipped into, came to nothing: however, I shall insert what I find of it in the registers, as a specimen of the trouble gentlemen were now brought to, who were presbyterians, and favourers of them. " Information being given, that Mr. Hugh M'Kail, chaplain to Sir James Stuart of Kirkfield, did of late, in a sermon preached in one of the kirks of Edinburgh, most maliciously inveigh against, and abuse his sacred majesty, and the present government in church and state, to the great offence of God, and stumbling of the people; and that the said Sir James Stuart, and Walter Stuart his second son, were present when the said sermon was preached, at least were certainly informed thereof; yet, notwithstanding thereof, did entertain him in their family: as also that the said Walter Stuart has emitted some speeches tending towards sedition, especially, that within these few weeks, he, at the smithy of ———, upon the occasion of a discourse anent public differences, said, that before businesses went as they are going, a hundred thousand in the three kingdoms would lose their lives; therefore macers are ordered to cite them both before the council against the 11th instant."

" November 11th, reported, that Sir James Stuart and his son had been cited to answer this day; and it being informed by some of the members, that Sir James can clear himself, the lords appoint the earl of Morton and lord Tarbet, to examine Sir James, and report. Walter Stuart his son appeared, and denied the foresaid speeches charged against him. Witnesses being called and examined, the council find he uttered some things tending to sedition, and imprison him in the tolbooth till further order."

Every thing which savoured of a sense of liberty, or expressed any dislike at bishops, was now reckoned seditious speaking. This excellent and religious young gentleman was soon dismissed, and died not very long after this, not without some very remarkable forenotices of his dissolution, to himself and excellent father; and having run fast, came soon to his eternal prize. We shall afterward hear of worthy Mr. Hugh M'Kail, and find him sealing the truth with his blood after Pentland. It was, as I take it, after this faithful and free sermon, wherein it was pretended he reflected on the king, because he preached the scriptural doctrine upon church government, that he went abroad, and accomplished himself in travelling for some years. When he came home, he was the more qualified to be the object of the prelates' spite.

Upon the same day, November 6th, the reverend Mr. John Brown, minister at Wamphray in the south, was before the council. Whether he had been brought in by letters desiring him to converse with the managers, or by a formal citation, I cannot say; but this day's act about him runs, " Mr. John Brown of Wamphray being convened before the council, for abusing and reproaching some ministers for keeping the diocesan synod with the archbishop of Glasgow, by calling them perjured knaves and villains, did acknowledge that he called them false knaves for so doing, because they had promised the contrary to him. The council ordains him to be secured close prisoner in the tolbooth till further order."—I need not enter upon the character of this great man; his abilities were so well known to the prelates, that he must not be suffered any longer, and so his freedom that he used with some of his neighbouring ministers, for complying with the prelates contrary to the assurances they had given him, was made a handle of for this end. He was a man of very great learning, warm zeal, and remarkable piety. The first he discovers in his works printed in Latin, against both Socinians and

Cocceians, which the learned world know better than to need any account of them from me. I have seen likewise a large Latin MS. history of his of the church of Scotland, wherein he gives an account of the acts of our assemblies, and the state of matters from the reformation to the restoration; to which is subjoined a very large vindication of the grounds whereupon presbyterians suffered. The "Apologetical Relation" appears to be an abbreviate of this in English. His letters he wrote home to Scotland, and the pamphlets and books he wrote, especially upon the indulgence, manifest his fervency and zeal; and the practical pieces he wrote and printed, discover his solid piety, and acquaintance with the power of godliness: such a man could not easily now escape.

I meet not with him again till December 11th, when, after Mr. Livingstone and others received their sentence, the council come to this conclusion about him. "Anent a petition presented by Mr. John Brown, minister at Wamphray, now prisoner in Edinburgh, showing, That, for some speeches rashly and inconsiderately uttered against some neighbour ministers, he has been kept close prisoner these five weeks bypast; and that seeing, that by want of free air, and ordinary necessaries for maintaining his crazy body, he is in hazard to lose his life, humbly therefore desiring warrant to be put to liberty, upon caution to enter his prison in person when he shall be commanded; as the petition bears. Which being at length heard and considered, the lords of council ordain the supplicant to be put at liberty forth of the tolbooth, he first obliging himself to remove and depart off the king's dominions, and not to return without license from his majesty and council, under pain of death.

I need not observe this unusual severity against this good man: the utmost he could be charged with, was a reproof given to his (once) brethren, for their apostasy; and for this he is cast in prison, and, when there, deprived of the very necessaries of life; and when, through ill treatment, he is brought near death, and offers bail to re-enter when commanded, cannot be permitted to have the benefit of the free air, till he sign a voluntary banishment for no cause. However, it seems his present danger brought this good man to these hard conditions: and December 23d, I find him petitioning for some more time to stay in the country; which is granted. "Anent a petition by Mr. John Brown, late minister at Wamphray, desiring the time of his removal off the kingdom may be prorogate, in regard that he is neither as yet able to provide himself of necessaries, and the weather so unseasonable that he cannot have the opportunity of a ship, as the petition at length bears: which being heard, read, and considered, the lords of council do grant liberty to the petitioner to remain within this kingdom for the space of two months after the 11th of December last, he carrying himself in the meantime peaceably, and acting nothing in prejudice of the present government." Next year this good man went to Holland, and lived there many years, but never, that I hear of, saw his native land after this.*

1662.

---

* Mr. John Brown was unquestionably one of the most eminent divines Scotland has yet produced, as his numerous writings, still carefully sought after by solid and judicious Christians, fully evince. That he was firmly attached to the true presbyterian principles of the church of Scotland, his history of the Indulgence abundantly demonstrates; and the clear and scriptural ardency of his piety, from his well known Treatise on Prayer, is equally apparent. Though he was thus unjustly and illegally driven from his native country, he was not allowed, by his merciless persecutors, to rest in that country, Holland, which had most cordially adopted him. This, our historian, when he comes to the case of colonel Wallace, has noticed, but he seems to have supposed, that his persecutors failed in their efforts with the Dutch government to disturb him. The following extract from Dr. M'Crie's notices of colonel Wallace, sets the whole transaction in a very clear light, and, inserted here, will supersede the necessity of a Note when we come to the author's notice of that gentleman.

"For several years colonel Wallace was obliged to wander from one part of the continent to another, for the sake of security. For the same reason he assumed the name of Forbes In the year 1670 he was on the borders of Germany. When he thought the search after him had relaxed, he took up his residence at Rotterdam, but he was not allowed to remain there undisturbed. On the 27th of June, 1676, Charles II. wrote to the states-general, requiring them, agreeably to an article in a treaty between the two countries, to cause Wallace, with Mr. Robert Macward, and Mr. John Brown, ministers, to remove from their terri-

1662. At this time the council have before them the case of William Dobbie, weaver in Glasgow, who might have been overlooked, being really crazed, had it not been the severity of the time. He is accused for slanderous speeches

tories, as persons guilty of lese-majesty against the king of Great Britain. Mr. Brown, in a paper of information which he gave into the states-general, after referring to the refusal of the states to comply with a similar demand in 1676, mentions, that the present application had been instigated by one Henry Wilkie, whom the king had placed at the head of the Scottish factory at Campvere, who was displeased because many of his countrymen, with the view of enjoying the ministry of Messrs. Macward and Brown, had repaired to Rotterdam, and brought their shipping there, in preference to Campvere, by which means his salary was impaired. Mr. Brown denies that either he or his colleague was ever convicted of treason, and begs the states to require from Sir William Temple, the English ambassador, a copy of the sentence pronounced against them, as this would shew, that the article in the treaty did not apply to them, and might be the means also of freeing Mr. Wallace from a prosecution which had commenced principally on their account; ' but,' continues he, ' it may be hinted to Sir William Temple, that James Forbes, *alias* Wallace, is a brave and skilful soldier, and may create more trouble to the king at home in Scotland, if he be forced to remove hence, than he can do by remaining here in the Netherlands, and discharging the office of an elder in the Scottish church at Rotterdam.' The states-general were satisfied that they were not bound by the treaty to remove the ministers, and they instructed lord Benningen, their ambassador at the court of England, to represent to his majesty, that they hoped he would not require them to put away persons who had complied with the sentence of banishment pronounced against them, and to wave, in the best and discreetest manner, the forementioned matter, as being in the highest degree prejudicial to their country. But instead of the affair being dropped, other letters were sent from England, repeating the demand in still stronger language, and Sir William Temple left Nimeguen, where he was employed in the negotiations for a peace then going on, and came to the Hague, for the express purpose of urging a categorical and speedy answer. Upon this, the states-general, to prevent a quarrel with Great Britain, judged it prudent to yield; but they failed not to represent their sense of the injustice of the claim made upon them. In their letter of the 22d of January, 1677, they say:—' We are willing to testify how sensible we are of the honour of your friendship and good-will, and that we prefer it to all other considerations, assuring your majesty, that we will not fail to cause the said Macward, Brown, and Wallace, to depart within the time mentioned in the treaties, from the bounds of this country. We find ourselves, however, obliged to represent to your majesty, that we believe you will agree with us, that the obligation of the treaties is reciprocal, and that, according to the laws of this country, we cannot by our letters declare any person fugitive, or a rebel, unless he has been recognised as such by a sentence or judgment of the ordinary criminal court of justice, and that your majesty could not pay any regard to any letters of ours making a similar declaration, unless accompanied by such sentence or judgment. And as thus, we cannot require of your majesty to remove any one from your kingdoms, as a rebel or fugitive, on a simple declaration made by our letters; so we assure ourselves, Sir, that your majesty will not in future require us, by simple letters, to remove any persons from our territories before he be declared a fugitive or rebel according to the ordinary forms of the laws and customs of your majesty.'

" The following is the resolution to which the states-general came, as translated from an authenticated copy of the original in Dutch:— ' By the sesumpt delivered on the report of M. M. van Heuckelom and others, their high mightinesses, commissioners for foreign affairs, having, in compliance with, and for giving effect to that resolution commissorial of the 16th instant, examined and discussed the memorial of Sir ——— Temple, baronet, envoy extraordinary of his majesty the king of Great Britain, requesting their High M. would be pleased to enter into a conference with him, as also a missive of the king of Great Britain, dated at Whitehall, the 29th of December last, *stilio Angliæ*, respecting his majesty's former letters of the 27th June, and 18th of November before, concerning three Scotsmen, James Wallis, Robert Macward, and John Brown, and having conversed with the said Amb. Ext. Temple, regarding the contents of it, and having also seen the *retroacta*, and exhibited and heard read a draught of a missive, drawn out and committed to paper by the commissioners of their H. M. for an answer to the missives of his majesty of Great Britain, of the 27th of June, 18th of November, and 29th of December last, respecting the said Scotsmen: it is found good to declare, that although the foresaid three Scotsmen—have not only not behaved and comported themselves otherwise than as became good and faithful citizens of these states, but have also given indubitable proofs of their zeal and affection for the advancement of the truth, which their H. M. have seen with pleasure, and could have wished that they could have continued to live here in peace and security;—considering the risk they run, however, and considering with what pressing earnestness his majesty has repeatedly insisted by three several missives, and verbally through his envoy extraordinary, and with great reason apprehending a breach between his majesty and these states, as Sir ——— Temple has expressed himself in terms that cannot be mistaken, they feel themselves necessitated, in order to obviate so great an evil at this conjuncture, to cause the foresaid three Scotsmen—withdraw from this country, and that, consequently, notice shall be given to the foresaid James Wallis, Robert Macward, and John Brown, in order that they may be able to avail themselves of the good intentions of their H. M. in having their property properly disposed before the 5th of March next—and for this end, an extract of this resolution of their H. M. shall be sent to the counsellors of the states of Holland and Westvriesland, in order

against the commissioner, and remitted to the criminal court; and his is the only process, for alleged disaffection, I find in the justiciary books before Pentland. December 14th, witnesses prove some expressions against the king and commissioner, and present church settlement, and declare he had been distempered once. There is no sentence, and he continues in prison a long time.

1662.

But to return to ministers: it had been customary for the managers for some months, by private fair letters, to call before them a good many of the old presbyterian ministers,

---

that due notification may be given, and the foresaid James Wallis, &c. may regulate their proceedings accordingly. They shall also find enclosed for this behoof separate instruments, *ad omnes populos*, word for word with the following, which shall be sent to the foresaid commissioners of the council of the H. and M. the states of Holland, to be put into the hands of the foresaid James Wallis,' &c. The instrument or testimonial referred to in the preceding decree runs in the following terms:—' The states-general of the United Netherlands, to all and every one who shall see or read these presents health. Be it known and certified, that James Wallace, gentleman, our subject, and for many years inhabitant of this state, lived among us highly esteemed for his probity, submission to the laws, and integrity of manners. And therefore we have resolved affectionately to request, and hereby do most earnestly request the emperor of the Romans, and all kings, republics, princes, dukes, states, magistrates, or whomsoever else our friends, and all that shall see these presents, that they receive the said James Wallace in a friendly manner whensoever he may come to them, or resolve to remain with them, and assist him with their counsel, help, and aid; testifying, that for any obliging, humane, or kindly offices done to him, we shall be ready and forward to return the favour to them and their subjects, whensoever an opportunity offers. For the greater confirmation whereof, we have caused these presents to be sealed with our seal of office, and signed by our secretary in our assembly, the sixth day of the month of February, in the year one thousand six hundred and seventy-seven."—Notices of Colonel Wallace, by Dr. M'Crie's Life of William Veitch, &c. pp. 362—369.

This was highly complimentary, and it must have been greatly cheering to these venerable exiles to find that fatherly protection in a strange land, and from a strange government, that was denied them by their own. Mr. Brown, from the ill state of his health, attested by physicians, was allowed, Dr. M'Crie informs us, to remain in the country, and he thinks it probable, that after a temporary concealment, Macward did the same; but colonel Wallace was under the necessity of removing. He, however, soon returned, for he died at Rotterdam in the end of the year 1678. That he was greatly respected by Mr. John Brown, is evident from the circumstance of his having by testament, dated the 2d of April, 1676, bequeathed to the poor of the Scots congregation there 100 guineas, and by a codicil, dated 11th of September the same year, appointing the above sum to be "put into the hands of Mr. Wallace, to be given out by him to such as he knoweth indigent and honest." For a token to Mr. Macward, he left his Complutensian Bible, six vols. and the half of his remanent gold, the other half to Mr. Wallace. Having survived Mr. Wallace, he has drawn his pen through Mr. Wallace's bequest. That he was also an object of great affection to Mr. Macward, is evident from the following extract of a letter from that great man to Mr. Bleketer concerning his death, December 5-15, 78.

" I doubt not but you have heard of the removall of worthy and great Wallace, of whom I have no doubt it may be said, he hath left no man behind him in that church, minister nor professor, quho hath gone thorow such a varietie of tentations, without turning to the right hand or to the left. He died in great serenity of soul. He had lived abroad such an ornament to his profession, as he was not more lamented by us than by all the serious English and Dutch of his acquaintance (who were many), as having lost the man who, as a mean, was made use of by the Lord to keep life amongst them: yea, the poor ignorant people of the congregation of Rotterdam (besides the more serious and knowing amongst them) bemoan his death, and their loss, as of a father. And they have good reason, for I must say he was the most faithfull, feckfull, compassionate, diligent, and indefatigable elder in the work of the Lord that ever I knew at home or abroad; and as for his care, solicitude, and concernedness in the work and people of God, I may say, the care of all the churches lay more upon him than upon hundreds of us; so that the church of God hath lost more in the removeall of that man, than most will suffer themselves to believe. Onely we who know it have this to comfort ourselves, that the residue of the Spirit is with Him quho made him such, and that the great Intercessour lives to plead his own cause, and the causes of his people's soul. I forgot to tell you, that when the cause for which he suffered was mentioned, when it was scarce believed he understood or could speake, there was a sunshine of serene joy looked out of his countenance, and a lifting up of hands on high, as to receive the confessor's crown, together with a lifting up of the voice, with an *aha*, as to sing the conqueror's song of victorie. And to close, I must tell you also, he lived and died in a deep detestation of that wretched indulgence, and of all the ways of supporting it, and this abrupt account of his death you may give to his friends. In a word, as a compound of all, he fell asleep in the furnace, walking with the Son of God, and now his bones will rise up with the bones of the other great witnesses buried in a strange land, as a testimony against the wrong done to Christ, and the violence used against his followers by this wicked generation, whom the righteous Lord in his time, from him who sitteth upon the throne, to the meanest instrument that hath put the mischiefs he framed into a law in execution, will make a generation of his wrath, of special wrath, which must answer and keep proportion unto the wrongs done to the Mediator."—Appendix to M'Crie's Life of Veitch, &c. &c.—*Ed.*

1662. ordained before the (year) 1649, and keep them hanging on at Edinburgh for some months; and if they got liberty to return to their families, it was with an express charge not to preach. We have had many instances already, and this method was taken also with Mr. Alexander Dunlop and others. Now they came to a shorter way with a considerable number of them, and November 18th, after they write for all absent members, the council give the following orders.

" Information being given of the seditious carriage of Mr. John Livingstone at Ancrum, Mr. Samuel Austin, Mr. John Nave, minister at Newmills, Mr. John Carstairs, Mr. Matthew Mowat, Mr. Robert Trail, Mr. James Nasmith, Mr. Andrew Cant, elder, Alexander Cant his son, Mr. John Menzies, Mr. George Meldrum at Aberdeen, Mr. Alexander Gordon, minister at Inveraray, Mr. J. Cameron, minister at Kilfinnan, Mr. James Gardiner, minister at Saddle: order the said persons, and every one of them, immediately, upon intimation made unto them, to repair to Edinburgh against the 9th of December next, and make their compearance before the council the said day, as they will be answerable at their utmost peril; and for that effect ordain letters to be direct to the noblemen and others underwritten, and that a double of this act be enclosed in these several letters. Likewise information being given of the turbulent and seditious practices of Mr. Gilbert Rule and Mr. John Drysdale, ordered that their persons be secured, and presented to the council, as follows, viz. That the magistrates of Kirkaldy shall secure the said Mr. Gilbert Rule, and bring him alongst with themselves, and present him to the council on Friday next; and the following letter be writ to them for that effect."

" Loving friends,
" You will perceive by the enclosed order, what commands the council have laid upon you, which you are immediately to execute, and come yourselves to attend the council on Friday next, as you will be answerable.
GLENCAIRN, Chancellor."

Follows the order, that the magistrates of Kirkaldy secure the person of Mr. Gilbert Rule, and present him to the council. And that I may give all which relates to this in this place: November 21st, the magistrates of Kirkaldy appear, and report that Mr. Rule was gone out of their bounds before the council's orders came, and could not be found, and that they had no hand in his being employed to preach; which excuse was sustained. " And the said magistrates having also reported that there were some in their council who refused to subscribe the declaration, appointed by the parliament to be taken by all such persons as bear public office or charge: ordered, that the magistrates cause all their members to subscribe the same, or declare them incapable of all public trust within their burgh. And because it is informed that several disaffected ministers reside there, who study to alienate the hearts of the people from the present government of church and state; therefore ordain the said magistrates to warn them to remove forth of their bounds within fourteen days, and report against the next council day." A report is accordingly made, that the orders were obeyed. We shall afterward meet with the reverend Mr. Rule, and there I shall give a larger account of his sufferings during this period.

To return to the procedure against the rest of the ministers; November 18th, the council orders the earl of Eglinton by himself or his deputes, sheriffs of Renfrew, to cause seize the person of Mr. John Drysdale, minister at Paisley, and send him in to the council against the 9th of December; and that he cause intimate the above mentioned act to Mr. Alexander Dunlop, minister at Paisley. A letter is likewise sent to the magistrates of Aberdeen, to intimate the act to Messrs. Menzies and Meldrum, and command them to appear the said day: another to the magistrates of Edinburgh, as to Mr. Trail: another to duke Hamilton, as to Messrs. Nasmith and Carstairs: one to the sheriff of Teviotdale, as to Mr. Livingstone: one to the sheriff of Nithsdale, as to Mr. Austin; and one to the marquis of Montrose, in regard there is not a sheriff or deputes in Argyle, as to Mr. Alexander Gordon and Mr. John Cameron, ministers in Argyle, and Mr. James Gardiner. November 27th, it is reported that Mr. Robert Trail cannot be personally apprehended; and the council order their macers to cite him at his dwelling-house, and by open proclamation at the cross of Edinburgh, to compear before the council, December 9th, to answer to such things as shall be laid to his charge, under the pain of rebellion. I find no letters writ about Mr. Nave, Mr. Cant, and his son; yet we shall find them present afterwards; nor for Mr. Matthew Mowat, who was not before the council, as far as I have observed in the registers, and probably was overlooked, as we saw Mr. Wylie, and it may be some others, who were at first in the list. Mr. Drysdale is not before the council either, having absconded, and perhaps gone to Ireland. The rest we shall just now meet with before the council, December 11th, and the after-diets. In the registers I find no sederunt, December 9th, to which the ministers were cited. It would seem that day either a committee of council met, before whom Mr. Livingstone and others were, or the council themselves; but coming to no issue till December 11th, there is nothing in the council-books. Those worthy and excellent persons were pitched upon from all corners of the country, the south, west, and north, as those that must either comply with the bishops, or be sent off the nation. And indeed they were all of them bright and shining lights in this church, and the attack made upon them was designed to fright presbyterian ministers to a compliance in all corners. I come now to give as distinct an account as I can of their several cases and processes.

I begin with the reverend and learned Mr. John Livingstone, who, among these worthies now under process, was first before the council; and because I have the fullest accounts of him from his Life writ by himself, out of this I shall give a pretty large detail of the council's method with him; and probably many of the same things were proposed to the rest. A large abstract of this excellent person's life, I know, would be useful and entertaining to the reader; and it is certainly a great loss to this church that we want a biography of our eminent ministers and Christians, done by some good hand, when there yet remain a good many materials for such a work, which may in some time be lost: but I shall only make a remark or two as to this singular person, and then come to his sufferings, which is my province.

1662.

Mr. John Livingstone was one remarkably honoured of the Lord, to be an instrument of the conversion of thousands. While yet only a probationer he was the honoured and happy mean of that remarkable conversion, upon Monday after the communion, at the Kirk of Shots, 1630. From Mr. Livingstone's sermon in the west side of the church-yard there, upon Ezek. xxxvi. 26., "A new heart also will I give you, and a new spirit will I put within you, and I will take away the stony heart out of your flesh, and give you a heart of flesh;" about five hundred persons dated their saving change. Such another, and yet a more plentiful effusion of the Spirit, attended a sermon of his at a communion at Hollywood in Ireland, if I mistake not, in the year 1641, where about a thousand were begotten unto Christ. Besides, he was blessed with very much success through the ordinary tract of his ministry. Perhaps few ministers since the apostles' days were more remarkably countenanced from heaven in their work than Mr. Livingstone. The prelates' violent pushing to be rid of such a man as he, gives occasion to make severer reflections than I am willing to insert here.

He was one of the three ministers, who, with some from the state, were sent over to the king at Breda: and after the treaty was finished, before his majesty landed in Scotland, Mr. Livingstone was pitched upon; and accordingly in the ship tendered the covenant to the king. His faithful freedom with his majesty at that time, with his declared dissatisfaction with the manner of carrying on and concluding of that treaty, probably were not altogether forgot now. When at London, in the year 1656, in a very public auditory, before Oliver Cromwell, and even to his face, Mr. Livingstone asserted the king's right and title to those three kingdoms. He was in his opinion a protester, but very moderate; and I find

1662. him in his Life heavily lamenting and regretting the sad breaches and extremities in that divided time. Every body owned his modesty and sweetness of temper.

Upon the king's return, and through the summer 1660, he with many others had very melancholy impressions of the approaching ruin coming upon the work of reformation in this church. The last communion he had at Ancrum, was upon the 12th of October this year, 1662, at which great multitudes of serious and godly persons were gathered from all corners of the country. Upon the Monday, at the close of the work, Mr. Livingstone had more than ordinary liberty in discoursing to the people about the grounds and encouragements to suffer for the truths at present controverted in Scotland; and in a manner took his farewell of his people, reckoning that would be the last communion he would have in that place. In his Life he remarks, that at this time he knew nothing of what was hatching against him, nor of his designed persecution, which followed so soon. His extemporary discourse, October 13th, this year, was taken from his mouth in characters, and is what would be acceptable to a good many of my readers, in its popular and homely dress, just as it was delivered, to be sure without the least thoughts of its appearing in print; but it is so large that I must not insert it. After he had, with Elijah, eaten before a great journey, and as the disciples did, had communicate before he entered upon suffering, he had notice in a little time of the council's procedure against him and others: and before the summons could reach him, Mr. Livingstone went in to Edinburgh, and lurked a while there, till he got certain information of the council's designs. Had he found them about to have proceeded against their lives, and treat them as Mr. Guthrie was dealt with last year, he was resolved to retire and hide himself the best way he might, and the rather that he was not cited nor apprehended personally: but finding their design only to be banishment, he resolved to appear with his brethren. Accordingly, December 11th, he was before the council. I cannot give an account of the procedure there, and his carriage, so well as in his own words, and therefore I here insert his own account from his Life.

An Account of what passed when Mr. John Livingstone appeared before the council, in the lower council house, Edinburgh, December 11th, 1662.

" As soon as he appeared, the chancellor (whom for shortness I design by *Ch.*) said, you are called here before his majesty's secret council, for turbulency and sedition. You, Sir, have been in all the rebellions and disobedience to authority that have been those many years; and though his majesty and the parliament have granted an indemnity for what is past, you continue in the same courses. Mr. Livingstone (whom I express by *Mr. L.*) answered, ' My lords, if I shall not be so ready in my answers as were requisite, or if in any thing through inadvertency I shall offend, I crave to be excused, in regard of my unacquaintedness with such ways. I am now towards sixty years, and was never till now called in such sort before such a judicatory. I am a poor servant of Jesus Christ, and have been labouring to serve him and his people in the ministry of the word, and it is a grief to me to be so charged by your lordships. I am not conscious to myself of any turbulency or sedition. There are some things anent the government and officers of the church, wherein I confess my judgment and principles differ from what is presently maintained, but I have laboured to carry myself with all moderation and peaceableness, with due respect to authority, and have lived so obscurely, that I wonder how I am taken notice of. *Ch.* ' You have transgressed two acts of parliament; one appointing the 29th of May, a day of commemoration of his majesty's happy restoration, and another appointing synods to be kept. Did you preach on the 29th of May ?' *Mr. L.* ' There are witnesses in town who will testify I preached the last 29th of May.' *Ch.* ' Did you keep the day, as it is appointed, in obedience to the act of parliament ?' *Mr. L.* ' I dare not say that I did so. It was my ordinary lecture day; yet the place of scripture which was my ordinary, gave occasion to speak somewhat of the benefit and

CHAP. III.] OF THE CHURCH OF SCOTLAND. 311

advantage of magistracy.' *Ch.* 'But will you publicly, as others, acknowledge the Lord's mercy in restoring the king?' *Mr. L.* 'I have done so, my lord, both at first and sometime since.' *Ch.* 'But what is the reason you do not keep the day appointed by the parliament?' *Mr. L.* 'My lord, I have not that promptness of judgment, or expression that were requisite for surprising questions, and would beg, if your lordships please, to be forborne.' *Ch.* 'Can you not give a reason why you keep it not?' *Mr. L.* 'My lord, even as to the laws of God there is a great difference between a man's doing of that which God hath forbidden, and the not doing of a thing, for want of clearness that God hath commanded it; and much more this holds in the laws of men.'— *Ch.* 'But you kept holydays of your own; you kept a day of thanksgiving for the battle of Long-marston Muir, and several days of fasting in the time of the engagement. Did you not keep the day for Long-marston Muir?' *Mr. L.* 'So far as I know, I did; but these days were not called holydays, but only appointed upon some special occasions. And besides, one may scruple if any have power to appoint anniversary holydays.'— *Ch.* 'But will you keep that day hereafter?' *Mr. L.* 'My lord, I would desire first to see an issue of this wherein I am now engaged, by this citation, before I am urged to answer for the time to come.' *Ch.* 'Well, because of your disobedience to these two acts, the council look upon you as a suspect person; and therefore think it fit to require you to take the oath of allegiance. You know it, and have considered it?' *Mr. L.* 'Yes, my lord.' *Ch.* 'The clerk shall read it to you. (He reads it) Now that you have heard it read, are you free to take the oath?' *Mr. L.* 'I do acknowledge the king's majesty (whose person and government I wish God to bless) to be the only lawful supreme magistrate of this and all other his majesty's dominions, and that his majesty is the supreme civil governor over all persons, and in all causes as well ecclesiastic as civil; but for the oath, as it stands *in terminis*, I am not free to take it.' *Ch.* 'I think you and we agree as to the oath?' *Lord Advocate.* 'My lord chancellor, your lordship doth not observe that he useth a distinction, ' That the king is the supreme civil governor,' that he may make way for the co-ordinate power of presbytery.' *Mr. L.* ' My lord, I do indeed believe and confess that Jesus Christ is the only head of his church, and that he only hath power to appoint a government and discipline for removing of offences in his house, which is not dependant on civil powers, and no ways wrongs civil powers: but withal, I do acknowledge his majesty hath a cumulative power and inspection in the house of God, for seeing both the tables of the law kept; and that his majesty hath all the ordinary power that was in the kings of Israel and Judah, and in the Christian emperors and kings since the primitive times, for reforming, according to the word, what is amiss.' *Ch.* ' We do not say that the king hath power to ordain ministers, or to excommunicate; and therefore are you not free to take the oath?' *Mr. L.* ' My lord, in the terms that I have expressed I am free to take it, but I know not if it would be well taken off my hand, to add one word, or give an explication of the oath which the right honourable the estates of parliament have set down.' *Ch.* ' Nay, it is not in the power of the council so to do?' *Mr. L.* ' I have likewise been of that judgment, and am, and will be, that his majesty is supreme governor, in a civil way, over all persons in all causes.' *Lord Commissioner.* ' You may not say that you have been always of that judgment, for you have been opposite to the king, and so have many here, and so have I been; but now it is requisite we profess our obedience to him, and would wish you to do so. You would consider that there is a difference betwixt a church to be constitute, and a church constitute; for where it is to be constitute, ministers and professors may do their work upon their hazard; but when a church is constitute with consent of the civil magistrate, who hath power to appoint the bounds of parishes and stipends, he may appoint the bishops his commissioners, and ordain them to keep synods, and ordain ministers to come to those synods.' *Mr. L.* ' May it please your grace, I hope the

1662.

312 THE HISTORY OF THE SUFFERINGS [BOOK I.

1662. churches that are mentioned in the Acts of the Apostles, were constitute churches, although they had not the concurrence of the civil magistrate.' *Ch.* ' You have heard many things spoken, will you take some time to advise whether you will take the oath or not ?' *Mr. L.* ' I humbly thank your lordship ; it is a favour, which, if I had any doubt or hesitation, I would willingly accept : but seeing, after seeking of God, and advising anent the matter, I have such light as I use to get in such things, if I should take time to advise, it would import I have unclearness and hesitation, which I have not ; and I judge it were a kind of mocking your lordships, to take time, and then return your lordships the same answer.' *Lord Commissioner.* ' Then you are not for new light ?' *Mr. L.* ' Indeed I am not, if it please your grace.' *Ch.* ' Then you will remove yourself.' Being removed, and called in again, the chancellor said, ' Mr. Livingstone, the lords of his majesty's council have ordained, that within two months you remove out of his majesty's dominions, and that within forty-eight hours you remove out of Edinburgh, and go to the north side of Tay, and there remain till you depart forth out of the country.' *Mr. L.* ' I submit to your lordships' sentence ; but I humbly beg I may have a few days to go home and see my wife and children.' *Ch.* ' By no means ; you cannot be suffered to go to that country.' *Mr. L.* ' Against what time must I go to the north of Tay, my lord ?' *Lord Commissioner.* ' You may be there against Saturday come sennight.' *Mr. L.* ' Well, although it be not permitted to me to breathe in my native air, yet I trust, whatsoever part of the world I go unto, I shall not cease to pray for a blessing to these lands, to his majesty and the government, and the inferior magistrates thereof, but especially to the land of my nativity.' *Ch.* ' You must either go to the tolbooth, or subscribe a few words of acquiescence to your sentence.' *Mr. L* ' My lord, rather than go to the tolbooth, I will subscribe the same.' And accordingly he did it ; and the tenor of it was,

' I Mr. John Livingstone, late minister at Ancrum, bind and oblige me, that I shall remove myself forth of his majesty's dominions, within the space of eight weeks after the date hereof, and that I shall not remain within the same hereafter, without license from his majesty or privy council, under the pain of death ; and that I shall depart from Edinburgh to the north side of Tay, and there remain while my departure, and that my going off from Edinburgh shall be within forty-eight hours after the date hereof. Subscribed at Edinburgh, Dec. 11th, 1662.

' Jo. Livingstone.'

Lord Commissioner. ' You must see that you keep no conventicles, nor preach in churches or houses.' To this Mr. Livingstone answered nothing."

Mr. Livingstone remarks, That he cannot say this is all that either he or they spoke, but it is as far as his memory served him ; that he could not so punctually repeat their speeches as his own, but as near as he remembers this is what passed. He further observes, that his difficulty as to the oath, was not only that it was conceived in general and ambiguous terms, as might import a receding from the covenants and work of reformation ; but upon the matter, the imposers' unlawful sense of the general terms, was determined and fixed by their rejecting the only safe sense offered by the west country ministers lately, as we have seen. He adds likewise, he was afraid his taking time, when offered him, to consider the oath, after he had thoroughly pondered it, might lay him open to temptations, and offend and weaken the hands of others. However, he apprehended his refusing their offer, grated the council, and made them sharper upon him than others.

According to this sentence, Mr. Livingstone went out of Edinburgh to Leith, in the prefixed time ; where I find him petitioning the council, December 23d, which I give in the words of the registers. " Anent the petition presented by Mr. John Livingstone, showing, That in regard of his age and infirmity, his going beyond Tay in such a season of the year, might be dispensed with, and he permitted to go to the south, and see his wife and children, and dispose of his affairs ; and by this means, he expects, within the two months prefixed, to get a more ready and shorter passage from Newcastle, and in better vessels than can be looked for out of the Firth; which being at length heard and considered, the lords of privy council do allow the petitioner to remain at Leith during the time that is granted him to abide in Scotland, he behaving and carrying himself peaceably in the meantime." He insisted for liberty only of a few days to go home and take his farewell of his excellent wife and children, but that would not be allowed. He further remarks, that by no means would the council allow him a copy of his sentence, though he petitioned once and again for it. One would think they had cause so to do, and they might be ashamed if it should appear abroad in the reformed churches, whither he was retiring. After he had stayed some time at Leith, toward the beginning of April, he was accompanied with a good many of his friends to a ship, in which he got safe to Rotterdam, where he found his dear brethren formerly banished, and lived till August, 1672, when he entered into the joy of his Lord, in a good old age. While in Holland, he spent his time in reading the scripture, and forming a new Latin translation of the Old Testament, being very well seen in all the eastern tongues. This was revised and approven by Voetius, Essenius, Nethenus, Leusden, and other eminent lights of that time. At his death it was put into the hands of the last, in order to be printed, but was never published; and now I fear it is lost.

Since Mr. Livingstone was not permitted to see his dear flock at Ancrum, he wrote a letter to them before his leaving Scotland, which breathing much of this holy man's excellent temper, and containing many things suitable to this time, and not being, as far as I know, printed, as another letter of his to them is, I have subjoined it, in a note. *

I return to the rest of the ministers at this time before the council. 1662. That same day, December 11th, Mr. James Gardiner was called upon; and, after some questions proposed to him, much of the nature with these to Mr. Livingstone, and the tendering him the oath, which he refused, he was banished; and his act, as the title of it is in the registers, follows.

" I Mr. James Gardiner, late minister of Kintyre, oblige me to remove myself out of the king's dominions, within a month after the date hereof, and not to be seen within the same under the pain of death; and that in the meantime I shall not repair to any place within the bounds of the diocese of Glasgow, Galloway, or Argyle. Subscribed at Edinburgh, December 11th, 1662.
JA. GARDINER."

The same day Mr. Robert Trail was before them. This good man had used freedom in his sermons, and very much displeased the managers and prelates. After the parliament had turned him over to the council, and he had, upon his liberation, retired sooner than the rest of his brethren at Edinburgh, he stayed some time in Preston-grange House. There some of the family being detained by sickness, and several relations of the family being there at the time, Mr. Trail was prevailed upon to expound a piece of scripture, at family worship, on the Lord's day afternoon. This was mightily aggravated as a conventicle, and he cited in peremptory terms, as we have heard, and banished with the other two. I shall give it from the council books.

" Mr. John Livingstone, Mr. James Gardiner, and Mr. Robert Trail, being cited, and compearing personally, who being examined and the oath of allegiance offered to be taken and subscribed; which they having refused, the lords of council ordain the

---

* Mr. John Livingstone's letter to his parish, 1663.
To the flock of Jesus Christ in Ancrum, light, life, and love, and the consolation of the Holy Ghost be multiplied.
Well-beloved in the Lord,
That which our sins, even yours and mine, have been a long time procuring, and which hath been often threatened, but never well believed, is now come, even a separation. How long it may continue, it is in the Lord's hand; but it will be our part, to search out, and mourn for these sins that have drawn down such a stroke. It is not needful to look much to instruments; I have from my heart forgiven them all, and would wish you to do the like, and pray for them, that it be not laid to their charge; but let us look to him, without whose doing there is no evil in a city, for he hath torn, and he will heal us, he hath smitten, and he will bind us up. Let

1662. said persons to be banished forth of his majesty's dominions, and to enter their persons in prison within the tolbooth of Edinburgh, while they be conveniently transported off the kingdom, or otherwise act themselves to that effect. Likeas they enact

us neither despise his chastening, nor faint when we are rebuked of him. It may be, we shall not suddenly find out every controversy he hath against us, but if there be upright dealing in such things as are obvious, and an impartial dealing, for discovery of what is hid, he will reveal even that to us. Neither is there any greater hinderance of repentance, than a secure desperate questioning, whether he will accept of us or not? Christ hath been, and will be in all ages, a stone of stumbling, and rock of offence to such as stumble at the word, and refuse to receive his rich offer; but to others a foundation, and a corner-stone, elect and precious, and he that believeth on him shall not be confounded. We have reason to believe, that whatever he doth, is only best. " God saw all that he had made, and behold, it was very good." That word will hold through to the world's end. For my part, I bless his name, I have great peace in the matter of my suffering. I need not repeat, you know my testimony of the things in controversy. Jesus Christ is a King, and only hath power to appoint the officers and government of his house. It is a fearful thing to violate the oath of God, and fall into the hands of a living God. It could not well be expected, but there having been so fair and so general professions through the land, the Lord would put men to it, and it is like it shall come to every man's door, that when every one, according to their inclinations, have acted their part, and he seems to stand by, he may come at last and act his part, and vindicate his glory and truth. I have often showed you, that it is the greatest difficulty under heaven, to believe that there is a God, and a life after this; and have often told you, that for my part, I could never make it a chief part of my work to insist upon the particular debates of the time, as being assured, that if a man drink in the knowledge, and the main foundations of Christian religion, and have the work of God's Spirit in his heart, to make him walk with God, and make conscience of his ways, such a one (except he be giddy with self-conceit) shall not readily mistake Christ's quarrel, to join either with a profane atheist party, or any fanatic atheist party; but the secret of the Lord will be with them that fear him, and he will show them his covenant: and I have thought it not far from a sure argument, that a course is not approven of God, when generally all they that are godly, and all profane men turning penitent, scunner at it, and, it may be, cannot tell why, and generally all the profane, at the first sight, and all that had a profession of piety, when they turn loose, embrace it, and, it may be, cannot tell why. There may be diversity of judgment, and sometimes sharp debates among them that are going to heaven; but certainly a spirit guides the seed of the woman, and another spirit the seed of the serpent; and " blessed are they that know their Master's will, and do it; blessed are they that endure to the end." Both you and I have great cause to bless the Lord, howbeit I be the unworthiest of all that ever spake in his name, yet my labour amongst you hath not been altogether in vain, but some hath given evidence of a real work of the Spirit of grace upon their heart and life, of which number some are already in glory, and others wrestling through an evil world, and I trust, some that have not yet given great evidence of a real work of the Spirit of God upon their heart, may have the seed of God in them, that may in due time bud forth, at least at their death. But ah! what shall be said of them, in whom yet an evil spirit of drunkenness, of greed and falsehood, of malice, of licentiousness, of wilful ignorance and neglect of prayer, and all the means of salvation, is still reigning and raging, who possibly will now be glad that they get loose reins to run to all wickedness, yea, may be carried on to open apostasy and persecution These and all of you, I request in the bowels of our Lord Jesus Christ, yea, I obtest and charge you, in the name and authority of him that shall judge the quick and the dead, that you turn speedily to the Lord, and make conscience of prayer, morning and evening, and read, or cause read to you some of his word, where you will find all things necessary for faith and conversation. It is true, snares and temptations are many and strong from Satan, from the world, and from the mind and heart within, but faith in God, and diligent seeking of him shall overcome them all. Shall not the care of your immortal souls go beyond the love of this life, or any thing in this world? Oh! that you would but taste and see the goodness of the Lord, and take an essay for a while of sincere serving of him, and prove him, if he will not open the windows of heaven, and pour out a blessing. Let me obtain this of you, as a recompense of all the labour I have had amongst you, and as an allaying of all my sufferings. I am put to that, after you read this, you will set some time apart each of you alone, or in your families, as you have conveniency, to think on these directions have been formerly given you from the word of God, and deal earnestly with him, that you may remember and obey them, and engage your hearts to him, that in his strength you will walk in his ways; and if any should stubbornly neglect such a wholesome counsel, that comes from an earnest desire of your salvation, I will be forced to bear witness against you, yea, these words you now hear read shall bear witness against you in the day of the Lord, that light was holden out to you, and you loved darkness rather than light; but I desire to hope better things of you. If the Lord see it good, we may see the day we may meet again, and bless his name solemnly, that although he was angry, his anger is turned away; but if not, the good will of the Lord be done. I think I may say, I could have been well content, although it had been with many discouragements and straits, to have gone on and served you all, as I could, in the Gospel of Jesus Christ; but the prerogative royal of Jesus Christ, and the peace of a man's own conscience, are not to be violated on any consideration, neither hath there been a blessing on ought that is done against these. I was very desirous, and used means, that I might have come and seen you, and at least, in a private way, bidden you farewell ere I had gone; but wise providence hath otherwise ordered it, yet,

themselves in the manner underwritten." We have had Mr. Livingstone's and Mr. Gardiner's; follows Mr. Trail his act:—

"I Mr. Robert Trail, late minister at Edinburgh, bind and oblige me to remove forth of the king's dominions, within a month after the date hereof, and not to remain within the same hereafter, under the pain of death. In witness whereof, I have subscribed these presents, at Edinburgh, December 11th, 1662.

"Ro. Trail."

December 23d, the council prorogate his time of continuance in Scotland. "Anent a petition of Mr. Robert Trail, sometime minister at Edinburgh, showing, that by an act of council of the 11th day of this instant, the petitioner is ordained to remove out of this kingdom, within a month after the date thereof; to which sentence, as he did then, so he does now humbly submit: but seeing the season is now tempestuous, and that hardly can he have the occasion of a ship in that time, and that the petitioner is towards the age of sixty years, if not more,

---

howsoever, I carry your names alongst with me in my book, yea, shall carry them in my heart whithersoever I go, and begs your mutual prayers for me, that I may be kept faithful, and fruitful, and blameless, even to the end, and that, if it be his will, I may be restored to you. In the meantime, love and help one another. Have a care to breed your children to know the Lord, and to keep themselves from the pollutions of an evil world. I recommend to you above all books (except the blessed word of God) the Confession of Faith and Larger Catechism. Be grounding yourselves and one another, against the abominations of popery, in case it should prove the trial of the time, as I apprehend it may. Let a care be had of the poor and sick; there is left as much in an ordinary way as will suffice for meat and money, a year and more. I cannot insist on the several particulars wherein possibly you would crave advice: the word is a lamp, and the Spirit of Christ will guide into all truth. The light that comes of the unfeigned humiliation, and self-denial, and earnest prayer, and search of the scriptures, is a sure light. I know that my word and writ is of small value; yet I could not forbear, but, in a few words, salute you before I went. And now, dearly beloved and longed for, farewell. The Lord of all grace, who hath called us unto his eternal glory by Jesus Christ, after you have suffered a while, make you perfect, stablish, settle, strengthen you. To him be glory and dominion for ever and ever. Amen.

By your loving servant and pastor
in the Lord,
John Livingstone.
Leith, April 3d, 1663.

---

and so cannot well undertake removing at such a season, without evident hazard of his life; therefore humbly desiring that the said space, appointed for the supplicant's removal, may be prorogate for some longer time. Which petition being at length heard, read, and considered, the lords of his majesty's privy council do allow and grant warrant to the supplicant to remain within this kingdom for the space of a month after the —— day of January next to come, and ordain him to confine himself within his own house, where his family is, during that space, except the last eight days, which is allowed to him for making way for his transportation."

Those three took up the council at that diet; and the rest, who were cited, being called, were continued, and appointed to continue in town, and attend the next meeting of council. Accordingly, December 16th, "Mr. John Menzies, and Mr. George Meldrum being called, compeared personally, and being examined, did declare their readiness to comply with the government of the church, as the same is presently established by archbishops and bishops, and most cordially did take and subscribe the oath of allegiance, in presence of the lords of council; wherefore they do seriously recommend their condition and case to the archbishop of St. Andrews, in order to their restitution." This is all I find about them in the registers. We shall afterward meet with the learned Mr. Menzies in the progress of this history, and see how burdensome this compliance with prelacy was unto him, before his death. The reverend and learned Mr. Meldrum, upon misrepresentations cast upon him in print, did at the end of Doctor Rule's Second Vindication of the Church of Scotland, publish an account of this, and other parts of his carriage during prelacy; of which I will here give the reader an abstract, that this great man's memory may have all the justice I can do him.

"He was ordained minister of the gospel by the presbytery of Aberdeen, 1659. When prelacy was introduced he was stopt in the exercise of his ministry, by the act of council, which laid aside divers hundreds of worthy ministers of this church, and obliged them to retire twenty miles from their parishes, because they received not presentation from the patron, and collation from th bishop, the condition of which was the oath of canonical obedience. At first Mr. Meldrum did offer submission, and to join in presbyteries and synods, supposing this was but the same that worthy men have done before the (year) 1638, and not discerning, as others who suffered did, the difference betwixt the state of things, anno 1662, and before the (year) 1638.

" This stop in the exercise of his ministry was fourteen days before the bishop of Aberdeen's first diocesan synod; at which, when he passed the sentence of deposition against the learned and pious Mr. Menzies, for not subscribing the oath of canonical obedience, though he offered submission, as said is, the bishop joined Mr. Meldrum in the sentence, though neither present nor cited to be present. Nothing moved with this sentence of deposition, Mr. Meldrum retired to the country, twenty-eight miles from Aberdeen, in compliance with the council's act. Yet in the beginning of December, he and Mr. Menzies got a citation to appear before the council, as was said, by the procurement of the bishop of Aberdeen, who alleged he could not appear in the streets of that city, for fear of the people irritated, as was alleged, by their pastors whom they had lost.

" When they appeared before the council, the commissioner and the rest of the counsellors, finding them willing to join in presbyteries and synods, did by their act recommend them to the bishop of St. Andrews to be restored to their places. When this was presented to the bishop, he readily promised to obey it, but never spoke to them one word of the oath of canonical obedience. And when in his letter to the bishop of Aberdeen, he signified that we were willing to own the government, Mr. Meldrum refused to receive it unless he added this qualification, ' so far as to join in presbyteries and synods;' to which the primate agreed, when they would take it in no other terms.

" When Mr. Menzies and Mr. Meldrum returned, bishop Mitchel ordered Doctor Keith to read that paper publicly in Aberdeen, thinking thereby to lessen their esteem: but the design failed; none of them were present at the reading of it. But next Lord's day, when Mr. Meldrum appeared first in the pulpit, he told his hearers, and the bishop of Ross was one of them, that he conceived he had yielded to nothing, but what at first he had offered, viz. to join in synods and presbyteries. Mr. Meldrum adds, that Mr. Menzies's compliance was grievous to that learned and pious man at his death, and to himself several years before, and tells the world that he repents for the subscribing that paper of submission to join in presbyteries and synods, and asserts he never took the oath of canonical obedience.

" He confesses that afterward he did sit in presbyteries and synods, thinking himself free to join in those duties, to which he was authorized by his office, although there had not been one bishop in the world; yet adds, if any can show me wherein I have complied contrary to my principles, or to the just offence of others, which I have not confessed already, I am ready to acknowledge it was my fault: but this I can say, the bishops themselves did not judge me a favourer of prelacy; and my intimates knew me to be presbyterian in my principles, and I did never wittingly desert those principles. He adds, that it was a manifest untruth that he took the declaration when he was admitted rector in the Marishal college of Aberdeen, and appeals to the records, and declares he never took it then, or at any other time. He says, that it was none of the least causes of his refusing the test, that he was obliged thereby to declare that there lay no obligation upon him to endeavour any alteration in the government of the church, and professes he judged it duty in his station, and according to his power did endeavour, to promote the alteration and removal of it, and prays that it may never return."

This truly great man, and ornament to this church, Mr. George Meldrum, is so well known, and his memory so savoury, that I need say nothing of him to the most yet alive; and his works show abundantly his eminent abilities. He was remarkably useful in Aberdeen, with his excellent colleague Mr. Menzies, against the quakers, and the cunning Jesuits, till the self-contradictory test turned him out of that city: and with many other pious and learned ministers he was persecuted, and silenced till the toleration; a little after which he was settled at the parish of Kilwinning, where he was soon called to more public service. He had an invitation from the university of Glasgow, to be colleague in the profession of divinity with the reverend Mr. James Wodrow; and a call to the city of Edinburgh, to which he was transported, and preached many years to great edification, and was a mighty master of the holy scriptures, and blessed with the greatest talent of opening them up, or lecturing, of any I ever heard. After the death of that great light, the reverend Mr. George Campbell, Mr. Meldrum was brought to the chair of divinity at Edinburgh, which how well he filled, many of the ministers of this church can testify. By a prudent and faithful sermon of his against episcopacy, he was led into a public debate with some of the abettors of it; and how generally useful he was to stop the design, 1703, to introduce toleration and patronages in this church, is well enough yet remembered; and what he printed upon the nice subject of toleration, led him into a paper war with Mr. Sage, and some others of the episcopal clergy, where he had an open field to display the great talents of learning, prudence, and zeal his Master had bestowed on him. Should I speak of his singular usefulness in church judicatories, his modest and healing temper, his solidity in teaching, his success in preaching, his excellent conversation, and abounding in alms and charity, I would not soon end. He will make a bright figure whenever we shall have the benefit of the lives of our Scots ministers: and his compliance at this time, we see, was matter of deep repentance to himself. I go forward to the rest of the ministers, who being called, were continued till the next council-day.

Accordingly, December 23d, Mr. John Neave or Nevoy compeared, and was examined, and, upon his refusal of the oath of allegiance, he was banished, and enacted himself as follows.

" I Mr. John Neave, late minister of the gospel at Newmills, bind 1662. and oblige me to remove myself forth of the king's dominions, and not to return, under the pain of death, and that I shall remove before the first of February; and that I shall not remain within the dioceses of Edinburgh or Glasgow in the meanwhile. Subscribed at Edinburgh, December 23d,

" JOHN NEAVE."

This excellent man was the earl of Loudon's minister, and very much valued by his lordship, and therefore must be attacked now: he was a person of very considerable parts, and bright piety. There is a handsome paraphrase of his upon the Song of Solomon, in Latin verse, printed; and I have seen some accurate sermons of his upon Christ's temptations, which I wish were published. He obeyed the sentence, and died abroad.

Mr. John Cameron next appeared, " Who being examined, and heard to express himself as to his principles towards the present government in church and state, the lords of council ordain him forthwith to remove himself with all convenient diligence from the place of his present dwelling, and confine himself within the bounds of Lochaber, and not to remove forth thereof without license from his majesty or the privy council, as he will be answerable at his utmost peril." He was a singularly pious and religious person, and he got this favour, if it may be so called, not to have the oath put to him, by the interposition of his chief the laird of Lochiel, who was caution for Mr Cameron's peaceable behaviour, and his keeping his confinement. He continued some time at the deserted garrison of Inverlochie, where he preached to Lochiel's family; and the people about came in and heard him. He lived a good many years after this, and had several remarkable communications of the Lord's mind as to the events a coming in this church.

That same day, " Mr. James Nasmith, and Mr. Samuel Austin, compeared personally, were referred by the lords of council to the commissioner his grace, that he may take such course and order with them as he thinks fit; and they appointed to attend and wait his pleasure." He was not long after this in the country, and it would seem the

1662. commissioner put back Mr. Nasmith upon the council; for I find, January 6th, next year, Mr. Nasmith appears before the council, and they ordain him, "To confine himself within the bounds of the sheriffdom of Merse, till further order, and that he demean himself in the meantime peaceably. I have no more of Mr. Austin."

At that diet, January 6th, Mr. Alexander Dunlop, minister at Paisley, was before them; "Who being examined, and the oath of allegiance offered to him to be taken and subscribed, and he refusing the same, the lords of council ordain him to be banished forth of his majesty's dominions, reserving to themselves to prefix the time of his removal; and in the meantime ordain him to confine himself within the bounds of the dioceses of Aberdeen, Brechin, Caithness, or Dunkeld; and allow him the space of ten days to go home and order his business and affairs." He was a person of eminent piety, and extraordinary diligence and learning, and singular prudence and sweetness of temper. He has left behind him, among other valuable papers, collections towards a system of divinity in English, which had he been able to have put in order, would have been one of the most valuable bodies of divinity which hath been drawn up.

I find nothing in the registers about Mr. Alexander Gordon, the marquis of Argyle his minister at Inveraray: the reason is, he was under a dangerous fever when cited before the council. The magistrates of that place sent up a testificate under the physicians' hands, which the council could not but accept. He was a while forgot as dead, and indeed he was very near death, but the Lord had more work for him; and he upon his recovery continued some years preaching in bishop Fletcher's time: but when Scrogie succeeded to that bishopric, Mr. Gordon fell into very great hardships, and sore persecution, of which he told me he had drawn up a large account, but I have not been able yet to come by it. This good man was a member of the assembly 1651, and I have a very distinct and accurate account of their procedure, writ by him at the time, which he gave me. He lived to a great age, and died in the Lord, 1714.

No accounts have come to my hand about Messrs. Andrew and Alexander Cants, who were present upon citation. This is all I have of those excellent men, marked out in all the corners of the church. Mr. Dunlop was banished, but came to be overlooked. Messrs. Trail, Livingstone, Brown, Nevoy, and Gardiner, went over to Holland beginning of next year, being turned out of their native country, merely for refusing the oath of allegiance, though all of them were willing to take it in the very sense the managers said they had themselves taken it in. Mr. Trail returned, and died in Scotland. Mr. Gardiner, through his tedious exile, fell under some melancholy, and ventured home likewise, and was overlooked. The rest, with Mr. M'Vaird and Mr. Simpson, died in a strange land. We shall meet with a good many more presbyterian ministers attacked next year, but we may well reckon these spoken of in this chapter, among the first worthies.

SECT. VI.

Of some few other remarkables this year, 1662.

I COME now to conclude this chapter with a few other incidental matters this year, that came not in so well upon the general heads in the former sections, and yet tend a little to enlighten the history of this period I am now upon; and I give them just in the order of time in which they offer.

The council pass their act and proclamation for keeping of Lent, February 6th, and the curious reader may desire to have the tenor of it.

"The lords of his majesty's privy council, taking to their consideration the great advantage and profit which will redound to all the lieges of this kingdom, by keeping the time of Lent, and the weekly fish days, viz. Wednesday, Friday, Saturday, and discharging all persons to eat flesh during that time, and upon the said days, or to kill and sell in markets any sort of fleshes which are usually bought at other times; whereby the young brood and store will be preserved, so that thereafter the hazard of scarcity and dearth may be prevented; and the fishes, which, by the mercy of God abound in the salt and fresh waters of this kingdom, may be made use of for the food and entertainment of the lieges, to the profit and encouragement of many poor families, who live by fishing; the improvement of which has not been looked unto these many years bygone, which hath been occasioned by the universal allowance of eating flesh, and keeping of markets for it at all ordinary times without any restraint; against which many laudable laws have been made, and acts of parliament, prohibiting the eating of flesh during the said time of Lent, or upon the said fish days, under the pains therein contained: ordain and command that the time of Lent for this year, and yearly hereafter, shall begin and be kept as before the year of God 1640, and that the said weekly fish days be strictly observed in all time coming; and that no subject of whatsoever quality, rank or degree, except they have a special license under the hand of the clerk of the council, presume to eat flesh during the said space of Lent, or upon the three said weekly fish days; and that no butchers, cooks, or ostlers, kill, make ready, or sell any flesh, either publicly in markets, or privately in their own houses, during the said time, or upon the said days, under the penalties following, to be exacted with all rigour, viz. for the first fault ten pounds, for the second twenty pounds, for the third forty pounds, and so to be multiplied according to the oft contravening of the said act, to be exacted and paid, the one half to the king's majesty, the other half to the delaters. Likeas for the surer exacting of the said pains, they give power and warrant to all magistrates within burghs, and all sheriffs, stewarts, and bailies, within their several jurisdictions, to inquire after the contraveners, and to pursue them before the lords of council, or such others as shall be appointed or delegate for that effect. And ordain publication hereof to be made at the market cross of Edinburgh, and all other places needful, that none pretend ignorance."

This proclamation was merely a requisition of a civil keeping of Lent, and the weekly fish days, for the preservation of the young bestial, and the consumption of our fish, which the Lord has so bountifully given us; and had the council seen to the execution of this good act, as well as they did the severe and bloody acts against presbyterians, it had been much for the interest of the lieges :* but we shall find them so much taken up to satisfy the prelates, and execute their desires against presbyterians, that so useful an act as this is (was) very much neglected, and, as far as I know, came to nothing.

1662.

This same month the articles of marriage, betwixt the king and princess Katharine of Portugal, came to be made public: and with a view to have our nobility present at her reception, the parliament as we heard, was adjourned from February to May. The articles of that marriage differed much from these in the projected match with Spain, and the real marriage of Charles I. with France: and, as I find them in papers come to my hand, the chief are, " That the queen be of the protestant religion, which I do not know if ever any care was taken about. That she bring no priests with her. That the half of the silver mines the king of Portugal hath, belong to Britain. That after the decease of the king of Portugal's son, if he die without heir, the kingdom of Portugal shall belong to England." Those were the articles given out here in

---

* We confess, that we do not see this act exactly in the light in which our historian seems to have viewed it. If it was intended to promote purposes merely civil, its provisions were preposterous and absurd. If it was intended to have also a religious reference, which we cannot help strongly suspecting, they were at the same time impious. We do not believe that compulsory labour, or compulsory diet, can be established in any country with advantage. Ignorant indeed must that people be, who, if left to their own discretion, cannot discover what species of industry will bring them in the largest returns, and that kind of diet, which is most suitable to their palates and their purses; and those principles of religion, which require haddocks and herring for so long a period of the year, and for so many days of the week, to preserve them in healthful operation, cannot possibly have any connexion either with morality or common sense. Such, however, has been and still is the religion of the far greater portion of the world called Christian; and so long as this shall be the case, it will be impossible to vindicate (extraordinary cases and circumstances excepted) any enactment of the kind referred to from having, at least, " the appearance of evil."—*Ed.*

1662. Scotland, whether they hold I do not know.

This year the usual solemnities were kept up in all cities and burghs, in celebrating of the 29th of May; and we have heard the non-observance of it as an anniversary holyday, was matter of great trouble to presbyterian ministers: but the town of Linlithgow signalized themselves, by mixing in with their solemnity a most horrid, irreligious, and unaccountable treatment of our solemn covenants, which was a matter of grief unto all who had any regard to religion and sacred things, and a terrible guilt and stain upon poor Scotland. The account given by the profane and impious actors of this abominable jest upon sacred things, when at this time they gloried in their shame, I shall give here from a paper writ this year, which follows.

" Our solemnity at Linlithgow, May 29th, 1662, was performed after this manner. Divine service being ended, the magistrates a little thereafter repaired to the earl of Linlithgow his lodging, to invite his lordship to honour them with his presence at the solemnity of that day; which he did. Then coming to the market-place, where a table covered with confections was placed, they were met by the minister of the place, who prayed to them, and sung a psalm; after which, eating a little of the confections, they threw the rest among the people.

" Meanwhile the fountain did run plentifully with French and Spanish wine, and continued so for two or three hours. The earl of Linlithgow, and the magistrates, drank the king and queen, and the royal family and progeny, their healths.

" At the cross was erected an arch, standing upon four pillars: on the one side of the arch was placed a statue in form of an old hag, having the covenant in her hand, with this superscription, A GLORIOUS REFORMATION. On the other side, there was another statue, in a Whigmuir's habit, having the remonstrance in his hand, with this inscription, NO ASSOCIATION WITH MALIGNANTS. On the top of the arch was placed a statue, representing the devil as an angel of light, with this label at his mouth, STAND TO THE CAUSE.

" The arch was beautifully adorned with several draughts of rocks, reels, and kirk stools upon the pillar beneath the covenant: and upon the pillar beneath the remonstrance were drawn brechams, cogs, and spoons.

" Within the arch, upon the right hand, was drawn a committee of estates, with this superscription, ACT FOR DELIVERING UP THE KING. On the left hand, was drawn a commission of the kirk, with this inscription, ACT OF THE WEST KIRK. In the middle of the arch hung a tablet with this litany,

" From covenanters with uplifted hands,
From remonstrators with associate bands,
From such committees as governed this nation,
From kirk commissions and their protestation.
    Good Lord deliver us.

" Upon the back of the arch was drawn the picture of rebellion, in a religious habit, with eyes turned up, and other fanatic gestures: in its right hand holding LEX REX, that infamous book, maintaining, among other absurd tenets, defensive arms; and in its left hand holding that pitiful pamphlet, THE CAUSES OF GOD'S WRATH. Round about her were lying acts of parliament, acts of committees of estates, acts of general assemblies, and commissions of kirk, with their protestations and declarations during those twenty-two years' rebellion. Above her was this superscription, REBELLION IS AS THE SIN OF WITCHCRAFT.

" At drinking the king's health, fire was put to the frame, and the fire-works about it gave many fine reports, and suddenly all was consumed to ashes; which being consumed, straightway there appeared a tablet supported by two angels, bearing this inscription.

" Great Britain's monarch on this day was born,
And to his kingdoms happily restored:
The queen's arrived, the mitre now is worn;
Let us rejoice, this day is from the LORD.

Fly hence, all traitors who did mar our peace,
Fly hence, schismatics who our church did rent,
Fly, covenanting remonstrating race;
Let us rejoice that God this day hath sent.

" Then the magistrates accompanied the earl of Linlithgow to the palace, where the earl had a magnificent bonfire, and drank with the magistrates the king's, queen's, and other loyal healths. When they had taken their leave of the earl, the magistrates, accompanied with a great many of the inhabitants, made their procession through the town, saluting every person of account."

Reflections upon this mean mock of the work of reformation, and appearances for religion and liberty, are obvious. Whatever the different sentiments of sober and any way serious persons might have been at this time, as to our covenants, yet, I persuade myself, such impious and scurrilous treatment of those solemn and national ties and engagements, wherein the holy and fearful name of the Lord our God was called upon, hath been, and is matter of deep abhorrence to all who have any reverence for that holy and sacred name. Indeed, if this public reproach upon, and burning of the covenants, could have loosed their obligation, one would think this profane work was necessary upon these anniversary days, really contrary to the reformation we are bound down to by them; but that was beyond their power. This wicked attack, not only upon our religious ties, which were the glory of Scotland, but also upon the appearances made for recovering and preserving our civil liberty, was chiefly managed by Robert Miln, then bailie of Linlithgow, and Mr. James Ramsay, at this time minister of the town. The first in some time thereafter came to great riches and honour, but outlived them and the exercise of his judgment too, and died bankrupt in miserable circumstances at Holyrood-house. The other, for this meritorious act of loyalty, after he was made dean of Hamilton, came at length to be bishop of Dunblane, where we shall afterwards meet with him, in no good terms with his superior the primate. Both of them, some few years ago, had solemnly entered into, and renewed these covenants, with uplifted hands to the Lord. This vile pageantry was not required by any law, or order from the government, and so I hope is not chargeable upon the public, any further than it was not punished: and as it had no precedent in Scotland, so there was no appointment for it, or approbation of it by the town-council of Linlithgow. It was then both officiously and impiously perpetrate, and comes very near Belshazzar's quaffing in the holy vessels. Those people would outrun others in wickedness, and by this bold insult upon religious matters, for what I know, without parallel in the whole world, avowed themselves perjured, and left a blot upon their memory in after times.

1662.

Some time in June or July this year, the commissioner stooped so low, as to procure an order of parliament, for the razing of the reverend Mr. Alexander Henderson his monument in the Grayfriars' church-yard, Edinburgh. After his death, August 18th, 1646, a monument was erected for him, with a pyramid, and inscription, wherein some mention was made of the solemn league and covenant. Indeed so great and useful a man as he was, whose character I shall leave to the writers of the history of this church, from the (year) 1637, to his death, when he had so great a share in all public ecclesiastical transactions, deserved to be had in remembrance. Now the letters and inscription must be razed, and the memory of this extraordinary person stained as much as might be. Yet, after all this, the abettors of prelacy, sensible of the great endowments of Mr. Henderson, would fain have him brought over to their side at his death; and palm upon the world most groundless stories of his changing his principles at his last hours.

I omitted to observe, that the council, immediately after the rising of the parliament, September 10th, " ordain the act of parliament, intituled, Act concerning the declaration to be signed by all persons in public trust, to be signed by all who have not subscribed the same, in the presence of any one of the lords of his majesty's privy council: and that thereafter they cause their deputes, clerks, stewarts, or commissaries, their deputes and their clerks, magistrates, and members of council in burghs, justices of peace and their clerks, within their respective bounds, subscribe the said declaration, conform to the said act of parliament, in all points; and that they make a report of their diligence in the premises to the council." The pushing of this order brought a vast deal of trouble to the country, of which we shall have instances afterwards.

1662. After the election of magistrates in Edinburgh this year, all the ministers of the town, as we have heard, were discharged preaching, save Mr. Robert Lawrie. I find one, who is no enemy to the change in church government, observing, "That sermons were taught by strangers in all the kirks, but they were not well liked; the people went from kirk to kirk, and many wandered to other kirks, and the Monday's preaching was either disused or discharged."

Upon the 5th of November, Mr. Joseph Meldrum minister at Kinghorn, Mr. John Robertson parson of Dysart, and Mr. Archibald Turner minister at North Berwick, were received ministers of Edinburgh. Mr. Robertson had a sermon to the people, and after it, came down to the elders' seat, and placed himself with the other two, who sat there with the magistrates and elders. Then the bishop of Edinburgh went up to the pulpit, and, in a short discourse, declared those three ministers were called and chosen; and they were received by the elders and magistrates, who afterwards feasted the company. So the ministers of Edinburgh at this time fixed, were those three; Mr. Robert Lawrie continued; Mr. John Paterson, formerly minister of Ellon, and afterward bishop, first of Galloway, next of Edinburgh, and last of Glasgow, was received minister there, the first Sabbath of January next year: and upon the first Sabbath of February, Mr. William Annand, formerly a minister in England, and chaplain to the earl of Middleton, was received minister there. They were six in number, and some were joined to them as helpers. How vast a difference must every body allow to have been betwixt them, and Messrs. Hutcheson, Douglas, Trail, Smith, Stirling; and yet those are turned out to make room for them.

Now the ministers who comply have double stipends allowed them, when they are translated to better posts, upon consideration of their alleged loyalty; when, I am sure, the presbyterian ministers who are turned out, and deprived of the stipends of these very years for which they had served the cure, had much more appeared for the king's interest. Thus I find, December 11th, when they are harassing presbyterian ministers, " The council taking to their consideration, that Mr. James Chalmers, late minister of Cullen of Boyn, and now minister of Dumfries, has been at a great deal of charges and pains in pursuance of his majesty's interest and government, both in church and state; have therefore ordained, and by these presents ordain, that the present year's stipend, 1662, due to the late minister at Dumfries, be paid to the said Mr. James Chalmers; and that the heritors, feuars, farmers, tenants, possessors, and others liable, make ready and thankful payment of the same to him, or any having his order; and, if need be, ordain letters of horning to pass hereupon as effeirs: and this is without prejudice to the said Mr. James, of the said year's stipend, 1662, due to him from the parish of Cullen."

December 25th, being yule-day, was kept this year with much solemnity at Edinburgh. The bishop preached himself, and the commissioner, with a good many of the nobility, and the magistrates, came to the new church; and the magistrates, by tuck of drum, advertised all the inhabitants of the town to observe the remainder of that day as a holyday; and discharged any shop to be opened, or any market to be in the streets, under the pain of twenty shillings scots. And I know not, but this was the last time ever Middleton heard sermon in Scotland; for in a few days after, upon a call, he went up to court, where we shall meet with his treatment next year.

I shut up this chapter with remarking, while prelacy is set and setting up in Scotland, that severe proclamation in England is emitted, commonly called, the Bartholomew act, whereby some thousands of churches were, August 24th, this year, laid desolate, and multitudes of people deprived of their pastors; and a set of ministers, who were equal to any of their number in all the protestant churches, were laid aside, for not doing what was really impossible to most of them to do, though they had been, as they were not, satisfied as to the lawfulness of what was required. The reverend and learned Dr. Calamy has done them justice, and set this matter in its due light, by his excellent abridgment of Mr. Baxter's

Life; which supersedes my observing the inconsistency of this procedure with the declaration at Breda; and the great and undeniable share the English presbyterians had in the king's restoration. In short, the same prelatic spirit of persecution, and oppressing people in their consciences and liberty, was raging through the whole island.

CHAP. IV.

OF THE STATE AND SUFFERINGS OF PRESBYTERIANS, DURING THE YEAR 1663.

1663. We have now seen the scriptural institution of church government overturned in Scotland, and prelacy established, and the foundations laid of turning out all the presbyterian ministers, and many of them confined and banished. This same work is carried on this year, and the few remaining old presbyterian ministers and others, are attacked and harassed. The council hath the greatest part of this sad work in their hand; and from their books I am to give a distinct account both of their more general acts, and particular prosecutions of ministers, gentlemen, and great numbers of country people, for their affection to their outed ministers.

This summer the hands are changed in Scotland, and a considerable turn of managers in England also: chancellor Hyde there, and Middleton here, the great abettors and introducers of prelacy in all its heights, are turned out; and Lauderdale comes to Scotland, and the parliament sits down, where some new acts are made against presbyterians. The act for balloting is rescinded, and Lauderdale and his party have the entire management in their hands for many years.

During the sitting of parliament, the excellent lord Wariston is executed; and though he be the only person suffering unto death, yet we shall have abundance of others sorely oppressed this year. The accounts of these will afford matter for five or six sections, much in the order I have used in the former years.

SECT. I.

Of the ejection of near four hundred ministers, the dismal effects thereof, with the general state of the west and south country this year, 1663.

HAVING, upon the former year, laid before the reader the act of the council at Glasgow, and what followed upon it toward the end of the year, by which such multitudes of ministers were cast out, I thought this as proper a place as I could find, to give him some further view of this melancholy scene and its consequents, especially in the west and south of Scotland, since what was begun in the close of the last year, was completed in the beginning of this. We shall indeed afterwards meet with the mile act, and that discharging alms and charity, and some others about presbyterian ministers: but those formerly mentioned were the great foundation of scattering these multitudes of worthy ministers. By the act of Glasgow, more than a third part of the ministers of the church of Scotland were cast out of their charges, merely for conscience' sake, because they would not take the oath imposed upon all who received presentations, and the oath of canonical obedience, a necessary requisite to collation; and because they could not, contrary to their light, subject to bishops. Scotland was never witness to such a sabbath as the last those ministers preached; and I know no parallel to it, save the 17th of August, 1662, to the presbyterians in England. It was not now as it came to be afterwards in the year 1689, when the episcopal ministers left their congregations, the people in many places through the west and south, obliging them to promise they should never return to them: but when those I am now speaking of took their leave of their dear flocks, it was a day not only of weeping but howling, like "the weeping of Jazer, as when a besieged city is sacked."

This I take to be a very proper place to record the names of the presbyterian ministers of this church, who were thrown out of their churches by the spite and enmity of

1663. the bishops. Most part of them were cast out by that act at Glasgow, October 1st, and that December 23d last year. Some indeed continued preaching for some time at their peril; and several of the elder ministers, who were ordained before the year 1649, were not so directly reached by those acts. But I have put together all the ministers ejected at this time, and formed the best account I could give from several papers come to my hand, of such as were cast out from their charges now, and in a very little after. The list I give is as complete as now, after threescore of years, I could have it. Probably there may be some mistakes in some of their names, their parishes or presbyteries where they resided, because this account is made up in part from the verbal notices given by old ministers, and taken out of several old lists which I have seen. And, which I more lament, there are some parishes out of which I know ministers were ejected, and yet I can by no means recover their names. But I persuade myself this is the most exact list that yet hath been framed, and the best I could give from the helps in my hand. I have added it at the bottom of the page, * and, as far as I could recover them, have added the names of such as conformed to prelacy, that the advocates for that government may see whom they have to glory in, especially in the west and south. And to make this list of nonconformists to prelacy as full as might be, I have added an account of such presbyterian ministers in the north of Ireland, who refused conformity to episcopacy there, and suffered severely enough for it; because I have always found the elder presbyterian ministers in Ireland reckoning themselves upon the same bottom with, and as it were a branch of the church of Scotland. It stands below, † as it comes to my hand, under the correction of the reverend ministers of that kingdom; and the reader may see a full list of the ejected and nonconformist ministers in England, in the Abridgment of Mr. Baxter's Life, formerly mentioned.

The ejecting near four hundred such worthy ministers, was the greater hardship, that, generally speaking, they were persons of remarkable grace and eminent gifts. They were pious, painful, and a great many of them learned and able ministers of the gospel, and all of them singularly dear to

---

* A roll of ministers who were nonconformists to prelacy, and were banished, turned out from their parishes, or confined; with some account of those who conformed to prelacy.

Those marked with R. were alive at the revolution; those marked with G. were outed by the act of council at Glasgow, 1662; those marked with C. were confined to their parishes; those marked with P. were outed by particular sentences of parliament or council; and those marked with S. were outed by the diocesan synod.

I. SYNOD OF LOTHIAN AND TWEEDDALE.

1. *Presbytery of Edinburgh.*
Messrs. Robert Douglas of Edinburgh, P.
Robert Trail of Edinburgh, banished.
John Smith of Edinburgh, P.
Thomas Garvan of Edinburgh, P.
James Hamilton of Edinburgh, P.
George Hutchison of Edinburgh, P.
John Stirling of Edinburgh, P.
David Dickson, professor of theology, P.
David Williamson of West Kirk, G. R.
Alexander Hutchison of Canongate.
John Hogg of South Leith,
James Knox of North Leith,
William Dalgleish of Cramond,
Robert Hunter of Corstorphin,
John Charters of Currie,
William Tweedie,

William Thomson,
Thomas Crawford,
John Hume.
Conformists.
Messrs. Robert Leighton, principal of the college,
Robert Lawrie of Edinburgh,
James Nairn of Canongate.

---

† A list of the nonconformed ministers of the synod of Bellimenoch in Ireland.

PRESBYTERY OF NEWTON IN THE CLANDIBOYES.
Messrs. Andrew Stuart,
Gilbert Ramsay,
John Gray,
William Reid,
John Drysdale,
James Gordon,
Thomas Peebles,
Hugh Wilson,
Michael Bruce,
William Richardson,
John Fleming,
Alexander Hutchison,
Henry Livingstone,
Henry Hunter,
James Campbell,
Andrew M'Cornick.

CHAP. IV.] OF THE CHURCH OF SCOTLAND. 325

their people. Many of them were but young men, who had but a small share in the actings in the late times of reformation, so much reproached now Most of them had suffered under the usurpation, for their loyalty to the king, and 1663.

2. *Presbytery of Linlithgow.*
Messrs. William Weir of Linlithgow, R.
Gilbert Hall of Kirkliston, P.
Alexander Hamilton of Dalmeny, R.
John Primrose of Queensferry,
Robert Steedman of Carridden, R.
William Crichton of Bathgate, R.
Patrick Shiels of West-Calder,
Hugh Kennedy of Mid-Calder, R.
William Wishart of Kinnoul, R.
Robert Row,
Robert Semple.
Conformists.
Messrs. James Ramsay of Linlithgow,
Patrick Shaw,
John Wauch.
3. *Presbytery of Biggar.*
Messrs. Alexander Livingstone of Biggar, P.
Anthony Murray of Coulter,
James Donaldson of Dolphington,
Patrick Anderson of Walston, R.
James Bruce,
Archibald Porteous,
Alexander Barton,
John Rae,
John Crawford,
William Dickson,
John Greg of Skirling,
Robert Brown.
4. *Presbytery of Peebles.*
Messrs. Robert Elliot of Linton, R.
Richard Brown of Drumelzier, R.
Patrick Fleming of Stobo.
In another list.
Messrs. Robert Brown of Lyne,
Hugh Craig of Kelly, conformist,
David Thomson of Dask,
Patrick Purdie of Newlands,
John Hay of Peebles.

But I am uncertain whether some of those conformed.
5. *Presbytery of Dalkeith.*
Messrs. George Johnston of Newbottle, G. R.
James Cunninghame of Lasswade, G.
Robert Mowat of Temple, G.
Thomas Paterson of Borthwick, G.
James Kirkpatrick of Carrington, G. R.
Alexander Heriot of Cranston, G.
John Sinclair of Ormiston G.
Conformists.
Messrs. John Logan of Falla,
William Calderwood of Heriot,
Adam Penman of Cockpen,
Oliver Colt of Musselburgh and Inverask,
Robert Carsan of Newton,
Gideon Penman of Crichton,
Robert Alison of Glencorse,
William Dalgarnock of Pennycuik.
6. *Presbytery of Haddington.*
Messrs. Robert Ker of Haddington,
John Macghie of Dirlton,
Thomas Kirkaldy of Tranent.
7. *Presbytery of Dunbar.*
Mr. John Baird of Innerwick.

II. SYNOD OF MERSE AND TEVIOTDALE.
1. *Presbytery of Dunse.*
Messrs. John Jamison,
John Burn.
2. *Presbytery of Churnside.*
Messrs. William Johnston,
Thomas Ramsay of Mordingston and Lamerton, C. R.
Edward Jamison of Swinton,
Daniel Douglas of Hilton, R.
David Hume of Coldingham.
3. *Presbytery of Kelso.*
Messrs. Robert Boyd of Linton, G. R.

THE CONFORMED MINISTERS WERE,
Messrs. Mungo Bennet,
George Wallace,
Robert Rowan,
Andrew Rowan,
Donald M'Neil.
PRESBYTERY OF ANTRIM.
Messrs. William Kays,
James Shaw,
Robert Cunningham,
Thomas Hall,
Patrick Adair,
James Fleming,
Gilbert Simpson,
Anthony Kennedy,
Thomas Crawford,
Robert Hamilton,
Robert Dewart,
John Schaw.
PRESBYTERY OF ROUT.
Messrs. David Bittel,
William Cumming,
John Douglas,
Robert Hogsberd,
Gabriel Cornwal,
Thomas Stulton,

John Crooks,
Thomas Boyd.
James Ker,
John Law.
PRESBYTERY OF DUNGENAN.
Messrs. Robert Auld,
Archibald Hamilton
Robert Keith,
Thomas Kennedy,
Thomas Govan,
John Abernethie,
Alexander Osburn,
James Johnston,
PRESBYTERY OF LAGAN.
Messrs. Robert Wilson,
William Moorcraft,
John Wooll,
William Semple,
John Hart,
John Adamson,
John Crookshank,
Thomas Drummond,
Robert Craighead,
Hugh Cunningham,
Hugh Peebles,
Adam White, and Wm. Jack.

1663. their refusing the tender. Those persons were not only deprived of their livings in time to come, but of the last year's stipend, for which they had served; and in the winter season obliged with sorrowful hearts and empty pockets to wander,

John Somerwel of Ednam, S.
Samuel Row of Sprouston, S.
Conformists.
Messrs. Richard Waddel of Kelso,
Thomas Inglis put in Sprouston,
David Stirk of Stitchel,
William Turnbull of Mackerston,
William Penman of Morbottle,
John Halyburton of Roxburgh,
John Clapperton of Yetholm.
4. Presbytery of Jedburgh.
Messrs. James Ainsley of Minto, G. R.
John Scot of Hawick, G. R.
James Gillon of Cavers, G.
Hugh Scot of Bedrule, G.
Gavin Elliot of Kirkton,
James Ker of Abbotsrule, C.
John Scot of Oxnam, C.
John Langlands of Wilton, C.
John Davidson of Southden, C.
Robert Martin of Eckford, C.
John Livingstone of Ancrum, banished, and died in Holland.
Conformists.
Messrs. Peter Blair of Jedburgh,
John Douglas of Crellon and Nisbet,
Thomas Abernethy of Hownam,
Andrew Pringle of Cassilton,
James Douglas of Hopkirk.
5. Presbytery of Ersilton.
Messrs. James Kirkton of Merton, G. R.
John Hardie of Gordon, G. R.
James Fletcher of Newthorn, G.
William Calderwood of Legerwood, G.
Thomas Donaldson, of Smelholm, C.
John Veitch of Westeruther, R.
John Cleland of Stow, C. but in some lists he is blotted out.
Conformists.
Messrs. Henry Cockburn of Ginglekirk,
James Doze of Ersilton,
David Forrester of Lauder.
6. Presbytery of Selkirk or Melrose.
Messrs. Robert Cunningham of Askirk, G. R.
Thomas Lowes of Gallashiels, G. R.
John Shaw of Selkirk, C.
William Elliot of Yarrow, C.
Andrew Dunkison of Maxton, C.
William Wilkie of Lilliesleafe, C.
Alexander Cunningham of Ettrick.
Conformists.
Messrs. David Fletcher of Melross,
John Colt of Roberton,
John Somerwel of St. Boswell,
James Knox of Bowdon.

III. SYNOD OF DUMFRIES.
1. Presbytery of Middleby.
Messrs. William Bailie of Annan,
Robert Law,
James Pringle of Westerkirk,
John Linlithgow of Ewes, R.
Hugh Scot of Middleby,
Alexander Crawford.
Conformists.
Messrs. James Craig of Hoddam,
Thomas Allan
William Graham,
David Laing, at Graitney,

2. Presbytery of Lochmaben.
Messrs. John Brown of Wamfrey, banished, died in Holland,
James Wellwood of Tindergirth,
William Boyd of Dalton,
James Porter of Kirkpatrick-juxta,
John Menzies of Johnston,
Alexander M'Gowan of Mouswell, C.
Alexander Forester of Castlemilk, C.
Another list adds,
Messrs. Archibald Inglis of Moffat,
John Lawrie,
Thomas Thomson,
But another list puts them among the Conformists.
Conformists.
Messrs. Thomas Henderson of Lochmaben,
John Lawrie of Halton,
Thomas Thomson of Applegirth, at Drysdale,
Gavin Young of Ruthwell.
3. Presbytery of Dumfries.
Messrs. Hugh Henderson of Dumfries, P.
George Campbell of Dumfries, G. R.
John Campbell of Thorthorald, G.
William Shaw of Garran, G.
William Hay of Holywood, G.
Robert Archbald of Dunscore, G. R.
John Welsh of Irongray, G.
Robert Paton of Terreagles, G. R.
John Blaccader of Traquair, G.
Anthony Murray of Kirkbean, G.
William Mean of Lochrutton, G. R.
Alexander Smith of Cowend, G.
Gabriel Semple of Kirkpatrick, Durham, G. R.
William M'Joir of Carlaverock, C.
Francis Irvine of Kirkmahoe, C. R.
George Gladstones of Orr, C.
James Maxwell of Kirkgunion, C.
Some lists make him Thomas Maxwell.
Some lists add Mr. James Wallace.
Conformists.
Messrs. John Brown of Tinward,
Ninian Paterson.
4. Prebytery of Penpont.
Messrs. Samuel Austin of Penpont,
James Brotherstones of Glencairn,
Alexander Strang of Dorisdeer, R.
John Liddersdale of Tindram,
Adam Sinclair of Morton,
Thomas Shiels of Kirkbride,
John Carmichael of Kirkonnald and Sanquhar.
One list puts the two following among the nonconformists, and others among the conformists.
Messrs. John Wisheart of Keir,
William Black of Closburn.

IV. SYNOD OF GALLOWAY.
1. Presbytery of Kirkcudbright.
Messrs. Thomas Wylie of Kirkcudbright, P.
Thomas Warner of Balmaclellan, G. R.
Adam Kay of Borgue,
John Semple of Carsfairn,
John Macmichan of Dalry,
John Cant of Kells, R.
John Duncan of Rerick and Lundrennan,
John Wilkie of Twynam,
Adam Alison of Balmaghie,
John Mean of Anwoth,

OF THE CHURCH OF SCOTLAND.

I know not how many miles, with their numerous and small families, many of them scarce knew whither. But the Lord wonderfully provided for them and theirs, to their own confirmation and wonder. And should I set down here 1663.

James Fergusson of Keltoun,
James Bugloss of Corsmichael,
William Erskine of Girton, R.
Thomas Thomson of Partan,
Samuel Arnot of Tongland,
Robert Fergusson of Buttle.
  2. *Presbytery of Wigton.*
Messrs. Archibald Hamilton of Wigton, R.
George Waugh of Kirkinder, R.
Alexander Ross of Kirkowan,
William Maitland of Whithorn.
Alexander Fergusson of Mochrum,
William Maxwell of Monygaff,
Patrick Peacock of Kirkmabrick, R.
  One list adds,
Robert Ritchie of Sorbie.
  3. *Presbytery of Stranraer.*
Messrs. James Lawrie of Stonykirk, R.
John Park of Stranraer,
James Bell of Kirkcolm, R.
Thomas Kennedy of Kirkmaiden, R.
Another list makes this Lisward.
John Macbroom of Portpatrick,
James Wilson of Inch,
Another list makes it Kirkmaiden.
Alexander Peden of New Glenluce.
One list adds John Dick.
  V. SYNOD OF GLASGOW AND AYR.
  1. *Presbytery of Ayr.*
Messrs. William Eccles of Ayr, G. R.
William Adair of Ayr, C.
Anthony Shaw of Colmanel, G.
Gilbert Kennedy of Girvan, G.
John Osburn of Kirkoswald, G.
John Hutchison of Maybole, G. R.
Fergus M'Alexander of Kirkdoming or Bar, G. R.
John Ross of Culton, G.
Hugh Crawford of New Cumnock, G. R.
Hugh Campbell of Muirkirk, G. R.
Andrew Dalrymple of Auchinleck, G.
John Guthrie of Tarbolton, G.
David Brown of Craigie, G.
Hugh Campbell of Riccarton, G. R.
James Inglis of Dallie, C.
William Cockburn of Kirkmichael, C.
William Fullarton of St. Quivox, C.
Robert Maxwell of Monkton, C.
John Gembil of Symmington, C. R.
Gabriel Maxwell of Dundonald, C.
John Cunningham of Cumnock, C.
Alexander Stevenson of Dalmellington, C. R.
Alexander Blair of Galston, P.
James Veitch of Mauchline, P. R.
John Campbell of Sorn,
Robert Miller of Ochiltree.
In lists of this presbytery I find named as nonconformists,
Messrs. John Reid of Muirkirk,
John Blair of New Kirk, Mauchlin,
Hugh Black,
Robert Ritchison,
Andrew Miller of Dallie.
  Conformists.
Messrs. Robert Wallace of Barnwell,
David M'Queen of Straiton, of Balentree.
  2. *Presbytery of Irvine.*
Messrs. John Nevoy of Newmills or Loudon, P.
Matthew Mowat of Kilmarnock, P.

James Rowat of Kilmarnock, P. R.
George Ramsay of Kilmaurs, G.
John Spaldy of Dreghorn, G. R.
John Wallace of Largs, G. R.
Andrew Hutchison of Stewarton, G.
William Castlelaw of Stewarton, C.
James Fergusson of Kilwinning, C.
Alexander Nisbet of Irvine, C.
John Grant of Irvine, G.
William Guthrie of Fenwick, S.
Gabriel Cunningham of Dunlop, R.
William Russel of Kilbirnie,
Robert Bell of Dalry,
John Bell elder of Stevenson,
John Bell younger of Ardrossan, R.
William Cunningham of Kilbride,
Patrick Colvil of Beith,
Robert Aird of Combray.
In some lists I find Mr. Thomas Boyd mentioned in this presbytery.
  3. *Presbytery of Paisley.*
Messrs. Alexander Dunlop of Paisley, P. outed by a particular act.
John Drysdale of Paisley, P. by a particular act.
James Stirling of Paisley, G.
John Stirling of Kilbarchan,
Patrick Simpson of Renfrew, G. R.
Hugh Smith of Eastwood, G.
William Thomson of Mearns.
William Thomson of Houston, G.
James Hutchison of Kilallan, R.
James Alexander of Kilmacolm, C. G.
Hugh Peebles of Lochgunnoch, G. R.
James Wallace of Inchinnan, C. R.
William Houston of Erskine, G.
Hugh Walker of Nelston, G.
John Hamilton of Innerkip.
I hear he conformed after.
  Conformed.
Mr. James Taylor of Greenock.
  4. *Presbytery of Hamilton.*
Messrs. James Nasmith of Hamilton, P.
John Inglis of Hamilton, G. R.
James Hamilton of Blantyre,
Robert Fleming of Cambuslang, R.
John Burnet of Kilbride,
William Hansilton of Glassford, C.
John Oliphant of Stonehouse, R.
James Currie of Shotts,
Ludowick Somerwel of New Monkland,
Hugh Weir of Old Monkland,
Matthew Mackail of Bothwell, C.
John Lauder of Dalziel, R.
Hugh Archibald of Strathaven.
  Conformed.
Mr. James Hamilton of Cambusnethan.
  5. *Presbytery of Lanark.*
Messrs. William Jack of Carluke, G.
William Brown of Carnwath, G.
William Somerwel of Pitenen, G.
John Hamilton of Carmichael, G.
Nicholas Blackie of Roberton, G. R.
Peter Kid of Douglas, G.
Gilbert Hamilton of Crawford or Crawfordmuir, G.
William Somerwel of Crawfordjohn, C.
Robert Lockhart of Dunsyre, C.
Robert Birnie of Lanark,
John Lindsay of Carstairs,

1663. many accounts I have from very good hands, of the remarkable interpositions of kind providence in their straits, they might tend to the conviction of unbelievers: but they are too many to come in here, some of them will fall in afterwards.

William Morton of Wiston,
Thomas Lawrie of Lesmahago.
  6. *Presbytery of Glasgow.*
Messrs. Patrick Gillespie, principal of the College of Glasgow, P.
Robert Macwaird of Glasgow, banished, and died in Holland,
John Dickson of Rutherglen, P. R.
John Carstairs of Glasgow, P.
Donald Cargil of Barony, P.
Ralph Rogers of Glasgow, G. R.
Alexander Jamison of Govan, G.
James Blair of Cathcart, G.
Agdrew Morton of Carmunnock, G. R.
James Hamilton of Eaglesham, C.
Thomas Melville of Calder, G.
John Law of Campsie, G R.
Henry Forsyth of Kirkintilloch,
Thomas Stuart of Cumbernauld or Easter Lenzie.
  Conformed.
Messrs. Hugh Blair of Glasgow,
John Young of Glasgow,
Gabriel Cunningham of Kilsyth or Monieburgh.
  7. *Presbytery of Dumbarton.*
Messrs. James Walkinshaw of Badernock, G.
Adam Gottie of Rosneath, G.
Robert Mitchell of Luss, G.
Robert Law of New or Wester Kilpatrick, G.
Matthew Ramsay of Old or Wester Kilpatrick, C.
David Elphinstone of Dumbarton, C.
Mr. James Glendonyng is added to this presbytery in some lists.
  Conformed.
Messrs. Allan Fergusson of Drimmen,
John Stuart,
James Craig of Killearn,
William Stirling of Baltron,
Robert Watson of Cardross,
Thomas Mitchel.
  VI. SYNOD OF ARGYLE.
  1. *Presbytery of Dunoon.*
Messrs. John Cameron of Kilfynan,
Hugh Cameron,
Archibald Maclean of Killen, R.
  Other lists add to this presbytery,
Messrs. Donald Morrison,
Neil Cameron.
  Conformed.
Mr. Colin M'Lauchlan.
  2. *Presbytery of Kintyre or Campbelton.*
Messrs. Edward Keith of Lochead,
John Cunison of Kilbride in Arran, R.
James Gardiner of Caddel, P.
David Simpson of Southrud,
Dugald Darroch.
  3. *Presbytery of Inverary.*
Messrs. Alexander Gordon of Inverary, P. R.
Archibald M'Callum,
Patrick Campbell of Inverary, R.
John Duncanson, R.
Dugald Campbell of Knapdale North,
Duncan Campbell of Knapdale South, R.
Robert Duncanson of Dalawich, R.
Andrew Maclean.
  Conformed.
Mr. John Lindsay.

  4. *Presbytery of Lorn or Kilimore.*
All conformed, as far as I find.
  5. *Presbytery of Sky.*
All Conformed.
  VII. SYNOD OF PERTH AND STIRLING.
  1. *Presbytery of Dunkeld.*
Messrs. Robert Campbell,
Thomas Lundy,
Patrick Campbell of Kilinnie,
John Anderson of Auchtergavan,
James Strachan,
John Murray.
  Another list adds,
Messrs. Thomas Glass of Little Dunkeld,
Robert Campbell of Moulin.
  2. *Presbytery of Perth.*
Messrs. Alexander Pitcairn of Dron, P. R.
David Orum or Orme of Forgondenny,
George Halyburton, younger of Duplin,
John Crookshanks of Rogerton, slain at Pentland,
Robert Young.
  3. *Presbytery of Dunblane.*
Messrs. Andrew Rind,
John Forrest, younger.
  4. *Presbytery of Stirling.*
Messrs. James Guthrie of Stirling, executed 1661.
Robert Rule of Stirling, R.
James Simpson of Airth, P.
Thomas Hogg of Lorbert and Dunipace,
John Blair of Bothkenner,
Richard Howieson of Alva, R.
  5. *Presbytery of Auchterarder.*
Mr. George Murray.
  VIII. SYNOD OF FIFE.
  1. *Presbytery of Dunfermline.*
Messrs. William Oliphant of Dunfermline, G
Andrew Donaldson of Dalgety, C. R.
George Belfrage of Carnock, C.
Robert Edmonston of Culross,
John Gray of Orwell, R.
Matthew Fleming of Culross, C.
  Conformists.
Messrs. Robert Binnie of Aberdour,
Walter Bruce of Inverkeithing,
James Sibbald of Torriburn,
Robert Rae of Dunfermline,
John Anderson of Saline,
Henry Smith of Beath,
James Haxton of Cleish,
George Loudon.
  2. *Presbytery of Kirkcaldy.*
Messrs. Alexander Moncrief of Scoonie, P. R.
Patrick Weems of Abbotshall, G.
George Nairn of Burntisland, G.
James Simpson of Kirkaldy, C.
Thomas Melvile of Kingcassie, C.
Thomas Black of Lesley, C.
James Wilson,
Mr. Frederick Carmichael of Markinch is added in one list.
John Chalmers added in one list.
  Conformists.
Messrs. Kenneth Logie of Kirkcaldy,
Robert Honnyman of Dysart,
Henry Wilkie of Weems,
Robert Mercer of Kennoway,
George Ogilvie of Portmoak,

All this was for no other fault in them, save a firmness to their known and professed principles. They are deprived of their ministry, which of all things on earth was dearest to them, without ever being summoned, called, or heard; no libel was given them, neither were they ever heard upon the reasons of their nonconformity. This severe procedure with so many excellent men was the foundation of many of

1663.

Andrew Walker of Auchtertule,
William Lindsay of Auchterderren,
Robert Bruce of Ballingrie,
John Ramsay of Scoonie.
    3. *Presbytery of Cupar.*
Messrs. John Macgill of Cupar, G.
Thomas Arnot of Cupar, G.
James Wedderburn of Monzie, G.
George Thomson of Kilmonie, G.
William Tullidaff of Dunboig, G. R.
John Alexander of Creich, G.
George Dishingtoun of Cults, G.
Walter Greg of Balmerinoch, C.
William Row of Ceres.
    Conformists.
Messrs. William Livingstone of Falkland,
John Ramsay of Kettle,
David Orme of Monnymeal,
Alexander Balfour of Abdie,
Lawrence Oliphant of Newburgh,
John Ridge of Strathmiglo,
James Martin of Auchtermuchty,
David Rait of Darsie,
William Myles of Flisk,
John Littlejohn of Collesy,
Henry Pitcairn of Logie.
    4. *Presbytery of St. Andrews.*
Messrs. Samuel Rutherford of St. Andrews,
Robert Blair of St. Andrews, P.
James Wood of St. Andrews, P. Provost of the Old College,
George Hamilton of Pittenween, G.
George Hamilton, younger of Newburn, G. R.
Robert Weems of Ely, G.
Alexander Wilson of Cameron, G. R.
John Wardlaw of Kemback, G.
William Violant of Ferrypartoncraigs, G. R.
David Forret of Kilconquhar, C.
James Macgill of Largo, C. R.
David Guthrie of Anstruther Wester, C.
Colin Anderson of Anstruther Easter, C.
Robert Bennet of Kilreny, C.
Henry Rymer of Carnbee, C. R.
Alexander Wedderburn of Forgon, C.
Robert Wilkie of St. Monans, C.
    Another list adds in this presbytery,
Messrs. William Campbell,
James Bruce.
    Conformists.
Messrs. James Sharp, Professor of Divinity, P.
Andrew Honnyman of St. Andrews,
Walter Comry of St. Leonards,
Alexander Udwar of Crail,
    Middleton of Leuchars.

    IX. SYNOD OF ANGUS AND MEARNS.
    1. *Presbytery of Meigle.*
Mr. John Robertson.
    2. *Presbytery of Forfar.*
Mr. Alexander Robertson.
    3. *Presbytery of Dundee.*
Messrs. John Minniman of Aberynte,
John Semple,
Andrew Wedderburn of Liste,
John Campbell of Tilen.

    4. *Presbytery of Aberbrothock.*
Mr. Andrew Spence. In several lists he is put in Brechin.
In one list James Fithie in Brechin.
    5. *Presbytery of Brechin.*
All conformed.
    6. *Presbytery of Mearns or Fordon.*
Mr. David Campbell of St. Cires.
    X. SYNOD OF ABERDEEN.
    1. *Presbytery of Aberdeen.*
Messrs. Andrew Cant, elder, of Aberdeen,
John Mercer of Kinneller,
    Mitchel in another list.
    2. *Presbytery of Kincardine.*
Messrs. Alexander Cant,
William Alexander,
John Young.
    3. *Presbytery of Alford.*
All conformed.
    4. *Presbytery of Garioch.*
Mr. George Telfer.
    5. *Presbytery of Ellon.*
All conformed.
    6. *Presbytery of Deer.*
Messrs. Robert Keith,
Nathanael Martin,
Duncan Forbes,
Alexander Irvine,
William Scot,
William Ramsay,
John Stuart.
    7. *Presbytery of Turreff.*
Mr. Arthur Mitchel.
    8. *Presbytery of Fordyce.*
All conformed.

    XI. SYNOD OF MURRAY.
    1. *Presbytery of Strathbogie or Keith.*
Mr. George Meldrum of Glass, R.
    2. *Presbytery of Abernethy.*
All conformed.
    3. *Presbytery of Elgin.*
Messrs. James Park,
Thomas Urquhart,
    4. *Presbytery of Forres.*
Mr. James Urquhart of Kinloss.
    5. *Presbytery of Inverness.*
Mr. Alexander Frazer of Daviot, R.
    XII. SYNOD OF ROSS AND SUTHERLAND.
    1. *Presbytery of Chanonrie.*
Messrs. Hugh Anderson of Cromarty, R.
John M'Culloch of Ardersier, R.
    2. *Presbytery of Dingwall.*
Messrs. Thomas Hogg of Kiltearn,
John Mackilligen of Alves,
Thomas Ross.
    3. *Presbytery of Tain.*
Mr. Andrew Ross.

    XIII. SYNOD OF CAITHNESS.
    1. *Presbytery of Dornoch.*
Mr. John M'Culloch.
    2. *Presbytery of Kirkwall.*
Messrs. Alexander Lennox of Kirkwall,
Arthur Murray.
One list adds Hugh Sinclair.

1663. the distractions and troubles, until the happy revolution. In the north parts of Scotland, many places of the Highlands and Isles, a good many ministers conformed; so that this stroke lay heaviest where people had most of the gospel and knowledge of real religion, which made it the worse to bear. And it was the more distressing to the people, that their ministers suffered so hard things, merely for their adhering to the doctrine, worship, discipline, and government, of this reformed church, and the covenants which they themselves had sworn solemnly, and often renewed.

I find those worthy ministers blamed for leaving their congregations so easily, and going out at the first publication of the council's pleasure. At this distance I reckon the most part of my readers must be very much unacquainted with circumstances of this hour and power of darkness, and wonder why so many excellent persons, in good terms with their God, their conscience, and their people, did so easily part with their charges. Therefore, besides what I have already given from Mr. Robert Douglas upon this head, I think it not improper to give the reader a taste of the circumstances things stood in at this time, and leave him to form a more favourable judgment of the conduct of so many presbyterian ministers, than some have done.

Preaching after the first of November last was declared a seditious conventicle, and some forbore to hear the presbyterian ministers who continued to preach, notwithstanding of the act of Glasgow; so fickle and uncertain are the sentiments of a multitude, that some were ready even to have jealoused (suspected) the ministers, had they continued at their posts, as secretly in collusion with the bishops, as afterwards did appear in the reproaches cast on some this way. Upon the other hand, the most solid and judicious, and far greater part of their people, encouraged ministers at this time to enter upon suffering: so far were they from censuring them for quitting their charges, that they rejoiced in their honesty and firmness to the principles and covenants of this church. None of the ministers questioned the magistrate's power over their persons and families, or that upon just grounds, which indeed were not in this case, he might banish and confine them, as well as imprison or put them to death. And to be sure it was impossible for them to maintain themselves against the persecuting state in the issue; and the benefit arising to their flock by continuing at their work a few Sabbaths, till force should be employed to dispossess them, they were of opinion would never have balanced the penalties of the acts, a minister's ruin, and at best his banishment.

Further, they had the example of multitudes of worthy ministers in neighbouring churches, to lead them into the method they took. In England presbyterian ministers took this same course, when absolutely discharged the exercise of their ministry; whereas here, this was only done by consequence. And if we may reason from events, and the issue of this their practice, it is plain, that if the ministers had continued at their work publicly, until they had been gradually turned out one by one in a way of violence, which was bishop Sharp's scheme, and their room had been still filled up as the prelates had leisure, the change had neither been so sensible and affecting as it was to many, nor the opposition to bishops by far so considerable as it came to be. But now this uniform course so many ministers jointly fell into, was the first and a very remarkable and clear stand against prelacy, a fair testimony against this horrid invasion made upon the church, and did mightily alienate the nation from the bishops. Indeed this wound, made by such a general act of passive obedience, and cheerful suffering, was what the bishops could never heal in the west and south of Scotland. Let me only add, that as the violence of the time was such as they had no probable prospect of standing out against it, so the ministers judged it would be more for the interest of their people, to be left in some measure to be useful now and then to them privately, in visiting, conversing, and preaching, than that, by absolute disobedience to the acts, they should be entirely deprived of them.

The reader will easily perceive, that the

circumstances of conscientious presbyterians were most deplorable, by the ejecting of so many worthy ministers. Last winter and this spring were the heaviest, presbyterians, that is, the bulk and body of the people in Scotland of the greatest piety and probity, ever saw. Parish churches, generally speaking, through the western and southern shires, were now waste and without sermon, which had not happened in Scotland since the reformation from popery; and the brighter and sweeter the light had been formerly, the blacker and more intolerable was this sudden and general darkness. The common people now had leisure, as well as ground enough, to heighten their former aversion at the bishops the authors of all this calamity. In many places they had twenty miles to run before they heard a sermon, or got the spiritual manna, which of late fell so thick about their tents. Some went to the elder ministers, not directly touched by the act of Glasgow. Such who could not reach them, frequented the family worship and exercises of the younger ministers, now outed of their churches. And so great were the numbers who came to their houses, that some were constrained to preach without doors, and at length to go to the open fields. This was the original of field meetings in Scotland, which afterwards made so much noise, and in some few years was made death by law, first to the minister, and then to the hearers.

At this time began the barbarous and unchristian abuses, committed upon the Lord's holy day by the rude soldiers, which shall be afterwards noticed. When people flocked to the churches of the few remaining presbyterian ministers, parties of armed men went up and down upon the Sabbath, to exact the fine imposed upon such as did not keep their own parish church, by the proclamation, December 23d last: this, we shall find, turned frequent in a little time; and upon the road, and at the churches of the old presbyterian ministers, they plundered and abused such as would not presently swear they were parishioners in that place.

As the presbyterians in Scotland suffered in a most sensible part, by the loss of their own dear pastors, who had been so useful among them; so they reckoned themselves in some sort yet more oppressed by thrusting in upon them a company of men, who were not only useless, but hurtful unto them, and really the authors of most of the harassings and persecution of the common people to be narrated. Those underlings of the bishops were called by the country people curates, a name rather odious than proper; for the most part of them were both unfit for, and very much neglected the cure of souls. The prelates, strictly speaking, were *sine-cures,* and few or none of them preached, save at extraordinary occasions. Those substitutes of theirs were set to the care and cure of souls; but as their care was about the fleece, so they rent and wounded the sheep and lambs, instead of curing them.

1663.

That the reader may have some view of the manner of their coming in at this time, and somewhat of their character; he would remember that the bishops' diocesan meetings last year were very ill kept; in some places there were not so many ministers came as there had been presbyteries in the diocese, and I find it observed, that some prelates had none at all. Wherefore this winter and spring, the bishops were busied in levying a crew of those curates to fill up the now multitudes of vacant parishes. They were mostly young men from the northern shires, raw, and without any stock of reading or gifts: these were brought west, in a year or two after they had gone through their philosophy in the college, and having nothing to subsist upon, were greedily gaping after benefices. To such the common people were ready to ascribe all the characters of Jeroboam's priests; and it must be owned great numbers of them were as void of morality and gravity, as they were of learning and experience, and scarce had the very appearance of religion and devotion. They came into parishes, much with the same views a herd hath when he contracts to feed cattle; and such a plenty of them came from the north at this time, that it is said a gentleman of that country cursed the presbyterian ministers heartily; for, said he, " since they have been turned out, we cannot have a lad to keep our cows." Those,

1663. with some few elder expectants, who, by reason of their scandal and insufficiency, could have no encouragement. under presbytery, were the persons forced in upon people in room of the outed ministers In many places the patrons, some from principle, and others because they were under a necessity to please the bishop in their nomination, refused to present; so the right of presentation devolved into the bishops' hands. Indeed the whole of the curates were of the prelates' choice; and perhaps it may a little excuse them, that really they had no better, among such as would subject to them, to fix upon.

Certainly this was a very ruining step to the interests of prelacy in Scotland; and some, when too late, saw so much. I know some of that persuasion do endeavour to reproach presbyterians after the revolution, for taking the same false step; but their information, to say no more, is ill. If any insufficient ministers have been at any time brought in by presbyterians to congregations, I shall blame it in them as well as the other side; and more, because they in other things are agreeable to the Divine institution, and ought not to take the liberty others do: but that I may set this matter in its due light, presbyterian ministers at the revolution, wished they had found more labourers at first to send into the Lord's vineyard; and yet they had a considerable number of godly and learned youths, very ripe for the holy ministry. I shall not say, but in the morning of the church's recovery, some few here and there, who had not that time they would have desired for study, were put to work in the Lord's vineyard: but then accurate care was taken, that any insuperable defects this way should be supplied by a shining piety, seriousness, and diligence. And whatever outcry some of the episcopal party make as to the hasty filling of churches after the revolution, presbyterians are willing a parallel be drawn betwixt the entrants to the holy ministry after the (year) 1688, and those after the (year) 1661, and are no way afraid of the issue.

Indeed there was never a more melancholy change made in a church, than when presbyterian ministers were thus turned out, and the bishops with their curates came in. This will be more than evident, if we consider the state of the church of Scotland in the preceding years, and compare it a little with the lamentable circumstances it is now falling into. Before the reintroduction of prelacy last year, every parish in Scotland had a minister, every village a school, every family, and in most places each person, had a Bible; the children were all taught to read, and furnished with the Holy Scriptures, either at their parents' or the parish charge: every minister professed and obliged himself to adhere to the protestant reformed religion, and owned the Westminster Confession, framed by the divines of both nations, and were regulate by our excellent acts of assemblies. Most part of ministers did preach thrice a week, and lecture once, to say nothing of catechising, and other pastoral duties, wherein they abounded according to the proportion of their ability and faithfulness. None of them were scandalous, insufficient, or negligent, as far as could be noticed, while presbyteries continued in their power. A minister could not be easy himself without some seals of his ministry, and evidences of the Divine approbation in the souls of his people, of which there were in that period not a few. One might have lived a good while in many congregations, and rode through much of Scotland, without hearing an oath. You could scarce have lodged in a house where God was not worshipped, by singing, reading the word, and prayer; and the public houses were ready to complain their trade was broke, every body now was become so sober.

As soon as the prelates and their curates were thrust in, one would have met with the plain reverse of all this, which was the heavier, that it resembled king Saul's change, a bad spirit after a good. Some two years ago there was scarce a minister or expectant in this church, but professed himself a covenanted presbyterian; and so the bishops and curates in the eye of the common people came in with perjury, written in their foreheads, where holiness to the Lord should have been; and one need not wonder at the opposition made to them.

When the curates entered their pulpits, it

CHAP. IV.] OF THE CHURCH OF SCOTLAND. 333

was by an order from the bishop, without any call from, yea contrary to the inclinations of the people. Their personal character was black, and no wonder their entertainment, was coarse and cold. In some places they were welcomed with tears in abundance, and entreaties to be gone: in others with reasonings and arguments, which confounded them; and some entertained them with threats, affronts, and indignities, too many here to be repeated. The bell's tongue in some places was stolen away, that the parishioners might have an excuse for not coming to church. The doors of the church in other places were barricaded, and they made to enter by the window literally. The laxer of the gentry easily engaged to join in their drinking cabals, which with all iniquity did now fearfully abound, and sadly exposed them: and in some places the people, fretted with the dismal change, gathered together, and violently opposed their settlement, and received them with showers of stones. This was not indeed the practice of the religious and more judicious; such irregularities were committed by the more ignorant vulgar, yet they were so many evidences of the regard they were like to have from the body of their parishioners. Such who were really serious mourned in secret, as doves in the valleys, and from a principle could never countenance them, and others dealt with them as hath been said.

This opposition to the settlement of the curates, occasioned severe inquiries and prosecutions before the council; and we shall meet with instances of it just now from Irongray and Kirkcudbright this year, and more instances will offer from many other parishes of the kingdom. The punishment became very severe, banishment to America, cruel scourgings, and heavy finings. Thus the effects of forcing the curates in upon congregations were confusion, and every evil work, and the first fruit of the prelates' ministers was the scattering of their congregations.

Towards the beginning of this year I am now upon, that question sprang up among the people, which was the occasion of so much hot persecution afterwards, " Whether they might hear the curates?" They were looked upon as coming in over the belly of solemn oaths and covenants 1663. the kingdom was under to the Lord; and the people did not find their conscience relieved from these by the act of parliament introducing prelacy; and it is not much to be wondered at, that there were scruples to hear men put into pulpits by military force, and kept in by so many banishments, fines, and so much cruelty.

The longer they continued, and the better they were known, the more they were loathed for their dreadful immoralities. If that party were to be dealt with in their own coin, a black list might be given of scandals, unheard of except among popes and Romish priests, about this time breaking out among them: but I do not love to rake into this unpleasant subject. Some of them, alas too many, were heard swearing very rudely in the open streets. And this was but of a piece with the doctrine taught in their pulpits, that to swear by faith, conscience, and the like, were innocent ways of speaking. And they used to adduce bishop Andrews, as of those sentiments. Instances were sadly common of their staggering in the streets, and wallowing in the gutters, even in their canonical habits; and this needs be no surprise, when many were witnesses to bishop Wishart's preaching publicly, that he was not to be reckoned a drunkard, who was now and then overtaken with wine or strong liquor, but he only who made a trade of following after strong drink. If I should speak of the uncleanness and vile practices of Mr. Bruce, curate at Balmerino, bishop Sharp's chaplain; Chisholm of Lilliesleaf, Mr. John Paterson, afterwards bishop, who was chastised by the reformed bishop; Mr. Keith in Ginglekirk, Mr. Thomas Hamilton at Carnwath; the accounts would stun the reader, and offend modest ears. Mr. Archibald Beith curate in Arran, of whom we shall hear afterwards, and one Duncan near Perth, were processed, and the last executed for murder. Mr. Edward Thomson at Anstruther, and Mr. Gideon Penman at Creighton, were charged with crimes yet of a higher nature. The first made a terrible exit, either by his own hands or the devil's; and the last, though

1663. delated by many confessing witches, escaped what he deserved.* I find all those taken notice of, as things notourly known in this period I am describing, in the papers of a worthy minister; and multitudes might be added; but indeed this is

---

* " Mr. Edward Thomson, curate of Anstrudder, was the son of a godly father, a minister, who bred his son in the knowledge of the truth and profession of godliness; and when the honest father died, he straitly charged this his son to follow his father's way, and in any case to beware of conforming to the course of the bishops. This course he follows for some time, but wearying of the purity of the presbyterian nonconformists, he went to one of their mock presbyteries, and there entered upon his tryals. The report went that, when he was upon his tryals his father appeared to him, and threatened him for engaging in such a course, whereupon he desisted for some time, but the same tentation returning, he once more engaged with the bishops, entered upon his tryals, and, having passed, settled at Anstrudder. He had while he was there wife and children; afterwards, being a widow, he continued in his ministry, but at length became very sad and heavy. Ane Saturday at night he went to make a visit, and stayed out very late, and as he returned homeward the wench that bare his lanthorn, as they passed a bridge, affirmed the bridge shoke, also that she saw something like a black beast pass the bridge before him. This made some suspect he meddled with the devil, and he was known to have a brother that was a diabolick man. However, home he came very late, and after he had lyen a while in bed, rose early upon Sabbath morning and threw himself into the river, when he was taken up dead, to the great astonishment of his poor neighbours.

" Mr. Gideon Penman, curat at Creighton, was well known to be a witch. Divers eye-witnesses deponed they had many times seen him at the witches' meetings, and that the devil called him ordinarily, ' Penman, my chaplain.' Also, upon a time when Satan administered his communion to his congregation, Penman sat next the devil's elbow, and that when their deacon had served the table with wafers in the popish fashion, when there remained two wafers more than served the company, the deacon laid down his two wafers before the devil, which two the devil gave to Penman, and bade him goe carrie these to the papists in Winton. But he escaped without punishment."—Kirkton's History of the Church of Scotland, pp. 188—191.

" Eight or ten witches, all (except one or two) poor miserable like women, were pannelled, some of them were brought out of Sir Robert Keith's lands, others out of Ormiston, Creighton, and Pencaithland parishes. The first of them were delated by these two who were burnt in Salt Preston, in May, 1678, and they divulged and named the rest, as also put forth seven in the Lonehead of Lasswade; and if they had been permitted, were ready to file by their delation sundry gentlewomen and others of fashion, but the justices discharged them, thinking it either the product of malice, or melancholy, or the devil's deception in representing such persons as present at their *field meetings*, who truly were not there. However, they were permitted to name Mr. Gideon Penman, who had been minister at Creighton, and for sundry acts of uncleanness and other crimes was deprived. Two or three of the witches constantly affirmed that he was present at their meetings with the devil, and then when the devil called for him, he asked, ' Where is Mr. Gideon, my chaplain?' and that ordinarily Mr. Gideon was in the rear of all their dances, and beat up these that were slow. He denied all, and was liberate on caution."—Fountainhall's Decisions, p. 14.

Such is the testimony of a divine of great celebrity, and of the highest civil tribunal in the nation, by which our historian is borne out in his statement on this subject, a statement which to many modern readers will be, we have no doubt, sufficiently repulsive, though it is in perfect unison with the belief of the best and the wisest statesmen and lawyers, as well as divines, of that day, which we could demonstrate by an array of quotations larger than the volume we are attempting to illustrate. The belief of such things may be safely stated to have been at that period nearly universal, and it was certainly carried to an extent warranted neither by reason nor revelation. At the same time, we hesitate not to affirm, that no man who believes the Bible to be a book divinely inspired, can possibly doubt of a connexion and an intercourse between the material and the spiritual worlds much more extensive and more frequent than the philosophy of the present day will admit, nor, after all the attempts that, by translation, modification, and explanation have been made to change the meaning of the words, that by witchcraft, sorcery, enchantments, &c. &c.—attempts of a highly criminal character, have been made to command that intercourse, though he may be just as little able to comprehend the modus or manner of these attempts as that of many other crimes, which, though unknown among Christians, if any credit be due to classic moralists, were common in the heathen world. In that code of jurisprudence given by God himself to the children of Israel, we find these things made the subjects of special and particular statutes; and, in the succeeding history of that people, we find them charged upon individuals as particular and special crimes, on account of which they were visited with most signal judgments, so that there is no alternative but either to believe them, or so far to reject the authority of the Scriptures.

We hope that no one from this will rashly or uncandidly suppose that we mean to demand, or that we say the Scriptures demand, his assent to that growing but shapeless mass of absurdity and fable, the monstrous spawn of imposture and guilty fear, which tradition, the easy handmaiden of credulity, is perpetually busied in rolling along from one generation to another; and because the magicians of Egypt cast down their rods, beside that of Moses before Pharaoh, and they became serpents, or because, along with that wonder-working prophet, they were instrumental in turning the waters of their country into blood, and in bringing up upon it the plague of frogs, he is to believe that, by the assistance of the devil, any decrepit, or envious, or avaricious old woman in his neighbourhood can transform herself into a hare or

a subject I do not love to enlarge upon. Those and many other things gave ground to people, to form a very black idea of those persons now thrust in upon this church. And if all be true which at this time was believed of Primate Sharp, one needs not wonder such persons were brought in, and overlooked notwithstanding of their prodigious wickedness. Indeed though the curates had been freer than they were of those gross immoralities, they had work upon their hand, ready enough of itself to give people bad impressions of them. They were to subdue the people of Scotland to the hated bishops, yea, to persuade them to alter their religion and principles in some measure. The way of their coming in, and this carriage when in, helped the odium forward.

When a presbyterian minister came in by the hearty choice of the people, and recommended himself by faithfulness and painfulness in his Master's work, and a humble dependance upon the Lord, there was no need of soldiers to force people to him; hearers came unconstrained: but the curates

---

a cat; sail the seas in a sieve or an eggshell; transport herself through the air upon a broom; collect at her pleasure, and by invisible means, all the milk in her neighbourhood; or, by a few knotted straws, and a misshapen image of clay stuck full of pins, destroy his cattle and himself. No. The very reverse of this is the fact. The Bible utterly forbids any such ascription of power to human beings, and all communication with such as pretend to it, further than to punish them as transgressors of the positive statutes of Jehovah, impious intermeddlers with his peculiar prerogatives, and at least the intentional murderers of their fellow men.—While it every where proceeds upon the assumed fact, that there are rulers of the darkness of this world, spiritual wickednesses in high places, with whom the Christian, though he would, cannot avoid a perpetual warfare, it forbids any external acknowledgment of them, either in themselves or their pretended agents, otherwise than, in continual dependance upon Divine providence in the use of all appointed means of grace, to guard against being by them inwardly seduced from that reposing of the soul upon its Creator and Redeemer, in which the essence of religion consists, and from those acts of humble and holy obedience by which it is especially manifested. The observing of times or days, as fortunate or unfortunate, of circumstances, as lucky or unlucky—all attempts at divination, though it should be by the Bible itself—all rejecting or using of meats and drinks for occult purposes, are by the Bible declared to be doctrines of devils, and all who practise them must be, by the enlightened reader of that book, regarded as so far worshippers of devils.—*Ed.*

were settled by the secular arm, compulsion and violence; and the wonder must be the less that their doctrine was unacceptable, and themselves loathed. The apostle of the Gentiles recommended himself to the consciences of those he dealt with, " by pureness, by knowledge, by longsuffering, by kindness, by the Holy Ghost, by love unfeigned, by the word of truth, by the power of God, by the armour of righteousness." Now another course must be taken, since those things were not to be found. The curates were commended " by fines imprisonments, banishments, relegation and selling for slaves, scourging, stigmatizing, and bloody executions."

1663.

Most part of presbyterians did agree in the conclusion and practice of forbearing to hear the curates, when they were thus forced in upon this church; but the grounds they went upon were very different, as may be seen in the papers upon this head, both in print and writ, which were pretty throng at this time and afterwards. There were some who thought the curates' ministry null and illegal, because their authors, the bishops, ordination was void, inasmuch as they were fallen from their office, by open violation of their own and the land's solemn covenant, nullified their former regular and scriptural ordination by re-ordination, and now derived any power they claimed from the supremacy entirely. Many thought the curates had no relation to the congregations where they entered, and upon that score refused to join in with them, without dipping into the validity of their ministerial actings: and indeed it is undeniable, they came in by force almost every where, and not only without the invitation, but against the inclination of the people; and refusing to hear them for a while, was the only testimony the most sober and judicious had to give against this unaccountable intrusion; and, one would think, a very modest and proper testimony. Some could not hear, because they observed the bulk of them so immoral and profane, that they were ashamed to haunt their company, much less could they own them as their ministers; and those who were smooth and blameless, which was the case of a few in more eminent posts, many of these were

1663. erroneous in their principles, and their doctrine pelagian, and very much tending to popery. All of them were settled among them by bishops, by virtue of the king's absolute supremacy ecclesiastical; and it was what stuck much with a good many that by joining with, and subjecting to their ministry, they concurred all they could in their private capacity, in owning that iniquitous and burdensome imposition. In short, the generality did reckon themselves, bound by the oath of God's covenant, against prelates, and their underlings: and since both were obtruded upon them by an oppression in their civil liberties and reformation rights, they could not prevail with themselves actively to concur in the deformation now established, or by countenancing it, to bind it down upon themselves and their posterity. And lastly, a good many forbear hearing, because it was offensive and stumbling to many serious and religious people.

Those things prevailed with the generality, at this time, to refuse to countenance the curates. Indeed some now, but especially many years after this, when the whole presbyterian ministers were silenced and banished, and they had no other way of public worshipping of God, and not daring to call entirely in question the validity of their mission, and having no sinful terms of holding communion, as they thought, imposed upon them, did hear, especially a little before the liberty, when circumstances were not a little altered from what they were at this time I am upon. And such as withdrew now, alleged many things in their own vindication, which I shall not here enter into the detail of. They advanced instances in other churches; the practice of the Christians in Chrysostom's case, when, by the emperor unjustly turned out of his charge, his people would not subject to such who came in his room; the practice of many worthy persons in Holland, when several worthy ministers there were turned out by the Barnavest faction, and Arminians put in their place, they would neither hear nor submit to their ministry, but went and joined in word and sacraments with the Calvinist ministers remaining among them. Further they alleged, that Scripture, primitive practice, and the method of this church of Scotland since the Reformation, gave them ground to withdraw from such who were settled in congregations, not only *renitente*, but even *contradicente ecclesia:* and they declared, that in such cases they could never see where the pastoral tie, and ministerial obligation was bottomed; and in some of those reasonings they brought the judgment of some of the best writers in the English church itself to support them.

Those reasonings I only relate as a historian: the consequence of so many gravelling scruples, and the nonconformity which followed upon them, was first empty churches. The ministers forced in upon the west and south, in several places, for some time had bare walls, and nobody to preach unto; and many had scarce twenty or thirty hearers; yea, in very numerous congregations not above fifty. And in the next place, a grievous persecution, till vast numbers of the more ignorant and meaner sort, were compelled by force, and even too many others were brought by violence to do what was against their profession, and the light of their own conscience. This was a long and fiery trial.

It will be noticed now, upon every turn, by the reader, without my help, that all the branches of the persecution now growing so hot, were merely for conscience' sake, and not upon any real disregard to the king and government, which they did heartily own and submit to, in all civil and lawful things. Indeed the whole of the persecution I am entering upon this year, and the two following, was barely upon the score of nonconformity to prelates and curates; and no other reason can be assigned for the severities during this year, or the rigour and terrible heights of the high commission, and heavy oppression of the country, which issued in the rising at Pentland; as will appear fully in the sequel of this book.

SECT. II.

Of the more general acts and proceedings of the council, this year, 1663.

WE shall meet with very severe persecutions of many ministers, gentlemen, and country people, by the privy council this year: but, before I come to them, let me take a view of the acts of that court, and the parliament, in as far as they concern suffering presbyterians; and I lay them before the reader from the registers, and begin with those of the council.

The act of fines, made last session of parliament, and the earl of Middleton his endeavours to have a share of the fines, turned about to his ruin. Those fines concern presbyterians so much, and the procedure of the managers about them being but very little known, I shall give a detail of what I meet with in the council registers about them this year altogether, and then go on to other matters which took up that court. This matter will stand best in its own light, from the principal papers themselves, which are not very long. February 12th, the council receive and read a letter from the king, of the date, January 23d, last; which follows.

"Right Trusty, &c.—We have considered that late act of the last session of parliament, intituled, on the back of that copy sent to us, 'anent persons excepted forth of the indemnity,' bearing date at Edinburgh, the 9th of September, 1662, which act hath not the names of the persons, nor the proportions of the fines imposed: yet we have lately received a list of the names, and those proportions, which we have not as yet taken into our consideration. In the meantime, seeing this act appoints the sums imposed to be paid, the one half at one term, the other at another, (both which terms are blank in the copy transmitted to us) with this express certification, that whoever of the fined persons shall not make payment of the respective sums imposed upon them, betwixt and the above-mentioned terms, they are from thenceforth to lose the whole benefit of our pardon and indemnity: and the said days being past, and the sums not paid, it is now as then, and then as now declared, that they have no share in our pardon, but are excepted therefrom, and their estates, rents, and goods to be sequestrate and raised for our use, their persons secured, and they punished as guilty of sedition, usurpation, and rebellion. And that you, our privy council, and others of our ministers and magistrates, are ordained to see this act put in due, exact, and punctual execution, conform to the tenor thereof, as you will be answerable. And seeing we are informed, that the first term's payment is at Candlemas first, upon serious consideration of the whole matter, we have, for reasons importing the good of our service, thought fit to suspend the first term's payment of the said fines, until our further pleasure be signified thereanent; likeas, We do by these presents suspend the first term's payment. As also by our royal prerogative we do dispense with all the penalties contained in the said certification, which the non-payers should have incurred by their not payment at the term foresaid. And we do hereby require you to make public proclamation of this our command, for the suspending of the first term's payment of the fines, until we shall declare our further pleasure concerning the same; as also our dispensing with the penalties, as aforesaid, by open proclamation, and all other ways requisite; to the end our good subjects may take notice of the same. And further, if any person be, or is empowered to be receiver of the fines, you shall in our name discharge him to receive any of them till our further pleasure shall be declared. We also require you to registrate this our letter in the council books: and to these our commands we expect your ready obedience, and a speedy account. Given at our court at Whitehall, the 23d of January, 1662-3, and of our reign the fourteenth year.

"By his majesty's command,

"LAUDERDALE."

The same day the council draw up a proclamation, intimating the suspension of the first term's payment of the fines, and the penalties incurred, just in the terms of the above letter, and so it needs not be repeated; and order the macers to pass to the market-cross of Edinburgh, and intimate so much. *Subscribitur.*

Glencairn, chancellor, Hamilton, Eglinton, Linlithgow, Roxburgh, Southesk, Callander, Halkerton, Ballenden, Jo. Gilmour, Ja. Lockhart, Kinnaird, Geo. Mackenzie, Wauchop, Robert Murray.

1663. But next day, February 13th, I find in the registers as follows. "There being a letter directed from the lord commissioner his grace, of the date the 7th of this instant, bearing, 'that if you have not published any thing relating to the fines, I do, in his majesty's name, desire that nothing may be done; for his majesty's commands are obeyed by the not publication of the act for fines.' Therefore the lords of his majesty's privy council ordain the proclamation subscribed, anent the fines, of the date the 12th of this instant, be not published until further order; and recommend to the lord chancellor to write to the lord commissioner, to give an account thereof to his majesty.

" GLENCAIRN, Chanc. I. P. D."

Thus matters stood till March 17th, when I find the proclamation agreed upon February 12th, was published by the chancellor in the interval of council days, upon his receiving the letter just now to be spoke of; and next council day, March 24th, his majesty's letter directed to the council, anent the fines, was read; the tenor whereof follows.

"Right trusty, &c. Upon consideration of an act of the last session of our parliament, intituled, anent persons excepted forth of the indemnity, bearing the date of the 9th of September, 1662, we did, by our letter of the 23d of January last, command you to make public intimation of our pleasure for suspending of the first term's payment of the fines, until we shall declare our further pleasure thereanent; as also for dispensing with the penalties, and that by open proclamation, and all other ways requisite, to the end all our good subjects might take notice of the same: this letter we commanded you to registrate in our council books, and to these commands we did require ready obedience, and a speedy account. In pursuance of which letter, we were informed that you gave order for a proclamation upon the 12th of February last: but we wondered to hear, that by the 13th of February, you did ordain by an act, that that proclamation should not be published until further order; yet, not having heard any thing from you concerning that sudden change, we did forbear the declaring of our pleasure concerning the same, till we should see an extract of the said act. And now finding, by a subscribed extract of that act, that a letter was directed by the earl of Middleton, our commissioner, to our chancellor, in these words, ' That if you have not published any thing relating to the fines, I do in his majesty's name desire that nothing may be done:' we have again thought fit to let you know, that we do again require you to obey our said letter of the 23d of January last, according to the tenor of it. So expecting a speedy account of these our renewed commands, we bid you heartily farewell. Whitehall, March 10th.

"By his majesty's command,
" LAUDERDALE."

When the chancellor presented the above letter to the council, he acquainted them, that upon the receipt of it he had immediately given orders to the clerk to make publication of the proclamation at the cross of Edinburgh. " The lords of his majesty's privy council do approve of the lord chancellor's proceedings, and give him hearty thanks for his diligence and care in prosecuting his majesty's commands. And considering that part of his majesty's letter, January 23d, requiring persons empowered to receive the fines, not to uplift them; therefore do discharge all who have been, or shall be appointed, to intromit with the said fines, or to uplift the same or any part thereof, while his majesty's further pleasure be known; and ordain intimation hereof to be made to Sir Alexander Durham, Lyon, and others having interest." This is all I meet with in the registers as to the fines this year. The reader will easily perceive where the stop of the king's letters being execute, lay; and this was a very considerable article against Middleton, who had, it seems, kept up some orders, formerly sent him, delaying the execution of the fines. In the following years we shall find the king's pleasure declared, and the fines severely exacted.

March 3d, the council, in prosecution of the former acts of parliament, ordaining

CHAP. IV.] OF THE CHURCH OF SCOTLAND. 339

vacant stipends to be uplifted, having named Mr. John Wilkie to collect them, write the following letter to the several bishops through the kingdom.

" My Lord,
" The lords of privy council having heard a petition presented by Mr. John Wilkie, collector of the vacant stipends, did recommend to me to write to your lordship, that you make trial what churches have been vacant within your diocese, how long they have vaiked, and the true quantity of the stipends; as also what of the said vacancies have been uplifted by the said Mr. John Wilkie, that the case of the said vacancies may be truly known, and all obstructions removed that may hinder the ingetting of what is resting, to be employed to the uses for which the same are destinate: and that with your conveniency you may make a report thereof to the parliament, or privy council. I am, &c.
" GLENCAIRN, Chancellor."

I find no more upon this head. Many were the vacancies made by the late acts of council and parliament, and there would be a round sum to distribute among such as they called sufferers in late times, whereas presbyterian ministers were among the greatest sufferers, and now are brought to a new scene of suffering.

That same diet of council, " The lords of council finding it most necessary and expedient upon very grave and good considerations, that the diet of the diocesan meeting of the synod of Galloway, should be continued while the 2d Wednesday of May next, have thought fit, and hereby do continue the same till that day, and ordain macers or messengers at arms, to make publication hereof at the market-cross of Edinburgh, Kirkcudbright, and other places needful." The reason of this was, few or none of the ministers in that synod did comply with prelacy, and none were expected at this synod. Most part of the ministers of that country, as we shall hear, were cited in February before the council, either to frighten them into a compliance, or in order to a banishment.

While the council are persecuting presbyterian ministers, and the very day the Galloway ministers are before them, March 24th, they have such accounts of the terrible increase of popery, as draw out the following letter to each of the bishops.

1663.

" Right reverend father in God.
" The lords of his majesty's privy council, having received frequent informations of the great increase of popery within this kingdom, and the insolent and bold carriage of many of that profession, who not only make open avowance of the same, though contrary to law, but make it their work to pervert and seduce his majesty's good subjects into that sinful and wicked way, and to corrupt them thereby both in their religion, obedience and allegiance: and finding themselves obliged, in conscience and duty, to prevent the further growth of this evil, have therefore thought fit by those to desire your lordship to take some effectual course at the next meeting of your synod, or any other way you shall think fit, that an exact account of the number, quality, and names of all persons within your diocese, who profess popery or are popishly affected, and upon that account withdraw from the public ordinances, and that with all diligence you send in the same to his majesty's council; and that in the meantime all means be used for bringing them to conformity; and in case of their obstinacy, that the censures of the church be execute against them. Herein expecting the fruits of your care and diligence, we rest your lordship's affectionate friends.
" GLENCAIRN, Ch. &c. ut in Sederunt."

In the progress of this history we shall find the bishops backward to this work, and nothing done in it to purpose, though one would think there was no great difficulty in it, had their zeal against papists been equal to that against presbyterian ministers.

That same day they give the following order about private meetings.—" Information being given that there are several persons who study to keep up private meetings and conventicles, in several parts of the kingdom, studying to alienate the hearts of

1663. the subjects from the present government in church and state; the lords of council do recommend to the lord chancellor to write to Sir James Turner, or any other whom he shall think fit, to take notice of all such persons, and to give account thereof to the council." What is meant here by private meetings, I shall not determine; I take them to relate to the meetings in the outed presbyterian ministers' houses for worship, when they were turned out; or to the meetings among good people for prayer and conference, in this black and sinful time. This I know, that at neither of them was there any alienating people from the king's government; and if their complaints to God against the invasions upon the church by introducing prelates and curates, and confession of their own and the land's sins, alienate peoples' hearts from the prelatical government of the church, this they avowed, and could not but pour out their soul before the Lord in the distress this church was at this time under. I only further remark, that prelatic men in this church, and prelates, have ever been against meetings for prayer and Christian societies this way; and even during presbytery, towards the (year) 1640, and afterwards, Mr. Henry Guthrie, and other malignants among the ministry, who had continued at their charges under presbytery, but were for prelacy in their judgment, made a terrible sputter against private meetings and societies for prayer: but Messrs. Rutherford, Dickson, and Douglas took up that matter, and were so happy as to fall upon an act of assembly, that did much to heal the rent that was like to rise upon this head. The Lord, it is certain, did wonderfully countenance private meetings for prayer in this period I am describing.

The council, April 14th, make the following appointment. " The chancellor having declared to the council, that he received a letter from a sure hand, that there was great abuse committed by several heritors and parishioners in Galloway, (I am of opinion it ought to be in Renfrew or Ayrshire, and I observe here, the registers are not so exactly writ as to the names of persons and places as I could wish) especially those of the parish of Nielston, tending highly to the disquiet of the government, both of church and state, without present remedy be provided; the lords of council, upon consideration thereof, appoint the marquis of Montrose, the earl of Eglinton, and lord Cochran, and the lord chancellor to be supernumerary, if his affairs can permit, to meet at such times and places as they shall think fit, and to call the persons, who have been either the committers or assisters to that abuse, before them, and, after hearing them, to examine witnesses, if need be, for proving what shall be laid to their charges; and if, after examination of witnesses and parties, there shall be just ground found, that the said lords shall either cause secure their persons in firmance, or cause them find sufficient caution to answer before the council with all diligence; and that a report thereof be made to them." —Very probably this letter was from the archbishop of Glasgow; and it shows how ready the council were to serve the prelates, when, upon one letter from them, or others, they straight appoint such a committee as this is. I find no more about this affair, and suppose nothing was made of it. Another evidence of this is, what follows in the registers. " The chancellor having declared, that there were several ministers, and preaching expectants, who inveighed highly against his majesty's government, ordered that letters be direct to cite all such ministers, or preaching expectants, as the lord chancellor shall give order for, to compear before the council next council day, to answer for their misdemeanors."

Little further remarkable of a general nature offers until the 13th of August, when the council pass their act and proclamation of this day's date, which may be termed " The Scots Mile act." I have added it at the foot of the page.* The council had had

---

* Act of Council, Edinburgh, August 13th, 1663.

Forasmuch as it doth appear, that divers ministers, who, by the law, have no right to preach or remain in those parishes which did belong to their cure, do notwithstanding presume to assemble his majesty's subjects in churches and elsewhere, to preach, administer the sacraments, and to keep conventicles and disorderly meetings; and do go about to corrupt

considerable numbers of presbyterian ministers before them, for the refusing obedience to the act of Glasgow, as we shall see in the fifth section. It had been endless work to have called the vast numbers from all corners before them, who were recusants to their former acts; and therefore, after they had, to terrify the rest, brought not a few before them, and banished them benorth Tay, they come to a shorter way, and comprise them all in this act.

It deserves our remark in the entry, that it was not formed, as most of other proclamations are, upon letters from the king, but at Edinburgh, without any orders from his majesty about it: and it is the first act of general concern made after the two archbishops are admitted counsellors; and indeed it savours much of their fiery persecuting spirit. The reader will further notice, that it was made during the sitting of parliament, the proper legislature. Whether the prelates dreaded the parliament would not come in to so unreasonable an act, or whether the council inclined to assume this power, properly parliamentary, under their nose, and, from their connivance at such a practice, plead a right to make laws for the subjects, when the parliament was not sitting, with a better grace, I do not determine.

By this act, presbyterian ministers entered since the (year) 1649, not receiving presentation and collation, are to remove with their families from their parishes in three weeks, and must not reside within twenty miles of the same, or six miles of Edinburgh, or any cathedral church, or three miles to any burgh royal in the kingdom, under pain of sedition. All heritors or householders are discharged to receive them, but in the above terms; and the ministers ordained before the (year) 1649, who attend not the diocesan synods, are to be proceeded against as contemners of his majesty's authority; as the act itself more fully bears. From this act we may see that the bishops would have

and dissuade the people from that affection, duty, obedience, and gratitude they owe to his majesty's government, the laws and authority established, under which the kingdom doth enjoy this great tranquillity and the blessings thereof: as likewise, that many subjects do countenance and join in these unlawful meetings, contrary to the acts of parliament prohibiting the same. Therefore, the lords of his majesty's privy council, in discharge of the trust reposed in them, for preserving the public peace and the laws in their authority and vigour, and that turbulent and disaffected ministers may not have such opportunity, as they have hitherto had, to continue their evil practices in seducing too many people into ways of schism, separation, and sedition, tending to the disquieting and overturning of the established government of the state, as well as that of the church; and in pursuance of what is recommended by his majesty and his estates of parliament, in the late act of the tenth of July, intituled, "act against separation and disobedience to ecclesiastical authority," do hereby command and charge all ministers, who are or shall be found to preach seditiously against the government of church and state, who entered in or since the year 1649, and have not since obtained presentations from their lawful patrons, and collations and admissions from their ordinary, and have notwithstanding continued to preach or exercise any duty, proper to the function of the ministers, either at these parish churches where they were incumbents, or at any other place, house, or family, to remove themselves, their families, and goods belonging to them, within twenty days after publication hereof, out of these respective parishes where they were incumbents, and not to reside within twenty miles of the same. nor within six miles of Edinburgh or any cathedral church, or three miles of any burgh royal within this kingdom; with certification, that if they fail to remove themselves, as said is, and to give exact obedience hereunto, (unless they have the permission of the lords of privy council, or of the bishop of the diocese) they are to incur the penalties of the laws against movers of sedition, and to be proceeded against with that strictness that is due to so great contempts of his majesty's authority over church and state. And do hereby inhibit and discharge all heritors and householders in burgh or land, to give any presence or countenance to any one or more of these ministers, removed by this act, to preach or exercise any act of the office of a minister; with certification, if they, after publication hereof, shall presume so to do, they are to be proceeded against according to law. And being likewise informed, that divers ministers who were entered by lawful presentations before the year 1649, and do still continue in their exercise of their ministry, do yet forbear to attend ecclesiastical meetings appointed by authority, and to exercise discipline in their parishes, without giving any account of their administrations, to the great detriment of the order and peace of the church: therefore they command and charge all those ministers to keep the diocesan synods, and other ecclesiastical meetings appointed by authority; with certification, that if, after publication hereof, they fail so to do, and disobey the acts of parliament and council made thereanent, they are to be proceeded against as contemners of his majesty's authority. And ordain these presents to be printed, and published at the Market-cross of Edinburgh, and other places needful, that none pretend ignorance.

PET. WEDDERBURN,
Cl. Secr. Concilii

1663. none of the presbyterian ministers so much as breathing air near them. "The five mile act" in England was reckoned abundantly severe, but this runs far higher; and all along we shall find our prelates screw every thing higher than the English laws go. In part I have already taken notice of the hardships in this rigid act, and the bare reading of it will discover them. Every body must see what charges and trouble it puts poor ministers to, as well as their small families. They are removed merely for conscience' sake, far from their beloved people, from whom at least they might have been allowed some commiseration in their distress: but the bishops, in as far as lies in their power, deprived them of any thing which might in the least alleviate their sufferings, and very barbarously send them to make the best they can of a hard lot among strangers. Presbyterian ministers had been already thrice punished for their simple nonconformity; and this is indeed the fourth proclamation and punishment for the same pretended crime of mere nonsubjection to bishops, and their adherence to the reformation rights of Scotland, and their own known principles: and where the equity of this procedure lies, the reader must judge. According to the episcopal principles, at least the profession of many of them, and sure, according to the very laws of this time, the government of the church is ambulatory, a matter indifferent, and entirely at the disposal of the magistrate. At the worst that can be made of the ministers' practice, they were only guilty of an omission in a matter indifferent; and it is at best grievous oppression to violent (treat with violence) men at such a rate, and to force them to run counter to their own light, in a thing of such a nature, according to the prelatists' own principles.

By former laws none but one minister must reside in one congregation; and I am of opinion, the nicest geographer will scarce find room for near four hundred ministers to live in separate congregations, provided they keep by all the conditions in this act, twenty miles from their own parish, six miles from Edinburgh, and from every cathedral, and three from every burgh royal. Several of the outed ministers had relations and friends in towns and burghs, and the industry of their families was now the only means of their subsistence, and there they had the best occasion of employing themselves. By this act they were almost deprived of the means of educating their small children, at least they must be at double charges this way, and have them removed from their inspection when at schools. In a word, it was every way unprecedented, as well as unreasonable, to oblige poor ministers to remove themselves and families the third time in less than the space of one year. Yet such are the tender mercies of the wicked.

Upon the 7th of October, another ill-natured act is passed in council. The bishops were fretted that any of the presbyterian ministers of Ireland should have a shelter in Scotland, and no less grated that such multitudes withdrew from hearing the curates; and therefore to reach both, this act is framed, which being the foundation of very much persecution, and not having seen it in print, I shall insert it here though it be pretty long.

"*Apud Edinburgh*, 7th October, 1663.

"Whereas his majesty, with advice and consent of his estates of parliament, by their act and proclamation bearing date the 22d day of February, 1661, finding, that many seditious and turbulent persons, ministers, and others, in the kingdom of Ireland, who by reason of their fanatic principles could not comply with the administration of his majesty's authority and government so happily established in that kingdom, were coming over, expecting shelter here, that they might be the more able to carry on their designs in perverting the allegiance of the subjects, and subverting the peace of the kingdom · and it did much concern the public peace, that such wasps and unworthy persons, enemies to all lawful authority, and to whom it is natural to stir up sedition, and undermine the peace wherever they are, should have no countenance in this kingdom; did therefore declare, that no persons whosoever coming from Ireland, without a sufficient pass and testimonial in writ from the lord lieutenant, or from the lords of council, or some having power from them, or the sheriff of the county, or mayor of the city where these persons lived, of their peaceable carriage and conformity to the laws, should be allowed any residence, receit, and stay within this kingdom; but it should be lawful, likeas all magistrates and justices of the peace, are hereby required to seize upon, and imprison such persons wanting such testimony, who should not willingly remove out of the kingdom within fifteen days after the intimating of the said proclamation to them (excepting all ordinary known trafficking merchants) likeas, by the said act it is ordained, that all such persons, who should come over with any such testimony, should within fifteen days after their landing make their appearance before the parliament, or in case of their not sitting, before his majesty's privy council, or such as shall be warranted by them, and make known the reasons of their coming hither, and give security, such as shall be thought fit, for their peaceable carriage, otherwise to remove off the country in fifteen days; wherein if they should fail, magistrates, sheriffs, and other public ministers, are by the said act empowered to apprehend, secure, and imprison them, till course shall be taken with them as with seditious and factious persons.

" And seeing the said act and proclamation was only to endure for a year after the date thereof, and longer as the privy council should think fit; and seeing the same has not yet been renewed or prorogated, neither as yet have any person or persons been nominated and empowered, before whom those coming from Ireland in manner foresaid, should be examined, and make known the reasons of their coming hither, and to whom they should find caution for their peaceable carriage in manner mentioned in the said act; by reason whereof several ministers have presumed to come from Ireland to this kingdom, without either acknowledging the authority of his majesty's parliament, or privy council, their authority, civil or ecclesiastic, some of which have been so bold as to preach publicly in churches, and others privately do watch their own opportunities, to stir up the subjects to sedition, and alienate their minds from the government so happily established in church and state: the lords of his majesty's privy council have renewed, and by those presents do renew the said act and proclamation, and ordain the same to stand in full force, strength, and effect, and to be put to due execution against the contraveners thereof, and for that effect have nominated, appointed, and empowered, and by these presents nominate, appoint, and empower, William, earl of Glencairn, lord chancellor, Hugh, earl of Eglinton, the earl of Galloway, William, lord Cochran, the provost of Glasgow for the time, the provost of Ayr for the time, Maxwel of Munshes, the provost of Wigton for the time, and Stuart of Taudergie, or any of them, to call before them all such persons coming from Ireland, wanting sufficient testimonies and passes from the lord lieutenant, or other persons mentioned in the said act and proclamation, who shall not willingly remove off the kingdom within fifteen days after the publication of those presents, and to secure their persons till his majesty's council be acquainted therewith; with power also to the forenamed persons or any of them, to examine all such persons as shall come over from Ireland, having such testimony, concerning their reasons of coming hither, and to take such caution and security of them for their peaceable carriage, as they shall think fit; and, in case they shall not find the said security, to cause them to remove off the country within fifteen days, otherwise to apprehend, imprison, and secure them, until they be proceeded against as seditious persons, and disturbers of the public peace.

1663.

" Moreover, the lords of his majesty's privy council taking to their consideration, that notwithstanding of the acts of parliament and council, published for the preventing and suppressing the seeds of separation and disobedience to authority, divers persons in several parishes presume to withdraw and separate themselves from attending upon the ordinary meetings for divine worship, in those parishes where ministers are legally planted, to the scandalous contempt of the laws, and great increase of disorder and licentiousness, and

1663. that some do pervert the true meaning of the act of parliament against separation and disobedience to ecclesiastical authority (of which we shall hear in the next section) which appoints every minister to give admonition in presence of two witnesses, to such persons as shall be given up to the council as transgressors of the said act; therefore the lords of his majesty's privy council, for explanation of that clause of the said act, according to the true meaning and intent thereof, do declare that those persons shall be proceeded against by the council as transgressors of the act, who withdraw from their parish church after three public admonitions given by the ministers of the respective parishes out of the pulpit, in the church, upon the Lord's day, after divine service, and that the minister's attestation under his hand, that in the presence of two or more sufficient witnesses, he hath from the pulpit upon three Lord's days intimated the names of such who ordinarily and wilfully absent themselves from the ordinary meetings for divine worship in their own parish church, shall give a sufficient ground of proceeding against such persons as transgressors of the said act. For putting of which into the more effectual execution, as they do discharge such persons, who under the pretext of their being elders in kirk sessions formerly, do go about to leaven the people with dissatisfaction and disobedience to the laws and ecclesiastical authority, upon the pain of being proceeded against as seditious persons; so they do require such persons as shall be called by the ministers legally planted, to assist them for suppressing of sin and disorders in the parish, to give their concurrence for that effect. And further they do command and require, and hereby authorize and warrant all noblemen, sheriffs, magistrates of burghs, justices of peace, and all officers of the standing forces, as they tender his majesty's service and the peace of the country, to give their assistance and effectual concurrence to ministers in their respective bounds in the discharge of their office, and to put the law in execution, and to execute the penalties which are expressed in the acts of parliament and council, from all and every person who are transgressors in every parish, unless the minister of the parish where the transgressor does reside, shall give a sufficient reason why the said person or persons should not be proceeded against; and to take care that the said penalties be employed for the relief of the poor, and other pious uses within the respective parishes. And further, all magistrates, sheriffs, and other public ministers, are hereby ordained, as they will be answerable upon their duty, to put this present act and proclamation, with the acts of parliament and council, hereby renewed and explained, to due execution, against the contraveners thereof, in manner therein expressed, and ordain those presents to be printed and published."

This act speaks for itself. I know not but the noise about Blood's plot, which was about this time, might occasion a greater severity in the first part of this proclamation, than otherwise perhaps might have been; but none of the ministers who came here many months ago, were in the least concerned in any thing disloyal, and the sedition talked of here, is only their dislike at prelatical government. What I remarked upon the former act, as to the council's procedure during the sitting of parliament, comes in upon this; for the parliament was yet sitting: and what an arbitrary step must it be in them, to explain and enlarge, yea, alter some of the branches of an act of this present parliament, even when they themselves are sitting? After this, I confess, we need not be surprised to find few parliaments, except upon some very special occasions, since the council take their power to themselves, even when sitting In short, the reader no doubt hath observed, that the execution of this act, and the uplifting of the fines, afterward called church-fines, for absence from the parish church, are put in the hands of the army. Indeed noblemen and others are named, but it is only *pro more*, and the army were the uplifters of the penalties; and the curates, we see, the informers, and witnesses in their own cause, which certainly was very impolitic, as well as unreasonable.

Towards the end of this year, the council are at much pains to press the declaration imposed by the parliament, and it became matter of sore suffering to multitudes. I shall give what I find in the registers about it altogether. November 17th, the whole lords of "privy council present, viz. chancellor, St. Andrews, Dunfermline, Roxburgh, Tweeddale, Kincardin, Halkerton, president, register, justice-clerk, Hatton, Niddry, Sir Robert Murray, did subscribe the declaration appointed by act of parliament to be taken by all persons in public trust; and recommend it to the president of the session, to see that the same be taken by all the members of the college of justice." That same day, the following letter was ordered to be directed to whole sheriffs of shires and stewarts.

" Assured friends,

" Seeing it is recommended to the council, by the parliament, to see their act concerning the declaration, to be taken by all persons in public trust, put in execution, and receive obedience conform to the tenor of the said act, and that a speedy account be returned thereof, immediately after the expiring of the terms appointed for that effect; we have thought fit to give you timous notice thereof, that your deputes and clerks subscribe, and be careful to require all those within your shire to subscribe the declaration, who are appointed to take the same, according as is appointed by the said act of parliament, whereof we have sent you a printed copy, with the ' declaration annexed; and that you give an account of your diligence immediately after the first of January next to come.

" And because we are informed likewise, that the late act of council concerning ministers that have entered since the year 1649, and have not obtained collation from their ordinary, has been openly and avowedly disobeyed, the said ministers still remaining in those places prohibited by the said act; therefore we require you to take trial what ministers within your bounds and jurisdictions have disobeyed the foresaid act, where they live and reside, and give advertisement to the clerk of council, to be communicate to us, that further order may be taken thereanent. We rest

" Your assured friend
" Ut in Sederunt.

Another letter is directed to the burghs, and a copy of the act and declaration is sent, of the same tenor with that above; only that part about ministers is not insert in it, now that ministers are discharged from all burghs. And as to the burghs where seaports are, this addition is made. " We being informed, that the pestilence is raging at Hamburgh and Amsterdam, so that the keeping commerce with these places may endanger this kingdom; therefore you are to take care that no ships, persons, and goods from thence, be suffered to enter your harbour, till they abide the ordinary trial of forty days, during which time you are to cause them keep apart by themselves." And December 2d, " The lords of council considering, that many reports from the burghs, anent the subscribing the declaration, are informal, do therefore appoint and ordain the whole shires and burghs to return to the clerks of council in writ, the very words of the declaration, subscribed by those who are appointed to take the same; and that the clerk of the court do testify, the same is truly subscribed by the whole persons whose names are subjoined; and where any refuses, that the names of the refusers be returned under the hands of the magistrates of burghs, sheriffs of shires, and their clerks."

We see the exact care taken about the subscription of this declaration, whereby the covenants were renounced; and in the beginning of the next year, we shall find more efforts used this way. Great numbers refused this declaration, and severals left their places and offices. I find it remarked by no enemy to this imposition, "that in December, Sir James Dalrymple of Stair, Sir James Dundas, and Sir George Mackenzie of Tarbet, refused the signing of this declaration, among the lords of session; but in a little time my lord Stair repented, and signed it."

November 24th, the council finding the army making some misimprovement of the general powers granted them by the pro-

1663. clamation, October 7th, give an explication and restriction of it, to the penalty of twenty shillings Scots for absence, perhaps to quicken them to persecute, by binding them down to this particular. Their order runs, "forasmuch as the lords of council, in prosecution of the acts of parliament and council, for settling church government, and for preventing and suppressing the seeds of separation and disobedience to authority, did emit an act and proclamation, of the 7th of October last, and, by a clause of the said act, did give warrant to all noblemen, &c. and officers of the standing forces, to give their assistance and effectual concurrence to ministers, in their respective bounds, in discharge of their office, and to put the laws in execution, and to exact the penalties expressed in the acts of parliament and council, from all persons transgressors thereof, within their respective parishes: the said lords, for the explanation of the foresaid act, and for clearing the power thereby given to the officers of the army, anent the exacting the penalties contained therein, do declare that the said officers of standing forces, shall have no power to exact any of the penalties contained in the said acts, except allenarly the penalty of twenty shillings Scots, from every person who stay from their own parish churches upon the Sabbath-day; which they are to exact in manner, and for the use contained in the act of council." Wolves will not be tamed; and when the soldiers were once let loose, we shall find they soon got over their restrictions, and no notice was taken of them for so doing. This year the council had many particular ministers, gentlemen and others before them; but those will afford matter for a section by themselves, if once I had given some account of the parliament this year.

SECT. III.

Of the acts of parliament, in as far as they relate to the church, with some account of Middleton's fall this year, 1663.

THE former two sessions of parliament had done so much in overturning the reformation, government, and discipline of this church, that very little was left to this session to do. And because I am to be very short upon the proceedings of this court, I shall begin with the change of their commissioner, the earl of Middleton, who had managed the two former sessions very much to the prelates' satisfaction.

The history of a church under the cross, can scarce be well given without intermixing something relating to the state, especially when the cross comes from the state, supporting corrupt churchmen; yet I have given, and shall insist upon as little of the civil history of this period, as is consistent with the reader's understanding the springs and circumstances of presbyterians' sufferings.

Towards the close of the last year, the earl of Middleton hastes up to London, and quits the stage of Scotland, upon which he had acted a severe, rough, and unacceptable part, never to return to his native country again, as I am informed a country woman told him at Coldstream, when he passed by; from what art she had her information I know not, but she assured him, he would never have any more power in Scotland.

When he came to London, the king welcomed him with that angry question, "whether he was sent to Scotland to be a check upon the king, and control his orders?" The reason of this is, what was remarked before, his concealing letters writ to him, and stopping the proclamation anent the fines.

In a little time I find Lauderdale gave in a libel and charge of high treason against him, consisting of many particulars. One of them, I hear, was, that he had taken bribes from some of the greatest criminals in Scotland, to keep them out of the exceptions from the act of fines. The king was pleased to keep the issue of this controversy betwixt those two great men in his own breast, until the time of the parliament drew near. At length his patent for being king's commissioner is recalled; and, as we shall hear, the earl of Rothes is put in his room. And in December, after the parliament is up, and the act of ballotting rescinded, his commissions, as governor of Edinburgh castle, and general of the forces in Scotland, are recalled, and he resigned all his places to his majesty's hands. The causes of this disgrace at this time were said to be, the act of fines, and the illegal manner of contriving it; the act that none should address themselves to his majesty in any matter, without first applying to the commissioner or council; the ballotting act incapacitating twelve persons of honour, from all places of trust and power; his uplifting and misapplication of some months' cess imposed by the usurper; his misemploying the cess and excise, to the value of forty thousand pounds sterling; a missive letter of his to a certain delinquent in the late times, requiring him to pay a great sum of money to one of his friends, otherwise assuring him he should abide the highest pains of law; a letter of his to the duke of Ormond, lord lieutenant in Ireland, desiring correspondence and mutual assistance, when there was need in either kingdom, without any warrant; which letter, it is said, the duke sent over to his majesty: and lastly, his stopping the proclamation for prorogating the payment of the fines. Those were alleged as the grounds of this great man's fall; some of them are certain, the rest I give as I find them in the memoirs of this period. Since the writing of this, I find the earl of Lauderdale's charge and Middleton's answer, are both printed in Brown's Miscellanea Aulica, 8vo. London, 1702, where the curious reader may see them. *

Middleton had for his patrons 1663. the duke of York, chancellor Hide, and the bishops of England, whom he had so much served in Scotland. It fared no doubt the worse with Middleton, that a party in England was about this time a forming against the chancellor; and in July, this year, the earl of Bristol and others in parliament managed a charge of high treason against him, and carried their point so far, as he in some time resigned his places. Thus the grand introducers of prelacy in Britain, began to fall about the same time. Lauderdale was a complete courtier, and had very much of his master's good graces, and stood much by the interest he had with Barbara Villiers, first Mrs. Palmer, and then dutchess of Cleveland, the king's she-favourite.

The earl of Middleton, in his own rough way, uttered some expressions of his regard to the duke of York, which were wanting in that respect he owed to the king: those Lauderdale failed not to improve. After a long and considerable struggle, Middleton, notwithstanding of his great friends and remarkable services, fell before his rival, for whom the king had a personal kindness and regard: and he was obliged to live obscurely enough, until the governor's place of Tangier fell vacant by the death of the lord Rutherford; and as an honourable sort of banishment, the king was prevailed with to bestow this post upon him as a reward of his establishing prelacy in Scotland. Our Scots history makes it evident, that all, who, since our

---

* This struggle for superiority between these unprincipled minions of tyranny, is related at great length by Sir George Mackenzie, a man as unprincipled as either of them, though possessed of much more external decency of manners. Lauderdale's speech against Middleton he declares to have been the great masterpiece of his life, but it is far too long to be inserted here. It is sufficiently seasoned with encomiums upon his majesty, and the illimitable nature of his prerogative, upon which, with a great deal of art, it insinuates that Middleton had in a number of instances encroached. The act of billeting, however, was the great object of the speaker's aversion, he being by it excluded from office, and he characterises it in the following manner:—" By billeting, any man's honour, his life, his posterity may be destroyed without the trouble of hearing him, calling him, hearing his answer, nay, without the trouble of accusing him. Billeting hath the wonderful power to destroy any man, and yet the collective body of that judicature who use it shall never be troubled with his name, till it come to be executed. This is a stranger engine than white powder which some fancy, for sure this shoots without any noise at all. But, blessed be God, this dreadful engine was never known as to punishments among any people, heathen or Christian, who had the blessing to live under monarchy. Some republics use the billet, or the ballot, in giving places, but I never so much as read of any thing like it as to punishment, except the ostracism among the Athenians, who were governed by that cursed sovereign lord the people; and by their oystershell billeting, I read of the banishment of Themistocles, after his two famous victories of Salamis and Thermopylæ. I read also that Aristides was so billeted, a man whose eminent justice is turned

1663. reformation by presbyters, put hand to build the hierarchy in Scotland, were turned out of their estates and honours, into a proverb. Yet, billeting was once attempted to have been brought into Scotland. It was, Sir, in the year 1641, when your blessed father's royal prerogative of naming officers of state was wrested from him, and subjected to the approbation of parliament. Then was billeting struggled for, but vigorously opposed by your royal father. And even in that sad time, such was the justice and strength of reason with which he opposed it, as it was never heard of in Scotland till now, that billeting, even in punishment, is touched with the royal sceptre by the earl of Middleton, and so endeavoured to be made a law. Now, Sir, let me humbly beg your patience a little, to open to you how, as I am informed, this billeting was brought in at this time. It was not first moved in articles, the most usual place for proposing laws. It was first moved in the committee of fines, as I am told, and by the fittest man to impose on your parliament this effectual way of it, who had imposed incapacitating itself on your majesty; and this was Sir George Mackenzie. As soon as moved, it was opposed, and then your commissioner appeared not for it; but when it was better prepared, it is moved in the articles, and again vigorously opposed, but then your commissioner appearing for it, it was, I think, believed he had good warrant for it, and so it passes. Now, in the last place, I come to the ways of carrying on the names of those who were to be billeted. This was done more in the dark; yet I shall discover what light I have got, but it must be with a gentle hand, for they say I am one of them, and I am apt to believe it, Sir, for to me it is no new thing. Six times have I been excepted; twice for life and estate, twice for my estate, and twice thus. Yet I bless God, five of the times was during rebellion, and by usurpers, for serving your royal father and yourself, and this last I hope will be found to be done neither by your majesty nor by your parliament. If by your sacred majesty, I lay myself at your feet—your breath shall easily destroy the work of your hands, without any such engine as billeting. And sure it is not by your parliament, for my name was never named by your parliament but when they honoured me with an obliging letter, and when they acknowledged your worthy choice of me as secretary, (so they are pleased to call it, and here I have it signed by your clerk register, as an act of parliament,) and none can make me believe that this so just a parliament would without accusation or hearing, so severely condemn a poor man whom they had so much honoured. But I am not worthy your majesty's trouble. The names inserted in the billets were well known, as I believe, to the earl of Middleton. I am informed the earl of Newburgh at his table read his list, and desired to make no secret of it, as a noble lord here will justify. I shall not now insist on my informations of diligent solicitings by men of quality, and in whose names they solicited, nor what meetings were kept at Masterton's tavern, and elsewhere, for carrying that which was called the right list, for it is time to end this too great trouble. If your majesty as might be shown at great length; and this last builder, after he had banished so many worthy and excellent ministers from their shall think the persons concerned worth so much consideration, you will easily discover every step for compassing this affront put on them in the face of all Europe. And such is the loyalty of the members of parliament, that when your pleasure shall be made known, no one circumstance will be concealed from you. How your honour, and the honour of your parliament is here engaged, I do humbly leave to your royal wisdom."

Middleton went through all these charges one by one at great length, and equally with Lauderdale devoted to his majesty, concluded thus:—" Having with great ingenuity made these returns to the earl of Lauderdale's paper, I humbly lay them with my life and honour at your feet, and do desire to live no longer than I have the esteem of being, Sir, your majesty's most faithful, most humble, and most obedient subject and servant." Middleton had exposed himself much for the king, and had many friends who interested themselves strongly in his behalf; and but for an unfortunate circumstance, might, after all, still have kept his place. He had succeeded in procuring a pardon for Sir John Swinton, that he might deprive Lauderdale of the estate which he had already secured, and of which, notwithstanding of Sir John's pardon, he kept possession till his death; and now Lauderdale, in return, that he might deprive Middleton of the rich harvest he expected to reap from the fines, and at the same time ingratiate himself with the people, procured, while their quarrel was yet unsettled, a letter from the king to the Scottish council, discharging by his prerogative royal, the payment of the first moiety of the fines till farther orders. Middleton, alarmed both for the loss of his share of the fines, and of his power at the same time, made application to Clarendon, that he might interpose his influence with the king to have the proclamation for the payment of the fines continued. The privy council of Scotland being for the most part Middleton's friends, raised at the same time a controversy, whether or not they could properly, while there was a lord commissioner in office, receive and execute any order from the king that had not been transmitted through the commissioner. While this was occupying the council, Middleton having the approbation of Clarendon, obtained, or at least writ to the council that he had obtained, an order from the king, that no proceeding should be made upon his own letter, and that of course the fines should be uplifted, according to the proclamation. This occasioned a new debate in the council, where it was affirmed by some that the letter of the king could not be countermanded but by another from his own hand. The council, as a measure of safety, wrote to the king, that they might have his own mind upon the subject. The king, on receiving this letter, was greatly out of humour, and his chagrin was heightened by Lauderdale, who told him, that since Middleton by his own private could recall his majesty's public warrant, he was, to all intents, king of Scotland. "Middleton," says our historian, Mackenzie, " de-

native country, was himself sent to die in a strange land. In Tangier he lived but a short while in contempt, till death seized him; and by a fall he broke the bone of his right arm, and the broken bone, at the next tumble down a pair of stairs, went into his side and wounded him, so as he turned first stupid, and very quickly died. I have it from good hands, that in times of taking the covenant, such was his forward zeal for it, that coming out of the place where he and others had taken it, he said to some gentlemen and others about him, "That this was the pleasantest day ever he had seen, and if ever he should do any thing against that blessed work he had been engaging into, holding up his right arm, he wished to God that might be his death." Whether he had his wish at Tangier, he now knows best.

This was the fate of the great overturner of our reformation establishment in Scotland, and, as hath been hinted, chancellor Hide's, who acted much the same part in England, was not much better. The attack began upon him this year, and after he was disgraced at court, in a little time he was forced, to escape the punishment of what was charged against him, to flee his native country, and died in a strange land after a seven years' exile: so dangerous a thing is it to meddle with the church of Christ! 1663.

The dependance of these debates betwixt these two great men, made the parliament to be adjourned more than once: at length it is determined it shall meet, and a new commissioner must be provided. Lauderdale now has all Scots affairs entirely in his hand, and finds it not convenient to fill that post himself, but pitches upon the earl of Rothes, afterwards duke; and to make all sure in Scotland against a new rival, and that he might be at the bottom of Middleton's plot against him, he comes down to Scotland with him, and brings a remission to the lord Lorn, as we shall hear; and Rothes hath a multitude of places heaped upon him; and the earl of Tweeddale, whose son married Lauderdale's daughter, is made president of the council.

Upon June 15th, the commissioner comes down to Holyrood-house, and June 18th, the parliament sat down. The bishop of Aberdeen had a sermon before this session opened, and the commissioner and chancellor had speeches, which I have not seen: and the formerly absent members took the oaths. The chief business of this parliament seems to have been to inquire into the act of balloting, and the design formed during the last session against Lauderdale, which I leave to civil historians. The lords of the articles were changed, and Middleton's party left out in the nomination. I find it remarked, that after all the search was made into this plot against the secretary, it was found mostly to land on Middleton, Lennox, and Newburgh. The former sessions had left very little to this meeting of parliament, to do in favour of the prelates, unless it was to guard them against the spite of the country, and to lay the foundations of a more

---

fended himself by alleging Clarendon's report to him of his majesty's pleasure, which answer satisfied not the king, but hastened Middleton's ruin. For, after the king had commanded the council by a new letter to issue out the proclamation, he recalled Middleton's commission, and declared his place of general and captain of the castle of Edinburgh void, and bestowed the captain of the castle's place upon the earl of Lauderdale." "Middleton," says Burnet, "always stood upon it that he had the king's order by word of mouth for what he had done, though he was not so cautious as to procure an instruction under his hand for his warrant. It is very probable that he spoke of it to the king when his head was full of somewhat else, so that he did not mind it, and that to get rid of Middleton he bid him do whatsoever he proposed, without reflecting much on it, for the king was at that time so distracted in his thoughts, that he was not at all times master of himself. The queen mother had brought over from France one Mrs. Stewart, reckoned a very great beauty, who was afterwards married to the duke of Richmond. The king was believed to be deeply in love with her. Yet his former mistress kept her ground still; and what with her humours and jealousy, and what with this new amour, the king had very little quiet between both their passions and his own."—Mackenzie's History of Scotland, pp. 78—112. Burnet's History of his Own Times, 12mo. edit. pp. 295, 296. Kirkton on this business remarks, "Lauderdale knew well what the king's delights were; he choosed for his patron neither statesman nor prince. Barbara Villiers, first Mrs. Palmer, then dutchess of Cleveland, was his choice; and before her bedside he would have kneeled for ane hour at ane time to implore her friendship with the king, because he knew well what influence his miss had upon him, and with these weapons he prevailed."—History of the Church of Scotland, p. 158.—Ed.

1663. open and universal persecution, than ever Scotland saw since popish prelates were removed.

Slavish principles as to civil rights and liberty, still lead the van to persecution for conscience' sake; and therefore, though indeed it hath little reference to the church, I could not but notice the tenor of the first act of this session anent the lords of articles.* By this act the king in a manner hath the whole of the business of the parliament in his hand; the prelates being the creatures of the court, and having the choice of the nobility who were to be members of the committee, would not readily fix upon any who were not acceptable to the court. The nobility, who chose members from the bishops, could scarce go wrong, they being all absolute creatures of the king's making: and those two together chose the barons and burgesses, who indeed could not miss to be right chosen of their own kidney; and they were on the matter but ciphers, the officers of state being supernumerary, and the chancellor president always. By this committee, every matter which was not agreeable to the court, was effectually kept out of the house, be it never so much for the good of the country. This was certainly one of the highest encroachments possible upon the privileges of the subject, as well as the Christian; and one of the most slavish acts that could be well made, limiting the supreme power, and making the king as absolute almost as he can wish; and the parliament must fall in with every thing proposed. They were a mere shadow, and as Sir George Mackenzie somewhere calls them, "the king's baron court."† The narrative of this act appeared to me odd enough when I read it. The commissioner is brought in representing that it is his majesty's express will and pleasure, that in this and all succeeding parliaments, the way used in choosing the lords of articles in the year 1633, shall be observed; and then it is added, " the parliament in all humble duty acquiesced thereunto." One must take it for a jest to call this an act of parliament; it was the king's will and pleasure, and that was to be the rule of their actions, as this parliament, in their eccentric loyalty to the king, are pleased to express themselves in their printed letter to his majesty, at the end of this session, to be seen in the printed acts. Thus they tamely fall in with the old maxim of tyrants, before the restoration truly a stranger in Scotland, *sic volo, sic jubeo, stat pro ratione voluntas*. This being their rule, let us see what was his majesty's will and pleasure, signified to them in their following acts, as to church affairs.

We need not doubt but the prelates and their adherents were chagrined by the general opposition made to their curates through the west and south, and many other parts of the kingdom. To bear down this as far as they can, they make their second act "against separation and disobedience to ecclesiastic authority." This act was termed, "The bishops' dragnet," and all alongst this reign it was altered, amended, and confirmed in their favours, as their *magna charta*; and therefore I have added it in a note.‡ Many remarks might be made upon it, but they fall much in with what hath been said on the acts of the former sessions. The parliament begin with a heavy libel against presbyterian government, as the fountain of the

---

* The folio edition, 1663, wants this, but the 8vo. 1683, has it, and the numbers of the acts are as here. In the other edition the 1st act is against separation, &c. The reason of this difference I know not.

† This servility on the part of the Scottish parliament was no new trait in its character; for we find James VI. in one of his hectoring speeches to the parliament of England, boasting that the parliament of his native country was entirely subservient to his will. "This," he goes on, "I must say for Scotland, and I may truly vaunt it, here I sit and govern it with my pen; I write, and it is done; and by a clerk of the council I govern Scotland now, which others could not do by the sword.—For here I must note unto you the different nature of the two parliaments in these two kingdoms; for there they must not speak without the chancellor's leave, and if any man do propound or utter any seditious or uncomely speeches, he is straight interrupted and silenced by the chancellor's authority; whereas here, the liberty for every man to speak what he list, and as long as he list, was the only cause he was not interrupted."— Works of King James VI. pp. 520, 521.—*Ed.*

‡ Act against separation and disobedience to ecclesiastical authority.

Forasmuch as the king's majesty, considering the prejudices which did ensue to the church and protestant religion, to the prerogative of the crown, to the authority of parliament, to the liberties of the subject, and to the public laws and peace of the kingdom, by the invasions made upon episcopal government, during the

evils in the late times. If we suppose this enacted as the king's pleasure signified to them, which now, it seems, must be their rule as to truth as well as practice, 1663.

late troubles; and finding that government, to be the church government most agreeable to the word of God, most convenient and effectual for preservation of truth, order, and unity, and most suitable to monarchy, and to the peace and quiet of the state; hath therefore, with advice and consent of his estates of parliament, by several acts passed in the second session of this parliament, restored the church to its ancient and right government, by archbishops and bishops, and hath redintegrated the estate of bishops to the exercise of their episcopal function, and to all the privileges, dignities, jurisdictions, and possessions due, and formerly belonging thereunto. And in further order to the settlement of the church, and bringing the ministers to a due acknowledgment of, and compliance with the government thereof, thus established by law, his majesty, with advice foresaid, hath also statute and ordained, that all these ministers, who entered to the cure of any parish, without right or presentations from the lawful patrons, in and since the year one thousand six hundred and forty-nine, and should not, betwixt and the twentieth of September last, obtain presentations from their several patrons, and collation from the bishop of the diocese where they lived, should have no right to the uplifting the rents of any benefice or stipend for the year one thousand six hundred and sixty-two, but that their places, benefices, and kirks should be, *ipso jure*, vacant: and that whatever ministers should, without a lawful excuse to be admitted by their ordinary, absent themselves from the diocesan assembly, or who should not concur in all the acts of the church discipline, as they should be thereunto required by the archbishop or bishop of the diocese, should be for the first fault suspended from their office and benefice till the next diocesan meeting; and if they amend not, should be deprived, and the church and benefice to be provided as in other cases of vacancies. And the king's majesty, having resolved to conserve and maintain the church in the present state and government thereof, by archbishops and bishops, and others bearing office therein, and not to endure nor give way or connivance to any variation therein in the least, doth therefore, with advice and consent of his estates convened in this third session of his parliament, ratify and approve the aforementioned acts, and all other acts and laws made in the two former sessions of parliament, in order to the settling of episcopal dignity, jurisdiction, and authority within this kingdom; and ordains them to stand in full force as public laws of the kingdom, and to be put to further execution in all points, conform to the tenor thereof. And in pursuance of his majesty's royal resolution herein, his majesty, with advice aforesaid, doth recommend to the lords of his majesty's privy council, to take speedy and effectual course, that these acts receive ready and due obedience from all his majesty's subjects; and for that end, that they call before them all such ministers, who, having entered in or since the year one thousand six hundred and forty-nine, and have not as yet obtained presentations and collations, as aforesaid, yet dared to preach in contempt of the law, and to punish them as seditious persons, and contemners of the royal authority. As also, that they be careful, that such ministers, who keep not the diocesan meetings, and concur not with the bishops in the acts of church discipline, being for the same suspended or deprived, as said is, be accordingly, after deprivation, removed from their benefices, glebes, and manses; and if any of them shall, notwithstanding, offer to retain the possession of their benefices or manses, that they take present course to see them dispossessed; and if they shall thereafter presume to exercise their ministry, that they be punished as seditious persons, and such as contemn the authority of church and state. And as his majesty doth expect, from all his good and dutiful subjects, a due acknowledgment of, and hearty compliance with his majesty's government, ecclesiastical and civil, as it is now established by law within this kingdom, and that in order thereunto, they will give their cheerful concurrence, countenance, and assistance to such ministers, as by public authority are or shall be admitted in their several parishes, and attend all the ordinary meetings for divine worship in the same; so his majesty doth declare, that he will, and doth account a withdrawing from, and not keeping and joining in these meetings, to be seditious, and of dangerous example and consequence. And therefore, and for preventing the same for the future, his majesty, with advice and consent of his estates in parliament, doth hereby statute, ordain, and declare, that all and every such person or persons, who shall hereafter ordinarily and wilfully withdraw and absent themselves from the ordinary meetings of divine worship, in their own parish church, on the Lord's day, (whether upon account of popery, or other disaffection to the present government of the church) shall thereby incur the pains and penalties underwritten; viz. each nobleman, gentleman, and heritor, the loss of a fourth part of ilk year's rent, in which they shall be accused and convicted; and every yeoman, tenant, or farmer, the loss of such a proportion of their free moveables, (after the payment of their rents due to their master and landlord) as his majesty's council shall think fit, not exceeding a fourth part thereof; and every burgess to lose the liberty of merchandising, trading, and all other privileges within burgh, and fourth part of their moveables. And his majesty, with advice foresaid, doth hereby authorize and require the lords of his majesty's privy council, to be careful to see this act put to due execution; and for that end, to call before them all such persons as, after admonition of the minister, in presence of two sufficient witnesses, and by him so attested, shall be given up to the council as transgressors of this act, in withdrawing from their parish churches, as aforesaid; and the same, after hearing of the parties, being duly found, to decern, and inflict the censures and penalties above-mentioned, and such other corporal punishment as they shall think fit, and direct all execution necessary for making the same effectual, and to do every other thing they shall find necessary, for procuring obedience to this act, and putting the same to punctual execution, conform to the tenor and intent thereof.

1663. every body will not acquiesce in it, and to be sure it was no infallible rule.

They next resume their former acts last session, which have been considered; only this act speaks out the design of some of the preceding more plainly than many at first believed, to bring all ministers to subject to bishops. Then the king is made to engage his royal word *pro futuro* to maintain the prelates, and not to endure or give any connivance to the least variation from prelacy. It had been better to have used softer terms, than afterwards, in a kind of contradiction to this, when there appeared an absolute necessity to grant indulgences, and to travail in accommodations to please some of the bishops. Next they give us to understand, that the acts of the first, as well as the second session of this parliament, were made to settle the episcopal dignity, though the contrary was at first pretended: but the fashion now was, to make acts in general and dubious expressions, and in a year or two after, fully to extend their meaning, when king and council had practically explained their sense. Accordingly, the council, in the next place, are made the bishops' executioners, and the execution of all laws and acts relative to the church, is put into their hands: this clause was of great use to the prelates, and for many years that court served them vigorously. But generals are not sufficient, therefore more particularly the council is required to begin the persecution of ministers who dared to fulfil the ministry they had received from Christ Jesus, without the bishops' collation, and patrons' presentation, and to punish them as seditious, and contemners of royal authority.

The following clause is in favours of the contemned curates, who are pretty singularly described, ministers by public authority admitted to parishes. This kind of ministers, I dare say, the Christian church was unacquainted with for three hundred years after Christ. Ministers they were literally of the king and bishops, and not the people, the *sacra plebs*, their choice, settled by public authority, and the reader may add, by military force, and not by consent, and consequently servants of men, and not of Christ, or his people for his sake. Further,

all are required to subject to those ministers as his majesty's government ecclesiastical now established; and the not hearing of those creatures of the king and bishops, is declared to be of seditious and dangerous example and consequences, and punishable by the fines specified in the act. Indeed the uplifting of those fines drew prodigious sums of money from the country; but constrained worship cannot be conscientious. In a parenthesis the papists are cast in with the presbyterians, and made censurable for withdrawing from their parish church: but I never heard of any of them troubled by our zealous protestant bishops! In the next session of parliament, this clause is expunged, and the papists left to their own freedom, and the anger of the government levelled only against religious protestants.

Toward the close of the act, the honourable privy council are *de novo*, that all might be sure, constitute executioners of this act, and empowered not only to exact the fines from all whom the curate shall delate, but further corporally to punish them, as they shall think fit. How far corporal punishment in law extends, I am not to determine; but they seem empowered by this to make poor people's life a bitterness to them. Last of all, the council are warranted to do all things necessary for procuring obedience to this act, in the intent thereof. How far this goes, I know not; but it looks very like the spirit of the treaty we heard of since in another persecuting country: we need not doubt that the bishops, in this case both judges and parties, sufficiently extended the intent of the act. In a word, this act contains a rule and canon, I cannot call it ecclesiastical, but it is sufficiently so to prelates, when to suspend and deprive ministers of the gospel. We have seen the council very soon explaining and enlarging this act; and the first persecution of country people, which was any way general, began upon this; and indeed it was the foundation of much severity.

Their 3d act specifies the time of signing the declaration, appointed last year to be subscribed by all persons in public trust, which hath been insert, and needs not be repeated. All are required to sign betwixt and the 11th of November, and make returns to the council against the 1st of January next to come; and it is recommended to the council to be careful it be put in execution, which, as we have seen, and shall have ground to observe further, they were careful to do. At this time a new clause is added unreasonable enough: if persons be elected counsellors or magistrates, and refuse to sign the declaration, they are not only for ever declared incapable of being magistrates, but are to "forfeit all the privileges of merchandising and trading." The remark is so obvious, that we need not be surprised that this was called "the mark in the right hand," without which none might "buy or sell." This was highly unjust. A party in a town that had a mind to be rid of a man, who, it may be, was their rival in trade, and knew he could not declare "the covenants to be in themselves sinful," had no more to do but to get him chosen a counsellor or magistrate; and then, though otherwise he was not obliged to take the declaration, yet now, by pique and party, he must be turned out of all his trade and business. This declaration comes pretty near the sacramental test, annexed to civil places and military posts in some nations; upon the account of which we are so much abused by the papists, for prostituting that holy ordinance, contrary to our own protestant principles, and the nature of the institution. For refusing this declaration imposed last year, John earl of Crawford, lost his office of lord treasurer, and Sir James Dundas of Arniston, his post of one of the lords of session. The lord Stair, and Sir George Mackenzie of Tarbet, since earl of Cromarty, after some difficulties, came at length to sign it.

Their fifth act is for establishing a national synod, which, because it concerns church affairs, though never put in execution, I have annexed it, below.* The bishops who framed this act, and with whose concurrence, and at their desire it was passed, took effectual care to prevent the convocating any such synod; and we shall afterwards hear of some debate upon this head among the clergy. By this act, and consequently by the bishops, it is declared, "that it is necessary for the honour of God, and good of souls, there be a national synod." And if the act be true, our prelates had neither of these before their eyes. By this act, besides other members constituent of this synod, (the dignified clergy, and some from universities, but none from burghs) a power is lodged "in the meeting for exercise, to send one to the synod who is a presbyter." These meetings which, for what I can find, were very unfrequent, they will not call by the name of presbyteries. The power of this synod is very much narrowed, that it may be as near the English convocation as possible. Here indeed they differed, that in Scotland, "the king or his commissioner behoved always to be present;" and without him there can be no national synod. This looks as if no restrictions could bound them, neither a perpetual president, nor the king's will expressly signified to them, from time to time, by the archbishop of St. Andrews, but the king or his commissioner behoved always to be present. 1663.

How far the frame of this act agrees with the foundation of Scots prelacy, where all church power is lodged in the persons of the bishops, as creatures of the regal supremacy, and the king's delegates in church affairs, I shall not spend time in considering. By this act the jurisdiction seems to me to be lodged in the plurality of the meeting, and the vote of the meanest presbyter goes as far as the vote of the bishops, and one of the archbishops. Indeed the president hath a negative, and though the plurality of the meeting, yea the whole bishops and

---

* Act for the establishment and constitution of a national synod.
Forasmuch as the ordering and disposal of the external government of the church, and the nomination of the persons, by whose advice matters relating to the same are to be settled, doth belong to his majesty, as an inherent right of the crown, by virtue of his prerogative royal, and supreme authority in causes ecclesiastical: and in prosecution of this trust, his majesty, considering how fit and necessary it is, for the honour and service of Almighty God, the good and quiet of the church, and the better government thereof in unity and order, that there be a national synod and assembly duly constitute within this kingdom, hath therefore appointed and declared, and by these presents appoints and declares, that there shall be a national synod

1663. the other archbishop should vote a matter yet if the primate, the constant president of this synod, go not in, it cannot pass into an act or canon; and thus it was pity the primate set not up the claim of infallibility, which seems necessary to such a power as is lodged here in his hands. But I shall leave those things to be debated and determined by the friends of this frame of government in Scotland; only things are here upon a very different plan from the make of the diocesan synods, where presbyters were only allowed a consultative voice; and if they fall not in with their bishop, they may be prosecute as seditious persons, and deprived.

This session of parliament continued long, and did very little; the reason was, the act of balloting was to be rescinded, and the commissioner and Lauderdale resolved to be at the bottom of it; and the searching into the authors and promoters thereof took up very much time: at length the state of that affair was drawn up, and sent to his majesty, by Sir William Bruce, clerk to the bills, that the king's pleasure thereanent might be had; and till that came, the parliament was adjourned from day to day. At length, as will best appear from the printed act rescinding this balloting act, it was declared, "a way never formerly practised under monarchy, or any government, to punish men without making known their names to the parliament, who gave sentence, and what was contrary to his majesty's honour and interest, and after which none could be secure in their honour, estate, liberty, or life," and so rescinded.

September 23d, the parliament order a levy to be made, if need be, of twenty thousand foot, and two thousand horse, for the preservation of Christendom against the Turks. It was never made, but their army had certainly been much better employed this way, than in persecuting protestants. This session rose, October 9th, and the parliament was rode from the house to the Abbey, but it was very thin, many of the nobility being absent. Bishop Fairfoul lived not long after this parade, as we shall hear. When the parliament was up, many of our great folks went to court: the earl of Rothes was well received by the king, and made a member of the privy council in England. The rest of the acts of this parliament relate to civil matters, and as far as I have observed, have nothing in them relative to the history I have now in hand; and so we have done with parliaments for more than six years' time. I come now to the

---

of the church of Scotland; and that this synod, for the lawful members thereof, shall consist and be constitute of the archbishops of St. Andrews and Glasgow, and the remanent bishops of these two provinces, of all deans of cathedral churches, archdeacons, of all the moderators of meetings for exercise, allowed by the bishops of the respective dioceses, and of one presbyter or minister of each meeting, to be chosen and elected by the moderator and plurality of presbyters of the same, and of one or two from the university of St. Andrews, one from Glasgow, one from the King's College, one from Marshal's college of Aberdeen, and one from the college of Edinburgh; and this synod, thus constitute, is to meet at such times and places, as his majesty, by his proclamation, shall appoint; and is to debate, treat, consider, consult, conclude, and determine upon such pious matters, causes, and things, concerning the doctrine, worship, discipline, and government of this church, as his majesty shall from time to time, under his royal hand, deliver, or cause be delivered, to the archbishop of St. Andrews, president of the said national assembly, to be by him offered to their consideration. The estates of parliament do humbly recognosce and acknowledge his majesty's royal power and prerogative aforesaid, with the piety, justice, and prudence of his majesty's resolution herein; likeas, his majesty, with their advice and consent, doth hereby establish, ratify, and confirm this constitution of a national assembly, as the lawful constitution of the national synods and assemblies of this church, his majesty, or his commissioner, (without whose presence no national synod can be kept) being always present: and declares, that no act, canon, order, or ordinance, shall be owned as an act of the national synod of the church of Scotland, so as to be of any effect, force, or validity in law, to be observed and kept by the archbishops and bishops, the inferior clergy, and all other persons within this realm, (as far as lawfully, being members of this national church, it may concern them) but that which shall be considered, consulted, and agreed upon, by the president, and major part of the members above specified. It is always hereby provided, that nothing be enacted or put in execution, by authority of a national synod within this kingdom, which shall be contrary to his majesty's royal prerogative, or the laws of the kingdom; and that no act, matter, or cause, be debated, consulted, and concluded upon, but what shall be allowed, approven, and confirmed by his majesty or his commissioner present at the said national synod.

sufferings of particular persons this year, and the sealing the laws of this and former sessions, with the blood of the excellent lord Warriston.

SECT. IV.

Of the sufferings and martyrdom of the lord Warriston, July 22d, 1663.

HAVING thus got through the general rules and acts, which were the foundation of the particular sufferings of presbyterians, I come to the hardships which gentlemen, ministers, and others were brought under this year; and before I give a detail of these, the singular case of the good lord Warriston deserves a section by itself, and I place it here, because he was executed in time of parliament, as all our three first worthies were. I might have brought in the account of this excellent person upon the second chapter, with that of his dear friends and fellow-martyrs, the noble marquis of Argyle, and Mr. James Guthrie, both because these three are the chief instances of suffering unto death in this first book, though we shall meet with multitudes in the following books; and it was fully determined that my lord's life should have been taken at the same time, but he was not catched: and the manner of dealing with his lordship, was much the same with that taken with his fellow-sufferers unto death, if not more base, though less seen; and the cause was much the same he died upon, though his circumstances, in some things, differed from the former two; yet I thought it most proper to keep to the order of time in which he suffered, as much as might be. As the foundations of prelacy in Scotland, attended with the destruction of our civil liberty, were soaked with the blood of one of the best of our noblemen, and one of the most eminent of our ministers, so the walls now fast building, and pretty far advanced, behoved to be cemented with the blood of this excellent gentleman; so this godly and innocent person must fall as a third sacrifice.

In the 1st chapter it hath been already observed, that the king by his letter ordered major-general Morgan to seize Sir Archibald Johnston of Warriston, lord register. The day upon which his two excellent friends, Sir John Chiesly of Carswel, and Sir James Stuart of Priestfield, were seized, my lord Warriston knowing nothing of the orders, was providentially out of town visiting a friend. When in his return, just entering the town, he got notice of the warrant for apprehending him, and turned his horse, and retired a while from the storm. For some time he was very narrowly hunted up and down, till, after his escaping many imminent hazards, at length he got off the kingdom in the habit and character of a merchant.

In the second chapter we have heard that his persecutors, during the first session of parliament, got passed two acts against him: by the first they declare him incapable of all public trust and office, after, by a proclamation, he had been declared fugitive. By their next they pass a sentence of forfeiture and death upon him, in absence; the grounds of which we already heard. The first was as unnecessary as the last was unjust. Meanwhile this excellent person is obliged to lurk very closely, sometimes in the Low Countries, sometimes in Germany, and mostly at Hamburgh. I find in the preface to the Apologetical Narration, that when he was at Hamburgh, and under sickness, Doctor Bates, one of king Charles's physicians, being, as was said, hired either to kill or distract him, did give him poison in his physic, and took from him upwards of sixty ounces of blood, whereby he was brought to the gates of death, and so far lost his memory, that he could not remember what he had done a quarter of an hour before.

After Warriston had wandered a part of two years, he most unadvisedly went into France, the unsafest place he could go to. The king or some body about him at London got some hints of this, and caused seize one Major Johnston, and bring him before him, expecting more particular accounts from him, it seems, than any he could think upon. The major was imprisoned and threatened with death, if he would not discover where

1663 Warriston was. What he told I cannot positively say, but when dismissed and gone to his lodgings, he never came any more abroad, but pined away in grief, till in a few days he died. Those circumstances, and a good part of what is in this section, I have from the papers of a reverend minister, who lived at this time, and had a particular occasion to know the state of my lord's sufferings.

In the meantime one Alexander Murray, commonly called crooked Murray, is despatched over to France, where notice had been got my lord Warriston was: the messenger, they say, was not unfit, and it was believed, as he lived, so he died an atheist. This man, when he went over, found means to trace out the lady Warriston, and by noticing her narrowly, at length he came to discover my lord at Roan. In that city, a very little after he was come to that lodging, he was seized, when at secret prayer, which duty he was much exercised in. Murray applied to the magistrates to send over Warriston to England, producing the king's commission to him for that effect. They put my lord into custody, and sent up an account of the affair to the French king and council, before they would take any further steps. I hear the question was put in council, whether the prisoner should be retained or delivered up? and the most part were for his being kept in France, at least till more reason was shown for giving him up than yet appeared. But that king, to whose influence in part we owe many of the bloody measures, and destructive steps to good men and religion, fallen into during the reigns of the two brothers, determined he should be delivered up. Accordingly, in January this year he was brought over prisoner, and put in the Tower of London; and in the beginning of June he is sent down to Edinburgh, to be executed with the greater solemnity, when the parliament is sitting. By the council registers I find that, June 2d, " The lords of council having received certain intelligence, that Archibald Johnston, sometime of Warriston, is coming home, and that in a few days he is to arrive at Leith, do therefore ordain the magistrates of Edinburgh to provide a sufficient guard to receive him at the shore of Leith when he is landed; and that he be brought up from thence on foot bareheaded to the tolbooth of Edinburgh, where the magistrates of Edinburgh are to secure his person in close prison, without suffering his wife or children, or any others, to have access to speak with him, while further order from the council or lord chancellor"

June 8th, he landed at Leith, and was brought up under a guard, and dealt with as above. June 9th, the council meet, and the king's letter about him is read. "Right trusty, &c.—You shall give order to receive into our prison, the body of Archibald Johnston, sometime of Warriston, whom we have sent into that our kingdom, to the end that he may be proceeded against according to law and justice. Given, &c. May 16th, 1663." —That same day the council give the following order, about the desire of my lord Warriston's friends. " The council having considered the desire of several friends of Archibald Johnston, late of Warriston, desiring they may have liberty to speak with him, do grant liberty to any one of his relations or friends, to have access unto him, at any time betwixt eight of the clock in the morning and eight at night, and do discharge the magistrates of Edinburgh and keeper of the tolbooth, to suffer any more persons to enter the prison but three at once; and those three to stay no longer than an hour, or two at farthest, and ordain the keeper of the tolbooth by himself, or those he shall intrust, to wait upon the chamber where he is, to take care of the security of his person, that he escape not in disguise or otherwise; and continue to determine the time and manner of his execution, till next council day."

It would seem from this, that at first it was projected that the council should name the time and place of his public death, upon the old sentence passed by the parliament: but afterwards it was resolved to bring him before the parliament, and to have his sentence solemnly pronounced at the bar. Accordingly, July 8th, he is brought before the parliament. I suppose their forms in his circumstances did not make any indictment necessary, at least I have heard of none, nor of any lawyers allowed him. When he appeared at the bar, he was so evidently weakened in his memory and judgment, by the vile methods taken with him, that every body lamented the vast change upon him. My lord Warriston was once in case to have reasoned before the greatest assembly in Europe, yea, to have presided in it; but now he could scarce speak to any purpose in his own case. The primate and bishops, now members in parliament, pleased with this vast change in this great man, scandalously and basely triumphed over him, and mocked him in the open house. No sober man could refuse him a great deal of compassion in such circumstances, and, it seems, most of the members of parliament were inclinable to spare his life. This began to appear in the vote upon this question, " Whether the time of his execution should be just now fixed, or delayed ?" When the rolls were called, at first a great number of members were for a delay. Which Lauderdale observing, and knowing he needed scarce return to his master if Warriston were spared, contrary to all order and form, in the middle of the calling of the rolls, rose up and had a very threatening harangue for his present execution. And thus upon the proceeding in the rolls, sentence was pronounced against him, that he should be hanged at the cross of Edinburgh the 22d day of July, and after he was hanged dead, that his head be severed from his body, and put up upon the Netherbow Port, beside his dear friend Mr. James Guthrie's. It is said, with what certainty I know not, that the bishops would have had the day of his execution to have been the 23d day of July, as a kind of expiation for what was done against their predecessors in office, July 23d, 1637, when the first open opposition was made to their innovations and the service book : but they were not humoured in this.

I regret that I can give so little account of this great man's Christian and affecting carriage while in prison. A person of very great worth, who was several times with my lord while in the tolbooth, hath left this account of him, " That when there he was sometimes under great heaviness and distress, and borne down with bodily weakness and melancholy, yet he never came in the least to doubt of his eternal happiness, and used to say, 'I dare never question my salvation, I have so often seen God's face in the house of prayer.' " It was certainly a most remarkable appearance of providence in behalf of this good, and once great, man, that the very morning before his execution, notwithstanding for some time formerly, he had, as it were, lost the exercise of those extraordinary parts and talents he once enjoyed, and his memory for some time was almost quite gone, yet like the sun at his setting, after he has been for a while under a cloud, he shone most brightly and surprisingly, and so in some measure the more sweetly. That morning he was under a wonderful effusion of the spirit of sons, as great perhaps as many have had since the primitive times. With the greatest confidence and holy freedom, and yet the deepest humility, he repeated that, " Father, Father, Abba, Father," the savour of which did not wear off the spirits of some who were witnesses for many days.*

1663.

---

* We have the following account of this eminent man's last appearance, from the pen of Sir George Mackenzie :—" He was brought up the street discovered, and being brought into the council house of Edinburgh, where the chancellor and others waited to examine him, he fell upon his face roaring and with tears entreated they would pity a poor creature who had forgot all that was in the Bible. This moved all the spectators with a deep melancholy, and the chancellor, reflecting upon the man's [*great parts*] former esteem, and the great share he had in all the late revolutions, could not deny some tears to the frailty of silly mankind. At his examination he pretended that he had lost so much blood by the unskilfulness of his chirurgeons that he lost his memory with his blood; and I really believe that his courage had indeed been drawn out with it. Within a few days he was brought before the parliament, where he discovered nothing but much weakness, running up and down upon his knees begging mercy. But the parliament ordained his former sentence to be put to execution, and accordingly he was executed at the cross of Edinburgh. At his execution he showed more composure than formerly, which his friends ascribed to God's miraculous kindness for him, but others thought that he had only formerly put on this disguise of madness to escape death in it, and that finding the mask useless, he had returned, not to his wit, which he had lost, but from his madness which he had counterfeited. However it cannot be denied but he had been a man of [*eminent parts and more eminent devotion*] some parts and devotion ; but his natural choler being kindled by his zeal, had been fatal first to this kingdom, and then to himself."—History of Scotland, pp. 134, 135.
It is probable that by writing such descrip

1663. The day of his execution, a high gallows or gibbet was set up at the cross, and a scaffold made by it. About two of the clock he was taken from prison: many of his friends attended him in mourning. When he came out he was full of holy cheerfulness and courage, and in perfect serenity and composure of mind as ever he was. Upon the scaffold he acknowledged his compliance with the English, and cleared himself of the least share in the king's death. He read his speech with an audible voice, first at the north side and then the south side of the scaffold: he prayed next with the greatest liberty, fervour, and sense, of his own unworthiness, frequently using the foresaid expression. After he had taken his leave of his friends, he prayed again in a perfect rapture, being now near the end of that sweet work he had been so much employed about through his life, and felt so much sweetness in.

Then the napkin being tied upon his head, he tried how it would fit him, and come down and cover his face, and directed to the method how it should be brought down when he gave the sign. When he was got to the top of the ladder, to which he was helped because of bodily weakness, he cried with a loud voice, " I beseech you all who are the people of God, not to scar at sufferings for the interests of Christ, or stumble at any thing of this kind falling out in those days; but be encouraged to suffer for him; for I assure you in the name of the Lord he will bear your charges." This he repeated again with great fervour, while the rope was tying about his neck, adding, " The Lord hath graciously comforted me." Then he asked the executioner if he was ready to do his office, who answering he was, he bid him do it, and crying out, " O, pray, pray, praise, praise!" was turned over, and died almost without a struggle, with his hands lift up to heaven. He was soon cut down, and his head struck off, and his body carried to the Grayfriars' church-yard. His head was put up upon the Nether-bow Port; but in a little time, by the interest and moyen of lieutenant general Drummond, who married one of his daughters, it was permitted to be taken down and buried with the body. His speech upon the scaffold is printed in Naphtali; and there he declares, that what he had prepared to have said at his death, was taken from him, but he hoped it should be preserved to be a testimony to the truth. In what is printed he speaks his very heart, touching his own soul's state, his sins and infirmities, the public, and his poor family, and present sufferings; and though it hath been often printed, I could not but insert it in a note,*

---

tions as the above, Sir George Mackenzie had fortified himself against the reproaches of conscience, and imposed on his own understanding to that degree, as to be perfectly serious when he wrote his defence of the government of that period, in which he affirms that no man, under the government of Charles II. died for or on account of religion.

Burnet, who was Warriston's nephew, says, " He was so disordered both in body and mind, that it was a reproach to any government to proceed against him. His memory was so gone, that he did not know his own children."—History of his Own Times, Edinburgh edit. p. 297.

Laing, who was certainly no fanatic, says, " He was a man of more than common understanding or genius; of an active, violent, and disinterested spirit; of a quick and vivid invention; of an extensive and tenacious memory; incapable of repose; indefatigable in application; ever fertile in expedients; endowed with a vehement, prompt, and impressive elocution; and at a time when the nobility themselves were statesmen, his political talents raised him from an obscure advocate, to a level with the prime nobility, in affairs of state."—History of Scotland, vol. iv. p. 36.—*Ed.*

* Lord Warriston's speech, July 22d, 1663, with some account of his carriage.

Right honourable, much honoured, and beloved auditors and spectators, that which I intended and prepared to have spoken at this time, and in this condition, immediately before my death, (if it should be so ordered that this should be my lot) is not at present in my power being taken from me when apprehended; but I hope the Lord shall preserve it to bear my testimony more fully and clearly than now I can in this condition, having my memory much destroyed through much sore and long sickness, melancholy, and the excessive drawing of my blood: yet, I bless the Lord, (that notwithstanding all these forementioned distempers) I am in any capacity to leave this weak and short testimony.

1. I desire, in the first place, to confess my sins, so far as is proper to this place and case, and to acknowledge God's mercies, and to express my repentance of the one, and my faith of the other, through the merits of our Lord Jesus Christ, our gracious Redeemer and Mediator. I confess that my natural temper hath been hasty and passionate, and that in my manner of going about and prosecuting the best pieces of work and service to the Lord,

CHAP. IV.] OF THE CHURCH OF SCOTLAND. 359

with some account of his carriage before and at his death, printed at this time.

Many things are laid to this great man's charge most falsely, of which he was perfectly innocent, particularly his accession to the king's murder, as to

1663.

and to my generation, I have been subject to my excess of heat, and thereby to some precipitations, which hath no doubt offended standers by and lookers on, and exposed both me and the work to their mistakes, whereby the beauty of that work hath been much obscured. Neither have I, in following the Lord's work, his good work, been altogether free of self-seeking, to the grief of my own conscience, which hath made me oftentimes cry out with the apostle, "O wretched man that I am, who shall deliver me from this body of death?" and to lie low in the dust, mourning and lamenting over the same, deprecating God's wrath, and begging his tender mercies to pardon, and his powerful grace to cure all these evils. I must confess withal, that it doth not a little trouble me, lie heavy upon my spirit, and will bring me down with sorrow to the grave, (though I was not alone in this offence, but had the body of the nation going before me, and the example of persons of all ranks to ensnare me) that I suffered myself, through the power of temptations, and too much fear anent the straits that my numerous family might be brought into, to be carried into so great a length of compliance in England with the late usurpers, which did much grieve the hearts of the godly, and made those that sought God ashamed and confounded for my sake; and did give no small occasion to the adversary to reproach and blaspheme, and did withal not a little obscure and darken the beauty of several former actings about his glorious and blessed work of reformation, so happily begun, and far advanced in these lands; wherein he was graciously pleased to employ, and by employing, to honour me to be an instrument, (though the least and unworthiest of many) whereof I am not at all ashamed this day, but account it my glory, however that work be now cried down, opposed, laid in the dust, and trode upon; and my turning aside to comply with these men, was the more aggravated in my person, that I had so frequently and seriously made profession of my averseness from, and abhorrency of that way, and had showed much dissatisfaction with others that had not gone so great a length: for which, as I seek God's mercy in Christ Jesus, so I desire that all the Lord's people may, from my example, be the more stirred up to watch and pray that they enter not into temptation.

2. I dare not deny, on the other hand, but must testify, in the second place, to the glory of his free grace, that the Lord my God hath often showed, ensured into, and engraven upon my conscience, the testimony of his reconciled mercy, through the merits of Jesus Christ, pardoning all my iniquities, and assuring me that he would deliver me also, by the grace of his Holy Spirit, from the spite, tyranny, and dominion thereof, and hath often drawn forth my spirit to the exercise of repentance and faith, and hath often engraven upon my heart, in legible characters, the merciful pardoning, and gracious begun cure thereof, to be perfected thereafter to the glory of his name, salvation of my own soul, and edification of his own church.

3. I am pressed in conscience to leave here at my death, my true and honest testimony, in the sight of God and man, unto and for the national covenant, the solemn league and covenant, the solemn acknowledgment of our sins, and engagements to our duties, and to all the grounds and causes of fasts and humiliations, and of the Lord's displeasure and contendings with the land, and to the several testimonies given for his interests, by general assemblies, commissions of the kirks, synods, presbyteries, and other faithful ministers and professors.

4. I am also pressed to encourage his doing, suffering, witnessing people, and sympathizing ones with those that suffer, that they would continue in their duties of mourning, praying, believing, witnessing, and sympathizing with others, and humbly to assure them, in the name of the Lord our God, the God of his own word, and work of his covenant, cause and people, that he will be seen, found, and felt in his own gracious way and time, by his own means and instruments, for his own honour and glory, to return to his own truths, interests, and servants, to revive his name, his covenant, his word, his work, his sanctuary, and his saints in this nation, yea, even in these three covenanted nations, which were by solemn bonds, covenants, subscriptions, and oaths, given away and devoted to himself.

5. I exhort all those that have been or are enemies, or unfriendly to the Lord's name, covenant, or cause, word, work, or people in Britain and Ireland, to repent and amend before these sad judgments that are posting fast, come upon them, for their sinning so highly against the Lord, because of any temptations of the time on the right hand or on the left, by baits or straits whatsoever, and that after so many engagements and professions of not a few of themselves to the contrary.

6. I dare not conceal from you who are friendly to all the Lord's precious interests in Britain and Ireland, that the Lord (to the commendation of his grace be it humbly spoken) hath several times, in the exercise of my repentance and faith, (during my troubles) and after groans and tears upon these three notable chapters, viz. the ninth of Ezra, the ninth of Nehemiah, and the ninth of Daniel, together with other suitable scriptures, even in the very nick of humble and fervent prayers and supplications to him, for reviving again of his name, covenant, cause, word, and work of reformation, in these covenanted nations, particularly in poor Scotland, (yea, O dear Scotland!) which solemnly re-engaged unto him, to the good example and encouragement of his people in the other two nations, to covenant with him also; that the Lord, I say, hath several times given me good grounds of hope, and lively expectations of his merciful, gracious, powerful, and wonderful renewing, reviving again of all his former great interests in these covenanted nations, and that in such a way, by such means and instruments, with such antecedents, concurrents, consequences, and effects, as shall wonderfully rejoice his mourning friends, and astonish his contradicting and contra-acting enemies.

1663. which he vindicates himself in his printed speech. The one thing which he himself heavily lamented, frequently to his dying day, and which was the only reasonable pretext for this severe sentence, was his compliance with the English,

7. I do earnestly recommend my poor afflicted wife and children, and their posterity, to the choicest blessings of God, and unto the prayers and favours of all the Lord's children and servants, in their earnest dealings with God and man in their behalf, that they may not be ruined for my sake, but that, for the Lord my God's sake, they may be favoured, assisted, supplied, and comforted, and may be also fitted of the Lord for his fellowship and service, whom God himself hath moved me often in their own presence, and with their own consents, to dedicate, devote, resign, alike, and as well as I devoted and resigned my own soul unto him, for all time and eternity.

8. Now here, I beseech the Lord to open the eyes of all the instruments of my trouble, who are not deadly irreconcilable enemies to himself and his people, that they may see the wrong done by them to his interest and people, and to me and mine, and may repent thereof, return to the Lord, and more cordially maintain, own and adhere unto all his interests in time to come. The Lord give unto them repentance, remission and amendment, which is the worst wish I do, and the best wish I can wish unto them; for I can wish no better to myself.

9. I do most humbly and earnestly beg the fervent prayers of all his praying children, servants, and instruments, wheresoever they be, whether absent or present, to be put up in behalf of his name, cause, covenant, work, and people, and also in behalf of my wife and children, and their posterity, and that the Lord would glorify himself, edify his church, encourage his saints further, and accomplish his good work by all his doings and dealings, in substance towards all his own.

10. Whereas I hear, that some of my unfriends have slandered and defamed my name, as if I had been accessory to his late majesty's death, and to the making the change of the government thereupon; I am free, as I shall now answer before his tribunal, from any accession by counsel or contrivance, or any other way, to his late majesty's death, or to their making that change of the government; and the Lord judge between me and mine accusers: and I pray the Lord to preserve the present king his majesty, and to pour his best blessings upon him and his royal posterity; and the Lord give unto them good and faithful counsellors, holy and wise counsels, and prosperous success, to God's glory, and the good of his interest and people and to their own honour and happiness.

11. I do here submit and commit my soul and body, wife and children, and their children's children, from generation to generation, for ever, with all others our Lord's friends and followers, and all his doing, suffering, witnessing, and sympathizing ones, in the present and subsequent generations, unto the Lord's choicest mercies, graces, favours, services, employments, impowerments, enjoyments, improvements, and inheritaments in earth, and in heaven, in time and eternity: all which suits, with all others which he hath at any time, by his Spirit, moved and assisted me to make, and put up according to his will, I leave before the throne, and upon the Father's merciful bowels, and the Son's mediating merits, and the Holy Spirit's compassionating groans, for now and for evermore. Amen.

Short narrative of his carriage before and after his last discourse above.

His carriage all the time from his coming from London, was most convincingly Christian, full of tenderness of spirit, and meekness towards all, so that all who were in his company, both in the ship and at other times, asserted, they were never in the company of a more godly, sincere, fervent seeker of God, and one that was most sensible of the least tenderness exercised towards himself. Before he came out of the ship he prayed for a blessing upon his majesty, and upon state and kirk, and when landed at Leith he inquired for the ministers of Edinburgh; to which it was answered, they are all silenced, and put out of the town. Well (said he) their silence does preach, and truly Mr. Douglas, &c. might have preached either before state or kirk.

During the whole time of this imprisonment the Lord kept him in a most spiritual tender frame, even to the conviction of some that hated him formerly. The great thing he most desired, was gracious through-bearing which he said was only to be had through the supply of the Spirit, and intercession of the saints; and the thing he most feared, was fainting in the hour of trial, and for that cause did earnestly desire, that prayer might fervently be put up to God for him, which was indeed done in all parts of the land, which had its good success in God's own way.

When he received his sentence, he did receive it with exceeding great meekness, to the admiration of all, desiring the best blessings of heaven to be upon his majesty, and upon state and kirk, whatever befell himself, and that God would give his majesty true and faithful counsellors, &c.

The nearer he was to his death he was the more quieted in his mind, which had been discomposed by poison, and the drawing of threescore ounces of blood, the physicians intending hereby to distract him, or make him an ideot fool. The night before his death he slept very sweetly, and in the morning was very full of comfort, uttering many sweet expressions as to his assurance of being clothed with a long white robe before night, and of getting a new song of the Lamb's praise put in his mouth. He dined very cheerfully, hoping to sup in heaven, and to drink the next cup fresh and new in his Father's kingdom. Thereafter he was alone till the time of his being brought forth. When he was going to the scaffold he said frequently to the people, "your prayers, your prayers." The Lord kept him very composed under some disturbances in the streets. When come up to the scaffold, he said to the people, "I entreat you quiet yourselves a little, till this dying man deliver his last words among you." He likewise desired them not to be offended that he made some use of his paper to help his memory, so much wasted by long sick.

in taking the office of clerk register, and sitting and presiding in some meetings at London, after Cromwell's death. In the year 1657, after many and long struggles against Cromwell's usurpation, when he was sent up from Scotland about some important affairs, he was prevailed upon to re-enter upon his former office of the clerk register, by Cromwell, who was abundantly sensible how much it would be for his interest to have so bright a person gained over to him. During five years and more, he wrestled and acted with the utmost vigour for the king's interest, and being a man of great resolution, he both spoke very openly, and wrote against Scotsmen's submitting to take offices under the usurper. I have it from good hands, that in the meeting at Edinburgh, which sent him up to London upon business, he reasoned against, and to his utmost opposed his being sent up. With great ingenuity he acquainted them with what he thought was his weak side, and that he was sensible of the easiness of his temper, and that he could not resist importunity, and begged he might not be sent among snares; but after all he was peremptorily named. My lord's family was numerous, and very considerable sums were owing him, which he had advanced for the public service, and a good many years of bygone salaries: and when no other way appeared to recover what was justly his, he was, through importunity, prevailed upon to fall in with the usurper, there being now no other door open for his relief. Thus he fell before the temptation that all flesh, even the best, may appear to be, grass. After his compliance he was observed to be generally sad and heavy, and not what he had been formerly; neither did his outward affairs thrive much upon his hand. But it is certain enough, that it was neither his lamented compliance under the usurpation, nor his great activity in the work of reformation, both which the government now were pretty much above; but a personal prejudice and pique at this good man, for his freedom in reproving vice, was at bottom of this bitter persecuting him to the death. This was what could never be forgot or forgiven, either to him or the marquis of Argyle, as was pretty plainly intimated to the earl of Bristol, when interceding for my lord Warriston. I have an account of this holy freedom my lord used, from a reverend minister not many years ago dead, who was his chaplain at the time, and took the freedom to advise my lord not to adventure upon it: yet this excellent person having the glory of God, and the honour of religion more in his eye than his own safety, went on in his designed reproof; and would not for a compliment quit the peace he expected in his own conscience, be the event what it would by disburdening himself. He got a great many fair words, and all was pretended to be taken well from my good lord register, but as he was told by his well-wishers, it was never forgot.

1663.

To shut up this section, my lord Warriston was a man of great learning and eloquence, of very much wisdom, and extraordinary zeal for the public cause of religion and reformation, in which he was a chief actor; but above all, he was extraordinary in piety and devotion, as to which he had scarce any equal in the age he lived in. One who was his intimate acquaintance says, he spent more time, notwithstanding the great throng of public business upon his hand, in prayer, meditation, and close observation of providences, and self-examination, than any ever he knew or heard of: and as he was very diligent in making ob-

---

ness and malice of physicians; then he delivered the above discourse, and repeated it again on the other side of the scaffold. After this he prayed with the greatest fervour and humility, beginning thus, " Abba, Abba, Father, Father, accept this thy poor sinful servant, coming unto thee through the merits of Jesus Christ," &c. After he had taken his leave of his friends, he prayed again at the foot of the ladder, cheerfully resigning God's interests and his own soul into the hands of his heavenly Father. There were no ministers allowed to be with him, but a person present observed, that there was no missing of ministers there, and the Lord made good those blessed words, Phil. iv. 19. and 2 Cor. i. 5. The executioner came to him desiring his forgiveness, to whom he said, "the Lord forgive thee, poor man, which I also do," and gave him some money, and bade him do his work right. He was helped up the ladder by some of his friends in deep mourning: as he ascended, he said, "your prayers, your prayers; I desire your prayers in the name of the Lord;" so great at all times was his esteem of prayers. The other circumstances of his death have been already noticed in the history.

1663. servations of the Lord's way, so he was visited with extraordinary discoveries of the Lord's mind, and very remarkable providences. He wrote a large diary, which yet remains in the hands of his relations, an invaluable treasure of Christian experiences and observations; and, as I am told by one who had the happiness to see some part of it, there is mixed in sometimes matters of fact very little known now, which would bring a great deal of light to the history of Scots affairs, in that period wherein he lived. There he records his sure hopes after wrestling, in which he was mighty, that the church of Scotland would be mercifully visited, and freed from the evils she fell under after the restoration. His numerous family he left upon the Lord's providence cheerfully, who provided as well for most of them, as they could have expected though he had continued in his outward prosperity. But it is time to come forward to other particular sufferers this year.

SECT. V.

Of the particular hardships and suffering of great numbers of ministers, gentlemen, and others, this year, 1663.

HAVING delayed the accounts of the severe persecution of vast numbers of presbyterian ministers, gentlemen, and people this year, especially before the council, to this place; I come now to give them altogether, mostly from the records of that court, and that much in the order of time they lie in.

The council are scarce ended with the west country ministers last year, and their banishing good numbers to foreign places, yea, even before the banished ministers went off, but they begin, February 24th, a new process against a greater number of ministers in Galloway. Few or none in that synod had conformed, and, we have heard, the bishop's diocesan meeting was adjourned, because there were few or none to wait upon it: therefore, probably at his instigation, the council pass the following act.

" The lords of his majesty's privy council being informed, that there are several ministers in the diocese of Galloway, who not only contrary to the order of council, dated at Glasgow, October 1st last, do continue at their former residences and churches, but in manifest contempt thereof, and contrary to the indulgence granted them by the late act, dated December 23d last, do yet persist in their wicked practices, still labouring to keep the hearts of people from the present government in church and state, by their pernicious doctrine; and more particularly that Messrs. Archibald Hamilton minister at Wigton, William Maitland at Whitthorn, Robert Richardson at Mochrum, George Wauch at Kirkindair, Alexander Ross at Kirkowan, Alexander (it ought to be Fergusson) Hutcheson at Sorbie, ministers in the presbytery of Wigton; Messrs. Alexander Pedin at the Muirchurch of Glenluce, John Park at the Shappel, Thomas Kennedy at Liswald, James Lawrie at Stainkirk, James Wilson at Kirkmaiden, John M'Broom at Portpatrick, ministers within the presbytery of Stranraer; Messrs. Patrick Peacock at Kirmabreck, William Erskine minister at Garston, Adam Kay minister at Borg, Robert Fergusson at Boittil, Samuel Arnot at Tongland, John Wilkie at Twinam, James Buglos minister at Corsmichael, Thomas Warner at Balmaclelland, John Cant at Kells, Adam Alison at Balmagie, John M'Michan at Dalry, John Duncan at Dundrenean and Rerick, and Thomas Thomson minister at Parton, ministers in the presbytery of Kirkcudbright; and Mr. Alexander Smith at Cowend and Siddick, are chief instruments in carrying on that wicked course: have therefore ordained letters to be directed against the forenamed persons, charging and commanding them, and every one of them, to remove themselves, wives, bairns, servants, goods and gear, forth and from their respective dwellingplaces and manses, and out of the bounds of the presbytery where now they live, betwixt and the 20th day of March next; and that they do not take upon them to exercise any part of the ministerial function: and also charging them to appear before the council, the 24th of March next to come, to answer for their former disobedience; with certification as is above specified."

CHAP. IV.] OF THE CHURCH OF SCOTLAND. 363

In the registers there are five or six of those ministers' names blank; and only the name of the parishes, which I have filled up from another list I have before me; by which I find, that Mr. Robert Fergusson and Mr. James Lawrie were ordained before the (year) 1649, and so in law came not under the two acts it is alleged they broke. Upon the 24th of March, I find Messrs. Maitland, Kay, Wilkie, Wauch, Lawrie, Cant, Alison, M'Gachan, and Smith, "being called, compeared personally, and being severally examined upon their obedience to the late acts of parliament and council, anent their obedience and submission to the government of the church, as the same is presently established by law, declared, they were not yet clear to give obedience thereunto; but they were ready and willing, likeas they then judicially promised to obey the said acts, for removing from their manses and parishes, and desisting from preaching, conform to the same in every point. In consideration whereof, the lords declare, that they do continue [i. e. delay,] to insist against them for their former carriages, while they be of new cited." The others who did not compear, were obliged to leave the manses and kirks; and I find no more about them this year in the registers. We shall meet with Mr. Samuel Arnot, Mr. John Park, and Mr. Thomas Warner, and some others of them, under new hardships, in the progress of this work.

At that same diet the council cite another considerable number of ministers before them. " The lords of his majesty's privy council being informed, that several ministers in the diocese of Dunkeld, who not only contrary to the order of council, dated at Glasgow, October 1st last, do continue at their former residence and churches; but in manifest contempt thereof, and contrary to the indulgence granted to them by the late act, December 23d, do persist in their wicked courses, still labouring to keep the hearts of the people from the present government of church and state, by their pernicious doctrine; and more particularly, that Messrs. Patrick Campbell minister at Kilinnie, John Anderson at Auchtergavan, Francis Pearson at Kirkrauchael, David Graham at Forgondenny, George Halyburton at Duplin, Richard Ferret at Ava, John Miniman at Abernytie, David Campbell, at Minnimore, Thomas Lundy at Rattray, Robert Campbell, at Mullen, John Cruikshanks at Rogertoun, Thomas Glassie at Little Dunkeld, Andrew Donaldson at Dalgety, and Thomas Black at Lesley, are chief instruments in carrying on these wicked courses: therefore the lords of council ordain letters to be directed to charge the forenamed persons to remove (as above, with relation to the Galloway ministers) and that they take not upon them to exercise any part of the ministerial function, either privately or publicly. As also command them and every one of them to compear before the council the   day of   to answer for their former disobedience. With certification." I find no more about those ministers in the registers. I am ready to think, that they obeyed the charge to remove from their kirks and manses, and their compearing before the council was not insisted upon. The bishops at present were pressing to have the churches vacated of those who did not wait on their synods; and we have heard, that by the acts of parliament and council this year, a general course was taken with the whole nonconformist ministers, and they removed at such and such distances from their congregations. 1663.

It hath been noticed already, with what reluctancy a great many parishes in the south and west, permitted the curates to enter among them, when presbyterian ministers were turned out. In some places open opposition was made to them, especially in Irongray near Dumfries, and Kirkcudbright. The tumults in those two places, as they were the first of this kind, so they were severely noticed by the council; and I shall give as distinct an account of this as I can, from the registers; if once I had set down an abbreviate of it, I find in the papers of a worthy minister who lived at the time.

" The first open opposition to the settlement of the curates, I have heard of, was at Irongray, where Mr. John Welsh was minister. The curate at first not finding peaceable access, returned upon them with an armed force. None ventured to appear

1663. openly save women, and those of the meaner sort. However, the women of Irongray, headed by one Margaret Smith, opposed a party of soldiers who were guarding the curate, and fairly beat them off with stones. Margaret was afterwards brought in to Edinburgh, and banished to Barbadoes: but when before the managers, she told her tale so innocently, that they saw not fit to execute the sentence. In April 1663, or about that time, ten women were brought in to Edinburgh from Kirkcudbright, for a tumult there, and were for some time kept in prison, and afterwards pilloried, with papers on their foreheads signifying their fault." But I come to give the detail of this matter, as I have it in the council books.

May 5th, the chancellor having written a missive letter to the magistrates of Kirkcudbright, for finding out the persons most guilty of the tumult lately there, and ordained them to be cited before the council this day; and if any women be guilty, that their husbands, fathers, masters, or such as have the charge of them, be cited. In obedience thereunto, at the magistrates' instance, compeared Adam Gumquhen, John Halliday, John M'Staffen, Alexander Maclean, ———— Renthoun, John Carsan, Alexander M'Key, indwellers in the said burgh, who being examined, denied any hand in the tumult. M'Staffen and Maclean are ordained to find caution to produce their wives before the council, and the rest to enter their persons in the tolbooth of Edinburgh, till they exhibit their wives who were present at the said tumult; and ordain James Hunter in Kirkcudbright, cited and not compearing, to be denounced: but the council in their great zeal in this matter, go further, and appoint a committee to go and inquire into that affair in the south, and send in part of the army with them. The act and commission is as follows.

" The lords of his majesty's privy council, being certainly informed of the very great insolencies committed in the burgh of Kirkcudbright, and parish of Irongray, by the tumultuary rising of divers persons within the same, and in a barbarous manner opposing the admission of certain ministers who were appointed and came to serve there, and their offering and committing several abuses and indignities upon the persons of the said ministers, to the high and great contempt of his majesty's authority, and the disquieting of the government both of church and state; as also that there is no settled magistracy and government within the said burgh, as has been within the same, and that severals who have been chosen to exerce the office of the magistracy, do refuse to accept of the same; whereby the said town is left desolate of civil policy and the inhabitants at liberty to do what they please: the said lords of council, in consideration thereof, and of the great trust reposed in them by his majesty, do appoint and commissionate the earls of Linlithgow, Galloway, and Annandale, the lord Drumlanerk, and Sir John Wauchop of Niddry, or any two of them, to repair to those places, at such times as they shall think fit, and to call all the persons who have been either plotters of, committers, or assisters to, or connivers at the insolencies and abuses foresaid; and after hearing of them to examine witnesses, and receive all other needful probation for proving what shall be laid to their charge; and if thereafter, the said commissioners, or quorum foresaid, shall find just ground, that they secure their persons, and send such of them to Edinburgh, as they shall think fit, to that effect, or take sufficient caution from them, to answer before the lords of council, the   day of   under such penalties as the commissioners shall think fit. And also, that they examine and try upon what account, and for what cause there are not magistrates in the said burgh, who exerce their offices as formerly; and if they see it meet and just, that they either incarcerate, or take bond under caution and penalty, of such as they shall find to have been obstructers of a civil and lawful government, as formerly, within the said burgh, or such as have been lawfully chosen, and refuse to accept and exerce their offices without just cause. And siclike, that they see a formal and legal election, according to the custom of the said burgh, of others loyal and faithful persons, for supplying the places of such as are wanting, or who refuse to accept: otherwise, by the advice of such as are well affected within the said burgh, to nominate such persons as they shall think fit, for discharging the office of magistracy, and ruling the people within the said burgh, till further order. As also, that the said commissioners, if they shall see cause, call for the charters, rights, and securities, made and granted in favours of the said burgh, and concerning their privileges and liberties, to the effect they may be secured and exhibited before the parliament or council. And likewise, to be aiding and assisting to the bishops of the respective dioceses, for settling such ministers in those places, as they shall ordain and appoint.

"And for the more exact performance of the premises, that the said earl of Linlithgow cause march alongst with him, an hundred horse, and two hundred foot of his majesty's guards, or such other number as he shall think fit, to the effect such as will not willingly submit and give obedience, may be forced thereunto. And for the entertaining the said horse and foot, the said earl is hereby empowered, either to take free quarters within the said burgh, and parish of Irongray, or then, with concourse of the magistrates of the said burgh, or such others in the said places as he shall call for, to raise so much money off the burgh and and parish, as will satisfy the said horsemen and footmen, at thirty shillings Scots to each horseman, and twelve shillings to each footman *per diem*, during their abode there, by and attour the paying the officers their ordinary pay. With power also to the said commissioners, by force of arms, to suppress all meetings or insurrections of the people, if any shall happen. And, if need be, that the said commissioners shall call to their aid and assistance, the sheriffs, stewarts, heritable bailies, and others within the sheriffdom of Galloway, and stewartry of Kirkcudbright, and all noblemen, gentlemen, stewarts, heritable bailies, and others his majesty's good subjects within those bounds, with command to them readily to answer, obey, assist, and concur with the said commissioners, to the effect foresaid, as they shall be required. And that the said commissioners make report to the council or parliament of their diligence in the premises, betwixt and the —— day of June next to come.

1663.

" Glencairn chancellor, Morton, Sinclair, J. Gilmour, Primrose, Jo. Fletcher, Geo. Mackenzie, Sir Rob. Murray."

When this commission is granted, the council join with it an order, that five hundred pounds sterling be advanced by the receivers of the excise to the soldiers, as part payment of their pay; with one hundred and twenty pounds sterling to the earl of Linlithgow, and fifty pounds to the laird of Niddry, for bearing their charges.

That such a sputter should be made because a few women in two parishes had put some affronts upon the curates, when forced in upon them, may seem odd enough, and could not fail to increase the dislike the people in the southern shires had against them. I scarce know what could have been done further, if the highest acts of treason had been committed: but the general aversation of that part of the country from prelacy, and the complaints of the bishops upon that score, put them on those harsh measures; and we shall after this meet with a constant tract of oppression and devastation in that corner, till they were forced to the rising in Pentland. And for about twenty-four years, the west and south of Scotland were the continual scene of such severities: but I go on to the procedure of these commissioners. June 9th, they make their report to the council, and it is very large; I shall give as short and distinct an abstract of it as I can, that we may have some view of this first public step of heavy oppression of country people, for their adherence to their principles, and aversion to prelacy. Their report was given in in writ, and is in short.

" At *Kirkcudbright, May 25th*, 1663.

" In obedience to our commission, we having met at sundry diets, and caused convene before us such persons as were committers of, or assisters at the tumult at Kirkcudbright, to wit, Agnes Maxwell, and about thirty-two women, (most of them

1663. widows and servants, who need not be named here) with John lord Kirkcudbright, John Carsan of Sennick, and John Euart; and after hearing depositions and confessions, find Agnes Maxwell, Christian M'Cavers, Jean Rennie, Marion Brown, and Janet Biglaw, are guilty of, and have been most active in the said abuse, and ordain their persons to be carried prisoners under a guard to Edinburgh, to answer before the council. And Bessie Lawrie, with thirteen others, have been accessory thereto; and ordain them to be imprisoned till they find caution to appear before the council, under the pain of a hundred pounds sterling each. Helen Crackin, and some others are found absent, and left to the sheriff of Wigtoun and magistrates of Kirkcudbright, to apprehend and imprison. And finding by John lord Kirkcudbright's own confession, and the depositions of witnesses, that he said, ' If the minister came in there, he should come in over his belly and that he should lose his fortune,' or some such words, ' before he should be preacher there;' and that by his own confession, he acknowledges the receipt of my lord chancellor's letter before the tumult, and that he refused to compesce the same; and that he declared, ' if the minister had come in by his presentation, he should have commanded as many men as would have compesced the tumult, and bound them hand and foot;' and therefore we declare him guilty of the insurrection, and ordain him to be carried prisoner to Edinburgh by a guard. The said John Carsan of Sennick, being lately provost of the said burgh, and having great interest therein, and being with the lord Kirkcudbrigth in the town in the time of the tumult, and desired by James Thomson commissary to go with the rest to compesce the tumult, said scornfully, ' by what authority could he go?' and when the commissary offered his authority, he said, ' his authority was more over the dead than over the living:' as also, that he being a commissioner of the assize, refused his advice or concurrence to compescing the tumult; therefore we declare him to have had accession to the tumult, and ordain his person to be carried prisoner to Edinburgh under a guard. And finding by deposition of witnesses, that John Euart, late provost of Kirkcudbright, being desired to give his advice for compescing the tumult, he refused the same, alleging he was not a counsellor. We find that at the last election he was chosen provost, and without any just cause refused to accept of his office, whereupon we declare him to be the chief cause why the magistrates did not exerce their office for the said burgh: and finding, that notwithstanding of his foresaid refusal, he has sitten as a commissioner of the excise, and having tendered to him the declaration of parliament, he refused to subscribe it; wherefore we ordain him likewise to be carried to Edinburgh under a guard. They add, that, according to the set of the burgh, a new council was chosen, and magistrates, Mr. William Euart provost, John Newall and Robert Glendonyng bailies, and John Livingstone treasurer, who accepted in terms of law; and they signed a bond in their own name, and of the haill inhabitants of the place, binding and obliging them, and ilk one of them, conjunctly and severally, during their public trust, that they and all their inhabitants within their public liberties, should from the day and date thereof behave themselves loyally and peaceably, and in all things conform to his majesty's laws made and to be made, both in civil and ecclesiastical affairs; and that they should with all diligence execute any commands that are or should be directed to them, during the said time, that flow from any authority derived from the sacred majesty of our dread sovereign: as also, that they should protect the lord bishop of Galloway, and the minister of their burgh, who should be established there, and any other ministers that are or shall be established by authority; and that they should fulfil all the above particulars, under the penalty of eighteen thousand merks Scots, to be paid by them, or any of them, within a month after they shall be declared guilty by the lords of his majesty's privy council. Which was subscribed in our presence, and the presence of the community of the said burgh, and delivered to us."

"At Dumfries, May 30th, 1663.

"In pursuance of the foresaid commission, as to the trial of the abuse lately at Irongray, we caused cite before us William Arnot of Littlepark, George Rome of Beoch, and several other persons said to be concerned therein; and after we had examined witnesses, we found that there had been several unlawful convocations of the people of that place, for the opposing of the admission of Mr. Bernard Sanderson to be preacher at the said parish, especially against the serving of his edict, and thereafter hindering Mr. John Wisheart to preach, who was to have admitted the said Mr. Bernard. By the said depositions we find, that the said William Arnot did keep several meetings before the tumult; and that, when he was desired and required by the messengers who went to serve the edict, to assist to hold the women off them, he declared, he neither could nor would do it; that he drew his sword and set his back to the kirk door, and said, "let me see who will place a minister here this day." Therefore we find him guilty of the said tumult, and ordain him to be sent into Edinburgh under a guard. We find George Rome of Beoch accessory, as being present upon the place, and not concurring for compescing of the tumult, and ordain him to go to prison until he find caution, under five thousand merks, to appear before the council when called. And as to the rest of the persons, we find there hath been a great convocation and tumult of women; but, by reason there is no special probation of any persons particular miscarrying, more than their being there present at the tumult, we thought fit to ordain the whole party of horse and foot to be quartered upon the said parish of Irongray, upon free quarters, until Monday next; and that the whole heritors of the said parish give bond, upon the penalty of one hundred pounds sterling, for their future loyal behaviour, conform to the bond given at Kirkcudbright: and recommended to the sheriff of Nidsdale, to apprehend and try some who had not compeared, and report to the parliament or council betwixt and the 28th of June. And they order ten pounds sterling to their two clerks, as much to three messengers, and twenty shillings to an officer who waited on them, to be paid by the heritors of Irongray, if the council think fit.

" ANNANDALE,   GALLOWAY,
   DRUMLANERK,   J. WAUCHOP."
   LINLITHGOW,

1663.

This day the council do no more upon the giving in of this report, save the appointing of a committee to examine the earl of Linlithgow's accounts of his charges in the said commission. And five of the inhabitants of Kirkcudbright, who had been imprisoned, when appearing for their wives, as we heard, are set at liberty by the council, their wives having found caution at Kirkcudbright, after they had found caution in the council books, "to live peaceably and submissively to the present government in church and state, and give all due deference to the bishop of the diocese, the magistrates and minister of the place, and keep their parish kirk, and if any tumults be, that they shall endeavour to compesce the same."

No more offers about this matter till July 14th. The council having considered the report, and the instructions of the earl of Linlithgow and the commissioners, find, "that they have proceeded diligently and legally in execution of the trust reposed in them, performed good service to his majesty and the kingdom, and approve and ratify what they have done, and render them thanks; particularly to the said earl, who has by the troops under his command, ended the tumults, and left a party of guards at the town of Kirkcudbright to keep the peace, and recommend him for his expenses to the exchequer; and add the earls of Montrose and Eglinton to those formerly appointed, to consider of the business of Kirkcudbright and Irongray, to consider the temper and disposition of the prisoners, with power to call before them the laird of Earlston, who is under bond to compear, and report."

August 13th, the lords having considered several petitions of the prisoners from Kirkcudbright and Irongray, and the report of the commissioners sent to that country

1663. do find, "John Carsan of Sennick, John Euart, late provost of Kirkcudbright, and William Arnot of Littlepark in Irongray, to have been most guilty of the abuses and disorders there, and fine John Carsan in the sum of eight thousand merks, and the said William Arnot in the sum of five thousand merks; and them to find caution before they depart from prison, to pay the said sums to his majesty's exchequer betwixt and Martinmas next, with certification if they fail, they shall be banished out of the kingdom: and ordain and command the said William Arnot, betwixt and the 25th of October next to come, to make public acknowledgment of his offences two several Sabbaths at the kirk of Irongray before that congregation. Likeas the said lords do banish the said John Euart forth of this realm for his offence, and ordain and command him forth of the same betwixt and this day twenty days, not to be seen therein at any time hereafter, without license from his majesty or the council, at his highest peril.

" And the said lords finding Agnes Maxwell, Marion Brown, Jean Rennie, Christian M'Cavers, and Janet Biglaw, to have been most active in the said tumult, do ordain them, betwixt and the 15th day of September next to come, to stand two several market days at the market-cross of Kirkcudbright, ilk day for the space of two hours, with a paper on their face, bearing their fault to be for contempt of his majesty's authority, and raising a tumult in the said town; and ordain them before they depart out of prison, to enact themselves in the books of council, to give obedience to this; and the magistrates of Kirkcudbright to execute the sentence; and if they fail or delay so to do, that they cause whip them through the said town, and banish them forth of the same, and the liberties thereof."

August 25th, John Euart petitions the council that his sentence may be mitigated, by reason of his ill state of health, after twelve weeks' imprisonment, the circumstances of his wife and family; and that the only ground of his sentence was his keeping his house in the time of the tumult. The lords prorogate the execution of his sentence while the first day of March next to come, and give warrant for his liberation, on his giving bond to keep his majesty's peace in the meantime. The same day John Carsan supplicates for a mitigation of his fine, seeing he was not present at the tumult, nor had his residence for a long time in the burgh of Kirkcudbright; and that he being in no public employment for many years, did not conceive himself concerned to meddle in that particular; and such a fine would be the ruin of his family. The council mitigate the fine to four thousand merks, and ordain him to be liberate upon his giving bond to pay the same at Martinmas next. William Arnot of Littlepark petitions for a mitigation, in regard he has not so much in all the world as the fine, and his acting in the late disorders at Irongray, was not from any disloyalty to his majesty, for whom he had appeared and suffered not a little in his worldly interests under the usurpation, as the noblemen and gentlemen about him know. The lords mitigate the fine to a thousand merks, and continue his public appearances after divine worship in the church of Irongray, as above.

This is all I meet with in the registers upon this head. The rest of the men, who were imprisoned for their wives' alleged accession to the tumult, after sixteen weeks' imprisonment at Edinburgh, were liberate, upon giving bond to live peaceably. I find nothing further about the lord Kirkcudbright, neither know I what course was taken with him. I find my lord Kirkcudbright joining with the lord Warriston, Mr. Andrew Cant, and others, 1652, in giving in reasons why they could not own that assembly till they had a conference, even before the choice of a moderator; and his being among the protesters, probably made it fare the worse with him now.

It was when those commissioners from the council were in the south, that the troubles of that worthy gentleman, the laird of Earlston began. All I have upon this, save what follows afterwards from the registers, I shall give from the original papers, communicated lately to me by his grandchild, the present laird of Earlston. The commissioners knew Earlston's firmness to presbyterian principles, and were willing to bring him either to comply in settling an episcopal minister at Dalry, where he was patron, or if he refused, which they had reason to expect he would, to bring him to trouble. Accordingly they write the following letter to him, which I give from the original.

"Kirkcudbright, 21st May, 1663.
" Sir,
" We doubt not but you heard, that the lords of his majesty's privy council have commissionate us to come to this country, as to take course with the seditious tumult raised in this place, so to do every thing that may contribute to the settling of the peace here, and to be assisting to the bishop for planting of other vacant churches, by the withdrawing of the respective ministers: and finding the church of Dalry to be one of those, and that the bishop hath presented an actual minister, Mr. George Henry, fit and qualified for the charge, now being, according to the act of parliament, fallen into his hand, *jure devoluto*, and that the gentleman is to come to your parish this Sabbath next to preach to that people, and that you are a person of special interest there; according to the power and trust committed to us, we do require you to cause his edict be served, and the congregation convene, and to countenance him so as he be encouraged to prosecute his ministry in that place. In doing whereof, as you will witness your respect to authority, so oblige us to remain,

" Sir,
" Your loving friends and servants,
" LINLITHGOW, ANNANDALE,
GALLOWAY, DRUMLANERK."

Earlston presently gave them a return, which I transcribe from the copy he kept, under his own hand.

" For the right honourable, and his very noble lord, my lord Linlithgow, and remanent nobles at Kirkcudbright.

" Earlston, May 22d, 1663.
" Right honourable,
" And my very noble lords, I received this day an express from your lordships, by Mr. George Henry; whereunto for answer, as to what relates to the bearer, I humbly entreat your lordships will be pleased to look upon me as one who has been educated from my youth hitherto, to know my duty to God, and all such whom he has placed in authority over his people. I am not ignorant, my lords, that my allegiance obligeth me (beside other engagements) to serve the king's majesty with my person and fortune, and I trust your lordships will permit me (because it is my duty) to keep in all things a good conscience towards God: yet, if these should thwart in any case, I have ever judged it safest to obey God, and stand at a distance with whatsomever doth not tend to God's glory and the edification of the souls of his scattered people, of which that congregation is a part. And besides, my lords, it is known to many, that I pretend and lay claim to the right of patronage of that parish, and has already (before the time appointed, by the last parliament did prescribe) determined therein with consent of the people, to a truly worthy and qualified person, and an actual minister, if he may be admitted to exercise his gift among that people; and for me to condescend to countenance the bearer of your lordships' letter, were to procure me most impiously and dishonourably to wrong the majesty of God, and violently to take away the Christian liberty of his afflicted people, and enervate my own right. Wherefore, please your lordships, believe me it is grievous to me that I am not in capacity in the present case to give your lordships that hearty obedience and real observance, that otherwise I am most free to perform to the meanest in whom any of your lordships may be concerned, seeing I have ever hitherto made it my study to testify my duty to your lordships, as my superiors whom God has established as judges over me under his majesty, to whose authority I shall (as hitherto) be most ready to witness all due respects, as doth become,

" My noble lords,
" Your lordships' most real friend, and humble servant."

1663. Upon this he is cited before the council; and we shall afterward see what unprecedented hardships he met with there, from the council books. I now return to the sufferings of other persons this year.

We have seen by the former acts, that the ministers who were not reached by the act at Glasgow, were restricted and confined to their own parishes, as a large prison; and many others confined to particular places, which was very uneasy to them. They behoved, upon every civil affair, to apply to the council for liberty to come out of their confinement. An instance or two of this will suffice.—May 24th, "Anent a petition presented by Mr. James M'Gill, late minister at Largo, showing, that umquhile James viscount of Oxenford has nominated him with several others, tutors testamentars to his children; and a meeting of the said tutors is appointed at Edinburgh next week, and letters are come to the petitioner to keep that meeting precisely, which he cannot do being under restraint, and therefore craves warrant for that effect. The council allows him to repair to Edinburgh, or any where else, for doing of his necessary affairs, for the space of one month, and hereby take off his restraint during that time."—That same day, "The lords of council having considered a petition from Mr. John M'Gill, late minister at Coupar, and now doctor of medicine, desiring, that the restraint put upon him not to return to this kingdom for a year, might be taken off: the lords of council take it off, and grant the said Mr. John liberty to return, he obliging himself to appear before them, and give them satisfaction for his peaceable behaviour."

In July, I find the council going on in their prosecution of the presbyterian ministers, in several corners of the country, whom the bishops behoved to be rid of. July 14th, " The lords of his majesty's privy council taking to their consideration, that Mr. James Wood, late principal of the college of St. Andrews, did, without any lawful call or warrant, intrude himself upon that charge, and as yet does continue to exerce the same, notwithstanding of all the acts of parliament or council made thereagainst, do ordain messengers to charge the said Mr. James to appear before them the 23d instant, to answer to the premises, or what else should be laid to his charge, under the pain of rebellion."—Mr. James Wood was provost of the old college of St. Andrews, and minister there, and one of the brightest lights we had in this church during this period, a person of eminent learning, piety, and solidity, and his printed books show his abilities. I have been informed he left some very valuable manuscripts behind him, particularly a complete refutation of the Arminian scheme of doctrine, ready for the press. Mr. Sharp was indebted to Mr. Wood for any reputation he had, and was under as great obligations to him, as one man could be to another. They had been more than ordinarily familiar, and now the primate could not bear his continuing at St. Andrews, and so caused cite him before the council. July 23d, Mr. Wood compears. He was asked how he came to be provost at St. Andrews. When he began to answer, he was interrupted in a very huffing manner, and commanded to give his answer in a word. The archbishop and some others present could not bear his telling them some truths he was entering upon; and when he saw it was fruitless to insist, he told them, he was called by the faculty of that college, at the recommendation of the usurpers, as some here, added he, meaning bishop Sharp, very well know. Whereupon he was removed, and in a little called in, and his sentence intimated to him, which thus stands in the council books: "Mr. James Wood being called to answer for intruding himself upon the office of principality of the old college of St. Andrews, without any lawful call, and as yet continuing to exercise the same, compeared personally, and declared, that he had deserted that charge upon Friday last. In respect whereof, and that it was found by the said Mr. James his own confession, that he had no right but a pretended call from the masters of that college, and an act of the late usurpers, for exercising that office, the lords of council, for present, do declare the said place vacant, and ordain and command him to confine himself within the city of Edinburgh, and not to depart forth thereof while further order. When his sentence was intimate to him, he told them, 'he was sorry they had condemned a person without hearing him, whom they could not charge with the breach of any law."

September 30th, a petition is presented by Mr. Wood, showing, that in obedience to the council's act, he had remained those divers weeks at Edinburgh, and is content still to continue there; but by reason his father is extremely sick, and that he hath several necessary affairs to do at St. Andrews, humbly therefore desiring liberty and warrant for that effect. "Which petition being read, with a testificate of the petitioner his father's infirmity, the council grant license to the petitioner to go to St. Andrews to visit his said father, and performing his other necessary affairs, he always returning when he shall be called by the council." This is all I find about this worthy person: next year, we shall hear, he gets to the joy of his Lord, and some bustle is made about him after his death.

At the same diet of the council, July 14th, an attack is made, at the bishop of Glasgow his instigation, against some worthy presbyterian ministers in the west and south. "The lords of his majesty's privy council, being informed of the turbulent and seditious carriage of the persons underwritten, Messrs. Alexander Livingstone, late minister at Biggar, Matthew M'Kail at Bothwell, John Guthrie at Tarbolton, John Blair at Mauchlin, John Schaw at Selkridge, George Johnston at Newbottle, John Hardy at Gordon, Archibald Hamilton at Wigton, George Wauch at Kirkinner, and Anthony Murray at Kirkbean; ordain macers, or messengers at arms, to charge the said persons to appear before them the 23d instant, to answer to such things as shall be laid to their charge, under the pain of rebellion."—July 23d, I find Messrs. Hardy, M'Kail and Livingstone compear, and are "continued till next council day, and in the meantime ordained and commanded to confine themselves within the city of Edinburgh, and not depart therefrom without license, and that they do not presume in the meantime to keep private meetings and conventicles."

That same day the council "appoint the lords archbishops of St. Andrews and Glasgow, the marquis of Montrose, the lord secretary, and register, to wait on the lord commissioner his grace, to think on a general course, what shall be done as well anent those ministers that were admitted before the (year) 1649, and carry themselves disobediently to the laws of the kingdom, as those who were admitted since; and to report their opinion."— Whether it was from this meeting that the following prosecution came, or not, I know not; but July 30th, "The lords of his majesty's privy council, being informed of the factious and seditious carriage of several ministers in the west, and particularly of Mr. Matthew Ramsay, late minister at Old Kirkpatrick, Mr. James Walkinshaw at Badernock, Mr. Hugh Smith at Eastwood, Mr. James Hamilton at Blantyre, or Eglisham, Mr. James Blair at Cathcart, who, in manifest and open contempt of the laws and acts of parliament and council, have taken upon them to convocate great multitudes of his majesty's subjects, for hearing their factious and seditious sermons, to the great scandal of religion, and prejudice to the government of the church: wherefore they ordain a charge to be given them personally, and failing that, at the head burgh of the shire and its market-cross, where they live, and at their late manses and dwelling-houses, and at the market-cross of Edinburgh, to answer for their contempt, under pain of rebellion; with certification they shall be denounced rebels." Many of those ministers now cited, and Mr. M'Kail formerly cited, lay pretty near the city of Glasgow, and the people flocked out to hear them, which grated the archbishop and those he had put in under him, and so they resolved to have them banished at some distance from them. This was the case likewise of Mr. James Cuningham minister at Lasswade, a little from Edinburgh, who, I find, was brought to trouble at this time, but I have not met with him in the council books.

July 30th, "Mr. John Hardy, minister of Gordon, being cited to answer for his contempt of the law, in preaching after he was

1663. discharged" (this is a good commentary upon the factious and seditious carriage of the ministers now cited) "compeared, and having, in face of council, acknowledged that he had done so: the lords of council find, that he hath highly contemned his majesty's laws and authority; and therefore do declare his place vacant, and ordain him within fourteen days to remove himself and family twenty miles distant from the said parish of Gordon, and discharge him to reside within six miles of any cathedral church, or three miles of a royal burgh, in time coming. With certification if he fail, he shall be pursued and punished as a seditious person, and contemner of his majesty's authority." This is a prelude to the mile act we have formerly heard the council passed next council day, August 13th, which pretty much spared them the trouble of any more particular prosecutions. And that act would seem to be the issue of that meeting, just now narrated, of the two archbishops, secretary, and commissioner; however they go on with such as had been cited before them.

August 18th, Mr. Matthew M'Kail and Mr. Alexander Livingstone, late ministers, confined within the city of Edinburgh, being called, compeared. The lords after hearing of them, ordain the said Mr. Matthew to wait on the lord commissioner's grace, and Mr. Livingstone on the archbishop of Glasgow, for giving them satisfaction as to their behaviour and carriage. I am told the archbishop had vowed, Mr. M'Kail should never preach again in Bothwell, but it did not hold. I think the bishop himself scarce ever saw Glasgow again; for in a few days after his riding the parliament, at its rising, he died.* And Mr. M'Kail being remitted to the commissioner, he went up to London without doing any thing in his affair; and Mr. M'Kail ventured back to Bothwell, and escaped for some time. I hear, that Mr. Livingstone was confined to his parish till further orders. Mr. George Johnstoun and Mr. James Cuningham were reached by the act of Glasgow, yet connived at by the influence of persons of note; but now with Mr. Blair are confined to the north side of Tay. I have nothing further about them in the registers.

That same day, "Mr. John Blair, late minister, compeared, and, being examined, acknowledged, that notwithstanding he had been admitted since the year 1649, he had, contrary to the law, exercised the ministerial function, by preaching, baptizing, and marrying. The lords do discharge him to exercise any part of the ministry in time coming, without warrant from his ordinary where he shall reside; and ordain and command him, within twenty days, to remove himself and his family from the new kirk of Mauchlin where he did last preach, and to remove himself beyond the river of Ness, betwixt and the first day of October next to come, and discharge him to transgress the bounds of his confinement, under the highest peril.—Messrs. Matthew Ramsay, Hugh Smith, and James Walkinshaw, compeering this day to answer for their contempt of authority, in preaching and keeping conventicles contrary to law, the council remit Mr. Ramsay to the archbishop of Glasgow, to give him satisfaction, and intimated the late act of council of the 13th of this month to Messrs. Smith and Walkinshaw, and ordain them to obey it at their peril." This is all I find about ministers this year, and we shall meet with few of them after this before the

---

* This was Fairfoul, "a very pleasant and facetious man, insinuating and crafty; but he was a better physician than a divine. His life was scarce free from scandal, and he was eminent in nothing that belonged to his own function. He had not only sworn the covenant, but had persuaded others to do it; and when one objected to him that it went against his conscience, he answered there were some very good medicines that could not be chewed, but were to be swallowed down without any further examination. Whatever the matter was, soon after the consecration his parts sunk so fast, that in a few months he who had passed his whole life long for one of the cunningest men in Scotland, became almost a changeling, upon which it may be easily collected what commentaries the presbyterians would make. Sharp lamented this to me as one of their great misfortunes: he said it began in less than a month after he came to London."—Burnet's History of his Own Times, 12mo. Ed. vol. i. p. 192.

" The commissioners and all the estates rode from the palace of Holyrood-house to the parliament house, in triumph and grandeur; and among the rest the loathsome archbishop Fair-

council, the mile act this year, comprehending them all, and the high commission next year take some of the council's work off their hand.

This year the laird of Earlstoun his trouble and oppression begins. He was a religious gentleman of good parts, and a great support to the presbyterians in that country, and we shall meet with him almost every year till the rising at Bothwell, when he got to heaven. July 30th, The lords of council order letters to be direct to charge William Gordon of Earlstoun to compear before them the ―――― day of ―――― next to come, to answer for his factious and seditious carriage, that is, his refusing to hear the curates, and hearing and favouring outed presbyterian ministers. And November 24th, the council being informed that the laird of Earlstoun keeps conventicles and private meetings in his house, notwithstanding the laws and acts of parliament and council made in the contrary, do ordain letters to be direct against him, to compear before the council the ―――― day of ―――― to answer for his contempt, under the pain of rebellion. We shall meet with him next year.

I shall end this section with some account of the sending the forces to the west and

---

foul finished his stinking office of bishop. He began it with stink, for he broke wind as he bowed to the altar when he was to be consecrate, and two days before this glorious day he hade taken physic, (as the report was,) which fell a working upon him as he was riding up the way that the bearer of his train, when he alighted from his horse, was almost choaked; no man could sit near him in the parliament house, so he was forced to rise and go home a footman, as he came a horseman, and so he made but the half of this miserable triumph; and after he was got home he never came abroad; and because he would never believe the physician, who assured him death was at hand, he died by surprisal and ·undesired, perishing like his own dung. He was so greedy he never reapt the profit of his benefice, for because he refused a reasonable composition to enter his vassals, therefore in his short time he had very little, and left the profits to his successor. His poor children were vagabonds and runagate, turning popish for a piece of silver and a morsel of bread; and such was the end of his tragedy."—Kirkton's History of the Church of Scotland, pp. 177, 178.

Such was the character of this bishop drawn by a bishop and by a plain presbyter. Either of these sketches is sufficiently repulsive, and there cannot be a doubt, but like the greater part of his brethren, the Scotish bishops, he was not only unprincipled, but at the same time a most contemptible individual.—*Ed.*

south country, to quarter there, and uplift the fines for not keeping the parish churches, which was the beginning of much oppression to those shires for some years.—October 13th, " The lords of his majesty's privy council do hereby give order and warrant to George, earl of Linlithgow, with all conveniency to cause so many of the six foot companies under his command to march to Kirkcudbright, as with the foot there already may make up the number of eightscore footmen with their officers, and to quarter there till further order."—That same day, " The council give order and command to Sir Robert Fleming, with all conveniency, to march to the west two squades of his majesty's lifeguard, and to quarter one squade thereof at Kilmarnock, and another at Paisley, till further order."

1663.

It seems Sir James Turner had the command of the forces in the south, and was very active in raising the fines for absence from the parish church, and I doubt not but the guards sent to Kilmarnock and Paisley were abundantly active this way; however, Sir James gets the thanks of the council for his diligence. November 24th, " The lords of his majesty's privy council recommend it to the earl of Linlithgow to write a letter of thanks to Sir James Turner, for his care and pains taken in seeing the laws anent church government receive due obedience: and withal to acquaint him, that he advise with the bishop of Galloway, and send a note to the council of the names of such ministers as are come in from Ireland to that country, or others who transgress, by preaching or otherwise, the acts of parliament and council anent the government of the church; to the effect that the council may take such course therein as they shall think meet. And that also Sir James acquaint those ministers who are debarred from the possession of their churches and manses, that they make their address to the lords of privy council or session, who will grant them letters of horning, upon sight of their presentations and collations, against the possessors of the said manses. And withal my lord is to acquaint Sir James, that the council have directed letters to cite Earlstoun to compear before them.

1663. Sir James Turner we shall frequently meet with in the progress of this history. He had been in the late times a great servant of the covenanters, and at the restoration found it convenient to go over to the other side, with the same zeal. He was a person of a forward active temper, and had somewhat of harshness mixed with it; but was endued with a considerable stock of learning, and very bookish. This person was abundantly ready to execute the orders here given him with rigour; but was obliged to go even beyond his inclinations to satisfy the bishop of Galloway, who was severe and cruel, as all apostates use to be, and the rest of the prelates. The council finding the body of the west and south of Scotland most dissatisfied with the late change in the church, and having put the uplifting of the fines in the hands of the army, send west a good body of the forces, and with them the strictest orders, to oblige all persons to subjection to the bishops and their curates. By this a large foundation is laid for most grievous oppression and exactions, under colour of law. The process was very short in cases of nonconformity. The curate accused whom he pleased to Sir James, or any of the officers of the army, yea, many times to a private sentinel. The soldier is judge, no witnesses are led, no probation is sought, the sentence is summarily pronounced; and the soldier executes his own sentence, and he would not see the less to this, that the money, generally speaking, came to his own pocket; and very frequently the fine upon some pretext or other, far exceeded the sum liquidate by law. Vast contributions were under this colour raised in the west and south: the soldiers really carried as if they had been in an enemy's country, and the oppression of that part of the kingdom was inexpressible. If a tenant or master of a family was unwilling, or really unable to pay, the soldiers are sent to quarter upon him, till it may be, he pay ten times the value of the fine; and indeed many were totally eaten up. And, as if this was not enough, when poor families were no longer able to sustain the soldiers, their stuff and goods were distrained and sold for a trifle.

In those quarterings the ruffian soldiers were terribly insolent. Family worship was mocked at, and people disturbed when at it, as if it had been a conventicle and contrary to law. Multitudes were cruelly beat, and dragged to church or prison with equal violence. By such methods hundreds of poor religious families in the west and south were scattered, and reduced to extreme necessity, and the masters of them were obliged either to lurk or leave the country.

Sir George Mackenzie's vindication of all this is, p. 10. "that it is impossible to answer for all the extravagancies of soldiers, and Sir James Turner was laid aside, which was all the state could do." We shall afterwards hear the procedure of the council against Sir James, and find it was upon other grounds than his quartering his soldiers at this time: we shall just now find him put on the high commission, and sent once and again to harass the west and south; and he himself made it out to the west country men, who made him prisoner, that he was far from going the length of his commission, notwithstanding the heights we shall see he ran to. And we shall afterward find, that when, April 17th, 1683, John Wilson, writer in Lanark, was before the council, and speaks of the council's condemning Sir James for his cruelty, he is answered in face of council, and none contradicted it, that Sir James went not the length of his commission. And as to the common extravagancies of soldiers, the reader will easily judge whether this be a defence for what now passed. Sir James understood the military law sufficiently, and had spirit enough to have limited his men; and I should not reckon Sir James worthy of the command he had, if he was not able to restrain his soldiers from going beyond his commission. And had he been guilty of this, as Sir George insinuates, his masters should have not only displaced, but punished him, at least they did so with far better men for less faults. Even Cromwell's officers were made to answer for the extravagancies of their soldiers, though foreigners, enemies, and conquerors; and it is strange if the like could not be done in time of peace, and under a just government, as Sir George calls that. But all this is an insufficient defence; only no better offered, the matter did not bear it.

In order to facilitate the soldiers' work, the curates formed in most parishes a roll of their congregations, not for any ministerial work they gave themselves the trouble of, but to instruct their parishioners with briers and thorns by their army; and in order to the soldiers visiting their families, and examining their people's loyalty. Sermons were all the curates' work, and these short and dry enough. And after sermon the roll of the parish was called from pulpit, and all who were absent, except some favourites, were given up to the soldiers; and when once delated, no defences could be heard, their fine behoved either presently to be paid, or the houses quartered upon; and some who kept the church were some time quartered upon, because the persons who last term lived there, were in the curates' lists as deserters of the church.

Another part of the severe oppression of the country, by the soldiers at this time sent west, was at the churches of the old presbyterian ministers. Such of those who continued either by connivance, or at their hazard, or by the interest of some considerable person in the parish, had very throng auditories, which grated the bishops and their underlings; so orders were sent to the soldiers, to go to their churches likewise. The method was, as a good many living witnesses can yet testify, the party of soldiers sat drinking, revelling, and carousing, in some public-house in the parish, till public worship was near over; and then came armed to the church door, or church-yard gates, and guarded those, caused the people pass out one by one, and interrogate them upon oath, if they were one of that congregation? If they could not say they were parishioners, though it may be the congregation they lived in was vacant, and no curate settled in it, the soldiers immediately fined them, and any money they had was taken from them. If they had no money, or not so much as was required, then their Bibles, the men's coats, and women's plaids were taken from them. You would have seen the soldiers returning on the Lord's day, from one of these churches, laden with spoil, as if they had come from a battle where they had stripped the slain, or the sacking and plundering a city.

1663.

In some places there was yet sadder work, though this was not so common as the former. The soldiers would come in companies in arms to the presbyterian ministers' churches, and without any ceremony, enter the same by force, and interrupt divine worship. One party would stand at the one door, and a second party at the other, and guard them so as let no body get out; and a third party would enter the church, and obliged the people to go out all by one door, and these that would not presently swear they belonged to that parish, they rifled them of all they had, and sometimes forced them to go with them to prison. Dreadful was the confusion and profanation of the Lord's day, and several were wounded, and others sorely beat. Many instances of those abuses, in this and the following years, might be given through the west and south, were there need; particularly at the churches of Eaglesham, Stewarton, Ochiltree, Irvine, Kilwinning, and other places, too long to be narrated here. And after all, the soldiers were so insolent and severe, as to force people, for fear of worse, to declare under their hand, that after all those and many other outrages, they were kindly dealt with and used, and engage to make no complaints; and when they had forced this from some people, they thought themselves secure. Indeed it is but a lame idea can be framed of the nature and severities of those quarterings, now at this distance: but from this short hint it is evident, the procedure of the managers this year, with that of the high commission next year, and the following severities in the year after, naturally paved the way for all confusions and extremities the country fell into afterwards, and may be reckoned the real causes of them.

SECT. VI.

Of several other occurrences this year, 1663.

As I have done upon the former years, so I shall end this, by taking notice of several

1663. incidental things which may tend to clear the history of this period, and yet come not in upon the former sections; and I shall run very quickly through them.

February, this year, died Mr. David Mitchel, who had been minister of Edinburgh before the (year) 1638, and, as we heard, was made first bishop of Aberdeen, after the restoration, though his character did not merit any elevation in the church; and he was succeeded by bishop Burnet.

We heard before, that an application was made to the council, for a license to print Mr. David Dickson's Therapeutica Sacra, in English, and it was remitted to Mr. Fairfoul to revise. As he was a very unfit hand to come after the reverend and learned Mr. Dickson, so I doubt, if, during his life, any application was further made; but now that excellent person having got to his reward, a new application is made, March 24th. " The council having considered the desire of the petition presented by Mr. Alexander Dickson, professor of Hebrew in the college of Edinburgh, son to umquhile Mr. David Dickson, professor of divinity there, for a license to print his father's Therapeutica Sacra, in English; do find it reasonable, and recommend to, and require the bishop of Edinburgh, or such as he shall think fit, to revise the said book and translation thereof; and if he or they shall find it useful for the public, and give testimony thereof under their hand, the lords give warrant to his majesty's printer to cause print the same." This excellent book is upon a subject the managers needed not be afraid of, and did not in the least concern politics, or their government in church and state, but was entirely calculate for the promoting of real godliness and practical religion, and hath been singularly useful unto thousands. Whether it was put into the hands of the bishop or not, I cannot say: but October 13th, I find there is a license granted for publishing it, without any restrictions. " The lords of council do hereby licentiate and give warrant to the printing of a book called Therapeutica Sacra, translated out of Latin into English, by Mr. David Dickson, and discharge all printers to print the same, except Christopher Higgins his Majesty's printer, as they will be answerable, without the special license of Mr. Alexander Dickson, son to the said Mr. David."

It may perhaps be thought foreign to this history, and I shall but just name it, to notice, that the duke of Monmouth and dutchess of Buccleugh were married, April 24th, and in a few weeks I find a patent, creating them duke and dutchess of Buccleugh, read in council and recorded:* we shall afterwards meet with his grace the king's natural son in the progress of this history.

Upon the 26th of April, the lyon king at arms died, and Sir Charles Erskine, brother to the earl of Airly, succeeded him in that post, who, September 26th, is crowned in presence of the parliament; but I do not find the formality of a sermon used, as was at the coronation of the former king at arms.—June 2d, the council pass the following act with relation unto quakers :

" The lords of his majesty's privy council, taking to their consideration the great abuse committed by these people who take upon them the profession of quakers, whereby both church and state is and may be prejudged, to the great scandal of the gospel ; and being most willing to remedy the same,

---

* From Mackenzie's History of Scotland, we learn that this marriage arose out of the struggle between Lauderdale and Middleton. The earls Marischal and Rothes were tools in the hands of the former, and " Rothes the more to insinuate himself in his majesty's favour, and to mix himself in the royal family by a near alliance, did propose a match between his niece the dutchess of Buccleuch, and James, natural son to the king, which produced the desired effect, for this gave him occasion to converse much with the king, and his conversation warmed the king into new degrees of friendship for him. Nor did the dutchess's mother, Rothes' sister, contribute a little towards the promoving of this kindness, being a person of much wit and subtilty; and to persuade the king yet more, that all Middleton's procedures were illegal, Lauderdale caused call up his friend Sir John Gilmour, president of the session, upon pretence of consulting the contract of marriage, who, being warmed with a kind collation, did complain to his majesty with tears, of Middleton's rash and illegal actions, which had the greater effect upon his majesty that he was figured to the king as a person who had been an eminent royalist and sufferer, and that he wept for joy when he spoke to his majesty."—History of Scotland, pp. 113, 114 —*Ed.*

they do appoint the lord advocate, the lord Tarbet, and Sir Robert Murray, to meet and call before them John Swinton, sometime of that ilk, Anthony Hedges of Burnside, and Andrew Robertson, and examine them, and the papers that have been intercepted, passing betwixt them and some others, and what correspondence they have had, either with those in England, or elsewhere, to the prejudice of the church or state; and for this effect give power to cite and receive witnesses, and all other manner of probation, and to report to the council. And because it is certainly informed, that there are several meetings of quakers in Edinburgh, both on the week-day and Sabbath, in time of divine worship, who seduce many to follow after mischievous practices; therefore, for preventing the same in time coming, they do ordain and require the magistrates of the burgh of Edinburgh, to cause a strict inquiry to be made after the dwelling places or houses where those persons resort, and that they call for the landlords or heritors of the said houses, and cause them take such course as there be no meetings of such persons any more within their houses; and, if need be, that they take the keys of their houses from them: and withal, that they take care that no heritor, landlord, or others, set any house to such persons, as they shall be answerable, in time coming."

Had this good act been prosecute with the same vigour those against presbyterians were, we might, in this land, soon been freed from that dangerous sect; but as soon as the bishops come into the council, in a few days after this, I observe little more done against them. They gave the council so much to do against presbyterian nonconformists, that for some years I meet with little further against the quakers; and any thing that was done was so little prosecute, that they spread terribly during this reign.*

June 9th, there is read a letter from the king to the council, relative to the plot, commonly called Blood's plot, bearing, "That by an express of the 29th of May, before this time they had received his majesty's letter, declaring his pleasure for discharging the two commissions formerly granted to the earl of Middleton, and requiring them to adjourn the parliament to the 18th of June, and that they had received the earl of Rothes's commission, that it might pass the seals: but now having received information of a damnable plot in the kingdom of Ireland, to surprise the Castle of Dublin, and raise a rebellion, which is now in a good measure prevented, and some of the principal persons secured; yet because it is informed, Gilbert Ker was engaged in that treasonable design, and escaped, and because there is reason to think he and some others, involved in that guilt, may endeavour an escape through the kingdom of Scotland, the council are required to give immediate orders, that all persons, come over in ten days before the date of this, be strictly examined, and dealt with as they deserve." A copy of the Irish proclamation is sent enclosed. This letter is dated the 1st of June. The council gives orders accordingly. For any thing I can learn, no accession to this plot could ever be fixed on colonel Ker.†

1663.

---

* Notwithstanding our historian's approbation of this act, we cannot help thinking it was sanguinary and unjust, and had it been rigorously executed, instead of atoning for the cruelties exercised upon the presbyterians, could only have involved the nation in deeper guilt, and rendered the government more disgustingly hateful. There may be reasons found for restraining in some degree the public exercise of certain forms of religious worship, or even for interfering with its private rites, when they are, as they have often been, scandalous and immoral; but to proscribe a man for his religious opinions, and forbid towards him the exercise of the common duties of humanity, is utterly repugnant both to reason and revelation.—*Ed.*

† The principal leader of this plot was colonel Thomas Blood, who had fought during the civil war under the standard of Charles I. After the ruin of the royal cause, falling in on his way to Ireland, his native country, with some of the presbyterian ministers in Lancashire, who were then writing against the violence which the sectarian army had done to the king and parliament, he became a convert to their views. He lived in Ireland quietly, and performed the duties of justice of the peace, with great approbation, till the restoration, when the government having forfeited the pledge which it gave in the declaration from Breda, he took an active part in a conspiracy formed by some members of parliament who had been deprived of their lands. The following is the declaration the conspirators put forth on this occasion:—" Having long expected the securing unto us of our lives,

1663. June 15th, the earl of Rothes's commission, to be commissioner to the parliament, is read and recorded in council, and likewise his commission to be lord high treasurer, in the room of the earl of Crawford, who had demitted that place,

liberties, and estates, as but a reasonable recompense of that industrie and diligence exercised by the protestantis of this kingdome, in restoring of his majesty to the exercise of his royal authority in his kingdomes, in steid therof, we find ourselfes, our wyfes and children, without mercy delyvered as a prey unto these barbarous and bloodie murderers, whose inhuman cruelty is registrated in the blood of 150,000 poor protestantis at the beginning of the war in this kingdom, all which doth appear by these insueing sad and infallible simptomes:—

"First. That notwithstanding of all the obligations of oathes and covenantis lyeing on his majesty for the extirpation of poperie, prelacie, and such grand malignancie, he hath suffered himself to be so far seduced by evil counsellors, that even the aforesaid bloodie papists that were deluders of the people unto that barbarous masaker, were now the first that tasted of his royal clemencie, in setling them in their justlie forfalted estates at his first comeing in, by paper ordores, taken from the protestantis illegallie, and confirmed on them, and they that had them not had sallaries out of the exchequer, untill they wer restored, although the poor suffering protestantis despoyled by them, never had any recompence for their losses.

" Secondly. That these vast soumes of money given by the protestantis for relief of that armie, which under God is the meanes of our preservatione from thair bloodie attempts, is disposed of to gratifie the aforesaid inhumane butchers of the poor protestantis, whilst the said armie parish for want of pay.

" Thirdly. That the lord lieutenant, to whose protection we are committit, doeth not onlie execute and practise, bot hath owned his keeping a correspondence with several of the said murderers, during their hostilitie, as appeareth by his certificates in their behalf to the court of clames, to which may be added, the hous of commones of thir kingdome's apprehensione, declared in the speaker's speech to the duk, by all which circumstances, we may undoubtedlie as David did, conclude that evill is determined against us, and before it be too late, stand upon our just and necessar defence, and use all our endeavours for our self-preservatione, and like the people with Saull, when he intended to requyte the incomparable desertis of Jonathan with death, to stand up without the sanctuarie and say, ' As the Lord liveth, Jonathan shall not die.' And to the end, no well mynded protestantis in the three kingdoms, may be afraid to stand be us in this our just quarell, we doe declar we will stand for that libertie of conscience proper to everie one as a Christian, for establishing the protestant religion in puritie, according to the tenor of the Solemn League and Covenant; the restoring each person to his lands as they held them in the year 1659; the discharging the armies arreirs; and the repairing the breaches maid upon the liberties and privileges of the corporationes in the three kingdoms. In all which, we doubt not bot the Lord of Hosts, the mighty God of Jacob, will strengthen our weik handis."

This plot being discovered prematurely, many of the persons concerned were apprehended, but Blood with many others escaped, some to Scotland, others to England. In this latter country, Blood took up the medical profession, and under the assumed names of Dr. Allan, and Dr. Clark, appears to have lived unmolested. He was unquestionably a very extraordinary character, and possessed of the most daring courage. Illustrative of this, Mr. William Veitch relates a circumstance of which he himself was the subject. He had preached a sermon in London, for a Mr. Nichol Blackie, who had been ejected from the parish of Roberton, and had found an asylum and a congregation in London. Mr. Veitch had concluded his sermon, and had pronounced the blessing, when some government spies started up and cried, "treason, treason!" which greatly alarmed both ministers and people, but the famous colonel Blood, who went then under the name of Allan, with some of his accomplices, sitting near the only door of the meeting-house, while the others who cried were on the far side of the pulpit, stands up, saying, " Good people, what are these that cry treason, treason, we have heard nothing, but reason, reason. You that are in the passage there, stand still, and you who are betwixt and the pulpit, make way for the minister to come to me, and I'll carry him safe to his chamber." " And so he did," adds Veitch, "and we heard no more of that business."—Life of Veitch.

Blood gave other demonstrations of his courage, not quite so honourable as that we have just noticed. His attempt to carry off the crown from the Tower of London, in which he had nearly succeeded, is familiar to every reader of history, and having no connexion with the subject of our present discussion, it would be impertinent here to insert it. But the following account of him is too curious to be omitted. " To give some account of Blood, I shall briefly say here, that the duke of Ormond, when he was lord lieutenant of Ireland, having caused some of Blood's complices to be hanged, who intended to surprise the Castle of Dublin, Blood swore he would revenge their deaths. For this purpose, Blood followed the duke of Ormond into England when he was recalled, and watched him so well, that with the assistance of seven or eight persons on horseback, he stopped his coach in the night as he was going to Clarendon-house, where he lived, knocked down his footman, and forced the duke up behind one of the horsemen, in order to carry him to Tyburn, and hang him there with a paper pinned on his breast, to show the cause of this execution. But the duke forcibly throwing himself off the horse, with the villain who had tied the duke fast to him, defeated the design, and the authors could never be discovered till after Blood's attempt upon the crown. This attempt was very extraordinary, but the king's conduct on that occasion was still more surprising. For, having a curiosity to examine Blood himself, he ordered him to be brought to Whitehall, and put several questions to him, which the villain

because he could not sign the declaration formed by parliament last year, and ordered to be taken by all in public trust. I am told, that this noble person was particularly in Middleton's eye, when the declaration was penned, and he readily went into it at the bishop's instigation, that he might have the post for himself or one of his friends. And it is said, he was put in hopes that the earl of Lauderdale might boggle at it: and the earl of Lauderdale said to my lord Crawford, that he wanted not some difficulties as to the declaration, and wished it had not been passed; but since it was passed, he would come over them, and be avenged upon his enemy Middleton. At the same time a considerable addition was made to the council. The earl of Lauderdale took his place: his brother Mr. Charles, master and general of the mint, was added to the council, by a letter from the king; we shall afterward meet with him under the style of the lord Hatton; and John Hume of Renton is, by another letter, admitted counseller; as also the two archbishops, the letter relative to them deserves a room here, and follows: " Right trusty &c.—We greet you well. Being most confident of the fidelity and affection to our service, of the most reverend fathers in God, the archbishops of St. Andrews and Glasgow, we have thought fit to add them

1663.

---

answered with astonishing boldness, confessing all, and unconcernedly relating the circumstances of the thing. Then the king asked him, whether he knew the authors of the attempt upon the duke of Ormond? Blood confessed it was himself. Not content with this, he told the king he had been engaged to kill him with a carabine from out the reeds, by the Thames-side above Battersea, where he often went to swim. But that when he had taken his stand in the reeds for that purpose, his heart was checked with an awe of majesty, and did not only relent himself, but diverted his associates from the design. He also told the king he was prepared to suffer death, as having deserved it, but must tell his majesty that he had hundreds of complices, who had bound themselves by a horrible oath to revenge the death of any of the fraternity, upon those who should bring them to justice, which would expose his majesty and all his ministers, to the daily fear and expectation of a massacre. But on the contrary, if he spared the lives of a few persons, his own would be secure. The king was surprised, and probably intimidated by Blood's discourse, and thought doubtless, the attempt of this villain on the duke of Ormond, to revenge the death of his complices, might be imitated in revenge of his death, by his surviving comerades. However this be, the king sent the earl of Arlington to the duke of Ormond, to desire him not to prosecute Blood, which the duke could not refuse. Afterwards he gave him his pardon, and not content with saving his life, conferred on him five hundred pounds a year in land in Ireland. From this time Blood was continually at court, and the king treated him with that freedom and familiarity, that many persons applied to him for favours to the king. This gave occasion to the king's cronies to say, that he kept this villain about him to intimidate those who should dare to offend him in things which were not punishable by law, as had been practised in the case of Sir John Coventry, for some railleries upon him in the house of commons."

In 1680, he was accused of a conspiracy against the duke of Buckingham, and while he was preparing for his trial, fell sick and died. But the terror which he had inspired in life, did not cease at his death, his burial was looked upon as a trick, the body was disinterred, and after a strict examination, was at last identified by the uncommon size of the left thumb. Having connected himself with the presbyterians, and advocated the covenant, though he had never had any thing to do with the duke of Ormond or the crown, it was impossible that in the estimation of the adulatory herd of historians, who, for such a length of time, had almost exclusively secured the attention of the public, Blood could be any thing but a desperate villain. The credulous and Jacobitical Carte exclaims against " his matchless impudence, in pretending to godliness or tenderness of conscience." Evelyn, in his Memoirs, says " he had not only a daring, but a villanous unmerciful look, a false countenance, but well spoken, and dangerously insinuating." But Evelyn saw him only after the attempt upon the crown, on which account, he would be prepared before hand to see all that he has recorded. Baxter, who probably knew him much better than Evelyn, and was unquestionably a better judge of character, seems to have entertained a favourable opinion of his character. A modern writer has observed with great propriety, that in the singular circumstances in which persons are placed in the convulsions of civil discord, we need not be surprised at inconsistencies real or apparent in the conduct of men, whose character in the ordinary course of affairs had been unimpeachable. Many actors in such scenes, stand in need of the liberal treatment which Cromwell receives at the hand of the celebrated Burke. " Cromwell," says he, " was a man in whom ambition had not wholly suppressed, but only suspended the sentiments of religion, and the love, as far as it could consist with his designs of fair and honourable reputation.—The country was nearly as well in his hands as in those of Charles II., and in some points much better. The laws in general, had their course, and were admirably administered. Blood," continues our author, " was of a restless disposition, and desperate courage, but it is not so evident that he was cruel, perfidious or altogether devoid of a sense of religion."—M'Crie's Life of Veitch, Tindal's England, &c. &c.—*Ed.*

1663. to our council: these are therefore to require you to receive them to our privy council, in the ordinary way; for which this shall be your warrant. Whitehall, June 4th.

"LAUDERDALE."

That same day an order is given to liberate the lord Lorn from the Castle of Edinburgh.

"Those are to require and command Robert Straiton, captain of the Castle of Edinburgh, immediately upon sight hereof, to put at liberty forth of the Castle of Edinburgh, Archibald Campbell, eldest son to the late marquis of Argyle, for which these shall be a warrant.

"ROTHES."

Middleton's projects against the noble family of Argyle were now at an end, and the earl of Lauderdale had taken care to convince the king, that the sentence passed against the lord Lorn was upon no solid grounds, and had been procured from particular designs of the earl of Middleton. And so after the parliament was up, in a few days came down a patent restoring the lord Lorn to all his grandfather's estate; and because his father the marquis died under a great burden of debt, it was ordained that the lord Lorn should have fifteen thousand pounds per annum paid to him out of the estate, and the rest of the estate was ordered to go to the payment of the debts and creditors, of which the lord Lorn and his two sisters were first to be satisfied. And the restoration of this noble person was indeed a piece of justice done him, as well as a grateful acknowledgment of his services to, and sufferings for the king under his exile.

At this time likewise the earl of Tweeddale was made president of the privy council in Rothes's room, and a remission was passed for George Campbell, sheriff-depute of Argyle, father to that great light of this church, the reverend Mr. George Campbell, professor of divinity at Edinburgh since the revolution, whom we shall meet with in the progress of this work.

I omitted a pretty singular order of council, which might have come in upon the former section, which no doubt came from the bishops now in council, with respect to the prisoners from Kirkcudbright. June 23d, "The lords of council being informed, that ministers and other persons visit the prisoners for the riot at Kirkcudbright, now in the tolbooth of Edinburgh, and not only exhort, but pray for the said persons to persist in their wicked practices, affirming that they are suffering for righteousness' sake, and assure them God will give them an outgate; recommend it to the keeper to notice who visits them, and what their discourse and carriage is when with them." Those idle censures of the prayers of such as visited the prisoners, were unworthy of the notice of the council. John Euart and some of the prisoners were eminent Christians, and no doubt suffering for their regard to the gospel. However, it is well the council went no further, and discharged all visits to them.

This summer, as we heard, a great many were vexed and harassed for not subjecting to the ministry of the episcopal clergy, and not waiting upon ordinances dispensed by them. Some had freedom to hear the conformist ministers, yet, when they had opportunity, they choosed far rather to join with the few remaining presbyterian ministers, especially in the dispensation of sacraments. And some had no freedom to hear the curates, or receive sacraments from them, till they gave a testimony or protestation against what they judged wrong in them, for exonerating of themselves, that they did not by joining with them approve of it. This was insisted upon by some, not only of the more common people, but even of better rank. That worthy and learned physician, doctor Silvester Rattray, well enough known in the learned world, was upon Thursday the 23d of July, this year, called before the meeting of the episcopal ministers at Glasgow, to receive a censure for his taking one of his children out of town, to be baptized by a presbyterian minister; and having this opportunity of exonering himself, he gave in the following paper signed with his hand:

"I declare unto you, sir, before this meeting, that really I am of the presbyterian persuasion and judgment; and that, not only because I was bred and brought up under it, but also being convinced by clear evidence from scripture, that it is the only government Christ and his apostles did leave behind them, whereby the church should be ruled to the end of the world: as also, because of the many obligations, ties, and vows, yet recent upon my spirit for adhering unto it: as also I am convinced that prelacy is a human invention, which derives its rise only from some antiquated customs in the church. And albeit the Lord in his holy and sovereign providence hath suffered this hedge of presbytery to be broken down, wherein ye have borne deep shares to your power, I do declare that I will not separate from the church of God, but will participate of the ordinances so long as they remain pure among us, only with this *proviso*, that this my participating of the ordinances do not infer my approving any unlawful or unwarrantable practice in you, or any other of the dispensers of the ordinances.

" Doctor S. Rattray."

Afterwards, when the bloody and cruel scheme of oppression and persecution opened out, such declarations as this were not received, and though they had, could scarce have been a sufficient salvo for joining with the courses and defections of this lamentable time. However, great numbers, some upon one pretext, some upon another, were brought to much trouble for their nonconformity with the clergy now set up.

During the sitting of parliament, and I think by order of it, Angus and Neil M'Leod were denounced and put to the horn, being, as was alleged, the persons who had taken the marquis of Montrose, May 1650. This was done, August 17th, this year.

September 29th, Mr. Thomas Sideserf, minister at Edinburgh, and bishop of Galloway, before the year 1638, and now, as we heard, bishop of Orkney, died at Edinburgh.*

He was buried honourably there, October 4th, being a Sabbath: his 1663. corpse lay in state in the isle of the Eastkirk, and Mr. William Annand had a sermon before their interment, wherein he described, with abundance of parade, the family, birth, piety, learning, travels, life, and sufferings, for the sake of the gospel, of the deceased prelate. This is the second bishop dies this year, and just now we shall hear of a third.

In September, the council write to the king about some new impositions put upon Scotsmen in France, in their traffic, as follows:

" Most sacred sovereign,

" We are informed by several merchants of this kingdom who traffic with France, and some who reside there who are your majesty's native subjects, that there being of late some impositions put upon the vessels and merchant-goods belonging to foreigners, by the French king; the general farmers of those taxes upon that pretext, have encumbered the goods and vessels of your majesty's subjects belonging to this kingdom, so that they are in hazard to be reduced to the condition of strangers, and lose the benefit of those ancient privileges which for many years they have enjoyed during the reigns of your majesty's glorious predecessors of blessed memory, until the time of the late usurpers, during which, your majesty's subjects of this kingdom did exceedingly suffer in their privileges and immunities in France, and other foreign kingdoms, for want of your majesty's protection.

" And seeing it can be made appear, that in the year 787, by a treaty betwixt Achaius, then king of Scotland, and Charles the great, then emperor and king of France, confirmed thereafter in the time of Alexander II. many great privileges were secured unto this your majesty's ancient kingdom; and that in the year 1558, when the dolphin of France, was married to Mary, then queen of Scotland, there was a reciprocal naturalization of the subjects of either kingdom, ratified and recorded here in parliament, and the great council of France, which has been punctually observed; and that whensoever any of your majesty's subjects were troubled in France, for taxes put upon strangers, they were

---

* Bishop Burnet says, " He died a little more than a year after his translation; he had died in more esteem, if he had died a year before it."—History of his Own Time, vol. i. p. 191.—*Ed*

1663. declared free by sentences of those judicatories, to which they were liable, conform to several declarations of the French kings from time to time, particularly in the year 1639, by a declaration and arrest of the council of state of France, whereby all Scottish men living in France, and their descendants, are declared free of all taxes put upon strangers. We found it our duty humbly to offer the condition of those your majesty's subjects, and their sufferings and hazard to your consideration, and take the boldness to implore in their behalf, that your majesty would be graciously pleased to interpose with the French king, for relief from their present encumbrances, and the security of their ancient privileges for the future, and to put a present stop to any levying of taxes from them. And if your majesty think fit to employ any of your subjects of this kingdom to negotiate that affair, we shall be ready to furnish him authorities and originals fit for that purpose. We are, &c." I find no more of this till in king James's reign, the recovery of our privileges in France is brought in to be a bait to come into the repeal of the penal laws against papists.

That same day the council considering the vacancy of St. Salvator's college in St. Andrews, recommend to the lord archbishop as chancellor of that university, to name a person to oversee the masters, regents, and scholars, exercising discipline, and enjoying the privileges, and uplifting the emoluments of the provost of that college: and the council require the person named by his grace to accept. We may see the archbishop had some reason for pushing the removal of the reverend Mr. James Wood, of which before.

As soon as the parliament rose, a good many went up to court. The commissioner who was well received, Lauderdale, the earl of Dumfries, lord Bellenden, treasurer-depute, Sir John Fletcher advocate. The primate goes not up at first, but in a little time followed them, and brought down the warrant for the high commission next year.

November 2d, archbishop Fairfoul died in his lodgings at Edinburgh. Since his riding the parliament in pomp and state, he was not well, and continued till this time when he died. Upon the 11th instant, his corpse were carried to St. Giles's east church, now the new church in Edinburgh, and laid in mourning before the pulpit. The bells rang for the funeral sermon at four in the afternoon. Mr. John Hay, parson at Peebles, now archdean at Glasgow, preached from Eccles. xii. 5. When sermon was over, the corpse were put into a mourning coach, and carried to Holyrood-house, with the nobility and principal gentry in town; the magistrates, the lords of session in coaches, and the rest on foot, with trumpets sounding, and two heralds, and two pursuivants with coats displayed before the corpse, with great numbers of torches; the chancellor with his purse after the corpse, and the archbishop of St. Andrews and other bishops in coaches; and the body was interred in the east end of the Abbey church. Thus three of our bishops are carried off, and bishop Burnet from Aberdeen, is translated to Glasgow. Doctor Scougal succeeds him there; and Mr. Andrew Honeyman is made bishop of Orkney, as we shall hear, next year.

I shall end this year with remarking, that the council are very careful to supply the alleged necessities of bishops and their clergy. The bishop of the isles was not satisfied with his rent as bishop, and so they allow him the stipend of the parish where he had been minister, and they allow a good large sum out of the vacant stipends to Mr. Annand, though his stipend was not despicable at Edinburgh. I shall give both as they stand in the registers.

November 10th, "Anent a petition presented by the bishop of the isles, showing that the provision of the bishopric of the isles is so mean that unless his majesty shall be pleased to take some course for helping of it, the petitioner shall not be able to subsist by it, by reason of the distance of the place, and the extraordinary expenses he is put to in visiting his diocese; and seeing the stipend of Barnwel, where the supplicant served last twenty-two years, is vacant this year, notwithstanding of all endeavours used for planting thereof; humbly therefore desiring, that in consideration of the extraordinary expenses and pains that he is put to, the said year's stipend may be allowed him for his present supply, as the petition bears. Whilk being at length read, heard, and considered, the lords of his majesty's council, give warrant and power to the supplicant to uplift the stipend of the said parish of Barnwel the said year 1663, and ordain the heritors, feuars, and liferenters, and others liable, to make due and thankful payment; and if need be, ordain letters to be direct hereupon in form as effeirs."

The same day, "Anent a petition of Mr. William Annand minister at Edinburgh, showing, that whereas the petitioner's father, in consideration of his sufferings, was appointed two hundred pounds sterling, out of the vacant stipends, notwithstanding whereof, his father, during his lifetime, received nothing thereof; humbly therefore desiring the same locality might be assigned to the petitioner, for payment of the said sum, or else that he may be recommended to the lord St. Andrews his grace, for that effect. The lords of council recommend him to the archbishop of St. Andrews, to appoint a locality for the said sum, and ordain letters of horning to be direct upon the localities so to be granted."

CHAP. V.

OF THE STATE AND SUFFERINGS OF PRESBYTERIANS, DURING THE YEAR 1664.

1664. WE are now got through the most considerable transactions of the period which is the subject of this first book : we are to have no more parliaments for some years ; and the extensive and large acts of council, with the severe execution of them, already described, leave little room for much further to be done by the managers, until the rising at Pentland is taken hold of for a handle to further severities. However, the laws made by the three last sessions of parliament, now begun to be rigorously executed by the army, did not satisfy the cruel bishops. The people in Scotland, when episcopacy was forced upon them, had ill enough impression of them and their curates; but the barbarity of the soldiers, 1664. hounded out by the prelates, and under the direction of the curates; brought the west and south of Scotland, now mostly the scene of their severities, perfectly to loath the bishops. Nevertheless, when they perceived that they could not be loved and esteemed as fathers of the church, they resolve to be feared, as tyrants ordinarily do; and therefore they prevail to get a high commission court set up, effectually to bring this about.

This terrible court is the chief and most remarkable thing in this year I am now entering upon; and because very little, either as to its nature or proceedings, hath, as far as I know, been published, I shall give the larger accounts of it in this chapter. The work of the privy council was pretty much abridged by this frightsome court; and yet we shall find them going on to put in execution the act of Middleton's parliament concerning the fines, and pushing the declaration formerly spoken of, and, at the instigation of the bishops, making some new and very unaccountable acts against presbyterian ministers, and others of that persuasion. Besides, they are going on against some more particular gentlemen and ministers, and putting them to new trouble. Those, with some other incidental matters that tend to clear the history of this year, will afford matter for five sections; and I begin with the high commission court.

SECT. I.

Of the erection and powers of the high commission court, with some reflections upon the same.

WHEN the plan of prelacy was perfected and set up in Scotland, the king was made to expect, that his prerogative would be strengthened in Scotland, and his power and pleasures every way secured. No doubt somewhat as to both was done for him, but in reality the bishops were a dead weight on his authority, and a clog upon his actings ; and as they dethroned him in the hearts of the best of his subjects, so they were perpetually teasing and vexing him

1664. with new demands, dishonourable for his majesty to go into, and very burdensome to his subjects and the poor country. Thus the archbishop of St. Andrews, in the end of December, last year, comes up to court to make new demands, and use his interest for filling up the vacant bishoprics, but especially for erecting the high commission court.

The chancellor, and some other of our noblemen here, were not for running altogether so fast as our prelates would have them; and Glencairn, in particular, was highly dissatisfied with the pride and overdriving of the archbishop and other prelates. I am informed, he went so far as to say to the earl of Rothes, before his going up to court last year, "That it was noblemen's interest and concern to bear down the growing power of bishops, otherwise they were like to be treated now by them, as they had been before the (year) 1638." This coming to the ears of bishop Sharp, I am told he treated the chancellor with indiscretion abundance, and plainly threatened to disgrace and discourt him. When he got up to court, he made heavy complaints of the backwardness of many noblemen in executing the laws made for the interest of the church; and prevailed with the king, by the help of the English bishops, and the highfliers, to grant a commission for erecting a high commission court in Scotland, made up of churchmen and laymen, to execute the laws concerning church affairs; and it was in every point modelled according to his mind.* The nature of this court will best appear from the king's commission brought down by the archbishop; which is as follows:

Commission for executing the laws in church affairs.

" Our sovereign lord ordains a commission to be passed and expede under his majesty's great seal for the kingdom of Scotland, making mention, that in consideration of the multiplicity and weight of the affairs of the state incumbent upon the lords of privy council, so as they cannot attend the due execution of the laws against popery, separation, and disobedience to ecclesiastical authority; and to the effect that the disorders and contempt of authority and the laws in the provinces of St. Andrews and Glasgow, may be timously suppressed, and the scandalous and disobedient may not through impunity and connivance be emboldened to violate and affront the laws, create disturbances, foment sedition and disaffection to the government of the church and state, under pretext of any engagements : his majesty by virtue of his royal prerogative in all causes, and over all persons, as well ecclesiastic as civil, has given and granted, likeas by the tenor hereof, gives and grants full power and commission to the archbishop of St. Andrews, the lord chancellor, the lord treasurer, the archbishop of Glasgow, duke Hamilton, the marquis of Montrose, the earls of Argyle, Athol, Eglinton, Linlithgow, Hume, Galloway, Annandale, Tweeddale, Leven, Murray; the bishops of Edinburgh, Galloway, Dunkeld, Aberdeen, Brechin, Argyle, and the Isles; the lords

---

* " Sharp went up to London to complain of the lord Glencairn, and of the privy council, where he said there was such remissness, and so much popularity appeared on all occasions, that unless some more spirit were put in the administration, it would be impossible to preserve the church. That was the word always used, as if there had been a charm in it. He moved that a letter might be writ, giving him the precedence of the lord chancellor. This was thought an inexcusable piece of vanity, for in Scotland, when there was no commissioner, all matters passed through the lord chancellor's hands, who, by act of parliament, was to preside in all courts, and was considered as representing the king's person; he also moved that the king would grant a special commission to some persons for executing the laws relating to the church. All the privy counsellors were to be of it, but to these he desired many others might be added, for whom he undertook, that they would execute them with zeal. Lord Lauderdale saw that this would prove a high commission court, he gave way to it, though much against his own mind. Upon these things I took the liberty, though then too young to meddle in things of that kind, to expostulate very freely with him. I thought he was acting the earl of Traquair's part, giving way to all the follies of the bishops, on design to ruin them. He, upon that, ran into a great deal of freedom with me; he told me many passages of Sharp's past life; he was persuaded he would ruin all, but he said he was resolved to give him time, for he had not credit enough to stop him, nor would he oppose any thing that he proposed, unless it were very extravagant. He saw the earl of Glencairn and he

Drumlanerk, Pitsligo, Frazer, Cochran, Halkerton, and Bellenden; the president of the session, the register, the advocate, Sir John Hume, justice-clerk, Mr. Charles Maitland, the laird of Philorth elder, Sir Andrew Ramsay, Sir William Thomson; the provosts of St. Andrews, Aberdeen, Glasgow, Ayr, and Dumfries; Sir James Turner, and the dean of guild of Edinburgh, or any five of them, an archbishop or bishop being one of the number, to use their utmost endeavour that the acts of parliament and council, for the peace and order of the church, and in behalf of the government thereof by archbishops and bishops, be put in vigorous and impartial execution against all and every one within the kingdom of Scotland, who presume to violate, contemn, or disobey, those acts and the ecclesiastical authority now settled; to summon and call before them at whatsoever time and place they shall appoint, all popish traffickers, intercommuners with, and resetters of Jesuits and seminary priests, all who say or hear mass, all obstinate contemners of the discipline of the church, or for that cause suspended, deprived, or excommunicated; all keepers of conventicles, all ministers who, contrary to the laws and acts of parliament or council, remain or intrude themselves on the function of the ministry in these parishes and bounds inhibited by those acts; all such who preach in private houses, or elsewhere, without license from the bishop of the diocese; all such persons who keep meetings at fasts, and the administration of the sacrament of the Lord's supper, which are not approven by authority; all who speak, preach, write, or print, to the scandal, reproach, and detriment, of the estate or government of the church or kingdom, as now established; all who contemn, molest, or injure, the ministers who are orderly and obedient to the laws; all who do not orderly attend divine worship, administration of the word and sacraments, performed in their respective parish churches, by ministers legally settled for taking care of these parishes in which those persons are inhabitants; all such, who, without any lawful calling, as busybodies, go about houses and places, for corrupting and disaffecting people from their allegiance, respect, and obedience, to the laws; and generally, without prejudice to the particulars above mentioned, all who express their disaffection to his majesty's authority, by contravening acts of parliament or council in relation to church affairs. With power to the said commissioners, or any five of them, an archbishop or bishop being one of the number, to appoint ministers to be censured with suspension or deposition, and to punish by fining, confining, committing to prison, and incarcerating them and all other persons, who shall be found transgressors, as aforesaid, according as they shall judge the quality of their offence to deserve, they always not exceeding the fines and punishments enjoined by the acts of parliament and council. Commanding the captains of his majesty's guards, the officers of the standing forces and militia, sheriffs, deputes, bailies of regalities, justices of the peace, and provosts and bailies of burghs, to search, seek, take, and apprehend, all such delinquents, and present them before the commissioners, upon the warrant of any five of them, as aforesaid. Commanding likewise the constables and commanders of his majesty's castles, keepers of prisons, and other places of firmance, to receive and detain those that shall be directed to them by the commissioners, upon the said warrant, as said is, as they will answer upon their obedience, or utmost peril. Ordaining further the lords of his majesty's privy council, upon any certificate subscribed by the said commissioners, or any five of them, as aforesaid, to direct letters of horning for payment of the fines imposed by the said commissioners, in case of the delinquents' disobedience and refusal to compear before them; of which letters of horning, no suspension or relaxation shall be granted

1664.

---

would be in a perpetual war, and it was indifferent to him how matters might go between them, things would run to a height, and then the king would of himself put a stop to their career. For the king said often, he was not priest-ridden, he would not venture a war, nor travel again for any party. This was all that I could obtain from the earl of Lauderdale. I pressed Sharp himself to think of more moderate methods. But he despised my applications, and from that time he was very jealous of me."—Burnet's History of his Own Times, vol. i. pp. 301, 302.—*Ed.*

1664. without the certificate of the archbishop or bishop, bearing their obedience to the said commissioners, and satisfaction to the laws. And his majesty doth make, constitute, and ordain, Mr. Thomas Young, clerk to the commission for plantation of kirks, to be clerk to this commission, with power to him to appoint officers, and other attendants necessary, and to direct summons and precepts in his majesty's name, for citing whatsoever parties or persons, in any of the cases aforesaid; whilk precepts shall be sealed by the signet, and subscribed by the said clerk; with power to summon witnesses, under the pains prescribed by law and practice; and if the said witnesses refuse to compear, or the said persons decerned in any fine, refuse or delay to make payment of the same, his majesty ordains the lords of secret council to direct letters and charges upon the certificate of the said commissioners, as is above specified. Of the which fines, to be collected and uplifted by Alexander Keith, under-clerk to the council, one half shall be employed for defraying the necessary charges of the said commission, at the sight of the said commissioners; and the other half shall be employed for pious uses, as his majesty shall appoint. And generally the commissioners aforesaid are authorized and empowered to do and execute what they shall find necessary and convenient for his majesty's service in the premises, for preventing and suppressing of schism and separation, for planting of vacant churches, and for procuring of reverence, submission, and obedience, to the ecclesiastical government established by law. And to the end that a business of so much importance to the peace and well being of the church and kingdom, may take a speedy and successful effect, as his majesty hath thought fit to make choice of such persons, in whose judgment and affection to his majesty's service and the church's good he doth repose special trust, so it is his pleasure that this his commission shall endure to the first of November, 1664, and after, until it be discharged by his majesty: and that the first meeting thereof be kept at Edinburgh the first Wednesday of March next to come; and after meetings shall be appointed in such places, and as often as shall be found necessary for obtaining the end of the said commission. And his majesty doth expect an exact account of their proceedings from time to time, as of a service whereof he will take special notice, and it succeeding well will be very acceptable to him. Commanding lastly, all his majesty's lieges who are or may be concerned, to answer and obey the said commissioners, or any five of them, an archbishop or bishop being one of the number, under all highest pains that may after follow. And ordains these presents to be an effectual warrant to the director of the chancellary, for writing the same, to the great seal, and to the lord chancellor for appending the seal thereunto, without any further order or warrant. Given at our court at Whitehall, January 16th, 1664, and of our reign the 15th year."

This commission is so very extensive and large, that it affords matter for many remarks The ground alleged for appointing of this new court, by many termed the "Crail court," being the contrivance of the primate, once minister there, with the best advice he could have in Scotland and England, is " the multiplicity of affairs lying before the privy council." But it is well enough known, the council spent much of their time before this in maintaining the prelates, and bearing down such as would not subject to them, and, bating church affairs, their business was not so very great; besides, when the high commission sat, the council could not sit, at least ply any business of moment, since the leading and managing members were on both these courts. So this reason is a mere pretext. The real grounds of erecting this court, were, that there might be room for the members, deriving immediately from the king's supremacy, to act with larger powers, in a more severe and general way than even the council itself could well do. The quorum picked out by the bishops, would go greater lengths, than the council would in their full meetings. By this means the bishops had occasion to rid themselves of some members of council, who were not altogether for their heights. They were empowered to meet in places where the council was not easily to be called; their influence this way was more diffusive, and a small quorum of this commission would effectuate the bishops' business more quickly, and in a more extensive way, by travelling up and down the country for harassing and persecuting the presbyterians, than could be done in the former channel.

It is pretended in the commission, the design of this court in the first place, is, "Against papists, and to execute the laws against popery:" but in reality, popery in this case is a mere cipher to fill up the current style. Presbytery was levelled at, under the name of separation; whereas, strictly speaking, and according to the natural and ordinary signification of words, the prelatic party were in Scotland the separatists, our reformation establishment being undoubtedly by presbyters, and contemners of the ecclesiastical authority, that is, such as refused to subject to bishops. The actings of the prelates is the best commentary on this grant, and it is notour, never one papist was called before them, or prosecute before this court. Their designs lay not that way, and indeed all things were ripening for the introduction of popery to these lands.

The dioceses of St. Andrews and Glasgow are named, both to extend their power through the whole kingdom, and, as their present particular level was, against some ministers and gentlemen in Fife and the west country.—The covenants are made a special ground of prosecution before this court, under the style of pretended engagements. The prelates had a particular grudge against these, as what they themselves had broken scandalously, and they could not well bear that their obligations should be owned by any. His majesty's royal prerogative is made the basis of this court, and by virtue of his supremacy over all persons and causes ecclesiastical and civil, this rampant commission is granted. Indeed nothing else could be the parent of so monstrous a birth. This being their foundation, and their being of such a constitution, made severals to scruple to appear before them, who could not homologate this supremacy.—

The archbishop of St. Andrews is put in front of this commission, and placed before the chancellor and other officers of state, by virtue of a letter from the king, of which notice shall be taken afterwards, giving him the precedency.—In this commission there are nine bishops to about thirty-five laymen : but the bishops are made necessary members, and four with any one prelate are to be a quorum; and they might be sure enough to find four in three dozen, who would do as they pleased. This was a very small quorum of so numerous a meeting, and so much the fitter for the purposes now in hand.

1664.

The chief work of this high commission, is to maintain the bishops, and to use the utmost endeavours that the acts of parliament and council be executed. What an untowardly and ill-thriving weed was prelacy in this kingdom! And what pains and force must be used to plant and maintain it! The authority of parliament, it seems, is not enough, the executions of the privy council do not suffice, even when supported with the quarterings of the army: the prelates must have this new court set up for their support, and to put the laws, made in their favour, to execution. In proportion to the difficulties justly expected in the maintenance of bishops in Scotland, the powers of this commission are extended. Every man in the nation may be called before this high and mighty court, at any time or place they shall please to appoint. The bishops of Brechin, Dunkeld, Argyle, and the Isles, with Sir James Turner, or to put the matter a little otherwise, three provosts of burghs, a dean of guild, and the inconsiderable bishop of Brechin, may bring the greatest peer in the land to their bar, fine, confine, incarcerate, at their pleasure.

I need scarce go through the lists of criminals against whom this commission is directed. Papists and popish recusants are made a cover for their rigorous powers against the presbyterians: meanwhile Jesuits, sayers, and hearers of mass, and all good catholics are very easy under our protestant bishops, and never one of them molested. After the clause about papists, all that follows points at the poor whigs : beside the

1664. ordinary crimes of conventicles, and presbyterian ministers their continuing at their Master's work, all such are cast in who keep meetings at fasts, and the sacrament of the Lord's supper, which are not approven by authority. It was a strange opposition to serious religion that brought people this length, as to arraign persons meeting together for prayer on fast-days and about communion times, when so much wrestling ought to be about all the members of Christ's mystical body. No doubt, private fasts in families, and private societies, at this time so very necessary, are by this clause made faults. The bishops had no mind to have their guilt, apostasy, and oppression, mourned over by others, and complained of before the Lord; some of their consciences probably smote them, and they were afraid, and not without ground, of the joint prayers and supplications of the Lord's people.

The next class of criminals is extensive with a witness. " All who write, speak, preach, or print, to the detriment of the government of the church." It is pity they took no notice of the dissenters in England, and protestants abroad, for their excellent books against prelacy and popery. Nevertheless, it was good they put not in *thinking* likewise; but this was reserved till some years afterwards, when they examined and interrogate people upon their thoughts, opinions, and inward sentiments of disputable matters; yet without this they have rope enough allowed them to make most of the subjects in Scotland offenders.

Just now I took notice of the smallness of the quorum, for so great a work, and such vast numbers of offenders; five only, whereof a bishop must be one, and all the five might be bishops for any thing I see; and it was proper, at least safest for them, since the work was theirs, and it was their interest and nobody's else was carrying on. Well, the four laymen and one bishop have power ecclesiastical and civil lodged in them, censures of suspension and deposition, as to churchmen, and fining, confining and imprisonment, for them, or others who shall be made transgressors. Indeed they are limited to the acts of parliament and council, and the penalties there; but it will be just now evident they exceeded those boundaries, though pretty wide. The whole army and inferior magistrates through the kingdom, are to be their terriers, and to search for, seek, take, and apprehend all they shall give orders about; yea, the privy council itself is in some sort subjected to this exalted court, those mighty five, and must direct letters of horning, and other diligence, for paying the impositions laid upon poor people by them; and no relaxation or suspension must be granted without warrant from a bishop. A very surprising clause is added in the commission, whereby the five are made their own carvers, and empowered " to do and execute what they shall find necessary and convenient for his majesty's service in the premises." And what will the prelates not find convenient for securing themselves and underlings, if we may judge by what they ventured on already? The poor country found to their sad cost, how extensively such general clauses were executed in this period. A clause of this nature, making the bishops absolute tyrants, and such as were parties supreme judges in their own cause, is such a stretch against equity and reason, as none but bishop Sharp would have proposed, and a parallel cannot be given, unless it be some posterior acts in the following years I am to describe.

His majesty is next made to give a high encomium to the members of this court, as persons to whom he could well commit such important matters, and in whom he put entire confidence: and so he might, as to the bishops, the cause was their own, and undoubtedly they would look after it with care enough. Thus the wolf gets the wethers to keep, and will give a good account of them; and yet they are encouraged to this work as " a service the king will take special notice of." And in the last place, all the king's lieges are required to submit to every thing done by this commission, under the highest penalties, without any appeal, or reclaiming to any other court.

From those things, the reader may have some view of this extraordinary court of the primate's contrivance; and cannot but observe the affinity of the hierarchy in the church, and arbitrary impositions and burdens upon the subject. It may be indeed (thought) strange, that the king granted such exorbitant powers, or that persons of honour ever joined with the prelates in such a court: at present the bishops' cravings were a rule, but our noblemen in a little time wearied to follow them in their heights. Perhaps this was an experiment of what was projected for the whole three kingdoms, in state and church. Things were fast working to bring matters in Britain up to the pattern the king saw, and kept his eye upon in France, where the king was turning tyrant, and made use of the bigoted high-flying clergy to help this on, and every thing was modelling plainly enough, towards the eastern absolute prerogative and power.

Let me finish this subject with some more general remarks upon the erection of this court. We have seen the powers and constitution of it from the king's warrant. Every one must see that this high commission in its very erection, casts a slur upon the privy council, either as remiss in the execution of the acts of parliament expressly committed to them, or wanting power or inclination to execute them to the satisfaction of the bishops. It is certain the council were not blameworthy as to any thing proper for them to do, yea, they really exceeded their powers in some cases, to gratify the bishops. But these behoved to have more, and the council generally sat at Edinburgh, and so were alleged not to be a sufficient bridle upon the presbyterians up and down the country: and therefore an itinerant sort of court, made up of a few zealots, whom the bishops should at their pleasure pick out to travel up and down, and overawe the people who disliked the church settlement, was reckoned a better expedient, especially when clothed with the highest power the king could put in their hand. This high commission in former times of prelacy, had been the last resort and plight-anchor of bishops in the reigns of James VI. and Charles I.

Whenever the nobility, gentry, and commons in Scotland came to have any sense of liberty, and awaked out of their sleep, this court was complained of, and petitioned against, as most arbitrary and oppressive, and one of the greatest grievances subjects could be under. But the truth of the matter was, such measures as those were still found absolutely necessary to support the hierarchy in Scotland. What is contrary to the constitution and inclinations of a people, must still be maintained and carried through by violent, rigorous, and illegal methods. However, in a year or two, our nobility and gentry fell into a dislike of this arbitrary court, and matters again returned to their own channel, the secret council, which indeed was a judicatory abundantly severe and arbitrary. The English nation, who, when at themselves, are vigorous asserters of the liberty of the subjects, at the restoration, in the heat of their loyalty, run to great enough lengths in the surrender they made to the king; and yet when they gave back the whole of the dignities and prerogatives possessed by their sovereigns formerly, some of which had been reckoned not very agreeable to the liberty of the subject, and constitution of England, some few years before; yet they could not hear of a high commission: and, as far as I have observed, it was never allowed, though sometimes attempted, during the reign of king Charles II. Indeed when a papist mounted the throne, and all things pointed towards popery, and consequently to slavery, this court was set up there; but any thing was welcome now to our managers in Scotland, which came from the royal prerogative, and was demanded for the support of prelacy.

1664.

Somewhat has been already said as to the members of this court; and from the list of them in the commission, the reader will have remarked, that it is of a heterogeneous nature: most of the members were laymen, by their commission empowered to judge of ministers' doctrine, and suspend and deprive (them) of both benefice and office. The churchmen in the commission had power of corporal punishment, and cognoscing upon civil matters. Thus it was a very native product of the royal supremacy, which works wonders in Scotland: it confounds, yea, alters the co-ordinate power of the state and church, and makes a layman

1664. of a churchman, and a churchman of a layman, without any difficulty. What can be more agreeable to so mighty a parent as the civil pope? Thus his holiness at Rome commits the sword and the keys to the high court of the inquisition, who yet are so discreet as to make the fashion of turning over their pannels to the secular arm, a little before their death.

An ingenious writer compares this Crail court unto the old lion in the cave. There were abundance of footsteps, and tracks of beasts' feet going to the cave, but none returning; which when cunning reynard observed, he stopped at the entry, and went no farther. Thus many came to this court, but very few returned; all almost were devoured who came within their clutches. I cannot so much as find one who appeared before them, that came off without punishment; so exact were they in their citations of guilty persons, or else made all guilty who came before them. Indeed their procedure was abundantly summary. When a pannel came before them, they used not the formalities of a libel, or witnesses; whoever the prelates pleased were cited, and upon their appearance, a captious question or two was asked, and upon their silence, or answering, for both were much the same before this court, who were determined to punish all that appeared, they presently judge him. It was but seldom they troubled any witnesses. The taking the oath of supremacy was the only thing that could save such as appeared; but I hear of few before them whose throats were wide enough for that. Frequently they doubled the fine imposed by the act of parliament, upon some pretext or other; and not satisfied with the punishment appointed by law, added somewhat of their own, further than what the king and parliament had annexed to the alleged crimes before them, such as confinement, relegation to some of the plantations, or some remote place of the kingdom, some hundred miles distant; and some were gifted away, and actually sold for slaves, which is against scriptural and natural law and light.

I find it remarked by a minister who lived at this time, that although their powers were very ample and wide, and they had abundance of room to make many offenders, yet their powers and commission were more than once enlarged, and that with an eye to particular circumstantiate cases, and many of their sentences exceeded the largest of their powers. I have not seen any other copies of their commission than that insert, and it is very large. In short, their arbitrary and tyrannical procedure frighted people from coming before them, and it was found more eligible to undergo a voluntary banishment, than to be sold as a slave. And in some time, the violent procedure of the prelates made the noblemen unwilling, and some way ashamed to sit with them; and in about a year and a half's time, our bishops could neither find judges to join with them, or parties to appear before them, and so were constrained to give over: and after near two years, this contrivance of bishop Sharp's came to an end, and those heavy harassings, joined with the oppressions of the army, opened the door to the country to rise in arms, as we shall hear in the beginning of the next book. It remains I now give some more particular account of the actings of this inquisition now set up.

SECT. II.

Of the actings of the high-commission court, and the persecution of gentlemen and others before them, 1664.

IN this section I do not pretend to give any full account of the actings and procedure of this terrible court. I have been at some pains to inquire for their records, if they kept any, but cannot fall upon them; if these could be recovered, or a particular and distinct account now had, it would make a dismal figure, and afford a large heap of materials for this history. It is only a very few instances of their procedure with gentlemen and ministers, some of which I have from the persons themselves, that I can set down as proofs of the iniquity and severity of this court; and from those some judgment may be formed of the rest of their procedure. Some more hints of what they

CHAP. V.] OF THE CHURCH OF SCOTLAND. 391

did next year may fall in on the following chapter.

Their commission bears them to sit down in March this year. Whether the primate came down by that time or not, I know not, but I don't meet with him in the sederunt of council till April; and I find they sat down at Edinburgh, April 15th. And I have it observed by one who writes at this time, " that they ordered Mr. James Wood, professor of divinity at St. Andrews, his declaration to be burnt, and some ministers, accessory thereunto, were put in prison in the tolbooth of Edinburgh, and the west country recusants were fined in a fourth part of their rent and yearly income." We shall afterwards meet with the trouble Mr. Carstairs and some others were brought to, upon the score of a paper left by the Reverend Mr. Wood, upon another section, since I cannot give any distinct account of the procedure of this court on this affair: and the west country recusants, here·spoken of, were the gentlemen who refused to give full conformity to the church government now set up. But I come forward to some particular instances of the hardships several worthy persons were brought to this year, probably at different meetings of this court, as I have them very well attested.

James Hamilton of Aikenhead, near Glasgow, yet alive, at a good old age when I write this, and attesting the account I am giving, was among the first brought before the high commission; and I shall give the whole detail of his sufferings at this time here. We shall meet with him more than once under hardships in the progress of this history. All that could be laid to this gentleman's charge, was his not hearing Mr. David Hay, curate in Cathcart parish, where Aikenhead hath his estate and house. The occasion of his deserting his parish church was this; Mr. Hay was extremely rigorous in exacting his stipend, and particularly hard upon Aikenhead's tenants in Langside, and violently pressed some of them to join with him in his session; upon which, one day a squabble fell in betwixt Hay and some of them, wherein the curate threatened them, and gave them ill names; and they did not spare to give him some returns of the same

nature. Mr. James Blair, the presbyterian minister of the parish, happened to be upon the place, and by his interest with the people protected Mr. Hay, else matters had gone further. When the fray was over, Mr. Blair dealt with Mr. Hay, and showed him how far it was contrary to his own interest, to inform against his parishioners for their disorders; and Mr. Hay promised to him, with more than ordinary assurances, to follow his advice, and never to delate any of them, and thanked him for his help and advice. Yet, notwithstanding his promise, in a little time he went in to Glasgow, and delated them to the bishop, who ordered out Sir James Turner, at this time in the west, with a party of soldiers, who came and apprehended some of the country people. Aikenhead was abroad at the time, and when he came home, and was informed of Mr. Hay's carriage, his cruelty, and prevarication, after that, he for ever disowned him, as unworthy to be a minister, and indeed never called to that congregation. When he comes before the high commission, he is fined in a fourth part of his yearly rent. Some time after, he is again called before them, to liquidate his rent; which he did, and gave in an account of it, and frankly acknowledged he heard not, and never designed to hear Mr. Hay, and gave the court so pointed, and well vouched an account of the injuries done him, and his tenants by the curate, as the archbishop of Glasgow promised, in open court, he should be removed from that parish.

1664.

The commission then urged the gentleman to engage judicially to hear and subject unto the minister whom the bishop should plant there in Mr. Hay's room. Aikenhead thought it soon enough to engage when he had heard him, and knew what and who he was, and peremptorily refused all such previous contracts. Hereupon, though he had some relations in the court, he is fined in another fourth part of his yearly rent, and remitted to the archbishop of Glasgow to give him satisfaction as to his loyal and peaceable behaviour. It seems bishop Burnet was not satisfied, and therefore, by a new information from him, he is cited, and

1664. actually compeared before the high commission court at Edinburgh, November 8th, this year. There he was charged with keeping up the session book of Cathcart, and the utensils of the church, from the curate; which he knew nothing about, and offered to depone he knew not where they were. He was further charged for refusing to assist his minister in session, when called, and suffering some of his family to absent from the church. The earl of Rothes told him, that he had seen him before several courts formerly, and never for any thing that was good and loyal, and therefore required him now to testify his loyalty, by taking the oath appointed by law. Aikenhead answered, his loyalty was never questioned before, yea, it was so well known, that he could not but reckon it was a tash (slur) upon him to put him to declare it by oath; that for his part he had no difficulty to take the oath of allegiance, but he knew there was mixed with it an oath of supremacy. Bishop Sharp interrupting, said, that was the common cant, but it would not do. He added, that he was willing to take it, as it was an oath of allegiance, providing they allowed him to declare against the clause relative to the supremacy. The president took him up very sharply, and told him, he ought to be hanged.

Upon Aikenhead's refusing the supremacy in the oath, and because he would not presently enter himself surety in the books of the court for all his tenants, that they should subject to ordinances, and live regularly, the court fined him in the sum of three hundred pounds sterling, and ordered him to go to prison till he paid it; and then to transport himself to the town of Inverness, which is about one hundred and fifty miles from his own house, and there to remain under confinement during pleasure, which was about a year and a half. He paid the half of his fine, and his estate was sequestrate for the rest of it; and, according to his sentence, in three weeks presented himself to the magistrates of Inverness, and continued there till his confinement was taken off. And to give all his sufferings in this period together, when at length he was allowed to come home, he was confined anew for six months, to his own house at Aikenhead, and a mile round it. And before these were elapsed, *brevi manu* he was one day carried in to Edinburgh tolbooth, without any reason or libel given him, and there he lay prisoner nineteen weeks. After he had been in prison some weeks, he found all they had now to lay to his charge, was his harbouring, and lodging some rebels, as they were called, at the break of Hamilton, about fourteen years ago, when some soldiers laid down their arms, and would not fight till they had some satisfaction given them as to what was then termed the remonstrance:* he could not depone that none of them had been lodged in his house, and so was continued in prison, till, by the payment of eighty guineas, he at length got out.

Another instance of the injustice of this court I have in the case of John Porterfield, laird of Duchall, in the shire of Renfrew, which is attested by his successor and grandchild the laird of Porterfield, of that ilk, an ancient and honourable family in the said shire. We shall frequently meet with this worthy person in the following parts of this history, and find him dealt with in a way peculiar to this period; I only here notice his treatment before the high commission. This excellent and religious gentleman was brought before that court in July this year, for his not hearing the curate in the parish of Kilmalcom, where his dwelling-house and his estate lay. He had very good grounds to withdraw from him as his pastor, since, besides the ordinary blemishes of those of his gang, his intruding himself without, yea, contrary to the inclinations of the people of that place, he had abused Duchall with groundless, base, and injurious reproaches. The court could not well get by the sustaining of this defence as relevant, and at his desire admitted it to probation. The very first witness he adduced, deponed all the gentleman alleged, and much more. The court finding he would vindicate himself, if law and equity took

---

* This was the attack upon general Lambert, where colonel Ker was made prisoner, and where Govan, who was executed along with Mr. James Guthrie, was charged with having treacherously laid down his arms.—Baillie's Letters, vol. ii. p. 364.—*Ed.*

place, interrupted the examination of witnesses, and required Duchall to take the oath of allegiance, well enough knowing the supremacy in it would choke him. This he peremptorily refused, unless they would allow him to give in an explication before his taking of it. Whereupon they proceeded straight to a sentence, and fined him in the sum of five hundred pounds sterling, and ordered his estate to be sequestrate until it should be paid, and confined him in the town of Elgin in the shire of Murray: there he continued about four years. Reflections upon such procedure are almost needless. Here was plain injustice, in refusing to permit the gentleman to vindicate himself, after they had allowed his exculpation. They go beyond the acts of parliament and council, which allow of no such exorbitant fines for nonjurancy. Those hardships for simple nonconformity did very much prejudge his estate and family, and yet we shall find he met with heavier things afterward.

But their procedure with the reverend Mr. Alexander Smith, minister at Cowend, was perfectly tyrannical, antichristian, and barbarous. We heard before that he was turned out of his charge, and at present he was residing at Leith. This worthy and religious person is called before them, and charged with preaching privately in his own house, or, in the present style, for keeping of conventicles. He compeared before them; and when charged with conventicling, his examination was oddly enough interrupted. In answering some interrogatories bishop Sharp put to him, Mr. Smith did not give him his titles, and called him only Sir. The earl of Rothes asked him, If he knew to whom he was speaking? Mr. Smith answered, Yes, my lord, I do, I speak to Mr. James Sharp, once a fellow-minister with myself. This was reckoned a high crime, and without any further inquiry into the affair of conventicles, Mr. Smith was immediately ordered to be laid in the irons, and cast into that nasty place, commonly called, the thieves' hole, where he had for his company only a poor furious distracted man. There he continued for some time, until the kindness and respect of the people of the town of Edinburgh to Mr. Smith, made the bishops ashamed of this unaccountable step. So he was removed to another room in the prison, where, through cold and other pieces of harsh treatment, he sickened, and was in the hazard of his life; yet, such was their cruelty, he could not get a few days' liberty from prison. In some time, by another sentence, he was banished to one of the isles of Shetland, where he continued many years. I am told, that for four years he lived alone in a wild desolate island, in a very miserable plight; he had nothing but barley for his bread, and his fuel to ready it with was sea-tangle and wreck, and had no more to preserve his miserable life.

1664.

Their treatment of some of the parishioners of Ancrum, deserves likewise our notice. When worthy Mr. Livingstone, as above we have heard, had been taken from them, one Mr. James Scott, who had been excommunicated about twenty years ago, and continued still under the sentence, was presented to that charge, although he possessed two benefices elsewhere. Upon the day named for his induction and settlement at Ancrum, a great many people convened to give him that welcome loathed and forced ministers use to receive. A country woman desired earnestly to speak with him, hoping to dissuade him from engaging in the charge of that congregation, who were so averse from him; but he would not stay to speak with her. She in her coarse rude way pulled him by the cloak, praying him to hear her a little; whereupon, not like one of Paul's bishops, who were not to strike, he turned and beat her most cruelly with his staff. This treatment provoked two or three boys to cast some stones at him, which touched him not, nor any of his company. This was presently found to be a treasonable tumult, and the sheriff and country magistrates thereabout fined and imprisoned some of them. This, one would think, might have atoned for a fault of this nature. But our high commission behoved to have those criminals before them: so four boys, and this woman, with two brothers of hers, of the name of Turnbull, are brought into Edinburgh prisoners. The four boys are brought before the court, and

1664. confessed, that upon Scott's beating the woman, they had thrown each their stone. The commissioner told them, hanging was too little for them. However, the sentence of this merciful court was, that they should be scourged through the city of Edinburgh, and burnt in the face with a hot iron, and then sold as slaves to Barbadoes. It is a question, if the Spanish inquisition would have gone further. That excellent lawyer Sir John Gilmour told them they had no law for this cruel sentence; but when they wanted law they resolved to make a practick, which would be as good as a law to them in their after-procedure against presbyterians. The boys endured their punishment like men and Christians, to the admiration of multitudes. The two brothers are banished to Virginia, for no other crime I can hear of, but their protecting their sister, though they had small families to subsist by their labour. The poor woman was, in great clemency, ordered to be scourged through the town of Jedburgh. Bishop Burnet was applied unto that she might be spared, seeing perhaps she might be with child. The answer he was pleased to give was, That he would cause claw the itch out of her shoulders.

Several presbyterian ministers were before them, of whom I have but short and imperfect accounts. Mr. George Hamilton, since the revolution minister at Edinburgh, and some other ministers in Fife, were cited, and when they appeared, were discharged to celebrate the sacrament of the supper in their parishes. I know no account can be given of this, save that when the holy communion was celebrate, great numbers gathered from other places to participate in that ordinance; which fretted the bishops. Mr. John Scott, minister at Oxnam, Mr. James Donaldson, and other two ministers were brought before them, being of the number of six or seven who had been at a communion, which was reckoned contrary to law. What was done with them I have not learned. Some who were cited to appear before this court, had no freedom to compear, unless it had been to have declined their authority. Others reckoned it a mere civil court, and in civil things merely, not to be declined.

When this court sat at Glasgow, I find Sir William Cuningham of Cuninghamhead before them. He was obliged to produce his chaplain Mr. John Hattridge, since the revolution an able and useful gospel minister for many years in the north of Ireland. This excellent person, when he came before them, intended to say somewhat by way of testimony against the nature and constitution of that court, and addressed himself thus to them. " My lords, I hope none of you will take it ill, that I declare before you some things that are pressures to my conscience." At this the primate started, and interrupted him, saying, " What have we to do, sir, with the pressures of your conscience? go to the door presently." And as he was removing, he called to him, without ever consulting the court, " Sir, you are discharged to preach without the archbishop of Glasgow's license," and so he was no more called.

At one of their meetings at Edinburgh, they had Pringle of Greenknows before them, merely for nonconformity; and when they could prove nothing against him, the oath of allegiance was tendered to him. He told them, he had no difficulty as to it, except in the clause relative to the supremacy, and offered to take that according to bishop Usher's explication, approven by James VI. But because the gentleman would not instantly take it in the terms offered, without any explication, they fined him in some hundred pounds sterling.

I find nothing in the council registers for a good while as to this court; and indeed it was not so consistent with their credit, as hath been noticed already. At length, July 7th, no doubt, upon application made to them from the high commission, " the lords of his majesty's privy council ordain letters of horning to be direct for payment of all fines imposed, and to be imposed by decreets of the commission for church affairs, upon sight of production of the said decreets to the clerk of council." And, November 9th, " the lords of privy council ordain letters of poinding to be directed upon all decreets pronounced, or to be pronounced by the commissioners for regulating church affairs, whereby any persons are, or shall be fined in liquidate sums of money, whereanent these presents shall be a sufficient warrant

CHAP. V.] OF THE CHURCH OF SCOTLAND. 395

to the clerk of council." Through this year and the following, I observe but little in the council-books relative to the subject of this history; and the two archbishops are still present in the sederunts, when any thing of this nature comes in. It is observed in some papers before me, that towards the end of this year the primate got the powers of this high commission court, termed likewise, the commission for church or ecclesiastical affairs, enlarged, and full powers to them to banish, stigmatize, and inflict all kinds of punishment, save death. However, it seems, they have assumed those powers before they were conferred upon them.

These short hints of the procedure of this court, are all I have met with. From them we may easily guess, what a black figure a full history of this tyrannous inquisition-court would make, could it be now at this distance recovered; and the reader is left to form a judgment of their cruelty from this taste of their procedure, though indeed those are but the smallest part of their actings.

SECT. III.

Of the more general acts and procedure of the council against presbyterians, this year, 1664.

ALTHOUGH the high commission court, during this year, took a good part of the ordinary work of persecution out of the hands of the council, yet we shall meet with several things before them, which call for a room in this history. The great thing before them is the pushing the declaration, and putting the act about fines in execution. We shall likewise meet with some further new and severe acts passed against presbyterians.

We have seen, upon the last year, how matters stood as to the declaration appointed by the parliament to be taken by all persons in office and trust: this year the council go on in pushing it. January 5th, a letter from the king upon this subject, directed to the chancellor, is read, the tenor whereof follows:—

" Right trusty, &c.
" We greet you well. We have been informed, that the lords of our privy council, and the senators and other members of our college of justice, have readily signed the declaration, viz. concerning the covenant. And though we are well pleased that those who were present, gave obedience to the law; yet lest any should shift that duty, by absenting themselves, and so delay their subscription, we thought fit to require you to acquaint our privy council, that it is our pleasure, that with all convenient speed they do return us an account of the subscription or refusal of their absent members, and of all sheriffs, magistrates of burghs, justices of the peace, and all others who by the act are required to subscribe. You shall also in our name require the senators of our college of justice, to appoint a set day on which the absent senators and other members may either subscribe or refuse, to the end we may take care for supplying the places of such as shall on that account forsake their station, and that both the lords of council and session respectively do declare the places of the refusers void; and that upon no terms, neither of them admit any written explication or declaration upon the subscription of any; which would look so like the stating of a party, that we shall never endure it. So expecting an account of these our commands, we bid you farewell. Given, &c. December 19th, 1663.
1664.

" LAUDERDALE."

These caveats and commands, no doubt, refer to the scruplers at this declaration we heard of before. Upon this letter, the earl of Linlithgow is required to see the earl of Wigton subscribe, because at present he is indisposed; and the council order a letter to be writ to the haill shires and burghs through the kingdom, " acquainting them with his majesty's letter above, and requiring an account of their diligence in this affair 'twixt and the 18th of February next to come, or sooner if possible; adding, that if they be not punctual in discharging their duty in this particular, the council will look on them as neglecters of his majesty's service, and proceed accordingly; and requiring them

1664. presently to deprive all refusers of their offices, and punish them otherwise conform to the act of parliament." And January 19th, the council ordain the magistrates of Edinburgh to make a formal report anent their subscribing the declaration in manner prescribed by act of council, and to give in a list of their names to the council, who refuse to subscribe betwixt and the 26th instant peremptorie. The council, February 23d, when they had waited for returns from the shires and burghs to whom they wrote, come to give the king an account of their diligence in the following letter

" Most sacred sovereign,
" We have delayed hitherto to answer your majesty's letter of December 19th, till we should be able to give an account of our obedience to your majesty's commands concerning the declaration. We did order all sheriffs and magistrates of burghs to offer the same to all within their jurisdictions, and have sent herewith to your majesty's secretary, a paper, bearing their particular returns. It will thereby appear, that all the royal burghs have given obedience, except some few who are not considerable. And upon the desire of some of their magistrates, we have given warrant to make a new election of their magistrates, consisting of such as are willing to subscribe; whereof we expect a good account. As for the shires, many of them have excused themselves for not returning so good an account of their obedience at present, by reason that the justices of peace are not yet settled, which will now be done in a very short time. We believe, the lords of session will make their own return to your majesty, for themselves and all the members of the college of justice. As for us of your majesty's privy council, all who reside in this kingdom have subscribed.—We have issued a proclamation in your majesty's name, discharging all in public trust, who shall not subscribe betwixt and the 14th of April next, to exercise any place of office, under the pain to be proceeded against as usurpers of your majesty's authority. And in all other your majesty's concerns, we shall be most willing to give such obedience to your majesty's royal commands, as may witness us to be,
" Most sacred sovereign,
" your majesty's most humble and
" faithful subjects and servants,
" Glencairn, chancellor, Hamilton, Linlithgow, Dunfermling, Southesk, Kincardine, Halkertoun, Bellenden, J. Gilmour, A. Primrose, J. Hume, J. Lockhart, Sir Robert Murray."

The proclamation they speak of follows in the registers, which being in print, and the substance of it narrated, needs not be insert. Those peremptory letters and proclamation, produced a pretty general giving in to this declaration: a great many in burghs through the west and south, demitted their offices, and this brought the managers under new difficulties how to get a council and magistracy in several places, who would take the declaration, when those who had been brought in to it, were to go off. That the reader may have all which relates to this head together, I shall subjoin the council's acts as to this, with relation to the burghs of Ayr and Irvine.

" September 14th, the lords of his majesty's privy council being informed of the prejudice that the burgh of Ayr is like to sustain, by reason that many persons within the same have not taken the declaration appointed to be subscribed by persons in public trust, and so cannot be elected magistrates and counsellors this ensuing year: as also, that they want a town-treasurer: therefore do ordain the magistrates and town council to elect persons, who have subscribed the said declaration, to be magistrates and counsellors this ensuing year: but if they shall not find fit persons who have taken it, the lords ordain the present magistrates and council to continue in place for the space of two months, and longer, during the council's pleasure, and until they consider what course to take anent the said burgh: and in the meantime give power to them to choose a treasurer."

The same case almost falls before them from the town of Irvine, and they take much the same method, only order a prosecution against the recusants. November 3d, "Anent a petition presented by Robert Cuningham, provost of the burgh of Irvine, and Henry Lynn, one of the bailies of the same for the last year, in name of themselves and the said burgh, showing, That having met on the last day of September last, and conform to the order observed in that burgh, elected the persons following to be of the council, to wit, John Porter, Gilbert Wylie, John Reid, elder, John Gray, Alexander Gardiner, Ninian Holmes, and some others who were out of the kingdom; the forenamed persons who were present, did all refuse to accept, because they were not clear to subscribe the declaration appointed by law, as instruments taken thereupon, and produced, bear; so that thereby the said burgh is like to be altogether disappointed of magistrates for the ensuing year: humbly therefore desiring warrant to the effect underwritten. The lords of his majesty's privy council, having heard and considered the foresaid petition, do hereby give warrant to the said magistrates and counsellors, to continue in the exercise of their offices, till the council give further orders. And in the meantime ordain letters to be directed for citing the above named persons, who refused to accept as counsellors, to compear before the council, the —— day of —— next to come, to answer therefore, and to cite witnesses."

I find no more about them this year in the registers. Some of those cited, I know, were worthy and religious persons, and stuck at the declaration from a real scruple of conscience. Thus we may see how this affair of the declaration stands during this year. I go on now to give some account of the council's procedure this year, upon the act of fines. February 16th, a letter is read in council from the king, upon this subject; which is as follows:—

" Right trusty, &c.

" We greet you well. Whereas, about a year ago, we did, by our letter, appoint a proclamation to be issued for suspending of the payment of the fines imposed by the second session of our parliament, until we should declare our further pleasure, suspending also the penalties for nonpayment in the interim: these are therefore to require and authorize you to issue a new proclamation, in our name, in due and ordinary form, requiring and commanding all such fined persons, as shall be charged in the name of our treasurer, or treasurer-depute, or advocate, betwixt the date of the proclamation, and the first day of August 1664, to make payment to such as we shall authorize, of the first half of the fines imposed by the act of parliament for fines, betwixt and the feast and term of Martinmas next, this year 1664, under the pains and penalties contained in the said act: as also, the same persons who shall be charged to pay the second moiety of the fines, at or before the term of Candlemas next following, in the year 1665, under the same pains. For the which proclamation this shall be your sufficient warrant. Given, &c. February, 1663-4.

" LAUDERDALE."

Next council day, February 18th, the draught of a proclamation is brought in, approven, and ordered to be published at the cross of Edinburgh, and they declare the same to be as sufficient as if proclamation were made at the head-burghs of this kingdom. It is sustained in terms above mentioned, and printed, so it needs not be added.

July 30th, the payment of the fines is prorogate a little longer. The following letter from the king is read, and recorded.

" Right trusty, &c.

" Whereas, by our letter dated the 6th of February, we gave order, that such of the fined persons who should be charged, were to pay in their first moiety of the fines, betwixt and the term of Martinmas next, and the second betwixt and Candlemas 1665, and because none are yet charged, we do, by these presents, authorize and require you to issue out a proclamation in due and ordinary form, requiring such as shall be charged betwixt and the last day of August next, to make ready their first moiety at or before the 11th of December next, under the same certifications contained in our

1664. former proclamation, and the second moiety at or before the 2d of March 1665. Also declaring in this proclamation, That citations at the market-crosses of the respective shires where the fined persons reside, shall be a sufficient citation. For all which this shall be your warrant. Given, &c. July 26th, 1664.

"LAUDERDALE."

Accordingly, that day, a proclamation is issued out in the terms of the letter, and ordered to be printed. What the reason was of this delay, I cannot tell. It may be the courtiers were not yet agreed about dividing the spoil, to be raised from many good persons by the execution of this act of fines. Indeed the west and south were sufficiently drained by the army now among them: but what is delayed is not forgiven, and the fines are coming on slowly, but surely. At length, when matters are fully concerted at London, and in Scotland also, as we may gather from the long delay of the producing the following letter, near seven weeks after its date, this matter of uplifting the fines is brought to an execution. Accordingly, the following letter is read and recorded in council. November 3d, "His majesty's letter direct to the council, anent the fines, is read, and ordered to be registrate; the tenor whereof follows."

"Right trusty, &c.

"The calling in of the fines being upon some considerations hitherto forborn, we have now thought fit, that without further delay they be called for; and for that end have signed the enclosed warrant for a proclamation, which you shall cause speedily to be published, in due and legal form, at the market-cross of Edinburgh; or if you find not that proclamation sufficient, we do allow and require you to cause send a just double thereof to the market-cross of the head burgh of every shire, with the names of the persons only which belong to that shire, and the several sums they should pay, to be with all diligence published there: and so we bid you heartily farewell. Given at our court at Whitehall, September 17th, 1664."

"LAUDERDALE."

Follows the enclosed warrant:—

"Charles, by the grace of God, king of Scotland, England, France, and Ireland, defender of the faith; to our lovits, —— messengers, or sheriffs, in that part specially constitute, greeting. Forasmuch as, during the late troubles, divers of our subjects of that our ancient kingdom, have fallen under and involved themselves in many great crimes, faults, and offences of omission and commission, did thereby become obnoxious to the law, and rendered themselves liable to the pains of treason, and other high pains: yet we being desirous to reclaim, if it were possible, the worst of our subjects to their duty, by acts of mercy and grace, did resolve to grant a general act of indemnity, pardon, and oblivion. But considering, that by their troublous and rebellious courses, many of our good subjects have been under great sufferings and liable to great losses for their loyalty and affection to us, and our royal father, of blessed memory: therefore, in order to their reparation, and for divers important considerations of state, we with advice and consent of our estates of parliament, convened at Edinburgh upon the 9th day of September 1662, thought fit to burden our pardon and indemnity with the payment of some small fines, and so far to except the persons after mentioned from the benefit of our royal pardon, with this express certification, That whoever of the persons foresaid should not deliver and pay the sums respectively imposed on them, to any person or persons who should be appointed by us to receive the same, and that and betwixt the terms appointed in the said act; and when bypast, they should from thence forfeit and lose the whole benefit of our pardon and indemnity, and should have no share therein, but be excepted therefrom, and their estates, rents and goods forthwith to be sequestrate and raised for our use, their persons to be secured, and themselves further punished, as persons guilty of usurpation and rebellion. Likeas, for the assurance of such as should duly make payment of the sums thus imposed upon them, it was declared by us, with advice of our parliament, that upon due payment of the sums aforesaid, the payers thereof were from thenceforth to enjoy the benefit of our pardon and indemnity, to all intents and purposes. And albeit, upon divers good considerations, we have hitherto forborn to require the calling in of those sums, so that the persons liable in payment thereof, have had two years to provide themselves; yet, now considering the great burdens and pressures many of our best subjects are lying under, and the extremities they and their families are reduced unto, by their sufferings for their loyalty and service to us, and our royal father, we find ourselves obliged in conscience and honour to be zealous and careful of any means offered for their supply and relief: and therefore, in pursuance of those courses, which, in order to their reparation, have been condescended and agreed to by our parliament, we have thought fit that the sums imposed by the foresaid act, should now be called for, and paid in to the persons appointed by us to receive the same. Our will is herefore, and we charge you strictly, that incontinent, thir our letters seen, you pass to the market-cross of Edinburgh, and other places needful, and there by open proclamation, you do make intimation unto, and charge the persons particularly named in the list underwritten, and the heirs and executors of such of them as are dead, to make payment to Sir William Bruce knight, clerk of the bills, whom we have appointed our receiver for that effect, of the several sums of money after mentioned, imposed upon each of them by the said act; the one half of the said sums to be paid betwixt and Candlemas next to come, in the year 1665, and the other half in full and complete payment of the whole, betwixt and the term of Whitsunday thereafter, in the said year 1665, under the pains, and with certification above mentioned, contained in the said act, which shall be inflicted and executed without favour, upon such as shall fail in due payment of the said sums, at the terms foresaid.

"By his majesty's command,

"LAUDERDALE."

The list spoken of here, is that which formerly upon the third chapter was insert; and I take the first and greatest part of this warrant to be just a resumption of the act of parliament about fines, and therefore though many remarks might be made upon it, yet I shall only make an observe or two, to set matters, which seem here misrepresented, in their due light.

1664.

This warrant, or the act narrated in it, supposes the persons fined to have been guilty of great crimes; whereas the matter of fact is, they were guilty of no other thing than what the managers themselves and the whole nation was guilty of, a necessary subjection to the English; here they are represented as liable to the pains of treason.* It is hard indeed to define what treason is in this and the following reign, when every thing almost is made treason: but this I affirm, that nothing treasonable could be charged on them, save their compliance with the usurpers, when forced to it, and it was nationally come in to. Besides, even this ought to have been proven upon them, and some acts of it produced, wherein they had exceeded others who were not put into this list; and not in a partial clandestine manner, a set of the best people in the nation culled out, without any probation or reason, and dealt in another way with than others: while in the meantime it was certain, a great many of them were less involved with the English than those not put in this list, yea, a good many of them were remarkable for their steadfast adherence to the king's interests, when at the lowest. But whatever is pretended here, the true reason of marking out those persons named in the act of fines was, they were esteemed firm presbyterians, and averse from the change in church government now established, as hath been observed.

Again it is alleged, many of the king's subjects were brought to sufferings for their

---

* The law of Scotland was so execrable, that it was the easiest of all possible undertakings to convict any person of treason. When a murder was to be perpetrated, and the intended murderer or murderers wished to cover it with the forms of justice, and to have it entered in the national records as legal, the absurd and wicked statute of leasing-making was always at hand, from the provisos of which no one could escape, if he had at any one time of his life ventured a single speculation on public affairs.—*Ed.*

1664. loyalty to the king and his father, and their losses were to be made up out of those fines. This is mere allegation without proof. Had an open and legal process been raised, and the fact fairly proven, that the fined persons by their disloyalty had brought those hardships upon those who were to share in the fines, there might have been some colour of reason for this procedure; but nothing of this was done. Neither was this in the least the rule Middleton and his agents went by in drawing up the list. Besides, it is well enough known, that the fines were neither distributed, nor ever designed to be distributed to such as were sufferers for their adherence to the king, otherwise presbyterian ministers would have come in for their large share. Middleton designed them for himself and his creatures; these who succeeded him would willingly enough have shared them among themselves: but unforeseen things fell in their way, and they were applied to uses quite different from the projectors' design, as we shall afterwards see; so that all this is mere grimace, and it was a bitter satire upon the king to make him say, he found himself obliged in conscience to uplift those fines. Many things further might be noticed here, but I shall not enlarge. It was a jest to call them some small fines, and one needs only look back to the list of them to see their exorbitancy. The pretext is as groundless, that two years' delay made them easier to be paid. The people concerned might rather, from the delay, conclude, the managers were so far convinced of the unreasonableness of the imposition, as they would be dropt altogether. But I come forward to what the council do on this letter and warrant.

" The lords of his majesty's privy council, in obedience to his majesty's letter of the 17th of September last, commanding a proclamation to be published, for calling in of the fines, at the head burghs of the several shires, stewartries, and regalities, where any of the persons to be charged do reside, the said persons' names and several fines being first insert conform to his majesty's warrant and order, and a particular list to be given to the clerk of the council; for that effect give power and warrant to the said clerk to fill up the names of such persons as are to be charged, with their particular fines, conform to the said list, in the several proclamations to be sent to the several shires, stewartries, and regalities, and to subscribe the doubles thereof, and to signet the same with the signet of the privy council, which is declared to be a sufficient warrant to messengers or macers, for making publication thereof at the head burghs, and to subscribe the doubles thereof, and signet the same: and that the said proclamation at the head burgh of every shire, stewartry and regality, shall be a sufficient intimation to all persons therein named, for making payment of their respective fines and proportions therein contained; and in case of their disobedience, to make them liable to the certification, penalties, and pains contained in the same." This was put in execution, as we shall hear afterwards, with the utmost severity. And thus we have a view of this oppressive step of uplifting so many fines, imposed upon great numbers of the best of the nation, in the most arbitrary manner. I return now to some other acts of council this year, gravaminous enough.

In such a time as this, presbyterian ministers and others used frequently to meet together for prayer in private houses: and information being given of this by the bishops and their underlings, who could not well bear the prayers of the people of God, the council emit the following act. It is indeed only with respect to Edinburgh, but no doubt it was designed for a check upon them in other places likewise. February 23d, " The lords of council being informed, that there are several private meetings and conventicles within the city of Edinburgh, by some late ministers, and others, contrary to law; these are to give warrant to the magistrates of Edinburgh, to cause search be made anent the keeping of any such meetings; and that they acquaint the lord chancellor with what they discover, and the persons' names, that order may be taken about the same."

April 29th, the council publish an act discharging the giving charity, and making contributions in favour of suffering ministers and others, the parallel of which,

CHAP. V.] OF THE CHURCH OF SCOTLAND. 401

I believe, we shall meet with no where. I give it as it stands in the registers.

" The lords of his majesty's privy council being informed, that without any public warrant or authority, some disaffected persons to the present establishment, presume and take upon them to require contributions from such persons as they please, and do collect sums of money, which are or may be employed for carrying on of their private designs, prejudicial to the peace of the kingdom and his majesty's authority; and considering that such courses and underhand dealing may strengthen seditious persons in their practices and designs to disturb the peace, if they be not timously prevented: therefore, in his majesty's name, they do prohibit and discharge all persons whatsomever, to seek or demand any contributions or supply, or to receive any sums of money. As likewise discharge all persons to grant or deliver any contributions to any persons, whosoever shall require the same, unless it be upon such occasions as have been publicly allowed and known, and heretofore practised; and that they have a special warrant and allowance of the lords of privy council, or lords of the clergy within whose dioceses these collections are to be made. With certification, that, if they contravene, they shall be proceeded against as persons disaffected to the present government, and movers of sedition. And ordain these presents to be printed and published at the market-cross of Edinburgh, and other places needful, that none pretend ignorance.

" GLENCAIRN, Chanc. I. P. D."

This proclamation is a full evidence of the virulence and malice of the prelates, and how little of the spirit of Christianity and compassion was in them, when they proposed and pushed such an act. The pretext, that they are disaffected persons to the government, who were employed in those contributions, is a mere blind. They might be disaffected to the government, in the church, but they were not to the state; and so it is a mere jest to say, that such contributions might be prejudicial to the peace of the kingdom, unless the preserving the lives of

the presbyterian ministers and families, now by oppression and violence brought to a starving condition, could endanger the same. It is a hard pass poor sufferers are brought to, when they are discharged to meet together, and pray to God in their distresses, and all subjects are expressly discharged to relieve them in their distresses, without the bishops' warrant.

1664.

June 23d, the council send a party of soldiers to compel the parish of Dreghorn, in the shire of Ayr, to comply with the episcopal minister who had been thrust in upon them. I know no more of this, but what is contained in the act. " The lords of his majesty's privy council being informed, that the heritors and whole inhabitants of the parish of Dreghorn, do, in manifest contempt of his majesty's authority, and the government of the church established by law, withdraw themselves altogether from the said parish church, for hearing the word, and receiving the sacraments, to the scandal of the Christian profession; do therefore ordain a party of soldiers to be forthwith sent to quarter upon that parish, with power to them to uplift the penalty of twenty shillings Scots, conform to the late act of council, *toties quoties*, from every person residing in the said parish, who shall withdraw from the said kirk, and recommend it to the chancellor to name the number and commander."—This method of dragooning people to the church, as it is contrary to the spirit of Christianity, so it was a stranger in Scotland, till Bishop Sharpe and the prelates brought it in. If the party uplifted the fines for bygones, since the date of the council's act last year, how terrible a sum must they exact from that parish; or if they stayed there some weeks, and we suppose them to be eight hundred in number, even as to the time to come, they shall uplift more every week than is yearly paid to the minister. But such procedure wants no reflections. I shall end this section with another proclamation of council, of a piece with those we meet with now so frequently: and, because I have not seen it in print, I give it here from the registers, November 17th, this year.

3 E

1664. "Forasmuch as it is notour, that divers ministers, who have gone off their charges or are outed by law, do ordinarily repair to Edinburgh, and other burghs and places expressly forbid by acts of council, and do there, in open contempt of his majesty's authority and acts of parliament and council, hold their meetings, and keep seditious correspondences, and use contrivances for seducing and debauching his majesty's subjects, from the duty and obedience they owe to the laws and authority established, to the scandal of religion, and endangering the public peace and quiet: therefore, the lords of his majesty's privy council ordain a macer to pass to the market-cross of Edinburgh, and, in his majesty's name and authority, to command and charge all those persons who have been removed from the charge of the ministry since the first of January, 1661, to remove themselves forth of the burgh of Edinburgh, within forty-eight hours after the publication hereof, and not to remain or reside therein, or in any other places prohibited by act of council, dated August 13th, 1663, unless they ask and obtain license to go about their lawful business, from the lords of his majesty's privy council, or from the bishop of the diocese. With certification, that if, after the publication hereof, they be found to repair to, or reside in Edinburgh, or other forbidden places foresaid, they shall be seized upon, and put in sure firmance, until they receive the punishment provided by law, against the movers of sedition. And ordain these presents to be printed and published, that none pretend ignorance."

I cannot but observe here, and it holds in a good many acts of this time, that the managers not only lay the severest hardships upon presbyterian ministers, hinder them to pray to God, to get relief from men, and see to the education of their children at schools, unless they will own the bishops so far as to take a warrant from them; but, in their acts, load them without any ground and reason, or permitting them to answer for themselves, and charge them with crimes of a very deep nature, of which they were entirely innocent; or at best, misrepresent things, so as they might be reckoned seditious and scandalous persons. Their reasonable repairing to Edinburgh and other burghs, for overlooking their children at schools, and other necessary business, is pretended to be for seditious correspondences and meetings, for purposes not named. I know no correspondence they entertained, unless it was in letters, for strengthening one another in their suffering lot, and these they might write without being in burghs. They were all of them loyal in their practices, and never had any share in any thing seditious. This was another punishing proclamation for one, or rather no fault, mere nonconformity in presbyterian ministers: and the number of punishments inflicted for this one reason is now growing so great, that I do reckon it up. Some at this time remarked, that all the former proclamations proceeded from the prelates' fear of, or hatred to presbyterian ministers: but this proceeds from pure envy: and the true reason of it was, the bishops and their curates were uneasy at the respect and kindness evidenced to ministers in the streets of Edinburgh. When Mr. Douglas, Mr. Hutcheson, or other known presbyterian ministers, were in town, they had so many salutations and caps, that it galled those of the other side, who were but little regarded except from fear. And no great wonder, for their practice, conversation, and doctrine, the great things which ought to create respect to a minister, commanded but very little to them. In short, it was evidently hard and unreasonable to banish presbyterian ministers from the town of Edinburgh, and other burghs. Popish priests, and professed papists, were entirely at their liberty, while some of the king's subjects, who had done no fault, but stood to their known principles against bishops and prelacy, are discharged to be seen in royal burghs, and within six miles of a bishop's house, however necessary their affairs were. The reader must conclude without my remarking it, that as the taking away of civil liberty, paves the way, and makes room for church-tyranny, so this ecclesiastical tyranny, like a kindly child of such a parent, encourages slavery, and removes the small remains of any thing like liberty. I go on to the hardships of particular persons this year,

SECT IV

Of the Sufferings of particular presbyterian ministers, gentlemen, and others, this year, 1664.

THE actings of the high commission court this year, were the most considerable branch of the church of Scotland's cross, and, together with the acts of council with their procedure, have, in some measure, been laid before the reader upon the former sections; and it remains that I give the accounts come to my hand, of the trouble some other particular persons were brought under; and I begin with that of ministers.

Since the general ejection of the younger presbyterian ministers, by the act of Glasgow, the bishops endeavoured to weed out the elder presbyterian ministers, one after another gradually, that they might possess the house alone. Indeed those worthy aged men were, upon many accounts, eyesores to them. Wherever an old minister, settled before the year 1649, was found, summons was sent him to appear before the bishop in his diocesan meeting. I find none who obeyed the citation after the first diocesan meetings, when, alas! more than might have been expected, both elder and younger, did conform. When ministers did not obey, and remained at their charge, the bishops, piece by piece, as they best might, without disobliging noblemen and other heritors concerned, deposed the minister in absence. In some places the prelate made the fashion of calling the roll of his curates at their meeting, that they might give their assent unto the presbyterian minister's deposition, which they were not backward to; but this was only a form they used, or not, at their pleasure. In the dioceses of St. Andrews and Edinburgh, the curates were told, without any ceremony, that they had no share in the government. And when some of the inferior clergy began to grumble, they were reprimanded by the bishop of Edinburgh, and made to know, that the power of jurisdiction was lodged in his sole person. The number of old ministers, this way cast out of their churches, was but small in comparison of such who were laid aside, as being ordained since the year 1649, and so the instances of their sufferings must be fewer. The hardships of two of this kind offer themselves this year, with pretty singular circumstances, and they were both very great men, on different sides in the former unhappy breaches; Mr. James Wood, divinity professor, at St. Andrews, and Mr. William Guthrie, minister of Fenwick, in the shire of Ayr, and presbytery of Irvine. The account of them will let us understand somewhat more of the methods, temper, and spirit of the time I am describing; and then I shall give the hardships of some other particular persons, and their sufferings, from the council books.

Towards the beginning of this year, the learned, grave, and singularly pious Mr. James Wood, exchanged this present life for the crown of righteousness. We have had somewhat of him before. Under presbytery he had been colleague to Mr. James Sharp, and as, after the restoration, he lamented much that he had been deceived by this unhappy man, so he regretted that he had been led into some heights on the side of the public resolutions; for which, when things opened out, and appeared in their true state, he was much grieved. The bishop at first did not much harass Mr. Wood; he was an old dying man, and his heart broken with the change brought in upon this once beautiful church, and the primate expected to be soon rid of him; yet he behoved to be turned out, as we have seen.

But if Mr. Wood suffered not in his body, as some of his brethren did, yet the archbishop, it seems, was resolved he should be wounded in his name and reputation after his death, if not sooner. In order to this, the primate saw good once or twice to give Mr. Wood a visit, when on his deathbed in St. Andrews. He was now extremely low in his body, and spoke very little to Mr. Sharp, and nothing at all about the changes made, or the state of public affairs. However, the consequent

1664. of those visits was, the primate spread a report, that Mr. Wood, being now under the views of eternity, and near to death, professed himself very much indifferent as to church government, and declared himself as much for episcopacy as presbytery. The bishop talked in all companies, that Mr. Wood, in conversation with him, had acknowledged presbyterian government to be indifferent, and alterable at the pleasure of the magistrate, and other falsehoods of this sort; yea, he had the impudence to write up accounts of this to court, even before Mr. Wood's death. When the knowledge of these reports came to Mr. Wood's ears, they added grief to his sorrow; and he could find no rest till he vindicated himself, by a solemn testimony against such wicked calumnies, subscribed, as well as dictated, by himself, and that before two witnesses and a public notar. It deserves a room here, and follows, as taken off the original written from his mouth.

" *St. Andrews, March 2d,* 1664.

" I Mr. James Wood, being now shortly, by appearance, to render up my spirit to the Lord, find myself obliged to leave a word behind me, for my just vindication before the world. It hath been said of me, that I have, in word at least, resiled from my wonted zeal for the presbyterian government, expressing myself concerning it, as if it were a matter not to be accounted of, and that no man should trouble himself therefore, in matter of practice. Surely any Christian that knows me, in this kirk, will judge that this is a wrong done to me. It is true, that I being under sickness, I have said some times, in conference about my soul's state, that I was taken up about greater business than any thing of that kind; and what wonder I said so, being under such wrestlings anent my interest in Jesus Christ, which is a matter of far greater concernment than any external ordinance? But for my estimation of presbyterian government, the Lord knoweth, that since the day he convinced my heart, which was by a strong hand, that it is the ordinance of God, appointed by Jesus Christ, for governing and ordering his visible church, I never had the least change of thought concerning the necessity of it, nor of the necessity of the use of it. And I declare before God and the world, that I still account so of it; and that however there may be some more precious ordinances, yet that is so precious, that a true Christian is obliged to lay down his life for the profession thereof, if the Lord shall see meet to put him to the trial. And for myself, if I were to live, I would account it my glory to seal this word of my testimony with my blood. Of this my declaration, I take God, angels, and men, to be my witnesses; and have subscribed thir presents at St. Andrews, the 2d day of March, 1664, about seven hours in the afternoon, before Mr. William Tullidaff minister at Dumbog, and Mr. John Carstairs my brother-in-law, and John Pitcairn writer hereof.

" Mr. Ja. Wood.
" Mr. William Tullidaff,
" Mr. John Carstairs,
" John Pitcairn."

I have in my hands a pretty large account of the dying words and exercise of this eminent saint of God, drawn up by several worthy persons at this time with him, which contains some further hints of the bishop's injustice to him, and a large vindication of himself; but the substance of it being insert in the above testimony, I shall not swell this work with it. It contains many sweet parts of his attainments and experiences, when drawing near the end of his race, till he came to make a pleasant, happy, and glorious exit, March 15th, this year.

When Mr. Wood's testimony came to be propaled, the primate raged terribly, and caused summon Mr. Carstairs, Mr. Tullidaff, and the notar, before the high commission court. The bishop alleged, yea, spread the report pretty publicly, that the notar had informed himself, that when Mr. Wood was in great weakness, Mr. Carstairs had imposed upon him, and made him subscribe that paper he had formed for him. We have heard some ministers were in prison some time upon this account, and brought before the high commission. I have not seen any large account of their procedure with them, only I find, that when Mr. Tullidaff and the notar came before them, both of them declared, that Mr. Wood had dictated the above written testimony, word by word, and that the notar wrote it at his desire, and attested it, as was his office to do. Here the primate once more got the lie given him to his face; and when they had continued in prison some time, and nothing worthy of death or bonds could be fixed upon them, the bishop was forced to dismiss them without any further punishment, having shown his malice, and got shame for his reward.

Mr. Carstairs thought fit, on many considerations, to abscond, and did not compear: only that his noncompearance might not wrong the cause, nor be imputed to his disloyalty, or contumacy against any who bore commission from the king, he wrote a letter to the chancellor at this time, a copy of which is before me, too long to be insert here: however, I shall give some passages of it, because they will set the circumstances of presbyterian ministers, and this affair, in some further light. After an apology for his taking upon him to write to the chancellor, he says, " Some days ago I received a citation to appear before the commission, designing no particular day or place, to answer for some misdemeanours, as keeping conventicles, and disturbing the public peace. As for keeping conventicles, I suppose it will be difficult, if not impossible, for my accusers, to prove me guilty of any contravention of the law, even in their sense of conventicles: and for disturbing the public peace, I hope none who know me will look upon me as so disposed; whereof this may be some evidence, that since I was outed of my ministry at Glasgow, which is now two full years, I have had so little pleasure to see any person, or to be seen, let be to meddle towards the disturbing the public peace, that I have been sometimes three, sometimes six weeks, sometimes two full months, that I have never come out of doors—so abstract have I been from meddling, that famous Mr. Wood, my brother-in-law, now at his rest, was sick some ten or twelve weeks before I did certainly know how it was with him, as your lordship may know from the enclosed from him to me. When he earnestly importuned me to see him, considering our near relation, and the concerns of my only sister, and her six children now to be orphans, I could not refuse to satisfy him, being under no interdiction to the contrary. Mr. Wood finding himself under a necessity to leave a testimony behind him, I did with some others, subscribe a witness to the truth of this deed, as done by him; which, being present at the time, I could neither in conscience nor ingenuity refuse, especially since it was so well known to all the world who knew him, that that was his fixed judgment, and that when a dying it did so much afflict him, that any report to the contrary should have gone of him. And whereas it is like it will be said by some, that it is forgery, and not his own deed, or at best extorted from him when he knew not what he did or said, I shall for my own, and especially for the worthy dead man's just vindication, beg leave to say a few things." Here Mr. Carstairs enlargeth at a considerable length, upon all the circumstances of Mr. Wood's forming that testimony, and declares, the motion of it was not suggested to him by himself or others, but he formed it most spontaneously, sedately, and deliberately; that he at that time was ordering his other affairs, and the physicians did not despair of his recovery; that in conversation he did more than once express himself at large upon the head of presbyterian government, and more fully than in his testimony; that he dictated it, and caused scroll it, and read it over, and transcribe it; and after he again heard it read, signed it; and that he was most distinct and edifying after that, and to his death, as to his soul's exercise and state. After this Mr. Carstairs adds, " So that if it were otherwise convenient for me to appear before the commission, it would be no difficulty humbly to justify my carriage all the time I was at St. Andrews. Neither doth my necessary not compearing proceed from any the least contempt of his majesty's authority,

1604.

1664. which I desire highly to reverence, and wish his sacred person to be every way most eminently blessed of God; nor out of disrespect to your lordship the lord high chancellor of the kingdom, nor to the lord treasurer, nor to any of the meanest under his majesty, called to rule over me, nor to any of his courts of judicature, to which, notwithstanding of the greatest apparent hazard, I have always on the first call, as it well became me, come; and on which I have patiently and submissively waited, days, weeks, and months, as your lordship well knoweth: but it is for other reasons, which I hope will not offend your lordship. I shall only presume to add, as to these reverend brethren cited with me, that Mr. Henry Rymer was not at St. Andrews with Mr. Wood, all the time I was there, neither did I see Mr. Alexander Wedderburn with him, neither did any of the rest, to my best knowledge, desire him to write this testimony. Hoping your lordship will pardon this trouble, I am, my noble lord, your lordship's very humble servant in the Lord,

" MR. JOHN CARSTAIRS."

By this letter we find, some other worthy ministers were brought to trouble in this matter; but I have seen no accounts concerning them. We shall just now meet with Mr. Carstairs cited before the council. This is all I have met with as to the reverend Mr. Wood, who stands entire in his reputation, notwithstanding of all the base artifices of the primate to darken it.

The other instance I promised as to the sufferings of old ministers this year, is that of the reverend, and singularly useful Mr. William Guthrie, minister of the gospel at Fenwick. This extraordinary person I have particular opportunities to have certain and distinct accounts of. I heartily wish some proper hand would give the public a just narrative of this great man's life, which might, I persuade myself, be very useful. The broken hints we have, before the last edition of his excellent Saving Interest, at London, 1705, are lame and indistinct, and were writ without the knowledge of his remaining relations, who could have given more just and larger accounts: I shall therefore here give the more particular history of his suffering at the time, and his being forced to part with his dear flock.

By the interest of several noblemen and others, to whom Mr. Guthrie was very dear, he enjoyed a connivance, and was overlooked for a considerable time, when he continued at his Master's work, though in his sermons he was more than ordinarily free and plain. But soon after doctor Alexander Burnet was brought from the see of Aberdeen to that of Glasgow; he and the few remaining ministers about him were attacked; such as, Mr. Livingstone at Biggar, Mr. M'Kail at Bothwell, Mr. Gabriel Maxwell at Dundonald, Mr. Gabriel Cuningham at Dunlop, and Mr. Andrew Hutcheson and Mr. William Castlelaw, ministers at Stewarton; and perhaps the chancellor's death about this time, helped to pave the way for the greater severity against these worthy persons. The archbishop had been addressed by some of the greatest in the kingdom, in behalf of Mr. Guthrie, and treated them very indiscreetly: by no importunity would he suffer himself to be prevailed upon to spare him any longer. When means and intercession could not prevail, Mr. Guthrie was warned of the archbishop's design against him, and advised by persons of note, his friends, to suffer no resistance to be made to his dispossession of the church and manse; since his enemies wanted only this for a handle to process him criminally for his zeal and faithfulness in the former times: such was their spite against this useful man of God.

Under the prospect of parting with his beloved people, Wednesday the 20th of July, this year, was set apart by him for fasting and prayer with his congregation. The text he preached from was, Hos. xiii. 9. "O Israel! thou hast destroyed thyself." His sermon was afterwards printed very unfairly and indistinctly, from an uncorrect copy. From that Scripture, with great plainness and affection, he laid before them their sins, and those of the land, and of that age; and indeed the place was a Bochim. At the close of that day's work, he intimate sermon upon the next Lord's day very early, and his own people and many others met him at the church of Fenwick betwixt four and five in the morning, where he preached twice to them from the close of his last text, "But in me is thine help." And as he used upon ordinary Sabbaths, he had two sermons, and a short interval betwixt them, and dismissed the people before nine in the morning. Upon this melancholy occasion, he directed them unto the great Fountain of Help, when the gospel and ministers were taken from them; and took his leave of them, commending them to this great God, who was able to build them up, and help them in the time of their need. His people would willingly have sacrificed all that was dear to them, in defence of the gospel, and adhering to him. Indeed Mr. Guthrie had some difficulty to get their affection to him so far moderated, as to keep them from violent proceedings against the party who came to dispossess him: they would have effectually prevented the church its being declared vacant, and were ready to have resisted even to blood, striving against sin, if they had been permitted: but Mr. Guthrie's peaceable disposition, his great regard to lawful civil authority, with his prudent foresight of the consequences of such a procedure, both as to the interests of the gospel, his people, and himself, made him lay himself out, and use the interest he had in the people, which was very great, to keep the peace; and there was no disturbance which could be made a handle of by adversaries.

When the archbishop of Glasgow resolved upon dispossessing him, he dealt with several of his curates, to intimate his sentence against Mr. Guthrie, and as many refused it. There was an awe upon their spirits, which scarred them from meddling with this great man; besides, they very well knew it was an action would render them for ever odious to the west country, and they feared the consequences. At last he prevailed with one who was curate of Calder, as I am told, and promised him five pounds sterling for his reward: but poor man! it was the price of blood, the blood of souls, and neither he nor his had much satisfaction in it. Upon the 24th of July, this man came with a party of twelve soldiers to Fenwick church on the Lord's day, and, by commission from the archbishop, 1664. discharged Mr. Guthrie to preach any more at Fenwick, declared the church vacant, and suspended him from the exercise of his ministry. The commanders of the party and the curate, leaving the soldiers without, came into the manse. The best account I can at this distance give of what passed in the manse, is by inserting a short minute of this, left among the small remains of a valuable collection of papers belonging to Mr. Guthrie; which were taken away, as we shall afterwards hear, some years after this, by violence, and against all the rules of equity, from his widow, and fell into the hands of the bishops. The paper was drawn up at the time to keep up the remembrance of this affair, without any design of its being published, and I give it in its own native and plain dress

The sum of the curate's discourse when he came and intimated Mr. William Guthrie's sentence of suspension, with Mr. Guthrie's answer to him.

"The curate showed, that the bishop and committee, after much lenity shown to him for a long time, were constrained to pass the sentence of suspension against him, for not keeping of presbyteries and synods with his brethren, and his unpeaceableness in the church; of which sentence he was appointed to make public intimation to him, for which he read his commission under the archbishop of Glasgow his hand."

Mr. Guthrie answered, "I judge it not convenient to say much in answer to what you have spoken: only, whereas you allege there hath been much lenity used towards me, be it known unto you, that I take the Lord for party in that, and thank him for it; yea, I look upon it as a door which God opened to me for preaching this gospel, which neither you nor any man else was able to shut, till it was given you of God. And as to that sentence passed against me, I declare before those gentlemen (the officers of the party) that I lay no weight upon it, as it comes from you, or those who sent you; though I do respect the civil authority, who by their law laid the ground for this sentence: and were it not for the

1664. reverence I owe to the civil magistrate. I would not surcease from the exercise of my ministry for all that sentence. And as to the crimes I am charged with, I did keep presbyteries and synods with my brethren; but I do not judge those who now sit in these to be my brethren, but men who have made defection from the truth and cause of God; nor do I judge those to be free or lawful courts of Christ, that are now sitting. And as to my unpeaceableness, I know I am bidden follow peace with all men, but I know also I am bidden follow it with holiness; and since I could not obtain peace without prejudice to holiness, I thought myself obliged to let it go. And as for your commission, sir, to intimate this sentence, I here declare I think myself called by the Lord to the work of the ministry, and did forsake my nearest relations in the world, and give up myself to the service of the gospel in this place, having received an unanimous call from this parish, and been tried and ordained by the presbytery; and I bless the Lord he hath given me some success, and a seal of my ministry upon the souls and consciences of not a few that are gone to heaven, and of some that are yet in the way to it. And now, sir, if you will take it upon you to interrupt my work among this people, as I shall wish the Lord may forgive you the guilt of it, so I cannot but leave all the bad consequences that follow upon it, betwixt God and your own conscience. And here I do further declare before these gentlemen, that I am suspended from my ministry for adhering to the covenants and work of God, from which you and others have apostatized."

Here the curate interrupting him, said, "That the Lord had a work before that covenant had a being, and that he judged them apostates who adhered to that covenant; and that he wished that not only the Lord would forgive him (Mr. Guthrie) but, if it were lawful to pray for the dead, (at which expression the soldiers did laugh) that the Lord would forgive the sin of this church these hundred years' bygone."—" It is true, answered Mr. Guthrie, the Lord had a work before that covenant had a being; but it is as true, that it hath been more glorious since that covenant, and it is a small thing for us to be judged of you in adhering to that covenant, who have so deeply corrupted your ways, and seem to reflect on the whole work of reformation from popery these hundred years bygone, by intimating that the church had need of pardon for the same. As for you, gentlemen, added he, directing himself to the soldiers, I wish the Lord may pardon you for countenancing of this man in this business." One of them scoffingly replied, " I wish we never do a greater fault." " Well, but said Mr. Guthrie, a little sin may damn a man's soul."

When this had passed, Mr. Guthrie called for a glass of ale, and craving a blessing himself, drank to the commander of the soldiers; and after they had been civilly entertained by him, they left the house. I have it confidently reported, that Mr. Guthrie at parting did signify to the curate, that he apprehended some evident mark of the Lord's displeasure was abiding him, for what he was now a doing, and seriously warned him to prepare for some stroke a coming upon him very soon. Mr. Guthrie's relations, and a worthy old minister yet alive when I write this, who was that day at Fenwick with him, from whom I have part of this account, do not mind to have heard any thing of this denunciation; but it might have been without their hearing, since none of them were present at parting. Whatever be in this, I am well assured the curate never preached more after he left Fenwick. He came into Glasgow, and whether he reached Calder, but four miles from it, I know not; but in a few days he died in great torment of an iliac passion, and his wife and children died all in a year, or thereby; and none belonging to him were left: so hazardous a thing it is to meddle with Christ's sent servants. When they left the manse, the curate went into the church of Fenwick with the soldiers his guard, and now his hearers, and preached to them not a quarter of an hour, and intimated from pulpit the bishop's sentence against Mr. Guthrie. Nobody came to hear him, save the party who came with him, and a few children and boys, who created him some disturbance, but were chased off by the soldiers. Mr. Guthrie continued in the parish, but preached no more in the church, where, as far as I can learn, there was no curate ever settled. Upon the 10th of October next year, this excellent person died in Angus, whither he went to settle some affairs relating to his estate of Pitforthy there. Thus by the malice of the prelates, this bright and eminent light of the west of Scotland was put under a bushel, and extinguished.

I shall only add here, that the procedure of the prelates was of a piece in all the corners of the church, and give another instance from the diocese of Dunkeld, relative to Mr. Andrew Donaldson minister at Dalgety. Many yet alive have a most savoury remembrance of this worthy person; and a minister at present in that neighbourhood, who had the happiness of his acquaintance for some years before his death, writes to me, " That he was singular for a heavenly and spiritual temper, and very much of a holy tenderness and ardent love to Jesus Christ at all times, discovered themselves in every thing he did: that many religious persons, since the revolution, in that country, at their death, owned, that Mr. Donaldson was the mean of their conversion and edification. In a word, he was not only eminent in holiness, and the faithful discharge of his office, but likewise a person of a very solid judgment, and great wisdom and prudence." Such a person as he was, could not well escape the malice of the bishops at this juncture, and therefore I shall here give a hint of the trouble he met with from attested accounts, and an original letter of the bishop of Dunkeld sent to him, October this year, lately come to my hand. We shall have some other hints concerning this good man in our progress, but here I shall give a general view of his sufferings altogether, from narratives before me very well vouched.

Mr. Andrew Donaldson was admitted minister at Dalgety, in the year 1644, and continued in the exercise of his ministry there twenty years. He had the favour of remaining longer at his Master's work than many of his brethren, by the interest of Charles, earl of Dunfermline, then lord privy seal. This year 1664, when the earl was called up to London, the primate in his absence pushed the bishop of Dunkeld, within which diocese Dalgety lies, to deprive him. Accordingly the bishop wrote to him to attend the presbyteries, under pain of suspension: which Mr. Donaldson did not regard, but continued at his work till the diocesan meeting in October, when the bishop deposed him, and wrote the following letter to him, which the reader hath from the original in mine eye.

" Sir,

" These five synods past, your brethren of the synod of Dunkeld have waited upon your presence to have concurred with them in all ministerial duties that relate to discipline, according to the strict acts of parliament and council enjoining the same, and the acts of your synod requiring your presence, and enjoining your keeping of session, presbytery and synod. Notwithstanding, you have still seditiously contemned the laws of the state, in not keeping your synod, though you knew the ordinary diets as well as others; and against the law and practice of the church, and your peaceable brethren, has still schismatically divided yourself from your brethren, in session, presbytery, and synod: and well considering their own patience and slowness to proceed against you, having formerly suspended you, and yet unwilling even to intimate that, causing it only come to your ear, hoping that their kindly forbearance should in end gain your submission to an union with them; yet still meeting with nothing from you, but obstinate and ungrate continuance in your seditious and schismatic way, they unanimously, at the last meeting of the synod, holden at Dunkeld, the 4th of October, 1664, did think and vote you worthy of deposition from your ministerial function. Likeas, I did in the name, and by the authority of Jesus Christ, and in the name, and with the consent of all my brethren, actually at that time depose you; which I now do declare, you Mr. Andrew Donaldson, sometime minister at Dalgety, deposed from all charge, not only there, but from all the parts of ministerial function within any diocese, or the kirk of Scotland.

1664. assuring you, if you shall insist on that charge, either at Dalgety, or elsewhere, after you shall be acquaint with this sentence, that immediately, with the consent of my synod, we will proceed against you with the highest censure of this kirk. In verification of all the premises, I have subscribed them, and sent them express to you for your warning, that you may not pretend ignorance, but may yield obedience, and not contravene. Perth, 10th October, 1664.

" GEORGE DUNKELD."

So careful was the bishop of Mr. Donaldson's knowing this sentence, that another letter in the very same words, only dated October 11th, came to his hand likewise. But more effectual methods were taken, and the primate procured a party to be sent to eject him from the kirk of Dalgety, who came on a Lord's day when the people were gathered to hear him. It was Mr. Donaldson's prudence which prevented a scuffle; and, upon the government their orders to remove, he compromised the matter with the soldiers, and got leave to preach that day, upon his promise to leave that place. When my lord Dunfermline, now at London, got notice of this, he procured a warrant from the king, reponing Mr. Donaldson to Dalgety during life; which his lordship brought down very soon, and showed it to the primate, complaining he had taken the occasion of his being absent, to deprive him of his minister whom he valued so much. The archbishop knew well to dissemble, and professed a great regard to the earl, and said, the king behoved to be obeyed, but craved, as a favour, that the earl would do nothing for three weeks in it, till he considered how to provide a young man now settled at Dalgety: which my lord yielded to. Meanwhile the primate, by his interest at court, in the earl's absence, procured a warrant under the king's hand, and got it down, per express, before the three weeks elapsed, discharging all outed ministers to come back to their charges. This galled the earl sufficiently, but there was no help for it.

For many years Mr. Donaldson continued to preach, with very great success, at a gentleman's house in that country where he lived, till, through the instigation of the prelates, he was about the year 1676, as we shall hear, intercommuned. When he removed, and had no small difficulties, and very remarkable preservations, and singular communications from his Master, in the year 1677, he was seized when he came to visit his family, and carried prisoner to Linlithgow tolbooth, were he continued till the general liberation of presbyterian ministers, after the defeat at Bothwell. I have before me an attested account of a very observable judgment of God upon the commander of the party who seized him, and his dying under horror for his hand in this worthy person's persecution; and of a very singular warning the Lord led Mr. Donaldson to give the earl of Argyle in April, or May 1679, of his after-sufferings and death, for the cause and interests of religion, which was exactly fulfilled; which that noble person told to severals when in the castle of Edinburgh, a little before his martyrdom. The circumstantiate and well vouched accounts of those are too large here to be insert. Mr. Donaldson continued under trouble, till, with many other worthy persons, he was freed by the toleration in the year 1687.

I shall conclude this account of the bishops' treatment of ministers this year, with the trouble another old worthy minister met with at this time, Mr. Robert Maxwel, minister at Monkton, in the presbytery of Ayr. Being settled before the (year) 1649, he continued in the exercise of his ministry, till he was suspended by the presbytery, February 14th, 1665. He was a grave, pious, useful minister in that place for near twenty-five years, and very much beloved of his people; but there was no continuing longer among them, when armed force put in execution those sentences. His suspension was intimate to him, February 18th, being Saturday, and next day he preached his farewell-sermon, from Eccles. v. 4. and had a very moving discourse to them at this sorrowful parting, which is before me, but too large to insert here. In the diocesan meeting, October this year, archbishop Burnet pushed and carried his deposition, for nothing less than the utmost rigour would satisfy him. From the original extract of the sentence in my hands, I give here the tenour of it.

"*Glasgow, October 11th, 1665.*

"The which day, the archbishop and synod taking to their serious consideration the process led and deduced by the presbytery of Ayr, against Mr. Robert Maxwel minister at Monktoun, and finding by the said process, that the said Mr. Robert Maxwel continues obstinate in refusing to join with the rest of his brethren, to sit in presbytery and synods for the exercise of discipline, censuring of scandals, and other uncontroverted duties; notwithstanding that the said Mr. Robert has been frequently conferred with by his brethren of the presbytery of Ayr, in order to his satisfaction, and that he either shuns all debating, or refuses to receive satisfaction when offered by them, showing them positively that he is fully resolved not to submit; as likewise, that he confessed that he had married other persons in other parishes without testimonial from their several ministers: and finding by the said process, that he has been thrice lawfully summoned to compear before the presbytery, and that he never compeared; and being by the presbytery referred to the archbishop and synod for censure: as likewise for these crimes he was formerly suspended from the office of the ministry, by the presbytery of Ayr, the 13th of February last; and finding by the execution of the summons produced and read in synod, the said Mr. Robert is legally cited to this day; and he being called at the most patent door of the high church, compeared not, but absolutely refused either to give satisfaction for those crimes, or to give any reason why he cannot or will not concur with his brethren, and so finding there is no hopes of gaining him: wherefore the archbishop and synod think fit that the said Mr. Robert Maxwel be deposed, and by these presents do depose him from the office and function of the ministry, at the said church of Monktoun, or in any place else; and ordain the presbytery of Ayr to intimate his sentence to him with their first conveniency, and make report thereof to the next committee. Extracted by

"LUD. FAIRFOUL, Cl."

1664.

We see he was proceeded against for mere refusing to subject to the bishop, by power from whom their presbyteries and synods met. His baptizing and marrying complained of, was only such persons as were in their consciences straitened to join with the curates. We shall afterwards meet with this good man under more trouble. Many other accounts might be given of the maltreatment of presbyterian ministers at this time, had they been carefully preserved, but these two are what I have particularly vouched, and they may serve as a specimen of the manner of the treatment these worthy servants and witnesses of Christ met with.

The people of the presbyterian persuasion were now everywhere harassed, and the methods I hinted at on the former chapter continued. Every day the soldiers grew more and more insolent at the churches where any old presbyterian ministers ventured to continue. And through the west and south multitudes of families were scattered, and the soldiers acted much in the same manner, as the French dragoons did some years after, among the protestants there. Sir James Turner, I find this year, is acting a very severe part in the western and southern shires; and next year also he is sent by the managers a second or third time to force people to comply with the church government, and ministers now established; and he executed his orders exactly enough. I do not enter upon particulars, since they fall in so much with what has been narrated; and accounts of the detail of the actings of those booted apostles would be endless. I come now to a few more accounts of the sufferings of particular persons this year, as they lie in order of time in the council-registers. We have had the reason formerly why we meet with so little of this nature in them, this and the following year. January 26th, it is recommended to the chancellor to write to Sir James Turner; which he does as follows:—

"Sir,

"Upon information given to his majesty's privy council, of some treasonable speeches uttered by one John Gordon burgess in Stranraer, for which he is now prisoner in that burgh, they order you to send him in prisoner, with as many soldiers as may be sufficient for that purpose, that the council may take such course with him, as they shall think fit. I am, &c."—The lords of justiciary were proper judges in this supposed case. Whether this information, as many which were now given by the clergy, was found groundless, I know not. No more offers about him in the registers; and I am ready to think, that all he could be charged with, was some reflections upon the change now made in affairs, by the establishing bishops by the supremacy.

March 1st, the council pass an act against the worthy gentleman formerly mentioned, the laird of Earlstoun. " The lords of his majesty's privy council, having considered several accusations exhibited against Mr. William Gordon of Earlstoun, for keeping of private meetings and conventicles, contrary to the laws and acts of parliament, with his own judicial confession, that he had been at three several conventicles, where Mr. Gabriel Semple, a deposed minister, did preach, viz. one in Corsack wood, and other two in the wood of Airds, at all which there were great numbers of people; and that he did hear Mr. Robert Paton, a deposed minister, expound a text of Scripture, and perform other acts of worship, in his mother's house; and that Mr. Thomas Thomson, another deposed minister, did lecture in his own house to his family on a Sabbath day; and that being required to enact himself to abstain from all such meetings in time coming, and to live peaceably and orderly conform to law, he refused to do the same: do therefore order the said Mr. William Gordon of Earlstoun, to be banished, and to depart forth of the kingdom within a month, after the date hereof, and not return under pain of death; and that he enact himself to live peaceably and orderly during the said month, under the pain of ten thousand pounds, or otherwise to enter his person in prison."—We shall afterwards, in the detail of this history, have occasion to speak more of these conventicles now a beginning, and to give the reasons why gentlemen and others could not bind themselves to abstain from them, and I shall not anticipate it; neither shall I make any remark upon the council's making the expounding of a place of Scripture, a part of divine worship; the bishops now with them ought to have rectified such a blunder. It was much worse in them to banish so excellent a gentleman, for mere hearing of presbyterian ministers, and, for what I can observe, exceeded any laws yet made.

April 29th, " The council ordain letters to be directed to a macer, to cite Mr. John Carstairs before the council, to answer to the crimes for which he was convened before the parliament, and all other emergent crimes by him sensyne (subsequently) committed." I find no more in the registers this year about him. I imagine, when he declined appearing before the high commission court, by his letter to the chancellor, he had this citation sent him to appear before the council; but the dropping the affair of Mr. Wood's testimony, and the chancellor's death falling in within a little, perhaps made him to be dropped.

June 23d, " The council being informed of the seditious and factious doctrine and practices of Mr. John Crookshanks, and Mr. Michael Bruce, pretended ministers, fugitives from Ireland,* and of their preaching in several places of this kingdom, without license, contrary to the laws, ordain letters, charging them at the market-cross of Edinburgh, and pier and shore of Leith, to appear the 27th of July next; and give power to the officers and commanders of the forces to seize them." Those were two worthy presbyterian ministers come from Ireland.

---

* These two ministers were obliged to leave Lochend on account of Blood's plot. Mr. Crookshanks was shortly after killed at Pentland.—*Ed.*

This is the first time that I have observed the phrase of pretended ministers used by the council. I do not find they appeared upon this charge. All their fault was preaching the gospel, and it is a question, if they got notice of this citation. We shall afterward meet with Mr. Bruce, who was a very useful minister, and did much good, by his awakening and rousing gift, in many places.

August 9th, I find, that upon a desire given in to the council, they prorogate John Swinton, once of that ilk, his liberation out of prison for a month longer, and order him to return to prison, September 9th. I find no more about him for some time, and at length he came to be overlooked, though he was a very active quaker.

November 3d, William Dobbie, weaver, petitions the council, that whereas by an act of council, August 18th, which I do not observe in their books, he was allowed to go out of prison from eight in the morning till eight at night, to his work; that now having been so long in prison, he may be relieved. The council order his liberation, six burgesses in Glasgow, formerly his cautioners, being caution for his re-entry when called. Middleton was now removed, and they did not think him worth any further notice.

That same day, Mr. Thomas Wylie, formerly spoken of, presents a petition to the council, " That whereas the petitioner being confined by act of council, October 1662, to reside benorth the River of Tay, with his family, to which sentence he hath submitted in all humility, as becometh; and ever since hath behaved himself peaceably and inoffensively, becoming a loyal subject, as a testimony herewith produced, under the hands of the magistrates and ministers of Dundee, will testify; and that seeing now for a long time it hath pleased the Lord to visit the said petitioner his bedfellow with great sickness and indisposition of body, often to the endangering her life, which, according to the opinion of her physicians, is judged to proceed from the climate of the place, where she and the petitioner hath been living, as will appear by a testificate under the hands of the doctors and chirurgeons of Dundee, herewith produced; and that the petitioner is purposed, wherever your lordships shall order his residence, that he and his family shall continue in a peaceable and inoffensive behaviour. May it therefore please your lordships, in consideration of the premises, to take off the said restraint from him, and grant him liberty, with his wife and family, to reside besouth the River of Forth, in any place of Lothian, which is more than fifty miles from the place where the petitioner had charge as a minister, and he shall ever pray." The council order his former bond to be given up, and that he give a new bond, for his peaceable behaviour where he is now confined.

1664.

December 18th, the council pass an act about Mr. Spreul, formerly mentioned in the first chapter, which I shall insert as I find it, knowing no more about this good man.—" The lords of council considering, that Mr. John Spreul, late town-clerk in Glasgow, having been cited before the commission for church affairs, to answer for his disobedience to the laws, and disaffection to the government thereby established, he, for eviting the sentence of the said judicatory, did for some time withdraw himself forth out of the country, and having privately returned, did carry himself most suspiciously by travelling secretly from place to place, in the night time; for which being apprehended and brought before the council, and the oath of allegiance being tendered to him, he refused the same, alleging he had not freedom to sign the same, by reason of the tie that lay upon him by the oath of the covenant: wherefore the said lords judging it unjust, that any person should have the benefit of the protection of his majesty, and enjoy the liberties of a free subject, who refuse to give their oath of allegiance, ordain the said Mr. John Spreul to enact himself under the pain of death, to remove out of the kingdom against the 1st of February next, and not to return without license, and find caution to behave peaceably till then, under the pain of two thousand pounds, and not to go within six miles of Glasgow."— This good man was forced to wander from his native country for some years; and we shall afterward meet with him in this history.

1664. That same day, the reverend Mr. Alexander Moncrief, formerly spoken of, in Reddy, petitions the council, "That in regard he hath an action of count and reckoning, which needs his personal presence at Edinburgh, as is attested by two of the senators of the college of justice, and by the late act the supplicant cannot come to Edinburgh without license, he humbly craves it. The council grant him license till the 24th instant, upon bond to live peaceably and loyally during that time." This is what I have observed most remarkable as to particular sufferings this year.

SECT. V.

Of some other remarkables, and incidental matters, this year 1664.

I SHALL end the history of this year with some few incidents that fall in, some of which relate directly enough to the history of the sufferings; and others of them falling in in the papers which have come to my hand, and tending to clear the state of things in this period, I thought they deserved a room here.

January 26th, the king's letter comes down to the council, ordering the archbishop of St. Andrews to have the precedency of the chancellor, and all other nobility and officers of state. It is dated the same day with the warrant for the high commission, and came down at the same time; but the council registers take no notice for some months of the high commission, for reasons above narrated: nevertheless, they record the king's letter about the primate's precedency; the tenor whereof follows.

" Right trusty, &c.

" We greet you well. Whereas our royal father of blessed memory, did, by his letter, dated at Whitehall, July 12th, 1626, signify to his privy council, that having considered, according to the custom of all civil and Christian kingdoms, what place and dignity is due unto the church, the precedency of whose chief ruler should procure the more respect thereunto; to the end that the archbishop of St. Andrews, primate and metropolitan of that our kingdom, may enjoy the privileges belonging to his place, we were pleased to name him first in the commission of our council; and our pleasure is, that he have the first place both at our council, and at all other public meetings before our chancellor, and all other our subjects within that our kingdom; as one from the eminency of whose place, we will have none to derogate in any way, but shall ever contribute what we can to the advancement thereof, in so far as is lawful and expedient. And we being also desirous to maintain the honour of the church, and that dignity, in the person of this archbishop of St. Andrews, and his successors, have thought fit to renew our blessed father's command; and to the end it may be punctually observed, we command you to registrate this our letter in the books of council; and so we bid you heartily farewell. Given at our court at Whitehall, the 16th of January 1663-4, and of our reign the 15th year.

" LAUDERDALE."

Thus Mr. James Sharp arrived at the very utmost of his ambition, and higher he could not desire to be.* This was the

---

* If we may credit Burnet, Mr. Wodrow was here in a mistake. Sharp had not yet, and never did, arrive at that dignity which was the object of his ambition. Precedence of the chancellor was no doubt highly gratifying to his vanity and pride, but his great object was the chancellorship itself; and the death of the chancellor Glencairn in the month of May following, seemed to pave the way for his immediate elevation to that so much desired precedency. " This event," Burnet remarks, " put him on new designs. He apprehended that the earl of Tweeddale might be advanced to that post, for in the settlement of the dutchess of Buccleugh's estate, who was married to the duke of Monmouth, the best-beloved of all the king's children, by which, in default of issue by her, it was to go to the duke of Monmouth, and the issue he might have by any other wife ; the earl of Tweeddale, though his children were the next heirs, who were by this deprived of their right, had yet given way to it in so frank a manner, that the king was enough inclined both to oblige and to trust him. But Sharp had great suspicions of him, as cold in their concerns. So he writ to Sheldon, that upon the disposal of the seals, the very being of the church did so absolutely depend, that he begged he would press the king very earnestly in the matter, and that he would move that he might be called up before that post should be filled. The king bid Sheldon assure

OF THE CHURCH OF SCOTLAND. 415

verifying of what Lauderdale threatened to Glencairn three years ago, that since he and Middleton would have bishops, they should have them with a vengeance: and agreeable to what a worthy presbyterian minister said to the earl of Glencairn, when he pressed him to come in to prelacy, and made some insinuations, as if he might be archbishop of St. Andrews. My lord, said he, if I be archbishop of St. Andrews, I will be chancellor too; alluding to the last archbishop, who enjoyed both offices.

This letter did not a little chagrin our nobility, especially the chancellor. In king Charles I. his reign, I find the earl of Kinnoul, then chancellor, would never yield the precedency to primate Spotiswood; but now matters are changed, and all behoved to stoop to Mr. Sharp; and, sore against his mind, the chancellor yields the door and tablehead, lest he should get the purse too.

The curious reader will be satisfied, 1664. that I add in this place a passage from Sir James Balfour, lyon king at arms, his annals in king Charles I. his reign, relative to this precedency of the archbishops of St. Andrews to the chancellor, p. 653, of the manuscript before me. "July 12th, 1626, the king by his letter commanded, that the primate of Scotland, the archbishop of St. Andrews, should take place of the chancellor: but chancellor Hay would never suffer him to do it all the days of his life, do what the king would. Sir James adds, that at the king's coronation, 1663, that morning the king called me, as lyon king at arms, and sent me to the earl of Kinnoul, at that time chancellor, to show him that it was his majesty's will and pleasure, that only for that day he would cede and give place to the archbishop. The earl returned by me this brisk answer,

---

him, he should take a special care of that matter, but that there was no occasion for his coming up; for the king, by this time, had a very ill opinion of him. Sharp was so mortified with this, that he resolved to put all to hazard, for he believed all was at stake, and he ventured to come up. The king received him coldly, and asked him if he had not received the archbishop of Canterbury's letter. He said he had, but he would choose rather to venture on his majesty's displeasure, than to see the church ruined through his caution or negligence. He knew the danger they were in in Scotland, where they had but few and cold friends, and many violent enemies. His majesty's protection, and the execution of the law, were the only things they could trust to; and these so much depended on the good choice of a chancellor, that he could not answer it to God and the church if he did not bestir himself in that matter. He knew many thought of him for that post, but he was so far from that thought, that if his majesty had any such intention, he would rather choose to be sent to a plantation. He desired that he might be a churchman in heart, but not in habit, who should be raised to that trust. These were his very words, as the king repeated them. From him he went to Sheldon, and pressed him to move the king, for himself, and furnished him with many reasons to support the proposition, a main one being, that the late king had raised his predecessor Spotiswoode to that trust. Sheldon upon that, did move the king with more than ordinary earnestness in it. The king suspected Sharp had set him on, and charged him to tell him the truth. The other did it, though not without some uneasiness. Upon that the king told him what he had said to himself; and then it may be easily imagined in what a style they both spoke of him. Yet Sheldon prayed the king, that whatsoever he might think of the man, he would consider the archbishop and the church which the king assured him he would do. Shel-

don told Sharp, that he saw the motion for himself did not take, so he must think on somewhat else. Sharp proposed that the seals might be put in the earl of Rothes' hands, till the king should pitch on a proper person. He also proposed that the king would make him his commissioner, in order to the preparing matters for a national synod, that they might settle a book of common prayer, and a book of canons.—

"All this was easily agreed to, for the king loved the lord Rothes, and the earl of Lauderdale would not oppose his advancement, though it was a very extravagant thing, to see one man possess so many of the chief places of so poor a kingdom. The earl of Crawford would not abjure the covenant, so Rothes had been made lord treasurer in his place; he continued to be still what he was before, lord president of the council; and upon the earl of Middleton's disgrace, he was made captain of a troop of guards, and now he was both the king's commissioner and, upon the matter, lord chancellor. Sharp reckoned this was his masterpiece. Lord Rothes being thus advanced by his means, was in all things governed by him. His instructions were such as Sharp proposed, to prepare matters for a national synod; and in the meanwhile to execute the laws that related to the church with a steady firmness. So when they parted from Whitehall, Sharp said to the king, that he had now done all that could be desired of him for the good of the church, so that if all matters went not right in Scotland, none must bear the blame, but either the earl of Lauderdale or Rothes; as they came to Scotland, where a very furious scene of illegal violence was opened. Sharp governed lord Rothes, who abandoned himself to pleasure; and when some censured this, all the answer that was made, was, a severe piece of raillery, that the king's commissioner ought to represent his person."—Burnet's History of his Own Times, vol. i. pp. 305--307 —*Ed.*

1664. "That since his majesty had been pleased to continue him in that office, which by his means his worthy father, of happy memory, had bestowed upon him, he was ready in all humility to lay it at his majesty's feet; but since it was his royal will, he should enjoy it with the known privileges of the same, never a st——d priest in Scotland should set a foot before him as long as his blood was hot. When I had related this answer to the king, he said, Well, Lyon, let us go to business, I will not meddle further with that old cankered goutish man, at whose hands there is nothing to be gained but sour words."

That same day, January 26th, another letter is read from the king to the council, acquainting them he had made choice of the persons who were to be commissioners for plantation of kirks, and ordered the register to insert them in the commission of parliament past thereupon, and requires them to advertise them to attend the diets of that commission, which he will have kept every week during session-time: whereupon the council write to all the members, to attend.

Some notice hath been taken already of the new made bishops this year. In January, Mr. Alexander Burnet is admitted to be archbishop of Glasgow, in room of Mr. Fairfoul deceased; and Mr. Scougal is his successor at Aberdeen, who was reckoned among the devoutest of that order; and Mr. Andrew Honeyman is made bishop of Orkney, in room of Sideserf deceased.

April 29th, by a letter from the king, the archbishop of Glasgow and Archibald earl of Argyle are added to the council, and take the oaths, and their places at that board. The same day a proclamation is published against that known and celebrated treatise of the great ornament of Scotland, Mr. George Buchanan, *De jure regni apud Scotos*, which deserves a room here.

" Forasmuch as, notwithstanding it hath pleased the almighty God, to restore the kingdom to the great blessings of peace and prosperity, under the protection of his majesty's royal government, after the late grievous sufferings and bondage under usurpers; yet some seditious and disaffected persons endeavour to infuse the principles of rebellion in the minds of many good subjects, of purpose to dispose them to new troubles; and for that end have endeavoured to translate into the English tongue, an old seditious pamphlet, entituled, *De jure regni apud Scotos*, whereof Mr. George Buchanan was the author, which was condemned by act of parliament 1584, during the reign of his majesty's grandfather of blessed memory, and have dispersed many copies of the said translation, which may corrupt the affections of the subjects, and alienate their minds from their obedience to the laws, and his majesty's royal authority, and the present government, if it be not timously prevented: therefore the lords of his majesty's privy council, in his majesty's name and authority, command and charge all subjects of what degree, quality or rank soever they be, to bring and deliver to the clerk of council, all copies they have of the said pamphlet or book, translated, as said is, and that none presume hereafter to double any of the said copies, or disperse the same: with certification, that the contraveners shall be proceeded against as seditious persons, and disaffected to monarchical government, conform to the laws, with all rigour: and ordain those presents to be printed, and published at the market-cross of Edinburgh, and all other places needful, that none pretend ignorance.

" GLENCAIRN, Chanc. I. P. D. Con."

This proclamation is every way singular: for any thing that appears, this translation of that known piece of the celebrated Buchanan, was not printed, but only, it seems, handed about in manuscript; while in the meantime thousands of copies of it, in the Latin original, were in every body's hands. It had been more just to have ordered an answer to have been formed to the solid arguments in that dialogue, against tyranny and arbitrary government, and the courses at this time carrying on; and more reasonable, than to make such a needless noise about a paper we must suppose to be in the hands but of a very few.

Upon the 30th of May this year, the earl Glencairn, lord high chancellor of Scotland, died at Boltoun in East-Lothian, of a high fever, in a few days sickness.* He was reckoned a wise statesman, and a brave soldier, and had made gallant appearances for the king, and the freedom and liberty of his country. In several things since the restoration, he was driven beyond his inclinations by the prelates. We have seen that he was abundantly active in the establishment of bishops; and it was evident enough that he had no satisfaction in this part of his conduct, when he came to die. The pride of the archbishop of St. Andrews, and his getting himself into the precedency of the chancellor, and the other officers of state, were no way agreeable to this nobleman, who was of a very ancient descent, and could not well bear the heights of our Scots prelates; and indeed it may appear strange, that our ancient nobility could so easily bow their necks to the yoke and tyranny of bishops. I am well informed from the person, to whom the chancellor had the expression, upon the rumours of Middleton's fall, that he was pleased to say, " If Middleton fall, people will infer that it is an accursed thing to bring in bishops to Scotland: for captain James Stuart, who set up the Tulchan bishops, died a lamentable death; the earl of Dunbar, who brought them in upon the union of the crowns, was the first and last of that house; and now if Middleton fall, people will comment upon it."—Some hot words, as hath been noticed, were said to have passed betwixt the chancellor and the primate, which stuck to the earl, who still declared himself to be only for a moderate episcopacy: but he felt to his sad experience, the prelates now brought in to be very far from moderation.

1664.

At his death, my lord inclined much to have presbyterian ministers with him. He earnestly desired Mr. Robert Douglas, but he was in Fife when the earl sickened: some others were sought in Edinburgh, and could not be had. And before Mr. Robert Ker could be brought from Haddington, my lord was so low, that he could not speak to him. I have been likewise well informed, that the chancellor showed a great concern to have a meeting with the primate before he died, that he might have dealt plainly with him; and an express was sent, but the archbishop had no mind to meet with the earl. The earl of Rothes, afterwards duke, and the earl of Annandale, and many others of our noblemen and gentlemen, how much soever in their life they had been hard upon presbyterian ministers, yet at their death they sought to have them with them, and got them; which made the duke of York one day say, he believed that Scotsmen, be what they would in their life, were all presbyterians at their death. July 28th, the earl of Glencairn was buried with a great deal of pomp and solemnity, in St. Giles's church in Edinburgh. He had done great services to the king, and he was pleased to be at the charges of the funerals. Doctor Burnet, archbishop of Glasgow, was the preacher of his funeral sermon. And August 1st, the great seal was depositate in the archbishop's hands, till a chancellor should be named.

This year, June 3d, the earl of Tweeddale, now president of the council, was made one of the extraordinary lords of session: and the earl of Argyle, as we heard formerly, was restored to that earldom, and to

---

* The following is Kirkton's account of this event :—" This spring also, the chancellor left the world, and his short-lived honour. He died at Bolton in East-Lothian, of a fever, of five days; and though he had lived among the bishops and curates, yet he desired earnestly to die among presbyterians; and therefore as soon as he apprehended death, he posted away a messenger for Mr. Robert Douglas, who sojourned then at Preston, but was not to be gotten being absent in Fife. Then he sent for Mr. Robert Ker, in Haddington, but before he could come, the dying man had lost his senses, and so he was reproved in his sin, though he had made his last choice of those whom he had sore persecute. And so did many of our grandees, when they had their eyes opened with the terrors of death, particularly the duke of Rothes and earl of Annandale; and many more. Many a time the chancellor cried out, ' O, to have my last three years recalled!' but it would not be granted."—History of the Church of Scotland, pp. 203, 204.

Mr. Wodrow, in additions and amendments, printed in the 2d vol. of his History, informs us, " That the king was pleased to be at the charges of the earl of Glencairn's burial; and I am warranted to say, so muchfrom his majesty's letter to the council declaring so much : but I am since well informed, that the great charges of the funeral were never (for what reason I know not) refunded to that noble family, notwithstanding the singular services they had done the king."—Ed.

1664. all and sundry the lands, lordships, and baronies thereunto belonging, fallen into the king's hands by the forfeiture of his father; and to all and haill the mails, farms, and entries of all crops and years bygone and coming; to all debts and sums of money pertaining to the late marquis, and contained in his predecessors' infeftments. And, June 8th, the excellent marquis's head was taken down from the tolbooth, early in the morning, about five of the clock, by a warrant from the king, and was conveyed to his body. Thus the earl continued in favour, till his noble appearance for the protestant religion, at the duke of York's parliament, as we shall afterward hear.

This summer, Sir John Fletcher, king's advocate, was obliged to quit that post, not much the richer for all he had got in it. He was a creature of Middleton's, and went up to court in the end of the last year, but did not succeed in his endeavours to keep his post, when his patron was discarded. July 14th, I find a letter from the king to the council read, giving license to Mr. Patrick Oliphant advocate, to pursue his majesty's advocate before the council; and they order the said Mr. Patrick to exhibit and give in his accusation the 26th. I find no more about him in the registers, till September 14th, when, " The lords of his majesty's privy council, in obedience to his majesty's commands, signified to them by the lord treasurer, do discharge any further procedure in the process at Mr. Patrick Oliphant's instance against Sir John Fletcher; and ordain either party's part of the process to be delivered back unto them, and his majesty's letter, which was the ground thereof, to be taken to his majesty by the lord treasurer, the same not being as yet booked." By other papers of this time, I find this process before the council was long and litigious. The advocate was libelled for bribery, partiality, and malversation in his office. The lords who tried him did not find his answers and defences relevant or satisfying; and finding matters going thus, he signified his inclinations to demit in the king's hands, and so the matter was transferred to London and Sir

John permitted to go up; and there, not being able satisfyingly to vindicate himself in several points, he demitted, and Sir John Nisbet succeeded. People could not but observe, that the earl of Middleton, the chancellor, and Sir John Fletcher, who had been so active in the introduction of prelacy, did not long continue in their posts, neither had the satisfaction Mr. Sharp proposed to them, in that lamentable change made in this church.

August 9th, I find an act of council against the venting and spreading the excellent lord Warriston's speech. " The lords of his majesty's privy council being informed, that there is a seditious pamphlet, called Warriston's speech, published in print, and publicly printed and sold by booksellers and boys in the streets, do therefore give power and warrant to Sir Robert Murray of Cameron, to try and examine how these pamphlets come to be sold without authority and warrant; where the same has been printed; who have been the printers, importers, or principal venders and dispersers thereof; and for that effect to call before him and examine all booksellers and boys; and, if he shall see cause, to commit them to prison, till they discover the true way and means by which the said pamphlets are so published and sold, and what persons have had the chief hand therein, and report."—I find no more about it: the reader hath seen that there was no sedition in this speech; and the selling of it in public was soon stopt.

In August this year, the earl of Rothes, and the archbishop of St. Andrews, by a letter from court, go up to London.* The matter of the fines, the chancellor's post, and the advocate's, were to be concerted. Accordingly they went up; and, October 22d, the earl of Rothes returns to Holyroodhouse, loaden with posts and offices. November 3d, I find the patents for some of them read and recorded in council. His commission to represent the king in the national synod, to sit May next year, being what the curious reader may be desirous to

---

* See note, p. 217.

CHAP. V.] OF THE CHURCH OF SCOTLAND. 419

see, I have insert at the bottom of the page.* That synod did not indeed sit, but was put off time after time, by the influence of the primate, of which I cannot give so distinct and particular accounts, as I could wish, and so say no more of it. Some years after, we shall find a struggle of a good many of the clergy, for the sitting of this synod, but in vain. After the reading of this commission, "His grace his majesty's high commissioner nominates and appoints the lord archbishop of St. Andrews his grace, to be preses of the council for the time." And, November 24th, in the primate's absence, the lord commissioner "nominates the lord archbishop of Glasgow to be president of the council." Then a letter from the king in Latin, approving the lord commissioner his conduct in the last session of parliament, is read and recorded; and after this a letter from the king, appointing him keeper of the great seal, and to enjoy all the profits thereof till his majesty nominate a chancellor. The council give warrant to append the seal to both those. By other papers, I find that he had twenty pounds sterling a day, as king's commissioner, till the synod should sit, and fifty pounds per day while it sat. He continued lord high commissioner for a good while; besides, he was lord high treasurer, general of the forces by sea and land, and extraordinary lord of session, commander of his majesty's life-guard, and principal

1664.

---

* Rothes's Patent to be commissioner to the national synod, October 14th, 1664.

Carolus Dei gratia, Scotiæ, Angliæ, Franciæ, et Hiberniæ Rex, fideique defensor, omnibus probis hominibus suis ad quos præsentes literæ pervenerint, salutem. Sciatis quandoquidem ordinatio et dispositio externi regiminis ecclesiæ, et nominatio personarum quarum consilio res et negotia eo spectantes stabiliantur, nobis tanquam jus coronæ nostræ innatum, virtute regalis nostræ prærogativæ, et supremæ authoritatis in causis ecclesiasticis, hærent et incumbunt; et quia nobis expediens et necessarium videtur, in honorem et servitium divini numinis, emolumentum et tranquillitatem ecclesiæ, et gubernationem ejusdem in ordine et unione, ut nationalis synodus in antiquo nostro regno Scotiæ, in omnibus ejus membris debite constituatur, secundum quartum actum tertiæ sessionis novissimi nostri parliamenti, cujus titulus est, Actum pro stabiliatione et constitutione nationalis synodi. Quam quidem synodum sic constitutam, nos decrevimus Edinburgi convocatum iri, die Mercurii tertio mensis Maii proxime futuri, anno Domini 1665, inque hunc finem, regalem nostram proclamationem debito tempore expeditum iri; et quia nulla nationalis synodus teneri vel observari potest absque nostra præsentia, vel nostri delegati seu commissionarii authoritate nostra in hunc finem muniti. Cumque nos gravissimis regni nostri Angliæ negotiis impediti, dictæ generali synodo et conventui in sacra nostra persona adesse nequeamus; idcirco commissionem nostram viro cuidam eximiæ virtutis et fidelitatis demandare decrevimus, qui regalem nostram personam sustineat et repræsentet, cum ante convocationem prædictæ synodi, pro necessariorum communicatione et præparatione, cum in ipsa synodo convocata, tum etiam interea temporis pro debita obedientia legum nostrorum ecclesiam spectantium procuranda, ut enormiter et proterviter viventes supprimantur; cumque multis testimoniis compertum habeamus, amorem, animi dotes, et fidelitatem prædilecti et fidelissimi nostri consanguinei et consiliarii nostri Joannis comitis de Rothes, Lesliæ et Bambreich, &c. nostri thesaurarii principalis, ejusque zelum et promptitudinem, tum in agendo tum in patiendo pro nobis, ante felicem nostram instaurationem et restitutionem, speciatim vero egregium specimen ejus fidelitatis, prudentiæ et animi candoris, in exequenda excelsa provincia nostri commissionarii, in ultima sessione novissimi nostri parliamenti, in qua quidem obeunda, præclarum et egregium servitium nobis in ecclesiæ et regni nostri emolumentum edidit: Igitur dedimus et concessimus, tenoreque præsentium damus et concedimus, plenam potestatem et commissionem memorato fidelissimo et dilectissimo nostro consanguineo et consiliario, Joanni comiti de Rothes,&c. nostram sacram personam et authoritatem sustinendi, tum ante convocationem prædictæ synodi, tum in ipsa synodo sequente convocata, et in cunctis conventibus ejusdem, ac in omnibus aliis quæ ecclesiæ bonum, pacem et gubernationem dicti antiqui regni nostri Scotiæ, tum in ecclesia tum in statu, (prout nunc legibus stabilitur) et nostri servitii propagationem, in universis et singulis administrationibus ejusdem, tanquam nostro commissionario spectare poterint. Quin etiam tenore præsentium, præfatum comitem authoritate et potestate nostra regali munimus, ut sit noster commissionarius, omniaque et singula peragat ad potestatem et provinciam nostri commissionarii spectantia, non minore juris libertate et amplitudine, in omnibus respectibus, quam quicumque alius commissionarius fecit, seu de jure facere potuit; firmum et ratum habemus et habituri sumus, totum et quodcunque prædictus comes, in obeunda et exequenda dicta commissione et ejusdem documentis,fecerit et præstiterit. Mandamus porro omnibus nostris officiariis status, consiliariis, judicibus, et cunctis nostris subditis, et peculiariter officiariis copiarum nostrarum, in antedicto regno nostro, ut debita obedientia afficiant, agnoscant, et morem gerant dicto comiti, tanquam nostro commissionario, regalem nostram personam et authoritatem repræsentanti, ad effectus, et in modo in eadem commissione specificato. Quam quidem commissionem ad finem usque et dimissionem synodi sequentis durare et vim habere volumus. In cujus rei testimonium, præsentibus magnum sigillum nostrum, una cum privato nostro sigillo, (quia ipse comes est magni nostri sigilli pro tempore custos) appendi præcipimus. Apud Whitehall, decimo quarto mensis Octobris, 1664, et regni nostri decimo sexto. Per signaturam S. D. N. Regis superscriptum.

1664. collector of the fines; and Sir William Bruce, as we heard, was under him. But I imagine this last came to his share as lord treasurer. About this same time I find it observed as a singular thing, that the archbishop of Glasgow was made an extraordinary lord of session.

That same day, November 3d, Sir John Nisbet's patent to be king's advocate, is read and recorded in council. He was reckoned an able lawyer, and we shall frequently meet with him afterward. Those changes among the managers, and alterations of hands, made little change in the sufferings of presbyterians. They were all as yet hearty enough supporters of the bishops, and by them put on the severities we shall hear of. This year the plague raged in Holland, and the council take great care about ships from thence. A purple fever was common in Scotland, and all things were ripening for a war with Holland.

the rest of the managers were pushed into by the prelates.

The first accounts I find in the council books of a war with the states general, is in a proclamation published by them, May 3d, for a national fast, which I have insert, in a note.* The copy of the proclamation comes down from London, with an order to the commissioner to publish it, which is accordingly done. What cause the English had to engage in a war with Holland, I shall leave to other historians; but this I may venture to say, they had no great honour by it in the issue. In Scotland some private persons made themselves rich by caping or privateering upon the Dutch, but the public had no great cause of boasting. I find it observed by a friend of the present administration, that our seamen were pressed, and

CHAP. VI.

OF THE STATE AND SUFFERINGS OF PRESBYTERIANS, DURING THE YEAR 1665.

1665. With this chapter I am to shut up this book, which hath swelled upon my hand far beyond my first design; and I shall not increase it further by subdividing this into sections, but give what hath come to my hand this year, all together as shortly as may be. The former courses were carried on up and down the country, and people harassed for their nonconformity. The high commission had some persons before them, but were now in the wane, and the council pass some more acts against presbyterians. I shall give what I have, just in the order of time, as much as I can.

We have seen the earl of Rothes loaded with places of trust and power; and under the direction of Lauderdale he is chief manager in Scotland. He was much milder than Middleton, and scarce ever severe, except when in the high commission court, where he did not act like himself. During this year of his management, we shall not find so much severity as afterwards he and

---

* A proclamation for a public general fast throughout the realm of Scotland.

Charles, by the grace of God, king of Scotland, England, France, and Ireland, defender of the faith, &c. To all and sundry our good subjects, greeting: forasmuch as we, by the great injuries and provocations from the states of the United Provinces, have been forced, for the just defence and vindication of our own and our subjects' rights, to prepare and set out naval forces, and to engage into a war, upon most important reasons of honour and justice: and we, out of our religious disposition, being readily inclined to approve of an humble motion made to us, for commanding a general fast to be kept throughout this our whole kingdom, for imploring the blessing of almighty God, upon our councils and forces employed in this expedition; have thought fit, by this our proclamation, to indict a general and public fast, and day of humiliation for the end foresaid. Our will is herefore, and we straitly command and charge, that the said fast be religiously and solemnly kept throughout this our whole kingdom, by all our subjects and people within the same, upon the first Wednesday of June, being the seventh day thereof: requiring hereby the reverend archbishops and bishops, to give notice hereof to the ministers in their respective dioceses, that upon the Lord's day immediately preceding the said seventh day of June, they cause read this our proclamation from the pulpit, in every parish church, and that they exhort all our loving subjects, to a sober and devout performance of the said fasting and humiliation, as they tender the favour of Almighty God, the duty they owe to us, and the peace and preservation of their country; certifying all those who shall contemn or neglect such a religious and necessary work, they shall be proceeded against, and punished as contemners of our authority, and persons disaffected to the honour and safety of their country. Given at Edinburgh, the third day of May, 1665, and of our reign the seventeenth year.

God save the king.

our trade almost ruined, and the poverty of the country very much increased by this Dutch war. It may be more proper to the design of this history to observe, that I find none of the few remaining presbyterian ministers who kept their churches, had any difficulty to keep this fast appointed by the council: their proclamation was not burdened with any straitening clauses. They found much ground for public fasting, and did not dip into the justice or injustice of this war: but in the intimation of this fast, they condescended upon a great many grounds of humiliation, which were not named in the proclamation, and kept the day named. I have before me the form and words in which Mr. James Fergusson, yet connived at in his church at Kilwinning, intimated this fast appointed by the council, too long here to be insert; I shall only give a short abstract of it, that the reader may have some view of the manner he used in this case.—Mr. Fergusson begins his intimation: "Beloved, you see there is a pressing necessity of a fast, in respect of the threatened judgments; and therefore since it is appointed by the secret council, let us go about it. But we missed one thing in the proclamation, which is a very considerable one, to wit, the mentioning of the particular sins which have procured those judgments. I shall put this favourable construction upon it, that they left it to the discretion of ministers to intimate the causes of the fast; and I shall give you some passages of scripture." He names Hos. iv. 1—4. Levit. xxvi. 23—27. Jer. xxxiv. 13—18. Zech. v. 1—5. Isa. v. 8—13. then he adds, " the sin of all ranks is so multiplied, that a minister can hardly know where to begin. I shall reduce them all to this one general, the contempt of the glorious gospel. And he runs out upon the streams that run out from this fountain, lukewarmness, and indifferency, rough handling of the messengers of Christ, laying desolate multitudes of congregations, contempt of the Sabbath, atheistical contempt of ordinances, gross profanity of all kinds, aggravated by a wonderful deliverance from the usurpation; and yet, immediately upon the back of it, we have done contrary to what we had vowed with a high hand to the Lord: the Lord make us sensible of the hand you and I have in the provocation." Then he particularly insists upon the pestilence they were threatened with, and before prayer directs them what they are to be most concerned about in wrestling on their Fast-day. And in his sermon, from Jonah iii. 8. he insists at great length upon those sins and strokes he had pointed at in this intimation.

1665.

Towards the beginning of this year the pestilence broke out in England; and many remarkable signs were observed to precede and accompany that awful arrow of the Lord. In the end of the last year, appeared a very large comet. This winter there was so violent a storm of frost and snow, that there was no ploughing from December till the middle of March. In March another comet appeared in the heavens. Whatever natural causes may be adduced for those alarming appearances, the system of comets is yet so uncertain, and they have so frequently preceded desolating strokes and turns in public affairs, that they seem designed in providence to stir up sinners to seriousness. Those preachers from heaven, when God's messengers were silenced, neither prince nor prelate could stop. I find it noticed, that May 3d this year, the planet Venus appeared most clearly all the day long, to the amazement of many at Edinburgh. Much about this time the pestilence broke out at Westminster. I find it taken notice of, in several papers written at this time, that the appearance of a globe of fire was seen above that part of the city where the solemn league and covenant was burnt so ignominiously by the hand of the hangman. Whatever was in this, it seems certain that the plague broke out there, and it was observed to rage mostly in that street, where that open affront had been put upon the oath of God, and very few were left alive there.

The raging of the plague in England, which put many to wander from their houses and friends, as some thousands of Christ's faithful ministers in England and Scotland, had been forced to do a little before, the Dutch war, and some other things which fell in, made our managers in Scotland not

1665. quite so violent against presbyterians as formerly. Our nobility began to be weary of the prelates' cruelties, and their own drudgery to them. And the prelates began to jealous some of our noblemen, as not quite so hearty in their interests as formerly. Some little favours now and then are granted to presbyterian ministers and gentlemen. Thus, May 3d, "anent a petition of Walter Pringle of Greenknows, showing, that since the 10th of March last, the petitioner hath been imprisoned within the tolbooth of Elgin, by virtue of an act of the high commission; and seeing he is a person most valetudinary, and if detained in prison, his life will be undoubtedly in hazard; humbly therefore desiring liberty and warrant to the effect underwritten: the lords of his majesty's privy council, having considered the above written petition, do grant the petitioner the liberty of the said town of Elgin, and the bounds of a mile round about it, during the council's pleasure; and for that effect ordain the magistrates of Elgin to set him at liberty out of prison, he finding caution to remain within the said bounds during the time of his liberty, under the pain of ten thousand pounds Scots." That same day, liberty is granted to Mr. Smith, minister, I suppose, of Edinburgh, to come to that place, "anent a petition presented by Mr. John Smith, minister, showing, that the petitioner being exceedingly diseased, and troubled with colic, gravel, and a complication of other diseases, and in so dangerous a condition thereby, that his physicians think it necessary he come to Edinburgh for counsel and assistance; the lords of council grant him liberty to come to Edinburgh, and reside there for the space of three months after the date of this."

Towards the end of May, there fell out a mutiny in the west-kirk parish of Edinburgh. I give it in the words of a writer, who was no enemy to conformist ministers. "May 28th, there fell out a mutiny betwixt the parishioners of the west-kirk and Mr. William Gordon, minister there, who, they alleged, was for keeping of festivals, and had been the prime author of the removal of their minister Mr. David Williamson, a good and able teacher. The people railed on him, and closed up the kirk door. Some of them were put in the thieves' hole, and a man and a woman were scourged through Edinburgh." No more about this hath come to my hand. Several persons in Dumfries, were about this time imprisoned, for not hearing the ministers put in by the bishops, and refusing to give obedience to the bishops' orders sent them; but I have no particular accounts who they were.

This summer, I find orders are given for disarming the west and south of Scotland; and Sir James Turner and others, with a good many soldiers, are raging up and down that country, pressing conformity, and assisting the uplifting of the fines. That part of the nation, having every day more and more reason to be dissatisfied with the changes in church government, behoved to be oppressed and borne down, and now, to satisfy the idle fears of the prelates, disarmed. For what I remember, this is the first time our Scots history affords us an instance of a Scots king's disarming his subjects in the time of profound peace at home. Perhaps the king might be made to apprehend, the affections of his subjects in those shires bore some proportion to his, or rather the managers their actions, and the obligations they had put upon them. Indeed had this been the rule, their respect would have been smaller for his majesty, than really it was: but under all their hardships and oppressions, presbyterians continued to have all due regard to the king. The violent seizure of their arms, was a very great loss to the country. Formerly our sovereigns reckoned it their safety to have good subjects, in case to defend themselves and the government, upon attacks made or threatened; and till of late, the method of standing forces, and armies in time of peace, were strangers in Scotland. There were few families but had some arms; and the forcible taking those away, without a fault, and without payment, was unprecedented and arbitrary. The silly pretext was, that the fanatics, now the modish way of expressing the presbyterians, and all who would not renounce the covenants, were to rise and join the Dutch against the king. *Credat Judæus appella!* This was another of the primate's fetches, and mightily pleased the prelates, who now thought themselves secure, and at liberty to do as they would. Those oppressions, with what followed, did but further irritate the country, and tended to expose them and their curates, to what, without ground, they pretended to be afraid of.

June 1st, 2d, and 3d, the engagement happened betwixt the English and Dutch fleets, of which a very favourable account, upon our side, was printed. And June 20th, the council publish the king's proclamation sent them from London, for a thanksgiving; which not having seen in print, I shall give the abstract of here.

"Charles, &c. Forasmuch as our royal navy, under the command of our dearest brother the duke of York, hath, upon the 3d instant, obtained a glorious victory of the fleets set out by the states of the United Provinces: and we finding it suitable, that a solemn return of praise be paid to Almighty God, by whose special hand, in a signal appearance for us and the justice of our cause, this great salvation hath been wrought; have judged fit, by this our proclamation, to indite a general thanksgiving for the aforesaid cause. Our will is herefore, and we straitly command and charge, that the said thanksgiving, and solemn commemoration of the goodness of God, manifested by the conduct and management of this late action, be religiously and solemnly observed through this our whole kingdom, upon the 2d Thursday of July next, being the 13th day thereof. Given at Whitehall, June 10th." The bishops are required to intimate the same to the ministers in their respective dioceses, and cause this proclamation to be read from the several pulpits, with exhortations to all loving subjects, to a cheerful and devout performance of so becoming a duty, owing to the name of the Lord God, who has done those great and auspicious things for us. I think I have somewhere read, that a thanksgiving was also appointed in Holland, the states apprehending the victory was upon their side. I shall only further remark, that Mrs. Trail, wife of Mr. Robert Trail, who, we heard, was banished, and now is in Holland, was imprisoned about this time, for writing to her husband, and receiving letters from him, though they concerned nothing but their mutual health, and family concerns.

1665.

June 22d, the council grant liberty to Mr. John Stirling, late minister, to come to Edinburgh, and stay about his necessary affairs for twenty days. And, July 20th, upon a new petition he is permitted to continue in Edinburgh for his health, till September 1st. We see what unnecessary trouble and charges those worthy ministers were put to, in so frequent petitioning for a thing no subject ought to be restricted in, without a crime proven against them. July 6th, "Anent a petition presented by Mr. John Cameron, showing, that in the year 1662, he was confined to the bounds of Lochaber, under which confinement he hath been ever since; and seeing his wife, for several weeks, hath been afflicted with a most dangerous disease, and, without the comfort and help of the petitioner and physicians, is in hazard of losing her life; humbly therefore desiring he may be liberate of his confinement for some space: the lords of his majesty's privy council discharge him of his confinement in Lochaber, and, in place hereof, do hereby confine him to the city of Glasgow, and two miles about the same, till the 1st of November next, he finding sufficient caution to live peaceably and legally in the meantime, and to retire to the place of his confinement, whenever he shall be required by the archbishop of Glasgow."

August 2d, a convention of estates meet at Edinburgh, by virtue of a proclamation published for that end, June 22d, which needs not be insert here. The design of this meeting was, to raise money for his majesty to support him in the Dutch war. Those conventions, merely to raise money from the subjects, had been but very little used in Scotland; and indeed it was scarce worth the king's while to insist upon it. What this poor and oppressed nation could advance, was but little, and it was but an insignificant part of it that ever was applied to the ends for which it was imposed. And because Rothes was keeper of the seal, and there was no chancellor, the archbishop of St. Andrews was chosen preses, and had a long harangue to them; and, in his cold way, urged, that the people might contribute willingly and cheerfully for the king's service. The king's commissioner was present, and could have delivered a speech of this nature, with a far better grace; but, it seems, this was also for the honour of the church, that a bishop should be at the head of this convention. By other accounts I find a taxation was laid upon the kingdom, of about a million of merks Scots, as it was calculated.

I find, that this summer an order was issued by the council, but I have observed nothing of it in their books this year, appointing all scholars who have university degrees conferred upon them, to take the oath of allegiance and supremacy, otherwise that they be not admitted to receive their degrees. We shall afterwards meet with acts of this kind. The design of the prelates in this is plain enough, and in the after addition that was made of the declaration, imposing it upon all who should receive their degrees, to corrupt the youth of the kingdom, and secure episcopacy to after generations. In this point, as well as many others, now Scotland must be of a piece with England, where the youth are most unreasonably clogged with party oaths, before they can well understand the importance and weight of an oath. This is a base bar upon learning, and what no universities in Europe, as far as I can hear of, save those under the influence of prelates, do burden students with. The honorary degrees ought certainly to be bestowed according to the progress students make in learning, and not as they are addicted to such a party and opinion. However, by this and subsequent acts, a great many of the most deserving youths of the nation were excluded from their degrees; and some were involved in perplexities of mind, when afterward they came to reflect upon what they had done hastily, and without consideration. It appears to me every way unaccountable, to put boys of fifteen or sixteen years of age, to attest the great God in matters of this kind, which they could not fully understand. And it gradually disposed the rising generation to swallow down the multitude of declarations, and dubious and self-contradictory oaths, which, in the progress of this spiritual tyranny over consciences, came to be imposed.

Conformity was pressed with the greatest warmth by the bishops this summer, through the west and south; it was in Galloway, where some of the outed ministers preached, most openly. This galled the bishops, and that country was sorely harassed by Sir James Turner and the soldiers at their instigation. I find likewise, several persons in the parish of Stewarton are brought to trouble about this time, for hearing a presbyterian minister; some were fined, and others imprisoned; but I have not a particular account of their trouble. Great numbers of persons, almost every where upon the south of Tay, were cited before the high commission court; but very few now compeared, choosing rather to live under an uncertain outlawry, than to be certainly ruined; and this mighty inquisition-court, from which the prelates expected so much, gradually weakened, and scarce lived out this year. Yet some were necessitated to compear before them.

This summer, Mr. Hugh Peebles, minister at Lochwinnoch, in the shire of Renfrew, was sisted before the high commission. He was a worthy, pious, and prudent person, and all the crime he was charged with, was, that he preached one Sabbath night in his own house, to some people who came to hear him. When he came before them, he used as much freedom, as might have probably sent him to banishment at least, had they not been a little upon the decline. Very frankly he told them, he did not know what to make of their court, he could reckon it scarce either civil or ecclesiastic; yet since his majesty's commissioner had commanded him, and self-defence was *juris naturalis*, he had appeared innocently to defend himself, and to give accounts of plain matter of fact. He told them, that ever since he was a minister, he had exercised in his family upon the Sabbath evenings, and the people who lived near him, generally came to hear him. He alleged, that the law did not militate at all against this, if the reason of the law be considered. The reason of their law behoved to be, either to prevent people's leaving the public worship, which could have no place in this case; or, to prevent people's being alienated from the minister of the congregation, which could have no room either, since there was no minister settled where he lived: and since his preaching to his neighbours, whom he could not exclude from his house, did not thwart with the *ratio legis*, it could not be said to thwart with the law itself. After all he could say, though never so reasonable, the archbishop of Glasgow was resolved to be rid of him; and so he was ordered to leave the west country, and to confine himself to the town of Forfar, which is, I suppose, near a hundred miles distant from the place where he lived and had an estate.

When the high commission court came to fall short of answering the designs of the prelates, they fall upon other measures, and give in groundless suggestions, innuendoes, and insinuations, against a great many excellent gentlemen, mostly in the west country, to such who found means to procure an order from the king to imprison them. And towards the beginning of September, an order comes down to the commissioner, to seize, imprison, and confine several of the most considerable and best gentlemen in the kingdom. Such were pitched upon who were suspected to have greatest aversion to the prelatic way, and indeed no other thing could they be charged with, and were as peaceable and loyal subjects as the king had. There were few in the kingdom equalled many of them, in piety, peaceableness, and good sense; and, generally speaking, they were persons of ancient and opulent estates, and very great influence and interest where they lived. It seems the prelates and their supporters reckoned it their interest to have them out of the way. Many of themselves could never learn the ground of their imprisonment, and so it is no wonder I cannot account for it any further than I have just now said: and I shall not determine, whether the prelates, and others now in the government, inclined to have their estates, or whether they were attacked just to terrify the country. I find nothing about their imprisonment in the council books; and several things were now done by direct orders from court, without communicating them to the privy council. It is pity we have no more distinct and particular accounts from those who can give them, of the unjust and illegal treatment those excellent persons met with. They were, without the least previous notice, seized by a written order from the commissioner, and had not the least reason given them. Their names, as far as I can now recover them, were, major-general Robert Montgomery, brother to the earl of Eglinton, Sir William Cunningham of Cunninghamhead, Sir George Maxwell of Nether-Pollock, Sir Hugh Campbell of Cesnock, Sir William Muir of Rowallan, major-general Holburn of Menstri, Sir George Monro, colonel Robert Halket, brother to Sir James Halket of Pitfiran, Sir James Stuart late provost of Edinburgh, Sir John Chiesly of Carswell, James Dunlop of that ilk, William Ralston of that ilk. I find some others named in some papers, as imprisoned at this time, such as Sir Patrick Hume of Polwart, and others; but not being certainly informed about them, I have omitted them. Those excellent persons when brought into Edinburgh, without any libel, accusation, or cause given them, were most arbitrarily imprisoned in the castles of Edinburgh, Stirling, Dumbarton, and other places, where a good many of them lay for many years. We shall in the progress of the history have some further accounts of their hardships and frequent removes.

The matter of the act of fines hath been pretty largely accounted for in the former part of this book. It was all mystery at first, and took several turns, as we have seen; and now it takes another shape when, October 3d, it comes before the council. I am not so well acquaint with the secret springs of this affair, as fully to account for it: but I shall set down the proclamation published by the council this day; and the rather, because it does not appear to have been printed.

" Charles by the grace of God, &c. to our lovits, &c. greeting: forasmuch as by an act of the second session of our late parliament, of the date of the 9th day of September 1662, entituled, act anent persons excepted forth of the act of indemnity; several of

1665. our lieges were fined in the particular sums of money therein expressed, and as to those sums were excepted out of the said general act: and albeit, we did not only suspend the payment of the foresaid sums for some time, but did prorogate the terms of payment thereof, until the 11th of December, 1664, for the first moiety, and the 11th of March last, for the second moiety: with certification, that such, as being charged at the instance of our treasurer, treasurer-depute, or advocate, should not pay in their respective sums, should incur the pains contained in the said act of our parliament, as our proclamation of the 13th of July 1664, bears: and notwithstanding that both the said terms of payment are long since elapsed, and that many of those who have been charged, have failed in payment of their first moiety; nevertheless, such is our royal goodness and clemency, that we resolve only to put in execution the said act of parliament, in manner, and upon condition following. Our will is, and we charge you straitly, and command, that incontinent these our letters seen, ye pass to the market cross of Edinburgh, and other market-crosses of the head burghs of the shires of this kingdom, and there in our name and authority command and charge all persons who are charged by the said act of parliament, excepting such to whom we have been graciously pleased to grant a suspension, as also such as have not been charged heretofore, for paying any of their said moieties, to pay in their respective proportions of the first moiety, in case it be not already paid, to Sir William Bruce, collector, betwixt and the first day of December next to come, which is the diet appointed for those that live besouth the North Water of Esk, and the first day of January, which is the diet appointed for those who live benorth the said water: with certification, if they fail, they shall for ever forfeit the benefit of our said act of indemnity and oblivion, and incur all other pains therein contained, to be executed with all rigour: as also, that ye make public intimation at the market-crosses foresaid to all concerned, that it is our gracious will and pleasure to remit and forgive the second moiety of the said fines, to all persons nominate in the said act, of whatsomever quality or degree they be of, the first being paid by such as are ordained to pay the same, who shall come in and take the oath of allegiance in the ordinary form, and shall subscribe the declaration as it is set down in the 5th act, session 2d, and act 2d, of the 3d session of our late parliament, in presence of our commissioner, or such of the lords of council as he shall call, or in the presence of the lords of our council met together; and that betwixt and the respective days foresaid, according to their residence: as also, that ye in our name and authority make lawful proclamation, as said is, to all persons to whom we granted a suspension of their fines, or who have not hitherto been charged for payment of any part thereof, to come in and take the said oath of allegiance, and subscribe the declaration the foresaid days respective, according to their residence: with certification, if they fail, they shall be liable for both the moieties of the said respective fines; and that, immediately after the running out of the said respective days, they shall be charged for payment thereof to our said collectors, under the pains contained in the foresaid act of parliament anent fines. Given under our signet at Edinburgh, the third day of October, 1665, and of our reign the seventeenth year."

Remarks upon this proclamation I shall not stay upon. Who these were who had their fines suspended, I know not. Some few up and down had paid the first moiety; but, it seems, there were but few. The king and some of the managers were willing enough to have waved this matter of the fines, but the prelates and others of them had no mind to part with so fat a morsel; and so the blind is fallen upon, which might expose the refusers in the king's eyes, and the view of those who knew not how matters stood, and effectually secure them in the fines of such who were really presbyterians. I need scarce observe, that this is a new proof that the fines were designed principally against presbyterians; and it was no ease to them at all to have the second moiety forgiven them, upon their paying the first half, and taking the oath and declaration, since both were flatly against their principles: and therefore it was but very few named in the act of fines, who embraced the terms offered; and that the primate and others expected. This, as the reader will have more than once occasion to observe, was one of the unhappy methods of this reign, first, to lay on illegal and oppressive impositions, and then to require absolute conformity to the church establishment, as an alleged reasonable thing to get rid of those impositions. This presbyterians found in many of the turns in those two reigns.

The council, November 23d, make some further regulations as to the fines. " And considering, that several persons, through age and infirmity of body, and other necessary impediments, may not be able to come in to Edinburgh, to take the oath and declaration, in the terms of the proclamation, give warrant to the clerk to issue out commissions under his hand, to such persons as shall make address for that effect, to the sheriffs of the respective shires where they live, or privy counsellors to administrate the same to them, providing his majesty's commissioner be first acquainted with their names, and satisfied with the reason wherefore they are craved." And further, considering several of the said fined persons are dead, they order the heirs and executors of the said defunct persons, claiming the benefit of the said proclamation, to take the oath of allegiance, and subscribe the declaration, if of lawful age, and willing to do the same." " And several of the fined persons being under captions for civil debts, and so cannot repair to Edinburgh, as the proclamation requires; the council grant warrant to the clerk to subscribe personal protections to such as shall make addresses for that effect, to continue till January next." After all those baits, to pay at least one moiety of the fines, it was not very many who paid it, and then Sir James Turner and the army were sent to uplift them by military force, which brought much trouble to many, as we shall see, next year.

The pushing of the declaration brings new difficulties this year in the election of magistrates in some burghs; and so I find two acts of council, October 4th, and December 7th, about the magistracy of Ayr. By 1665. the first, the present magistrates, and eight or nine others who have signed the declaration, are empowered to elect the magistrates and council for the ensuing year, providing William Cunningham continue provost; and the earl of Eglinton, with advice of the archbishop of Glasgow, is to see this act put in execution. By the other, the matter is left to the old magistrates, and such of the council as have taken the declaration.

By this time many of the old presbyterian ministers, who had seen the glory of the former temple, were got to their rest. The 10th day of October this year, brought the reverend Mr. William Guthrie to his father's house: I shall only add the remark made upon his lamented death, by the worthy minister his contemporary, whom I cited before, when I spoke of him. " This year the presbyterians in Scotland lost one of their pillars, Mr. William Guthrie, minister of the gospel at Fenwick, one of the most eloquent, successful, popular preachers, that ever was in Scotland.* He died a sufferer, for he was deposed by the bishop, but in hope, that one day the Lord would deliver Scotland from her thraldom." Many others of the old ministers of this church died about this time in peace, being taken away from the evil to come, and fast coming on in great measures, and departed under the solid and firm hope of a glorious deliverance coming to this poor church.

Others of them were harassed by the prelates. This year, in October, Mr. Matthew Ramsay minister at Kilpatrick Wester, in the presbytery of Dunbarton, a person of the most shining piety, stayed gravity, of the greatest eminency of gifts, extraordinary sweetness of temper, and of a most peaceable behaviour, was by the bishop in synod deposed at Glasgow, without any other cause so much as alleged, but his not attending their prelatical synods and presbyteries.

---

* Mr. Guthrie's little book, " The Trial of a Saving Interest in Christ," a book with which, to this day, we believe almost every pious Scottishman is familiar, bears ample testimony to the extent of his talents and to the pure and pious spirit wherewith he was animated.—*Ed.*

1665. Together with him, Mr. Robert Mitchel, minister of Luss, in the same presbytery, a person of most eminent ministerial qualifications, was for the same crime suspended, in order to be deposed next year.

October 14th, I find George Porterfield and John Graham, late provosts of Glasgow, were cited, as usual in such cases, to appear and answer before the council, to what should be charged against them, upon pain of death. They were two excellent persons, who had been singularly active in the late work of reformation; and after they had been brought to some trouble by the committee of estates, in the year 1660, retired to Holland, where they were living peaceably, under a voluntary exile: and, December 19th, they were both, upon their noncompearance, declared rebels and fugitives. It was pretended, without the least proof, that they were guilty of treasonable practices in Holland, merely because they continued there during the war; when indeed, whether there had been peace or war, they would not willingly have come home, to involve themselves in unnecessary trouble, and the persecution now so much raging against all presbyterians.

In the beginning of November this year, the earl of Rothes commissioner, made a tour to the west country, in great pomp and splendour, with the king's guards waiting on him, and a great train of attendants. He was at Hamilton, Glasgow, Eglinton, Paisley, Dunbarton, and Mugdock. That part of the country behoved to be overawed, if possible, from their aversion to the courses now carrying on. Whether information was taken of the circumstances and estates of the excellent gentlemen in that neighbourhood, now in prison, in order to some following designs, I cannot say; but as some severe acts against presbyterian ministers accompanied Middleton's circuit, so we shall just now meet with some more of that kind. The commissioner returned to Edinburgh towards the end of the month.

November 30th, the council having considered the report made by the committee appointed to consider what course should be taken with quakers, " find, that they are guilty, and may be reached as contraveners of the acts of parliament against separation, the 1st act of the 3d session of the late parliament, and the proclamation emitted by his majesty and parliament, against quakers, January 22d, 1661, and that they be punished by fining, confining, imprisonment, and such other corporal and arbitrary punishments as the council think fit; and that these now in prison, Anthony Hodges, and Andrew Robertson, be brought before the council, and a libel be given them by his majesty's advocate to see and answer." The laird of Swinton is dropped, and I find very little effectually done as to others of them: so that in this reign they got deep rooting, especially in the northern shires.

The council go more closely to work against presbyterian ministers and people; and next council day, December 7th, pass some severe acts and proclamations against them. The high commission was now expiring, and the privy council return to their former work. Their first act at this diet extends their former acts, chiefly pointing at the younger presbyterian ministers, unto all of them, as may be seen in the act itself, at the foot of the page.* The act

---

* Act of council against ministers, Edinburgh, December 7th, 1665.
The lords of his majesty's privy council finding it now, after a long and tender forbearance, necessary, that their acts of the third of December, one thousand six hundred and sixty-two, and thirteenth of August, one thousand six hundred and sixty-three years, against such ministers as entered in, or since the year one thousand six hundred and forty-nine, and had not since obtained presentations from their lawful patrons, and collations and admissions from their ordinaries, be, upon some weighty grounds and considerations therein mentioned, extended against all such other ministers, who being entered before the year forty-nine, have, since the restitution of the government of the church by archbishops and bishops, relinquished their ministry, or been deposed therefrom by their ordinary; do therefore command and charge all such ministers, within forty days after publication hereof, and all such ministers as shall hereafter relinquish their ministry, or be deposed therefrom by their ordinary, (within forty days after their relinquishing and deposition) to remove themselves, their families and goods belonging to them, out of these respective parishes where they were incumbents, and not to reside within twenty miles of the same, or within six miles of Edinburgh or any cathedral church, or three miles of any burgh royal within this kingdom, or to reside two of them within one parish: with certification, if they fail to

begins with a declaration, "That the council after a long and tender forbearance," (after what we have now seen in the preceding part of this book, some readers will be ready to say, " The tender mercies of the wicked are cruel") " Find it necessary their former acts, December 23d, 1662, and August 13th, 1663, be extended to the ministers who entered in before the year 1649, and have relinquished their ministry, and been deposed by their ordinary." There was no new fault pretended, and nothing charged, but a firm adherence to their principles; and yet these worthy old men are sent a wandering from their flocks and friends. The hardships put on them by this proclamation, have been above considered as they relate to the younger ministers; and they are very much accented, and the barbarity of the prelates pushing this, aggravated, in extending them to a very few old dying men, living most

---

remove themselves as said is, and to give exact obedience hereunto, (unless they have the permission of the lords of the privy council, lords of his majesty's commission for church affairs, or of the bishop of the diocese) they are to incur the penalties of the laws made against movers of sedition, and to be proceeded against with that strictness which is due to so great contempt of his majesty's authority over church and state. And do hereby inhibit and discharge all heritors and householders in burgh or land, to give any presence or countenance to any one or more of these ministers, removed by this present act, to preach or exercise any act of the office of a minister: with certification, if they, after publication hereof, shall presume so to do, they are to be proceeded against according to law: and commanding and requiring all sheriffs, stewarts, magistrates of burghs, and justices of peace, to make diligent search and inquiry within their respective jurisdictions, if any such ministers, as fall within the compass of this or the other two acts of council aforesaid, do reside within the bounds therein prohibited, and to seize upon and imprison their persons, ay and while they find sufficient caution to compear before the lords of his majesty's council or commission, betwixt and such a short day, as the said sheriffs, stewarts, magistrates of burghs, and justices of peace, shall, upon consideration of the distance of the place, judge convenient: and in case of not meeting of the council or commission at the day foresaid, to compear the next meeting day thereafter; certifying all sheriffs, magistrates of burghs, and justices of peace, that his majesty will account their neglect and remissness in this affair, an high contempt of his authority and commands, and punish the same accordingly. And ordain these presents to be printed and published, that none pretend ignorance.

Pet. Wedderburn, Cl. Secr. Concilii.

---

quietly and peaceably, of whom, in 1665. the ordinary course of nature, they would very quickly have been rid without this cruelty. A door is left open to the council, the high commission court, or any one bishop, to tolerate them; which was not sought, at least from the two last, as far as I hear of. All heritors and householders are forbid to give them any countenance in their preaching, or exercising any part of the ministerial office; and all magistrates, and other executors of the law, are empowered to imprison them, if they keep not within the bounds appointed by this proclamation. Some interpreted the clause with relation to heritors and householders, as discharging all to set a house to any presbyterian minister; but I cannot see so much in the letter of the act, without stretching it. However, it was improven by their adversaries, so as they had no small difficulties in many places where to fix, and it was really impossible for all of the presbyterian ministers in Scotland, to continue in it, if they kept precisely to the terms in those acts, as hath been noticed. All this severity against those worthy old men, was according to archbishop Burnet's maxim, which he openly enough propaled as his real sentiments, " That the only way to deal with a fanatic, was to starve him." I am told, that the earl of Kellie, no great friend to presbyterians, upon the publishing of the acts and proclamations agreed to this day, said, " It was his opinion, presbyterian ministers ought to be obliged to wear a badge of distinction from other men, that every body might know them, otherwise he might ignorantly set them some of his houses and lands, and so fall under the lash of the law." This is another persecuting proclamation against presbyterian ministers, for the old fault of bare peaceable nonconformity; I have forgot their number, but they are near a dozen now, and every new one hath some severe clause added. Thus the wicked wax worse and worse.

In the next place they order a proclamation to be published and printed against conventicles, and meetings for religious exercises; which I have insert

1665. below.* It speaks for itself, and is so plain as it scarce needs a commentary. The former acts since the year 1660, against subjects' convening without the king's authority, are narrated; and this is termed a very dangerous and unlawful practice. Thus the heathen writers and their emperors used to talk, during the first three centuries after Christ; and yet the primitive Christians met at their hazard, notwithstanding of such edicts as this. In a little we shall find it the ordinary cant of this period which follows, that these meetings for religious exercises are the seminaries of separation and rebellion. That they were a separation from prelates and their curates, every body perceived; but still the question remains, whether these had not sinfully separated from the reformation of the church of Scotland, and given just ground to ministers and people to withdraw from them? And

---

* Proclamation against conventicles, Edinburgh, December 7th, 1665.

Charles, by the grace of God, king of Great Britain, France, and Ireland, defender of the faith to our lovits, heralds, pursuivants, macers, and messengers at arms, our sheriffs in that part conjunctly and severally, specially constitute, greeting: forasmuch as the assembling and convening our subjects, without our warrant and authority, is a most dangerous and unlawful practice, prohibited and discharged by several laws and acts of parliament, under the pains against such as unlawfully convocate our lieges; and notwithstanding thereof, and that it is the duty of all our good and faithful subjects to acknowledge and comply with our government ecclesiastic and civil, as it is now established by law within this kingdom, and in order thereto, to give their cheerful concurrence, countenance, and assistance to such ministers, as by public authority are, or shall be admitted in their several parishes, and to attend the ordinary meetings for divine worship of the same. And by the first act in the third session of our late parliament, it is declared, that the withdrawing from, and not joining in the said public and ordinary meetings for divine worship, is to be accounted seditious: and siklike, by an express clause of the first act of the third session of our said parliament, all such ministers as have not obtained presentations and collations, and all such as should be suspended or deprived, and yet should dare to presume to exercise their ministry, are to be punished as seditious persons. Nevertheless, divers persons, disaffected to our authority and government, do not only withdraw from the public meetings of divine worship in their own parish churches, but under the pretence of religion assemble themselves: likeas, some of the foresaid pretended ministers presume to preach, lecture, pray, or perform other acts belonging to the ministerial function, contrary to the foresaid acts of parliament, and to many other acts of parliament, made by our royal ancestors, and revived by ourself, against such seditious practices. And albeit it is our royal resolution to give all due encouragement to piety and pious persons, in the worship and service of God, in an orderly way; yet, considering that conventicles and unwarrantable meetings and conventions, under pretence and colour of religion, and the exercises thereof, have been the ordinary seminaries of separation and rebellion, and are in themselves reproachful to our authority and government ecclesiastic and civil, and tending to the alienating of our subjects' hearts and affections from the same, and ministering opportunities for infusing those pernicious and poisonous principles, the consequences whereof threaten no less than the confusion and ruin of church and kingdom. Our will is herefore, and we charge you strictly and command, that, incontinent these our letters seen, you pass, and in our name and authority, inhibit and discharge all conventicles, conventions, and other meetings, of what number soever, for, and under the pretence of the exercise of religion, except such meetings for divine worship, and other relating hereunto, as are allowed by authority; certifying all such persons as shall be present at such unlawful meetings, they shall be looked upon as seditious persons, and shall be punished by fining, confining, and other corporal punishments, as our privy council, or such as have, or shall have our commission for that effect, shall think fit; and also certifying all such ministers as shall dare to perform any acts of the ministerial function, contrary to the foresaid acts, and all such as shall reset any of these disorderly persons, known to be such, or who shall have any hand in contriving of, or enticing others to keep the said conventicles, or shall suffer the same to be kept within their houses, where they are dwelling for the time; that they shall, after due conviction, be liable not only to the foresaid pains but also to the highest pains which are due to, and may, by the laws of this kingdom, be inflicted upon seditious persons. And for the better preventing of all such unlawful meetings, we do hereby command and require all sheriffs, stewarts, magistrates of burghs, bailies of regalities, justices of peace, constables, and other our public ministers, to make exact search from time to time in all places, where any such meetings have been, shall, or may be suspected, and to apprehend every such person, who shall keep or frequent these meetings, and to commit them to the next prison, therein to remain till further order be taken with them, by such as have, or shall have our authority for that effect: and ordains you to make publication hereof at the market crosses of our royal boroughs, and at every parish church within the kingdom, on the Lord's day, wherethrough none pretend ignorance thereof, as ye will answer to us thereupon. The which to do, we commit to you, conjunctly and severally, our full power by these our letters, delivering them by you duly execute and indorsed again to the bearer. Given at Edinburgh, the seventh day of December, and of our reign the seventh year, 1665.

in the determination, scripture, reason, and the practice of this church, since we came out from Babylon, must come in; and not the king. and council's laws and acts. Whatever extremities might be afterward run to, at some conventions for religious exercises, if any such were, the unparalleled severity and oppression justly lodged at the prelates' door, forced people into them: yet there was nothing now at them, that in any native way of speaking, can be termed rebellion; the covenants indeed were owned, and their obligation asserted sometimes, and other truths, the owning of which was now made treason and rebellion, by iniquity established by a law.

As to the doctrine taught by presbyterian ministers at those meetings, termed in the next clause of the proclamation, "infusing poisonous and pernicious principles;" I wish the world had a specimen of the ordinary doctrine preached by the curates,* and a parallel betwixt it and that of presbyterians at conventicles, and they would soon perceive on which side the poison lies. If smoothing over oppression and tyranny, weakening the very common principles of morality and natural religion, gross pelagian errors, and plain popery, be poisonous, many instances can be given in the ministers established by authority, as now the style goes. Those meetings are discharged under the "pains of sedition, fining, confining, and such other corporal punishments as shall appear fit to the council, or any having the king's authority, whether he be officer of the army, bishop, or even a private sentinel; every body present at them, are thus to be treated: but ministers, or any who have a hand in contriving and enticing people to such meetings, or suffer the same to be kept in their houses, are made liable to the highest pains due unto, and which by law may be inflicted upon seditious persons. And all magistrates and others, are required presently to apprehend the contraveners, and imprison them. Here is a broad foundation for the army to act upon, and they did it to purpose next year.

Upon this proclamation we have another instance of the ignorance of the English writers in our Scots affairs. The author of the Complete History of England, vol. iii. says, "This year, 1665, the parliament of Scotland issued out a severe proclamation against conventicle preachers, as movers of sedition." Being much a stranger to the methods of our Scots parliaments, it is not to be wondered that he knew not, that save in some extraordinary and temporary cases, proclamations were never issued by parliament, and were ordinarily the deed of the executors of the law: but one would have expected, that from our printed acts of parliament, he might have noticed there was no Scots parliament sat from the year 1663, to the year 1669. From his mistaking the parliament for the council, we may guess how far he is out in the reason he gives for the proclamation, which very justly he terms severe, "being provoked by the insolence of Mr. Alexander Smith, a deposed minister." His story of Mr. Smith's carriage before the high commission, is quite misrepresented, and was no ways the reason of this proclamation. Mr. Smith was before the high commission many months before this proclamation: his crime there, as we have heard, was only his refusing the primate his titles; and the barbarous treatment of this good man, is one of the black stains upon this administration. Mr. Eachard copies here again after the former, and follows him in all his mistakes.

In the papers of a reverend minister, who understood well how matters went, I find that this same day an act was passed in favour of the curates, and for the constituting presbyteries; though that word must not now be used, yet the curates continued it in many places for their own credit among the people. But not finding this act in the council books, though I know several things of importance are now done,

---

* Of these curates we have the following character from the pen of Bishop Burnet:—"They were the worst preachers I ever heard: they were ignorant to a reproach, and many of them were openly vicious. They were a disgrace to their orders, and to the sacred functions; and were indeed the dregs and refuse of the northern parts."—History of His Own Times, vol. i. p. 229.—*Ed.*

1665. and that sometimes by order from the commissioner, and sometimes by advice of the council, which are not booked, neither having seen the act at large, I shall not insist much upon it. The abstract of this act or order before me, falls much in with what we have had formerly, and perhaps this day the council recommended their former acts and proclamations to be observed; and it is declared, "that his majesty, with advice of his council, by virtue of his supremacy, allows the bishops to depute such a number of their curates as they judge qualified, to convene for exercise, and to assist in discipline, as the bishop shall direct them. But the whole power of ecclesiastical censures is reserved to the bishop, except parochial rebukes, and he only must suspend, deprive, or excommunicate." In short, those meetings in effect were nothing else but the bishops' spies, and informers up and down the country: and this seems to have been the shape and make of the prelatical presbyteries. The bishop under his hand granted a deputation to so many of his curates as he pleased, to meet in such a precinct, and gave them their instructions and limitations, beyond which they must not go. The number of those meetings for exercise, was but small in many places. Elders and inspectors of the manners of the people, must not be now named in this kind of presbyteries. At this time the church of Scotland might groan out that, "How is the gold become dim, and the most fine gold changed!" Alas! what a poor shadow and skeleton was this of the judicatory Christ himself instituted, and the presbyteries the apostles themselves joined in! This plant had for its root the king's supremacy, its stock was the bishop acting as the king's servant and depute, the curates were its branches; and its fruit certainly could not be holiness, reformation, or the edification of the body of Christ; but destruction, wormwood, and gall to the bulk of the religious people in Scotland. And I find very little they did, but consulted how to inform against, and promote the work of persecution upon presbyterians.

This same diet the council grant a commission for discipline, and empower ministers in each congregation to choose persons, whom they will not call elders, that they may join with them for suppressing of sin. Of this and the consequents of it, for further trouble to presbyterians who could not join with the curates, I shall give some further account upon the next year, when it came to be put in execution. And to end the account of this remarkable sederunt of council, the same day they pass an act concerning the prisoners among their hands. "The privy council considering, that there are several prisoners within the tolbooth of Edinburgh, who of their own accord are desirous to be transported to Barbadoes, ordain the magistrates to set all at liberty, who are content of their own free will to go to Barbadoes, and ordain them to be delivered to George Hutcheson, merchant in Edinburgh, in order to transportation." Who they were is not specified, nor the crimes for which they were incarcerate; but by other papers I find they were the remains of such who had been imprisoned by the high commission court, and sent in prisoners for their nonconformity and opposition to the curates: and several of them chose rather to go to the plantations, than to abide for ever in prison at home. In the progress of this work we shall afterwards find, that transportation was not left to prisoners' choice.

Little further remarkable offers this year. March 1st, the bishop of Argyle petitions the council, "that whereas by an act of the last session of parliament, dated September 17th, eight expectants who have passed their course of philosophy, and eight scholars to be trained up at schools and colleges, are to be entertained out of the vacant stipends of that diocese, each of which are to have two hundred merks yearly for their subsistence, a collector be named, and letters direct at his instance." The council empower the bishop to name a collector, and grant the desire of the petition.

October 3d, the council having received his majesty's commands, ordain the lord marquis of Huntley to be educated in the family of the lord archbishop of St. Andrews, to whose tender care they recommend him, and that no person popishly inclined have liberty to attend him or serve him: and ordain the earls of Linlithgow and Tweeddale, to acquaint his mother and himself, and call a meeting of his curators, to provide all things necessary and suitable to one of his rank; and that he enter the archbishop's family against the 27th of October instant. We shall afterwards meet with this nobleman created the duke of Gordon, and living in the profession of popery. What care the primate took to prevent this, I know not.*

November 30th, a proclamation is published, ordering a voluntary collection to be gathered through all the churches of the kingdom, for the relief of the distressed churches in Poland and Bohemia, to be delivered to Paul Hartman, their commissioner. It comes down from London, and is ordered to be published. I find it further remarked, that Yule was not so solemnly kept this year, as during the former; and at Edinburgh there was no proclamation by the magistrates discharging the opening of shops, and going about people's ordinary work; only Mr. William Annand preached a sermon suited to the occasion.

1665.

Thus I have gone through the lamentable circumstances of Presbyterians, during the first six years of their furnace, in as far as what papers I could have access to, would carry me. It is indeed but a very lame account can be given at this distance; and yet from the original papers, and acts of parliament and council, with the vouched instances of their rigorous execution, the reader may form some notion of the severities of this period: and harder things are coming upon presbyterians in the succeeding years. There is not much further matter offers, as the subject of this history, till the end of the next year, when the rising and unsuccessful attempt made by some presbyterians for recovering of their liberty, and shaking off the heavy yoke of oppression they groaned under, brought upon them a new and very dreadful scene of sufferings. Any thing noticeable as to their state and sufferings, during the former part of the year 1666, I shall leave to the second book, where it natively falls in, to prepare the way for the account of the rising, which was dissipate at Pentland.

---

* Of this affair we have the following account from Burnet. After having stated that there had been a convention in the year 1665, in which Sharp had presided, he continues: "In the winter, 1666, or rather in the spring, 1667, there was another convention called, in which the king, by a special letter, appointed duke Hamilton to preside. And the king, in a letter to lord Rothes, ordered him to write to Sharp to stay within his diocese, and to come no more to Edinburgh. He upon this was struck with so deep a melancholy, that he showed as great an abjectness under this slight disgrace, as he had showed insolence before when he had more favour. Sharp finding he was now under a cloud, studied to make himself popular by looking after the education of the marquis of Huntly, now the duke of Gordon. He had an order long before from the king to look to his education, that he might be bred a protestant, for the strength of popery within that kingdom lay in his family, But though this was ordered during the earl of Middleton's ministry, Sharp had not all this while looked for it. The earl of Rothes' mistress was a papist, and nearly related to the marquis of Huntly. So Sharp, either to make his court the better, or at the lord Rothes' desire, had neglected it these four years: but now he called for him. He was then above fifteen, well hardened in his prejudices by the loss of so much time. What pains were taken on him I know not. But after a trial of some months, Sharp said he saw he was not to be wrought on, and sent him back to his mother. So the interest that popery had in Scotland was believed to be chiefly owing to Sharp's compliance with the earl of Rothes' amours."—Burnet's History of His Own Times, vol. i. pp. 351, 352.—*Ed.*

END OF VOLUME FIRST.

GLASGOW:
PRINTED BY W. G. BLACKIE, & CO.,
VILLAFIELD.

OTHER SOLID GROUND TITLES

We recently celebrated our seventh anniversary of uncovering buried treasure to the glory of God. During these seven years we have produced nearly 200 volumes. A sample is listed below:

Biblical & Theological Studies: *Addresses to Commemorate the 100th Anniversary of Princeton Theological Seminary in 1912* by Allis, Machen, Wilson, Vos, Warfield and many more.

Notes on Galatians by J. Gresham Machen

The Origin of Paul's Religion by J. Gresham Machen

A Scientific Investigation of the Old Testament by R.D. Wilson

Theology on Fire: *Sermons from Joseph A. Alexander*

Evangelical Truth: *Sermons for the Family* by Archibald Alexander

A Shepherd's Heart: *Pastoral Sermons of James W. Alexander*

Grace & Glory: *Sermons from Princeton Chapel* by Geerhardus Vos

The Lord of Glory by Benjamin B. Warfield

The Person & Work of the Holy Spirit by Benjamin B. Warfield

The Power of God unto Salvation by Benjamin B. Warfield

Calvin Memorial Addresses by Warfield, Johnson, Orr, Webb…

The Five Points of Calvinism by Robert Lewis Dabney

Annals of the American Presbyterian Pulpit by W.B. Sprague

The Word & Prayer: *Classic Devotions from the Pen of John Calvin*

A Body of Divinity: *Sum and Substance of Christian Doctrine* by Ussher

The Collected Works of James H. Thornwell

A Puritan New Testament Commentary by John Trapp

Exposition of the Epistle to the Hebrews by William Gouge

Exposition of the Epistle of Jude by William Jenkyn

Lectures on the Book of Esther by Thomas M'Crie

Lectures on the Book of Acts by John Dick

To order any of our titles please contact us in one of three ways:

Call us at **1-866-789-7423**
Email us at **sgcb@charter.net**
Visit our website at **www.solid-ground-books.com**

www.ingramcontent.com/pod-product-compliance
Lightning Source LLC
Chambersburg PA
CBHW020810100426
42814CB00001B/14